Insurance Handbook for the Medical Office

MARILYN TAKAHASHI FORDNEY, CMA-AC, CMT

Formerly
Instructor of Medical Insurance, Medical Terminology,
Medical Machine Transcription, and Medical Office Procedures
Ventura College
Ventura, California

Insurance Handbook for the Medical Office

5th edition

W.B. Saunders Company
A Division of Harcourt Brace & Company
Philadelphia London Toronto Montreal Sydney Tokyo

W.B. Saunders Company
A Division of Harcourt Brace & Company

The Curtis Center
Independence Square West
Philadelphia, Pennsylvania 19106

Library of Congress Cataloging-in-Publication Data

Fordney, Marilyn Takahashi.
Insurance handbook for the medical office / Marilyn Takahashi Fordney.—5th ed.

p. cm.

Includes bibliographical references and index.

ISBN 0–7216–6987–5

1. Insurance, Health—United States—Handbooks, manuals, etc.
2. Medical offices—Management—Handbooks, manuals, etc.
I. Title. [DNLM: W 39 F712i 1997]

HG9396.F67 1997 368.38′0024′61—dc21

DNLM/DLC 96–48722

Insurance Handbook for the Medical Office, 5th Edition ISBN 0–7216–6987–5

Printed in the United States of America.

Last digit is the print number: 9 8 7 6 5 4 3

This book is dedicated to my husband, ALAN
and to the memory of my parents, MARGARET O'BRIEN TAKAHASHI and
TOSHIO JAMES TAKAHASHI,
and of my brother, JAMES MARTIN "POOPSIE" TAKAHASHI

Preface

When this book made its first appearance in 1977, few people were aware of how important the subject of health insurance would become. *Insurance Handbook for the Medical Office* has since gained wide acceptance abroad as well as nationally. A vast number of changes have occurred since the previous edition, making major revision and expansion necessary. It has been challenging and exciting to put the fifth edition together. Because changes take place in the insurance industry on a daily basis, *Insurance Handbook for the Medical Office* will be revised every two years to keep the information current.

PURPOSE

The goals of this text are to increase efficiency and streamline administrative procedures for the most exasperating aspect of the doctor's office routine: insurance billing. To develop a good relationship with patients and meet ever-increasing competition, management consultants recommend that medical offices submit the insurance claims for their patients. Even offices that do not routinely complete insurance claims for patients will make exceptions for those patients who suffer from mental incompetence, illiteracy, diminished eyesight, or a poor command of the English language. When the bill is for hundreds or thousands of dollars or when a surgical report is required, the physician's office should submit the bill for maximum reimbursement. Those who administer the federal government's Medicare program increasingly promote electronic transmission of insurance claims. Because of these factors, as well as the requirement to document care, the amount of paperwork has increased by leaps and bounds, becoming burdensome and unwieldy. Figures throughout the text feature generic forms created to simplify billing procedures.

In recent years, the community and health care professionals have witnessed emergence of an administrative medical specialty known either as insurance billing specialist, medical biller, or reimbursement specialist. Certification is being offered by several national organizations, and the career is quickly achieving recognition and professionalism. Health care reform means an explosion of jobs in the medical field, especially for those trained to process insurance claims manually as well as transmit them electronically. It is not uncommon to find medical practices either undercharging or not charging for billable services from lack of knowledge by office personnel.

A number of community colleges have established one-year certificate programs for those interested in a career as an insurance billing specialist, and many existing programs offer medical insurance as a full-semester, 18-week course. Community college extension divisions also offer community service classes in this subject. The text may be used as a learning tool in vocational or commercial training institutes, as well as for welfare-work programs. It also serves as a text for in-service training in the private medical office. It may be used for independent home study if no formal classes are available in the community. The lay reader not pursuing a career in the medical field will find it useful when working with a claims assistance professional or for billing his or her insurance plans. Insurance companies and their agents have found this a valuable reference book.

Many types of insurance coverage are available in the United States. Those types most commonly encountered in physicians' offices and clinics have been emphasized in this text in simple, nontechnical explanations and tables. Primarily the text is designed for the student who plans to seek employment in a physician's office or clinic or wishes to establish an independent billing business and needs a good understanding of the reimbursement process. This fifth edition has been enhanced with a chapter entitled "Hospital Billing" because of the need for basic training for those interested in employment in an inpatient setting. In addition, this new material is of great value to those involved with billing for hospital outpatient clinics. Finally, it may be used as a stand-alone reference source or as an educational tool to increase the knowledge of someone presently working as an insurance billing specialist in a private medical office.

CONTENT

In the previous edition, each chapter was reviewed by several experts so improvements in content, clarity of topics, and deletions could be considered. For this fifth edition, each chapter has been updated to reflect 1996 policies and procedures. Objectives are presented at the beginning of each chapter to guide the instructor in preparing lecture material and inform the reader about what will be presented. By reviewing the key terms introducing each chapter, the student is alerted to important words for the topic. An entirely new first chapter explains in detail the career and professionalism of the insurance billing specialist and the many directions an individual may take after learning the skills of procedural and diagnostic coding and insurance claims completion. Basic health insurance information and coding problems have been added for the person who needs to study for a certification examination. In recent years, insurance forms and electronic transmission formats have become more standardized, and most private companies and state and government fiscal agents or carriers now accept the HCFA-1500 Health Insurance Claim Form, as discussed in Chapter 6. A separate chapter on managed-care systems and how they affect various government and state programs, as well as issues about health care reform, is presented. Helpful billing tips and guidelines for submitting insurance claims are given for each type of insurance covered. Many specific quick-action solutions for insurance problems, tracing delinquent claims, and appealing denied claims are mentioned. Special emphasis is placed on correct and incorrect procedural codes and explaining appropriate documentation—the keys to obtaining maximum reimbursement. Thorough up-to-date coverage is presented for Medicare, Medicaid, CHAMPUS, the Blue Plans, workers' compensation, managed care plans, disability income insurance, and disability benefit programs. Chapter 7, Electronic Data Interchange, explains electronic claims transmission as well as computer claim systems—carrier direct or clearinghouse. The text is leavened with cartoons, amusing approaches, and quotes. A final chapter provides information pertinent to seeking a position as either an insurance billing specialist, a claims assistance professional, or an electronic claims processor.

At the back of the book is an extensive glossary of basic medical and insurance terms and abbreviations. Appendix A lists addresses for insurance claim's offices and insurance commissioners by state, territory, or Canadian. Appendix B is a comprehensive reference resource of available audiotapes, books, newsletters, periodicals, software, and videotapes designed to assist the insurance billing specialist. Addresses and toll-free telephone numbers are listed at the end to assist the reader in locating a special item, if desired. With this edition, Appendix C has been added for those working in California and in need of information on submission of Medi-Cal claims and other documents.

SUPPLEMENTS

Workbook

For the learner, the *Workbook* that accompanies the text is a practical approach to learning insurance billing, progressing from easy to more complex issues within each chapter. Chapter outlines serve as a lecture guide. Each chapter's performance objectives for assignments clue the student about what will be accomplished. Key terms are repeated for quick reference when studying. Patients' medical records, ledgers, and encounter forms are presented exactly as they might appear in the doctor's files, so the student may learn how to abstract information to complete claim forms properly and accurately. Many contain physicians' handwritten notes. For this edition, the patient records and ledgers have been completely updated and reworded to correspond with the 1996 procedural and diagnostic code books. Easily removable insurance claim forms and other sample documents are included in the *Workbook* for typing practice. Some assignments give students hands-on experience in typing forms for optical character recognition (OCR) computer equipment, which is used in many states for insurance claims processing and payment. Current procedural and diagnostic code exercises are used throughout the *Workbook* to facilitate and enhance coding skills for submitting a claim or posting to an itemized billing statement. Review questions are presented for each chapter of the textbook, with some critical thinking problems for certain sections.

Tests are provided at the end of the *Workbook* to provide a complete competency-based educational program. Special appendices appear at the end of the *Workbook* that include a mock Medicare fee schedule with codes and fees and a Medicare Level II Health Care Financing Administration nationally designated alphanumeric code list. The appendices may be used as reference tools to complete the procedural code problems.

Software

Because most medical practices now use a computer to perform financial operations that were formerly completed manually, an additional tool for the learner has been developed in the form of user-friendly computer software. Software features are programmed to go along with the textbook and workbook. The textbook glossary plus definitions and questions are integrated into the chapters for comprehension and retention of textbook material. To give the student a hands-on approach, practical application exercises for diagnostic and procedural coding and insurance claims completion are incorporated into the software with printing capabilities. A simulated electronic transmission of an insurance claim is also included. An ongoing summary of scores achieved on completed assignments may be brought up on screen to keep the student and teacher informed of progress made. Detailed scoring reports may be printed out so that the instructor has access to the information from time to time. Employment of this overall practical applications approach makes possible an easier transition from classroom to workplace.

INSTRUCTOR'S MANUAL

An *Instructor's Manual* is available for use with the text to assist in establishing a course in medical insurance, to give ideas on how to use the text as an adjunct to a medical office procedures course, and to obtain the answers to the *Workbook* review questions, assignments, and tests. Rationale, optional codes, and further explanations have been provided for some of the codes given in the answer keys. A selection of illustrations suitable for making overhead transparencies is incorporated into the manual. If an instructor is interested in establishing a one-year certificate program for insurance billing specialists and wishes networking and other information on how other schools have set up a program for this career field, write to or e-mail the author, using the mailing address in the manual.

Textbook learning objectives, *Workbook* performance objectives for all assignments, use of the text with reinforcement by workbook assignments, and incorporation of classroom activities and suggestions from the *Instructor's Manual* provide a complete competency-based educational program.

COMPUTERIZED TEST BANK

A test bank of 1000 questions with answers is provided on computer disk to assist the instructor in test construction. It gives a variety of testing formats, such as multiple choice, true and false, mix and match, completion of blanks, and quizzes on illustrations.

SUMMARY

Escalating costs of medical care, the impact of technology, and the explosion of managed care plans have affected insurance billing procedures and claims processing as well as requiring new legislation for government and state programs. Therefore, it is essential that all medical personnel handling claims continue to update their knowledge by reading bulletins from state agencies and regional insurance carriers and speaking with their representatives or by attending insurance workshops offered at local colleges or local chapters of professional associations, such as those mentioned in Chapter 1. It is hoped that this text will resolve any unclear issues pertaining to current methods and become the framework upon which the insurance billing specialist builds new knowledge as understanding and appreciation of the profession are attained.

Marilyn T. Fordney, CMA-AC, CMT
Oxnard, California

Acknowledgments

During my 14 years as a medical assistant and 19 years of teaching and writing, hundreds of students, physicians, friends, colleagues, and instructors have contributed valuable suggestions and interesting material for this book. I wish to express my thanks to all of them, with special emphasis to the following.

Lois C. Oliver, retired Professor, Pierce College, Woodland Hills, California, helped me organize my first medical insurance class in 1969 and offered assistance and encouragement throughout the preparation of the first edition of the *Handbook.*

Marcia O. "Marcy" Diehl, CMA-A, CMT, retired instructor, Grossmont Community College, El Cajon, California, generously shared her knowledge, ideas, and class materials.

Members of the *California Association of Medical Assistant Instructors (CAMAI)* contributed suggestions for improving the text and gave me motivation from time to time to continue the project.

Mary E. Kinn, CPS, CMA-A, retired Assistant Professor, Long Beach City College, Long Beach, California, provided a perceptive review of my syllabus. Without her positive endorsement, the first edition of this book might not have been published.

I gratefully acknowledge the artist involved with the design of the cover and text, Steven Stave, Design Department, W.B. Saunders Company. I am also grateful to the artists who produced the cartoons featured throughout the text: Deborah McKillop, Illustrator, Deborah McKillop Design Studio, Ventura, California; Roman Yslas, Graphic Illustrator, Oxnard, California; and Gail Niebrugge, Graphic Illustrator and Fine Artist, Palmer, Alaska.

I also wish to thank the Print Shop Staff, Publications Department, Ventura College, Ventura, California, who printed the first California syllabus of this text.

I am indebted to many individuals on the staff of the W.B. Saunders Company for encouragement and guidance. I express particular appreciation to Margaret M. Biblis, Senior Acquisitions Editor, and her assistant, Christa Fratantoro; Helaine A. Barron, Developmental Editor; and Agnes Byrne, Copy Editor, for expert editing and coordination of the entire project. My thanks go also to Linda R. Garber, Senior Production Manager.

Numerous supply companies were kind enough to cooperate by providing forms and descriptive literature of their products, and their names will be found throughout the text and workbook figures.

But colleagues, production staff, and editors working alone do not quite make a book; there are others to whom I am deeply indebted. I wish to thank my husband, Alan, who offered support, encouragement, a sense of humor, and motivation throughout the preparation of each edition and understanding of the priority it had on my time. Special thanks to my two assistants, Linda French, CMA-C, and Nina Janis, for without their day-to-day help I would not have been able to meet the deadlines.

Many of the ideas, comments, and suggestions by the reviewers of the fourth edition have been retained in this edition and continued appreciation is extended to them. Additionally, thanks and appreciation are extended to Eugenia Mills Fulcher, RN, BSN, Med, Swainsboro Technical Institute, Swainsboro, Georgia, and Brenda Mack, BA, Ross Technical Institute, Ann Arbor, Michigan who graciously reviewed elements for the new Chapter 16, Hospital Billing.

Last, and most importantly, I must express overwhelming debt and enduring gratitude to the consultants who reviewed each chapter or who provided vital information about private, state, and federal insurance programs. Without the knowledge of these advisers, the massive task of compiling an insurance text truly national in scope might never have been completed. Although the names of all those who graciously assisted me are too numerous to mention, I take great pride in listing my principal consultants for this fifth edition.

PRINCIPAL CONSULTANTS AND REVIEWERS

Judy Capko
Owner
Professional Management Concepts
Newbury Park, California

Michelle R. Carter
Associate Consultant, Marketing Programs
Blue Cross Blue Shield Association
Federal Employee Program
Washington, D.C.

Kay Cavanaugh, ART
Medical Records Consultant
ParaMedical Services, Inc.
Anaheim, California

George S. Conomikes and Staff
President
Conomikes Associates, Inc.
Los Angeles, California

Kathryn Dokas
Executive Director
National Association of Claims Assistance Professionals
Downers Grove, Illinois

Deborah Emmons, CMA
President
S.T.A.T. Transcription Service
Port Hueneme, California

Sharon Ferrell
President
Rx Managed Care Reimbursement
Danville, California

Ronna Jurow, MD
Active Staff and Attending Physician in Obstetrics, Gynecology and Infertility
Community Memorial Hospital
Ventura, California

Anne L. Lilly, RN, BSN, MA, CPC
Instructor
Santa Rosa Junior College
Santa Rosa, California

Lucille M. Loignon, MD, FACS
Diplomate American Board of Ophthalmology
Oxnard, California

Kathy A. McCall, CMA-AC, BS, MA
Professor of Allied Health
Community College of Allegheny County
Pittsburgh, Pennsylvania

Jane E. McCaw
Product Specialist
SYCOM
Madison, Wisconsin

Oscar Melendez
State Compensation Insurance Fund
Ventura, California

Fran Muller, BS, MeD
Department of Medical Assisting
Guilford Technical Community College
Jamestown, North Carolina

Susan K. Nagy
Ombudsman
Aetna Government Health Plans
CHAMPUS Division
San Diego, California

Gregory J. Payette
Personnel Director
Smith-Glynn-Callaway Clinic, Inc.
Springfield, Missouri

Joan Robinson
Manager
BlueCard Operation
Blue Cross Blue Shield Association
Chicago, Illinois

Vicki Sanders
University of Alabama at Birmingham
School of Health Related Professions
Birmingham, Alabama

Cynthia L. Shaff
President, Shaff and Associates
Los Angeles, California

Walter A. Shaff
President
CPR
Lake Oswego, Oregon

Lita Starr
Office Manager for William E. Starr, MD, FACS
Oxnard, California

Sue Stratton
Vice President, Health Care Services
Medical Administrative Consultants Inc.
Agoura Hills, California

Carolyn Talesfore
Ad and Promo Manager
Bibbero Systems, Inc.
Petaluma, California

Christopher R. Traube
Manager, Medicare Liaison
Medicare Review and Educational Services
Blue Shield of California
San Francisco, California

Ann G. Uniack, RRA
Ann G. Uniack and Associates
San Anselmo, California

Judy Vasquez
Information Coordinator
Media Relations
Blue Cross Blue Shield Association
Chicago, Illinois

Special thanks go to the following people who graciously reviewed various elements of this book.

REVIEWERS

Jerri Adler, CMA, CMT, BA
Health Occupations
Lane Community College
Eugene, Oregon

Gloria Ahern, RRA, BS
Central Oregon Community College
Bend, Oregon

Terri A. Beagan
Katherine Gibbs School
Warwick, Rhode Island

Judith S. Bell, BA
Midstate College
Peoria, Illinois

Geneva M. Burch, AAS, BS, MS
West Virginia Northern Community College
Benwood, West Virginia

Julie L. Curry, BS
Wallace Community College
Dothan, Alabama

Eugenia Mills Fulcher, RN, BSN, Med
Swainsboro Technical Institute
Swainsboro, Georgia

Theresa J. Gavazzi, AAS, BS
Broane Community College
Binghamton, New York

Linda Lindsey
San Antonio College of Medical and Dental Assistants
San Antonio, Texas

Brenda F. Mack, BA
Ross Technical Institute
Ann Arbor, Michigan

Thomas W. Owen
Billings Business College
Park City, Montana

Karen Paulin, BA, CMA
Buckeye Joint Vocational School
Carrollton, Ohio

Brenda Potter
Northwest Technical College
Fargo, North Dakota

Vicki Prater, CMA
Concorde Career Institute
San Bernardino, California

Marilyn Ryser, AAS, CMA
Ivy Technical College
Columbus, Indiana

Pamela Sue Wiebelhaus
T.H. Pickens Technical Center
Highlands Ranch, Colorado

Brief Contents

UNIT 1
Career Role and Responsibilities

CHAPTER 1
A Career as an Insurance Billing Specialist 3

CHAPTER 2
Legal Issues Affecting Insurance Claims and Medical Records 19

UNIT 2
The Claim Process

CHAPTER 3
Basics of Health Insurance 43

CHAPTER 4
Procedural Coding 65

CHAPTER 5
Diagnostic Coding 107

CHAPTER 6
The Health Insurance Claim Form 125

CHAPTER 7
Electronic Data Interchange (EDI) 159

CHAPTER 8
Tracing Delinquent Claims and Insurance Problem Solving 177

UNIT 3
Health Care Payers

CHAPTER 9
Managed Care Systems and Special Plans 203

CHAPTER 10
Blue Cross and Blue Shield Plans 227

CHAPTER 11
Medicaid and Other State Programs 247

CHAPTER 12
Medicare 259

CHAPTER 13
CHAMPUS, CHAMPVA, and TRICARE 297

CHAPTER 14
Workers' Compensation 329

CHAPTER 15
Disability Income Insurance and Disability Benefit Programs 369

UNIT 4
Inpatient and Outpatient Billing

CHAPTER 16
Hospital Billing 389

UNIT 5
Employment

CHAPTER 17
Seeking a Position as an Insurance Billing Specialist 419

APPENDICES

APPENDIX A
Addresses for Submitting Claims and Other Information 445

APPENDIX B
Reference List of Audiotapes, Books, Newsletters, Periodicals, Software, and Videotapes 487

APPENDIX C
Medi-Cal 503

GLOSSARY 521

INDEX 535

Detailed Contents

UNIT 1
Career Role and Responsibilities

CHAPTER 1
A Career as an Insurance Billing Specialist 3

Objectives
Key Terms
INTRODUCTION 3
EDUCATIONAL AND TRAINING REQUIREMENTS 4
CAREER ADVANTAGES 5
PERSONAL QUALIFICATIONS 5
MEDICAL ETIQUETTE 8
MEDICAL ETHICS 8
Confidentiality 11
PROFESSIONALISM 15
Personal Image 15
Certification 15
KEEPING CURRENT 17

CHAPTER 2
Legal Issues Affecting Insurance Claims and Medical Records 19

Objectives
Key Terms
INTRODUCTION 19
EMPLOYER LIABILITY 20
INSURANCE POLICIES (CONTRACTS) 20
PATIENT/PHYSICIAN CONTRACTS AND FINANCIAL RESPONSIBILITY 21
PHYSICIAN AND MANAGED CARE CONTRACTS 21
CONFIDENTIALITY 21
Medical Records 21
Principles for Release of Information 25
Retention of Records 27
SUBPOENA 28
INSURANCE CLAIMS 29
Guarantor 29
Assignment 29
Time Limits 29
Signature Authorization 29
INSURANCE CLAIM FRAUD AND ABUSE 30
Forgery 33
Claim Audits and Review 33
EMBEZZLEMENT 34
CREDIT AND COLLECTION LAWS 35
APPEALS 35
STATUTE OF LIMITATIONS 35
Prevention Commandments of American Medical Association Committee on Medicolegal Problems 36
Physician/Patient Agreement 39
Termination of a Case 39
MEDICOLEGAL REFERENCES 40
INSURANCE COMMISSIONERS 40
STATE BOARDS OF MEDICAL EXAMINERS 40

UNIT 2
The Claims Process

CHAPTER 3
Basics of Health Insurance 43

Objectives
Key Terms
INTRODUCTION 43
HISTORY 44
THE INSURANCE POLICY 44
Policy Application 44
Policy Provisions 44
Coordinator of Benefits 45
General Policy Limitations 45
CHOICE OF HEALTH INSURANCE 47
TYPES OF HEALTH INSURANCE COVERAGE 47
EXAMPLES OF INSURANCE BILLING 51
BASIC STEPS IN PROCESSING AN INSURANCE CLAIM 52
HANDLING INSURANCE CLAIMS 56
First Visit: Patient Information Sheet 56
Submitting and Tracing the Claim 60
Insurance Claims Register 61
KEEPING UP-TO-DATE 61

CHAPTER 4
Procedural Coding 65
Objectives
Key Terms
INTRODUCTION 65
CODING OF PROCEDURES 66
Current Procedural Terminology (CPT) 66
Relative Value Studies (RVS) 67
METHODS OF PAYMENT 67
VOCABULARY USED IN CODING 69
EVALUATION AND MANAGEMENT SECTION 69
Unlisted Procedures 71
Basic Life and/or Disability Evaluation Services 76
DOCUMENTATION 76
Documentation Guidelines for Evaluation and Management Services 76
General Principles of Medical Record Documentation 77
Documentation of History 77
Internal Audit 79
Crib Sheets 81
SURGERY SECTION 81
HOW TO USE THE CPT CODE BOOK 82
Code Book Symbols 82
Code Modifiers 83
How to Code Effectively 84
Coding Tips 86
RELATIVE VALUE STUDIES VARIANCES 95
Determining Relative Value Studies Conversion Factors 95
COMPREHENSIVE LIST OF MODIFIER CODES 100
MEDICARE CODING 104
LABORATORY ABBREVIATIONS 104

CHAPTER 5
Diagnostic Coding 107
Objectives
Key Terms
INTRODUCTION 107
CODING DISEASES 108
History 108
ICD-9-CM 108
ICD-10 109
ICD-9-CM CONTENTS 109
HOW TO USE THE DIAGNOSTIC CODE BOOKS PROPERLY 109
Coding Instructions 109
Handy Hints in Diagnostic Coding 114
E Codes 114
V Codes 115
RULES FOR CODING SIGNS, SYMPTOMS, AND ILL-DEFINED CONDITIONS 116
Rules for Coding Circulatory System Conditions 118
Rules for Coding Diabetes Mellitus 118
Rules for Coding Pregnancy, Delivery, or Abortion 120
Rules for Coding Admitting Diagnoses 120
Rules for Coding Burns 120
Rules for Coding Injuries and Late Effects 120
DIAGNOSTIC CODING AND THE PHYSICIAN'S FEE PROFILE 121

CHAPTER 6
The Health Insurance Claim Form 125
Objectives
Key Terms
INTRODUCTION 125
TYPES OF CLAIMS 128
ABSTRACTING FROM MEDICAL RECORDS 129
MEDICAL AND DIAGNOSTIC TERMINOLOGY 129
PROCEDURES FOR USE OF THE HEALTH INSURANCE CLAIM FORM HCFA-1500 137
General Guidelines 137
COMMON REASONS WHY CLAIMS ARE REJECTED OR DELAYED 140
COMPLETING AN OPTICALLY SCANNED FORM 142

Optical Character Recognition 142
Optical Character Recognition or Intelligent Character Recognition Guidelines 142
COMPLETING THE HEALTH INSURANCE CLAIM FORM (HCFA-1500) 143
EXPLANATION OF BENEFITS 155

CHAPTER 7
Electronic Data Interchange (EDI) 159
Objectives
Key Terms
BACKGROUND 159
COMPUTER 160
COMPUTER CLAIMS SYSTEM 161
Carrier-Direct 161
Clearinghouse 162
Electronic Claims Processor 162
ELECTRONIC DATA INTERCHANGE 163
Carrier Agreements 164
Signature Requirements 164
Workers' Compensation 164
Encounter Forms 165
Crib Sheets 166
Eligibility Verification 166
Keying Insurance Data 166
Electronically Completing the Claim 166
Electronic Inquiry or Claims Status Review 170
Remittance Advice 171
Statements 172
COMPUTER CONFIDENTIALITY 172
Confidentiality Statement 172
Prevention Measures 172
RECORDS MANAGEMENT 174
Data Storage 174

CHAPTER 8
Tracing Delinquent Claims and Insurance Problem Solving 177
Objectives
Key Terms
CLAIMS PROVISIONS 177
STATE INSURANCE COMMISSIONER 178
Commission Objectives 178
Types of Problems 178
Commission Inquiries 178
CLAIM MANAGEMENT TECHNIQUES 180
Insurance Claims Register 180
Insurance Company Payment History 180
Tickler File 180
PROBLEM CLAIMS 181
Types of Problems 181
Delinquent, Pending, or Suspense 181
Lost Claims 183
Rejected Claims 184
Denied Claims 184
Down Coding 185
Partial Payment 186
Payment Paid to the Patient 186
Two-Party Check 186
Overpayment 187
REBILLING 187
Claim Inquiries 187
REVIEW AND APPEAL PROCESS 188
Blue Cross and Blue Shield Review and Appeal Process 189
Champus Review and Appeal Process 190
Reconsideration 190
Medicare Review and Appeal Process 190
Medigap 200

UNIT 3
Health Care Payers

CHAPTER 9
Managed Care Systems and Special Plans 203
Objectives
Key Terms
HISTORY 203
Prepaid Group Practice Health Plans 203
Health Care Reform 205
MANAGED CARE SYSTEMS 206
Health Maintenance Organizations 206
Individual (or Independent) Practice Association (IPA) 206
Preferred Provider Organizations 207
Champus and Managed Care Programs 207
Medicare and Managed Care Programs 209
Medicaid and Managed Care Programs 209
Point of Service Plans 209
Physician Provider Groups 210
Triple Option Health Plan 210
Foundations for Medical Care 210

MEDICAL REVIEW 211
- Professional Review Organizations 211
- Utilization Review or Management 211

MANAGEMENT OF PLANS 211
- Contracts 211
- Precertification or Prior Authorization 211
- Laboratory and X-ray Tests 213
- Managed Care Guide 213
- Plan Administration 213

FINANCIAL MANAGEMENT 219
- Statement of Remittance 219
- Accounting 219
- Fee for Service 219
- Capitation and Year-End Evaluation 219

BANKRUPTCY 221

SPECIAL PLANS 221
- Individual Responsibility Plan 222
- Optometric Service Plans 222

CHAPTER 10

Blue Cross and Blue Shield Plans 227

Objectives
Key Terms

INTRODUCTION 227

HISTORY AND PURPOSE 228

SPECIAL CLAUSES AND BENEFITS 228

TYPES OF BLUE CROSS AND BLUE SHIELD CONTRACTS 229
- Service Benefit Contracts 229
- Indemnity Benefit Contracts 229

METHODS OF PAYMENT 229
- Usual, Customary, and Reasonable (UCR) Payment Program 229
- Payments under UCR 230
- Fee Schedules 230

PHYSICIAN PARTICIPATION CONCEPT 230
- BlueCard Program 231

CENTRAL CERTIFICATION AND CENTRAL SITE PROCESSING 231

IDENTIFYING INFORMATION 231

BLUE CROSS/BLUE SHIELD AND MEDICARE CLAIMS 233
- Local Blue Shield Plan Is Medicare Part B Carrier 233

MANAGED CARE 233
- Preferred Provider Organizations 233
- Health Maintenance Organizations 233
- Point of Service Programs 233

MEDICAL NECESSITY PROGRAM 233

TECHNOLOGY ASSESSMENT 233

PREADMISSION TESTING, AMBULATORY SURGERY, AND SECOND OPINIONS 234

STANDARD BLUE PLANS CLAIMS PROCEDURE 234
- Manual Completion of HCFA-1500 Claim Form 234
- Electronic Claims Submission 237
- Following Up on Delinquent Claims 238
- Blue Cross/Blue Shield State Insurance Addresses 238
- Reference Books 238

EXPLANATION OF BENEFITS 238

PROVIDER NUMBER 238

FEDERAL EMPLOYEE HEALTH BENEFITS PROGRAM 238
- Nonbenefits 238
- Identification Card 240
- Claims Procedure 240
- Time Limit 240
- Explanation of Benefits 245

CHAPTER 11

Medicaid and Other State Programs 247

Objectives
Key Terms

HISTORY 247
- Medicaid Qualified Medicare Beneficiaries Program 248
- Medicaid Reform 248

MEDICAID ELIGIBILITY 249
- Benefits 250

CLAIM PROCEDURE 250
- Identification Card 250
- Copayment 251
- Prior Approval 251
- Time Limit 251
- Reciprocity 251
- Claim Form 251
- Remittance Advice 253
- Appeals 253
- Third Party Liability 253
- Medicaid and Managed Care Plans 253
- Medicaid and CHAMPUS/CHAMPVA 253
- Medicaid and Medicare 253
- Medicaid and Aliens 253

HANDY HINTS 255

MATERNAL AND CHILD HEALTH PROGRAM (MCHP) 256
- Eligibility 256
- Claims Procedure 256

CHAPTER 12
Medicare 259

Objectives
Key Terms

INTRODUCTION 259
MEDICARE PROGRAM 260
- Eligibility Requirements 260
- Fiscal Intermediaries and Fiscal Agents 260
- Aliens on Medicare 265
- Beneficiary Representative/ Representative Payee 265

MEDICARE PAYMENTS 266
- Civil Monetary Penalties Law 267
- Medicare Health Insurance Card 269

COVERAGE 270
- Hospital Benefits 270
- Medical Benefits 270
- Railroad Retirement Benefits 270
- Physician Self Referrals 270
- Employed Elderly Health Care Coverage 270

MEDICARE SUPPLEMENTAL INSURANCE 274
- MEDIGAP 275
- Medicare Secondary Payer (MSP) 275
- MEDIGAP and MSP Guidelines 275
- MEDIGAP and MSP Claims 276

MEDICARE AND PREPAYMENT PLANS 276
- Health Maintenance Organizations 276
- Copayments 281
- Carrier-Dealing Prepayment Organization 281

AUTOMOBILE OR LIABILITY INSURANCE COVERAGE 281
BILLING FOR A DECEASED PATIENT 284
MEDICARE/MEDICAID (Medi-Medi) 284
- Benefits 284
- Claim Procedure 284

UTILIZATION AND QUALITY CONTROL 284
- Peer Review Organization Program 284

PRIOR AUTHORIZATION OR PRECERTIFICATION 288
MEDICARE CODING TIPS 288
- Medicare and Medicaid Coverage Data Bank 289
- Medicare Claim Form 290
- Electronic Claims Submission 290
- Medicare Fraud and Abuse 290
- Medicare Review and Appeal Process 290
- Posting Medicare Payments 290

CHAPTER 13
CHAMPUS, CHAMPVA, and TRICARE 297

Objectives
Key Terms

BACKGROUND 297
- CHAMPUS 297
- CHAMPVA 298

CHAMPUS PROGRAM 298
- Eligibility 298
- Defense Enrollment Eligibility Reporting System 299
- Providers of Health Care 299
- CHAMPUS and CHAMPVA Identification Cards 299
- Inpatient and Outpatient Benefits and Coverage 300

CHAMPVA PROGRAM 300
- Eligibility 300
- Preauthorization 305

PRIVACY ACT OF 1974 305
NONAVAILABILITY STATEMENT 305
CLAIMS PROCEDURE 306
- CHAMPUS/CHAMPVA 306
- Claims Offices 306
- Participating Providers 306
- Nonparticipating Providers 309
- Summary Payment Voucher 313
- CHAMPUS/CHAMPVA and Other Insurance 313
- Claim Submission 313
- Dual or Double Coverage 313
- Medicaid or Medigap 313
- CHAMPUS and Medicare 313
- CHAMPVA and Medicare 315
- Third Party Liability 315
- Workers' Compensation 315
- Claims Inquiries and Appeals 315
- Additional Information 315

CHAMPUS/TRICARE MANAGED CARE PROGRAMS 315
- Tricare Prime 321
- Benefits 321
- Enrollment 321
- Identification Cards 321
- Primary Care Manager 321
- Copayments 322

TRICARE EXTRA 322
- Identification Card 322

Copayments 322
Network Provider 322
Referrals and Precertification 323
Tricare Prime/Tricare Extra Nonavailability Statements 324
Quality Assurance 325
Claims Procedure 325
TRICARE STANDARD 327

CHAPTER 14
Workers' Compensation 329
Objectives
Key Terms
HISTORY 329
Benefits 330
Purposes of Workers' Compensation Laws 330
Workers' Compensation Reform 330
Self-Insurance 331
Managed Care 331
COVERAGE OF FEDERAL LAWS 331
COVERAGE OF STATE LAWS 332
Funding 332
Minimum Number of Employees 332
Waiting Periods 336
Types of State Compensation Benefits 336
TYPES OF STATE CLAIMS 337
Nondisability Claim 337
Temporary Disability Claim 337
Permanent Disability Claim 341
Rating 341
FRAUD AND ABUSE 342
Employee 342
Employer 342
Insurer 342
Medical Provider 342
Lawyer 344
OCCUPATIONAL SAFETY AND HEALTH ADMINISTRATION (OSHA) ACT OF 1970 344
Background 344
Coverage 344
Regulations 344
Filing a Complaint 344
Inspection 344
Recordkeeping, Posting, and Reporting 344
SPECIAL CIRCUMSTANCES 345
Third Party Subrogation 345
Medical Testimony 345
Depositions 345
Liens 346
Second-Injury Fund (Subsequent Injury Fund) 348
Unemployment Compensation Disability and Workers' Compensation 349
MEDICAL REPORTS 349
Confidentiality 349
Documentation 349
Recordkeeping 349
Terminology 349
Information to be Included in Detailed Progress or Re-examination Reports 358
BILLING CLAIMS 358
Financial Responsibility 358
Fee Schedules 358
Helpful Billing Tips 360
Electronic Claims Submission 361
Out-of-State Claims 361
INSTRUCTIONS FOR COMPLETING THE DOCTOR'S FIRST REPORT OF OCCUPATIONAL INJURY OR ILLNESS 361
DELINQUENT CLAIMS 363

CHAPTER 15
Disability Income Insurance and Disability Benefit Programs 369
Objectives
Key Terms
INTRODUCTION 369
HISTORY 370
DISABILITY INCOME INSURANCE 370
Individual 370
Group 372
FEDERAL DISABILITY PROGRAMS 372
Workers' Compensation 372
Disability Benefit Program 372
STATE DISABILITY INSURANCE 376
Background 376
Funding 376
Eligibility 376
Benefits 376
Time Limits 379
Medical Examinations 379
Limitations 379
Voluntary Disability Insurance Plan 379
INSTRUCTIONS AND PROCEDURES FOR CLAIMS SUBMISSION 379
Disability Income Claims 379

Federal Disability Claims 380
Veterans Administration Disability Outpatient Clinic Claims 383
State Disability Claims 386

UNIT 4
Inpatient and Outpatient Billing

CHAPTER 16
Hospital Billing 389

Objectives
Key Terms
INTRODUCTION 389
Reimbursement Methods 391
MEDICOLEGAL 392
Confidentiality 392
BILLING ERRORS 393
Duplicate Statements 393
Double Billing 393
Phantom Charges 393
Posting Errors 394
HOSPITAL BILLING PROCESS 394
Electronic Data Interchange 394
Payments 395
OUTPATIENT INSURANCE CLAIMS 395
INPATIENT INSURANCE CLAIMS 396
Private Insurance (Group or Individual) 396
Blue Plans 396
Workers' Compensation 396
Managed Care 396
Medicare 397
Medicaid 397
CHAMPUS, CHAMPVA, and TRICARE 397
DIAGNOSTIC CODING 397
ICD-9-CM Volume 3 Procedures: Tabular List and Alphabetic Index 397
Tabular List 397
Alphabetic Index 398
Special Points to Remember in Volume 3 398
Diagnostic Coding Handy Hints 399
PROCEDURAL CODING 399
Current Procedural Terminology 399
Procedural Coding Hospital Billing Handy Hints 399
Health Care Finance Administration Common Procedure Coding System 399
HOSPITAL BILLING CLAIM FORM 399
Uniform Bill Inpatient and Outpatient Claim Form 399
Instructions for Completing the UB-92 Claim Form 399
DIAGNOSIS-RELATED GROUPS 408
History 408
The DRG System 409
Diagnosis Related Groups and the Medical Assistant/Insurance Billing Specialist 410
Handy Hints for the Physician's Practice 411
Diagnostic Related Groups and Medical Records 412
Outpatient Classifications 414
Utilization Review 414
PEER REVIEW ORGANIZATION 414
APPROPRIATENESS EVALUATION PROTOCOLS 415

UNIT 5
Employment

CHAPTER 17
Seeking a Position as an Insurance Billing Specialist 419

Objectives
Key Terms
EMPLOYMENT OPPORTUNITIES 419
JOB SEARCH 428
Insurance Billing Specialist 428
On-Line Job Search 428
Electronic Resume 429
Claims Assistance Professional 429
Electronic Claims Professional 430
Application 430
Letter of Introduction 430
Resume 433
Interview 437
SELF-EMPLOYMENT OR FREE-LANCING 438
Setting Up An Office 438
Finances 439
Equipment 439
Insurance 439
Marketing, Advertising, Promotion, and Public Relations 441
Contracts or Agreements 441
Documentation 441
Statements and Pricing 441
Networking 442

APPENDICES

APPENDIX A
Addresses for Submitting Claims and Other Information 445

APPENDIX B
Reference List of Audiotapes, Books, Newsletters, Periodicals, Software, and Videotapes 487

APPENDIX C
Medi-Cal 503

GLOSSARY 521

INDEX 535

UNIT 1

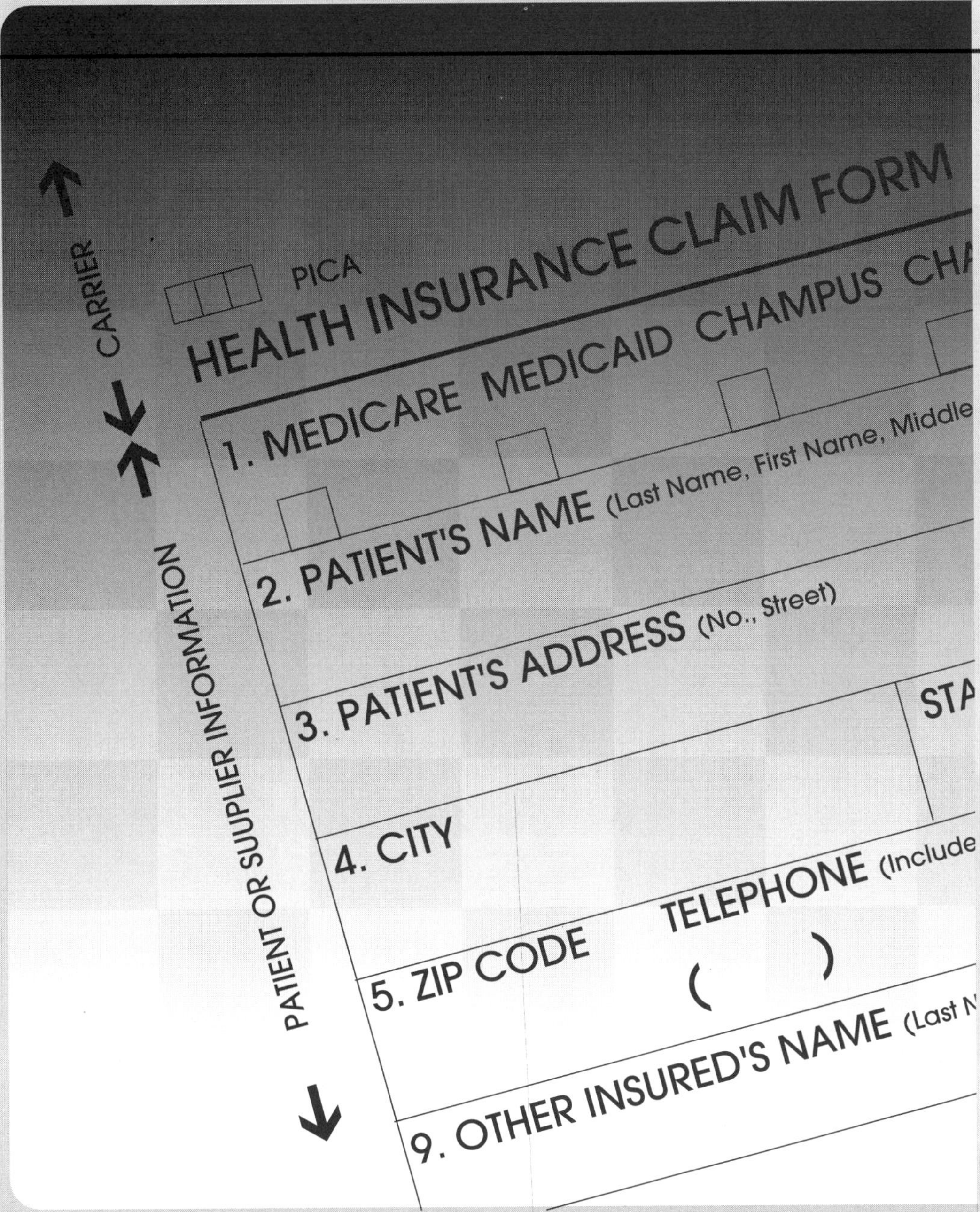

Career Role and Responsibilities

Objectives*

THE INSURANCE BILLING SPECIALIST WILL BE ABLE TO:

- Identify the background and importance of insurance claims completion, coding, and billing.
- Name at least three skills possessed by insurance billing specialists.
- Describe the variety of career possibilities and areas of specialization open to those trained as insurance billing specialists.
- List personal qualifications and skills to be acquired by an insurance billing specialist.
- State the personal image to be projected.
- Explain the educational requirements for a job as an insurance billing specialist and as a coder.
- Explain how insurance knowledge and medical knowledge can be kept current.
- Determine the differences between medical ethics and medical etiquette.
- Define privileged communication.
- Describe the difference between privileged and nonprivileged information.
- State types of certification and registration available to insurance billing specialists, coding specialists, and administrative medical assistants.

Key Terms

American Academy of Procedural Coders (AAPC)
American Association of Medical Assistants, Inc. (AAMA)
American Association for Medical Transcription (AAMT)
American Health Information Management Association (AHIMA)
American Medical Association (AMA)
certification
Certified Claims Assistance Professional (CCAP)
Certified Coding Specialist (CCS)
Certified Electronic Claims Professional (CECP)
Certified Medical Assistant (CMA)
Certified Procedural Coder (CPC)
Claims Assistance Professional (CAP)
continuing education (CE)
ethics
etiquette
group practice
insurance billing specialist
National Association of Claims Assistance Professionals, Inc. (NACAP)
nonprivileged information
privileged communication
privileged information
Professional Association of Health Care Office Managers (PAHCOM)
recertification
Registered Medical Assistant (RMA)
reimbursement specialist

* Performance objectives and exercises for hands-on practical experience for this chapter appear in the *Workbook*.

CHAPTER 1

A Career as an Insurance Billing Specialist

Introduction

In the past, a medical assistant working in a physician's office performed both administrative and clinical duties. Then, as decades passed, he or she performed either one or the other. Now, various medical assisting job tasks have become specialized. It is commonplace to find administrative duties shared by a number of specialists: office manager, receptionist, file clerk, administrative medical assistant, transcriptionist, bookkeeper, insurance billing specialist, coding specialist, and so on. In some work settings, an insurance billing specialist may be known as an electronic claims processor, a medical biller, or a reimbursement specialist. In clinics and large practices, it is not uncommon to find many people who make up a billing department, and within the department each person is a specialist: Medicare billing specialist, Medicaid billing specialist, and so on.

Some medical practices and clinics contract with management services organizations (MSOs), which perform a variety of business functions, such as accounting, billing, coding, collections, computer support, legal advice, marketing, payroll, and management expertise. An insurance billing specialist may find a job working for an MSO as a part of this team.

Cost pressures on health care providers are forcing employers to reduce personnel costs by hiring multiskilled health practitioners (MSHPs). The knowledge of insurance claims completion and coding enhances skills so an individual can offer more flexibility to someone hiring in a medical setting.

There are also people called claims assistance professionals (CAPs), who work for the consumer and help patients organize, file, and negotiate health insurance claims of all types. Their primary goals are to assist the consumer in obtaining maximum benefits and to tell the patient what checks to write to providers to make sure there is no overpayment. A number of states require CAPs to be licensed depending on the services rendered to clients. CAPs who perform only the clerical function of filing health insurance claims do not have to be licensed except in Florida. CAPs who review, analyze existing or potential policies, and render advice, counseling, recommendations, and information may or may not require a license.

It is advisable to check with your state's insurance commissioner (see Chapter 8 and Appendix A) to make certain you are adhering to the licensing requirements of your state.

Front office duties have gained in importance for a number of reasons. First, documentation is vital to good patient care. It must be done comprehensively for proper reimbursement. Second, diagnostic and procedural coding must be performed accurately. Third, insurance claims must be filed promptly. Without money coming in, overhead expenses cannot be met and a practice would fold. Some offices have a collection manager or an insurance billing specialist who answers routine inquiries related to account balances and insurance file dates, assists patients in budgeting, and follows up on delinquent accounts by telephone and correspondence.

In large medical practices, an insurance billing specialist may act as an insurance counselor who takes the patient to a private area of the office to discuss the treatment and insurance coverage and negotiate a reasonable payment plan. The counselor finds out the deductible amount and verifies with the insurance company whether any predetermination, precertification, or second-opinion requirements exist. Counseling helps obtain payment in full when expensive procedures are completed.

A collection manager must have current knowledge of state and federal laws related to medical collections. Usually, clinical responsibilities are handled by a clinical medical assistant or shared with a registered nurse. This book focuses on the insurance billing and coding specialist.

Educational and Training Requirements

Generally, a high school diploma is required for an insurance billing and coding specialist. Additional education in medical and insurance terminology, insurance claims completion, procedural and diagnostic coding, anatomy and physiology, computer skills, and medicolegal knowledge is necessary. For one who seeks a job as a coder, completion of an accredited program for coding certification or an accredited health information medical record technology program is necessary.

For one who seeks a job as an insurance billing specialist, experience in coding and insurance claims completion and/or completion of a 1-year insurance specialist certificate program at a community college is preferred. The curriculum that might be offered in a 1-year certificate program is shown in Figure 1–1. Some community colleges have found the need in their communities for beginning 1-year certificate programs as either insurance/reimbursement or coding specialists. A 2-year educational course can result in obtaining an Associate degree. The training prepares an individual for a number of employment opportunities. If you are planning to become an electronic claims processor, then knowledge of computer hardware and software, electronic data transmission requirements, and health care claim reimbursement is necessary.

In 1990, the American Health Information Management Association (AHIMA) published diagnostic coding guidelines for outpatient services and diagnostic coding and reporting requirements for physician billing (Fig. 1–2). In 1992, coding guidelines known as the International Classification of Diseases, 9th Revision, Clinical Modification (ICD-9-CM) were approved by the cooperating parties (American Hospital Association, AHIMA, Health Care Financing Administration, and National Center for Health Statistics) (Fig. 1–3). A reading of these guidelines illustrates the knowledge and expertise one must acquire to become a coder.

If your goal is to become a claims assistance professional, it is necessary to have a moderate-to-high degree of knowledge of the health insurance business. In addition to insurance terminology, claims procedures, and coding, you must know commercial insurance carrier and Medicare policies and regulations. You will also need business skills, including marketing and sales expertise.

To reach a professional level, certification is available from eight national associations, depending on the type of certification desired.

MEDICAL INSURANCE SPECIALIST PROGRAM

CATALOG DESCRIPTION OF NEW CURRICULUM:

The Medical Insurance Specialist Program is a two-semester certificate program to prepare students for employment as medical insurance specialists in physicians' offices, hospital billing, outpatient departments, and insurance companies and also to upgrade the skills of persons presently employed in the medical field. Although this is planned as a full-time program, students may enroll in one or more daytime or evening courses per semester and proceed at their own pace to complete the requirements.

The following courses are included in this program:

First Semester

Medical Terminology	3 Credits
Medical Assistant I	4 Credits
Human Biology in Health and Diseases	5 Credits
Typewriting I or Keyboarding	3 Credits
	TOTAL 15 Credits

Second Semester

Principles and Applications of Medical Insurance	3 Credits
Current Issues in Medical Insurance	3 Credits
Medical Financial Management	3 Credits
Word Processing	3 Credits
English Composition 1	3 Credits
	TOTAL 15 Credits

FIGURE 1-1
Example of a 1-year medical insurance specialist certificate program offered at a community college. Basic coding is taught as a part of Medical Assistant I, and advanced coding is covered in Principles and Applications of Medical Insurance. (Reprinted with permission from Community College of Allegheny County, Pittsburgh, Pennsylvania.)

Career Advantages

Jobs are available in every state, ranging from nonmanagement to management positions. Insurance billing specialists can receive from $5,000 to $50,000 or more per year depending on knowledge, experience, locale, and size of the employing institution. Jobs are available in consulting firms, clinics, hospitals, multispecialty medical groups, and private physicians' practices and as instructors or lecturers. You can be your own boss by either setting up a business in your home or establishing an office.

Many people establish self-owned and operated businesses within their communities for insurance claim completion or electronic claim submission, or they work as a claims assistance professional. However, the responsibilities are greater in this area, because you have to set up the business, obtain clients, and advertise and market the business.

Personal Qualifications

Insurance claims competition is a skill. One needs a working knowledge of medical terminology, including anatomy and physiology, as well as disease and treatment (e.g., surgical, drug, laboratory)

AMERICAN HEALTH INFORMATION MANAGEMENT ASSOCIATION

ICD-9-CM AND CPT-HCPCS AMBULATORY CARE CODING COMPETENCIES

ICD-9-CM - International Classification of Diseases - 9th revision, Clinical Modification, Volumes 1 and 2, Superintendent of Documents, US Government Printing Office, P. Box 371954, Pittsburgh, PA 15250-7954, (202) 783-3238.
Volume 3, American Health Information Management Association, 919 N. Michigan Avenue, Suite 1400, Chicago, IL 60611, (312) 787-2672.
CPT - Current Procedural Terminology, American Medical Association 515 N. State St., Chicago, IL 60610, (800) 621-8335.
HCPCS - HCFA *[Health Care Financing Administration] Common Procedure Coding System-Level Two* Superintendent of Documents, US Government Printing Office, Washington, DC 20402. (202) 783-3238

ICD-9-CM DIAGNOSTIC CODING

1. Read and interpret medical record documentation to identify all diagnoses, conditions, problems, or other reasons for the ambulatory care encounter/visit.
2. Assess the adequacy of medical record documentation to ensure that it supports the diagnoses, conditions, problems, or other reasons for an ambulatory care encounter/visit assigned codes.
3. Clarify conflicting or ambiguous information appearing in a medical record by consulting the appropriate physician.
4. Apply the Basic Coding Guidelines for Outpatient Services* and Diagnostic Coding and Reporting Requirements for Physician Billing* to select and sequence diagnoses, conditions, problems, or other reasons which require coding in an ambulatory care encounter/visit.
5. Exclude from coding diagnoses, conditions, and problems which are no longer being treated or which have no bearing on the management of the current ambulatory care encounter/visit.
6. Apply knowledge of ICD-9-CM instructional notations and conventions to locate and assign the correct diagnostic codes and sequence them correctly.
7. Apply knowledge of anatomy, clinical disease process, and diagnostic terminology to assign accurate codes to each individual diagnosis, condition, problem, or other reason for encounter/visit.
8. Apply knowledge of disease processes to assign non-indexed medical terms to the appropriate class in the classification system.
9. Conduct quality assessment to ensure continuous improvement in ICD-9-CM coding and collection of quality health data.

CPT/HCPCS PROCEDURAL CODING

1. Read and interpret medical record documentation to identify all services and procedures performed during the ambulatory care encounter/visit.
2. Assess the adequacy of medical record documentation to ensure that it supports the procedures and services assigned codes.
3. Clarify conflicting, ambiguous, or non-specific information appearing in a medical record by consulting the appropriate physician.
4. Apply knowledge of CPT format, guidelines, and notes, to locate the correct codes for all services and procedures performed during the encounter/visit and sequence them correctly.
5. Apply knowledge of the HCPCS-Level Two (alphanumeric) coding system, if applicable, to locate the correct procedural codes and sequence them correctly.
6. Apply knowledge of anatomy and procedural terminology to assign accurate codes to procedures.
7. Apply knowledge of procedural terminology to recognize when an unlisted procedure code must be used in CPT.
8. Refuse to unfairly maximize reimbursement by unbundling services and codes that do not conform to CPT basic coding principles and payer reimbursement guidelines.
9. Apply knowledge of payer reimbursement guidelines to ensure optional reimbursement.
10. Conduct quality assessment to ensure continuous improvement in CPT/HCPCS-Level Two coding.

* *Diagnostic Coding Guidelines for Outpatient Services* and *Diagnostic Coding and Reporting Requirements for Physician Billing* were published in the First Quarter 1990 *Coding Clinic for ICD-9-CM* (Vol. 7, No. 1), a quarterly publication of the Central Office on ICD-9-CM at the American Hospital Association and the October 1990 *Journal of the American Medical Record Association.*

January 1, 1992

FIGURE 1–2
Diagnostic coding guidelines for outpatient services and diagnostic coding and reporting requirements for physician billing. (Reprinted with permission from the American Health Information Management Association, Chicago, Illinois, as published in the First Quarter 1990 *Coding Clinic for ICD-9-CM* [Vol. 7, No. 1].)

AMERICAN HEALTH INFORMATION MANAGEMENT ASSOCIATION

ICD-9-CM INPATIENT CODING COMPETENCIES

ICD-9-CM - International Classification of Diseases - 9th revision - Clinical Modification, Volumes 1 and 2, Superintendent of Documents, US Government Printing Office, PO Box 371954, Pittsburgh, PA 15250-7954, (202) 783-3238.

Volume 3, American Health Information Management Association, 919 N. Michigan Avenue, Suite 1400, Chicago, IL 60611, (312) 787-2672.

1. Read and interpret medical record documentation to identify all diagnoses and significant procedures that affect the current inpatient stay.
2. Assess the adequacy of medical record documentation to ensure that it supports all diagnoses and procedures assigned codes.
3. Clarify conflicting, ambiguous or non-specific information appearing in a medical record by consulting the appropriate physician.
4. Apply Uniform Hospital Discharge Data Set definitions to select the principal diagnosis, principal procedure, complications and comorbid conditions, other diagnoses and significant procedures which require coding.
5. Exclude from coding diagnoses or procedures related to an earlier episode of care which have no bearing on the current episode of care.
6. Exclude from coding nonsurgical, noninvasive procedures which carry no operative or anesthetic risk.
7. Exclude from coding information, such as symptoms or signs characteristic of the diagnosis, findings from diagnostic studies, or localized conditions, which has no bearing on the current management of the patient.
8. Apply knowledge of ICD-9-CM instructional notations and conventions to locate and assign the correct diagnostic and procedural codes and sequence them correctly.
9. Apply knowledge of current approved* ICD-9-CM coding guidelines to assign and sequence the correct diagnosis and procedure codes.
10. Apply knowledge of anatomy, clinical disease processes, and diagnostic and procedural terminology to assign accurate codes to diagnoses and procedures.
11. Select the appropriate principal diagnosis for episodes of care in which determination of the principal diagnosis is not clear-cut because the patient has multiple problems.
12. Apply knowledge of disease processes to assign non-indexed medical terms to the appropriate class in the classification system.
13. Facilitate comprehensive retrieval by recognizing when more than one code is required to adequately classify a given condition.
14. Apply knowledge of prospective payment system to confirm DRG assignment which ensures optimal reimbursement.
15. Refuse to fraudulently maximize reimbursement by assigning codes that do not conform to approved coding principles/guidelines.
16. Conduct quality assessment to ensure continuous improvement in ICD-9-CM coding and collection of quality health data.

* ICD-9-CM coding guidelines approved by the cooperating parties (American Hospital Association, American Health Information Management Association, Health Care Financing Administration, and National Center for Health Statistics) are published in *Coding Clinic for ICD-9-CM*, a quarterly publication of the Central Office on ICD-9-CM at the American Hospital Association.

January 1, 1992

FIGURE 1–3

ICD-9-CM Inpatient Coding Competencies. (Reprinted with permission from the American Health Information Management Association, Chicago, Illinois, as published in *Coding Clinic for ICD-9-CM,* January 1, 1992.)

terms to be proficient in completing insurance claims. The individual learns billing and collection techniques. In addition, the insurance billing specialist works to become an expert in using procedural and diagnostic code books.

Medicolegal knowledge is important to avoid filing fraudulent claims. It is vital to know the legalities of collection on accounts to avoid lawsuits. Basic mathematics is necessary because fees entered on the claim are totaled and, if necessary, ledgers are adjusted. It is essential that these figures be accurate. Because the industry is increasingly heading toward electronic claims submission, basic typing or keyboarding and computer skills are needed; handwritten claims are a format of the past.

Medical Etiquette

Before beginning work as an insurance billing specialist, it is wise to have a basic knowledge of medical etiquette as it pertains to the medical profession, the insurance industry, and the coder. *Medical etiquette* has to do with the customs, rules of conduct, courtesy, and manners of the medical profession. It can be expressed in three simple words: *consideration for others.*

Several points about medical etiquette bear mentioning:

1. Never keep another physician waiting longer than necessary in the reception room. Usher him or her into the physician's office as soon as the latter is free.
2. Always connect another physician on the telephone to your physician immediately without asking the reason for the call. The only exception to this is if you know the physician calling is treating one of your patients and you wish to verify the name to pull the chart for your physician.
3. Follow the basic rules of etiquette with coworkers while working in the office, such as acknowledging people who enter your office or come to your desk by saying "I'll be with you in a moment."
4. Identify yourself to callers and to those you call.
5. Do not be too casual by using first names until you know it is appropriate to do so.
6. Keep a professional demeanor and maintain a certain amount of formality when interacting with others. Remember to be courteous and always project a professional image.

Medical Ethics

The earliest written code of ethical principles and conduct for the medical profession originated in Babylonia about 2500 B.C. and is called the Code of Hammurabi. Then, in about the fifth century B.C., Hippocrates, a Greek physician who is known as the Father of Medicine, conceived the Oath of Hippocrates (Fig. 1–4).

In 1980, the American Medical Association (AMA) adopted a modern code of ethics called the Principles of Medical Ethics for the benefit of the health professional and to meet the needs of changing times. The following Principles of Medical Ethics of the AMA guides physicians' standards of conduct for honorable behavior in the practice of medicine.

Preamble:

The medical profession has long subscribed to a body of ethical statements developed primarily for the benefit of the patient. As a member of the profession, a physician must recognize responsibility not only to patients, but also to society, to other health professionals, and to self. The following Principles adopted by the American Medical Association are not laws, but standards of conduct which define the essentials of honorable behavior for the physician:

I. A physician shall be dedicated to providing competent medical service with compassion and respect for human dignity.

II. A physician shall deal honestly with patients and colleagues, and strive to expose those physicians deficient in character or competence, or who engage in fraud or deception.

III. A physician shall respect the law and also recognize a responsibility to seek changes in those requirements which are contrary to the best interests of the patient.

IV. A physician shall respect the rights of patients, of colleagues, and of other health professionals, and shall safeguard patient confidences within the constraints of the law.

V. A physician shall continue to study, apply and advance scientific knowledge, make relevant information available to patients, colleagues, and the public, obtain consultation, and use the talents of other health professionals when indicated.

VI. A physician shall, in the provision of appropriate patient care, except in emergencies, be free to choose whom to serve, with whom to associate, and the environment in which to provide medical services.

VII. A physician shall recognize a responsibility to participate in activities contributing to an improved community.

Medical ethics are not laws but rather are standards of conduct generally accepted as a moral guide for behavior by which an insurance billing or

The Oath of Hippocrates

I swear by Apollo, the physician, and Aesculapius and health and all-heal and all the Gods and Goddesses that, according to my ability and judgment, I will keep this oath and stipulation:

TO RECKON him who taught me this art equally dear to me as my parents, to share my substance with him and relieve his necessities if required; to regard his offspring as on the same footing with my own brothers, and to teach them this art if they should wish to learn it, without fee or stipulation, and that by precept, lecture and every other mode of instruction, I will impart a knowledge of the art to my own sons and to those of my teachers, and to disciples bound by a stipulation and oath, according to the law of medicine, but to none others.

I WILL FOLLOW that method of treatment which, according to my ability and judgment, I consider for the benefit of my patients, and abstain from whatever is deleterious and mischievous. I will give no deadly medicine to anyone if asked, nor suggest any such counsel; furthermore, I will not give to a woman an instrument to produce abortion.

WITH PURITY AND WITH HOLINESS I will pass my life and practice my art. I will not cut a person who is suffering from a stone, but will leave this to be done by practitioners of this work. Into whatever houses I enter I will go into them for the benefit of the sick and will abstain from every voluntary act of mischief and corruption; and further from the seduction of females or males, bond or free.

WHATEVER, in connection with my professional practice, or not in connection with it, I may see or hear in the lives of men which ought not to be spoken abroad I will not divulge, as reckoning that all such should be kept secret.

WHILE I CONTINUE to keep this oath unviolated may it be granted to me to enjoy life and the practice of the art, respected by all men at all times but should I trespass and violate this oath, may the reverse be my lot.

FIGURE 1-4
The Oath of Hippocrates.

coding specialist may determine the propriety of his or her conduct in a relationship with patients, the physician, coworkers, the government, and insurance companies. Acting with ethical behavior means to carry out responsibilities with integrity, honesty, competence, respect, fairness, trust, and courage. Early in 1991 the National Association of Claims Assistance Professionals, Inc. formed an association and developed a code of ethics for claims assistance professionals, as shown in Figure 1-5. In a 1990 newsletter, the California Health Information Association published a statement of ethical coding principles (Fig. 1-6 A and B).

It is the coder's responsibility to inform administration or his or her immediate supervisor if unethical or possible illegal coding practices are taking place. Illegal activities are subject to penalties, fines, and/or imprisonment and can result in loss of morale, reputation, and the goodwill of the community. It is *illegal* to report incorrect information to government-funded programs, such as Medicare, Medicaid, and CHAMPUS. However, it is *unethical*, not illegal, to report incorrect information to private insurance carriers because this can possibly damage the individual and the integrity of the database, may allow reimbursement for services that should be

NACAP

NATIONAL ASSOCIATION *of* CLAIMS ASSISTANCE PROFESSIONALS, INC.

Code of Ethics

PREAMBLE: Those engaged in health insurance claims processing occupy the unique position of liaison between the purchaser, the supplier and the provider of health care services. In this role, it is the professional duty of a member of the National Association of Claims Assistance Professionals to voluntarily endorse and abide by the **NACAP** Code of Ethics.

I Believe It Is My Responsibility To:

Provide accurate and honest information essential to my client.

Protect the personal, medical and financial information supplied by my client and use such information only to the betterment of my client.

Obtain written consent for the disclosure of personal, medical or financial information from my client or their representative.

Provide client information only to those insurers, government agencies, health care providers, facilities or other entities specified by my client and deemed necessary for the resolution and payment of health insurance claims for my client.

Never willingly or knowingly be party to the submission of fraudulent claims information to insurers, government agencies or health care providers.

Serve as agent for my client and solely represent my client's interests.

Advance my knowledge through continuing education.

Raise the standards of my profession through the ethical conduct of my business, including the explanation of services I will render and the disclosure of fees for such services and fees for additional services in advance of performing them.

Avoid conflict of interest situations by disclosing to my client any affiliations I have with an insurance company.

Maintain current knowledge of applicable laws and regulations and observe them in the practice of my profession.

Cooperate with other professionals whose services relate to meeting the needs of my client.

KNOWLEDGE IS POWER

FIGURE 1–5
Code of Ethics of the National Association of Claims Assistance Professionals, Inc. (NACAP), Downers Grove, Illinois. Reprinted with permission.

RESOLUTION

Statement of Ethical Coding Principles

WHEREAS, various coding and classification systems (e.g., *ICD-9-CM, CPT, DSM-IIIR,* etc.) are being used for reimbursement of healthcare, evaluation of quality of care, strategic planning, and medical research, and are reported to state data commissions, payors, and other agencies;

WHEREAS, Health Information/Medical Record Professionals and/or Certified Coding Specialists (hereinafter referred to as Health Information Professionals) identify the following coding practices as ethical behavior:

Following published national and state coding guidelines (provided that state guidelines do not conflict with published national coding guidelines);

Selecting or sequencing codes, according to approved coding guidelines, and not on a basis solely to maximize reimbursement potential;

Recording codes only for diagnoses or procedures documented in the health care record.

IT IS HEREBY RESOLVED THAT

Health Information Professionals have an obligation to inform their immediate designated authority within their organization when they are aware that unethical coding practices are occurring;

Health Information Professionals are responsible for assuring that coding which they perform or which is performed by personnel under their direction occurs in an ethical fashion.

PREPARED BY: Coding and Reimbursement Committee *January 29, 1992*
ADOPTED BY: House of Delegates *May 31, 1992*

FIGURE 1–6A
Statement of Ethical Coding Principles. (Courtesy of the California Health Information Association, Fresno, CA, 1996.)

paid by the patient, or can deny payment that should be made by the insurance company.

Some examples of illegal or unethical coding are

1. Violating guidelines by using code numbers or modifiers to increase payment when the case documentation does not warrant it.
2. Coding procedures for payment that were not performed at your facility.
3. Unbundling services provided into separate codes when one code is available.
4. Failure to code a relevant condition or complication when it is documented in the medical record.
5. Coding a service for it to be covered when it usually is not covered.
6. Coding another condition as the principal diagnosis when the majority of the patient's treatment is for a preexisting condition.

In 1985, the AHIMA adopted a code of ethics for those who handle medical records (Fig. 1–7). Because some insurance billing specialists also have medical assistant responsibilities, the American Association of Medical Assistants, Inc. (AAMA) has established a code of ethics that is appropriate for medical assistants regardless of whether they are members of the association (Fig. 1–8).

CONFIDENTIALITY

Like anyone working with medical records of patients, the insurance billing specialist must be responsible for maintaining confidentiality of privileged communication. Privileged communication is a confidential communication that may be disclosed only with the patient's permission. Everything you see, hear, or read about patients remains confidential and does not leave the office. Never talk about patients or data contained in medical records where others may overhear. Some employers require employees to sign a confidentiality agreement (Fig. 1–9).

If a telephone inquiry is made about a patient, ask

RESOLUTION

Responsibility for Coding of Clinical Data

WHEREAS, various coding and classification systems (e.g., *ICD-9-CM*, *CPT*, *DSM-IIIR*, etc.) are being used for reimbursement of healthcare, evaluation of quality of care, strategic planning, and medical research, and are reported to state data commissions, payors, and other agencies;

WHEREAS, the linkage of coded clinical data with financial data is increasingly important for financial planning, technology assessment, and market development; and

WHEREAS, coding of diagnoses and procedures is complex and requires technical skills;

IT IS HEREBY RESOLVED THAT

Coding of diagnoses and procedures should be performed only by Health Information/Medical Record Professionals and/or Certified Coding Specialists (hereinafter referred to as Health Information Professionals);

When coding by Health Information Professionals is impractical, coding shall be done only by personnel who have been trained by Health Information Professionals;

Health Information Professionals shall ensure that:

Coding of diagnoses and procedures is based on a review of the complete medical record;

Assignment and sequencing of codes are done according to approved coding guidelines;

Inquiries regarding the accuracy of codes are reviewed and corrective action taken;

The confidentiality of the coded clinical data is protected.

The California Health Information Association shall support data quality assurance by:

Filling position statements with appropriate health care organizations, government agencies, third-party payors, fiscal intermediaries, etc., asserting that they should accept clinical data coded only by Health Information Professionals, Certified Coding Specialists, or personnel trained by Health Information Professionals;

Making available coding training programs to assure that sufficient training is provided to personnel at all levels of healthcare;

Providing in its publications and training programs the latest coding information, references and resource materials;

Promoting the Health Information Professional's efforts to enhance coding skills and training at the highest professional level.

PREPARED BY: Coding and Reimbursement Committee *January 29, 1992*
ADOPTED BY: House of Delegates *May 31, 1992*

FIGURE 1-6B
Responsibility for Coding of Clinical Data. (Courtesy of the California Health Information Association, Fresno, CA, 1996.)

the caller to put the request in writing and include the patient's signed authorization. If the caller refuses, have the physician return the call. If a relative telephones asking about a patient, have the physician return the call. It is important never to discuss patient information other than with the physician or an insurance company that has been authorized by the patient. When telephoning a patient about an insurance matter and voice mail is reached, use care in the choice of words when leaving the message in the event the call was inadvertently received at the wrong number.

Do not discuss a patient's condition within hearing distance of others. Do not discuss a patient with

AMERICAN HEALTH INFORMATION MANAGEMENT ASSOCIATION

CODE OF ETHICS

Preamble: The health information management professional abides by a set of ethical principles developed to safeguard the public and to contribute within the scope of the profession to quality and efficiency in health care. This code of ethics, adopted by the members of the American Health Information Management Association, defines the standards of behavior which promote ethical conduct.

1. The health information management professional demonstrates behavior that reflects integrity, supports objectivity, and fosters trust in professional activities.
2. The health information management professional respects the dignity of each human being.
3. The health information management professional strives to improve personal competence and quality of services.
4. The health information management professional represents truthfully and accurately professional credentials, education, and experience.
5. The health information management professional refuses to participate in illegal or unethical acts and also refuses to conceal the illegal, incompetent, or unethical acts of others.
6. The health information management professional protects the confidentiality of primary and secondary health records as mandated by law, professional standards, and the employer's policies.
7. The health information management professional promotes to others the tenets of confidentiality.
8. The health information management professional adheres to pertinent laws and regulations while advocating changes which serve the best interest of the public.
9. The health information management professional encourages appropriate use of health record information and advocates policies and systems that advance the management of health records and health information.
10. The health information management professional recognizes and supports the Association's mission.

Amended December, 1991

FIGURE 1-7
Code of Ethics of the American Health Information Management Association, Chicago, Illinois (a national organization). Reprinted with permission.

acquaintances—yours or the patient's. Do not leave patients' records or appointment books exposed on your desk. If confidential documents are on your desk that patients can see easily as they walk by, either flip the documents over or lock them in a secure drawer when you leave your desk, even if you are gone for only a few moments. If patient information is on your computer, save it on disk, lock the disk away, and clear the information from the screen. Properly dispose of notes, papers, and memos by using a shredding device. Be careful when using the copying machine because it is easy to forget to remove the original insurance claim or medical record from the document glass. Use common sense and follow the guidelines mentioned in this chapter to help you keep your professional credibility and integrity.

The few exceptions to the right of privacy and

Members of this association dedicated to the conscientious pursuit of their profession, and thus desiring to merit the high regard of the entire medical profession and the respect of the general public which they serve, do pledge themselves to strive always to:

1. Render service to humanity with full respect for the dignity of person.
2. Respect confidential information gained through employment unless legally authorized or required by responsible performance of duty to divulge such information.
3. Uphold the honor and high principles of the profession and accept its disciplines.
4. Seek to continually improve the knowledge and skills of medical assisting for the benefit of patients and professional colleagues.
5. Participate in additional service activities which aim toward improving the health and well-being of the community.

FIGURE 1-8
Principles of medical ethics for medical assistants as established by the American Association of Medical Assistants, Inc., Chicago, Illinois. Reprinted with permission.

privileged communication are patient records of physicians employed by insurance companies (industrial cases); reports of communicable diseases; child abuse; gunshot wounds, and stabbings resulting from criminal actions; and diseases and ailments of newborns and infants. Also, any medical information obtained by a Medicare insurance carrier is subject to disclosure to the beneficiary to whom that information pertains. Medical information *cannot* be accepted by a Medicare insurance carrier from physicians on a confidential basis, either expressed or implied. Even if medical information is marked "Confidential," the Medicare insurance carrier must still disclose it to the beneficiary or his representative on request, either directly or through designated professional medical personnel.

Nonprivileged information consists of ordinary facts unrelated to treatment of the patient. This might include the patient's name, city of residence, and dates of admission or discharge. The patient's authorization is not needed *unless* the record is in a specialty hospital or in a special service unit of a general hos-

EMPLOYEE CONFIDENTIALITY STATEMENT

As an employee of ______________________________(employer), and having been trained as an insurance billing specialist with employee responsibilities and authorization to access personal medical and health information, I recognize that violation of confidentiality statutes and rules may lead to immediate dismissal from employment and, depending on state laws, criminal prosecution. I understand that such violation may cause irreparable damage to my employer, and the employer and any other injured party may seek legal action against me. I acknowledge that this signed document will be placed in my personnel file at this facility.

______________________ Signature

______________________ Witness signature

______________________ Print Name

______________________ Date

FIGURE 1-9
An example of an employee confidentiality agreement that may be used by an employer when he or she is hiring an insurance billing specialist.

pital, such as the psychiatric unit. Professional judgment is required, and the information is disclosed on a legitimate "need-to-know" basis.

Privileged information is related to the treatment and progress of the patient. The patient must sign an authorization to release the information or selected facts and not the entire record. Some states have passed laws allowing test results to be placed separate from the patient's medical record. A special authorization form to release this information (e.g., test results disclosing the presence of the human immunodeficiency virus [HIV] or alcohol or substance abuse) is used.

Some additional principles of ethics for the medical assistant and insurance billing specialist are as follows:

- Never make critical remarks about a physician to a patient.
- Be neat, clean, and dignified; do not belittle patients.
- If you discover that a patient of your physician employer is under the care of another physician for the same ailment, it is your duty to notify your physician because it is unethical for two physicians to treat the same patient for the same condition.
- Maintain a dignified, courteous relationship with all persons in the office—patients, staff, and the physician—as well as with insurance adjusters, pharmaceutical representatives, and others who come into or telephone the office.
- Do not collect payment from another physician or members of his or her family for services unless your employer tells you to do so.
- Do not make critical statements about the treatment given a patient by another physician.

Professionalism

PERSONAL IMAGE

To project a professional image, be attentive to apparel and grooming. If a person works at home, the tendency is to dress casually (e.g., blue jeans, sneakers, shorts, tank tops, etc.). However, in a work setting, business attire that is conservative and stylish but not trendy is appropriate. For women, this includes a business suit or dress, knee-length or longer skirts; slacks; sweaters; blouses; and dress shoes; for men, a business suit, shirt, tie (optional), and dress shoes are appropriate.

It is important that hair be clean and in a style that flatters. Because fragrances can be offensive to some clients and patients, they should be used minimally. Fingernails should be carefully manicured. For a woman, subdued eye makeup is appropriate for day use. Long artificial nails are generally not considered to be part of a professional image; clear or muted polish without glued-on designs or rhinestones is acceptable.

For either sex, jewelry should be simple, and dangling earrings are avoided. A professional pin is frequently worn at professional functions.

CERTIFICATION

During 1996, a national organization for individuals that bill for physicians and clinics was in formative stages. One of its goals is to establish a national certification program for medical billers. Information on membership may be obtained by writing or calling:

American Association of Medical Billers (AAMB)
642 South Sunset, Suite B
West Covina, CA 91790
Telephone: 1-888-BILLERS

A number of certifications are available on a national level, depending on how you wish to specialize. For further information on membership and how to obtain titles such as a Certified Claims Assistance Professional (CCAP) or Certified Electronic Claims Professional (CECP), contact:

National Association of Claims Assistance Professionals, Inc. (NACAP)
5329 S. Main Street, Suite 102
Downers Grove, IL 60515-4845
Telephone: 708-963-3500

If you decide to specialize as a coder, certification by examination from two national associations is available. For further information regarding membership, independent study programs, and becoming either a Certified Procedural Coder (CPC) or Certified Coding Specialist (CCS), contact the following organization:

American Academy of Procedural Coders (AAPC)
145 West Crystal Avenue
Salt Lake City, UT 84115
Telephone: 1-800-626-CODE

American Health Information Management Association (AHIMA)
P.O. Box 97349
Chicago, IL 60690-7349
Telephone: 1-800-621-6828

To become a member of the AHIMA Society for Clinical Coding (SCC), write or telephone (1-800-574-1027) for an application and datasheet.

Individuals who become certified by any of these associations must participate in an ongoing program of continuing medical education in health information management to increase their knowledge of coding and the changes taking place in various insurance programs (e.g., Medicare, Medicaid, CHAMPUS, and so on). Depending on the policies of the certifying association, the individual recertifies either annually or every 3 to 5 years by meeting established requirements. For example, AAPC's annual renewal requires 18 continuing education credits and payment of a fee, whereas NACAP requires renewal every 5 years.

In some medical practices, job duties may overlap (i.e., a front office assistant might carry out receptionist responsibilities as well as billing and coding duties). Many of these assistants obtain certification or become registered by national associations. In some states, there may be certification by a state organization. To become a Certified Medical Assistant (CMA), one must have worked in the field for 1 year or have graduated from an accredited school recognized by the AAMA and then apply to take the national certifying examination in medical assisting. Applications, membership, and further information may be obtained from

American Association of Medical Assistants, Inc. (AAMA)
20 N. Wacker Drive
Chicago, IL 60606
Telephone: 1-800-228-2262

To become a Registered Medical Assistant (RMA), one must take the certification examination offered by the American Medical Technologists (AMT). For further information, contact

Registered Medical Assistant/AMT
710 Higgins Road
Park Ridge, IL 60068
Telephone: 847-823-5169

Some medical transcriptionists type as well as code and complete insurance claims. To obtain additional information on membership and how to become a Certified Medical Transcriptionist (CMT), write to

American Association for Medical Transcription (AAMT)
P.O. Box 576187
Modesto, CA 95357
Telephone: 1-800-982-2182

Another national, state, and regional organization is the American Guild of Patient Account Management (AGPAM). This organization promotes the recognition of patient account managers who are responsible for the management of patient accounts in hospitals and in physicians' practices. A certification program is offered for hospital and medical business office personnel in either managerial or technical (nonmanagerial) careers. The AGPAM self-study course leads to designation as any one of the following: Certified Patient Account Technician (CPAT), Certified Clinic Account Technician (CCAT), Certified Patient Account Manager (CPAM), or Certified Clinic Account Manager (CCAM). Standard examinations are administered twice a year. For information on eligibility requirements, application forms, and information, write to

American Guild of Patient Account Management (AGPAM)
National Certification Examination Program
1101 Connecticut Avenue, NW, Suite 700
Washington, D.C. 20036
Telephone: 202-857-1179

If working in a managerial or supervisory capacity, you may wish to become a member of a national association for medical office managers of small-group and solo practices. For further information about the examination to obtain credentials as a Certified Medical Office Manager (CMOM), write to

Professional Association of Health Care Office Managers (PAHCOM)
461 E. Ten Mile Road
Pensacola, FL 32534-9714
Telephone: 1-800-451-9311

A national organization that supports the development of medical practice administration is Medical Group Management Association (MGMA). Membership is available to persons working in the group management field. It has groups that are focused by specialty and profession, for example, an individual may belong to the Cardiovascular and Thoracic Surgery group as well as the Financial Management group. An affiliated organization is American College of Medical Practice Executives (ACMPE). It is a professional organization for group practice administrators with three levels of membership. The primary or entry level is called nominee. After successfully completing a 6 to 7 hour examination, a nominee moves to certified member and is eligible to use the initials CMPE after his or her name. The final level is fellow and requires the completion of either a mentoring project or thesis. It offers a professional certification process that aims at personal development and provides the employer with a baseline when searching for candidates for a new position. Information may be obtained from the following:

Medical Group Management Association (MGMA)
104 Inverness Terrace East
Englewood, CO 80112
Telephone: 303-799-1111
Fax: 303-643-4427
Web site http://www.mgma.com

American College of Medical Practice Executives (ACMPE)
104 Inverness Terrace East
Englewood, CO 80112
Telephone: 303-397-7869
Fax: 303-643-4427

An organization established in 1992 for professional billing businesses or services that support the billing services industry is the International Billing Association, Inc. (IBA). This trade association has been formed to promote the general welfare of the billing industry. IBA is working to give the billing industry a unified voice and to structure effective communication with the Health Care Financing Administration and the health care industry. Members agree to abide by a strict code of ethics. A pilot certification program will be offered by the California chapter in the latter part of 1996, and it will be a model for a national certification program. After completing a comprehensive program and taking the proficiency test, a passing candidate receives the title Certified Medical Billing Associate (CMBA). For complete information about eligibility requirements for membership and its benefits, contact

International Billing Association, Inc.
7315 Wisconsin Avenue, Suite 424 East
Bethesda, MD 20814
Telephone: 301-961-8680

For information about certification, contact

California Chapter of International Billing Association, Inc.
917 San Ramon Valley Boulevard, Suite 290
Danville, CA 94526
Telephone: 510-837-7254

Keeping Current

Membership in any of the aforementioned organizations helps in keeping up to date and increases the benefits of networking with those working in the field. Most of these associations have student as well as active and associate membership categories. You can inquire whether there is a local chapter or state organization affiliated with the national association. Benefits of belonging to a professional organization in addition to certification include problem solving and employment opportunities through networking. Local meetings can keep you knowledgeable by providing guest speakers on topics of current interest. The newsletters and journals published by these organizations keep you abreast of current trends either as a subscriber or as a benefit when becoming a member. For further information on networking, see the end of Chapter 17. See Appendix B for a list of publications that will assist you in your work as an insurance billing or coding specialist.

TO THE STUDENT

Read Introduction in the *Workbook,* which explains how you will be working as an insurance billing specialist during this course. Study Chapter 1 and then answer the review questions in the *Workbook* to reinforce the theory learned in this chapter and to help prepare you for a future test. As you proceed through the assignments in the *Workbook,* you will broaden your knowledge of medical terminology as well as gain an entry-level skill in diagnostic and procedural coding and insurance claims completion. Assignment 1 is offered to help develop critical thinking and writing skills. For further knowledge and understanding, the key terms at the beginning of the chapter appear in the Glossary at the end of this textbook so you can look up the pertinent terms.

Objectives*

THE INSURANCE BILLING SPECIALIST WILL BE ABLE TO:

- Translate the Latin phrase *respondeat superior.*
- State four concepts of a valid insurance contract.
- Explain the difference between an implied and expressed physician-patient contract.
- Explain the techniques used for fax confidentiality.
- Identify the principles for release and retention of medical records.
- Respond appropriately to the subpoena of a witness and records.
- List four actions to prevent problems when given signature authorization for insurance claims.
- List various types of insurance fraud.
- Define abuse under the Medicare program.
- State components necessary for an audit trail.
- Explain arbitration.
- Formulate a procedure for termination of a case.
- Prepare legally correct medicolegal forms and letters.
- Describe how to prevent malpractice claims.
- Define key legal terms.

Key Terms

abuse
arbitration
assumption of risk
bonding
breach of confidential communication
breach of contract
breach of duty
civil law
embezzlement
felony
fraud
grievance committee
invasion of privacy
libel
litigation
medical record
negligence
phantom billing
qui tam action
respondeat superior
statute of limitations
subpoena
subpoena duces tecum

* Performance objectives and exercises for hands-on practical experience for this chapter appear in the *Workbook.*

CHAPTER 2

Legal Issues Affecting Insurance Claims and Medical Records

Introduction

Before developing the skill of coding and completing insurance claim forms, it is necessary to know some of the legal situations that might be encountered and how to handle them. The role of an insurance billing specialist is to complete the insurance claim accurately and to facilitate claims submission so reimbursement is received quickly. However, legal situations are encountered daily in the performance of these job duties and involve confidentiality of medical documents, insurance contracts, release of medical records, insurance claim completion, fraud and abuse, credit and collection laws, and so on. An insurance billing specialist cannot escape liability by pleading ignorance. It cannot be overemphasized that keeping up-to-date on health care plan policies and procedures is essential.

A claims assistance professional (CAP) acts as an informal representative of patients (policyholders and Medicare beneficiaries) and does not interpret insurance contracts or act as an attorney. The legal ability of a CAP to represent a policyholder is limited. When a claim cannot be resolved after a denied claim has been appealed to the insurance company, the CAP must be careful in rendering a personal opinion or advising clients that they have a right to pursue legal action. In some states, a CAP could be acting outside the scope of the law by giving advice to clients on legal issues even if licensed as an attorney but not practicing law full time. If the client wishes to take legal action, it is his or her responsibility to find a competent attorney specializing in contract law and insurance.

In some states, giving an insured client advice on purchase or discontinuance of insurance policies is construed as being an insurance agent. The National Association of Claims Assistance Professionals, Inc., advises CAPs to contact the state department of insurance to determine whether the state laws require licensure.

The first half of this chapter discusses legalities dealing specifically with insurance claims and medical records. Most legal issues of health insurance claims fall under civil law. Insurance is regulated by state laws and is not considered a federally regulated industry. The second half of this chapter emphasizes some malpractice issues as well as measures for preventing medical professional liability (malpractice) as it relates to this specific career field. The information is intended only as a general outline of the various legal matters in which the insurance billing specialist may be involved. It is not a substitute for legal advice, and the physician and his or her insurance billing specialist should always seek the counsel of an attorney about specific questions of law as they relate to medical practice.

Employer Liability

As mentioned in Chapter 1, insurance billing specialists can be either self-employed or employed by physicians, clinics, or hospitals. Physicians are legally responsible for their own conduct and for any actions of their employees performed within the context of their employment. This is referred to as vicarious liability, also known as *respondeat superior,* which literally means "let the master answer." However, this does not mean that an employee cannot be sued or brought to trial. Actions of the insurance billing specialist may have a definite legal ramification on the employer depending on the situation. For example, if an employee knowingly submits a fraudulent Medicare or Medicaid claim at the direction of the employer and subsequently the business is audited, the employer and the employee can be brought into litigation by the state or federal government. All insurance billing specialists should check with their physician employers to see whether the specialist is included in the medical professional liability insurance policy. If they are not included, they could be sued as individuals. It is up to the physician to make certain that all staff members are protected.

If you are working as a CAP who does not handle checks or cash, inquire about an errors and omissions insurance policy by contacting the National Association of Claims Assistance Professionals, Inc.* *Errors and omissions insurance* is protection against loss of monies due to failure through error or unintentional omission on the part of the CAP.

Insurance billing specialists and CAPs who handle checks or cash should be bonded and insured.

If you are employed as a medical assistant who is submitting insurance claims, further information on professional liability insurance is available through the American Association of Medical Assistants, Inc.†

Insurance Policies (Contracts)

The first legal item in the business of handling medical insurance is the insurance contract. There is no standard health insurance contract. Individuals who take out a policy receive an original document composed by the insuring company.

There are four considerations involved in drawing up a valid insurance contract:

1. The person must be a mentally competent adult and not under the influence of drugs or alcohol.
2. The insurance company must make an offer (the signed application), and the person must accept the offer (issuance of the policy), without concealment or misrepresentation of facts on the application.
3. An exchange of value (the first premium payment) submitted with the application, known as a *consideration,* must be present.
4. A legal purpose must exist, which, in the case of a health insurance policy, is an insurable interest. This means the policyholder expects to continue in good health, but if an accident or illness strikes, the insurance policy provides something of value.

* 4724 Florence Avenue, Downers Grove, IL 60515.
† 20 N. Wacker Drive, Chicago, IL 60606.

When a fraudulent statement is made by the subscriber, a policy can be challenged. A *challenged policy* means that coverage may not be in effect. After a policy has been in force for 2 years (3 years in some states), a policy becomes *incontestable* (may not be challenged). If a policy is guaranteed renewable and the time limit has passed, the policy becomes incontestable even if false statements were made on the application. Further information and additional insurance terminology concerning contracts are provided in detail in the next chapter.

Patient/Physician Contracts and Financial Responsibility

A physician and his or her staff must be aware of the physician's obligations to each patient, the physician's liabilities in regard to his or her service, and the patient's obligations to the physician. The physician-patient contract begins when the physician accepts the patient and agrees to treat the patient. This action can be either an implied or expressed contract. An *implied contract* is defined as not manifested by direct words but implied or deduced from the circumstance, the general language, or the conduct of the patient. For example, if Mary Johnson goes to Dr. Doe's office and Dr. Doe gives Ms. Johnson professional services that she accepts, this is an implied contract. *Expressed contracts* can be verbal or written. However, most physician-patient contracts are implied.

Even though a patient carries medical insurance, the contract for treatment is between the physician and the patient, who is liable for the entire bill. An exception to this is a person injured on the job, in which case the matter is referred to workers' compensation; this is also referred to as an industrial accident. Then, the contract exists between the physician and the insurance company as far as bills are concerned. If a physician is treating federal or state government employees or a Medicare recipient, he or she may lose the fee if government guidelines are not followed. When a physician is under contract to a managed care plan to render medical services to enrolled individuals, the contract for treatment occurs when the patient is first seen. If the physician no longer wishes to treat an HMO or a PPO patient, termination is handled according to the same method that is used when discharging patients who are insured under private insurance or state or government programs.

Most laws governing financial responsibility state that a husband is responsible for his wife's debts; a wife is not always responsible for her husband's debts. However, this would always depend on the way the contractual application reads. A father is ordinarily responsible for his children's debts if they are minors and are not emancipated. An *emancipated minor* is a person under 18 years of age who lives independently, is totally self-supporting, and possesses decision-making rights. Children may or may not be responsible for the debts of their parents, depending on the circumstances.

Physician and Managed Care Contracts

Contractual and legal obligations between the physician and preferred provider organizations (PPOs), health maintenance organizations (HMOs), and other insurance entities are discussed in Chapter 9, Managed Care Systems and Special Plans, as well as in chapters dealing with the various health care programs—Medicare, Medicaid, CHAMPUS, and so on. The insurance billing specialist should be able to understand billing and collection requirements, track reimbursement or capitation payments, and read and interpret health insurance contracts. (*Capitation* is a system of payment used by managed care plans in which physicians and hospitals are paid a fixed, per capita amount for each patient enrolled over a stated period of time, regardless of the type and number of services provided.) However, if the specialist is unable to interpret these matters, professional assistance from the physician's attorney should be sought.

Confidentiality

MEDICAL RECORDS

A *medical record* can be defined as written or graphic information documenting facts and events during the rendering of patient care. Some states use different terminology, such as medical information, health record, hospital record, or health care records. Complete documentation and well-organized patient records can protect a physician in a medical professional liability suit or in an audit by state or federal officials. If a patient fails to keep an appointment or to follow the physician's medical advice, a letter should be sent to the patient. The patient record and any photographs are confidential documents unless an authorization form to release information has been signed by the patient (Fig. 2–1).

Confidentiality is automatically waived in the following situations:

1. When the physician examines a patient at the request of a third party who is paying the bill, as in workers' compensation cases;
2. When the patient is suing someone, such as an employer, who must protect herself or himself; and
3. When the patient's records are subpoenaed or there is a search warrant.

Other exceptions to the confidentiality requirement include when state law requires the release of information that is for the good of society, such as cases of child or, in some states, elder abuse, certain highly contagious or infectious diseases, gunshot wounds, and so on.

In regard to computer use and confidentiality, refer to Chapter 7.

AUTHORIZATION FOR DISCLOSURE OF CONFIDENTIAL INFORMATION

I hereby authorize and request Dr. ________________ to furnish

information or copy of my medical records to:

____

____

____

about medical findings and treatment about my illness and/or treatment

during the period from ________________to________________

I understand that this is a required consent and I must voluntarily and knowingly sign this authorization before any records may be released, and that I may refuse to sign, but in that event the records will not be released.

I further release my physician from any liability arising from the release of information to the individual(s)/agency designated herein.

Signed________________________ Witness________________________

Address________________________ Date________________________

____

Optional statements may include:
I agree that a photocopy of this form may be used in lieu of the original.

This authorization will automatically expire one year from the date signed or is effective until________________________.

FIGURE 2–1
Authorization for Disclosure of Confidential Information. (Reprinted with permission from Diehl MO, Fordney MT: Medical Keyboarding, Typing, and Transcribing Techniques and Procedures. Philadelphia, W. B. Saunders, 1997.)

Facsimile (Fax) Communication

The common term *fax* is derived from the word *facsimile.* Faxes have become an important communication tool. Fax transmission is a system of sending and receiving copies of information instantly over telephone lines. It is used in the medical insurance business to transmit claims data directly to an electronic claims processor, resubmit an unpaid insurance claim, send further documentation on a claim to insurance carriers, obtain preauthorization for surgery on a patient, network with other insurance billing specialists, and send medical reports between offices and to other medical facilities across the country. Original documents can be typewritten or handwritten with pen or pencil or a graphic illustration. When a fax is used to send records, the patient must sign a release allowing it. The American Health Information Management Association (AHIMA), formerly the American Medical Record Association (AMRA), advises that fax machines should not be used for *routine* transmission of patient information and that documents should be faxed *only* when hand or mail delivery will not meet the needs of immediate patient care.

From the legal standpoint, protecting the patient's confidentiality in the fax process is critical. If, due to circumstances, a medical report must be faxed, you should have the patient sign an authorization to release information via facsimile equipment. Documents containing information on sexually transmitted diseases, drug or alcohol treatment, or human immunodeficiency virus (HIV) status should not be faxed. Fax machines should be located in secure or restricted access areas. To ensure protection, a cover sheet should be used for all transmissions. This can be a half sheet, full sheet, or small self-adhesive form attached to the top of the first page. It should contain the following information: name of recipient, name of sender, date, total number of pages including the transmittal page, fax and telephone numbers in case of transmittal problems (e.g., lost page, dropped line), and the statement that it is personal, privileged, and confidential medical information intended for the named recipient only (Fig. 2–2). A helpful hint to retain confidentiality is to ask the receiving party for a patient reference number (i.e., the patient's Social Security number). Blank out the patient's name and write in the reference number on the document before faxing it. Also ask other providers to fax records by reference number rather than by patient name.

Make arrangements with the recipient for a scheduled time for transmission or send it to a coded mail box. If neither of these is possible, do not fax it. Coded mail boxes require the sender to punch in a code indicating the individual to whom the fax is addressed and the receiver to then punch in his or her own code to activate the printer.

Never fax a patient's financial data. In court, faxing medical information can be justified on the basis of medical necessity, but faxing financial information cannot be justified. Psychiatric records should not be faxed except for emergency requests. Place a telephone call to the requesting physician's office approximately 15 minutes after faxing patient records to verify receipt, or request that the authorized receiver sign and return the attached receipt form at the bottom of the cover sheet on receipt of the faxed information. Noise or interference from telephone lines can be severe enough to garble a fax message, so it is necessary to verify receipt.

Consult an attorney to make sure whether documents (i.e., contracts, proposals, insurance claims) requiring signatures are legal if faxed. You might consider editing your release of records authorization form to allow for its transmittal by fax because it is acceptable to honor an authorization transmitted by fax. If a fax is misdirected, telephone or fax a request to destroy the information that has been erroneously sent. Note the incident, along with the misdialed number, in the patient's medical record. Program frequently used numbers into the fax machine to avoid misdirecting faxed communications.

In regard to Medicare patients, check with your Medicare fiscal intermediary on whether faxing of claims and documents is acceptable. The use of a fax transmittal system requires that the physician retain the original facsimile with the signature on it.

To prevent deterioration, ensure that fax transmissions on thermal paper are photocopied onto regular paper before they are put in medical records.

Medical Record Guidelines

The following are some guidelines for the insurance billing specialist for handling medical documents and patient records.

1. Keep the patient records accurate, detailed, and neat.
2. Keep all records until you are positive they are no longer needed.
3. Do not release confidential information.
4. When correcting an entry on a patient's record, use a legal copy pen, cross out the incorrect entry with a single line and write the correct one, and then date and initial the entry. Never

FAX TRANSMITTAL SHEET

To: ______________________________ Date ____________

Fax Number: ______________________ Time ____________

Number of Pages (including this one): ______________________

From: ____________________________ Phone ____________

Note: This transmittal is intended only for the use of the individual or entity to which it is addressed, and may contain information that is privileged, confidential, and exempt from disclosure under applicable law. If you are not the intended recipient, any dissemination, distribution, or photocopying of this communication is strictly prohibited. If you have received this communication in error, please notify this office immediately by telephone and return the original FAX to us at the address below by U. S. Postal Service. Thank you.

Remarks: ____

____

____

If you cannot read this FAX or if pages are missing, please contact:

PRACTON MEDICAL GROUP, INC.
4567 Broad Avenue
Woodland Hills, XY 12345-4700
Tel. 013/486-9002
Fax No. 013/488-7815

INSTRUCTIONS TO THE AUTHORIZED RECEIVER: PLEASE COMPLETE THIS STATEMENT OF RECEIPT AND RETURN TO SENDER VIA THE ABOVE FAX NUMBER.

I, ____________________, **verify that I have received** ____________
(no. of pages including cover sheet)

from ______________________
(sending facility's name)

FIGURE 2-2
Example of a fax cover sheet for medical document transmission.

erase, white out, or use self-adhesive paper over any information recorded on a patient record.

Incorrect: 1~~8~~0/~~9~~0 Correct: 190/70 ~~150/90~~ 1/2/9X mtf

Incorrect: right leg is ~~markedly~~ slightly edematous. . .

Correct: right leg is ~~markedly~~ slightly edematous. . . 1/2/9X mtf

Correctly typed: right leg is slightly edematous . . .
11-23-9X mtf

5. Keep a record of a patient's failure to return for needed treatment. Post it in the medical record, in the appointment book, and on the financial record or ledger card and see that a letter is sent to the patient advising him or her that further treatment is indicated.
6. Do not attempt to interpret a report or to give any information regarding the outcome of laboratory tests to the patient. Let the physician do it.
7. Examine insurance reports carefully before sending them out. Be absolutely certain that the insurance form is complete because an in-

surance firm can sue a physician for incomplete records.

8. If the authorization form containing the signature of the patient is a photocopy, it is necessary to state that the photocopy is approved by the patient, or write to the patient and obtain an original signed document.

PRINCIPLES FOR RELEASE OF INFORMATION

Some situations may require the insurance billing specialist to release medical information to or for a patient, such as when a patient is seeking a second medical opinion, wishes to acquire insurance, needs it for personal recordkeeping or upcoming surgery, is transferring to another physician, or is relocating to another city. Some general guidelines follow:

1. Requests from physicians concerned with patient care may be honored only with the written consent of the patient.
2. Requests from insurance companies, attorneys, and others concerned from a financial point of view may be honored *only* with the written authorization of the patient.
3. When litigation is involved, information should *not* be released in the absence of a subpoena unless authorized by the patient.
4. Government and state agencies may have access to records pertaining to government- and state-sponsored programs. See Chapter 13 for an explanation of the Privacy Act of 1974. In regard to Medicaid, members of a state attorney general's staff or the Department of Public Welfare may review Medicaid records without the patient's release to verify billing information and determine whether the services provided were medically necessary. The information in the records may be used only for the audit and may not be released.
5. Information of a psychiatric nature presents special and frequently delicate problems. Usually the psychiatrist or another attending physician concerned with the case should be consulted before records are released. Depending on state law, a therapist may be required to report cases of child abuse. If a patient threatens to harm himself or herself, someone else, or the therapist, the patient may lose the confidentiality privilege when he or she files litigation in which mental distress is claimed.
6. Special care should be exercised concerning the release of any information to an employer, even with the authorization of the patient.
7. To avoid misunderstanding of technical terms, it is preferable not to allow lay persons to examine records.
8. Care must be exercised in the release of any information for publication because this also constitutes an invasion of the patient's right to privacy and can result in legal action against the physician or health facility releasing such information.
9. When working in a hospital, the insurance billing specialist should check with the supervisor at all times to make sure his or her actions conform with hospital policy. Whether working in a hospital or for a physician, do not hesitate to ask for clarification of matters that are unclear. If you are employed by a health facility that has a policy manual or office procedure manual, familiarize yourself with its rules regarding the release of information.
10. Telephoned requests can be handled in two ways. Ask the caller to put the request in writing and to include the patient's signature for release of information, or obtain the name and telephone number of the caller and relationship to the patient and have the physician return the call.
11. Seek legal counsel if a patient has a positive test for HIV or acquired immune deficiency syndrome (AIDS), applies for life or health insurance, and requests that the physician send medical records to the insurance company. Some state laws allow AIDS information to be given only to the patient's spouse. Release of information must be carefully handled because the results of tests may be found in several sections of the medical record. ICD-9-CM diagnostic code 795.8 reflects a positive HIV test and must be considered confidential.

The AHIMA suggests the use of a consent for release of information form (Fig. 2–3). On this form, it is important to list the extent or nature of the information to be released (e.g., HIV test results of diagnosis and treatment with inclusive dates of treatment). Keep a signed authorization to release information in the medical record, noting exact information released, date of release, and signature of person who released the information. Stamp all information released about a patient who has an HIV infection with a statement prohibiting redisclosure of the information to another party without prior consent of the patient. The party receiving the information also should be requested to destroy the information after the stated need is fulfilled.

NAME OF FACILITY
Consent for Release of Information

DATE ____________________

1. I hereby authorize ________________________ to release the
Name of Institution
following information from the health record(s) of
____
Patient Name
____
Address
covering the period(s) of hospitalization from:
Date of Admission ______________________________
Date of Discharge ______________________________
Hospital # ____________________ Birthdate ______________
2. Information to be released:
▯ Copy of (complete) health record(s) ▯ Discharge Summary
▯ History and Physical ▯ Operative Report
▯ Other ______________________________________
3. Information is to be released to ______________________
____
4. Purpose of disclosure __________________________
____
5. I understand this consent can be revoked at any time except to the extent that disclosure made in good faith has already occurred in reliance on this consent.
6. Specification of the date, event, or condition upon which this consent expires:
____
7. The facility, its employees and officers, and attending physician are released from legal responsibility or liability for the release of the above information to the extent indicated and authorized herein.

Signed ______________________________________
(Patient or Representative)
____
(Relationship to Patient)
____
(Date of Signature)

FIGURE 2-3
Consent for Release of Information form. (Reprinted with permission from the American Health Information Management Association [AHIMA], Chicago.)

12. Under the Confidentiality of Medical Information Act, if a minor patient is legally capable of consenting to medical treatment, *only* the minor patient may sign an authorization for disclosure. In all other cases, the authorization must be signed by the minor's parent, guardian, or other legal representative.

13. Under the federal regulations governing the confidentiality of alcohol and drug abuse information, a minor patient may sign an authorization for disclosure where state law permits the minor to apply for and obtain alcohol or drug abuse treatment. Only the minor may authorize disclosure.

14. Remember, when in doubt about the release of any information, obtain the patient's authorization in writing.

RETENTION OF RECORDS

Medical Records

Preservation of medical records is governed by state and local laws. Individual states generally set a minimum of 7 to 10 years for keeping records, but it is the policy of most physicians to retain medical records of their patients indefinitely. Proof materials for the establishment of evidence, such as x-rays, films, laboratory reports, and pathologic specimens probably should be kept indefinitely. Calendars, appointment books, and telephone logs should also be filed and stored. Cases that involve radiologic injury claims (e.g., leukemia from radiation) may begin running the statute of limitations after discovery of the injury, which may occur 20 or 30 years after radiation exposure.

In some states a minor may file suit, after he or she has attained legal age, for any act performed during childhood that the person believes to be wrong or harmful. Sometimes a suit may be permitted even 2 to 3 years after the child has reached legal age. Thus, it is important to keep records until patients are 3 to 4 years beyond the age of majority.

A person's medical record may be of value not only to himself or herself in later years but also to the person's children.

Deceased patients' charts should be kept for at least 5 years. Shred documents that are no longer needed. Some practices prefer to put records on microfilm before disposal. Maintain a log of destroyed records showing the patient's name, Social Security number, date of last visit, and treatment.

Accounting Records

According to income tax regulations on record retention, accounting records should be kept a minimum of 4 years (following the due date for filing the tax return or the date the tax is paid, whichever is later). Always contact an accountant before discarding records that may determine tax liability. Suggested retention periods are shown in Table 2–1.

A federal regulation mandates that assigned claims for Medicaid and Medicare be kept for 7 years; the physician is subject to auditing during that period.

TABLE 2-1
Records Retention Schedule

Temporary Record	Recommended Retention Period (Years)
Accounts receivable ledger cards	4
Appointment sheets	1
Balance sheets	5
Bank deposits and statements, reconciliations	6–8
Cash receipt records	10
Contracts and leases (expired)	7
Contracts with employees	6
Copies of estimated tax forms	6
Correspondence, general	1–5
Deceased patients' medical records	5
Depreciation schedules	3
Duplicate bank deposit slips	1
Employee time cards/sheets and schedules	5
Employment applications	3
Expense reports	7
Inventory records	3
Invoice and billing records	7
Medicare records	7
Payroll records	7
Petty cash vouchers	3
Postal and meter records	1
Permanent Record (Retained Indefinitely)	
Accounts payable ledgers	
Balance sheets	
Bills of sale for important purchases	
Canceled checks and check registers	
Capital asset records	
Cashbooks	
Certified financial statements	
Charts of accounts	
Correspondence, legal	
Credit history	
Deeds, mortgages, contracts, leases, and property records	
Equipment records	
Inactive patient medical records purged from active files	
Income tax returns and documents	
Insurance policies and records	
Journals	
Magnetic tapes and disks	
Patients' medical records, including x-ray films	
Professional liability insurance policies	
Property appraisals	
Tax returns	
Telephone records	

Reproduced by permission. Fordney MT, Follis JJ: *Administrative Medical Assisting*, ed 3. By Albany, NY, Delmar Publishers, 1993.

Subpoena

Subpoena literally means "under penalty." In legal language, it is a writ requiring the appearance of a witness at a trial or other proceeding. Strictly defined, a *subpoena duces tecum* requires the witness to appear and to bring and/or send certain records "in his possession." Frequently, however, only the records may be sent, and the physician is not required to appear in court.

A subpoena is a legal document signed by a judge or an attorney in the name of a judge. In cases in which a pretrial of evidence or deposition is set up, the subpoena may be issued by a notary public, in which event it is called a *notary subpoena.* If an attorney signs it, he or she must attest it in the name of a judge, the court clerk, or other proper officer.

A subpoena must be personally served or handed to the prospective witness. Neither civil nor criminal subpoenas can be served via the telecopier (fax) machine. The acceptance of a document by someone authorized to accept it is the equivalent of personal service. The subpoena cannot be left on a counter or desk. In a state civil case, a witness fee and payment for travel to and from court are given, if demanded, at the time a subpoena is served. The fee is discretionary in criminal cases. In some states, provision is made for substitute service by mail or through newspaper advertisements. This is permitted only after all reasonable efforts to effect personal service have failed.

The insurance billing specialist should be courteous at all times to the deputy serving the subpoena. He or she should request the fee when the subpoena is served. Never accept a subpoena without the fee because in the absence of the fee, the subpoena is not legally valid and may be refused.

The medical office should designate one person as keeper of the medical records. If the subpoena is for medical records only, the representative for the specific doctor can then usually accept it, and the physician will not be called to court. Another employee cannot accept a subpoena for records, however, because the subpoena is served on the keeper of the records.

The medical office is given a prescribed time in which to produce the records. It is not necessary to show them at the time of service of the subpoena unless the court order so states. Call the attorney who sent the subpoena and ask if the records can be mailed. If they can be mailed, send them by registered mail with return receipt requested. Retain a copy of the records released. You will have to appear in court if specified in the subpoena. If you do not appear, you may be in contempt of court and subject to several days in jail.

Remember never to accept a subpoena or to give records to anyone without the physician's prior authorization. Before releasing records, make certain that you have a release of records form signed by the patient. Read the record to see that it is complete and that signatures and initials are identifiable.

In the case of a partnership or other multiple-physician situations, find out from the deputy to which physician the subpoena is addressed. Then determine the custodian of records for that physician if you are not the custodian. If the deputy is uncooperative, state that you cannot help unless you see the subpoena so that you know what action to take. If the deputy is antagonistic, ask one of the other physicians what to do.

If a physician is on vacation, explain that you are not authorized to accept a subpoena on his or her behalf—if that is indeed the case. Tell the deputy you understand the problem but that the physician is not here and cannot be served. Suggest that the deputy contact the physician's attorney and relay this information to the attorney. Discuss the subpoena problem with one of the other physicians in the office for advice or management.

When the witness fee has been given and the subpoena has been served, the insurance billing specialist may then pull the chart, placing the chart and the subpoena on the physician's desk for review. Willful disregard of a subpoena is punishable as contempt of court. After receiving the subpoena, verify with the court that the case is actually on the calendar.

If you are not mailing the records, remove them to a safe place, preferably under lock and key, so that they cannot be taken away or tampered with before the trial date. Make photocopies of the records if you are in doubt about their safety. This may be expensive, but it will prevent a total loss of the records and facilitate discovery of any altering or tampering while they are out of your custody. Number the pages of the records so that you will know if a page is missing when the person copying the records has finished.

On the day of your court appearance, comply with all instructions given by the court. *Do not* give up possession of the records unless instructed to do so by the judge. *Do not* permit examination of the records by anyone before their identification in court. *Do not* leave the chart in the court unless it is in the possession of the judge or jury and a receipt for it has been obtained.

If you have any other questions, call the physician's attorney.

Insurance Claims

GUARANTOR

A *guarantor* is an individual who promises to pay the medical bill by signing a form agreeing to pay or who accepts treatment, which constitutes an expressed promise. Usually, a patient is the guarantor and must be of legal age (18 or 21 years, depending on state law). If the patient is unconscious when treatment is rendered, treatment is based on an implied-in-fact contract. Most of the time an agreement is obtained by having the patient sign an assignment of insurance benefits form.

ASSIGNMENT

The general definition of *assignment* is the transfer, after an event insured against, of an individual's legal right to collect an amount payable under an insurance contract. Many health insurance claims forms contain a provision that, when signed by the insured, directs the insurance company to pay benefits directly to the provider of care on whose charge the claim is based. However, because the definition of assignment can vary depending on whether one is submitting claims to a private third party payer, Blue plan, federal Medicare program, or state Medicaid program, this will be discussed in each chapter concerning those topics.

An assignment of benefits becomes a legally enforceable document but must refer to specific hospitalization, course of treatment, or office visit(s). Each course of treatment needs to have an assignment document executed by the patient except when automobile or homeowners' liability insurance is involved. In third party liability cases, the physician needs to negotiate with the insurance company to make sure benefits are paid to him or her directly. In workers' compensation cases, when there is a dispute as to whether the injured party was hurt at work, a form must be signed by the patient, as shown in Chapter 14, Figure 14–14.

TIME LIMITS

Each program or plan has variable time limits for submitting claims. This is a legal issue because claims can be denied for payment if submitted after the time limit. Because these time periods vary depending on the program, this topic is discussed within the chapters on Medicare, Medicaid, CHAMPUS, and so on.

SIGNATURE AUTHORIZATION

Most third party payers will accept a completed insurance claim with no signature as long as the physician's name is preprinted on the form. However, state and government programs and Blue Cross and Blue Shield Plans require a signature, except that the Blue plans will send you a form for authorization to use a facsimile signature.

Some medical practices use a facsimile signature stamp so the staff can process checks, insurance forms, and other paperwork without interrupting the physician or waiting for her or his signature. For an authorization of this type, a document should be typed and signed before a notary (Fig. 2–4). However, use of this stamp can lead to problems, because it is possible to stamp unauthorized checks, transcribed medical reports, prescriptions, third party insurance claims, or credit card charge slips. If such a stamp is used infrequently, then delete the practice. If one is used regularly, prevent problems by doing the following:

1. Make only one stamp
2. Allow only long-term, trusted, bonded staff members to have access to the stamp.
3. Keep the stamp in a location with a secure lock.
4. Limit access to the stamp.

Sometimes a physician gives signature authorization to one person on the staff to sign insurance claims. For an authorization of this type, a document should be typed and signed before a notary (Fig. 2–5). This means that whoever signs the form is attesting to it because it is a legal document. If the medical practice is ever audited and fraud or embezzlement is discovered, then the person who had signature authorization can be brought into the case as well as the physician. If this involves a Medicare case, the federal government will prosecute. If a Medicaid case is involved, the state prosecutes.

An *electronic signature* is defined as an individualized computer access and identification system (i.e., a series of numbers, letters, electronic writing, voice, computer key and fingerprint transmission [biometric system]).

Federal law requires physicians' signatures in a medical record for a hospital to comply with the Medicare Conditions of Participation to qualify for reimbursement under the prospective payment system (PPS). Authentication may include signature, initials, or computer entry. The hospital must main-

PROVIDER'S NOTARIZED SIGNATURE AUTHORIZATION

State of __________________)
)ss
County of __________________)

Know all persons by these presents:

That I, ______________________have made, constituted and appointed and by these presents do make, constitute and appoint__________________________my true and lawful attorney-in-fact for me and in my name place and stead to sign my name on claims, for payment for services provided by me submitted to the ____________________________________. My signature by my said attorney-in-fact includes my agreement to abide by the full payment concept and the remainder of the certification appearing on all ________________claim forms. I hereby ratify and confirm all that my said attorney-in-fact shall lawfully do or cause to be done by virtue of the power generated herein.

In witness whereof I have hereunto set my hand this ________day of __________________19_____.

____
(Signature)

Subscribed and sworn to before me this______day of_________19___.

____
Notary Public

My Commission Expires_________________________.

FIGURE 2-4
Example of a provider's signature authorization form that can be completed, notarized, and sent to the insurance carrier after a copy is retained for the physician's records.

tain a list of computer codes and written signatures and adequately safeguard the codes against unauthorized access and use. The Medicare fiscal intermediary must approve of the system before use.

The Joint Commission on the Accreditation of Healthcare Organizations (JCAHO) requires entries into a medical record authenticated by written signature, initials, or computer key. A rubber stamp is permitted if the physician executes a statement of exclusive possession of the stamp.

In regard to transcribed medical reports, JCAHO and the Medicare guidelines require that signatures, electronic or other, be written or entered by the physician and not be delegated.

For information on state laws, contact your state legislature at your state capitol.

Insurance Claim Fraud and Abuse

Fraud is *knowing* and *intentional* deception (lying) or misrepresentation that could result in some unauthorized benefit to the deceiver or some other person. It is a felony, and if detected, financial or prison penalties can be imposed, depending on the laws of the state. If a Medicare or CHAMPUS case is involved, then fraud becomes a federal offense and federal laws apply. Claims are audited by state and federal agencies as well as private insurance companies.

Usually fraud involves careful planning. Some examples include the following:

PROVIDER'S NOTARIZED FACSIMILE OR STAMP SIGNATURE AUTHORIZATION

State of ___________________)
)ss
County of ___________________)

___________________________being first duly sworn, deposes and says:

I hereby authorize the____
(Name of Fiscal Administrator)

to accept my facsimile or stamp signature shown below

____
(Facsimile or Stamp Signature)

as my true signature for all purposes under the____________________
(Name of Insurance Program)

in the same manner as if it were my actual signature, including my agreeing to abide by the full payment concept and the remainder of the certification normally signed by the source of care as it appears on all ____________________claim forms.

____
(Signature)

Subscribed and sworn to before me this _______________day of_______________________19_____.

____
Notary Public in and for

____________County, State of________________________

(SEAL)

My Commission expires___________________________

FIGURE 2–5
Example of a provider's facsimile or stamp signature authorization form that can be completed, notarized, and sent to the insurance carrier after a copy is retained for the physician's records.

1. Billing for services or supplies not provided (phantom billing or invoice ghosting) or for an office visit if a patient fails to keep an appointment
2. Altering fees on a claim form to obtain higher payment
3. Forgiving the deductible or copayment for a Medicare patient or for any health care plan. This is illegal and is considered fraud. The insurance billing specialist must attempt to collect the copayment before asking the physician if he or she wishes to write it off. The reasoning behind this is that it makes the insurer pay 100% of what the physician will accept instead of the 80% that it is obligated to pay. It costs the insurance carrier money by encouraging overuse of medical services. It has a tendency to eliminate the incentive for

the patient to watch medical expenditures closely. If there is a special circumstance surrounding the case and the physician wishes to accept the insurance reimbursement as payment in full, then disclose this fact to the insurance company. Obtain a hardship waiver from the patient explaining why he or she cannot pay. Retain copies of the waiver and any documentation of attempts to collect from the patient in case of an audit or investigation.

4. Altering medical records to generate fraudulent payments
5. Leaving relevant information off a claim (e.g., failing to reveal whether a spouse has health insurance coverage through an employer)
6. Upcoding (e.g., submitting a code for a complex fracture when the patient had a simple fracture)
7. Shortening (e.g., dispensing less medication than billed for)
8. Split billing schemes (e.g., billing procedures over a period of days when all treatment occurred during one visit)
9. Using another person's insurance card in obtaining medical care
10. Changing a date of service
11. Using the adjustment process to generate fraudulent payments
12. Soliciting, offering, or receiving a kickback, bribe, or rebate in return for referring a patient to a physician, physical therapist, or pharmacy or for referring a patient to obtain any item or service that may be paid for in full or in part by Medicare or Medicaid
13. Rewording the diagnosis to obtain insurance benefits or better payment
14. Deliberately applying for duplicate payment (billing Medicare and the beneficiary for the same service or billing Medicare and another insurer in an attempt to get paid twice)
15. Unbundled or exploded charges (e.g., billing a multichannel laboratory test as if individual tests were performed)
16. Collusion between a physician and a carrier employee when the claim is assigned (if the physician deliberately overbilled for services, adjustments could be generated with little awareness on the part of the Medicare beneficiary)
17. Billings based on gang visits (e.g., a physician visits a nursing home and bills for 20 visits without furnishing any specific service to, or on behalf of, individual patients)

These actions constitute fraud unless the physician has medical test results to warrant rewording a diagnosis as proof that the statements are true. Two types of intent must be proved: intent to agree to practice a fraudulent act and intent to commit the substantive offense. When an insurance billing specialist bills for a physician and completes the insurance claim form with information that does not reflect the true situation, then he or she may be found guilty of conspiring to commit fraud. It is not necessary to receive monetary profit from a fraudulent act to be judged guilty in participating in a criminal conspiracy.

Unintentional fraud may occur when completing the HCFA-1500 insurance claim form. For example, in a Medicare case, if the statement "signature on file" or "patient's request for payment on file" is inserted in Block 12 and the records do not contain the patient's authorization to file the claim on his or her behalf, this is a federal violation. The insurance billing specialist must verify that the authorization is for the insurance company in question. To prevent this problem from occurring in Medicare cases, obtain a lifetime authorization for the Medicare fiscal intermediary as well as for the patient's Medigap insurance company.

A coder or biller who has knowledge of fraud or abuse should take the following measures:

1. Notify the provider both personally and with a dated, written memorandum.
2. Document the false statement or representation of the material fact.
3. If no change is made, a memorandum should be sent to the office manager or employer stating your concern.
4. Keep a written audit trail with dated memorandums.
5. Do not discuss the problem with anyone who is not immediately involved.

Abuse means incidents or practices by physicians, not usually considered fraudulent, that are inconsistent with accepted sound medical business or fiscal practices. Medicare defines abuse as involving payment for services when there is no legal entitlement to payment and the physician has not knowingly and intentionally misrepresented the facts to obtain payment. This can mean that if an inadvertent error is made when billing and inappropriate payment is received, then the persons involved may be subject to civil penalties. Coding and billing mistakes resulting in overpayments are no longer considered negligence but qualify as abuse cases. Some examples are

Excessive referrals to other providers for unnecessary services, also called *ping-ponging*

Excessive charges for services or supplies
Claims for services not medically necessary, such as performing a battery of diagnostic tests when only a few are required, also called *churning*
Violating Medicare's physician participating agreement
Calling patients back for repeated and unnecessary follow-up visits, also called *yo-yoing*
Billing Medicare beneficiaries at a higher rate
Submitting bills to Medicare instead of to third party payers (e.g., claims for injury from an automobile accident, in a store, or the workplace)
Breaching assignment agreement
Failure to make required refunds when services are not reasonable and necessary
Requiring patients to contract to pay their physician's full charges, in excess of the Medicare charge limits
Requiring a patient to waive rights to have the physician submit claims to Medicare and obligating a patient to pay privately for Medicare-covered services
Requiring patients to pay for services not previously billed, including telephone calls with the physician, prescription refills, and medical conferences with other professionals.
Requiring patients to sign a global waiver agreeing to pay privately for all services that Medicare will not cover, and using these waivers to obligate patients to pay separately for a service that Medicare covers as part of a package of related procedures but not individually

The Federal False Claims Amendments Act of 1986 offers financial incentives of 15% to 25% of any judgment to informants who report physicians suspected of defrauding the federal government. This is called a *qui tam* action. The laws are intended to help catch Medicare and Medicaid cheaters. The health insurance companies that process Medicare claims have a Medicare fraud unit whose job is to catch people who steal from Medicare. The Office of the Inspector General (OIG), Department of Health and Human Services, is the law enforcement agency that investigates and prosecutes people who steal from Medicare. The OIG works closely with Medicare insurance companies, the Federal Bureau of Investigation (FBI), the Postal Inspection Service, and other federal law enforcement agencies. If the physician is on an optical disk retrieval (ODR) A-1000 system, it is possible to obtain procedure codes that show comparison billing with peers in the area. The Health Care Financing Administration alerts regional offices of whom to investigate.

Insurance carriers receive complaints of fraud and abuse from patients who misunderstand the billing process. Therefore, it is important to tell the patient how services will be billed to avoid possible fraud and abuse audits. For example, a hospitalized patient is not always aware that their attending physician has requested a consultation, which will result in a separate bill, or that a simple invasive procedure done in the physician's office may be referred to as a surgical procedure on the monthly statement because the code number is obtained from the surgical section of the procedure code book.

For information on fraud and abuse in the workers' compensation program, see Chapter 14.

FORGERY

The following situations are indicators that there may be forgery:

- The beneficiary or provider states that he or she did not receive the check but the insurance company shows it as being cashed.
- The endorsement on the back of the payment check does not match the name on the front.
- A beneficiary or provider indicates that he or she never received monies for which a check was both issued and cashed. The payee claims that the signature is not his or hers.

CLAIM AUDITS AND REVIEW

Many insurance companies have installed antifraud telephone hotlines or billing question telephone lines for patients. Investigations can result from such calls, depending on the circumstances. Insurance companies have computer software programs capable of editing and screening insurance claims to identify billing excesses or potential abuses before payment is rendered. Most insurance companies perform routine audits on unusual billing patterns or excessive payment amounts.

Another area commonly reviewed is documentation in medical records. Physicians who charge excessive fees are routinely audited by most carriers. Insurance carriers hire undercover agents to visit physicians' offices if overuse and abuse of procedure codes are suspected. Carriers spot check by sending questionnaires to patients, asking them if they received medical care from Dr. Doe and to verify the services rendered. The answers are then compared with what the physician billed. Tips also come from peer review organizations, state licensing boards, whistle-blowing physicians, and ex-staff members and patients. If there is any suspicion of fraud, the insurance company will notify the medical practice, specifying a date and time at which they will come to the office and the records they wish to audit. Investigators question the patient, look at the documentation in the medical record, and interview the staff, other physicians, and medical personnel.

In 1984, Michigan signed into law the Health Care False Claim Act with felony penalties ranging to 10 years in prison and fines of up to $50,000 per count for attempting to defraud an insurance company. Other states are following suit in establishing such laws. To avoid being audited, use multiple levels of service when billing office or hospital visits and consultations. Carriers accept a variety of levels of service; if only one or two levels are consistently listed, this will attract attention and, possibly, an audit. If the diagnosis does not match the service provided, the claim will be thrown out by the editing capabilities of the computer program.

Therefore, it is vital to be as correct as possible in your choice of diagnostic and procedural codes with modifiers. It is equally important that everything involved in patient care be well documented and that records be complete. In subsequent chapters, you will learn what needs to be documented and the basics of coding. Additional information on the Civil Monetary Penalties Law to prosecute cases of Medicare and Medicaid fraud can be found in Chapter 12.

Once an individual has been found guilty of committing a Medicare or Medicaid program–related crime, exclusion from program participation is mandatory under Sec. 1128(a) of the Social Security Act. An individual can be anyone who participates in fraud or abuse (e.g., physician, nurse, home health aide, insurance billing specialist, claims assistance professional, electronic claims processor, medical assistant, and so on).

Embezzlement

Embezzlement means to steal money that has been entrusted in one's care. Bonding of employees who handle cash or checks is imperative because embezzlement can occur in any practice by an associate, office manager, accountant, or other employee. A practice that carries a fidelity or *honesty* bond means that an insurance company will prosecute any guilty employees. *Bonding* is an insurance contract by which a bonding agency guarantees payment of a certain sum to a physician in case of a financial loss caused by an employee or some contingency over which the payee has no control. There are three bonding methods that are effective for a practice with three or more office employees:

- *Position-schedule bond.* This covers a designated job, such as a bookkeeper or nurse, rather than a named individual. If one employee in a category leaves, the replacement is automatically covered.
- *Blanket-position bond.* This provides coverage for all employees regardless of job title.
- *Personal bond.* This provides coverage for those who will be handling large sums of money. A thorough background investigation is required.

Such insurance contracts may be obtained from a casualty insurance agent or broker. Bond coverage should be reviewed periodically with the insurance agent to ensure that coverage is keeping pace with the expansion of the business.

In many cases of insurance claims embezzlement, the physician is held as the guilty party and has to pay huge sums of money to the insurance carrier when false claims are submitted by the employee. If an undiscovered embezzler leaves the employer and you are hired to replace that person, you could be accused some months down the line of doing something that you did not do.

As a precautionary measure, always type your initials at the bottom of the claims that you submit so you will know who did the work. Always retain the Explanation of Benefits or Remittance Advice documents that accompany checks from insurance companies. If poor bookkeeping and record keeping are noticed, bring this to your employer's attention. Encounter forms, transaction slips, and cash receipts should be prenumbered. If a mistake is made when completing one, void it and keep the slip as part of the financial records. It is especially imperative to have prenumbered insurance forms if the physician's practice allows the use of a signature stamp when submitting claims. Thus, filing of fictitious insurance claims can be totally eliminated. All insurance payment checks should be immediately stamped "For Deposit Only." The bank should be given instructions never to cash a check made payable to the physician.

Ask the physician or supervisor to initial all entries about adjustments, discounts, and write-offs on either the day sheet, transaction slip, or ledger card. If a patient owes money to the physician that is uncollectable, be sure the physician dates and initials the ledger that shows the closed account. Ask the physician to occasionally check an entire day's

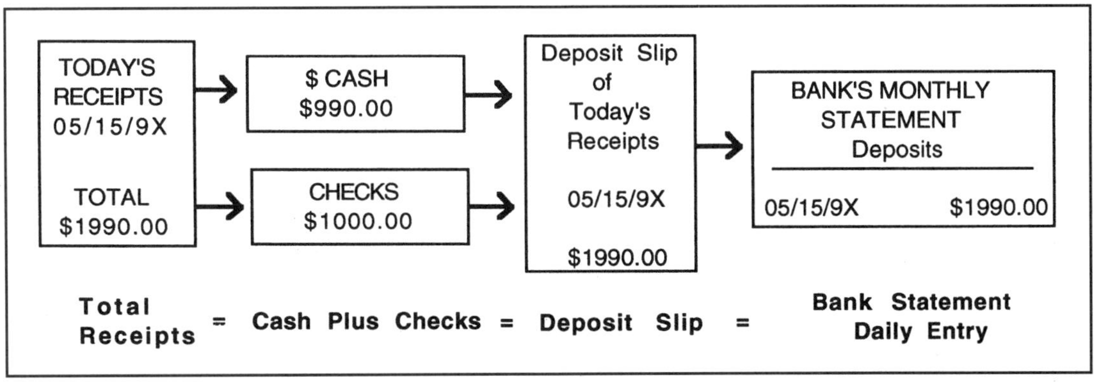

FIGURE 2-6
Explanation of an audit trail to review monies received by a medical practice and monies deposited into a bank account.

records (the patient sign-in log and appointment schedule) with the day sheet, ledger cards, and transaction and cash receipt slips. A daily trial balance of accounts receivable and daily banking of checks and cash can assist in reviewing monthly income and aid in discovering embezzlement. If there are no deposit receipts, review the monthly bank statement to verify that the deposits tally with the receipts for each business day (Fig. 2–6).

Only a few of the many precautions for protection are mentioned here; embezzlement can occur in accounts payable, with petty cash and use of computers, and in various other aspects of a medical practice.

Credit and Collection Laws

The legalities of collecting from delinquent accounts and insurance claims are not discussed here. For information on that topic, see Chapter 8, Tracing Delinquent Claims and Insurance Problem Solving.

Appeals

In some cases, a claim can be denied payment and a physician may wish to have the claim receive a multistep review and arbitration and possibly be appealed. This legal subject will be discussed in detail for CHAMPUS and Medicare in Chapter 8. In a workers' compensation case, an injured person declared permanent and stationary may appeal (see Chapter 14). Individuals who have applied for federal disability benefits and been denied may appeal (see Chapter 15).

Statute of Limitations

There are time periods during which an insured may sue the insurance company to collect the amount the claimant believes is owed. An insured may not initiate a legal action against the insurer until 60 days after the initial claim has been submitted. An insured must bring a suit against the insurer within 3 years of the date the initial claim was submitted for payment. Tracing of delinquent claims is discussed in Chapter 8.

Medical Professional Liability Prevention

The term *malpractice* can be defined as any misconduct or unreasonable lack of skill of a professional person that occurs within that person's field of expertise and results in injury or loss to the recipient of those services. While acting within the scope of his or her duties, the insurance billing specialist is the agent of the physician, and the physician is charged with the consequences of his or her conduct under *respondeat superior*. However, this does not mean that the insurance billing specialist could not be brought into litigation regarding a financial matter. Remember to always be polite and courteous to patients when discussing billing and filing of claims, regardless of the circumstances. It is unwise for an insurance billing specialist to tell the patient whether the physician carries medical professional liability insurance. The mere mention of this fact may plant the seed of a lawsuit in the mind of a patient who is dissatisfied with the bill or the outcome of treatment given. If a professional liability claim is filed against a health care provider, keep correspondence with the insurance carrier and with the defense attorney in a separate location from the patient's treatment record.

To further expand your legal knowledge, information will be presented here on some aspects of medical professional liability that may be of some help to an insurance billing specialist. To aid in medical professional liability claims prevention, the prevention commandments set forth in 1963 by the American Medical Association Committee on Medicolegal Problems are provided. Any special instructions to the insurance billing specialist are given in parentheses after the commandment.

PREVENTION COMMANDMENTS OF AMERICAN MEDICAL ASSOCIATION COMMITTEE ON MEDICOLEGAL PROBLEMS

1. *The physician must care for every patient with scrupulous attention given to the requirements of good medical practice.* In other words, the patient must receive the attention that is or her symptoms demand.
2. *The physician must know and exercise his or her legal duty to the patient.*
3. *The physician must avoid destructive and unethical criticism of the work of other physicians.* The present physician cannot know the circumstances or condition at the time of prior treatment. (Patients sometimes invite criticism of the methods or results of former physicians. Remember that you are hearing only one side of the story. Do not discuss the other physician with the patient.)
4. *The physician must keep records that clearly show what was done and when it was done, that clearly indicate that nothing was neglected, and that demonstrate that the care given met fully the standards demanded by the law. If any patient discontinues treatment before he or she should or fails to follow instructions, the records should show it; a good method is to preserve a carbon copy of the physician's letter advising the patient against an unwise course.* See Figures 2–7 and 2–8 for proper wording of forms.
5. *The physician must avoid making any statement that constitutes or might be construed as constituting an admission of fault on his or her part. He or she should instruct employees to make no such statements.* (Remember that the insurance billing specialist's position in lawsuits is to say nothing to anyone except as required by the attorney of the physician or by the court. If the physician is doing something illegal, the insurance billing specialist can be held responsible for being silent.)
6. *The physician must exercise tact as well as professional ability in handling his or her patients and should insist on a professional consultation if the patient is not doing well, if the patient is unhappy and complaining, or if the family's attitude indicates dissatisfaction.* (The insurance billing specialist should tell the physician immediately if he or she learns that a new patient is still under treatment by another physician and did not give this information to the physician during the initial interview. If a physician feels a specialist is necessary, he or she is expected to make referral.)
7. *The physician must refrain from overly optimistic prognoses.* (The insurance billing specialist should not compare the respective merits of various forms of therapy and should refrain from discussing patients' ailments with them. Patients come to talk to the physician about their symptoms, and you may give them incorrect information. Let the physician make the diagnosis. Otherwise, you may seriously embarrass the physician, yourself, or both.)
8. *The physician must advise his or her patients of any intended absences from practice and recommend, or make available, a qualified substitute. The patient must not be abandoned* (see Fig. 2–2).
9. *The physician must unfailingly secure an "informed" consent (preferably in writing) for medical and surgical procedures and for autopsy.* (The insurance billing specialist should not refer to surgical consent forms or other forms as "releases." They are acknowledgment or authorization forms. Help your physician remember that he or she needs written consent from parents or a legal guardian before any surgery is performed on a minor.)
10. *The physician must carefully select and supervise assistants and employees and take great care in delegating duties to them.*
11. *The physician must keep abreast of general medical and scientific progress.* (The duty to keep informed also applies to the insurance billing specialist in the handling of insurance matters.)
12. *The physician should limit practice to those fields that are well within his or her qualifications.* Two legal phrases commonly heard are:
    a. *Standard of reasonable care:* This means that the physician is required to use the same knowledge and skill as other physicians in good standing and of the same general training in the same or similar communities under similar circumstances.

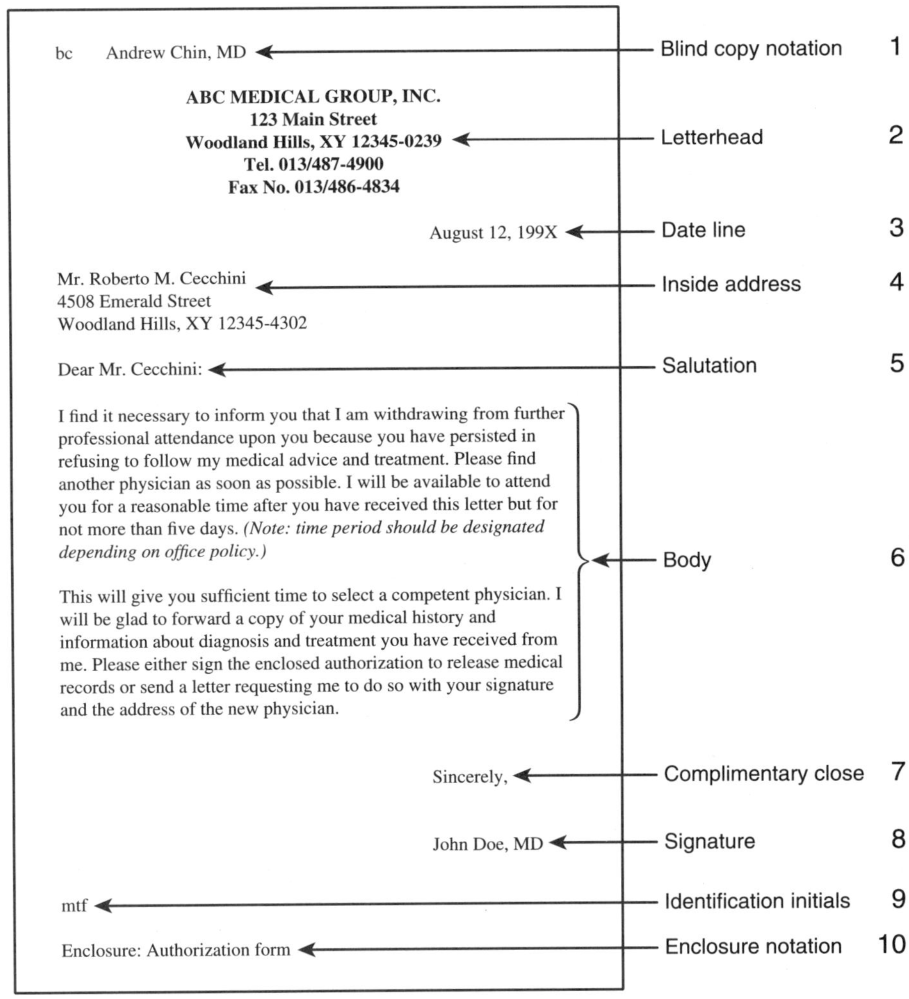

bc Andrew Chin, MD

ABC MEDICAL GROUP, INC.
123 Main Street
Woodland Hills, XY 12345-0239
Tel. 013/487-4900
Fax No. 013/486-4834

August 12, 199X

Mr. Roberto M. Cecchini
4508 Emerald Street
Woodland Hills, XY 12345-4302

Dear Mr. Cecchini:

I find it necessary to inform you that I am withdrawing from further professional attendance upon you because you have persisted in refusing to follow my medical advice and treatment. Please find another physician as soon as possible. I will be available to attend you for a reasonable time after you have received this letter but for not more than five days. *(Note: time period should be designated depending on office policy.)*

This will give you sufficient time to select a competent physician. I will be glad to forward a copy of your medical history and information about diagnosis and treatment you have received from me. Please either sign the enclosed authorization to release medical records or send a letter requesting me to do so with your signature and the address of the new physician.

Sincerely,

John Doe, MD

mtf

Enclosure: Authorization form

FIGURE 2–7
Example of letter of withdrawal from a case that is typed in modified-block style with closed punctuation and special notations (i.e., placement of parts of letter).

b. *Standard procedure:* This means any treatment commonly performed by most physicians of similar training.

13. *The physician must frequently check the condition of his or her equipment and make use of every available safety installation.* (The insurance billing specialist should be alert to hazards that may cause injury to the physician, the patients, or himself or herself. Watch for telephone and light cords, rugs or carpets that curl at the edges, wobbly chairs, objects that protrude, and so on. If you have linoleum floors, they must not be slippery. Do not let equipment get run down.)
14. *The physician should make every effort to reach an understanding with patients in the matter of fees, preferably in advance of treatment.* (If the insurance billing specialist handles the problem of the fee to be charged, he or she should be sure that the patient understands what services will be received and what the "extras" may be. In regard to hospital cases, it is advisable to explain that the fee your physician charges is for his or her services only and that the operating room, laboratory, anesthesia, and so on will be charged for in addition to the bed charge.)
15. *The physician must realize that it is dangerous to diagnose or prescribe by telephone.*
16. *The physician should not sterilize a patient solely for the patient's convenience, except after a reasonably complete explanation of the procedure, its risks, and possible complications and after obtaining a signed consent from the patient and the patient's spouse, if the patient is married. Such sterilization is a crime in Connecticut, Kansas, and Utah and should not be performed in those states. Eugenic sterilization should be performed only in conformity with the law of the state, if any exists. Sterilization for therapeutic purposes may lawfully be performed with the informed consent of the patient and preferably with the informed consent of the patient's spouse, if the patient is married.* Voluntary nontherapeutic surgical sterilization is lawful in California and in

XYZ MEDICAL CLINIC
459 South Elm Street
Woodland Hills, XY 12345-4309
Tel. 013/487-9870
Fax No. 013/486-3400

September 3, 199X

Mrs. Gregory Putnam
4309 North E Street
Woodland Hills, XY 12345-4398

Dear Mrs. Putnam

This will confirm our telephone conversation today during which you discharged me from attending you as your physician in your present illness. In my opinion, your medical condition requires continued treatment by a physician. If you have not already obtained the services of another physician, I suggest you do so without further delay.

You may be assured that, upon your written authorization, I will furnish your new physician with information regarding the diagnosis and treatment you have received from me.

Very truly yours

Mary Doe, MD

mtf

FIGURE 2-8
Example of letter to confirm discharge by patient that is typed in modified-block style with open punctuation.

many other states, and such operations are permissible for the purpose of family limitation motivated solely by personal or socioeconomic considerations. It is recommended that for every such procedure the physician obtain from the patient and the spouse, if any, a signed, written recognition of

a. The lack of any guarantee of successful sterilization.
b. The necessity for supplementary contraceptive measures until sterilization can be reasonably assured (particularly after vasectomies).
c. The risk of tissue breakdown and recanalization with subsequent fertility.

17. *Except in an actual emergency situation that makes it impossible to avoid doing so, a male physician should not examine a female patient unless an assistant or a nurse, or a member of the patient's family, is present.*
18. *The physician should exhaust all reasonable methods of securing a diagnosis before embarking on a therapeutic course.* (A legal phrase commonly used is *negligent diagnosis*, which means failure to make necessary tests, take essential x-rays, and observe all unusual conditions as the physician's colleagues do under similar circumstances. In dealing with fractures, x-rays should usually be taken before and after reduction, immediately after surgical intervention, and after surgery,

during healing, to check position and progress. Failure to order sufficient x-rays can create tremendous difficulties in defending a malpractice case. On the other hand, it is also prudent to avoid taking too many x-rays because some physicians have been sued for exposing the patient to excessive radiation. In the treatment of the patient, there must be no experimentation without the explicit and informed consent of the patient and then only when there is sufficient reason to believe that such experimentation offers greater potential for benefit to the patient than currently acceptable modes of treatment.)

19. *The physician should use conservative and less dangerous methods of diagnosis and treatment whenever possible in preference to highly toxic agents or dangerous surgical procedures.*
20. *The physician should read the manufacturer's brochure accompanying a toxic agent to be used for diagnostic or therapeutic purposes and, in addition, ascertain the customary dosage or usage in this area.*
21. *The physician should be aware of all the known toxic reactions to any drug he or she uses, together with the proper methods for treating such reactions.*

PHYSICIAN/PATIENT AGREEMENT

Arbitration is an alternative legal method, provided by statute in some states, by which the patient and physician agree to resolve any controversy arising between them before an impartial panel, sometimes referred to as a grievance committee. In some states, disputes involving a relatively small amount of money (less than $10,000) are subject to arbitration.

The *arbitration agreement* is a contract between patient and physician prepared by legal counsel for use in the medical office. A *legal agreement* covers all present or future claims or disputes of any kind between patient and physician for which the patient might sue the physician or for which the physician might sue the patient, including collection of the physician's fees. However, the loser may appeal the decision in court. Arbitration is thus a fairer, faster, and less expensive way of handling disagreements arising in the patient-physician relationship.

The patient is free to sign the agreement or not. He or she does not have to sign to be seen by the physician or to receive continuing medical treatment. If the patient does sign and subsequently changes his or her mind within 30 days, the signature can be revoked by giving written notice to the physician stating withdrawal from the arbitration agreement.

Some arbitration contracts, particularly those used in hospitals, include a box that the patient may check to indicate that he or she is unwilling to accept arbitration but feels forced to sign. This provision may be made when the rules of the hospital specify that the patient must sign an arbitration agreement to be admitted. In this instance, the patient may disavow the agreement at a later date. A court may set aside the contract on the grounds that the patient was ill at the time of admission and on that basis unable to make a rational judgment.

The two kinds of arbitration agreements are preclaim agreements and postclaim agreements. In a *preclaim agreement*, the patient agrees before the service is rendered that if a controversy arises concerning the service, it will be settled through arbitration and not litigation. Some HMOs and some insurance plans have preclaim agreements as an option or requirement of the plan. A *postclaim agreement* is transacted after a dispute occurs; both sides agree to arbitrate rather than litigate.

The tact with which the physician's employee presents the arbitration agreement to the patient and the willingness with which he or she answers the patient's questions can have considerable bearing on whether the court upholds the contract. When the physician's employee "speaks for the physician," any representations that he or she makes can be held against the physician.

An arbitration agreement in no way affects payment by the patient's health insurance. If a claim for professional negligence arises, immediately notify the physician's insurance carrier. Include a copy of any arbitration agreement relating to the patient's care and request that arbitration be invoked. Failure to assert the right to arbitration at the outset can result in a waiver of the arbitration agreement.

TERMINATION OF A CASE

A physician may wish to withdraw formally from further care of a patient because the patient discharged the physician, did not follow instructions, did not take the recommended medication, or failed to return for an appointment. A physician may terminate a contract by

1. Sending a letter of withdrawal to the patient by registered or certified mail with return of signature card requested so that proof of termination is available in the patient's medical record.
2. Sending a letter of confirmation of discharge when the patient states that he or she no longer wishes care. This should also be sent registered or certified with return receipt requested.

3. Sending a letter confirming that the patient left the hospital against the advice of the physician. If there is a signed statement in the patient's hospital records to this effect, it is not necessary to send a letter. If a letter is sent, a copy of the letter and return receipt card from the post office must be filed with the patient's records.

See Figures 2–7 and 2–8 for the proper wording of letters to patients for termination of a case.

Medicolegal References

To keep up-to-date and well informed in the medicolegal field, you might read some journals that come to the physician's office, which frequently have excellent articles, as well as the journals and newsletters published by the many professional organizations mentioned in Chapter 1. Refer to Appendix B for titles of legal books and their sources.

Insurance Commissioners

Contact your state insurance commissioner for assistance or information regarding the laws in your state (see Appendix A).

State Boards of Medical Examiners

Because state laws vary, you should write to the state board of medical examiners and ask for information regarding medicolegal laws or ordinances in your state (see Appendix A for state addresses).

TO THE STUDENT

Study Chapter 2 and then answer the review questions in the *Workbook* to reinforce the theory learned in this chapter and to help prepare you for a future test. For further knowledge and understanding, the key terms at the beginning of the chapter appear in the Glossary at the end of this textbook so that you can look up the pertinent terms. Refer to the *Workbook,* Assignment 2, for hands-on experience in preparing medicolegal form letters.

UNIT 2

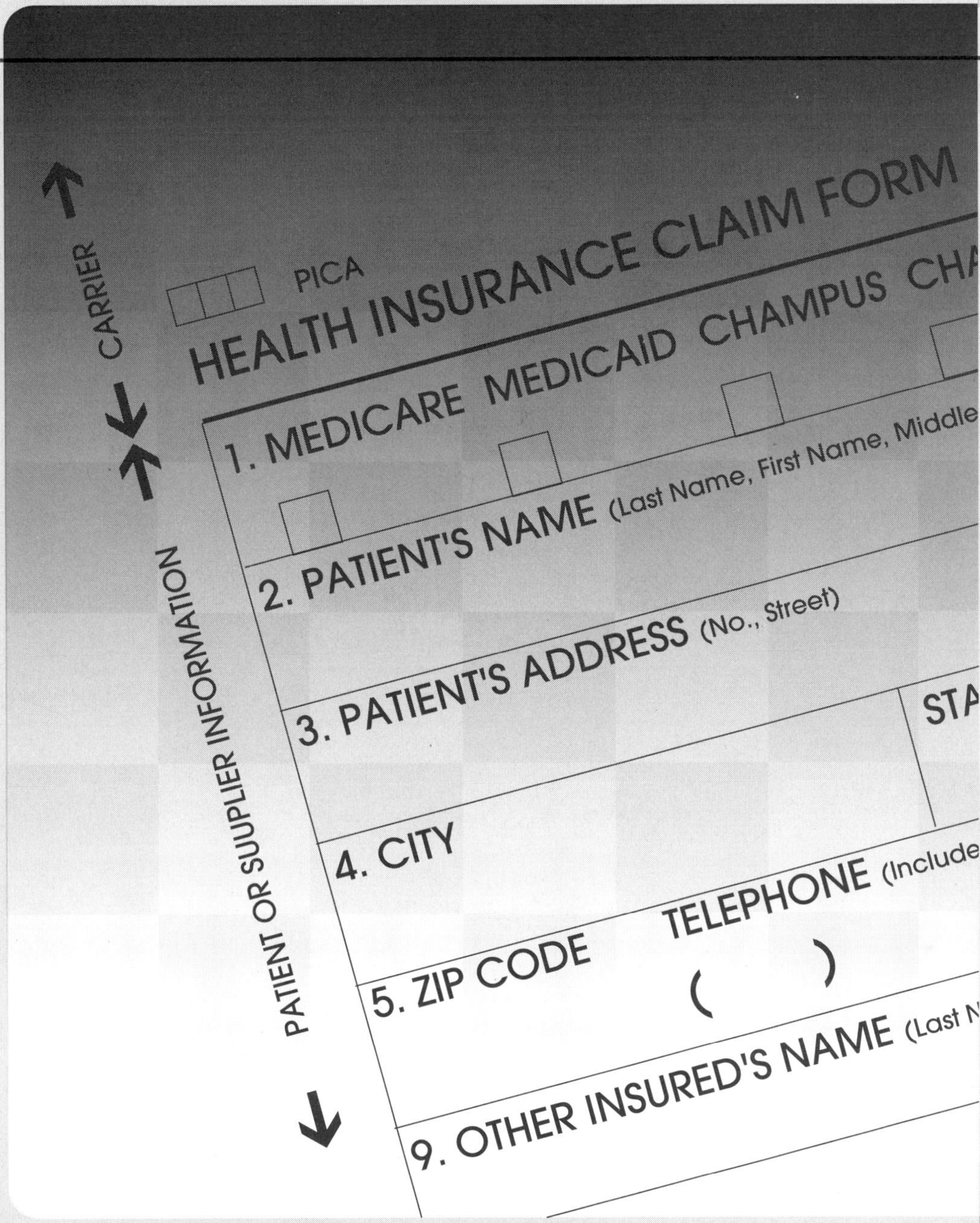

The Claims Process

Objectives*

THE INSURANCE BILLING SPECIALIST WILL BE ABLE TO:

- Distinguish between the three major classes of health insurance contracts.
- Describe in general terms the important federal, state, and private health insurance plans.
- Define common insurance terms.
- Handle insurance claims in the physician's office to minimize their rejection by insurance carriers.
- Explain the basic steps in processing an insurance claim from the physician's office, to the insurance carrier, and after the payment is received.
- Establish an insurance claims register or log.
- Determine the appropriate questions to ask a patient for a complete patient record.
- List the functions of a tickler file.

Key Terms

applicant
blanket contract
Blue Cross (BC)
Blue Shield (BS)
CHAMPUS
CHAMPVA
claim
coinsurance
Competitive Medical Plan (CMP)
conditionally renewable
contract
disability income insurance
exclusion
exclusive provider organization (EPO)
Foundations for Medical Care (FMC)
guaranteed renewable
health insurance
Health Maintenance Organization (HMO)
high risk
indemnity
Independent Practice Association (IPA)
insured
Maternal and Child Health Programs (MCHP)
Medicaid
Medicare (M)
member
noncancelable policy
optionally renewable
personal insurance
preauthorization
precertification
predetermination
Preferred Provider Organization (PPO)
subscriber
Unemployment Compensation Disability (UCD) or State Disability Insurance
Veterans Administration (VA) Outpatient Clinic
Workers' Compensation Insurance

*Performance objectives and exercises for hands-on practical experience for this chapter appear in the *Workbook*.

CHAPTER 3

Basics of Health Insurance

Introduction

It is important for an insurance billing specialist to know some basic insurance terms and to have a working knowledge of medical terminology. Insurance policies are complex and contain a great deal of technical jargon. This can cause misunderstanding by patients or anyone trying to obtain information from the policy. To give you a working knowledge of insurance, some of the basic words in this chapter have been italicized for emphasis; additional terms will be introduced and explained in subsequent chapters. See the Glossary at the end of this textbook for a comprehensive list of terms, with detailed definitions to broaden your knowledge.

This chapter focuses on basic insurance concepts, and Chapter 9 discusses health care reform, national health insurance policies and procedures, and various types of managed care.

History

The insurance industry is among the world's largest businesses. In the 1800s, life insurance came to be widely offered. Because anyone can have an accident or become ill unexpectedly, leading to large expenses, health insurance began to be available in the early part of this century. Health insurance is designed to help offset some of the high costs accrued during sickness or when an injury occurs.

During the Renaissance, when Italian traders insured valuable cargo to be shipped across the Mediterranean, they recorded the insurance agreement on a piece of folded paper called a *polizza*. English merchants adapted the term to their insurance practices, modifying the pronunciation to suit the Anglo-Saxon tongue, resulting in the word *policy*.

Because individual needs vary, each patient has a different type of health insurance policy with various benefits, or a patient may be covered under a different type of private, state, or federal program. In the last decade, medical care costs have escalated, forcing insurance companies to reduce their forms of coverage and the federal government to adopt cost-containment policies for the Medicare, Medicaid, and CHAMPUS programs.

The Insurance Policy

Basic health insurance coverage includes benefits for hospital, surgical, and other medical expenses. *Major medical* or *extended benefits* contracts are designed to offset large medical expenses caused by prolonged illness or serious injury. Some of these policies include coverage for *extended care* or *skilled nursing facility* benefits. The insured is known as a *subscriber* or, in some insurance programs, a *member*. The *insured* is known as a *policyholder* or *recipient* in some insurance programs and may or may not necessarily be the patient seen for the medical service. The insured is the individual (enrollee) or organization protected in case of loss under the terms of an insurance policy. The insured is not necessarily the *risk*, the person whose risk of loss from accident or sickness is protected against. In group insurance, the employer is the insured, and the employees are the risks. Generally, the Blue Plans refer to a *contract holder* as a *subscriber* or *member*. A policy might also include *dependents* of the insured. Generally, this term refers to the spouse and children of the insured, but under some contracts, parents or other family members may be dependents.

POLICY APPLICATION

Before a policy is issued, the insurance company decides whether it will enter into a contract with the *applicant* who is applying for the insurance coverage. Information is obtained about the applicant so the company can decide whether to accept the risk. Generally, the application form has two sections: part one contains basic information about the application, and part two concerns the health of the individual.

An insurance policy is a legally enforceable agreement, or *contract*. If a policy is issued, the applicant becomes part of the insurance contract or plan. The policy becomes effective only after the company offers the policy and the person accepts it and then pays the initial premium. If a premium is paid at the time the application is submitted, then the insurance coverage can be put into force before the policy is delivered. Depending on the laws in some states, the applicant can also have temporary conditional insurance if the agent issues a specific type of receipt.

POLICY PROVISIONS

Health insurance policies may have renewal provisions written into the policy stating the circumstances when the company may refuse to renew, may cancel coverage, or may increase the premium. There are five classifications: (1) cancelable, (2) optionally renewable, (3) conditionally renewable, (4) guaranteed renewable, or (5) noncancelable.

- A renewable provision in a *cancelable* policy grants the insurer the right to cancel the policy at any time and for any reason. The company notifies the insured the policy is canceled and refunds any advance premium the policyowner has paid. In some states, this type of policy is illegal.
- In an *optionally renewable* policy, the insurer has the right to refuse to renew the policy on a date (premium due or anniversary date) specified in the contract and may add coverage limitations or increase premium rates.
- *Conditionally renewable* policies grant the insurer a limited right to refuse to renew a health insurance policy at the end of a premium payment period. Reasons stated in the policy may be age and/or employment status but not because of the insured's health.
- The *guaranteed renewable* classification is desirable because the insurer is required to renew the policy as long as premium payments are

made. However, these policies may have age limits of 60, 65, or 70 years, or they may be renewable for life.

- In a *noncancelable* policy, the insurer cannot increase premium rates and must renew the policy until the insured reaches the age specified in the contract. Some disability income policies have noncancelable terms.

It is the patient's responsibility to give a written notice of *claim* to the insurance company within a certain number of days, known as a *time limit*. However, in some cases, the claim is filed for the patient by the medical assistant or insurance billing specialist. Thus, it becomes important to be able to abstract proper information from the patient record to the insurance form, to code the diagnoses, to code the services rendered by the physician, to complete an insurance claim, to make entries on the patient's ledger card, and to follow up on unpaid claims by contacting the claims representative, called an *adjuster*. If any of these procedures is not done properly, correct reimbursement or payment (also called *indemnity*) from the insurance *carrier* will not be generated. The payment might be too small or too large. If the payment is to go directly from the insurance company to the physician, then the patient must sign an *assignment of benefits* form granting permission.

Health insurance policies consider an *accident* to be an unforeseen and unintended event. Some policies cover accidents occurring from the first day the policy is in force. Others may contain an *elimination period* or a *waiting period* before benefits for sickness or accident become payable. Many policies do not provide benefits for conditions that existed and were treated before the policy was issued, called *preexisting conditions*. In some instances, such conditions might be covered after a specified period of time following the issuance of the policy.

COORDINATION OF BENEFITS

A *coordination of benefits* statement is included in most policies. When the patient has more than one insurance policy, this prevents duplication or overlapping of payments for the same medical expense.

Most state legislatures have adopted the *birthday law,* a change in the order of determination of coordination of benefits regarding primary and secondary carriers for dependent children. Rather than the father's insurance being primary, the father's *or* mother's carrier may be primary. The health plan of the person whose birthday (month and day, not year) falls earlier in the calendar year will pay first, and the plan of the other person covering the dependent will be the secondary payer. If both mother and father have the same birthday, the plan of the person who has had coverage longer is the primary payer. If one of the two plans has not adopted this birthday rule (i.e., if one plan is in another state), the rules of the plan without the birthday rule determine which plan is primary and which is secondary. In cases of divorce, the plan of the parent with custody of the children is the primary payer.

Unions and companies that self-insure their employees do not fall under this birthday law. The states that do not have birthday laws are Georgia, Hawaii, Idaho, Massachusetts, Mississippi, Vermont, Virginia, and Washington, D.C.

GENERAL POLICY LIMITATIONS

Health insurance policies also contain *exclusions*—some more than others. If a person has an injury or illness that is excluded in his or her policy, then there is no insurance coverage. These exclusions or limitations of the policy could be such factors as losses resulting from military service, attempted suicide, or self-inflicted injuries; losses due to an injury on the job; pregnancy; and so on. Some policies have a *waiver,* which is an attachment to a policy that excludes certain illnesses or disabilities that would otherwise be covered. Generally, waivers are used to eliminate benefits for specific preexisting conditions.

To keep the insurance in force, a person must pay a monthly, quarterly, or annual fee called a *premium*. If the premium is not paid, a *grace period* of from 10 to 30 days is usually given before insurance coverage ceases. In addition, usually a *deductible* (a specific amount of money) must be paid each year before the policy benefits begin. The higher the deductible, the lower is the cost of the policy.

Case Management Provisions

Many private insurance carriers and prepaid health plans require *precertification* or *predetermination* before they will approve certain hospital admissions, inpatient or outpatient surgeries, and elective procedures. The carrier can refuse to pay part or all of the fee if this requirement is not met.

Precertification refers to discovering whether a treatment (surgery, hospitalization, tests) is covered under a patient's contract. *Preauthorization* relates not only to whether a service or procedure is covered but also to finding out whether it is medically necessary. *Predetermination* means discovering the

Insurance Precertification Form

Insurance Carrier ______________________________
Admission Certification ______________ Outpatient _____ Inpatient _____
Surgery Certification ______________

Patient's Name ______________ Date of Birth ______________
Patient's Address ______________
____

Insured's Name ______________ Policy Group/ID No. ______________
Insured's Address ______________
____

Admitting Physician ______________ Admission Date ______________
Physician's Provider No. ______________
Name of Hospital ______________

Diagnosis ______________________________
Approximate length of hospital stay ______________
Complicating conditions to substantiate need for inpatient hospitalization ______________
____

Second Opinion obtained _____ Yes _____ No

Certification Approved _____ Yes _____ No
Reason(s) for denial ______________

Telephone precertification:
Name of representative certifying ______________
Direct-dial telephone number of representative ______________
Certification approved _____ Yes _____ No Certification approval No. ______________

Emergency situation:
Who must notify the insurance company? ______________
To whom must the notification be made? ______________
How many hours may elapse before notification? ______________
After-hours telephone number for reporting emergencies ______________

FIGURE 3–1
Insurance Precertification Form. This form can be sent to the insurance company or used when telephoning to find out if a particular treatment is covered under a patient's insurance policy.

maximum dollar amount that the carrier will pay for primary surgery, consulting services, postoperative care, and so on.

Obtain precertification or predetermination when a procedure is tentatively scheduled. The information that may be required to obtain precertification approval by mail or telephone is shown in Figure 3–1. To obtain predetermination by mail, use the form shown in Figure 3–2. This form can also be used to document the information received when verifying the patient's insurance coverage by telephone. It can become part of the patient's record and be used for reference when billing future insurance claims.

After the information is received from the insurance carrier, give the patient an estimate of fees for the proposed surgery. An example of suggested wording for a letter is given in Figure 3–3. This procedure makes collection quicker and easier.

Choice of Health Insurance

There are three ways in which a person can obtain health insurance: (1) take out insurance through a group plan (contract or policy), (2) pay the premium on an individual basis, or (3) enroll in a prepaid health plan.

Group Contract

A *group contract* is any insurance plan by which a group of employees (and their eligible dependents) or other homogeneous group is insured under a single policy issued to their employer or leader, with individual certificates given to each insured individual or family unit. A group policy usually provides better benefits, and the premiums are lower. However, the coverage for each person in the group is the same.

Many physicians can obtain comprehensive group coverage through plans sponsored by the professional organizations to which they belong. Sometimes this is called a *blanket contract*. If the person leaves the employer or organization or the group contract is terminated, the insured may continue the same or lesser coverage under an individual policy if the group contract has a *conversion privilege*.

Usually, conversion from a group policy to an individual policy increases the premium and reduces the benefits. However, if the person has a condition that would make him or her ineligible for coverage or is a *high-risk* case, it is advantageous to convert to an individual policy because no physical examination is required; therefore, a preexisting condition cannot be excluded.

Under the Consolidated Omnibus Budget Reconciliation Act of 1985 (COBRA), when an employee is laid off from a company with 20 or more workers, federal law requires that the group health insurance coverage be extended to the employee and their dependents at group rates for up to 18 months. This also applies to those workers who lose coverage because of reduced work hours. In the case of death of a covered employee, divorced or widowed spouse, or employee entitled to Medicare, the extension of coverage may be for 36 months. However, the employee must pay for the group policy; this is known as *income continuation benefits*. COBRA requires that third party payers reimburse for certain care rendered in government-run veterans and military hospitals. This act made private employer health plans primary to Medicare for active workers and their spouses who also have Medicare coverage. For additional information on this topic, see the section on COBRA in Chapter 12.

Individual Contract

Any insurance plan issued to an individual (and dependents) is called an *individual contract*. Usually, this type of policy has a higher premium, and often the benefits are less than those obtainable under a group health insurance plan. Sometimes this is called *personal insurance*.

Prepaid Health Plan

This is a program of health care in which a specified set of health benefits is provided for a subscriber or enrolled group of subscribers who pay a yearly fee or fixed periodic payments. For additional information on this topic, refer to Chapter 9.

Types of Health Insurance Coverage

Many forms of health insurance coverage are currently in effect in the United States. A brief explanation of the programs to be discussed in this text is given here. For an in-depth study, refer to the appropriate chapters that follow.

Blue Cross and Blue Shield Plans ■ Independent, generally nonprofit community service organizations that contract with hospitals, physicians, and other health care providers to give prepaid health care services to their subscribers. Some Blue Plans

INSURANCE PREDETERMINATION FORM

Patient:________________________ Policy: ________________________
Address________________________ ( ) Group # ____________________
City____________State________ZIP____ ( ) Individual #________________
Tel. No.______________ Date of Birth____________ Soc. Sec. #____________
Insurance Company______________________ Relation to insured: self ( )
Insurance Co. Address____________________ spouse ( )
Tel. No.______________________________ child ( )
Employer:______________________________ other ( )
Insurance Representative
Releasing Information:______________________Date:________Time:________
(Name) (Title)
Copy of insurance card attached? Yes_____ No. _____
BENEFITS
Major Medical: Yes _____ No _____ % Payable:______________
Deductible: Yes _____ No _____ Amount: $______________
time interval: Year _____ Month _____ Other:______________
per family: Yes _____ No _____ Per Person: Yes___ No___
Co-insurance: Yes _____ No _____ Amount: $______________

COVERAGE: 1. Office Visits: Yes _____ No _____ Amount $____________

2. Office X-rays & Lab: Yes _____ No _____ Amount $____________

3. Hospital surgery: Yes _____ No _____ Limit $ __________ UCR
Second opinion required: Yes _____ No _____
Preadmission hospital and surgical authorization: Yes_____ No _____

4. Office surgery: Yes _____ No _____ Limit $__________ UCR

5. General anesthesia: Yes _____ No _____ Per hr. $_____ Limit $_____

FEE SCHEDULE:
1. RVS Yes_____ No _____ 1974 1989 1993 conversion factor:____________
2. Other:____

DEPENDENT COVERAGE:
1. Spouse: Yes _____ No _____ Same?________________________
2. Children: Yes _____ No _____ Same?________________________

Prior Authorization____
IS YOUR FEE SCHEDULE FOR A ____________________THE SAME AS OTHER
(Physician's Specialty)
MEDICAL SPECIALISTS? Yes______ No _____
WHEN CAN I EXPECT PAYMENT AFTER SUBMISSION?____________________

REVIEW COPY SENT TO: ____________________ DATE:________________
(Name)
PERSON VERIFYING:______________________ DATE:________________

FIGURE 3-2
Insurance Predetermination Form. This form can be sent to the insurance company to find out the maximum dollar amount that will be paid for primary surgery, consulting services, postoperative care, and so forth.

COLLEGE CLINIC
4567 Broad Avenue
Woodland Hills, XY 12345-0000

Phone: 013/486-9002 **Fax: 013/590-2189**

Current date

Patient's name
Address
City, State, ZIP code

Dear

This letter gives you an estimate of the fees for your proposed surgery. Verification of coverage and benefit information has been obtained from your insurance company. Listed are your benefits for the proposed surgical expenses and the estimated balance after your insurance carrier pays.

Surgical Procedure ______________________________
Date of Surgery ______________________________
Name of Hospital ______________________________
Hospital Address ______________________________

		Insurance Pays	Estimated Balance
Surgeon's Fee	____________	____________	____________
Hospital Visits	____________	____________	____________
Follow-up Office Visits	____________	____________	____________

You have a policy deductible of $________which____has ____has not been met.

The surgery requires the use of an anesthesiologist, an assistant surgeon, and a pathologist. These physicians will bill you separately for their services. The hospital will also bill you separately.

This office will file your insurance claim for the surgical procedure, so the insurance payment should come directly to us. If the insurance carrier sends you the payment, then you are responsible to forward the payment to this office within 5 days. Your balance after surgery should be approximately $______. You are responsible for any remaining balance after our office receives the insurance payment.

Thank you for choosing our medical practice. If you have any questions, please call me.

Sincerely,

Karen Martinez, CMA
Administrative Medical Assistant

FIGURE 3-3
Sample letter to a patient supplying an estimate of the fees for proposed surgery.

have merged and have begun converting to for-profit status by forming publicly traded for-profit, managed-care subsidiaries (see Chapter 10).

CHAMPUS (Civilian Health and Medical Program of the Uniformed Services) ▪ This government-sponsored program provides hospital and medical services for dependents of active service personnel, retired service personnel and their dependents, and dependents of members who died on active duty (see Chapter 13).

CHAMPVA (Civilian Health and Medical Program of the Veterans Administration) ▪ The Veterans Administration shares the medical bills of spouses and children of veterans with total, permanent, service-connected disabilities or of the surviving spouses and children of veterans who died as a result of service-connected disabilities (see Chapter 13).

Competitive Medical Plan (CMP) ▪ A type of managed care organization created by the 1982 Tax Equity and Fiscal Responsibility Act (TEFRA), federal legislation for enrollment of Medicare beneficiaries into managed care plans (see Chapters 9 and 12).

Disability Income Insurance ▪ A form of health insurance that provides periodic payments to replace income when the insured is unable to work as a result of illness, injury, or disease (see Chapter 15).

Exclusive Provider Organization (EPO) ▪ A type of managed health care plan in which subscriber members are eligible for benefits only when they use the services of a limited network of providers. EPOs are regulated under state health insurance laws (see Chapter 9).

Foundation for Medical Care ▪ An organization of physicians, sponsored by a state or local medical association, concerned with the development and delivery of medical services and the cost of health care (see Chapter 9).

Health Maintenance Organization (HMO) ▪ An organization that provides a wide range of comprehensive health care services for a specified group at a fixed periodic payment. An HMO can be sponsored by the government, medical schools, hospitals, employers, labor unions, consumer groups, insurance companies, or hospital-medical plans (see Chapter 9).

Independent Practice Association (IPA) ▪ A medical capitation plan that provides a number of basic medical services at no charge, with additional charges for more costly procedures. Generally, *capitation* is characteristic of HMOs and is a method of payment for health services by which an individual or institutional provider is paid a fixed, per capita amount for each person served without regard to the actual number or nature of services provided to each person. Subscribers to IPA plans have limited or no choice of physician. Treatment is delivered via a clinic, an IPA, or IPA physicians who practice in their own offices and continue to see their fee-for-service patients. This is also called an individual practice association (see Chapter 9).

Maternal and Child Health Programs (MCHP), formerly Crippled Children's Services (CCS) ▪ A state and federal program for children who are under 21 years of age and have special health care needs. It assists parents with financial planning and may assume part or all of the costs of treatment, depending on the child's condition and the family's resources (see Chapter 11).

Medicaid ▪ A program sponsored jointly by the federal government and by state governments for people eligible for public assistance and for some other low-income people. Coverage and benefits vary widely from state to state. In California, this program is known as *Medi-Cal* (see Chapter 11).

Medicare (M) ▪ The hospital insurance system and supplementary medical insurance for those over 65 years of age, created by the 1965 Amendments to the Social Security Act and operated under the provisions of the act. Benefits are also extended to certain disabled people (e.g., totally disabled or blind) as well as coverage and payment for those requiring kidney dialysis and kidney transplant services (see Chapter 12).

Medicare/Medicaid (Medi-Medi) ▪ This program covers those persons protected under both Medicare and Medicaid (or Medi-Cal) (see Chapter 12).

Point-of-service (POS) Plan ▪ An HMO consisting of a network of physicians and hospitals that provides an insurance company or employer with discounts on its services (see Chapter 9).

Preferred Provider Organization (PPO) ▪ A form of contract medicine by which a large employer (e.g., hospitals or physicians) or any organization that can produce a large number of patients (e.g., union trusts, insurance companies, and so on) contracts with a hospital or a group of physicians to offer medical care at a reduced rate (see Chapter 9).

State Disability or Unemployment Compensation Disability (UCD) ▪ Insurance that covers off-the-job injury or sickness and is paid for by deductions from a person's paycheck. This program is administered by a state agency (see Chapter 15).

Veterans Administration (VA) Outpatient Clinic ▪ A clinic where medical and dental services are rendered to a veteran who has a service-related disability (see Chapter 15).

Workers' Compensation Insurance ▪ A contract that insures a person against on-the-job injury or illness. The employer pays the premium for his or her employees (see Chapter 14).

Examples of Insurance Billing

Sometimes, it is difficult to comprehend the full scale of insurance billing. As an example of total medical billing, six cases are presented to help you understand the entire billing picture from simple to complex.

CASE 1: **A new patient comes in with complaints of a sore throat and an infected nail.**

Physician's office bills for:

- Evaluation and Management services
- Penicillin injection
- Office surgery for infected nail
- Sterile surgical tray (may or may not be billed depending on carrier)

CASE 2: **A patient comes in because of an accident and has complaints that require Evaluation and Management services, x-rays, and laboratory studies performed in the physician's office.**

Physician's office bills for:

- Evaluation and Management services
- X-ray and laboratory studies, including interpretation (varies according to carrier; Medicare may not pay for interpretation)

CASE 3: **A patient is seen by the family physician after office hours in the hospital emergency department.**

A. Physician's office bills for:
   Evaluation and Management services

B. Hospital bills for:
   Hospital (outpatient) emergency department services (use and supplies)

CASE 4: **A patient is seen in the office and is immediately or 1 week later hospitalized for surgery.**

A. Physician's office bills for:
   Initial hospital admission, Evaluation and Management services, or presurgical consultation
   Surgical procedure, e.g., hysterectomy (physician is surgeon)

B. Assistant surgeon bills for:
   Hysterectomy (assists the surgeon) (some carriers do not allow)

C. Anesthesiologist bills for:
   Hysterectomy (anesthetizes the patient)

D. Hospital (inpatient) bills for:

Hospital room	Also could include:
Operating room	Blood for transfusions
Anesthesia supplies	Electrocardiogram (ECG)
Medications	Electroencephalogram (EEG)
X-rays	Electromyogram (EMG)
Laboratory studies	Radiation therapy
Medical and surgical supplies (dressings, IV lines, and so on)	Physical therapy
	Speech therapy
	Respiratory therapy
	Occupational therapy

CASE 5: **A patient is sent to a local hospital for an upper gastrointestinal (GI) series. A privately owned radiologic group takes the films in the hospital and does the interpretation.**

A. Hospital bills for:
   Upper GI series x-rays (technical component)

B. Radiologic group bills for:
   Upper GI series x-ray interpretation

CASE 6: **A physician sends a Medicare patient's Papanicolaou smear to a private clinical laboratory. (Note: Because of the Clinical Laboratory Improvement Amendment [CLIA] of 1988, federal standards, quality, and safety measures must be met or fines are levied whether a laboratory test performed is billed or not. This has had an impact on office laboratories, and many physicians send patients to independent laboratories for tests [blood counts, cytology specimens, cultures]. However, some physicians prefer to draw blood from a patient, particularly if the patient has a history of difficult veins. Physicians may not send patients to laboratories in which they have a proprietary interest. Physicians billing patients for outside laboratory work may charge the patient only what the laboratory charges [based on a fee schedule], plus any additional services the physician provides, e.g., drawing blood, handling, shipping, and interpretation of the blood, or the office visit.)**

A. The physician bills for:
   Evaluation and Management services

B. The laboratory bills for:
   Papanicolaou smear

A medical assistant or insurance billing specialist in the offices of the attending physician, assistant surgeon, anesthesiologist, radiologic group, and private clinical laboratory will submit an itemized statement and/or insurance claim form or give the patient the necessary information to submit his or her own claim to the insurance company. Exception: Generally, Medicare patients may not submit their own claims for physician or hospital services. Exceptions are mentioned in Chapter 12.

In the hospital and hospital emergency department, a hospital insurance clerk or patient representative prepares the itemized statement and submits the claim to the insurance carrier.

Basic Steps in Processing an Insurance Claim

There are four basic methods of preparing and processing insurance claims: manual claims submission, in-office electronic filing by fax or computer, contracting with an outside service bureau to prepare and submit the claims manually or electronically, or use of a telecommunications networking system. The fourth method is a system in which a computer is networked via modem (telephone line) to another computer at another site so that the patients' insurance information is available to generate the insurance claim. This method is used when a medical practice has two or three offices and all billing is accomplished at one site.

In the use of any of these methods, the basic steps (Fig. 3–4) in processing an insurance claim are as follows:

1. A patient service slip (also called a transaction, charge, or fee slip or encounter or router form) is attached to the patient's medical record (Fig. 3–5). This contains the patient's name, date, and, in some instances, the previous balance due.
2. After examination and treatment, the physician completes the patient service slip by checking off the service(s) and treatment(s) codes and diagnosis code and inserting the fee(s). The physician signs the slip and indicates whether the patient needs another appointment.
3. The patient carries the patient service slip to the reception desk and is given the opportunity to pay and make a future appointment.
4. The medical assistant or insurance billing specialist uses a copy of the patient service slip to post charges and payments to the patient's ledger card and day sheet (Fig. 3–5).
5. Generally, someone in the physician's office completes the insurance claim forms for the following cases: (1) all hospitalized (both surgical and medical) patients, (2) all claims where the benefits are assigned to the physician, and (3) special procedures (minor surgery or extensive testing). In these cases, the medical assistant/insurance billing specialist completes the HCFA-1500 insurance form, makes sure the assignment of benefits is signed by the patient, and mails the form to the insurance company.

   If an insurance claim form is mailed or brought in by the patient at the time of the office visit, the form is checked to be sure the patient has signed the release of information statement. The claim form is date stamped.

   Patients who are expected to submit their own insurance claim will be given two copies of the patient service slip. The patient retains one copy for personal records, attaches the second copy to the proper insurance claim form, and forwards it to the insurance company. This type of patient service slip (encounter or router form) used to be referred to as a *superbill* because it is an itemized billing statement and gives all pertinent information so that the patient can bill the insurance company directly. Many insurance companies no longer accept superbills. However, medical practices continue to use the encounter form as a communications tool (routing sheet) or as an invoice to the patient. When used as a routing sheet, it becomes a source document for insurance claim data. The encounter form's procedure and diag-

BASIC STEPS IN PROCESSING AN INSURANCE CLAIM

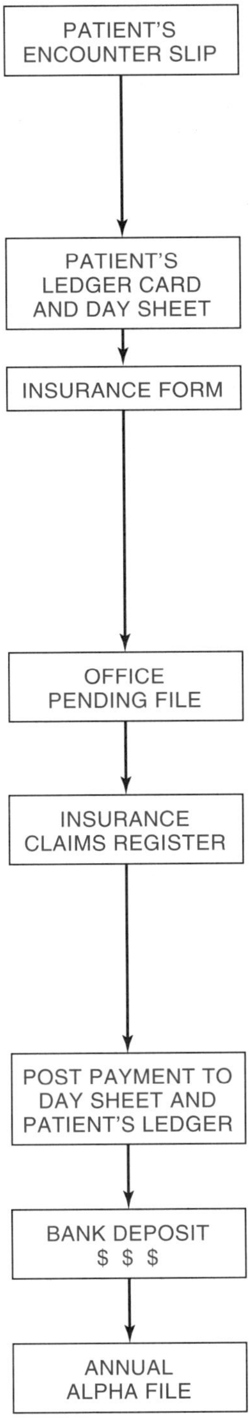

1. Patient encounter slip attached to patient's medical record. Slip contains patient's name, date, and, possibly, balance due.

2. Physician completes patient encounter slip by checking all service and diagnostic codes. Physician signs slip and indicates if patient needs return appointment. Fees are then determined.

3. Patient takes encounter slip to reception desk to make future appointment and to pay.

4. Insurance billing specialist uses copy of encounter slip to post charges and payments to patient's ledger card and day sheet.

5. Insurance form is completed and routed to the physician, who reviews it for accuracy and signs it.
   Generally physician's offices complete insurance claim forms for:
   a. All hospitalized (both surgical and medical) patients.
   b. All claims where benefits are assigned to the physician.
   c. Special procedures (minor surgery and/or extensive testing).
   The patient is given two copies of the patient encounter slip (i.e., superbill) to submit his or her own insurance claim, or the insurance billing specialist completes an insurance form with a signed assignment of benefits or attaches a copy of the encounter slip to the insurance form.
   d. If an insurance form is mailed or brought into the office by the patient, the form is date stamped and logged into the insurance claims register.

6. A duplicate claim is put in the office pending file. Insurance billed and date submitted are noted on the patient's ledger card and recorded into the insurance register (see Figure 3-6).

7. Envelope is addressed and insurance claim form is mailed to insurance carrier.
   Insurance carrier's processing:
   a. Claim form is scanned for identification of patient and policy number.
   b. Procedure code numbers are matched with the policy's master benefits list.
   c. Procedure codes are cross-matched with diagnostic code numbers.
   d. Claim form is checked against common data file.
   e. Determination is made of "allowed or approved" charges.
   f. Patient's deductible amount is determined.
   g. Copayment or coinsurance requirement is determined.
   h. Explanation of benefits (EOB) or remittance advice form is generated.
   i. EOB and insurance payment check are mailed to provider.

8. When proper payment is recieved, the payment is posted to the patient's ledger card and current day sheet.

9. The payment check received is entered on a bank deposit slip.

10. A duplicate copy of the insurance claim is pulled from the pending file, attached to the EOB, and filed in an annual alpha file or in the patient's financial record. If an annual alpha file is maintained, the records should be retained for 3 years before purging.

11. Bill the patient for the balance due, if any.

FIGURE 3–4
Basic steps in processing an insurance claim in a physician's office, to the insurance carrier, by the insurance company, and after payment is received.

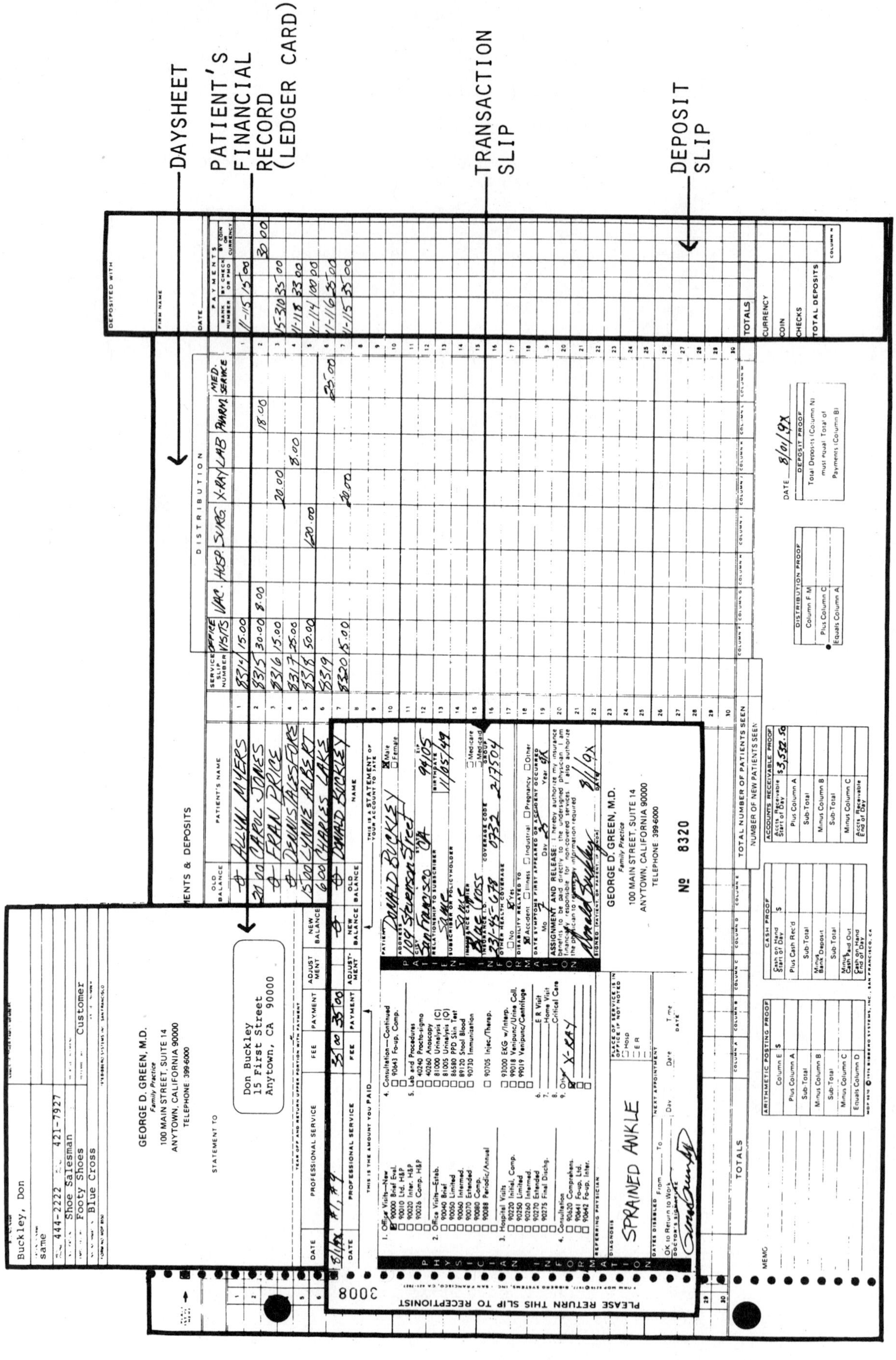

FIGURE 3–5
Pegboard bookkeeping system illustrating a ledger card, transaction slip, deposit slip, and day sheet. (Courtesy of Bibbero Systems, Inc., Petaluma, California. Phone: 800-242-2376; FAX: 800-242-9330.)

nostic codes should be updated annually with correct descriptions. Remove all codes not used or seldom used and revise and add current valid commonly used codes for the practice; do not print large quantities because codes change annually. Some practices develop encounter forms for different services (e.g., surgical services, office services [within the facility], and out-of-office services [hospital visits, emergency, outpatient facility, nursing home, or house calls]). Examples of encounter forms are shown in Chapter 9, Figures 9–6 and 9–7.

The minimum information required by third party payers is

- What was done (services and procedures)
- Why it was done (diagnoses using ICD-9-CM codes, discussed later)
- When it was performed (date)
- Where it was received (place of service)
- Who did it (provider number)

6. The completed insurance form is routed to the physician, who reviews it for accuracy and signs it.
7. A duplicate of the claim is retained in the office pending file in the event payment is not received and the claim must be followed up. This file may also be referred to as a suspense, follow-up, or tickler file. The term "tickler" came into existence because it tickles or jogs the memory at certain dates in the future (Fig. 3–6). Note on the patient's ledger card to whom the claim was sent and the submission date.
8. File an office copy of the claim form and record the submission in the insurance claims register (Fig. 3–7).
9. An envelope is addressed and the claim form is mailed to the insurance carrier. Refer to Figure 3–4 for the nine phases of processing by an insurance carrier of a claim form for payment.
10. Payment from the insurance carrier should be received in 4 to 8 weeks. The duplicate claim form is pulled from the file to verify the payment received with the amount due. When proper payment is received, the duplicate copy of the insurance claim is pulled out of the pending file and filed in an annual alpha file. Some medical practices file claim forms at the back section of the patient's medical record after payment is received and accepted (optional but not preferred system). The payment is posted (credited) to the patient's

3

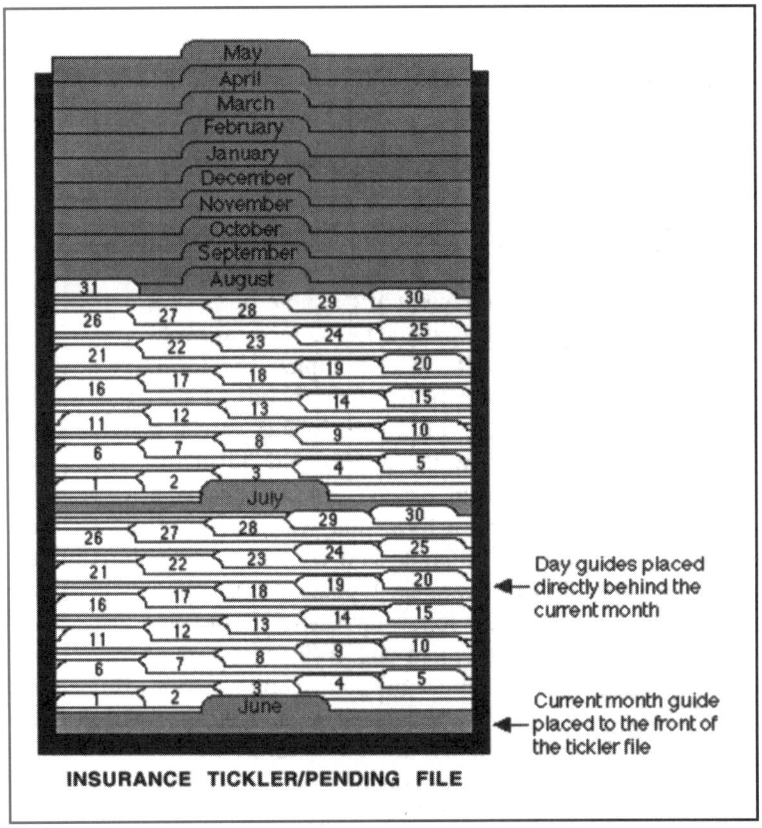

FIGURE 3–6
Example of a 30- to 60-day pending or tickler file for following up on unpaid insurance claims.

INSURANCE CLAIMS REGISTER Page No. _____

Claim No.	Patient's Name Group/Policy No.	Name of Insurance Company	Claim Submitted		Follow-Up Date	Claim Paid		Difference
			Date	Amount		Date	Amt	

FIGURE 3–7
Insurance Claims Register. An example of how a form can be set up to establish an easy way to follow up on insurance claims.

ledger card and current day sheet. The check is then entered on a bank deposit slip and may be deposited at the bank.

11. The patient is billed for the balance due, if any.

When insurance claims are sent in on a monthly basis, the balance due on the patient's ledger card may differ from the balance due on the insurance claim form. This occurs when a patient is given professional services each month and insurance claims are sent in on a monthly basis.

If an annual alpha file is maintained, the records should be retained for 3 years before purging, to meet the requirements of the Internal Revenue Service. The Internal Revenue Service can request tax records for the 3 years preceding an audit. The audit can include records for the previous 6 years if taxpayers fail to report more than 25 per cent of their gross income. There are no time limitations if taxpayers file a fraudulent return or fail to file a return.

Improper payments received and claims that become delinquent are discussed in Chapter 8.

Handling Insurance Claims

To maintain a harmonious patient-physician relationship, always be friendly and courteous when handling insurance claims. If the patient feels free to discuss personal financial problems at any time and is educated regarding the physician's fees, collections can often be significantly improved and simplified. The value of maintaining careful records of all insurance matters cannot be overemphasized. The following hints will help you handle insurance claims properly.

FIRST VISIT: PATIENT INFORMATION SHEET

1. A patient information sheet is also called a patient registration record (Fig. 3–8). This form should be completed by the patient at the time of the initial office visit. If the patient has a medical problem that makes it difficult to complete the form, such as rheumatoid arthritis of the hands

3

PATIENT INFORMATION
FOR
MEDICARE AND OTHER MEDICAL RECORDS **DATE:**

Please Print *GROUP PLAN OR INS. CO. NAME______

#1 CHECK APPROPRIATE BLOCK(S)
☐ MEDICARE (Medicare No) ☐ MEDICAID (Medicaid No) ☐ CHAMPUS (Sponsor's SSN) ☐ CHAMPVA (VA File No) ☐ GROUP HEALTH PLAN:* (SSN or ID) ☐ PRIVATE INS. CO.:* ☐ FECA BLK LUNG (SSN) ☐ OTHER (ID)

1a. INSURED'S I.D. NUMBER (From Block #1)

2. PATIENT'S NAME (Last Name, First Name, Middle Initial)

3. PATIENT'S BIRTH DATE MM | DD | YY SEX MALE ☐ FEMALE ☐

4. INSURED'S NAME (Last Name, First Name, Middle Initial)

5. PATIENT'S ADDRESS (No., Street)

6. PATIENT RELATIONSHIP TO INSURED Self ☐ Spouse ☐ Child ☐ Other ☐

7. INSURED'S ADDRESS (No., Street)

CITY | STATE

8. PATIENT STATUS Single ☐ Married ☐ Other ☐ Employed ☐ Full-Time Student ☐ Part-Time Student ☐

CITY | STATE

ZIP CODE | TELEPHONE (Include Area Code) ( )

ZIP CODE | TELEPHONE (Include Area Code) ( )

9. OTHER INSURED'S NAME (Last Name, First Name, Middle Initial)

10. IS PATIENT'S CONDITION RELATED TO:

11. INSURED'S POLICY GROUP OR FECA NUMBER

a. OTHER INSURED'S POLICY OR GROUP NUMBER

a. EMPLOYMENT? (CURRENT OR PREVIOUS) ☐ YES ☐ NO

b. INSURED'S DATE OF BIRTH MM | DD | YY SEX MALE ☐ FEMALE ☐

b. OTHER INSURED'S DATE OF BIRTH MM | DD | YY SEX MALE ☐ FEMALE ☐

b. AUTO ACCIDENT? PLACE (State) ☐ YES ☐ NO

b. INSURED'S EMPLOYER'S NAME OR SCHOOL NAME

c. OTHER INSURED'S EMPLOYER'S NAME OR SCHOOL NAME

c. OTHER ACCIDENT? ☐ YES ☐ NO

c. INSURED'S INSURANCE PLAN NAME OR PROGRAM NAME

d. OTHER INSURED'S INSURANCE PLAN NAME OR PROGRAM NAME

CHECK IF APPROPRIATE: ☐ MEDIGAP POLICY ☐ RETIREE COVERAGE

d. IS THERE ANOTHER HEALTH BENEFIT PLAN? ☐ YES ☐ NO *If yes,* complete items 9 a-d.

12. PATIENT'S OR AUTHORIZED PERSON'S SIGNATURE. I authorize the release of any medical or other information necessary to process this claim. I also request payment of government benefits either to myself or to the party who accepts assignment below.

SIGNED ______ DATE ______

13. INSURED'S OR AUTHORIZED PERSON'S SIGNATURE. I authorize payment of medical benefits to the undersigned physician or supplier for services described below.

SIGNED ______

SUPPLEMENTAL INFORMATION

REASON FOR THIS VISIT: ______

ONSET DATE OF CURRENT ILLNESS (1ST SYMPTOM), INJURY (ACCIDENT), OR PREGNANCY (LMP)____/____/____

IF SAME OR RECURRING ILLNESS, ENTER DATE OF INCEPTION____/____/____

LIST DATES IF UNABLE TO WORK AT CURRENT OCCUPATION DUE TO CONDITION FROM ____/____/____ TO ____/____/____

NAME OF REFERRING PHYSICIAN OR OTHER SOURCE______

(FOR OFFICE USE ONLY) IF REFERRING OR ORDERING PHYSICIAN, ENTER UPIN______

▼ IF SOMEONE OTHER THAN PATIENT OR PERSON(S) LISTED ABOVE IS RESPONSIBLE FOR PAYMENT PLEASE COMPLETE THIS SECTION

NAME OF RESPONSIBLE PARTY ______ ADDRESS CITY STATE ZIP

WHAT IS THEIR RELATIONSHIP TO THE PATIENT? ______ SOCIAL SECURITY NUMBER ______

EMPLOYED BY ______ WORK PHONE ( ) ______ HOME PHONE ( ) ______

▼ IF YOUR INJURY IS JOB RELATED

NAME OF PERSON WHO CAN AUTHORIZE TREATMENT______

PHONE (OFFICE) ______ EXT. ______ HOME PHONE: ______

COMPANY'S INSURANCE CARRIER ______ ADDRESS

INSURANCE CARRIER PHONE NUMBER ( ) ______ OK'D BY ______

▼ PLEASE SIGN AND RETURN TO RECEPTIONIST

INSURED OR GUARDIAN SIGNATURE	PATIENT'S SIGNATURE

58-8407 1990 BIBBERO SYSTEMS, INC. • PETALUMA, CA 11/90 (MB-CO) # 8-12 (REV. 7/92) TO REORDER CALL TOLL FREE: (800) BIBBERO — (800 242-2376)

FIGURE 3-8

Patient registration record showing a comprehensive listing of personal and financial information to be obtained from the patient on his or her first visit to the office. (Courtesy of Bibbero Systems, Inc., Petaluma, California. Phone: 800-242-2376; FAX: 800-242-9330.)

PATIENT INFORMATION UPDATE

Welcome, we are delighted to see you again!
Please take a few minutes to help us update our records.

Name ______________________________ Today's Date ______________
FIRST MIDDLE LAST

1. Has your name changed since your last visit here? ______ Yes ______ No
   If yes, what was the old name? ______________________________
   What name do you use for health insurance if different than above? ______________________________
   ____
2. If you have a new or different address since your initial visit here, please indicate below:
   ____
   ____
   ____
3. Has your marital status changed? ______ Yes ______ No
4. Has your telephone number changed? ______ Yes ______ No
   Please indicate your correct telephone number ______________________________
5. Has your employment changed? ______ Yes ______ No
   Please indicate your new employer name and address:
   ____
   ____
   ____
   New employer telephone #: ______________________________
6. Have you changed health insurance companies? ______ Yes ______ No
   If yes, please indicate your new health insurance carrier and address.
   Primary ______________________ Secondary ______________________
   ______________________ ______________________
   ______________________ ______________________
   Group Nos. ______________________ Group Nos. ______________________
   Subscriber Nos. ______________________ Subscriber Nos. ______________________
7. Who is responsible for this bill? ______________________________
8. Please note any changes in your health since your last visit.
   Illness ______________________________
   Accident ______________________________
   Allergies ______________________________
   Medications being taken ______________________________
   ____
   Other ______________________________
   ____
   ____
9. Signature ______________________________

F202B/REV. 2/90 Professional Filing Systems, Inc. 1-800-477-7473, In Atlanta 404/396-4894

PATIENT INFORMATION UPDATE

FIGURE 3–9
Patient Information Update form showing questions to ask the patient for updating a previous Patient Registration Record. (Courtesy of Professional Filing Systems, Inc., Atlanta, Georgia.)

or limited vision, then the insurance billing specialist may have to interview the patient and fill in the necessary data. Obtain *complete* information on a new patient by using a form that will contain information pertinent to credit and collections. This information must be *accurate*. Update the form annually, as this makes follow-up easier should the account become delinquent (Fig. 3–9).

There are two kinds of patient information sheets:

a. A personalized record sheet developed by the physician (perhaps in conjunction with the insurance billing specialist) for his or her own use. See Figure 3–8 as well as examples shown throughout the *Workbook*.
b. A form furnished the physician by a collection agency or malpractice insurance company. An arbitration agreement is sometimes printed on this sheet. Arbitration is a legal method, provided for by statute in certain states, by which patient and physician agree to resolve any controversy that may arise between them before an impartial panel. The advantages of arbitration are speed of settlement and reduction of expense (see Chapter 2).

2. The following facts should be recorded:
   a. Name: first, middle initial, and last. (Some pediatric patients do not have the same last name as their parents or stepparents. An insurance check is usually received with the policyholder's name, and it is time consuming to find and give credit to the patient's account. If using a computer system, cross-reference the name or Social Security number so that when you call up the policyholder's name, the patient's name will also appear. If a manual system is used, keep an alphabetical card index of parental or billing names that also lists each patient's name.)
   b. Address and telephone number.
   c. Business address, telephone number, and occupation.
   d. Date of birth. (This is now recorded on insurance forms as six digits because many insurance forms are processed by computer. January 2, 1936, is written as 01-02-36.)
   e. Person responsible for account or insured's name.
   f. Social Security number.
   g. Spouse's name and occupation.
   h. Whether a patient is referred by another physician or patient.
   i. Driver's license number.
   j. Close relative or friend (name, address, and telephone number).
   k. Insurance billing information.
3. Obtain the names, addresses, and policy and group numbers of *all* insurance companies insuring the patient. This is important because of the coordination of benefits clause written into some health insurance policies. Elderly patients are given the option of joining managed care programs and are allowed to switch every 30 days. Always ask each elderly patient whether he or she is covered by traditional Medicare or a Medicare HMO (health maintenance organization). A good patient information sheet will have space where this information can be written in by the patient. The patient obtains this information from his or her insurance identification card(s).
4. Always copy front and back sides of the patient's insurance card and date the photocopy. Sometimes the reverse side of the card provides information, such as deductible, copayment, preapproval provisions, and insurance company address and telephone number. A copy produces error-free insurance data. On a return visit, ask to see the card and check it with the data on file. If it differs, photocopy both sides and write the date on the copy, using this as the base for revising data on file. An insurer can have several different health plans, each with different copayments.
5. Recheck insurance policy or group numbers every 6 months because these numbers can change.
6. If the physician is submitting an insurance claim for the patient, the patient must sign a release of information form (also known as an authorization or consent form) before information can be given to an insurance company, attorney, or other third party regardless of whether the physician wishes to accept assignment. If the physician wishes to accept assignment, the patient signs information release and assignment of benefits forms for each insurance company. Many insurance forms, such as the universal Health Insurance Claim Form (HCFA-1500), contain boxes for the patient's signature with authorization for release of information and assignment of benefits (Fig. 3–10).

Assignment is the transfer of one's right to collect an amount payable under an insurance contract. In completion of the HCFA-1500 insurance claim form, information about assignment is printed in blocks 12, 13, and 27. The date and patient's signature must appear in blocks 12 and 13.

When using an insurance claim with no printed assignment, attach a signed patient authorization (signature-on-file) form with "Bene-

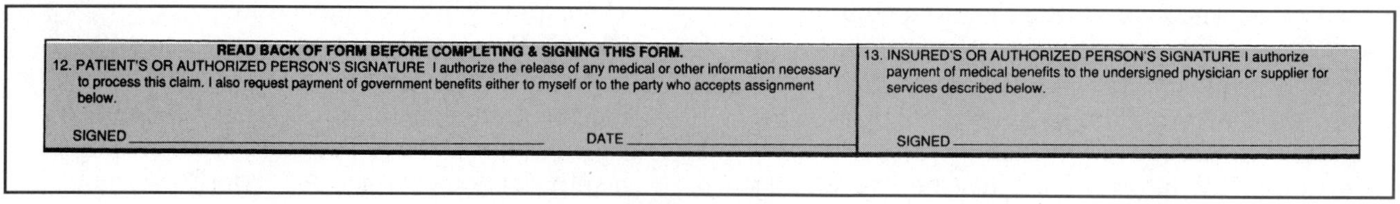

READ BACK OF FORM BEFORE COMPLETING & SIGNING THIS FORM.

12. PATIENT'S OR AUTHORIZED PERSON'S SIGNATURE I authorize the release of any medical or other information necessary to process this claim. I also request payment of government benefits either to myself or to the party who accepts assignment below.

SIGNED ______ DATE ______

13. INSURED'S OR AUTHORIZED PERSON'S SIGNATURE I authorize payment of medical benefits to the undersigned physician or supplier for services described below.

SIGNED ______

FIGURE 3–10

Sections 12 and 13 from the Health Insurance Claim Form HCFA-1500, illustrating authorization for release of information and assignment of benefits.

fits assigned; see attachment" or "Patient's request for payment on file" typed on the form. Attachments to insurance forms may be lost after their arrival at the insurance company. Some insurance billing specialists make two copies of the assignment (one for the insurance company and one for the physician's office) and then stamp or type on the insurance claim, "The above patient has signed the attached assignment of benefits; the XYZ insurance company will be liable for payment of this bill." This indicates that the insurance company should make out the check to the physician who rendered the professional services.

With a patient on a federal program such as CHAMPUS or Medicare (see Chapters 12 and 13), acceptance of assignment means not only that the check will come to the physician but also that the physician will accept what the federal program will allow as a "reasonable charge." The federal program will pay 75% or 80% of this reasonable charge, and the patient will pay the remaining 25% to 20%. This is called *coinsurance,* which is a cost-sharing requirement under some health insurance programs or is written into some policies that provide that the insured assumes a percentage of the costs of covered services.

Instructions on how to complete the HCFA-1500 health insurance claim form are given in Chapter 6.

SUBMITTING AND TRACING THE CLAIM

1. Date stamp *all* incoming insurance forms, whether brought in by the patient or received by mail. This will permit you to remind the patient when the form was received in the office, in the event that the patient's own records are incomplete.
2. Group together all the ledgers and charts from patients who have the same type of insurance and bill them all at one time. This cuts down on errors and makes completing the forms easier. Mail claims in batches to each carrier to save on postage. Use no-carbon-required health insurance claim forms (HCFA-1500) so that you do not have to photocopy claims after completion; just retain the file copies. Or, if your office handles a large volume of claims, divide the unpaid claims into four groups, one for each of the three largest insurers and the fourth for all others. Work on one group each week so the work is spread out over the 4 weeks in the month.
3. Do not bill one fee to the insurance company and a different fee to the patient.
4. *Optional:* Establish an insurance claims register (tracing file) to keep track of the status of each case that has been billed (see Fig. 3–6).
5. Post the insurance payments on the patient's ledger card. This is a control factor for the doctor, patient, and accountant. Show the date billed, name of insurance company, amount, and name of the patient if the ledger includes the names of more than one family member.
6. Usually, claims are submitted as soon as possible after professional services are rendered except for patients receiving continuing care. However, there are time limits (from 30 days to 1 1/2 years) for filing an insurance claim. This can vary depending on the private insurance carrier, the federal or state program, and whether the claim is for an illness or accident. If the claim is filed after the time limit, payment can be denied. Some offices prefer daily or weekly billing.

Losses from delay can occur in the following instances. If a patient has had a long-term illness, insurance benefits can run out before a claim is processed. If several physicians treat the same patient, some insurance companies pay only one of the physicians (typically, whoever files the claim first is paid first). Submit hospitalized patients' insurance forms twice a month (on the 15th and 30th) regardless of discharge.

For easy and quick access, some practices

prefer to keep the patients' financial records separate from their medical records. The financial record should contain all billing information, completed patient information form, patient authorization or signature-on-file form, copies of insurance identification cards, responsible-party authorization, insurance correspondence, explanation of benefits or remittance advice documents, and a log of all telephone conversations and actions taken regarding insurance disputes or collection activities.

For further information on tracing a claim, see Chapter 8.

INSURANCE CLAIMS REGISTER

To reduce collections, it is wise to establish a follow-up procedure on insurance claims. As each form is completed and sent from the physician's office, perform the following steps or use the optional methods.

1. Log the claim on an insurance claims register form (see Fig. 3–7). The insurance billing specialist handling the insurance forms can see at a glance which claims are becoming delinquent and the amounts owed to the physician.
2. Keep two copies of each claim for the physician's records, one to be filed by patient name and the other by carrier name.
3. *Or* simply record the name of the insurance company on each patient's ledger card and keep a file by carrier name only. Then, all inquiries may be included in a single letter to the insurance company, eliminating having to write to the same company three or four times in a 2-day period.
4. *Or* establish a pending or tickler file for each month of service, retaining all unpaid claims. This method is easy for 30- to 60-day follow-up (see Fig. 3–7). Write a follow-up letter to the insurance company asking for payment and enclose a copy of the original claim form. Then, attach a copy of the follow-up letter to the file copy of the claim form and put it into the tickler file in a folder for 30- to 60-day follow-up. For additional information about how to set up a tickler file, see Chapter 8.
5. Notify the patient on the monthly statement, "Insurance company billed for above charge. You will be notified of any balance due."
6. Appeal every incorrect payment. Always check every private, Blue Shield, CHAMPUS, Medicare, and Workers' Compensation payment against the fee schedule or customary profile to determine whether the benefits were allowed correctly.

Instead of writing a letter, you may want to make a telephone call to the insurance company. It may save time and money, and you may reach an expert who is able to solve the problem. Here are some basic guidelines to follow.

1. Assemble all documents needed (e.g., patient's medical record, copy of the insurance claim form, explanation of benefits or remittance advice documents, and so on).
2. Remain courteous at all times.
3. Obtain the name and extension number of the insurance claims representative or adjuster, and keep this with your telephone records. After developing rapport, you may wish to call on him or her in the future for help. Ask for any toll-free numbers that the company may have, and keep these for future reference.
4. Listen carefully. Jot down the date and take notes of how to solve the problem. This may be of help if another problem of the same type occurs again.

Keeping Up-to-Date

- Make up a folder or binder of pertinent insurance information. Obtain information booklets and manuals from the local offices of the various insurance companies. Obtain sample copies of all the forms required for the insurance plans most used in your physician's office and samples of completed claim forms.
- Keep well informed by reading your Medicaid (Medi-Cal), Medicare, CHAMPUS, and local medical society bulletins. Maintain a chronologic file on each of these bulletins for easy reference, always keeping the latest bulletin on top. This will also help you keep this *Handbook* up to date.
- Attend any workshops offered in your area on insurance in medical practice because changes occur daily and monthly. The American Association of Medical Assistants* has chapters in many states that feature educational workshops and lectures.
- Become a member of the National Association of Claims Assistance Professionals, American

* 20 N. Wacker Drive, Chicago, IL 60606.

Academy of Procedural Coders, American Association of Medical Billers, and/or American Health Information Management Association. Each of these associations distributes journals or newsletters on a monthly basis featuring current information.

TO THE STUDENT

Study Chapter 3 and then answer the review questions in the *Workbook* to reinforce the theory learned in this chapter of the text and to help prepare you for a future test. For further knowledge and understanding, the key terms at the beginning of the chapter appear in the Glossary at the end of this textbook so that you can look up the pertinent terms. Refer to the *Workbook,* Assignment 3, to help reinforce the basic steps in submitting an insurance claim form.

CHAPTER 4

Procedural Coding

Objectives*

THE INSURANCE BILLING SPECIALIST WILL BE ABLE TO:

- Explain the purpose of coding for professional services.
- Use procedure code books properly.
- Define procedure code terminology.
- Explain the importance and usage of modifiers in procedure coding.
- Code after completing the procedure code problems in the *Workbook.*
- Describe the differences between CPT and RVS coding systems.
- Describe various methods of payment by insurance companies and state and federal programs.
- Explain the reasons medical documentation is required.

Key Terms

actual charge
asterisk procedures
coding creep
conversion factor
crib sheet
Current Procedural Terminology (CPT)
customary charge
documentation
down coding
global fee
Health Care Financing Administration Common Procedure Coding System (HCPCS)
modifier
prevailing charges
procedure codes
relative value studies (RVS)
SOAP
special report
unbundling
upcoding
usual, customary, and reasonable (UCR)

* Performance objectives and exercises for hands-on practical experience for this chapter appear in the *Workbook.*

CHAPTER 4

Procedural Coding

Introduction

This chapter deals with procedural coding for professional services. Chapter 5 deals with coding diagnoses. Proper coding can mean financial success or failure in a medical practice.

With the use of the computer to produce insurance claims and the use of telecommunications, magnetic tape billing, or optical scanning equipment to process payment of these claims, more emphasis is placed on the transformation of verbal descriptions of diseases, injuries, and procedures into numeric designations (coding) by the physician rendering medical care. Coding must be correct if claims are to be paid promptly. Every individual diagnosis and procedure or service must be assigned correct and complete code numbers. Because of the complexity of diagnostic and procedural coding, a working knowledge of medical terminology, including anatomy and physiology, is essential.

Two coding systems are used in physicians' offices—(1) for diagnoses: *International Classification of Diseases*, Ninth Revision, *Clinical Modification* (ICD-9-CM), updated each October; and (2) for services and procedures: *Physicians' Current Procedural Terminology*, fourth edition (CPT),* published annually by the American Medical Association (AMA). Another rating scale, called relative value studies (RVS) is also used for services and procedures (see later).

Institutions (within a facility), pathologists, and those involved with generating medical reports and billing for laboratory medicine procedures use a system for retrieving types of diagnoses. These codes are found in a book entitled *Systematized Nomenclature of Human and Veterinary Medicine (SNOMED International)*, Volumes I through IV.† In addition, this system is used for managing patient records, teaching medical information science (informatics), and indexing and managing research data.

Coding of Procedures

Various books are available for coding procedures for physicians. In some states, medical societies and medical specialty associations publish books for this purpose. The Blue Shield Plans use code numbers, and usually each district office can be contacted to obtain a Blue Shield manual (see Appendix B).

Almost all states use some method of procedural coding, and many states recommend CPT. CPT emerged as the procedural coding of choice when the federal government developed the Health Care Financing Administration Common Procedure Coding System (HCPCS) for the Medicare program. The Medicare HCPCS consists of three levels of coding:

- Level I: the AMA CPT codes and modifiers (national codes)
- Level II: Health Care Financing Administration (HCFA) designated codes and alpha modifiers (national codes)
- Level III: Codes inherent to fiscal intermediary or individual insurance carrier and not already found in the first two levels (regional codes)

Examples of the second level may be found at the end of Appendix B of the Student Workbook for the *Insurance Handbook for the Medical Office*. The HCPCS is updated each spring. (See Chapter 12 for additional information on coding for Medicare cases.)

In some states, the CHAMPUS and Medicaid programs accept CPT codes. In most states, Blue Shield uses CPT, and most third party payers have adopted the CPT system.

The procedure codes are used to standardize codes and precisely describe the services provided by physicians and allied health professionals. This then allows claim forms to be optically scanned by insurance companies. The general acceptance of the codes by insurance carriers and government agencies assures the physician who uses this coding system that the services and procedures he or she performs can be objectively identified and priced.

Some managed care plans develop a few "plan codes" for use by the plan only. Sometimes, the codes are used for tracking; other times, they are used to provide reimbursement for a service not defined with CPT.

CURRENT PROCEDURAL TERMINOLOGY (CPT)*

The first edition of *Physicians' Current Procedural Terminology* appeared in 1966, and the book was subsequently revised in 1970, 1973, and 1977. Since 1984, *Physicians' Current Procedural Terminology*, fourth edition (CPT) has been updated and revised annually. Code numbers are added or deleted as new procedures are developed or other procedures are modified. Without revision, physicians would use a single procedure number and procedure description for several services instead of for just one service.

CPT uses a basic five-digit system for coding services rendered by physicians, plus two-digit add-on modifiers or separate five-digit numbers representing the modifiers to indicate complications or special circumstances. Code numbers represent diagnostic and therapeutic *procedures* on medical billing statements and insurance forms.

* Available from Book and Pamphlet Fulfillment—OP-3416, American Medical Association, P.O. Box 10946, Chicago, IL 60610-0946.

† Available from the College of American Pathologists, 325 Waukegan Road, Northfield, IL 60093-2750.

*** CPT codes, descriptions, and two-digit numeric modifiers only are from CPT 96 copyright 1995 American Medical Association. All Rights Reserved.**

Example: A physician providing diagnostic or therapeutic radiology, ultrasound, or nuclear medicine services in a hospital would use either modifier -26 or 09926 to report the professional component.

74430-26	Cystography + professional component
OR	
74430 and 09926	Cystography + professional component

The five-digit modifiers are useful when claim forms, especially electronic claims, cannot accommodate more than five digits in any one space. Modifiers will be discussed in detail later in this chapter.

RELATIVE VALUE STUDIES (RVS)

In 1956, the California Medical Association Committee on Fees published the first edition of the *California Relative Value Studies* (CRVS). It was subsequently revised and published in 1957, 1960, 1964, 1969, and 1974. RVS is sometimes referred to as relative value scale, or schedule. It is a coded listing of procedures with unit values that indicate the relative value of the various services performed, taking into account the time, skill, and overhead cost required for each service.

The units in this scale are based on median charges of all physicians during the time period in which the RVS was published. Conversion factors are used to translate the abstract units in the scale to dollar fees for each service.

Example: Code No. 10060, Incision & Drainage of cyst, 0.8 units

Using a hypothetical figure of $153/unit, this procedure would be valued at $122.40.

The RVS became a very sophisticated system for the coding and billing of professional services. After the successful use of the California RVS, many state and medical specialty associations adopted the same method of coding for professional services. In 1975, the Federal Trade Commission (FTC) challenged the legality of using the RVS as a fee schedule. Since that time, many medical societies and medical specialty associations have issued new publications that omit unit values for the procedures listed, retaining the procedure code portion of RVS.

Some states have passed legislation mandating the use of RVS codes for procedures and the unit values as the schedule of fees for workers' compensation claims. In these states, the conversion factor to be used in applying the units is also stated in the law. The insurance carrier pays a specific dollar amount for each unit listed for each procedure in the RVS code book.

An insurer or other third party could devise an RVS based on its own data. This RVS would not be created by physicians desiring to regulate their own fees and, therefore, would be acceptable to the FTC. One such book available is *Relative Values for Physicians* (RVP) (refer to Appendix A for information on where to obtain this book). A national RVS developed under a government contract may be acceptable and would not be in violation of antitrust laws.

Resource-Based Relative Value Scale (RBRVS) is an RVS developed for the HCFA by William Hsiao and associates of the Harvard School of Public Health. HCFA used it to devise the Medicare fee schedule that was phased in from 1992 through 1996. For further information, see Chapter 12, Medicare.

4

Methods of Payment

Private insurance companies and federal and state programs adopt different methods of basing their payments on claims; they are (1) fee schedules; (2) RVS (scales or schedules); (3) usual, customary, and reasonable; and (4) diagnosis-related groups.

A *fee schedule* is simply a listing of accepted charges or established allowances for specific medical procedures. A medical practice can have more than one fee schedule unless specific state laws restrict this practice. The following situations can occur:

1. A provider participating in the Medicare program would typically have a fee schedule for Medicare patients and one for non-Medicare patients.
2. If a practice is not participating in Medicare, then the physician's office typically has two fee

schedules. One is based on the limits set by the Medicare program, and one is used for non-Medicare patients.

3. If a practice has a contractual arrangement with a managed care plan (e.g., health maintenance organization, individual practice association, or preferred provider organization), additional fee schedules may be in use.
4. If a substantial part of the practice is taking care of those who have sustained industrial or workers' compensation injuries, then a separate fee schedule may be used for these bills.

Section 1128(b) of the Social Security Act says a physician may risk exclusion or suspension from Medicare if his or her Medicare charges are "substantially in excess of such individual's or entity's usual charges." Options are to either raise private rates to the Medicare fee schedule amount or charge Medicare a lower private rate. An exception to this are the charges made with managed care contracts which are not considered the physician's usual charges. Thus, it is possible in that scenario that Medicare patients would be charged more than managed care patients.

The physician may want to evaluate one of the fee schedules to increase his or her fees as a result of a rise in the cost of living or on an annual basis. A sampling of procedures could be listed and evaluated as shown in the illustration below.

Payments based on RVS are discussed in the preceding section.

Usual, customary, and reasonable (UCR) is a complex system in which three fees are considered in calculating payment. UCR is used mostly in reference to fee-for-service reimbursement. The *usual fee* is the fee that a physician usually charges (submitted fee) for a given service to a private patient. A fee is *customary* if it is in the range of usual fees charged by providers of similar training and experience in a geographic area (i.e., the history of charges for a given service). The *reasonable fee* is the fee that meets the aforementioned criteria or is, in the opinion of the medical review committee, justifiable considering the special circumstances of the case. Reimbursement is based on the lower of the two fees (usual and customary) and determines the approved or allowed amount. In a UCR system, payment can be extremely low for a rarely performed but highly complex procedure because there may be no history of billed charges from other physicians on which to base payment. Many private health insurance plans use this method and will pay a physician's full charge if it does not exceed UCR charges. Depending on the insurance company policy, the UCR system is updated periodically. If the physician has a UCR that is significantly lower than those of other practices in his or her area, document this and ask the insurance carrier for a review and possible adjustment. Increasing numbers of plans are beginning to discontinue the UCR system and are adopting the Medicare RBRVS method for physician reimbursement.

Two other factors that Medicare takes into consideration are *actual charge* and *prevailing charge*. The actual charge is the amount a physician actually bills a patient for a particular medical procedure or service. The prevailing charge is a charge that falls within the range of charges most frequently used in a locality for a particular medical service or procedure. Note that this is a general definition of UCR, and other programs define it in a different way. For example, in Chapter 10, UCR is discussed in greater detail, including how this differs between Blue Shield and Medicare Part B payments.

Diagnosis-related groups (DRGs) is a patient classification scheme that categorizes patients who are medically related with respect to diagnosis and treatment and are statistically similar in length of hospital stay. Hospitals are reimbursed in a lump sum with a fixed fee payment based on the diagnoses rather than on time or services rendered. Refer to Chapter 16 for an in-depth discussion.

Evaluation of Fee Schedule

Procedure	Fee	CPT Code	Relative Value	Customary	Medicaid Allowable	Conversion Factor	New Fee	Follow-up Days
Total OB care	$1850	59400	18.5	$1850	$650	$100	$2035 (10% increase)	45 (established via RVS)

Vocabulary Used in Coding

The insurance billing specialist must become familiar with the terminology in the procedure code books to use them efficiently. This provides for accurate descriptions of services rendered and maximum payment from insurance carriers.

In procedure coding, two categories of patients are considered: the new patient or the established patient. A *new patient* is one who has **not received** any professional services from the physician or another physician of the same specialty who belongs to the same group practice within the past 3 years. An *established patient* is one who **has received** professional services from the physician or another physician of the same specialty who belongs to the same group practice within the past 3 years.

General definitions of additional terms used when coding are as follows:

Concurrent care is the providing of similar services (e.g., hospital visits) to the same patient by more than one physician on the same day. Usually, such cases involve the presence of a physical disorder (e.g., diabetes) at the same time as the primary admitting diagnosis, and this may alter the course of treatment or lengthen recovery time for the primary condition. When concurrent care is provided, no special reporting is required. (See discussion on page 9.)

Critical care means the care of critically ill patients in a variety of medical emergencies requiring constant bedside attention by a physician (e.g., cardiac arrest, shock, bleeding, respiratory failure, postoperative complications, a critically ill neonate, and so on). Critical care may sometimes, but not always, be rendered in a critical care area, such as a coronary care unit, intensive care unit, respiratory care unit, or emergency care facility.

Emergency care differs from critical care in that it is given by the physician in a hospital emergency department, codes 99281 through 99285. Code 99288 is used when advanced life support is required during emergency care. If office services are provided on an emergency basis, code 99058 is used when billing private insurance cases, and any additional services are coded. Medicare does not pay when code 99058 is used. For further information on emergency care, see pages 93–94.

In the Medicare program, an emergency medical condition is currently defined as a medical condition manifesting itself by acute symptoms of sufficient severity (including severe pain) such that the absence of immediate medical attention could reasonably be expected to result in placing the patient's health in serious jeopardy, serious impairment to bodily functions, or serious dysfunction of any body organ or part.

Counseling is a discussion with a patient, family, or both concerning one or more of the following: diagnostic results, impressions, recommended diagnostic studies; prognosis; risks and benefits of treatment options; instructions for treatment and/or follow-up; importance of compliance with chosen treatment options; risk factor reduction; and patient and family education.

4

A *consultation* includes services rendered by a physician whose opinion or advice is requested by another physician or agency in the evaluation or treatment of a patient's illness or a suspected problem. Consultations may occur in a home, office, hospital, extended care facility, and so on. A physician consultant may initiate diagnostic or therapeutic services. A consulting physician must submit a written report to the requesting physician. Codes for consultations are as follows:

- Office or other outpatient consultations (new or established patient)
  99241 through 99245
- Initial inpatient consultations (new or established patient)
  99251 through 99255
- Follow-up inpatient consultations (established patient)
  99261 through 99263
- Confirmatory consultations (new or established patient)
  99271 through 99275

A *referral* is the transfer of the total or specific care of a patient from one physician to another. It is *not* a consultation. As a courtesy, the physician may send a thank you note for the referral with comments about the patient's condition.

Evaluation and Management Section

The Evaluation and Management (E/M) section of CPT has categories and subcategories that have from three to five levels for reporting purposes. These levels are based on key components, contributory factors, and face-to-face time with the patient and/or family. To begin the coding process, the in-

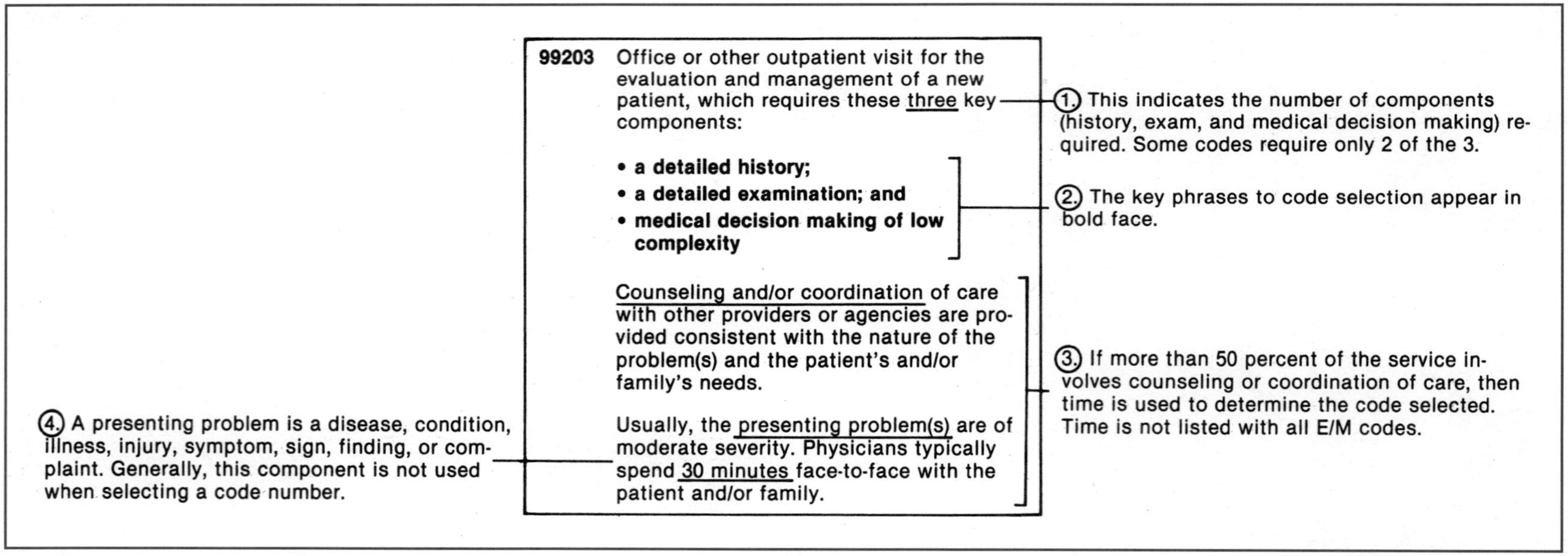

FIGURE 4–1
Evaluation and Management code 99203 defining the main words and phrases. This code is used for a new patient seen in the office or in an outpatient or ambulatory setting. (CPT codes, descriptions, and two-digit numeric modifiers only are from CPT 96 copyright 1995 American Medical Association. All Rights Reserved.)

surance billing specialist must identify the category (e.g., office, hospital inpatient or outpatient, consultation, and so on) and then select the subcategory (e.g., new patient, established patient, and so on). Read the description thoroughly to note the *key* components (e.g., history, examination, medical decision making) and the *contributory factors* (e.g., counseling, coordination of care, nature of the presenting problem), and also note the face-to-face time of the service. Review the sample in Figure 4–1 illustrating an E/M code for a new patient seen in the office or in an outpatient or ambulatory setting.

Because key components are clinical, it is important that **the physician give these factors** and document them in the patient's record to assist in coding each case. In a case in which counseling and coordination of care dominate (more than 50%) the face-to-face physician/patient encounter, then *time* is considered the key to qualify for a particular level of E/M services. Tables 4–1 and 4–2 give a concise view of the components for each code number.

Many physicians began ranking the E/M codes on a scale of from 1 to 5, with 5 as the highest, most-complex level, and 1 as the lowest, least-complex level. It is common to hear a physician say, "Ted Brown was seen for a level 4 today." This terminology may appear on encounter forms with five-digit CPT code numbers and be referred to as levels I through V. Alternately, this terminology may be abbreviated as L-1, L-2, and so on or written out as level one, level two, and so on, depending on the complexity of the case. The following is a breakdown of the levels with code numbers.

	Office Visits		Consultations	
	New	Established	Office	Hospital
Level 1	99201	99211	99241	99251
Level 2	99202	99212	99242	99252
Level 3	99203	99213	99243	99253
Level 4	99204	99214	99244	99254
Level 5	99205	99215	99245	99255

In some billing cases, it is necessary to use a two-digit modifier or a separate five-digit code to give a more accurate description of the services rendered. This is used in addition to the procedure code.

The modifiers in the E/M section are as follows:

- -21 Prolonged E/M services
- -24 Unrelated E/M service; same physician during postoperative period
- -25 Significant, separate, identifiable E/M service by the same physician on the day of a procedure or other service
- -32 Mandated services
- -52 Reduced services
- -57 Decision for surgery

UNLISTED PROCEDURES

When a service is rendered that is not listed in the code book, use a code with a description stating "unlisted":

Example: 99429 Unlisted preventive medicine service.

However, there are certain guidelines to be followed to obtain payment:

- Always send supporting documentation with the claim that clearly identifies the procedure

Text continued on page 76

TABLE 4-1
Selection of Evaluation and Management Codes

Code	History	Examination	Medical Decision Making	Problem Severity	Coordination of Care and Counseling	Time Spent (avg)
Office or Other Outpatient Services (Includes Hospital Observation Area)						
New Patient*						
99201	Problem focused	Problem focused	Straightforward	Minor or self-limited	Consistent with problem(s) and patient's needs	10 min face to face
99202	Expanded problem focused	Expanded problem focused	Straightforward	Low-to-moderate	Consistent with problem(s) and patient's needs	20 min face to face
99203	Detailed	Detailed	Low complexity	Moderate	Consistent with problem(s) and patient's needs	30 min face to face
99204	Comprehensive	Comprehensive	Moderate complexity	Moderate to high	Consistent with problem(s) and patient's needs	45 min face to face
99205	Comprehensive	Comprehensive	High complexity	Moderate to high	Consistent with problem(s) and patient's needs	60 min face to face
Established Patient*†						
99211	—	—	Physician supervision, but presence not required	Minimal	Consistent with problem(s) and patient's needs	5 min face to face
99212	Problem focused	Problem focused	Straightforward	Minor or self-limited	Consistent with problem(s) and patient's needs	10 min face to face
99213	Expanded problem focused	Expanded problem focused	Low complexity	Low to moderate	Consistent with problem(s) and patient's needs	15 min face to face
99214	Detailed	Detailed	Moderate complexity	Moderate to high	Consistent with problem(s) and patient's needs	25 min face to face
99215	Comprehensive	Comprehensive	High complexity	Moderate to high	Consistent with problem(s) and patient's needs	40 min face to face
99217	—	—	—	—	—	—
99218	Detailed or comprehensive	Detailed or comprehensive	Straightforward or low complexity	Low	Consistent with problem(s) and patient's needs	

99219	Comprehensive	Comprehensive	Moderate complexity	Moderate	Consistent with problem(s) and patient's needs	—
99220	Comprehensive	Comprehensive	High complexity	High	Consistent with problem(s) and patient's needs	—
			Hospital Inpatient Services			
			Initial Care‡			
99221	Comprehensive	Comprehensive	Straightforward or low complexity	Low	Consistent with problem(s) and patient's needs	30 min unit/floor
99222	Comprehensive	Comprehensive	Moderate complexity	Moderate	Consistent with problem(s) and patient's needs	50 min unit/floor
99223	Comprehensive	Comprehensive	High complexity	High	Consistent with problem(s) and patient's needs	70 min unit/floor
			Subsequent Care‡§			
99231	Problem focused interval	Problem focused	Straightforward or low complexity	Stable, recovering or improving	Consistent with problem(s) and patient's needs	15 min unit/floor
99232	Expanded problem focused interval	Expanded problem focused	Moderate complexity	Inadequate response to treatment; minor complication	Consistent with problem(s) and patient's needs	25 min unit/floor
99233	Detailed interval	Detailed	High complexity	Unstable; significant new problem or complication	Consistent with problem(s) and patient's needs	35 min unit/floor
99238	Hospital discharge day management					

* Key component: For new patients for initial office and other outpatient services, all three components (history, physical examination, and medical decision making) are essential in selecting the correct code. For established patients, at least two of these three components are required.

† Includes followup, periodic reevaluation, and management of new problems.

‡ Key components: For initial care, all three components (history, physical examination, and medical decision making) are essential in selecting the correct code. For subsequent care, at least two of these three components are required.

§ All subsequent levels of service include review of the medical record, diagnostic studies, and changes in the patient's status, such as history, physical condition, and response to treatment since the last assessment.

Reprinted with permission from *St. Anthony's Coding for Physician Reimbursement*, St. Anthony Publishing, Alexandria, Virginia, January 1992 and updated 1996.

TABLE 4–2
Code Selection Criteria for Consultations

E/M Code	History*	Examination	Medical Decision Making*	Problem Severity	Coordination of Care; Counseling	Time (avg)
Office and Other Outpatient						
99241	Problem focused	Problem focused	Straightforward	Minor or self-limited	Consistent with problem(s) and patient's needs	15 min face to face
99242	Expanded problem focused	Expanded problem focused	Straightforward	Low	Consistent with problem(s) and patient's needs	30 min face to face
99243	Detailed	Detailed	Low complexity	Moderate	Consistent with problem(s) and patient's needs	40 min face to face
99244	Comprehensive	Comprehensive	Moderate complexity	Moderate to high	Consistent with problem(s) and patient's needs	60 min face to face
99245	Comprehensive	Comprehensive	High complexity	Moderate to high	Consistent with problem(s) and patient's needs	80 min face to face
Initial Inpatient†						
99251	Problem focused	Problem focused	Straightforward	Minor or self-limited	Consistent with problem(s) and patient's needs	20 min unit/floor
99252	Expanded problem focused	Expanded problem focused	Straightforward	Low	Consistent with problem(s) and patient's needs	40 min unit/floor
99253	Detailed	Detailed	Low complexity	Moderate	Consistent with problem(s) and patient's needs	55 min unit/floor
99254	Comprehensive	Comprehensive	Moderate complexity	Moderate to high	Consistent with problem(s) and patient's needs	80 min unit/floor
99255	Comprehensive	Comprehensive	High complexity	Moderate to high	Consistent with problem(s) and patient's needs	110 min unit/floor

Follow-Up Inpatient†						
99261	Problem focused	Problem focused	Straightforward or low complexity	Stable, recovering or improving	Consistent with problem(s) and patient's needs	10 min unit/floor
99262	Expanded problem focused interval	Expanded problem focused	Moderate complexity	Inadequate response to treatment; minor complication	Consistent with problem(s) and patient's needs	20 min unit/floor
99263	Detailed interval	Detailed	High complexity	Unstable; significant new problem or significant complication	Consistent with problem(s) and patient's needs	30 min unit/floor
Confirmatory						
99271	Problem focused	Problem focused	Straightforward	Minor or self-limited	Consistent with problem(s) and patient's needs	—
99272	Expanded problem focused	Expanded problem focused	Straightforward	Low	Consistent with problem(s) and patient's needs	—
99273	Detailed	Detailed	Low complexity	Moderate	Consistent with problem(s) and patient's needs	—
99274	Comprehensive	Comprehensive	Moderate	Moderate to high	Consistent with problem(s) and patient's needs	—
99275	Comprehensive	Comprehensive	High	Moderate to high	Consistent with problem(s) and patient's needs	—

*Key component: For office and initial inpatient consultations, all three components (history, physical examination, and medical decision making) are crucial for selecting the correct code. For follow-up consultations, two of these three components are required.

†These codes also are used for residents of nursing facilities.

Reprinted with permission from *St. Anthony's Coding for Physician Reimbursement—Special Supplement,* St. Anthony Publishing, Alexandria, Virginia, March 1992 and updated 1996.

performed and the medical necessity for it. If detailed documentation cannot be electronically submitted, then send a paper claim in a large envelope so it is not folded. Do not use paper clips, staples, or tape to affix the attachments to the claim. Mark each attachment with the patient's name, insurance identification number, date of service, page number of the attachment, and total number of pages submitted (e.g., page 2 of 3). This helps the claims processor match the documentation to the claim in the event they become separated.

- If the physician does this procedure frequently, ask the insurance carrier to assign a temporary local code so that it is not necessary to submit supporting documentation each time. This avoids manual processing and delays.
- File unlisted procedure coded claims in a separate "tickler" file. Follow up about the status of the claim if there is no response within 1 month.

BASIC LIFE AND/OR DISABILITY EVALUATION SERVICES

When reporting examinations done on patients for the purpose of trying to obtain life or disability insurance, use code 99450. For work-related or medical disability examinations, codes 99455 and 99456 may be used. Additional information about life or disability insurance examinations is given in Chapter 6.

Documentation

Medical documentation is a chronologic recording of pertinent facts and observations about a patient's health. The key to substantiating procedure and diagnostic code selections for appropriate reimbursement is a supporting medical record. Proper documentation can prevent refund requests should the physician's practice be reviewed or audited.

The first document obtained is the patient information form, which is used primarily for administrative purposes (see Chapter 3, Fig. 3–8). It is of vital importance that every patient seen by the physician have comprehensive legible documentation regarding what occurred during the visit for the following reasons:

1. Insurance carriers have become stricter in enforcing accurate coding substantiated by documentation. It is not uncommon for prepayment and postpayment random audits or reviews by Medicare carriers to monitor accuracy of physicians' use of evaluation and management procedural codes. The Blue plans, health maintenance organizations (HMOs), preferred provider organizations (PPOs), and all private carriers have the right to claim refunds in the event of accidental (or intentional) miscoding. However, Medicare has the power to levy fines and penalties and exclude practices from Medicare programs. If improper coding patterns exist and are not corrected, then the provider of service will be penalized. Insurance carriers go by the rule "If it's not documented, then it was not performed," and they deny reimbursement.
2. If a treatment is questioned as to medical necessity, the payment may be delayed or denied. As a rule, medically necessary services mean consistent with the diagnosis, in accordance with standards of good medical practice, and the proper level of care provided in the most appropriate setting. However, insurers differ on this definition and may or may not cover the services, depending on the benefits of the plan.
3. It is possible for a state investigator to subpoena patient records and then file administrative charges against the physician, not because of the practice of shoddy medicine but rather because the case was inadequately documented for the treatment provided.
4. A professional liability claim could be filed by a patient, but good documentation helps establish a strong defense.

DOCUMENTATION GUIDELINES FOR EVALUATION AND MANAGEMENT SERVICES

The AMA and HCFA developed documentation guidelines for CPT evaluation and management services. These were released to Medicare carriers by HCFA in November 1994. The guidelines were developed because

- Medicare has an obligation to those enrolled to ensure that services paid for have been provided and are medically necessary.
- During audits, it was discovered that some medical practices should improve their quality of documentation.

Physicians are not required to use these guidelines. However, Medicare claims processors and auditors may use them when reviewing documentation to determine whether the reported services were actually rendered and the level of service was provided. A variety of formats of documentation (e.g., SOAP notes) are accepted by Medicare fiscal intermediaries, as long as the information is discernible. When significant aberrant reporting patterns are detected, a review will be conducted.

The following is a brief overview of the guidelines to acquaint you with some of the terminology.

GENERAL PRINCIPLES OF MEDICAL RECORD DOCUMENTATION

1. The medical record should be complete and legible.
2. The documentation of each patient encounter should include the following:
   - Reason for the encounter and relevant history, physical examination findings, and prior diagnostic test results
   - Assessment, clinical impression, or diagnosis
   - Plan for care
   - Date and legible identity of the observer
3. If not documented, the rationale for ordering diagnostic and other ancillary services should be easily inferred.
4. Past and present diagnoses should be accessible to the treating and/or consulting physician.
5. Appropriate health risk factors should be identified.
6. The patient's progress, response to and changes in treatment, and revision of diagnosis should be documented.
7. The CPT and ICD-9-CM codes reported on the health insurance claim form or billing statement should be supported by the documentation in the medical record.

DOCUMENTATION OF HISTORY

The levels of E/M services are based on four types of history (problem focused, expanded problem focused, detailed, and comprehensive). Each type of history includes some or all of the following elements:

Chief Complaint (CC) ▪ The CC is a concise statement describing the symptom, problem, condition, diagnosis, physician-recommended return, or other factor that is the reason for the encounter. *This is required for all levels of history.*

History of Present Illness (HPI) ▪ The HPI is a chronologic description of the development of the patient's present illness from the first sign and/or symptom or from the previous encounter to the present. It includes location, quality, severity, duration, timing, context, modifying factors, and associated signs and symptoms.

Review of Systems (ROS) ▪ An ROS is an inventory of body systems obtained through a series of questions that is used to identify signs and/or symptoms that the patient might be experiencing or has experienced. For an ROS, the following systems are recognized: constitutional symptoms (e.g., fever, weight loss), eyes, ears, nose, mouth, throat, cardiovascular, respiratory, gastrointestinal, genitourinary, musculoskeletal, integumentary (skin and/or breast), neurologic, psychiatric, endocrine, hematologic/lymphatic, and allergic/immunologic.

Past, Family, and Social Histories (PFSH) ▪ The PFSH consists of a review of three areas:

- Past history (the patient's past experiences with illnesses, operations, injuries, and treatments)
- Family history (a review of medical events in the patient's family, including diseases that may be hereditary or place the patient at risk)
- Social history (an age-appropriate review of past and current activities).

Physical Examination (PE) ▪ The levels of E/M services are based on four types of examination, as follows:

Problem focused: A limited examination of the affected body area or organ system.

Expanded problem focused: A limited examination of the affected body area or organ system and other symptomatic or related organ system(s).

Detailed: An extended examination of the affected body area(s) and other symptomatic or related organ system(s)

Comprehensive: A general multisystem examination or complete examination of a single organ system.

The extent of the examination and what is documented depend on clinical judgment and the nature of the presenting problem(s). They range from limited examinations of single body areas to general multisystem or complete single-organ system examinations. For purposes of examination, the following body areas and organ systems are recognized.

Body Areas	**Organ Systems**
Head, including the face	Constitutional (vital signs, general appearance)
Chest, including breasts and axillae	Eyes
Abdomen	Ears, nose, mouth, and throat
Genitalia, groin, buttocks	Cardiovascular
Back, including spine	Respiratory
Each extremity	Gastrointestinal
	Genitourinary
	Musculoskeletal
	Skin
	Neurologic
	Psychiatric
	Hematologic/lymphatic/immunologic

Complexity of Medical Decision Making ▪ The levels of E/M services represent four types of medical decision making (*straightforward, low complexity, moderate complexity,* and *high complexity*). Medical decision making refers to the complexity of establishing a diagnosis and/or selecting a management option as measured by:

- The number of possible diagnoses and/or the number of management options that must be considered.
- The amount and/or complexity of medical records, diagnostic tests, and/or other information that must be obtained, reviewed, and analyzed.
- The risk of significant complications, morbidity, and/or mortality, as well as comorbidities, associated with the patient's presenting problem(s), the diagnostic procedure(s), and/or the possible management options. Note: *Comorbidities* means underlying diseases or other conditions present at the time of the visit.

Number of Diagnoses or Management Options ▪ This is based on the number and types of problems addressed during the visit, the complexity of establishing a diagnosis, and the management decisions made by the physician.

Amount and/or Complexity of Data to Be Reviewed ▪ This is based on the types of diagnostic testing ordered or reviewed. A decision to obtain and review old medical records and/or obtain history from sources other than the patient increases the amount and complexity of data to be reviewed.

Risk of Significant Complications, Morbidity, and/or Mortality ▪ This is based on other conditions (i.e., the risks) associated with the presenting problem(s), the diagnostic procedure(s), and the possible management options (treatment rendered—surgery, therapy, drug management, services, and supplies). Note: In addition, any reasons for not examining a particular body area or system should be listed.

Additional Principles of Documentation ▪ Although not stated in the AMA and HCFA documentation guidelines, these policies should also be followed regarding the keeping of patient records.

1. Standardize charting procedures for progress notes and include response to treatment, change in treatment, change in diagnosis, and patient noncompliance. A method called the SOAP style is popular, and it matches the E/M keys for procedure code format. This format is as follows:

S (subjective statements of symptoms and complaints)	=	history
O (objective findings)	=	data from physical examination, x-rays, laboratory and other diagnostic tests
A (assessment of subjective and objective parts of the chart note) and		
P (plans—diagnostic and therapeutic and instructions to the patient)	=	medical decision making

2. Treatments should be written out and medications should be listed specifying frequency and dosage. If the patient is referred for a consultation, this must be stated. Also include patient/family education and specific instructions for follow-up. Treatment must be consistent with the working diagnosis.
3. Each chart entry should be dated and signed, including the title or position of the person signing. In some situations, the physician's initials are acceptable. In regard to paperless documents, if passwords are used for restricted access, electronic signatures may be acceptable.
4. Before coding, obtain hospital reports if the patient was an inpatient or was seen in the emer-

gency or outpatient department. In some cases, coding from hospital reports can increase reimbursement. Because this can delay submission of claims, contact the hospital's medical record department either 10 days after outpatient treatment or 4 weeks after a patient's discharge.

It is the physician's responsibility to handwrite or dictate the documentation for transcription. Entries for no-show appointments, prescription refills, and telephone calls must always be entered in patients' medical records by the receptionist. The insurance billing specialist's responsibility is to bring any substandard documentation to the physician's attention. If a case involves continuity of care (e.g., a patient who received previous treatment for a condition referred by another physician for treatment for the same condition), the insurance billing specialist must obtain summaries or records of the patient's previous treatment.

INTERNAL AUDIT

The degree of documentation depends on the complexity of the service and the specialty of the physician. For example, a "normal chest examination" means different things to a cardiologist and an orthopedic surgeon. Figure 4–2 is an example of insufficient versus acceptable documentation.

As a help to the medical practice, a coder or insurance biller may be asked to perform an internal audit to determine whether there is a lack of documentation. To accomplish this, pull at random 15 to 20 medical records from the same time period for the last four to six months. Use a form similar to the Audit Form shown in Figure 4–3. Compile information from the patient's record, laboratory reports, pathology reports, x-ray reports, operative reports, and other diagnostic tests. On another form like the Audit Analysis Form (see Fig. 4–3) record the analysis and report to the physician the results of the audit. If the physician is coding properly, the E/M

Scenario: a 35-year-old woman complains of frequent sore throats. A brief history and pertinent review of systems is performed. A problem-focused examination of the ears, nose, and throat is performed. A working diagnosis is made and treatment chosen.

E/M component	Insufficient documentation	Acceptable documentation
		Date of service
Presenting problem	Sore throat.	Frequent sore throats.
History	Review of systems head/neck negative.	Patient complains of having similar sore throats every 6–9 months for the past 3–4 years. Has never been examined or treated for this problem. Pertinent review of head/neck systems. Patient denies: -trouble swallowing -swelling of lymph nodes -ear infections -allergies -exposure to dust particulates or fumes
Exam	Negative except redness of throat.	Head/neck exam: -sinuses: nontender -tympanic membranes: flat and pearly w/o redness -oropharynx: no focal lesions; general erythemia in posterior oropharynx; tonsils not enlarged -neck: palpable cervical lymph nodes bilaterally
Medical Decision Making	Rule out strep sore throat. Culture.	Assessment: patient with history of chronic upper respiratory problems, without prior medical evaluation. Most likely etiology: streptococcal. Other, less likely etiologies include: -allergic (no history, non-seasonal, no pets) -external irritants (nonsmoker, no industrial exposure) -viral (unlikely with pattern and frequency) -inflammatory condition (unlikely without more systemic involvement or family history) Treatment plan: throat culture and sensitivity. If culture is positive for strep, will begin penicillin prophylaxis. If negative, will assume viral etiology for now and re-examine in one week.—*Physician signature*

MEDICODE

MED-INDEX IS A DIVISION OF MEDICODE, INC.

FIGURE 4–2

Example of insufficient versus acceptable documentation. (Reprinted with permission from Med-Index Reimbursement Update, Vol. 8, No. 2, Med-Index Publications, Salt Lake City, Utah, 1993.)

AUDIT FORM

PHYSICIAN ______________________________

PATIENT NAME ______________________ DATE OF SERVICE ____________

TYPE OF SERVICE REVIEWED ______________________________

1. HISTORY

Chief Complaint ______________________________

History of Present Illness or Problem	Brief ______
	Extended ______
System review	Problem pertinent ______
	Extended ______
Past, family and/or social history	Pertinent ______
	Complete ______
Extent of history	Problem focused ______
	Expanded problem focused ______
	Detailed ______
	Comprehensive* ______

**Needs complete ROS (review of system), past medical, family and social history and extended history of present illness.*

2. EXAMINATION

Extent of exam	Problem focused ______
	Expanded problem focused ______
	Detailed ______
	Comprehensive ______

3. MEDICAL DECISION MAKING/ASSESSMENT

Amount/complexity of data reviewed ______________________________

Number of diagnosis/MGT options ______________________________

Risk of complications/mortality ______________________________

PLAN:

Tests ordered and why ______________________________

Counseling and/or coordination of care ______________________________

Management/Treatment recommended ______________________________

Level 5 services require "high complexity" medical decision making.

Levels of components must meet or exceed the level billed.

AUDIT ANALYSIS

PHYSICIAN NAME ______________________ SPECIALTY ____________

Number of records reviewed	______	New patients	______
Number of claims submitted	______	Established patients	______
Total charges submitted	$ ______		

Level	OV	Consults	$ Billed	$ Should Have Billed	$ Difference
Minimal	____	____	____	____	$____
Level 1	____	____	____	____	$____
Level 2	____	____	____	____	$____
Level 3	____	____	____	____	$____
Level 4	____	____	____	____	$____
Level 5	____	____	____	____	$____
Hospital			____	____	$____
Critical Care			____	____	$____
Radiology			____	____	$____
Laboratory			____	____	$____
Other			____	____	$____
Total	____	____	____	____	$____

FIGURE 4–3

An audit and an audit analysis form. (From Duston, GR: Coding expert. American Academy of Procedural Coders, Salt Lake City, Utah, Spring 1994.)

codes should reveal a bell curve. For additional information on claims audits and reviews, refer to Chapter 2. A booklet detailing the complete guidelines entitled "Documentation Guidelines for Evaluation and Management Services" (OP924095) may be ordered from the AMA (address is given at the back of Appendix B). Because documentation guidelines will be updated and refined periodically, it is important to read the local fiscal intermediary's Medicare bulletins.

CRIB SHEETS

Because of the complex nature of the E/M coding rules, some physicians have designed or purchased crib sheets for their specialty (Fig. 4–4). A *crib sheet* is a summary form listing key components of the E/M codes. Because such sheets are abbreviated and not in detail, they cannot be used in place of documentation and may not withstand an audit. Physicians and coders should be well trained in the E/M definitions before using crib sheets. However, the sheets can make the job of coding and billing quicker, easier, and more error free.

Surgery Section

In the surgery section of CPT, the insurance billing specialist will encounter some miscellaneous

MC2 CHARGE SLIP

NAME: DATE:

CODE	HIST EXAM DEC	CODE	HIST EXAM DEC
99201	* NEW PAT. OFF.	99261	+ F.UP CONSULT INPATIENT
99202	* EPF EPF SF	99262	+ EPF EPF MC
99203	* D D LC	99263	+ D D HC
99204	* C C MC	99281	* EMERG.DEP.
99205	* C C HC	99282	* EPF EPF LC
99211	+ EST.PAT.OFF.	99283	* EPF EPF L-MC
99212	+ PF PF SF	99284	* D D MC
99213	+ EPF EPF LC	99285	* C C HC
99214	+ D D MC	99291	CRITIC.CARE 1st Hr.
99215	+ C C HC	99292	ADDIT. 30 MIN
99221	* INIT.HOSP.VIS NEW or ESTAB.	99301	* NURSING FACIL.
99222	* C C MC	99302	* D C M-HC
99223	* C C HC	99303	* C C M-HC
99231	+ SUBSQ.HOSPIT.	99311	+ SNF SUBSEQ.
99232	+ EPF EPF LC	99312	+ EPF EPF MC
99233	+ D D HC	99313	+ D D M-HC
99238	HOSPIT.DISCH.	99341	* HOME SERVICES NEW PAT.
99241	* CONSULT.OFF.	99342	* PF PF SF-LC
99242	* EPF EPF SF	99343	* EPF EPF MC
99243	* D D LC	99351	+ ESTAB.PATIENT
99244	* C C MC	99352	+ EPF EPF MC
99245	* C C HC	99353	+ D D HC
99251	* INIT.CONSULT. INPATIENT	DIAGNOSES:	CPT CODES:
99252	* EPF EPF SF		
99253	* D D LC		
99254	* C C MC		
99255	* C C HC		

KEY: PF:Probl.Foc. EPF:Expand.Probl.Foc D:Detail. C:Comprehens. LC:Low Complex. MC:Moder.Complex. HC:High Complex.

Requirem.: *: 3 Key Components req. +: 2 out of 3 Key Compon. req.

FIGURE 4–4
Example of a crib sheet. This system of abbreviations has cut in half the time the physician spends in choosing the correct Evaluation and Management CPT codes. The format shown here can be adapted to any specialty. (Reprinted with permission from Helmut O. Haar, M. D., Ventura, California.)

terms. Lacerations require either *simple, intermediate,* or *complex* repairs. Simple lacerations are superficial, whereas intermediate and complex lacerations involve deeper layers of the skin and may require reconstructive surgery. Repairs are coded according to the sum of the length of the repairs in centimeters (cm) rather than in inches. The words "unilateral" and "bilateral" appear in this section, and it is important to know which one to use when coding. *Unilateral* refers to one side only, whereas *bilateral* refers to both sides.

When multiple wounds are repaired, add the lengths of wounds in the same classification and report them as a single item. If the wounds are listed separately, the first code will be given the highest payment, and the payments for the subsequent codes will be decreased substantially. Therefore, to get maximum payments, use one code number. When billing for office surgery and supplies used, employ a check list sheet for the items on the sterile tray (Fig. 4–5*A*), as well as a check list for determining complete and incomplete records (Fig. 4–5*B*).

A

MINOR OPERATING ROOM INSTRUMENT TRAY CHECK LIST

1 Adson Brown tissue forceps	____
1 Adson tissue forceps with teeth	____
1 long tissue forceps	____
2 mosquito clamps	____
1 Peck Joseph dissecting scissors	____
1 Kahn dissecting scissors	____
1 Reynolds dissecting scissors	____
1 Stratte needle holder	____
1 Webster needle holder	____
4 small piercing towel clips	____
2 double-skin hooks	____
2 single-skin hooks	____
1 knife handle	____
1 #15 blade	____
10 4 x 4s	____
2 cotton-tipped applicators	____
1 small basin	____
3 sterile towels (drapes)	____
1 Bovie pencil	____
Sutures: ____ ____ ____	
Dressings: 1/2 inch Steri-Strips	____

B

OFFICE SURGERY CHART CHECK LIST

Patient Information Sheet	____
H & P or Progress Note	____
Consent Form	____
Diagnostic Studies	____
Pathology Report(s)	____
Anesthesia Record	____
Circulating Nurse's Note	____
Doctor's Orders	____
Discharge Note	____
Operative Report	____
Signature/Operative Report	____

FIGURE 4–5
A, Check list to document supplies used when billing for office surgery. This list can be kept with the patient's medical record. *B,* Check list for identifying complete and incomplete medical records used for a patient receiving office surgery. As each item or document is completed, it is checked off so that the person reviewing the chart can see at a glance what needs to be finalized.

How to Use the CPT Code Book

The following are guidelines for the 1996 edition of CPT. This code book is a systematic listing of five-digit code numbers with no decimals. It is divided into six code sections with categories and subcategories. They are:

1. Evaluation and Management (E/M)	99201 to 99499
2. Anesthesia	00100 to 01999, 99100 to 99199
3. Surgery	10040 to 69979
4. Radiology, Nuclear Medicine, and Diagnostic Ultrasound	70010 to 79999
5. Pathology and Laboratory	80002 to 89399
6. Medicine	90700 to 99199

Within each of the main sections are categories and subcategories divided according to anatomic body systems, procedure, condition, description, and specialties.

CODE BOOK SYMBOLS

With each new issuance of CPT, new codes and description changes are added. It is important to become familiar with the new codes and any description changes for the specialized areas that will be used. To help you identify new codes and description changes, the following symbols are used:

Service includes surgical procedure only

10080* Incision and drainage of pilonidal cyst; simple

New code

●20100 Exploration of penetrating wound (separate procedure); neck

Revised code

▲ 81000 Urinalysis, by dip stick or tablet reagent for bilirubin, glucose, hemoglobin, ketones, leukocytes, nitrite, pH, protein, specific gravity, urobilinogen, any number of these constituents; nonautomated with microscopy

Highlight what is new or what is deleted from codes marked with a triangle. This will save time in trying to figure out what was changed and will prevent using these codes incorrectly. When using a new code, remember that it may take as long as 6 months before an insurance carrier has a mandatory value assignment; therefore, reimbursements will be received in varying amounts during that time. Appendices B and C in the code book provide a summary of the additions, deletions, and revisions.

In the Surgery section, a star (*) next to a procedure number means all of the following.

a. The listed service is for the surgical procedure only.
b. All postoperative care is added on a service-by-service basis (e.g., office or hospital visit, cast change, and so on).
c. Complications are added on a service-by-service basis, as with all surgical procedures.
d. Preoperative services are considered as one of the following:
   i. When the starred (*) procedure is carried out at the time of the initial office visit and constitutes the major service provided at that visit, identify the procedure by listing the surgical procedure and using code number 99025.

Example: This CPT coding shows that the surgical procedure constitutes the major service. Two entries are required.

99025	Initial new patient visit	$00.00
10060*	Incision and drainage of abscess	$00.00

   ii. When the starred (*) procedure is carried out at the time of the initial office or other visit involving significant identifiable services (e.g., removal of a small skin lesion at the time of a comprehensive history and physical examination), list the appropriate visit, the starred (*) procedure, and all follow-up care.
   iii. When the starred (*) procedure is carried out during an established patient visit and constitutes the major service at that visit, the office visit would not usually be charged.
   iv. When the starred (*) procedure requires hospitalization, both the hospital visit and the starred (*) procedure should be listed, as well as all follow-up care.

CODE MODIFIERS

The use of CPT modifiers permits the physician to indicate circumstances in which a procedure as performed differs in some way from that described by its usual five-digit code. When using a modifier, if necessary, append an operative, pathology, x-ray, or special report to justify why it is being used. Modifiers give a more accurate description of the services rendered. However, not every modifier is used with every section of the code book. In other words, specific modifiers are used with certain sections.

Modifiers may be used to indicate that

- A service or procedure has both a professional and a technical component.
- A service or procedure was performed by more than one physician or in more than one location.
- A service or procedure has been increased or reduced.
- Only part of a service was performed.
- An adjunctive service was performed.
- A bilateral procedure was performed.
- A service or procedure was provided more than once.
- Unusual events occurred.*

In certain cases, it is important to use modifiers so that the physician's profile will not be affected as the result of fees and/or services being reduced. The physician's profile is a compilation of each physician's charges and the payments made to him or her through the years for each specific professional service rendered to a patient. As charges are increased, so are payments, and the profile is then updated through the use of computer data. There are two types of profiles: *individual customary profile* and *prevailing profile.* Inquire from each insurance carrier whether the carrier will update the physician's profile on an annual basis. If so, send in an annual updated fee profile to those third party payers who implement this policy.

Here are a few instances to illustrate the use of a modifier so the profile is not affected.

Example 1: If surgery is begun but not completed because of the patient's condition, the procedure code number would be listed with the modifier -52, or 09952. A copy of the operative report should accompany the completed insurance claim, documenting why the procedure was incomplete.

Example 2: If a bilateral procedure is described in CPT but the procedure is being done on one side, the bilateral procedure code number would be listed with the modifier -52 or 09952, indicating it was not performed in its entirety.
For modifer -52, submit full fee and let payer reduce payment.

When listing a surgical fee with a modifier, it might be wise to use two lines to state the situation so that the claims adjuster clearly understands the case and maximum payment is generated. If an insurance company's input system accepts only five digits, then it is always necessary to use five-digit modifiers when submitting claims. If in doubt, ask the insurance companies to express their desire of one form (two digits) over the other (five digits).

Example:

65710	Keratoplasty, corneal transplant
65710-20	Employment of operating microscope

Besides CPT and RVS modifiers when submitting insurance claims for Medicare patients, Level 2 Medicare codes have alpha two-digit modifiers.

Example: When taking x-rays of both feet, the billing portion of the insurance claim would appear as follows:

05/06/9X	73620	RT	$00.00
05/06/9X	73620	LT	$00.00

Multiple Modifiers

If a procedure requires more than one modifier code, use a multiple two-digit code (-99) after the usual five-digit code number, all typed on one line, or a separate five-digit code (09999) in addition to the basic five-digit procedure code number typed on two different lines. Some insurance companies require just -99 with a separate note explaining the multiple modifiers. Remember to ask the insurance company which format is preferred when submitting claims.

Example:* A physician sees a patient who is grossly obese. The operative report documents that a bilateral sliding-type inguinal herniorrhaphy was performed, and the procedure took 2 hours 15 minutes.

49525-00	Repair sliding inguinal hernia
09950	Bilateral procedure
09922	Unusual services requiring 2 hours 15 minutes
OR	
49525-99 -50 -22	Bilateral repair sliding inguinal hernia requiring 2 hours 15 minutes

HOW TO CODE EFFECTIVELY

Follow these procedures:

1. Always read the introductory section at the beginning of the code book because this changes from one edition to the next edition/year.

* Examples shown in this chapter reflect wording pertinent to coding a specific diagnosis and are missing chart entries; therefore, there is a gap of information for the reader.

2. Read the *guidelines* at the beginning of each of the six sections of the book. These give general information and instructions on coding certain procedures within each main section and will help you understand the application of the codes.
3. Read the *notes* and special subsection information throughout the Surgery, Radiology, Pathology, and Medicine sections.
4. Use the index at the back of the book to locate a specific item by generalized code numbers, NOT by page numbers. Listings are given in four primary classes of main entries:
   a. Procedure or service
      Example: Endoscopy; Anastomosis; Splint
   b. Organ or other anatomic site
      Example: Tibia; Colon; Salivary Gland
   c. Condition
      Example: Abscess; Entropion; Tetralogy of Fallot
   d. Synonyms, eponyms, and abbreviations
      Example: EEG; Bricker operation; Clagett procedure

   If the procedure performed is not listed, check for the organ involved. If the procedure or organ is difficult to find, look up the condition. Key words, such as synonyms or eponyms, and abbreviations will help you find the appropriate code.
5. Locate the code number in the code section and read through the narrative description to locate the most appropriate number to apply to the patient's procedure. A semicolon (;) separates common portions from subordinate designations, and subterms are indented (Fig. 4–6). Any terminology after the semicolon has a subordinate status, as do the subsequent indented entries. In Figure 4–6 you see that 11044 should read as follows: Debridement; skin, subcutaneous tissue, muscle, and bone. Using Figure 4–7, take an example of a patient who has had six lesions cauterized. On the insurance claim, it would appear as follows:

11050	Paring or curettement of benign lesion with cauterization; single lesion	$00.00
11051	two to four lesions	$00.00
11052	fifth and sixth lesions	$00.00

Remember, always list the highest dollar figure first.

6. If you are trying to locate an E/M code, identify the place or type of service rendered. Then locate the category or subcategory. Review any guidelines or instructions pertaining to the category or subcategory. Read the descriptors of the levels of E/M service. Identify the requirements necessary for code assignment. Make sure the components required were performed by the physician, and then assign the E/M code.
7. Transfer the descriptor wording and five-digit code number to the claim form exactly as given for each procedure in the book. Be careful not to transpose code numbers.
8. Add the two-digit add-on modifiers or separate five-digit numbers representing the modifiers whenever they are required, because these can either increase or decrease the physician's fee. If modifiers are not used, this can drastically affect the physician's fee profile to the extent of possibly reducing payment to the physician.
9. Parentheses ( ) tell where other services are located (Fig. 4–8).
10. Measurements throughout the code book are based on the metric system (Fig. 4–9).
11. In some cases, a code number cannot be found for a procedure done by the physician. Go to the end of the section or subsection in which you are trying to locate a code, where you will find a five-digit code for "unlisted procedures" that ends in -99. A copy of a report documenting and detailing the procedure should be attached to the insurance claim when billing for an unlisted procedure.
12. All anesthesia services are reported by use of the five-digit anesthesia code plus a physical status

FIGURE 4–6
Use of a semicolon. (CPT codes, descriptions, and two-digit numeric modifiers only are from CPT 96 copyright 1995 American Medical Association. All Rights Reserved.)

11040	**Debridement; skin, partial thickness**
11041	**skin, full thickness**
11042	**skin, and subcutaneous tissue**
11043	**skin, subcutaneous tissue, and muscle**
11044	**skin, subcutaneous tissue, muscle, and bone**

PARING OR CURETTEMENT

11050*	Paring or curettement of benign hyperkeratotic skin lesion with or without chemical cauterization (such as verrucae or clavi) not extending through the stratum corneum (e.g., callus or wart) with or without local anesthesia; single lesion
11051	two to four lesions
11052	more than four lesions

FIGURE 4–7
Procedure codes from the Surgery Section of Physicians' Current Procedural Terminology. (CPT codes, descriptions, and two-digit numeric modifiers only are from CPT 96 copyright 1995 American Medical Association. All Rights Reserved.)

modifier. The use of other modifiers to explain a procedure further is optional. *Example:* Patient is a healthy 23-year-old white woman. Anesthesia is given for a vaginal delivery. The procedure code would be 00946-P1.

13. The Surgery section has subsections and subheadings. It is important to be able to break down a procedure.

Example: Closed manipulative treatment of a clavicular fracture.

Section:	Surgery, Musculoskeletal System
Anatomic subheading:	Shoulder
Condition:	Fracture and/or Dislocation
Code:	23505

Thus, when completing an insurance claim, the billing portion would appear as follows:

01/07/9X	23505	Closed manipulative tx, clavicular fracture	$00.00

Note: The description of the procedure might not appear on claim forms when only code numbers are required.

Example:

50300	Unilateral kidney transplant
09966	Surgical team See attached operative report
OR	
50300-66	Unilateral kidney transplant See attached operative report

CODING TIPS

Every medical practice has billing problems and questions unique to its specialty. You must become a detective and discover what maximum reimbursements apply in your specialty. The best way is to experiment and try out some new coding options and note how you are reimbursed. Coding takes expertise. It is an art, not an exact science. Each insurance company sells slightly different policies. The following ideas and variations will help you obtain maximum reimbursement for each service rendered.

Bundled Codes

When related to insurance claims, the phrase *bundled code* means to group codes together that are re-

BIOPSY

11100	Biopsy of skin, subcutaneous tissue and/or mucous membrane (including simple closure), unless otherwise listed (separate procedure); single lesion
11101	each separate/additional lesion
	(For biopsy of conjunctiva, see 68100; eyelid, see 67810)

FIGURE 4–8
Use of parentheses in the Surgery Section of Physicians' Current Procedural Terminology. (CPT codes, descriptions, and two-digit numeric modifiers only are from CPT 96 copyright 1995 American Medical Association. All Rights Reserved.)

FIGURE 4-9
Metric measurements from the Surgery Section of Physicians' Current Procedural Terminology. (CPT codes, descriptions, and two-digit numeric modifiers only are from CPT 96 copyright 1995 American Medical Association. All Rights Reserved.)

13150	Repair, complex, eyelids, nose, ears and/or lips; 1.0 cm or less
	(See also 40650-40654, 67961-67975)
13151	1.1 cm to 2.5 cm
13152	2.6 cm to 7.5 cm

lated to a procedure. In the Medicare program, a number of services may be affected because HCFA considers the services bundled. When listing starred (*) procedures, for example, a sterile tray for minor surgery is bundled with the service unless a second tray is needed owing to complications. For unstarred procedures, CPT code 99070 is not recognized by Medicare for supplies but Level 2 alpha numeric codes must be used. The cost of some services and most supplies are bundled into evaluation and management codes, for example, telephone services, reading of test results, and surgical dressings. However, Medicare will pay for slings, splints, rib belts, cast supplies, Hexelite and light casts, pneumatic ankle-control splints, and prosthetics, but a supplier number is needed to bill for take-home surgical supplies and durable medical equipment (DME). Claims for supplies and DME go to one of four regional carriers whose addresses are listed in Appendix A. A reference book published by St. Anthony Publishing has comprehensive lists of the codes that HCFA considers bundled for the Medicare program (see Appendix B for further information).

When dealing with private insurance, an Explanation of Benefits document may print out with a statement, "Benefits have been combined," which means the same thing as bundling. Whenever appealing a claim, a great deal of time may be spent on paperwork only to discover that the code is bundled and denial is imminent. Whenever in doubt about whether services are combined or not, contact the insurance carrier and ask.

Down Coding

CPT and RVS codes have been emphasized in this chapter because they are the most commonly accepted, depending on what type of case you are billing—private, federal, state, or industrial. Approximately 35 different procedural coding systems are used in various regions across the United States. Generally, only three to five procedural coding systems are in use in any one given region at the same time. Down coding occurs when the coding system used on a claim submitted to an insurance carrier does not match the coding system used by the company receiving the claim. The computer system converts the code submitted to the closest code in use, but the payment generated may be less than if the claim was not down coded. To prevent down coding, always monitor reimbursements and monitor down codes to become knowledgeable about which codes are affected. Then call the insurance carrier and find out which code system is in use and obtain a reference so you can code using the appropriate system.

Incorrect Coding:

20010 Incision of abscess with suction irrigation

(Note: 20010 is not listed in CPT and would result in down coding.)

Correct Coding:

20005 Incision of abscess, complicated

Down coding also occurs when the claims examiner must convert the CPT code submitted to a code in the RVS being used by the carrier. When there is a choice between two or three somewhat similar codes, the claims examiner will choose the lowest-paying code. Find out which RVS system is being used by the carrier before billing, and find the best match for the CPT code.

Down coding also occurs when a claims examiner compares the code used with the written description of the procedure if a document is attached. If the two do not match, the carrier will reimburse according to the lowest-paying code that fits the description given. For additional information and solutions to down coding, see Chapter 8.

Incorrect Coding:

11400 Excision of bone lesion, benign

Correct Coding:

27635 Excision of bone tumor of tibia, benign

Upcoding

This term is used to describe deliberate manipulation of CPT codes for increased payment. This practice can be spotted by Medicare fiscal intermediaries and insurance carriers using prepayment and postpayment screens or stop alerts built into computer software programs. Intentional upcoding is when a physician selects one level of service code for all visits with an attitude that it evens out. This opens the door to audits and in the end may cost the practice money. Upcoding can occur unintentionally when the coder is ill informed or does not keep current.

When multiple office or hospital visits occur on a single day, assess the total service rendered and code correctly. Note that codes (99231-99233) for subsequent hospital care identify each day's service.

Unbundling

Unbundling is coding and billing numerous CPT codes to identify procedures that are usually described by a single code. It is also known as *exploding* or *à la carte* medicine.

Example:

Unbundled claim	Claim coded correctly
58150 Total abdominal hysterectomy with removal of tubes and with removal of ovary ($1894)	58150 Comprehensive code for all three services ($1894)
58700 Salpingectomy ($271)	
58940 Oophorectomy ($271)	
Total **charge:** $2436	Total **payment:** $1218

Some practices do this unwittingly, but if it is done intentionally, it is considered fraud. Unbundling can lead to downward payment adjustments and possible audit of claims submitted.

Types of unbundling are:

- Fragmenting one service into component parts and coding each component part as if it were a separate service.
  Example:
  43235 Upper GI endoscopy and 43600 Biopsy of stomach (incorrect)
  43239 Upper GI endoscopy with biopsy of stomach (correct)
- Reporting separate codes for related services when one comprehensive code includes all related services.
  Example:
  58150 total abdominal hysterectomy with or without removal of tubes, with or without removal of ovary, 58700 Salpingectomy, and 58940 Oophorectomy (incorrect if using these 3 codes together)
  58150 total abdominal hysterectomy with or without removal of tubes, with or without removal of ovary (correct)
- Code bilateral procedures as two codes when one code is proper.
  Example:
  76090-RT Right mammography and 76090-LT Left mammography (incorrect)
  76091 Bilateral mammography (correct)
- Separating a surgical approach from a major surgical service.
  Example:
  49000 Exploratory laparotomy and 44150 total abdominal colectomy (incorrect)
  44150 Total abdominal colectomy (correct since it includes exploration of the surgical field)

Insurers use special software that detects unbundling. To avoid this problem, always use up-to-date CPT and RVS code books, because the use of outdated codes often inadvertently results in unbundling. Find out from insurers what edition they are using and always use the same edition as the insurer, especially during a transition period at the first of the year. When a new technology or technique is developed, it may have its own code, but as it becomes commonplace it may be bundled with another code. If the practice uses a billing service, request in writing that its computer system include no unbundling programming.

Code Monitoring

Determine which codes are used most often in the physician's practice. Many computer programs can generate a list of codes, ranking them according to frequency of use. If the practice does not have a computer, take a sampling of the charge slips to find out the prevalent codes. Once the high-volume codes are known, focus on coding strategies for maximum reimbursement.

Monitor every Medicare Remittance Advice document that comes to you directly or via the patients. Every private, Medicare, Medicaid, and CHAMPUS payment received should be checked for accuracy to see whether it is consistently the same or down coding has occurred. Incorrect payments need to be appealed as well as any code that is not what you submitted. Be sure to appeal every payment that is less than half of what your physician bills. An example of a code and payment tracking log to help monitor payments received is shown in Figure 4–10.

Office Visits

When an established patient comes in for an office visit and incidentally the medical assistant takes the patient's blood pressure per the physician's order, then the physician would include that service with the appropriate level of service code number (i.e., 99213, 99214, and so on). If the medical assistant takes the blood pressure and the patient is not seen by the physician but the physician reviews the results, then the appropriate code number is 99211 (minimal). No modifier is required in either situation.

Some insurance policies allow only two moderate- or high-complexity office visits per patient per year. Therefore, it is important to contact the insurance company to learn whether there are any limitations.

4

Consultations

Some insurance policies will pay for only one consultation per patient per year. Consultations require a written report to be generated after this type of visit. If a second opinion is necessary, refer to code numbers 99241 through 99255.

Drugs and Injections

If the insurance claim has a description section, give the name, amount, and strength of the medication as well as how it was administered. This data must be documented in the patient's medical record. If a drug is experimental or expensive, in-

CODE/PAYMENT TRACKING LOG					Date: 1-95
CPT Code	Practice Fee	Medicare Date & Amount Paid	Medicaid Date & Amount Paid	CHAMPUS Date & Amount Paid	Blue Shield Date & Amount Paid
99201	$00.00	11-94 $00.00	8-94 $00.00	7-94 $00.00	4-94 $00.00
99202	$00.00	12-94 $00.00	9-94 $00.00	10-94 $00.00	6-94 $00.00
99211	$00.00	12-94 $00.00			11-94 $00.00
99212	$00.00				12-94 $00.00
99221	$00.00				
99231	$00.00				
99232	$00.00				
99241	$00.00				

FIGURE 4–10
Example of a code/payment tracking log.

clude a copy of the invoice when sending in the insurance claim. Codes for injections are 90700 through 90749 and 90782 through 90799. If a single injection contains two agents, use one code. Two separate injections require two separate codes. If an anesthetic agent is being used, determine whether it is diagnostic/therapeutic or prophylactic for pain.

Administrative or Add-On Codes

These codes are referred to in CPT as Special Services and Reports and fall under the category of Miscellaneous Services. They are important to consider when billing because these codes can be added to the basic professional services rendered. The circumstances that are covered under these codes (99000 to 99090) include handling of laboratory specimens, telephone calls, seeing patients at odd hours, emergency services, supplies and materials, special reports, travel, and educational services rendered to patients. If there is room on the insurance claim, explain the circumstances or attach a report to justify the use of these codes. Some insurance companies will pay, but others will not.

Surgeries

Obtain a copy of the patient's operative report from the hospital. Make a photocopy that you can write on as you make notes. When scanning the report, use a ruler or highlighter pen. Use the ruler to read the report line by line for key words, such as

bilateral, or unilateral
biopsy
blood loss of over 600 ml
complete, partial, or total
complicated by
debridement
endoscopy
excision or incision
extensive
graft
hemorrhage
incision and drainage
initial or subsequent
ligation
multiple
open treatment
prolonged procedure due to
reconstructive
repair
surgical
unusual findings or circumstances
very difficult

On the other hand, you may note words such as "ordinary," "simple," or "uncomplicated." Look up any unfamiliar terms, and write the definition in the margin. Major errors can occur when a coder is not familiar with the medical terms being used. Ask the physician to clarify the case because medical terminology is very technical and can puzzle even the most knowledgeable of insurance billing specialists. If in doubt about the meaning of a word, always look it up in a good medical dictionary. This may help in locating the right code. Highlighted words can remind you that a modifier may be needed.

Do not code from only the physician's procedural statement. Code only the operations that were actually documented in the report. Read the report before coding to see whether additional procedures were performed and whether they were part of the main procedure, performed independently, or unrelated. If multiple procedures are done that are not inherent in a major procedure, modifier -51 can be used. Terms such as *undermining* (cut in a horizontal fashion), *take down* (to take apart), or *lysis of adhesions* appear in many operations but should not be coded separately.

Reread the report to make certain that all procedural and diagnostic codes have been identified. Compare the content with the codes you are using. You cannot code circumstances the physician relays to you verbally. The postoperative diagnosis is the primary diagnosis. If there were extensive complications, be sure the words "extensive complications" are in the report. If there was a lesion and a pathology report is involved in the case, read it to see whether the biopsied specimen was benign or malignant because this will affect the diagnostic code and reimbursement.

Note the *position* (lithotomy, dorsal) of the patient during the operation because this clue helps indicate the correct code to use. Also note the *surgical approach* (vaginal, abdominal) that was used, which helps with proper code selection.

If more than one surgeon is involved, clarify for whom you are billing by using two-digit modifiers (-62, co-surgeon; -66, team surgery; -80, assistant at surgery; -81, minimum assistant surgeon; or -82, assistant surgeon).

When using a computer program, if you have difficulty in determining whether an operative report needs to be submitted for a procedure, mark the specific codes with a special note or code letter as a clue. If you are submitting an operative report with the insurance claim, type the patient's insurance identification number on the report in the event it becomes separated during processing.

If you add the modifier -22 for unusual services, then the operative report must state that unusual services were performed within the context of the normal procedure. Encourage your physician to use appropriate descriptions in the report, and call these words to his or her attention. Most insurance carriers send an insurance claim to medical review before payment is made if modifier -22, indicating unusual services, appears on the claim. Comprehensive documentation will obtain 20% to 30% more reimbursement for the basic procedure. However, some Medicare carriers routinely deny any claim with modifier -22. An appeal for review can be made in such denials. See Chapter 8 for details on the Medicare review and appeal process. Because payments may be delayed, it is important to be cautious when using this modifier. Three guidelines follow: (1) the complications cannot be indicated by a separate code; (2) the procedure is lengthy and unusual; and (3) the services provided by the physician are increased because of unusual circumstances or complexities.

Documentation should list the length of time spent on the procedure, especially if of unusual duration. This should be stated somewhere in the report. If the surgeon has spent a prolonged period of time waiting for his or her turn to operate or perform a necessary service, this time should be coded.

Documentation should list the length (in centimeters) of all incisions and layers of involved skin (subcutaneous, fascia, muscle, grafts) so that you can determine the correct codes for excisions of lesions, simple and complex repairs, and so on.

Use of code numbers that describe a part of the body treated may increase reimbursement (e.g., suturing of a facial laceration will pay a higher rate than suturing of laceration on the arm).

If special instruments are used, such as an operating microscope, document the equipment as well as the time spent using it. If the equipment is not usual to the procedure, use modifier -20.

When coding therapeutic or cosmetic surgical procedures, break down the surgery into two categories. State how much of the procedure was functional and how much was cosmetic or therapeutic. Generally, the insurance carrier will pay for the functional portion of the procedure even if there is no coverage for cosmetic or therapeutic procedures.

The use of modifiers -57 or -58 requires accurate and complete documentation of events leading up to surgeries and any subsequent surgeries. It is only possible to modify procedures if the coder has all of the relevant facts and circumstances.

Above all, be sure the report findings agree with the procedure codes on the claim. *(Remember the rule: Not documented, not done.)*

Concurrent Care

When a patient goes into the hospital for extensive inpatient procedures involving other specialists or other providers, the attending physician should telephone or send a letter to all involved in the case who are billing from different offices. This will better insure that the correct code numbers with modifiers will appear on the insurance claims, thus eliminating denials for attending physicians. A telephone call or letter might include the following:

Dear Ms. Insurance Claims Specialist:

Dr. (Medical) appreciates the care given by Dr. (Surgeon) to our patient (Jane Doe) during her (June 4–6), 199x, hospital stay.

To insure a cooperative billing effort in this case and to obtain the maximum insurance reimbursement for the patient, we are giving you the patient's insurance data, including the diagnosis and procedure codes that we plan to submit to the insurance company (see enclosed copy of HCFA-1500 form).

Please review the codes for pre- and postoperative medical follow-up visits, exclusive of surgery, where we have used -55 and -56 code modifiers. This will allow you to use the proper modifier (-54) to code your surgery claim.

If you have any questions regarding this case, please call me.

Sincerely,

Dr. (Medical)

Medicare has a list that includes 62 specialties and subspecialties (two-digit codes) to help carriers more accurately judge whether care by two physicians on the same day, known as concurrent care, is necessary. For example, if two internists (a general internist and a cardiologist) see the same patient on the same day and the second doctor is not identified in carrier records as a cardiologist, the claim may be denied. This is because the services appear to be concurrent care by physicians of the same specialty. Periodically, physicians should check with the carrier's provider services representative to see if they have updated their subspecialty status so claims are not denied in cases of concurrent care.

Follow-Up Days

A variable number of follow-up days are allowed after surgery at no additional charge. The code book does not specify how many days should be given. Most states use an RVS for workers' compensation cases, so obtain the RVS used in your state because it will list the follow-up days allowed for most surgical procedures. Another source that lists a global fee period* for each surgical procedure is Appendix B (the Medicare Fee Schedule) in the ninth column, December 8, 1994, *Federal Register*.

If the patient has to be seen beyond the normal time period, justify this on the claim by documenting the reason. If the physician does not wish to make a charge, use CPT code number 99024 to indicate No Charge. This code should always be used on itemized billing statements, as this lets the patient know how many office visits after surgery are being billed at no charge. Code number 99024 has no value, is unbundled with other codes, and is used for tracking purposes. There is no Medicare guideline for this code. Generally, it is not necessary to list this code when completing an insurance claim unless the insurance carrier has specific instructions requesting that it be shown.

Surgical Package

A phrase in the Surgery section commonly encountered when billing is "surgical package." Procedures not followed by a star (i.e., unstarred) include the "package" concept. Generally, a surgical procedure includes the operation, local infiltration, digital block or topical anesthesia, and normal, uncomplicated postoperative care (follow-up hospital and/or office visits). This is referred to as a "package" for surgical procedures, and one fee covers the whole package. The majority of surgical procedures are handled in this manner. Preoperative services such as consultations, office visits, and initial hospital care are often billed separately. Payment of these services depends on third party payment policy. The basic five-digit code number plus a two-digit add-on modifier or a separate five-digit code number should be used. For complex cases, a copy of the operative report itemizing services, personnel, and equipment may be attached to the claim.

In regard to preoperative visits, there are variations among insurance policies and managed care plans in regard to what is included in the package fee. Plans may include all visits from 6 weeks before surgery or include only visits from 1 day before the surgery. A common question asked when an office consultation is done is whether a charge may be made for the consult and admission if done on the same day. In most cases, the admission should be charged listing inpatient visit codes 99221-99223. However, for surgeons the guidelines are different. For example, if a surgeon sees a patient in consultation and recommends that the patient receive immediate transfer of case and admission for surgery, then global surgery rules apply. The consult that resulted in the decision for surgery may be billed, adding modifier -57 (Decision for surgery) to the consult code number. The surgeon may not charge for an admit because all E/M services provided within 24 hours of surgery are bundled into the global surgical fee.

Medicare has a global surgery policy for major operations, which became effective January 1, 1992. Included in the package are

a. Preoperative visits (1 day before surgery)
b. Intraoperative services that are a usual and necessary part of the surgical procedure
c. Complications after surgery that do not require additional trips to the operating room (medical and surgical services)
d. Postoperative visit (variable postoperative period: **0**, **10**, or **90** days)

In addition, procedures in the global period column may show one of the following:

MMM means a service furnished in uncomplicated maternity cases that include prenatal care, delivery, and postnatal care.
XXX means there is no global period, so visits, procedures, and follow-up services may be charged separately.
YYY indicates that the global period will be determined by the local Medicare carrier because the code is for an unlisted procedure.
ZZZ means the code is part of another service and falls within that service's global period.

Services to a Medicare patient not included in the global surgery package are the following:

a. Initial consultation or evaluation
b. Visits unrelated to the diagnosis for which the surgical procedure was performed (modifier -24)

*Medicare global fee period is the postoperative days (0, 10, or 90) included in the fee for the surgery. Medicare global fee is a single fee for all necessary services normally furnished by the surgeon before, during, and after the procedure.

c. Treatment required to stabilize a seriously ill patient before surgery
d. Diagnostic tests and procedures
e. Treatment for postoperative complications that require a return trip to the operating room (modifier -78)
f. Immunosuppressive therapy after transplant surgery

Medicare Global Package

If a Medicare patient is discharged from one hospital facility and admitted to a different hospital or facility on the same day, a provider can get paid for both depending on the circumstances of the case. A low-level admission code, such as 99221, is used for the second hospital admit. A higher-level admission code may be used when the patient goes from a regular room to a specialized hospital of some type. Two separate claim forms, one for the discharge and another for the admission, must be used.

Prolonged Services, Detention, or Standby

Code numbers 99354 through 99360 should be used to indicate prolonged services, e.g., the physician has spent time beyond the usual amount allotted the service (i.e., 30 to 60 minutes). This may be either with or without face-to-face contact or involving standby service. Prolonged service that is less than 30 minutes should not be billed using these codes because the time is included in the total work of the E/M codes. The time should be documented in the medical record to justify use of these codes. Reimbursement for prolonged detention in the hospital is higher than payment for many other types of care, and reimbursement for critical care is even higher.

Some insurance programs or plans (e.g., Medicare, Blue Shield) do not pay for operative standby, so be sure to check before surgery to see whether the commercial carrier will pay. The charge is based on what the physician feels is the value of an hour of her or his time. An example is when a cardiologist performing an angioplasty that may not work asks a cardiovascular surgeon to be ready to do a coronary bypass, or when a pediatrician is on standby during a cesarean section on a pregnant woman. Code 99360 is used for each 30 minutes of standby.

Critical Care

Another area of billing is critical care. This is usually, but not always, given in a critical care area, such as the coronary care unit (CCU), intensive care unit (ICU), respiratory care unit (RCU), or the emergency department (ED), also called the emergency room (ER). These codes are 99291 and 99292. Add-on codes 99050 through 99054 can be used, depending on the hour at which the patient is seen in critical care. Other add-on codes under Miscellaneous Services may be applicable for a patient receiving critical care, so be sure to scrutinize these carefully. The key to obtaining the highest level of reimbursement lies in selecting ICD-9-CM codes that convey the critical nature of the patient's condition.

Emergency Hospital Care

When a physician is reporting services performed in the emergency department, code numbers 99281 through 99288 should be used. When a physician spends several hours attending to a patient, coding for prolonged services (modifier -21), in addition to an E/M emergency department code, might be indicated.

Emergency Office Visits

If a patient comes into the office requiring emergency care and you bill for the office visit, suturing of the laceration, and the surgical tray, most insurance carriers will pay only for the tray and suturing, i.e., the patient will have to pay for the office visit. However, if you code the claim for office services provided on an emergency basis, most carriers will reimburse for the office visit.

Incorrect Coding:

99201	Office visit, intermediate, new pt
12001	Suture of scalp 2.5 cm
99070	Surgical tray (itemized)

Correct Coding:

99058	Office services provided on an emergency basis
12001	Repair of 2.5-cm scalp laceration
99070	Surgical tray (itemized)

Add-on codes 99050 through 99054 can be used depending on the hour at which the patient is seen as an emergency in the physician's office. Other add-on codes under Miscellaneous Services may be applicable for a patient receiving emergency care, so be sure to scrutinize these carefully.

All-Inclusive Codes

In most instances, itemizing supplies works best, but in some circumstances it is best to use an all-inclusive single charge and a single code number. Treatment of long bone fractures is a good example, because the insurance carrier will pay more than one-third more if the correct coding is used.

Incorrect Coding:

99213	Initial office visit, extended
73090	X-rays and interpretation
29075	Application of cast (fractured radius)
99070	Plaster and supplies (itemized)

Correct Coding:

99213-57	E/M code with modifier to tell carrier of decision to perform a major surgical procedure. Fracture care is considered "surgery" because it is located in the Surgery section of the CPT book.
25560	Treatment of closed radial shaft fracture; without manipulation (includes application of the initial cast)
73090	X-rays and interpretation

Note: For a Medicare case, HCPCS Level 2 code A4590 may be submitted for the fiberglass material used in creating the cast if it was applied in the medical office. If the cast was applied and x-rays were taken at the hospital, the facility will charge for those items.

Repair of Lacerations

If multiple lacerations are repaired with the same technique and are in the same anatomic category, the surgeon should add up the total length of all the lacerations and report one code to obtain maximum reimbursement. If the patient had three repairs and each was listed with a different code, the second and third codes would be down coded, so a smaller payment would be generated.

Incorrect Coding:

12011	Repair 2.5 cm laceration of face
12013	Repair 2.7 cm laceration of face
12013	Repair 3 cm laceration of face

Correct Coding:

12015	Repair 8.2 cm laceration of face

Multiple Lesions

The descriptions for the lesion surgical codes can cause confusion when billing for more than one lesion. Use the following examples as guides to obtain maximum reimbursement for surgery of multiple lesions.

Incorrect Coding:

10060*	Incision and drainage, 7 lesions
OR	
10060 × 7	Incision and drainage, 7 lesions

Correct Coding:

10060*	Incision and drainage of one lesion
10061	Incision and drainage, complicated or multiple

Note: This is a starred (*) procedure, so in addition, procedure number 99025 or an E/M code for an initial office visit may be listed.

Delay submission of the insurance claim for removal of a lesion or lesions until the pathology report is received. Usually, a malignant lesion is reimbursed at a higher rate because of the more-detailed nature of the procedure.

Relative Value Studies Variances

RVS code books are published in a number of states for use in billing workers' compensation (industrial) cases. This code system uses a basic five-digit system plus two-digit or five-digit add-on modifiers. RVS and CPT code books are basically the same with regard to the sections and index. There are different modifiers for each code book, and these will be given later in this chapter. Another difference is that RVS code books have unit values listed for each procedure in each of the sections.

The same terminology is used in both code systems (i.e., new patient, established patient, and levels of service).

A term used in the surgery section of the RVS that might be encountered when billing is *global fee*. This term does not involve starred (*) procedures. A *global fee* is associated with many surgical procedures, obstetric procedures, and some highly complex procedures requiring several physicians of different specialties, such as a surgical team. In this instance, a single, global fee for the total service is billed. The services included in the global charge vary widely from place to place. Some insurance carriers consider the office visit before surgery, the admission history and physical examination, and the surgery to be paid as a global fee.

Some RVS code books have stars (*) next to surgical procedures and some code books do not. However, when a starred (*) surgical procedure is carried out at the time of the initial office visit and constitutes the *major service* provided at that visit, it would be listed as well as procedure number 99025 in lieu of the usual E/M initial visit code.

Example:

*10060	Incision and drainage of sebaceous cyst	$00.00
99025	Initial new patient visit	$00.00

Check the book used in your area and read the detailed instructions regarding any additional rules pertaining to the star (*).

Follow-up days are usually listed after each surgical description. If your code book has such a listing, it is important to look at that column to know which follow-up office visits after a surgical procedure are allowed at no charge so as not to inadvertently bill the patient.

A base value for general anesthesia, if required, is listed after each surgical description.

An interim relative value is designated by a box and the letter (I) and may be treated as though the relativity of one procedure to another has not been established (RNE). When using a code with this designation, the code should be substantiated by a report. Some procedures flagged with an interim value may have a date stamp (e.g., 1-94). This means that the procedure is new and considered to be technically difficult, that physicians may require special training to perform the procedure, and that the value of the procedure will automatically decline at the end of the year of the date stamp.

4

DETERMINING RELATIVE VALUE STUDIES CONVERSION FACTORS

If a physician's fees are too high or too low, they can be adjusted. But how to do this can present a problem. Determining the conversion factor can be of great assistance in realigning fees or setting a fee for a procedure for which the physician has not previously billed. Because there are several code divisions (Surgery/Anesthesia, Radiology, Pathology, Medicine, Evaluation and Management), it is necessary to figure out the conversion factor for each division separately. Once the unit values are known and you discover the RVS being used by the insurance carriers that you bill, you can monitor the reimbursements to make sure the payments are correct. It is legal to use an RVS guide for setting, realigning, or evaluating fees as long as the physician does not enter into any price-fixing agreements. To set fees based on an RVS, obtain an RVS and make up a set of separate conversion factors in the Surgery/Anesthesia, Radiology, Pathology, Medicine, and Evaluation and Management sections. The workers' compensation board or the insurance commissioner in your state can supply you with an RVS, or you can obtain a copy of *Relative Values for Physicians.*

Physicians who take x-rays in their offices and bill for them will find an RVS radiology book to be of value. See Appendix B for information on how to obtain the code books mentioned in this chapter.

Use the following four steps to determine conversion factors:

1. Choose 10 or more procedures in the *same* section (Surgery/Anesthesia, Radiology, Pathology, Medicine, or Evaluation and Management) and put down the code numbers and fees you presently use.

Text continued on page 100

TABLE 4-3
Current Procedural Terminology Modifier Codes*

Modifier Code	Explanation
-20	**Microsurgery:** When the surgical service is performed using the techniques of microsurgery, including the aid of an operating microscope, modifier -20 may be added to the surgical procedure, or the separate five-digit modifier code 09920 may be used. The use of this modifier is not warranted when surgery is done with the aid of a magnifying loupe, whether attached to the eyeglasses or on a headband. A special report may be appropriate to document the necessity of the microsurgical approach.[1] **Example:** *65275 Repair of laceration; cornea, nonperforating, with removal foreign body* *65275-20 Use of operating microscope* *See attached copy of operative report for details. Sometimes listing on two separate lines emphasizes the procedure and payment may be more precise. Modifier -20 indicates an increase in payment for the surgical procedure.*
-21	**Prolonged Evaluation and Management Services:** When the service(s) provided is prolonged or otherwise greater than that usually required for the highest level of evaluation and management service within a given category, it may be identified by adding modifier -21 to the evaluation and management code number or by use of the separate five-digit modifier code 09921. A report may also be appropriate.[2] **Example:** *A physician spends an hour with a spouse and hospital inpatient, then an additional hour reviewing laboratory studies and x-ray films and reports, setting up a treatment plan with nurses, and coordinating care by two other specialists.*
-22	**Unusual Services:** When the services provided are greater than that usually required for the listed procedure, they may be identified by adding modifier -22 to the usual procedure number or by using the separate five-digit modifier code 09922. A report may also be appropriate.[2] **Example:** *Removal of foreign body from stomach, which usually takes about 45 minutes, takes 4 hours on a particular patient; use modifier -22. A discharge summary or specially dictated statement should be attached to the claim form. This modifier increases the payment.*
-23	**Unusual Anesthesia:** Occasionally, a procedure that usually requires either no anesthesia or local anesthesia must be done under general anesthesia because of unusual circumstances. This circumstance may be reported by adding the modifier -23 to the procedure code of the basic service or by using the separate five-digit modifier code 09923.[1] **Examples:** *A proctoscopy might require no anesthesia. A skin biopsy or excision of a subcutaneous tumor might require local anesthesia.*
-24	**Unrelated Evaluation and Management Service by the Same Physician During a Postoperative Period:** The physician may need to indicate that an evaluation and management service was performed during a postoperative period for a reason(s) unrelated to the original procedure. This circumstance may be reported by adding the modifier -24 to the appropriate level of E/M service, or the separate five-digit modifier 09924 may be used.[3] **Example:** *A patient seen for a postoperative visit after an appendectomy complains of a lump on the leg. The physician spends 10 minutes taking a history of the complaint, family history of incidence of cancer, and an examination of the site. The patient receives 20 minutes of counseling, and a biopsy is scheduled. Therefore, -24 is added to the E/M code for unrelated service rendered during a postoperative period and 99024 is used for the post surgery exam.*
-25	**Significant, Separately Identifiable Evaluation and Management Service by the Same Physician on the Day of a Procedure:** The physician may need to indicate that on the day a procedure or service identified by a CPT code was performed, the patient's condition required a significant, separately identifiable E/M service above and beyond the other service provided or beyond the usual preoperative and postoperative care associated with the procedure that was performed. This circumstance may be reported by adding the modifier -25 to the appropriate level of E/M service, or the separate five-digit modifier 09925 may be used. Note: This modifier is not used to report an E/M service that resulted in a decision to perform surgery. See modifier -57.[3] **Example:** *A diabetic patient is seen and the physician discovers two moles on the right arm, which are removed. The physician makes a minor adjustment of the oral diabetes medication. This illustrates a significant E/M service provided on the same day as a procedure, so -25 is added to the E/M code and code 11050 and 11051 are used for removal of the moles (verrucae).*
-26	**Professional Component:** Certain procedures are a combination of a physician component and a technical component. When the physician component is reported separately, the service may be identified by adding the modifier -26 to the usual procedure number or by using the five-digit modifier code 09926.[2]

*Reprinted with permission from the American Medical Association, Chicago, Illinois.

TABLE 4-3
Current Procedural Terminology Modifier Codes *(Continued)*

Modifier Code	Explanation
	Note: *The physician may wish to submit a charge for the professional component of a procedure and not the technical component. The professional component comprises only the professional services performed by the physician during radiologic, laboratory, and other diagnostic procedures. These services include examination of the patient, supervision of patient examinations by other health personnel, interpretation of the results of such examinations, and consultation with referring physicians. The technical component includes personnel, materials, including usual contrast media and drugs, film or xerograph, space, equipment, and other facilities but excludes the cost of radioisotopes. When billing for the technical component, use only the usual five-digit procedure number without a modifier.* Examples: *70373-26 Laryngography, contrast; supervision and interpretation only* *70373 Laryngography, contrast; complete procedure* *31708 Instillation of contrast material for laryngography without catheterization*
-32	**Mandated Services:** Services related to *mandated* consultation and/or related services (e.g., PRO, 3rd party payer) may be identified by adding the modifier -32 to the basic procedure, or the service may be reported by use of the five-digit modifier 09932.[3] Example: *A patient is referred to the physician by an insurance company for an unbiased opinion regarding permanent disability after a year of treatment following an accident. Add modifier -32 to the E/M code because of mandated consultation.*
-47	**Anesthesia by Surgeon:** Regional or general anesthesia provided by the surgeon may be reported by adding the modifier -47 to the basic service or by using the separate five-digit modifier code 09947 (this does not include local anesthesia).[1] ***Note:*** *Modifier -47 or 09947 would not be used for anesthesia procedures 00100 through 01999.*
-50	**Bilateral Procedure:** Unless otherwise identified in the listings, bilateral procedures requiring a separate incision performed during the same operative session should be identified by the appropriate five-digit code describing the first procedure. The second (bilateral) procedure is identified either by adding modifier -50 to the procedure number or by using the separate five-digit modifier code 09950. Use of this modifier will eventually eliminate many of the bilateral procedure numbers now listed separately by five-digit codes.[2] ***Note:*** *Most of the bilateral procedures listed in the Surgery and Radiology sections as five-digit procedure codes have been deleted. It is important to read each description carefully for the word bilateral.* Example A: *71060 Bronchography, bilateral would be listed with no modifier* Example B: *19200-50 Bilateral radical mastectomy* *or* *19200 Left radical mastectomy* *19200-50 Right radical mastectomy* Example C: *Bilateral inguinal hernia repair would be typed as:* *49520-50 Repair right and left inguinal hernia*
-51	**Multiple Procedures:** When multiple procedures are performed on the same day or at the same session, the major procedure or service may be reported as listed. The secondary, additional, or lesser procedure(s) or service(s) may be identified by adding the modifier -51 to the secondary procedure or service code(s) or by using the separate five-digit modifier code 09951. This modifier may be used to report multiple medical procedures, a combination of medical and surgical procedures, or several surgical procedures performed at the same operative session. If a second incision is made, do not use -51. Use -51 when additional surgery is done in the same incision.[2] ***Note:*** *It may be necessary to attach a report to the claim outlining each procedure and its clinical indications. Always list the procedure of highest dollar value first.* Example: *Patient had herniated disk in lower back with stabilization of the area where the disk was removed.* *63030 Lumbar laminectomy with disk removal* *22612-51 Arthrodesis* *(modifier used after the lesser of the two procedures)*

Table continued on following page

TABLE 4-3
Current Procedural Terminology Modifier Codes *(Continued)*

Modifier Code	Explanation
-52	**Reduced Services:** Under certain circumstances a service or procedure is partially reduced or eliminated at the physician's election. Under these circumstances the service provided can be identified by its usual procedure number and the addition of the modifier -52, signifying that the service is reduced. This provides a means of reporting reduced services without disturbing the identification of the basic service. Modifier code 09952 may be used as an alternative to modifier -52.[4] ***Note:*** *This means there will be no effect on the physician's fee profile in the computer data. It is not necessary to attach a report to the claim when using this modifier, since it indicates a reduced fee. When a physician performs a procedure but does not charge for the service, such as a postoperative follow-up visit that is included in a global service, remember to use code 99024. Some physicians prefer to bill the insurance carrier the full amount and accept what the carrier pays as payment in full. In such cases, a modifier would not be used. If only part of a procedure is performed and the physician feels a reduction in the service is warranted, to develop a reduced fee try calculating the reduced service by time. Calculate the amount (cost) per minute of the complete procedure by dividing the amount (cost) by the usual time it takes to complete the procedure. To determine how long the reduced procedure took, times the amount (cost) per minute by the time it took to do the reduced procedure.*
-54	**Surgical Care Only:** When one physician performs a surgical procedure and another provides preoperative and/or postoperative management, surgical services may be identified by adding the modifier -54 to the usual procedure number or by using the separate five-digit modifier code 09954.[2] ***Note:*** *Since many surgical procedures encompass a "package" concept that includes normal uncomplicated follow-up care, the surgeon should show a reduced fee when using this modifier.*
-55	**Postoperative Management Only:** When one physician performs the postoperative management and another physician performs the surgical procedure, the postoperative component may be identified by adding the modifier -55 to the usual procedure number or by using the separate five-digit modifier code 09955.[2] ***Note:*** *The fee to list would be approximately 30% of the surgeon's fee.*
-56	**Preoperative Management Only:** When one physician performs the preoperative care and evaluation and another physician performs the surgical procedure, the preoperative component may be identified by adding the modifier -56 to the usual procedure number or by using the separate five-digit modifier code 09956.[1] ***Note:*** *Explain to the insurance carrier that your physician is doing the preoperative care only. If the surgeon was paid the entire surgical fee by the insurance carrier because of the "package" concept, the carrier should issue your physician a check and handle the problem of overpayment to the surgeon.*
-57	**Decision for Surgery:** An evaluation and management service that resulted in the initial decision to perform the surgery may be identified by adding the modifier -57 to the appropriate level of E/M service, or the separate five-digit modifier 09957 may be used.[3] **Example:** *A patient is referred for a consultation to determine whether surgery is necessary. The patient consents to surgery. The surgeon bills the E/M consultation code and adds the -57 modifier. By adding this modifier, the third party payer is informed that the consultation is not part of the global surgical procedure. Medicare will pay if it is for major surgery that requires a 90-day postoperative follow-up but not for a minor surgical procedure (0- to 10-day postoperative follow-up).*
-58	**Staged or Related Procedure or Service by the Same Physician During the Postoperative Period:** The physician may need to indicate that the performance of a procedure or service during the postoperative period was (a) planned prospectively at the time of the original procedure (staged); (b) more extensive than the original procedure; or (c) for therapy following a diagnostic surgical procedure. This circumstance may be reported by adding the modifier -58 to the staged or related procedure, or the separate five-digit modifier 09958 may be used.[3] ***Note:*** *This modifier is not used to report the treatment of a problem that requires a return to the operating room. See modifier -78.* **Example:** *A patient has breast cancer, and a surgeon performs a mastectomy. During the postoperative global period, the surgeon inserts a permanent prosthesis. The -58 modifier is added to the code for inserting the prosthesis, indicating that this service was related to the initial operation. If the modifier is not used, the insurance carrier may reject the claim because surgery occurred during the surgery's global period.*
-62	**Two Surgeons:** Under certain circumstances the skills of two surgeons (usually with different skills) may be required in the management of a specific surgical procedure. Under such circumstances the separate services may be identified by adding the modifier -62 to the procedure number used by each surgeon for reporting his or her services. Modifier code 09962 may be used as an alternative to modifier -62.[2]

TABLE 4-3
Current Procedural Terminology Modifier Codes *(Continued)*

Modifier Code	Explanation
	Example: *Lumbar laminectomy for herniated disk performed by a neurosurgeon and an orthopedic surgeon: 63030-62 or 63030 and 09962. The fees are approached by mutual agreement between the two surgeons.*
-66	**Surgical Team:** Under some circumstances, highly complex procedures (requiring the concomitant services of several physicians, often of different specialties, plus other highly skilled, specially trained personnel and various types of complex equipment) are carried out under the "surgical team" concept. Such circumstances may be identified by each participating physician with the addition of the modifier -66 to the basic procedure number used for reporting services. Modifier code 09966 may be used as an alternative to modifier -66.[2] Examples: *A kidney transplant, requiring use of a vascular surgeon, urologist, anesthesiologist, nephrologist, and pathologist, or open heart surgery using perfusion personnel, anesthesiologist, and three cardiologists.*
-76	**Repeat Procedure by Same Physician:** The physician may need to indicate that a procedure or service was repeated subsequent to the original service. This circumstance may be reported by adding modifier -76 to the repeated service or by using the separate five-digit modifier code 09976.[3] Example: *When there is no visualization of the gallbladder on the first examination or during the endoscopy, the procedure cannot be completed and is repeated the following day. A report should be attached to the insurance claim when using this modifier.*
-77	**Repeat Procedure by Another Physician:** The physician may need to indicate that a basic procedure performed by another physician had to be repeated. This situation may be reported by adding modifier -77 to the repeated service or by using the separate five-digit modifier code 09977.[3]
-78	**Return to the Operating Room for a Related Procedure During the Postoperative Period:** The physician may need to indicate that another procedure was performed during the postoperative period of the initial procedure. When this subsequent procedure is related to the first, and requires the use of the operating room, it may be reported by adding the modifier -78 to the related procedure or by using the separate five-digit modifier 09978. (For repeat procedures on the same day, see -76.)[1] Example: *A patient has an open reduction with fixation of a fracture of the elbow. While still hospitalized, the patient develops an infection and is returned to surgery only to discover the patient is suffering an allergic reaction to the pin and it is removed. A code would be listed for the open treatment of the fracture. Because of complications, modifier -78 would be added to the code for removal of the pin.*
-79	**Unrelated Procedure or Service by the Same Physician During the Postoperative Period:** The physician may need to indicate that the performance of a procedure or service during the postoperative period was unrelated to the original procedure. This circumstance may be reported by using the modifier -79 or by using the separate five-digit modifier 09979. (For repeat procedures on the same day, see -76.)[3] Example: *A patient in the hospital has surgery and is discharged home. After 7 days, the patient develops acute renal failure, is hospitalized, does not recover renal function, and hemodialysis is ordered. A nephrologist inserts a cannula for the dialysis. When billing for the nephrologist, the code for hemodialysis is shown with a -79 modifier indicating that this is unrelated to the initial surgery. If -79 is not used, the insurance carrier may not realize the service is not related to the initial surgery and may reject the claim.*
-80	**Assistant Surgeon:** Surgical assistant services may be identified by adding the modifier -80 to the usual procedure number(s) or by using the separate five-digit modifier code 09980.[2] **Note:** *Some insurance policies do not include payment for assistant surgeons, such as for 1-day surgery, but do pay for major or complex surgical assistance. In some instances, prior approval may be indicated owing to the patient's physiologic condition. Medicare will not pay assistant surgeons for operations that are not life threatening. Therefore, Medicare supplemental insurance will not pay on this service since the service is nonallowable. Assisting surgeons usually charge 16% to 30% of their normal fee for performing the surgery alone.*
-81	**Minimum Assistant Surgeon:** Minimum surgical assistant services are identified by adding the modifier -81 to the usual procedure number or by using the separate five-digit modifier code 09981. **Note:** *Payment is made to physicians but not registered nurses or technicians who assist during surgery.*[2]
-82	**Assistant Surgeon:** (When qualified resident surgeon is not available.) The unavailability of a qualified resident surgeon is a prerequisite for use of modifier -82 appended to the usual procedure code number(s) or the separate five-digit modifier code 09982.[2] **Note:** *This modifier is usually used for services rendered at a teaching hospital.*

Table continued on following page

TABLE 4-3
Current Procedural Terminology Modifier Codes *(Continued)*

Modifier Code	Explanation
-90	**Reference (Outside) Laboratory:** When laboratory procedures are performed by a party other than the treating or reporting physician, the procedure may be identified by adding the modifier -90 to the usual procedure number or by using the separate five-digit modifier code 09990.[3] ***Note:*** *Use this modifier when the physician bills the patient for the laboratory work and the laboratory is not doing its own billing.*
-99	**Multiple Modifiers:** Under certain circumstances, two or more modifiers may be necessary to delineate a service completely. In such situations modifier -99 should be added to the basic procedure, and other applicable modifiers may be listed as part of the description of the service. Modifier code 09999 may be used as an alternative to modifier -99.[3] **Example:** *57270-99 Repair of enterocele* *-22 Extensive hemorrhaging* *-76 Procedure had to be repeated* *See attached operative report*

[1] This modifier may affect reimbursement, depending on the payer.
[2] This modifier may have an effect on reimbursement.
[3] Modifier is informational in nature. Do not ask for an adjustment in reimbursement. Monitor reimbursement when using this modifier.
[4] This modifier affects reimbursement but not the physician's fee profile.

2. Take each procedure and divide the fee you presently charge by the procedure's unit value. The unit value is listed next to the code number and procedure description in the RVS. Because some procedure descriptions change from year to year, be sure that the description of the service is the proper definition for the service you are giving for that particular fee. Divide each procedure's fee in the sampling you have chosen by its individual unit value.
3. Look at all the dollar figures in the section that you have determined. They should fall within the same general range. If they do not, then some of the fees that are too high or too low may have to be re-evaluated and readjusted depending on the service descriptions and competition. Go through this procedure with all sections.
4. Add all the conversion factors in the Medicine section. Divide the sum by the total number of procedures in that sampling. This is the conversion factor for the Medicine section. Remember this is only a guideline, and the physician may elect to use the highest, lowest, or median figure depending on his or her own judgment and circumstances. Repeat these four steps with each of the sections to obtain at least five conversion factors. Once you have determined the conversion factors for the Surgery/Anesthesia, Radiology, Pathology, Medicine, and Evaluation and Management sections, you can determine a dollar figure for a new procedure within the same general grouping by multiplying the unit value by the dollar conversion factor. This will give an approximate cost of each procedure's relative worth.

Comprehensive List of Modifier Codes

Listed values for most procedures may be modified under certain circumstances. The modifying circumstance should be identified by adding the appropriate two-digit modifier code number (including the hyphen) after the usual five-digit procedure code number or by using the separate five-digit modifier code on a separate line. Table 4–3 lists modifiers used in CPT. Editorial comments and examples are shown in italics following each modifier. Important footnotes about physician reimbursement are located at the end of the list. Only certain modifiers are used for specific sections of CPT and are not common to all six sections.

Although the modifier codes seen in CPT may be the same as those seen in RVS code books, there may be a slight variation in the description of usage. The modifier codes are used in addition to those shown on the previous pages (Table 4–4). These have been

TABLE 4-4
Relative Values for Physicians' Modifier Codes

Modifier Code	Explanation
-10	**Endoscopic Surgery:** When the surgical procedure is performed through any type of endoscope for which there is no endoscopic code, attach this modifier to the open surgery procedure code. (This modifier is not CPT compatible.) Attachment of this modifier should warrant no reduction or increase in value for the interim. Values established for laparoscopic procedures will be given a separate listing in the *body* of RVP. Please check the code range for both the correct open procedure and codes 56300 through 56399 for possible CPT-compatible codes.
-27	**Technical Component:** Under certain circumstances, a charge may be made for the technical component alone. (This modifier is not CPT compatible.)
-28	**Debridement and/or Decontamination** are considered of additional value when appreciable amounts of devitalized or contaminated tissue are removed. Report required. (This modifier is not CPT compatible.)
-29	**Services Provided by Other Than Physician:** When a service is performed by a licensed physician assistant or personnel other than the physician under direct supervision of a physician. (This modifier is not CPT compatible.)
-30	**Anesthesia Services:** Add this modifier for normal, uncomplicated anesthesia. Medicare and some other carriers may require reporting of a specific anesthesia code section. Otherwise, use the value indicated in the anesthesia column. (This modifier is not CPT compatible.)
-48	**Reduced Anesthesia Value for Supervision:** When the anesthesiologist is supervising the services of the nurse anesthetist and is involved in medical direction of the patient, including preoperative and postoperative evaluation and care, but is not personally administering the anesthesia. (This modifier is not CPT compatible.)
-49	**Distinct Service/Procedure:** This modifier is used to indicate a service/procedure provided by the physician that is significant and distinct from other services provided. When a procedure/service is normally considered a composite part of another procedure (e.g., separate procedure), is provided through a separate surgical invasion on a separate organ system, or is significantly greater in time and intensity than that which is normal due to the present circumstance and not the physician's performance, modifier -49 may be attached to the code. In such cases, normal multiple procedure guidelines are applicable (see surgical guidelines). When a service/procedure is provided at a separate site or a separate operative setting on the same day, modifier -49 should be attached to the second procedure in conjunction with other appropriate modifiers (-78, related procedure in operating room; -76, repeat procedure; -79, unrelated procedure; -58, staged or related; -68, related procedure in office setting). Payment/billing should follow payment guidelines listed under the secondary modifier. (This modifier is not CPT compatible.)
-52	**Reduced Values:** Under certain circumstances, the listed value for a procedure is reduced or eliminated because of common practice or at the physician's election. Use this modifier to identify such procedures.
-53	**Add-On Procedure:** Procedures which are indicated by an editor's note following the code indicates the service is an add-on procedure and therefore is already reduced by multiple procedure rules. Identify by adding the modifier -53 to the code. Bill at 100% of the previously reduced value. (This modifier is not CPT compatible.) Some payers require reporting of these procedures with no modifier.
-59	**Significant, Separately Identifiable Evaluation and Management Service by the Same Physician During a Preoperative Period and Before the Day of a Procedure:** The physician may need to indicate that during a preoperative period and before the day of a procedure or service identified by a CPT code was performed, the patient's condition required a significant, separately identifiable E/M service above and beyond the usual preoperative care associated with the procedure that was performed. This circumstance may be reported by adding the modifier -59 to the appropriate level of E/M service. The use of the modifier requires substantiation by report, and 100% of the listed value should be allowed. (This modifier is not CPT compatible.)
-68	**Related Procedure Performed During the Postoperative Period in the Office or Outpatient Setting (Non–Operating Room):** The physician may need to report another procedure that was performed during the postoperative period of the initial procedure. When this subsequent procedure is related to the first, it may be reported by adding -68 to the related procedure. In these circumstances, 70% of the listed value is warranted. (This modifier is not CPT compatible.)
-75	**Concomitant Care:** Services rendered by more than one physician. When the patient's condition requires the services of more than one physician, each physician may identify services by adding this modifier to the basic service he or she performed. (This modifier is not CPT compatible.)

* Reprinted with permission from *Relative Values for Physicians* (RVP). New York, McGraw-Hill Healthcare Management Group, 1993.

TABLE 4-5
Laboratory Abbreviations

Abbreviation	Definition
AcG	factor V (AcG or pro-accelerin); a factor in coagulation that converts prothrombin to thrombin
ACTH	adrenocorticotropic hormone
AFB	acid-fast bacilli
A/G ratio	albumin-globulin ratio
AHB	alpha-hydroxybutyric dehydrogenase
AHG	antihemophilic globulin; antihemolytic globulin (factor)
ALA	aminolevulinic acid
ALT	alanine aminotransferase (see SGPT)
AMP	adenosine monophosphate
APT test	aluminum-precipitated toxoid test
AST	aspartate aminotransferase (see SGOT)
ATP	adenosine triphosphate
BSP	bromsulfonphthalein (Bromsulphalein; sodium sulfobromophthalein) test
BUN	blood urea nitrogen
CBC	complete blood count
CNS	central nervous system
CO	carbon monoxide
CPB	competitive protein binding; plasma
CPK	creatine phosphokinase
CSF	cerebrospinal fluid
D hemoglobin	hemoglobin fractionation by electrophoresis for hemoglobin D
DAP	direct agglutination pregnancy (Gravindex and DAP)
DEAE	diethylaminoethanol
DHT	dihydrotestosterone
DNA	deoxyribonucleic acid
DRT	test for syphilis
EACA	EACA control (epsilon-aminocaproic acid is a fibrinolysin)
EMIT	enzyme-multiplied immunoassay technique (for drugs)
ENA	extractable nuclear antigen
esr, ESR	erythrocyte sedimentation rate (sed rate)
FDP	fibrin degradation products
FIGLU	formiminoglutamic acid
FRAT	free radical assay technique (for drugs)
FSH	follicle-stimulating hormone
FSP	fibrinogen split products
FTA	fluorescent-absorbed treponema antibodies
Gc, Gm, Inv	immunoglobulin typing
GG, gamma G- A,D,G,M nephelometric	gamma-globulin (immunoglobulin fractionation by electrophoresis)
GG, gamma G E, RIA	immunization E fractionation by radioimmunoassay
GGT	gamma-glutamyl transpeptidase
GLC	gas liquid chromatography
GMP	guanosine monophosphate
G6PD	glucose-6-phosphate dehydrogenase
HAA	hepatitis-associated agent (antigen)
HBD, HBDH	hydroxybutyrate dehydrogenase
HCT	hematocrit
hemoglobin, electrophoresis (includes A_2, S, C, etc.)	letters of the alphabet used for different types or factors of hemoglobins
Hgb	hemoglobin, qualitative
HGH	human growth hormone
HI	hemagglutination inhibition
HIA	hemagglutination-inhibition antibody
HIAA	hydroxyindoleacetic acid (urine), 24-hour specimen
HIV	human immunodeficiency virus
HLA	human leukocyte antigen (tissue typing)
HPL	human placental lactogen

TABLE 4-5
Laboratory Abbreviations *(Continued)*

Abbreviation	Definition
HTLV-III	antibody detection; confirmatory test
HVA	homovanillic acid
ICSH	interstitial cell stimulating hormone
IFA	intrinsic factor, antibody (fluorescent screen)
IgA, IgE, IgG, IgM	immunoglobulins; quantitative by gel diffusion
INH	isonicotinic acid hydrazide
LAP	leucine aminopeptidase
LATS	long-acting thyroid-stimulating hormone
LDH	lactic dehydrogenase
LE Prep	lupus erythematosus cell preparation
L.E. factor	antinuclear antibody
LH	luteinizing hormone
LSD	lysergic acid diethylamide
L/S ratio	lecithin-sphingomyelin ratio
MG *(Streptococcus)*	antibody titer
MIC	minimum inhibitory concentration
NBT	nitro-blue tetrazolium test
OCT	ornithine carbamyl transferase
PAH	para-aminohippuric acid
PBI	protein-bound iodine
pCO_2	arterial carbon dioxide pressure (or tension)
PCP	phencyclidine piperidine
pcv	packed cell volume
pH	symbol for expression of concentration of hydrogen ions (degree of acidity)
PHA	phenylalanine
PIT	prothrombin inhibition test
PKU	phenylketonuria–a metabolic disease affecting mental development
pO_2	oxygen pressure
P & P	prothrombin-proconvertin
PSP	phenolsulfonphthalein
PT	prothrombin time
PTA	plasma thromboplastin antecedent
PTC	plasma thromboplastin component; phenylthiocarbamide
PTT	prothrombin time; partial thromboplastin time (plasma or whole blood)
RBC, rbc	red blood cells (count)
RIA	radioimmunoassay
RISA	radioiodinated human serum albumin
RIST	radioimmunosorbent test
RPR	rapid plasma reagin test
RT3U	resin triiodothyronine uptake
S-D	strength-duration (curve)
SGOT	serum glutamic oxaloacetic transaminase
SGPT	serum glutamic pyruvic transaminase
STS	serologic test for syphilis
T_3	triiodothyronine (uptake)
TB	tubercle bacillus, tuberculosis
TBG	thyroxine-binding globulin
T & B differentiation, lymphocytes	thymus-dependent lymphs and bursa-dependent lymphs
THC	tetrahydrocannabinol (marijuana)
TIBC	total iron-binding capacity, chemical
TLC screen	thin layer chromatography screen
TRP	tubular reabsorption of phosphates
UA	urinalysis
VDRL	Venereal Disease Research Laboratory (agglutination test for syphilis)
VMA	vanillylmandelic acid
WBC, wbc	white blood cells (count)

abstracted from the 1996 edition of *Relative Values for Physicians* (RVP). These modifiers are not CPT compatible.

Medicare Coding

During the late 1980s, an RBRVS approach to fees was developed to redistribute Medicare dollars most equitably among physicians. This information, as well as the three levels of Medicare coding used to obtain correct payment for a procedure or service, is provided in Chapter 12, Medicare.

Laboratory Abbreviations

Frequently, the physician orders a laboratory test, such as a complete blood count (CBC), by abbreviation only. Table 4–5 will help the insurance billing specialist translate the abbreviation and thereby locate the correct code number in either CPT or RVS.

TO THE STUDENT

For further knowledge and understanding, the key terms at the beginning of the chapter appear in the Glossary at the end of this textbook so that you can look up the pertinent terms. Study Chapter 4 and then answer the review questions in the *Workbook* to reinforce the theory learned in this chapter of the text and to help prepare you for a future test. Assignments 4 through 11 will assist you in hands-on practical experience in procedural coding as well as learning medical abbreviations.

CHAPTER 5

Diagnostic Coding

Objectives*

THE INSURANCE BILLING SPECIALIST WILL BE ABLE TO:

- Explain the purpose and importance of coding diagnoses.
- Use diagnostic code books properly.
- State the meaning of basic abbreviations and symbols in the code books.
- Define diagnostic code terminology.
- Give the history of diagnostic coding.
- Perform CPT (procedure) coding and ICD-9-CM (diagnostic) coding accurately after completing the problems in the *Workbook.*

Key Terms

combination code
complication
E codes
eponyms
etiology
International Classification of Diseases, Ninth Revision, Clinical Modification (ICD-9-CM)
italicized code
late effect
Not elsewhere classifiable (NEC)
Not otherwise specified (NOS)
primary diagnosis
principal diagnosis
slanted brackets
V codes

* Performance objectives and exercises for hands-on practical experience for this chapter appear in the *Workbook*.

CHAPTER 5

Diagnostic Coding

Introduction

Now that you have learned some basics of procedural coding, the next step is to learn how to code diagnoses. Again, a working knowledge of medical terminology and a course in anatomy and physiology are essential to become a topnotch coder of diagnoses. The coding must be accurate because in some instances, such as a patient under the Medicare program, payment for hospitalizations is based on the diagnosis. All diagnoses that affect the current status of the patient may or may not be assigned a code depending on the insurance carrier involved. This includes conditions that exist at the time of the patient's initial contact with the physician as well as conditions that develop subsequently that affect the treatment received. Diagnoses that relate to a patient's previous medical problem and that have no bearing on the patient's present condition are excluded.

Codes must be sequenced correctly on an insurance claim so that the chronology of patient care events and severity of disease can be understood. When submitting insurance claims for patients seen in a physician's office or in an outpatient hospital setting, the *primary diagnosis,* which is the underlying cause of the condition, must be listed first. The secondary diagnosis, listed subsequently, is that which may contribute to the condition but is not the underlying cause. The *principal diagnosis* is the illness or injury that prompted the hospitalization or office visit. It is possible that the primary and principal diagnosis codes may be the same but not in all cases. For example, if a diabetic patient comes in for management of oral insulin therapy, a diagnosis code for diabetes would be used as both the primary and principal diagnoses. But if a diabetic patient comes in with a complaint of blood in the urine, the diagnosis code for hematuria would be listed first and the diagnosis code for diabetes would be second.

Diagnostic coding was developed for the following reasons:

1. Tracking of disease processes
2. Classification of medical procedures
3. Medical research
4. Evaluation of hospital utilization

Some medical practices do not use diagnostic codes on insurance claims, preferring to name the diagnosis. The consequences of not using ICD-9-CM codes are many. For example, it affects the physician's level of reimbursement, claims can be denied, fines or penalties can be levied, and sanctions can be imposed. It is important to use diagnostic codes on all claims, and, if correctly done, payments are accurate and prompt.

Occasionally an insurance company will reply to an insurance claim with an explanation of benefits or remittance advice, stating "This procedure/item is not payable for the diagnosis as reported." The procedures that are diagnosis related include most imaging services (x-rays, computed tomograms [CTs], and magnetic resonance images [MRIs]), cardiovascular services (electrocardiograms, Holter monitors, echocardiography, Doppler and stress testing), neurologic services (electroencephalography and noninvasive ultrasound), some laboratory services, and vitamin B_{12} injections. For example, a patient has an MRI of the brain. Medicare will not reimburse an MRI for a transient ischemic attack (TIA) or Alzheimer's disease but will pay for one for cerebral insufficiency. So it is important to know the procedures that are diagnosis related and exactly which diagnosis relates to the procedure being billed. A reference book helpful in this situation is *St. Anthony's Guide to Code Linkage,* see Appendix B.

Because health care costs have escalated in the 1980s and 1990s, insurance premiums have risen with higher deductibles and copayments. The Medicare program is approaching the brink of bankruptcy. Prospective payment, diagnosis-related groups (DRGs), utilization review, and the Medicare freeze are some of the cost containment measures affecting mainly hospital reimbursement. These measures have failed to keep the costs down, and the nation is in the beginning years of a national health system reform. DRGs are discussed in Chapter 16, Hospital Billing. If records are comprehensive, statistics can be gathered to make future payments more realistic for the physician in private practice.

Coding of Diseases

HISTORY

From the beginnings of medicine, people have tried to name and classify diseases. Although many attempts have been made to systematize and clarify disease terminology, no one method has ever been accepted by the entire medical community.

About 1869, the American Medical Association prepared the *American Nomenclature of Diseases.* Then, in 1903, the *Bellevue Hospital Nomenclature of Diseases* was published. It was subsequently replaced by the *Standard Nomenclature of Diseases and Operations.* In the 1960s, the American Medical Association published *Current Medical Information and Terminology* (CMIT), which used a computer format to make frequent revisions easier. The medical terms were alphabetically arranged with detailed descriptions of the diseases and two- and four-digit code numbers. This book ceased publication in 1991.

ICD-9-CM

The *International Classification of Diseases* (ICD) had its beginnings in England during the 17th century. The United States began using the ICD toward the latter half of the 19th century to report causes of death and prepare mortality statistics. Hospitals began using ICD in 1950 to classify and index diseases. The ninth revision of the *International Classification of Diseases* (ICD-9), published by the World Health Organization, is now being used by state health departments and the United States Public Health Service for mortality reporting.

In 1978, the *International Classification of Diseases, Ninth Revision, Clinical Modification* (ICD-9-CM) was published by the Commission on Professional and Hospital Activities in the United States. It has three volumes. Volume 1 is Diseases: Tabular (numerical) List. Volume 2 is Diseases: Alphabetic Index. Volume 3 is Procedures: Tabular List and Alphabetic Index, used primarily in the hospital setting. The systematized arrangement in these books makes it possible to encode, computerize, store, and retrieve large volumes of information from the patient's medical record. ICD-9-CM is used by hospitals and other health care providers to code and report clinical information required for participation in various government programs, such as Medicare, Medicaid, and professional standards review organizations.

Volumes 1 and 2 are used in physicians' offices to complete insurance claims. These two volumes are completely compatible with the original international version (ICD-9). The code numbers have from three to five digits. Although abbreviated versions of ICD-9-CM are available, it is preferable to obtain the complete ninth revision of Volumes 1 and 2. Computer readouts of these volumes are difficult to read, and errors can be made in coding.

The annual update of ICD-9-CM occurs each October 1, and the changes are published in three publications—*Coding Clinic,* published by the American Hospital Association; the *American Health Information Management Association Journal,* published by the American Health Information Management Association; and the *Federal Register,* published by the U.S. Government Printing Office. Coding from an out-of-date manual can delay payment or cause costly mistakes that can lead to financial disaster. Many insurance carriers do not use the new codes until they have a chance to update their computer systems. It is important to verify with each carrier exactly when it plans to begin using the new codes. Refer to Appendix B to learn the names and addresses of several companies that publish ICD-9-CM.

Psychiatric disorders are coded using the *Diagnostic and Statistical Manual of Mental Disorders,* Third Edition (DSM III). This coding is not discussed in this text. Refer to Appendix B to find out where to obtain this code book.

ICD-10

ICD-10 Volume 1: Tabular List was published by the World Health Organization in 1992. This code book differs from ICD-9-CM in the following ways.

1. There is a replacement of the traditional numeric coding system with an alphanumeric scheme. This stabilizes the coding system and minimizes disruption for revisions.
2. Old injury (800–999) codes have been changed to S and T codes.
3. Explanatory notes and instructions for use have been greatly expanded.
4. The dagger-and-asterisk system of dual classification has been considerably expanded.
5. The E and V codes in ICD-9-CM are now Chapters XX and XXI.
6. Many new categories and chapters have been added.

Volume 2 provides definitions, standards, and rules for the tabular list. Volume 3 is an alphabetic index. Because ICD-10 has not yet been adopted or approved for use nationally by private insurance carriers or state or federal programs, this chapter stresses the instruction and use of ICD-9-CM codes. A video offering a clear, well-organized presentation of how the new coding methodology will benefit health care is mentioned in Appendix B.

ICD-9-CM CONTENTS

5

Table 5–1 is an outline of Volumes 1 and 2 of ICD-9-CM. Volume 1 contains a classification of diseases and injuries grouped by etiology and anatomic systems and a numeric index. In Chapter 16, Hospital Billing, an outline is provided for Volume 3 because this reference is used primarily in the hospital setting. Information on how to find codes in Volume 3 is also presented in that chapter.

How to Use the Diagnostic Code Books Properly

To become a proficient coder, it is important to develop an understanding of the conventions and terminology of ICD-9-CM. Read all of the information at the beginning of Volumes 1 and 2 before coding. In Volume 1, the Tabular List for the disease classifications makes use of certain abbreviations, punctuation, symbols, and other conventions as follows.

In Volume 2, the Alphabetic Index for both the disease and procedure classification uses the symbol of slanted brackets (*[]*) to indicate the need for another code. In the Alphabetic Index, a code will be given after a listing followed by slanted brackets enclosing an additional code. Record both of these codes in the same sequence as indicated in the index.

Italicized codes in the Tabular List and codes in *slanted brackets* in the Alphabetic Index may never be sequenced as principal diagnoses. Codes in slanted brackets must be sequenced in the order specified in the Alphabetic Index.

CODING INSTRUCTIONS

Code only the conditions or problems that the physician is actively managing at the time of the visit. However, some insurance carriers have restrictions on accepting codes and may allow only one or two codes per claim. In those situations, it

TABLE 5-1. Outline of Volumes 1 and 2 of ICD-9-CM

	Volume/Chapters	Codes
1	Infectious and Parasitic Diseases	001–139
2	Neoplasms	140–239
3	Endocrinologic, Nutritional, and Metabolic Diseases and Immunologic Disorders	240–279
4	Diseases of the Blood and Blood-Forming Organs	280–289
5	Mental Disorders	290–319
6	Diseases of the Nervous System and Sense Organs	320–389
7	Diseases of the Circulatory System	390–459
8	Diseases of the Respiratory System	460–519
9	Diseases of the Digestive System	520–579
10	Diseases of the Genitourinary System	580–629
11	Complications of Pregnancy, Childbirth, and the Puerperium	630–676
12	Diseases of the Skin and Subcutaneous Tissue	680–709
13	Diseases of the Musculoskeletal System and Connective Tissue	710–739
14	Congenital Anomalies	740–759
15	Certain Conditions Originating in the Perinatal Period	760–779
16	Symptoms, Signs, and Ill-Defined Conditions	780–799
17	Injury and Poisoning	800–999
	Supplementary Classification	
	Classification of Factors Influencing Health Status and Contact with Health Service	V01–V82
	Classification of External Causes of Injury and Poisoning	E800–E999
	Appendices	
A	Morphology	
B	Glossary of Mental Disorders	
C	Classification of Drugs by American Hospital Formulary Service List Number and Their ICD-9-CM Equivalents	
D	Classification of Industrial Accidents According to Agency	
	Volume 2 Contents	
Index to Diseases and Injuries, alphabetic		
Table of Drugs and Chemicals		
Index to External Causes of Injuries and Poisonings		

may not be possible to code all active problems. Always use both Volume 2, the Alphabetic Index, and Volume 1, the Tabular (numerical) List. Never use just one volume. Begin with the Alphabetic Index to locate the main entry term and then find and read the code section in the Tabular List. The primary arrangement of the Alphabetic Index is by *condition* in the disease index. If you cannot find the condition listed, consider rearranging the roots. *Example:* crypt orchid/o or orchido-crypt/o. Then substitute a similar suffix. *Example:* Fx (fracture) lumbar vertebra due to senile osteoporosis is an Fx, vertebra, pathologic (any site) 733.13.

Volume 2 elements are structured as follows:

Main terms appear in **bold face** type.
Subterms are indented two spaces to the right under main terms.
Carry-over lines are indented more than two spaces from the level of the preceding line.
Subterms of subterms are indented two spaces to the right under the subterm.

A three-digit code may be used only when the diagnostic statement cannot be further subdivided. When a three-digit code has subdivisions, the appropriate subdivision must be coded. Some insurance carrier computer systems kick out the lower-level codes (three-digit codes) and hold these claims for medical review, thereby delaying payment. If the CPT code indicates a lower-level office visit, the claim may not be rejected if a three-digit ICD-9-CM code was used. If the claim was for a higher-level office visit, the three-digit code would not justify the medical necessity of this level of service. The addition of a zero to a code number that does not

Abbreviations

NEC Not Elsewhere Classifiable (in the coding books). The category number for the term including NEC is to be used only when the coder lacks the information necessary to code the term in a more-specific category.

> **Example:**
> **Adherent**
> Scar (skin) NEC 709.2

NOS Not Otherwise Specified (by the physician). This abbreviation is the equivalent of "unspecified."

> **Example:**
> **153.9 Colon, unspecified**
> Large intestine NOS

Punctuation

[] Brackets are used to enclose synonyms, alternative wordings, or explanatory phrases.

() Parentheses are used to enclose supplementary words that may be present or absent in the statement of a disease or procedure without affecting the code number to which it is assigned.

: Colons are used in the Tabular List after an incomplete term that needs one or more of the modifiers that follow to make it assignable to a given category.

} Braces are used to enclose a series of terms, each of which is modified by the statement appearing at the right of the brace.

Symbols

□ The lozenge symbol printed in the left margin preceding the disease code indicates that the content of a four-digit category has been moved or modified.

§ The section mark symbol preceding a code denotes the placement of a footnote at the bottom of the page that is applicable to all subdivisions in that code.

require an additional digit can cause a claim to be denied.

Example:

Invalid code due to zero added	Valid code
373.20	**373.2**
496.0	**496**

Five-digit codes can appear

At the beginning of a chapter
At the beginning of a section
At the beginning of a three-digit category
In a four-digit subcategory

Near the end of this chapter, accompanying Rules for Coding Diabetes Mellitus, is another example illustrating the use of five digits. *The use of five digits is NOT optional;* therefore, a handy hint would be to go through the entire classification to highlight all four-digit subcategories that require a fifth digit or to purchase code books that have the categories marked. Unless you take this precaution, it is easy to overlook fifth digits. Although the code books show decimal points, these are not required on optically scanned insurance claims. When the fourth or fifth digit is missing, the code is not complete and technically is not a code but rather a category.

> **Example:**
>
> §645 Prolonged pregnancy
> [0, 1, 3] Post-term pregnancy
> Pregnancy which has advanced beyond 42 weeks of gestation.
>
> The section mark requires a fifth digit; valid digits are in [brackets] under each code. Use 0 as the fourth digit for this category.

Do not arbitrarily use a zero as a filler character when typing a diagnostic code number because this may be interpreted as indicating a different disease.

When you are billing Medicare, you will find that some diagnostic codes are designated as invalid from year to year. If you work in a medical practice, it is essential to read the regional Medicare bulletins to keep abreast of these changes.

Basic Steps in Coding

Follow these steps for the first diagnosis, eliminating any shortcuts. For each subsequent diagnosis in a patient's medical history, repeat these steps.

Step 1. Locate the main term in the Alphabetic Index, Volume 2.
- a. Refer to any notes under the main term.
- b. Read any terms enclosed in parentheses following the main term.
- c. Refer to any nonessential modifiers of the main term.
- d. *Do not* skip over any subterms indented under the main term.
- e. Follow any cross-reference instructions.

Step 2. Verify the code number in the Tabular List, Volume 1.
- a. Read and be guided by any instructional terms in the Tabular List.
- b. Assign the code.

Now use a step-by-step approach and refer to each volume in the following examples.

Example: Chronic alcoholic liver *disease.*

Step 1. Look under *disease* (the condition) in Volume 2.
Find the heading "liver."
Locate the subheading "alcoholic."
Look for the second subheading *chronic*. The correct code number is 571.3.

Step 2. Look for the code number—*not* the page number—in Volume 1.
Notice the wording "571.3 Alcoholic Liver damage, unspecified." The code and its title refer to any liver damage caused by alcoholism, without specification as to the nature of the disorder. Because there are no exclusion notes, this is the correct code.

Refer to the Tabular List, Volume 1, to *verify* that the code number selected is in accord with the desired classification of the diagnosis. Never code directly from the Alphabetic Index because important instructions often appear in the Tabular List. Watch for exclusion notes, which refer to terms or conditions that are not included within the code and title under which the note appears and which direct the coder to the correct ICD-9-CM code assignment. Code to the highest specificity.

If there were an exclusion note, the proper code would be indicated, and this code should again be checked in the Tabular Listing.

Example: The patient's diagnosis is dyspepsia and heartburn, code number 536.8.

Step 1. Look for the code number–*not* the page number–in Volume 1.

Step 2. Notice that there is an exclusion note for heartburn indicating the code number 787.1.

Step 3. Be sure to check code number 787.1 in the Tabular Listing.*

536.8 Dyspepsia and other specified disorders of function of stomach

Achylia gastrica
Hourglass contraction of stomach
Hyperacidity
Hyperchlorhydria
Hypochlorhydria
Indigestion

Excludes: *achlorhydria (536.0)*
heartburn (787.1)

In listing this diagnosis on the insurance claim, you would write the following:

536.8	dyspepsia
787.1	heartburn

The use of a medical dictionary at any one of the preceding stages will aid in accurate coding. Research any unfamiliar terminology. *Examples:* Amaurotic idiocy with severe mental retardation; impaludism.

Certain conditions are classified according to *etiology* (cause) of the disorder. In these cases, you should find the etiology before assigning the code. Words to look for in the diagnostic statement include "transmissible" and "not transmissible," "congenital" and "acquired," "traumatic" and "nontraumatic," and "obstetric" and "nonobstetric."

*The samples from the *International Classification of Diseases,* Ninth Revision, *Clinical Modification* (ICD-9-CM) that follow are reproduced with the permission of the Commission on Professional and Hospital Activities of the World Health Organization.

When the patient's medical record states a "versus" diagnosis, such as "peptic ulcer versus gastroesophageal reflux," code the presenting symptoms. When a specific condition is stated in the diagnosis as both acute (or subacute) and chronic and the Alphabetic Index provides separate codes at either the third-, fourth-, or fifth-digit level for acute and chronic, use both codes with the acute code given first.

Example: Acute and chronic pelvic inflammatory disease

Condition:	Disease	
Subcategories:	Pelvis, Pelvic	
Subsubcategory:	Inflammatory	
	Acute	614.3
	Chronic	614.4

Although the code books show decimal points, these are not required on optically scanned insurance claims. Therefore, type "5713."

Four-digit subcategories .8 and .9 are usually, but not always, reserved for "other" specified and "unspecified" conditions, respectively. "Other" and "unspecified" subcategories are referred to as residual subcategories. Residual subcategories are used for conditions that are specifically classified there and are NOT to be used because you are unfamiliar with the terminology used in diagnostic statements.

Research the medical record to see if there is a qualifying statement in the physician's progress notes or history and physical report that will allow you to use a more specific diagnostic code.

Diagnostic codes must match the age and gender of the patient. If an adult female patient with breast cancer is seen, a code from 174.0 through 174.9 must be used. If a male with breast cancer is treated, a code from 175.0 through 175.9 must be chosen. Some codes apply only to newborn infants, such as code 775.1 for neonatal diabetes mellitus.

Special Points to Remember in Volume 1

Use two or more codes if necessary to describe completely a given diagnosis. *Example:* Arteriosclerotic cardiovascular *disease* (429.2) with congestive heart *failure* (428.0).

Follow the instructions to "code also underlying disease." This means the patient is being treated for a condition that has an underlying cause, and both conditions should be coded.

Two diagnoses or a diagnosis with an associated secondary process (manifestation) or complication is sometimes classified with a single code number called a *combination code.*

> ***713.1 Arthropathy associated with gastrointestinal conditions other than infections***
>
> *Code first underlying disease as:*
> regional enteritis (555.0-555.9)
> ulcerative colitis (556)

Category codes (three-digit codes) are used only if there are no subcategory codes (fourth-digit subdivisions).

> **430 Subarachnoid hemorrhage**
>
> Meningeal hemorrhage
> Ruptured:
> berry aneurysm
> (congenital) cerebral aneurysm NOS
>
> *Excludes:* *syphilitic ruptured cerebral aneurysm (094.87)*

Special Points to Remember in Volume 2

Appropriate sites and/or modifiers are listed in alphabetic order under the main terms, with further subterm listings as necessary. Examine all modifiers that appear in parentheses next to the main term. Check for modifiers that apply to any of the qualifying terms used in the statement of the diagnosis found in the patient's medical record.

> **Obesity** (constitutional) (exogenous) ← Nonessential modifiers
> (familial) (nutritional) (simple) 278.0
> adrenal 255.8
> due to hyperalimentation 278.0
> endocrine NEC 259.9
> endogenous 259.9
> Fröhlich's (adiposogenital dystrophy) 253.8
> glandular NEC 259.9
> hypothyroid (*see also* Hypothyroidism) 244.9
> of pregnancy 646.1
> pituitary 253.8
> thyroid (*see also* Hypothyroidism) 244.9

Eponyms appear as both main term entries and modifiers under main terms such as "disease" or "syndrome" and "operation." The main term entries of surgical and other procedures include standard procedural terms and eponyms. Eponyms for operations are accompanied by either a parenthetic explanation or by a sublisting of different operations associated with the eponym.

Eponym → **Cushing's**
basophilism, disease, or syndrome
(iatrogenic) (idiopathic) (pituitary basophilism) (pituitary dependent) 255.0 p. 154

Basophilism (corticoadrenal) (Cushing's) (pituitary) (thymic) 255.0 p. 86

Cross-referencing to synonyms, closely related terms, and code categories are indicated by *see* and *see also*.

Inflammation, inflamed, inflammatory
(with exudation) - *continued*

spinal
cord (*see also* Encephalitis) 323.9
late effect—*see* category 326
membrane—*see* Meningitis
nerve—*see* Disorder, nerve

HANDY HINTS IN DIAGNOSTIC CODING

If your ICD-9-CM code books are not color coded, mark italicized codes with a colored highlighter pen (i.e., 608.81 [italicized code]). This will remind you **to always code the underlying disease first.**

Many times you locate a diagnostic code in Volume 2 only to find that the cross-referenced code is the same when verified in Volume 1. Highlight these codes in Volume 2 with a colored highlighter pen to remind you that this code is correct, saving the time you would use going to Volume 1.

Keep a list of diagnostic and CPT procedure codes that go well together. It may be difficult for you to determine the reason behind the codes for some primary diagnoses, but if you know the ones that match with CPT codes, you solve a basic problem. The American Medical Association publishes a list of the most common diagnostic codes at the end of each of their mini-specialty code books. See Appendix B for other reference books that contain such data.

E CODES

E codes are a supplementary classification of coding in which you look for external causes of injury rather than disease. E codes are given in a separate section of Volume 1, Tabular List. In Volume 2, the E codes are in a separate section, Index to External Causes. E codes are also used in coding adverse reactions to medications.

INDEX TO EXTERNAL CAUSES

Heat (apoplexy) (collapse) (cramps) (effects of) (excessive) (exhaustion) (fever) (prostration) (stroke)—*continued*
due to—*continued*
weather (conditions) E900.0
from
electric heating apparatus causing burning E924.8
nuclear explosion in war operations E996
generated in, boiler, engine, evaporator, fire room of boat, ship, watercraft E838
inappropriate in local application or packing in medical or surgical procedure E873.5
late effect of NEC E989

E codes may be used for insurance claims submitted by physicians' offices, and the instructions are included here to aid the student if they are required when sending in insurance claims for industrial accidents, automobile accident, or school insurance company claims. The use of an E code after the primary or other acute secondary diagnosis tells the insurance carrier what caused the injury. The cause of the injury should be written on the encounter slip to alert the biller to code and include it on the insurance claim form as the last diagnosis.

Read the Foreword at the beginning of the Table of Drugs and Chemicals in Volume 2. This table contains a classification of drugs and other chemical substances for identifying poisoning states and external causes of adverse effects. Each of the substances listed in the table is assigned a code according to the poisoning classification (960 through 989). These codes are used when there is a state of poisoning, overdose, wrong substance given or taken, or intoxication.

Adverse effect is defined as an adverse or a pathologic reaction to a drug that occurs when appropriate doses are given to humans for prophylaxis, diagnosis, and therapy. *Poisoning* is defined as a condition resulting from an overdose of drugs or chemical substances or from the wrong drug or agent given or taken in error. *Intoxication* is defined as an adverse effect rather than a poisoning when drugs such as digitalis, steroid agents, and so on are involved.

Table of Drugs and Chemicals

Substance	Poisoning	External Cause (E Code) Accident	Therapeutic Use	Suicide Attempt	Assault	Undetermined
Acetylsalicylic acid	965.1	E850.3	E935.3	E950.0	E962.0	E980.0

Step 4. The correct number is 983.2.
Step 5. Now look for the correct E code number by choosing the *Accident* column. (If the poisoning was a suicide attempt, the result of assault, or of undetermined nature, then you would choose a different column for the E code.) In this example, the correct E code number is E861.4.

Example: Coding an adverse effect.
The patient had an adverse effect (ventricular fibrillation) to the medication digoxin, which was prescribed by her physician.

Step 1. Refer to the Table of Drugs and Chemicals in Volume 2 and look up "digoxin."
Step 2. Because this medication was for therapeutic use, locate the correct E code number under that column.
Step 3. The correct number is E942.1.
Step 4. Locate "fibrillation" in the index to diseases.
Step 5. Find the subheading "ventricular."
Step 6. The correct code number is 427.41.
Step 7. Be sure to check the code number 427.41 in Volume 1, Tabular Listing.

With an adverse effect (i.e., drug reaction, hypersensitivity, drug intolerance, idiosyncratic reaction, and so on), the diagnosis is assigned to the code that classifies the specific reaction (e.g., dermatitis, syncope, tachycardia, urticaria), and the E code identifying the agent involved is taken solely from the Therapeutic Use column.

Example: Coding a poisoning.
Baby Kathy got into the kitchen cabinet and ingested liquid household ammonia.

Step 1. Refer to the Table of Drugs and Chemicals in Volume 2 and locate "ammonia."
Step 2. Find the subheading "liquid (household)."
Step 3. Locate the correct code number under the *Poisoning* column.

V CODES

V codes are also a supplementary classification of coding located in a separate section of Volume 1, Tabular List. In Volume 2, the Alphabetic Index, the V codes are included in the major section Index of Diseases.

V codes are used when a person who is not currently sick encounters health services for some specific purpose, such as to act as a donor of an organ or tissue, to receive a vaccination, to discuss a problem that is not in itself a disease or an injury, to seek consultation regarding family planning, or to request sterilization. These types of encounters are among the more common encounters for hospital outpatients and patients of private practitioners, health clinics, and others. V codes are also used when some circumstance or problem is present that influences the person's health status but is not in itself a current illness or injury, such as when the person is known to have an allergy to a specific drug. In this instance, the V code should be used only as a supplementary code and should not be selected for use in primary, single-cause tabulations.

Example: Supervision of first *pregnancy*, normal.

Step 1. Find the heading "pregnancy" in Volume 2.
Step 2. Look for the subheading "supervision."
Step 3. Look for the second subheading "normal" and a further subheading "first," which gives you the code V22.0.
Step 4. Find V22.0 in Volume 1, Tabular List, and you will see "Supervision of normal first pregnancy."

Example: Routine annual physical *examination.*

Step 1. Look up "examination," and notice "routine" in parentheses and the code V70.9.
Step 2. Find V70.9 in Volume 1, Tabular List, and the wording "Unspecified general medical examination."

Additional code numbers are given for occupational health examinations, so depending on the circumstances you may have to be more specific when coding a physical examination.

Sometimes a patient receives a consultation for a preoperative medical evaluation as an inpatient or outpatient, and the majority of the results are negative for chronic or current illness. A good-health diagnosis code will trigger a rejection by the insurance carrier. Use an evaluation, not a treatment, V71.x code series for "Observation and evaluation for suspected conditions."

Example: A patient to have surgery for gallstones is sent to a cardiologist for evaluation of suspected cardiovascular disease.

Step 1. In Volume 2, look up "observation (for) disease, cardiovascular" and the code V71.7 as the reason for the consultation. Verify it in Volume 2.
Step 2. Code the reason for the surgery—574.xx, cholelithiasis.
Step 3. Code any cardiac findings.

Be cautious when using V codes as second or third diagnoses. For example, Medicare regards V70.1 and V70.3 through V70.7 (healthy patient examination codes) as primary diagnoses over all other diagnoses, even if placed in the second or third positions, and will automatically reject the claim.

Rules for Coding Signs, Symptoms, and Ill-Defined Conditions

Chapter 16 of ICD-9-CM, Symptoms, Signs, and Ill-Defined Conditions (codes 780.0 to 799.9), contains many but not all codes for symptoms. If the final diagnosis at the time of discharge is qualified by any of the following terms ("suspected," "suspicion of," "questionable," "likely," "probable," or "rule out"), do not code these conditions as if they existed or were established. Instead, document the condition(s) to the highest degree of certainty for each encounter or visit (e.g., signs, symptoms, abnormal test results, or other reason for the visit). This is contrary to coding practices used by hospital and medical record departments for coding the diagnoses of hospital inpatients. If one were to follow those guidelines and the patient was, for example, suspected of having AIDS, this would be interpreted as a confirmed case of AIDS. Instead, code the chief complaint or final diagnosis. The same would hold true for "possible epilepsy." If the patient had a convulsion and epilepsy has not been proved, code the convulsion. For possible carcinoma, do not use the "unspecified" column, as this is for unspecified tumor type by the pathologist. If a tumor is suspected and not confirmed, use "mass." For example, a breast mass would be coded 611.72.

If the statement "ruled out" is used, *do not code.* Do not type "ruled out" on the insurance claim. This condition was suspected at one time but was ruled out after study and is no longer an active diagnosis. *Example:* Diabetes mellitus, ruled out.

The following are instances in which sign and symptom codes can be used:

- No precise diagnosis can be made.

Example: The patient has an enlarged liver, and further diagnostic studies may or may not be done. Use code 789.1 for hepatomegaly.

Example: The patient complains of painful urination, and urinalysis is negative. Use code 788.1 for dysuria.

- Signs or symptoms are transient, and a specific diagnosis was not made.

Example: The patient complains of chest pain on deep inspiration. On examination, the physician finds nothing abnormal and tells the patient to return in 1 week. When the patient returns, the pain has ceased. Use code 786.52 for painful respiration.

- Provisional diagnosis for a patient who does not return for further care.

Example: On examination, the physician documents abnormal percussion of the chest. The patient is sent for a chest x-ray and asked to return for a recheck. The patient does not have the x-ray and fails to return. Use code 786.7 for abnormal chest sounds.

- A patient is referred for treatment before a definite diagnosis is made.

Example: A patient complains of nausea and vomiting and is referred to a gastroenterologist. Use code 787.01 for nausea with vomiting.

- Symptoms are present that indicate a more intensive condition, which needs classification as well as the known cause.

Example: A controlled insulin-dependent diabetic patient is seen because of spreading cutaneous gangrene. Use both code 250.71 for diabetes and code 785.4 for cutaneous gangrene.

Rules for Coding Sterilization

If the sterilization is purely elective, code V25.2 will suffice as a single code for the diagnosis. If the sterilization is performed for contraceptive purposes during a current admission for obstetric delivery, use code V25.2 as an additional code. If the sterilization is the end result of a hysterectomy performed because of injury or damage to the uterus during delivery, do not use code V25.2 but instead code the condition and/or procedure. The code V25.2 is used only when the sterilization is performed for the major purpose of contraception rather than being an incidental result of the treatment of a disease.

Rules for Coding Neoplasms

Neoplasms are new growths, and they may be benign or malignant tumors. A *benign tumor* is one that does not have the properties of invasion and metastasis (i.e., transfer of disease from one organ to another) and is usually surrounded by a fibrous capsule, whereas a *malignant tumor* has the properties of invasion and metastasis. Cysts and lesions are *not* neoplasms. Carcinoma *in situ* means cancer confined to the site of origin without invasion of neighboring tissues. A *primary* tumor means the original tumor site. A *secondary* tumor means a site of metastasis. If the diagnosis does not mention metastasis, then code the case as primary except for codes 200 through 202, lymph and liver. These are assumed to be secondary, unless specified as primary.

Example:

Neoplasm of liver, NOS	155.2 secondary
Neoplasm of liver, specific	155.0 primary

5

The diagnostic statement "metastatic from" indicates primary stage carcinoma, whereas "metastatic to" indicates secondary stage carcinoma. If the diagnostic statement is "malignant neoplasm spread to," then code the primary site spread to the secondary site. The phrase "recurrent malignancy" is a new primary neoplasm.

The main entry "Neoplasm" contains a table with the column headings Malignant, Benign, Uncertain Behavior, and Unspecified. (The table begins approximately midway into Volume 2.) Code numbers for neoplasms are given by anatomic site. For each site, there are six possible code numbers, indicating whether the neoplasm in question is malignant, benign, carcinoma *in situ*, of uncertain behavior, or of unspecified nature. The description of the neoplasm often will indicate which of the six code numbers is appropriate (e.g., malignant melanoma of skin, benign fibroadenoma of breast, carcinoma *in situ* of cervix uteri, and so on). When coding a neoplasm, ask yourself the following questions:

- What is it now?
- Where did it start?
- What happened to it?

Anatomic sites marked with an asterisk (*) are always considered to be neoplasms of the skin.

Example: *Adenocarcinoma* of the breast with metastases to the pelvic bone.

Step 1. Look up "adenocarcinoma" in Volume 2. *Do not* use the morphology code, M814013. Notice it states "see also Neoplasm, by site, malignant."

Step 2. Locate "neoplasm" in the table in Volume 2. At the top of the page notice the Malignant heading with the subheadings Primary, Secondary, and Ca *In Situ*. *Primary* means the first site of development of the malignancy. *Secondary* means metastasis from the primary site to a second site. *Ca In Situ* means cancer confined to the epithelium of the site of origin without invasion of the basement membrane tissue of the site.

Step 3. Find the site of the adenocarcinoma (in this case the breast), and look under the Malignant and Primary headings. Note that the code given is 174.9.

Step 4. Next, find "bone" as a secondary site and look for a subheading "pelvic." Now look at the three columns under Malignant and, using the Secondary column, find the correct code number 198.5. In listing these diagnoses on the insurance claim, you would give the following: 174.9 and 198.5.

In Appendix A of the Tabular List of Volume 2, there is a section entitled Morphology of Neoplasms, which gives M codes. These codes are not used for billing insurance claims by physicians' offices.

RULES FOR CODING CIRCULATORY SYSTEM CONDITIONS

Diseases of the circulatory system are difficult to code due to the variety and lack of specific terminology used by physicians in stating the diagnoses. Carefully read all inclusion, exclusion, and "use additional code" notations contained in the Tabular List of Volume 1.

The lay term high blood pressure is medically termed *hypertension*. Hypertension can *cause* various forms of heart and vascular disease or it can be mentioned with some heart conditions. In fact, there is a syndrome called *malignant hypertension* that has nothing to do with tumor formation. This is a symptom complex of markedly elevated blood pressure (diastolic pressure of more than 140 mm Hg) associated with papilledema. *Benign hypertension* refers to high blood pressure that runs a relatively long and symptomless course. When the diagnostic statement indicates a cause by stating "heart condition *due to* hypertension" or "hypertensive heart disease," use codes 402.0 through 402.9. If the diagnostic statement reads "*with* hypertension" or "cardiomegaly *and* hypertension," you will need two separate codes. Elevated blood pressure without mention of hypertension is coded 796.2. Secondary hypertension is coded 405.XX, and the cause of the hypertension should be coded when specified.

A separate three-digit category (412) is provided for old myocardial infarction, healed myocardial infarction, or myocardial infarction diagnosed on ECG. Myocardial infarction of 8 weeks' duration or less is considered acute, if not specified otherwise. Symptoms of more than 8 weeks' duration are coded 414.8, Other Forms of Chronic Ischemic Heart Disease.

The conditions presumed to be rheumatic fever are as follows:

mitral valve of unspecified etiology 394
mitral valve insufficiency 394.1
mitral valve and aortic valve disorders of unspecified etiology 396
mitral stenosis 394.0

The following condition is *not* presumed to be rheumatic fever:

aortic valve of unspecified etiology 424

In regard to a patient who has a diagnosis of arteriosclerotic cardiovascular disease (ASCVD), use code 429.2. If you refer to code 440.9, it excludes ASCVD because it is in conflict with the note given for 429.2. Code 429.2 is primary when the additional code 440.9 is needed. However, a patient with artiosclerotic heart disease (ASHD) would be assigned code 414.0. In your copy of Volume 1, at code 429.2, write in "see code 440" following "use additional code to identify, if desired, the presence of arteriosclerosis." To distinguish between ASCVD and ASHD, cardiovascular means pertaining to heart and blood vessels throughout the body, whereas ASHD means acute or chronic heart disability resulting from an insufficient supply of oxygenated blood to the heart.

RULES FOR CODING DIABETES MELLITUS

There are two types of diabetes, type I and type II. The following are the clinical features important in the classification of diabetes.

Type I Diabetes	Type II Diabetes
Insulin dependency	Non–insulin dependency
Patients must be treated with insulin	Patients may be treated with insulin
Insulin levels are very low	Insulin levels may be high, "normal," or low
Ketosis prone	Nonketosis prone
Patients are usually lean	Patients are usually obese
Usually "juvenile onset" (peak onset at early puberty)	Usually "adult onset," although occasionally seen in children
Often little family history of diabetes mellitus	Often strong family history of diabetes mellitus

Because of the types and complications that may accompany this disease, coding may require as many as five digits. Here is the way this classification appears in ICD-9-CM, Volume II.

Fifth-digit subclassification with code 250 is not based on severity or age grouping of the case. It is a *type grouping;* use the following:

250.00 for non–insulin-dependent diabetes
- Adult onset
- Type two, Type II
- Non–ketosis prone
- Stable

250.01 for insulin-dependent diabetes
- Juvenile onset
- Growth onset
- Type one, Type I
- Ketosis prone

When a medical record contains the statement "discharged on insulin" with no further explanation of the type of diabetes, always ask the physician for further clarification. Do not assume that a patient taking insulin has insulin-dependent diabetes.

Do not use code 250.0 if the diabetes is stated with delivery of a child or as a complication of pregnancy. Use code 648.01.

Chapter heading → 3. ENDOCRINE, NUTRITIONAL AND METABOLIC DISEASES, AND IMMUNITY DISORDERS (240-279)

Section title → DISEASES OF OTHER ENDOCRINE GLANDS (250-259)

Main term → **250 Diabetes mellitus**

Excludes: *gestational diabetes (648.8)*
hyperglycemia NOS (790.6)
neonatal diabetes mellitus (775.1)
nonclinical diabetes (790.2)
that complicating pregnancy, childbirth, or the puerperium (648.0)

The following fifth-digit subclassification is for use with category 250:

0 type II [non-insulin dependent type] [NIDDM type] [adult-onset type] or unspecified type, not stated as uncontrolled
1 type I [insulin dependent type] [IDDM type] [juvenile type], not stated as uncontrolled
2 type II [non-insulin dependent type] [NIDDM type] [adult-onset type] or unspecified type, uncontrolled
3 type I [insulin dependent type] [IDDM type] [juvenile type], uncontrolled

Subterm → **250.0 Diabetes mellitus without mention of complication**

Subterm to subterm → Diabetes mellitus without mention of complication or
Carry over line → manifestation classifiable to 250.0–250.9
Diabetes (mellitus) NOS

250.0 Diabetes with ketoacidosis

Diabetes:
acidosis } without mention of coma
ketosis }

RULES FOR CODING PREGNANCY, DELIVERY, OR ABORTION

The following main sections are included:

630–633 Ectopic and Molar Pregnancy
634–639 Other Pregnancy with Abortive Outcome
640–648 Complications Mainly Related to Pregnancy (*five-digit subclassification must be used*)
650–659 Normal Delivery, and Other Indications for Care in Pregnancy, Labor, and Delivery
660–669 Complications Occurring Mainly in the Course of Labor and Delivery (*five-digit subclassification must be used*)
670–676 Complications of the Puerperium (*five-digit subclassification must be used*)

1. Code 650 is used for a completely *normal* delivery. This means normal spontaneous delivery, cephalic (vertex) presentation of one liveborn fetus, full-term gestation, with or without episiotomy, no manipulation required, and no laceration.
2. An additional code should be used to provide greater detail about a *complication* of abortion, pregnancy, childbirth, or the puerperium when information is available, such as the presence of anemia, diabetes mellitus, or thyroid dysfunction. Categories 647 and 648 are used. Complication of the puerperium is a complication within 6 weeks after labor.

Example:

648.01		Pregnancy with diabetes mellitus
648.2	282.60	Pregnancy with sickle cell anemia

3. A multiple gestation (twins, triplets, and up) is a complication of pregnancy and is considered high risk. When a patient delivers and experiences both antepartum and postpartum complications, different fifth digits may be applied on the codes to describe the episode of care.

Example:

651.11 Triplet pregnancy (delivered)
675.02 Infection of nipple (postpartum)

RULES FOR CODING ADMITTING DIAGNOSES

Some diagnosis codes are considered questionable when used as a principal diagnosis on admittance of a patient to the hospital (e.g., 278.0 obesity, 401.1 benign hypertension). The inpatient admission diagnosis may be expressed as one of the following:

1. One or more significant findings (symptoms or signs) representing patient distress or abnormal findings on examination.
2. A "possible" diagnosis based on significant findings (working diagnosis).
3. A diagnosis established on an ambulatory care basis or on a previous hospital admission.
4. An injury or poisoning.
5. A reason or condition not classifiable as an illness or injury, such as pregnancy in labor, follow-up examinations, and so on.

When your employer physician makes hospital visits, code the reason for the visit, which may *not* necessarily be the reason the patient was admitted to the hospital.

RULES FOR CODING BURNS

Burns are always coded using two codes. The first code is for the exact site and degree of the burn. The second code describes the percentage of body surface area burned. A fifth digit is required to identify how much of the total body surface had third-degree burns. Think of the body as a whole and not the body part as a whole. The adult body is divided into regions: head, 9%; arms, 9% each; trunk, 18% front and 18% back; legs, 18% each; and perineum, 1%. Children's and infants' bodies have different regional percentages. Burn codes should be sequenced with the highest-degree burn first, followed by the other burn codes (Fig. 5–1).

RULES FOR CODING INJURIES AND LATE EFFECTS

Codes 800 through 959 include fractures, dislocations, sprains, and other types of injury. Injuries are coded according to the general type of injury and broken down within each type by anatomic site. Injuries are often associated with late effects, which must be coded.

Late effects mean "the usually inactive residual

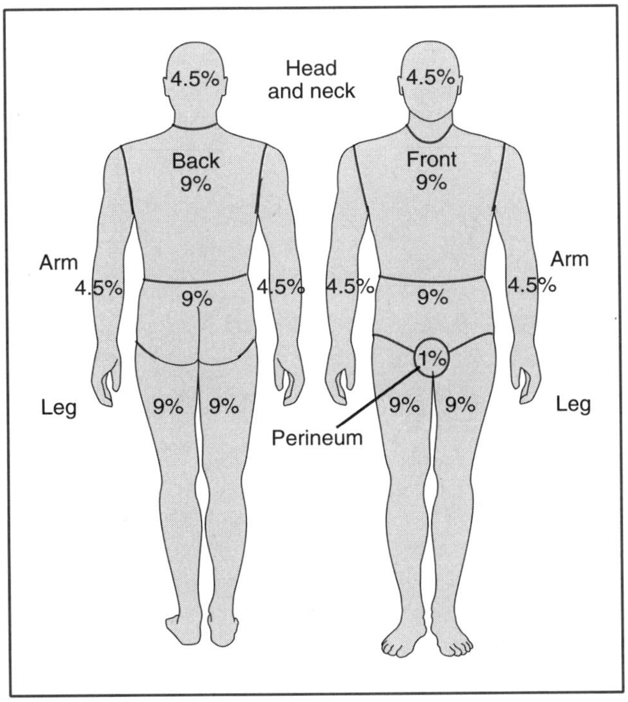

FIGURE 5-1
Illustration of rule of nines.

effects of indefinite duration after termination of the acute phase of the illness or injury." An effect is considered to be late if the diagnosis reads "due to an old injury," "late," "due to previous illness or injury," or "due to an injury or illness that occurred 1 year or more before the current admission of encounter" or if time has passed between the occurrence of the acute illness or injury and the development of the residual effect, such as scarring. Both residuals and causes are coded.

In the following examples of late effects, residuals are shown in italics and the causes are shown in bold print.

Malunion **fracture,** right tibia
Traumatic *arthritis* following **fracture** of right knee
Hemiplegia following **cerebrovascular thrombosis** 1 year ago
Scarring due to third-degree **burn** of right arm
Contracture of right heel tendons due to **poliomyelitis**

Use the following guides for coding injuries:

1. Decide whether a diagnosis represents a current injury or a late effect of an injury.

Example:

824.8	Current injury: Fracture, left ankle
733.81 and 905.4	Late effect: Malunion, fracture left ankle

2. Fractures are coded as closed if there is no indication of whether the fracture is open or closed.
3. Code the most severe degree of burns when several burns are stated to be at the same site but are of different degrees.
4. Code 948 may be used to code the percentage of body surface involved with burns. For third-degree burns, a fifth digit is included in this category.
5. When multiple injury sites are given, the word "with" indicates involvement of both sites, and the word "and" indicates involvement of either one or two sites.

Example:

806 Fracture of the vertebral column *with* spinal cord injury
813 Fracture of radius *and* ulna

Diagnostic Coding and the Physician's Fee Profile

Generally, medical practices use numeric procedural coding, such as CPT, and descriptive diagnoses (*no* numeric coding). These descriptive diagnoses can, at times, be nonspecific and vague, which places the physician's practice at considerable risk regarding the development of his or her fee profile.

Because insurance processors code the diagnostic statement as given without the aid of the medical record, they may code diagnoses inaccurately or use nonspecific coding, both of which become part of the physician's diagnostic profile. Every claim form filed with Medicare or any other third party payer is entered into permanent computerized records and may be used in the future as the basis for the physician's fee profile if the Prospective Payment System is expanded to include reimbursement of physician's charges.

To ensure accuracy of future profiles, it is important that the medical assistant/insurance billing specialist use diagnostic ICD-9-CM coding routinely and accurately rather than leave the coding to the insurance keypunch operators, who work only from the material presented on the claim form. The coding must be accurate and precise if profiles are to be established for realistic payments.

TO THE STUDENT

Study Chapter 5 and then answer the review questions in the *Workbook* to reinforce the theory learned in this chapter of the text and to help prepare you for a future test. In addition, refer to the *Workbook* Assignments 12 through 14 to gain hands-on practical experience in diagnostic coding. Assignments 15 and 16 will assist you in procedural and diagnostic coding.

CHAPTER 6

The Health Insurance Claim Form

Objectives*

THE INSURANCE BILLING SPECIALIST WILL BE ABLE TO

- Give the history of the Health Insurance Claim Form (HCFA-1500).
- State when the HCFA-1500 claim form may or may not be used.
- Expedite the logging and processing of the HCFA-1500 claim form.
- Define two types of claims submission.
- Explain the difference between clean, pending, rejected, incomplete, and invalid claims.
- Abstract from the patient record relevant information for completing the HCFA-1500 claim form.
- Define common medical and diagnostic terms.
- Describe reasons why claims are rejected.
- Minimize the number of insurance forms returned because of improper completion.
- Record proper information in financial records or on the patient's ledger card after claim submission.
- Identify techniques required for optically scanned insurance claims.
- Recognize general guidelines for completing the HCFA-1500 claim form.

Key Terms

clean claim
digital fax claim
dingy claim
dirty claim
electronic claim
employer supplemental insurance
HCFA-1500 claim form
incomplete claim
intelligent character recognition (ICR)
invalid claim
Medigap policy
optical character recognition (OCR)
ordering physician
"other" claims
paper claim
pending claim
physically clean claim
referring physician
rejected claim

*Performance objectives and exercises for hands-on practical experience for this chapter appear in the *Workbook*.

CHAPTER 6

The Health Insurance Claim Form

Introduction

In 1958, the Health Insurance Association of America (HIAA) and the American Medical Association (AMA) attempted to standardize the insurance claim form by jointly developing the Standard Form. It was not universally accepted by all third party payers, and as the types of coverage became more variable, new claim forms were instituted that required more information than the original Standard Form. The form eventually became known as COMB-1, or Attending Physician's Statement. In 1968, the HIAA decided to revamp the form so that it would be more adaptable to electronic data processing.

In April 1975, the AMA approved a "universal claim form" called the Health Insurance Claim Form, or HCFA-1500, that could be used for both group and individual claims. The HCFA-1500 form answered the needs of many health insurers processing claims manually. The National Association of Blue Shield Plans Board of Directors adopted a motion supporting the concept of a uniform national claim form.

Then, in 1990, the HCFA-1500 was revised and printed in red ink that would allow claims to be optically scanned by the insurance carriers (Figs. 6–1 and 6–2). Beginning on May 1, 1992, all services for Medicare patients from phy-

PLEASE DO NOT STAPLE IN THIS AREA

Prudential Insurance Company
5450 Wilshire Boulevard
Woodland Hills, XY 12345-0000

CARRIER

PICA **HEALTH INSURANCE CLAIM FORM** PICA

1. MEDICARE (Medicare #) ☐ MEDICAID (Medicaid #) ☐ CHAMPUS (Sponsor's SSN) ☐ CHAMPVA (VA File #) ☐ GROUP HEALTH PLAN (SSN or ID) ☐ FECA BLK LUNG (SSN) ☐ OTHER (ID) [X]

1a. INSURED'S I.D. NUMBER (FOR PROGRAM IN ITEM 1): GC-1117

2. PATIENT'S NAME (Last Name, First Name, Middle Initial): FOREHAND HARRY N

3. PATIENT'S BIRTH DATE MM DD YY: 01 06 36 SEX M [X] F ☐

4. INSURED'S NAME (Last Name, First Name, Middle Initial): SAME

5. PATIENT'S ADDRESS (No., Street): 1456 MAIN STREET

6. PATIENT RELATIONSHIP TO INSURED: Self [X] Spouse ☐ Child ☐ Other ☐

7. INSURED'S ADDRESS (No., Street)

CITY: WOODLAND HILLS STATE: XY

8. PATIENT STATUS: Single ☐ Married [X] Other ☐

CITY STATE

ZIP CODE: 12345-0000 TELEPHONE (Include Area Code): (013) 490-9876

Employed [X] Full-Time Student ☐ Part-Time Student ☐

ZIP CODE TELEPHONE (INCLUDE AREA CODE) ( )

9. OTHER INSURED'S NAME (Last Name, First Name, Middle Initial)

10. IS PATIENT'S CONDITION RELATED TO:

11. INSURED'S POLICY GROUP OR FECA NUMBER

a. OTHER INSURED'S POLICY OR GROUP NUMBER

a. EMPLOYMENT? (CURRENT OR PREVIOUS) ☐ YES [X] NO

a. INSURED'S DATE OF BIRTH MM DD YY SEX M ☐ F ☐

b. OTHER INSURED'S DATE OF BIRTH MM DD YY SEX M ☐ F ☐

b. AUTO ACCIDENT? PLACE (State) ☐ YES [X] NO

b. EMPLOYER'S NAME OR SCHOOL NAME

c. EMPLOYER'S NAME OR SCHOOL NAME

c. OTHER ACCIDENT? ☐ YES [X] NO

c. INSURANCE PLAN NAME OR PROGRAM NAME

d. INSURANCE PLAN NAME OR PROGRAM NAME

10d. RESERVED FOR LOCAL USE

d. IS THERE ANOTHER HEALTH BENEFIT PLAN? ☐ YES ☐ NO *If yes*, return to and complete item 9 a-d.

READ BACK OF FORM BEFORE COMPLETING & SIGNING THIS FORM.

12. PATIENT'S OR AUTHORIZED PERSON'S SIGNATURE I authorize the release of any medical or other information necessary to process this claim. I also request payment of government benefits either to myself or to the party who accepts assignment below.

SIGNED Harry N. Forehand DATE March 3, 199x

13. INSURED'S OR AUTHORIZED PERSON'S SIGNATURE I authorize payment of medical benefits to the undersigned physician or supplier for services described below.

SIGNED Harry N. Forehand

PATIENT AND INSURED INFORMATION

14. DATE OF CURRENT: ILLNESS (First symptom) OR INJURY (Accident) OR PREGNANCY(LMP) MM DD YY: 03 03 9x

15. IF PATIENT HAS HAD SAME OR SIMILAR ILLNESS. GIVE FIRST DATE MM DD YY: 03 03 9x

16. DATES PATIENT UNABLE TO WORK IN CURRENT OCCUPATION FROM MM DD YY TO MM DD YY

17. NAME OF REFERRING PHYSICIAN OR OTHER SOURCE: NICK E CUTFORTH MD

17a. I.D. NUMBER OF REFERRING PHYSICIAN: 000654321

18. HOSPITALIZATION DATES RELATED TO CURRENT SERVICES FROM MM DD YY TO MM DD YY

19. RESERVED FOR LOCAL USE

20. OUTSIDE LAB? ☐ YES [X] NO $ CHARGES

21. DIAGNOSIS OR NATURE OF ILLNESS OR INJURY. (RELATE ITEMS 1,2,3 OR 4 TO ITEM 24E BY LINE)

1. 382 . 9   3. ___ . __

2. ___ . __   4. ___ . __

22. MEDICAID RESUBMISSION CODE ORIGINAL REF. NO.

23. PRIOR AUTHORIZATION NUMBER

24.	A DATE(S) OF SERVICE From MM DD YY	To MM DD YY	B Place of Service	C Type of Service	D PROCEDURES, SERVICES, OR SUPPLIES (Explain Unusual Circumstances) CPT/HCPCS | MODIFIER	E DIAGNOSIS CODE	F $ CHARGES	G DAYS OR UNITS	H EPSDT Family Plan	I EMG	J COB	K RESERVED FOR LOCAL USE
1	03 03 9x		11	1	99213	1	40 00	010				
2												
3												
4												
5												
6												

25. FEDERAL TAX I.D. NUMBER: 95-3664021 SSN [X] EIN ☐

26. PATIENT'S ACCOUNT NO.

27. ACCEPT ASSIGNMENT? (For govt. claims, see back) [X] YES ☐ NO

28. TOTAL CHARGE $ 40 00

29. AMOUNT PAID $

30. BALANCE DUE $ 40 00

31. SIGNATURE OF PHYSICIAN OR SUPPLIER INCLUDING DEGREES OR CREDENTIALS (I certify that the statements on the reverse apply to this bill and are made a part thereof.)

SIGNED Concha Antrum MD DATE 3-3-9x

32. NAME AND ADDRESS OF FACILITY WHERE SERVICES WERE RENDERED (If other than home or office)

33. PHYSICIAN'S, SUPPLIER'S BILLING NAME, ADDRESS, ZIP CODE & PHONE #
CONCHA ANTRUM MD 013-486-9002
4567 BROAD AVENUE
WOODLAND HILLS XY 12345-0000

PIN# GRP#

PHYSICIAN OR SUPPLIER INFORMATION

(APPROVED BY AMA COUNCIL ON MEDICAL SERVICE 8/88) APPROVED OMB-0938-0008

PLEASE PRINT OR TYPE

FORM HCFA-1500 (12-90) FORM OWCP-1500 FORM RRB-1500

ref initials

FIGURE 6–1

Front side of the scannable (red ink) Health Insurance Claim Form approved by the AMA Council on Medical Service. This form is also known as the HCFA-1500 and is shown illustrating completion to an insurance company. Third party payers, state, and local guidelines vary and may not always follow the visual guide presented here.

6

BECAUSE THIS FORM IS USED BY VARIOUS GOVERNMENT AND PRIVATE HEALTH PROGRAMS, SEE SEPARATE INSTRUCTIONS ISSUED BY APPLICABLE PROGRAMS.

NOTICE: Any person who knowingly files a statement of claim containing any misrepresentation or any false, incomplete or misleading information may be guilty of a criminal act punishable under law and may be subject to civil penalties.

REFERS TO GOVERNMENT PROGRAMS ONLY

MEDICARE AND CHAMPUS PAYMENTS: A patient's signature requests that payment be made and authorizes release of any information necessary to process the claim and certifies that the information provided in Blocks 1 through 12 is true, accurate and complete. In the case of a Medicare claim, the patient's signature authorizes any entity to release to Medicare medical and nonmedical information, including employment status, and whether the person has employer group health insurance, liability, no-fault, worker's compensation or other insurance which is responsible to pay for the services for which the Medicare claim is made. See 42 CFR 411.24(a). If item 9 is completed, the patient's signature authorizes release of the information to the health plan or agency shown. In Medicare assigned or CHAMPUS participation cases, the physician agrees to accept the charge determination of the Medicare carrier or CHAMPUS fiscal intermediary as the full charge, and the patient is responsible only for the deductible, coinsurance and noncovered services. Coinsurance and the deductible are based upon the charge determination of the Medicare carrier or CHAMPUS fiscal intermediary if this is less than the charge submitted. CHAMPUS is not a health insurance program but makes payment for health benefits provided through certain affiliations with the Uniformed Services. Information on the patient's sponsor should be provided in those items captioned in "Insured"; i.e., items 1a, 4, 6, 7, 9, and 11.

BLACK LUNG AND FECA CLAIMS

The provider agrees to accept the amount paid by the Government as payment in full. See Black Lung and FECA instructions regarding required procedure and diagnosis coding systems.

SIGNATURE OF PHYSICIAN OR SUPPLIER (MEDICARE, CHAMPUS, FECA AND BLACK LUNG)

I certify that the services shown on this form were medically indicated and necessary for the health of the patient and were personally furnished by me or were furnished incident to my professional service by my employee under my immediate personal supervision, except as otherwise expressly permitted by Medicare or CHAMPUS regulations.

For services to be considered as "incident" to a physician's professional service, 1) they must be rendered under the physician's immediate personal supervision by his/her employee, 2) they must be an integral, although incidental part of a covered physician's service, 3) they must be of kinds commonly furnished in physician's offices, and 4) the services of nonphysicians must be included on the physician's bills.

For CHAMPUS claims, I further certify that I (or any employee) who rendered services am not an active duty member of the Uniformed Services or a civilian employee of the United States Government or a contract employee of the United States Government, either civilian or military (refer to 5 USC 5536). For Black-Lung claims, I further certify that the services performed were for a Black Lung-related disorder.

No Part B Medicare benefits may be paid unless this form is received as required by existing law and regulations (42 CFR 424.32).

NOTICE: Any one who misrepresents or falsifies essential information to receive payment from Federal funds requested by this form may upon conviction be subject to fine and imprisonment under applicable Federal laws.

NOTICE TO PATIENT ABOUT THE COLLECTION AND USE OF MEDICARE, CHAMPUS, FECA, AND BLACK LUNG INFORMATION
(PRIVACY ACT STATEMENT)

We are authorized by HCFA, CHAMPUS and OWCP to ask you for information needed in the administration of the Medicare, CHAMPUS, FECA, and Black Lung programs. Authority to collect information is in section 205(a), 1862, 1872 and 1874 of the Social Security Act as amended, 42 CFR 411.24(a) and 424.5(a) (6), and 44 USC 3101;41 CFR 101 et seq and 10 USC 1079 and 1086; 5 USC 8101 et seq; and 30 USC 901 et seq; 38 USC 613; E.O. 9397.

The information we obtain to complete claims under these programs is used to identify you and to determine your eligibility. It is also used to decide if the services and supplies you received are covered by these programs and to insure that proper payment is made.

The information may also be given to other providers of services, carriers, intermediaries, medical review boards, health plans, and other organizations or Federal agencies, for the effective administration of Federal provisions that require other third parties payers to pay primary to Federal program, and as otherwise necessary to administer these programs. For example, it may be necessary to disclose information about the benefits you have used to a hospital or doctor. Additional disclosures are made through routine uses for information contained in systems of records.

FOR MEDICARE CLAIMS: See the notice modifying system No. 09-70-0501, titled, 'Carrier Medicare Claims Record,' published in the Federal Register, Vol. 55 No. 177, page 37549, Wed. Sept. 12, 1990, or as updated and republished.

FOR OWCP CLAIMS: Department of Labor, Privacy Act of 1974, "Republication of Notice of Systems of Records," Federal Register Vol. 55 No. 40, Wed Feb. 28, 1990, See ESA-5, ESA-6, ESA-12, ESA-13, ESA-30, or as updated and republished.

FOR CHAMPUS CLAIMS: PRINCIPLE PURPOSE(S): To evaluate eligibility for medical care provided by civilian sources and to issue payment upon establishment of eligibility and determination that the services/supplies received are authorized by law.

ROUTINE USE(S): Information from claims and related documents may be given to the Dept. of Veterans Affairs, the Dept. of Health and Human Services and/or the Dept. of Transportation consistent with their statutory administrative responsibilities under CHAMPUS/CHAMPVA; to the Dept. of Justice for representation of the Secretary of Defense in civil actions; to the Internal Revenue Service, private collection agencies, and consumer reporting agencies in connection with recoupment claims; and to Congressional Offices in response to inquiries made at the request of the person to whom a record pertains. Appropriate disclosures may be made to other federal, state, local, foreign government agencies, private business entities, and individual providers of care, on matters relating to entitlement, claims adjudication, fraud, program abuse, utilization review, quality assurance, peer review, program integrity, third-party liability, coordination of benefits, and civil and criminal litigation related to the operation of CHAMPUS.

DISCLOSURES: Voluntary; however, failure to provide information will result in delay in payment or may result in denial of claim. With the one exception discussed below, there are no penalties under these programs for refusing to supply information. However, failure to furnish information regarding the medical services rendered or the amount charged would prevent payment of claims under these programs. Failure to furnish any other information, such as name or claim number, would delay payment of the claim. Failure to provide medical information under FECA could be deemed an obstruction.

It is mandatory that you tell us if you know that another party is responsible for paying for your treatment. Section 1128B of the Social Security Act and 31 USC 3801-3812 provide penalties for withholding this information.

You should be aware that P.L. 100-503, the "Computer Matching and Privacy Protection Act of 1988", permits the government to verify information by way of computer matches.

MEDICAID PAYMENTS (PROVIDER CERTIFICATION)

I hereby agree to keep such records as are necessary to disclose fully the extent of services provided to individuals under the State's Title XIX plan and to furnish information regarding any payments claimed for providing such services as the State Agency or Dept. of Health and Humans Services may request.

I further agree to accept, as payment in full, the amount paid by the Medicaid program for those claims submitted for payment under that program, with the exception of authorized deductible, coinsurance, co-payment or similar cost-sharing charge.

SIGNATURE OF PHYSICIAN (OR SUPPLIER): I certify that the services listed above were medically indicated and necessary to the health of this patient and were personally furnished by me or my employee under my personal direction.

NOTICE: This is to certify that the foregoing information is true, accurate and complete. I understand that payment and satisfaction of this claim will be from Federal and State funds, and that any false claims, statements, or documents, or concealment of a material fact, may be prosecuted under applicable Federal or State laws.

Public reporting burden for this collection of information is estimated to average 15 minutes per response, including time for reviewing instructions, searching existing date sources, gathering and maintaining data needed, and completing and reviewing the collection of information. Send comments regarding this burden estimate or any other aspect of this collection of information, including suggestions for reducing the burden, to HCFA, Office of Financial Management, P.O. Box 26684, Baltimore, MD 21207; and to the Office of Management and Budget, Paperwork Reduction Project (OMB-0938-0008), Washington, D.C. 20503.

FIGURE 6–2

Back side of the Health Insurance Claim Form HCFA-1500 approved by the AMA Council on Medical Service.

sicians and suppliers except for ambulance services had to be billed on the scannable HCFA-1500 form. The form may or may not have a bar code in the top left corner.

The revised form was adopted by the Office of Civilian Health and Medical Program of the Uniformed Services (OCHAMPUS), and it received the approval of the AMA Council on Medical Services. The HIAA endorses and recommends that their members, who are private insurance companies, accept the form. If the form suits the private carrier's business needs by containing information routinely required, the carrier may supply the form, if desired, to clients. In some states, the Medicaid program, as well as industrial (workers' compensation) cases, uses this form to process claims.

Widespread use of this form will save time and simplify processing of claims for both physicians and carriers, because it eliminates having to complete many various insurance forms brought into the office by patients. The insurance billing specialist simply completes the HCFA-1500 and attaches it to the patient's form, making sure, however, that the patient's and employer's portions of the private insurance form are complete and accurate and that the patient has signed the release of information box and the assignment, if applicable. Both forms go directly to the insurance carrier. If the patient is insured with two companies, the assistant obtains assignments for both insurance carriers and bills both.

Insurance carriers with various computer programs and equipment that optically scan claims may have instructions on completion of the form that will vary from locality to locality and program to program. Always contact local representatives of insurance carriers to find out whether the form is acceptable before submitting any claims. If the form is processed by the insurance carrier through scanning equipment, a photocopy is not acceptable. Quantities of the HCFA-1500 can be purchased from many medical office supply companies as well as the American Medical Association, 515 North State Street, Chicago, IL 60610.

In this chapter, how to complete a claim manually for submission via mail is emphasized. The federal government prefers electronic claims submission to reduce costs and make reimbursement faster. Chapter 7 takes you through the intricacies of that system of claims processing as well as the do's and don'ts of transmitting a digital fax claim.

Types of Claims

Claims are either paper or electronic and can be designated as clean, pending (in suspense), invalid, incomplete, or rejected. You may come across the term "encounter record." This is a new buzz term for claim.

A *paper claim* is one that is submitted on paper, including optically scanned claims that are converted to electronic form by insurance companies.

An *electronic claim* is one that is submitted to the insurance carrier via a central processing unit (CPU), tape diskette, direct data entry, direct wire, dial-in telephone, digital fax, or personal computer download or upload. A digital fax claim is sent to the insurance carrier via fax but never printed on paper. The fax is encoded while in electronic form via optical code reader, is electronically entered into the claims processing system, and is considered an electronic claim.

A *clean claim* means that the claim was submitted within the program or policy time limit and correctly completed (contains all necessary information so it can be processed and paid promptly). To be physically clean means there are no staples or highlighted areas, and the bar code area has not been deformed. In the Medicare program, a clean claim means the following:

1. The carrier does not need to investigate outside of the carrier's operation before paying the claim,
2. The claim has no deficiencies, passes all electronic edits,
3. The claim is investigated on a postpayment basis, meaning a claim is not delayed before payment and may be paid. However, all paid claims may be subject to audit if fraud or abuse is ever suspected,
4. The claim is subject to medical review with attached information or forwarded simultaneously with electronic medical claim (EMC) records.

Participating provider submissions are processed within approximately 14 days of receipt, and nonparticipating providers are processed within approximately 27 days of receipt.

Dingy claims happen when the Medicare contractor cannot process a claim for a particular service or bill type. The claims are held until the necessary systems changes are implemented to pay the claim correctly.

Dirty claims are claims submitted with errors or those requiring manual processing for resolving problems or rejection of payment. Pending or suspense claims are placed in this category because something is holding the claim back from payment, perhaps for review or some other problem.

Rejected claims are those that require investigation and need further clarification and possibly answers to some questions. Such a claim may need to be resubmitted.

An *incomplete claim* is any Medicare claim missing required information. Such claims are identified to the provider so they can be resubmitted.

An *invalid claim* is any Medicare claim that contains complete, necessary information but is illogical or incorrect (e.g., listing an incorrect provider number for a referring physician). Invalid claims are identified to the provider and may be resubmitted.

If the patient is a Medicare beneficiary with Medigap insurance coverage, a claim may need development for Medicare Secondary Payer (MSP) information. Refer to Chapter 12 for information on completing the HCFA-1500 for MSP cases.

Abstracting from Medical Records

You may be asked to abstract technical information from patient records in either of two situations: (1) when you file a health insurance claim after professional services are rendered; or (2) when a patient applies for life, mortgage, or health insurance for the first time. In this instance, the insurance company may require a physical examination, or information may be requested from the patient's private physician. Abstracting for insurance claims will be discussed in detail in subsequent chapters. In the following paragraphs, abstracting medical information for insurance applications is briefly considered.

On some application forms (Fig. 6–3), the release of medical information signed by the patient may appear as a perforated attachment or as a separate sheet. The insurance company will send a request to the attending physician along with a check (Fig. 6–4). The amount of the check may vary, depending on how much information is requested. If the check is not included, the physician should request a fee based on the length of the report before sending in the completed report form. You must have the fee before completion of the form, or you may not receive it.

If you are asked to abstract medical information from the patient's record, be extremely accurate. Be certain that you understand abbreviations on the chart. Give only the information requested. If the form has questions about high blood pressure (higher than 130/85), kidney infection, or heart problems, you can prohibit a patient from obtaining life, health, or mortgage insurance if your answers are derogatory. If the urine shows albumin or sugar, a person can also be denied insurance. If a patient has had pulmonary tuberculosis, ask the physician if a euphemism can be substituted. A euphemism is a word or phrase substituted for one considered offensively explicit. (*Example:* "remains" for "corpse.") If a patient tests positive for HIV, legal counsel may be necessary because some state laws allow AIDS information to be given only to the patient's spouse.

In some states, it is illegal to require a blood test for HIV antibodies, a urinalysis for HIV, or an HIV antigen test as a condition of coverage or to question applicants about HIV status or prior symptoms of and treatment for AIDS or other forms of immune deficiency. Sometimes, private group plans allow medical coverage for people testing positive for HIV or an AIDS-related illness through a state major risk medical insurance program. However, if the maximum enrollment number is reached, the waiting period may exceed 1 year.

Sometimes, a narrative report dictated by the physician is preferable to filling in the form, especially if there are long columns to check and no space for comments. It may even be necessary to attach a copy of an operative, pathology, laboratory, electrocardiogram (ECG) tracing, or x-ray report. ECG tracings mounted upside-down have resulted in rejections of insurance applications.

Place a "Please Read" note on the form to have the physician check it over thoroughly before signing it, to make sure that the information is accurate and properly stated.

An insurance company may ask a copy service to come to your office to photocopy the patient's record. This is usually done at your convenience, and an appointment should be made. Remind the insurance company that you must have a release of medical information form signed by the patient. Charge accordingly and quote the fee at the time of the telephone request. The physician should review the records in advance to see that they are in proper order.

Medical and Diagnostic Terminology

If a lay term appears on a patient record, the correct medical term should be substituted if narrative description is required on an insurance claim (Table 6–1). Some physicians write Imp (impression) or Dx (diagnosis) on the patient's record, which usually serves as the diagnosis when completing the claim. If the diagnosis is not on the chart and there is any doubt at all, always attach a note to the insurance form for the physician to see before he or she signs the form. If the patient has been in the hospital, look

Text continued on page 136

PART II of Application to the MASSACHUSETTS INDEMNITY AND LIFE INSURANCE COMPANY

PROPOSED INSURED OR ANNUITANT: .... Date of Birth .... Mo. Day Year

1. a. Name and address of your personal physician? ....
   (*If none, so state*)
   b. Date and reason last consulted? ....
   c. What treatment was given or medication prescribed? ....

	Yes	No
2. Have you ever been treated for or ever had any known indication of:		
a. Disorder of eyes, ears, nose, or throat?	☐	☐
b. Dizziness, fainting, convulsions, recurrent headache, speech defect, paralysis or stroke, mental or nervous disorder?	☐	☐
c. Shortness of breath, persistent hoarseness or cough, blood spitting, bronchitis, pleurisy, asthma, emphysema, tuberculosis or chronic respiratory disorder?	☐	☐
d. Chest pain, palpitation, high blood pressure, rheumatic fever, heart murmur, heart attack or other disorder of the heart or blood vessels?	☐	☐
e. Jaundice, intestinal bleeding, ulcer, hernia, appendicitis, colitis, diverticulitis, hemorrhoids, recurrent indigestion, or other disorder of the stomach, intestines, liver or gallbladder?	☐	☐
f. Sugar, albumin, blood or pus in urine, venereal disease, stone or other disorder of kidney, bladder, prostate or reproductive organs?	☐	☐
g. Diabetes, thyroid or other endocrine disorders?	☐	☐
h. Neuritis, sciatica, rheumatism, arthritis, gout, or disorder of the muscles or bones, including the spine, back, or joints?	☐	☐
i. Deformity, lameness or amputation?	☐	☐
j. Disorder of skin, lymph glands, cyst, tumor or cancer?	☐	☐
k. Allergies, anemia or other disorder of the blood?	☐	☐
l. Excessive use of alcohol, tobacco, sedatives, or any habit-forming drugs?	☐	☐
3. Are you now under observation or taking treatment?	☐	☐
4. Have you had any change in weight in the past year?	☐	☐
5. *Other than above,* have you within the past 5 years:		
a. Had any mental or physical disorder not listed above?	☐	☐
b. Had a checkup, consultation, illness, injury, surgery?	☐	☐
c. Been a patient in a hospital, clinic, sanatorium, or other medical facility?	☐	☐
d. Had electrocardiogram, X-ray, blood sugar, basal metabolism, other diagnostic test?	☐	☐
e. Been advised to have any diagnostic test, hospitalization, or surgery which was not completed?	☐	☐
6. Have you ever had military service deferment, rejection or discharge because of a physical or mental condition?	☐	☐
7. Have you ever requested or received a pension, benefits, or payment because of an injury, sickness or disability?	☐	☐
8. Family History: Tuberculosis, diabetes, cancer, high blood pressure, heart or kidney disease, mental illness or suicide?	☐	☐

	Age if Living?	Cause of Death?	Age at Death?
Father			
Mother			
Brothers and Sisters No. Living No. Dead			

DETAILS of "Yes" answers. (IDENTIFY QUESTION NUMBER, CIRCLE APPLICABLE ITEMS: Include diagnoses, dates, duration and names and addresses of all attending physicians and medical facilities.)

(For non-medical cases only)

Height .... Weight ....

9. Females only:	Yes	No
a. Have you ever had any disorder of menstruation, pregnancy or of the female organs or breasts?	☐	☐
b. To the best of your knowledge and belief are you now pregnant?	☐	☐

I HEREBY DECLARE that, to the best of my knowledge and belief, the statements and answers in Part II of this Application are full, complete, and true. These statements and answers are to be considered as the basis for any insurance written hereon.

Signed at: (City & State) .... Dated: .... 19 ....

.... **X** ....

Signature of Witness Signature of PROPOSED INSURED

Form MD (70)a

FIGURE 6–3
The prospective insured completes this side of the insurance application form.

6

PART III—PHYSICIAN'S EXAMINATION REPORT

Acct. No.__________ District or Agency __________ Name of Agent __________

Date __________ Name of Insuring Company __________

PROPOSED INSURED: __________ Date of Birth __________

Last Name | First Name | Middle Initial | Mo. | Day | Year

10a.	Height (In Shoes)	Weight (Clothed)	Chest (Full Inspiration)	Chest (Forced Expiration)	Abdomen, at Umbilicus
	___ ft. ___ in.	___ lbs.	___ in.	___ in.	___ in.

Details of "Yes" answers. (Identify item.)

b. Did you weigh? ..... ☐ Yes ☐ No Did you measure? .... ☐ Yes ☐ No

c. Is appearance unhealthy or older than stated age? .... ☐ Yes ☐ No

11. Blood Pressure (Record ALL readings)

Systolic			
Diastolic 4th phase			
Diastolic 5th phase			

12. Pluse:	At Rest	After Exercise	3 Minutes Later
Rate			
Irregularities per min.			

13. Heart: Is there any:

Enlargement .... ☐ Yes ☐ No Dyspnea .... ☐ Yes ☐ No

Murmur(s) .... ☐ Yes ☐ No Edema .... ☐ Yes ☐ No

(describe below—if more than one, describe separately)

Location		
Constant	☐	☐
Inconstant	☐	☐
Transmitted	☐	☐
Localized	☐	☐
Systolic	☐	☐
Presystolic	☐	☐
Diastolic	☐	☐
Soft (Gr. 1-2)	☐	☐
Mod. (Gr. 3-4)	☐	☐
Loud (Gr. 5-6)	☐	☐
After Exercise:		
Increased	☐	☐
Absent	☐	☐
Unchanged	☐	☐
Decreased	☐	☐

Indicate:

Apex by X

Murmur area by ○

Point of greatest intensity by O

Transmission by ➧

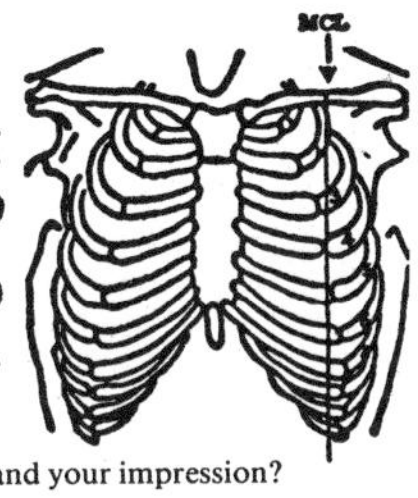

For comments and your impression?

14. Is there on examination any abnormality of the following: (Circle applicable items and give details.)	Yes	No
(a) Eyes, ears, nose, mouth, pharynx? ______ (If vision or hearing markedly impaired, indicate degree and correction.)	☐	☐
(b) Skin (incl. scars); lymph nodes; varicose veins or peripheral arteries?	☐	☐
(c) Nervous system (include reflexes, gait, paralysis)?	☐	☐
(d) Respiratory system?	☐	☐
(e) Abdomen (include scars)?	☐	☐
(f) Genitourinary system (include prostate)?	☐	☐
(g) Endocrine system (include thyroid and breasts)?	☐	☐

	Yes	No
(h) Musculoskeletal system (include spine, joints, amputations, deformities)? .... (A confidential report may be sent to the Medical Director)	☐	☐
15. (a) Are there any hernias?	☐	☐
(b) Any hemorrhoids?	☐	☐
16. Are you aware of additional medical history?	☐	☐
17. Was the examination conducted in the English language?	☐	☐
If No, complete the following:		
a. Was an interpreter used?	☐	☐
b. What language was used? ______		
c. Relationship of interpreter to proposed insured? ______		

Urinalysis: Specific Gravity	Albumin	Sugar

Is specimen being sent? .... ☐ Yes ☐ No

If Yes, where? __________

Send Specimen: (Details according to Company) __________

Date: __________ Time: _____ A.M. P.M. City: __________ State: __________

Signature of Medical Examiner: __________ M.D. Physical Measurements Information. __________

PMI-188R—1-88

FIGURE 6–4

Sample of a life insurance application form with the check to the physician omitted. The physician completes this side of the form at the time of the examination of the patient, the prospective insured.

TABLE 6-1
Medical Terminology

Lay Term	Medical Term	Pronunciation
Acute	Use "acute" when referring to a condition that runs a short but relatively severe course	ah-KŪT
Allergy	Allergic asthma	ah-LER-jik AZ-ma
	Allergic bronchitis	ah-LER-jik brong-KI-tis
	Bronchial asthma	BRONG-kē-al AZ-ma
Appetite loss (abnormal)	Anorexia nervosa	an"o-REK-se-ah ner-VO-sa
Athlete's foot	Pedal epidermophytosis	PED-al ep"i-der" mō-fī-TŌ-sis
	Tinea pedis	TIN-e-ah PED-is
Bad breath	Halitosis	hal-i-TO-sis
Balance, sense of	Equilibrium	E-kwe-LIB-rē-um
Baldness	Alopecia	al"o-PĒ-shē-ah
Bedsore	Decubitus ulcer	de-KŪ-bi-tus UL-ser
Bed-wetting	Enuresis	en"u-RE-sis
Belching	Eructation	ē-ruk-TĀ-shun
Bleeder's disease	Hemophilia	he"-mo-FIL-e-ah
Bleeding	Hemorrhage	HEM-or-ij
Blood blister	Hematoma	hem"ah-TO-mah
Blood clot	Thrombus	THROM-bus
Blood, in stools	Melena	MEL-e-nah or me-LĒ-nah
Blood, in urine	Hematuria	hēm"ah-TŪ-re-ah
Blood poisoning	Septicemia	sep"ti-SĒ-mē-ah
Blood, spitting up of	Hemoptysis	he-MOP-tĭ-sis
Bloody vomitus	Hematemesis	hem"ah-TEM-ĕ-sis
Blue skin	Cyanosis	sī"ah-NŌ-sis
Boil	Furuncle	FU-rung-k'l
Bowel movement	Defecation	def"e-KA-shun
Bowleg	Genu varum	JE-nu VA-rum
Breathing, cessation of	Apnea	ap-NĒ-ah
Breathing, difficult	Dyspnea	DISP-nē-ah or disp-NĒ-ah
Breathing, normal	Eupnea	ūp-NĒ-ah
Breathing, rapid	Tachypnea	tak"ip-NĒ-ah
Breathing, slow	Bradypnea	brad"ip-NĒ-ah
Breathing, upright position only	Orthopnea	or"thop-NĒ-ah
Bruise or injury not involving sutures	Contusion	kon-TŪ-zhun
	Echymosis(ses)	ek"i-MŌ-sis(sēz)
	Hematoma	hem"ah-TŌ-mah
	Extravasation	eks-trav"ah-SĀ-shun
Bulging of eyes	Exophthalmos	ek"-sof-THAL-mōs
Burning or cauterizing	Use "surgical removal of"	
Canker sore	Aphthous stomatitis	AF-thus sto-mah-TI-tis
Cardiac arrest	Cardiac asystole	KAR-de-ak ah-SIS-to-le
	Cardiac standstill	KAR-de-ak STAND-stil
Chafing	Intertrigo	in"ter-TRI-gō
Change of life	Menopause	MEN-ō-pawz
	Climacteric	kli"mak-TER-ik
Chest pain with ECG but not cardiac case	Intercostal neuritis	in"ter-KOS-tal nu-RĪ-tis
	Neurasthenia	nu"ras-THĒ-nē-ah
Chickenpox	Varicella	var"i-SEL-ah
	Variola crystallina	vah-RI-ō-lah kris"tah-LĪ-nah
Chronic	Use "recurrent"	
Clubfoot	Talipes	TAL-i-pēz
Cold	Coryza	ko-RĪ-zah
Cold sore; fever blisters on lips	Herpes simplex	HER-pēz SIM-plex
Cold with runny nose	Coryza with motor rhinitis	ri-NĪ-tis
Collapsed lung	Pneumothorax	nu"mo-THO-raks
Corn	Clavus	KLĀ-vus
	Heloma molle	he-LO-mah MOL-le

TABLE 6-1
Medical Terminology *(Continued)*

Lay Term	Medical Term	Pronunciation
Cross-eye	Convergent strabismus	kon-VER-jent strah-BIZ-mus
	Esotropia	es″o-TRO-pe-ah
Cut	Laceration (give location, length, depth)	las″er-Ā-shun
Cutting into	Incision of	in-SIZH-un
Cutting out	Excision of	ek-SIZH-un
Dandruff	Seborrhea capitis	seb″o-RĒ-ah CAP-i-tis
Degenerative joint disease	Osteoarthritis	os″te-o-ar-THRI-tis
Dim vision	Amblyopia	am″blē-Ō-pē-ah
Dizziness	Vertigo	VER-ti-go or ver-TI-go
Dog bite	Dog bite (one or more abrasions, give location and description)	
Double vision	Diplopia	di-PLŌ-pē-ah
Drooping eyelids	Ptosis	TŌ-sis
	Blepharoptosis	blef″ah-ro-TO-sis
Ear discharge	Otorrhea	o″to-RĒ-ah
Ear procedure involving opening of ear	Myringotomy	mir″in-GOT-ō-mē
Earache	Acute otitis	ah-KŪT o-TĪ-tis
	Otitis media	o-TĪ-tis MĒ-dia
	Otalgia	o-TAL-jē-ah
	Neuralgic pain in ear (left or right)	nū-RAL-jik
Eardrum	Tympanic membrane	tim-PAN-ik MEM-brān
Earwax removal	Cerumen syringed	see-ROO-men si-RINJD
Enlarged heart	Cardiomegaly	kar″de-o-MEG-ah-le
Excessive eating	Polyphagia	pol″ē-FĀ-je-ah
Excessive thirst	Polydipsia	pol″ē-DIP-sē-ah
Eye examination if more than just a check for eyeglasses	Refraction and eye examination	re-FRAK-shun
Fainting	Syncope	SIN-ko-pē
Farsightedness	Hyperopia	hi″per-Ō-pe-ah
Fat	Obese	o-BĒS
	Exogenous obesity	eks-OJ-e-nus o-BĒS-i-te
Felon	Paronychia	par″o-NIK-e-ah
Fever	Pyrexia	pi-REK-se-ah
Fever blister	Lesion of herpes simplex	HER-pēz SIM-plex
Fibroid of uterus	Leiomyoma	li″o-mi-O-mah
Fit	Convulsion	kon-VUL-shun
Flatfeet	Pes planus	pes PLA-nus
Flu	Influenza	in″flu-EN-zah
	La grippe	lah GRIP
Freckle	Lentigo	len-TI-go
	Ephelis	e-FĒ-lis
Gallstone	Cholelithiasis	ko″le-li-THI-ah-sis
Gas pain	Borborygmus	bor″bo-RIG-mus
Gas, passing	Flatulence	FLAT-u-lens
Gastrointestinal case that is not a duodenal ulcer	Gastroenteritis	gas″tro-en-ter-i-tus
German measles	Rubella	roo-BEL-ah
Glands, swollen	Diffuse lymphadenitis	dif-FŪS lim-fad″e-NĪ-tis
Grippe; flu	Influenza	in″flu-EN-zah
	La grippe	la GRIP
Hammer toe	Hallux malleus	HAL-uks MAL-leus
Hangnail	Agnail	AG-nāl
Hardening of the arteries	Arteriosclerosis	ar-te″-re-o-skle-RO-sis
Harelip	Cleft palate	kleft PAL-at
	Cleft lip	kleft lip
Hay fever	Allergic rhinitis	ah-LER-jik rī-NĪ-tis
	Rhinallergosis	rīn″al-er-GŌ-sis

Table continued on following page

TABLE 6-1
Medical Terminology *(Continued)*

Lay Term	Medical Term	Pronunciation
Headache	Acute cephalalgia	ah-KŪT sef″ah-LAL-jē-ah
	Cephalgia	se-FAL-jē-ah
Heart attack	Coronary thrombosis	KOR-ŏ-na-re throm-BO-sis
	Coronary occlusion	KOR-ŏ-na-re ŏ-KLOO-zhun
Heart wave (tracing)	Electrocardiogram (ECG), (EKG)	e-lek″tro-KAR-de-o-gram
Heartburn	Pyrosis	pī-RŌ-sis
Hiccough; hiccup	Singultus	sing-GUL-tus
High blood pressure	Hypertension	hi″per-TEN-shun
Hives	Urticaria	ur″ti-KĀ-rē-ah
Hoarseness	Laryngitis	lar″in-JI-tis
	Dysphonia	dis-FO-ne-ah
Housemaid's knee	Prepatellar bursitis	pre″pah-TEL-ar ber-SI-tis
Humpback; hunchback	Kyphosis	ki-FO-sis
Incontinence of urine	Enuresis	en″u-RE-sis
Indigestion	Dyspepsia	dis-PEP-se-ah
Injury	Trauma	TRAW-mah
Itching	Pruritus	proo-RĪ-tus
Jaundice	Icterus	IK-ter-us
Kidney stone	Nephrolithiasis	nefro-li-THI-ah-sis
	Renal calculus	RE-nal KAL-ku-lus
Knock knees	Genu valgum	JE-nu VAL-gum
Lockjaw	Tetanus	TET-ah-nus
Loss of appetite	Anorexia	an″o-REK-se-ah
Loss of hearing	Deafness	DEF-nes
Loss of voice	Aphonia	ah-FO-ne-ah
Low blood pressure	Hypotension	hi″po-TEN-shun
Malnutrition, general ill health	Cachexia	kah-KEK-sē-ah
Marble bones	Osteosclerosis	os″te-o-skle-RO-sis
Measles	Rubeola	roo-BĒ-ō-lah
Measles, German	Rubella	roo-BEL-ah
Milk leg	Phlebitis	fle-BĪ-tis
Miscarriage	Abortion (AB)	ah-BOR-shun
Mole(s)	Nevus(vi)	NĒ-vus(vī)
Mongolism	Down's syndrome	downz SIN-drōm
Monthly period	Menses	MEN-sēz
	Menstruation	men″stroo-A-shun
Mumps	Contagious parotitis	kon-TĀ-jus par″ō-TĪ-tis
Muscle wasting	Muscular atrophy	MUS-kular AT-rō-fe
Muscular weakness	Atony	AT-o-ne
Nearsightedness	Myopia	mi-O-pe-ah
Nosebleed	Epistaxis	ep″i-STAK-sis
	Rhinorrhagia	rī″nō-RĀ-jē-ah
Overweight	Exogenous obesity	eks-OJ-e-nus o-BĒS-i-tē
Painful periods	Dysmenorrhea	dis″men-o-RE-ah
Painful urination	Dysuria	dis-U-re-ah
Pap smear	Papanicolaou smear	pap″ah-nik″-o-LA-ōō smēr
Piles	Hemorrhoids	HEM-o-roids
Pinkeye	Acute contagious conjunctivitis	ah-KŪ-T kon-TĀ-jus kon-junk″ti-VĪ-tis
Pneumonia	If both lungs are involved, use "bilateral pneumonitis"	bi-LAT-er-al nu″mō-NĪ-tis
Poison ivy; poison oak	Rhus toxicodendron sensitivity	rus tok″si-kō-DEN-dron sen″si-TIV-i-tē
	Rhus dermatitis	rus der″mah-TĪ-tis
Postnasal drip (PND)	Catarrh	kah-TAHR
Protrusion of eyeballs	Exophthalmos	ek″sof-THAL-mos
Pus, full of	Purulent	PU-roo-lent, PUR-u-lent
Pus, in urine	Pyuria	pī-Ū-rē-ah
Question of	Use "possible" or "probable"	

TABLE 6-1
Medical Terminology *(Continued)*

Lay Term	Medical Term	Pronunciation
Rabies	Hydrophobia	hi"dro-FO-be-ah
Residual inquiry(ies)	Sequela(ae)	se-KWE-lah(lē)
Ringing in ears	Tinnitus	TIN-i-tus
Rule out (R/O)	Use "possible" or "probable"	
Ruptured spleen	Splenorrhexis	sple"no-REK-sis
St. Vitus' dance	Chorea	kō-RĒ-ah
Scar	Cicatrix	sik-A-triks, SIK-ah-triks
Sciatica	Sciatic neuritis	si-AT-ik nu-RI-tis
Scraping of uterus	Dilatation and curettage (D & C)	dil-ah-TA-shun and ku"rĕ-TAHZH
Sebaceous cyst	Steatoma	ste"ah-TO-mah
	Wen	wen
Shingles	Herpes zoster	HER-pez ZOS-ter
Sleeping sickness	Encephalitis	en"sef-ah-LĪ-tis
Slipped disc	Herniated intervertebral disc	HER-ne-āt"ed in"ter-VER-tĕ-bral disc
Slow heart rate	Sinus bradycardia	SI-nus-brad"e-KAR-de-ah
Smallpox	Variola	vah-RI-o-lah
Sore throat	Laryngitis	lar"in-JĪ-tis
	Pharyngitis	far"in-JĪ"-tis
	Tonsillitis	ton"si-LĪ-tis
	Alpha-hemolytic streptococcus (milder strep)	AL-fah hē"mō-LIT-ik strep"tō-KOK-us
	Beta-hemolytic streptococcus (real strep throat)	BĀ-tah hē"mō-LIT-ik strep"tō-KOK-us
	Acute sore throat for any kind of sore throat unless it is strep	ah-KŪT sōr thrōt
Speaking difficulty	Dysphonia	dis-FŌ-nē-ah
Spinal fusion	Arthrodesis	ar"thro-DE-sis
Squint	Strabismus	strah-BIZ-mus
Stiff joint	Ankylosis	ang" kĭ-LO-sis
Stiff neck; wryneck	Torticollis	tor"ti-KOL-is
Stomach ache	Tonic abdominal spasm	TON-ik ab-DOM-i-nal spazm
	Gastritis	gas-TRĪ-tis
	Gastroenteritis	gas"trō-en-ter-Ī-tis
Stone(s)	Calculus (li)	KAL-kū-lus(lī)
Stroke	Apoplexy	AP-o-plek"se
	Cerebral hemorrhage	SER-e-bral HEM-or-ij
Stye	Hordeolum	hor-DE-o-lum
Swallowing difficulty	Dysphagia	dis-FĀ-je-ah
Swayback	Lordosis	lor-DŌ-sis
Tarry stool	Melena	mĕ-LE-nah
Tennis elbow	Radiohumeral bursitis	ra"de-o-HU-mer-al ber-SĪ-tis
Tic douloureux	Trigeminal neuralgia	tri-JEM-ĭ-nal nu-RAL-je-ah
Tongue tie	Ankyloglossia	ang"kĭ-lo-GLOS-e-ah
Trench mouth	Acute neurotizing ulcerative infection	ah-KŪT nek-ro-TI-zing UL-ser-ah-tiv in-FEK-shun
	Vincent's angina	VIN-sents an-JI-nah
Undescended testicle	Cryptorchism	krip-TOR-kizm
	Cryptorchidism	krip-TOR-kĭ-dizm
Undulant fever	Brucellosis	broo"sel-LO-sis
Urination, excessive	Nocturia (night)	nok-TŪ-rē-ah
	Polyuria	pol"e-Ū-rē-ah
Urination, involuntary	Enuresis (bed-wetting)	en"ū-RĒ-sis
Urination, painful	Dysuria	dis-Ū-rē-ah
Urine, scanty	Oliguria	ol"i-GŪ-rē-ah
Urine, sugar in	Glycosuria	gli"ko-SU-re-ah
Vomiting of blood	Hematemesis	hem"-ah-TEM-e-sis
Wall eye	Divergent strabismus	di-VER-jent strah-BIZ-mus
	Exotropia	ek"so-TRO-pe-ah
Wart(s)	Verruca(cae)	ve-ROOH-kah(sē)

Table continued on following page

6

TABLE 6-1
Medical Terminology *(Continued)*

Lay Term	Medical Term	Pronunciation
Water on the brain	Hydrocephalus	hi-dro-SEF-ah-lus
Water on the knee	Prepatellar bursitis	prē"pah-TEL-ar bur-SĪ-tis
Wen	Sebaceous cyst	sĕ-BA-shus sist
	Steatoma	ste"ah-TO-mah
Whooping cough	Pertussis	per-TUS-is
Womb	Uterus	U-ter-us
Wristdrop	Carpoptosis	kar"pop-TO-sis
Writer's cramp	Graphospasm	GRAF-o-spazm
Wryneck	Torticollis	tor"tĭ-KOL-is

for a copy of the hospital's admitting diagnosis or impression at the end of the physician's report, or call the medical records department of the hospital and request a copy of the discharge summary, which contains the admitting and discharge diagnoses.

Official American Hospital Association policy states that "abbreviations should be totally eliminated from the more vital sections of the record, such as final diagnosis, operative notes, discharge summaries, and descriptions of special procedures." Many physicians are not aware of this policy, and the final diagnosis may appear as an abbreviation on the patient's record. Use your medical dictionary (most list abbreviations alphabetically with the unabbreviated words) and spell out the medical term on the insurance claim when listing the diagnosis. Frequently, an abbreviation translates to several meanings. (If you are using the *Student Workbook for the Insurance Handbook for the Medical Office,* see the detailed list of common medical abbreviations in the chapter entitled "Instruction Guide to the Workbook.")

An eponym (term including the name of a person) should not be used when a comparable anatomic term can be used in its place. *Example:* "Graves' disease" is an eponym; the comparable anatomic term is "exophthalmic goiter."

The word "acute" refers to a condition that runs a short but relatively severe course. The word "chronic" means persisting over a long period of time. However, the word "recurrent" should be used instead of chronic. For example, "chronic asthma" should be written as "recurrent asthma" when completing an insurance claim. A "bruise" is usually referred to as a "contusion." Whenever the words "question of," "rule out," or "R/O" are used in connection with a disease or illness, substitute the words "possible" or "probable." These are just a few of the many terms used in documentation for payment. For a comprehensive reference list of correct diagnostic, procedural, symptomatic, and treatment terms with their lay equivalents, see Table 6-1. This list may be helpful to a person not well versed in medical terminology.

Some terms commonly used to describe injuries shown in Figure 6-5 (regions or quadrants of the abdomen) are:

Right Upper Quadrant (RUQ) or Right Hypochondriac. Contains the liver (right lobe), gallbladder, part of the pancreas, parts of the small and large intestines.

Epigastric. Contains upper middle region above the stomach.

Left Upper Quadrant (LUQ) or Left Hypochondriac. Contains the liver (left lobe), stomach, spleen, part of the pancreas, parts of the small and large intestines.

Right and Left Lumbar. Contain middle right and left regions near the waist.

Umbilical. Contains central region near the navel.

Right Lower Quadrant (RLQ) or Right Inguinal. Contains parts of the small and large intestines, right ovary, right uterine (fallopian) tube, appendix, right ureter.

Hypogastric. Contains middle region below the umbilical region.

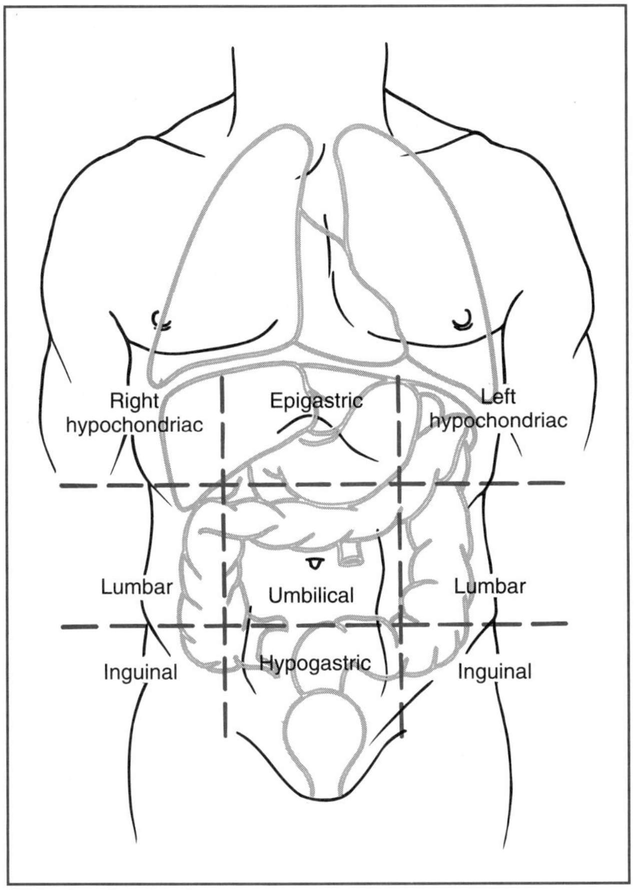

FIGURE 6–5
Regions of the abdomen. (Redrawn with permission from Anderson, P. D.: *Clinical Anatomy and Physiology for Allied Health Sciences*. Philadelphia, W. B. Saunders Company, 1976.)

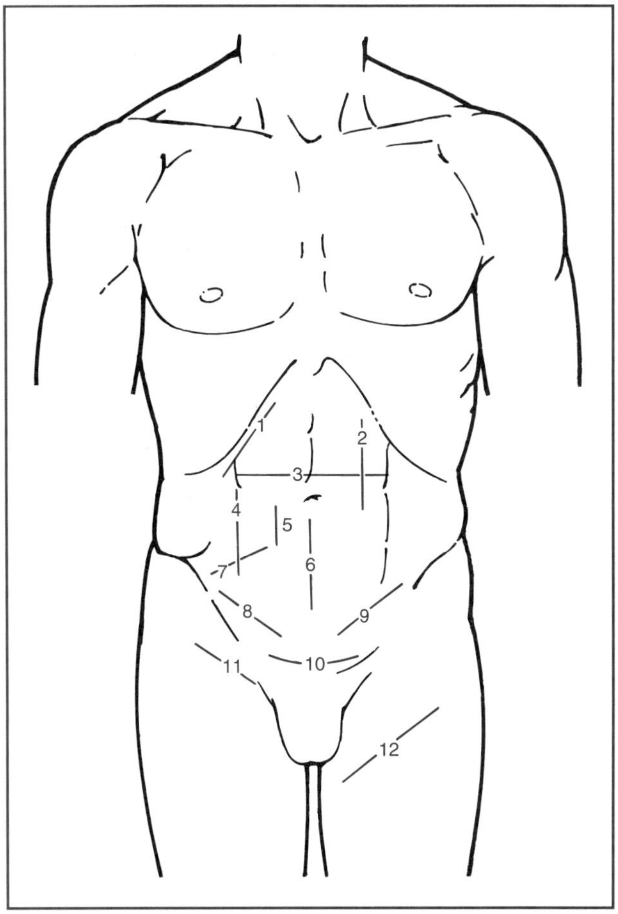

FIGURE 6–6
Operational incisions. Anterior (front) view. 1, Subcostal incision; 2, paramedian incision; 3, transverse incision; 4, upper right rectus incision; 5, midrectus incision; 6, midline incision; 7, lower right rectus incision; 8, McBurney or right iliac incision; 9, left iliac incision; 10, suprapubic incision; 11, hernia incision; 12, femoral incision.

Left Lower Quadrant (LLQ) or Left Inguinal. Contains parts of the small and large intestines, left ovary, left uterine tube, left ureter. Additional words used to detail accidents and injuries are shown in Chapter 14, Figures 14–10 through 14–13.

Other terms commonly used to describe injuries are shown in Figure 6–5 (regions of the abdomen) and in Chapter 14, Figures 14–10 through 14–13. If you type reports to be attached to insurance claims to help justify the claim, you should also become familiar with the terms for various operational incisions (Fig. 6–6). If you would like a more thorough discussion of medical terminology, many good books are available.*

*E.g., Chabner, D. E.: *The Language of Medicine*, 5th ed. Philadelphia, W. B. Saunders Company, 1996; Leonard, P. C.: *Building a Medical Vocabulary*, 3rd ed. Philadelphia, W. B. Saunders Company, 1993.

Procedures for Use of the Health Insurance Claim Form, HCFA-1500

GENERAL GUIDELINES

1. File a claim form whenever you are asked to do so by the patient, even though you think there is no coverage, unless the patient accepts your tactful suggestion that he or she is not covered. An official rejection from the insurance company is the best answer to present to the patient in this instance.
2. Use the Health Insurance Claim Form, also known as the HCFA-1500 form, as often as possible. The universal Health Insurance Claim Form is accepted by nearly all general insurance carriers as well as Blue Cross, Blue

Shield, CHAMPUS, Medicare, Medicaid, and Medi-Cal. Some insurance companies require answers to questions other than those included on the Health Insurance Claim Form. In these instances, you might include an additional information sheet listing the following items that may be pertinent to the case:

a. Date on which your physician's services were terminated.
b. When the services of a nurse (RN) or allied health professional were required.
c. Address of a referring physician, if any.

3. As mentioned previously, when a patient brings in a form from a private insurance plan that is not like the HCFA-1500, have him or her sign it, as well as reading the front and back sides and signing the Health Insurance Claim Form in two places (the Assignment of Benefits and Release of Information boxes). Make sure the patient's portion of the private insurance form is complete and accurate. Mail them together to the insurance carrier. Some companies allow staples and some do not. Some prefer paperclips or no clips.
4. When a patient has group insurance through an employer, make sure the employer has completed the employer section. If it is not completed, send the private insurance form to the employer before completing the physician's section of the Health Insurance Claim Form. If the employer has completed the section, send both forms directly to the insurance carrier.
5. When the coverage is not group insurance, send both forms directly to the insurance company. It is not recommended to let patients direct their own forms to insurance companies or employers. Patients have been known to lose or alter data on documents before mailing, forget to send them, or mail them to an incorrect address.
6. As previously stated, if the patient has insurance with more than one company (sometimes called dual coverage), be sure to obtain assignments for both insurance companies and bill both.
7. If a form is not optically scanned by the insurance carrier, then it is a good idea to answer all questions on the form. If any are unanswerable, indicate as suggested in "b" below. Here are some good reasons why all questions on insurance forms should be completed:
   a. Because of possible tampering.
   b. So that when the physician checks the form before signing it and sees that you have written DNA (or Does not apply) or NA or N/A (or Not Applicable) or have simply put a dashed line where a question is unanswerable, he or she knows that you have gone over the form thoroughly and have not forgotten or overlooked anything.

      If a claim is optically scanned by the insurance company, do NOT put any comments in those blanks that are unanswerable, since the computer scanner will kick out the claim.
   c. Because an insurance firm can sue a physician for incomplete records.
8. In the space for the Diagnosis, insert all accurate diagnostic codes. Some physicians write Imp (impression) or Dx (diagnosis) on the chart. Either usually suffices as an abbreviation for diagnosis. Never send in a diagnosis without the physician's approval. Be certain the diagnosis agrees with the treatment. Use the words "possible" or "probable" instead of "rule out," and code the symptoms. Use correct medical terminology for finding the correct diagnostic code. See Table 6–1 for further information on medical terminology.

   Diagnostic codes and how to use them are discussed in Chapter 5. The ICD-9-CM diagnostic coding system has been developed for use on computerized billing and insurance forms. Sometimes, the code appears on the billing statement without terminology. There are several good reference books describing this coding system (see Appendix B).
9. Do not ditto dates for services performed.
10. To avoid confusion, it is best to list only one illness or injury and its treatment per form, unless there are concurrent conditions.
11. Office visits may be grouped if each visit is consecutive, uses the same procedure code, and results in the same fee.

    For example,

    10-4-98 to 10-8-98   99211 $75.00

    would be shown. However, if there is a difference in fee and several visits must be indicated on the claim, processing may be speeded up if the office visits are itemized and each charge is listed separately.
12. If more than one office visit is required per day, on a separate sheet state times of visits and justification for additional visits, so that the claims clerk will know that separate procedures were done at different times and why they were performed.
13. Some insurance companies now write policies that include coverage for annual physi-

cals. In these instances, you may code for an "Annual physical examination" on the diagnosis portion of the form. However, if the patient comes into the office after a year's absence with a definite symptom (e.g., gastrointestinal complaint or chronic headache), always ask the physician for a specific diagnosis, even if a complete annual checkup was performed. In this way the examination may be covered, even if the patient's policy is not written to include an annual physical.

14. Itemize laboratory work separately from office calls regardless of whether the physician is billing for work done in an outside laboratory or in his or her own laboratory. Some states have passed legislation stating that the exact fee charged by the laboratory must be the fee billed to the patient by the physician, and the name and address of the clinical laboratory must be listed on the insurance claim.
15. Some policies do not allow injections on an outpatient basis. Medication is covered only when the patient is in the hospital as an inpatient. However, if the service is itemized on the claim as an Evaluation and Management service and injection, credit can be given because an office call for the purpose of administering an injection is covered.

Example:

09-12-95	992xx Evaluation and Management	$00.00
09-12-95	90788 Inj IM 3.6 mL Rocephin 1 gm penicillin	$00.00

Document in the patient's medical record the amount, name of medication, and how the injection was administered.

16. When listing injections, if the medication is expensive send a copy of the invoice received from the supply house or pharmacy to obtain maximum reimbursement. If the insurance claim form has space to list the details about the injection, then state the name of the medication, amount of injection in cubic centimeters (cc), milligrams (mg), or milliliters (mL), and whether the injection was intramuscular (IM), intravenous (IV), subcutaneous (SC, SQ), intradermal (ID), or parenteral (parent). Whether detailed on the claim form or not, such documentation about the injection should appear in the medical record.
17. X-rays must also be itemized separately, coding the part of the body filmed, number of views, and type of view: anteroposterior (AP), lateral (Lat), oblique (Obl), and so on. If the procedure was complicated, it is a good idea to include a copy of the radiology report.
18. Hospital visits may be grouped if consecutive and if each visit resulted in the same fee. For example,

    10-4-98 to 10-8-98 99231 $150.00

    would be shown.
19. When listing a laceration, the code number should indicate length in centimeters (cm), exact location, and whether the repair was simple, intermediate, or complex.
20. When listing a tumor, code the location and, if possible, attach a copy of the pathology report. Put the patient's insurance identification number on the report in the event it becomes separated during processing.
21. If a sterile surgical tray is used for office surgery, itemize the contents on a separate sheet and give a separate fee. The same procedure should be followed for cast materials, burn dressings, and the like.
22. Do not submit items that have no charge unless the patient requests you to send it in.
23. For a treatment not listed in the *Current Procedural Terminology* (CPT), send in a detailed report, giving the nature, extent, and need for the services if the claim is submitted on paper. If possible, send a copy of the operative report from the hospital, the discharge summary, and any other pertinent medical reports. Be sure to use the proper code number for unlisted services or procedures. (*Example:* Unlisted Allergy Testing Procedure 95199.) Usually the codes for unlisted services end in "99." If the claim is submitted electronically, the description should be typed in the narrative field.
24. If your preprinted claim forms do not have the physician's IRS number (also known as employer ID number or tax ID number) or Social Security number, you must type it in the appropriate block. Sometimes the physician's state license number or Medicare or Medicaid fiscal agent (provider) numbers are also required on insurance claim forms. If the physician or supplier is employed by a health maintenance organization, he or she will be assigned an ID (identifying) number.

Section 6109 of the Internal Revenue Code of 1954 requires that the IRS number be furnished. IRS Ruling 69-595, supplemented by 70-608, requires all insurance carriers to report certain payment information using Form 1099. Therefore, on certain checks that your physician receives, you will be required to type the Social Security or IRS number in the space immediately over the physician's name on the face of the draft.

25. Have the physician sign the insurance claim form. A stamped signature is allowed in some instances, and these are discussed in subsequent chapters. Always type the physician's name under the signature if the name is not preprinted. Make a red check mark where the physician should sign the claim. This will help the physician locate the correct area, since every form has a different location for the signature.
26. To avoid confusion as to who in your office typed the insurance form, place your initials in the bottom left or top right corner. Be consistent in where you place this reference.
27. File the office copy of the insurance form in the back of the patient's medical chart, or maintain a separate alpha file for insurance claim copies.
28. Avoid submitting claim forms or attachments containing holes or tears, because these can jam or tear further in the insurance processor's microfilm equipment.
29. The patient's eligibility is determined by the physician's diagnosis and the treatment rendered. The patient may be unaware of major medical credits accrued because of nonpayment of benefits from a basic plan. It is feasible to bill for services rendered even though the patient may not think that he or she is covered.
30. Proofread every claim, especially larger, more complex claims, as they involve greater sums of money and are more difficult to complete. Proofread for transposition of numbers (group, policy, claim, physician's ID, CPT codes, ICD-9-CM codes), misspelled name, missing date of birth, blanks, and attachments.
31. Do not submit charges for services rendered in different months or in different years on the same claim form. Sometimes such practices can be affected by deductible and eligibility factors, thereby delaying reimbursement.
32. As you learned in Chapter 5, the appropriate ICD-9-CM diagnostic code number(s) should be included on each claim.

Common Reasons Why Claims Are Rejected or Delayed

For quicker claim settlements and to reduce the number of appeals, it is wise to be aware of common billing errors and how to correct them (Fig. 6–7). This may help avoid additional administrative burdens, such as telephone calls, resubmission of claims, appeal letters, and so on. The following is a list of some reasons why claims are rejected or delayed and some solutions.

1. Patient has not answered all questions on his or her portion of the form. **Solution:** Educate patients on data requirements at the time of their first visit to the physician's office.
2. The patient's insurance number is incorrect or transposed (especially in Medicare and Medicaid [Medi-Cal] cases). **Solution:** Proofread numbers carefully.
3. Patient's name and insured's name are entered as the same when the patient is a dependent.
4. Incorrect gender identification, resulting in a diagnosis code that is inconsistent with patient's gender.
5. Incomplete entry for other insurance coverage.
6. Failure to indicate whether patient's condition is related to employment or an accident.
7. Patient's signature is missing.
8. Omitted dates of onset of illness or injury.
9. Failure to identify referring physicians on claims for consultations.
10. Diagnostic code is missing, incomplete, invalid, or not in standard nomenclature (e.g., missing fourth or fifth digit) or does not correspond with the treatment (CPT procedure code) rendered by the physician. **Solution:** Verify and submit correct diagnosis codes by referring to an updated diagnostic code book.
11. Omitted, incorrect, overlapping, or duplicate dates of service. **Solution:** Verify that all dates of service, especially the year, are listed and accurate. Date spans for multiple services must be adequate for the number and types of services provided.
12. Missing place of service code for Medicare, Medicaid, and CHAMPUS. **Solution:** Verify that the place of service is correct for the submitted procedure code(s).
13. Missing type of service code for CHAMPUS and Medicaid to indicate where services were rendered.

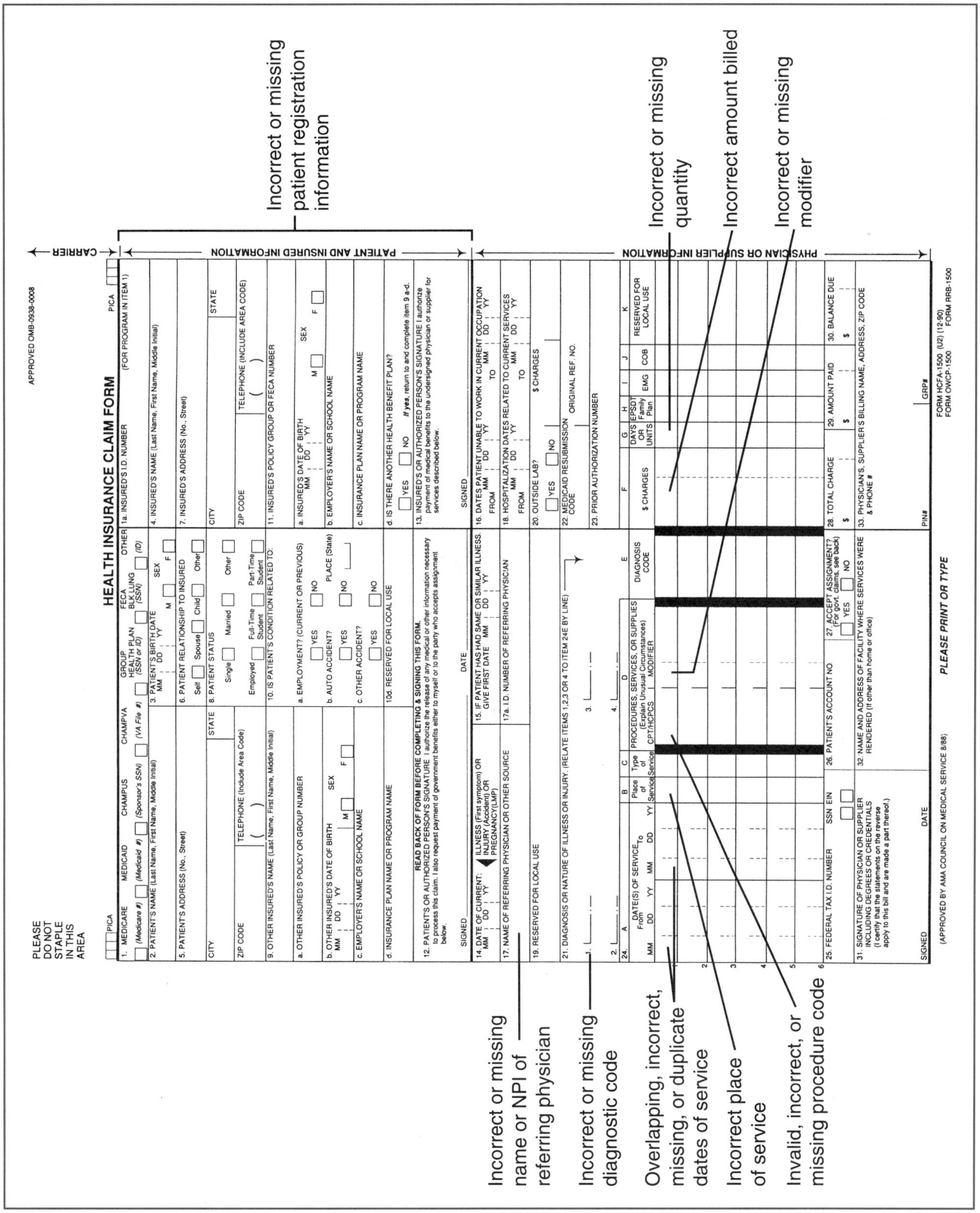

FIGURE 6–7 Explanations and locations of common errors on the HCFA-1500 Health Insurance Claim Form.

14. Procedure codes are incorrect, invalid, or missing. **Solution:** Verify and submit correct procedure code(s) by referring to a current CPT code book or for Medicare patients and/or HCPCS manual for HCFA national and local procedure codes.
15. Incorrect or missing modifier(s). **Solution:** Verify and submit valid modifiers with the correct procedure codes for which they are valid.
16. Reasons for multiple visits made in 1 day are not stated on an attachment sheet.
17. Identical procedures filed on separate claims. **Solution:** Bill identical same-date-of-service procedures on the same claim unless specific instructions have been issued by the insurance carrier. Surgical procedures performed on the same day should be billed on the same claim. Code them on separate lines of the claim form.
18. Incorrect quantity billed. **Solution:** Verify charge amounts. Make sure that the quantity billed is equal to the date span when more than one date of service is billed. When a service is billed multiple times on the same day, make sure that Block 24g of the HCFA-1500 claim form accurately reflects the number of services or the units of services for multiple service field.
19. Omitted or incorrect amount billed or charges and total amounts do not equal amounts itemized. **Solution:** Be certain the fee column is filled in, and total the charges for each claim.
20. Provider's address or license number is missing. When a patient is seen by a psychologist (marriage and family counselor), identifying data are required.
21. Physician's signature is missing.
22. Attachments (e.g., prescription, operative report, manufacturer's invoice) or Medicaid verification (e.g., labels, identification numbers) are missing. **Solution:** Submit all information required for pricing or coverage on 8.5 × 11–inch paper with the patient's name and insurance identification number on each attachment (enclosure). Type the word "ATTACHMENT" in Block 10d. Never staple or clip documentation to a claim.
23. There is no record of the claim, or the claim form submitted is illegible. **Solution:** Type or electronically transmit insurance claims.
24. The claim was submitted to the secondary instead of the primary insurer. **Solution:** Obtain data from patient during first office visit as to which company is the primary insurer depending on illness, injury, or accident.
25. Untimely or lack of response to claim development letters. **Solution:** Pay close attention to the due date shown in the letter and reply to development letters as soon as possible.

See Chapter 8 for information on solutions to denied or delayed claims as well as prevention measures.

Completing an Optically Scanned Form

OPTICAL CHARACTER RECOGNITION

Optical character recognition (OCR) or intelligent character recognition (ICR) devices (scanners) are being used more frequently across the nation in the processing of insurance claims because of their speed and efficiency. A scanner can transfer the text directly from printed or typed pages, magnetic ink codes on checks, and bar codes to a computer's memory. Scanners are also used to digitize handwriting. This eliminates the need to key in the information and cuts costs because scanners can read more than five typewritten pages a minute, thus decreasing processing time.

The use of OCR reduces coding errors, because the claim is entered exactly as coded by the insurance billing specialist. Depending on the program or carrier receiving the claim, the patient's signature may have to be on file.

OPTICAL CHARACTER RECOGNITION OR INTELLIGENT CHARACTER RECOGNITION GUIDELINES

The HCFA-1500 form was developed so insurance carriers could process claims efficiently by OCR or ICR. Typing a form for OCR scanning requires different techniques than preparing one for standard claims submission. The insurance billing specialist should follow these guidelines:

1. Always use original claim forms printed in red ink; photocopies cannot be scanned.
2. *Do not* handwrite information on the document. Use clean equipment (typewriter, word processor, computer printer) and letter quality matrix printers, if possible, not single dot matrix. Clean line printers frequently. Adjust

hammer density to prevent shadows and satellites. Monitor phase adjustment to ensure character clarity side to side and top to bottom.

3. If an optically scanned form has a delete field, then lines, marks, or characters entered in a delete field will cause the entire line to be deleted.
4. Align the typewriter or printer correctly so characters appear in the proper fields. Enter all information within the designated fields and on the same horizontal line.
5. Enter information via machine printing (e.g., typewriter or impact, quality matrix, or laser printer). For best results, use pica Courier 10 or Courier 12 type.
6. Enter all information in upper case (CAPITAL) letters. Keep the characters within the borders of each field and do not touch the box lines. *Do not* type in the shaded areas of the claim form.
7. Use black typewriter ink, NOT red; high carbon content one-time Mylar; or OCR printer ribbons, which provide clear print quality. Handwritten claims require manual processing.
8. *Do not* strike over any errors when correcting or crowd preprinted numbers; OCR equipment does not read corrected characters on top of correction tape or correction fluid. If the claim form used has a per line delete box, indicate a deletion for such a line and go on to the next line to insert the data.
9. *Do not* use highlighter pens or colored ink on claims because OCR equipment will not pick these up.
10. Use alpha or numeric symbols. *Do not* use symbols such as $, #, −, /, periods (.), ditto marks, parentheses, or commas (,), nor decimals in the money columns.
11. *Do not* use narrative descriptions of procedures, modifiers, or diagnoses; the code numbers are sufficient.
12. *Do not* use N/A or DNA. Leave the space blank when information is not applicable.
13. *Do not* fold or spindle forms when mailing because they will not feed into OCR equipment properly if creased or torn.
14. *Do not* use script, slant, minifont, or italicized fonts. If typing on a typewriter, use an OCR or Manifold typing element so that shifting for capitals is unnecessary. Do not use expanded, compressed, bold, or proportional print. Use only typefaces that have the same width for each character.
15. *Do not* use stickers or rubber stamps, such as those that print "tracer" or "corrected billing" or give the provider name and address.
16. *Do not* use paperclips, cellophane tape, or staples. *Do not* staple over the bar code area of the claim form.
17. Enter date formats: MM/DD/YY or 06/01/95.
18. *Do not* overtrim or undertrim forms when bursting. Use care in separating forms.
19. Keep signatures within the signature block. Rubber stamps are acceptable if they produce complete, clean images, without smudges or missing letters. However, do not use rubber stamps to print comments or messages (e.g., "tracer" or "resubmitted") on the claim form.

6

Completing the Health Insurance Claim Form (HCFA-1500) (See Figures 6–1 and 6–2 and *Workbook* Assignments 17, 18, 19, and 20)

The Health Insurance Claim Form is divided into two major sections: patient information and physician information. The Patient and Insured (Subscriber) Information section contains 11 data elements and two spaces for signatures. The Physician or Supplier Information section consists of 22 elements.

The instructions are straightforward and contain all pertinent information needed to complete a claim. However, much information on specific coverage guidelines, program policies, and practice specialties could not be included here.

A brief description of each element and its applicability to the requirements of Medicare (Fig. 6–8), Medicaid, and CHAMPUS (Fig. 6–9) and general guidelines for third party payers and workers' compensation cases are presented. For more specific information, consult your local intermediary or third party carriers as well as Chapters 10 through 14. Because guidelines for completing the HCFA-1500 form for Medicare, Medicaid, the Blue Plans, CHAMPUS, third party payers and workers' compensation cases may vary at the state and local level, telephone those you send claims to regarding their requirements. For those completing Medi-Cal claims in California, see Appendix C.

The Health Care Financing Administration has indicated to fiscal intermediaries the blocks of the HCFA-1500 form that *must be filled out* (required data fields), blocks that *may be filled out* depending

PLEASE DO NOT STAPLE IN THIS AREA

BASIC MEDICARE CASE
NO OTHER INSURANCE COVERAGE

APPROVED OMB-0938-0008

Name and address
of insurance carrier

CARRIER

PICA **HEALTH INSURANCE CLAIM FORM** PICA

1. MEDICARE [X] (Medicare #) MEDICAID [ ] (Medicaid #) CHAMPUS [ ] (Sponsor's SSN) CHAMPVA [ ] (VA File #) GROUP HEALTH PLAN [ ] (SSN or ID) FECA BLK LUNG [ ] (SSN) OTHER [ ] (ID)

1a. INSURED'S I.D. NUMBER (FOR PROGRAM IN ITEM 1): 123 45 6789A

2. PATIENT'S NAME (Last Name, First Name, Middle Initial): HUTCH BILL

3. PATIENT'S BIRTH DATE MM DD YY: 05 07 10 SEX M [X] F [ ]

4. INSURED'S NAME (Last Name, First Name, Middle Initial)

5. PATIENT'S ADDRESS (No., Street): 8888 MAIN STREET

6. PATIENT RELATIONSHIP TO INSURED: Self [X] Spouse [ ] Child [ ] Other [ ]

7. INSURED'S ADDRESS (No., Street)

CITY: WOODLAND HILLS STATE: XY

8. PATIENT STATUS: Single [X] Married [ ] Other [ ]; Employed [ ] Full-Time Student [ ] Part-Time Student [ ]

CITY STATE

ZIP CODE: 12345 TELEPHONE (Include Area Code): (013) 732-1544

ZIP CODE TELEPHONE (INCLUDE AREA CODE) ( )

9. OTHER INSURED'S NAME (Last Name, First Name, Middle Initial)

10. IS PATIENT'S CONDITION RELATED TO:

11. INSURED'S POLICY GROUP OR FECA NUMBER: NONE

a. OTHER INSURED'S POLICY OR GROUP NUMBER

a. EMPLOYMENT? (CURRENT OR PREVIOUS) [ ] YES [X] NO

a. INSURED'S DATE OF BIRTH MM DD YY SEX M [ ] F [ ]

b. OTHER INSURED'S DATE OF BIRTH MM DD YY SEX M [ ] F [ ]

b. AUTO ACCIDENT? [ ] YES [X] NO PLACE (State)

b. EMPLOYER'S NAME OR SCHOOL NAME

c. EMPLOYER'S NAME OR SCHOOL NAME

c. OTHER ACCIDENT? [ ] YES [X] NO

c. INSURANCE PLAN NAME OR PROGRAM NAME

d. INSURANCE PLAN NAME OR PROGRAM NAME

10d. RESERVED FOR LOCAL USE

d. IS THERE ANOTHER HEALTH BENEFIT PLAN? [ ] YES [ ] NO *If yes, return to and complete item 9 a-d.*

READ BACK OF FORM BEFORE COMPLETING & SIGNING THIS FORM.

12. PATIENT'S OR AUTHORIZED PERSON'S SIGNATURE I authorize the release of any medical or other information necessary to process this claim. I also request payment of government benefits either to myself or to the party who accepts assignment below.

SIGNED ______ DATE ______

13. INSURED'S OR AUTHORIZED PERSON'S SIGNATURE I authorize payment of medical benefits to the undersigned physician or supplier for services described below.

SIGNED ______

PATIENT AND INSURED INFORMATION

14. DATE OF CURRENT: MM DD YY ◀ ILLNESS (First symptom) OR INJURY (Accident) OR PREGNANCY(LMP)

15. IF PATIENT HAS HAD SAME OR SIMILAR ILLNESS. GIVE FIRST DATE MM DD YY

16. DATES PATIENT UNABLE TO WORK IN CURRENT OCCUPATION FROM MM DD YY TO MM DD YY

17. NAME OF REFERRING PHYSICIAN OR OTHER SOURCE: ROBERT SMITH MD

17a. I.D. NUMBER OF REFERRING PHYSICIAN: 765432

18. HOSPITALIZATION DATES RELATED TO CURRENT SERVICES FROM MM DD YY TO MM DD YY

19. RESERVED FOR LOCAL USE: 123456

20. OUTSIDE LAB? [ ] YES [X] NO $ CHARGES

21. DIAGNOSIS OR NATURE OF ILLNESS OR INJURY. (RELATE ITEMS 1,2,3 OR 4 TO ITEM 24E BY LINE)

1. 487 . 0
2. ___ . __
3. ___ . __
4. ___ . __

22. MEDICAID RESUBMISSION CODE ORIGINAL REF. NO.

23. PRIOR AUTHORIZATION NUMBER

24.

	A DATE(S) OF SERVICE From MM DD YY	To MM DD YY	B Place of Service	C Type of Service	D PROCEDURES, SERVICES, OR SUPPLIES (Explain Unusual Circumstances) CPT/HCPCS MODIFIER	E DIAGNOSIS CODE	F $ CHARGES	G DAYS OR UNITS	H EPSDT Family Plan	I EMG	J COB	K RESERVED FOR LOCAL USE
1	03 10 9X		11		99205	1	145 00					
2												
3												
4												
5												
6												

25. FEDERAL TAX I.D. NUMBER: 95-234789 SSN [ ] EIN [X]

26. PATIENT'S ACCOUNT NO.

27. ACCEPT ASSIGNMENT? (For govt. claims, see back) [X] YES [ ] NO

28. TOTAL CHARGE: $ 145 00

29. AMOUNT PAID: $

30. BALANCE DUE: $ 145 00

31. SIGNATURE OF PHYSICIAN OR SUPPLIER INCLUDING DEGREES OR CREDENTIALS (I certify that the statements on the reverse apply to this bill and are made a part thereof.)

JOHN DOE MD

SIGNED DATE 3/10/9X

32. NAME AND ADDRESS OF FACILITY WHERE SERVICES WERE RENDERED (If other than home or office)

33. PHYSICIAN'S, SUPPLIER'S BILLING NAME, ADDRESS, ZIP CODE & PHONE #

JOHN DOE MD
4567 BROAD AVENUE
WOODLAND HILLS XY 12345
013-432-1001

PIN# GRP# 0004

PHYSICIAN OR SUPPLIER INFORMATION

(APPROVED BY AMA COUNCIL ON MEDICAL SERVICE 8/88) ***PLEASE PRINT OR TYPE*** FORM HCFA-1500 (U2) (12-90) FORM OWCP-1500 FORM RRB-1500

reference initials

FIGURE 6–8

Example of a completed HCFA-1500 Health Insurance Claim Form for a basic Medicare case with no other insurance coverage. Shaded blocks do not need to be completed for a Medicare case that has no other insurance coverage.

PLEASE DO NOT STAPLE IN THIS AREA

APPROVED OMB-0938-0008

CHAMPUS (PRIMARY)
OTHER INSURANCE (SECONDARY)

Name and address of insurance carrier

CARRIER

PICA **HEALTH INSURANCE CLAIM FORM** PICA

1. MEDICARE (Medicare #) MEDICAID (Medicaid #) CHAMPUS [X] (Sponsor's SSN) CHAMPVA (VA File #) GROUP HEALTH PLAN (SSN or ID) FECA BLK LUNG (SSN) OTHER (ID)

1a. INSURED'S I.D. NUMBER (FOR PROGRAM IN ITEM 1): 234 67 4523

2. PATIENT'S NAME (Last Name, First Name, Middle Initial): THROAT ROSE E

3. PATIENT'S BIRTH DATE MM DD YY: 04 15 70 SEX M [ ] F [X]

4. INSURED'S NAME (Last Name, First Name, Middle Initial): THROAT RED

5. PATIENT'S ADDRESS (No., Street): 110 VOCAL AVENUE

6. PATIENT RELATIONSHIP TO INSURED: Self [ ] Spouse [X] Child [ ] Other [ ]

7. INSURED'S ADDRESS (No., Street): 1ST WING GR

CITY: SINGER STATE: XY

8. PATIENT STATUS: Single [ ] Married [X] Other [ ]

CITY: POINT MUGU STATE: XY

ZIP CODE: 12340 TELEPHONE (Include Area Code): (013) 123-4567

Employed [X] Full-Time Student [ ] Part-Time Student [ ]

ZIP CODE: 12345 TELEPHONE (INCLUDE AREA CODE): (013) 456-7890

9. OTHER INSURED'S NAME (Last Name, First Name, Middle Initial)

10. IS PATIENT'S CONDITION RELATED TO:

11. INSURED'S POLICY GROUP OR FECA NUMBER: NONE

a. OTHER INSURED'S POLICY OR GROUP NUMBER

a. EMPLOYMENT? (CURRENT OR PREVIOUS) [ ] YES [X] NO

a. INSURED'S DATE OF BIRTH MM DD YY: 11 20 65 SEX M [X] F [ ]

b. OTHER INSURED'S DATE OF BIRTH MM DD YY: 11 20 65 SEX M [ ] F [ ]

b. AUTO ACCIDENT? [ ] YES [X] NO PLACE (State)

b. EMPLOYER'S NAME OR SCHOOL NAME: USAF

c. EMPLOYER'S NAME OR SCHOOL NAME

c. OTHER ACCIDENT? [ ] YES [X] NO

c. INSURANCE PLAN NAME OR PROGRAM NAME: UNITED AMERICAN

d. INSURANCE PLAN NAME OR PROGRAM NAME: UNITED AMERICAN

10d. RESERVED FOR LOCAL USE

d. IS THERE ANOTHER HEALTH BENEFIT PLAN? [X] YES [ ] NO *If yes*, return to and complete item 9 a-d.

READ BACK OF FORM BEFORE COMPLETING & SIGNING THIS FORM.

12. PATIENT'S OR AUTHORIZED PERSON'S SIGNATURE I authorize the release of any medical or other information necessary to process this claim. I also request payment of government benefits either to myself or to the party who accepts assignment below.

SIGNED ______ DATE ______

13. INSURED'S OR AUTHORIZED PERSON'S SIGNATURE I authorize payment of medical benefits to the undersigned physician or supplier for services described below.

SIGNED ______

EXAMPLE ONLY

PATIENT AND INSURED INFORMATION

14. DATE OF CURRENT: MM DD YY ILLNESS (First symptom) OR INJURY (Accident) OR PREGNANCY(LMP)

15. IF PATIENT HAS HAD SAME OR SIMILAR ILLNESS. GIVE FIRST DATE MM DD YY

16. DATES PATIENT UNABLE TO WORK IN CURRENT OCCUPATION FROM MM DD YY TO MM DD YY

17. NAME OF REFERRING PHYSICIAN OR OTHER SOURCE: CLARENCE V MC NULTY MD

17a. I.D. NUMBER OF REFERRING PHYSICIAN: 234567

18. HOSPITALIZATION DATES RELATED TO CURRENT SERVICES FROM MM DD YY TO MM DD YY

19. RESERVED FOR LOCAL USE: 654321

20. OUTSIDE LAB? [ ] YES [X] NO $ CHARGES

21. DIAGNOSIS OR NATURE OF ILLNESS OR INJURY. (RELATE ITEMS 1,2,3 OR 4 TO ITEM 24E BY LINE)

1. 493 . 9
2. ___ . ___
3. ___ . ___
4. ___ . ___

22. MEDICAID RESUBMISSION CODE ORIGINAL REF. NO.

23. PRIOR AUTHORIZATION NUMBER

24.	A DATE(S) OF SERVICE From MM DD YY	To MM DD YY	B Place of Service	C Type of Service	D PROCEDURES, SERVICES, OR SUPPLIES (Explain Unusual Circumstances) CPT/HCPCS	MODIFIER	E DIAGNOSIS CODE	F $ CHARGES	G DAYS OR UNITS	H EPSDT Family Plan	I EMG	J COB	K RESERVED FOR LOCAL USE
1	06 01 9X		11	1	99203		1	70 00					465354
2	06 01 9X		11	1	99070		1	30 00					465354
3	06 01 9X		11	2	57100		1	225 00					465354
4	06 01 9X		11	2	64435		1	65 00					465354
5													
6													

25. FEDERAL TAX I.D. NUMBER: 95-123456 SSN [ ] EIN [X]

26. PATIENT'S ACCOUNT NO.

27. ACCEPT ASSIGNMENT? (For govt. claims, see back) [X] YES [ ] NO

28. TOTAL CHARGE $ 390 00

29. AMOUNT PAID $

30. BALANCE DUE $ 390 00

31. SIGNATURE OF PHYSICIAN OR SUPPLIER INCLUDING DEGREES OR CREDENTIALS (I certify that the statements on the reverse apply to this bill and are made a part thereof.) PHILLIP E TUBES MD

SIGNED ______ DATE ______

32. NAME AND ADDRESS OF FACILITY WHERE SERVICES WERE RENDERED (If other than home or office)

33. PHYSICIAN'S, SUPPLIER'S BILLING NAME, ADDRESS, ZIP CODE & PHONE #
PHILLIP E TUBES MD 013-486-9008
921 YELLOWBIRD AVENUE
SINGER XY 12340
PIN# GRP# 00006

PHYSICIAN OR SUPPLIER INFORMATION

(APPROVED BY AMA COUNCIL ON MEDICAL SERVICE 8/88) *PLEASE PRINT OR TYPE* FORM HCFA-1500 (U2) (12-90) FORM OWCP-1500 FORM RRB-1500

reference initials

FIGURE 6–9

An example of a completed HCFA-1500 Health Insurance Claim Form for a CHAMPUS case with other insurance coverage. Shaded blocks do not need to be completed for a CHAMPUS case.

6

on the completion of other blocks (conditional data fields), and blocks that *are not required to be completed.*

Required Data Blocks	**Conditional Data Blocks**
1, 1A, 2, 3, 5, 10A B, C, 11, 12, 21, 24A, 24B, 24D, 24E, 24F, 24G, 28, 29, 31, and 33	4, 6, 7, 9, 9A, 9C, 9D, 11B, 11C, 13, 14, 16, 17, 17A, 18, 19, 20, 23, 24K, 25, and 32

As a first step in learning about the claim form, use a blank HCFA-1500 form, and mark the blocks that must be completed with a red highlighter pen and the conditional blocks with a yellow highlighter pen. Put the highlighted form in your personal insurance notebook for ready reference when completing claims for Medicare patients.

Some carriers process claims for more than one state, and this means they may not always follow the instructions presented here.

When generating paper claims via computer, many software programs insert the insurance carrier's name and address in the top right corner of the HCFA-1500 claim form. If typing a claim form, it is suggested that this same procedure be followed.

Important blocks and information are marked with one or more of four icons to emphasize areas of the form that require special attention. Remember to give special attention to the areas in which these icons appear. ICR and fax icons apply to insurance carriers that process claims using facsimile and ICR technology. Check with local carriers to see whether that technology is used.

This Icon	Will Tell You This
(hand icon)	Completion of this block of the form is either mandatory or follows detailed instructions.
ICR	Completion of this block of the form is important to the ICR system.
FAX	Completion of this block of the form is important to claims submitted via fax.
FAX (crossed out)	This block of the form cannot be completed for claims submitted via fax.

The following numbers correspond to the numbers on the Health Insurance Claim Form (see Fig. 6–1).

BLOCK 1 FAX Check the type of health insurance coverage applicable to the claim. **Medicare:** Check for patient who receives Medicare benefits. If a Medicare patient has insurance primary to Medicare coverage, check "Medicare" and "Group Health Plan"; if the patient has supplemental or Medigap coverage, check "Medicare" and "Other." **Medicaid:** Check for person receiving Medicaid benefits. **CHAMPUS:** Check for individual receiving CHAMPUS benefits. **CHAMPVA:** Check for individual receiving CHAMPVA benefits. **Group Health Plan:** Check this box for those under any group contract insurance; for patients who receive services paid by managed care programs (e.g., HMOs, PPOs, IPAs, and so on), for individuals under group Blue Plans. **FECA Black Lung:** Check this box for patients who receive black lung benefits under the Federal Employee Compensation Act. For additional information, see Chapters 14 and 15, pp. 331 and 372. **Other:** Check this box for a patient who is covered under an individual Blue Plan, who has an individual policy from a third party payer, or who is a workers' compensation case.

BLOCK 1A ICR FAX **Medicare:** Enter the patient's Medicare Health Insurance Claim (HIC) number from the patient's Medicare card regardless of whether Medicare is the primary or secondary payer. **Medicaid:** Medicaid number. Do not enter dashes or other special characters in this block. **CHAMPUS:** Enter sponsor's Social Security number. If the patient is a NATO beneficiary, enter "NATO." If the sponsor is a security agent, enter "Security." **CHAMPVA:** Enter the Veterans Affairs file number (omit prefix or suffix) or sponsor's Social Security number. Do not use any other former service numbers. **Third party payers:** Enter the patient's policy and/or group number. **Blue Plans:** Enter patient's subscriber and group numbers. **Workers' compensation:** Enter the claim number. If none is assigned, enter the employer's policy number or patient's Social Security number.

BLOCK 2 ICR FAX **Medicare, Medicaid, CHAMPUS, and third party payers:** Enter the last

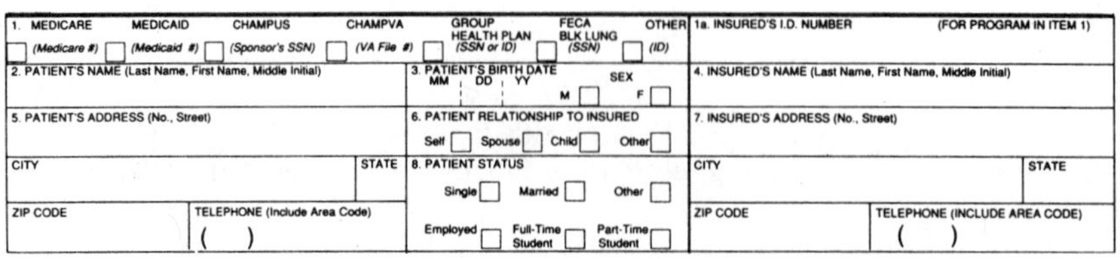
1. MEDICARE (Medicare #) MEDICAID (Medicaid #) CHAMPUS (Sponsor's SSN) CHAMPVA (VA File #) GROUP HEALTH PLAN (SSN or ID) FECA BLK LUNG (SSN) OTHER (ID)
1a. INSURED'S I.D. NUMBER (FOR PROGRAM IN ITEM 1)
2. PATIENT'S NAME (Last Name, First Name, Middle Initial)
3. PATIENT'S BIRTH DATE MM DD YY SEX M F
4. INSURED'S NAME (Last Name, First Name, Middle Initial)
5. PATIENT'S ADDRESS (No., Street)
6. PATIENT RELATIONSHIP TO INSURED Self Spouse Child Other
7. INSURED'S ADDRESS (No., Street)
CITY STATE
8. PATIENT STATUS Single Married Other Employed Full-Time Student Part-Time Student
CITY STATE
ZIP CODE TELEPHONE (Include Area Code) ( )
ZIP CODE TELEPHONE (INCLUDE AREA CODE) ( )

name, first name, and middle initial of the patient–**in that order**—as shown on the patient's identification card, even if it is misspelled. Do not use nicknames. Do not use commas. If a name is hyphenated, a hyphen may be used. Examples: SMITH-WHITE, MACIVERSON, ELLIS III JOHN.

BLOCK 3 ICR FAX **Medicare, Medicaid, CHAMPUS, and third party payers:** Enter the patient's birth date using six digits (012776) and sex. If left blank, this block defaults to "female."

BLOCK 4 FAX **Medicare:** If Medicare IS the primary insurance, leave blank. Type the name of the insured (last name first) if the patient's primary insurance is not Medicare. Enter "SAME" when the insured is also the patient. **Medicaid:** Enter name of the insured if the patient is also covered by third party liability. **CHAMPUS:** Enter the sponsor's full name, not a nickname. Do not complete if "self" is checked in Block 6 (e.g., retirees). **CHAMPVA:** Enter the veteran's name. **Third party payers:** Type the name of the insured (last name first). **Workers' compensation:** Enter employer's name. If the employer is a large corporation, enter the insured's name, (e.g., Harcourt Brace is an insured corporation but the employer W. B. Saunders Company would be typed in Block 11B).

BLOCK 5 ICR FAX **Medicare, Medicaid, CHAMPUS, and third party payers:** Enter the patient's mailing address and telephone number. On the first line, enter the street address; on the second line, the city and two-character state code; e.g., AZ = Arizona; on the third line, enter the ZIP code and residential telephone number. Punctuation is not necessary (e.g., in St Louis, no period after St). **CHAMPUS/CHAMPVA:** An APO/FPO address should not be used unless that person is residing overseas.

BLOCK 6 FAX **Medicare and third party payers:** Enter the patient's relationship to the insured when block 4 is completed. If billing for an organ donor, do not indicate "self" because services are billed to the organ recipient's insurance. If the patient is the insured, check "self." **Medicaid:** If there is third party coverage, check the appropriate box. **CHAMPUS:** Check the patient's relationship to the sponsor. If the patient is the sponsor, check "self", e.g., retiree. **Workers' compensation:** Check "Other."

BLOCK 7 FAX **Medicare, Medicaid, and third party payers:** Complete this block only if Blocks 4 and 11 are completed. If Block 4 is blank, leave this block blank. Only the address and telephone number of the person in Block 4 should be put here. If the address is the same as in Block 5, type "SAME." **CHAMPUS:** Enter the sponsor's address, including ZIP code, e.g., an APO/FPO address. If address is the same as that of the patient, enter "SAME." **Workers' compensation:** Enter employer's address.

BLOCK 8 Medicare, CHAMPUS, and third party payers: Check the appropriate box or boxes for the patient's marital status and whether employed or a student, e.g., a beneficiary may be employed, a student, and married. For individuals between the ages of 19 and 23, some insurance carriers require documentation from the school verifying full-time student status. This may be obtained as a signed letter from the school or by using a special form supplied by the insurance company. The "other" box should be checked when a patient is disabled or covered under his or her children's health insurance plan. In some locales, this block is not required by Medicare. **Medicaid:** Leave blank. **Workers' compensation:** Leave blank.

BLOCK 9 ICR FAX **Medicare:** Only participating physicians and suppliers may complete Blocks 9 through 9D. The Medicare beneficiary must approve assignment of Medigap benefits. *Medigap* is health insurance from a private insurance carrier to supplement Medicare, and Medicare is billed first. *Employer supplemental insurance* is a policy that a Medicare beneficiary has through a former employer, and the supplemental insurance is billed first.

9. OTHER INSURED'S NAME (Last Name, First Name, Middle Initial)
a. OTHER INSURED'S POLICY OR GROUP NUMBER
b. OTHER INSURED'S DATE OF BIRTH MM DD YY — SEX M ☐ F ☐
c. EMPLOYER'S NAME OR SCHOOL NAME
d. INSURANCE PLAN NAME OR PROGRAM NAME

Enter information in Blocks 9 through 9D only if requested by the beneficiary. Enter the last name, first name, and middle initial of the Medigap enrollee if it differs from that in Block 2. If it is the patient, type "SAME." If no Medigap benefits are assigned, leave blank and no signature is required in Block 13.

Do not list other supplemental coverage on the Medicare claim. Beneficiaries are responsible for filing a supplemental claim if the private insurer does not contract with Medicare to send claim information electronically. **CHAMPUS/CHAMPVA and third party payers:** Enter the full name of the person with other health insurance that covers the patient.

BLOCK 9A **Medicare/Medigap; Medigap and Employer-Supplement:** Enter the policy and/or group number of the Medigap enrollee, preceded by the word "MEDIGAP." Do not abbreviate. For graphic examples, see Chapter 12, pp. 277–278. **Employer Supplement:** Enter EMPLOYER-SUPP and the insured's policy or group number. **Medigap and Medi-Cal:** Enter MEDIGAP and the insured's policy number and the patient's Medi-Cal number in Block 11. If the primary insurance is in Block 11, put the Medi-Cal information on a claim attachment. **Medi-Cal and Employer-Supp:** Enter EMPLOYER-SUPP and the insured's policy number in this block, with the patient's Medi-Cal number in Block 11. If the primary insurance information is in Block 11, put the Medi-Cal information on a claim attachment. **Medi-Cal:** Enter MEDI-CAL and the patient's Medi-Cal number. It must contain 14 digits, so if necessary, add 00000 (5 zeros) to the beginning of the patient's Social Security number. **CHAMPUS/CHAMPVA and third party payers:** Enter the policy or group number of the other insured's insurance coverage. **Workers' compensation:** Leave blank.

BLOCK 9B **Medicare:** Enter the Medigap enrollee's birthdate, using six digits (e.g., 030670), and gender. If same as patient, leave blank. **Medicaid:** Leave blank. **CHAMPUS/CHAMPVA and third party payers:** Enter the other insured's date of birth. **Workers' compensation:** Leave blank.

BLOCK 9C **Primary Medicare Second Payer (MSP); Primary and Medi-Cal; Medicare and Medigap; Medi-Cal and Medigap; Medi-Cal and Employer-Supp:** An explanation of MSP may be found in Chapter 12. Enter the Medigap insurer's claims processing address. Ignore "employer's name or school name." Abbreviate the street address to fit in this block by deleting the city, and using the two-letter state postal code and ZIP code. For example, 1234 Wren Drive, Any City, Pennsylvania 19106 would be typed "1234 WREN DR PA 19106." If a HCFA-assigned payer identifier (PayerID) number for a Medigap insurer appears in Block 9D, then Block 9C may be left blank. **Medigap and Employer-Supp:** Enter the Medigap insurer's address and list the EMPLOYER-SUPP information on an attachment. **Medicaid or Medi-Cal:** Leave blank. **CHAMPUS/CHAMPVA and third party payers:** Give name of the other insured's employer or name of school. **Workers' compensation:** Leave blank.

BLOCK 9D **Medicare:** Enter either the name of the Medigap enrollee's insurance company or the Medigap insurer's nine-digit PAYERID number if known. Medigap plans are identifiable by the numbers "99" in the seventh and eighth digits of the PayerID. If you are a participating provider, all the information in Blocks 9 through 9D *must* be complete and correct or the Medicare carrier cannot forward the claim information to the Medigap insurer. For multiple insurance information, enter ATTACHMENT in Block 10D and provide information on an attached sheet. **Medicaid:** Name of other insurance, not Medicaid or Medicare. **Medicaid and CHAMPUS/CHAMPVA:** Give the name of the insured's other health insurance program. **Workers' compensation:** Leave blank.

BLOCK 10A–10C **Workers' compensation:** Leave blank. **Medicare:** Checking YES in Blocks 10A through 10C indicates there may be other insurance primary to Medicare. In a Medicare case, if the patient's condition is due to an "other accident," file the claim with the other insurance. Then, send a copy of the response and file the secondary claim with Medicare. List the abbreviation of the state in which the accident took place (e.g., CA). Use Block 11 to identify primary insurance information. **CHAMPUS:** If a third party is involved in the accident, the beneficiary must complete Form DD 2527 (Statement of Personal Injury—Possible Third-Party Liability) and attach it to the claim. **Third party payers:** Check yes or no.

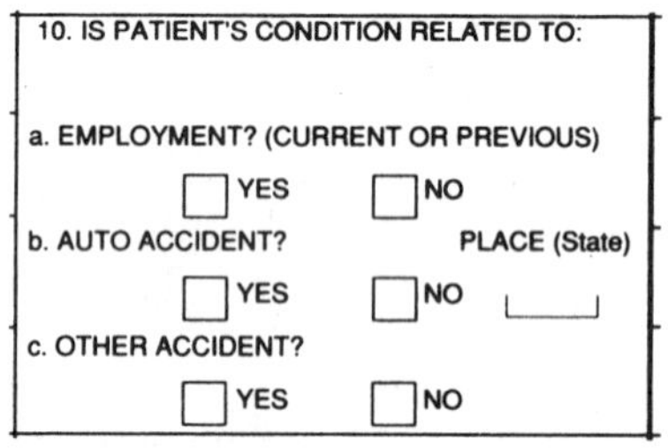
10. IS PATIENT'S CONDITION RELATED TO:

a. EMPLOYMENT? (CURRENT OR PREVIOUS)

☐ YES ☐ NO

b. AUTO ACCIDENT? PLACE (State)

☐ YES ☐ NO

c. OTHER ACCIDENT?

☐ YES ☐ NO

BLOCK 10C "Other accident" is checked when the patient's condition is related to an accident other than automobile or employment.

BLOCK 10D **Medicaid:** Generally, this block is used exclusively for Medicaid. Enter the patient's Medicaid (MCD) number preceded by "MCD." Note, however, that this guideline is under discussion, so carriers may not yet notify providers of a usage change for this block. Some carriers state that if more than one type of other insurance applies to the claim, show the identifiers for each type–e.g.,

Medigap and Medicaid coverage	=	MG/MCD
Medigap and Employer-Supp coverage	=	MG/SP
Medicaid and Employer-Supp coverage	=	MCD/SP

Primary (MSP) and Medicaid secondary coverage	=	MSP/MCD
Two primary insurance plans	=	2MSP

CHAMPUS/CHAMPVA: Generally, leave blank unless regional fiscal intermediary gives special guidelines. If Block 11D is checked "yes," the mailing address of the insurance carrier must be attached to the claim form, and in this block enter "ATTACHMENT." **Workers' compensation:** Leave blank.

10d. RESERVED FOR LOCAL USE

BLOCK 11 **Medicare:** This block *must* be completed. By completing this block, the physician/supplier acknowledges having made a good faith effort to determine whether Medicare is the **primary** or secondary payer. If insurance is primary to Medicare, enter the insured's policy or group number and complete Blocks 11A through 11C. If other insurance is not primary to Medicare, enter NONE and go to Block 12. If the insured's status has changed (e.g., due to retirement), enter NONE and complete Block 11B (e.g., enter RETIRED and the retirement date). Submit paper claims with a copy of the primary payer's Remittance Advice (RA) document to be considered for Medicare Secondary Payer benefits. Instances when Medicare may be secondary include the following:

- Group health plan coverage
  - Working aged
  - Disability (large group health plan)
  - End-stage renal disease
- No fault and/or other liability
  - Automobile
  - Homeowner
  - Commercial
- Work-related illness/injury
  - Workers' compensation
  - Black lung
  - Veterans' benefits

11. INSURED'S POLICY GROUP OR FECA NUMBER

a. INSURED'S DATE OF BIRTH MM | DD | YY SEX M ☐ F ☐

b. EMPLOYER'S NAME OR SCHOOL NAME

c. INSURANCE PLAN NAME OR PROGRAM NAME

d. IS THERE ANOTHER HEALTH BENEFIT PLAN?

☐ YES ☐ NO *If yes,* return to and complete item 9 a-d.

Medicaid: Enter a rejection code if the patient has other third party insurance coverage and the claim was rejected. **CHAMPUS:** Indicate "CHAMPUS" in this field if the patient has Medicare, or enter NONE and go to Block 12. Blocks 11 through 11C usually relate to the sponsor. **CHAMPVA:** Show the three-digit number of the VA station that issued the identification card. **Third party payer:** If no other insurance, leave blank Blocks 11 through 11D. **Workers' compensation:** Leave blank.

BLOCK 11A **Medicare:** Enter the insured's date of birth and gender if different from Block 3. **Medicaid:** Leave blank. **CHAMPUS/CHAMPVA:** Enter the sponsor's date of birth and gender, if different from Block 3.

BLOCK 11B **Medicare:** Enter the employer's name, if applicable. Use this block to indicate a change in the insured's insurance status (e.g., RETIRED and the retirement date). **Medicaid:** Leave blank. **CHAMPUS/CHAMPVA:** Indicate the sponsor's branch of service. **Workers' compensation:** If a large corporation's name is listed in Block 4, enter the name of the patient's local employer.

BLOCK 11C **Medicare:** Enter the nine-digit PAYERID number of the primary insurer. If no PAYERID number exists, then enter the complete name of the insurance plan or program. Include the primary payer's claim processing address directly on the EOB. Block 11C no longer indicates whether the insured has supplemental or other insurance. **Medicaid:** Leave blank. **CHAMPUS/CHAMPVA:** Indicate the name of the supplemental insurance, if applicable. **Blue Cross/Blue Shield:** Give the name of the state or geographic area, e.g., Blue Shield of Pennsylvania. **Workers' compensation:** Leave blank.

BLOCK 11D **Medicare:** Generally, leave blank; some regions require "yes" or "no" checked, so verify this requirement with your local fiscal intermediary. **Medicaid:** Leave blank. **CHAMPUS/CHAMPVA and third party payers:** If Block 11D is checked yes, Blocks 9A through 9D must be completed. **Workers' compensation:** Leave blank.

BLOCK 12 **Medicare, CHAMPUS, and third party payers:** Have the patient or the authorized representative sign and date this block. If the patient has signed an authorization form, "Signature on File" or "SOF" can be typed here. The form must be current, may be lifetime, and must be in the physician's file. When the patient's representative signs, the relationship to the patient **must** be indicated. If the signature is by mark (X), a witness must sign his or her name and enter the address next to

READ BACK OF FORM BEFORE COMPLETING & SIGNING THIS FORM.
12. PATIENT'S OR AUTHORIZED PERSON'S SIGNATURE I authorize the release of any medical or other information necessary to process this claim. I also request payment of government benefits either to myself or to the party who accepts assignment below.

SIGNED ____________ DATE ____________

the mark. A signature here authorizes payment of benefits to the physician (if the physician accepts assignment) and release of medical information for claims processing. **Medicaid:** Leave blank. **Workers' compensation:** No signature is required.

BLOCK 13 FAX **Medicare/Medigap:** Block 13 should list the signature of the patient or authorized representative, or the signature should be on file as a *separate* Medicare or Medigap authorization. The signature authorizes payment of "mandated" Medigap benefits when required Medigap information is included in Blocks 9 through 9D. **Medicaid:** Leave blank. **CHAMPUS or third party payers:** When benefits are assigned, have the patient sign this block. **Workers' compensation:** Leave blank. All payment goes directly to the physician.

13. INSURED'S OR AUTHORIZED PERSON'S SIGNATURE I authorize payment of medical benefits to the undersigned physician or supplier for services described below.

SIGNED ____________

BLOCK 14 FAX **Medicare, CHAMPUS, or third party payers:** Enter the date of the patient's current illness, injury, or pregnancy (date of last menstrual period). For chiropractic treatment, enter the date that treatment began; enter the x-ray date in Block 19. **Medicaid:** Leave blank. **Workers' compensation:** Enter first date of injury; it should coincide with the Doctor's First Report of Injury.

14. DATE OF CURRENT: MM | DD | YY ◀ ILLNESS (First symptom) OR INJURY (Accident) OR PREGNANCY(LMP)

BLOCK 15 FAX **Medicare:** Leave blank. **Medicaid:** Leave blank. **CHAMPUS or third party payers:** Enter date if appropriate. **Workers' compensation:** Complete if appropriate.

15. IF PATIENT HAS HAD SAME OR SIMILAR ILLNESS. GIVE FIRST DATE MM | DD | YY

BLOCK 16 FAX **Medicare or third party payers:** Enter dates patient is employed but cannot work in current occupation. An entry in this block may indicate employment-related insurance coverage. **Medicaid:** Leave blank. **Workers' compensation:** May be completed but is not mandatory and must be verified with what appears in Doctor's First Report of Injury.

16. DATES PATIENT UNABLE TO WORK IN CURRENT OCCUPATION FROM MM | DD | YY TO MM | DD | YY

BLOCK 17 ICR FAX **Medicare:** Enter the name of the referring or ordering physician on all claims for Medicare-covered services and items resulting from a physician's order or referral. This block must be completed when a physician orders nonphysician services (i.e., referral for consultation, diagnostic radiology/laboratory/pathology tests, pharmaceutical services, durable medical equipment [DME], parenteral and enteral nutrition, or immunosuppressive drugs). Use a separate claim form for each referring and/or ordering physician. A surgeon must complete this block when a physician refers the patient. When the ordering physician is also the performing physician (e.g., in-office laboratory tests), the performing physician's name and assigned UPIN number must appear in Blocks 17 and 17A. **Medicaid:** Enter complete name and degree of referring physician. **CHAMPUS or third party payers:** Indicate name of referring provider. Do not use any commas or dashes. **Workers' compensation:** If appropriate, complete.

17. NAME OF REFERRING PHYSICIAN OR OTHER SOURCE

BLOCK 17A ICR FAX **Medicare, Medicaid, or third party payers:** Enter the HCFA-assigned seven-digit base number, one-digit check digit, and two-digit locator code National Provider Identifier (NPI) of the referring or ordering physician. Although the NPI appears as a single block of 10 characters, the first seven characters are the NPI root base; the eighth character is a check digit; and the last two characters identify the provider's location. This understanding may help resolve disputes about statements that the NPI is 7, 8, or 10 characters in length.

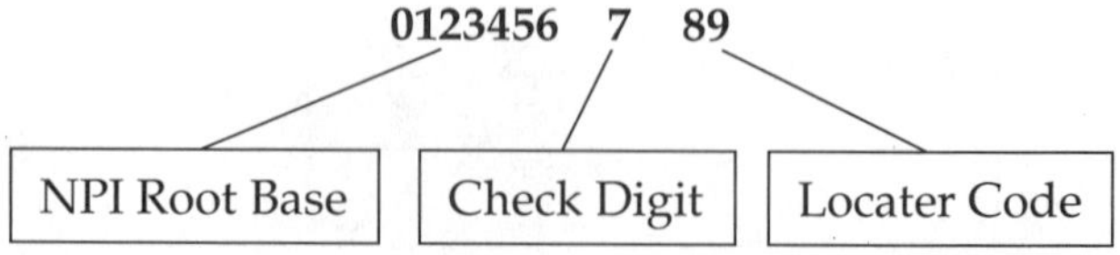

Do not confuse the NPI with the group practice number. If the claim involves both a referring and an ordering physician, enter the referring physician information in Blocks 17 and 17A, and enter the ordering physician information in Block 19. If there are multiple referring and/or ordering physicians, type the word "ATTACHMENT" in Block 17. Complete separate HCFA-1500 forms when there are multiple ordering/referring physicians. Enter one of the following "surrogate" NPIs:

RES00000	Residents
INT00000	Interns
RET00000	Retired physicians
NPP00000	Nonphysicians working in rural areas (nurse practitioners, clinical nurse specialists, other state licensed nonphysicians)
VAD00000	Veterans Administration/US Armed Services
PHS00000	Public Health/Indian Health Services
OTH00000	Any physician not meeting the above criteria for a surrogate

CHAMPUS: Enter the referring physician's federal tax identification number or Social Security number. **Workers' compensation:** Leave blank.

17a. I.D. NUMBER OF REFERRING PHYSICIAN

BLOCK 18 FAX **Medicare, Medicaid, third party payers, or CHAMPUS:** Complete this block when a medical service is furnished as a result of, or subsequent to, a related hospitalization, skilled nursing facility, or nursing home. Enter admitting and discharge dates. If the patient is still hospitalized at the time of the billing, enter zeros in the "TO" field. If services were provided in a facility other than the patient's home or physician's office, enter name and address in Block 32. **Workers' compensation:** Complete, if appropriate.

18. HOSPITALIZATION DATES RELATED TO CURRENT SERVICES
FROM MM | DD | YY TO MM | DD | YY

BLOCK 19 ICR FAX **Medicare:** Although the block is labeled "Reserved for Local Use," HCFA guidelines state it may be completed in a number of different ways depending on the circumstances of the services provided to the patient.

- Enter the attending physician's NPI and the date of the patient's latest visit for claims submitted by physical or occupational therapist, psychotherapist, chiropractor, or podiatrist.
- For chiropractic services, enter the x-ray date.
- When submitting a claim for Not Otherwise Classified (NOC) drugs, enter the drug's name and dosage.
- For *unlisted procedures,* describe the procedure. If there is not sufficient room in this block, send an attachment.
- When modifier −99 is used in Block 24D, enter all applicable modifiers. If −99 appears with more than one procedure code, list the line number (1, 2, 3, and so on) for each −99 listed. Example: Line 1 shows modifiers −99, −24, −26, and −50, and this would be shown as 1 = 24 26 50.
- Enter "Homebound" when an independent laboratory renders an ECG tracing or collects a specimen from a patient who is homebound or institutionalized.
- When a Medicare beneficiary refuses to assign benefits to a participating provider, enter the statement "Patient refuses to assign benefits." No payment will be made on the claim in this case.
- When submitting a claim to obtain an intentional denial from Medicare as the primary payer for hearing aid testing and a secondary payer is involved, enter "Testing for hearing aid."
- For dental examinations, enter the specific surgery for which the examination is being performed.
- When billing for low osmolar contrast material, for which there is no Level 2 HCPCS code, enter the name and dosage.
- When codes 63750 and/or 63780 are used, enter whether a "Pump" or a "Reservoir" is used.
- For global surgery claims when providers share postoperative care, each provider should enter the assumed and relinquished dates of care.
- When a physician gives service to a hospice patient but the hospice in which the patient resides does not employ the physician, enter the statement "Attending physician, not hospice employee." **CHAMPUS:** Indicate referral number. **Workers' compensation:** Leave blank.

BLOCK 20 FAX **Medicare, CHAMPUS, and third party payers:** Complete when billing diagnostic tests (ECG, X-rays) subject to purchase price limitations. Enter "No" if no purchased tests are included on the claim. Enter Yes and complete Block 32 if the diagnostic test was performed outside of the entity billing for the service. Enter the purchase

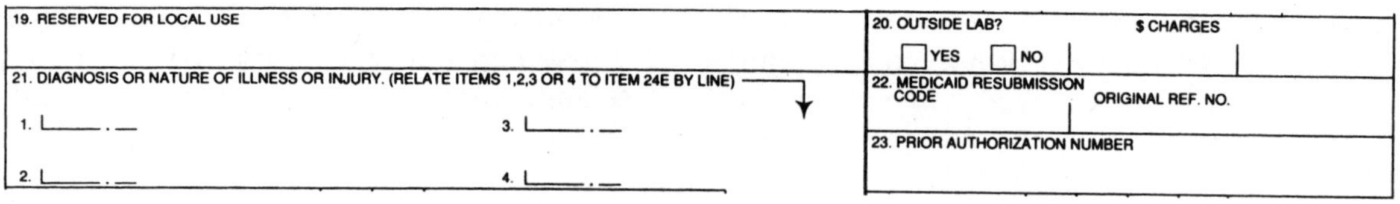

19. RESERVED FOR LOCAL USE

20. OUTSIDE LAB? $ CHARGES

YES NO

21. DIAGNOSIS OR NATURE OF ILLNESS OR INJURY. (RELATE ITEMS 1,2,3 OR 4 TO ITEM 24E BY LINE)

1. ___ . ___ 3. ___ . ___

2. ___ . ___ 4. ___ . ___

22. MEDICAID RESUBMISSION CODE ORIGINAL REF. NO.

23. PRIOR AUTHORIZATION NUMBER

price under "$Charges." Clinical laboratory services rendered in a physician's office must be billed to Medicare on an assigned basis; Block 27 must be completed. **Medicaid:** Check No, outside laboratory must bill direct.

BLOCK 21 ICR FAX **Medicare, Medicaid, CHAMPUS, and third party payers:** Physicians must use an ICD-9-CM code to enter the patient's diagnosis or condition in priority order (primary, secondary condition) and carried out to their highest degree of specificity. Independent laboratories must enter a diagnosis only for limited coverage procedures. Do not use decimal points or add any code narratives unless required in your locale. **Also note** the diagnosis code "pointers" (1–4) for each ICD-9-CM code entered. For Medicare claims only one diagnosis is accepted per claim. For other programs and third party payers, if a patient has more than four diagnoses, use another claim form. The second claim form should contain the additional diagnoses. It is important to check with the insurance carrier if more than one diagnosis is accepted per procedure.

BLOCK 22 FAX **Medicare:** Leave blank. **Medicaid:** Complete. **Workers' compensation:** Leave blank.

BLOCK 23 FAX **Medicare, Medicaid, and CHAMPUS:** Enter the Professional (Peer) Review Organization (PRO) 10-digit prior authorization or precertification number for procedures requiring PRO prior approval. If billing for an investigational device, enter the Investigational Device Exemption (IDE) number.

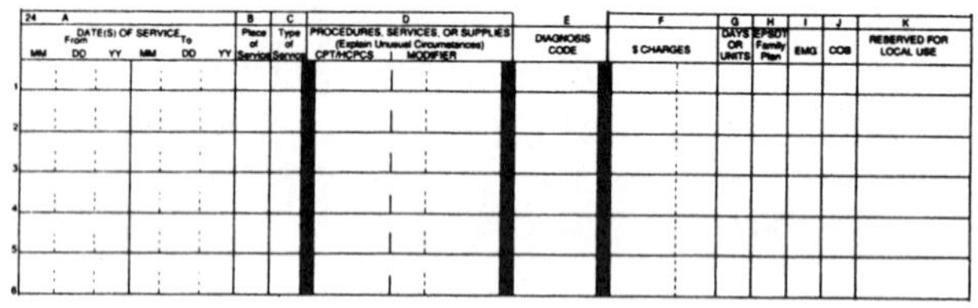

Note: Blocks 24A through 24K may not contain more than six detail lines. If the case requires more than six detail lines, put the information on a separate claim form. Claims cannot be "continued" from one to another. Each claim must be separate. Do not list a procedure on the claim form for which there is no charge.

BLOCK 24A ICR FAX **Medicare, CHAMPUS, and third party payers:** Enter the month, day, and year (six digits) for each procedure, service, or supply reported in Block 24D. Make sure the dates shown are no earlier than the date of the current illness shown in Block 14. If the "from" and "to" dates are the same, enter only the "from" date. Enter the "to" date when reporting a consecutive range of dates. Use a separate line for each month.

> **Example:** For service provided from November 30 through December 4, 1996, report as follows:
>
> Line 1 = 113096
> Line 2 = 120196 120496

Note: In preparation for the year 2000, Medicare and some third party payers are changing requirements for date format to

Example: 12041997

The HCFA-1500 claim form does not have sufficient spaces to allow for the year in four digits. Keep abreast of this requirement by reading all bulletins.

Medicaid: Do not bill for consecutive dates. Enter the month, day, and year for each service.

BLOCK 24B ICR FAX **Medicare, Medicaid, CHAMPUS, third party payer, and workers' compensation:** Enter the appropriate Place of Service code from the following list. Identify by location where the item is used or the service is performed. Use the inpatient hospital code when a service is provided to a hospital inpatient. Show the name and address of the hospital in block 32.

PLACE OF SERVICE CODES

- 11 Office
- 12 Home
- 21 Inpatient hospitalization
- 22 Outpatient hospitalization
- 23 Emergency room–hospital
- 24 Ambulatory surgical center
- 25 Birthing center
- 26 Military hospital or clinic
- 31 Skilled nursing facility
- 32 Nursing facility
- 33 Custodial care facility
- 34 Hospice
- 41 Ambulance, land
- 42 Ambulance, air or water
- 50 Federally qualified health center
- 51 Inpatient psychiatric center
- 52 Psychiatric facility, partial hospitalization
- 53 Community mental health center
- 54 Intermediate care center/mentally retarded
- 55 Residential substance abuse treatment facility
- 56 Psychiatric residential treatment center
- 61 Comprehensive inpatient rehabilitation facility
- 62 Comprehensive outpatient rehabilitation facility
- 65 End-stage renal disease treatment facility
- 71 State or local public health clinic
- 72 Rural health clinic
- 81 Independent laboratory
- 99 Other unlisted facility

BLOCK 24C FAX **Medicare and third party payers:** Leave blank. These codes are used on the Medicare Remittance Advice (RA) document and electronic claims.

CHAMPUS, MEDICAID AND WORKERS' COMPENSATION SERVICE CODES

These codes should be selected depending on the procedure code used on each line.

- 1 Medical care
- 2 Surgery
- 3 Consultation
- 4 Diagnostic X-ray
- 5 Diagnostic laboratory dialysis
- 6 Radiation therapy
- 7 Anesthesia
- 8 Assistance at surgery
- 9 Other medical service
- 0 Blood or packed red cells
- A Used DME
- F Ambulatory surgical center
- H Hospice
- L Renal supply in home
- M Alternate payment for maintenance
- N Kidney donor
- V Pneumococcal vaccine
- Y Second opinion on elective surgery
- Z Third opinion on elective surgery

BLOCK 24D ICR FAX **Medicare, CHAMPUS, Medicaid, and third party payers:** Enter CPT (Level 1), HCFA Common Procedure Coding System (HCPCS) (Level 2 or 3), and local codes and modifiers for procedures, services, and supplies without a narrative description. Medicare requires submission of documentation for selected procedure codes. Include a narrative description in Block 19 for unlisted procedure codes (e.g., 99499, "Unlisted Evaluation and Management service"). If it does not fit in the block, include an attachment. When entering an unlisted surgery code, submit the operative notes with the claim as an attachment. When procedure codes do not require modifiers, leave modifier area blank—do not enter 00 or any other combination. For multiple or bilateral surgical procedures, list the highest fee first. Failure to use modifiers when billing for Certified Registered Nurse Anesthetist (CRNA) or Health Professional Shortage Area (HPSA) services may reduce the level of Medicare reimbursement. **Workers' compensation:** Enter RVS codes used in your state or region.

BLOCK 24E ICR Enter only one diagnosis code reference "pointer" number per line item, as shown in Block 21. When multiple services are performed, enter the corresponding reference number for each service. (e.g., 1, 2, 3, or 4). Ask non-Medicare payers whether they are adopting this rule; since it is contrary to ICD-9-CM coding guidelines for manifestations, they might not. DO NOT USE ACTUAL ICD-9-CM CODES IN THIS BLOCK. **Medicaid:** In some states, completion may not be required. **Workers' compensation:** May use more than one line item per procedure. Place commas between more than one diagnosis reference pointer on the same line.

BLOCK 24F Enter the fee for each listed service. DO NOT ENTER DOLLAR SIGNS OR DECIMAL POINTS. ALWAYS INCLUDE CENTS. For multiple services, list the separate fee for each service in this block and the number of units or days in Block 24G. Do not bill a flat fee for multiple dates of service on one line.

BLOCK 24G Enter the number of days or units. This block is commonly used for multiple visits, number of miles, units of supplies including drugs, anesthesia minutes, or oxygen volume. Initially, this block was a three-digit block showing 1 service as 010 and 2.5 services as 025. Guidelines indicate it to be completed showing one service as 1. Or when billing for a two-view chest x-ray taken three times on the same day, use code 71020 and list the number of units as 3. Enter the total minutes of elapsed time required for anesthesia procedures. Convert hours into minutes. For example, 1 hour 10 minutes would be 070. See the Medicare Manual for rounding out figures when billing gas and liquid oxygen units. **Medicaid:** List the number of visits in 1 day. List services on different days separately.

BLOCK 24H **Medicare, third party payers, and workers' compensation:** Leave blank. **Medicaid:** EPSDT means early, periodic, screening, diagnosis, and treatment, and this refers to a Medicaid program service. Enter "E" for EPSDT services or "F" for family planning.

BLOCK 24I **Medicare, third party payers, and workers' compensation:** Leave blank. EMG stands for the word "emergency" and means that the service was rendered in a hospital emergency department. **Medicaid:** Enter "X" if there was emergency care in an emergency department.

BLOCK 24J **Medicare, CHAMPUS, third party payers, and workers' compensation:** See note under BLOCK 24K. **Medicaid:** COB means coordination of benefits. Check if applicable.

BLOCK 24K **Medicare, CHAMPUS, and third party payers:** If there are multiple referring/ordering physicians, file a separate claim form for each. Enter the HCFA-assigned National Provider Identifier (NPI) when the performing physician/supplier is in a group practice. An individual physician's NPI is not required if he or she is in solo practice. **Workers' compensation:** Leave blank.

Note: *Enter the first two digits of the NPI in Block 24J. Enter the remaining eight digits of the NPI in Block 24K, including the two-digit location identifier.*

BLOCK 25 **Medicare, CHAMPUS, Medicaid, third party payers, and workers' compensation:** Show the physician's federal tax I.D. This number may be the Employer Identification number (EIN) or Social Security number (SSN). The physician's federal tax I.D. number is required for Medigap transfer.

BLOCK 26 Optional: Enter the patient's account number assigned by the physician's accounting system. Do not use dashes or slashes. When Medicare is billed electronically, this block *must be completed.*

BLOCK 27 **Medicare or CHAMPUS:** Check YES or NO to indicate whether the physician accepts assignment of benefits. If yes, then the physician agrees to accept the amount paid by the third party as payment in full, and any copay or deductible. Payment on an assignment basis also applies to the following provider/supplier services only:

- Clinical diagnostic laboratory services
- Services of physician assistants, nurse practitioners, clinical nurse specialists, nurse midwives, certified registered nurse anesthetists, clinical psychologists, clinical social workers
- Ambulatory surgical center services
- Home dialysis supplies and equipment paid under Method II (monthly capitation payment)

Physicians wishing to accept assignment on clinical laboratory services but not other services should submit two separate claims, one "assigned" for other services. **Medicaid:** Check YES. **Medicare/Medicaid:** YES must be checked. **Workers' compensation:** Leave blank. **Blue Cross/Blue Shield:** It is not necessary to check "yes" or "no" because member physicians are paid directly; nonmember physicians must bill the patient and collect directly from the patient.

BLOCK 28 **Medicare, Medicaid, CHAMPUS, third party payers, and workers' compensation:** Enter total charges for services listed in Block 24F. If more than one unit is listed in Block 24G, the total should reflect a computation of all charges.

25. FEDERAL TAX I.D. NUMBER SSN EIN	26. PATIENT'S ACCOUNT NO.	27. ACCEPT ASSIGNMENT? (For govt. claims, see back) YES NO	28. TOTAL CHARGE $	29. AMOUNT PAID $	30. BALANCE DUE $
31. SIGNATURE OF PHYSICIAN OR SUPPLIER INCLUDING DEGREES OR CREDENTIALS (I certify that the statements on the reverse apply to this bill and are made a part thereof.) SIGNED DATE	32. NAME AND ADDRESS OF FACILITY WHERE SERVICES WERE RENDERED (If other than home or office)		33. PHYSICIAN'S, SUPPLIER'S BILLING NAME, ADDRESS, ZIP CODE & PHONE # PIN# GRP#		

BLOCK 29 ICR FAX **Medicare:** On assigned claims, enter only the amount paid by the patient for the charges listed on the claim, with the exception of the 20 per cent coinsurance and deductible. **Medicaid:** Enter payment by a third-party payer, excluding Medicare. **CHAMPUS:** Amount paid by patient or other carrier for the charges listed on the claim. **Third party payer:** Not mandatory.

BLOCK 30 FAX Enter the balance due (Block 28 less Block 29). **Medicare:** May be left blank.

BLOCK 31 FAX **Medicare, CHAMPUS, Medicaid, third-party payers and workers' compensation:** Show the signature of the physician, or her or his representative, and the date the form was signed. Most insurance carriers will accept a stamped signature, but the stamp must be completely inside the block. Type the provider's name below the signature or stamp. *Do not* type the name of the association or corporation.

BLOCK 32 FAX **Medicare, CHAMPUS, Medicaid, third party payer:** Enter the name and address of the facility if other than home, office, nursing facility, or community mental health center. For durable medical equipment, enter the location where the order is taken. Enter SAME if the facility furnishing services is the same as that of the biller listed in Block 33. Enter the six-digit, FDA-approved certification number if the supplier is a mammography screening center. Complete Block 32 for all supplier and laboratory work. Physicians must identify the supplier's name, address, and HCFA-assigned NPI when billing for purchased diagnostic tests. When more than one supplier is used, list each name and HCFA-assigned NPI. For independent laboratories, enter the place where the test was performed.

BLOCK 33 ICR FAX **Medicare, Medicaid, CHAMPUS, and third party payer:** Enter the name, address, and telephone number for the physician or supplier. Enter the ten-character HCFA-assigned NPI, for a performing physician or supplier who is *not* a member of a group practice. Enter the Group number for a performing physician or supplier who belongs to a group practice. Enter the Medicaid provider number in the lower righthand section of the block. Use a 10- to 12-pitch pica font when entering this information. **Medicaid:** Enter name, address, telephone number of the provider, and, in the lower right section of the block, the NPI number. **Workers' compensation:** Enter the name, address, and telephone number of the physician.

Explanation of Benefits

After an insurance carrier processes a claim, the insurance billing specialist can put the claim in a suspense (pending), rejected, denied for payment, or, it is hoped, payment issued file. If the claim is paid, a document known as an Explanation of Benefits (EOB) is usually issued to the patient (insured), and the physician receives one along with a payment check if benefits have been assigned. If the claim has not been assigned, payment goes to the patient and the physician may have a difficult time in obtaining this payment.

In regard to Medicare claim response, a Remittance Advice (RA) document formerly known as an Explanation of Medicare Benefits (EOMB) used to be sent to a participating physician and the patient received a Beneficiary RA. RAs are no longer mailed to providers and have been replaced by a nationally standardized "Medicare Remittance Advice" document, also called the Medicare Summary Voucher. Offices transmitting claims electronically receive an Electronic Remittance Advice (ERA) showing payment data and this is automatically uploaded into the office computer system. The ERA electronically posts payments and the provider does not have to manually post them. Paper and electronic remittance notices have the same format. Explanations as to why a claim may not have been paid in full is shown in reason codes that are the same nationwide. If the patient has Medigap coverage, the "other payer" statement will say whether the claim has been transferred to the supplemental insurer. Nonparticipating physicians also receive remittance notices with payment information about unassigned claims. The remittance notice will separate payment information about assigned claims from unassigned claims to avoid posting errors by the practice.

6

MEDICARE REMITTANCE ADVICE

PHYSICIAN OR SUPPLIER NAME	DATES OF SERVICE FROM MMDD	TO MMDDYY	SEE BACK SERV TYPL	SUB CODE (ALWCODE)	BILLED AMOUNT	AMOUNT APPROVED	SEE ** ACT CDE	BENEFICIARY OBLIGATION DEDUCTIBLE	CO-INS	MEDICARE PAYMENT TO BENEFICIARY	PROVIDER
BENEFICIARY: BILL HUTCH						HIC NUMBER: 5432-112-34					
CONTROL NO: 92106-30810-00			DE/MI: 2121D52								
John Doe MD	0310	031095	D03	120101	145.00	105.00	101	100.00	1.00	0.00	4.00
					145.00	105.00		100.00	1.00		4.00

FIGURE 6–10
Example of a Medicare Remittance Advice (RA) document showing claim payment for the example shown in Figure 6–8. In this example, Medicare applied the patient's full $100 deductible amount to the claim, reducing the payment to $4.

CHAMPUS EXPLANATION OF BENEFITS

PROVIDER NO 235467890183928000
PATIENT ACC # 0000000000000601

PATIENT NAME	SPONSOR NO	CLAIM NO
ROSE E THROAT	234-67-4523	1904593847 2357

SPONSOR NAME RED THROAT

PROVIDER	SERVICE DATES	PROCED	MOD	NO	TYP	BILLED	ALLOWED	CODE
TUBES PHILLIP E MD	06/01/9X	99203	00	01	01	70.00	43.40	003
		99070	00	01	01	30.00	30.00	
		57100	00	01	02	225.00	92.20	003
		64435	00	01	02	65.00	41.20	003
			TOTAL			390.00	206.80	

DEDUCT	OTHER INS. PAID	COST SHARE	PAID BY PATIENT	TOTAL PAYABLE	NET PAYMENT
** 0.00	211.80	51.70	0.00	145.20	145.20

REMARKS
THE COST SHARE HAS BEEN PAID BY OTHER INSURANCE.
CODE 003 SEE ITEM FIVE ON REVERSE OF PAGE 1. IF YOU ARE NOT SATISFIED WITH OUR DETERMINATION, YOU HAVE THE RIGHT TO REQUEST A REVIEW WITHIN 90 DAYS OF THE DATE OF THIS NOTICE. SEE ITEM ONE ON REVERSE OF PAGE 1

************************************** VOUCHER SUMMARY ***

TOTAL PAYABLE	NET PAYMENT
145.20	145.20

FIGURE 6–11
Example of an Explanation of Benefits for the CHAMPUS case shown in Figure 6–9 with a total billed amount of $390 and a net payment of $145.20.

Reading and interpreting an EOB has become a complicated procedure because of a number of situations. If many claims were filed with one insurance carrier, the EOB may include information on all of them. The physician may have signed a contract agreeing to discounted fees with a number of insurance carriers and managed care plans, so payment amounts may vary.

At first glance, the form may seem difficult to understand. Unfortunately, there is no standardization of format for EOBs from one carrier to the next, but information contained in each one is usually the same. If you read one line at a time, you can easily understand the calculations for each patient. The EOB breaks down how payment was determined and contains the following information:

1. Patient's name and policy number
2. Provider of services
3. Dates of services
4. Date claim received
5. Services or procedures
6. Amount billed by the physician
7. Amount allowed (allowable charge) by the insurance carrier
8. Disallowed, nonallowed, or not eligible for payment
9. Less deductible amount
10. Copayment or coinsurance amount due from the patient
11. Total amount paid by the insurance carrier
12. Comments (remarks or notes) giving reasons payment was denied, asking for more information to determine coverage and benefits, or amount of adjustment because of payment by another insurance company (coordination of benefits.)

Refer to Figures 6–10 and 6–11, illustrating EOBs and RAs for a private insurance carrier, Medicare beneficiaries, and CHAMPUS beneficiaries. Read through each one line by line and see if you can interpret the meanings. On receipt of an EOB in the physician's office, pull the claim(s) and check every payment against any managed care contract to find out whether the amount is correct. If services are reimbursed and are not clear as to what they refer on patients' accounts for posting purposes, ask the patients to send you copies of the EOBs or RAs they receive from their carriers. These often have better explanations of what was or was not paid.

In federal or state programs, check the payment against the fee schedule to determine whether the benefits are for the correct amount. On each claim form, note the amount of payment, RA processing date, and batch number.

Claims paid with no errors are put into a file for closed assigned claims. An EOB for a single payment may be stapled to the claim form and then filed with the closed assigned claims. EOBs that have many patients' payments listed may be filed in an EOB file. Some offices prefer to make copies of each EOB and attach it to each patient's financial record. In a subsequent chapter, you will learn what steps to take if an error is found on an EOB.

TO THE STUDENT

You are now ready to complete the review questions and Assignments 17 through 21 in the *Workbook.* The assignments will give you hands-on experience in abstracting information from case histories and ledger cards as well as completing insurance claim forms. In addition, you will be shown a claim example and asked to point out the errors based on the instructions you have been given in this chapter. Take a look at this claim and see how many errors you can find! For further knowledge and understanding, the key terms at the beginning of the chapter appear in the Glossary at the end of this textbook so you can look up the pertinent terms.

Objectives*

THE INSURANCE BILLING SPECIALIST WILL BE ABLE TO:

- State differences between manual and electronic claim submission.
- State the job duties of an electronic claims professional.
- Learn what is needed when adopting a computer system.
- Identify components of a computer system.
- Explain the difference between carrier-direct and clearinghouse electronically transmitted claims.
- Describe the use of patient encounter forms and crib sheets.
- Indicate some computer transmission problems.
- Define computer terminology and interpret abbreviations.
- Name some types of interactive computer transactions.
- List prevention measures to retain computer confidentiality.
- Explain how to manage and store computer data.

Key Terms

audit trail
back up
batch
bit
bug
byte
carrier-direct system
central processing unit (CPU)
clearinghouse system
data base
debug
disk
down time
electronic claims processor (ECP)
electronic claims submission (ECS)
electronic data interchange (EDI)
encounter form
encryption
file
format
hard copy
hardware
input
interactive transaction
interface
K
keypad
memory
modem
network
on-line system
output
password
program
prompts
RAM
retrieve
ROM
soft copy
software
terminal
time-sharing
video display terminal (VDT)
virus

* Performance objectives and exercises for hands-on practical experience for this chapter appear in the *Workbook*.

CHAPTER 7

Electronic Data Interchange (EDI)

Background

In the 1960s and early 1970s, large hospitals began submitting electronic claims for payment to insurance carriers. This transmission became known as electronic data interchange (EDI). This is a process by which understandable data items are sent back and forth via computer linkages between two or more entities that function alternatively as sender and receiver. In the mid-1970s, the Medicare program expanded, thereby increasing the number of covered individuals. To reduce the number of paper claims and administrative costs, the Health Care Financing Administration (HCFA) began to emphasize electronic claims submission (ECS). This system of transmission was practical only for hospitals and large medical practices, because some carriers required 25 or more claims per batch. A *batch* is a group of claims for different patients from one facility.

As mentioned in the previous chapter, an electronic claim is one that is submitted to the insurance carrier via a central processing unit (CPU), tape diskette, direct data entry, direct wire, dial-in telephone, digital fax, or personal computer download or upload. Each insurer has had different software, making maintenance of software expensive for physicians, unwieldly to use, and time-consuming to operate. *Software* represents the program (computer instructions) required to make hardware perform a specific task. *Hardware* represents the physical components of a computer system (e.g., display screen, hard disk, keyboard, mouse, and so on).

In 1981, the National Electronic Information Corporation (NEIC) was formed by 11 major insurance companies. This provided a national network to receive, process, edit, sort, and transmit claims to insurers electronically for payment in 2 weeks or less. In comparison, claims submitted manually by mail are usually paid within 4 to 6 weeks.

The NEIC system allowed the physician to use one version of software to communicate with different insurers. Claims can be submitted directly to NEIC for routing or through a network of independent software vendors, clearinghouses, and billing centers. A *clearinghouse,* also referred to as third party administrator (TPA), is an entity that receives transmission of claims, separates the claims, and sends each one to the correct insurance payer.

Almost 90% of all insurance companies participate in electronic claims submission to eliminate costs of overhead. Claims sent electronically require no signing or stamping, no searching for an insurance carrier's address, no postage fees or trips to the post office, and no storing or filing of claim forms in a file cabinet. Also, they leave an audit trail. Generally, cash flow is improved, allowing more time for patient education, collection efforts, and so on. Because information is going from one computer to another, this reduces labor costs and human error. It eliminates the insurance carrier's excuse, "We never received the claim, please resubmit," because a proof of receipt is generated at the carrier's end. The office is notified of rejected claims faster, which allows quicker follow-up with the use of accurate data.

By late 1998, HCFA plans to have the Medicare Transaction System (MTS) in place, ending separate Part A and Part B claims processing. This system will replace the 14 software processing programs presently used by Medicare's 84 claims contractors with a national electronic standard program. The system will be used for nearly all Medicare transactions, including claims submission, payment, online eligibility verification, coordination of benefits, and claims status.

Computer

A *computer* is a machine that uses electricity to maneuver information according to programmed instructions in a larger volume and at a lower cost than can be done by hand (Fig. 7–1). Besides hardware and software, a computer has a *central processing unit* (CPU), which acts as the brain of the computer system. It includes the computing capability and working memory. Data must be *input* using a *keypad,* which resembles a typewriter keyboard, and a mouse or a scanning device.

A computer contains two types of memory: *read-only memory* (ROM) and *random access memory* (RAM). Data stored in ROM can be read but not changed. ROM usually contains a permanent program. RAM allows data to be stored randomly and retrieved directly by specifying the address location. Data can be saved on a hard disk or floppy disk (Fig. 7–2.)

The computer has a television-like screen attached to it, called a *monitor* or *video display terminal* (VDT), that displays the output of data, or *soft copy.* It is also known as a cathode ray tube (CRT). The computer *interfaces* with the printer, the computer *output* device, which produces *hard copy* of data in readable form. Printer output can be either dot matrix or laser-generated copy, or it can be produced by ink jet.

Input, output, and storage units are attached to the CPU by cables known as *peripherals.* Storage capacity (K) of the computer is measures in *bytes,* each of which consists of a group of eight bits (BInary digiT), the smallest unit of storage possible. One byte of storage capacity will hold one piece of information. Memory capacity is measured in kilobytes or megabytes. One kilobyte will store 1,024 characters, and one megabyte is equal to 1,000 kilobytes.

Numerous machine language codes have been developed over the years.

A medical practice wishing to use an in-office computer or an individual wishing to set up his or her own business should consider the following:

1. What is the cost of the basic equipment and will it be purchased or leased?
2. What accessories will be needed, and what are their costs?
3. How much space will be needed for the equipment and accessories?
4. If the computer is on a time-sharing system with other users, how much will the telephone line cost when communicating on-line or directly to the computer?
5. What initial software will be required, and will there be compatibility with the next larger system to keep down costs of any future conversion?
6. Will installation require special electrical work?
7. What are the software maintenance costs, and who will provide this maintenance?
8. What forms will be used as output from the computer? Also, their design, acquisition, storage, wastage, obsolescence, and inventory finance should be considered.

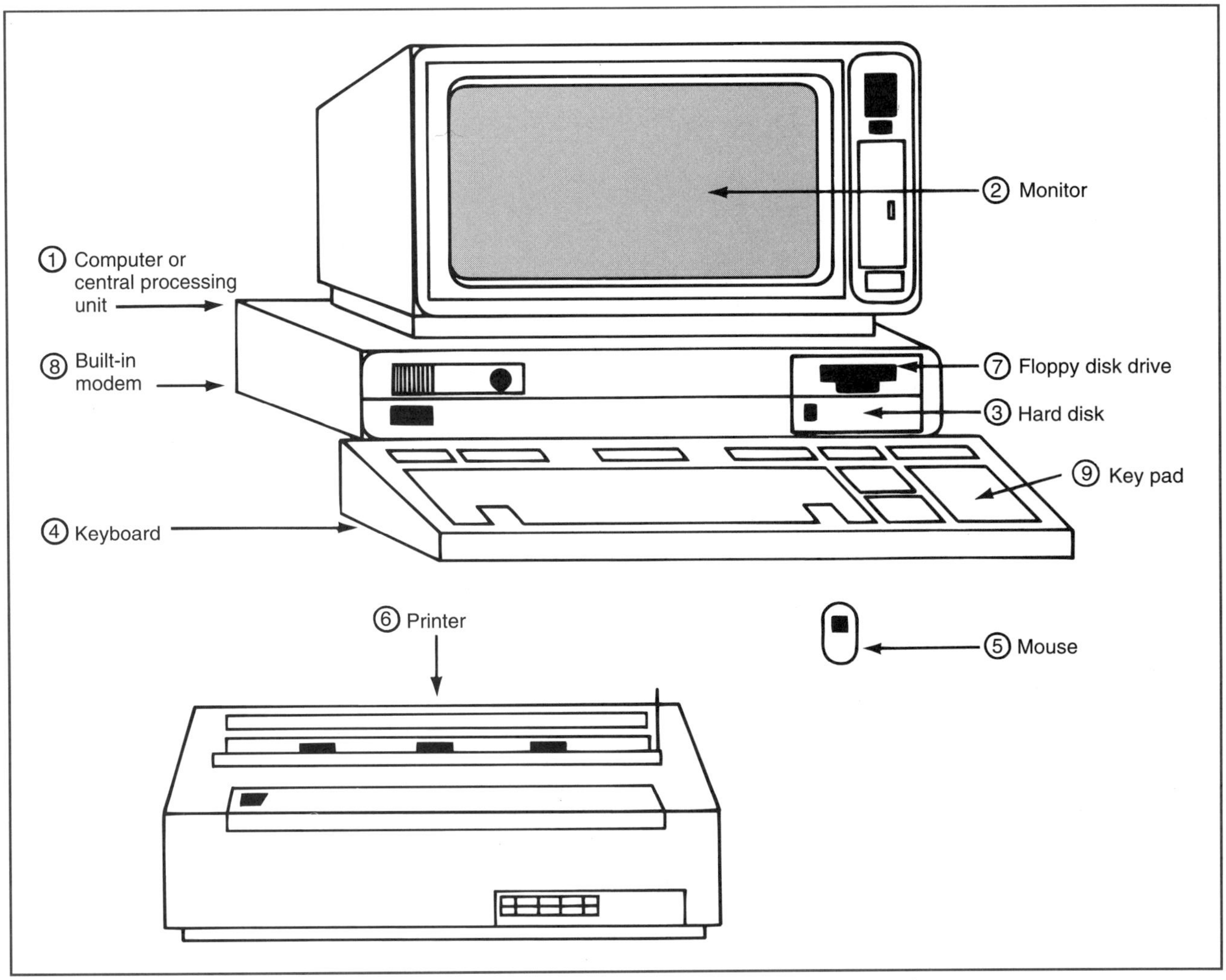

FIGURE 7-1

Illustration of the hardware components of a computer system. The system consists of input devices (keyboard [4], keypad [9], and mouse [5]), a central processing device (inside system unit) [1], output devices (monitor [2] and printer [6]), auxiliary storage devices (disk drives [3,7], also located within the system unit), and a transmission device or modem (inside the system unit) [8].

9. What are the hardware maintenance costs, and who will do the repairing?
10. What supplies will be needed and their costs?
11. How much electrical energy will be used, and how much will it cost?
12. How many on the staff will operate the computer? Other factors to consider are recruitment and training time.
13. Will there be financing when the equipment is purchased?
14. Will there be insurance and a warranty on the system?
15. What will the consulting costs amount to?
16. What will the response level (work the computer handles) cost?
17. What is the response time when there is a system crash (software or hardware)? Who will respond to software problems, and who will respond to hardware problems?
18. How much time will it take to convert the present accounting system to the computerized system?

Computer Claims Systems

CARRIER-DIRECT

There are two types of systems: *carrier-direct* and *clearinghouse.* Fiscal agents for Medicare, Medicaid, CHAMPUS, Blue Cross/Blue Shield, and many private insurance carriers use the carrier-direct system. With this system, either the medical practice must

7

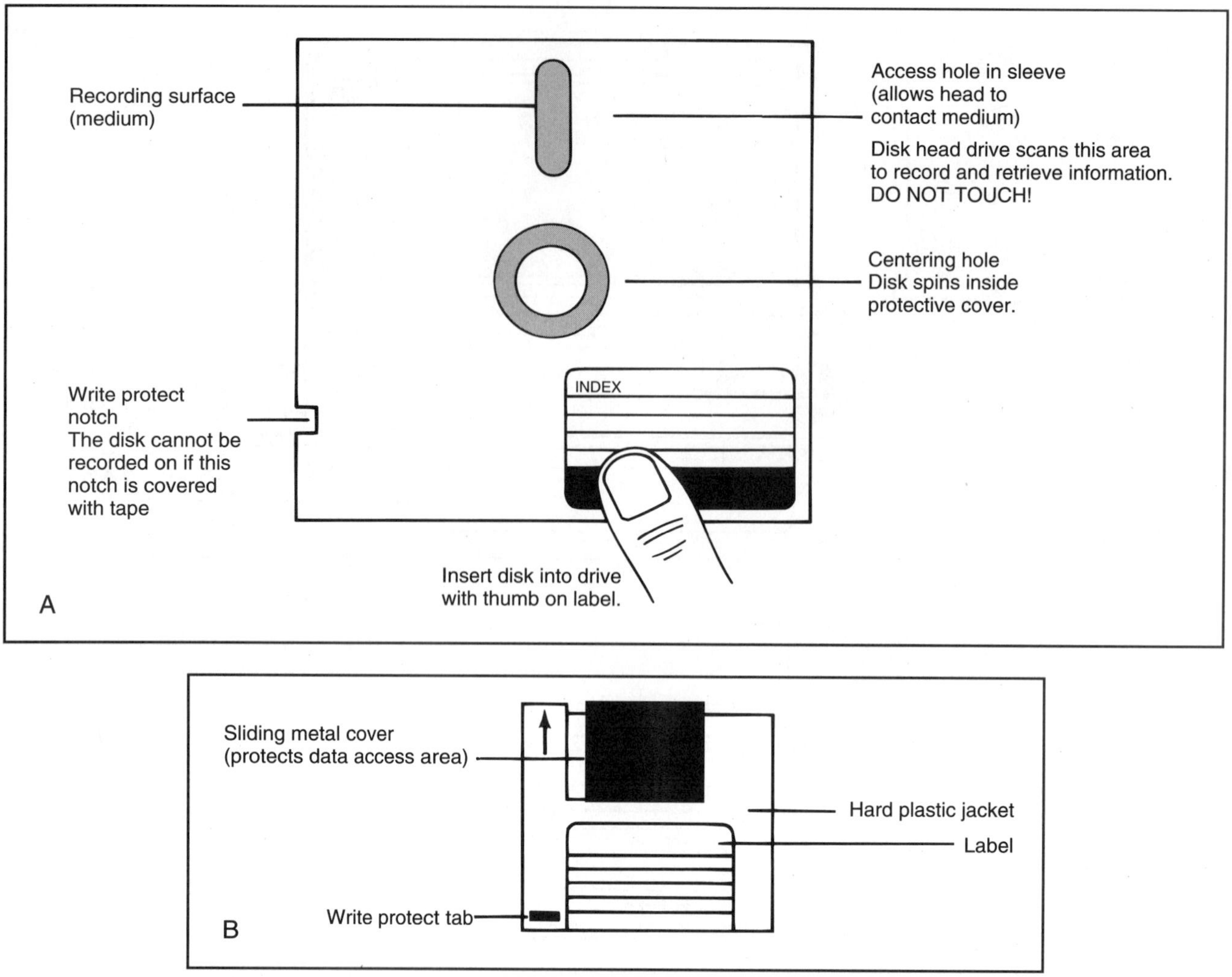

FIGURE 7–2
A, Illustration of the components of a 5.25-inch disk and information on how to insert it into the disk drive. *B*, Components of a 3.5-inch disk.

have its own computer and software or the physician must lease a terminal from the carrier or key-in claim data directly and transmit via modem over a dedicated telephone line.

CLEARINGHOUSE

As mentioned previously, when using the clearinghouse system the medical practice submits either paper claims or telecommunications-submitted claims every day or once a week, dictated by need or volume, to one company (the clearinghouse, sometimes referred to as the third party administrator [TPA]), which then redistributes the claims to various insurance carriers and fiscal agents for Medicare. The insurance carrier checks the claim for completeness and accuracy and either writes a check, returns the claim for more information, or sets it aside for manual review. Rejected claims can be telecommunicated to the physician's computer terminal, printed in the physician's office, or mailed to the physician.

Figure 7–3 outlines an electronic claim submission. The error-edit process in the carrier-direct system is an important advantage of electronic claims submission (ECS), since the insurance billing specialist will know of an error immediately and can make a correction.

ELECTRONIC CLAIMS PROCESSOR

An electronic claims processor (ECP) is an individual who converts insurance claims to standardized electronic format and transmits electronic claims data through an electronic network to help the physician receive payment. This individual can work in a physician's office or clinic setting, or a billing center, or be self-employed. A knowledge-

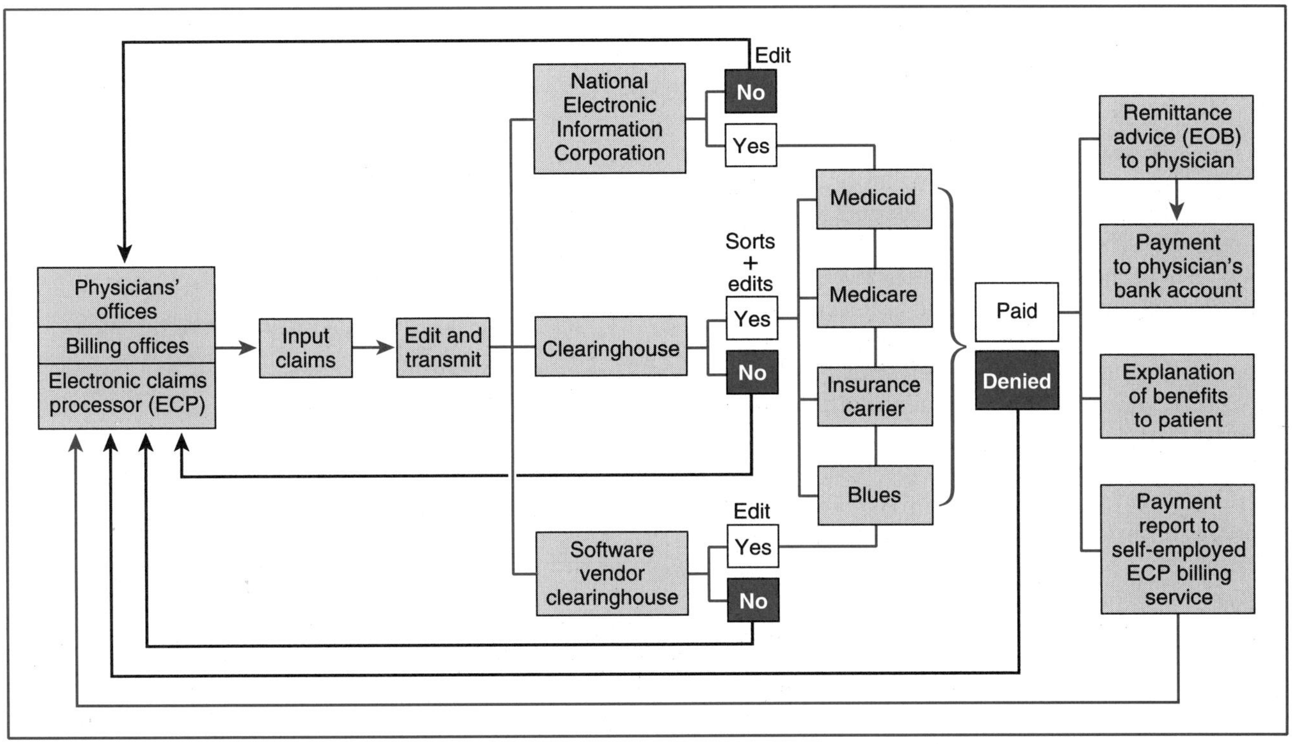

FIGURE 7–3
Outline of an electronic claim transmission system.

able and efficient ECP can reduce the number of rejected claims. One of the duties of an ECP is to perform a front-end edit (on-line error checking) before the claim is transmitted to the insurance carrier to correct any errors. A good software program can edit claims and flag areas where data are missing.

Computer software programs can be purchased or leased. An important responsibility of an ECP is to make sure the software is always updated on transaction sets, diagnostic coding, and procedural coding changes to ensure that claims submissions are always correct. Failure to do this can result in refused claims.

"I give up – everything I tell you anymore just goes in one gear and out the other!"

As mentioned in Chapter 1, the National Association of Claims Assistance Professionals (NACAP) offers an examination to those eligible; those who pass receive the title certified electronic claims professional (CECP). If you decide to set up a business to transmit claims, obtain the NACAP publication entitled *Electronic Claims Professional Manual*.

Electronic Data Interchange

A physician who plans to begin electronic billing must contact the Medicare carrier and major insurers for a list of vendors approved to handle ECS. The carriers know which systems can meet their criteria and are compatible in format. Each one has special electronic billing requirements. Medicare carriers provide the software and training free of charge. It is important to find out from the Medicare carrier how to bill for a Medicare patient who is covered by another insurer. The most common claim format is the HCFA-1500.

If the physician's system cannot be linked with the insurance carrier, then the physician may use a clearinghouse, which forwards a batch of claims to the insurers. Some insurers do not accept claims directly from physician's offices. They may ask that the claims be sent on diskette or tape to a clearinghouse, which then reformats the claims, transmits them to the carrier, and charges the physician a fee. Some clearinghouses have additional services, such as mailing claims to carriers that are not on line. This means that every claim can be sent electronically rather than processing half electronically and printing and mailing the rest. Sufficient volume must exist with a particular insurer to make using a clearinghouse cost-effective. Clearinghouses may charge a flat fee per claim or charge a percentage of dollar volume. Some clearinghouses will advance a certain amount per service before the carrier has paid the claims and then keep whatever it recovers.

CARRIER AGREEMENTS

It is important to have a signed agreement with each carrier so claims can be electronically submitted to many different carriers. Any exclusions in the agreement will not be accepted by ECS, so look over the agreement carefully.

SIGNATURE REQUIREMENTS

Physician

The physician's signature on the agreement is a substitute for his or her signature on the claim form.

Patient

In regard to assignment of benefits and release of information, each patient's signature must be obtained once a month or on a one-time basis, depending on the case, since there are no signatures on electronic claims. For a monthly authorization form, the HCFA-1500 Health Insurance Claim form may be used, and the patient should sign in Block 12 for Medicare and in Block 13 for Medigap. Or physicians may devise their own form for such purposes but must include the statement shown in Figure 7–4*A*. A physician dealing with a regular patient whose condition will require treatment over an extended period of time may instead obtain the patient's signature on a one-time basis. The patient must sign a brief statement, as shown in Figure 7–4*B*. When the computer prepares the claim, it will indicate "Signature on file."

Signatures must be maintained on file in the physician's records for 72 months after the month in which the claim was submitted. Some Medicare fiscal intermediaries require annual renewal of signatures, so check with the local carrier.

WORKERS' COMPENSATION

Uniform data processing codes and universal electronic injury report forms have been developed by the American National Standards Institute (ANSI) and the International Association of Industrial Accident Boards and Commissions (IAIABC). ANSI is a national organization founded in 1918 to coordinate the development of voluntary business standards in the United States. Texas is one of the first states to establish an insurance regulation requiring workers' compensation carriers to use universal electronic transmission for first report of injury forms and subsequent reports developed by IAIABC.

Electronic Data Systems, Inc. (EDS) in Dallas, Texas, and Insurance Value-Added Network Services (IVANS) in Greenwich, Connecticut, have introduced the nation's first coast-to-coast electronic claims processing and report-filing network, called Workers' Compensation Reporting Service. EDS processes all claims and follow-up reports. IVANS provides the network service and marketing of software to employers. By the end of the 1990s, the network is expected to be operational in California, Florida, Illinois, Michigan, Minnesota, New York, Texas, and many more states.

Some insurance companies are using telephone reporting of claims. Employees report injuries occurring on the job by calling a toll-free number. Calls go to a regional center where service representatives document the first report of injury and electronically transmit it to the local claim office handling the workers' compensation insurance. Employers avoid tardiness of reporting when using this system. In the past, employers neglecting prompt report of injuries could delay payments to physicians.

Because workers' compensation is operated under state laws, each state is required to report financial data, statistics on injuries and illnesses, and other reports to state insurance regulators. In the states that use this reporting service, workers' compensation payers use the system to reduce the paper processing costs that have escalated out of proportion and improve administrative efficiency.

PATIENT'S MEDICARE ELECTRONIC SIGNATURE MONTHLY AUTHORIZATION FORM

I authorize any holder of medical or other information about me to release to the Social Security Administration and Health Care Financing Administration or its intermediaries or carriers any information needed for this or a related Medicare claim. I permit a copy of this authorization to be used in place of the original, and request payment of medical insurance benefits either to myself or to the party who accepts assignment.

____________________________ ________________

Signature of Patient Date

A

PATIENT'S MEDICARE ELECTRONIC SIGNATURE ONE-TIME AUTHORIZATION FORM

I request that payment of authorized Medicare benefits be made either to me or on my behalf to ____________________ for services furnished me by that physician or supplier. I permit a copy of this authorization to be used in place of the original and authorize any holder of medical information about me to release to the Health Care Financing Administration or its agents any information needed to determine these benefits or the benefits payable for related services.

____________________________ ________________

Signature of Patient Date

B

FIGURE 7–4

Examples of patients' Medicare electronic signature authorization forms. *A*, Monthly form. *B*, One-time form.

ENCOUNTER FORMS

Patient encounter forms (also known as transaction forms, charge slips, or routing slips) are personalized and custom-printed to the practice of the physician. Formerly, when used with a pegboard bookkeeping system, they were called patient visit slips or super bills. Figure 9–6 in Chapter 9 is an example of an encounter form used in a managed care plan or fee-for-service setting. This form is used for recording information regarding services performed during a patient visit (i.e., current fees, description of services, treatment codes, diagnostic information, patient data, insurance requirements). It is the key to a successful computer billing system and triggers everything automatically for third party paperwork.

After the patient's name is written on the form, it is clipped to the outside of the patient's file folder before the physician sees the patient. After the visit, the physician simply checks boxes for services, charges, and diagnoses and makes appropriate clinical notations in the comment space. The form is then routed to the front desk. The patient arranges for payment, which can be marked on the form, makes a follow-up appointment if necessary, and the form is further processed for submitting an insurance claim. Each January, the encounter form should be reviewed for possible updating to reflect any new procedural or diagnostic codes. Whenever fees or office requirements change, it should be revised.

CRIB SHEETS

In 1992 when the CPT Evaluation and Management procedure codes made their appearance, another method used as a routing slip was developed. This is done in abbreviated style and is known as a crib sheet or charge slip (see Chapter 4, Fig. 4–4). The physician circles the codes, and the insurance billing specialist can easily take that information and enter it into the computer system.

ELIGIBILITY VERIFICATION

Smart and Swipe Cards

Cards similar to plastic credit cards are beginning to make their way into the insurance scene. A *smart card* is a wallet-sized, machine-readable card containing a computer chip that allows the card to store a variety of information, such as payer, coverage, eligibility, and precertification requirements. As an extra service, some hospitals make up cards for patients containing the patient's medical record and history. This service is especially helpful for patients who have heart conditions, serious allergies, special medication, and so on. These cards can hold two chips, one for memory and one for microprocessing.

A *swipe card* is a plastic, machine-readable wallet-sized card with a magnetic stripe containing a small capacity, 200-byte microchip. This card is used to hold small amounts of information, such as patient's eligibility and coverage.

Computer Verification

Some insurance carriers as well as Medicare can give information electronically about who is truly eligible. Simply type certain information about a patient into the computer and push a button. The information received on the computer screen is what the insurance company's employee uses to read about the patient's eligibility, insurance coverage, and benefits.

KEYING INSURANCE DATA

When using computer technology, *prompts* for claim information appear on the monitor as if you were completing a paper form. Because there are prompts for each item, there is less chance for error or omitting an important item. The program checks to see that data are complete and in proper format.

Some entries are made with just one keystroke, and this technique is known as a *macro*. Here are some guidelines for keying in data:

- Do not use special characters (dashes, spaces, or commas).
- Use the contract numbers to differentiate between patients with similar names.
- Use correct numeric locations of service code, valid CPT, or HCPCS (HCFA Common Procedure Coding System) procedure codes.
- Do not bill codes using modifiers -21 or -22 electronically unless the carrier receives documents via facsimile transmission. Usually such claims must be manually completed and sent with documentation attached to justify more payment.
- Perform a front-end edit (on-line error checking) before the claim is transmitted to the insurance carrier to correct any errors.
- Request electronic-error reports from the insurance carrier to make corrections to your system.

ELECTRONICALLY COMPLETING THE CLAIM

Coding

Medicare HCPCS national and regional procedural codes for services, supplies, and procedures; CPT codes with modifier; and ICD-9-CM diagnostic codes are required when electronically transmitting insurance claims. Medicare and many insurers require the physician to be responsible for assigning diagnostic and procedural codes. Refer to Appendix B for the names and addresses of publishers of the code books.

Because the insurance billing specialist inputs the codes, claims examiners do not need to recode. This eliminates any miscoding of transmitted claims. During the edit/error process, software code editors identify invalid codes, age conflicts, sex conflicts, procedural and diagnostic conflicts, and other data before issuing payment. In other words, immediate feedback is received regarding the status of an electronically transmitted claim. If certain information is submitted incorrectly (the patient's name or Medicare identification number is incorrect; a diagnosis code is missing a fifth digit; or a provider's identification number is omitted), the claim is rejected and must be resubmitted with correct data the day it was originally sent. Incorrect coding may be keying errors, or it may be a deliberate attempt to obtain fraudulent payment.

Beginning April 1, 1996, Medicare requires certain information when submitting paper and electronic claims for some blocks of the HCFA-1500 claim form or carriers may return claims. A list of mandatory information and conditional requirements is shown in Table 7–1.

Physicians may revise coding on the medical record and on the claim to reflect more accurately the services up until the time at which the claim is submitted for payment. Submission of a revised claim is usually rejected as a duplicate request for payment unless documents warrant a review or appeal of the claim. Therefore, it is imperative that coding be accurate in reflecting the services performed and documentation in the medical records. As mentioned in Chapter 4, *documentation* is a chronologic recording of pertinent facts and observations about a patient's health.

It is the insurance billing specialist's responsibility to engage in an ongoing process of keeping up-to-date with procedural and diagnostic codes as well as changes in program policies. The new codes must be entered manually until the software program is updated.

Computer Electronic Transmission

Medical practices that see a large number of patients transmit their claims on a daily basis. Physi-

TABLE 7–1
Medicare Requirements When Submitting Paper and Electronic Claims

Block No.	Paper Claims	Electronic Claims
Mandatory Information		
1A.	Insured ID number	Insured ID number
2.	Patient name	Patient last and first names
11.	Insured's policy group number	Group number/Source of payment
13.	Patient signature source	Patient signature source/Release of information indicator
24a.	Dates of service	Services from/through dates
24b.	Place of service	Place of service
24d.	Procedures, services, and so on	HCPCS procedure code
24f.	$ charges	Line charges
24g.	Days or units of service	Units of service
31.	Provider signature indicator	Provider signature indicator
33.	Provider's billing name and address	Provider last and first names
		Payer organization, name
		Provider Medicare number (batch level)
		Provider's pay-to address 1
		Provider's pay-to city
		Provider's pay-to state
		Provider's pay-to Zip code
		Provider's pay-to telephone number
Conditional Requirements		
4.	Insured name	Insured last and first names
6.	Patient relationship to insured	Patient relationship to insured
7.	Insured's address	Insured address-Line 1 Insured city, state, Zip code and telephone number
9c.	Employer's or school name	Insured employer name
9d.	Insurance plan or program name	Group name
14.	Date of current illness, and so on	Accident/symptom date
17.	Name of refer/ordering	Refer/ordering provider last name
17a.	ID no. of refer/ordering	Refer/ordering provider NPI, Referring provider NPI
19.	Reserved for local use	Date last seen, supervising provider NPI, date of last x-ray
20.	Outside lab	Laboratory indicator, lab charges, purchased service indicator, purchased service charge
21.	Diagnosis	Diagnosis 1, 2, 3, 4
24d.		HCPCS modifier 1, 2, 3, 4
24k.	Reserved for local use	Rendering provider NPI
32.	Facility name and address	Facility/laboratory name and/or facility/laboratory NPI number, mammography certification no.

cians seeing a small number of patients per day may decide to transmit their claims once a week.

Some problems can occur in electronic claims submission. Data transmission problems arise periodically owing to hardware or software problems. An error in a program is called a *bug;* removing the error is *debugging.* A static telephone line can impair transmitted claims by delaying transmission and can result in rejected claims. Sometimes the computer is malfunctioning, resulting in a period known as *down time.* Peakload problems may occur, delaying access to the insurance carrier's computer. Submit claims early in the morning or after hours to avoid "traffic jams" (logjams).

Usually a weekly status report of claims is sent electronically (Fig. 7–5).

Facsimile Communication Transmission

Presently, claims sent by fax are considered to be "electronically submitted." However, beginning

JOHN DOE M D
1234 MAIN STREET
WOODLAND HILLS
XY 12345-0000

XYZ INSURANCE COMPANY
MEDICARE ADMINISTRATION

ELECTRONIC CLAIMS ACKNOWLEDGMENT REPORT

DATE: 02-28-96

SUBMITTER CODE: 000002469

RECEIPT DATE: 02-28-96

THERE WERE NO EDIT ERRORS DETECTED AND THE CLAIMS WERE PASSED TO OUR CLAIMS PROCESSING SYSTEM.

YOU SHOULD BE INFORMED OF THE STATUS OF ALL CLAIMS ON THE NEXT OUTPUT REPORT YOU RECEIVE FROM US.

FOLLOWING ARE STATISTICS RELATED TO THE PROCESSING OF YOUR BATCH:

TOTAL CLAIMS SUBMITTED	50
TOTAL CLAIMS ACCEPTED	50
TOTAL CLAIMS REJECTED	0
TOTAL CLAIMS ACCEPTED WITH ERRORS	0
% OF ERRORS TO CLAIMS EDITED	0%
TOTAL CHARGES ACCEPTED:	$15,267.00
TOTAL ASSIGNED CHARGES:	$4,289.00
TOTAL NON-ASSIGNED CHARGES:	$0.00
TOTAL CROSSOVER CHARGES:	$10,978.00
TOTAL CHARGES REJECTED:	$0.00
TOTAL BATCHES TRANSMITTED	1
TOTAL DETAIL LINES SUBMITTED	146

A

FIGURE 7–5
A, Weekly status report (Electronic Claims Acknowledgment Report) of electronically transmitted claims.

XYZ INSURANCE COMPANY
MEDICARE ADMINISTRATION

ELECTRONIC CLAIMS BILLER OUTPUT REPORT ** DUE TO SYSTEM CHANGES THIS REPORT SHOWS ONLY ASSIGNED CLAIMS THIS WEEK **

CURRENT DATE: 03/04/93

SUBMITTER CODE: 000002469 MAIL

TAPE VOL. SER. NO.:

	ASSIGNED (NOT CROSSOVER)	ASSIGNED CROSSOVER	NOT ASSIGNED	TOTAL
CLAIMS:	105	114	0	219
TOTAL CHARGES	$47,647.00	$14,551.00	$0.00	$62,198.00
COMPLETED CLAIMS:	93	106	0	199
CLAIMS SETTLED BUT NOT PAID	0	0	0	0
CLAIMS PAID	88	51	0	139
CLAIMS APPLIED TO DEDUCTIBLE	5	2	0	7
CLAIMS DENIED	0	0	0	0
CLAIMS TRANSFERRED	0	0	0	0
CLAIMS SENT TO MEDI-CAL	0	53	0	53
TOTAL AMOUNT PAID	$15,493.57	$5,817.48	$0.00	$21,311.05
PENDING CLAIMS:	12	8	0	20
CLAIMS PENDING MANUAL REVIEW	9	4	0	13
CLAIMS PENDING CWF RESPONSE	0	4	0	4
CLAIMS PENDING DEVELOPMENT	3	0	0	3
TOTAL AMOUNT PENDING	$6,005.00	$1,500.00	$0.00	$7,505.00

INSURANCE BILLING COMPANY
2300 MAIN STREET, SUITE J
WOODLAND HILLS XY 12345-0000

B

FIGURE 7-5

Continued. B, Weekly report (Electronic Claims Biller Output Report) of assigned claims.

January 1, 1996, "digital fax" claims will no longer be considered as electronic claims. Digital fax is a claim that arrives at the insurance carrier via fax but is never printed on paper. The fax is encoded when in electronic form by OCR and electronically entered into the claims processing system, bypassing manual data entry.

Although most procedure codes no longer require reports, a few codes still need them. If the claim is transmitted electronically, indicate "Report Sent" or "Report Faxed" in the "Comments" field of the EMC claim format. Then immediately mail or fax the documentation to the insurance carrier.

Some insurance carriers set up a fax line specifically for electronic billers and may require an agreement form completed and signed (Fig. 7–6). Insurance claims as well as supporting documentation on a claim may be sent to the carrier via a fax machine if the carrier's guidelines allow this. Even clearer transmission is accomplished if the office computer has fax capabilities. The process is simple, fast, and accurate.

After receiving the claims, some carriers send a faxback report verifying acceptance of the submitted claims (Fig. 7–7). However, the fax machine needs to be left on to ensure receiving the report. This means that payment will be quicker than a paper claim via mail. Some carriers require the medical office to complete a short test phase and, after approval, claims may be faxed and processed. Some carriers do not require a cover sheet and might not allow multipage claims or claims with attachments.

For legal information in regard to faxing documents and confidentiality issues, see Chapter 2.

Here are some general fax guidelines for insurance claims.

- Use light blue-green or white unlines—NOT red—versions of the HCFA-1500.
- Use dark, distinct print—NOT photocopies containing claim form lines.
- Use a fixed pitch font, such as sans serif, with a font size of between 10 and 14 points.
- Properly align and center claim data.
- Do not use stamps or stickers or handwrite information on the claim.

PROVIDER AGREEMENT

This Agreement is made by and between Blue Shield of California, herein called "Carrier" and ______________________________, herein called "Provider".
(Provider Name/Provider Number)

It is understood that this Agreement is subject to modification, revision, or termination due to changes in the prime contract between the Carrier and the Department of Health and Human Services or changes in federal laws or regulations pertaining to Medicare. This Agreement will be deemed modified, revised, or terminated, to comply with any change in the federal law or regulations or change in the aforesaid prime contract on the effective date of such change.

consideration of the Carrier agreeing to permit Provider to Fax claims in lieu of written requests for payment, Provider agrees:

(1) That claims will be submitted to the Carrier in the specific format required by the carrier, as is described in the Blue Shield of California instructions to billers as they may be amended from time to time.

(2) That the Secretary of Health and Human Services, his or her designee(s) or agent(s), or the Carrier has the right to audit and confirm for any purposes any information submitted by the Provider and shall be permitted access to claim documentation records and original source documentation. including patient signatures, medical and financial records in the office of the Provider or any other place for that purpose. Any and all incorrect payments discovered, as a result of such audit, will be adjusted according to the applicable provisions of Title XVIII of the Social Security Act, as amended, Federal Regulations, or Supplementary Medical Insurance (Medicare Part B) Guidelines.

(3) That the Provider accepts responsibility for any and all Medicare claims submitted to the Carrier to research and correct any and all billing or claim discrepancies submitted under this agreement and that the Carrier will be held harmless for any claims, costs, or damages incurred as a result of such discrepancies.

FIGURE 7–6
Example of a fax agreement between a physician and an insurance carrier.

- Do not submit claims on continuous feed paper unless the pages are separated.

ELECTRONIC INQUIRY OR CLAIMS STATUS REVIEW

Interactive transaction is back-and-forth communication between user and computer and occurs during on-line real time. It can involve inquiries, status of claims, eligibility verification, and other insurance claim data.

An on-line transaction about the status of a claim is called an *electronic remittance notice.* This gives information on charges paid or denied and automatically posts the information to patients' accounts. The computer tests the claims computer data against various guidelines or parameters known as *screens.* If the services billed on the claim exceed the screens, the claim is either denied, returned to the physician for more information, or sent for review. If a claim is denied or rejected, the ECP receives a printout stating the reason. Simply add or correct the missing, miscoded, or incomplete information and resubmit the claim instead of remaining on a telephone on hold or resubmitting a claim via mail.

The patient's deductible status can be tracked from all providers the patient has seen during the year. Information can be accessed such as limiting charges, fee schedules, procedure codes, and post-

(4) That all original source documents and source records (e.g., medical/financial records and/or billing statements) will be maintained in such a way that all faxed claims can be readily associated and identified by source documents, including patient's signatures or signatures on behalf of patient. All original source documents will be retained for a period of seventy-two months following the date of submission to the Carrier. Medical records shall be retained pursuant to applicable state law.

(5) That all claims represent services or supplies actually furnished by the provider identified on the faxed claims; that all claims have corresponding original source documents as referenced in this Agreement; and that no claims will be submitted to the Carrier which the Provider knows or has reason to know conflict with the Social Security Act, as amended, Federal Regulations, or Medicare Guidelines.

(6) That the submission of a faxed claim to the Carrier is a claim for Medicare payment, and that anyone who misrepresents or falsifies any record or other information essential to that claim or that is required pursuant to this Agreement may, upon conviction, be subject to fine and imprisonment under Federal law. That the required patient signatures or appropriate signatures on behalf of patients are on file in accordance with prescribed procedures. If assignment is accepted, the Provider agrees to accept the reasonable charge, as determined by the Carrier, as the full charge for services on the claim and to bill the patient for deductible, co-insurance, and noncovered services.

PROVIDER NAME ____________ PROVIDER NUMBER ____________

PROVIDER ADDRESS ____________ TELEPHONE NUMBER ____________

____________ PROVIDER FAX NUMBER ____________

BY ____________

DATE ____________

FIGURE 7–6 *Continued*

operative days for certain procedures. Medicare provides access to information on assigned pending and paid claims. Additional information that may be determined includes whether the patient's Medicare deductible has been met, whether the individual has other coverage, and whether this carrier should be billed prior to billing Medicare. In addition, some Medicare carriers will deposit payments into the physician's bank account automatically via electronic funds transfer (EFT).

REMITTANCE ADVICE

The Medicare electronic Remittance Advice (RA), formerly known as Explanation of Medicare Bene-

BLUE SHIELD OF CALIFORNIA FAX SUBMISSION DATE: 01/19/94
450 W EAST AVE, CHICO, CA 95926
916-896-7195

PROVIDER RID (FAX) NUMBER: xxx-xxxx

CONTROL NUM	PATIENT NAME	HIC NUMBER	DATES OF SVC	TOTAL AMOUNT	PHYSICIAN
1094003000000	Herman, Louise	123456789A	120193123193	161.10	xxAxxxxxxx
1094003000010	Hope, Hortense	951847623B	120193121793	91.29	xxAxxxxxxx
1094003000020	Kamb, Charles	753869421C1	122993122993	128.88	xxAxxxxxxx

FIGURE 7-7
Example of a faxback report verifying receipt of three transmitted insurance claims.

fits (EOMBs) is based on the American National Standards Institute (ANSI) Accredited Standards Committee X12 (ASCX12) Health Care Claim Payment/Advice (835), or "ANSI 835." ASCX12 is an accredited standards committee of ANSI, founded in 1979. Its goal is to develop standards for common business transactions such as purchase orders and invoices. A subcommittee, X12N, has developed standards for a variety of transactions between third party payers and health providers, including insurance claims and remittance advice.

The use of ANSI 835 generates an electronic Medicare remittance advice instead of the paper RA. The payment can be posted directly to the patient's accounting data without data entry if the software has this feature. To improve cash flow, ANSI 835 also allows EFT of Medicare payments to the physician's bank account, which is called *direct deposit.*

STATEMENTS

Statements sent to Medicare patients must have written or stamped on them: "Do not use this bill for claiming Medicare benefits. A claim was submitted to Medicare on your behalf." Medicaid patients cannot be billed for any unpaid balance. Patients who belong to a preferred provider organization (PPO) or a health maintenance organization (HMO) may have different bookkeeping and reporting needs.

Computer Confidentiality

CONFIDENTIALITY STATEMENT

A great deal of information in office medical records and physicians' financial records is considered confidential and sensitive. Employees who have access to such computer data should be well chosen. To emphasize to employees the degree of their responsibility and accountability, it is wise to have those handling sensitive computer documents sign an annual confidentiality statement, as recommended by the National Association of Claims Assistance Professionals (Fig. 7–8). In this way, the statement can be updated when an individual's responsibilities increase or decrease. The statement should contain the following:

- Written or oral disclosure of information pertaining to patients is prohibited.
- If information is disclosed without consent of the patient, there is a serious penalty (e.g., immediate dismissal).

An additional example of an employee confidentiality agreement that may be used by an employer when hiring an insurance biller is shown in Chapter 1, Figure 1–9.

PREVENTION MEASURES

Employees can take a number of preventive measures to maintain computer security. Follow these guidelines:

1. Obtain a software program that stores files in coded form. *Encryption* is to assign a code to represent data and is done for security purposes. In encrypted (encoded) versions, the data look like gibberish to unauthorized users and must be decoded to be used or read.
2. Never leave disks or tapes unguarded on desks or anywhere else in sight.
3. Use a privacy filter over the computer monitor so data may be read only when one is directly in front of the computer and it cannot be seen from the side.

YOUR COMPANY NAME
ADDRESS
PHONE/FAX

CONFIDENTIALITY STATEMENT

I, ______________________________, understand and acknowledge that as a
(Type in individual's name)

principle / employee of (company name) ______________ my position as (job title) ______________ requires that I access and use computer equipment and software applications owned or leased by company name ______________.
I understand that my position as a principle / employee of this company obligates me to abide by the purchase, lease or rental agreements applicable to this equipment and software.

I understand and acknowledge that my position may require that I handle information regarding the physicians and medical suppliers who are clients of company name ______________. I understand and acknowledge that such client information, including financial data, fees, corporate structure, etc., is privileged and confidential and that I am not at liberty to divulge or discuss such information with unauthorized individuals within this company or to anyone outside this company.

I understand and acknowledge that my duties may require me to access and/or process specific patient data for individuals under the care of company name ______________ client physicians and/or medical suppliers. I understand and acknowledge that all patients data is protected under Federal privacy legislation and that discussion or release of this information in any form without the patient's express permission is prohibited by federal law and subject to procecution and civil money penalties for any violation.

I further understand that violations of this confidentiality agreement will result in termination of employment with company name ______

My signature below is to verify my understanding and acceptance of the above data confidentiality requirements and to signify my explicit agreement to abide by these requirements.

______________________________ ______________ Date
Signature

______________________________ ______________
Type name Title

FIGURE 7-8

Sample of confidentiality statement for an employee using computer equipment and software. (Reprinted with permission from the National Association of Claims Assistance Professionals, Inc., Downers Grove, IL.)

4. Always log off the computer terminal before leaving a work station, especially if working in a local area network (LAN) environment.
5. Never download public domain software files from electronic bulletin boards or other communication systems because a virus could get into the office system. A *virus* is a destructive program that attaches and copies itself to other programs in the computer system. Some viruses destroy programs and data after a precise lapse of time.
6. Never bring in diskettes from outside the office.
7. Check and double check the credentials of any consultant hired.
8. Read the manuals for the equipment, especially the sections entitled "Security Controls," and follow any directions given.
9. Store confidential data on diskettes rather than in the computer's hard drive. Diskettes should be stored in a locked, secure location, preferably one that is fireproof.

10. Always turn off the modem when the office is closed. This can keep amateurs, but not professional hackers, from accessing your electronic system. Hackers can access digital copiers, laser printers, fax machines, and other electronic equipment that have internal memories. Some offices transmit and receive data during low-cost, low-volume hours. This means the modem would be on. In that case, develop passwords and access codes to protect the data. A *password* is a combination of letters and numbers that each individual is assigned to access the system. Passwords should be changed at regular intervals and never written down. Delete obsolete passwords from the system. Change any passwords known by an employee who is fired or resigns. Individuals with their own passwords allow the employer to distinguish work done by each employee. If errors or problems occur, focus may then be directed toward correcting the individual user who can learn from the mistakes.

Records Management

DATA STORAGE

A paperless office requires an organized and efficient system for backing up files to protect records against accidental destruction. When keyboarding data, it is wise to *back up* (save data) frequently. Always back up files at the end of the day or several times a week so information is not lost during a power spike, computer breakdown, or head crash. *Head crash* is when the read-write head on a disk drive strikes the surface of the disk, causing damage at the point of impact.

Plugging in equipment to power surge suppressors prevents computer and data file damage. Even better is to have the entire office protected by a surge suppressor installed near the circuit breaker panel of the electric service. This device is called an all-office or whole-office surge suppressor.

To prevent a virus from infecting the computer, install software designed to display a warning message when an infected disk has been inserted. Antiviral software programs must be updated from time to time. Automated back up is possible, and the computer regularly initiates the process. Most financial software programs display a screen prompt instructing the operator to back up before quitting the program.

About once a week a verification process should be done that compares the original records with the copies. This can take 20% to 30% longer than ordinary back up, but if a comparison is not made there is no way to ensure that the data have been backed up. Store back-up copies away from the office in case of fire, flood, or theft. Keep track of files so they can be located quickly.

In summary, here are some basic tips to help develop a well-organized records management system.

1. Keep financial records on permanent disks or tapes, and store these disks/tapes in a secure spot.
2. Always make daily back-up copies of the records or keep a log of when you backed up last. A power failure or a surge in electricity while you are working on the computer could destroy an important document in a fraction of a second.
3. Maintain a notebook of the documents you have on your permanent disks/tapes with an index located at the front of the book. Be sure another employee knows where this notebook is kept and is familiar with how to track down files through this system.
4. Note the code for accessing these documents.
5. If you update old documents, date your revisions.
6. Store your disks/tapes in an area that does not have temperature extremes or magnetic fields.

TO THE STUDENT

Study Chapter 7 and then answer the review questions in the *Workbook* to reinforce the theory learned in this chapter and to help prepare for a future test. For further knowledge and understanding, the key terms at the beginning of the chapter appear in the Glossary at the end of this textbook so that you can look up the pertinent terms. Refer to the *Workbook,* Assignment 22, to correct insurance claims that have been transmitted and rejected with errors.

CHAPTER 8

Tracing Delinquent Claims and Insurance Problem Solving

Objectives*

THE INSURANCE BILLING SPECIALIST WILL BE ABLE TO:

- State three health insurance payment policy provisions.
- Name three claim management techniques.
- Identify purposes of an insurance company history reference file.
- Define terminology pertinent to problem claims.
- State time limits for receiving payment for manually versus electronically submitted claims.
- Identify reasons for claims inquiries.
- State solutions for problem claims.
- Describe situations for filing appeals.
- Determine which forms to use for the Medicare review and appeal process.
- Identify reasons for rebilling a claim.
- List four objectives of state insurance commissioners.
- Mention seven problems to submit to insurance commissioners.
- Name three levels of review under the CHAMPUS appeal process.
- State six levels of review and appeal in the Medicare program.

Key Terms

appeal
delinquent claim
denied claim
inquiry
lost claim
overpayment
payments
peer review
rebill
rejected claim
review
tracer

* Performance objectives and exercises for hands-on practical experience for this chapter appear in the *Workbook*.

CHAPTER 8

Tracing Delinquent Claims and Insurance Problem Solving

Claims Provisions

Individual health insurance policies have provisions relating to insurance claims. One provision mentions the insurance company's obligation to pay benefits promptly when a claim is submitted. However, time limits in the provision vary from one company to another. In addition, there is a provision that the claimant has an obligation to notify the insurance company of a loss within a certain period of time or the insurer has the right to deny benefits for the loss. If the insured is in disagreement with the insurer for settlement of a claim, a suit must begin within 3 years after the claim was submitted. Another provision states that an insured person cannot bring legal action against an insurance company until 60 days after a claim is submitted to the insurance company. If a payment problem develops and the insurance company is slow, ignores, denies, or exceeds time limits to pay a claim, then it is prudent to contact the state insurance commissioner to see whether he or she can take action to improve the situation.

State Insurance Commissioner

COMMISSION OBJECTIVES

The insurance industry is protected by a special exemption from the Federal Trade Commission (FTC) under the McCarran Act (named for the late Senator Pat McCarran of Nevada). Under this exemption, the FTC cannot attack unfair or deceptive practices if there is any state law regarding such practices. The regulations vary widely from state to state, and by no means are all 50 states equally strict. If a complaint arises about an insurance policy, medical claim, or insurance agent or broker, contact the insurance department of the state or the state where the insurance company's corporate office is headquartered. Sometimes this department is referred to as the insurance commission of the state. State insurance departments usually have various objectives, including the following:

- To make certain that the financial strength of insurance companies is not unduly diminished.
- To monitor the activities of insurance companies to make sure that the interests of the policyholders are protected.
- To verify that all contracts are carried out in good faith.
- To make sure that all organizations authorized to transact insurance, including agents and brokers, are in compliance with the insurance laws of that state.

Additional services the insurance commission renders are

- To release information on how many complaints have been filed against a specific insurance company in a year.
- To help explain correspondence related to insurance company bankruptcies and other financial difficulties.
- To assist if a company funds its own insurance plan and help is needed to resolve insurance conflicts.

The insurance commissioner can hold a hearing to determine whether licensed insurers, agents, or brokers are in compliance with the insurance laws of the state, but the commissioner does not have the authority vested in a court of law to order an insurance company to make payment on a specific claim.

The insurance commissioner will review the policy to see whether the denial of a claim by the insurance company was based on legal provisions of the insurance contract and will advise the patient if there is an infraction of the law. If there is an infraction, the patient should consult an attorney to determine whether the claim should be submitted to a court of law.

TYPES OF PROBLEMS

The types of problems that should be submitted to the insurance commissioner are as follows:

1. Improper denial of a claim or a settlement of an amount less than that indicated by the policy.
2. Delay in settlement of a claim.
3. Illegal cancellation or termination of an insurance policy.
4. Misrepresentation by an insurance agent or broker.
5. Misappropriation of premiums paid to an insurance agent or broker.
6. Problems about insurance premium rates.
7. Two companies cannot determine which is primary.

COMMISSION INQUIRIES

Requests to the insurance commissioner must be submitted in writing. An example of an insurance complaint form showing pertinent information required when making a request for assistance from the state insurance commissioner is shown in Figure 8–1. In some states, the insurance commissioner requires that the complaint come from the patient even if an assignment of benefits form has been signed. Prepare a letter or form for the patient to sign and then send it in. Depending on the situation of the case, you may wish to send copies to the state medical association and/or an attorney. Mail may be sent certified, return receipt requested. The request should contain the following information:

1. The inquiring person's name, address, and telephone number.
2. The policyholder's name and address if he or she is not the person inquiring.
3. The name and address of the insurance company, agent, or broker. If the premium was financed, the name and address of the finance company.
4. The policy period.

INSURANCE COMPLAINT FORM

To: State Insurance Commissioner
Address
City, State, ZIP code

Your Name________________ ________________
(Agent or Company Complaint Against)

Address________________ Policy No.________________

________________ Date of Loss:________________

Day Telephone No.________________ Claim or File No.________________

Insured:________________

Is this the only complaint you have filed with the insurance commissioner concerning this matter?
Yes______ No______

Have you taken up this problem with an official of the company, agent, or broker? If yes, give name, address, and title. Yes______ No______

____

____

The following is a brief statement of what the agent or company has done, or failed to do:

________________ ________________
Signature of Patient Date

Attach a copy of the insurance policy, related documents, correspondence, etc.

FIGURE 8–1
Insurance Complaint Form, showing pertinent information required when making a request for assistance from the state insurance commissioner.

5. The policy or claim number.
6. The date of loss.
7. A statement of the complaint including, if possible, a copy of the policy, medical bills, unpaid medical insurance claim, canceled checks, and any correspondence from the company pertaining to the claim.
8. Because the commissioner's responsibility is to the patient (the consumer), not the physician, any letter must include the patient's signature, address, and telephone number.

If an insurance company pays the patient directly, even though the physician has sent in an Assignment of Benefits form with the claim, file a complaint with the state insurance commissioner. After receiving the physician's complaint, the commissioner will write to the insurance company and request a review of the claim. If the insurance company admits that there is an assignment of benefits and that they inadvertently paid the patient, the insurance company must pay the physician within 2 to 3 weeks and honor the assignment even before they recover their money from the patient. The insurance company will then file for payment from the patient.

If an insurance company is continually a slow payer, a method to speed up payments is to include a note to the carrier that reads:

"Unless this claim is paid or denied within 30 days, a formal written complaint will be filed with the state insurance commissioner."

Or, a letter may be sent to the insurance commissioner with a copy notation inserted at the end to the insurance company. It might read:

"The attached claim has been submitted to the XYZ Insurance Company. It has not been paid or denied. Please accept this letter as a formal written complaint against the XYZ Insurance Company."

Insurance companies are rated according to the number of complaints received about them, so they do not want the insurance commissioner to be alerted to any problems. Some states have information available to the public on how many claims have been submitted against a company if you need this data. To contact the state insurance commissioner for assistance or information regarding state laws, refer to Appendix A.

Claim Management Techniques

INSURANCE CLAIMS REGISTER

In Chapter 3 you learned to establish a follow-up procedure for insurance claims by logging the claims completed onto an insurance claims register (see Fig. 3–7). Use a loose-leaf notebook indexed according to the various insurance companies. Place a copy of the insurance claims in a pending file labeled for each month of service so that the unpaid claims can be retrieved for easy follow-up. Or, place a copy of the insurance claim by insurance company name. This method permits an inquiry on multiple outstanding claims in one letter each month rather than many letters covering individual claims.

When referring to this register, you can quickly locate delinquent claims by simply looking through the book under the Date Claim Paid column. If that column is blank, check the Date Claim Submitted column. You can request a tracer on a claim when no payment has been received from the insurance company.

When a payment is received, pull out the copies of claims that correspond with the payments and dispose of them. Post payment received to the patient's ledger and to the day sheet, and deposit the payment check in the physician's bank account. Draw a line through the pertinent information but do not obscure data. When all claims on the page have been paid, draw a diagonal line across the page. Pages may be retained for future reference. This will also help you keep track of payments not received.

INSURANCE COMPANY PAYMENT HISTORY

Make a file of 3″ × 5″ index cards or 8-1/2″ × 11″ three-hole punched sheets in a loose-leaf binder listing the insurance companies or managed care plans that send claim payments directly to the physician. Every time a payment is received, pull out the card or the loose-leaf sheet for that company and update the information. The card should contain the following information:

Insurance company name and regional office addresses
Names of patients covered and their policy numbers
Claims filing procedures
Payment policies for each plan

If the patients' names and group policy numbers are listed, this file will be of help when discussing with the patient what the insurance company may be expected to pay on a claim. Remember, group numbers may change annually when employers increase insurance coverage so employees receive more benefits. Be sure to keep the policy numbers current. This insurance company payment history system can help avoid potential problems and pinpoint requirements that must be met to ensure prompt payment.

TICKLER FILE

A *tickler file,* also called a *suspense* or *follow-up file,* is used to remind patients of upcoming or missed appointments as well as to track submitted pending or resubmitted insurance claims (see Chapter 3, Fig. 3–6). Tickler files can also be set up in computer systems to prompt the insurance billing specialist to telephone or send inquiries about unpaid insurance claims.

To set up this reminder system, divide active claims by month and file them in chronologic order. Subdivisions can also be made by patient name or in numerical order by account number. Some large group practices prefer to subdivide claims by month and date of treatment. Maintain the active file by calendar year and put inactive resolved claims (older than 1 year) in storage that is accessible.

To begin using this system, print two completed HCFA-1500 claim forms and send the original to the payer and file a copy in the tickler file. After receiving the Medicare Remittance Advice (RA), formerly known as Explanation of Medicare Benefits (EOMB) form, and payment check, post the payment to the financial record and pull all claims noted on the RA from the tickler file. Compare the charges made on each claim to the payments listed on the RA. If a patient has received many services and the claim was submitted on several forms, determine whether services on all forms were processed for payment. After performing this reconciliation process, attach a copy of the RA to the claim and put it in a paid file.

Copies of claims remaining in the tickler file exceeding the time limits for manual or electronic submission should be resubmitted to the payer for reconsideration. Complete the form shown in either Figure 8–2 or send a letter as shown in Figure 8–3 and attach it to the copy. Keep copies of the documents in the tickler file indicating the date of second submission and write "second request" on the copies.

Problem Claims

TYPES OF PROBLEMS

There are many types of problem claims, such as delinquent, denied, rejected, partial payment, down coding, claims in suspense (pending), payment lost in the mail, payment paid to patient, overpayment, and so on. These problems require some type of follow-up action. When transmitting claims electronically, claim status may be quickly and easily accessed via computer or teledigital response systems, thus speeding up inquiry time. See Chapter 7 for information on electronic remittance notices.

To prevent repeated claims errors, the office manager should identify the source of the errors within the medical office. Often, a claim may be denied because of an error that occurred at the front desk, at check-out time, or when posting was done. The individual handling the front desk must update insurance information routinely (e.g., insurance identification number, address, and so on). The person posting to accounts must be certain that supplemental insurers are billed after the primary insurance carrier has paid; amounts may be posted to the wrong account. Identified errors should be brought to the attention of the individual(s) responsible to improve outgoing claims and avoid future problems.

DELINQUENT, PENDING, OR SUSPENSE

The term *delinquent* in reference to an insurance claim means payment is overdue from a nonpayer. The nonpayer can be an insurance company, a managed care plan, or an intermediary for the Medicare, Medicaid, or CHAMPUS programs. Sometimes

8

INSURANCE CLAIM TRACER

INSURANCE COMPANY NAME____________ DATE____________

ADDRESS:____________

PATIENT NAME____________ INSURED:____________

POLICY/CERTIFICATE NUMBER____________ GROUP NAME/NUMBER____________

EMPLOYER NAME AND ADDRESS:____________

DATE OF INITIAL CLAIM SUBMISSION____________ AMOUNT:____________

An inordinate amount of time has passed since submission of our original claim as described above. We have not received a request for additional information and still await payment of this assigned claim. Please review the attached duplicate and process for payment within seven (7) days.

If there is any difficulty with this claim, please check one of these below and return this letter to our office.

Claim pending because:____________
Payment of claim in process:____________
Payment made on claim: Date:____________ To Whom:____________
Claim denied: (Reason)____________
Patient notified: Yes_____ No_____
Remarks:____________

Thank you for your assistance in this important matter. Please contact ____________ in our office if you have any questions regarding this claim.

Office of:____________ M.D.

Address: ____________

____________ TELEPHONE NUMBER:____________

FIGURE 8–2
Insurance Claim Tracer. An example of how a form may be set up to follow up on a delinquent claim.

ABC MEDICAL GROUP, INC.
123 Main Street
Woodland Hills, XY 12345-0239
Tel. 013/487-4900
Fax No. 013/486-4834

September 12, 199X

Ms. Jane Hatfield
Appeals Division
XYZ Managed Care Plan
100 South H Street
Anytown, XY 12345-0001

Dear Ms. Hatfield:

Re: Claim number: A0958
Patient: Carolyn B. Little
Dates of service: August 2-10, 199X

Recently I received a denied claim from your office (see enclosure). A review of the contract I have with your managed care plan shows that these services should have been approved.

Enclosed is a photocopy of my chart notes for the professional services rendered to the patient on these dates. I have seen Ms. Hatfield five times in the last nine days and each service was medically necessary by the specific complaints expressed by the patient.

On examination, I found the complaints by the patient were valid.

If after review of this claim you still feel reimbursement is not appropriate, please forward this request to the Peer Review Committee for a final determination.

If you need additional information, please telephone, fax, or write my office.

Sincerely,

John Doe, MD

mtf

Enclosures

FIGURE 8–3
Example of a letter asking for a review about a claim submitted and denied by a managed care plan.

nonpayment is due to a claim in review or in *suspense (pending)* due to an error or need for additional information. To keep on top of delinquent claims, use claim management techniques (i.e., insurance claims register, insurance company payment history, tickler file), so that follow-up can be accomplished in a timely manner. It is possible that payment can be received even after a claim has been denied in whole or in part.

If it becomes necessary to contact an insurance company about a delinquent claim, complete and send in the form shown in Figure 8–2. State laws require insurance companies to notify the insured of a denial and why the claim was denied. With regard to Medicare, federal laws require that an explanation must be given for each denied service. A Medicare claim may be appealed by requesting a review in writing.

The time limit for receiving insurance reimbursement can vary depending on the insurance carrier or program (Table 8–1). It is reasonable to expect payment as follows:

TABLE 8–1
Time Limit for Receiving Insurance Reimbursement

Program	From Date Claim Was Manually Submitted	From Date Claim Was Electronically Submitted
Private insurance companies	4 to 6 weeks by mail	2 weeks or less
Blue Cross / Blue Shield	4 to 6 weeks by mail	2 weeks or less
CHAMPUS	8 to 12 weeks by mail	2 weeks or less
Medicare	4 to 6 weeks by mail	2 1/2 weeks for participating physicians 3 1/2 weeks for nonparticipating physicians
Worker's compensation	4 to 8 weeks by mail	2 weeks or less

8

If the insurance carrier is slow in paying, write to the carrier and ask why the claim has not been paid. Mail a copy of the correspondence to the insurance commissioner in your state; the addresses are given in Appendix A.

Managed care plans usually process claims on a daily basis, but some plans release payments quarterly. Some plans withhold a percentage that is reserved in a pool and distributed at the end of the fiscal year. Because these plans vary considerably in paying policies and how they are administered, Chapter 9 details how to followup on claims for services and problem solving.

LOST CLAIMS

- When an insurance claim is received by the insurance company, the claim is date stamped usually within 24 hours, assigned a claim number, and logged into the payer system. However, if there is a backlog of claims, it may take 7 to 15 days or longer to be logged into the system. If you call to find out the status of the claim during that time, you may be told it has not been received or lost.
  Solution: Ask if there is a backlog of claims because this will indicate to you that it probably has not been logged into the system. If it is determined to be lost, then submit a copy of the original claim, marking it "copy of the original claim submitted on ____________." Before sending it, be sure you have the correct mailing address, post office box number, zip code, and so on. If you have had several problems with the same insurance company, send it by certified mail with return receipt. If you have verifiable information of a lost claim, call or write to the provider relations department or member services and explain the problem. You may want to check the contract with the payer. Some contracts have a clause that specifies any claims not paid within a certain number of days (e.g., 30 days) after receipt will be paid at an increased rate or in full.

- Claim is not received.
  Solution: Verify that the patient is insured by the insurance carrier and is covered for the benefits claimed. Then resubmit the insurance claim.

REJECTED CLAIMS

In Chapter 6, you learned some common reasons why claims are rejected or delayed. A *rejected claim* is one submitted that does not follow Medicare instructions or contains a technical error. Such claims may be disproved or discarded by the system and returned to the biller. Technical errors consist of missing or incorrect information and are found via computer edits, screening processes, and claim data accuracy. Claim rejections occur because of the following:

- Transposed numbers
- Missing, invalid, or incorrect procedure codes and modifiers
- Missing or invalid place of service
- Mismatch of place of service to type of service
- Missing referring physician when billing tests or missing provider
- Number when the patient was referred
- Missing or invalid provider number
- Incorrect, invalid, nonspecific, or missing diagnostic code numbers
- Incorrect dates of service
- Incorrect year of service
- Incorrect number of days in the month (i.e., February)
- Code description does not match services rendered
- Duplicate dates of service
- Duplicate charges
  Solution: Always double check the initial claim for accuracy before it has left the office. However, if the claim is rejected and returned, add the missing or incomplete information and resubmit the claim for regular claims processing. Do not send a corrected claim for review or appeal.

- Claim submitted for several services and one service is rejected for incomplete information and services not rejected are paid.
  Solution: Resubmit the rejected services on a new HCFA-1500 claim form.

- Insurance carrier requests further information or information about another carrier.
  Solution: Call or mail the information to the insurance company.

- Claim resubmitted is returned a second time.
  Solution: Review the explanation of benefits (EOB) statement or remittance advice to see if there is a denial code or narrative explanation. Examine the claim for missing, incomplete, or incorrect information. Determine if a specific appeal form must be submitted. Submit a detailed summary or a copy of the operative or pathology report to clearly identify the procedure. Enclose a cover letter with the resubmitted data.

DENIED CLAIMS

Insurance companies save money when a claim is denied, and only a small percentage of individuals pursue appeals. Some reasons why claims are not paid because of denial are because of the following:

- Payable for selected diagnoses
- Frequency limitations or restrictions per benefit period
- Procedure performed by ineligible specialty provider (e.g., a podiatrist would not be paid for neurosurgery)
- Bundled with other services
- Payable in certain locations (e.g., outpatient only)
- Prior approval needed and not obtained
- Diagnosis did not justify the service or procedure rendered

You cannot simply change the information and resubmit. A *denied claim* is one that may be denied due to medical coverage policy issues or program issues. Some additional examples with suggested solutions are as follows:

- Service was not a policy or program benefit (e.g., routine physical examination, routine tests, routine foot care, routine dental care, cosmetic surgery, custodial care, eye or hearing examinations for glasses or hearing aids, some immunizations, and so on). Plastic surgery may be considered a general exclusion in many insurance policies.
  Solution: Send the patient a statement with a notation of the response from the insurance company on the bill.

- Treatment given for a pre-existing condition (currently some policies do not include this exclusion).
  Solution: When a patient is referred, ask the referring physician to forward information on all pre-existing conditions that may be relevant to the surgery to be performed. Request verification of insurance coverage from the insurer for the procedure with regard to pre-existing conditions. If authorization is denied, have the physician discuss other treatment/payment options with the

patient (e.g., rendering minimum level of interim care until the pre-existence period has expired). If the physician believes that the patient's condition is not pre-exisitng, send an appeal to the insurance company. Otherwise, bill the patient, noting the insurance company's response on the statement.

- Insurance coverage canceled when service had been given.
  Solution: Send the patient a statement with notation of the insurance information on the bill.

- Insurance coverage lapsed beyond renewal date when service was rendered.
  Solution: Send the patient a statement with notation of the response from the insurance company on the bill.

- Service given before coverage was in effect.
  Solution: Send the patient a statement with notation of the response from the insurance company on the bill.

- Service given when patient was no longer a member of a group plan.
  Solution: Send the patient a statement with notation of the response from the insurance company on the bill.

- Service was not medically necessary.
  Solution: The problem may be that the diagnostic code does not properly support the procedural codes being reported. It is vital that the physician's documentation be specific enough to support the necessity of the services provided. If the physician believes the patient's condition was medically necessary, send an appeal for review to the insurance company, explaining in detail the reasons why. Otherwise, bill the patient, noting the insurance company's response on the statement. Make a list of codes that have been denied and if and how they were paid. Consider asking patients to sign a "Waiver of Liability" form—if payment is denied, then bill the patient.

- Service was for an injury that is being considered as compensable under workers' compensation.
  Solution: Locate the carrier for the industrial injury and send them a report of the case with a bill. Notify the patient's health insurance carrier monthly to let them know the status of the case.

- Service was not precertified for the surgery, hospitalization, or diagnostic procedure.
  Solution: Ask the patient to bring in his or her insurance policy for review to determine whether precertification was required for the service or whether any sanctions are imposed. If there were problems or difficulties about the case leading to why precertification was not obtained, write a letter of appeal.

When a claim is denied, notify patients by telephone or mail as soon as possible so that they keep well informed. Always retain the correspondence from the insurance company so it can be quickly retrieved in the event a patient inquires and has additional questions.

When a claim is denied, the recourse is to appeal and request a review in writing. In Medicare Part B hearing cases, carriers have been instructed to pay an appealed claim if the cost of the hearing process is more than the amount of the claim.

Remember, prevention measures to avoid denied claims are

1. Include progress notes and orders for tests for extended hospital services.
2. When ambulance transportation is used, include a letter from the prescribing physician documenting necessity.
3. Clarify the type of service (e.g., primary surgical services versus assist-at-surgery services).
4. Use modifiers to identify the exact service rendered.
5. Keep abreast of the latest policies for the Medicare, Medicaid, and CHAMPUS programs by reading local newsletters.
6. Obtain current provider manuals for Blue Cross and Blue Shield, Medicaid, Medicare, and CHAMPUS so these are available for quick reference. If bulletins or pages are received for these during the year, keep the manuals up-to-date by inserting the current material.

DOWN CODING

Lowered reimbursement is the result of down coding. As mentioned in Chapter 4, down coding occurs for several reasons. When the coding system used on a claim does not match the coding system used by the insurance carrier receiving the claim, computer software is designed to convert the code submitted to the nearest code in use. However, payment may be less. Down coding may also be due to insufficient diagnostic information on a claim.

Example: Maria Pironti undergoes surgery, a laparotomy, for diagnosis of abdominal pain. During surgery, a right ovarian cyst is discovered and removed. A second diagnosis is not listed on the claim.

When a more-extensive procedure is performed than that related to the operation, ask the physician whether more than one diagnosis is appropriate. Another reason for down coding is when too many diagnoses have the number "9" as the fourth or fifth digit. These codes indicate "unspecified" diagnoses. Routine use of too many nonspecific diagnostic codes results in denials or down coding, especially if extensive, or specific surgery is involved.

Solution: Monitor reimbursements and monitor down codes to discover which codes are affected. Then, telephone the insurance carrier and ask which code system is in use, obtain the book, and use the appropriate system.

Although Medicare is a federal program for seniors to receive uniform benefits, this is not always the case. Each fiscal intermediary prepares screening criteria within policies set by the Health Care Financing Administration to prevent overuse of certain diagnostic services. This causes variations in claims paid as well as claims being rejected. The variations can be caused by differences in medical practice, local population of patients, fraud, and differences in billing practices.

"I've got the papers to prove he's worth at least <u>twice</u> my bill..."

PARTIAL PAYMENT

If a check is received made out to both the physician and the hospital, call the insurance company and ask how much should be retained by the physician. Ask whose tax identification number will be used on the 1099 Form for reporting income to the Internal Revenue Service. The hospital's income should not be reflected on the physician's 1099 Form. To avoid another problem like this, inquire why the insurance company paid in this manner. Sometimes a participating agreement may exist that the physician did not know about.

If a claim is partially paid and the provider feels justified in requesting more payment, go through the review and appeal process mentioned at the end of this chapter.

PAYMENT PAID TO THE PATIENT

- Payment paid to patient. Sometimes, an insurance payment may be sent in error to the patient after an assignment of benefits has been signed and sent in with the insurance claim. In some cases, a clause may be in the insurance policy that payment may be made only to the insured.

  Solution: Call the insurance company to verify whether the payment was made and to whom. If the account is substantially overdue, ask for a copy of the endorsed check or EOB/RA statement that indicates where payment was sent. If the carrier refuses, ask for help from the supervisor of the provider or customer relations department. Call the patient explaining that the insurance company sent payment to him or her and ask when you can expect full payment. Document the commitment in the patient's financial record. If not able to reach the patient by telephone, send a letter by certified mail to the patient. If the patient still refuses to pay, inform the patient that the provider is forced to write off the debt, that the money is considered taxable income to the patient, and that you will report the undeclared income the patient received to the Internal Revenue Service on the 1099 form. This may assist in getting the debt paid.

TWO-PARTY CHECK

- Patient cashes a two-party check. An insurance company may issue a check made out to both the physician who provided care and the patient. Although not legal, the patient may be successful in cashing it without the endorsement of the physician.

Solution: Do not allow time to pass. Immediately advise the insurance company of the fraud so they can recover the money from whomever accepted the check without proper endorsement.

OVERPAYMENT

It is wise to develop an overpayment policy and procedure for each type of insurer, program, or managed care plan and for every type of overpayment situation that may occur. Scenarios that may occur are receiving more than your fee from an insurance carrier, receiving more than the contract rate from a managed care plan, receiving payments that should have been paid to the patient, receiving duplicate payments from two or more insurance carriers or from the patient and one or more third party payers, payment made for someone who is not the provider's patient, overpayments immediately discovered, overpayments called to your attention by the patient or insurance carrier, and overpayments not discovered for several months or years. In any type of overpayment problem, always cash the third party payer's check and make out a provider's refund check. In case of an audit, this establishes documentation showing that the problem has been resolved. If the patient pays and a third party pays and the overpayment must be refunded to the patient, always write a check—never refund in cash.

- Medicare. If you discover that an overpayment has been made, it is especially important to refund the money immediately. If it is not paid back, future claims may be held up and past claims may be reviewed. Check the billing and medical records to see whether the provider made any mistakes. If you feel an error has been made by the insurance carrier, send a letter with documentation to appeal and prove the provider's case.
- Commercial carriers. Usually a mistake made by a commercial carrier is the insurer's problem. If the provider is notified after 6 months to refund money, do not refund because trying to collect from the patient is almost impossible. If two or more insurance carriers send duplicate payments, write a letter to each explaining the situation and let them straighten it out. Then, send a refund to the correct insurance carrier after receiving a letter explaining who to refund the money to.
- Managed care plan. Develop a policy regarding overpayments and have it documented in the provider's contract. Allow the plan 60 days to audit their payments.

Rebilling

Generally, if a bill has not been paid, the physician rebills the patient every 30 days. However, there are many other instances for rebilling the insurance carrier, the patient, or both. If it is discovered that an error has been made in billing a case, send in a corrected billing and ask for an adjustment, or call the insurance company and ask the representative what to do. Some medical practices have found payment success in printing or stamping on insurance claims the statement:

"Unless this claim is paid or denied within 30 days, we will file a formal written complaint with the insurance commissioner."

To prevent having to rebill patients month after month, clearly identify that the insurance biller has submitted an insurance claim as well as what action is expected from the patient. Statements to patients may carry some of these notations:

"Your insurance carrier has been billed."

"Your insurance company has paid its share of your bill. This statement is for the amount payable directly by you."

"Your Medicare has been billed. This is for your information only."

"Your insurance has paid $________ for the above services. You are responsible for the copayment portion of $________."

CLAIM INQUIRIES

An inquiry, sometimes called a *tracer,* is made to an insurance company to locate the status of an insurance claim as a follow-up for something that is missing. As previously mentioned, claim status can be easily accessed via computer or teledigital response systems, thus speeding up inquiry time. Here are some reasons for making inquiries:

- Payment not received within the time limit for the plan or program.
- Carrier may be investigating a claim due to pre-existing conditions or possibly because the patient may have a work-related injury.

- Payment is received but the amount is incorrect.
- Payment is received but the amount allowed and the patient's responsibility are not defined.
- Payment received was for a patient not seen by the physician. It is possible to receive a payment check made out to a payee's name that is different from the patient's name. Making a call may quickly clarify whom the payment is for.

In addition to nonpayment or payment, there are other reasons for inquiries to an insurance company. These might include the following:

- EOB/RA shows that a professional or diagnostic code was changed from what was submitted.
- EOB/RA shows that the service was disallowed. The claim should be revised and resubmitted. Check to see whether the procedure codes were correct and that the services listed were described fully enough to justify the maximum allowable benefits.
- Error on the EOB/RA.
- Check received was made out to the wrong physician.

If any of these situations occur, inquire about the claim. Inquiries may be in writing or by telephone, depending on the case. If submitted in writing, some programs require special forms completed with a copy of the claim attached. Figure 8–3 is an example of a letter used when inquiring about a claim submitted to a managed care plan. If you need to have a claim reviewed after payment has been rendered, send in the letter as shown in Figure 8–4. When calling, document the name of the person spoken to and an outline of the conversation.

Review and Appeal Process

An *appeal* is a request for more payment by asking for a review of an insurance claim that has been inadequately or incorrectly paid or denied by an insurance company. Usually there is a time limit for appealing a claim, so it is important to know the variables for each plan or program. To find out this information, read the EOB/RA document or refer to provider manuals for the various programs.

There may be a discrepancy in the way the physician and insurance company interpret a coding guideline. If the provider determines that there is sufficient information to back up his or her claim, then do as follows:

- Send a letter explaining the reason why the provider does not agree with the claim denial listed on the EOB/RA or remittance advice.
- To back up the reason, abstract excerpts from the coding book and attach a photocopy of the article or pertinent information showing the name of the article, coding resource, and date of publication.
- Call the insurance company and speak to the individual responsible for appeals, explaining what you are trying to accomplish with the resubmission. Direct the correspondence to this person.
- Retain copies of the data for the physician's files.

If you win the appeal but must submit copies of the same documents each time this issue arises, ask the insurance carrier how future claims with the same issue may be handled.

If an appeal is not successful, the physician may want a peer review done. A *peer review* is a review done by a group of unbiased practicing physicians to judge the effectiveness and efficiency of professional care rendered. This group determines the payment for the case in question. Some insurance companies send a claim for peer review routinely for certain procedures that have been done for certain diagnoses.

An appeal would be filed in the following circumstances:

- Payment is denied and the reason for denial is not known.
- Payment is received but the amount is incorrect. Perhaps there was an excessive reduction in the allowed payment.
- Physician disagrees with the decision by the insurance carrier about a pre-existing condition.
- Unusual circumstances warranted medical treatments rendered that are not reflected in payment.
- Precertification was not obtained within contract provisions due to extenuating circumstances, and the claim was denied.
- Inadequate payment was received for a complicated procedure.

Appeals must be in writing, but some programs require special forms completed (see Fig. 8–4). Always send a copy of the original claim, EOB/RA, and any other documents to justify the appeal.

Remember, it is always important to keep track of the status after inquiry or appeal until payment for the case is resolved. Use the insurance claims register as shown in Chapter 3 or a separate active file labeled "Appeals Pending."

Cosmo Graff, M. D.
4567 Broad Avenue
Woodland Hills, CA 91364
213/486-9002

Committee on Physician's Services

Re: Underpayment
Identification No.: M 18876 782
Patient: Peaches Melba
Type of Service: Plastic & Rec. Surgery
Date of Service: 1-3-9X
Amount Paid: $ 75.00
My Fees: $180.00

Dear Sirs:

Herewith a request for a committee review of the above named case, since I consider the allowance paid very low having in mind the location, the extent, the type and the necessary surgical procedure performed: The skin graft, only one inch in diameter, included the lateral third of eyebrow and was full thickness to preserve hair follicles.

Operative report for the surgery has been sent to you with the claim.

Considering these points I hope that you will authorize additional payment in order to bring the total fee to a more reasonable amount.

Sincerely,

Cosmo Graff

Cosmo Graff, M. D.

mf

FIGURE 8-4
Appeal of Fee Reduction. This letter may be sent to an insurance company after payment has been received that the physician feels should be increased. This simple form requires little time and effort. It has helped physicians to win back many fee cuts made by insurers.

Additional information on tracing delinquent claims, appealing or reviewing a claim, or submitting a claim for a deceased patient can be found in the chapters on Medicaid, Medicare, CHAMPUS, and workers' compensation.

BLUE CROSS AND BLUE SHIELD REVIEW AND APPEAL PROCESS

The appeal procedure for the patient can be found in the Blue Plan coverage booklet. Most plans provide for an initial appeal by submitting a "Request for Administrative Review of Complaint" form that the patient may obtain by contacting the Member Services Department of his or her local Blue Plan. If the patient is not satisfied with the response, he or she may request an independent equity review by writing to the Blue Plan Consumer Affairs Department. Certain plans, such as employer-funded plans, may provide other appeal procedures. Appeals are normally resolved within 60 days. If additional time is needed, a written notification is sent to the patient. For complaints regarding health plans, the state insurance commissioner may be contacted. If the patient has a grievance against a health plan, he or she should first contact the plan and use the plan's grievance process.

CHAMPUS REVIEW AND APPEAL PROCESS

In the mid-1990s, the Defense Department's Coordinated Care Program was introduced nationwide and will replace some of the CHAMPUS test projects and special programs operating in specific areas. The appeals procedures applicable to such projects may vary from the procedures described here. For information on how to file reviews and appeals for test projects and special programs, ask the contracting insurance carrier for instructions and forms. Figure 8–5 shows an example of a form that may be used for inquiring about a CHAMPUS claim.

Three levels of review under CHAMPUS appeal procedures exist:

1. Reconsideration (conducted by the claims processor or other CHAMPUS contractor responsible for the decision in a particular case).
2. Formal review (conducted by CHAMPUS headquarters).
3. Hearing administered by CHAMPUS headquarters, but conducted by an independent hearing officer.

RECONSIDERATION

Participating providers may appeal certain decisions made by CHAMPUS, requesting reconsideration. Providers who do not participate may not appeal, but CHAMPUS patients and parents or guardians of patients under 18 years of age may file appeals. Providers who do not participate may not receive any information regarding a particular claim without the signed authorization of the patient or the patient's parent or guardian.

Appealable matters include the following:

1. Denials or partial denials of requests for preauthorization for certain services or supplies.
2. Notification that CHAMPUS will not pay for services after a certain date.
3. Disagreements regarding medical necessity, inappropriate care, level of care, investigational procedures.

Nonappealable matters include the following:

1. A specific exclusion of law or regulation.
2. Allowable charges for particular services.
3. Decisions by the claims processor to ask for additional information on a particular case.

The CHAMPUS department handling appeals collects and aggregates all information necessary to review the case effectively. Usually a determination decision is made within 60 days from receipt of the appeal. Disagreements regarding the amount allowed for a particular claim may be reviewed by the claims processor to determine whether it was calculated correctly. However, an individual cannot appeal the amount that the CHAMPUS contractor determines to be the allowable charge for a certain medical service.

Requests must be sent to the claims processor of the state in which services were provided and must be postmarked within 90 days of the date the provider receives the EOB/RA. Include photocopies of the claim, EOB/RA, and other supporting documents with the request form or letter. The claim identification number assigned by the claims processor should be included in any inquiry concerning payment of the claim. If CHAMPUS denies the initial request, then the other two levels of review, formal review and hearing, may be pursued.

Formal Review

A formal review must be done within 60 days from the date on the reconsideration decision notice. Include photocopies of the notice as well as any other information or documents to support why there is a disagreement in the CHAMPUS decision. The case will be reviewed again and a formal review decision will be issued. If the amount in dispute is less than $300, the formal review decision is final.

Hearing

If the amount in dispute is $300 or more, an independent hearing may be pursued. The request must be postmarked or received within 60 days from the date of the formal review decision. A hearing is conducted by an independent hearing officer, at a location convenient to both the requesting party and the government.

MEDICARE REVIEW AND APPEAL PROCESS

After payment or denial, a physician or beneficiary has the right to appeal a claim. The Medicare

CHAMPUS CLAIM INQUIRY

Date: ____________________

TO: CHAMPUS
Address of fiscal intermediary
City, State, Zip code

FROM: Provider's name
Address
City, State, Zip code

Telephone number
Fax number

RE: Sponsor's Social Security Number ____________________
Sponsor's Name ____________________
Patient's Name ____________________
Patient's Mailing Address:

____
Street City State Zip code

Dates of service of claim: ____________________
Total charges billed on claim: ____________________
Claim number that appears on CHAMPUS Explanation of Benefits (leave blank if the claim has not been paid and information is not available) ____________________

A. ________ I have submitted a claim, but have not received any payment or other notification from you.

B. ________ I have received notification or payment concerning the claim, but feel it may have been processed incorrectly.

C. ________ Deductible Status. Please confirm that individual and family deductibles have been applied correctly.

D. ________ Coverage for this patient is under
__________CHAMPUS __________CHAMPVA

E. ________ Additional information or explanation which will assist reviewing or processing the claim is attached to this letter or written in this area.

FIGURE 8-5
Example of a CHAMPUS claim inquiry form that may be completed to obtain a quick reply. Mail to the CHAMPUS fiscal intermediary for your region.

8

program has six levels and special guidelines for appealing. The levels are

- Inquiry
- Review
- Fair hearing
- Administrative law judge (ALJ) hearing
- Appeals council review
- Federal district court hearing

Table 8–2 illustrates the Medicare Part B appeals process.

Inquiry

If the claim was denied because of a simple error made by the insurance biller, such as omission of the National Provider Identifier (NPI) of the referring physician or a failure to code a diagnosis, then resubmit a corrected claim including only the denied services. In the event the insurance carrier made an error—for example, a procedure code was different from what was submitted or the date of service was entered incorrectly from the paper claim into the carrier's computer—then resubmit the claim with an attachment explaining the error. If response to the resubmission is that the claim has been "processed" previously, then go to the next appeal level.

Review

When a claim is assigned, the physician may ask for a review. The request must be within 6 months from the date of the original determination shown on the RA. Figure 8–6 shows Form HCFA-1964, which may be used in requesting a review of Medicare Part B claims. However, some carriers have developed their own request forms. Contact the carrier to find out the form required. Review the RA for the denial code or narrative stating why the claim has been denied. Check the claim for accuracy of ICD-9-CM, HCPCS, or CPT codes or missing modifiers as well as any other item that might be incorrect or missing.

If you are developing a form on the physician's letterhead, it must include the following information:

1. Current date
2. Medicare provider number
3. RA number or claim number
4. Date of RA
5. Patient's name
6. Patient's health insurance claim number (HICN)
7. Date of service
8. Place of service
9. Procedure code(s)
10. Amount billed
11. Amount approved
12. Amount paid
13. Denial reason (action code description from the RA)
14. Brief statement of why service should be reviewed.

With the review request, attach the following:

15. Copy of the original insurance claim

TABLE 8–2
Medicare Part B Appeals Process

Inquiry	Resubmit the claim	
Request for review	Time limit	6 months
	Amount in controversy	None
	Jurisdiction	Carrier
	Form	HCFA 1964
Fair hearing	Time limit	6 months
and	Amount in controversy	$100 for Hearing Officer or $500 for Administrative Law Judge (ALJ)
Administrative law judge hearing	Jurisdiction	Carrier (if less than $500) or Social Security's Bureau of Hearings and Appeals (BHA) (if more than $500)
	Form	HCFA 1965
Appeals council review	Time limit	60 days
	Amount in controversy	$500
	Jurisdiction	Bureau of Hearings and Appeals
	Form	HA 520
Judicial review (federal court system)	Time limit	60 days
	Amount in controversy	$1,000
	Jurisdiction	U.S. District Court

DEPARTMENT OF HEALTH AND HUMAN SERVICES
HEALTH CARE FINANCING ADMINISTRATION

Form Approved
OMB No. 0938-0033

REQUEST FOR REVIEW OF PART B MEDICARE CLAIM
Medical Insurance Benefits - Social Security Act

NOTICE—Anyone who misrepresents or falsifies essential information requested by this form may upon conviction be subject to fine and imprisonment under Federal Law.

1 Carrier's Name and Address	2 Name of Patient
	3 Health Insurance Claim Number

4 I do not agree with the determination you made on my claim as described on my Explanation of Medicare Benefits dated:

5 MY REASONS ARE: (Attach a copy of the Explanation of Medicare Benefits, or describe the service, date of service, and physician's name—NOTE.—If the date on the Notice of Benefits mentioned in item 3 is more than six months ago, include your reason for not making this request earlier.)

6 Describe Illness or Injury:

7 ☐ I have additional evidence to submit. (Attach such evidence to this form.)

☐ I do not have additional evidence.

COMPLETE ALL OF THE INFORMATION REQUESTED. SIGN AND RETURN THE FIRST COPY AND ANY ATTACHMENTS TO THE CARRIER NAMED ABOVE. IF YOU NEED HELP, TAKE THIS AND YOUR NOTICE FROM THE CARRIER TO A SOCIAL SECURITY OFFICE, OR TO THE CARRIER. KEEP THE DUPLICATE COPY OF THIS FORM FOR YOUR RECORDS.

8 SIGNATURE OF **EITHER** THE CLAIMENT **OR** HIS REPRESENTATIVE

Representative		Claimant	
Address		Address	
City, State, and ZIP Code		City, State, and ZIP Code	
Telephone Number	Date	Telephone Number	Date

Form HCFA-1964 (8-85)

(over)

CARRIER'S COPY

FIGURE 8–6
Request for Review of Part B Medicare Claim Form HCFA-1964. This form can be used by the Medicare beneficiary and/or physician when requesting a review of a submitted claim.

16. Copy of the RA showing the denial
17. Photocopy of other documents, such as operative or pathology report or detailed summary about the procedure with appropriate words highlighted to help the reviewer
18. Cover letter explaining the procedure, indicating justification for the services and why the provider should receive more reimbursement. Include the physician's NPI in the letter (Fig. 8–7)

Physician's Letterhead

January 2, 199x

Committee on Physician's Services
Medicare
Street address of fiscal intermediary
City, State, ZIP Code

Dear Madam or Sir:

Re: Underpayment

Identification No.:	1910-2192283-101
Patient:	Mrs. Sarah C. Nile
Type of Service:	Exploratory laparotomy
Date of Service:	December 1, 199x
Amount Paid:	$000.00
My Fees:	$000.00

Herewith a request for a Committee Review of the above-named case, since I consider the allowance paid very low having in mind the location, the extent, the type, and the necessary surgical procedure performed.

Enclosed is a photocopy of the operative report, the Medicare Remittance Advice, and the Medicare HCFA-1500 claim originally submitted.

Considering these points, I hope that you will authorize additional payment in order to bring the total fee to a more reasonable amount.

Sincerely,

Hugh R. Aged, M. D.

mf

Enclosures (3)

FIGURE 8–7
Example of a cover letter for a Medicare review request to be sent with photocopies of documents pertinent to a claim.

Mail the documents by certified mail with return receipt requested, and retain copies of all documents sent to the carrier in the provider's pending file.

If a claim is unassigned, the beneficiary can pursue the review or appoint the physician as an authorized representative. The patient completes forms HCFA-1964 and SSA-1696 (Fig. 8–8) and obtains the physician's acceptance signature. Decisions on unassigned claims are sent to the patient.

Send the request to the review department. Most insurance carriers have an address or post office box for review requests that is different from initial claim submissions, so be sure to send it to a correct current address. A review is usually completed by the insurance carrier within 30 to 45 days. Make a follow-up inquiry if no response is received in that time frame.

If certain procedures are consistently denied, ask the carrier what information is necessary to process the claim. If the provider is not satisfied with the results of the review, move to the next level and request a fair hearing.

Fair Hearing

If the physician feels the review is unfair and wishes to request a hearing, obtain and complete the HCFA-1965 form, Request for Hearing Part B Medicare Claim (Fig. 8–9) from either the Medicare carrier or local Social Security office. Two conditions must be met to proceed to this level.

- A fair hearing must be requested with 6 months from the date of the Medicare review determination letter.
- The amount in controversy (AIC) must be at least $100. This amount may represent a single claim or a combination of several smaller claims involving common billing issues.

The request for an appeal must include the patient's name, Medicare health insurance card number, all carrier control numbers involved, date of review determination, NPI, reason for requesting the hearing, and type of hearing (in-person, by telephone, or on-the-record). Address the request to the fair hearing officer (FHO) in care of the Medicare fiscal agent. The mailing address of the hearing is usually different from the review request address. The provider may request that a physician of his or her specialty review the case to offer advice or opinion to the FHO.

An acknowledgement should be received within 10 days, and the provider may either attend the hearing or waive the right to appear. When choosing the latter, inform the FHO in writing and enclose any additional documents that should be considered at the hearing. The FHO will send a written decision based on Medicare regulations, which may be full reversal of the initial claim ruling; adjustment of the review level decision giving more reimbursement; or denied. If not satisfied, proceed to the next level.

Administrative Law Judge Hearing

A request for a hearing before an administrative law judge (ALJ) may be made if the amount still in question is $500 or more (usually in combined claims). The request must be made within 60 days of receiving the FHO's decision. It may take 18 months to receive an ALJ assignment. Proof that this is an unusual case and warrants special consideration may lead to a successful conclusion. However, the decision might be reversed, might allow partial adjustment of the carrier's payment, or might deny payment. If the final judgment is not satisfactory, then proceed to the next level.

Appeals Council Review

The Appeals Council is part of the Office of Hearings and Appeals of the Social Security Administration. A request must be made within 60 days of the ALJ decision. Or, if there is a question that the final judgment was not made in accordance with the law, the council by its own election may review the ALJ decision. If the council denies a review, the provider may file a civil action for a federal district court hearing.

Federal District Court Hearing

At this highest level, the amount in controversy must be $1,000 or more, and an attorney must be hired to represent the provider and manage the case. The case may be filed where the physician's business is located. Contact the local medical society for suggestions of names of attorneys experienced at this level of the appeals process.

HCFA Regional Offices

One final suggestion, and this can be done with steps for a hearing or a review, is to write or telephone the medical director at one of the ten HCFA regional offices. Sometimes a regional officer will intercede or take steps to correct problems or inequities. HCFA regional office addresses with the states they serve are listed on page 199.

DEPARTMENT OF
HEALTH AND HUMAN SERVICES
SOCIAL SECURITY ADMINISTRATION

NAME (Claimant) (Print or Type)	SOCIAL SECURITY NUMBER
WAGE EARNER (if different)	SOCIAL SECURITY NUMBER

Section I APPOINTMENT OF REPRESENTATIVE

I appoint this individual ______________________________
(Name and Address)

to act as my representative in connection with my claim or asserted right under:

☐ Title II (RSDI) ☐ Title XVI (SSI) ☐ Title IV FMSHA (Black Lung) ☐ Title XVIII (Medicare Coverage)

I authorize this individual to make or give any request or notice; to present or elicit evidence; to obtain information; and tu receive any notice in connection with my pending claim or asserted right wholly in my stead.

SIGNATURE (Claimant)	ADDRESS
TELEPHONE NUMBER (Area Code)	DATE

Section II ACCEPTANCE OF APPOINTMENT

I, ______________________________, hereby accept the above appointment. I certify that I have not been suspended or prohibited from practice before the Social Security Administration; that I am not, as a current or former officer or employee of the United States, disqualified from acting as the claimant's representative; and that I will not charge or receive any fee for the representation unless it has been authorized in accordance with the laws and regulations referred to on the reverse side hereof. In the event that I decide not to charge or collect a fee for the representation, I will notify the Social Security Administration. (Completion of Section III satisfies this requirement.)

I am a / an ______________________________
(Attorney, union representative, relative, law student, etc.)

SIGNATURE (Representative)	ADDRESS
TELEPHONE NUMBER (Area code)	DATE

Section III (Optional) WAIVER OF FEE

I waive my right to charge and collect a fee under Section 206 of the Social Security Act, and I release my client (the claimant) from any obligations, contractual or otherwise, which may be owed to me for services I have performed in connection with my client's claim or asserted right.

SIGNATURE (Representative)	DATE

WAIVER OF DIRECT PAYMENT

I ONLY waive my right to direct certification of a fee from the withheld past-due benefits of my client (the claimant). I do NOT, however, waive my right to petition for and be authorized to charge and collect a fee directly from my client.

SIGNATURE (Representative)	DATE

Form **SSA-1696-U4** (3-88) *(See Important Information on Reverse)* FILE COPY

FIGURE 8–8
Form SSA-1696-U4 completed by a Medicare patient appointing the physician as his or her authorized representative.

HOW TO COMPLETE THIS FORM

Print or type your full name and your Social Security number.

Section I—APPOINTMENT OF REPRESENTATIVE

You may appoint as your representative an attorney or any other qualified individual. You may appoint more than one person, but see "The Fee You Owe The Representative(s)." You may NOT appoint as your representative an organization, the law firm, a group, etc. Example, you go to a law firm or legal aid group for help with your claim, you may appoint any attorney or other qualified individual from that firm or group, but NOT the firm or group itself.

Check the block(s) for the program in which you have a claim. Title II, check if your claim concerns disability or retirement benefits, etc. Title XVI, check if the claim concerns Supplemental Security Income (SSI) payments. Title IV FMSHS (Federal Mine Safety and Health Act), check if the claim is for black lung benefits. Title XVIII, check only in connection with a proceeding before the Social Security Administration involving entitlement to medicare coverage or enrollment in the supplementary medical insurance plan (SMIP). More than one block may be checked.

Section II—ACCEPTANCE OF APPOINTMENT

The individual whom you appoint in Section I above, completes this part. Completion of this section is desirable in all cases, but it is mandatory only if the appointed individual is not an attorney.

Section III—WAIVER OF FEE

This section may be completed by your representative if he/she will not charge any fee for services performed in this claim. If you had appointed a co-counsel (second representative) in Section I and he/she will also not charge you a fee, then the cocounsel should also sign this section or give a separate waiver statement.

GENERAL INFORMATION

1. When you have a representative:

   We will deal directly with your representative on all matters that affect your claim. Occasionally, with the permission of your representative, we may deal directly with you on the specific issues. We will rely on your representative to keep you informed on the status of your claim, but you may contact us directly for any information about your claim.

2. The authority of your representative:

   Your representative has the authority to act totally on your behalf. This means he/she can (1) obtain information about your claim the same as you; (2) submit evidence: (3) make statements about facts and provisions of the law; and (4) make any request (including a fee request). It is important, therefore, that you are represented by a qualified individual.

3. When will the representation stop:

   We will stop recognizing or dealing with your representative when (1) you tell us that he/she is no longer your representative; (2) your representative does any one of the following; (a) submits a fee petition, or (b) tells us that he/she is with-drawing from the claim, or (c) he/she violates any of our rules and regulations, and a hearing is held before an administrative law judge (designated as hearing officer) who orders your representative disqualified or suspended as representative of any Social Security claimant.

4. The fee you owe the representative(s):

   Every representative you appoint has a right to petition for a fee. To charge you a fee, a representative must first file a fee petition with us. Irrespective of your fee agreement, you never owe more than the fee we have authorized in a written notice to you and representative(s). (Out-of-pocket expenses are not included). If your claim went to court, you may owe an additional fee for your representative's service before the court.

5. How we determine the fee:

   We use the criteria on the back of the fee petition (Form SSA 1560-U4), a copy of which your representative must send you.

6. Review of the fee authorization:

   If you or your representative disagrees with the fee authorization, either of you may request a review. Instructions for filings this review are on the fee authorization notice.

7. Payment of fees:

   If past-due benefits are payable in your claim, we generally withhold 25 percent of the past-due benefits toward possible attorney fees. If no past-due benefits are payable or this an SSI claim, then payment of the fee we have authorized is your responsibility.

8. Penalty for charging an unauthorized fee:

   If your representative wants to charge and collect from you a fee that is greater than what we had authorized, then he/she is in violation of the law and regulations. Promptly report this to your nearest Social Security office.

Form **SSA-1696-U4** (3-88)

FIGURE 8–8 *Continued*

8

DEPARTMENT OF HEALTH AND HUMAN SERVICES
HEALTH CARE FINANCING ADMINISTRATION

Form Approved
OMB No. 0938-0034

REQUEST FOR HEARING - PART B MEDICARE CLAIM

Medical Insurance Benefits - Social Security Act

NOTICE—Anyone who misrepresents or falsifies essential information requested by this form may upon conviction be subject to fine and imprisonment under Federal Law.

Carrier's Name and Address	**1** Name of Patient
	2 Health Insurance Claim Number

3 I disagree with the review determination on my claim, and request a hearing before a hearing officer of the insurance carrier named above.
MY REASONS ARE: *(Attach a copy of the Review Notice. NOTE.—If the review decision was made more than 6 months ago include your reason for not making this request earlier)*

4 Check one of the Following:

☐ I have additional evidence to submit. *(Attach such evidence to this form or forward it to the carrier within 10 days.)*

☐ I do not have additional evidence.

Check Only One of the Statements Below:

☐ I wish to appear in person before the Hearing Officer.

☐ I do not wish to appear and hereby request a decision on the evidence before the Hearing Officer.

5 EITHER THE CLAIMANT OR REPRESENTATIVE SHOULD SIGN IN THE APPROPRIATE SPACE BELOW:

Signature or Name of Claimant's Representative ➡		Claimant's Signature ➡	
Address		Address	
City, State, and ZIP Code		City, State, and ZIP Code	
Telephone Number	Date	Telephone Number	Date

(Claimant should not write below this line)

ACKNOWLEDGMENT OF REQUEST FOR HEARING

Your request for a hearing was received on ______________________. You will be notified of the time and place of the hearing at least 10 days before the date of the hearing.

Signed	Date

Form **HCFA-1965** (8-79)

CARRIER COPY

FIGURE 8–9
Request for Hearing—Part B Medicare Claim Form HCFA-1965.

HCFA REGIONAL OFFICES

REGION I—BOSTON

Connecticut, Maine, Massachusetts, New Hampshire, Rhode Island, and Vermont

Associate Regional Administrator,
HCFA Program Operations
John F. Kennedy Federal Building
Government Center
Boston, Massachusetts 02203

REGION II—NEW YORK

New Jersey, New York, Puerto Rico, and Virgin Islands

Associate Regional Administrator,
HCFA Program Operations
Jacob K. Javits Federal Building
26 Federal Plaza
New York, New York 10278

REGION III—PHILADELPHIA

Delaware, District of Columbia, Maryland, Pennsylvania, Virginia, and West Virginia

Associate Regional Administrator,
HCFA Medicare
3535 Market Street
P.O. Box 7760
Philadelphia, Pennsylvania 19101

REGION IV—ATLANTA

Alabama, Florida, Georgia, Kentucky, Mississippi, North Carolina, South Carolina, and Tennessee

Associate Regional Administrator,
HCFA Program Operations
101 Marietta Tower
Atlanta, Georgia 30323

REGION V—CHICAGO

Illinois, Indiana, Michigan, Minnesota, Ohio, and Wisconsin

HCFA Program Operations
105 West Adams Street
15th Floor
Chicago, Illinois 60603-6201

REGION VI—DALLAS

Arkansas, Louisiana, New Mexico, Oklahoma, and Texas

Associate Regional Administrator,
HCFA Program Operations
1200 Main Tower
Dallas, Texas 75202

REGION VII—KANSAS CITY

Iowa, Kansas, Missouri, and Nebraska

Associate Regional Administrator,
HCFA Program Operations
601 East 12th Street, Room 242
Kansas City, Missouri 64106

REGION VIII—DENVER

Colorado, Montana, North Dakota, South Dakota, Utah, and Wyoming

Associate Regional Administrator,
HCFA Medicare
19th and Stout Streets, Room 1185
Denver, Colorado 80294

REGION IX—SAN FRANCISCO

Arizona, California, Nevada, Guam, Hawaii, and American Samoa

Associate Regional Administrator,
HCFA Program Operations
Federal Office Building
75 Hawthorne Street, 4th Floor
San Francisco, California 94105

REGION X—SEATTLE

Alaska, Idaho, Oregon, and Washington

HCFA Program Operations
2201 Sixth Avenue
Mail Stop RX-42
Seattle, Washington 98121

MEDIGAP

Only the state insurance commissioner can exert pressure on Medigap insurance companies. Insurance companies that sell Medigap policies must be certified before being allowed to sell in each state. The certification can be lifted from any insurer that does not honor its contract agreements. If payment is slow in coming in or is not received from a Medigap insurer, tell the insurer, "If I do not receive payment, I will have no alternative but to contact the state insurance commissioner."

Document complete follow-up information on each Medigap insurer (firm name, address, telephone number, and policy numbers of every patient seen).

TO THE STUDENT

Study Chapter 8 and then answer the review questions in the *Workbook* to reinforce the theory learned in this chapter of the text and to help prepare you for a future test. Refer to Assignments 24 through 26 to complete a form for tracing a delinquent claim, to locate errors on returned claims, and to complete a form to appeal a Medicare case. For further knowledge and understanding, the key terms at the beginning of the chapter appear in the Glossary at the end of this textbook so you can look up the pertinent terms.

UNIT 3

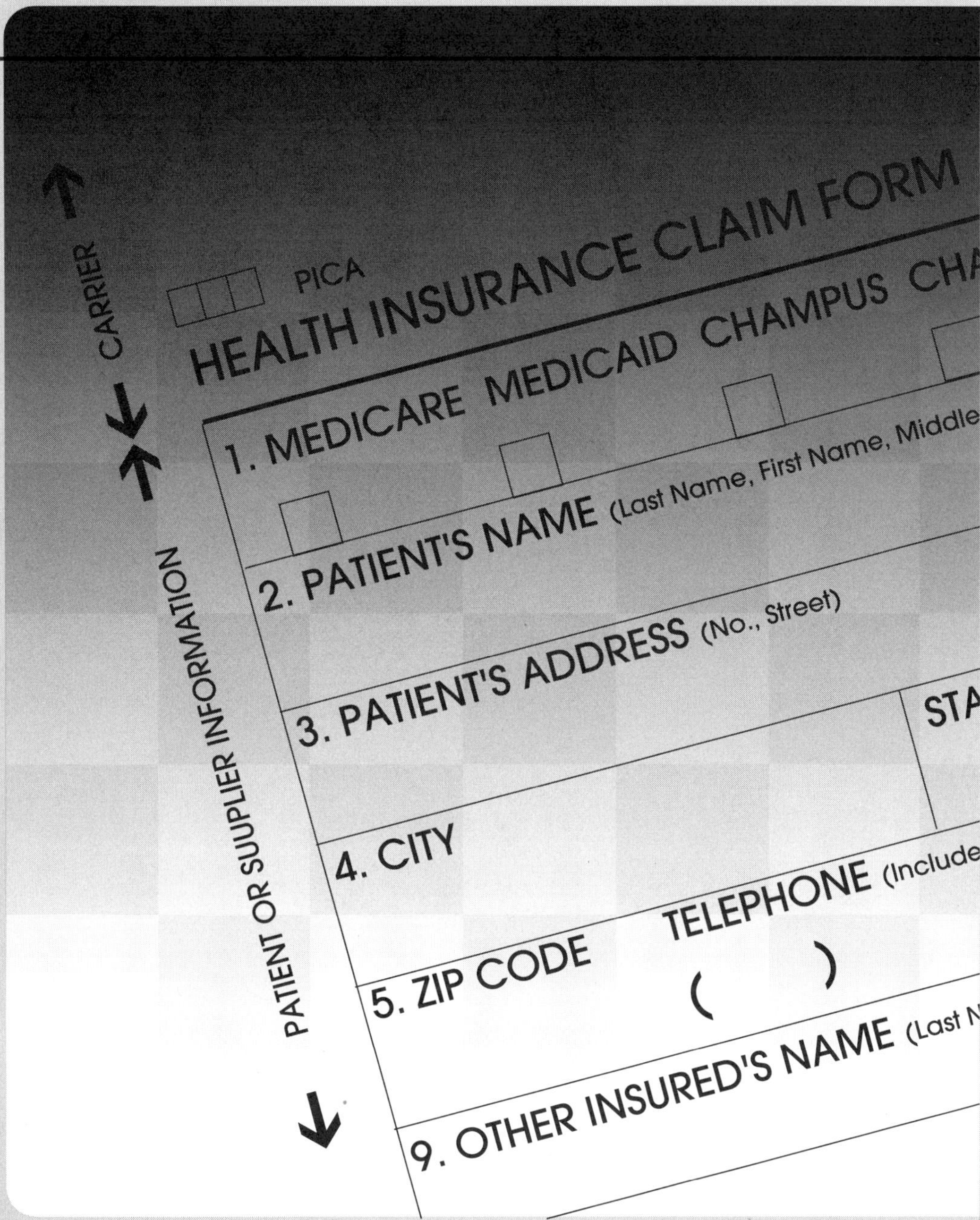

Health Care Payers

Objectives*

THE INSURANCE BILLING SPECIALIST WILL BE ABLE TO:

- Define a prepaid health plan (PHP).
- Identify types of prepaid health plans.
- Understand two different operations of foundations.
- Define the Health Maintenance Organization Act of 1973.
- Explain health maintenance organization benefits and eligibility requirements.
- State reasons for professional review organizations.
- Explain how managed care plans work with the Blue Plans, CHAMPUS, Medicaid, and Medicare.
- Define independent practice associations.
- Define preferred provider organizations.
- Explain an optometric service plan and its benefits.

Key Terms

ancillary services
buffing
capitated payment
capitation
churning
claims-review type of foundation
closed panel program
comprehensive type of foundation
copayment (copay)
deductible
disenrollment
encounter record
fee for service
foundations for medical care
gatekeeper
group model
health maintenance organization (HMO)
in-area
individual or independent practice association (IPA)
individual responsibility program (IRP)
managed care organization (MCO)
managed care system (MCS)
optometric service plan
out-of-area
participating physician
physician provider group (PPG)
point-of-service (POS) plan
preferred provider organization (PPO)
prepaid group practice plan
prepaid health plan (PHP)
primary care physician (PCP)
quality assurance
service area
staff model
stop-loss
tertiary care
turfing
utilization review (UR)
withhold

* Performance objectives and exercises for hands-on practical experience for this chapter appear in the *Workbook*.

CHAPTER 9

Managed Care Systems and Special Plans

History

PREPAID GROUP PRACTICE HEALTH PLANS

The *Ross-Loos Medical Group* in Los Angeles was America's oldest privately owned, prepaid medical group. It was founded in 1929 by Dr. Donald E. Ross and Dr. H. Clifford Loos and existed only in Southern California, where it expanded to 17 medical group locations. In 1975, the Ross-Loos Medical Group formed a corporation and received a federal grant to develop a health care system under the federal Health Maintenance Organization Act of 1973. In 1980, INA Healthplan, Inc., of Philadelphia merged with Ross-Loos. Ross-Loos is now known as *CIGNA Healthplans of California.*

Most CIGNA patients are served under a prepayment group plan by which they pay a monthly premium and receive hospital, surgical, and professional benefits from a CIGNA staff physician or CIGNA Health Care Center. Several thousand other CIGNA patients are private and are treated on a fee-for-service basis. In the case of an emergency when the patient is outside the area of a CIGNA Health Care Center, he or she may seek professional or hospital care in other facilities, but CIGNA must be notified as soon as possible. A dental plan and Medicare supplemental plan are also available through CIGNA.

Another pioneer of the prepaid group practice concept is the *Kaiser Permanente Medical Care Program.* It began in 1933, when Dr. Sidney R. Garfield and a few physicians working for him gave combined industrial accident and personal medical care to approximately 5000 workers building a fresh-water aqueduct across the California desert to Los Angeles. Dr. Garfield charged the insurance carriers $1.50 per man per month and the workers 5 cents a day. In return, he provided comprehensive health care. Then, in 1938, Henry J. Kaiser and his son, Edgar, started a joint venture to complete the Grand Coulee Dam in Washington and invited Dr. Garfield to form a medical group to furnish care to the workers for 7 cents a day prepaid by the employer. The group expanded to include the workers' wives and children.

Kaiser Permanente now has centers in 12 regions covering 16 states. Patients are served under a prepayment group plan and receive hospital, surgical, and professional benefits from physicians located at the Kaiser Permanente Medical Care Centers. In January 1994, Kaiser Permanente announced a venture with Pacific Mutual Life Insurance Company to give Kaiser's 4.6 million California patients the option of using physicians and medical facilities outside the vast Kaiser network. This is the first time that Kaiser has allowed all members of its two California health maintenance organizations to seek medical help from non-Kaiser physicians and is termed a *point of service* (POS) option.

Kaiser does not provide care on a fee-for-service or a cost-reimbursement basis. In emergency situations when patients are out of reach of a Kaiser Center, they may seek the services of outside facilities or physicians. The Kaiser Permanente Medical Plan is a *closed panel program,* which means it limits the patient's choice of personal physicians (a multispecialty medical group) to those practicing in one of the 12 geographic regions previously mentioned.

Health Maintenance Organization Act of 1973

In 1973, Congress passed the Health Maintenance Organization Act of 1973 (Public Law 93-222), creating authority for the federal government to assist health maintenance organization (HMO) development in a number of ways, including (1) providing grants, loans, and loan guarantees to offset the initial operating deficits of new HMOs that meet federal standards (i.e., are federally qualified) and (2) requiring most employers to offer the HMO to their employees as an alternative to traditional health insurance.

Basically, an HMO is a prepaid group practice that can be sponsored and operated by the government, medical schools, clinics, foundations, hospitals, employers, labor unions, community or consumer groups, insurance companies, the Blue Plans, hospital-medical plans, or the Veterans Administration.

Benefits

Benefits under the HMO Act fall under two categories: basic and supplemental health service, which are listed in the box.

HMO ACT BENEFITS

BASIC HEALTH SERVICES

- Physicians' services and consultant or referral services without time or cost limits
- Inpatient and outpatient hospital services
- Emergency health services in or out of the HMO service area
- Short-term (not to exceed 20 visits) ambulatory, evaluative, and crisis intervention mental health services on an outpatient basis
- Alcohol and drug abuse and addiction medical treatment
- Diagnostic laboratory and x-ray services and therapeutic radiology services
- Home health services
- Preventive health services (physical examinations for adults, vision and hearing tests for children through age 17 years, well-baby care, immunizations, health education, and so on)
- Family planning and infertility services
- Preventive dental services for children under age 12 years
- Health education and medical social services

SUPPLEMENTAL HEALTH SERVICES

- Prescription drugs
- Intermediate and long-term care (skilled care facilities and nursing homes)
- Long-term physical medicine and rehabilitative services, such as physical therapy
- Adult eye examinations
- Dental care and extended mental health services not included in basic benefits

Eligibility

Those who have voluntarily enrolled in the plan from a specific geographic area *("in-area")* or who are covered by an employer who has paid an established sum per person to be covered by the plan are eligible. The law states that an employer employing 25 or more persons may offer the services of an HMO clinic as an alternative health treatment plan for employees. Medicare and Medicaid beneficiaries may also join. The federal government reimburses the HMOs on a per capita basis, depending on the size of the enrollment. This means that a fixed amount is paid per month per patient, for which the patient is entitled to receive the prescribed benefits.

To qualify as an HMO, an organization must present proof of its ability to provide comprehensive health care. To retain eligibility, an HMO must render periodic performance reports to the offices of the Department of Health and Human Services. Thus, accurate and complete medical records are imperative to the survival and cost control of an HMO.

HEALTH CARE REFORM

Over the past 60 years, leaders of the United States from Presidents Roosevelt to Nixon have announced reforms of the health care system. Medical practices have made a transition from rural to urban, from generalist to specialist, from solo to group practice, from direct payment to a fee-for-service basis, including group or individual insurance, to a number of systems of health care delivery that try to manage the cost of health care. *Fee for service* was the usual method of billing by physicians in private practice. In other words, the professional service was rendered by the physician to the patient, and the physician expected to receive a fee at the time of the service. Indemnity insurance plans meant the subscriber could choose his or her physician or clinic, and the plan generally reimbursed 80% of the billed fees.

However, this scenario is changing. This chapter defines and explains the health care reforms of the past and present. In addition to HMOs, other types of *prepaid group practice plans* (prepaid health plans) are discussed that use a managed care approach (managed care system). Patients pay monthly medical insurance premiums through their employer or individually, the physician renders service to the patient, and the patient either does not pay any additional monies to the physician for the service or pays copayments and deductibles as required by the plan.

During the 1990s, a major restructuring of the United States health care system was needed because

- A growing percentage of Americans were not covered by private or government insurance.
- Employers were having to pay escalating health care premiums and did not want to cut wages. They wanted methods to decrease the cost of employee health care, thereby freeing more monies for research and development.
- The government needed to reduce the deficit by keeping down increases in the Medicare and Medicaid programs. This would also free some funds for other domestic problems.
- Physicians and hospital costs were soaring with no end in sight due to inflation, high-tech equipment, expensive medications, and so on. Patients were spending more and more money for less and less care and coping with a system riddled with inefficiency and fraud.

In the past decade, integrated health care delivery systems have formed in many states to reduce costs, i.e., managed care organizations (MCOs), physician-hospital organizations, and group practices without walls. These systems allow for better negotiations for contracts with large employers and managed care plans, as well as with suppliers for discounts. Each type of organization differs in ownership, purpose, governance, management, and type of services provided. Even before the government released its health care reform proposal, some states began establishing laws implementing managed care for the general populations as well as for Medicaid patients and those injured on the job (workers' compensation cases). Hawaii has had a statewide universal health insurance plan since 1974. In 1994, California put together a working alliance, the first in the nation, followed by Florida's voluntary purchasing group, the Community Health Purchasing Alliances. In California, the alliance is formally known as Health Insurance Plan of California. This allows firms with 5 to 50 workers to offer their employees a wide choice of different insurance programs. All plans must offer the same benefits, but some physicians and hospitals are more desirable than others. The company must pay an amount equal to at least half of the cost of the lowest-priced plan; the worker pays the remainder.

Many regions have large groups of Medicare-eligible people who have opted to belong to a health maintenance organization or other prepaid plan. In the future, it is foreseen that those on Medicaid, under age 65 years, and not receiving either Aid to Families with Dependent Children (AFDC) or Supplemental Security Income (SSI) will no longer be part of Medicaid. They might obtain their health

9

benefits like everyone else. AFDC and SSI recipients would be covered under the plans, but Medicaid would pay a capitated premium (payment per capita) to the alliance for each one. The recipient would pick a low-cost plan from the state alliance. Some states have pilot projects in certain communities to determine whether this is feasible for the entire state.

Managed Care Systems

HEALTH MAINTENANCE ORGANIZATIONS

The most popular of all the prepaid health plans are *health maintenance organizations* (HMOs). An HMO is a plan or program by which specified health services are rendered by participating physicians to an enrolled group of persons, with fixed periodic payments made in advance by or on behalf of each person or family. If a health insurance carrier is involved, it contracts to pay in advance for the full range of health services to which the insured is entitled under the terms of the health insurance contract.

Because of the increase in self-insured businesses and contracts that do not rely on prepayment, the definition of an HMO needs enhancing. Some HMO health plans withhold a percentage of the monthly capitation payment to physicians until the end of the year. This creates an incentive for limiting care by the gatekeeper to refer patients to specialists. If the physician or group of physicians exceeds utilization norms, then they do not receive it. They can cover all services or be specific to hospital care, laboratory/x-ray usages *(ancillary services)*, or specialty referrals. Some HMOs use primary care physicians as gatekeepers, whereas others do not. A *gatekeeper* is a physician who controls patient access to specialists.

Prepaid Group Practice Model ▪ There are important differences in the structure of different HMOs that influence the way physicians practice and, perhaps, the quality of medical care delivered. In Kaiser-Permanente and similar HMOs, physicians form an independent group (Permanente) and contract with a health plan (Kaiser) to provide medical treatment to members enrolled by the plans. Although the physicians work for a salary, it is paid by their own independent group, not by the administrators of the health plan. This is designed to permit the physicians to concentrate on medicine. Such a plan is called a *prepaid group practice model.* This HMO delivers services at one or more locations through a group of physicians who contract with the HMO to provide care or through its own physicians, who are employees of the HMO.

Staff Model ▪ A second type of HMO is the *staff model,* in which the health plan hires physicians directly and pays them a salary instead of contracting with a medical group.

Independent Practice Association ▪ The third type is the *independent* (or *individual) practice association* (IPA) or foundation model in which the physicians are not employees and are not paid salaries. Instead, they are paid fees for their services out of a fund drawn from the premiums collected by an organization that markets the health plan minus a discount of up to 30% withheld to cover operating deficits. At year's end, the physicians share in any surplus or pay part of any deficit. This risk-sharing incentive tends to keep medical costs down. An IPA makes contractual arrangements with physicians in the community, who treat HMO members out of their own offices. The physicians are paid on a per-patient basis as treatment is rendered. An IPA may not limit the number of participating physicians or restrict participating physicians to treating IPA patients only. See further discussion of this type of HMO in the next section.

Network HMO ▪ A fourth type is call a *network HMO,* which contracts with two or more group practices to provide health services.

For further information on HMOs, write to the Office of Health Maintenance Organizations.*

INDIVIDUAL (OR INDEPENDENT) PRACTICE ASSOCIATION (IPA)

This type of prepaid health plan is somewhat similar to an HMO. A group of physicians and sometimes other providers create a corporation to provide health care coverage for patients. The corporation collects a premium from the subscriber, union, or corporation. It then pays the physicians on a per-patient, fee-for-service basis. There is no limit on the number of participating physicians in the IPA. A participating physician may also treat non-IPA patients. A certain percentage is held out of the premium fund to pay for operating the IPA, and this is known as a *withhold.* If the budgeted services for the plan are not overused, the withhold plus interest is returned to the physician at the end of the plan year. However, if services are overutilized, the withhold is retained by the plan.

At the end of the year, the physicians share in any

*Health Care Financing Administration, Room 4360, Cohen Building, 330 Independence Avenue, S.W., Washington, D.C. 20201.

surplus or pay part of any deficit to keep the IPA running. This risk-sharing incentive tends to keep medical costs down. Unlike an HMO, an IPA does not have a central health care facility.

PREFERRED PROVIDER ORGANIZATIONS

A *preferred provider organization* (PPO) is a variation on the HMO theme. Like an HMO, a PPO contracts with a group of providers (designated as "preferred") to deliver care to members. Many of these plans are offered to employers for their employees. Unlike HMO members, PPO members have the freedom to choose any physician or hospital for services, but they receive a higher level of benefits if the preferred providers are used. There are usually copayments and deductibles, and claims have to be filed. Some PPOs pay 100% of the cost, but many do not. As with major medical policies, coinsurance requires the patient to pay 20 to 25% up to a certain point, and then the PPO pays 100% of the balance. Some PPOs may require predetermination of benefits, fee limits, quality control, and utilization review. Some hospital indemnity plans pay fixed fees for various services. If the charges are higher, the patient pays the difference.

If a plan says a test is not covered, bill the patient for it. However, inform the patient ahead of time about this cost. If a test is deemed "medically unnecessary" and the PPO denies payment, an appeal is necessary. The physician can present clinical reasons to the PPO's medical director for covering additional tests and expanding benefits for future patients.

Blue Cross/Blue Shield and Managed Care Programs

Preferred Provider Organizations

More than 76% of the United States population lives within the service areas of established Blue Cross and Blue Shield PPOs. Unlike most PPOs, which operate almost exclusively in urban areas, Blue Cross and Blue Shield PPOs serve suburban and rural as well as urban areas. Blue Cross and Blue Shield's national PPO program, Preferred Care USA, has 60 networks in 48 states, the District of Columbia, and Puerto Rico. It has over 17.5 million members, 480,000 participating physicians, and 3600 participating hospitals.

HMO Blue USA

The Blue Cross and Blue Shield HMO, HMO USA, is the largest HMO network in the country. It has more than 70 HMOs located in 43 states plus the District of Columbia, with almost 8.3 million members, 140,000 participating physicians, and 2200 participating hospitals.

Medicare Blue USA

Launched in 1996, Medicare Blue USA is a national network of Blue HMOs for medicare beneficiaries. One of its benefits is that it provides seniors with portable HMO out-of-area, managed care coverage nationally through the Away From Home Care^{SM} Program. This gives seniors access to hassle-free urgent and followup care, as well as access to the Guest Program, through the national Blue network when traveling away from home. The Guest Program enables a senior, who is residing in another geographic area from 30 days to 6 months, to register as a guest in an affiliate Medicare Blue USA HMO.

Point of Service Programs

In September 1996, Blue Shield of California introduced Access Plus, an HMO plan that allows patients to refer themselves to a specialist for a higher copayment. Many companies have a similar version for those that belong to point-of-service (POS) plans, but they are traditionally more expensive than HMOs.

9

CHAMPUS AND MANAGED CARE PROGRAMS

Beginning in January, 1988, CHAMPUS beneficiaries in California and Hawaii who were military retirees and their dependents had a choice of retaining their benefits under CHAMPUS or enrolling in a PPO called CHAMPUS Prime. Then, in January 1994, "TRICARE Standard" became the new terminology to be used for CHAMPUS Standard coverage (see Chapter 13). In addition, TRICARE Prime and TRICARE Extra made their appearance. CHAMPUS managed care programs continue to grow across the nation in other states (Illinois, Indiana, Maine, Massachusetts, Michigan, New Jersey, Pennsylvania) and may be known as CHAMPUS Prime or by both other names. TRICARE Prime is a health maintenance organization type of option. TRICARE Extra is a PPO type of option in which nonenrolled CHAMPUS-eligible beneficiaries may participate by seeking care from network providers. Those eligible for either of the two managed care programs are

- Dependents of active duty personnel
- Retirees and their dependents
- Dependents of active duty reservists (if called to duty for more than 30 days)
- Disabled beneficiaries under 65 years of age who have Medicare parts A and B and qualify under one of the above categories

A quality assurance program continually assesses the effectiveness of inpatient and outpatient care. The quality assurance department reviews providers' outpatient records on a random basis for clinical and administrative quality. Grievance procedures have been established for members and providers if any complaint arises from an administrative process, a service provided by a physician, or an issue involving quality of care. Through the appeal process, providers may request reconsideration of a denial of certification for coverage or of the amount paid for a submitted claim.

TRICARE Prime

A beneficiary must enroll for a minimum of 12 months and, once enrolled, may no longer use the TRICARE Standard program. The beneficiary selects a network provider (primary care manager) and must initiate all care through this provider except in an emergency. The beneficiary may not use a military treatment facility (MTF), NAVCARE or Primus clinic, except in emergencies and for pharmaceuticals, without completion of a referral from a Health Care Finder.

At *every* visit, in addition to checking the TRICARE Prime Member card, *always* check the military I.D. card for effective and expiration dates, make copies of the cards, and retain them in the patient's file. An illustration of the card is shown in Chapter 13, Figure 13–11. Always collect copayments at the time services are rendered. All admissions, ambulatory surgical procedures, and other selected procedures require precertification. Referral and precertification numbers are required claims information. Nonavailability Statements are required for certain inpatient and outpatient services if the beneficiary resides within the designated military treatment facility catchment area.

Additional benefits are available for preventive care, such as periodic physicals, immunizations, and annual eye examinations for dependent children of retirees. Providers must submit claims on HCFA-1500 forms. See Appendix A for the name and address of where to submit the claims and to obtain further information about this program.

TRICARE Extra

A nonenrolled CHAMPUS beneficiary wishing to use TRICARE Extra must receive care from an authorized network provider listed in the TRICARE Prime/TRICARE Extra directory. A nonenrolled beneficiary automatically becomes a TRICARE Extra beneficiary when care is rendered by a network provider. If a nonenrolled beneficiary receives care from a non-network provider, the services received are covered under TRICARE Standard. The military I.D. card indicates "Yes" in Box 15B (on the back side of the card) if the beneficiary is eligible. To verify eligibility, contact your local Health Care Finder for assistance. Beneficiaries using TRICARE Extra receive a reduction in the amount of copayment. Providers receive a contract rate for giving care.

There are certain referral and precertification requirements. All admissions, ambulatory surgical procedures, and other selected procedures require precertification. Nonavailability Statements are required for certain inpatient and outpatient services if the beneficiary resides within the designated military treatment facility catchment area. Providers must submit claims on HCFA-1500 forms for services given to beneficiaries, including cases where CHAMPUS is the secondary payer. Beneficiaries must submit claims to supplemental insurance carriers. See Chapter 13, Figures 13–3 and 13–4, for deductible amounts and outpatient and inpatient benefits. See Appendix A for the name and address of where to submit the claims and to obtain further information about this program.

CHAMPUS and HMO Coverage

CHAMPUS considers HMOs to be the same as any other primary health insurance coverage. CHAMPUS shares the cost of covered care received from an HMO (including the HMO's user fees), after the HMO has paid all it is going to pay, under the following conditions:

- Provider must meet CHAMPUS provider certification standards
- Type of care must be a CHAMPUS benefit and medically necessary

When an HMO has a limit on how much it will pay, CHAMPUS shares the cost of only that portion of the charge that the HMO does not cover. This includes emergency services received outside the HMO's normal service area.

CHAMPUS will not cost-share services an individual obtains outside the HMO, if the services are available through the HMO. For example, if an HMO provides psychiatric services but the patient does not like the HMO's psychiatrist and obtained services outside the HMO, then CHAMPUS would not pay anything on the claim.

MEDICARE AND MANAGED CARE PROGRAMS

There are two types of HMO plans that may have Medicare Part B contracts: HMO risk plans and HMO cost plans. Sometimes these plans may be referred to as HMO senior plans. Medicare cards are not forfeited and an elderly patient may show two cards leading to confusion about what and who they are covered by. As a condition of enrollment in an HMO risk plan, beneficiaries receive Medicare-covered services (except emergency, urgent need, and prior authorized services) only from providers who are contracted members of the HMO network. Enrollees of HMO risk plans are referred to as "restricted" beneficiaries. Usually services rendered by "out-of-plan" physicians are not covered when the same services are available through the organization unless a referral or prior authorization is obtained. The only exception is for emergency care. Under an HMO cost plan, beneficiaries receive Medicare-covered services from sources in the HMO network or outside the HMO network. Enrollees are referred to as "unrestricted" beneficiaries.

Claims for cost plan beneficiaries may be sent to the HMO plan or the regular Medicare carrier. Claims for HMO risk plan beneficiaries must be sent directly to the organization. Physicians should verify Medicare Part B coverage with beneficiaries to be sure claims are properly submitted either to the carrier or HMO plan. Claims may be denied or delayed if submitted to the wrong carrier or HMO organization.

If a nonmember physician treats a Medicare/HMO patient, the services are considered "out-of-plan" services. Submit the claim to the managed care plan, which will determine whether it is responsible to pay for the services. The conditions that must be met are

1. Service was an emergency and the patient was not able to get to an HMO facility or member physician (patient was out of the HMO area, or "out-of-area").
2. Service was one covered by Medicare.
3. Service was medically necessary.
4. Service was prior authorized or an approved referral.

Denied services can be billed to the patient (no more than the Medicare Fee Schedule or Limiting Charge) after the HMO Explanation of Benefits is received. If the managed care program determines there was no emergency and denies payment, the patient is responsible for the fee. The HMO reimburses according to the Medicare Fee Schedule Allowable amount, so the physician cannot bill the patient for the balance. If the physician does not receive 100% of the Allowable, steps must be taken through the HMO's appeals process. If this fails, contact the Medicare Managed Care department at your Medicare Regional HCFA Operations office.

If a Medicare patient has switched over to a managed care plan and wishes to disenroll, the following steps must be taken.

1. Patient must notify the plan in writing of disenrollment.
2. Patient must complete Medicare form HCFA 566, attach a copy of the disenrollment letter, and take it to the Social Security office.

It may take the plan 30 days for disenrollment, and Medicare may take as long as 60 days to re-enroll a patient. For further information on this subject, see Chapter 12, Medicare.

MEDICAID AND MANAGED CARE PROGRAMS

When filing a claim for a Medicaid patient who is also enrolled in a managed care program (HMO or PPO), send the bill to the program and not the Medicaid fiscal agent or carrier. The HMO receives payment for services rendered to eligible members via the capitation method. This means that the HMO is paid a fixed, per capita amount for each patient served without considering the actual number or nature of services provided to each person.

POINT OF SERVICE PLANS

The typical *point of service* (POS) program combines elements of an HMO and a PPO while offering some unique features. It is basically an HMO consisting of a network of physicians and hospitals that provides an insurance company or an employer with discounts on its services. In a POS program, members choose a primary care physician who manages specialty care and referrals. POS members may choose to use a nonprogram provider at any time. The POS program, however, pays members a higher level of benefits when they use program (network) providers. The key advantage of POS programs is the combination of HMO-style cost management and PPO-style freedom of choice.

The typical POS program within the Blue Cross and Blue Shield system works by offering comprehensive coverage for services such as preventive medicine, physician office visits, and outpatient and inpatient care through a network of participating providers. The member initially selects a primary care physician who delivers primary care services and manages specialty care and referrals. The member may use providers outside the network, but higher deductibles and coinsurance percentages for non-network services give members incentives to use network providers.

Blue Cross and Blue Shield POS programs are available through 46 networks in 35 states. They have 1.2 million members, 133,000 participating physicians, and almost 2000 participating hospitals. More than half of these POS programs use an existing HMO provider network as their core networks.

PHYSICIAN PROVIDER GROUPS

A *physician provider group* (PPG) is a physician-owned business entity that has the flexibility to deal with all forms of contract medicine and still offer its own packages to business groups, unions, and the general public. One division may function as an IPA under contract to an HMO. Another section may act as the broker or provider in a PPO that contracts with hospitals as well as other physicians to market services or medical supplies to employers and other third parties. And still another portion might participate in joint ventures with hospitals, such as the purchase of diagnostic equipment. The difference between an IPA and a PPG is that an IPA may not be owned by its member physicians, whereas a PPG is physician owned.

An advantage of PPGs is their ability to combine services (joint purchasing, marketing, billing, collections, attorneys and accountant fees), therefore cutting down on the cost of running a business. Each physician retains his or her own practice but may joint venture into freestanding imaging centers and laboratories, retail medical equipment as a corporate subsidiary, and so on. The sideline businesses do not pay dividends but provide income to make future assessments to participating physicians unnecessary. Patients call one telephone number to make appointments. The billing is done in one location. The physicians turn over a small percentage of their income to the PPG for expenses. Specialists are attracted to PPGs, because they can better compete with primary care physicians.

TRIPLE OPTION HEALTH PLAN

This plan combines indemnity insurance with HMOs and/or PPOs. Some of these plans allow the employee to change from an indemnity plan to HMO plan to PPO plan more often than under traditional arrangements. They incorporate cost containment measures (precertification for hospital admission and hospital stays and second surgical options).

FOUNDATIONS FOR MEDICAL CARE

A foundation for medical care (FMC) is an organization of physicians sponsored by a state or local medical association concerned with the development and delivery of medical services and the cost of health care. The first Foundation for Medical Care was established in 1954 in Stockton, California. Foundations have sprung up across the United States, and some comprehensive foundations have assumed a portion of the underwriting risk for a defined population and have provided comprehensive health services for a fixed yearly sum on a capitation basis, thereby qualifying as HMOs. Foundations deal primarily with employer groups, government groups, and county and city employees. Some plans are open to individual subscribers, but this usually is a small percentage of the foundation activity because the emphasis is on groups.

There are basically two different types of foundations for medical care operations: (1) a *comprehensive* type, which designs and sponsors prepaid health programs or sets minimum benefits of coverage, and (2) a *claims-review* type, which provides peer review by physicians to the numerous fiscal agents or carriers involved in its area, including the ones processing Medicare and Medicaid. *Peer review* is an evaluation of the quality and efficiency of services rendered by a practicing physician or physicians within the specialty group. This is done for an insurance claim or for services rendered to the patient that exceed local community guidelines for the fee and/or service.

A key feature of the foundation is its dedication to an incentive reimbursement system for participating physicians, by which income is received in direct proportion to the number of medical services delivered (i.e., fee for service). In some areas, foundation physicians agree to accept the foundation allowance as payment in full for covered services. The patient is *not* billed for the balance. However, the patient is billed for nonbenefit items and deductible coinsurance. Billing to the foundation may be done via computer and electronically transmitting data so paperwork is eliminated.

The patient may select any member or nonmember physician he or she wishes. Member physicians agree to bill the foundation directly, and a nonmember physician may wish to collect directly from the patient. Some foundations submit claims on the HCFA-1500 form. The foundation movement has a national society, the American Managed Care and Review Association,* which can give you further information on the foundation or foundations in your state.

Medical Review

PROFESSIONAL REVIEW ORGANIZATIONS

Practitioners in the HMO program may come under a peer review by a *professional review organization* (PRO) to determine quality assurance and operation of health care. In this type of peer review, one or more physicians working with the federal government under federal guidelines evaluate another physician in regard to the quality of professional care, to settle disputes on fees (see Fig. 8–4 in Chapter 8), or to examine evidence for admission and discharge of a hospital patient. PROs are not restricted to HMO programs but also play a role in Medicare inpatient cases.

UTILIZATION REVIEW OR MANAGEMENT

In a managed care setting, a management system called *utilization review* (UR) is necessary in order to control costs. In a performance-based reimbursement system, emphasis is placed on seeing a high volume of patients. When a physician sees a patient more than is medically necessary, this is termed *churning*. This is done to increase revenue through an increased number of services. Churning may be seen in fee-for-service as well as some managed care environments. *Turfing* means to transfer the sickest, high-cost patients to other physicians so the provider appears as a low utilizer. *Buffing* refers to a physician's making this practice look justifiable to the plan. All of these situations may affect utilization review.

The utilization review committee reviews individual cases in regard to medical care services for medical necessity. It also watches over how providers use medical care resources. If care is denied, then the patient must be informed of the need for the medical care and the risks of not having it. The reasons for denial, in writing, let patients know their rights to receive the service and their obligation to pay before any care is given.

*1227 25th Street, N.W., #610, Washington, D.C. 20037 (formerly known as American Association of Foundations for Medical Care).

Management of Plans

CONTRACTS

Before signing a contract with a managed care plan, a physician should have the contract reviewed by an attorney. To make a knowledgeable financial decision on how the plan will have an impact on an existing medical practice, it is important to obtain nationwide data from Medirisk, Inc.* Data supplied by this company can be used to evaluate existing fees, negotiate with managed care firms, and weigh practice expansions (i.e., add partners or a satellite office).

PRECERTIFICATION OR PRIOR AUTHORIZATION

Some managed care plans require preauthorization for certain services or when the patient must be referred to a subspecialist (Fig. 9–1). Patients may be unaware of this requirement of their plan. A good solution is to ask patients about insurance coverage at the time they call for an appointment. If they are a member of an HMO or a PPO, carefully review the patient's insurance coverage; if preauthorizations are required for certain situations, inform them of this before they see the physician. If the patients have the authorization forms, then remind them to bring the forms at the time of the scheduled visit. If an authorization is delayed and the patient comes in for the appointment, try to call the plan and obtain an authorization documenting the date, time, and name of the authorizing person; otherwise, the patient's appointment may have to be rescheduled. A referral recommendation must be documented in the patient's record and sent to the referring physician. A tracking system, such as a referral tracking log, needs to be in place for patients referred to a physician so they do not get lost in the system. Sometimes paperwork goes to the primary

*5901 Peachtree Dunwoody Road, N.E., Suite 455, Building B, Atlanta, Georgia 30328.

MANAGED CARE PLAN
TREATMENT AUTHORIZATION REQUEST

TO BE COMPLETED BY PRIMARY CARE PHYSICIAN OR OUTSIDE PROVIDER

Health Net	☐	Met Life	☐
Pacificare	☐	Travelers	☒
Secure Horizons	☐	Pru Care	☐

Patient Name: Louann Campbell Date: 7-14-9X

M___ F X Birthdate 4/7/52 Home telephone number (013) 450-1666

Address 2516 Encina Avenue, Woodland Hills, XY 12345-0439

Primary Care Physician Gerald Practon, MD Member ID# C14021-AT

Referring Physician Gerald Practon, MD Member ID# C14021-AT

Referred to Raymond Skelton, MD Address 4567 Broad Avenue

Woodland Hills, XY 12345-0001 Office telephone no. (013) 486-9002

Diagnosis Code 724.2 Diagnosis Low back pain

Diagnosis Code 722.10 Diagnosis Sciatica

Treatment Plan: Orthopedic evaluation of lumbar spine R/O herniated disc L4,5

Authorization requested for procedures/tests/visits:

Procedure Code 99244 Description New patient consultation

Procedure Code_____ Description_____

Facility to be used:_____ Estimated length of stay_____

Office ☒ Outpatient ☐ Inpatient ☐ Other ☐

List of potential consultants (i.e., anesthetists, assistants, or medical/surgical):

Raymond Skelton, MD - Orthopedic

Physician's signature *Gerald Practon, MD*

TO BE COMPLETED BY PRIMARY CARE PHYSICIAN

PCP Recommendations: See above PCP Initials *GP, MD*

Eligibility checked 7-14-9X Effective date 1-15-9X

TO BE COMPLETED BY UTILIZATION MANAGEMENT

Authorized_____ Not authorized_____

Deferred_____ Modified_____

Authorization Request #_____

Comments:_____

FIGURE 9–1
Example of a managed care plan treatment authorization request form completed by a primary care physician for preauthorization of a professional service.

care physician and not to the referring physician. Allow a 2-week turnaround time and follow-up.

If a managed care plan refuses to authorize payment for treatment, tests, or procedures, have the primary care physician send a letter to the plan that is worded similarly to that shown in Figure 9–2. Then, send a letter, such as that shown in Figure 9–3, to the patient informing him or her of this fact and asking the patient to appeal the denial of benefits.

When a primary care physician sends a patient to a specialist for consultation who is *not* in the managed care plan, the specialist bills the primary care physician and that office pays. This is done because the primary care physician receives a monthly capitation check from the plan, and any care for the patient must come from the capitation pool. This type of plan encourages primary care physicians to not refer patients because they want to retain their profits.

If a specialist recommends referral to another specialist *(tertiary care)*, be sure the recommendation is in writing. Call the specialist at the later date to see whether the recommendation was acted on. If the patient refuses to be referred, be sure this is documented. If a referral form is required, do NOT write a letter because the managed care plan may refuse payment if a form is not completed. When you receive a referral form, make a copy of the form for each approved office visit, laboratory test, or other procedure. Then use the form as a reference to bill for the service. When all copies are used, this indicates all the procedures or services that the patient's plan has approved are completed and you must ask the primary care physician for a new referral form for the patient.

LABORATORY AND X-RAY TESTS

Many managed care plans require that patients have laboratory tests and X-ray tests performed at plan-specified facilities. Always allow sufficient time to receive the test or X-ray results before a patient's scheduled appointment.

MANAGED CARE GUIDE

To assist you in keeping up with the growth of prepaid health plans in your area as well as knowing which physician belongs to which plan in the practice, create a reference sheet that at a glance will give you the specifics about alternate plan coverage (Fig. 9–4).

PLAN ADMINISTRATION

Some of the payment mechanisms in managed care plans can range from fee for service and capitation (fee paid usually monthly for each enrollee with the plan) to salaried physicians. Usually state laws dictate the time limit within which an HMO, a PPO, or an IPA must pay. These can vary from one plan to another or may not be regulated in terms of payments. Some contracts have a "stop loss" section, which means that if the patient's services go over a certain amount, then the physician can begin asking the patient to pay (fee for service); thus, in those instances, it is important to monitor each patient's ledger.

Screen patients when they call for appointments to determine whether they belong to the same prepaid health plan as the physician. Ask the patient to read from the insurance card to determine whether the physician participates in the plan. Keep on hand an alphabetical list of all plans with which the practice has signed. It might also be useful to have a list of plans to which the practice does not belong. If the patient still wishes to schedule a visit, tell him or her that payment of the regular fee at the time of the appointment is required.

9

Deductibles

Usually, there are no deductibles for managed care plans. However, if there is one, be sure to collect it in the early months of the year (January through April) by asking patients if they have met their deductibles.

Copayments

Most copayments are fixed dollar amounts or percentages. If you develop a quick reference sheet for managed care plans, this will provide the amount that is due. Always collect the copayment when the patient arrives for his or her appointment because billing is not cost effective and it is easy to forget to ask for payment when the patient is leaving the office.

Identification Card

Photocopy both sides of the patient's card because a copay may be listed on the back of the card showing amounts to be paid to the hospital, office, or emergency department.

**LETTER TO MANAGED CARE PLAN
FOR REFUSAL TO AUTHORIZE PAYMENT**

Ms. Jane Smith
Chairperson
Utilization Review Committee
ABC Managed Care Plan
111 Main Street
Anytown, XY 12345-0122

Dear Ms. Smith:

On _________ I prescribed ___________________________ for _______________.
(Date) (List treatment, test, procedure) (Patient's name)

On _________ you refused to authorize payment for that treatment. I find that I
(Date)
must take issue with your determination for the following reasons:

In my medical judgment, the treatment is a very important part of my overall care of _____ ____________. This patient suffers from ____________________. The treatment is
(Patient's name) (Describe condition)

necessary to __________________________. Failure to perform the treatment could
(Describe why necessary)

result in the following problem(s):

For these reasons, I urge you to reconsider your refusal to authorize payment for the procedure I have prescribed.

By copy of this letter to ________________ I am reiterating my suggestion that he/she
(Patient's name)

obtain the treatment despite your refusal to authorize payment, for the reasons I have set forth in this letter and in prior discussions with _______________.
(Patient's name)

Yours truly,

John Doe, MD

cc: (Name of patient)

FIGURE 9–2
Example of a letter to a managed care plan when there is a refusal to authorize payment for a treatment, test, or procedure.

LETTER TO PATIENT ABOUT INFORMED REFUSAL

Mr. Avery Johnson
130 Sylvia Street
Anytown, XY 12345-0022

Dear Mr. Johnson:

On _________ I prescribed _________________________ for you. On _______,
(Date) (Treatment, test, procedure) (Date)

__________________________ refused to authorize payment for same. On that basis,
(Name of Managed Care Plan)

you have informed me of your decision to forego the treatment I have prescribed. I expressed my concerns regarding your decision during our discussion on _______ (Date) about the potential ramifications of your refusal to undergo the treatment.

The purpose of this letter is to recommend that you appeal ________________________ (Name of Managed Care Plan's) denial of benefits and reconsider your decision to forego the treatment in light of the potential consequences of your refusal.

Should you wish to discuss this further, please do not hesitate to contact me.

Sincerely yours,

John Doe, MD

FIGURE 9-3
Example of a letter to inform the patient about refusal of payment for treatment, test, or procedure by the managed care plan.

Patient Information Letter

Tell your managed care subscribers what you expect from them and what they can expect from you by giving them a letter to read and sign that outlines possible restrictions, noncovered items, expectations for both sides, and names of the managed care plans in which your physician is presently participating. Put in a note saying that if the patient neglects to notify the office of any change regarding eligibility status in the plan, such as *disenrollment*, the patient is held personally responsible for the bill. Also, if hospitalization, surgery, or referral to a specialist is required, the patient must inform you if he or she belongs to a managed care plan; failure to do so would make the patient liable for noncovered charges because of restrictions.

Figure 9–5 is a sample letter of appropriate wording and content. File a copy of the letter in the patient's medical record. If the patient refuses to cooperate, document this in the medical record because reimbursement may depend on the documentation. Keep a profile of each plan within easy reach. Place colored stick-on dots on file labels or color code managed care files by using a different colored chart for each HMO, PPO, or Medicare case. This decreases confusion and saves time in identifying the plan and what is required as far as coverage, copayments, billing, authorizations, and so on are concerned.

Encounter Form

Many managed care plans use an internal document on which the services rendered to the patient

HMO/PPO QUICK REFERENCE GUIDE

Name of plan: Travelers Managed Care

Address: 540 Ralston St., Anytown, XY 12309 Phone No. (013) 540-9800

Name of contact person: Marjorie Macy Phone No. ( ) ____

PROFESSIONAL SERVICES:

*Limited dollar amount for test/procedure $ 500.00 Radiology

$ 50.00 Laboratory

Office visit co-pay amount $ 10.00 Deductible: Amt $ N/A

Preauthorization Phone No. (013) 450-9877

Precertification requirements: See attached list

Hospital Benefits

Inpatient surgery requirements

Second opinion: Yes X No ____

Outpatient surgery requirements Preauthorization required

Participating hospitals College Hospital

Participating laboratories ABC Laboratories

Participating x-ray providers 1) College Hospital

2) ABC Radiology

Participating physicians (put in location of directory or attach list)

COMMENTS: ____

*There may be a specific dollar limit per service before authorization is required, e.g., only radiology services over $500 need prior authorization.

FIGURE 9–4
HMO/PPO Quick Reference Guide to help keep efficient track of specifics for each managed care plan.

XYZ MEDICAL GROUP, INC.
1400 Avon Road, Suite 200
Woodland Hills, XY 12345

January 1, 199x

TO: OUR PATIENTS

RE: PREFERRED PROVIDER ORGANIZATIONS

The following is a list of the PPOs and health insurance plans that we are members of and, therefore, will bill for you:

1. Georgia County Foundation
2. VIP Health Plan
3. Blue Cross Prudent Buyer Plan
4. Georgia County PPO
5. Northwest PPO
6. Blue Shield PPO

We are participating providers in several different PPOs. In order that we may maintain proper records for referrals and/or hospitalization, we request that each patient who is enrolled in a specific PPO keep our office currently informed regarding his or her eligibility status in that plan. Each time you are in the office for a visit, please verify with the receptionist that we have the correct coverage information.

If you have not informed us of changes in the status of your eligibility within the plan, you will be held responsible for any outstanding balance on your account due to that change.

Additionally, when your physician feels it is necessary to either hospitalize you or refer you to another physician outside this group, it is your responsibility to inform your physician that you belong to a specific PPO, as there may be restrictions imposed by that PPO regarding admission and referrals. If you fail to inform your physician at the time of referral or admission, our group may not be held responsible for noncoverage charges due to these restrictions.

If you have any questions regarding the above, please ask to speak to our insurance specialist.

I have read and understand the above text.

Signed:____Date:____________________
Patient (subscriber)

FIGURE 9–5
Sample letter to HMO subscribers outlining restrictions and noncovered services.

are checked off (charge ticket, encounter form, routing slip). Some plans require an HCFA-1500 Health Insurance Claim form to be completed. Encounter reports document the number of services and are not necessarily used to generate payments. The document is then routed to the appropriate administrative office. Physicians who join an IPA, PPO, or staff model HMO might submit a billing statement, such as the one shown in Figure 9–6. The original is forwarded to the health plan, and one copy is retained in the physician's files. Some patients have a copayment for hospital, office, or emergency department and the copayment varies depending on where service is rendered. The copayment can also be based on the time of day at which the patient is seen so that one seen at the regular office hours is charged one fee and those at other times require a higher copayment fee. Sometimes a plan pays twice on the same patient; if so, a refund must be made. Monitor payments made from all managed care plans, and note whether the payment received is less than the agreed amount as stated in the contract. Send a letter to the plan citing, "As per contract see page ___ regarding the fee for the consultation."

Sometimes a procedure (e.g., angioplasty with an assistant) may be done and the plan will not pay for an assistant, stating that it is not usual practice. However, you discover that in your region the stan-

DATE		DESCRIPTION	CHARGES	PAYMENT (CREDITS)	ADJ. (CREDITS)	CURRENT BALANCE	PREVIOUS BALANCE	NAME

THIS IS YOUR **RECEIPT** FOR THIS AMOUNT ▲ ▲ THIS IS A **STATEMENT** OF YOUR ACCOUNT TO DATE

27361

Patient ______

1. OFFICE VISITS - New Patient

Code	History	Exam	Dec.	Nature/ Severe	Time	Diag.	FEE
99201	Prob. Foc.	Prob. Foc.	Straight	Minor	10 min.		
99202	Ex. Prob. Foc.	Ex. Prob. Foc.	Straight	Low-Mod.	20 min.		
99203	Detail	Detail	Low	Mod.	30 min.		
99204	Comp.	Comp.	Mod.	Mod.-High	45 min.		
99205	Comp.	Comp.	High	Mod.-High	60 min.		

2. OFFICE VISIT - Established Patient

Code	History	Exam	Dec.	Nature/ Severe	Time	Diag.	FEE
99211				Minimal	5 min.		
99212	Prob. Foc.	Prob. Foc.	Straight	Minor	10 min.		
99213	Ex. Prob. Foc.	Ex. Prob. Foc.	Low	Low-Mod.	15 min.		
99214	Detail	Detail	Mod.	Mod.-High	25 min.		
99215	Comp.	Comp.	High	Mod.-High	40 min.		

3. SURGERY

Anesthesia ☐ **None** ☐ **Local** ☐ **Topical**

Excision Surgery

	Benign	Malig.	FEE
Trunk, Arm, Leg			
0.6 to 1.0 cm	11401	11601	
1.1 to 2.0 cm	11402	11602	
2.1 to 3.0 cm	11403	11603	
Scalp, Neck, Feet, Hand, Genitalia			
0.6 to 1.0 cm	11421	11621	
1.1 to 2.0 cm	11422	11622	
2.1 to 3.0 cm	11423	11623	
Face, Ears, Eyelids, Nose, Lips			
0.5 cm or Less	11440	11640	
0.6 cm to 1.0 cm	11441	11641	
1.1 to 2.0 cm	11442	11642	
Curettement of			
Benign Lesion - Single		11050*	
Two to Four		11051	
More Than Four		11052	

4. OTHER SURGERY

			FEE
Single Lesion	17100*	17000*	
Second Lesion		17101	
Second and Third Lesion ea.		17102	
I & D Abscess, Simple		10060*	
I & D Bartholin's Gland Abscess		56420*	
Condyloma Accuminala, Simple		46900*	

5. WOUND REPAIR ☐ Curved ☐ Angular ☐ Stellate ☐ Straight

	Simple	Intermediate	FEE
Scalp, Axille, Trunk, Extremities			
2.5 cm or Less	12001*	12031*	
2.6 cm to 7.5 cm	12002*	12032*	
7.6 cm to 12.5 cm	12004*	12034	
Neck, Hands, Feet and or External Genitalia			
2.5 cm or Less	12011*	12041*	
2.6 cm to 5.0 cm	12013*		
5.1 cm to 7.5 cm	12014	12042	
7.6 cm to 12.5 cm	12015	12044	
Face, Ears, Eyelids, Nose, Lips, and or Mucous Membranes			
2.5 cm or Less		12051*	
2.6 cm to 5.0 cm		12052	

6. PROCEDURES

	Code	FEE
Thrombosed Hemorrhoid	46320*	
Foreign Body - Eye	65220*	
Removal Impacted Cerumen	69210	
EKG	93000	
Exam ______		
Proctosigmoidoscopy, Diagn.	45300	
Arthrocentesis, Small Jt.	20600*	

D412445

Date of Service ______

7. LAB & TESTING

	Code	FEE
CBC	85022	
Thyroid Panel	80070	
Blood Sugar	82947	
GTT	82952	
Hemaglobin	85018	
Mono Test	86300	
Pap Smear	88150	
Strep Test	87082	
Stool Blood, Occult	82270	
Urinalysis w/Micro	81000	
Urinalysis w/o Micro	81002	
Lipid Profile	80061	

8. INJECTIONS & SUPPLIES

	HCPCS.	DIAGN.	CPT	DIAGN.	FEE
Surgical Tray	A4550		99070		
Allergy Shot			95115		
Bicillin - CR Up to 600,000 U	J0530		90788		
Demerol HCL, Up to 100 Mg.			90782		
Decadron LA to 8 Mg.	J1100		90782		
Estrogen	J1410		90782		
Influenza			90724		
Tet. Tox. to 1 ML	J3180		90703		
Vistaril Up to 25 Mg.	J3410		90782		
Vitamin B-12	J3420		90782		
SUPPLIES			99070		

☐ Accept Assignment ☐ Do Not Accept Assignment

I hereby authorize payment directly to the below named doctor of the group insurance benefits otherwise payable to me.

Signed (Insured Person) ______ Date ______

TOTAL FOR SERVICES ON THIS STATEMENT

______ M.D.
Doctor's Signature

RETURN: ______ Days ______ Weeks ______ Months

NEXT APPT ______ Day ______ Month ______ Date ______ Time AM PM

COLLEGE CLINIC
4567 Broad Avenue
Woodland Hills, XY 12345-0001
Tel. 013-486-9002 Fax. 013-487-8976

Diagnosis: ______

1. ☐ 706.1 Acne
2. ☐ 493.00 Allergic Asthma
3. ☐ 477.__ Allergic Rhinitis
4. ☐ 565.0 Anal Fissure
5. ☐ 566 Anal/Rectal Abscess
6. ☐ 285.9 Anemia, Unspec.
7. ☐ 280.1 Anemia: Inadequate Iron Intake
8. ☐ 411.__ Angina Pectoris, Acute
9. ☐ 413.9 Angina Pectoris, Chronic
10. ☐ 300.4 Anxiety Depression
11. ☐ 300.02 Anxiety Disorder, Gen.
12. ☐ 300.00 Anxiety States
13. ☐ 540.__ Appendicitis
14. ☐ 719.4_ Arthralgia
15. ☐ 414.0 ASHD
16. ☐ 691.8 Atopic Dermatitis
17. ☐ 616.2 Bartholin's Gland Cyst
18. ☐ 616.3 Bartholin's Gland Cyst, Abscess
19. ☐ 490 Bronchitis
20. ☐ 491.__ Bronchitis, Chronic
21. ☐ 466.0 Bronchitis, Acute
22. ☐ 493.9_ Bronchitis, Asthmatic
23. ☐ 485 Bronchopneumonia
24. ☐ 726.__ Bursitis
25. ☐ 112.9 Candidiasis
26. ☐ 427.__ Cardiac Arrhythmia
27. ☐ 682.__ Cellulitis
28. ☐ 622.0 Cervical Erosion
29. ☐ 616.0 Cervicitis
30. ☐ 786.5_ Chest Pain
31. ☐ 052.9 Chicken Pox
32. ☐ 428.0 Congestive Heart Failure
33. ☐ 372.__ Conjunctivitis, Acute
34. ☐ 496 COPD
35. ☐ 918.1 Corneal Abrasion
36. ☐ 930.0 Corneal Foreign Body
37. ☐ 414.__ Coronary Heart Disease
38. ☐ 464.4 Croup
39. ☐ 595.__ Cyscitis
40. ☐ 300.4 Depression
41. ☐ 692.__ Dermatitis
42. ☐ 110.__ Dermatophytosis
    ☐ Diabetes/Mellitus
43. ☐ 250.00 w/o Complication -Adult or Unspec.
44. ☐ 250.01 w/o Complication-Juvenile Type
45. ☐ 562.10 Diverticulosis of Colon
46. ☐ 562.11 Diverticulitis of Colon
47. ☐ 532.__ Duodenal Ulcer
48. ☐ 625.3 Dysmenorrhea
49. ☐ 692.__ Eczema
50. ☐ 558.9 Enteritis
51. ☐ 604.__ Epididymitis
52. ☐ 530.5 Esophageal Spasm
53. ☐ 530.1 Esophagitis
54. ☐ 930.__ Foreign Body-External Eye
55. ☐ 536.9 Functional GI Distress
56. ☐ 680.__ Furuncle
57. ☐ 535.__ Gastritis
58. ☐ 098.__ Gonococcal Infection
59. ☐ 274.0 Gout Arthropathy
60. ☐ 784.0 Headaches
61. ☐ 307.81 Headaches, Tension
62. ☐ ______ Healthy Person
63. ☐ 455.__ Hemorrhoids
64. ☐ 054.__ Herpes Simplex
65. ☐ 053.__ Herpes Zoster
66. ☐ 553.3 Hiatal Hernia
67. ☐ 272.0 Hypercholesterolemia
68. ☐ 272.1 Pure Hyperglyceridema
69. ☐ 272.0 Pure Hypercholesterolemia
70. ☐ 272.4 Hyperlipidemia, Other
71. ☐ 401.9 Hypertension, Unspec.
72. ☐ 786.01 Hyperventilation
73. ☐ 703.0 Ingrown Nail
74. ☐ 380.4 Impacted Cerumen
75. ☐ 684 Impetigo
76. ☐ 487.__ Influenza
77. ☐ 626.__ Irregular Menses
78. ☐ 702.__ Keratosis
79. ☐ 590.__ Kidney Infection
80. ☐ 386.3_ Labyrinthitis
81. ☐ 464.20 Acute Laryngotracheitis
82. ☐ 724.2 Low Back Syndrome
83. ☐ 346.__ Migraine
84. ☐ 625.2 Mittelschmerz
85. ☐ 112.__ Monilia Infection
86. ☐ 729.1 Mytosis
87. ☐ 460 Naso-Pharyngitis
88. ☐ 729.2 Neuritis/Neuralgia
89. ☐ 216.__ Nevus
90. ☐ 932 Nose, Foreign Body
91. ☐ 110.1 Onychomycosis
92. ☐ 715.__ Osteoarthritis
93. ☐ 380.10 Otitis Externa
94. ☐ 381.0_ Otitis Media
95. ☐ 381.1_ Otitis Media, Chronic Serus
96. ☐ 462 Pharyngitis
97. ☐ 614.__ PID
98. ☐ 696.3 Pityriasis Rosea
99. ☐ 511.__ Pleursy
100. ☐ 512.8 Pneumothorax, Spontaneous
101. ☐ 569.49 Proctitis
102. ☐ 601.__ Prostatitis
103. ☐ 696.1 Psoriasis
104. ☐ 686.0 Pyoderma
105. ☐ 714.0 Rheumatoid Arthritis
106. ☐ 706.3 Seborrhea
107. ☐ 702.1 Seborrheic Keratosis
108. ☐ 345.__ Seizure Disorder
109. ☐ 780.3 Seizure/Convulsions
110. ☐ 616.__ Servicitis/Vaginitis
111. ☐ 473.9 Sinusitis
112. ☐ 780.2_ Sleep Disorder
113. ☐ 564.1 Spastic Colon
114. ☐ 454.1 Stasis Dermatitis
115. ☐ 528.__ Stomatitis
116. ☐ 034.0 Strep/Sore Throat
117. ☐ 308.3 Stress Reaction Acute
118. ☐ 785.0 Tachycardia
119. ☐ 727.__ Tendonitis
120. ☐ 307.81 Tension Headache
121. ☐ 455.7 Thrombosed Hemorrhoid
122. ☐ 451.__ Thrombophlebitis
123. ☐ 463 Tonsillitis
124. ☐ 111.0 Tinea Versacolor
125. ☐ 597.__ Urethritis
126. ☐ 599.0 Urinary Tract Infection
127. ☐ 465.__ URI
128. ☐ 708.0 Urticaria, Allergic
129. ☐ 995.2 Urticaria-Drug Reaction
130. ☐ 454.__ Vericose Veins, Lower Extremities
131. ☐ 780.4 Vertigo, Acute
132. ☐ 079.9 Viral Infection, Other
133. ☐ 078.1 Viral Wart

FIGURE 9–6
Encounter form or billing statement that is forwarded to the health plan administrative offices. One copy is retained in the physician's files. (Reprinted with permission from Professional Filing Systems, Inc., Atlanta, GA.)

dard practice is to always use an assistant for an angioplasty. When this is emphasized, the plan may remit additional payment.

If claims are not being paid promptly (30 days), take the following steps.

1. Take examples and statistics to the next renegotiating session when the physician's contract is expiring.
2. Send a statement to the director of the managed care plan notifying him or her that if the bill is not paid you will contact the employer's benefits manager or patient and alert that person to outstanding, slow-paying accounts. Say that this will prevent the physician from renewing the plan's contract, and ask the recipient to contact the plan's representative. The consumer has a choice of managed care plans; if the present plan does not fulfill the intent to pay, the HMO or PPO loses members because of dissatisfaction.
3. Write to the plan representative and list the claims paid in error or delayed.

In some states, laws such as California's Knox-Keene Health Care Service Plan Act of 1975 prohibit hospitals and physicians under contract to an HMO from billing patients. Other states do not have such protection but may have created emergency insurance funds to limit the financial liability of enrollees in bankrupt HMOs. If you write to the insurance commissioner, they will refer you back to the HMO. However, your letter makes insurance commissioners aware of problems that have developed.

Financial Management

STATEMENT OF REMITTANCE

A *statement of remittance* is also known as an Explanation of Benefits (EOB). Such statements are an explanation of services that have been rendered to patients and are usually sent out monthly by the plan to the physician, indicating the amount billed, amount allowed, amount paid, and whether there is any copayment to be made by the patient (Fig. 9–7). Some plans require copayment, depending on the type of service rendered. Generally, patients under managed care plans do not receive EOB.

ACCOUNTING

Because managed care plans vary in their financial reimbursement structure, careful accounting procedures are required. Accounting can become a confusing issue because the medical practice may have a combination of private patients and those in various managed care plans.

FEE FOR SERVICE

In some instances, you may wish to handle some accounts as you would for fee-for-service patients. If copayment is required at the time of service, enter the charge, the copayment figured on the percentage of the charge the plan allows, and whether there is any adjustment or disallowance to zero out the account (Fig. 9–8). If there is an overpayment by the patient, this would be shown as a refund or credit to the patient (Fig. 9–9).

CAPITATION AND YEAR-END EVALUATION

1. For managed care plans, when payment is made on a capitation basis rather than a fee-for-service basis, put records of all patients in one particular plan on one accounting sheet. When the capitation check is received, post the payment against the total month's charges to give you an accurate idea of whether payment is being received for the services the physician performed. At the end of the year, you will be able to assess the success of each capitation plan.
2. Monitor plan payments for profit or loss by comparing actual income from managed care patients with what would have been received if the patients were private payers. Make up a log with columns for date of service, services provided (procedures, injections, and laboratory work). In the charge for services column, list the total cost of the visit as the usual charge. These amounts can then be compared with the actual capitation checks received at the end of the month plus any copayment made at the time of services. Monitoring of this type will show whether there was a gain or loss as a result of treating a managed care patient.
3. A managed care plan that withholds a percentage must be tracked in the physician's accounts receivable so it is not prematurely written off as a bad debt. Post withhold adjustments to a ledger account for the particular managed care plan and do not write them off. This credit entry indicates that the plan owes the withheld amount, pending its year-end reconciliation. If and when the bonus arrives, the ledger can be compared with what was denied

STATEMENT OF REMITTANCE

PATIENT NAME (ID NUMBER)	SERVICE DATE MO. DAY YR	POS	NO SVC	PROCEDURE NUMBER AND DESCRIPTION	AMOUNT BILLED	AMOUNT ALLOWED	RISK WITHHELD	CO PAY	AMOUNT PAID	ADJ. CODE
380224171-01 ALAN E.				CLAIM NO. 62730406 ACCOUNT NO.						
	092695	03	1	81000 URINALYSIS-ROUTINE	1000	1000	100	0	900	
	092695	03	1	82270 OCCULT BLOOD ANY S	1200	1200	120	0	1080	
	092695	03	1	99243 COMPRE RE-EXAM OR	6500	6500	650	0	5850	
	092695	03	1	36415 VENIPUNCTURE W/CEN	1700	1700	170	0	1530	
				CLAIM TOTALS =	10400	10400	1040	0	9360	
558700321-01 RONALD B.				CLAIM NO. 62730407 ACCOUNT NO.						
	092595	03	1	90050 LIM EXAM EVAL A/O	3000	3000	300	300	2400	
				CLAIM TOTALS =	3000	3000	300	300	2400	
473760096-01 DORMA L.				CLAIM NO. 62730408 ACCOUNT NO.						
	092595	03	1	90050 LIM EXAM EVAL A/O	3000	3000	300	300	2400	
				CLAIM TOTALS =	3800	3800	380	300	3120	

VENDOR SUMMARY: TOTAL AMOUNT PAID $1,638.96 TOTAL WITHHELD $194.39
AMOUNT PAID YEAR-TO-DATE $42,411.95 AMOUNT WITHHELD YEAR-TO-DATE $5,109.94

Adjustment Code Legend
A = Adjusted: Billed amount exceeds VIP allowed.
O = Claim for service denied. Charges for this service included in other benefit payment. No patient liability.

FIGURE 9–7
An HMO Statement of Remittance or explanation of benefits indicating the amount billed, amount allowed, amount paid, and if any copayment is to be made by the patient.

STATEMENT

College Clinic
4567 Broad Avenue
Woodland Hills, XY 12345

Telephone: 013-486-9002 Fax: 013-487-8967

Jose Cervantes

DATE	PROFESSIONAL SERVICE DESCRIPTION	CHARGE	CREDITS		CURRENT BALANCE
			PAYMENTS	ADJUSTMENTS	
02-06-95	OV Level II	50.00	10.00		40.00
03-16-95	Ins. check		36.00		4.00
	Adj. and credit			5.00 (disallowed)	(1.00)

FIGURE 9–8
Example of posting a patient's ledger card. The plan allowed $45. The patient paid 20% of $50 rather than 20% of $45, resulting in a $1 credit and a $5 adjustment (disallowance).

during the year. The amount is adjusted off once withholds are settled (Fig. 9–10). Combine the final bonus with the managed care fees received for the year to determine whether it is worthwhile for the practice to participate in the plan. Compare the total receipts against the gross charges for actual HMO services as if they were fee for service. Some practices can use the information to renegotiate increased fees when the managed care contract is to be renewed.

In the previous chapter, information is presented on how to handle slow or delinquent managed care plan payers.

Bankruptcy

If an HMO declares bankruptcy, such as a Chapter 11 filing, it is obligated to pay for all bills incurred after the filing. If the patient had treatment before the filing, a delay in getting reimbursed may occur because the HMO cannot repay debts incurred before its filing until it has worked out a reorganization plan. Physicians under contract with the HMO are obligated to honor their contractual commitments. If their contracts expire or if they have escape clauses, they may be required to continue accepting patients depending on the contract provisions.

Some clauses in the contracts allow a physician to leave if the HMO is in bankruptcy proceedings for more than 4 months. However, bankruptcy courts have broad powers to prevent physicians from leaving HMOs in bankruptcy proceedings if the court deems such actions to be detrimental to the rehabilitation of the debtor.

Special Plans

The following plans are unrelated to HMOs, PPOs, IPAs, or foundations.

STATEMENT

College Clinic
4567 Broad Avenue
Woodland Hills, XY 12345

Telephone: 013-486-9002 Fax: 013-487-8967

Brian Wu

DATE	PROFESSIONAL SERVICE DESCRIPTION	CHARGE	CREDITS		CURRENT BALANCE
			PAYMENTS	ADJUSTMENTS	
04-07-95	Surgery	4000.00			
	Prepayment required		800.00		3200.00
05-15-95	Plan payment		2720.00		480.00
	Adj.			600.00 (disallowed)	(120.00)
	Refund to patient			(120.00)	0

FIGURE 9–9
Example of posting to a patient's ledger card showing charge, plan allowance ($3400), and copayment (20% of $4000 or $800) paid by the patient in advance. The managed care plan check of $2720 was received, which was 80% of $3400. Note the adjustment of $600 (disallowed) and the refund of $120 (20% of $3400 = $680) due to the patient.

INDIVIDUAL RESPONSIBILITY PLAN

In some states, a program has been established in which physicians accept all patients but do not bill and refuse to accept reimbursement from any third party, private, or government agency. They bill the patient directly, and the patient applies to the carrier or program for reimbursement. This is called an individual responsibility program (IRP).

OPTOMETRIC SERVICE PLANS

Some states have service plans that are not considered health insurance but that are very specialized in the area of optometric care. There is no national program and no standardization of forms or procedures. Member doctors are given a detailed instruction manual on processing and claims procedure. This form of prepaid group vision care program is available to group health and welfare trust funds as well as businesses with a certain number of full-time employees. The cost of the plan is paid by the employer as a fringe benefit.

Some plans cover both the employee and his or her dependents; others are limited and cover only members or employees. This type of coverage provides for a yearly eye examination and corrective glasses if necessary. Certain costs of frames may be included, as may contact lenses for certain conditions. Some plans may even cover vision therapy.

In some instances, there may be a small deductible to meet before the plan is effective. For further information contact The American Optometric Association.*

*243 North Lindbergh Boulevard, St. Louis, Missouri 63141.

CAPITATION ACCOUNTING SHEET

NAME OF PLAN ABC Managed Care Plan

DATE	PROFESSIONAL SERVICE DESCRIPTION	CHARGES		PAYMENTS	
		Services	Copay	Capitation	Copay
1997 1/15	Capitation (5 members) @ $8 ea			40.00	
2/15	Capitation (15 members)			120.00	
2/20	Sanchez OV/Copay	35.00	5.00		5.00
2/22	Jones OV/Copay	35.00	5.00		5.00
2/23	Davis OV/Copay	35.00	5.00		5.00
3/6	Evans OV/Copay	35.00	5.00		5.00
3/15	Capitation (30 members)			240.00	
4/10	Wu OV/Copay	35.00	5.00		5.00
4/15	Capitation (35 members)			280.00	
12/15	Capitation (80 members)			640.00	
12/31	Return of withhold			1000.00	
TOTALS:					

9

FIGURE 9-10

Example of an accounting sheet of a capitation plan from January through April showing members' service charges and capitation payments received by the medical practice. A return of the withhold at the end of the year is shown as a December entry. Service and capitation columns may be totaled at the end of the year to compare capitation with fee-for-service earnings.

TO THE STUDENT

Study Chapter 9 and then answer the review questions in the *Workbook* to reinforce the theory learned in this chapter and to help prepare you for a future test. Assignments 27 through 29 will give you hands-on experience in abstracting information from a medical record to complete treatment authorization forms for prepaid health insurance cases. For further knowledge and understanding, the key terms at the beginning of the chapter appear in the Glossary at the end of this textbook so you can look up the pertinent terms.

CHAPTER 10

Blue Cross and Blue Shield Plans

Objectives*

THE INSURANCE BILLING SPECIALIST WILL BE ABLE TO:

- Cite the essential features of Blue Cross and Blue Shield Plans and explain how the Plans came into existence.
- Identify which federal and state programs the Plans may administer.
- Explain the difference between usual, customary, and reasonable fees.
- Process claims for patients on Medicare with supplemental Blue Shield coverage.
- Explain the Federal Employee Program, including its benefits and nonbenefits.
- State the meaning of pertinent Blue Cross and Blue Shield Plan terminology and abbreviations.
- Explain the BlueCard Program.
- Name two processing methods used to administer benefits of companies with business locations in different states.
- List two reasons for the Medical Necessity Program.
- State important data abstracted from the patient's identification card(s).

Key Terms

adjustments
assignment of benefits
BlueCard Program
Blue Cross and Blue Shield Association (BCBSA)
Blue Cross and Blue Shield Plans
carrier
certificate number
complementary benefits
control plan
direct payment
Explanation of Benefits (EOB)
Federal Employee Health Benefits Program (FEHBP)
Federal Employee Program (FEP)
Federal Tax Identification Number
indemnity benefit contract
itemized bill
medical record number
member
national account
participating physician
Point of Service (POS) product
service benefit contract
subscriber
third party payer

*Performance objectives and exercises for hands-on practical experience for this chapter appear in the *Workbook* and on computer disk.

CHAPTER 10

Blue Cross and Blue Shield Plans*

Introduction

Because individual Blue Cross and Blue Shield Plans vary widely, only topics of a strictly general nature are discussed in this chapter and are not specific to one state. Blue Plans are unique in that they employ a large staff of professional and provider relations representatives for the express purpose of assisting physicians and their staffs in claims problems and helping providers when there are payment delays or use of incorrect codes. These representatives make personal calls at physicians' offices, conduct seminars for physicians and insurance billing specialists, and speak to hospital staff and local medical societies. They also work closely with local and state components of the American Association of Medical Assistants (AAMA) in various capacities.

Get to know and keep in regular contact with the professional and provider relations representative at the Blue Cross/Blue Shield office in your area. He or she will be able to give you specific information about your local Plan and will keep you informed about any procedural changes.

* The Blue Cross and Blue Shield Association, an association of independent Blue Cross and Blue Shield Plans, has authorized the display of the Blue Cross and Blue Shield name and mark in *Insurance Handbook for the Medical Office,* 5th edition, but by so doing is not verifying the accuracy of the description of benefits, exclusions, or general principles of the Program.

History and Purpose

Blue Cross and *Blue Shield,* which are registered service marks, are the names and symbols used by the 69 local, nonprofit community service organizations that contract with hospitals, physicians, and other health care providers to provide prepaid health care services to their subscribers. They are called *prepayment plans* because individuals pay in advance for the health services they may need. The Blue Cross and Blue Shield organization is not a single company but rather a nationwide federation of locally governed, autonomous corporations, each operating under state law as a nonprofit organization. Several plans are organized as nonprofit mutual insurance companies. In 1996, some Blue Plans began merging with other Blue Plans and some began converting to for-profit status by forming publicly traded for-profit managed-care subsidiaries.

The Blue Cross idea originated in Dallas, Texas, in 1929, when a group of teachers found the cost of hospital care a heavy load for an individual to bear. Each member agreed to pay Baylor University Hospital a small sum of money every month. In return, all members were guaranteed 21 days of hospitalization a year. The experiment worked, and soon hospitals in other cities tried a similar arrangement. The idea took on the Blue Cross name and was adopted by the American Hospital Association (AHA) as a public service. In 1972, the relationship between the Blue Cross Association (BCA) and the AHA was officially ended when the Blue Cross name and mark were turned over to BCA.

The origin of the Blue Shield organization can be traced to a number of county medical prepayment bureaus that came into existence shortly before the turn of the century in northwestern United States. These pioneer programs provided the foundation for the first Blue Shield–type plan founded in California in 1939, called California Physician's Service.

Blue Cross Plans were founded originally to cover hospital expenses. Blue Shield Plans were originally established primarily to cover physician services. Both types of Plans now cover hospital expenses, outpatient care, other institutional services, home care, and dental, vision, and outpatient benefits. In most areas, Blue Cross and Blue Shield Plans are a single corporation. In other areas, they are separate organizations and, in some cases, even compete with each other. On the national level, the Blue Cross and Blue Shield Association is a single corporation and speaks for the Plans in matters of national concern.

Blue Cross and Blue Shield Plans are nonprofit, which means that almost all the money they take in as premiums is paid out in benefits. A person becomes a member by entering into a contract with his or her local Blue Cross and/or Blue Shield Plan and by paying regular dues. He or she becomes a *subscriber,* not a policyholder, and retains a *certificate,* not a policy, that tells him or her what to expect from the contract when medical services are required.

When the Blue Cross and Blue Shield Plans serve as a Medicare contractor, the Blue Cross staff within the Plan handle Medicare Part A as the fiscal intermediary, and the Blue Shield staff within the Plan handle Medicare Part B as the carrier.

Blue Cross and Blue Shield programs across the country have developed health maintenance organizations, preferred provider organizations, dental care programs, and prescription drug programs.

Special Clauses and Benefits

Some Blue Cross and Blue Shield Plan contracts include a pre-existing conditions clause, which outlines a specific waiting period before benefits are payable for those conditions existing before the membership-effective date. The waiting period varies with the plan and the contract.

Coverage for emergency treatment is provided under many contracts if the treatment is rendered immediately after an accident within the time specified by the contract (usually within 24 to 72 hours).

When a Blue Cross/Blue Shield member has additional coverage from a commercial insurance carrier, benefits must be coordinated. As discussed in Chapter 3, a *coordination of benefits* clause written into some health insurance policies means that if the member has group hospital, medical, or dental coverage with another company, the Blue Plan* will take into account benefits payable by the other carrier in determining its own liability.

Second and third opinions to confirm the need for elective surgery are required in some health plans as a condition for full coverage. Contact the Blue Shield representative in your area for specific requirements.

---

*This can refer to Blue Cross or Blue Shield or both (i.e., Blue Cross/Blue Shield).

Types of Blue Cross and Blue Shield Contracts

There are two basic types of Blue Cross and Blue Shield contracts: service benefit contracts and indemnity benefit contracts.

SERVICE BENEFIT CONTRACTS

Service benefit contracts are offered by all Blue Cross and Blue Shield Plans that offer physician participation agreements. The contract provides the covered services themselves, rather than reimbursing the subscriber for some or all of the expenses incurred in obtaining covered services. Through *physician participation agreements,* a Blue Cross or Blue Shield Plan secures the performance of service benefits (i.e., covered services) on behalf of its subscribers.

INDEMNITY BENEFIT CONTRACTS

Indemnity benefit contracts cover some or all of the actual expenses of providing covered services but not more than the actual charges for a specific service. An indemnity benefit contract makes no promise to cover the full fee. A professional provider may bill the subscriber an amount in excess of the Plan's benefit allowance. The subscriber is responsible for any difference between the Plan's allowance and the professional provider's bill.

Methods of Payment

Blue Cross and Blue Shield Plans use several methods of payment: fee schedules, relative value studies (RVS), and usual, customary, and reasonable (UCR). A few contracts make payments under the diagnosis related group (DRG) system. The predominant method used to determine the level of physician payment is UCR, which is by far the most complicated. Regardless of the method of payment from Blue Cross and Blue Shield Plans, the subscriber is still responsible for payment of any deductible, coinsurance, and noncovered services.

USUAL, CUSTOMARY, AND REASONABLE (UCR) PAYMENT PROGRAM

Essentially, a UCR program means that payment is determined by (1) determining the usual fee that the doctor most frequently charges to the majority of patients for similar services, (2) considering the physician's geographic location and specialty, and (3) interpreting medical complications or unusual circumstances. The following definitions spell out these features in greater detail.

Usual fee — That fee normally charged for a given professional service by an individual physician to his or her patients (i.e., his or her own usual fee).

Customary fee — That fee which is in the range of usual fees charged by physicians of similar training and experience for the same services within the same specific and limited geographic area.

Reasonable fee — That fee which meets the two above criteria or by responsible medical opinion is justifiable considering special circumstances of the particular case in question.

Examples:

1. A surgeon's *usual* charge for a specific surgical procedure is $350.
   The *customary* level (usually the 90th percentile of all surgeons' charges for the procedure within the geographic area) is $350.
   The surgeon in point charges $400. This is $50 over the *usual* and the *customary* range. The Plan will determine whether the $400 charge is *reasonable* because of extenuating circumstances in this specific case. If, on investigation, the Plan deems the charge to be *reasonable,* the $400 will be paid in full. If, however, there are no indications of unusual circumstances, the Plan will reimburse the physician the *usual* charge of $350.
2. A surgeon's *usual* charge for a specific surgical procedure is $350.
   The *customary* level (usually the 90th percentile of all surgeons' charges for the procedure within the geographic area) is $400.
   The surgeon in point charges the *usual* fee of $350. The charge is paid in full because it is the *usual* charge and falls within the *customary* range.
3. The *usual* charge is $350, the *customary*

10

level is $400, and the surgeon in point bills for $375. This is screened against the *usual* level and is found to be $25 over the *usual* charge. However, it does not exceed the *customary* level and is, therefore, paid in full.

PAYMENTS UNDER UCR

1. The participating member physician will be paid a usual, customary, or reasonable fee and will accept this amount as *payment in full* for services rendered or may bill the patient for any unpaid balance, depending on the contract. Various appeal mechanisms are available to the physician for fees in question. Your local professional and provider relations representative can explain these to you.
2. Participating physicians are paid directly.
3. Payments to nonparticipating physicians vary with individual plans. Again, contact your professional and provider relations representative for further information.
4. *Copayment:* Some contracts provide for percentage (75%, 80%, or 90%) coverage of the UCR fee. The remaining 25%, 20%, or 10% up to the UCR maximum is the responsibility of the patient. The subject of fees should be discussed by the physician and patient before a professional service is rendered.

Table 10–1 illustrates similar (though not identical) terminology used in the Medicare Part B program.

In summary, under UCR, the Blue Shield payment to the physician is the lowest of the actual charge, the physician's usual charge, or the customary charge within the area. Third party payment will not exceed the customary allowance (except in individual consideration cases, i.e., Level III).

FEE SCHEDULES

Fee schedules designate the maximum level of third party payment for a specific service, with the physician's actual payment level being the lesser of the billed charge or the fee schedule level. Fee schedules are established on the basis of a survey of physicians' billed charges, by applying a conversion factor to a relative value scale, or through negotiations with medical specialty organizations. Fee schedules are not generally established solely by physicians and do not necessarily reflect existing physician charge patterns. Before Medicare, fee schedules were the predominant method of physician payment by third party payers.

Relative Value Studies

Refer to Chapter 4 for a discussion of this fee schedule based on RVS. Procedure codes and nomenclature in use by local plans vary widely. In addition to modifiers used in CPT and RVS coding systems, some Blue Cross and Blue Shield programs employ additional modifiers. For example, second and/or third opinions to confirm the need for elective surgery are required in some health plans as a condition for full coverage. If the physician provides a second or third opinion at the request of another physician, certain modifiers must be used to indicate this situation. A penalty is imposed if a second opinion is a requirement of the plan and is not obtained. Some plans pay 100% for the second opinion.

Physician Participation Concept

Service benefits are assured through the physician participation agreement or contract with the Blue Plans. The participation concept is similar to Medicare's physician assignment approach, except that under Medicare, the physician can choose to accept assignment on a case-by-case basis. Member physicians treating patients who are members of a Blue Cross and Blue Shield Plan participate under these guidelines:

TABLE 10–1
Fee Screen Levels

	Level I Screen, Individual Physician	Level II Screen, Geographic Area	Level III Screen, Reasonableness
BC/BS Plan	Usual	Customary	Reasonable
Medicare Part B	Customary	Prevailing	Reasonable

1. The physician will be paid usual and customary fees if the plan is based on the UCR payment method and may accept this as *payment in full* for services rendered or may bill the patient for any unpaid balance, depending on the contract. If a fee schedule, RVS, or DRG system is written into the plan, then payment is based on whichever method is pertinent to the plan.
2. The physician will be paid directly, regardless of assignment of benefits.
3. Mandatory arbitration is written into the Blue Plans contracts to protect both physician and patient. (For an explanation of arbitration, see Chapter 2.)

Physicians who are *not* participating physicians and who bill Blue Cross or Blue Shield fall under these guidelines:

1. The physician will be paid the reasonable fee if UCR is the payment method. If a fee schedule, RVS, or DRG system is written into the plan, then payment is based on whichever method is pertinent to the plan.
2. The payment will go directly to the patient, regardless of assignment of benefits.
3. The physician must collect the entire amount of the bill directly from the patient.

BLUECARD PROGRAM

The BlueCard Program has been put into effect to meet the needs of members who require health care when traveling or living in the area of another Blue Plan. It is a significant improvement over the plans of past years that have been known by various names, such as Inter-Plan Bank, Reciprocity, and Out-of-Area Programs. The Program, which initially provided inpatient, outpatient, and professional claims service for traditional benefit plans has been expanded beginning in 1996 to include a preferred provider organization (PPO) delivery capability that can be accessed when it is negotiated with an account. Blue Cross and Blue Shield of Western Europe is making its institutional provider network available through the BlueCard Program, and their subscribers, in turn, are eligible to access Plan networks in the United States.

Providers send claims for members who are out of the area to the local Plan electronically or on the local Plan's claim form. After adding information about the provider pricing arrangements, the local Plan forwards the claim to the member's own Plan for benefit adjudication (determination) and payment authorization. The local Plan pays its provider as authorized. Software tools, known as Inter-Plan Teleprocessing Services (ITS), standardize and help Plans manage the exchange of claims and payment information. In addition, providers may call a toll-free 800 number to be connected to the subscriber's Home Plan for eligibility verification, and subscribers may call an 800 number to obtain a selection of PPO providers near their location.

Always read local Blue Plan bulletins for additional BlueCard Program enhancements that will further improve the Program's value to Blue Cross and Blue Shield providers and customers.

Central Certification and Central Site Processing

Central certification and central site processing are methods used by the Blue Cross and Blue Shield system to administer benefits of companies (Plan corporate accounts) with business locations in several different states (national account). Such companies tend to have employees who travel or change locations frequently. In addition, these companies may have their personnel, payroll, and health coverage records in one place and require a high level of consistency in benefit administration that is best provided by a single processor.

Under central certification and central site processing arrangements, a single Blue Cross and/or Blue Shield Plan (called the control Plan) maintains all enrollment and claims history information for a company's employees. The control Plan is usually the Plan located in the company's headquarters city. The control Plan issues identification cards to all employees of that company, regardless of their location. These subscribers are treated like any subscriber of a local Blue Cross and Blue Shield Plan. The subscriber's identification card is accepted the same as a card from a local Plan.

10

Identifying Information

Identification cards for most Blue Cross and Blue Shield subscribers (Fig. 10–1) contain the subscriber's name and identification number with a three-character alpha(betic) prefix (e.g., DDD123456789). The alpha(betic) prefix is essential information and must be reported on claims filed with the local Plan. Contact the local Plan for more information about filing claims for subscribers who carry identification cards issued by Plans other than the local Plan.

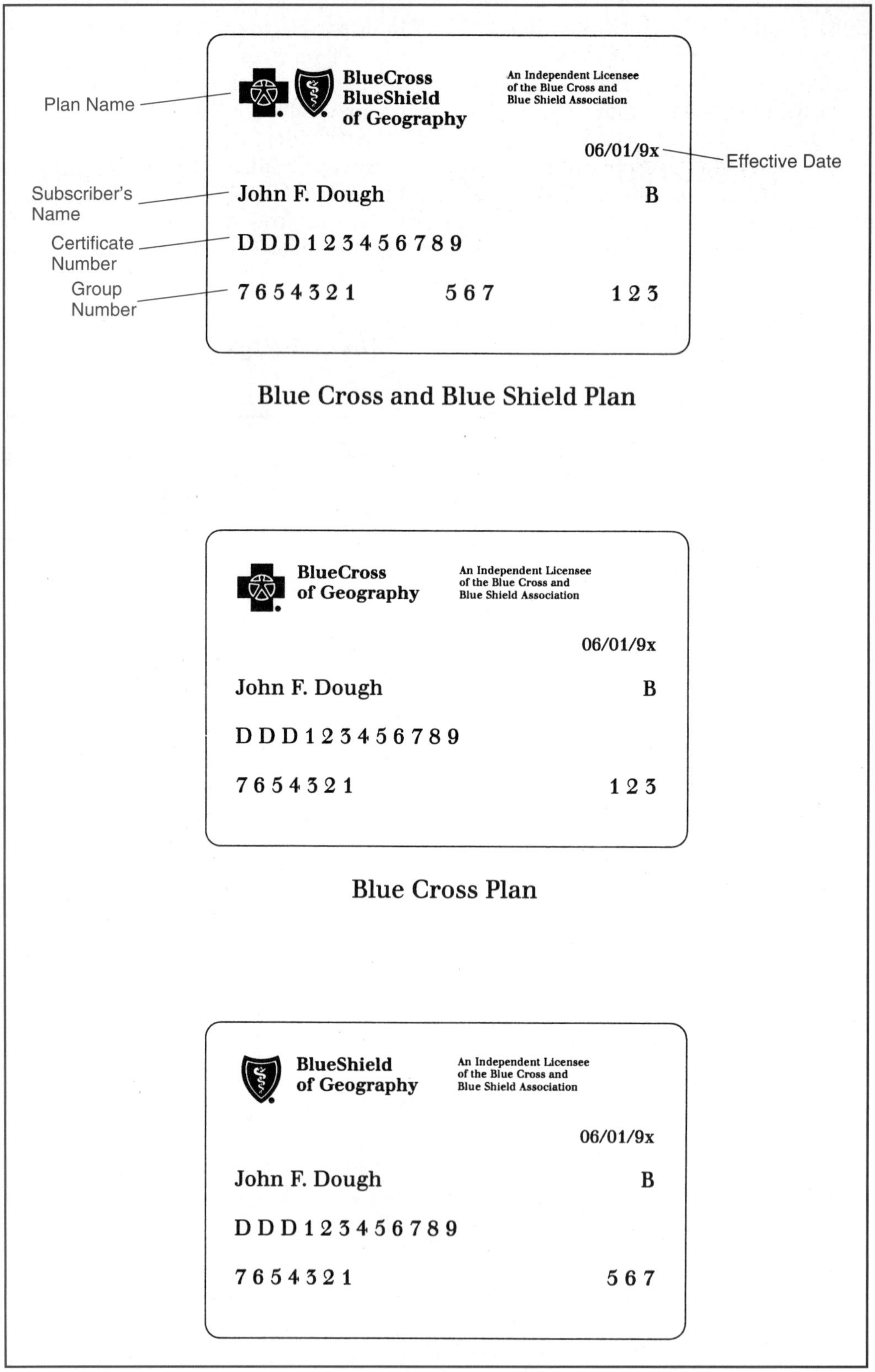

FIGURE 10–1
Typical Blue Cross and Blue Shield identification cards. Cards may be issued on either embossed plastic, nonembossed plastic, or a heavy paper stock. *Note:* All identification cards now carry an alpha(betic) prefix at the beginning of the identification number.

The Blue Cross and Blue Shield Association's electronic data interchange company (EDI-USA) has teamed up with National Data Corporation (NDC) to offer providers on-line, all-payer, interactive eligibility information.

Blue Cross/Blue Shield and Medicare Claims

Medicare recipients who are Blue Cross and Blue Shield BlueCard Program subscribers carry both a Blue Cross/Blue Shield card and a Medicare identification card for *complementary benefits*. The Blue Plan pays the deductible and copayment. However, on group plans, an itemized statement is needed. If the itemized bill contains Health Care Financing Administration (HCFA) Common Procedure Coding System (HCPCS) code numbers, you will have to substitute the Blue Plan code numbers used in your region for the procedure(s). Alternatively, you may include a narrative description so that the physician can receive payment on the claim from the Blue Plan.

LOCAL BLUE SHIELD PLAN IS MEDICARE PART B CARRIER

If the physician accepts assignment, include the identification numbers from the Blue Shield card in the appropriate space on the Medicare claim form. Forward the form to your local Blue Shield Plan.

Managed Care

PREFERRED PROVIDER ORGANIZATIONS

See Chapter 9 for information pertinent to Blue Cross and Blue Shield Plans that have PPOs.

HEALTH MAINTENANCE ORGANIZATIONS

Some areas served by a Blue Cross and Blue Shield Plan group practice health maintenance organization (HMO) or an individual practice association HMO have enrollees from large companies. Benefits include such services as routine office visits, immunizations, physical examinations, and a low prescription drug copayment. Because of these benefit incentives, HMO coverage may vary from one region to another. See Chapter 9 for in-depth information on HMOs and Blue Cross and Blue Shield Plans.

POINT OF SERVICE PROGRAMS

See Chapter 9 for information pertaining to Blue Cross and Blue Shield Plans and point of service (POS) programs.

Medical Necessity Program

The Medical Necessity Program was begun in 1976 as a quality management and cost control effort related to utilization review. The program ended routine payment for a number of surgical and diagnostic procedures that have been judged obsolete, outmoded, or of unproved value. These procedures were put on a list and providers were notified in local Blue Plan bulletins. The Blue Cross and Blue Shield Association has not issued any updates to this program since 1991. It is possible that local Blue Cross and Blue Shield Plans may have added procedures to the initial list generated by the Blue Cross and Blue Shield Association. The procedures listed are payable only upon satisfactory justification or require justification when performed for specific conditions. Consequently, it is important to obtain a current copy of the list of such procedures from your local Blue Cross and Blue Shield office for reference in the treatment of patients.

Also included in the Medical Necessity Program is the recommendation that Plans provide benefits for tests performed when a patient is admitted to a hospital only if such tests were ordered by the attending/admitting physician specifically for that patient.

Technology Assessment

Decisions about health care are being made every day by patients, physicians, health plan medical directors, and others. There is concern about benefits, risks, and outcomes. As health care becomes more technologically complex, these decisions will increasingly revolve around the technology itself.

The Blue Cross and Blue Shield Association's Technology Evaluation Center (TEC) offers technology assessment and information services to support medical decision making and policy development. Each year the TEC program evaluates 30 to 40 technologies and publishes the findings for its subscribers. A TEC subscription includes more than 30 technology assessments, the TEC Newsletter, access to the TEC telephone clearinghouse, and invitations to scientific forums. If you are interested in further information about the TEC program, call (312) 440-6080.

Preadmission Testing, Ambulatory Surgery, and Second Opinions

The Blue Cross and Blue Shield Plans encourage preadmission testing for patients having surgery, which often reduces the length of hospitalization by 1 or 2 days. A plan might pay 80% if the preadmission requirements are approved and only 50% if they are not approved. Therefore, it is important to contact Blue Cross and Blue Shield for this approval. The Plans also encourage and pay for surgical procedures performed on an outpatient basis, in either same-day surgery units at hospitals or free-standing ambulatory surgical centers.

Most Plans have started second opinion programs, under which the Plan will pay for consultations in advance of elective surgery as a means of reducing the incidence of surgery. A penalty can be imposed if a second opinion is a requirement of a plan as a condition for full coverage and is not obtained.

Standard Blue Plans Claims Procedure

1. Obtain the necessary information from the patient's identification card (see Fig. 10–1):
   a. Group number.
   b. Certificate number (also known as Agreement, Identification, Member, or Subscriber number). Often this is the patient's Social Security number. When the patient is a member of a federal or national group, the identification number is different (see the subsequent discussion on Federal Employee Programs and Fig. 10–4). A member can be the contract holder, the spouse, or a dependent.
2. Blue Plan claims should be submitted no later than 30 days after the physician's service is completed. On most contracts, Blue claims received more than 1 year after service is performed are not payable. Exact time limits vary with the local plan.
3. Submit the claim on the proper Blue Plan claim form. Many Plans are now adopting the universal or uniform Health Insurance Claim Form (see Chapter 6). However, there are variations in this form, depending on the Plan area. Be sure to check with your local Blue Plan office to determine the procedure in your area.
4. *Medicare and Blue Cross/Blue Shield:* Some Blue Shield or Blue Cross Plans offer a contract that supplements Medicare Part B coverage, including deductibles and a percentage of copay. In this instance,
   a. Bill Medicare first.
   b. Then bill Blue Cross or Blue Shield with the Medicare Remittance Advice (RA) formerly known as an Explanation of Medicare Benefits (EOMB) Form, indicating the Blue group and Subscriber Identification numbers on the RA. Submit the RA to the local Blue Plan.
5. Members of special groups, including trust funds and union locals, must work a specified number of hours per quarter to be eligible for benefits under some local Plans. If in doubt about a patient's eligibility, call his or her local union office to ascertain this information.
6. Sometimes a Blue Cross member is covered under two Blue Cross contracts, a situation known as duplicate coverage. When this occurs, bill Blue Cross under each coverage code or group number. This permits payment of the maximum amount under each coverage up to the total amount of the fee.
7. Because of the vast amount of paperwork in the physician's office, many Blue Cross and Blue Shield programs are developing claim forms for the subscriber (insured) to complete and submit. The subscriber attaches the bill(s) from the provider(s) of service. The patient should retain a photocopy of the itemized billing statement. The claim number should be listed on the retained copy in case the patient needs to inquire about a claim. If several members of a family are seen at the same time, a separate claim form must be completed for each member.

MANUAL COMPLETION OF HCFA-1500 CLAIM FORM

Instructions on how to complete the HCFA-1500 Claim Form for Blue Plans are presented here. However, regional offices may have different requirements, so always check with your local Blue Plan for their guidelines. Additional instructions for third party payers are presented in Chapter 6. Figure 10–2 shows an example of a completed Health Insurance Claim Form, HCFA-1500, for a Blue Cross and Blue Shield case.

Block	Instructions
1	Identify coverage by checking all appropriate boxes.
1a	Enter the insured subscriber's I.D. number exactly as on I.D. card.
2	Enter patient's full name in last name, first name, middle initial order.
3	Enter patient's date of birth (two-digit method, e.g., 05/07/42) and sex.
4	Enter name of insured subscriber exactly as it appears on the I.D. card.
5	Enter patient's complete current address and telephone number.
6	Enter patient's relationship to insured subscriber.
7	Enter insured subscriber's complete address and telephone number.
8	Check appropriate box.
9	If there is any other insurance company or insured party who may be responsible for any part of this bill, enter the insured person's name, and 9a Policy and/or group number; and 9b Date of birth and sex; and 9c Employer's name, if applicable; and 9d Insurance plan or program name.
10a–10c	Check *Yes* or *No* to indicate whether employment, auto, or other accident applies to one or more services described in Block 24.
11	Enter subscriber's group number exactly as it appears on I.D. card and 11a Insured's date of birth and sex; and 11b Employer's name, if applicable; and 11c Insurance plan or program code; and 11d Indicate if there is another health benefit plan. If *Yes*, complete fields 9–9d with other health benefit plan information.
12–13	Not applicable. *Note: Blue Shield will only make payment directly to physician members and participating health care professionals.*
14	Enter date of current illness, injury, or pregnancy.
15	Complete if applicable.
16	If applicable, enter dates patient is/has been unable to work. An entry in this field usually indicates workers' compensation–related coverage.
17–17a	Enter name and Blue Cross/Blue Shield provider I.D. number (PIN) of the referring physician.
18	Complete these dates when a medical service is furnished as a result of, or subsequent to, a related hospitalization.
19	Not applicable.
20	Enter *Yes* or *No* when billing diagnostic laboratory tests. *No* means the tests were performed by the billing physician/laboratory. *Yes* means that the laboratory test was performed *outside* the physician's office. (For a laboratory billing for tests performed by another affiliated laboratory, also check *Yes*.) If *Yes*, you must enter purchase price for the test in the Charges portion of this block. When laboratory procedures are performed by a party *other than* the billing physician/laboratory, identify procedures by adding the -90 modifier to the regular procedure code in Block 24D. Charges for these services cannot exceed the amount that the outside laboratory charged.
21	Enter up to four five-digit ICD-9-CM codes in priority order with the primary diagnosis in the first position. Do **not** add any diagnosis description.
22–23	Not applicable.
24	Itemize services rendered using appropriate *codes*, one line for each service. This area of the claim form may *not* contain more than six lines of service. If you need to report more lines for the same patient, do so on separate claims. Also, claims cannot be continued from one to another; each claim must be separate.
24A	Enter a six-digit *from* date (month, day, and year) for each service or supply. Leave *to* date blank—no date ranging.
24B	Enter the two-digit place of service code as follows: 11 Office 12 Patient home 21 Inpatient hospital 22 Outpatient hospital 23 Emergency department 24 Ambulatory surgery center 25 Birthing center 26 Military treatment center 31 Skilled nursing facility 32 Nursing home/facility 33 Custodial care facility 34 Hospice 41 Ambulance (land) 42 Ambulance

10

PLEASE DO NOT STAPLE IN THIS AREA — BLUE CROSS/BLUE SHIELD CASE

APPROVED OMB-0938-0008

BLUE CROSS/BLUE SHIELD
1901 MARKET STREET
WOODLAND HILLS, XY

CARRIER

PICA — **HEALTH INSURANCE CLAIM FORM** — PICA

1. MEDICARE (Medicare #) [ ] MEDICAID (Medicaid #) [ ] CHAMPUS (Sponsor's SSN) [ ] CHAMPVA (VA File #) [ ] GROUP HEALTH PLAN (SSN or ID) [ ] FECA BLK LUNG (SSN) [ ] OTHER (ID) [X]

1a. INSURED'S I.D. NUMBER (FOR PROGRAM IN ITEM 1): ATC 489 20 1201

2. PATIENT'S NAME (Last Name, First Name, Middle Initial): MACKINNON MARY JO

3. PATIENT'S BIRTH DATE MM DD YY — SEX M [ ] F [X]

4. INSURED'S NAME (Last Name, First Name, Middle Initial): MACKINNON HAROLD M

5. PATIENT'S ADDRESS (No., Street): 5430 BRACKEN STREET

CITY: WOODLAND HILLS — STATE: XY

ZIP CODE: 12345 — TELEPHONE (Include Area Code): (013) 423-1400

6. PATIENT RELATIONSHIP TO INSURED: Self [ ] Spouse [X] Child [ ] Other [ ]

7. INSURED'S ADDRESS (No., Street): SAME

CITY — STATE — ZIP CODE — TELEPHONE (INCLUDE AREA CODE) ( )

8. PATIENT STATUS: Single [ ] Married [X] Other [ ]; Employed [ ] Full-Time Student [ ] Part-Time Student [ ]

9. OTHER INSURED'S NAME (Last Name, First Name, Middle Initial)

a. OTHER INSURED'S POLICY OR GROUP NUMBER

b. OTHER INSURED'S DATE OF BIRTH MM DD YY — SEX M [ ] F [ ]

c. EMPLOYER'S NAME OR SCHOOL NAME

d. INSURANCE PLAN NAME OR PROGRAM NAME

10. IS PATIENT'S CONDITION RELATED TO:

a. EMPLOYMENT? (CURRENT OR PREVIOUS) [ ] YES [X] NO

b. AUTO ACCIDENT? [ ] YES [X] NO — PLACE (State)

c. OTHER ACCIDENT? [ ] YES [X] NO

10d. RESERVED FOR LOCAL USE

11. INSURED'S POLICY GROUP OR FECA NUMBER

a. INSURED'S DATE OF BIRTH MM DD YY — SEX M [ ] F [ ]

b. EMPLOYER'S NAME OR SCHOOL NAME

c. INSURANCE PLAN NAME OR PROGRAM NAME

d. IS THERE ANOTHER HEALTH BENEFIT PLAN? [ ] YES [X] NO *If yes*, return to and complete item 9 a-d.

READ BACK OF FORM BEFORE COMPLETING & SIGNING THIS FORM.

12. PATIENT'S OR AUTHORIZED PERSON'S SIGNATURE I authorize the release of any medical or other information necessary to process this claim. I also request payment of government benefits either to myself or to the party who accepts assignment below.

SIGNED NOT APPLICABLE DATE

EXAMPLE ONLY

13. INSURED'S OR AUTHORIZED PERSON'S SIGNATURE I authorize payment of medical benefits to the undersigned physician or supplier for services described below.

SIGNED NOT APPLICABLE

PATIENT AND INSURED INFORMATION

14. DATE OF CURRENT: ILLNESS (First symptom) OR INJURY (Accident) OR PREGNANCY(LMP) — MM DD YY: 08 15 9X

15. IF PATIENT HAS HAD SAME OR SIMILAR ILLNESS. GIVE FIRST DATE MM DD YY

16. DATES PATIENT UNABLE TO WORK IN CURRENT OCCUPATION FROM MM DD YY TO MM DD YY

17. NAME OF REFERRING PHYSICIAN OR OTHER SOURCE

17a. I.D. NUMBER OF REFERRING PHYSICIAN

18. HOSPITALIZATION DATES RELATED TO CURRENT SERVICES FROM MM DD YY TO MM DD YY

19. RESERVED FOR LOCAL USE

20. OUTSIDE LAB? [ ] YES [X] NO — $ CHARGES

21. DIAGNOSIS OR NATURE OF ILLNESS OR INJURY. (RELATE ITEMS 1,2,3 OR 4 TO ITEM 24E BY LINE)

1. 992 . 0
2. ___ . __
3. ___ . __
4. ___ . __

22. MEDICAID RESUBMISSION CODE — ORIGINAL REF. NO.

23. PRIOR AUTHORIZATION NUMBER

24.

	A DATE(S) OF SERVICE From MM DD YY	To MM DD YY	B Place of Service	C Type of Service	D PROCEDURES, SERVICES, OR SUPPLIES (Explain Unusual Circumstances) CPT/HCPCS	MODIFIER	E DIAGNOSIS CODE	F $ CHARGES	G DAYS OR UNITS	H EPSDT Family Plan	I EMG	J COB	K RESERVED FOR LOCAL USE
1	08 15 9X		11		99203		1	75 00	010				
2													
3													
4													
5													
6													

25. FEDERAL TAX I.D. NUMBER SSN EIN: 70 3459766 [ ] [X]

26. PATIENT'S ACCOUNT NO.

27. ACCEPT ASSIGNMENT? (For govt. claims, see back) [ ] YES [ ] NO

28. TOTAL CHARGE $ 75 00

29. AMOUNT PAID $

30. BALANCE DUE $ 75 00

31. SIGNATURE OF PHYSICIAN OR SUPPLIER INCLUDING DEGREES OR CREDENTIALS (I certify that the statements on the reverse apply to this bill and are made a part thereof.)

Gerald Practon, MD

SIGNED Gerald Practon MD DATE 8-16-9X

32. NAME AND ADDRESS OF FACILITY WHERE SERVICES WERE RENDERED (If other than home or office): Same

33. PHYSICIAN'S, SUPPLIER'S BILLING NAME, ADDRESS, ZIP CODE & PHONE #

GERALD PRACTON MD
4567 BROAD AVENUE
WOODLAND HILLS XY 12345
013-486-9002

PIN# — GRP# 3664021CC

PHYSICIAN OR SUPPLIER INFORMATION

(APPROVED BY AMA COUNCIL ON MEDICAL SERVICE 8/88) — ***PLEASE PRINT OR TYPE*** — FORM HCFA-1500 (U2) (12-90) FORM OWCP-1500 FORM RRB-1500

reference initials

FIGURE 10–2

Example of a completed Health Insurance Claim Form HCFA-1500 for a Blue Cross/Blue Shield case.

(air or water)
51 Inpatient psychiatric facility
52 Day-care facility/psychiatric facility
53 Community mental health center
54 Special treatment center/intermediate care
55 Residential treatment center/substance abuse
56 Psychiatric residential treatment center
61 Comprehensive inpatient rehabilitation facility
62 Comprehensive outpatient rehabilitation facility
65 Independent kidney disease treatment center
71 State or local public health clinic
72 Rural health clinic
81 Independent laboratory
99 Other

24C Leave blank. Completion of this block is not required.

24D Enter procedure, service, or supply using the appropriate HCPCS/CPT procedure code and up to two modifiers. For assistant at surgery or anesthesia, always be sure to include applicable modifiers. *Note: When you need to use more than two modifiers with a procedure code, enter modifier -99 in Block 24D and list applicable modifiers in Block 19.*

24E Enter diagnosis code reference pointer from Block 21 to relate date of service and procedures performed to appropriate diagnosis. A maximum of four diagnosis pointers may be referenced. Place commas between multiple diagnosis reference pointers on the same line.

24F Enter charge for the service performed. Do not enter dollar signs or decimal points. Always include cents.

24G When charge is for more than one item or service, enter number of items or services. This field is most commonly used for number of miles, units of supplies, anesthesia minutes, or oxygen volume.

Format: This is a three-digit block. The rightmost digit represents tenths, and the leftmost two digits represent whole items or units.

Example: 1 service: enter 010
2.5 services: enter 025
14 services: enter 140

If you need to report more than 99 services, you must use two lines.

Example: 100 Services billed: Enter first line as 990 and second line as 010

For anesthesia services, show elapsed time in minutes. Do not use time *units.*

Example: 1 hour and 10 minutes = 70 minutes
Enter as 070 (70 minutes)

24H–24J Not applicable.

24K Enter Blue Cross/Blue Shield of the performing physician or supplier. Several different physicians or suppliers may be involved in providing services billed on the claim. If several members of a group shown in Block 33 have furnished services, this item is used to distinguish them.

25 Show physician/supplier federal tax I.D. (employer identification number) or Social Security number.

26 Optional field to enhance patient identification by physician or supplier.

27 It is not necessary to check *Yes* or *No* because member physicians are paid directly; nonmember physicians must bill and collect directly from patients.

28 Enter total charge for services indicated in Block 24F. Do not enter dollar signs or decimal points. Always include cents.

29 Enter total amount paid by patient on submitted charges in Block 28.

30 Enter the balance due (Block 28 minus Block 29).

31 Show signature of physician/supplier or representative and the date form was signed.

32 Enter name and address of person; organization or facility performing services; and whether services were furnished in a hospital, clinic, laboratory, or any facility other than patient's home or physician's office.

33 Enter name, address, telephone number, and Blue Cross/Blue Shield–issued nine-digit PIN assigned to practice location for which bill is submitted. Show PIN on bottom line of this block.

ELECTRONIC CLAIMS SUBMISSION

The Blue Cross and Blue Shield Association's electronic data interchange company (EDI-USA) has teamed up with National Data Corporation (NDC) to offer providers on-line, all-payer, interactive eligibility information. EDI-USA is an electronic claims clearinghouse that will eventually provide for interactive and batch referrals and physician/pharmacy communications. To boost electronic claim submission, some Blue Plans, such as Blue Cross of California, assess a surcharge and a payment hold on paper-submitted claims. Refer to Chapter 7 for further information on this aspect of submission of claims.

FOLLOWING UP ON DELINQUENT CLAIMS

See Chapter 8 for information on how to follow up on Blue Cross and Blue Shield delinquent payments.

BLUE CROSS/BLUE SHIELD STATE INSURANCE ADDRESSES

Refer to Appendix A for the Blue Cross and Blue Shield address for your state.

REFERENCE BOOKS

Refer to Appendix B for names and sources of books relating to insurance, coding, and health insurance plans.

Explanation of Benefits

After an insurance claim is processed and payment is generated, a document called an Explanation of Benefits (EOB) (Fig. 10–3) is sent to the physician and/or patient along with the check. In this chapter, we present the simplest type of EOB you will encounter, showing payment made on one patient instead of a number of patients. Always check the patient's name, provider of services, dates of service, amount billed, and amount paid.

Indicate the payment received on the patient's ledger and the day sheet. If the bill is $40 and Blue Cross/Blue Shield pays $35, then adjust off the $5 if the provider is a participating physician as noted on the EOB. If there is an amount applied to the deductible, the patient pays this as well as the patient's total responsibility for the claim (copayment amounts and nonbenefit items).

Provider Number

In some regions, Blue Cross/Blue Shield issues a provider identification number (PIN) to member physicians, which enables the program to validate the fact that the provider is licensed. Often, the PIN for an unincorporated physician is his or her state license number. A single PIN can be issued to a medical group (or a group PIN can be issued to a physician corporation). A physician who employs other physicians should obtain a separate PIN for each provider (physician) or a group PIN.

If Blue Cross/Blue Shield does not issue provider numbers in your area, your physician can obtain one by applying, under a fictitious name, such as Main Street Medical Group, to the Board of Medical Examiners of your state, for fictitious name certification. This certification is then used to apply for a PIN.

Federal Employee Health Benefits Program

The Commission on the Health Needs of the Nation, established by President Truman in 1951, recommended that the federal government guarantee health care insurance for its employees. The Federal Employee Health Benefits Program (FEHBP) was founded for this purpose. In July 1960, the Blue Cross and Blue Shield Association established their Federal Employee Program (FEP) for federal government employees, which is a part of the FEHBP. The payroll deduction system is used for payment of prepaid health benefits. There are three types of health care insurance plans under the FEHBP:

- The Service Benefit Plan administered by Blue Cross and Blue Shield
- Employee organization plans
- Comprehensive medical plans

NONBENEFITS

Following are some of the services not covered under the FEHBP.

1. In-hospital private duty nursing
2. Hospitalization not requiring the acute facility
3. Charges in excess of usual, customary, and reasonable fees
4. Diagnostic tests unrelated to diagnosis of specific symptoms
5. Services or supplies that do not serve a medical purpose, but are primarily for comfort or convenience
6. Drugs or medications for use outside a hospital that do not require a prescription

BLUE SHIELD

P.O. BOX 7168 • SAN FRANCISCO, CA 94120

SECURITY PACIFIC NATIONAL BANK
SAN FRANCISCO, CALIFORNIA
11-4
1210

STANDARD BUSINESS ACCOUNT 0153
VOID 12 MONTHS FROM ISSUE DATE

PROVIDER NO.	CHECK NO.
	43080215

MO.	DAY	YEAR	PAY	DOLLARS	CENTS
01	10	9X	$VOID		VOID

PAY TO THE ORDER OF
FORDNEY M
3821 OCEAN DR
OXNARD CA 93030

AMOUNTS $10,000.00 AND OVER REQUIRE TWO SIGNATURES

*VOID*VOID*VOID*VOID*
*VOID*VOID*VOID*VOID*
*VOID*VOID*VOID*VOID*

⑈43080215⑈ ⑆121000044⑆928⑈979979⑈

C 11229 (1/84)

DETACH CHECK

DETACH CHECK

DETACH CHECK

BLUE SHIELD

P.O. BOX 3308 SONORA, CA 95370
(800)351-2466, (209)532-8513

CHECK NO.
43080215

EXPLANATION OF BENEFITS

Your claim has been processed in accordance with the subscriber's health plan coverage. Please see the reverse side for an important message.

FOR THE CLAIM RECEIVED ON 01/08/9X

PATIENT'S NAME	GROUP NO.	SUBSCRIBER NO.	CLAIM NO.	PROVIDER OF SERVICES	DATE
FORDNEY MARILYN	1901 0230	557469969	06861221211300	LOIGNON LUCILLE M MD	05 13 9X

770693040 05000 PHYSICIAN MEMBER - YES

SERVICES BILLED	PROCEDURE NUMBER	DATES OF SERVICE -DAYS- MO	FROM	TO	YEAR	NUMBER OF SERVICES	AMOUNT BILLED	AMOUNT ALLOWED	MESSAGE (SEE BELOW)	APPLIED TO DEDUCTIBLE	PATIENT'S COPAYMENT AMOUNT	AMOUNT PAID
PROF MEDICAL	9201452	03	03	03	9X	1	70.00	70.00		70.00		0.00
TOTALS							70.00	70.00		70.00		0.00

THE PATIENT'S TOTAL RESPONSIBILITY FOR THIS CLAIM IS $ 70.00

DEDUCTIBLE RECORD FOR 199X:

$ 70.00 HAS APPLIED TO THE $ 300.00 BASIC DEDUCTIBLE FROM THIS CLAIM.
AS OF 05 13 9X, $ 70.00 OF THIS DEDUCTIBLE HAS BEEN MET.

C 11230 (1-84)

C 11214 REVISION (1/84)

THIS IS NOT A BILL - RETAIN FOR PERSONAL TAX AND MEDICAL RECORDS

FIGURE 10-3
Example of a Blue Shield Explanation of Benefits Form indicating the amount billed, amount allowed, deductible, and amount paid on the insurance claim.

10

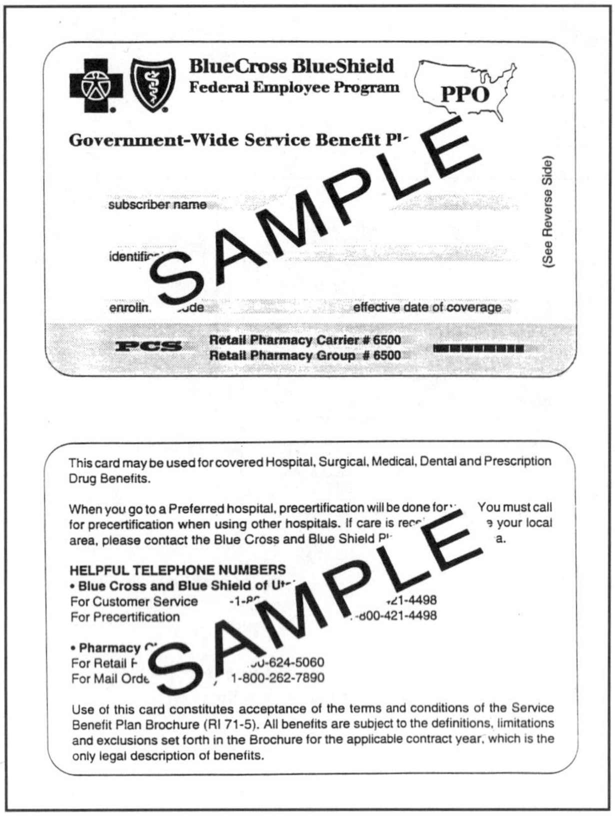

FIGURE 10–4

A, Front. *B*, Back. A sample of the Blue Cross and Blue Shield Service Benefit Plan identification card for an individual who receives Federal Employee Program (FEP) benefits. This is not considered a standard Federal Employee Health Benefits Program card because each carrier issues a card differing in appearance.

For complete details of benefits, definitions, limitations, and exclusions, including a description of covered charges, read the FEHBP's officially approved brochure which may be obtained from

Blue Cross Blue Shield Association
Federal Employee Program
1510 G Street, N.W.
Washington, D.C. 20005

IDENTIFICATION CARD

Persons enrolled in the Blue Cross and Blue Shield Service Benefit Plan, Federal Employee Health Benefits Program (FEHBP), receive an embossed plastic identification card (Fig. 10–4). All federal employee enrollment numbers start with "R" followed by eight digits. Coverage is indicated by one of the following enrollment code numbers:

- 101 represents "high-option, self only" coverage (covers only the federal employee or annuitant, the person whose name appears on the card)
- 102 is "high-option, self and family coverage" (covers the federal employee or annuitant and his or her eligible family members)
- 104, "standard option, self only"
- 105, "standard option, self and family"

CLAIMS PROCEDURE

Preferred hospitals, physicians, dentists (available only under Standard Option), and pharmacies may file claims for the patient, but this is not mandatory. The Blue Plans encourage most nonpreferred hospitals and physicians to submit claims for the patient. Sometimes, however, the patient may have to submit an FEHBP Health Benefits Claim Form for his or her covered services (Figs. 10–5 and 10–6). Along with the claim form, itemized bills for all covered expenses from the physician, nurse, or other health care provider must be included.

A separate claim form should be used for each covered member of the family. Fill out the claim form completely. Include the patient's full name, date of birth, and Social Security number (if available). Write in the patient's enrollment code and identification number found on the FEHBP card. Indicate the relationship of the patient to the contract holder. Give the member's name, address, and date of birth (if different from the patient's). Make sure the patient enrolled under the Blue Cross and Blue Shield Service Benefit Plan contract signs the claim form before it is sent to the address on the back of the form. Occasionally, an additional form or information may be required along with the claim form, so contact the local Blue Cross and Blue Shield Plan to obtain the form.

Itemized bills are an important part of submitting claims. Bills from health care institutions and professionals are the only ones accepted. Itemized bills on billing forms or letterhead stationery must show the name, address, and professional status of the health care professional who provided the service or supplies. The full name of the patient, date of service, type of service, and charge for each service must be listed separately. List the various types of services and supplies that a person received on the same form.

TIME LIMIT

For the FEHBP, claims must be submitted no later than December 31 of the calendar year following the year during which the services or supplies were received. For example, if a member received covered services on May 8, 1995, a claim for reimbursement

Text continued on page 245

BlueCross® BlueShield®

Federal Employee Program

Please review the instructions on the reverse side of this form before completing. PLEASE TYPE OR PRINT.

Health Benefits Claim Form

1. PATIENT INFORMATION

A ENROLLMENT CODE 1 0 — IDENTIFICATION NUMBER R — PATIENT'S SOCIAL SECURITY NUMBER ___ — __ — ____

B PATIENT'S NAME *(First, Middle Initial and Last)*

C PATIENT'S DATE OF BIRTH *Month Day Year*

D PATIENT'S SEX *Male* ☐ *Female* ☐

E NAME OF SUBSCRIBER OR POLICY HOLDER *(First, Middle Initial and Last)*

F DATE OF BIRTH *Month Day Year*

G PATIENT'S RELATIONSHIP TO SUBSCRIBER *Self* ☐ *Spouse* ☐ *Child* ☐

If the patient's last name is different from the subscriber's, please attach a statement explaining the relationship.

H SUBSCRIBER'S CURRENT ADDRESS *(Street, City, State and ZIP Code)* ***CHECK IF NEW ADDRESS*** ☐

2. OTHER HEALTH INSURANCE ***Is the patient covered by additional health insurance through an employer, a group such as a professional organization, or any other group health insurance, including other Blue Cross and/or Blue Shield Coverage?*** ☐ ***Yes*** ☐ ***No*** ***If yes, please complete this section.***

A NAME AND ADDRESS OF INSURING COMPANY *(Street, City, State and ZIP Code)*

B EFFECTIVE DATE *Month Day Year* TERMINATION DATE *Month Day Year*

C NAME OF POLICY HOLDER *(First, Middle Initial and Last)* AND HIS/HER EMPLOYER

D DATE OF BIRTH *Month Day Year*

E IDENTIFICATION NUMBER *(Include all letters and numbers)*

3. MEDICARE PLEASE COMPLETE THIS SECTION ON MEDICARE REGARDLESS OF THE PATIENT'S AGE

A MEDICARE PART A *(Hospital Insurance) If yes, effective date* *Yes* ☐ *No* ☐ *Month Day Year*

B MEDICARE PART B *(Medical Insurance) If yes, effective date* *Yes* ☐ *No* ☐ *Month Day Year*

C ***If the patient is eligible for Medicare due to End-Stage Renal Disease, please indicate the beginning date of renal treatment or transplant.*** *Month Day Year*

4. EMPLOYMENT A ***Is the patient presently employed?*** *Yes* ☐ *No* ☐ ***If the patient is retired from the Federal Government, but still employed, please complete the following:***

B NAME AND ADDRESS OF COMPANY OR GOVERNMENT AGENCY *(Street, City, State and ZIP Code)*

5. DIAGNOSIS ***Describe illness, injury or symptoms requiring treatment. If illness, injury or symptoms are related to an accident, please complete A, B and C.***

A DATE OF ACCIDENT *Month Day Year*

B TIME *AM* ☐ *PM* ☐

C LOCATION *At Home* ☐ *Motor vehicle accident* ☐ *At Work* ☐ *If so, what state* ______ *Other* ☐ *Please explain* ______

Was the accident caused by someone else? ☐ *Yes* ☐ *No* *Other* ______

6. CHARGES ***Please list below those charges that you are claiming for benefits. Use a separate line for each type of service or provider.***

PLEASE ATTACH ITEMIZED BILLS

NAME OF PROVIDER MAKING CHARGE *(Doctor, Hospital, etc. Two or more bills from the same provider may be entered on one line if they are for the same type of service.)*	DESCRIPTION OF CHARGE *(Office Visits, Therapy for Mental Conditions, etc.)*	DATE OF SERVICE OR PURCHASE *(If there is only one date, show it under "FROM".)* FROM	TO	CHARGE

I certify the above is complete and correct and that I am claiming benefits only for charges incurred by the patient named above. Authorization is hereby given to any provider of service, which participated in any way in my care, to release to the Blue Cross and/or Blue Shield Plan any medical information which they deem necessary to adjudicate this claim.

7. SIGNATURE ______ Signature of Subscriber or Patient — Date — Daytime telephone number including area code

Failure to sign this claim form may delay processing.

4F1-19049 - F Rev. 11/17/92

FIGURE 10-5

Federal Employee Program Health Benefits Claim Form used to apply for benefits from the FEHBP of Blue Cross/Blue Shield.

10

INSTRUCTIONS

Please complete a separate claim form for each patient, and remember to file all claims by December 31 of the calendar year after the one in which the covered care or service was provided. Since most of the information requested on this form is self-explanatory, we did not include specific instructions for each item. However, we ask that each item be completed. If the information requested does not apply to the patient, indicate N/A (NOT APPLICABLE).

Special care should be taken when completing the following items:

1A and 2E — These spaces are for the Blue Cross and Blue Shield Service Benefit Plan Enrollment Code and Identification Number (Item 1A) and other Health Insurance Identification Number (Item 2E). When completing these items, please ensure that these numbers and letters are exactly as they appear on your identification card(s). Also, please ensure that the patient's social security number is completed in 1A.

3A, B and C — Medicare covers persons age 65 and over and persons who qualify because of disabling conditions such as End-Stage Renal Disease. **THEREFORE, PLEASE COMPLETE ITEMS 3A AND B REGARDLESS OF THE PATIENT'S AGE.** Item C should be completed if applicable.

ITEMIZED BILLS FOR COVERED SERVICES OR SUPPLIES MUST BE ATTACHED TO THIS FORM AND MUST INCLUDE THE FOLLOWING:

- Name and address of the provider of the service or supply.
- Full name of the patient.
- Date and type of service or supply.
- Charge for each service or supply.
- Diagnosis.

Personal itemizations, cash register receipts and cancelled checks are not acceptable. Since itemized bills cannot be returned, please be sure to make copies for your records. In addition, bills for home nursing care must show the professional status, such as R. N. (Registered Nurse). Bills for all drugs and medicines dispensed by a physician, the outpatient department of a hospital or any other non-retail-pharmacy provider must show the name of each drug or medicine.

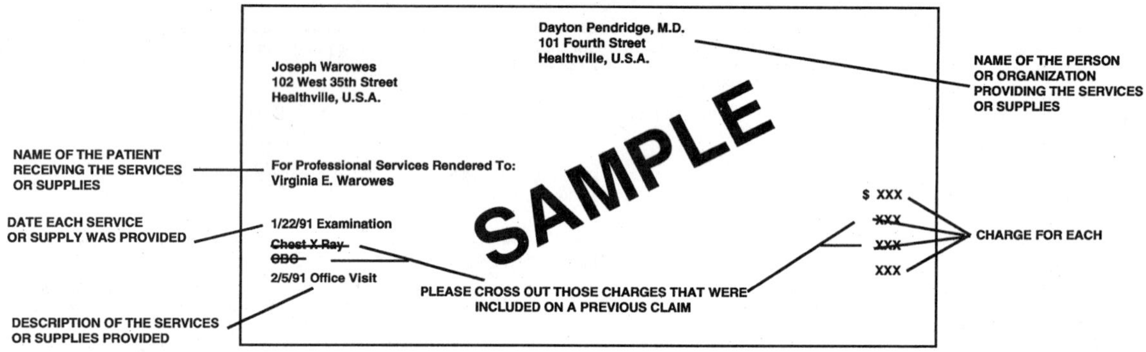

RETAIL PHARMACY PROGRAM

Prescription drugs purchased on and after January 1, 1993, in a retail pharmacy in the U.S. or Puerto Rico must be submitted to the Retail Pharmacy Program on the Retail Pharmacy Program claim form. Call 1-800-624-5060 for more information, claim forms and customer service assistance. The claim form provides detailed instructions for submission of the form and should be mailed to: Service Benefit Plan Retail Pharmacy Program, P.O. Box 52057, Phoenix, AZ 85072-2057.

SPECIAL SERVICES

Certain services such as physical, speech and occupational therapy, therapy for mental conditions, durable medical equipment, home nursing care and dental care resulting from an accidental injury may require additional information along with this claim form. Call your local Blue Cross and/or Blue Shield Plan before submitting your claim for such services; they will send you additional forms, if needed.

FOR PATIENTS COVERED BY MEDICARE

When the patient is covered by Medicare Part A (Hospital Insurance) and/or Medicare Part B (Medical Insurance) and incurs expenses which are covered by Medicare, if Medicare is primary (it pays first), your claim must be submitted to Medicare first **(See Note Below)**. After the Medicare payment has been made, a claim for the expenses not paid by Medicare, to include a copy of your **itemized bill,** can be submitted to your local Blue Cross and/or Blue Shield Plan, along with the appropriate forms from Medicare. For retail pharmacy prescription drug expenses, see the instructions above.

1. For Medicare Part A inpatient services, attach the "Explanation of Benefits" form from Medicare.
2. For Medicare Part B services, attach the "Explanation of Medicare Benefits" and/or the "Your Record of Part B Medicare Benefits Used" form furnished by the Medicare Carrier or Intermediary. Also, a copy of your itemized bill should be sent along with the Medicare Information.

NOTE: If the following conditions are met, the Blue Cross and Blue Shield Service Benefit Plan is primary (it pays first).

- If you are 65 or over and employed by the federal government and have Medicare Part A (or Parts A and B);
- If you or your spouse are employed by the federal government and your covered spouse is 65 or over and has Medicare Part A (or Parts A and B);
- If the patient (you or a covered family member) is under 65, eligible for Medicare benefits only because of End Stage Renal Disease (ESRD) and is within the first 18 months of eligibility to receive Medicare Part A benefits; or
- If the patient (you or a covered family member) is under age 65 and eligible for Medicare solely on the basis of disability, and you are employed by the federal government.

FOR PATIENTS COVERED BY OTHER HEALTH INSURANCE

When submitting charges for services or supplies that have been partially paid by other group health insurance, **attach a copy of the Notice of Payment or Explanation of Payment from the other health care insurer.**

THIS COMPLETED FORM, TOGETHER WITH ITEMIZED BILLS AND SUPPORTING MATERIAL, SHOULD BE SUBMITTED TO YOUR LOCAL BLUE CROSS AND/OR BLUE SHIELD PLAN.

FIGURE 10–6

Back of the Federal Employee Program Health Benefits Claim Form shown in Figure 10–5.

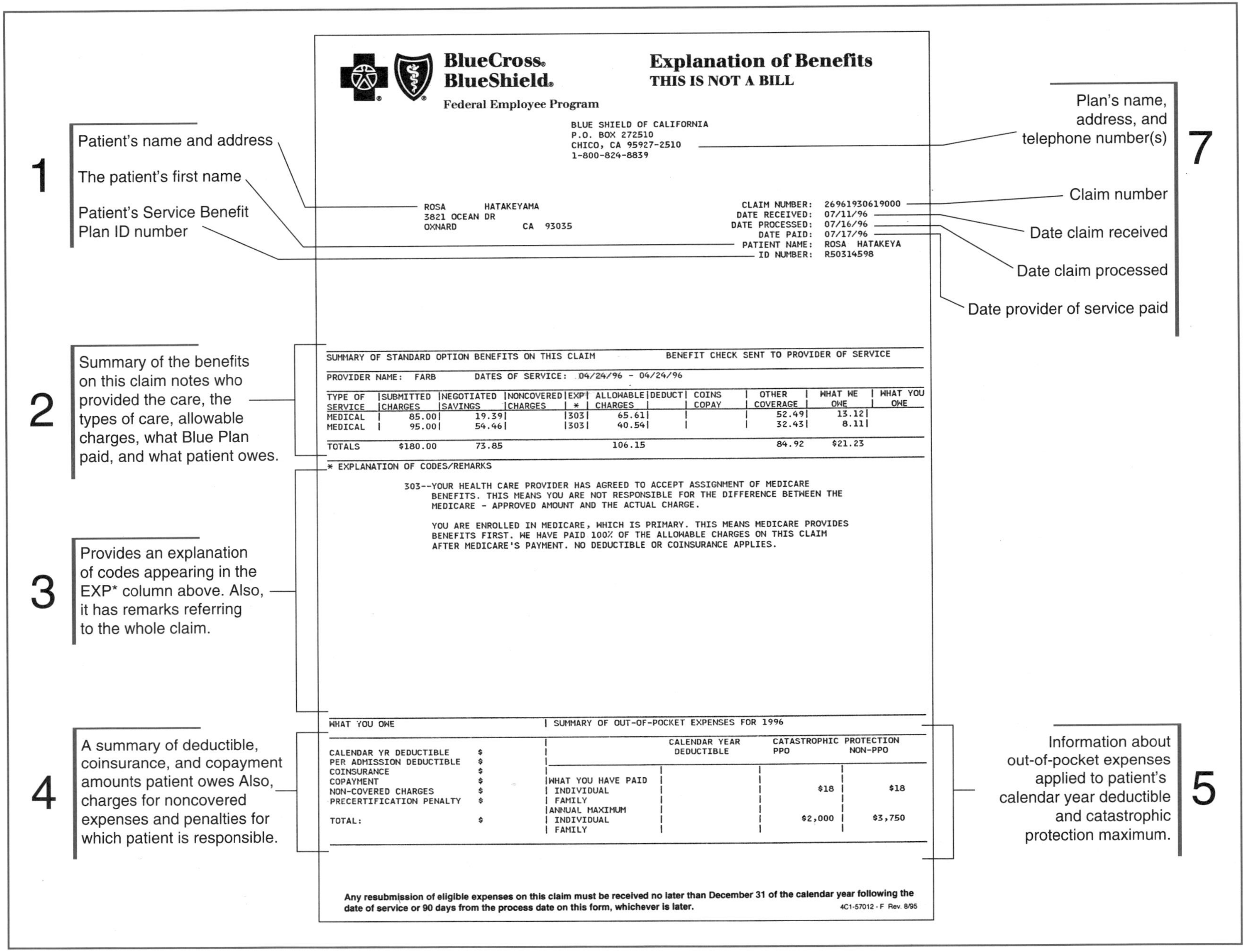

BlueCross. BlueShield.
Federal Employee Program

Explanation of Benefits
THIS IS NOT A BILL

BLUE SHIELD OF CALIFORNIA
P.O. BOX 272510
CHICO, CA 95927-2510
1-800-824-8839

ROSA HATAKEYAMA
3821 OCEAN DR
OXNARD CA 93035

CLAIM NUMBER: 26961930619000
DATE RECEIVED: 07/11/96
DATE PROCESSED: 07/16/96
DATE PAID: 07/17/96
PATIENT NAME: ROSA HATAKEYA
ID NUMBER: R50314598

SUMMARY OF STANDARD OPTION BENEFITS ON THIS CLAIM — BENEFIT CHECK SENT TO PROVIDER OF SERVICE

PROVIDER NAME: FARB — DATES OF SERVICE: 04/24/96 - 04/24/96

TYPE OF SERVICE	SUBMITTED CHARGES	NEGOTIATED SAVINGS	NONCOVERED CHARGES	EXP *	ALLOWABLE CHARGES	DEDUCT	COINS COPAY	OTHER COVERAGE	WHAT WE OWE	WHAT YOU OWE
MEDICAL	85.00	19.39		303	65.61			52.49	13.12	
MEDICAL	95.00	54.46		303	40.54			32.43	8.11	
TOTALS	$180.00	73.85			106.15			84.92	$21.23	

* EXPLANATION OF CODES/REMARKS

303--YOUR HEALTH CARE PROVIDER HAS AGREED TO ACCEPT ASSIGNMENT OF MEDICARE BENEFITS. THIS MEANS YOU ARE NOT RESPONSIBLE FOR THE DIFFERENCE BETWEEN THE MEDICARE - APPROVED AMOUNT AND THE ACTUAL CHARGE.

YOU ARE ENROLLED IN MEDICARE, WHICH IS PRIMARY. THIS MEANS MEDICARE PROVIDES BENEFITS FIRST. WE HAVE PAID 100% OF THE ALLOWABLE CHARGES ON THIS CLAIM AFTER MEDICARE'S PAYMENT. NO DEDUCTIBLE OR COINSURANCE APPLIES.

WHAT YOU OWE	
CALENDAR YR DEDUCTIBLE	$
PER ADMISSION DEDUCTIBLE	$
COINSURANCE	$
COPAYMENT	$
NON-COVERED CHARGES	$
PRECERTIFICATION PENALTY	$
TOTAL:	$

SUMMARY OF OUT-OF-POCKET EXPENSES FOR 1996	CALENDAR YEAR DEDUCTIBLE	CATASTROPHIC PROTECTION PPO	CATASTROPHIC PROTECTION NON-PPO
WHAT YOU HAVE PAID			
INDIVIDUAL		$18	$18
FAMILY			
ANNUAL MAXIMUM			
INDIVIDUAL		$2,000	$3,750
FAMILY			

Any resubmission of eligible expenses on this claim must be received no later than December 31 of the calendar year following the date of service or 90 days from the process date on this form, whichever is later.

4C1-57012 - F Rev. 8/95

FIGURE 10–7
Example of an FEHBP Blue Shield Explanation of Benefits Form for a Medicare case showing amount billed, amount allowed, Medicare payment, and FEHBP payment.

10

TERMS YOU SHOULD KNOW

So that you can better understand the information provided on the reverse side of this form, here are explanations of some important terms:

Type of Service: This is a general description of the service or supply your provider reported.

Submitted Charges: This is the amount the provider has billed.

Negotiated Savings: Local Blue Cross and Blue Shield Plans have agreements with certain providers to accept a negotiated fee. When such arrangements apply, the negotiated discounts or adjustments will be reported in this column.

Non-Covered Charges: This is an amount for which your Blue Cross and Blue Shield Service Benefit Plan coverage does not pay benefits. The column titled "Exp." lists a number or letter code referring to an explanation (shown on your form) or the reason the charge was not covered.

Allowable Charges: These are charges for covered services and the amount on which your covered benefits are based.

Deductible: Before the Plan pays benefits for certain types of services, you must first pay a portion of the Covered charges. The amount you pay is called a deductible.

Coinsurance: This is the percentage of Covered charges you are responsible for paying after you have met any applicable deductibles.

Copayment: This is a flat dollar amount you must pay as your share of costs before the Plan makes its payment.

Other Coverage: When you or a covered family member are covered by another benefit plan including Medicare, the amounts the other plan has paid will appear in the column titled Other Coverage.

Precertification Penalty: If you do not obtain precertification of inpatient hospital services when required, your benefits will be reduced by $500.

Catastrophic Protection: Your Service Benefit Plan coverage limits the amount of coinsurance, copayments and deductibles you pay. If you reach your catastrophic protection limit within a calendar year, the Plan will pay 100 percent of certain Covered charges for the remainder of the year. Please keep in mind that not all your out-of-pocket expenses will count toward meeting your catastrophic protection limit. See your Service Benefit Plan brochure for further details.

If you have questions, please refer to your Blue Cross and Blue Shield Service Benefit Plan brochure, or call your local Blue Cross and Blue Shield Plan at the telephone number shown on the front of this form.

HELP STOP FRAUD AND ABUSE!

IF YOU SUSPECT FRAUD OR ABUSE
CALL THE FEP ANTI-FRAUD HOTLINE:

1-800-FEP-8440 (337-8440)

4C1-57012 - B Rev. 8/95

FIGURE 10–8
Back of the Blue Cross/Blue Shield Federal Employee Program Explanation of Benefits Form shown in Figure 10–7.

must be submitted no later than December 31, 1996. Claims for long hospital stays or other long-term care must be submitted every 30 days.

EXPLANATION OF BENEFITS

An example of an FEHBP Blue Cross/Blue Shield EOB form for a federal employee is shown in Figure 10–7. When you look at the front of the EOB, you will notice it is divided into five sections. They are as follows:

1. The top section gives important member and enrollment information: where to write or call if there is a question concerning a claim, the provider's name, address, and Service Benefit Plan I.D. number, the patient's name, and the claim number.
2. The *Summary of Benefits on this Claim* section provides information about the types of care the patient has received and how benefits were determined—what was paid, the amount applied toward the deductible, an applicable coinsurance or copayment, what the Blue plan owes, and what the patient owes.
3. The processing of the claim is explained in the *Explanation of Codes/Remarks* section. If a code appears in the EXP* section of the Summary of Benefits on This Claim section, it refers to a specific amount in that line of information. For example, an explanation may be required to explain why a charge is not covered. This code will also appear in Explanation of Codes/Remarks section along with an explanation of the code. If a code does not appear in the EXP* section of the Summary of Benefits but an explanation appears, it applies to all the charges on the claim.
4. The deductible, coinsurance, and copayment amounts owed by the patient are indicated in the *What You Owe* section. In addition, the amount of charges not covered for which the patient is responsible is indicated in this section.
5. The *Summary of Out-of-Pocket Expenses* section provides a summary of amounts applied to the calendar year deductible and catastrophic protection maximums for the year this care was provided.

On the back of the EOB are definitions of terms used regarding explanation of payment and determination of benefits (Fig. 10–8).

TO THE STUDENT

Study Chapter 10 and then answer the review questions in the *Workbook* to reinforce the theory learned in this chapter of the text and to help prepare you for a future test. Assignments 30 through 34 will give you experience in abstracting from patients' medical records, posting to ledger cards, and completing insurance claim forms pertinent to the Blue Cross and Blue Shield Plans. For further knowledge and understanding, the key terms at the beginning of the chapter appear in the Glossary at the end of this textbook so you can look up the pertinent terms.

After completing the *Workbook* assignments, you may want additional practice on the concepts you have learned. Blue Cross/Blue Shield Case 1 is available on your computer diskette.

Objectives*

THE INSURANCE BILLING SPECIALIST WILL BE ABLE TO:

- Understand the benefits and nonbenefits of Medicaid.
- Define terminology inherent to Medicaid.
- Name the two Medicaid eligibility classifications.
- Minimize the number of insurance forms rejected because of improper completion.
- Define Medicaid abbreviations.
- List important information to abstract from the patient's Medicaid card.
- State those eligible for the Medicaid Qualified Medicare Beneficiaries program.
- Explain basic operations of a Medicaid managed care system.
- Describe basic Medicaid claim procedure guidelines.
- File claims for patients who have Medicaid and other coverage.
- State eligibility requirements and claims procedures for the Maternal and Child Health Program.

Key Terms

aid category
capitation fee
categorically needy
covered services
Early and Periodic Screening, Diagnosis, and Treatment (EPSDT)
emergency
family planning services
fiscal agent
fiscal year
Maternal and Child Health Program (MCHP)
Medicaid
Medi-Cal
medically needy
prior approval
recipient
Remittance Advice (RA)
share of cost
Supplemental Security Income (SSI)

*Performance objectives and exercises for hands-on practical experience for this chapter appear in the *Workbook* and on the computer disk.

CHAPTER 11

Medicaid and Other State Programs

History

Federal participation in providing medical care to needy persons began between 1933 and 1935 when the Federal Emergency Relief Administration made available funds to pay the medical expenses of the needy unemployed. The Social Security Act of 1935 set up the public assistance programs, and although no special provision was made for medical assistance, the federal government paid a share of the monthly assistance payments, which could be used to meet the costs of medical care. However, the payment was made to the assistance recipient rather than to the provider of medical care.

In 1950, Congress passed a law mandating that all states set up a program of assistance, which meant that the states had to meet minimum requirements. As a result of this mandate, the states set up Medicaid programs. Congress authorized *vendor payments* for medical care, i.e., payments from the welfare agency directly to physicians, health care institutions, and other providers of medical services. By 1960, four fifths of the states made provisions for medical vendor payments, and a new category of assistance recipient was established, the *medically needy aged*. The incomes of these people were too high to qualify them for cash assistance payments, but they needed help in meeting the costs of medical care. The federal government financially supports the *minimum assistance level,* and the states must wholly support any part of the program that goes beyond the federal minimum.

In 1965, Title XIX of the Social Security Act became federal law, and Medicaid legally came into being. It was, to a large extent, the result of various attempts over the previous 30 years to provide medical care to the needy. The program has always had somewhat of a split personality. On one hand, it is viewed as an attempt on the part of the government to provide comprehensive quality health care to those unable to afford it. On the other hand, Medicaid has been seen as merely a bill-paying mechanism whose purpose is to administer the provision of health care on the most efficient, economical basis possible.

Title XIX of the Social Security Act provides for a program of medical assistance for certain low-income individuals and families. The program is known as Medi-Cal in California and Medicaid in 48 states. Arizona is the only state without a Medicaid program like those existing in other states. Since 1982, it has received federal funds under a demonstration waiver for an alternative medical assistance program (prepaid care) for low-income persons called the Arizona Health Care Cost Containment System (AHCCCS).

Medicaid is administered by state governments with partial federal funding. Coverage and benefits vary widely from state to state because the federal government sets minimum requirements and the states are free to enact more benefits. Thus, each state designs its own Medicaid program within federal guidelines. The Health Care Financing Administration (HCFA) of the Bureau of Program Operations of the United States Department of Health and Human Services is responsible for the federal aspects of Medicaid. Medicaid is not so much an insurance program as an assistance program.

Since 1983, the trend in many states has been to expand Medicaid eligibility requirements and services. Changes in Medicaid eligibility allowing more people into the program were made by many states following the passage by the federal government of the Deficit Reduction Act of 1984 (DEFRA) and the Child Health Assurance Program (CHAP).

In 1982, the Tax Equity and Fiscal Responsibility Act (TEFRA) set down laws affecting those under the Medicare program as well as Medicaid medically needy recipients and certain other categories. These laws required certain Medicaid recipients to share in the cost of all services. Emergency care and pregnancy services are exempt by law from copayment requirements.

MEDICAID QUALIFIED MEDICARE BENEFICIARIES PROGRAM

The Medicaid Qualified Medicare Beneficiaries (MQMB) program was introduced via the Medicare Catastrophic Act of 1988 as an amendment to the Social Security Act. Then in 1990, the Omnibus Budget Reconciliation Act allowed for assistance to qualified Medicare beneficiaries (QMBs) who are aged and disabled and are receiving Medicare and have incomes below the federal poverty level.

Under this act, states must provide limited Medicaid coverage for QMBs. They must pay Medicare Part B premiums (and, if applicable, Part A premiums), along with required Medicare deductibles and coinsurance amounts. If an individual's annual income is below the national poverty level but he or she does not qualify for other financial assistance programs, the person may be eligible for the MQMB program. Eligibility also depends on what other financial resources an individual might have. Coverage is restricted to Medicare cost sharing unless the beneficiary qualifies for Medicaid in some other way.

States are also required to pay Part A premiums, but no other expenses, for qualified disabled and working individuals. It is optional for states to provide full Medicaid benefits to QMBs who meet a state-established income standard.

MEDICAID REFORM

As early as 1967, some states began bringing managed care to their Medicaid programs. In the past decade, many states have adopted pilot projects to see whether a managed care system will work and what benefits might be received. Mainly this has been done as an effort to control escalating health care costs by curbing unnecessary emergency department visits and emphasizing preventive care.

When the last state, Arizona, joined Medicaid, it began with prepaid care rather than the way most states have structured their programs. By then, most states had been struggling with Medicaid for nearly 20 years. Such systems work like this—the Medicaid recipient enrolls either in an existing or specifically formed plan similar to a health maintenance organization (HMO). Some plans are run by independent commissions appointed by county boards of supervisors. Usually the patient can either choose or be assigned a gatekeeper (primary care physician), who must approve all specialty care and inpatient or outpatient hospital treatment.

Patients can be cared for side by side with private-paying patients. Some states have adopted capitated (a flat fee per patient) rather than fee-for-service reimbursement. There may be a small co-payment for services. In programs run for a number of years, it has been found that if they are well managed, there is better access to primary health care and savings of monies in delivering the care.

Within the establishment of the American Health Security Act of 1993 that was introduced by President William Clinton, it is possible that the Medicaid program eventually may be phased out, as a result of reform as well as the learning experience by many states already using managed care in their Medicaid programs.

Medicaid Eligibility

Medicaid is available to certain needy and low-income people, such as the aged (65 years or older), the blind, the disabled, and members of families with dependent children deprived of the support of at least one parent and financially eligible on the basis of income and resources. The first classification, the *categorically needy group*, includes all cash recipients of the Aid to Families with Dependent Children (AFDC) program, certain other AFDC-related groups, most cash recipients of the Supplemental Security Income (SSI) program, and other SSI-related groups

For those individuals who may become *medically indigent* (MI) as a result of high medical care expenses and inadequate health insurance coverage, a number of states have adopted a State Program of Assistance for the Medically Indigent. This may be a component of a state's general assistance program for low-income people. This second category is sometimes referred to as the *medically needy class.* Some Medicaid recipients in this category must pay coinsurance and/or a deductible, which sometimes must be met within the eligibility month or other time frame before they can receive state benefits. For a clear, simple understanding of the classes and basic groups for Medicaid eligibility, see Figure 11–1.

If a person is eligible for Medicaid, he or she goes to the local welfare office and applies for benefits. After acceptance into the program, the patient brings a form or card to the physician's office that verifies the dates or month of eligibility. Each state decides what services are covered and what the payments are for each service.

In some cases, retroactive eligibility may be granted to a patient. If the patient has documentation or a retroactive card confirming this and has paid for any services during the retroactive period, then a refund must be made and Medicaid billed.

ELIGIBILITY FOR MEDICAID BENEFITS

Classes	
Categorically Needy	Medically Needy

Basic Groups

I. Families, pregnant women and children
   a) Aid to Families With Dependent Children (AFDC)-related groups
   b) Non-AFDC pregnant women and children

II. Aged and disabled persons
   a) Supplemental Security Income (SSI)-related groups
   b) Qualified Medicare Beneficiaries (QMBs)

III. Medically needy (indigent low-income individuals and families)

IV. Persons receiving institutional or other long-term care in nursing facilities (NFs) and intermediate care facilities (ICFs)

V. Medicaid purchase of COBRA coverage (low-income persons losing employer health insurance coverage)

FIGURE 11–1
Classes and basic groups of eligibility for Medicaid benefits.

Sometimes an unborn child can be issued an identification card that is used for services promoting the life and health of the fetus.

Individual physicians are likely to have their own office procedures for handling Medicaid patients. A patient can be on Medicaid 1 month and off the following month or on the program for several months or years; therefore, each case is different. The physician may accept or refuse to treat Medicaid patients and must make the decision on the basis of the entire Medicaid program, not an individual patient's personality or other discriminating factor.

If the physician decides to take Medicaid patients, he or she must accept the Medicaid allowance as payment in full. However, a small copayment is sometimes required from some patients. If a service is totally disallowed by Medicaid (denied claim), a physician is within legal rights to bill the patient. However, it is wise to have the patient sign a waiver of liability agreement if the service to be provided may be a denied service from known past claim submission experience. An example of a waiver of liability agreement is shown in Chapter 12, Figure 12–10. It is important that the patient receive quality care and be treated the same as the paying patient.

To obtain up-to-date information and details on the Medicaid program in your state, write or telephone your state agency (see Appendix A).

BENEFITS

Under Federal guidelines, the state Medicaid basic benefits offered to eligible recipients include the following types of services:

- Family planning
- Home health care
- Immunizations
- Inpatient hospital care
- Laboratory and X-ray
- Outpatient hospital care
- Physicians' care
- Screening, diagnosis, and treatment of children under 21 years of age
- Skilled nursing care
- Transportation to and from health care providers

In some states, additional services included might be the following:

- Allergy care
- Ambulance services
- Certain medical cosmetic procedures
- Chiropractic care
- Clinic care
- Dental care
- Dermatologic care
- Diagnostic, screening, preventive, and rehabilitative services (e.g., physical therapy)
- Emergency department care
- Eyeglasses and eye refractions
- Hospice care
- Intermediate care
- Occupational therapy
- Optometric services
- Podiatric care
- Prescription drugs
- Private duty nursing
- Prosthetic devices
- Psychiatric care
- Respiratory care
- Speech therapy

Another benefit of the Medicaid program is the Early and Periodic Screening, Diagnosis, and Treatment (EPSDT) service. This is a program of prevention, early detection, and treatment of welfare children (under age 21). In California (Medi-Cal), it is known as the Child Health and Disability Prevention (CHDP) program.

The EPSDT guidelines include a medical history and physical examination; immunization status assessment; dental, hearing, and vision screening; developmental assessment; and screening for anemia and lead absorption, tuberculosis, bacteriuria, and sickle cell disease and trait. States are required to provide necessary health care, diagnostic services, treatment, and other services to correct physical or mental defects found.

Claim Procedure

Because Medicaid state policies and claim procedures (identification cards, prior approval regulations, claim forms, time limits) vary from state to state, always consult your current Medicaid Handbook and/or state fiscal agent. See Appendix A for the name and address in your region. Only general guidelines for submitting claims are stated here.

For those working as an insurance billing specialist for a clinic or physician's practice in California, claim procedures and information on the Medi-Cal program are presented in Appendix C.

IDENTIFICATION CARD

A plastic or paper Medicaid identification card (or, in some states, coupons) is usually issued monthly. However, under certain classifications of eligibility, identification cards are issued in some states on the 1st and 15th of each month, every 2 months, every 3 months, or every 6 months. Obtain a photocopy of the front and back of the card. When professional services are rendered, the card must show eligibility for that month. Some states issue cards that contain adhesive labels, and a label must be used on the billing claim for payment.

Carefully check the expiration date of the card each time the patient visits the physician's office to see whether eligibility is indicated for the month of service. Note whether the patient has other insurance, copayment requirements, or restrictions or is eligible for only certain types of medical services.

For some states, the Potomac Group Inc. in Nashville, Tennessee has developed MediFAX. This is a machine that allows the user to verify coverage in seconds. It is available for more than 22 states. There are some states that provide their own electronic system for Medicaid verification via touch-tone telephone, modem, or specialized Medicaid terminal equipment.

COPAYMENT

Some Medicaid recipients must meet a copayment requirement each month before Medicaid benefits can be claimed. It is important to obtain this copay amount when the patient comes in for medical care.

PRIOR APPROVAL

Many times prior authorization is required for various services, except in a bona fide emergency. Some of these services might be

- durable medical equipment
- hearing aids
- hemodialysis
- home health care
- inpatient hospital care
- long-term care facility services
- medical supplies
- medications
- prosthetic/orthotic appliances
- surgical procedures
- transportation
- some vision care

Usually, prior authorization forms are completed to obtain permission for a specific service or hospitalization (Fig. 11–2) and sent to the Department of Health or a certain office in your region for approval. In some cases, it is not possible to obtain a prior authorization for the care needed so an immediate approval can be obtained via a telephone call to the proper department in your locale. Note the date the authorization was given, the name of the person who gave authorization, the approximate time of day authorization was given, and any verbal number given to you by the field office. Usually a treatment authorization form indicating that the service was already authorized must be sent in as follow-up to the telephone call.

TIME LIMIT

Each state has its own time limit for the submission of a claim. The time limit can vary from 2 months to 1 year from the date that the service was rendered. If a bill is submitted after the time limit, it can be rejected, unless there is some valid justification that the state recognizes. Prescription drugs and dental services are sometime billed to a different intermediary than services performed by a physician, depending on the state guidelines.

RECIPROCITY

Most states have reciprocity for Medicaid payments if a patient requires medical care while out of state. Contact the Medicaid intermediary in the patient's home state and ask for the appropriate forms. If the case was an emergency, state this on the form. File the papers with Medicaid in your patient's home state. Reimbursement will be at that state's rate.

CLAIM FORM

Either physicians submit a claim form to a fiscal intermediary, which might be an insurance company, or the bill is sent directly to the local Department of Social Services. Refer to Appendix A for the Medicaid fiscal agent's address for your state.

As of October 1, 1986, federal law mandates that Form HCFA-1500 be adopted for the processing of Medicaid claims in all states that do not optically scan their claims for payment. States that use optical scanners must adopt a form that is as close as possible to the format of the Form HCFA-1500.

Instructions for completing the HCFA-1500 claim form vary among all Medicaid intermediaries as of this printing. Therefore, refer to your local Medicaid intermediary for guidelines. Chapter 6 gives basic instructions on how to complete the HCFA-1500

STATE USE ONLY

SERVICE CATEGORY

3

TYPEWRITER ALIGNMENT Elite Pica

CONFIDENTIAL PATIENT INFORMATION

FOR F.I. USE ONLY

CCN

F.I. USE ONLY

TREATMENT AUTHORIZATION REQUEST

STATE OF CALIFORNIA DEPARTMENT OF HEALTH SERVICES

TYPEWRITER ALIGNMENT Elite Pica

(PLEASE TYPE) FOR PROVIDER USE (PLEASE TYPE)

VERBAL CONTROL NO.

TYPE OF SERVICE REQUESTED: DRUG / OTHER [X]

REQUEST IS RETROACTIVE?: YES / NO [X]

IS PATIENT MEDICARE ELIGIBLE?: YES / NO [X]

PROVIDER PHONE NO. (013) 555-1111

PATIENT'S AUTHORIZED REPRESENTATIVE (IF ANY) ENTER NAME AND ADDRESS:

PLEASE TYPE YOUR NAME AND ADDRESS HERE

PROVIDER NAME AND ADDRESS

SMITH, SUSAN MD
727 ELM BLVD
ANYTOWN, CA 90101

PROVIDER NUMBER HSC12345F

30 83

NAME AND ADDRESS OF PATIENT

PATIENT NAME (LAST, FIRST, M.I.) APPLEGATE, NANCY

MEDI-CAL IDENTIFICATION NO. 253971060

CHECK DIGIT

P

STREET ADDRESS 1515 RIVER ROAD

CITY, STATE, ZIP CODE SACRAMENTO, CA 95822

PHONE NUMBER (013) 545-1123

SEX F AGE 32 DATE OF BIRTH 0618 65

PATIENT STATUS: [X] HOME / BOARD & CARE / SNF/ICF / ACUTE HOSPITAL

FOR STATE USE

PROVIDER; YOUR REQUEST IS:

1 [X] APPROVED AS REQUESTED / DENIED / DEFERRED

2 APPROVED AS MODIFIED (ITEMS MARKED BELOW AS AUTHORIZED MAY BE CLAIMED) / JACKSON VS RANK PARAGRAPH CODE

By *John Doe* MEDI-CAL CONSULTANT

I.D. # 01 DATE 08209X REVIEW COMMENTS INDICATOR

COMMENTS/EXPLANATION

DIAGNOSIS DESCRIPTION: ENDOMETRIOSIS

ICD-9-CM DIAGNOSIS CODE 617.9

MEDICAL JUSTIFICATION:

VISTA HOSPITAL - 1200 MAPLE ST., ANYTOWN, CA

UNCONTROLLABLE ENDOMETRIOSIS

RETROACTIVE AUTHORIZATION GRANTED IN ACCORDANCE WITH SECTION 51003 (B)

1 2 3 4 5 6

LINE NO.	AUTHORIZED YES	AUTHORIZED NO	APPROVED UNITS	SPECIFIC SERVICES REQUESTED	UNITS OF SERVICE	PROCEDURE OR DRUG CODE	QUANTITY	CHARGES
1	X		3	DAYS: 3 HOSPITAL DAYS REQUESTED				$
2	X		1	HYSTERECTOMY	1	5815070	1	$ 1300.00
3								$
4								$
5								$
6								$

TO THE BEST OF MY KNOWLEDGE, THE ABOVE INFORMATION IS TRUE, ACCURATE AND COMPLETE AND THE REQUESTED SERVICES ARE MEDICALLY INDICATED AND NECESSARY TO THE HEALTH OF THE PATIENT.

Susan Smith SIGNATURE OF PHYSICIAN OR PROVIDER — MD TITLE — 8-10-9X DATE

AUTHORIZATION IS VALID FOR SERVICES PROVIDED FROM DATE 09019X TO DATE 09309X

TAR CONTROL NUMBER: OFFICE 12 SEQUENCE NUMBER 61240229 PI 0

NOTE: AUTHORIZATION DOES NOT GUARANTEE PAYMENT. PAYMENT IS SUBJECT TO PATIENT'S ELIGIBILITY. BE SURE THE IDENTIFICATION CARD IS CURRENT BEFORE RENDERING SERVICE. SEND TO FIELD SERVICES (F.I. COPY)

SEE YOUR PROVIDER MANUAL FOR ASSISTANCE REGARDING THE COMPLETION OF THIS FORM. 50-1 12/87

FIGURE 11-2
Example of a completed prior authorization form.

claim form for Medicare, CHAMPUS, and other third party carriers. Figure 11–3 is a template emphasizing basic elements and shaded blocks that do not require completion.

REMITTANCE ADVICE

A remittance advice (RA), formerly known as an explanation of benefits (EOB) form, accompanies all Medicaid payment checks to the physician. Sometimes five categories of adjudicated claims appear on an RA: adjustments, approvals, denials, suspends, and audit / refund (A / R) transactions, although this terminology may vary from one fiscal agent to another (Fig. 11–4). Adjustments occur from overpayments or underpayments. Approval is when an original claim or a previously denied claim is approved for payment. All denied claims are listed as denials on the RA. Claims in suspense for a certain period of time may be listed on the RA. A / R transactions are miscellaneous transactions as a result of cost settlements, state audits, or refund checks received. An RA for a Medicare / Medicaid case may be found in Chapter 12.

APPEALS

The time limit to appeal a claim varies from state to state, but it is usually 30 to 60 days. Most Medicaid offices consider an appeal filed when they receive it, not when you send it. Usually appeals are sent with a cover letter or special form along with photocopies of documents applicable to the appeal (i.e., claim form, explanation of benefits, preauthorization forms). Appeals go first to the regional fiscal agent or Medicaid bureau, next to the Department of Welfare, and then to an appellate court that evaluates decisions by local and government agencies. At each level, an examiner looks at the case and makes a decision. If not satisfied, the physician may ask for further review at the next level.

THIRD PARTY LIABILITY

It is possible that a person can be eligible for Medicaid and also have additional group health insurance coverage through an employer or other government program. If any entity is liable to pay all or part of the medical cost of injury, disease, or disability, this is called third party liability. In these cases, the primary carrier becomes the other program or insurance carrier and is sent the claim first. After receiving an RA from the primary carrier, Medicaid, being the secondary carrier, is billed next, enclosing a copy of the RA.

MEDICAID AND MANAGED CARE PLANS

Across the nation, many states have begun to shift Medicaid patients into managed care plans. These patients must use physicians, clinics, and hospitals participating in their assigned plan.

When filing a claim for a Medicaid patient who is also enrolled in a health maintenance organization (HMO or PPO), send the bill to the HMO and not the Medicaid fiscal agent. The HMO receives payment for services rendered to eligible members via the capitation method. This means that the HMO is paid a fixed, per capita amount for each patient served without considering the actual number or nature of services provided to each person. See Chapter 9 for further information on managed care plans.

MEDICAID AND CHAMPUS/CHAMPVA

For patients who receive benefits under the CHAMPUS or CHAMPVA programs and also have Medicaid, send the bill to the CHAMPUS fiscal agent servicing your region. Then bill Medicaid and attach the RA to the claim form. See Chapter 13 for further information on CHAMPUS/CHAMPVA.

MEDICAID AND MEDICARE

For information on how to process insurance claims for patients receiving both Medicaid and Medicare benefits, see Chapter 12.

MEDICAID AND ALIENS

Some aliens may have Medicare Part A or Part B or both (see Chapter 12, Aliens on Medicare). If an alien is more than 65 years old and on Medicaid and not eligible for Medicare benefits, bill the Medicaid processing agent and use the proper Medicaid claim form for your region. On the form indicate, "Alien is over 65 years and not eligible for Medicare benefits."

PLEASE DO NOT STAPLE IN THIS AREA

MEDICAID TEMPLATE

APPROVED OMB-0938-0008

Name and address of insurance carrier

CARRIER

PICA

HEALTH INSURANCE CLAIM FORM

PICA

1. MEDICARE (Medicare #) ☐ MEDICAID (Medicaid #) ☒ CHAMPUS (Sponsor's SSN) ☐ CHAMPVA (VA File #) ☐ GROUP HEALTH PLAN (SSN or ID) ☐ FECA BLK LUNG (SSN) ☐ OTHER (ID) ☐

1a. INSURED'S I.D. NUMBER (FOR PROGRAM IN ITEM 1)

2. PATIENT'S NAME (Last Name, First Name, Middle Initial)

3. PATIENT'S BIRTH DATE MM DD YY SEX M ☐ F ☐

4. INSURED'S NAME (Last Name, First Name, Middle Initial)
3rd party coverage

5. PATIENT'S ADDRESS (No., Street)

6. PATIENT RELATIONSHIP TO INSURED Self ☐ Spouse ☐ Child ☐ Other ☐

7. INSURED'S ADDRESS (No., Street)
3rd party coverage

CITY STATE

8. PATIENT STATUS Single ☐ Married ☐ Other ☐ Employed ☐ Full-Time Student ☐ Part-Time Student ☐

CITY STATE

ZIP CODE TELEPHONE (Include Area Code) ( )

ZIP CODE TELEPHONE (INCLUDE AREA CODE) ( )

9. OTHER INSURED'S NAME (Last Name, First Name, Middle Initial)

10. IS PATIENT'S CONDITION RELATED TO:

11. INSURED'S POLICY GROUP OR FECA NUMBER
3rd party insurance rejection code

a. OTHER INSURED'S POLICY OR GROUP NUMBER

a. EMPLOYMENT? (CURRENT OR PREVIOUS) ☐ YES ☐ NO

a. INSURED'S DATE OF BIRTH MM DD YY SEX M ☐ F ☐

b. OTHER INSURED'S DATE OF BIRTH MM DD YY SEX M ☐ F ☐

b. AUTO ACCIDENT? PLACE (State) ☐ YES ☐ NO

b. EMPLOYER'S NAME OR SCHOOL NAME

c. EMPLOYER'S NAME OR SCHOOL NAME

c. OTHER ACCIDENT? ☐ YES ☐ NO

c. INSURANCE PLAN NAME OR PROGRAM NAME

d. INSURANCE PLAN NAME OR PROGRAM NAME
other ins. not Medicaid or Medicare

10d. RESERVED FOR LOCAL USE
MCD number

d. IS THERE ANOTHER HEALTH BENEFIT PLAN? ☐ YES ☐ NO *If yes*, return to and complete item 9 a-d.

READ BACK OF FORM BEFORE COMPLETING & SIGNING THIS FORM.

12. PATIENT'S OR AUTHORIZED PERSON'S SIGNATURE I authorize the release of any medical or other information necessary to process this claim. I also request payment of government benefits either to myself or to the party who accepts assignment below.

SIGNED DATE

EXAMPLE ONLY

13. INSURED'S OR AUTHORIZED PERSON'S SIGNATURE I authorize payment of medical benefits to the undersigned physician or supplier for services described below.

SIGNED

PATIENT AND INSURED INFORMATION

14. DATE OF CURRENT: MM DD YY ILLNESS (First symptom) OR INJURY (Accident) OR PREGNANCY(LMP)

15. IF PATIENT HAS HAD SAME OR SIMILAR ILLNESS. GIVE FIRST DATE MM DD YY

16. DATES PATIENT UNABLE TO WORK IN CURRENT OCCUPATION FROM MM DD YY TO MM DD YY

17. NAME OF REFERRING PHYSICIAN OR OTHER SOURCE
name and degree of ref. doctor

17a. I.D. NUMBER OF REFERRING PHYSICIAN
Medicaid NPI

18. HOSPITALIZATION DATES RELATED TO CURRENT SERVICES FROM MM DD YY TO MM DD YY

19. RESERVED FOR LOCAL USE

20. OUTSIDE LAB? ☐ YES ☒ NO $ CHARGES

21. DIAGNOSIS OR NATURE OF ILLNESS OR INJURY. (RELATE ITEMS 1,2,3 OR 4 TO ITEM 24E BY LINE)

1. ___ . __
2. ___ . __
3. ___ . __
4. ___ . __

22. MEDICAID RESUBMISSION CODE ORIGINAL REF. NO.

23. PRIOR AUTHORIZATION NUMBER

24. A DATE(S) OF SERVICE From MM DD YY To MM DD YY	B Place of Service	C Type of Service	D PROCEDURES, SERVICES, OR SUPPLIES (Explain Unusual Circumstances) CPT/HCPCS MODIFIER	E DIAGNOSIS CODE	F $ CHARGES	G DAYS OR UNITS	H EPSDT Family Plan	I EMG	J COB	K RESERVED FOR LOCAL USE
1 No consecutive dates allowed										NPI
2										
3							E = EPSDT service F = family planning	X = emergency		
4										
5										
6										

PHYSICIAN OR SUPPLIER INFORMATION

25. FEDERAL TAX I.D. NUMBER SSN EIN ☐ ☐

26. PATIENT'S ACCOUNT NO.

27. ACCEPT ASSIGNMENT? (For govt. claims, see back) ☒ YES ☐ NO

28. TOTAL CHARGE $

29. AMOUNT PAID $ 3rd party other than Medicare

30. BALANCE DUE $

31. SIGNATURE OF PHYSICIAN OR SUPPLIER INCLUDING DEGREES OR CREDENTIALS (I certify that the statements on the reverse apply to this bill and are made a part thereof.)

SIGNED DATE

32. NAME AND ADDRESS OF FACILITY WHERE SERVICES WERE RENDERED (If other than home or office)

33. PHYSICIAN'S, SUPPLIER'S BILLING NAME, ADDRESS, ZIP CODE & PHONE #

PIN# GRP#

(APPROVED BY AMA COUNCIL ON MEDICAL SERVICE 8/88)

reference initials

PLEASE PRINT OR TYPE

FORM HCFA-1500 (U2) (12-90)
FORM OWCP-1500 FORM RRB-1500

FIGURE 11-3
A Medicaid template emphasizing basic elements and shaded blocks that do not require completion.

MEDICAID
REMITTANCE ADVICE

TO: ANYBODY, FERNANDO G.
1000 ELM STREET
ANYTOWN, XY 12345-0001

REFER TO PROVIDER MANUAL FOR DEFINITION OF RAD CODES

PROVIDER NUMBER	CLAIM TYPE	WARRANT NO	EDS SEQ NO	DATE	PAGE 1 of 1 pages
00AX65800	MEDICAL	39248026	20000617	06/01/9X	

RECIPIENT NAME	RECIPIENT MEDICAID I.D. NO.	CLAIM CONTROL NUMBER	SERVICE DATES FROM MMDDYY	TO MMDDYY	PROCED CODE MODIFIER	PATIENT ACCOUNT NUMBER	QTY	BILLED AMT	PAYABLE AMT			PAID AMT	RAD CODE
APPROVES (RECONCILE TO FINANCIAL SUMMARY)													
TORRES R	559978557	5079350917901	03079X	03079X	Z4802		0001	20.00	16.22			16.22	0401
		5079350917901	03079X	03079X	Z4802		0001	20.00	16.22			16.22	0401
						TOTAL		40.00	32.44			32.44	
CHAN B	561198435	5044351314501	02039X	02039X	Z4800		0001	30.00	27.03			27.03	0401
		5044351314501	02039X	02039X	Z4800		0001	20.00	16.22			16.22	0401
						TOTAL		50.00	43.25				
		****TOTALS FOR APPROVES						90.00	75.69			75.69	
												75.69	AMT PAID
DENIES (DO NOT RECONCILE TO FINANCIAL SUMMARY)													
GOMEZ M	624163192	5011340319001	12279X	12279X	Z4800		0001	30.00					0036
		TOTAL NUMBER OF DENIES					0001						
SUSPENDS (DO NOT RECONCILE TO FINANCIAL SUMMARY)													
HERN D	562416373	5034270703001	01059X	01059X	Z4802		0001	20.00					0602
MART E	623105478	5034270712305	01059X	01059X	Z4802		0001	20.00					0602
		5034270712305	01059X	01059X	Z4802		0001	20.00					0602
						TOTAL		40.00					0602
LOPEZ C	560291467	5034270712502	01249X	01249X	Z4802		0001	20.00					0602
		PAT LIAB 932.00 OTH COVG			0.00	SALES TX		0.00					
		TOTAL NUMBER OF SUSPENDS					0004	80.00					

EXPLANATION OF DENIAL/ADJUSTMENT CODES

0401 PAYMENT ADJUSTED TO MAXIMUM ALLOWABLE
0036 RESUBMISSION TURNAROUND DOCUMENT WAS EITHER NOT RETURNED OR WAS RETURNED UNCORRECTED, THEREFORE YOUR CLAIM IS FORMALLY DENIED
0602 PENDING ADJUDICATION

OHC CARRIER NAME AND ADDRESS
N049 NORTHWESTERN NATIONAL LIFE 111 WASHINGTON AVE. FL 3 MINNEAPOLIS MN 55401

FIGURE 11-4
Example of a Medicaid Remittance Advice form showing adjustments, cutbacks, denied claims, and claims in suspense.

Handy Hints

It is important to code accurately using the Current Procedural Terminology (CPT) code book and modifiers. However, this does not guarantee an increase in reimbursement, because of Medicaid budgetary problems from time to time. List modifiers in order of importance. Example: If multiple procedures were performed (modifier -51) and two surgeons were involved (modifier -62), the important Medicaid fact is that there were two surgeons involved, so list -62 ahead of modifier -51. ICD-9-CM diagnostic codes must correspond with CPT codes or the claim will be kicked out

11

of the system, and payment will be denied or delayed.

If claims ordinarily are sent electronically and the case is unusual, it is more efficient to send this claim manually. The reason is that if it is incorrectly paid electronically, then you must file an appeal, which can take a long time to resolve before payment.

If a claim is submitted with an error and paid accordingly (e.g., a physician removes multiple lesions but this procedure is entered on one line instead of being entered on multiple lines), payment is generated for one lesion. Then it is worth the time to resubmit a new claim that is completed correctly.

To keep up-to-date, always read the current bulletins on the Medicaid or Medi-Cal program published by the fiscal agent in your state. Obtain your state-published handbook with updates of its Medicaid rules. Read and implement the rule changes and updates to avoid rejected claims.

Maternal and Child Health Program (MCHP)

All states and certain other jurisdictions, including territories and the District of Columbia (56 programs total), operate Maternal and Child Health Programs (MCHP) with federal grant support under Title V of the Social Security Act. Although Title V has been amended on a number of occasions, notably between 1981 and 1987, no changes have been as sweeping as those in the Omnibus Budget Reconciliation Act (OBRA) of 1989. Federal funds are granted to states, enabling them

- To provide low-income mothers and children access to quality maternal and child health services.
- To reduce infant mortality and the incidence of preventable diseases and handicapping conditions among children.
- To increase the number of children immunized against disease and the number of low-income children receiving health assessments and follow-up diagnostic and treatment services.
- To promote the health of mothers and infants by providing prenatal, delivery, and postpartum care for low-income, at-risk pregnant women.
- To provide preventive and primary care services for low-income children.
- To provide rehabilitation services for the blind and disabled less than age 16 years.
- To provide, promote, and develop family-centered, community-based, coordinated care for children with special health care needs.

The state agency tries to locate mothers, infants, and children less than age 21 years who may have conditions eligible for treatment under the MCHP. The conditions are diagnosed and the necessary medical and other health-related care, hospitalization, and continuing follow-up care is given.

After a child is examined at an MCHP clinic and a diagnosis is made, the parents are advised about the treatment that will benefit the child. The state agency then helps them locate this care. If the parents cannot afford this care, the agency assists them with financial planning and may assume part or all of the cost of treatment, depending on the child's condition and the family's resources.

ELIGIBILITY

Each agency operates under a law passed by the state legislature. The state law either defines the conditions to be included or directs the children's agency to define them. All state laws include children who have some kind of handicap that needs orthopedic treatment or plastic surgery; a few states add other conditions. A list of both types of conditions follows:

Cleft lip
Cleft palate
Club foot
Chronic conditions affecting bones and joints
Paralyzed muscles
Cerebral palsy
Rheumatic and congenital heart disease*
Epilepsy*
Cystic fibrosis*
Vision problems requiring surgery*
Hearing problems*
Mental retardation*
Multiple handicaps*

CLAIMS PROCEDURE

Each jurisdiction operates its own MCHP with its own unique administrative characteristics. Thus, each has its own system and forms for billing and related procedures. The official plans and documents are retained in the individual state offices and

*Only some states include this item in their Maternal and Child Health Program.

are not available on either a regional or national office basis. For specific information about your state's policies, write to the MCHP state agency listed in Appendix A.

TO THE STUDENT

Study Chapter 11 and then answer the review questions in the *Workbook* to reinforce the theory learned in this chapter of the text and to help prepare you for a future test. Assignments 35 through 37 will give you experience in abstracting from case histories, posting to ledger cards, and completing forms pertinent to the Medicaid program in your state. For further knowledge and understanding, the key terms at the beginning of the chapter appear in the Glossary at the end of this textbook so you can look up the pertinent terms.

After completing the *Workbook* assignments, you may want additional practice on the concepts you have learned. Medicaid Case 2 is available on your computer disk.

Objectives*

THE INSURANCE BILLING SPECIALIST WILL BE ABLE TO:

- List the benefits and nonbenefits of both Medicare and Medi-Medi.
- Learn who is eligible for Medicare and Medi-Medi.
- Identify a Medicare patient's card.
- Know the proper service codes when submitting the Medicare claim.
- Minimize the number of insurance forms rejected because of improper completion.
- Learn how to post information on the patient's ledger after a Medicare payment has been received.
- State five exceptions when patients may submit their own insurance claim.
- State the three Medicare procedure coding levels.
- State the four instances when a physician participates in violations and can be penalized.
- Explain where the National Provider Identifier (NPI) is shown on the HCFA-1500 claim form.
- List steps in filing a claim when Medicare is the secondary payer.
- Name three conditions when an HMO patient can be seen by a nonmember HMO physician.
- Explain what steps to take and what documents are needed when a denied claim is taken to review.
- Define a Medicare-mandated prepayment screen.
- List the information about their employees an employer must report annually to the federal government from 1994 to 1997.
- Discover what blocks to complete on the HCFA-1500 claim form when filing for Medicare primary versus Medicare secondary payments.

Key Terms

allowed amount
assignment
benefit period
crossover claim
diagnostic cost groups (DCGs)
disabled
employer group health plan (EGHP)
end-stage renal disease (ESRD)
fiscal intermediary
Health Care Financing Administration (HCFA)
home health agency
hospice
hospital insurance
intermediate care facility
internal control number
limiting charge
medical necessity
Medicare
Medicare/Medicaid (Medi-Medi)
Medigap (MG)
national codes
nursing facility (NF)
participating physician program
peer review organizations (PRO)
premium
primary payer
prospective payment system (PPS)
reasonable fee
relative value unit (RVU)
Remittance Advice (RA)
resource based relative value scale (RBRVS)
respite care
secondary payer
short-stay hospital
supplemental insurer
Supplemental Security Income (SSI)
supplementary medical insurance (SMI)
volume performance standard (VPS)

*Performance objectives and exercises for hands-on practical experience for this chapter appear in the *Workbook* and on the computer disk.

CHAPTER 12

Medicare

Introduction

Individuals completing claims and working with Medicare patients will discover rapidly the frustration that is captured in writer David Chartrand's humorous poster "Medicare Laws."* Sometimes it is the constant changes in policies of the program.

There are no rules for properly coding reimbursement forms. There are only penalties for doing it wrong.

Or trying to deal with government regulations with the myriad of forms and authorizations needed.

Medicare will always revise its claim forms the week after you have purchased a year's supply of the current ones.

In addition, the patient may be hard of hearing and visually impaired or have poor memory retention or difficulty in getting around.

There is an inverse relationship between the hours spent treating a nursing-home patient and the fee Medicare thinks you should receive for doing it.

* To obtain David V. Chartrand's complete set of "Medicare Laws" in poster form, write him at 130 North Cherry Street, #202, Olathe, KS 66061-3460 or send a fax to (913) 768-4900.

Then there are telephone questions or inquiries from patients who are irritable because of illness or pain or anger because they are getting old.

When more than one supervisor at Medicare gives you the same incorrect information, no one will be at fault. If you feel you've finally figured out Medicare's rules, don't worry. The feeling will soon go away.

Finally, there are the denied, rejected, or returned claims and no payment.

Medicare, as a rule, will always expect you to know if the instructions you got from a Medicare representative were correct or incorrect. When the enforcement officer calls, you then will learn whether you guessed right.

Well, you probably guessed by now that everything in this section in bold face was written with a sense of humor. It is important to learn about the Medicare program but also just as vital to be able to laugh to relieve some of the pressures of stress in dealing with its intricacies. That is why this chapter begins on a humorous note.

Medicare Program*

ELIGIBILITY REQUIREMENTS

Medicare is a federal health insurance program for the following categories of people:

1. People 65 years of age or older who are retired on Social Security or railroad or civil service retirement
2. Blind individuals
3. Disabled individuals who are eligible for Social Security disability benefits† and are in the following categories:
   a. Disabled workers of any age
   b. Disabled widows of workers who are fully or currently insured through the federal government, civil service, Social Security Administration (SSA), supplemental security income (SSI), or the Railroad Retirement Act and whose husbands qualified for benefits under one of these programs
   c. Adults disabled before age 18 whose parents are eligible for or retired on Social Security benefits
4. Children and adults with end-stage renal disease (ESRD)
5. Kidney donors (all expenses related to the kidney transplantation are covered)

Medicare is run by the Health Care Financing Administration (HCFA). Local SSA offices take applications for Medicare and provide information about the program. The eligible person must apply to receive the benefits.

Those who apply for Social Security early (at age 62 years) do not receive Medicare but receive monthly reduced Social Security benefits. When they become 65, they are eligible for Medicare Parts A and/or B.

All persons who meet one of the previously stated eligibility requirements are eligible for Medicare Part A (hospital coverage). Those who qualify for full Medicare benefits may also elect to take Medicare Part B (outpatient coverage) by paying annually increasing basic premium payments to the SSA, and some pay a Medicare surtax on federal income tax payments. This premium may be automatically deducted from the patient's monthly Social Security check if he or she wishes. Those individuals not eligible for Medicare Part A (hospital insurance) at age 65 may purchase it from the SSA.

FISCAL INTERMEDIARIES AND FISCAL AGENTS

The National Blue Cross Association holds the fiscal intermediary contract for Medicare Part A; it, in turn, subcontracts it out to member agencies. Medicare Part B payments are handled by private insurance organizations under contract with the government. Organizations handling claims from hospitals, nursing facilities (formerly called skilled nursing facilities), intermediate care facilities (ICFs), long-term care facilities (LTCFs), and home health agencies are called *fiscal intermediaries*. Organizations handling claims from physicians and other suppliers of services covered under Medicare Part B are called *carriers* or *fiscal agents*. Because the policies regarding payments are different for Part A and Part B, different organizations process the claims of each part.

Prospective Payment System

On October 1, 1983, an important development in the Medicare Part A program, the Prospective Pay-

* For further information, booklets, pamphlets, and the annual *Medicare Handbook*, contact your nearest Social Security office.

† Note: In the disabled categories, a person must be disabled for 6 months before he or she receives disability payments. There is also a 24-month waiting period before Medicare benefits begin. See Chapter 15 for further information on this topic.

ment System (PPS), became effective. Under the regulations enacted by the Social Security Amendments of 1983, hospitals treating Medicare patients are reimbursed according to pre-established rates for each type of illness treated based on diagnosis. Payments to hospitals for Medicare services are classified according to 495 diagnosis related group (DRG) numbers. Beneficiaries (patients) cannot be billed beyond the pre-established DRG rate except for normal deductible and copayment amounts. (See Chapter 16 for an in-depth discussion of DRGs.)

Medicare Guidelines

The following are some basic guidelines about Medicare Parts A and B.

Medicare Part A

Part A of Medicare is hospital insurance benefits for the aged, disabled, and blind.

1. Funds for this health service come from special contributions from employees and self-employed persons, with employers matching contributions. These contributions are collected along with regular Social Security contributions from wages and self-employment income earned during a person's working years.
2. A benefit period begins the day a patient enters a hospital and ends when the patient has not been a bed patient in any hospital or skilled nursing facility (NF) for 60 consecutive days. It also ends if a patient has been in a skilled NF but has not received skilled nursing care there for 60 consecutive days. Hospital insurance protection is renewed every time the patient begins a new benefit period. There is no limit to the number of benefit periods a patient can have for hospital or nursing facility care. However, special limited benefit periods apply to hospice care.
3. Medicare Part A provides benefits to applicants in any of the following situations:
   a. A bed patient in a hospital (up to 90 hospital days for each benefit period). A patient can be hospitalized for more than one benefit period per year.
   b. A bed patient in an NF (up to 100 extended care days for each benefit period).
   c. A patient receiving home health care services.
   d. A terminally ill patient diagnosed as having 6 months or less to live who needs hospice care. A *hospice* is a public agency or private organization that is primarily engaged in providing pain relief, symptom management, and supportive services to terminally ill people and their families.
   e. A patient who needs care in a psychiatric hospital (up to 190 days in a lifetime).
   f. A terminally ill patient who needs respite care. *Respite care* is a short-term inpatient stay that may be necessary for the terminally ill patient to give temporary relief to the person who regularly assists with home care. Inpatient respite care is limited to stays of no more than 5 consecutive days for each respite period.
4. Due to the high cost of health care, the government has enforced many more cost containment features in the Medicare program. Figure 12–1 contains information on inpatient Medicare cost-sharing benefits.

Medicare Part B

Part B of Medicare is supplementary medical insurance benefits for the aged, disabled, and blind.

1. Funds for this program come equally from those who sign up for it and the federal government. Medical insurance premiums are automatically deducted from monthly checks for those who receive Social Security benefits, railroad retirement benefits, or a civil service annuity. Others pay premiums directly to the SSA.
2. Benefits to patients under Medicare Part B are shown in Figure 12–2.
3. Billing Medicare Part B
   a. *Assignment:* Under the participating physician program, the physician agrees to accept payment from Medicare (80% of the allowable) plus from the patient the remaining 20% of reasonable charges after the $100 deductible has been met (Fig. 12–3). The physician completes the HCFA-1500 (12-90) form (Fig. 12–4). The payment goes directly to the physician.

      Effective September 1, 1992, patients are not allowed to submit claims to Medicare (with five exceptions). Physicians, practitioners, and suppliers who fail to submit claims are subject to civil money penalties of up to $2,500 for each claim. Situations when a patient may file a claim are

      - Services covered by Medicare for which the patient has other insurance that should pay first;
      - Services not covered by Medicare for which the patient wants a formal Part B coverage determination;
      - Services provided by a physician who refuses to submit the claim;

12

MEDICARE (PART A): HOSPITAL INSURANCE-COVERED SERVICES FOR 1996

Services	Benefit	Medicare Pays	Patient Pays
HOSPITALIZATION Semiprivate room and board, general nursing and miscellaneous hospital services and supplies. (Medicare payments based on benefit periods.)	First 60 days	All but $736	$736
	61st to 90th day	All but $184 a day	$184 a day
	91st to 150th day[1]	All but $368 a day	$368 a day
	Beyond 150 days	Nothing	All costs
SKILLED NURSING FACILITY CARE Patient must have been in a hospital for at least 3 days and enter a Medicare-approved facility generally within 30 days after hospital discharge.[2] (Medicare payments based on benefit periods.)	First 20 days	100% of approved amount	Nothing
	Additional 80 days	All but $92 a day	Up to $92 a day
	Beyond 100 days	Nothing	All costs
HOME HEALTH CARE Part-time or intermittent skilled care, home health aide services, durable medical equipment and supplies, and other services.	Unlimited as long as Medicare conditions are met.	100% of approved amount; 80% of approved amount for durable medical equipment.	Nothing for services; 20% of approved amount for durable medical equipment.
HOSPICE CARE Pain relief, symtom management, and support services for the terminally ill.	If patient elects the hospice option and as long as doctor certifies need.	All but limited costs for outpatient drugs and inpatient respite care.	Limited cost sharing for outpatient drugs and inpatient respite care.
BLOOD	Unlimited if medically necessary.	All but first 3 pints per calendar year.	For first 3 pints.[3]

[1] This 60-reserve-days benefit may be used only once in a lifetime.
[2] Neither Medicare nor private Medigap insurance will pay for most nursing home care.
[3] To the extent the blood deductible is met under Part B of Medicare during the calendar year, it does not have to be met under Part A.

FIGURE 12-1
Five major classifications of Medicare Part A benefits. (Modified from *Your Medicare Handbook For Railroad Retirement Beneficiaries.* U.S. Government Printing Office, 1992.)

- Services provided outside the United States; and
- When durable medical equipment is purchased from a private source.

Reasonable charges means the amount that Medicare lists on the Remittance Advice (RA), formerly known as Explanation of Benefits (EOB), as an allowed (approved) charge for the procedure. This charge may be lower than the fee the physician lists on the claim. When a physician accepts assignment, he or she may bill the patient only 20% of what Medicare considers a reasonable (allowed) charge. Charging for completion and submission of a claim form on an assignment claim violates the terms of the assignment. Interest fees cannot be assessed to Medicare patients. Do not collect the Medicare copayment up front. It is permissible to collect the deductible.

Mandatory assignment laws have been adopted in several states, and legislation is under consideration and pending in many more states. These state laws would require physicians to accept the *reasonable* rate for their Medicare patients as a condition for being licensed to practice medicine in the state. Arkansas, Florida, Illinois, Maryland, Montana, and New Hampshire have rejected mandatory assignment proposals.

b. *Nonparticipating (non-par) physician:* A physician who does not participate has an option regarding assignment. The physician may not accept assignment for all services or has the option of accepting assignment for some services and collecting from the patient for other services performed at the same time and place. An exception to this policy is mandatory assignment for clinical laboratory tests and services by physician assistants. Usually a nonparticipating physician who is not accepting assignment collects the total fee from the patient but may bill no more than the Medicare limiting charge. Medicare sends the payment check to the patient. Limiting charge is a percentage limit on fees, specified by legislation, that non-par physicians may bill

MEDICARE (PART B): MEDICAL INSURANCE-COVERED SERVICES FOR 1996

Services	Benefit	Medicare Pays	Patient Pays
MEDICAL EXPENSES Physicians' services, inpatient and outpatient medical and surgical services and supplies, physical and speech therapy, ambulance, diagnostic tests, and other services.	Unlimited if medically necessary.	80% of approved amount (after $100 deductible). Reduced to 50% for most outpatient mental health services.	$100 deductible,[1] plus 20% of approved amount and limited charges above approved amount.[2]
CLINICAL LABORATORY SERVICES Blood tests, urinalyses, and more.	Unlimited if medically necessary.	100% of approved amount.	Nothing for services.
HOME HEALTH CARE Part-time or intermittent care, home health aide services, durable medical equipment and supplies, and other services.	Unlimited as long as patient meets conditions for benefits.	100% of approved amount; 80% of approved amount for durable medical equipment.	Nothing for services; 20% of approved amount for durable medical equipment.
OUTPATIENT HOSPITAL TREATMENT Services for the diagnosis or treatment of illness or injury.	Unlimited if medically necessary.	Medicare payment to hospital based on hospital cost.	$100 deductible, plus 20% of whatever the hospital charges.
BLOOD	Unlimited if medically necessary.	80% of approved amount (after $100 deductible and starting with 4th pint).	First 3 pints plus 20% of approved amounts for additional pints (after $100 deductible).[3]
AMBULATORY SURGICAL SERVICES	Unlimited if medically necessary.	80% of predetermined amount (after $100 deductible).	$100 deductible plus 20% of predetermined amount.

[1]Once the patient has had $100 of expenses for covered services in the year, the Part B deductible does not apply to any further covered services received for the rest of the year.
[2]See Figure 12–3.
[3]To the extent the blood deductible is met under Part A of Medicare during the calendar year, it does not have to be met under Part B.

FIGURE 12–2
Five major classifications of Medicare Part B benefits. (Modified from *Your Medicare Handbook For Railroad Retirement Beneficiaries.* U.S. Government Printing Office, 1996.)

Medicare beneficiaries above the fee schedule amount. This percentage changes each year. For assigned claims, non-par physicians may submit usual and customary fees. Non-par physicians maintain two fee schedules, one with usual fees and the other with limiting charges, because of these two situations.

c. *Patient's signature authorization:* Signatures are required on all HCFA-1500 claim forms except Medicare / Medicaid cases. When an illiterate or physically handicapped enrollee signs by mark (X), a witness should sign and enter his or her address next to the mark. If the claim is filed for the patient by another person, that person should enter the patient's name and write "By," sign his or her own name and address in the space, and show relationship to the patient and state why the patient cannot sign.

Sometimes it is not possible to obtain the signature of a Medicare patient because of confinement in a nursing facility or hospital or at home. In such cases, physicians can obtain a lifetime signature authorization from the patient. The lifetime beneficiary claim authorization and information release form shown in Figure 12–5 is an example that can be used for assigned and nonassigned Medicare claims and kept in the patient's medical record. The HCFA-1500 form should be submitted with the notation in the patient's signature block: "Patient's payment authorization on file." If the claim will be automatically crossed over and paid by a Medigap carrier, obtain a lifetime signature authorization for the Medigap carrier. If the patient has died, a survivor should contact the nearest Social Security office for information on what to do. If

Three Payment Examples

The annual Part B deductible has been met

	Doctor's Bill	Medicare Approved Amount *	Medicare Pays	Beneficiary Responsible For	Medicare Courtesy Adjustment**
Doctor A accepts assignment	$480	$400	$320 (80% of approved amount)	$80 (20% of approved amount)	$80
Doctor B does not accept assignment and charges no more than the limiting charge	$437	$380	$304 (80% of approved amount)	$133 (difference between the $437 actual charge–which is also the limiting charge–and Medicare payment)	None
Doctor C does not accept assignment and charges more than the limiting charge	$500	$380	$304 (80% of approved amount)	$133 (difference between the $437 limiting charge and Medicare payment)	$63

*The Medicare approved amount is less for non-participating physicians than for participating physicians.

**The courtesy adjustment is the amount posted to the patient's account to zero out the balance. The word "courtesy" implies that Medicare patients are treated well and is preferred to phrases like "not allowed" or "write off."

Note: If Medicare does not cover a service, e.g., cosmetic, hearing aid related, refractions, and so forth, the patient pays for the service whether the doctor accepts the assignment or not.

FIGURE 12–3

Example of a case showing a physician accepting an assignment versus not accepting an assignment, and the amount the patient is responsible for paying.

the insurance billing specialist is sending in the claim, he or she can sign as insurance billing specialist and state "Unable to obtain signature, patient is deceased."

d. The *time limit* for sending in claims is the end of the year following the year in which services were used. On assigned claims, the provider may file without penalty up to 27 months after providing service if reasonable cause for the delay is shown to the insurance carrier. Otherwise, there is a 10% reduction in the reimbursement. On unassigned claims, the provider may be fined up to $2000 and/or dropped from Medicare. Ask the fiscal intermediary for HCFA guidelines what is considered reasonable.

e. The form that physicians use to submit their claims to Medicare is HCFA-1500 (12-90). (See Chapter 6, Fig. 6–8.)

f. To obtain the mailing address for the Medicare claim form for your state or county, refer to Appendix A.

g. RA documents are received by the physician and patient, with the Medicare check going to the physician.

4. The following list shows the kinds of physicians' services that medical insurance Part B will help pay for.

   a. Medical and surgical services by a doctor of medicine (MD), doctor of osteopathy (DO or MD), or a doctor of dental medicine or dental surgery (DDS).

25. FEDERAL TAX I.D. NUMBER SSN EIN ☐☐	26. PATIENT'S ACCOUNT NO.	27. ACCEPT ASSIGNMENT? (For govt. claims, see back) ☒ YES ☐ NO	28. TOTAL CHARGE $	29. AMOUNT PAID $	30. BALANCE DUE $
31. SIGNATURE OF PHYSICIAN OR SUPPLIER INCLUDING DEGREES OR CREDENTIALS (I certify that the statements on the reverse apply to this bill and are made a part thereof.) SIGNED DATE	32. NAME AND ADDRESS OF FACILITY WHERE SERVICES WERE RENDERED (If other than home or office)		33. PHYSICIAN'S, SUPPLIER'S BILLING NAME, ADDRESS, ZIP CODE & PHONE # PIN# GRP#		

(APPROVED BY AMA COUNCIL ON MEDICAL SERVICE 8/88) **PLEASE PRINT OR TYPE** FORM HCFA-1500 (U2) (12-90) FORM OWCP-1500 FORM RRB-1500

FIGURE 12–4

Portion of the HCFA-1500 claim form, Block 27, marked with an X showing that the physician accepts Medicare assignment of benefits.

Hugh R. Aged, M.D.
1000 Any Street
Anytown, XY 12345
013/486-9002

LIFETIME BENEFICIARY CLAIM AUTHORIZATION AND INFORMATION RELEASE

Patient's
Name__________________________ Medicare I.D. number__________________________

I request that payment of authorized Medicare benefits be made either to me or on my behalf to (name of physician/supplier) for any services furnished me by that physician/supplier. I authorize any holder of medical information about me to release to the Health Care Financing Administration and its agents any information needed to determine these benefits or the benefits payable to related services.

I understand my signature requests that payment be made and authorizes release of medical information necessary to pay the claim. If other health insurance is indicated in Item 9 of the HCFA-1500 claim form or elsewhere on other approved claim forms or electronically submitted claims, my signature authorizes releasing of the information to the insurer or agency shown. In Medicare assigned cases, the physician or supplier agrees to accept the charge determination of the Medicare carrier as the full charge, and the patient is responsible only for the deductible, coinsurance, and noncovered services. Coinsurance and the deductible are based upon the charge determination of the Medicare carrier.

__________________________ __________________________
Patient's Signature Date

FIGURE 12–5
Lifetime Assignment of Benefits and Information Release.

b. Certain services by podiatrists (DPM).
c. Limited services by chiropractors (DC), such as subluxation of the spine.

ALIENS ON MEDICARE

An alien on Medicare may have both Part A and Part B coverage, or he or she may be eligible only for one part. To be eligible, the applicant must have lived in the United States as a permanent resident for 5 consecutive years. It is usually not necessary to state on the Medicare HCFA-1500 form that the patient is an alien. The only exception to this is when the alien is more than 65 years old and is on Medicaid (Medi-Cal) and is not eligible for Medicare benefits. In this case, the Medicaid processing agent must be billed on the proper Medicaid billing form, and it is best to state on the Medicaid form that this person is "over 65 years old and is not eligible for Medicare benefits—ALIEN."

12

BENEFICIARY REPRESENTATIVE/ REPRESENTATIVE PAYEE

Because Medicare beneficiaries may have memory impairment or may be confined to a wheelchair or bed, they have a legal right to appoint an individual to serve as their representative.

Claims assistance professionals (CAPs) act as a client representative. They have some legal standing and are recognized by Medicare to act on the beneficiary's behalf if the beneficiary completes a Beneficiary Representative Form SSA 1696. This form is available from the Social Security District Office. Copies of the completed form should be sent to the Medicare intermediary or carrier when appropriate.

In contrast, a representative payee is an individ-

Formula to Calculate Payment for Each Service

Example: HCPCS code 91000 Esophageal intubation
The medical practice location is Oakland, California.

	Work		Overhead		Malpractice	
RVUs	1.04		0.70		0.06	
GPCI*	× 1.028		× 1.258		× 1.370	
	1.07	+	0.88	+	0.08	= Total adjusted RVUs, 2.03

For 1997, the Conversion Factor for nonsurgical care is \$33.8454 × 2.03 = Allowed amount \$68.71

** Geographic practice cost indices*

FIGURE 12–6
Example of formula showing calculations to determine the fee for a specific procedure.

ual or organization chosen by the SSA to receive and administer SSA benefit funds on behalf of the beneficiary. Other duties consist of discharging the beneficiary's financial obligations for physical care and maintenance, housing, medical service expenses, and investing any surplus monies for the beneficiary's benefit. A representative payee is responsible for using payments received only for the benefit of the beneficiary, accounting for the benefits received upon request, and contacting SSA when anything affects eligibility for SSA benefits or prevents the representative payee's ability to perform these responsibilities.

Medicare Payments

For many years Medicare payments were based on reasonable charges, i.e., the amounts approved by the Medicare carrier (fiscal agents). Medicare paid 80% of the approved charge. In 1984, the Deficit Reduction Act established a participating physician program that offered incentives to participating physicians and froze the fees of nonparticipating physicians. After this, the 1987 Omnibus Budget Reconciliation Act (OBRA) introduced the maximum allowable actual charge (MAAC) formula, which developed the maximum fee a physician could charge Medicare patients for each service.

Next, a resource based relative value scale (RBRVS) system was established as a means to redistribute Medicare dollars among physicians more equitably. This became the basis for physicians' payments nationwide for a 5-year phase-in that began on January 1, 1992. This system consists of a fee schedule based on relative values. The formula for obtaining relative value units is somewhat complex and involves a bit of mathematics in computing three components: a relative value unit (RVU) for the service, a geographic adjustment factor (GAF), and a monetary conversion factor (CF).

$$\text{RVU} \times \text{GAF} \times \text{CF} = \text{Medicare \$ per service}$$

RVUs are based on the physician work RVU, the practice expense RVU, and the malpractice insurance RVU. To bring the fees in line for the region where the physician practices and to adjust for regional overhead and malpractice costs, each of the RVUs is adjusted for each Medicare local carrier by geographic practice cost indices (GPCIs), referred to as "gypsies."

To convert a geographically adjusted relative value into a payment amount, a CF is used. This CF is updated to a new amount each year. Figure 12–6 provides an example of calculating payment for one procedure code.

The figures to work out this formula in the chart for each service are published annually in the Federal Register.

RVUs help when determining cost accounting because they account for practice expense, malpractice expense, work effort, and cost of living. They are also helpful when negotiating the best contract available with managed care plans, so it is important for office managers or individuals assisting physicians to know and understand RBRVS data. A crosswalk is an effective way to see how the practice may be affected by an RBRVS contract. To develop one, make several columns using spreadsheet soft-

Example:

A	B	C	D	E	F	G	H
Code	Code Description	RBRVS /RVUs	Conversion Factor	Fee	Contract Conversion Factor	Contract Fee	% Contract Payment
99212	Ofc Visit	0.68	72.06	$49	64.71	$44.00	90%

ware. In column A, list common procedure codes used by the practice; column B, the code description; and column C, the RBRVS RVUs. Leave column D blank to insert a conversion factor. In column E, put in the present fee-for-service rate (rounded-out figure). Divide the fee in column E by column C to get the conversion factor. Leave a blank for column F to insert a conversion factor for the contract. List the managed care contract payment in column G. Divide column G by column C to get the conversion factor for column F. Then, to work out the percentage being paid at the contract rate, divide the plan's contract fee by the physician's fee for column H.

Beginning in 1996, each Medicare local carrier annually sends each physician a Medicare fee schedule for their area or region number listing three columns of figures: participating amount, nonparticipating amount, and limiting charge for each procedure code number. To see an example of this, refer to the Mock Fee Schedule shown in the *Student Workbook for the Insurance Handbook for the Medical Office.*

The federal government developed the Health Care Financing Administration Common Procedure Coding System (HCPCS) for the Medicare program. As mentioned in Chapter 4, to obtain correct payment for a procedure or service, a code number must be selected from three levels of Medicare coding. They are:

Level I ▪ The American Medical Association's *Current Procedural Terminology* codes and modifiers (national codes), referred to as CPT.

Level II ▪ Health Care Financing Administration's (HCFA) designated codes (national codes), referred to as HCPCS (pronounced "hick-picks").

HCFA developed the HCPCS to code those services, materials, drugs, and procedures that are not in the *CPT Code Book.* This second level is composed of alphanumeric codes from A0000 through V5999 and is a national code standard used by all regional Medicare fiscal agents or carriers. Special alpha modifiers, from -AA to -ZZ, have been developed by HCFA to clarify unusual services or procedures not fully described by HCPCS codes. The national HCFA alphanumeric code book can be ordered from the U.S. Government Printing Office.* Examples of this level are located at the end of Appendix B of the *Student Workbook for the Insurance Handbook for the Medical Office.*

Level III ▪ These alphanumeric codes are assigned and maintained by each Medicare fiscal agent or insurance carrier and are not found in Level I or II. They are known as regional or local codes. These range from W0000 through Z9999. Special alpha modifiers are used to further explain a given service. These alpha modifiers range from -WA through -ZZ. HCFA plans to phase out these codes, so you may see fewer of these in the future.

Figure 12–7 shows a list of the index/ranges contained in HCPCS. An alphabetic partial list along with alpha modifiers may be found in Appendix B of the *Student Workbook for the Insurance Handbook for the Medical Office.*

CIVIL MONETARY PENALTIES LAW

In 1983, the federal government passed the Civil Monetary Penalties Law (CMPL) to prosecute cases of Medicare and Medicaid fraud. The law carries three separate forms of sanction:

- A penalty of up to $2,000 for each item or service wrongfully listed in a payment request to Medicare or Medicaid.
- An assessment of up to twice the total amount improperly claimed.
- Suspension from the programs for whatever period the Department of Health and Human Services determines.

A physician may be penalized when participating in the following violations:

Billing more than once for the same service to obtain greater reimbursement.

*Superintendent of Documents, Washington, D.C. 20402. Ask for the *HCFA Common Procedure Coding System, Non-CPT-4 Portion,* Document Number 01706000 168-2. The cost is $12.50.

HCFA Common Procedure Coding System

Index/Ranges	
A0000–A0999	Transportation services including ambulance
A2000–A2999	Chiropractic services
A4000–A4999	Medical and surgical supplies
A9000–A9999	Miscellaneous and experimental
B4000–B4999	Enteral and parenteral therapy
D0100–D9999	Dental procedures
E0100–E9999	DME (durable medical equipment)
H5000–H9999	Rehabilitative services
J0000–J9999	Drugs administered other than oral method
L0100–L4999	Orthotic procedures
L5000–L9999	Prosthetic procedures
M0000–M0019	Office services
M0020–M0059	Hospital and other medical facilities visits
M0070–M0099	Other medical services
M0250–M0299	Otorhinolaryngologic services
M0300–M0399	Cardiovascular services
M0500–M0549	Special diagnostic services
M0600–M0649	Psychologic testing services
M0700–M0799	Physical medicine services
M0800–M0899	Allergy services
M0900–M0999	CRD (chronic renal dialysis) services
P0000–P0999	Automated laboratory tests
P2000–P4999	Chemistry and toxicology tests
P7001–P7999	Microbiology tests
P9000–P9999	Miscellaneous pathology and laboratory
R0000–R5999	Diagnostic radiology services
R6000–R6999	Diagnostic ultrasound services
T1000–T1999	Integumentary system surgical services
T2000–T2999	Musculoskeletal system surgical services
T3000–T3999	Hemic, lymphatic, endocrine surgical services
T4000–T4999	Digestive system surgical services
T5400–T5999	Male/female system surgical services
T6000–T6499	Nervous system surgical services
T6500–T6899	Eye surgical services
T6900–T6999	Ear surgical services
T7000–T9999	Other surgical services
V0000–V2799	Vision services
V5000–V5999	Hearing services

FIGURE 12–7
Index showing alpha-numeric ranges for the Health Care Finance Administration's Common Procedure Coding System (HCPCS).

Billing for services that were not provided.
Fragmenting billed services that could be accurately described by one procedural code.
Upgrading the reported level or complexity of services, over that of services actually furnished, to obtain greater reimbursement.

A physician who fails to practice due care to ensure the accuracy of Medicare and Medicaid claims prepared in his or her office risks enormous financial penalties. The CMPL makes no distinction between outright fraud and negligence in billing. Therefore, if an employee submits false billings that the physician knows nothing about, the physician may be held liable. Reckless disregard of federal and state regulations by the insurance billing specialist can affect the way claims are submitted and possibly cause a physician to incur a civil monetary penalty. Incorrectly coded procedures can affect the penalties imposed on a physician.

The insurance billing specialist should periodically attend Medicare and Medicaid training workshops to keep up-to-date and gain a better understanding of federal and state government claim requirements. Medicare and Medicaid manuals and bulletins should be kept up-to-date and accessible for quick reference. Keep documentation to support claims submission in the event of an audit. If a record is missing, make a written note that it has been lost or destroyed because it might be presumed that the physician deliberately destroyed the documents to conceal evidence. If a billing error is discovered after a claim submission or an overpayment is received, notify the fiscal agent or insurance carrier immediately.

Always document any meetings with representatives of the fiscal agent or state welfare department and include the advice given. If the advice later proves to be erroneous, such records can support the physician's good faith. The Office of the Inspector General of the Department of Health and Human Services and each state's Medicaid fraud control unit investigate violations. Notify the physician's attorney if the physician is advised that he or she is being investigated. Documents should be released only after the attorney's approval. Retain photocopies of all documents given to the investigator.

MEDICARE HEALTH INSURANCE CARD

The patient should show you his or her health insurance card (Fig. 12–8) because it indicates whether the patient has both hospital and medical insurance and when each started. When a husband and wife both have Medicare, they receive separate cards and claim numbers. This card is red, white, and blue, and cards issued after 1990 are plastic. A patient whose Medicare card claim number ends in "A" will have the *same* Social Security and claim numbers. A patient whose Medicare card claim number ends in "B" or "D" will have *different* Social Security and card claim numbers. A quick check between Social Security and card claim numbers may identify a submission error and forestall a claims rejection.

The letters following the Medicare number on the patient's identification card indicate the following (this is only a partial listing):

A = wage earner
B = husband's number (wife 62 years or older)
D = widow
HDA = disabled adult
C = disabled child
J, K1, or J1 = special monthly benefits, never worked under Social Security
T = uninsured and entitled only to health insurance benefits

These letters preceding the Medicare number on the patient's identification card indicate railroad retirees:

FIGURE 12–8
Medicare Health Insurance Claim Card. Cards issued since 1990 are plastic.

A	Retired railroad employee *Examples:* A 000000 (6 digits) A 000-00-0000 (9 digits)
MA	Spouse of a retired railroad employee
WA/WD	Widow or widower of deceased employee (age or disability) *Examples:* A 000000 (6 digits) A 000-00-0000 (9 digits)
CA	Child or student
WCA/WCD	Widow of retiree with child in her care or disabled child of deceased employee
PA/PD	Parent of deceased employee (male or female)
H	Railroad retirement board pensioner before 1937
MH	Wife of railroad retirement board pensioner before 1937
WH	Widowed wife of railroad retirement board pensioner before 1937
WCH	Widow of railroad retirement board pensioner with child in her care
PH	Parent of railroad retirement board pensioner before 1937
JA	Widow receiving a joint and survivor annuity
X	Divorced spouse's annuity, for use on forms AA-3 and AA-7 only

A telephone hotline or, in some states, a modem is available to verify the enrollment status because some patients can switch coverage on a month-to-month basis to a managed care plan. Most carriers also allow information on deductible status. The patient's numeric information (Medicare number and date of birth) is entered into the telephone, and the digital response indicates how much of the deductible has been satisfied. Contact the Medicare fiscal agent in your location for information about this service.

Coverage

HOSPITAL BENEFITS

As shown in Figure 12–1, five major classifications of hospital benefits for Medicare Part A are listed. However, miscellaneous hospital services and supplies might consist of intensive care unit (ICU) costs, blood transfusions, drugs, x-ray and laboratory tests, medical supplies (casts, surgical dressings, splints), use of wheelchair, operating room (OR) and recovery room costs, and therapy (physical, occupational, speech–language). There are no benefits for personal convenience items (television, radio, telephone), private duty nurses, or a private room unless it is determined medically necessary. Similar benefits also relate to NFs.

Benefits for hospice and respite care consist of nursing and physicians' services, drugs, therapy (physical, occupational, speech–language pathology), home health aide, homemaker services, medical social services, medical supplies and appliances, short-term inpatient care, and counseling.

MEDICAL BENEFITS

As shown in Figure 12–2, five major classifications of medical benefits for Medicare Part B are shown. In addition to medical and surgical procedures, x-rays, and laboratory tests, the benefits are a routine Papanicolaou test once every 3 years, mammograms every other year, vaccines (influenza, pneumococcal pneumonia, hepatitis B), ambulance service, therapeutic shoes for severe diabetic foot disease, rental or purchase of durable medical equipment for home use, prosthetic devices for internal body organs, artificial limbs and eyes, and braces (leg, arm, back, neck). Laboratories must be certified by Medicare.

Nonbenefits consist of routine physical examination, routine foot care, eye or hearing examinations, and cosmetic surgery unless because of injury or to improve functioning of a malformed part. A physician may bill a patient separately for noncovered services. Medicare also covers limited services by chiropractors and podiatrists. Dental care is covered only for fractures or surgery of the jaw. Optometric examinations are provided if a person has aphakia (absence of the natural lens of the eye).

There are many other benefits and nonbenefits, too numerous to list here. To find out whether a particular procedure qualifies for payment, contact your Medicare carrier.

RAILROAD RETIREMENT BENEFITS

Railroad Retirement Board offices take applications for Medicare and provide information about the program for railroad beneficiaries. Medical insurance premiums are automatically deducted from the monthly checks of people who receive railroad retirement benefits. Those who do not receive a monthly check pay their premiums directly or, in some cases, have premiums paid on their behalf under a state assistance program. The Medicare beneficiary's I.D. card has a claim number with nine digits and one to three letters before the digits. (*Examples:* A-000-00-0000 or WA-000-00-0000.) After a claim is submitted to the Medicare railroad retiree carrier a Remittance Advice (RA) document is generated, explaining the decision made on the claim and what services Medicare paid.

If the allowed fees differ from those allowed by your regular Medicare carrier, write or fax the Medicare railroad retiree carrier, asking that fees be based on fee data from your local carrier.

Railroad retirement beneficiaries are generally entitled to benefits for covered services received from a qualified American facility. However, under certain circumstances, a Medicare beneficiary may receive care in Canada or Mexico. Benefits and deductibles under Parts A and B are the same as for other Medicare recipients.

Some railroad retirees are members of a railroad hospital association or a prepayment plan. These members pay regular premiums to the plan and then can receive health services the plan provides without additional charges. In some plans, small charges are made for certain services, such as drugs or home visits. Many prepayment plans make arrangements with Medicare to receive direct payments for services they furnish that are covered under Medicare Part B. Some prepayment plans have contracts with Medicare as HMOs or competitive medical plans and can receive direct payment for services covered by either hospital or medical insurance.

A list of fiscal agents or carriers for Medicare railroad retirees appears in Appendix A.

PHYSICIAN SELF REFERRALS

Stark I and II Regulations

On January 1, 1992, federal legislation, Stark I, took effect, without regulations until they were published in 1995. This law prohibits a physician or his or her family who has a financial relationship with a laboratory from referring patients to that facility. Clinical laboratories must submit financial information to HCFA, including the names and identification numbers of physicians who hold a financial interest in the business. Stark II, an amendment, took effect on January 1, 1995, and expanded these regulations by prohibiting Medicare and Medicaid payments for treatment that results from the referral of a patient by a physician (or immediate family member of the physician) who has a financial relationship (ownership interest or compensatory arrangement) with providers of designated health services. It also prohibits the provider from billing for the designated health service. These services include:

- Clinical laboratory services
- Durable medical equipment and supplies
- Home health services
- Inpatient and outpatient hospital services
- Occupational therapy services
- Outpatient prescription drugs
- Parenteral and enteral nutrients, related equipment and supplies
- Physical therapy services
- Prosthetics, orthotics, and prosthetic devices and supplies
- Radiation therapy services and supplies
- Radiology services, including magnetic resonance imaging (MRI), computed tomography (CT) scans, and ultrasound services

Many states have passed laws and administrative rules that may apply the same principles to other private payers. Uncovered self-referral deceits or failure of a laboratory to report financial information can lead to hefty fines, sanctions, payment denials, and exclusion from the Medicare/Medicaid programs by the Office of the Inspector General, Department of Health and Human Services. There are some general exceptions related to ownership/investment and compensation arrangements, so it is important to obtain a complete description of this legislation for proper compliance.

EMPLOYED ELDERLY HEALTH CARE COVERAGE

To understand various types of scenarios that may be encountered when submitting claims for elderly individuals, it is important to know about several powerful federal laws that regulate health care coverage of those age 65 and older who are employed. Such individuals may have group insurance or a Medigap policy or may fall under billing categories of Medicare First Payer or Medicare Secondary Payer (all are reviewed in detail later in this chapter).

Omnibus Budget Reconciliation Act

The Omnibus Budget Reconciliation Act (OBRA) of 1981 required that, in the case of a current or former employee or dependent under age 65 and Medicare eligible solely because of end-stage renal disease (ESRD), the employer's group coverage is primary for up to 12 months. This act applies to all employers regardless of the number of employees. OBRA of 1986, effective in 1987, required that if an employee or dependent under age 65 has Medicare coverage due to a disability other than ESRD, the group coverage is primary and Medicare is secondary. This act applies only to large group health plans having at least 100 full- or part-time employees.

Tax Equity and Fiscal Responsibility Act

The Tax Equity and Fiscal Responsibility Act (TEFRA) of 1982 established that an employee or spouse aged 65 to 69 years is entitled to the same health insurance benefits offered under the same conditions to younger employees and their spouses. The group insurance is primary and Medicare is secondary.

Deficit Reduction Act

The Deficit Reduction Act (DEFRA) of 1984, effective 1985, was an amendment to TEFRA and stated that a spouse aged 65 to 69 years of an employee of any age is entitled to the same group health plan offered to younger employees and their spouses. The group's coverage is primary and Medicare is secondary.

Consolidated Omnibus Budget Reconciliation Act

The Consolidated Omnibus Budget Reconciliation Act (COBRA) of 1985, effective 1986, is another amendment to TEFRA eliminating the age ceiling of 69 years. An employee or spouse age 65 or over is entitled to the same group health plan offered to younger employees and their spouses. The group's coverage is primary and Medicare is secondary.

TEFRA, DEFRA, and COBRA apply to employers with at least 20 full- or part-time employees.

The Tax Reform Act was passed in 1986; it clarified certain aspects of COBRA. A spouse and dependents may elect to receive continued coverage even if the employee does not wish insurance coverage and terminates. However, the spouse and dependents must have been covered under the plan before the covered employee terminates. Spouses who are widowed or divorced while receiving continued coverage must report such changes to the benefit plan administrator within 60 days to determine how many additional months of coverage are available.

Effective October 1, 1987, under this act, a nonparticipating physician who does not accept assignment for an *elective surgery* for which the actual charge will be $500 or more must provide the beneficiary in writing (1) the estimated fee for the procedure, (2) the estimated Medicare-approved allowance for the procedure, and (3) the excess of the physician's actual charge over the approved allowance (Fig. 12–9). *Elective surgery* means a surgical procedure that can be scheduled in advance, is not an emergency, and is discretionary on the part of the physician and the patient. Failure to undergo elective surgery does not pose a mortality threat. Give a copy of this letter to the Medicare patient and keep the original for your files. Document the patient's acknowledgement by obtaining his or her signature at the bottom of the letter.

When a patient is to receive a service that might be denied for medical necessity by Medicare, it is wise to tell this to the patient and have him or her acknowledge this by agreeing to pay for the denied service. Have the patient sign a waiver of liability agreement or responsibility statement as shown in Figure 12–10.

Provider Identification Numbers

National Provider Identifier Program

Another requirement of this act was the establishment of identification numbers for each physician providing services paid by Medicare. However, the most common billing mistakes were the insertion of provider identification numbers (PINs), unique physician identification numbers (UPINs), clinic provider identification numbers (CPINs), and performing physician identifications (PPIs) in the wrong blocks on the HCFA-1500 claim form. As a solution, HCFA developed the national provider identifier (NPI) implemented by all providers on January 1, 1997. The NPI is a single block of 10 characters. The first seven characters are the NPI root base, the eighth character is a check digit, and the last two characters identify the provider's location.

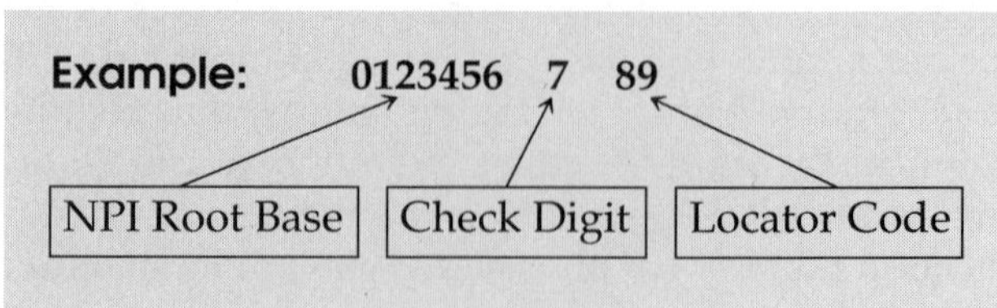

The NPI replaces the UPIN, PIN, CPIN, and PPI and is used for assigned or unassigned claims. It will be used by all federal insurers (CHAMPUS, Medicaid, Medicare). The first eight digits identify the physi-

WORKSHEET FOR
ESTIMATED MEDICARE PAYMENT FOR ELECTIVE SURGERY

1. Physician's actual fee $_________
2. Medicare approved or allowed amount $_________
3. Difference between physician's actual fee and Medicare approved or allowed amount (1 - 2 = □) -_________
4. Twenty per cent coinsurance (0.20 X 2 = □) +_________
5. Beneficiary's out-of-pocket expense (3 + 4 + □) $_________
   Assume the $100 deductible has been met

Items 1, 2, and 5 must be included in the letter to the beneficiary

A

Physician's Letterhead

Dear Patient:

Because I do not accept assignment for elective surgery, Medicare requires that I give you certain information before surgery when my charges are $500 or more.

The following information concerns the surgery we have discussed. These estimates assume that you have already met the $100 deductible.

Type of surgery_______________________________________
Estimated charge (Limiting charge) $_________________
Medicare estimated payment $_________________
Patient's estimated payment $_________________

This estimate is based upon our present expectations of what surgical procedure(s) will be required. Please remember that this is only an estimate of charges, we cannot be sure that additional procedures will or will not be necessary.

Sincerely,

John Doe, M. D.
Medicare Provider Number_______________

I understand the foregoing physician charges and my financial responsibility with respect to those estimated charges.

Patient's Signature______________________________ Date____________

B

FIGURE 12–9
Worksheet *(A)* and sample beneficiary letter *(B)* for estimated Medicare payment for elective surgery.

cian throughout his or her career (as did the UPIN) and the two-digit suffix identifies the service location (as did the PIN). The NPI is entered on the HCFA-1500 claim form in Block 17A for referring physicians. If more than one physician in a group is billing on the claim, it is inserted in Blocks 24K and 33. When billing for a group, the group provider number is placed in Block 33.

Name and address of physician

ADVANCE NOTICE MEDICARE BENEFICIARY AGREEMENT

If Medicare determines that a particular service, although it would be otherwise covered, is not reasonable and necessary under Medicare program standards, Medicare will deny payment for that service. In your case, Medicare might deny payment for:

1.____
2.____

for the following reasons:

Medicare does not usually pay for this:
__________many visits or treatments
__________service or this many services within this period of time
__________injection or this many injections
__________because it is a treatment that is yet to be proved effective
__________office visit unless it was needed because of an emergency
__________same services by more than one doctor during the same time period
__________equipment
__________laboratory test
__________visit since it is more than one visit per day
__________extensive procedure
__________same service by more than one doctor of the same specialty
__________nursing home visit since only one is allowed per month

Beneficiary Agreement

I have been notified by my physician that, in my case, Medicare might deny payment for the service(s) checked above. If Medicare denies payment, I agree to be personally and fully responsible for payment.

__________________________ __________________________
Beneficiary's Signature Date Signed

FIGURE 12–10
Example of an advance notice Medicare beneficiary agreement, which is also known as a waiver of liability agreement or responsibility statement.

To assist you with claims completion, compile a reference list of ordering and frequently referring physicians with their NPIs. To obtain the physicians' NPIs, call their offices or obtain them through your Medicare carrier.

If a physician supplies durable medical equipment (DME) to patients, a supplier number registered with one of four Medicare regional carriers is required. The claim is billed to the DME regional carrier and NOT the Part B carrier. See Appendix A for your state's DME regional carrier address.

Examples and additional information on this topic appear in the *Workbook* before Chapter 1, Introduction Guide to the *Workbook*.

Medicare Supplemental Insurance

Many people over the age of 65 years elect to purchase private insurance to supplement Medicare. It helps pay for some of the expenses that Medicare does not cover. There are two types of policies: service benefit, or incurred, type and indemnity benefit type.

Service benefit policies pay Medicare's Part A deductible and copayments as well as Part B's coinsurance requirements. This type of policy automatically adjusts with cost increases caused by inflation or changes in the Medicare Part A deductible. These policies only supplement what Medicare pays for covered services the patient has actually received; they do not cover Medicare expenses that are disallowed. However, a comprehensive insurance policy sometimes covers some things Medicare does not pay for, but usually requires that the patient pass a physical examination.

Indemnity benefit policies pay fixed-dollar benefits and do not necessarily keep up with inflation or changes in Medicare's deductible or copayments. Therefore, the patient has to purchase additional coverage from time to time.

There are also insurance policies that insure against specific diseases, such as cancer.

When a patient is in an NF and is declared *custodial,* meaning in need of long-term care and with little chance for improvement, Medicare will not pay, and most private health insurance will not pay. A few insurance policies are written specifically for custodial care only. There are three types of long-term care insurance policies:

1. Indemnity plans that pay a set amount per day for care;
2. Reimbursement policies that pay a percentage of services; and
3. Policies that combine indemnity and reimbursement.

MEDIGAP

Another specialized insurance policy devised for the Medicare beneficiary is called *Medigap* or *Medifill.* This type of policy covers the deductible and copayment amounts typically not covered under Medicare (e.g., 20% of the Medicare allowed amount). Benefits of these plans are predefined by the federal government and are the same for all Medigap policies. These plans are offered by private third party payers to Medicare beneficiaries. Medicare carriers are supposed to transmit Medigap claims electronically for participating physicians, thus eliminating the need to file an additional claim. This is called "claims transfer," or "crossover." Usually, the Medicare RA to the patient states, "This claim has been referred to your supplemental carrier for any additional benefits."

Medigap payments for benefits go directly to the participating physicians. See Chapter 10 for additional information on the Blue Cross and Blue Shield/Medicare Reciprocity Program.

MEDICARE SECONDARY PAYER (MSP)

Employer supplemental coverage is a plan that a Medicare beneficiary has through a former employer. Medicare calls these primary programs Medicare Secondary Payer (MSP). When an employee retires and Medicare becomes the primary coverage, the company's group health plan coordinates benefits with Medicare. These are known as *conversion policies.* Benefits can vary in these supplemental plans, and these policies are not considered "Medigap" as defined by federal law.

There are also insurance policies for individuals aged 65 years or over who are still employed. Employers with 20 or more employees are required to offer workers and their spouses aged 65 through 69 the same health benefits offered to younger workers. Workers may accept or reject the employer's health insurance plan. If they accept it, Medicare becomes the secondary insurance carrier. Thus, the employer's sponsored plan will be billed as primary (first) and Medicare second. Payments for these types of policies may not necessarily go to the physician but may go to the insured.

MEDIGAP AND MSP GUIDELINES

As you have learned, it is important to be able to identify when Medicare is primary or secondary and to know what additional benefits the patient might have. Suggested procedures are as follows:

1. Inquire whether the patient is
   a. working and covered under an employee group health plan
   b. covered by auto insurance for an auto accident
   c. injured or suffering a disease connected with employment (workers' compensation program or Federal Black Lung Program)
   d. injured or ill because of an automobile accident covered by liability insurance or no-fault insurance
   e. suffering from end-stage renal disease (ESRD) and covered by an Employer Group Health Plan (EGHP)
   f. aged 65 years or older and enrolled in an employer- or union-sponsored health plan
   g. entitled to disability benefits covered by a large group health plan (LGHP)

h. receiving benefits authorized by the Veterans Administration (VA)

If yes, this means Medicare is the secondary payer (MSP).

2. If Medicare is the primary payer, ask to see the Medicare card as well as any other insurance cards, and make photocopies of both sides of each card.
3. Ask the patient whether the supplemental coverage was carried over (conversion policy) from his or her employer.
4. Call the carrier if the type of plan is not clearly identified.
5. Generally, Medicare would be billed first unless it is a case of Medicare second payer (MSP). For Medigap cases, nonparticipating physicians may collect copayments and deductibles up to their limiting charge (unless the state forbids collection of more than the allowed amount) from patients at the time of service. Participating physicians *may not* collect copayments/deductibles from patients covered by Medigap if the patient requests the physician to submit the claim to the Medigap insurer. Collect copayments after receiving the Medicare (RA) document.
6. If not a Medigap and the secondary insurance carrier has not received any communication from the Medicare carrier after receiving the RA, write the patient's group and policy (or certificate) numbers on the RA and attach it to
   a. a copy of the original Health Insurance Claim Form HCFA-1500 showing the diagnosis and itemization of charges
   OR
   b. a copy of the billing statement of the physician (or other provider of service), showing date of treatment, description of service(s) rendered, fees, and diagnosis.

   If a photocopy is made of the RA, copy both the front and back sides because notations are frequently explained on the back.

MEDIGAP AND MSP CLAIMS

Completing the HCFA-1500 claim form for a Medicare patient who has supplemental insurance can be confusing. First decide whether the case is Medicare primary or secondary payer. After that is correct in your mind, then follow the directions on what should be entered in each box of the HCFA-1500 Health Insurance Claim Form, depending on the payer.

Some templates (Figs. 12–11 and 12–12) make it easier to learn which boxes to complete and which to ignore, depending on the primary and secondary payer. Figure 12–11 is used for submitting claims when Medicare is primary and the patient has a Medigap (supplemental) policy. Figure 12–12 is for billing other insurance and then Medicare after the primary insurance has paid. A copy of the primary insurance's Explanation of Benefits (EOB) document must be attached to this type of claim.

The notations used in the instructions in Table 12–1 for each box of the HCFA-1500 form are

P = Medicare primary
S = Medicare secondary, primary insurance has paid
P/S = Same data required whether Medicare is primary or secondary

For additional general instructions for completing claims in Medicare, Medigap, and Medicare Secondary Payer cases, see Chapter 6. For instructions on how to transmit a claim electronically, see Chapter 7.

Medicare and Prepayment Plans

HEALTH MAINTENANCE ORGANIZATIONS

During the spring of 1984, the Department of Health and Human Services published regulations giving Medicare enrollees the right to join and assign their Medicare benefits to health maintenance organizations (HMOs). HMOs had been in operation for nearly 50 years when they became available as an option for Medicare enrollees. Medicare pays the HMO directly on a monthly basis for Medicare enrollees who use the HMO option. Enrollees pay the HMO a monthly premium that covers the cost of Medicare deductibles and coinsurance for which the enrollee would be responsible. With a Medicare HMO, the patient does not need a Medicare supplemental insurance plan. Medicare HMO plans may also be referred to as HMO senior plans.

Some HMOs provide services not usually covered by Medicare, such as eyeglasses, prescription drugs, and routine physical examinations. Once a person has signed up with an HMO, he or she cannot go back to a former physician of personal choice and expect Medicare to pay the bill. If the patient wants to leave the HMO, he or she must give written notice. Until Medicare officially takes the patient off its rolls, he or she must continue to use the HMO. This may take as long as 2 months. Some hospitals contract with HMOs as the sole hospital facility for the HMO patient.

APPROVED OMB-0938-0008

PLEASE DO NOT STAPLE IN THIS AREA

MEDICARE/MEDIGAP—A CROSSOVER CLAIM
(primary) (supplemental)

PICA **HEALTH INSURANCE CLAIM FORM** PICA

CARRIER

1. MEDICARE [X] (Medicare #) MEDICAID [ ] (Medicaid #) CHAMPUS [ ] (Sponsor's SSN) CHAMPVA [ ] (VA File #) GROUP HEALTH PLAN [ ] (SSN or ID) FECA BLK LUNG [ ] (SSN) OTHER [X] (ID)

1a. INSURED'S I.D. NUMBER (FOR PROGRAM IN ITEM 1)
Medicare #

2. PATIENT'S NAME (Last Name, First Name, Middle Initial)

3. PATIENT'S BIRTH DATE MM DD YY SEX M [ ] F [ ]

4. INSURED'S NAME (Last Name, First Name, Middle Initial)

5. PATIENT'S ADDRESS (No., Street)

6. PATIENT RELATIONSHIP TO INSURED Self [ ] Spouse [ ] Child [ ] Other [ ]

7. INSURED'S ADDRESS (No., Street)

CITY STATE

8. PATIENT STATUS Single [ ] Married [ ] Other [ ]

CITY STATE

ZIP CODE TELEPHONE (Include Area Code)
BLOCKS 9-9D ONLY
PARTICIPATING PHYSICIAN

Employed [ ] Full-Time Student [ ] Part-Time Student [ ]

ZIP CODE TELEPHONE (INCLUDE AREA CODE) ( )

9. OTHER INSURED'S NAME (Last Name, First Name, Middle Initial)
Medigap policyholder name

10. IS PATIENT'S CONDITION RELATED TO:

11. INSURED'S POLICY GROUP OR FECA NUMBER
NONE

a. OTHER INSURED'S POLICY OR GROUP NUMBER
MEDIGAP + policy/grp #

a. EMPLOYMENT? (CURRENT OR PREVIOUS) [ ] YES [ ] NO

a. INSURED'S DATE OF BIRTH MM DD YY SEX M [ ] F [ ]

b. OTHER INSURED'S DATE OF BIRTH MM DD YY SEX M [ ] F [ ]

b. AUTO ACCIDENT? PLACE (State) [ ] YES [ ] NO

b. EMPLOYER'S NAME OR SCHOOL NAME

c. EMPLOYER'S NAME OR SCHOOL NAME
Medigap insurer claims address

c. OTHER ACCIDENT? [ ] YES [ ] NO

c. INSURANCE PLAN NAME OR PROGRAM NAME

d. INSURANCE PLAN NAME OR PROGRAM NAME
Medigap's name or carrier's unique identifer

10d. RESERVED FOR LOCAL USE

d. IS THERE ANOTHER HEALTH BENEFIT PLAN? [ ] YES [ ] NO *If yes*, return to and complete item 9 a-d.

READ BACK OF FORM BEFORE COMPLETING & SIGNING THIS FORM.

12. PATIENT'S OR AUTHORIZED PERSON'S SIGNATURE I authorize the release of any medical or other information necessary to process this claim. I also request payment of government benefits either to myself or to the party who accepts assignment below.

SIGNED ____ DATE ____

13. INSURED'S OR AUTHORIZED PERSON'S SIGNATURE I authorize payment of medical benefits to the undersigned physician or supplier for services described below.

SIGNED ____

PATIENT AND INSURED INFORMATION

14. DATE OF CURRENT: MM DD YY ILLNESS (First symptom) OR INJURY (Accident) OR PREGNANCY(LMP)

15. IF PATIENT HAS HAD SAME OR SIMILAR ILLNESS. GIVE FIRST DATE MM DD YY

16. DATES PATIENT UNABLE TO WORK IN CURRENT OCCUPATION FROM MM DD YY TO MM DD YY

17. NAME OF REFERRING PHYSICIAN OR OTHER SOURCE

17a. I.D. NUMBER OF REFERRING PHYSICIAN
NPI

18. HOSPITALIZATION DATES RELATED TO CURRENT SERVICES FROM MM DD YY TO MM DD YY

19. RESERVED FOR LOCAL USE

20. OUTSIDE LAB? [ ] YES [ ] NO $ CHARGES

21. DIAGNOSIS OR NATURE OF ILLNESS OR INJURY. (RELATE ITEMS 1,2,3 OR 4 TO ITEM 24E BY LINE)
1. ___ . ___ 3. ___ . ___
2. ___ . ___ 4. ___ . ___

22. MEDICAID RESUBMISSION CODE ORIGINAL REF. NO.

23. PRIOR AUTHORIZATION NUMBER

24. A DATE(S) OF SERVICE From MM DD YY To MM DD YY	B Place of Service	C Type of Service	D PROCEDURES, SERVICES, OR SUPPLIES (Explain Unusual Circumstances) CPT/HCPCS MODIFIER	E DIAGNOSIS CODE	F $ CHARGES	G DAYS OR UNITS	H EPSDT Family Plan	I EMG	J COB	K RESERVED FOR LOCAL USE
1										NPI
2										
3										
4										
5										
6										

PHYSICIAN OR SUPPLIER INFORMATION

25. FEDERAL TAX I.D. NUMBER SSN EIN [ ] [ ]

26. PATIENT'S ACCOUNT NO.

27. ACCEPT ASSIGNMENT? (For govt. claims, see back) [X] YES [ ] NO

28. TOTAL CHARGE $

29. AMOUNT PAID $

30. BALANCE DUE $

31. SIGNATURE OF PHYSICIAN OR SUPPLIER INCLUDING DEGREES OR CREDENTIALS (I certify that the statements on the reverse apply to this bill and are made a part thereof.)

SIGNED DATE

32. NAME AND ADDRESS OF FACILITY WHERE SERVICES WERE RENDERED (If other than home or office)
Facility name, address, and NPI

33. PHYSICIAN'S, SUPPLIER'S BILLING NAME, ADDRESS, ZIP CODE & PHONE #

PIN# GRP#

(APPROVED BY AMA COUNCIL ON MEDICAL SERVICE 8/88) ***PLEASE PRINT OR TYPE*** FORM HCFA-1500 (U2) (12-90) FORM OWCP-1500 FORM RRB-1500

reference initials

FIGURE 12–11

Example of a completed HCFA-1500 Health Insurance Claim Form for a Medicare/Medigap case. Shaded blocks do not need to be completed for this type of case.

12

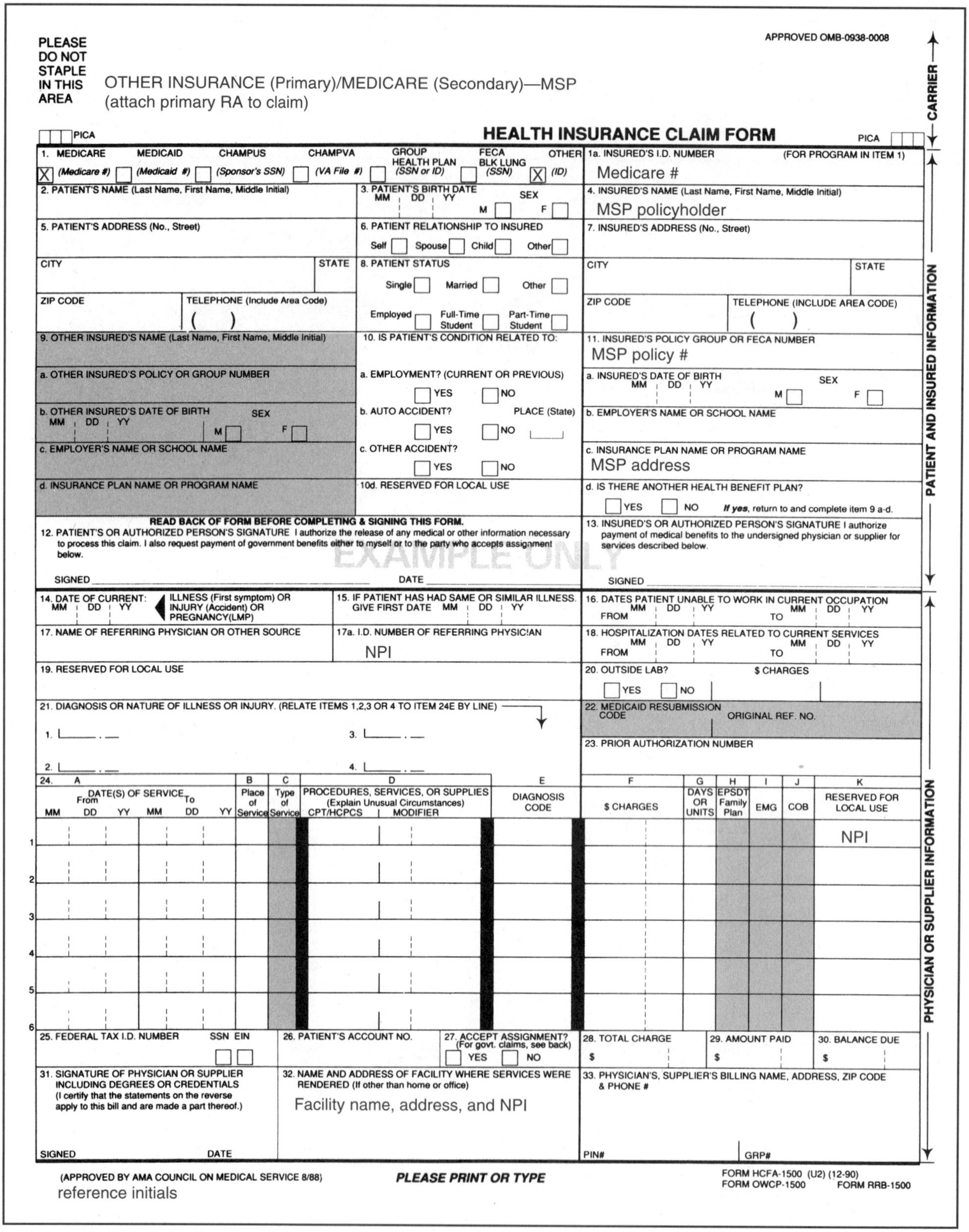

PLEASE DO NOT STAPLE IN THIS AREA

OTHER INSURANCE (Primary)/MEDICARE (Secondary)—MSP
(attach primary RA to claim)

APPROVED OMB-0938-0008

PICA

HEALTH INSURANCE CLAIM FORM

PICA

CARRIER

1. MEDICARE [X] (Medicare #) MEDICAID [ ] (Medicaid #) CHAMPUS [ ] (Sponsor's SSN) CHAMPVA [ ] (VA File #) GROUP HEALTH PLAN [ ] (SSN or ID) FECA BLK LUNG [ ] (SSN) OTHER [X] (ID)

1a. INSURED'S I.D. NUMBER (FOR PROGRAM IN ITEM 1): Medicare #

2. PATIENT'S NAME (Last Name, First Name, Middle Initial)

3. PATIENT'S BIRTH DATE MM DD YY SEX M [ ] F [ ]

4. INSURED'S NAME (Last Name, First Name, Middle Initial): MSP policyholder

5. PATIENT'S ADDRESS (No., Street)

6. PATIENT RELATIONSHIP TO INSURED Self [ ] Spouse [ ] Child [ ] Other [ ]

7. INSURED'S ADDRESS (No., Street)

CITY STATE

8. PATIENT STATUS Single [ ] Married [ ] Other [ ] Employed [ ] Full-Time Student [ ] Part-Time Student [ ]

CITY STATE

ZIP CODE TELEPHONE (Include Area Code) ( )

ZIP CODE TELEPHONE (INCLUDE AREA CODE) ( )

9. OTHER INSURED'S NAME (Last Name, First Name, Middle Initial)

a. OTHER INSURED'S POLICY OR GROUP NUMBER

b. OTHER INSURED'S DATE OF BIRTH MM DD YY SEX M [ ] F [ ]

c. EMPLOYER'S NAME OR SCHOOL NAME

d. INSURANCE PLAN NAME OR PROGRAM NAME

10. IS PATIENT'S CONDITION RELATED TO:

a. EMPLOYMENT? (CURRENT OR PREVIOUS) [ ] YES [ ] NO

b. AUTO ACCIDENT? PLACE (State) [ ] YES [ ] NO

c. OTHER ACCIDENT? [ ] YES [ ] NO

10d. RESERVED FOR LOCAL USE

11. INSURED'S POLICY GROUP OR FECA NUMBER: MSP policy #

a. INSURED'S DATE OF BIRTH MM DD YY SEX M [ ] F [ ]

b. EMPLOYER'S NAME OR SCHOOL NAME

c. INSURANCE PLAN NAME OR PROGRAM NAME: MSP address

d. IS THERE ANOTHER HEALTH BENEFIT PLAN? [ ] YES [ ] NO *If yes*, return to and complete item 9 a-d.

READ BACK OF FORM BEFORE COMPLETING & SIGNING THIS FORM.

12. PATIENT'S OR AUTHORIZED PERSON'S SIGNATURE I authorize the release of any medical or other information necessary to process this claim. I also request payment of government benefits either to myself or to the party who accepts assignment below.

SIGNED ______ DATE ______

EXAMPLE ONLY

13. INSURED'S OR AUTHORIZED PERSON'S SIGNATURE I authorize payment of medical benefits to the undersigned physician or supplier for services described below.

SIGNED ______

PATIENT AND INSURED INFORMATION

14. DATE OF CURRENT: MM DD YY ILLNESS (First symptom) OR INJURY (Accident) OR PREGNANCY(LMP)

15. IF PATIENT HAS HAD SAME OR SIMILAR ILLNESS. GIVE FIRST DATE MM DD YY

16. DATES PATIENT UNABLE TO WORK IN CURRENT OCCUPATION FROM MM DD YY TO MM DD YY

17. NAME OF REFERRING PHYSICIAN OR OTHER SOURCE

17a. I.D. NUMBER OF REFERRING PHYSICIAN: NPI

18. HOSPITALIZATION DATES RELATED TO CURRENT SERVICES FROM MM DD YY TO MM DD YY

19. RESERVED FOR LOCAL USE

20. OUTSIDE LAB? [ ] YES [ ] NO $ CHARGES

21. DIAGNOSIS OR NATURE OF ILLNESS OR INJURY. (RELATE ITEMS 1,2,3 OR 4 TO ITEM 24E BY LINE)

1. ___ . __ 3. ___ . __
2. ___ . __ 4. ___ . __

22. MEDICAID RESUBMISSION CODE ORIGINAL REF. NO.

23. PRIOR AUTHORIZATION NUMBER

24. A DATE(S) OF SERVICE From MM DD YY To MM DD YY	B Place of Service	C Type of Service	D PROCEDURES, SERVICES, OR SUPPLIES (Explain Unusual Circumstances) CPT/HCPCS MODIFIER	E DIAGNOSIS CODE	F $ CHARGES	G DAYS OR UNITS	H EPSDT Family Plan	I EMG	J COB	K RESERVED FOR LOCAL USE
1										NPI
2										
3										
4										
5										
6										

25. FEDERAL TAX I.D. NUMBER SSN EIN [ ] [ ]

26. PATIENT'S ACCOUNT NO.

27. ACCEPT ASSIGNMENT? (For govt. claims, see back) [ ] YES [ ] NO

28. TOTAL CHARGE $

29. AMOUNT PAID $

30. BALANCE DUE $

31. SIGNATURE OF PHYSICIAN OR SUPPLIER INCLUDING DEGREES OR CREDENTIALS (I certify that the statements on the reverse apply to this bill and are made a part thereof.)

SIGNED DATE

32. NAME AND ADDRESS OF FACILITY WHERE SERVICES WERE RENDERED (If other than home or office): Facility name, address, and NPI

33. PHYSICIAN'S, SUPPLIER'S BILLING NAME, ADDRESS, ZIP CODE & PHONE #

PIN# GRP#

PHYSICIAN OR SUPPLIER INFORMATION

(APPROVED BY AMA COUNCIL ON MEDICAL SERVICE 8/88) *PLEASE PRINT OR TYPE* FORM HCFA-1500 (U2) (12-90) FORM OWCP-1500 FORM RRB-1500

reference initials

FIGURE 12–12

Template for a case when other insurance is primary and Medicare is the secondary payer. After the primary insurance has paid, an HCFA-1500 claim form is sent with a copy of the Explanation of Benefits from the primary payer.

TABLE 12–1
Completing Form HCFA-1500 for Medicare/Medigap/Medicare Secondary Payer Patients

Block	Medicare Status	Data
1	P/S	Place an "X" in the Medicare block.
1a	P/S	Enter Medicare claim number with prefix/suffix.
2	P/S	Last, first name and middle initial.
3	P/S	Patient's birth date using 6 digits, sex.
4	P	Blank.
	S	MSP policy holder's name; if patient, enter SAME.
5	P/S	Patient's address: Line 1—street. Line 2—city, state. Line 3—ZIP code, phone number.
6	P	Blank.
	S	Indicate relationship to insured in Block 4.
7	P	Blank.
	S	Block 4 insured's address if insured is other than the patient, or SAME. (Used only when blocks 4 and 11 are completed.)
8	P/S	Check "single" if widowed or divorced; indicate whether employed or student.
9	P/S	For Medigap: policyholder name if different from Block 2, otherwise enter SAME. If no Medigap benefits are assigned, leave blank. *Note:* Only participating physicians and suppliers are to complete Block 9 and its subdivisions, and only when the beneficiary wishes to assign his/her benefits under a Medigap policy to the participating physician or supplier.
9a	P/S	The word MEDIGAP and policy/group number.
9b	P	Blank.
	S	Birth date, sex of Medigap enrollee.
9c	P/S	Claims processing address of Medigap insurer. May be left blank if the carrier-assigned Medigap identifier is reported in 9d.
9d	P/S	Medigap name, and carrier's unique identifier.
10a-c	P	Check all "no."
	S	If employment related, bill workers' compensation insurance company. If auto accident, bill auto insurance as primary. Report the post office two-character state abbreviation. If accident, bill other liability carrier as primary.
10d	P/S	Medicaid only. Report MCD and Medicaid number.
11		*This item must be completed. By completing this item, the physician/supplier acknowledges having made a good faith effort to determine whether Medicare is the primary or secondary payer.*
	P	If the patient has no insurance primary to Medicare, enter NONE. If recently retired, enter NONE and go to 11b.
	S	Complete policy/group number, if Medicare is secondary.
11a	P	Blank.
	S	Insured's date of birth (6 digits) and sex, if other than patient.
11b		*Note:* If there is a change in the insured's insurance status, e.g., retired, enter RETIRED and the retirement date.
	P	Blank.
	S	Employer's name for primary insurance.
11c	P	Blank.
	S	Primary insurance name.
11d	P/S	Blank.
12	P/S	Standard signature rules apply for "one time authorization" or "signature on file."
13	P/S	Signature authorizes Medicap payment to participating physician.
14	P/S	Date of current illness, or pregnancy.
15	P/S	Blank.
16	P/S	Entry could mean claim should be billed to workers' compensation insurance company.
17	P/S	Referring/ordering physician name.

Table continued on following page

12

TABLE 12–1
Completing Form HCFA-1500 for Medicare/Medigap/Medicare Secondary Payer Patients *(Continued)*

Block	Medicare Status	Data
17a	P/S	NPI of referring/ordering physician, must match name in Block 17. May use surrogate NPI for selected providers. May require NPI of physician submitting the claim. *Note:* When a patient is referred to a physician who also orders and performs a diagnostic service, a separate claim form is required for the diagnostic service.
18	P/S	Admit/discharge dates (6 digits) if services relate to hospitalization.
19	P/S	Used by special providers.
20	P/S	"No" indicates no purchased services are reported on the claim. If "yes," enter the purchase price. Name of laboratory performing the service must be reported in Block 32.
21	P/S	Enter up to four diagnosis codes, most significant first.
22	P/S	Blank.
23	P/S	Professional or peer review organization (PRO) 10-digit prior authorization number.
24a	P/S	Enter the month, day, and year (six digits) for each procedure, service, or supply reported in Block 24d. Make sure the dates shown are no earlier than the date of the current illness shown in Block 14. For OCR claims, if the "from" and "to" dates are the same, enter only the "from" date. Enter the "to" date when reporting a consecutive range of dates. Use a separate line for each month. Example: For service provided from November 30 through December 4, 1997 report as follows: Line 1: 113097 Line 2: 120197 120497
24b	P/S	Use the 2-digit place of service codes. (See Chapter 6.)
24c	P/S	Blank.
24d	P/S	Five-digit procedure code, up to two modifiers. If unlisted code, enter description.
24e	P/S	Enter diagnosis reference number from Block 21, ONLY ONE REFERENCE NUMBER PER LINE ITEM. When multiple services are performed, enter the corresponding reference number for each service. Check with the insurance carrier to see whether a guideline is implemented that allows more than one reference number per line item, as this rule may or may not be adopted. If allowed, place commas between more than one diagnosis reference pointer on the same line. Do not use actual ICD-9-CM diagnostic codes in this block.
24f	P/S	Enter regular fee if participating claim; limiting charge if nonparticipating physician.
24g	P/S	Enter the number of days or units.
24h	P/S	Blank.
24i	P/S	Blank.
24j	P/S	Blank.
24k	P/S	Enter carrier assigned performing physician's NPI number if billing with group provider.
25	P/S	Enter Federal Tax Employer Identification Number. Mark "EIN" box.
26	P/S	Enter patient account number, if desired.
27	P/S	Indicate accept or no accept on assignment if not participating. If participating physician, always mark accept. If left blank, accept is assumed.
28	P/S	Total all charges on this claim.
29	P/S	Report patient payments only. Attached vouchers will show payments by primary insurers.
30	P/S	Show balance due after patient payments, "0" if patient paid total charges.
31	P/S	Signature of physician/supplier or representative and date form was signed.
32	P/S	Use for hospital or facility name; also for source of purchased tests. Enter SAME if furnished in same facility as the biller's name and address shown in Block 33.
33	P/S	Physician's address; report HCFA-assigned NPI.

A system of Medicare reimbursement for HMOs with risk contracts is called diagnostic cost groups (DCGs). The HMO enrollees are classified into various DCGs on the basis of each beneficiary's prior 12-month history of hospitalization, and payments are adjusted accordingly. This payment system does not apply to disabled and hospice patients, those on renal dialysis, or those enrolled only in Medicare Part B. Patients are reclassified each year according to their previous year's use of hospital services.

If a noncontract physician treats a Medicare HMO patient, the services are considered "out-of-plan" services. Submit the claim to the HMO, and the HMO will determine whether it is responsible to pay for the services. The conditions that must be met are:

1. Service was an emergency and the patient was not able to get to an HMO facility or member physician (patient was out of the HMO area).
2. Service was one covered by Medicare.
3. Service was medically necessary.

Denied services can be billed to the patient (no more than the Medicare fee schedule or limiting charge) after the HMO Explanation of Benefits is received. If the HMO determines there was no emergency and denies payment, the patient is responsible for the fee. The HMO reimburses according to the Medicare Fee Schedule Allowable amount so the physician cannot bill the patient for the balance. If the physician does not receive 100% of the allowable, steps must be taken through the HMO's appeals process. If this fails, contact the Medicare Managed Care Department at your Medicare Regional HCFA Operations Office. See Chapter 9 on managed care systems for further information.

COPAYMENTS

When a patient belongs to a managed care plan that requires copayments, it is possible to obtain reimbursement for those copayments. This is to protect the Medicare patient from making a cash outlay for services that would usually be paid by Medicare as a secondary payer (MSP). An assigned MSP claim must be filed with Medicare for those copayments. When the reimbursement has been received, the provider must refund to the patient the amount previously collected. A nonparticipating physician must file an unassigned MSP claim. The patient will be directly reimbursed by Medicare and no refund is necessary. Because there is no EOB document to send since the practice is paid a capitated amount, have the patient sign a statement that explains the situation. Attach the statement and the copayment receipts to the claim. The statement may read as follows:

Patient name ______________________
Medicare number ______________________
There is no Explanation of Benefits documentation available for the attached billed services. I am currently enrolled with ____________ managed care plan for my health care. My physician, ________, MD, is paid on a capitated basis, and the copayment that I pay is $______ for each service or visit.
Patient's signature ______________________
Date ______________

CARRIER-DEALING PREPAYMENT ORGANIZATION

This is a prepayment organization that may be set up by a medical practice under contract to the government. It accepts Medicare assignment and agrees to deal with the Medicare carrier instead of HCFA. Patients sign a contract agreeing to pay a monthly fee (usually $20 to $25). This covers all Medicare copayments, deductibles, and nonreimbursable expenses (annual physical examinations and preventive care). The patient is not responsible to pay for noncovered services. The organization must furnish physicians' services through employees and partners, or under formal arrangement with medical groups, independent practice associations, or individual physicians. Part B services must be provided through qualified hospitals or physicians.

Such plans are considered a service contract rather than insurance. In the past, such plans were run by HMOs, but now practices of 12 to 15 physicians are opting to run their own plans. These organizations must be incorporated and have their own Medicare billing number. Physicians cannot be paid by fee-for-service but can be reimbursed in direct proportion to the amount of income each generates, with all the physicians sharing expenses.

Automobile or Liability Insurance Coverage

Payment may not be made under Medicare for otherwise covered services to the extent that payment has been made under an automobile or liability insurance policy or no-fault insurance. If Medicare payments have been made but should not have

FORM APPROVED OMB NO. 0938-0214

REPORT TO MEDICARE OF AUTOMOBILE OR LIABILITY INSURANCE COVERAGE

HEALTH INSURANCE CLAIM NUMBER	DATE	SEND COMPLETED FORM TO:

NAME OF PROVIDER, PHYSICIAN, OR SUPPLIER	DATE OF SERVICES FROM: TO:

NOTE: SEE REVERSE FOR PRIVACY ACT STATEMENT BEFORE COMPLETING FORM.

This refers to the services you received from the provider, physician or supplier named above.

We have information indicating that the expenses for these services may be payable under automobile insurance or under liability insurance (including automobile liability insurance). The law excludes Medicare payment for expenses which have been paid by such insurance or which such insurance can reasonably be expected to pay. All Medicare payments are made on the condition that the individual is responsible for refunding them if an automobile or liability insurer also makes payment.

Medicare may also recover its payments directly from an automobile or liability insurer or from anyone who has been paid by the insurer. Medicare can be a party to any claim by an individual against an insurer.

To help us determine whether Medicare must pay for these services, we need the information requested below. Please return the completed form in the enclosed self-addressed, postage paid envelope.

PLEASE ANSWER ALL QUESTIONS

1. DATE INJURY OCCURRED OR ILLNESS BEGAN

2. BRIEF DESCRIPTION OF ACCIDENT OR OTHER CAUSE OF INJURY OR ILLNESS

3. NAME, ADDRESS, AND TELEPHONE NUMBER OF ATTORNEY, IF YOU HAVE ONE

4. YOUR TELEPHONE NUMBER

5. MAY THE SERVICES YOU RECEIVED BE COVERED UNDER AN AUTOMOBILE MEDICAL OR NO FAULT INSURANCE POLICY OR PLAN?

☐ YES ☐ NO IF YES, GIVE: → NAME, ADDRESS AND TELEPHONE NUMBER OF INSURANCE COMPANY AND THE AUTOMOBILE INSURANCE CLAIM NUMBER

IF YOU HAVE RECEIVED A DECISION NOTICE FROM THE COMPANY, PLEASE SEND US A COPY.

6. IF YOU HAVE NOT FILED A CLAIM WITH AN AUTOMOBILE INSURER BUT BELIEVE YOU MAY BE ENTITLED TO DO SO, PLEASE EXPLAIN WHY YOU HAVE NOT FILED

A

(CONTINUED ON REVERSE)

FORM HCFA-L 365 (7-85)
PRIOR EDITIONS MAY BE USED

FIGURE 12–13
HCFA-L 365 Report to Medicare of Automobile or Liability Insurance Coverage Form. *A*, Front. *B*, Back.

7. DO YOU FEEL YOU HAVE A RIGHT TO BE COMPENSATED BY A PARTY WHO MAY HAVE CAUSED THE INJURY OR ILLNESS FOR WHICH THESE SERVICES WERE FURNISHED? ☐ YES ☐ NO	8. HAVE YOU FILED, OR DO YOU INTEND TO FILE, A LIABILITY CLAIM OR LAWSUIT IN CONNECTION WITH THIS INJURY OR ILLNESS? ☐ YES ☐ NO
9. IF YOU ANSWERED YES TO EITHER QUESTION 7 OR 8, PLEASE FURNISH THE FOLLOWING INFORMATION:	
A. NAME, ADDRESS AND TELEPHONE NUMBER OF ANY PARTY THAT YOU BELIEVE WAS RESPONSIBLE FOR INJURY OR ILLNESS	B. NAME, ADDRESS AND TELEPHONE NUMBER OF INSURANCE COMPANY OF PARTY NAMED IN A., AND CLAIM NUMBER ASSIGNED BY THAT INSURANCE COMPANY

If you have filed or have a right to file a liability claim or lawsuit against another party who you feel was responsible for this injury or illness, Medicare can pay for the services pending a decision on your liability claim. Do not settle your liability claim with the other party or his/her insurance company without first letting us know. If you do receive payment from a liability insurer, you will be responsible for paying Medicare back, or arranging for the insurance company to repay. The refund is the amount Medicare paid for this injury or illness up to the amount of the liability insurance payment less a part of your cost in procuring that payment. If Medicare is not repaid after you receive a liability insurance payment, the amount may be withheld from any social security benefits to which you are entitled.

If you do not at present intend to file a liability claim or lawsuit against any person or insurance company for this injury or illness but later change your mind, you are responsible for notifying us promptly of your decision.

CERTIFICATION: To the best of my knowledge and belief, the above answers are true.

DATE FORM COMPLETED	SIGNATURE OF BENEFICIARY OR REPRESENTATIVE	TELEPHONE NUMBER

12

PRIVACY ACT STATEMENT

We are authorized to collect this information by sections 205(a) and 1862(b) of the Social Security Act (42 USC 405a and 1395y). The information will be used to determine if the services you received are covered by Medicare or whether an automobile, no-fault, or liability insurer or any other person may be responsible for payment. Section 1877(a)(3) of the Social Security Act (42 USC 1395nn) provides criminal penalties for withholding this information.

B ★U S GPO:1985-0-540-136 FORM HCFA-L 365 (7-85)

FIGURE 12-13 *Continued*

been because the services are excluded under this provision, or if the payments were made on a conditional basis, they are subject to recovery. A Report to Medicare of Automobile or Liability Insurance Coverage Form HCFA-L 365 should be completed and sent to the fiscal agent (Fig. 12–13). The patient must sign and date the form. A copy of the notice of payment or denial form from the other insurer should be included when sending in Form HCFA-L 365, along with the HCFA-1500 claim form. Medicare is secondary even if a state law or a private contract of insurance states that Medicare is primary. The physician must bill the other insurer first. A claim for secondary benefits may be submitted to Medicare only after payment or denial has been made by the primary coverage.

Billing for a Deceased Patient

There are two ways in which to submit billing for a patient who has died. The first method, in which the physician accepts assignment on the claim form, will result in the quickest payment. No signature by a family member is needed on a form; in Block 6 where the patient's signature is required, type in "Patient died on (indicate date)."

The second method is when the physician does not accept assignment and bills Medicare. Nothing can be done about the open balance on the account until the estate is settled, and then Medicare will pay. If family members of a deceased Medicare patient need to request reimbursement for services for which they have already paid, the person(s) who paid the bill should complete Form HCFA-1660, shown in Figure 12–14.

Medicare/Medicaid (Medi-Medi)

Patients designated as Medi-Medi are on both Medicare and Medicaid (Medi-Cal) simultaneously. They are those who qualify for Old Age Security (OAS) assistance benefits (over age 65), the severely disabled, and the blind.

BENEFITS

Medi-Medi patients enjoy the benefits of Medicare as well as Medicaid. Because of this fact, the assignment on the claim form HCFA-1500 must *always* be accepted. If the physician does not accept assignment, then payment goes to the patient, and Medicaid (Medi-Cal) will not pick up the residual.

Prepare a preprinted form for your Medi-Medi patients for whom you do not accept assignment. Ask them to either send you the RA or telephone you, giving you the Medicare-approved amount, the coinsurance amount, and the deductible. Send this information to Medicaid and collect the difference between what Medicare pays and the Medicaid fee schedule. Generally, the Medicare payment exceeds the Medicaid fee schedule except when the patient has not met his or her annual Medicare deductible.

CLAIM PROCEDURE

In general, use the HCFA-1500 claim form. In some states the fiscal intermediary for a Medi-Medi claim may have a different address from that used for the processing of a person who is on Medicare only. Write or call your nearest Medicare fiscal intermediary for the guidelines pertinent to your state. Figure 12–15 is a reference template for completing an HCFA-1500 claim form for a Medicare patient who also has Medicaid.

The HCFA-1500 claim form will be processed automatically by Medicaid (Medi-Cal) after processing is completed by Medicare. The fiscal intermediary may refer to this as a *crossover claim.* It is not necessary to submit another form. Claims should be sent according to the time limit designated by the Medicaid program in your state.

Utilization and Quality Control

PEER REVIEW ORGANIZATION PROGRAM

A *peer review organization* (PRO) is a state-based group of physicians working under government guidelines reviewing cases for hospital admission and discharge, extended stay, or extended services emphasizing utilization review. The PRO evaluates physicians in regard to the quality and appropriateness of professional care and settles fee disputes. It is involved in implementing a quality of improvement plan using statistical data. Case review focuses on admission and discharge, invasive procedures, documentation, extraordinarily high costs (outlier costs), and limitation of liability determinations.

HCFA has assigned a point system for medical and documentation errors. If sufficient points ac-

DEPARTMENT OF HEALTH AND HUMAN SERVICES
HEALTH CARE FINANCING ADMINISTRATION

Form Approved
OMB No. 0938-0020

REQUEST FOR INFORMATION — MEDICARE PAYMENT FOR SERVICES TO A PATIENT NOW DECEASED

No further monies or other benefits may be paid out under this program unless this report is completed and filed as required by existing law and regulations (20 C.F.R. 405 1683).

When completed, send this form to:	Deceased patient
	Health insurance claim number of deceased patient

For Services Provided By:

PART I — PAID BILL (If The Bill Is Not Paid Go To Part II)

If bills for medical or other health services were paid by or for the deceased person, Medicare benefits may be due. We hope you will be able to help us determine who should receive payment. The person who paid the deceased's bill(s) has first right to any payment due. If the deceased or his estate paid the bill(s), benefits will be paid to the legal representative of the estate. If there is no legal representative, payment will be made to the person who stands highest in the list of relatives below. If the person who paid the bill(s) dies before being reimbursed, payment is also made to the person standing highest in the list of relatives. If there are no living relatives or legal representatives, no payment will be made. Please answer the questions, sign on the reverse side and return this form in the enclosed envelope.

ALWAYS INCLUDE EVIDENCE OF PAYMENT SUCH AS A RECEIPTED BILL OR OTHER RECEIPT

1. Who paid the deceased's bills for medical or other health services?

☐ The deceased or his estate *(Answer (2) below)*

☐ Yourself *(Sign on reverse side and return form)*

☐ Other person or organization. (Enter the person's or organization's name and address in item 4 below.) If there is more than one person or organization, attach a listing of names and addresses of these persons or organizations to this form.

2. Is there a legal representative of the estate?

☐ Yes *(If "Yes," print his name and address below, Sign on reverse side and return form).* If you are the legal representative, submit a copy of your appointment papers with this form.

☐ No *(If "No," answer item 3 below.*

3. This item is answered only if item 2 above is checked "No". Put a check in the box next to the living relative that stands highest on the following list and then write that relative's name and address in item 4 below. (If you check the box for child or children and there is more than one child, attach a listing of the names and address of all the children to this form.)

☐ Widow or widower living in the same household as the deceased at the time of death, or entitled to a monthly Social Security or Railroad Retirement benefit on the same earnings record as the deceased in the month of death.

☐ A child or children of the deceased entitled to monthly Social Security or Railroad Retirement benefits or the same earnings record as the deceased in the month of death. *(List the names and addresses of all entitled children of the deceased.)*

☐ A parent or parents of the deceased entitled to monthly Social Security or Railroad Retirement benefits on the same earnings record as the deceased in the month of death.

☐ A widow or widower who was neither living with the deceased at the time of death nor at that time entitled on the same earnings record to a Social Security or Railroad Retirement benefit.

☐ A child or children of the deceased who were not entitled in the month of death to monthly Social Security or Railroad Retirement benefits on the same earnings record as the deceased. *(List the names and addresses of all such children.)*

☐ A parent or parents not entitled in the month of death to monthly Social Security or Railroad Retirement benefits on the same earnings record as the deceased.

4. Name	Address

FORM HCFA-1660 (8-81) DESTROY PRIOR EDITIONS

Continued On Back

A

FIGURE 12–14

Medicare form HCFA-1660, Request for Information—Medicare Payment for Services to a Patient Now Deceased. This form is completed by the family of the deceased patient. *A*, Front. *B*, Back.

Illustration continued on following page

cumulate, penalty can lead to forfeiture of the physician's license. Therefore, it is extremely important that each patient's care be well documented from the care standpoint as well as for billing the claim.

A physician who receives a letter from a PRO regarding quality of care should consult his or her attorney before responding by letter or personal appeal.

12

PART II — UNPAID BILL (If The Bill Is Paid, Complete Part I)

When the beneficiary has died and a physician or supplier does not agree to accept the reasonable charge as the full charge, payment may be made on the basis of an unpaid bill to the person who has agreed to assume legal liability to pay the physician or supplier.

If you are assuming such legal liability and want to claim Medicare benefits for the services furnished to the deceased beneficiary, you must furnish the documents listed below to us and sign this form below. Your signature below certifies to the following statement:

I have assumed the legal obligation to pay the physician or supplier named below for services furnished to the deceased beneficiary on the date(s) indicated. I hereby claim any Medicare benefits due for these services.

Name of Physician or Supplier	Name of Deceased Beneficiary	Date(s) of Services

In addition furnish the following documents together with this form to us.

1. A completed form HCFA-1490S, PATIENT'S REQUEST FOR MEDICARE PAYMENTS. You must sign item 6 of the HCFA-1490S in lieu of the deceased beneficiary. (You may obtain a copy of the HCFA-1490S from a Social Security Office if you did not receive one with this form;) and
2. A signed statement from the physician or supplier which shows that the physician or supplier refuses to accept assignment for the bill; and
3. An itemized bill from the physician or supplier which identifies you as the person to whom the physician or supplier looks for payment.

Sign below and return this form together with the documents specified above to the address shown in the upper left portion of the form on the other side. If no carrier name and address is shown on the other side of this form request the proper addressee information from a Social Security Office.

I certify that if I receive the entire amount due, I will distribute it among other persons if they are legally entitled to it. Knowing that anyone making a false statement or representation of a material fact for use in determining the right to or the amount of Health Insurance benefits commits a crime punishable under the Federal law, I certify that the above statements are true.

If this statement has been signed by mark (X), two witnesses who know the claimant should sign below, giving their full addresses. The signature and title of a Social Security employee will suffice in lieu of signatures of two witnesses.	Name of claimant *(Please print)*
Name	Signature of claimant *(Write in ink)* **SIGN HERE ▶**
Address *(Number and Street, City, State and ZIP Code)*	Mailing Address *(Number and Street, P.O. Box or Route)*
Name	City, State and ZIP Code
Address *(Number and Street, City, State and ZIP Code)*	Date *(Month, Day and Year)* / Telephone number

If you wish assistance in completing this request, please take it to a Social Security Office. The people there will help you.

PLEASE RETURN THIS REQUEST IN THE ENCLOSED ENVELOPE

HCFA-1660 (8-81) ★ U.S.G.P.O.: 1986- 491-258/53795

B

FIGURE 12-14 *Continued*

If a physician is asking for payment for extended services from Medicare Part B, a clinical report must include the following:

1. A brief reference to the history of onset, duration, and progression of the illness.
2. A description of the degree of impairment or severity of the problem.
3. Physical or anatomic findings determined after the examination.
4. Records of all the diagnoses written in ICD-9-CM format.

APPROVED OMB-0938-0008

CARRIER

PLEASE DO NOT STAPLE IN THIS AREA

MEDICARE/MEDICAID—A CROSSOVER CLAIM
(primary) (secondary)

PICA

HEALTH INSURANCE CLAIM FORM

PICA

1. MEDICARE [X] (Medicare #) MEDICAID [X] (Medicaid #) CHAMPUS [ ] (Sponsor's SSN) CHAMPVA [ ] (VA File #) GROUP HEALTH PLAN [ ] (SSN or ID) FECA BLK LUNG [ ] (SSN) OTHER [ ] (ID)

1a. INSURED'S I.D. NUMBER (FOR PROGRAM IN ITEM 1)
Medicare #

2. PATIENT'S NAME (Last Name, First Name, Middle Initial)

3. PATIENT'S BIRTH DATE MM DD YY SEX M [ ] F [ ]

4. INSURED'S NAME (Last Name, First Name, Middle Initial)

5. PATIENT'S ADDRESS (No., Street)

6. PATIENT RELATIONSHIP TO INSURED Self [ ] Spouse [ ] Child [ ] Other [ ]

7. INSURED'S ADDRESS (No., Street)

CITY STATE

8. PATIENT STATUS Single [ ] Married [ ] Other [ ]

CITY STATE

ZIP CODE TELEPHONE (Include Area Code) ( )

Employed [ ] Full-Time Student [ ] Part-Time Student [ ]

ZIP CODE TELEPHONE (INCLUDE AREA CODE) ( )

9. OTHER INSURED'S NAME (Last Name, First Name, Middle Initial)

10. IS PATIENT'S CONDITION RELATED TO:

11. INSURED'S POLICY GROUP OR FECA NUMBER
NONE

a. OTHER INSURED'S POLICY OR GROUP NUMBER

a. EMPLOYMENT? (CURRENT OR PREVIOUS) [ ] YES [ ] NO

a. INSURED'S DATE OF BIRTH MM DD YY SEX M [ ] F [ ]

b. OTHER INSURED'S DATE OF BIRTH MM DD YY SEX M [ ] F [ ]

b. AUTO ACCIDENT? PLACE (State) [ ] YES [ ] NO

b. EMPLOYER'S NAME OR SCHOOL NAME

c. EMPLOYER'S NAME OR SCHOOL NAME

c. OTHER ACCIDENT? [ ] YES [ ] NO

c. INSURANCE PLAN NAME OR PROGRAM NAME

d. INSURANCE PLAN NAME OR PROGRAM NAME

10d. RESERVED FOR LOCAL USE
MCD + Medicaid #

d. IS THERE ANOTHER HEALTH BENEFIT PLAN? [ ] YES [ ] NO *If yes*, return to and complete item 9 a-d.

READ BACK OF FORM BEFORE COMPLETING & SIGNING THIS FORM.

12. PATIENT'S OR AUTHORIZED PERSON'S SIGNATURE I authorize the release of any medical or other information necessary to process this claim. I also request payment of government benefits either to myself or to the party who accepts assignment below.

SIGNED ____ DATE ____

EXAMPLE ONLY

13. INSURED'S OR AUTHORIZED PERSON'S SIGNATURE I authorize payment of medical benefits to the undersigned physician or supplier for services described below.

SIGNED ____

PATIENT AND INSURED INFORMATION

14. DATE OF CURRENT: MM DD YY ILLNESS (First symptom) OR INJURY (Accident) OR PREGNANCY(LMP)

15. IF PATIENT HAS HAD SAME OR SIMILAR ILLNESS. GIVE FIRST DATE MM DD YY

16. DATES PATIENT UNABLE TO WORK IN CURRENT OCCUPATION FROM MM DD YY TO MM DD YY

17. NAME OF REFERRING PHYSICIAN OR OTHER SOURCE

17a. I.D. NUMBER OF REFERRING PHYSICIAN
NPI

18. HOSPITALIZATION DATES RELATED TO CURRENT SERVICES FROM MM DD YY TO MM DD YY

19. RESERVED FOR LOCAL USE

20. OUTSIDE LAB? [ ] YES [ ] NO $ CHARGES

21. DIAGNOSIS OR NATURE OF ILLNESS OR INJURY. (RELATE ITEMS 1,2,3 OR 4 TO ITEM 24E BY LINE)

1. ___ . __
2. ___ . __
3. ___ . __
4. ___ . __

22. MEDICAID RESUBMISSION CODE ORIGINAL REF. NO.

23. PRIOR AUTHORIZATION NUMBER

24. A DATE(S) OF SERVICE From MM DD YY To MM DD YY	B Place of Service	C Type of Service	D PROCEDURES, SERVICES, OR SUPPLIES (Explain Unusual Circumstances) CPT/HCPCS MODIFIER	E DIAGNOSIS CODE	F $ CHARGES	G DAYS OR UNITS	H EPSDT Family Plan	I EMG	J COB	K RESERVED FOR LOCAL USE
1										NPI
2										
3										
4										
5										
6										

25. FEDERAL TAX I.D. NUMBER SSN EIN [ ] [ ]

26. PATIENT'S ACCOUNT NO.

27. ACCEPT ASSIGNMENT? (For govt. claims, see back) [X] YES [ ] NO

28. TOTAL CHARGE $

29. AMOUNT PAID $

30. BALANCE DUE $

31. SIGNATURE OF PHYSICIAN OR SUPPLIER INCLUDING DEGREES OR CREDENTIALS (I certify that the statements on the reverse apply to this bill and are made a part thereof.)

SIGNED DATE

32. NAME AND ADDRESS OF FACILITY WHERE SERVICES WERE RENDERED (If other than home or office)
Facility name, address, and NPI

33. PHYSICIAN'S, SUPPLIER'S BILLING NAME, ADDRESS, ZIP CODE & PHONE #

PIN# GRP#

PHYSICIAN OR SUPPLIER INFORMATION

(APPROVED BY AMA COUNCIL ON MEDICAL SERVICE 8/88) *PLEASE PRINT OR TYPE* FORM HCFA-1500 (U2) (12-90) FORM OWCP-1500 FORM RRB-1500

FIGURE 12–15
Template for a Medicare/Medicaid case. The HCFA-1500 claim form is sent to Medicare and then processed automatically by Medicaid.

12

5. Therapy given and the prognosis. Make sure all tests relate directly to diagnoses listed.
6. References to past history of operations pertinent to the treatment.
7. Necessity and review of functional test results (x-ray or laboratory) or second opinions. Explain why the procedure or test was required for therapeutic decision making.

A photocopy of the patient's medical record can be used to substantiate the claim if there is detailed clinical documentation.

Prior Authorization or Precertification

Many insurance carriers require prior authorization for surgical procedures when individuals are insured under some group plans or signed up with HMO senior plans. Some of these procedures are on a mandatory list, whereas others are chosen by the regional carrier as requiring authorization. The mandatory list is composed of such procedures as cataract extractions, cholecystectomy, carotid endarterectomy, joint replacements (hip, shoulder, knee), coronary artery bypass graft surgery, inguinal hernia repair, transurethral prostatectomy, complex peripheral revascularization, bunionectomy, hysterectomy, and so on. Sometimes precertification is based on the diagnosis.

Some carriers have an 800 toll-free line; some require that the request must be in writing; and some require a letter only if there is a dispute over claims payment. Check with your local carrier on its policy for preauthorization. The authorization number is used when billing the Medicare carrier and is entered into the HCFA-1500 claim form Block 23 (Fig. 12–16). If the procedure is not approved, the carrier sends a denial to the physician, the patient, and the hospital. If the procedure is done as an emergency, notify the carrier as soon as possible so a retrospective review can be arranged.

Medicare Coding Tips

When billing for injections, the drugs and other supplies must be billed separately, using the HCFA's HCPCS. The HCPCS codes allow you to reclaim your direct costs for materials supplied to Medicare patients.

Example:
Incorrect Coding

90782	Injection IM adrenalin

Correct Coding

90782	Therapeutic injection, intramuscular
J0170	Injection, adrenalin, epinephrine, up to 1 mL ampule

Whenever modifier -22 is attached to a code, the Medicare claim is usually sent for review, and this will delay payment. Modifier -22 should be used only with careful documentation. Some Medicare fiscal agents automatically deny claims with this modifier because physicians have abused the use of this modifier and can seldom document the "unusual services." Appeal such a denial, but make sure you can provide thorough documentation.

Some Medicare fiscal agents will not pay for any

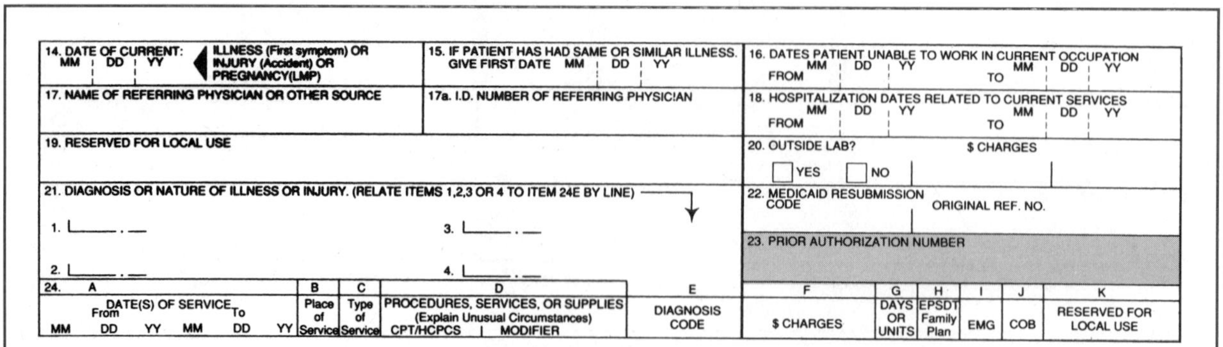
14. DATE OF CURRENT: MM DD YY ILLNESS (First symptom) OR INJURY (Accident) OR PREGNANCY(LMP)
15. IF PATIENT HAS HAD SAME OR SIMILAR ILLNESS. GIVE FIRST DATE MM DD YY
16. DATES PATIENT UNABLE TO WORK IN CURRENT OCCUPATION FROM MM DD YY TO MM DD YY
17. NAME OF REFERRING PHYSICIAN OR OTHER SOURCE
17a. I.D. NUMBER OF REFERRING PHYSICIAN
18. HOSPITALIZATION DATES RELATED TO CURRENT SERVICES FROM MM DD YY TO MM DD YY
19. RESERVED FOR LOCAL USE
20. OUTSIDE LAB? YES NO $ CHARGES
21. DIAGNOSIS OR NATURE OF ILLNESS OR INJURY. (RELATE ITEMS 1,2,3 OR 4 TO ITEM 24E BY LINE)
1. 2. 3. 4.
22. MEDICAID RESUBMISSION CODE ORIGINAL REF. NO.
23. PRIOR AUTHORIZATION NUMBER
24. A DATE(S) OF SERVICE From MM DD YY To MM DD YY | B Place of Service | C Type of Service | D PROCEDURES, SERVICES, OR SUPPLIES (Explain Unusual Circumstances) CPT/HCPCS MODIFIER | E DIAGNOSIS CODE | F $ CHARGES | G DAYS OR UNITS | H EPSDT Family Plan | I EMG | J COB | K RESERVED FOR LOCAL USE

FIGURE 12–16
Section of the HCFA-1500 claim form showing where to put a prior authorization number (Block 23) when permission has been granted for a procedure.

of the special 99 adjunct codes. The use of modifier -22 in place of a special 99 adjunct code may or may not work, depending on the Medicare fiscal agent in your area.

On some procedures, Medicare limits the number of times a given procedure can be billed during one year. This is known as a Medicare Prepayment Screen. These screens are meant to identify claims to review for medical necessity and compliance with other appropriate criteria. If the patient previously submitted a claim for the procedure performed in the same year by another physician and has met the limit for the year, then the claim will be down coded. Contact your local Medicare fiscal agent to find out the Medicare Prepayment Screens applicable in your area.

Some Medicare Mandated Prepayment Screens as of 1993 are shown in Table 12–2.

TABLE 12-2

Screen	Parameter
Routine foot care (excluding mycotic nails)	1 treatment every 60 days (HCPCS M0101)
Injections: joint	Joint injections, 3 injections per month (CPT 20600, 20605, 20610)
Mycotic nails	1 treatment every 60 days (CPT 11700, 11701, 11710, 11711)
Nursing home visits	1 per month (CPT 99331–99333)
Vitamin B_{12} injections	1 injection per month (HCPCS J3420)
Office visits	4 per month (CPT 99201–99215)
Holter monitoring	No more than 1 instance per 6 months (CPT 93224–93237)
Chiropractic care	12 per year (HCPCS A2000)
Concurrent care	Same date, different practitioner, similar specialty 31 per month (CPT 99221–99223; 99231–99233)
Hospital visits	31 days per 3 months (CPT 99231–99233)
Nursing facility (NF)	Subsequent care, 2 first week, 1 per week thereafter (CPT 99311–99313)
Postcataract lens replacement	1 per eye per year (HCPCS V2500–V2599)
Assistants at cataract surgery	None at routine surgery; prior approval by PRO required. (CPT 66820–66986) use modifier -80

For a complete list of prepayment screens, refer to your carrier's newsletters or bulletins.

If a surgeon assists in a teaching hospital, Medicare may disallow payment unless one of the following situations is apparent:

1. When a qualified resident is not available
2. In an emergency or life-threatening case
3. For complex procedures requiring a team of physicians, each performing a service different from that of the primary surgeon
4. When assisting a primary surgeon whose stated policy is never to involve residents in the preoperative, operative, or postoperative aspects of any patient's care

When billing for the assistant surgeon, type the following statement on the claim and have the assistant surgeon sign the form.

> "I understand that Section 1842(b)(6)(D) of the Social Security Act usually prohibits Medicare Part B reasonable charge payment of services of assistants at surgery in teaching hospitals when qualified residents are available to furnish such services. I certify that the services for which payment is claimed were medically necessary, and no qualified resident was available to perform the services. I understand these services are subject to postpayment review by the Medicare fiscal agent."

MEDICARE AND MEDICAID COVERAGE DATA BANK

As of January 1994, employers must report information about their employees annually through 1997. The purpose of this information is twofold: first, to identify and collect data on health care items and services to Medicare beneficiaries, and second, to collect, or assist in the collection of, amounts due from liable third parties for the reimbursement of costs incurred by any state plan under the Medicaid program.

The information employers must report is

- name and taxpayer identification number (TIN) of electing individual
- type of group health plan coverage (single or family) elected
- name, address, and identifying number of the group health plan elected by the employee
- name and TIN of each other individual (spouse and dependents) covered by the group plan
- period during which such coverage is elected
- name, address, and TIN of employer

MEDICARE CLAIM FORM

Refer to Chapter 6 for instructions on how to complete the Medicare HCFA-1500 claim form.

ELECTRONIC CLAIMS SUBMISSION

Refer to Chapter 7 on how to submit claims electronically to your Medicare carrier.

MEDICARE FRAUD AND ABUSE

See the section in this chapter on the Civil Monetary Penalties Law as well as Chapter 2 for further information on this subject.

MEDICARE REVIEW AND APPEAL PROCESS

As you have already read, Chapter 8 outlines in detail the steps to take for having a claim reviewed and the process of appealing a claim.

POSTING MEDICARE PAYMENTS

Usually a physician's charge is higher than the charge approved by the Medicare carrier or fiscal agent. This does not mean that his or her charges are unreasonable. As previously mentioned, payments are established using a fee schedule based on an RBRVS, a volume performance standard (VPS) for expenditure increases, and a limiting charge for nonparticipating physicians.

Because some services may be disallowed or the payments on them may be lower than those charged by the physician, it is important to know how to post payments to the patient's ledger card. Figure 12–17 illustrates how payments and courtesy adjustments are posted. The word "courtesy" implies that Medicare patients are treated well and is preferred to phrases like "not allowed" or "write off."

In regard to the patient's copayment, Medicare regulations require that a patient be billed for the copayment at least three times before the balance is adjusted off as uncollectible.

It is also important to realize that when a Remittance Advice (RA) is received, it may list many patients (Fig. 12–18). Do not post the entire payment made in a lump sum to the day sheet. Individually post each patient's name and the amount of payment on the day sheet and each patient's ledger card. To prevent funds from going astray, some offices prefer to post Medicare payments to a separate day sheet and deposit each multiple reimbursement check separately. This way, the day sheet totals will agree with the deposit slip totals. If a separate Medicare day sheet is not used, the medical assistant or insurance billing specialist should periodically check day sheets against the corresponding ledger cards.

It is wise to make up a list of all the procedures most commonly used in your physician's practice, the code for each procedure, your physician's fee, the amount approved by Medicare, and the amount Medicare is supposed to pay your physician. When the RA arrives, compare the actual payments with those on your Should Have Paid list. If there are any discrepancies, refile any incorrect claims with Medicare.

Many patients do not understand what is meant by *amount billed, approved amount, amount owed, deductible,* and *coinsurance.* Photocopy the RA, deleting the patient's name to ensure confidentiality. Then use the RA to illustrate to future patients what various terms mean. This will increase patient understanding and save time.

Figure 12–19A illustrates an example of a Medicare/Medicaid case after payment by Medicare. Medicare applied the patient's full $100 deductible amount to the claim, reducing payment to $4. The Medicaid RA (Fig. 12–19B) shows reimbursement of the coinsurance and deductible amounts dual-billed to Medicaid.

Calculations are as follows:

Medicare		**Medicaid**	
$105	Approved amount	$105	Medicare allowed or approved amount
−100	Deductible	− 32	Medicaid cutback
5		$ 73	Medicaid allowed
$ 4	Medicare paid 80%	− 4	Medicare paid
		$ 69	Medicaid payment

Overpayments can occur in the following situations: when the carrier processes the charge more than once, the physician receives duplicate payments from Medicare and a secondary payer, the physician is paid directly on an unassigned claim, the item is not covered but is paid, payment is made on erroneous information, and so on.

If you receive a check and know that it is an overpayment, deposit the check and then write to Medicare notifying them of the overpayment. Include a copy of the check and the RA. This overpayment

STATEMENT

College Clinic
4567 Broad Avenue
Woodland Hills, XY 12345
013/486-9002

Account No. 946
John Smith
100 Main Street
Any City, U.S.A.

DATE	PROFESSIONAL SERVICE DESCRIPTION	CHARGE	CREDITS: PAYMENTS	CREDITS: ADJUSTMENTS	CURRENT BALANCE
	BF				20 --
11-19-9x	OC Dx 582	40 --			60 --
11-20-9x	Medicare billed				
01-05-9x	Medicare payment		28 --		32 --
01-05-9x	Medicare courtesy (adjustment)			5 --	27 --
01-17-9x	No Co-insurance payment		0		
	MEDICARE AND CO-INSURANCE HAVE PAID THEIR PORTION OF THIS CLAIM. THE BALANCE IS YOUR RESPONSIBILITY. PLEASE REMIT				
2-15-9x	Surgery Dx 5637	800 --			827 --
2-17-9x	Medicare billed				
4-02-9x	Medicare payment		440 --		387 --
4-02-9x	Medicare courtesy (adjustment)			250 --	137 --
	AWAITING CO-INSURANCE PAYMENT YOUR BALANCE HAS BECOME PAST DUE. PLEASE REMIT				

Due and payable within 10 days. **Pay last amount in balance column** ⇧

CON – Consultation	HCD – House Call (Day)	LAB – Laboratory
CPX – Complete Phys Exam	HCN – House Call (Night)	NC – No Charge
E – Emergency	HV – Hospital Visit	OC – Office Call
EC – Error Corrected	INJ – Injection	OS – Office Surgery
ECG – Electrocardiogram	INS – Insurance	SE – Special Exam

FIGURE 12-17

Sample ledger card illustrating how payments and adjustments should be posted. If there is no adjustment column on the ledger, the figure should be entered under the charge column, putting it in parentheses, i.e., (5--).

12

Transamerica Occidental Life

MEDICARE REMITTANCE ADVICE

Transamerica Occidental Life Insurance Company

*22313 W3276 FAM PRAC MED SEP 19, 198

BENEFICIARY NAME / H.I.C. NO.	PERFORMING SUPPLIER / CONTROL NUMBER	SERVICE FROM MO-DAY	SERVICE TO DAY-YR	PLACE -TYPE	PROCEDURE CODE-MODIFIERS	AMOUNT BILLED	AMOUNT APPROVED	NOTE	DEDUCTIBLE	COINSURANCE	PAYMENT
	EX 544458	08-19	19-86	1 D	71020	61.00	43.30	56	**MEDI-CAL:5610-9499341487		
499-34-1487-A	6246-080-860			* *	**TOTALS***	61.00	43.30	106	0.00	8.66	34.29
L WILSON	EX 149	09-08	08-86	1 A	90050	28.00	26.00	56	**MEDI-CAL:5614-0375195050		
458-07-7080-A	6260-078-640			* *	**TOTALS***	28.00	26.00	106	0.00	5.20	20.59
M. MIRELE	EX 126	09-05	05-86	1 E	99000	17.00	3.00	6			
464-40-3930-A	6254-194-800			* *	**TOTALS***	17.00	3.00		0.00	0.60	2.38
M MIRELE	EX 915	08-25	25-86	1 A	90070	46.00	41.30	56			
464-40-3930-A		08-25	25-86	1 E	99000	17.00	3.00	6			
		08-25	25-86	1 E	81000-XL	10.00	5.75	56			
	6258-701-250			* *	**TOTALS***	73.00	50.05	209	0.00	8.86	40.78
R WALL	EX 126	09-08	08-86	1 A	90080-22	120.00	61.80	56			
042-16-3112-A		09-08	08-86	1 B	69210	38.00	25.00	56			
		09-08	08-86	1 E	99000	17.00	3.00	6			
		09-08	08-86	1 A	93000	42.00	42.00				
		09-08	08-86	1 E	81000-XL	10.00	5.75	56			
		09-08	08-86	1 D	71020	61.00	43.30	56			
		09-08	08-86	1 A	J0110	26.00	3.00	6			
		09-08	08-86	1 A	A4460	11.00	10.00	56			
	6254-194-790			* *	**TOTALS***	325.00	193.85	209	0.00	37.62	154.67

NOTE ------------------------------ EXPLANATION ------------------------------
209: CLINICAL LABORATORY PROCEDURES WERE PAID AT 100% OF THE APPROVED AMOUNT.

A NEW LAW HAS REDUCED YOUR MEDICARE PAYMENT BY 1% FOR SERVICES FROM 03/01/86 THROUGH 09/30/86

ON QUESTIONS RELATED TO THIS PAYMENT:

TOTALS	BILLED	APPROVED	CLAIMS	DEDUCTIBLE	COINSURANCE	PAYMENT
	504.00	316.20	5	0.00	60.94	252.71

№ 208044826

MCC-4 ED 4-86

1. Date of check and statement.
2. Patient's name and Medicare number.
3. Name of supplier performing services if not the same as the physician/supplier billing for the services.
4. Claim control number. Refer to this number when inquiring about a particular claim.
5. Medi-Cal number, or special notation, when applicable.
6. Procedure code-modifier. These codes and modifiers describe services rendered as billed by you or as listed in the California Standard Nomenclature.
7. Reductions or denials of charges can be explained by matching these numbers to the numbered explanations on the back of the EOMB. RA.
8. Deductible. This column lists any deductible applied for claims included on this statement.
9. Co-insurance. This column lists the 20% co-insurance amount for claims included on this statement.
10. Number of claims. This figure represents the total number of claims included on this statement.
11. Amount of check. This is the total amount of the check attached and represents payment for all claims included on this statement.
12. This is the check number on the payment issued for the claims included on this statement.

A

See legend on opposite page.

EXPLANATION OF NOTES

Additional notes may be listed on the front of this form.

1 — See enclosed letter.
2 — Claim was filed after the time limit.
4 — These bills are handled by a special intermediary.
5 — This payment is for an adjustment of a previous claim.
6 — Charges over the maximum Medicare allowance are not covered.
7 — Services before Medicare entitlement are not covered.
8 — Services after Medicare entitlement ended are not covered.
10 — Other charges submitted with this claim may be on a separate statement which you have received or will receive soon.
12 — Routine examinations and related services are not covered.
13 — Immunizations or other routine and preventative services are not covered.
16 — We need an itemization of this charge. Please resubmit your claim with this information.
17 — Prescription drugs are not covered.
18 — Charges for this physician/supplier are not covered.
19 — We need a full description of the service or supply to consider this charge. Please resubmit your claim with this information.
23 — We need a written report for this service. Please resubmit your claim with this information.
26 — More than $312.50 annual psychiatric expense is not covered.
27 — We need from the prescribing physician the specific length of time this medical equipment is needed. Please resubmit your claim with this information.
30 — This charge was previously considered.
37 — Claims for these services will be made by a home health agency or hospital.
39 — Equipment that is not medically necessary is not covered. (See Note 89)
42 — These supplies or services are not covered.
45 — Over 62½% of psychiatric expenses is not covered.
46 — Routine foot care is not covered.
47 — Routine eye examinations or eye refractions are not covered.
48 — Partial payment of this claim was made to the beneficiary.
49 — This service cannot be considered until the hospital makes the necessary arrangement with the carrier for its processing.
50 — The beneficiary is not responsible for this reduction/denial under the assignment agreement.
54 — Care before and/or after surgery is included in the surgery benefit. (See Note 50)
56 — This is the full charge allowed based upon the prevailing or usual and customary rate.
62 — Payment has been reduced because this test is commonly part of an automated test group. (See Note 50)
66 — This service is not covered when done by this laboratory.
70 — There were no charges or bills with your claim form. Please resubmit your claim with this information.
72 — We need a signed and dated prescription showing medical necessity and specific length of time needed. Please resubmit your claim with this information.
73 — Before another month's payment can be made, we need a new signed and dated prescription showing further necessity of the medical equipment and specific length of time needed.
80 — We need to know the place of service to consider this charge. Please resubmit your claim with this information.
83 — SSA advises us that they are unable to verify the patient's eligibility for Part B Medical Insurance Plan. For this reason, no payment can be made on this claim.
84 — The patient's HIC number shown on this claim was incorrect. Please use the correct HIC number on all future claims.
85 — The patient's name shown on this claim was incorrect. Please use the correct name on all future claims.
86 — Over 62½% of the allowable charges for psychiatric services is not covered.
89 — If you did not know that Medicare does not pay for this medical service, you may request a review of this decision. See below paragraph entitled "Your right to review of a case".
90 — This service by a chiropractor is not covered.
93 — Over $500.00 annual expense billed by a physical therapist is not covered.
95 — These specific services by this supplier are not covered.
96 — Please verify the date of this service. Resubmit your claim with this information.
99 — We need a complete diagnosis before the claim can be considered. Please resubmit your claim with this information.
106 — The Medicare covered services on this claim have been forwarded for additional processing under Medi-Cal.
107 — This claim was not forwarded for Medi-Cal processing. Please bill Medi-Cal directly and attach a copy of this statement.
108 — The bills for these services have been transferred to Blue Shield of California Medicare Claims, Chico, CA 95976. You will hear from them.
129 — Payment for services prior to July 1 is based on the previous year's payment rate.
131 — Payment for this physician service in a hospital department is reduced since this service is commonly performed in the physician's office. (See Note 50)
138 — This amount is more than Medicare pays for maintenance treatment of renal disease.
147 — This charge is not covered because an allowance for purchase of the same equipment was previously made.
151 — Your claim was transferred to a Health Maintenance Organization for processing.
153 — These are more visits (treatments) for this diagnosis than Medicare covers unless there were unusual circumstances. (See Note 89)
154 — This service is not covered for your patients reported condition. (See Note 89)
155 — Only one visit per month to a nursing home is covered unless special need is indicated. (See Note 89)
156 — This laboratory test for the reported condition and/or illness is not covered. (See Note 89)
158 — Procedures whose effectiveness has not been proven are not covered. (See Note 89)
161 — The frequency of services for this condition are not covered. (See Note 89)
162 — More than one visit per day for this condition are not covered. (See Note 89)
172 — This type of services billed by a psychologist are not covered.
179 — The amount for this service is included in the approved amount for the consultation/office/hospital visit.
181 — Payment for this service is included in the major surgical fee.
187 — We need the name and address of the individual doctor who performed this service. Please resubmit your claim with this information.
192 — Medicare benefits have been reduced because the patient's employer group health plan has paid some of these expenses.
198 — A claim must be sent to the patient's employer group health plan first. After the claim has been processed by that plan, resubmit this claim with the bills and the notice the other insurance company sent you.
203 — Clinical laboratory services, Blood Gas Studies and Rhythm Strips (1-3 leads) furnished in a hospital setting are reimbursed through the hospital.
205 — The date of this service is after the patient's expiration date provided to us by SSA. If service was rendered to this patient on this date, have the patient's estate contact the local Social Security Office for assistance.
206 — For payment, these services must be billed by the performing laboratory with the assignment accepted.
213 — We did not send this claim to Medicaid. Please send this statement and a copy of the claim to the agency that handles Medicaid in your area.
216 — This service or item cannot be processed until your application for a Medicare provider identification number is received and approved.
218 — Since you are Medicare participating, we have processed this claim as assigned. Future claims must be billed on assignment. If the bill was paid in full, you must immediately refund the amount due to the beneficiary.
219 — We need this charge submitted on your letterhead bill. Please resubmit your claim with this information.
221 — The name and Medicare number submitted on this claim do not match. Please verify for whom these services were rendered and provide the correct name and number on the claim and resubmit.
223 — We did not consider this for payment because you did not send the extra information we asked for. Payment can be requested again by sending us another claim form and all the information.
226 — Medicare will pay rent for the prescribed number of months or until the equipment is no longer needed, whichever occurs first. This is the first monthly rental payment.
227 — You will receive a notice each month when additional rental payments are paid.
231 — Medicare will no longer pay for rental on this item since the purchase price has been paid.
237 — The amount of this payment is the difference between the approved purchase allowance and the rental payments you have received.

YOUR RIGHT TO REVIEW OF A CASE

If you have a problem or question about the way a claim was handled or about the amount paid, please write Transamerica Occidental Life, Box 54905, Terminal Annex, Los Angeles, California 90054, within 6 months of the date of this notice. We will give your request full consideration.

Your Social Security office will help you file a request for review of a claim if it is more convenient for you.

WHERE TO SEND REFUNDS

When refunding a payment you should send a check with a letter of explanation. The letter should include your Transamerica Occidental/Medicare check number, beneficiary name and Medicare identification number (HIC No.), control number to which the payment relates and any other information which may be pertinent to the refund. Send this information to:

Transamerica Occidental Life
C/O Check and Payment Control
Box 54905, Terminal Annex
Los Angeles, CA 90054-0905

KEY TO CODES FOR PLACE AND TYPE OF SERVICE

Place of Service	Type of Service
1. Office	A. Medical Care
2. Home	B. Surgery (includes treatment of fractures)
3. Inpatient Hospital	C. Consultation
4. Skilled Nursing Facility	D. Diagnostic X-ray
5. Outpatient Hospital	E. Diagnostic Laboratory
6. Independent Laboratory	F. Radiation Therapy
7. Other	G. Anesthesia
8. Independent Kidney Disease Treatment Center	H. Assistance at Surgery
	I. Other Medical Service
	J. Whole Blood or Packed Red Cells

MCC-4 ED 4-86

B

FIGURE 12-18 *Continued*
Sample of Medicare Remittance Advice (RA) document. *A,* Front. *B,* Back. Insurance carriers are required to use Health Care Financing Administration messages for Medicare RA, but each carrier has its own code numbers to denote the messages.

will be deducted from your next Medicare payment and will be shown on the RA. If the physician wishes to repay a Medicare overpayment on the installment plan, form HCFA-379 may be used. This form is sent to the physician when the carrier notifies the physician that money is due back.

For additional information on what some private insurance carriers refer to as Explanation of Benefits, refer to Chapter 6.

MEDICARE REMITTANCE ADVICE
XYZ Insurance Company

Physician or Supplier Name	Dates of Service From MMDD	To MMDDYY	See Back Serv Typl	Sub Code (Alwcode)	Billed Amount	Amount Approved	See ** Act Cde	Beneficiary Obligation Deduc-tible	Co-Ins	Medicare Payment To Bene-ficiary	Provider

BENEFICIARY: BILL HUTCH HIC NUMBER: 5432-112-34
CONTROL NO: 92106-30810-00 DE/MI: 2121D52

John Doe MD	0310	031094	D 03	120101	145.00	105.00	101	100.00	1.00	0.00	4.00
A CLAIM TOTALS:					145.00	105.00	101	100.00	1.00	0.00	4.00

MEDICAID REMITTANCE ADVICE

RECIPIENT NAME	RECIPIENT MEDICAID ID NO.	CLAIM CONTROL NUMBER	SERVICE DATE MO DAY YR	PROCEDURE CODE	PATIENT ACCT. NO.	QTY.	MEDICARE ALLOWED	MEDICAID ALLOWED	PATIENT LIABILITY	COMPUTED MCR AMT.	MEDICAID PAID	EOB MESSAGE
BILL HUTCH	521345678	4006984891200	03 10 94	49555-80		001	105.00	73.00		4.00	.00	
		4006984891200	00 00 00			000	105.00	73.00		4.00	69.00	CUTBACK 443

B BLOOD DEDUCT 00 DEDUCTIBLE 100.00 COINSUR 1.00 CUTBACK 32.00

FIGURE 12–19
A, Example of a Medicare/Medicaid case after payment by Medicare. *B,* The Medicaid Remittance Advice (RA) shows reimbursement of the coinsurance and deductible amounts dual billed to Medicaid.

TO THE STUDENT

Study Chapter 12 and then answer the review questions in the *Workbook* to reinforce the theory learned in this chapter of the text and to help prepare you for a future test. Assignment 38 presents Medicare cases for computing mathematic calculations. Assignment 39 will give you hands-on experience in selecting HCPCS code numbers. Assignments 40 through 45 will give you experience in abstracting from patients' medical records, preparing ledger cards, and completing forms pertinent to the Medicare program. For further knowledge and understanding the key terms at the beginning of the chapter appear in the Glossary at the end of this textbook so you can look up the pertinent terms.

After completing the *Workbook* assignments, you may want additional practice on the concepts you have learned. Medicare Case 3 is available on your computer disk and will give you a mock experience of electronically transmitting a Medicare claim.

CHAPTER

13

CHAMPUS, CHAMPVA, and TRICARE

Objectives*

THE INSURANCE BILLING SPECIALIST WILL BE ABLE TO:

- State who is eligible for CHAMPUS, CHAMPVA, and CHAMPUS/TRICARE managed care plans.
- Understand the benefits and nonbenefits of these government programs.
- Define pertinent CHAMPUS and CHAMPVA terminology and abbreviations.
- Identify the difference between CHAMPUS, CHAMPVA, and CHAMPUS/TRICARE managed care plan cards.
- Identify and learn the forms used with these health care programs.
- Learn the claims procedure for the provider of services.
- State the circumstances when a nonavailability statement is required.
- State how to process claims for individuals who are covered by CHAMPUS, CHAMPVA, or CHAMPUS/TRICARE managed care plans.
- Learn the differences between CHAMPUS/TRICARE managed care plans and the standard CHAMPUS program.

Key Terms

allowable charge
authorized provider
CHAMPUS
CHAMPUS supplemental insurance
CHAMPUS/TRICARE
CHAMPVA
claims processor
cooperative care
coordination of benefits
cost-share
Defense Enrollment Eligibility Reporting System (DEERS)
fiscal intermediary (FI)
health benefits advisor (HBA)
Inpatient Nonavailability Statement (INAS)
medically (or psychologically) necessary
military treatment facility (MTF)
Nonavailability Statement (NAS)
nonparticipating provider
other health insurance (OHI)
Outpatient Nonavailability Statement (ONAS)
participating provider
partnership program
provider
sponsor
summary payment voucher
uniformed service hospitals

* Performance objectives and exercises for hands-on practical experience for this chapter appear in the *Workbook* and on computer disk.

CHAPTER 13

CHAMPUS, CHAMPVA, and TRICARE

Background

CHAMPUS

The U.S. Congress created CHAMPUS in 1966 under Public Law 89–614 because individuals in the military were finding it increasingly more difficult to pay for the medical care required by their families. CHAMPUS is the acronym for *Civilian Health and Medical Program of the Uniformed Services,* which is a congressionally funded comprehensive health benefits program. It is designed to provide families of uniformed services personnel and service retirees a supplement to medical care available from military and Public Health Service facilities (also known as uniformed service hospitals) as well as from civilian physicians and hospitals. A person who is retired from a career in the armed forces is known as a *service retiree* or *military retiree* and remains in this program until age 65, at which time the individual becomes eligible for the Medicare program. In the event that an active duty military person served from 4 to 6 years and then chose to leave the armed services, thereby giving up a military career, no further family benefits are provided.

CHAMPVA

The Veterans Health Care Expansion Act of 1973 (PL93–82) authorized a CHAMPUS-like program, CHAMPVA, for the spouses and children of veterans with total, permanent, service-connected disabilities or for the surviving spouses and children of veterans who have died as a result of service-connected disabilities. Individuals who qualify for CHAMPUS and CHAMPVA are known as *beneficiaries,* and the active duty service member is called the *sponsor.* A *veteran* is any person who has served in the armed forces of the United States, especially in time of war; is no longer in the service; and has received an honorable discharge. Examples of total, permanent disability are when an individual suffers an injury with paraplegic results, receives a bullet wound with neurologic damage, loses a limb, and so on. This contrasts to a service-connected disability, which might exist if an individual while in the Navy improperly lifts a heavy object, suffers a back injury with ongoing sporadic symptoms, and requires continuing medical care after leaving the service. Both scenarios present service-connected disabilities, but the first example illustrates a person permanently disabled, whereas the second example illustrates what may be a chronic or temporary disability.

The CHAMPVA program became effective on September 1, 1973. The acronym stands for *Civilian Health and Medical Program of the Veterans Administration* (now known as the Department of Veterans Affairs). People entitled to CHAMPUS benefits are excluded from CHAMPVA. The Veterans Administration (VA) elected to provide these beneficiaries with benefits and cost-sharing plans similar to those received by dependents of retired and deceased uniformed services personnel under CHAMPUS. CHAMPUS and CHAMPVA *are not insurance programs* in that they do not involve a contract guaranteeing the indemnification of an insured party against a specified loss in return for a premium paid. They are considered a service benefit program; therefore, there are no premiums.

CHAMPUS is governed by the Department of Defense Regulation 6010-8.R, which implements Chapter 55, Title 10, United States Code. As such, it is not subject to those state regulatory bodies or agencies that control the insurance business. The Department of Defense (DoD) and the VA have agreed to use the Office for the Civilian Health and Medical Program of the Uniformed Services (OCHAMPUS) and the CHAMPUS system of fiscal intermediaries and hospital contractors to receive, process, and pay CHAMPVA claims, following the same procedures currently used for CHAMPUS.

A *fiscal intermediary* (FI) is an organization under contract to the government that handles insurance claims for care received under the CHAMPUS or CHAMPVA programs. The contract for an FI comes up for renewal approximately every 3 years.

CHAMPUS Program

In the CHAMPUS program, beneficiaries may receive a wide range of civilian health care services, with a significant portion of the cost paid for by the federal government. Ordinarily these patients seek care from an Army or a Navy hospital near their home. If the service hospital that is managing the CHAMPUS patient cannot provide a particular service or needed medical supplies, the military physician may refer the patient to a civilian source. These services or supplies may be cost-shared by CHAMPUS under certain conditions, and this is known as *cooperative care.*

Another program that lets CHAMPUS-eligible persons receive inpatient or outpatient treatment from civilian providers of care in a military hospital, or from uniformed services providers of care in civilian facilities, is called a *partnership program.* Whether the partnership program is instituted at a particular military hospital is up to the facility's commander, who makes the decision if it is more economical than having local service families use the regular CHAMPUS program.

In addition, there are times when a CHAMPUS beneficiary may seek care through a private physician's office or hospital when there is no service hospital in the area. Delivery of care through the private physician will be emphasized in this chapter.

ELIGIBILITY

Those who are entitled to medical benefits under CHAMPUS are

- Dependents of active-duty personnel
- Retirees and their dependents
- Dependents of service personnel who have died in active duty

- Dependents of active-duty reservists (if called to duty for more than 30 days)
- Disabled beneficiaries under age 65 who have Medicare parts A and B and qualify under one of the aforementioned categories.

Those *not* eligible are

- Medicare eligible beneficiaries (except active-duty dependents over age 65 and those with end-stage renal disease)
- Active duty service members
- CHAMPVA beneficiaries

DEFENSE ENROLLMENT ELIGIBILITY REPORTING SYSTEM

All CHAMPUS-eligible persons must be enrolled in the Defense Enrollment Eligibility Reporting System (DEERS) computerized data base. CHAMPUS claims processors check DEERS before processing claims to verify beneficiary eligibility. A CHAMPUS beneficiary may check his or her status by contracting the nearest personnel office of any branch of the service or by calling the toll-free number of the DEERS center.

PROVIDERS OF HEALTH CARE

The following health care professionals may treat a CHAMPUS patient (authorized providers):

Doctor of Medicine (M.D.)
Doctor of Osteopathy
Doctor of Dental Surgery
Doctor of Dental Medicine
Doctor of Podiatric Medicine or Surgical Chiropody
Doctor of Optometry
Psychologist
Certified Nurse Midwife, Audiologist, Speech Therapist, registered nurse, licensed practical nurse, licensed vocational nurse, registered physical therapist, psychiatric or clinical social worker

CHAMPUS AND CHAMPVA IDENTIFICATION CARDS

All dependents 10 years of age or older are required to have a Uniformed Services (military) identification and privilege card for CHAMPUS and CHAMPVA. Figure 13–1 provides an example of a

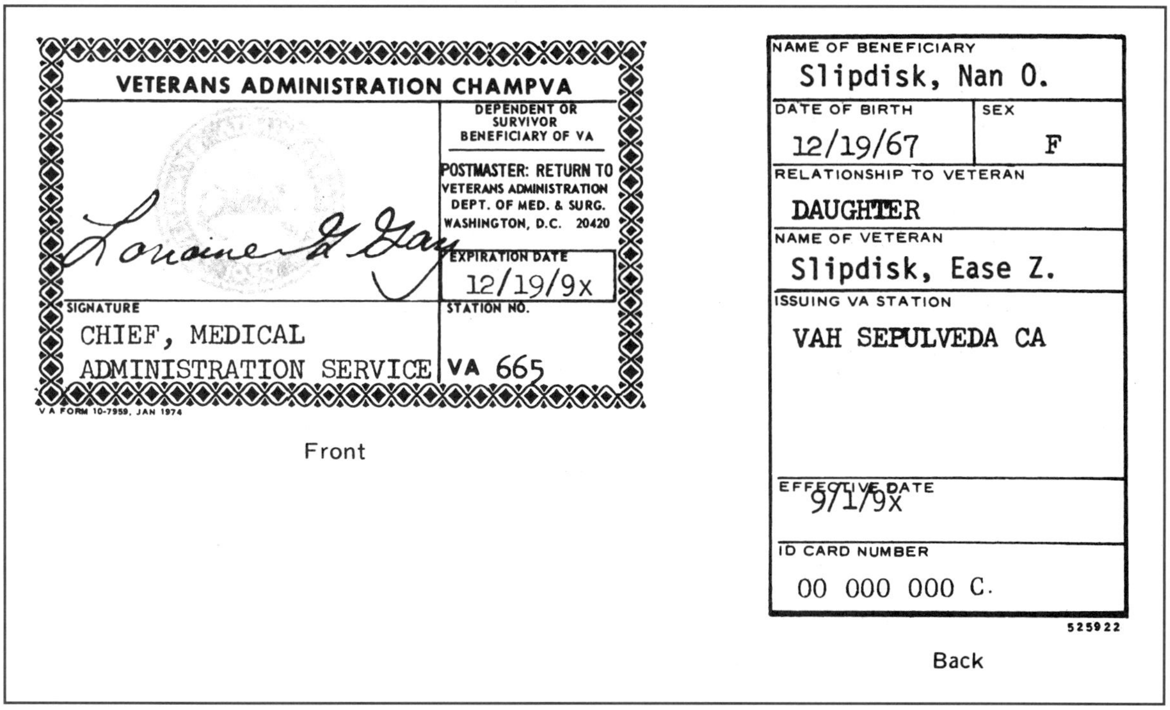

VETERANS ADMINISTRATION CHAMPVA
DEPENDENT OR SURVIVOR BENEFICIARY OF VA
POSTMASTER: RETURN TO VETERANS ADMINISTRATION DEPT. OF MED. & SURG. WASHINGTON, D.C. 20420
EXPIRATION DATE 12/19/9x
SIGNATURE
CHIEF, MEDICAL ADMINISTRATION SERVICE
STATION NO. VA 665
VA FORM 10-7959, JAN 1974

Front

NAME OF BENEFICIARY: Slipdisk, Nan O.
DATE OF BIRTH: 12/19/67
SEX: F
RELATIONSHIP TO VETERAN: DAUGHTER
NAME OF VETERAN: Slipdisk, Ease Z.
ISSUING VA STATION: VAH SEPULVEDA CA
EFFECTIVE DATE: 9/1/9x
ID CARD NUMBER: 00 000 000 C.
525922

Back

FIGURE 13–1
Sample CHAMPVA Card.

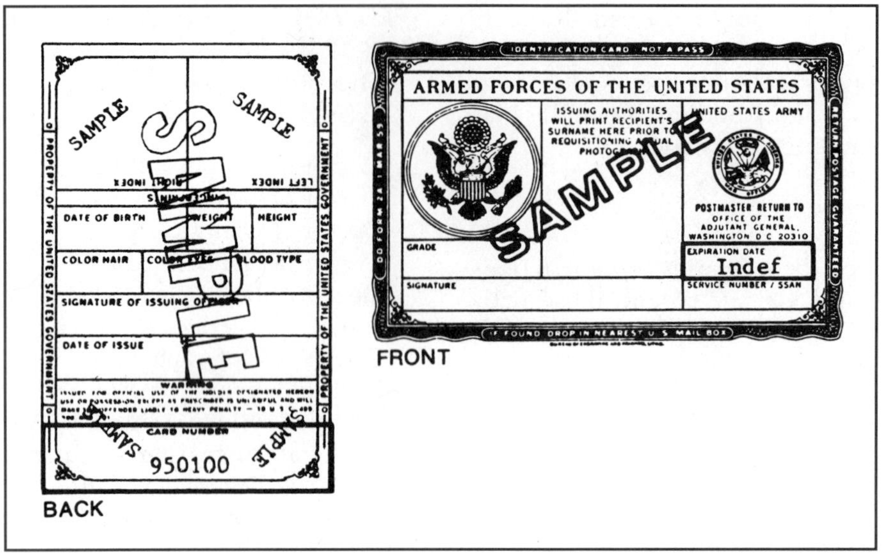

FIGURE 13–2
Sample CHAMPUS retiree's identification card (blue-gray in color), DD Form 2.

dependent's identification card, DD Form 1173, and Figure 13–2 is a representation of a retiree's identification card, DD Form 2. Dependents under 10 years of age are not normally issued Uniformed Services identification cards; information for their claims should be provided from either parent's card. Essential information must be abstracted from the front and back of the card, so photocopy both sides to retain in the patient's medical record.

INPATIENT AND OUTPATIENT BENEFITS AND COVERAGE

CHAMPUS beneficiaries have a broad range of inpatient and outpatient benefits. For CHAMPVA beneficiaries, the benefits are the same as those authorized for CHAMPUS beneficiaries who are dependents of retired or deceased personnel. In addition, cost sharing is the same as for CHAMPUS beneficiaries who are dependents of retired or deceased personnel.

Medical or psychologic services or supplies that are considered appropriate care and are generally accepted by qualified professionals to be reasonable and adequate for the diagnosis and treatment of illness, injury, pregnancy, and mental disorders, or that are reasonable and adequate for well-baby care, are referred to as *medically* or *psychologically necessary.*

To see the overall picture of CHAMPUS and CHAMPVA benefits which includes cost sharing (deductibles and copayments), read carefully through Figures 13–3 and 13–4.

CHAMPVA Program

ELIGIBILITY

The following persons are eligible for CHAMPVA benefits as long as they *are not eligible* for CHAMPUS and not eligible for Medicare Part A as a result of reaching age 65:

- The husband, wife, or unmarried child of a veteran with a total disability, permanent in nature, resulting from a service-connected injury.
- The husband, wife, or unmarried child of a veteran who died as the result of a service-connected disability or who, at the time of death, had a total disability, permanent in nature, resulting from a service-connected injury.
- The husband, wife, or unmarried child of an individual who died in the line of duty while on active service.

Children are those unmarried and under the age of 18 regardless of whether dependent or not, or up to the age of 23 if enrolled in a course of instruction at an approved educational institution.

Determination of eligibility is the responsibility of the Department of Veterans Affairs. The prospective beneficiary goes to the nearest VA hospital or clinic and, if eligible, receives a VA identification card. The issuing station's number appears on the identification card to identify the home station where the beneficiary's case file is kept. The identification card number is the veteran's VA file number with an alpha suffix. The suffix is different for each beneficiary

Text continued on page 305

Benefits and Coverage Chart

Inpatient Services — **Beneficiary Cost**

SERVICES	CHAMPUS or CHAMPVA
HOSPITALIZATION++ Semiprivate room (and when medically necessary, special care units), general nursing, and hospital service. Includes inpatient physician and their surgical services, meals including special diets, drugs and medications while an inpatient, operating and recovery room, anesthesia, laboratory tests, x-rays and other radiology services, necessary medical supplies and appliances, blood and blood products.	Active Duty Family Members: $25 copayment or $9.70* per day, whichever is higher. +Retirees and their Family Members and Survivors: copayment of $323* per day or 25% of billed charges, whichever is less, plus 25% of CHAMPUS allowable for separately billed professional charges.
MATERNITY++ Hospital and professional services (prenatal, postnatal).	
SKILLED NURSING FACILITY Semiprivate room, regular nursing services, meals including special diets, physical, occupational, and speech therapy, drugs furnished by the facility, necessary medical supplies, and appliances.	Active Duty Family Members: $25 copayment or $9.70* per day, whichever is higher. Retirees and their Family Members and Survivors: 25% of billed charges, plus 25% of CHAMPUS allowable for separately billed professional charges.
HOSPITALIZATION FOR MENTAL ILLNESS++ 18 and under, 45 days per year. 19 and older, 30 days per year as medically necessary. Up to 150 days for treatment in a Residential Treatment Center. The number of days may be subject to change pending new legislation.	
ALCOHOLISM++ 7 days for detoxification and 21 days for rehabilitation per 365 days. Maximum of one rehabilitation program per year and three per lifetime. Detoxification and rehabilitation days count toward 30-day limit for mental health benefits.	

* This figure is for Fiscal Year 1996 and is subject to change each October 1 at the beginning of each Fiscal Year. Effective October 1,1997 $_______.
This is only a summary description of CHAMPUS/CHAMPVA coverage. Refer to the CHAMPUS Handbook for more complete description of all terms and conditions. In addition, CHAMPUS regulations and the interpretations under those regulations are the final authority on covered services.
\+ Unlimited, with authorization, as medically necessary.
++ NAS Note: The patient must obtain a Nonavailability Statement if he or she lives within a designated service area around a military hospital.

For Active Duty Family Members, the maximum family liability (Catastrophic Cap Benefit) is $1000 for deductibles and cost-shares based on allowable charges for the Basic Program services and supplies received in a Fiscal Year. For all other beneficiary families, the Fiscal Year cap is $7500. After a Fiscal Year cap is met, the CHAMPUS-determined allowable amount shall be paid in full for all covered services and supplies under the Basic Program received through the end of that Fiscal Year. In order to get credit for all family expenditures allowed toward the catastrophic cap benefit, the beneficiary may be required to submit appropriate documentation (e.g., CHAMPUS Explanation of Benefits).

FIGURE 13-3
CHAMPUS and CHAMPVA Inpatient Benefits and Cost-sharing Chart.

Benefits and Coverage Chart

Outpatient Services — **Beneficiary Cost**

SERVICES	CHAMPUS or CHAMPVA*
ANNUAL DEDUCTIBLE* (Applied to Outpatient Services)	$150/person or $300/family per fiscal year.**
PHYSICIAN SERVICES*** Office visits; outpatient office-based medical and surgical care; consultation, diagnosis, and treatment by a specialist; allergy tests and treatment; osteopathic manipulation; medical supplies used within the office including casts, dressings and splints.	Active Duty Family Members: 20% of CHAMPUS allowable after deductible has been satisfied. Retirees and their Family Members and Survivors: 25% of CHAMPUS allowable after deductible has been satisfied.
LABORATORY and X-RAY SERVICES (Including Mammograms.)	
ROUTINE PAP SMEARS Frequency depends on physician recommendations based on the published guidelines of the American Academy of Obstetrics and Gynecology.	
AMBULANCE SERVICES When medically necessary as currently defined and covered by OCHAMPUS.	
EMERGENCY SERVICES Outpatient, both in and out of service area for emergency and urgently needed care.	
DURABLE MEDICAL EQUIPMENT, PROSTHETIC DEVICES, AND MEDICAL SUPPLIES PRESCRIBED BY PHYSICIAN AND WHEN A CHAMPUS BENEFIT (If dispensed for use outside of the office or after the home visit.)	
HOME HEALTH CARE Part-time skilled nursing care, physical, speech and occupational therapy as currently defined by OCHAMPUS (when medically necessary).	
FAMILY HEALTH SERVICES Family planning and well-baby care (up to 24 months of age). Certain exclusions apply as currently defined by OCHAMPUS.	
OUTPATIENT MENTAL HEALTH One hour of therapy no more than two times each week (when medically necessary). Outpatient Medication Management	

* CHAMPUS and CHAMPVA annual deductibles and cost shares subject to change.

** Except for families whose Active Duty sponsor's pay grade is E-4 and below, for whom the annual deductible is $50/person or $100/family.

This is only a summary description of the CHAMPUS and CHAMPVA coverage. See the CHAMPUS Handbook for a more complete description of all terms and conditions. In addition, CHAMPUS regulations and the interpretations under those regulations are the final authority on covered services. CHAMPUS fiscal year is October 1 to September 30.

*** An outpatient Nonavailability Statement (NAS) may be required. The patient must obtain a NAS if he or she lives within a designated service area near a military treatment facility if the care is not available at the facility. The patient should call the Health Care Finder.

FIGURE 13-4
CHAMPUS and CHAMPVA Outpatient Benefits and Cost-sharing Chart.

Benefits and Coverage Chart

Outpatient Services	Beneficiary Cost
SERVICES	**CHAMPUS or CHAMPVA***
ANNUAL DEDUCTIBLE* (Applied to Outpatient Services)	$150/person or $300/family per fiscal year.**
PRESCRIPTION DRUGS No charge for prescriptions at military treatment facility.	Active Duty Family Members: 20% of CHAMPUS allowable after deductible has been satisfied. Retirees and their Family Members and Survivors: 25% of CHAMPUS allowable after deductible has been satisfied.
EYE EXAMS One routine examination per year.	Active Duty Family Members: 20% of CHAMPUS allowable after deductible has been satisfied. Retirees and their Family Members and Survivors: Not Covered.
AMBULATORY SURGERY (same day)*** Authorized hospital-based or freestanding ambulatory surgical center that is CHAMPUS Certified.	Active Duty Family Members: $25 copayment for hospital charges. Retirees and their Family Members and Survivors: 25% of billed charges after deductible has been satisfied.
IMMUNIZATIONS Pediatric and adult immunizations as recommended by the American Academy of Pediatrics for children and by the U.S. Public Health Service for adults. If immunizations are needed for overseas travel, it is recommended the patient contact a military hospital or clinic and/or Public Health Department.	For official travel, PCS orders outside the U.S. only. Active Duty Family Members: 20% of CHAMPUS allowable after deductible has been satisfied. Retirees and their Family Members and Survivors: Not Covered.

* CHAMPUS and CHAMPVA annual deductibles and cost shares subject to change.
** Except for families whose Active Duty sponsor's pay grade is E-4 and below, for whom the annual deductible is $50/person or $100/family.
This is only a summary description of the CHAMPUS and CHAMPVA coverage. See the CHAMPUS Handbook for a more complete description of all terms and conditions. In addition, CHAMPUS regulations and the interpretations under those regulations are the final authority on covered services. CHAMPUS fiscal year is October 1 to September 30.
*** An outpatient Nonavailability Statement (NAS) may be required. The patient should call the Health Care Finder.
For active Duty Family Members, the maximum family liability (Catastrophic Cap Benefit) is $1000 for deductibles and cost-shares based on allowable charges for the Basic Program services and supplies received in a Fiscal Year. For all other beneficiary families, the Fiscal Year cap is $7500. After a Fiscal Year cap is met, the CHAMPUS-determined allowable amount shall be paid in full for all covered services and supplies under the Basic Program received through the end of that Fiscal Year. In order to get credit for all family expenditures allowed toward the catastrophic cap benefit, the beneficiary may be required to submit appropriate documentation (e.g., CHAMPUS Explanation of Benefits).

FIGURE 13-4 *Continued*

Benefits and Coverage Chart

Outpatient Services	Beneficiary Cost
SERVICES	**CHAMPUS or CHAMPVA ***
ANNUAL DEDUCTIBLE * (Applied to Outpatient Services)	$150/person or $300/family per fiscal year. **
PARTIAL HOSPITALIZATION FOR ALCOHOLISM TREATMENT Up to 21 days for rehabilitative treatment on a limited hour-per-day basis. Does not count toward the mental health inpatient limit, but does count toward 60-day partial hospitalization limit.	Subject to inpatient mental health copayment.
PARTIAL HOSPITALIZATION FOR PSYCHIATRIC TREATMENT Limited to 60 treatment days (whether a full day or partial day program) in a fiscal year or in an admission. Not counted toward the 30/45 day inpatient limit.	Subject to inpatient mental health copayment.
PERIODIC PHYSICAL EXAMINATIONS	Not covered.
PHYSICAL, OCCUPATIONAL, SPEECH AND RADIATION THERAPY	Active Duty Family Members: 20% of CHAMPUS allowable after deductible has been satisfied. Retirees and their Family Members and Survivors: 25% of CHAMPUS allowable after deductible has been satisfied.
WELLNESS CLASSES, COMMUNITY HEALTH SERVICES AND COMMUNITY RESOURCE COORDINATION	No charge of minimal cost.

* CHAMPUS and CHAMPVA annual deductibles and cost shares are subject to change.

** Except for families whose Active Duty sponsor's pay grade is E-4 and below, for whom the annual deductible is $50/person or $100/family.

This is only a summary description of the CHAMPUS and CHAMPVA coverage. See the CHAMPUS Handbook for a more complete description of all terms and conditions. In addition, CHAMPUS regulations and the interpretations under those regulations are the final authority on covered services.

For Active Duty Family Members, the maximum family liability (Catastrophic Cap Benefit) is $1000 for deductibles and cost-shares based on allowable charges for the Basic Program services and supplies received in a Fiscal Year. For all other beneficiary families, the Fiscal Year cap is $7500. After a Fiscal Year cap is met, the CHAMPUS-determined allowable amount shall be paid in full for all covered services and supplies under the Basic Program received through the end of that Fiscal Year. In order to get credit for all family expenditures allowed toward the Catastrophic Cap benefit, the beneficiary may be required to submit appropriate documentation (e.g., CHAMPUS Explanation of Benefits).

FIGURE 13-4 *Continued*

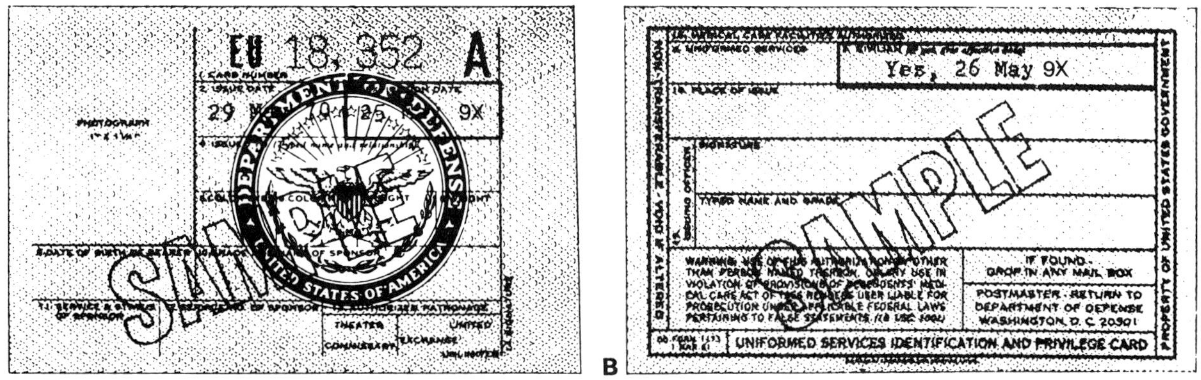

A FRONT

B BACK

FIGURE 13–5
Sample CHAMPUS family member dependent's Identification Card (orange in color), DD Form 1173, from which essential information must be abstracted. Dependents under 10 years of age are not normally issued identification cards; information on their claims should reflect that on either parent's card.

of a sponsor. These beneficiaries have complete freedom of choice in selecting their civilian health care providers. Figure 13–5 is a sample of a CHAMPVA identification card.

PREAUTHORIZATION

Certain types of health care services requiring prior approval from the CHAMPUS health contractor are dental care, mental health care, and purchase of durable medical equipment.

Privacy Act of 1974

This act became effective on September 27, 1975, and establishes an individual's right to review his or her medical records maintained by a federal medical care facility, such as a VA hospital, U.S. Public Health Service facility, or military hospital, and to contest inaccuracies in such records. The Act directs each agency to make its own rules establishing access procedures. Agencies are allowed to adopt special procedures when it is felt that direct access could be harmful to a person. The Act requires that an individual from whom personal information is requested be informed of (1) the authority for the request, (2) the principal purpose of the information requested, (3) routine use of the information, and (4) the effect on an individual who does not provide the information.

Another act, the Computer Matching and Privacy Protection Act of 1988, was established and permits the government to verify information by way of computer matches.

Both of these acts are mentioned on the back of the CHAMPUS HCFA-1500 claim form. It is important that CHAMPUS patients are made aware of this information by physicians who treat them, so they are knowledgeable about routine use and disclosures of medical data.

Patients may make a Privacy Act request in writing, in person, or by telephone. Individuals should call the facility to determine the required procedures to obtain access to the records and what to include in making a written request.

Nonavailability Statement

A Nonavailability Statement (NAS) is a certification from a military hospital stating that it cannot provide the care needed. This type of certification is required for all CHAMPUS and CHAMPVA beneficiaries (dependents of active duty, retired, and deceased personnel and retired members themselves) who wish to receive treatment as inpatients or outpatients at a civilian hospital and who live within a catchment area surrounding a Uniformed Services Medical Treatment Facility (USMTF). If this certification is not obtained, CHAMPUS may not share the costs. The catchment area is defined by ZIP codes and is based on an area of approximately 40 miles in radius surrounding each USMTF. Individuals whose home address ZIP code falls outside the local military hospital's service area do not need an NAS before they seek civilian health care under CHAMPUS. An inpatient NAS is needed for inpatient services and an outpatient nonavailability statement (ONAS) is needed for outpatient services.

Since October 1, 1991, the NAS system has been automated. This means that instead of a paper copy of the NAS being sent in with the CHAMPUS or CHAMPVA claim, the uniformed service medical facility enters the NAS electronically into the DEERS (Defense Enrollment Eligibility Reporting System) computer files. However, a hard (paper) copy of DD Form 1251 may be printed out if the patient needs one to show the hospital or physician (Fig. 13–6). Electronically filed NASs are the only ones accepted for processing claims, and there is no need to attach a copy of the NAS to the claim form. Always ask the patient if he or she is enrolled in DEERS.

Nonavailability statements are used for certain outpatient procedures and are valid for 30 days after being issued. Patients do not need an NAS to visit a physician to determine the need for these procedures. The NAS is required only when the procedure is actually performed. The procedures are

- Certain hernia repairs
- Breast mass or tumor removal
- Nose repair (rhinoplasty and septoplasty)
- Removal of tonsils or adenoids
- Cataract removal
- Strabismus repair
- Dilation and curettage
- Gastrointestinal endoscopy
- Myringotomy or tympanostomy
- Arthroscopy
- Gynecologic laparoscopy
- Cystoscopy
- Neuroplasty

An NAS is not needed for inpatient care in the following situations.

1. In a medical emergency when delay could cause death or serious threat to health.
2. When the patient has other non-CHAMPUS major medical insurance that pays first on the bills for CHAMPUS-covered care (i.e., when CHAMPUS is second pay).

Claims Procedure

CHAMPUS/CHAMPVA

Photocopy and abstract the correct information from front and back sides of the patient's identification card. Effective January 1, 1993, the time limit within which a claim must be filed is within 1 year from the date a service is provided or (for inpatient care) within 1 year from a patient's date of discharge from an inpatient facility. CHAMPUS and CHAMPVA claims must be billed on the HCFA-1500 claim form and submitted to the claims processor (fiscal intermediary), as shown in Figure 13–7. Refer to Chapter 6 and follow the CHAMPUS or CHAMPVA instructions for completing the HCFA-1500 claim form. If electing to complete the VA Form 10-1759A for a CHAMPVA case, refer to p. 309 for instructions in this chapter.

Do not file claims of active duty armed service patients to CHAMPUS. Claims for patients on active duty must be sent to the specific branch of service (i.e., Army, Navy, Air Force, Marines, and so on).

CLAIMS OFFICES

Refer to Appendix A for the address for filing a CHAMPUS or CHAMPVA claim for services rendered in your state. The U.S. government reviews the performance of fiscal intermediaries approximately every 3 years, so addresses are subject to change without notice. Contact the Health Benefits Advisor (HBA) at the nearest military treatment facility (MTF) to obtain a current CHAMPUS *Handbook* or to answer any questions about the name of the regional claims processor, benefits, nonbenefits, when a nonavailability statement is required, and so on.

PARTICIPATING PROVIDERS

For a CHAMPUS case, if the physician agrees to *accept assignment,* then the participating provider agrees to accept the CHAMPUS-determined allowable or reasonable cost/charge as payment in full. Providers may choose to accept CHAMPUS assignment on a case-by-case basis. Always accept assignment in cases when the service member is transferring within 6 months because this will avoid collection problems. The provider may then bill the patient for his or her cost-share or coinsurance (20% to 25% of these charges after the deductible has been met) and for any noncovered services or supplies but may not bill for the difference between the provider's usual charge and the allowable charge. Remember that the CHAMPUS fiscal year is different than other programs as far as the deductible is concerned and begins October 1 and ends September 30.

Beneficiaries pay only a certain amount each year

Text continued on page 309

NONAVAILABILITY STATEMENT
DEPENDENTS MEDICAL CARE PROGRAM
(AR 40-121, SECNAV INST 6320.8A, AFR 160-41, PHS GEN CIR NO 6)

(This Statement is Issued for your Immediate use)

THE ISSUANCE OF THIS STATEMENT MEANS:

1. The medical care requested is not available to you at a Uniformed Services facility in this area.
2. If you receive medical care from civilian sources and such care is determined to be authorized care under the Medicare Program, it will be paid for by the Government to the extent that the program permits.
3. If you receive medical care from civilian sources and it is determined that all or part of the care is not authorized under the Medicare Program, THE GOVERNMENT WILL NOT PAY for the unauthorized care.

The determination of whether medical care you may receive from civilian sources is authorized for payment cannot be made at this time because this determination depends, among other things, upon the care you actually receive. Further, no statement regarding your condition or diagnosis made hereon will be considered in any way determinative as to whether care rendered for such condition is payable under the Medicare Program.

The use of this statement is subject to the conditions and limitations set forth in the regulation issued under the Dependents' Medical Care Act as codified in 10 U.S.C. 1071-1085.

This form must be presented with your Uniformed Services Identification and Privilege Card (DD Form 1173), identified below, when you obtain civilian medical care.

DEPENDENT, SPOUSE OR CHILD, RESIDING WITH SPONSOR

DEPENDENT'S LAST NAME - FIRST NAME - MIDDLE INITIAL	UNIFORMED SERVICES IDENTIFICATION AND PRIVILEGE CARD (DD FORM 1173)			
	CARD NUMBER			EXPIRATION DATE
	PREFIX	NUMERICAL	SUFFIX	
DEPENDENT'S ADDRESS *(Complete mailing address)*				

SPONSOR MEMBER OF UNIFORMED SERVICES ON ACTIVE DUTY

SPONSOR'S LAST NAME - FIRST NAME - MIDDLE INITIAL		BRANCH OF SERVICE
SERVICE NUMBER	GRADE OR RANK	☐ ARMY ☐ NAVY ☐ AIR FORCE ☐ MARINE CORPS ☐ PUBLIC HEALTH ☐ COAST GUARD ☐ COAST & GEODETIC SURVEY
ORGANIZATION AND OFFICIAL DUTY STATION		

REMARKS

STATION AT WHICH PERMIT ISSUED	DATE ISSUED
GRADE OR RANK, AND POSITION OF ISSUING OFFICER Commanding Officer	SIGNATURE OF ISSUING OFFICER

DISTRIBUTION *(Three signed copies of this statement will be furnished the dependent for distribution as follows):*

DEPENDENT *(Original copy)* ATTENDING PHYSICIAN *(Duplicate copy)* CIVILIAN MEDICAL FACILITY *(Triplicate copy)*

FIGURE 13–6
CHAMPUS Nonavailability Statement DD Form 1251 for inpatient care rendered in a non-military hospital.

APPROVED OMB-0938-0008

PLEASE DO NOT STAPLE IN THIS AREA

BASIC CHAMPUS CASE

Type address of fiscal agent or intermediary here.

CARRIER

PICA

HEALTH INSURANCE CLAIM FORM

PICA

1. MEDICARE (Medicare #) ☐ MEDICAID (Medicaid #) ☐ CHAMPUS (Sponsor's SSN) ☒ CHAMPVA (VA File #) ☐ GROUP HEALTH PLAN (SSN or ID) ☐ FECA BLK LUNG (SSN) ☐ OTHER (ID) ☐

1a. INSURED'S I.D. NUMBER (FOR PROGRAM IN ITEM 1): 581-14-7211

2. PATIENT'S NAME (Last Name, First Name, Middle Initial): SMITH SUSAN J

3. PATIENT'S BIRTH DATE MM DD YY: 03 16 66 SEX M ☐ F ☒

4. INSURED'S NAME (Last Name, First Name, Middle Initial): SMITH WILLIAM D

5. PATIENT'S ADDRESS (No., Street): 420 MAPLE STREET

6. PATIENT RELATIONSHIP TO INSURED: Self ☐ Spouse ☒ Child ☐ Other ☐

7. INSURED'S ADDRESS (No., Street): SAME

CITY: WOODLAND HILLS STATE: XY

8. PATIENT STATUS: Single ☐ Married ☒ Other ☐

CITY STATE

ZIP CODE: 12345 TELEPHONE (Include Area Code): (013) 789-9898

Employed ☐ Full-Time Student ☐ Part-Time Student ☐

ZIP CODE TELEPHONE (INCLUDE AREA CODE) ( )

9. OTHER INSURED'S NAME (Last Name, First Name, Middle Initial)

10. IS PATIENT'S CONDITION RELATED TO:

11. INSURED'S POLICY GROUP OR FECA NUMBER: NONE

a. OTHER INSURED'S POLICY OR GROUP NUMBER

a. EMPLOYMENT? (CURRENT OR PREVIOUS) ☐ YES ☒ NO

a. INSURED'S DATE OF BIRTH MM DD YY SEX M ☐ F ☐

b. OTHER INSURED'S DATE OF BIRTH MM DD YY SEX M ☐ F ☐

b. AUTO ACCIDENT? ☐ YES ☒ NO PLACE (State)

b. EMPLOYER'S NAME OR SCHOOL NAME

c. EMPLOYER'S NAME OR SCHOOL NAME

c. OTHER ACCIDENT? ☐ YES ☒ NO

c. INSURANCE PLAN NAME OR PROGRAM NAME

d. INSURANCE PLAN NAME OR PROGRAM NAME

10d. RESERVED FOR LOCAL USE

d. IS THERE ANOTHER HEALTH BENEFIT PLAN? ☐ YES ☒ NO *If yes,* return to and complete item 9 a-d.

READ BACK OF FORM BEFORE COMPLETING & SIGNING THIS FORM.

12. PATIENT'S OR AUTHORIZED PERSON'S SIGNATURE I authorize the release of any medical or other information necessary to process this claim. I also request payment of government benefits either to myself or to the party who accepts assignment below.

SIGNED ______ DATE 2-22-9X

13. INSURED'S OR AUTHORIZED PERSON'S SIGNATURE I authorize payment of medical benefits to the undersigned physician or supplier for services described below.

SIGNED ______

EXAMPLE ONLY

PATIENT AND INSURED INFORMATION

14. DATE OF CURRENT: MM DD YY 02 21 9X ◀ ILLNESS (First symptom) OR INJURY (Accident) OR PREGNANCY(LMP)

15. IF PATIENT HAS HAD SAME OR SIMILAR ILLNESS. GIVE FIRST DATE MM DD YY

16. DATES PATIENT UNABLE TO WORK IN CURRENT OCCUPATION FROM MM DD YY TO MM DD YY

17. NAME OF REFERRING PHYSICIAN OR OTHER SOURCE

17a. I.D. NUMBER OF REFERRING PHYSICIAN: Fed Tx ID # or Soc. Sec. #

18. HOSPITALIZATION DATES RELATED TO CURRENT SERVICES FROM MM DD YY TO MM DD YY

19. RESERVED FOR LOCAL USE

20. OUTSIDE LAB? ☐ YES ☒ NO $ CHARGES

21. DIAGNOSIS OR NATURE OF ILLNESS OR INJURY. (RELATE ITEMS 1,2,3 OR 4 TO ITEM 24E BY LINE)

1. 382 . 0
2. ___ . __
3. ___ . __
4. ___ . __

22. MEDICAID RESUBMISSION CODE ORIGINAL REF. NO.

23. PRIOR AUTHORIZATION NUMBER

24.	A DATE(S) OF SERVICE From MM DD YY	To MM DD YY	B Place of Service	C Type of Service	D PROCEDURES, SERVICES, OR SUPPLIES (Explain Unusual Circumstances) CPT/HCPCS	MODIFIER	E DIAGNOSIS CODE	F $ CHARGES	G DAYS OR UNITS	H EPSDT Family Plan	I EMG	J COB	K RESERVED FOR LOCAL USE
1	02 21 9X		11	1	99213		1	45 00	1				A001234
2	02 21 9X		11	2	69420		1	100 00	1				A001234
3													
4													
5													
6													

25. FEDERAL TAX I.D. NUMBER: 93-0123456 SSN ☐ EIN ☒

26. PATIENT'S ACCOUNT NO.

27. ACCEPT ASSIGNMENT? (For govt. claims, see back) ☒ YES ☐ NO

28. TOTAL CHARGE $ 145 00

29. AMOUNT PAID $

30. BALANCE DUE $ 145 00

31. SIGNATURE OF PHYSICIAN OR SUPPLIER INCLUDING DEGREES OR CREDENTIALS (I certify that the statements on the reverse apply to this bill and are made a part thereof.) John Doe, MD

SIGNED DATE 2-22-9X

32. NAME AND ADDRESS OF FACILITY WHERE SERVICES WERE RENDERED (If other than home or office): Same

33. PHYSICIAN'S, SUPPLIER'S BILLING NAME, ADDRESS, ZIP CODE & PHONE #: SHORE CLINIC 013-567-0909 121 MINOR WOODLAND HILLS XY 12345

PIN# GRP# 0003

PHYSICIAN OR SUPPLIER INFORMATION

(APPROVED BY AMA COUNCIL ON MEDICAL SERVICE 8/88) **PLEASE PRINT OR TYPE** FORM HCFA-1500 (U2) (12-90) FORM OWCP-1500 FORM RRB-1500

reference initials

FIGURE 13–7

Example of a completed CHAMPUS Form HCFA-1500, used when billing for professional services.

for the cost-share and annual deductible. This amount is known as the *catastrophic cap*. After this cap is reached, CHAMPUS and CHAMPVA pay 100% of the allowable charges for the rest of the year. Attach a note to the claim when the patient has met the catastrophic cap, and this may help expedite claims processing and payment. After completing the claim and sending it to the fiscal intermediary, the payment will go directly to the physician.

NONPARTICIPATING PROVIDERS

CHAMPUS

If the physician is nonparticipating and *does not accept assignment*, the patient completes the top portion of the HCFA-1500 claim form, attaches the physician's itemized statement, and submits the claim. Alternatively, the patient may submit on the white CHAMPUS claim DD Form 2642 Patient's Request for Medical Payment. Patients and providers of care for health services in foreign countries must use DD Form 2520. The UB-92 form is used for inpatient hospital billing. When the physician does not accept assignment, the patient pays the deductible, 20% or 25% of the charges determined to be allowable, and any amount over the allowable charge. In other words, the patient is responsible for the total actual charge of the bill.

As of November 1, 1993, health care providers who choose not to participate in CHAMPUS may not bill the patient more than 115% of the CHAMPUS allowable charge. For example, if the CHAMPUS allowable charge for a procedure is $100, providers who decide not to participate in CHAMPUS may charge CHAMPUS patients no more than $115 for that procedure.

CHAMPVA

If the physician is nonparticipating and *does not accept assignment*, the patient completes Items 1 through 17 of the CHAMPVA Claim Form VA Form 10-7959A, attaches the physician's itemized statement or encounter form, and submits the claim. If an itemized statement is not attached, the physician completes Items 18 through 28 on the bottom half of the CHAMPVA Claim Form.

Figure 13–8 is an example of a completed CHAMPVA case on VA Form 10-7959A. The following are explanations of the items required on the claim form, which preferably should be typed by the insurance billing specialist or printed legibly if completed by the patient.

Instructions for Completing a CHAMPVA Claim Form

Item 1: Patient's last name, first name, and middle initial (do not use nicknames or abbreviations).

Item 2: Patient's Social Security number exactly as it appears on the Social Security card. If the patient does not have a Social Security number, print "NONE."

Item 3: Patient's complete address. If the patient's address has changed, place an "X" in the box.

Item 4: Patient's home telephone number. Include area code.

Item 5A: Enter the number from Item 6 of the patient's current CHAMPVA Authorization Card.

Item 5B: Enter the date from Item 4 of the patient's current CHAMPVA Authorization Card.

Item 5C: Enter the date from Item 5 of the patient's current CHAMPVA Authorization Card.

Item 6: Patient's date of birth.

Item 7: Patient's relationship to sponsor.

Item 8: Patient's sex.

Item 9: Sponsor's last name, first name, and middle initial (do not use nicknames or abbreviations).

Item 10: Enter sponsor's VA Claim/File Number.

Item 11: Sponsor's complete address (if different from the patient's).

Item 12A: Place an "X" in the appropriate box if the patient is covered under any other medical benefits plan or health insurance coverage.

CHAMPVA will not duplicate benefits of any other health insurance plan or program.

Item 12B: Place an "X" beside all applicable types of medical plans or other health insurance to which the patient is entitled.

Item 12C: Enter the name and address of the other insurance carrier.

Item 12D: If other health insurance is provided by the patient's employer, enter the name and address of the employer.

Text continued on page 312

13

OMB NC: 2900-
Estimated burden: 30 min

Department of Veterans Affairs

CHAMPVA CLAIM FORM

CHAMPVA CENTER, 4500 Cherry Creek Drive South, Box 300, Denver CO 80222

WARNING: IF YOU KNOWINGLY MAKE A FALSE STATEMENT OF ANY MATERIAL FACT IN OR IN CONNECTION WITH THIS CLAIM, YOU ARE SUBJECT TO PROSECUTION IN A U.S. COURT.

PART 1 - PATIENT INFORMATION (To be completed by the beneficiary, patient or sponsor)

1. PATIENT'S NAME (Last, first, middle initial): CHIEU, MARION W.

2. PATIENT'S SOCIAL SECURITY NUMBER: 742-11-0491

3. PATIENT'S ADDRESS (Street, City, State, ZIP) (Check if new address): 321 OAK STREET, WOODLAND HILLS, XY 12345

4. TELEPHONE NUMBER (include area code): (013) 492-7800

5A. CHAMPVA IDENTIFICATION CARD/AUTHORIZATION NUMBER: 49-467-081C

5B. EFFECTIVE DATE			5C. EXPIRATION DATE		
MONTH	DAY	YEAR	MONTH	DAY	YEAR
09	01	9X	12	19	9X

6. PATIENT'S DATE OF BIRTH (Month, day, year): 12-01-77

7. PATIENT'S RELATIONSHIP TO SPONSOR (Check one): ☒ SPOUSE ☐ CHILD

8. PATIENT'S SEX (Check one): ☐ MALE ☒ FEMALE

PART II - SPONSOR INFORMATION (To be completed by the beneficiary, patient or sponsor)

9. SPONSOR'S NAME (Last, first, middle initial): CHIEU, FRANK T.

10. VA CLAIM/FILE NUMBER: 421-05-0129

11. SPONSOR'S ADDRESS IF DIFFERENT FROM PATIENT'S (Street, City, State, ZIP)

PART III - PATIENT INSURANCE INFORMATION (To be completed by the beneficiary, patient or sponsor)

12A. IS PATIENT'S TREATMENT COVERED BY OTHER HEALTH INSURANCE
☐ YES ☒ NO IF YES, PLEASE COMPLETE ITEMS 12B THROUGH 12G BELOW

12B. TYPE OF COVERAGE
☐ GROUP HEALTH ☐ PRIVATE (NON-GROUP)
☐ MEDICARE ☐ CHAMPVA SUPPLEMENTAL
☐ MEDICAID ☐ WORKERS COMPENSATION
☐ OTHER ☐ NONE

12C. NAME AND ADDRESS OF INSURANCE CARRIER

12D. IF COVERAGE IS THROUGH WORK, NAME AND ADDRESS OF EMPLOYER

12E. POLICY IDENTIFICATION NUMBER

12F. INSURANCE AGENT'S NAME

12G. AGENT'S TELEPHONE NUMBER ( )

PART IV - TREATMENT INFORMATION (To be completed by the beneficiary, patient or sponsor)

13. TYPE OF CLAIM (Check one)
☐ INPATIENT ☐ DENTAL
☒ OUTPATIENT ☐ DME
☐ PHARMACY ☐ OTHER
☐ TRAVEL

14. WAS NEED OF TREATMENT DUE TO A PHYSICAL INJURY? ☐ YES ☒ NO
(If "Yes", briefly describe injuries and give a statement of circumstances)

15. I authorize the identified provider of service to disclose to CHAMPVA medical record information that pertains to the medical services described on this form. Unless limitations are shown below, this consent pertains to all of my medical records, including records related to treatment for medical or dental conditions, psychological or psychiatric impairments, drug or alcohol abuse, acquired immune deficiency syndrome (AIDS) or infection with the human immunodeficiency virus (HIV), and sickle cell disease.
The information will be used to process my CHAMPVA claim and determine my (or the patient identified above) eligibility for medical benefits. I also authorize the release of or obtaining of medical and/or other coverage information to and from another organization with which I have other medical benefits plan or health insurance coverage. I understand that I may revoke this authorization at any time, except to the extent that action has already been taken to comply with it. Without my express revocation, this consent will automatically expire: (1) upon satisfaction of the need for disclosure; (2) on February 2, 199x (date supplied by the beneficiary); or (3) under the following condition(s):

LIMITATIONS:

16. I assign payment to the provider(s) of these claimed services ☒ YES ☐ NO

17. I CERTIFY THAT THE ABOVE STATEMENTS AND ATTACHMENTS ARE CORRECT AND REPRESENT ACTUAL SERVICES, DATES AND FEES CHARGED TO ME OR MY ELIGIBLE DEPENDENTS.

17A. CLAIMANT'S SIGNATURE	17B. DATE	17C. RELATIONSHIP TO SPONSOR
	2-2-9X	WIFE

VA FORM 10-7959A
DEC 1990

Pg I

FIGURE 13-8
Example of a completed CHAMPVA Claim Form VA Form 10-7959A, used when billing for professional services.

PATIENT'S NAME (Last, first, middle initial)	SPONSOR'S NAME (Last, first, middle initial)
CHIEU, MARION W.	CHIEU, FRANK T.

PART V - PHYSICIAN/OTHER PROVIDER (To be completed by physician or other provider)

18. PROVIDER'S NAME	19. PROVIDER'S TAX I.D. NUMBER	20. NAME OF REFERRING PHYSICIAN OR OTHER SOURCE (e.g. public health agency)
DOE, JOHN M.D.	93-4267890	

21. WHEN SERVICES ARE RELATED TO A PERIOD OF HOSPITALIZATION, GIVE DATES — ADMITTED / DISCHARGED

22. NAME AND ADDRESS OF FACILITY WHERE SERVICES RENDERED (if other than home office)

23. DIAGNOSIS OR NATURE OF ILLNESS OR INJURY. RELATE DIAGNOSIS TO PROCEDURE BY USING PROCEDURE NUMBER IN COLUMN 24E BELOW

A. Dysfunctional uterine bleeding.

B.

C.

24A DATE OF SERVICE	24B * PLACE OF SERVICE	24C PROCEDURE CODE	24D DESCRIBE UNUSUAL SERVICE OR CIRCUMSTANCES	24E DIAGNOSIS CODE	24F CHARGES	24G DAYS OR UNITS	24H TYPE OF SERVICE
02-02-9X	0	99213	Ofc visit Eval & Mgmt Level 3	626.8	45 00		1

25. I certify that the statements on the reverse apply to this bill and are made a part hereto.

SIGNATURE OF PROVIDER — DATE 02-02-9X

26. PROVIDER'S SOCIAL SECURITY NO 272-49-5731

27. TOTAL CHARGES 45.00

28. PROVIDER'S ADDRESS, ZIP CODE AND TELEPHONE NUMBER
123 MAIN STREET, WOODLAND HILLS, XY 12345 013/486-9002

* PLACE OF SERVICE CODE FOR ITEM 24B

IN -INPATIENT HOSPITAL
OH -OUTPATIENT HOSPITAL
O -DOCTOR'S OFFICE
H -PATIENT'S HOME
DCF -DAY CARE FACILITY (PSY)
NCF -NIGHT CARE FACILITY (PSY)
NH -NURSING HOME
SNF -SKILLED NURSING FACILITY
AMB -AMBULANCE
OL -OTHER LOCATIONS
IL -INDEPENDENT LABORATORY
OF -OTHER MEDICAL/SURGICAL FACILITY
RTC -RESIDENTIAL TREATMENT CENTER
STF -SPECIALIZED TREATMENT FACILITY

PART VI - PHARMACY INFORMATION (To be completed by pharmacist) — PATIENT'S NAME

29A. NATIONAL DRUG CODE	29B. RX NUMBER	29C. PHARMACY NAME	29D. FILL DATE (Month, day, year)	29E. PHYSICIAN NAME	29F. CHARGES

30. TOTAL CHARGES —$

VA FORM 10-7959A
DEC 1990 reference initials

Pg II

FIGURE 13-8 *Continued*

Item 12E: Enter the policy identification number of the other health insurance carrier.

Item 12F: Enter the insurance agent's name. If this information is not known, enter "Unknown."

Item 12G: Enter the insurance agent's telephone number. If this information is not known, enter "Unknown."

Item 13: Check the appropriate box according to the type of medical care the patient received.

- Inpatient. For admission to a civilian hospital, check the Inpatient box.
- Outpatient. All eligible CHAMPVA beneficiaries will be provided medical care from civilian facilities unless otherwise authorized by the VA. Check the Outpatient box.
- Pharmacy. Only for claims for payment of drugs and medicines requiring a prescription by law. Check the Pharmacy box.
- Travel. Only for claims for ambulance travel to, from, or between hospitals to Inpatient care. Check Travel box.
- Dental. Dental care for which the patient has an approved preauthorization. Check the Dental box.
- DME. Only for claims for payment for durable medical equipment costing more than $100. Check the DME box.
- College Infirmary. Check the Other box.
- Other Inpatient Care. Check the Inpatient box for admissions to an approved nursing facility (including a Christian Science sanatorium).

Item 14: If the patient needs treatment for any kind of an injury (broken toe, sprained knee, lacerated forehead, back injury, etc.), check "YES" and briefly describe the injury and circumstances of how the patient was injured.

Item 15: Be sure to read the information contained in this item and complete the blanks, if appropriate.

Item 16: CHAMPVA is a benefit program. As such the patient (or sponsor) MUST assign their benefit to the provider of care if they wish the payment to be made to the provider. Otherwise, payment will be made to the patient.

Item 17: Every CHAMPVA claim must be signed by the patient 18 years of age or older. If the beneficiary is unable to sign on his or her own behalf, the sponsor (or other parent) may sign. In the absence of either parent, a guardian or fiduciary may sign. (*Note:* For privacy reasons, a patient under 18 years of age may sign his or her own claim form.) The claimant's relationship to sponsor is also required.

Part V: To be completed by physician or other provider

Top of page II: Enter patient and sponsor's last name, first name, and middle initial.

Item 18: Enter provider's (physician's) name.

Item 19: Enter provider's tax identification number.

Item 20: Enter the name of the referring physician.

Item 21: If patient is hospitalized, enter the admission and discharge dates.

Item 22: Enter the name and address of the facility where services were rendered if other than home or office.

Item 23: Enter diagnosis or nature of illness or injury.

Item 24A: Enter the date of service.

Item 24B: Enter the place of service using one of the codes shown midway down on this page of the form.

Item 24C: Enter the CPT procedure code number with modifier.

Item 24D: Insert a description of the service.

Item 24E: Enter the ICD-9-CM diagnostic code number for each diagnosis as described in Item 23.

Item 24F: Enter the fee for each service, procedure, or test.

Item 24G: Enter the number of days or units. This block is commonly used for multiple visits, number of miles, units of supplies including drugs, anesthesia minutes, or oxygen volume.

Item 24H: Enter the type of service code from the following list:

1 Medical care
2 Surgery
3 Consultation
4 Diagnostic x-ray
5 Diagnostic laboratory dialysis
6 Radiation therapy
7 Anesthesia
8 Assistance at surgery
9 Other medical service
0 Blood or packed red cells
A Used DME
F Ambulatory surgical center
H Hospice
L Renal supply in home
M Alternate payment for maintenance
N Kidney donor

V Pneumococcal vaccine
Y Second opinion on elective surgery
Z Third opinion on elective surgery

Item 25: Show the signature of the physician, or her or his representative, and the date the form was signed.
Item 26: Enter the provider's Social Security number.
Item 27: Total the charges.
Item 28: Enter the provider's street address, city, state, ZIP code, and telephone number, including area code.
Items 29A through 30 may be completed if the patient is receiving prescription drugs.

SUMMARY PAYMENT VOUCHER

For each CHAMPUS claim, the claims processor issues a Summary Payment Voucher (Fig. 13–9). When the provider participates (accepts assignment), the voucher is sent to him or her. The patient always receives a copy of the voucher, even if the provider receives payment directly from the fiscal intermediary. The voucher details the payment of the claim.

CHAMPUS/CHAMPVA AND OTHER INSURANCE

By law, CHAMPUS/CHAMPVA is usually second payer when a beneficiary is enrolled in other health insurance (OHI) or belongs to a health maintenance organization (HMO) or preferred provider organization (PPO). However, there are two exceptions, and they are

- When a plan is administered under Title XIX of the Social Security Act (Medicaid)
- When coverage is specifically designed to supplement CHAMPUS benefits (Medigap health plan)

CLAIM SUBMISSION

When the patient is submitting his or her own claim to the other insurance carrier, the procedure is as follows:

1. Bill the other insurance carrier with the form it has supplied.
2. After receiving payment and an explanation of benefits (EOB) from the other insurance company, bill CHAMPUS or CHAMPVA by completing the top section of the HCFA-1500. See Chapter 6, Figures 6–8 and 6–10, for an example of a completed CHAMPUS case with other insurance on the HCFA-1500 claim form and an explanation of benefits. Attach the physician's itemized statement, which must contain the following:
   a. Provider's name
   b. Date the services/supplies were provided
   c. Description of each service/supply
   d. Place of treatment
   e. Number/frequency of each service
   f. Fee for each item of service or supply
   g. Procedure code numbers
   h. Diagnostic code number or description of condition for which treatment is being received

   Not acceptable as itemized statements are billing statements showing only total charges, canceled checks, or cash register receipts (or similar type receipts).
3. Attach a photocopy of the EOB from the other insurance company.
4. Send the CHAMPUS or CHAMPVA claim to the local claims processor (fiscal intermediary).

DUAL OR DOUBLE COVERAGE

If a double coverage plan provides, or may provide, benefits for the services, a claim must be filed. Refusal by the beneficiary to claim benefits from other health insurance coverages will result in a denial of CHAMPUS benefits. In double coverage situations, CHAMPUS will pay the lower of:

- The amount of CHAMPUS allowable charges remaining after the double coverage plan has paid its benefits; or
- The amount CHAMPUS would have paid as primary payer.

So that there is no duplication of benefits paid between the double coverage plan and CHAMPUS, there must be coordination of benefits.

MEDICAID OR MEDIGAP

File CHAMPUS or CHAMPVA claims first if the beneficiary has Medigap supplemental health insurance or is a recipient of the Medicaid program.

CHAMPUS AND MEDICARE

CHAMPUS is considered secondary to Medicare for persons under age 65 who have Medicare Part

CHAMPUS/CHAMPVA SUMMARY PAYMENT VOUCHER

Blue Cross and Blue Shield of South Carolina
CHAMPUS/CHAMPVA Fiscal Intermediary

PAGE 1 8904

Provider Number	Check Number	Date of Voucher
	00115384	10/27/86

SERVICE CODES		
PLACE OF TREATMENT	TYPE OF SERVICE	
1 - INPATIENT HOSPITAL 2 - OUTPATIENT HOSPITAL 3 - PHYSICIAN'S OFFICE 4 - PATIENT'S HOME 5 - DAY CARE FACILITY 6 - NIGHT CARE FACILITY 7 - NURSING HOME 8 - SKILLED NURSING FACILITY 9 - AMBULANCE O - OTHER A - INDEPENDENT LABORATORY C - RESIDENTIAL TREATMENT CENTER D - SPECIALIZED TREATMENT FACILITY H - HOME HEALTH AGENCY P - PHARMACY	1 - BLOOD 2 - SURGERY 3 - MATERNITY 4 - ANESTHESIA 5 - X-RAY 6 - MEDICAL CARE 7 - DENTAL 8 - LAB PATHOLOGY 9 - CONSULTATION O - ASSISTANT @ SURGERY A - MEDICAL EMERGENCY B - CONCURRENT CARE C - PSYCHIATRIC D - PHYSICAL THERAPY	E - THERAPEUTIC X-RAY F - AMBULANCE G - EQUIPMENT PURCHASE H - EQUIPMENT RENTAL K - DRUGS L - NURSING P - PROFESSIONAL COMPONENT S - HOSPITAL CHARGES T - RADIOIMMUNOASSAY U - ORTHODONTIC W - SECOND OPINION SURGERY X - OTHER Y - DENTAL ACCIDENT

WOODLAND HILLS FAMILY PRACTICE
1234 MAIN STREET
WOODLAND HILLS XY 12345-0001

"Appeals must be filed within ninety (90) days of the receipt of this notice. See reverse."

Patient Account Number	Patient's Name/ Sponsor's Social Security Number or VA File Number	Admission or From Date	Discharge or Thru Date	No. of Ser.	Service Codes Type	Service Codes Place	Total Charges	Reason Codes	Allowed/ Covered Charges	Deduct-ible	Procedure Code CPT-4 / Cost Share	CHAMPUS/ CHAMPVA Payment
UNAVAILABLE	SMITH, MARY JO	09249x	09249x	001	6	1	138.00	P7001	110.00	.00	99433	110.00
UNAVAILABLE		09279x	09279x	001	6	3	30.00		30.00	.00	99391	24.00
	305827596 /005 62861156	1-00-00	CLAIM TOTALS	*****			168.00		140.00	.00	6.00	134.00

Total Charges	Total Other Carrier	Total Non-Covered Charges	Total Allowed/ Covered Charges	Total Previous Paid	Total Deductible	Total Cost Share	Total CHAMPUS/ CHAMPVA Payment
168.00	.00	28.00	140.00	.00	.00	6.00	134.00

Remarks:

P7001 CHARGES ARE MORE THAN ALLOWABLE AMOUNT.
*** NOTE NEW CHAMPUS CLAIM FILING ADDRESS ***
P.O. BOX 100502
FLORENCE, S.C. 29501-0502

FIGURE 13–9
Sample of a CHAMPUS Summary Payment Voucher.

A as a result of a disability and who have enrolled in Medicare Part B. Those eligible for Medicare Part A are *not* covered by CHAMPUS unless disabled. Claims should be submitted to Medicare, then to CHAMPUS with a copy of the Medicare RA. Services covered by CHAMPUS but not covered by Medicare, i.e., prescription medications, will be paid by CHAMPUS. Participating providers may obtain a CHAMPUS fee schedule by contacting their fiscal intermediary.

CHAMPVA AND MEDICARE

Effective December 5, 1991, CHAMPVA became secondary payer to Medicare for persons under age 65 who are enrolled in Medicare Parts A and B and who are otherwise eligible for CHAMPVA. Because CHAMPVA is secondary payer, claims must first be submitted to Medicare.

THIRD PARTY LIABILITY

If the patient is in an automobile accident or receives an injury that may have third-party involvement, the following two options are available for reimbursement:

Option 1 ▪ CHAMPUS Form DD 2527 (Statement of Personal Injury—Possible Third-Party Liability) must be sent in with the regular claim form for cost-sharing of the civilian medical care (Fig. 13–10). All five sections of the form should be completed by the patient. This form allows CHAMPUS to evaluate the circumstances of the accident and the possibility that the government may recover money for the medical care from the person who injured the patient. If an HCFA-1500 claim form is submitted without CHAMPUS Form DD 2527, a request will be made to complete it. This form must be returned within 35 days of the request, or the claims processor will deny the original and all related claims. Then the fiscal intermediary submits a claim to the third party for reimbursement or files a lien for reimbursement with the liability insurance carrier, the liable party, or the attorneys or court involved.

Option 2 ▪ The provider can submit claims exclusively to the third party liability carrier for reimbursement.

Claims submitted with ICD-9-CM diagnostic codes between 800 and 999 (Injury and Poisoning) trigger the fact that there might be third party litigation, and the claims processor may request the completion of DD Form 2527.

WORKERS' COMPENSATION

If a CHAMPUS or CHAMPVA beneficiary is injured on the job or becomes ill because of his or her work, this becomes a workers' compensation case, and the claim must be filed with the compensation insurance carrier. When all workers' compensation benefits have been exhausted, then CHAMPUS or CHAMPVA can be billed. In some cases, it can happen that the case is in the state of determining whether it is a work-related accident or illness and the claim might be sent to the CHAMPUS or CHAMPVA claims processor. In those instances, the claims processor files a lien with the workers' compensation carrier for recovery when the case is settled.

CLAIMS INQUIRIES AND APPEALS

See Chapter 8 for following up on delinquent claims.

ADDITIONAL INFORMATION

The CHAMPUS program is administered by the Office for the Civilian Health and Medical Program of the Uniformed Services (OCHAMPUS), which is located in Aurora, CO 80045-6900, but claims are not processed in Colorado. See Appendix A for the address of the claims processor for your state. Write to OCHAMPUS for additional information, *CHAMPUS Handbook*, booklets, bulletins, and pamphlets.

CHAMPUS/TRICARE Managed Care Programs

To control escalating medical costs and to standardize benefits for active-duty families, military retirees, and their dependents, CHAMPUS offers managed health care programs to 12 organized regions in the continental United States and Hawaii, with a total phase-in by 1998. Alaska and Europe will be considered separately. If a CHAMPUS/TRICARE program has begun in your area, telephone the contractor managing the plan for their guidelines, forms, bulletins, and booklets. Only CHAMPUS-eligible persons may enroll in the TRICARE managed care programs, and TRICARE must be in operation where the enrollee lives. Those under the Medicare or CHAMPVA programs are *not* eligible. Active-duty service members are enrolled automatically in TRICARE Prime and may be able to use local military providers and, when directed, the civilian portion of the TRICARE network. Individuals eligible for CHAMPUS/TRICARE benefits will find three options from which to choose: TRICARE Prime (HMO), TRICARE Extra (PPO), and TRI-

Text continued on page 321

STATEMENT OF PERSONAL INJURY - POSSIBLE THIRD PARTY LIABILITY CHAMPUS / CHAMPVA

SECTION I - GENERAL INFORMATION

1. SPONSOR

a. SPONSOR'S NAME *(Last, First, Middle Initial)*

b. SSN

c. GRADE / RANK

d. SPONSOR'S STATUS *(X one)*
☐ ACTIVE DUTY ☐ RETIRED ☐ VA ☐ DECEASED

e. BRANCH OF SERVICE *(X one)*
☐ USMC ☐ USA ☐ USN ☐ USAF ☐ USCG ☐ USPHS ☐ NOAA

f. MILITARY ADDRESS *(Active Duty Only)*

g. HOME ADDRESS *(Street, City, State, ZIP Code)*

TELEPHONE NO. *(Include Area Code)*

2. INJURED BENEFICIARY

a. INJURED BENEFICIARY'S NAME *(Last, First, Middle Initial)*

b. AGE

c. RELATIONSHIP TO SPONSOR *(X one)*
☐ FORMER SPOUSE ☐ NATURAL/ ADOPTED CHILD ☐ SELF ☐ SPOUSE ☐ STEPCHILD ☐ OTHER

d. HOME ADDRESS *(Street, City, State, ZIP Code)*

TELEPHONE NO. *(Include Area Code)*

e. NATURE OF INJURIES

SECTION II - REMARKS

Use this section to describe in your own words how you were injured.

DD Form 2527, NOV 91

Page 1 of 5 Pages

FIGURE 13-10
CHAMPUS Form DD 2527, Statement of Personal Injury—Possible Third Party Liability.

SECTION III - NON-VEHICULAR ACCIDENTS

Complete if injuries did not result from a motor vehicle accident. If injuries resulted from a vehicular accident, go to Section IV.

3. LOCATION

a. SITE OF INJURY *(Street/Place, City, County, State)*	b. TIME *(Hour)* ☐ A.M. ☐ P.M.	c. DATE *(YYMMDD)*
d. NAME AND ADDRESS OF OWNER OF PROPERTY WHERE INJURY OCCURRED	e. NAME OF OCCUPANT OF PROPERTY *(If different from Owner)*	

4. PERSONS INVOLVED

a. NAME *(Last, First, Middle Initial)*	b. ADDRESS *(Street, City, State, ZIP Code)* AND TELEPHONE NO. *(Include Area Code)*

5. WITNESSES

a. NAME *(Last, First, Middle Initial)*	b. ADDRESS *(Street, City, State, ZIP Code)* AND TELEPHONE NO. *(Include Area Code)*

6. POLICE INVESTIGATION

a. WAS AN INVESTIGATION CONDUCTED? *(If Yes, state by whom (e.g.,City/ State Police, Sheriff's Dept.)* ☐ YES ☐ NO	b. WAS ANYONE ARRESTED OR CITED AS CAUSING THE ACCIDENT? *(If Yes, give name and charge)* ☐ YES ☐ NO	c. DISPOSITION OF CASE *(e.g., Dismissal, Fine, Jail Sentence)*

d. EXPLAIN IN YOUR OWN WORDS WHO WAS AT FAULT AND WHY

e. WERE OTHER FAMILY MEMBERS INJURED IN THE ACCIDENT? *(If Yes, give name(s) and relationship)* ☐ YES ☐ NO	f. WAS THE ACCIDENT WORK RELATED? *(If Yes, state circumstances)* ☐ YES ☐ NO

7. INSURANCE

a. INSURANCE COMPANY OF OWNER OF PROPERTY WHERE INJURY OCCURRED *(e.g., Homeowner's Insurance Company)*	b. INSURANCE COMPANY OF PERSON WHO CAUSED ACCIDENT *(If different from Item a.)*	c. YOUR OWN INSURANCE COMPANY
(1) COMPANY NAME	(1) COMPANY NAME	(1) COMPANY NAME
(2) ADDRESS *(Include ZIP Code)*	(2) ADDRESS *(Include ZIP Code)*	(2) ADDRESS *(Include ZIP Code)*
(3) POLICY NO.	(3) POLICY NO.	(3) POLICY NO.
(4) AMOUNTS AND TYPES OF COVERAGE	(4) AMOUNTS AND TYPES OF COVERAGE	(4) AMOUNTS AND TYPES OF COVERAGE

SECTION IV - VEHICULAR ACCIDENT

A copy of an official police report may be substituted for Items 8 through 15 of this section.

8. LOCATION

a. SITE OF ACCIDENT *(Street/Place, City, County, State)*	b. TIME *(Hour)* ☐ A.M. ☐ P.M.	c. DATE

9. DIAGRAM *(Diagram the accident - indicate traffic signs, regulators, direction of travel, street names, traffic lane markings, etc.)*

DD Form 2527, NOV 91 Page 2 of 5 Pages

FIGURE 13-10 *Continued*

10. PASSENGERS IN YOUR VEHICLE *(Vehicle 1)*					
a. NAME *(Last, First, Middle Initial)*	b. ADDRESS *(Street, City, State, ZIP Code)* AND TELEPHONE NO. *(Include Area Code)*	c. INJURED *(X one)*		d. *(X one)*	
		YES	NO	CIVILIAN	MILITARY

11. WITNESSES *(Other than persons involved)*	
a. NAME *(Last, First, Middle Initial)*	b. ADDRESS *(Street, City, State, ZIP Code)* AND TELEPHONE NO. *(Include Area Code)*

12. POLICE INVESTIGATION	
a. WHAT POLICE AGENCY INVESTIGATED THE ACCIDENT? *(e.g., State/City Police, Sheriff's Dept.)*	b. TRAFFIC VIOLATIONS FOR WHICH TICKETS WERE ISSUED, AND TO WHOM ISSUED

13. ACCIDENT CONDITIONS

a. ROAD CONDITIONS *(X one)*	b. TRAFFIC CONDITIONS *(X one)*	c. WEATHER CONDITIONS *(X one)*
☐ PAVED ☐ GRAVEL ☐ DIRT ☐ DRY ☐ WET ☐ ICY ☐ NARROW ☐ WINDING ☐ SNOW COVERED ☐ OTHER *(Explain)*	☐ NORMAL ☐ LIGHT ☐ HEAVY ☐ CONGESTED ☐ OTHER *(Explain)*	☐ CLEAR ☐ FOGGY ☐ RAINING ☐ SNOWING ☐ OTHER *(Explain)*

14. TRAFFIC REGULATIONS

a. POSTED REGULATIONS *(X one)*	b. SIGNALS GIVEN BY VEHICLES INVOLVED *(X one)*		c. SPEED OF VEHICLES *(X one)*
DESCRIBE EXISTING REGULATIONS AT SCENE OF ACCIDENT	(1) DRIVER OF YOUR VEHICLE	(2) DRIVER(S) OF OTHER VEHICLE(S)	(1) YOUR VEHICLE
☐ STOP SIGN ☐ TRAFFIC LIGHT ☐ YIELD SIGN ☐ SCHOOL CROSSING ☐ NO PASSING ☐ RAILROAD CROSSING ☐ OTHER *(Specify)*	☐ HORN ☐ TURN SIGNALS ☐ BRAKE LIGHTS ☐ OTHER *(Specify)*	☐ HORN ☐ TURN SIGNALS ☐ BRAKE LIGHTS ☐ OTHER *(Specify)*	MILES PER HOUR YOU WERE TRAVELING LAWFUL POSTED MPH (2) DRIVER(S) OF OTHER VEHICLE(S) ESTIMATED MPH TRAVELING LAWFUL POSTED MPH

15. CONDITION OF DRIVERS

a. GIVE YOUR OPINION AS TO IMPAIRMENT OF DRIVING ABILITY OF ALL DRIVERS *(e.g., Sleepiness, Inexperience, etc.)*		b. WAS ANYONE DRIVING UNDER THE INFLUENCE OF ALCOHOL OR DRUGS? *(X one)*	
(1) DRIVER OF VEHICLE YOU WERE IN	(2) DRIVER(S) OF OTHER VEHICLE(S)	(1) DRIVER OF VEHICLE YOU WERE IN	(2) DRIVER(S) OF OTHER VEHICLE(S)
		☐ INTOXICATED ☐ UNDER INFLUENCE BUT NOT INTOXICATED ☐ NOT UNDER INFLUENCE	☐ INTOXICATED ☐ UNDER INFLUENCE BUT NOT INTOXICATED ☐ NOT UNDER INFLUENCE

DD Form 2527, NOV 91

Page 3 of 5 Pages

FIGURE 13–10 *Continued*

16. VEHICLE 1 *(Vehicle in which you were riding)*

a. VEHICLE	(1) YEAR OF VEHICLE	(2) MAKE AND MODEL OF VEHICLE	(3) VEHICLE LICENSE NO. AND STATE

b. DRIVER		c. OWNER *(Complete these blocks ONLY if different from driver of vehicle)*	
(1) DRIVER'S NAME AND DRIVER'S LICENSE NUMBER *(Include State)*		(1) OWNER'S NAME	
(2) DRIVER'S ADDRESS *(Include ZIP Code)* AND TELEPHONE NO. *(Include Area Code)*		(2) OWNER'S ADDRESS *(Include ZIP Code)* AND TELEPHONE NO. *(Include Area Code)*	
(3) DRIVER'S INSURANCE COMPANY		(3) OWNER'S INSURANCE COMPANY	
(4) INSURANCE COMPANY ADDRESS *(Include ZIP Code)*		(4) OWNER'S INSURANCE COMPANY ADDRESS *(Include ZIP Code)*	
(5) INSURANCE COMPANY TELEPHONE NO. *(Include Area Code)*	(6) POLICY NO.	(5) INSURANCE COMPANY TELEPHONE NO. *(Include Area Code)*	(6) POLICY NO.

17. VEHICLE 2 *(If more vehicles were involved, use additional sheets to list applicable information)*

a. VEHICLE	(1) YEAR OF VEHICLE	(2) MAKE AND MODEL OF VEHICLE	(3) VEHICLE LICENSE NO. AND STATE

b. DRIVER		c. OWNER *(Complete these blocks ONLY if different from driver of vehicle)*	
(1) DRIVER'S NAME AND DRIVER'S LICENSE NUMBER *(Include State)*		(1) OWNER'S NAME	
(2) DRIVER'S ADDRESS *(Include ZIP Code)* AND TELEPHONE NO. *(Include Area Code)*		(2) OWNER'S ADDRESS *(Include ZIP Code)* AND TELEPHONE NO. *(Include Area Code)*	
(3) DRIVER'S INSURANCE COMPANY		(3) OWNER'S INSURANCE COMPANY	
(4) INSURANCE COMPANY ADDRESS *(Include ZIP Code)*		(4) OWNER'S INSURANCE COMPANY ADDRESS *(Include ZIP Code)*	
(5) INSURANCE COMPANY TELEPHONE NO. *(Include Area Code)*	(6) POLICY NO.	(5) INSURANCE COMPANY TELEPHONE NO. *(Include Area Code)*	(6) POLICY NO.

18. MISCELLANEOUS

a. INJURED BENEFICIARY'S AUTOMOBILE INSURANCE COMPANY	b. INSURANCE COMPANY'S ADDRESS *(Include ZIP Code)*
c. INSURANCE COMPANY TELEPHONE NO. *(Include Area Code)*	

d. POLICY NO.	e. AMOUNTS AND TYPE OF COVERAGE			
	(1) LIABILITY $	(2) MEDICAL PAYMENT $	(3) UNINSURED MOTORIST $	(4) NO FAULT $

f. WAS ACCIDENT REPORTED TO YOUR INSURANCE COMPANY? *(If No, explain)*	g. HAS YOUR INSURANCE CO. ASSIGNED A CLAIM OR FILE NUMBER? *(If Yes, provide number)*	h. WAS ACCIDENT WORK RELATED? *(If Yes, state circumstances)*
☐ YES ☐ NO	☐ YES ☐ NO	☐ YES ☐ NO

SECTION V - MEDICAL TREATMENT

19. AMBULANCE SERVICE

a. WAS AN AMBULANCE USED TO TRANSPORT INJURED PARTY? *(If Yes, complete 19.b. and c.)*	b. NAME OF AMBULANCE SERVICE	c. ADDRESS OF AMBULANCE SERVICE *(Include ZIP Code)*
☐ YES ☐ NO		

20. CIVILIAN HOSPITALIZATION

a. IF YOU WERE HOSPITALIZED IN A CIVILIAN HOSPITAL OR EXPECT TO BE HOSPITALIZED, COMPLETE THE FOLLOWING:

(1) NAME OF HOSPITAL	(2) ADDRESS *(Include ZIP Code)*	(3) DATES HOSPITALIZED FROM	TO	(4) IS TREATMENT COMPLETED? *(X one)* YES	NO

DD Form 2527, NOV 91

Page 4 of 5 Pages

FIGURE 13-10 *Continued*

13

b. IF YOU HAVE SEEN CIVILIAN DOCTORS / DENTISTS IN CONNECTION WITH THE ACCIDENT, COMPLETE THE FOLLOWING:

(1) NAME OF DOCTOR / DENTIST	(2) ADDRESS *(Include ZIP Code)*	(3) IS TREATMENT COMPLETED? *(X one)* YES	NO

c. IF YOU HAVE INCURRED / RECEIVED MEDICAL BILLS FROM THIS ACCIDENT, COMPLETE THE FOLLOWING:

(1) NAME OF DOCTOR / DENTIST / HOSPITAL / AMBULANCE	(2) AMOUNT ($)	(3) PAYMENT OF THESE BILLS WILL BE MADE BY *(e.g., Insurance Company, CHAMPUS, Other)*

21. GOVERNMENT HOSPITALIZATION

a. IF YOU WERE HOSPITALIZED OR EXPECT TO BE HOSPITALIZED IN A GOVERNMENT HOSPITAL, COMPLETE THE FOLLOWING:

(1) NAME OF HOSPITAL	(2) ADDRESS *(Include ZIP Code)*	(3) DATES HOSPITALIZED FROM	TO	(4) IS TREATMENT COMPLETED? *(X one)* YES	NO

22. MISCELLANEOUS

a. WHEN DO YOU EXPECT TREATMENT TO BE COMPLETED?

b. DID YOU RECEIVE PHYSICAL THERAPY TREATMENT? *(If Yes, explain)*

☐ YES
☐ NO

c. IF THE INJURY LED TO DISCHARGE OR RETIREMENT, WHAT AMOUNT OF SEVERANCE PAY OR PENSION DID YOU RECEIVE FROM THE UNITED STATES?

(1) AMOUNT
$

(2) TYPE *(Pension, etc.)*

SECTION VI - MISCELLANEOUS

23. YOUR ATTORNEY

a. ATTORNEY'S NAME

b. ADDRESS *(Street, City, State, ZIP Code)*

c. TELEPHONE NO. *(Include Area Code)*

24. RELEASE / STATEMENTS

a. HAVE YOU FURNISHED ANYONE OTHER THAN THE POLICE A STATEMENT AS TO WHAT HAPPENED? *(If Yes, to whom was it given?)*

☐ YES
☐ NO

b. HAVE YOU SIGNED ANY RELEASE OR WAIVER OF RIGHTS? *(If Yes, to whom was it given?)*

☐ YES
☐ NO

c. HAVE YOU RECEIVED ANY OFFER OF SETTLEMENT FOR YOUR INJURY? *(If Yes, from whom?)*

☐ YES
☐ NO

d. HAVE YOU ACCEPTED ANY SETTLEMENT? *(If Yes, from whom and how much?)*

☐ YES
☐ NO

25. CERTIFICATION

I have completed this form and state that the information is true to the best of my knowledge and belief. Federal Laws (18 USC 287 and 1001) provide for criminal *penalties* for knowingly submitting or making any false, fictitious, or fraudulent statement or claim in any matter within the jurisdiction of any department or agency of the United States.

a. YOUR SIGNATURE

b. DATE SIGNED *(YYMMDD)*

DD Form 2527, NOV 91 ☆ U.S. GOVERNMENT PRINTING OFFICE: 1993—775-820 / M 8430 REGION NO. 8 **Page 5 of 5 Pages**

FIGURE 13-10 *Continued*

CARE Standard (the same as standard CHAMPUS). Here is a brief description of the uniform benefit-and-cost structure of each.

TRICARE PRIME

TRICARE Prime is an HMO type of option. Participation in TRICARE Prime is optional. Beneficiaries who are *not* enrolled as members in TRICARE Prime may continue to receive services through TRICARE Extra from network providers or through TRICARE Standard using non-network providers.

BENEFITS

Covered services are like those of standard CHAMPUS, plus additional preventive and primary care services. For example, periodic physical examinations are covered at no charge under TRICARE Prime but are not covered under TRICARE Extra or TRICARE Standard (CHAMPUS). Prime also covers certain immunizations that are not a benefit under Extra or Standard. A dental plan is available for an additional monthly premium.

The CHAMPUS/TRICARE hospice program is based on Medicare's hospice program. It is designed to provide care and comfort to patients who are expected to live less than 6 months if the terminal illness runs its normal course. Those persons who receive care under the hospice program cannot receive other services under the CHAMPUS/TRICARE basic program (treatments aimed at a cure) unless the hospice care has been formally revoked. There are a number of additional rules and limits to the hospice program, so call the health benefits advisor (HBA) at the nearest military medical facility and ask for a copy of the guidelines.

Outpatient or ambulatory surgery must be on the approved procedure list before it is performed. The list is in the CHAMPUS Policy Manual. An NAS may be needed for some types of surgery performed in approved ambulatory surgery centers or hospitals. Call the HBA at the nearest military medical facility to check out the procedure, the approved facility, and the need for an NAS before scheduling the surgery. If no authorization is obtained, a point-of-service (POS) option is available featuring an annual outpatient deductible and 50% cost-share. Patients may need advanced authorization for any nonemergency care received while away from the area in which they are enrolled.

Active-duty service members receive medically necessary outpatient care free, and there is a small daily subsistence fee charged for inpatient care. Permission must be obtained from the military to receive nonemergency care from civilian sources. Active-duty members will not gain any CHAMPUS benefits because of their enrollment in Prime.

ENROLLMENT

To become a TRICARE Prime member, an individual must complete an application and enroll for 1 year at a time. Annual re-enrollment is not required. There is an annual fee per person or per family. Enrollees normally receive care from within the Prime network of civilian and military providers. The beneficiary has the option of choosing or being assigned a primary care manager (PCM) for each family member, who furnishes most of the care and manages all aspects of the patient's health care including referrals to specialists. Active-duty families do not pay an annual enrollment fee, but others will. There are no annual deductibles. Copayments for services are reduced. Once enrolled, the beneficiary may no longer use the TRICARE Standard (CHAMPUS) program. Enrolled beneficiaries may no longer use a military treatment facility (MTF), except in emergencies or for pharmaceuticals, without a specific referral from a health care finder (HCF). The HCF is a medical professional, usually a registered nurse, with extensive medical, surgical, and/or mental health experience. However, the MTF remains the site of preference for all specialty and inpatient care.

IDENTIFICATION CARDS

Individuals who enroll are issued a TRICARE Prime identification card, as shown in Figure 13–11. This card does not guarantee CHAMPUS eligibility, so providers *must* call the local HCF or check the CHAMPUS Uniformed Services identification card for the effective and expiration dates. Always make copies of that card and the TRICARE Prime card and retain them in the patient's file. Remember, for TRICARE Prime patients, check both cards at *every* visit.

PRIMARY CARE MANAGER

The primary care manager (PCM) is a physician who is responsible for coordinating and managing all the beneficiary's health care unless there is an emergency. The PCM may refer the beneficiary for additional services, when necessary, but specific referral and precertification requirements must be

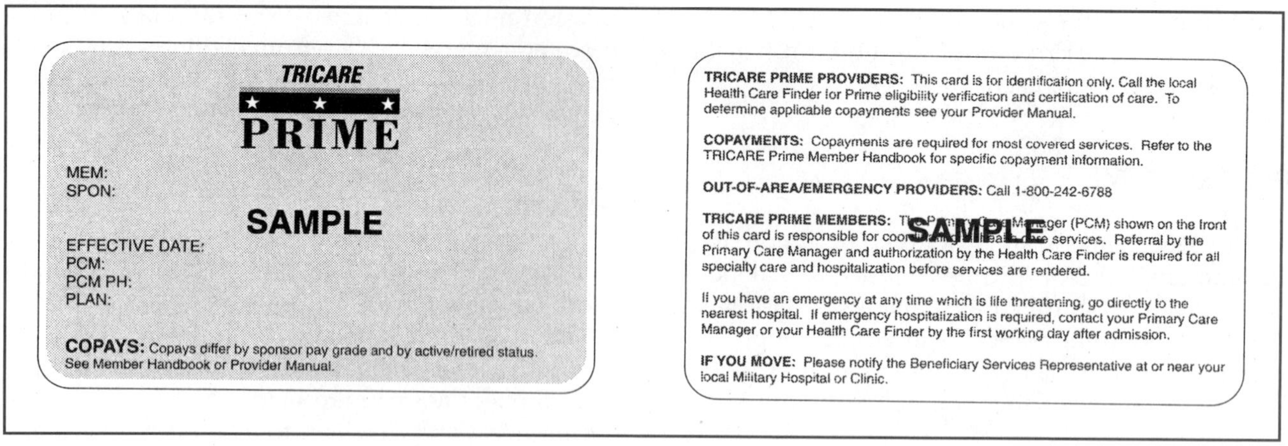

FIGURE 13–11
Sample TRICARE Prime identification card (red, white, and blue in color).

carried out. Referral patterns are evaluated to determine excessive or inappropriate referrals to specialists. A pattern of such referrals could result in termination of participation in TRICARE Prime. Referral authorizations are required when PCMs refer to specialists for consultations and when specialists refer to subspecialists for consultations. The insurance billing specialist should contact the health care finder at the military medical facility and the provider relations representative of the CHAMPUS carrier for a list of services and procedures with associated CPT codes, precertification requirements, and referral forms.

COPAYMENTS

TRICARE Prime copayments should always be collected at the time services are rendered. See Figures 13–12 and 13–13 for further clarification of benefits, deductibles, and copayments.

TRICARE Extra

In this option, the individual does not have to enroll or pay an annual fee. On a visit-by-visit basis, the individual may seek care from a provider who is part of the TRICARE Extra network and receive a discount on services and reduced cost-shares. A nonenrolled beneficiary automatically becomes a TRICARE Extra beneficiary when care is rendered by a network provider. The individual will not have to file any claim forms when using network providers. If a nonenrolled beneficiary receives care from a non-network provider, the services received are covered under TRICARE Standard.

IDENTIFICATION CARD

A TRICARE Extra beneficiary must present the military identification card when receiving care as proof of eligibility. The military identification card will indicate a "Yes" in Box 15B (back of card) if the beneficiary is eligible. Children under 10 years of age may use the sponsor's identification card (attach a copy of the card to the claim). Individuals over age 10 years must have their own identification card. To verify eligibility, contact the local health care finder.

Retirees carry a blue or gray military identification card (see Fig. 13–2).

Active duty and retiree dependents and survivors carry an orange/brown military identification card (see Fig. 13–1).

COPAYMENTS

Beneficiaries using TRICARE Extra receive a reduction in the required amount of copayment. See Figures 13–12 and 13–13 for further clarification of benefits, deductibles, and copayments.

NETWORK PROVIDER

The network provider is the physician who provides medical care to CHAMPUS beneficiaries under the TRICARE Extra program at contracted rates. Referrals from other network providers are coordinated through the HCF. The network provider refers the beneficiary for additional services, when necessary, following precertification requirements and completing a referral form.

Benefits and Coverage Chart

Inpatient Services — **Beneficiary Cost**

SERVICES	TRICARE PRIME	TRICARE EXTRA	TRICARE STANDARD
HOSPITALIZATION ++ Semiprivate room (and when medically necesary, special care units), general nursing, and hospital service. Includes inpatient physician and their surgical services, meals including special diets, drugs and medications while an inpatient, operating and recovery room, anesthesia, laboratory tests, x-rays and other radiology services, necessary medical supplies and appliances, blood and blood products.	+ Active Duty Family Members: No copayment. + Retirees and their Family Members and Survivors: No copayment for professional services. $75 per day to $750 maximum per admission.	+ Active Duty Family Members: No copayment. + Retirees and their Family Members and Survivors: copayment of $250 per day or 25% of plan allowable, whichever is less, plus 20% of separately billed professional charge at Plan allowable rate.	Active Duty Family Members: $25 copayment or $9.70*** per day whichever is higher. + Retirees and their Family Members and Survivors: copayment of $330*** per day or 25% of billed charges, whichever is less, plus 25% of CHAMPUS allowable for separately billed professional charges.
MATERNITY ++ Hospital and professional services (prenatal, postnatal).	↓	↓	
SKILLED NURSING FACILITY CARE Semiprivate room, regular nursing services, meals including special diets, physical, occupational, and speech therapy, drugs furnished by the facility, necessary medical supplies, and appliances.	↓	↓	Active Duty Family Members: $25 copayment or $9.70*** per day, whichever is higher. Retirees and their Family Members and Survivors: 25% of billed charges, plus 25% of CHAMPUS allowable for separately billed professional charges.
HOSPITALIZATION FOR MENTAL ILLNESS ++ 18 and under, 45 days per year. 19 and older, 30 days per year as medically necessary. Up to 150 days for treatment in a Residential Treatment Center. The number of days may be subject to change pending new legislation.	+++ Active Duty Family Members: $20 copayment for civilian hospital. +++ Retirees and their Family Members and Survivors: copayment of $40 per day or 25% of Plan allowable, whichever is less.	+++ Active Duty Family Members: $20 copayment for civilian hospital. +++ Retirees and their Family Members and Survivors: copayment of $40 per day or 25% of Plan allowable, whichever is less, plus 20% of separately billed professional charge at Plan allowable rate.	Active Duty Family Members: $25 copayment or $9.70*** per day, whichever is higher. Retirees and their Family Members and Survivors: 25% of CHAMPUS allowable billed charges, plus 25% of CHAMPUS allowable for separately billed professional charges.
ALCOHOLISM ++ 7 days for detoxification and 21 days for rehabilitation per 365 days. Maximum of one rehabilitation program per year and three per lifetime. Detoxification and rehabilitation days count toward 30-day limit for mental health benefits.			

*** This figure is for Fiscal Year 1996 and is subject to change each October 1 at the beginning of each Fiscal Year.
This is only a summary description of your coverage. Please see the Standard CHAMPUS Handbook and a TRICARE Prime member handbook for more complete description of all terms and conditions. In addition, CHAMPUS regulations and the interpretations under those regulations are the final authority on covered services.

\+ Unlimited, with authorization, as medically necessary.

++ NAS Note: You must obtain a Non-availability Statement if you live within a designated service area around a military hospital. This may be a restricted NAS requiring you to use TRICARE network providers.

+++ With authorization.

For Active Duty Family members, the maximum family liability (Catastrophic Cap Benefit) is $1000 for deductibles and cost-shares based on allowable charges for the Basic Program services and supplies received in a Fiscal Year. For all other beneficiary families, the Fiscal Year cap is $7,500. After a Fiscal Year cap is met, the CHAMPUS-determined allowable amount shall be paid in full for all covered services and supplies under the Basic Program received through the end of that Fiscal Year. In order to get credit for all family expenditures allowed toward the Catastrophic Cap Benefit, the beneficiary may be required to submit appropriate documentation (e.g. CHAMPUS Explanation of Benefits).

FIGURE 13–12
TRICARE Prime, Extra, and Standard Inpatient Services Benefits and Coverage Chart.

REFERRALS AND PRECERTIFICATION

When specialty care or hospitalization is required, the military treatment facility must be used if services are available. If services are not available, the health care finder will assist with the referral or precertification process. All admissions, ambulatory surgical procedures, and other selected procedures require precertification. Referral authorizations are required when primary care managers refer to specialists for consultations and when specialists refer to subspecialists for consultations.

Benefits and Coverage Chart

Outpatient Services **Beneficiary Cost**

SERVICES	TRICARE PRIME*	TRICARE EXTRA**	TRICARE STANDARD**
ANNUAL DEDUCTIBLE ** (Applied to Outpatient Services)	None	$150/person or $300/ Family per fiscal year.***	$150/person or $300/Family per fiscal year.***
PHYSICIAN SERVICES * + Office visits; outpatient office-based medical and surgical care; consultation, diagnosis, and treatment by a specialist; allergy tests and treatment; osteopathic manipulation; medical supplies used within the office including casts, dressings and splints.	$5 copayment per visit.*	Active Duty Family Members: 15% of Plan allowable after deductible has been satisfied. Retirees and their Family Members and Survivors: 20% of Plan allowable after deductible has been satisfied.	Active Duty Family Members: 20% of CHAMPUS allowable after deductible has been satisfied. Retirees and their Family Members and Survivors: 25% of CHAMPUS allowable after deductible has been satisfied.
LABORATORY and X-RAY SERVICES (Including Mammograms.)	$6 copayment. (No copayment if included in the office visit.)	↓	↓
ROUTINE PAP SMEARS Frequency depends on physician recommendations based on the published guidelines of the American Academy of Obstetrics and Gynecology.	$6 copayment per visit. (No copayment if included in the office visit.)	↓	↓
AMBULANCE SERVICES When medically necessary as currently defined and covered by OCHAMPUS.	$10, $15, or $20 copayment per occurrence, depending on pay grade.	↓	↓
EMERGENCY SERVICES Outpatient, both in and out of service area for emergency and urgently needed care.	$10, $20, or $30 copayment, depending on pay grade. $15 copayment for urgent care center use.	↓	↓
DURABLE MEDICAL EQUIPMENT, PROSTHETIC DEVICES, AND MEDICAL SUPPLIES PRESCRIBED BY YOUR PHYSICIAN AND WHEN A CHAMPUS BENEFIT (If dispensed for use outside of the office or after the home visit.)	10%, 15%, or 20%, depending on pay grade.	↓	↓
HOME HEALTH CARE Part-time skilled nursing care, physical, speech and occupational therapy as currently defined by OCHAMPUS (when medically necessary).	$6 or $12 copayment per visit, depending on pay grade.	↓	↓
FAMILY HEALTH SERVICES Family planning and well-baby care (up to 24 months of age). Certain exclusions apply as currently defined by OCHAMPUS.	$6 or $12 copayment per visit, depending on pay grade.	↓	↓
OUTPATIENT MENTAL HEALTH One hour of therapy no more than two times each week (when medically necessary).	$10 copayment for individual visits. $5 copayment for group visits.	↓	↓
Outpatient Medication Management.	$5 copayment per visit.	▼	▼

* No copayment for primary care or preventive services for family members of sponsors with pay grades of E-4 and below (both active duty and retired). The Fiscal Intermediary has the responsibility for defining primary care; some office visits are subject to copayment(s).

** Please note that TRICARE Extra and TRICARE Standard annual deductibles and cost shares are subject to change.

*** Except for families whose Active Duty sponsor's pay grade is E-4 and below, for whom the annual deductible is $50/person or $100/family.

This is only a summary description of your coverage. Please see the Standard CHAMPUS Handbook and a TRICARE Prime Member Handbook for a more complete description of all terms and conditions. In addition, CHAMPUS regulations and interpretations under those regulations are the final authority on covered services.

\+ Certain outpatient procedures require a Nonavailability Statement (NAS). You must obtain an NAS if you live within a designated service area near a military treatment facility if the care is not available at the facility. This may be a restricted NAS requiring you to use TRICARE network providers.

FIGURE 13–13
TRICARE Prime, Extra, and Standard Outpatient Services Benefits and Coverage Chart.

TRICARE PRIME/TRICARE EXTRA NONAVAILABILITY STATEMENTS

If the local military treatment facility cannot provide inpatient care or services for certain nonemergency outpatient procedures, an NAS is required if the beneficiary resides within the designated MTF catchment area. The beneficiary is responsible for obtaining the NAS. The NAS must be obtained before admission or rendering of outpatient service. Emergency admissions do not require an NAS.

Benefits and Coverage Chart

Outpatient Services — **Beneficiary Cost**

SERVICES	TRICARE PRIME*	TRICARE EXTRA**	TRICARE STANDARD**
ANNUAL DEDUCTIBLE** (Applied to Outpatient Services)	None	$150/person or $300/ Family per fiscal year.***	$150/person or $300/Family per fiscal year.***
PARTIAL HOSPITALIZATION FOR ALCOHOLISM TREATMENT Up to 21 days for rehabilitative treatment on a limited hour-per-day basis. Does not count toward the mental health inpatient limit, but does count toward 60-day partial hospitalization limit.	Subject to inpatient mental health copayment.	Subject to inpatient mental health copayment.	Subject to inpatient mental health copayment.
PARTIAL HOSPITALIZATION FOR PSYCHIATRIC TREATMENT Limited to 60 treatment days (whether a full day or partial day program) in a fiscal year or in an admission. Not counted toward the 30/45 day inpatient limit.	Subject to inpatient mental health copayment.	Subject to inpatient mental health copayment.	Subject to inpatient mental health copayment.
PERIODIC PHYSICAL EXAMINATIONS Conducted by Primary Care Manager for ages over 24 months. For well-baby care up to 24 months of age, see "Family Health Services."	Free	Not covered.	Not covered.
PHYSICAL, OCCUPATIONAL, SPEECH AND RADIATION THERAPY	$5 copayment per visit.	Active Duty Family Members: 15% of Plan allowable after deductible has been satisfied. Retirees and their Family Members and Survivors: 20% of Plan allowable after deductible has been satisfied.	Active Duty Family Members: 20% of CHAMPUS allowable after deductible has been satisifed. Retirees and their Family Members and Survivors: 25% of CHAMPUS allowable after deductible has been satisfied.
WELLNESS CLASSES, COMMUNITY HEALTH SERVICES AND COMMUNITY RESOURCE COORDINATION	No charge or minimal cost.	Not covered.	Not covered.

* No copayment for primary care or preventive services for family members of sponsors with pay grades of E-4 and below (both active duty and retired). The Fiscal Intermediary has the responsibility for defining primary care; some of fice visits are subject to copayment(s).

** Please note that TRICARE Extra and TRICARE Standard annual deductibles and cost shares are subject to change.

*** Except for families whose Active Duty sponsor's pay grade is E-4 and below, for whom the annual deductible is $50/person or $100/family .

This is only a summary description of your coverage. Please see the Standard CHAMPUS Handbook and a TRICARE Prime member handbook for a more complete description of all terms and conditions. In addition, CHAMPUS regulations and the interpretations under those regulations are the final authority on covered services.

++ An outpatient Nonavailability Statement (NAS) may be required. Consult your Health Care Finder . This may be a restricted NAS requiring you to use TRICARE network providers.

+++ With authorization.

For Active Duty Family Members, the maximum family liability (Catastrophic Cap Benefit) is $1000 for deductibles and cost-shares based on allowable charges for the Basic Program services and supplies received in a Fiscal Year. For all other beneficiary families, the Fiscal Year cap is $7,500. After a Fiscal Year cap is met, the CHAMPUS-determined allowable amount shall be paid in full for all covered services and supplies under the Basic Program received through the end of that Fiscal Year. In order to get credit for all family expenditures allowed toward the catastrophic cap benefit, the beneficiary may be required to submit appropriate documentation (e.g., CHAMPUS Explanation of Benefits).

FIGURE 13-13 *Continued*

13

QUALITY ASSURANCE

CHAMPUS managed care programs have a quality assurance program to assess continually the effectiveness of care and services rendered by providers. This includes inpatient and outpatient hospital care, mental health services, long-term care, home health care, and programs for the handicapped. Medical records are also reviewed on a random basis for both clinical and administrative quality. Providers are notified in writing when a potential quality issue has been confirmed as a breach of quality standards. Recommended corrective action plans are given, and noncompliance may lead to suspension or termination of a provider.

A provider who decides to participate in a managed care program goes through a credentialing process. This is done approximately every 2 years for all those who participate as providers.

CLAIMS PROCEDURE

The beneficiary does not file claims under TRICARE Prime or TRICARE Extra. A provider submits the claim to Aetna Government Health Plans.

Benefits and Coverage Chart

Outpatient Services **Beneficiary Cost**

SERVICES	TRICARE PRIME*	TRICARE EXTRA**	TRICARE STANDARD**
ANNUAL DEDUCTIBLE** (Applied to Outpatient Services)	None	$150/person or $300/ Family per fiscal year.***	$150/person or $300/Family per fiscal year.***
PRESCRIPTION DRUGS No charge for prescriptions at the military treatment facility.	$5 copayment per Rx up to a 30-day supply for Active Duty Family Members. $9 copayment per Rx up to a 30-day supply for Retirees, their Family Members, and Survivors.	Active Duty Family Members: 15% of Plan allowable. Retirees and their Family Members and Survivors: 20% of Plan allowable. The deduction is waived for prescriptions at a network pharmacy.	Active Duty Family Members: 20% of CHAMPUS allowable after deductible has been satisfied. Retirees and their Family Members and Survivors: 25% of CHAMPUS allowable after deductible has been satisfied.
EYE EXAMS One routine examination per year.	Active Duty Family Members: $6 copayment E4 and below; $12 copayment, E5 and above. Retirees and their Family Members, and Survivors 18 years of age and over: Not Covered.	Active Duty Family Members: 15% of Plan allowable after deductible has been satisfied. Retirees and their Family Members and Survivors: Not Covered.	Active Duty Family Members: 20 % of CHAMPUS allowable after deductible has been satisfied. Retirees and their Family Members and Survivors: Not Covered.
AMBULATORY SURGERY (same day)++ Authorized hospital-based or freestanding ambulatory surgical center that is CHAMPUS Certified.	+++Active Duty Family Members: $25 copayment. +++Retirees and their Family Members and Survivors: $5 copayment for primary surgeon only.	+++Active Duty Family Members: $25 copayment. +++Retirees and their Family Members and Survivors: 20% of Plan allowable after deductible has been satisfied.	Active Duty Family Members: $25 copayment for hospital charges. Retirees and their Family Members and Survivors: 25% of billed charges after deductible has been satisfied.
IMMUNIZATIONS Pediatric and adult immunizations as recommended by the American Academy of Pediatrics for children and by the U.S. Public Health Service for adults. If immunizations are needed for overseas travel, it is recommended you contact the military hospital or clinic and/or Public Health Department.	$5 copayment per visit up to 24 months of age. (See Family Health Services.) $5 copayment per immunization for over 2 years old.	For official travel, PCS orders outside the U.S. only. Active Duty Family Members: 15% of Plan allowable after deductible has been satisfied. Retirees and their Family Members and Survivors: Not Covered.	For official travel, PCS orders outside the U.S. only. Active Duty Family Members: 20% of CHAMPUS allowable after deductible has been satisfied. Retirees and their Family Members and Survivors: Not Covered.

* No copayment for primary care or preventive services for family members of sponsors with pay grades of E-4 and below (both active duty and retired). The Fiscal Intermediary has the responsibility for defining primary care; some of fice visits are subject to copayment(s).

** Please note that TRICARE Extra and TRICARE Standard annual deductibles and cost shares are subject to change.

*** Except for families whose Active Duty sponsor's pay grade is E-4 and below, for whom the annual deductible is $50/person or $100/family.

This is only a summary description of your coverage. Please see the Standard CHAMPUS Handbook and a TRICARE Prime member handbook for a more complete description of all terms and conditions. In addition, CHAMPUS regulations and the interpretations under those regulations are the final authority on covered services.

++ An outpatient Nonavailability Statement (NAS) may be required. Consult your Health Care Finder. This may be a restricted NAS requiring you to use TRICARE network providers.

+++ With authorization.

For Active Duty Family Members, the maximum family liability (Catastrophic Cap Benefit) is $1000 for deductibles and cost-shares based on allowable charges for the Basic Program services and supplies received in a Fiscal Year. For all other beneficiary families, the Fiscal Year cap is $7,500. After a Fiscal Year cap is met, the CHAMPUS-determined allowable amount shall be paid in full for all covered services and supplies under the Basic Program received through the end of that Fiscal Year. In order to get credit for all family expenditures allowed toward the catastrophic cap benefit, the beneficiary may be required to submit appropriate documentation (e.g., CHAMPUS Explanation of Benefits).

FIGURE 13–13 *Continued*

Electronic claims must be submitted within 6 months of the provider's contract effective date. When submitting claims for TRICARE Prime and TRICARE Extra, refer to Appendix A for the name and address.

For *outpatient* care, the claim must be *received by* your state's or region's CHAMPUS/TRICARE contractor within 1 year of the date the provider rendered the service to the patient. For *inpatient* care, the claim must be *received by* the contractor within

1 year from the date the patient was discharged from the facility. If the claim covers several different medical services or supplies that were provided at different times, the 1-year deadline applies to each item on the claim. When a claim is submitted on time, but the contractor returns it for more information, resubmit the claim along with the requested information so it is received by the contractor no later than 1 year after the medical services or supplies were provided or 90 days from the date the claim was returned to you, whichever is later. A contractor may grant exemptions from the filing deadlines for several reasons. Submit a request to the contractor including a complete explanation of the circumstances of the late filing, together with all available documentation supporting the request, along with the claim denied for late filing.

TRICARE Standard

This option is the same as the standard CHAMPUS program. It pays a share of the cost of covered health care services that the patient obtains from a non-network civilian health care provider. There is no enrollment in TRICARE Standard. The patient pays the normal CHAMPUS deductibles for outpatient care, and the cost-sharing percentages are the same as for regular CHAMPUS beneficiaries. If the provider does participate (also known as *accepting assignment*), he or she accepts the TRICARE Standard (CHAMPUS) allowable charge as the full fee for the services rendered and files the claim. If the provider does not participate, the patient pays the bill in full and, effective as of October 1, 1996, the physician is required to file the claim. Nonparticipating providers may charge no more than 15% above the CHAMPUS/TRICARE maximum allowable charge (CMAC) for their services.

TO THE STUDENT

For further knowledge and understanding, the key terms at the beginning of the chapter appear in the Glossary at the end of this textbook so you can look up the pertinent terms. You are now ready to complete the review questions and assignments in the *Workbook*. Assignment 46 presents three CHAMPUS cases for computing mathematic calculations. Assignments 47 through 49 will give you hands-on experience in completing CHAMPUS and CHAMPVA insurance claim forms and more proficiency in procedural and diagnostic coding.

After completing the *Workbook* assignments, you may want additional practice on the concepts you have learned. CHAMPUS Case 4 is available on your computer disk.

Objectives*

THE INSURANCE BILLING SPECIALIST WILL BE ABLE TO:

- Explain the development of workers' compensation from before the 1900s to the present.
- State the purpose of workers' compensation laws.
- Understand who is covered under federal workers' compensation laws.
- Understand who is covered under state workers' compensation laws.
- Learn the difference between workers' compensation insurance and employers' liability insurance.
- State the difference between compulsory and elective laws.
- Describe how funding is carried out in his or her state.
- Identify the exceptions to workers' compensation laws.
- Determine the waiting period in each state before benefits begin.
- Describe the types of compensation benefits.
- Define nondisability, temporary disability, and permanent disability claims.
- Explain OSHA's role in protecting employees.
- Define third party subrogation.
- Define second-injury fund.
- Learn what a medical report should contain, how to complete forms properly, and the deadline for submitting reports.
- Expedite billing in a workers' compensation case and know what to do about out-of-state claims.
- Define terminology and abbreviations pertinent to workers' compensation cases.
- List the advantages of filing a lien.
- List signs of fraud and abuse involving employees, employers, insurers, medical providers, and lawyers.
- State when to report a workers' compensation claim involving fraud or abuse.
- Describe workers' compensation recordkeeping methods.
- Understand terms and payment of medical testimony.
- Explain two ways in which depositions are used.
- Describe how to handle delinquent workers' compensation claims.

Key Terms

accident
adjudication
by report (BR)
compromise and release (C and R)
deposition
employers' liability insurance
extraterritorial
Federal Employees' Compensation Act (FECA)
fee schedule
independent medical examiner (IME)
injury
lien
limited duty
medical service order
nondisability (ND) claim
occupational illness (or disease)
Occupational Safety and Health Administration (OSHA)
Office of Federal Employees' Compensation (OFEC)
Office of Workers' Compensation Programs (OWCP)
permanent and stationary (P and S)
permanent disability (PD)
petition
second-injury fund
sub rosa films
subsequent injury fund (SIF)
temporary disability (TD)
third-party liability
third-party subrogation
waiting period (WP)
Workers' Compensation Appeals Board (WCAB)
workers' compensation (WC) insurance
work hardening

* Performance objectives and exercises for hands-on practical experience for this chapter appear in the *Workbook* and on computer disk.

CHAPTER 14

Workers' Compensation

History

Before the establishment of a workers' compensation program in the United States, the employer was responsible for any injury or death to his employees resulting from administrative negligence. *Employees* are individuals employed by another, generally for wages, in exchange for labor or services. A physician who is incorporated is considered an employee under workers' compensation laws.

Originally, the worker had to prove that injury was due to negligence on the part of the employer. However, by the close of the 19th century, federal and state legal provisions were required because the number of accidents increased and legal processes were uncertain. As an outcome, in the early 1900s employers' liability laws were adopted by many states, but there was still a great need for improvement. In 1911, the first workers' compensation laws were enacted allowing injured employees to receive medical care without first taking employers to court. Today, all states have workers' compensation laws.

BENEFITS

Workers' compensation coverage provides benefits to employees and their dependents if employees suffer work-related injury, illness, or death. An *accident* is an unplanned and unexpected happening traceable to a definite time and place causing *injury* (damage or loss) not due to any fault on the part of the person injured.

Workers' compensation accidents do not necessarily occur at the work site. For example, an individual may be asked to obtain cash for the petty cash reserve on the lunch hour; while walking to the bank, he or she missteps off the curb, suffering a fractured ankle. This person is considered to be working, although not at the work site, and the injury is covered under workers' compensation insurance.

Occupational illness is any abnormal condition or disorder caused by exposure to environmental factors associated with employment, including acute and chronic illnesses or diseases that may be caused by inhalation, absorption, ingestion, or direct contact. Occupational diseases usually become apparent soon after exposure. However, some diseases may be latent for a considerable amount of time. Some states, therefore, have extended periods during which claims may be filed for certain slowly developing occupational diseases. These diseases might be silicosis, asbestosis, pneumoconiosis, berylliosis, anthracosilicosis, radiation disability, loss of hearing, cumulative trauma, or repetitive motion illnesses (e.g., carpal tunnel syndrome). Workers' compensation benefits include medical care, disability income, and death benefits.

PURPOSES OF WORKERS' COMPENSATION LAWS

There are a variety of reasons for workers' compensation laws:

1. To provide the best available medical care necessary to ensure a prompt return to work of any injured or ill employee, as well as the achievement of maximum recovery.
2. To provide income to the injured or ill worker or to his or her dependents, regardless of fault.
3. To provide a single remedy and reduce court delays, costs, and work loads arising out of personal injury litigation.
4. To relieve public and private charities of financial drains resulting from uncompensated industrial accidents.
5. To eliminate payment of fees to attorneys and witnesses as well as time-consuming trials and appeals.
6. To encourage maximum employer interest in safety and rehabilitation through an appropriate experience-rating mechanism.
7. To promote the study of causes of accidents and reduce preventable accidents and human suffering rather than concealing fault.

Workers' compensation insurance is the most important of the coverages written to insure industrial accidents. Previously, this form of insurance was known as workmen's compensation. The term *workmen* was changed to *workers* for a more generic title and to avoid sexual bias in language. Employers still use employers' liability coverage occasionally to protect themselves when their employees do not come within the scope of a compensation law.

There are two kinds of statutes under workers' compensation: federal compensation laws and state compension laws. Federal laws apply to miners, maritime workers, and those who work for the government; they do not apply to state and private business employees. State compensation laws apply to employers and employees within each state, but the laws vary for each state.

WORKERS' COMPENSATION REFORM

By 1994 in many U.S. cities, dysfunctional workers' compensation systems were costing companies more than $65 billion annually, driving insurers to deny insurance to businesses and causing companies to close their doors. Some employers began moving their businesses to states requiring lower premiums. Widespread legal and medical corruption and abuse had evolved throughout the system in the form of record high medical treatment and legal expenses. Because of these problems, reforms of the compensation of health care workers became necessary. Reform laws have been introduced in a number of states. They deal with the following:

- Antifraud legislation and increased penalties
- Antireferral provisions (i.e., restrictions of physicians referring patients for diagnostic studies to sites where the physician has a financial interest)
- Proof of the medical necessity for treatment (or tests), as well as appropriate documentation, or the carrier may refuse to pay the entire charged fee (i.e., utilization review of inpatient and outpatient claims and treatment plans)
- Preauthorization for major operations and ex-

pensive tests, e.g., computed tomography and magnetic resonance imaging
- Caps on vocational rehabilitation and utilization of a disabled worker in another division of the company so that the person may be gainfully employed while not using the injured part of the body
- An increase in occupational safety measures
- Employers offering a variety of managed care plans from which employees can choose, with some of these restricting their choice of provider (i.e., HMOs, PPOs)
- Development of fee schedules
- Medical bill review (mandatory review by law or payers' voluntary review identifying duplicate claims and billing errors)
- Use of mediators instead of lawyers to reach agreement between employers and the injured employee
- Prosecuting physicians, lawyers, and employees who abuse the system

Although far from perfect or complete, much progress has been made toward reducing high costs by trimming reimbursement for medical services and minimizing abuses of the system.

SELF-INSURANCE

Another way of fighting high medical costs after an accident is self-insurance by employers. A very large employer can save money by self-insuring employees for a predetermined amount of money and then purchasing policies with large deductibles to cover catastrophic problems. A self-insuring company pays for medical expenses instead of insurance premiums. Benefits are variable from plan to plan, and precertification for certain services may be required. Generally, the state insurance commissioner does not have jurisdiction over such plans. Some states may have laws that regulate self-insurers. Physicians who care for individuals under such plans may wish to negotiate payment terms to be 60 days or less.

MANAGED CARE

Increasing numbers of employers are seeking managed care contracts with preferred provider organizations (PPOs) and health maintenance organizations (HMOs). Some states have adopted laws authorizing managed care programs, and other states are conducting pilot programs to test the effectiveness of managed care networks. Managed care contracts are not uniform and may limit the choice of providers, use fee schedule–based payments, require precertification for certain procedures, implement hospital and medical bill review, and incorporate utilization review of medical services.

COVERAGE OF FEDERAL LAWS

Employees who work for federal agencies are covered by a number of federal workers' compensation laws. The following three programs are administered by the United States Department of Labor, Office of Workers' Compensation Programs (OWCP). They are:

- *Workmen's Compensation Law of the District of Columbia.* This law became effective on May 17, 1928, and provides benefits for those working in Washington, D.C.
- *Federal Coal Mine Health and Safety Act.* This is sometimes referred to as the Black Lung Benefits Act and became effective on May 7, 1941. The act provides benefits to coal miners and is administered through the national headquarters in Washington, D.C.
- *Federal Employees' Compensation Act.* This act was instituted on May 30, 1908, to provide benefits for on-the-job injuries to all federal employees. The insurance is provided through an exclusive fund system. Many different claim forms are used, depending on the type of injury. Payment is based on a schedule of maximum allowable charges. The time limit for submitting a bill is by December 31 of the year following the year in which services were rendered (or by December 31 of the year following the year the condition was accepted as work compensable, whichever is later). For further information, contact the Office of the Federal Employees' Compensation Act (FECA) by writing to the nearest office as listed in Appendix A.

A fourth federal program is

- *Longshoremen's and Harbor Workers' Compensation Act (LHWCA).* This act became effective on March 4, 1927, and provides benefits for private or public employees engaged in maritime work nationwide. It is administered through regional offices in Boston, Chicago, Cleveland, Denver, Honolulu, Jacksonville, Kansas City,

New Orleans, New York City, Philadelphia, San Francisco, Seattle, and Washington, D.C. The type of insurance provided corresponds to that available through the private insurance system. For further information contact the nearest district office, as listed in Appendix A.

COVERAGE OF STATE LAWS

The state compensation laws cover those workers not protected by the previously mentioned federal statutes. Federal law mandates that states set up laws to meet minimum requirements. If an employer does not purchase workers' compensation insurance from a private insurance company, the employer must self-insure and have enough cash in reserve to cover the cost of medical care for all workers who suffer work-related injuries. In some instances, an employer may be reluctant to file a workers' compensation report with the state, preferring to pay medical expenses out of pocket because of not wanting premium rates to increase. It is illegal for an employer to fail to report a work-related accident when it is required by state law, and some states consider it a misdemeanor. Different penalties can be imposed, depending on state law, such as imprisonment or assessment of fines of from $50 to $2,500 or more.

State compensation laws are either compulsory or elective.

1. *Compulsory law.* Requires each employer to accept its provisions and provide for specified benefits.
2. *Elective law.* The employer may accept or reject the act. If the act is rejected, the employer loses the three common-law defenses, which are
   a. Assumption of risk
   b. Negligence of fellow employees
   c. Contributory negligence

In all 50 states and U.S. territories, statutes require compulsory workers' compensation and employers' liability insurance. However, coverage is still elective in three states: New Jersey, South Carolina, and Texas. This means that if an employer rejects the act, the employer loses the three common-law defenses.

FUNDING

Six states (Nevada, North Dakota, Ohio, Washington, West Virginia, Wyoming), two U.S. territories, and most provinces require employers to insure through a monopolistic state or provincial fund.

In 48 states and territories, employers may qualify as self-insurers. Puerto Rico and the Virgin Islands require employers to insure through a territorial fund.

A number of states permit employers to purchase insurance from either a competitive state fund or a private insurance company.

The workers' compensation statutes relieve the employer of liability for injury received or illness contracted by an employee except in gross negligence cases. They also enable the employee to be more easily and quickly compensated for loss of wages, medical expenses, and permanent disability. Before these statutes were passed, the employer could be found legally responsible for his or her employees' injuries or illnesses, and frequently there were delays in the employee's attempt to recover damages.

The employer pays the premiums for workers' compensation insurance, the amount depending on the employee's job and the risk involved in job performance. The physician usually must supply comprehensive information, and the requirements vary from state to state. To obtain instructions and proper forms, contact your state bureau or individual insurance carriers. State bureaus are listed in Appendix A; also see Table 14–1.

Minors are covered by workers' compensation, but in some states double compensation or added penalties are provided. In many states, minors also receive special legal benefit provisions.

If a worker's occupation takes him or her into another state, questions may arise as to which state's law determines compensation payable. Most compensation laws are *extraterritorial* (effective outside of the state) by either specific provisions or court decision.

Several states have laws to compensate civil defense and other volunteer workers, such as firemen, who are injured in the line of duty.

MINIMUM NUMBER OF EMPLOYEES

Table 14–2 shows the minimum number of employees required by each state before the state workers' compensation law comes into effect. There are exemptions in many states for certain occupations such as domestic or casual employees, laborers, babysitters, newspaper vendors or distributors, charity workers, and gardeners. Some states do not require compensation insurance for farm laborers or may need a larger number of farm employees than the number shown in the Table.

Text continued on page 336

TABLE 14-1
Employers' and/or Physicians' Report of Accidents[1]

Jurisdiction	Time Limit	Injuries Covered
Alabama	Within 15 days	Death or disability exceeding 3 days
Alaska	Within 10 days	Death, injury, disease, or infection
American Samoa	Within 10 days[2]	Injury or death
Arizona	Within 10 days	All injuries
Arkansas	Within 10 days and as required	Injury or death
California	Immediately[3] (employer) As prescribed Within 5 days	Death or serious injuries 1-day disability or more than first aid Occupational diseases or pesticide poisoning
Colorado	Immediately Within 10 days [4a]	Death All injuries causing lost time of 3 days or more[4b]
Connecticut	7 days or as directed	Disability of 1 day or more
Delaware	Within 48 hours[5] Within 10 days	Death or injuries requiring hospitalization Other injuries
District of Columbia	Within 10 days	All injuries
Florida	Within 24 hours[6] Within 7 days of carrier receipt of notice	Death All injuries
Georgia	Within 10 days[7]	All injuries requiring medical or surgical treatment or causing over 7 days of absence
Guam	Within 10 days[8]	Injury or death
Hawaii	Within 48 hours Within 7 working days	Death All injuries
Idaho	As soon as practicable but not later than 10 days after the accident[9]	All injuries requiring medical treatment or causing 1 day's absence
Illinois	Within 2 working days Between 15th and 25th of month As soon as determinable	Death or serious injuries Disability of over 3 days Permanent disability
Indiana	Within 7 days[10]	Disability of 1 day or more
Iowa	Within 4 days	Disability of more than 3 days, permanent partial disability, death
Kansas	Within 28 days[11] Within 28 days	Death Disability of more than remainder of day or shift
Kentucky	Within 7 days[12]	Disability of more than 1 day
Louisiana	Within 10 days or within 7 days of mediation[13]	Lost time over 1 week or death
Maine	Within 7 days	All injuries[14]
Maryland	Within 10 days	Disability of more than 3 days
Massachusetts	Within 7 days, except Sundays and holidays	Disability of more than 5 days
Michigan	Immediately	Death, disability of 7 days or more, and specific losses
Minnesota	Within 48 hours Within 14 days	Death or serious injury Disability of 3 days or more
Mississippi	Within 10 days	Death, disability of more than 5 days
Missouri	Within 10 days[15]	Death or injury
Montana	Within 6 days[16]	All injuries
Nebraska	Within 48 hours[17] Within 7 days	Death All injuries
Nevada	Within 6 working days after report from physician[18]	All injuries
New Hampshire	Within 5 calendar days	All injuries
New Jersey	Immediately[19]	All injuries
New Mexico	Within 10 days	Compensable injuries

Table continued on following page

14

TABLE 14-1
Employers' and/or Physicians' Report of Accidents *(Continued)*[1]

Jurisdiction	Time Limit	Injuries Covered
New York	Within 10 days	Disability of 1 day or more or requiring medical care beyond two first aid treatments
North Carolina	Within 5 days[20]	Disability of more than 1 day
North Dakota	Within 7 days	All injuries
Ohio	Within 1 week	Injuries causing total disability of 7 days or more
Oklahoma	Within 10 days or a reasonable time	All injuries
Oregon	Within 5 days	All compensable injuries[21]
Pennsylvania	Within 48 hours	Death
	After 7 days but not later than 10 days	Disability of 1 day or more
Puerto Rico	Within 5 days	All injuries
Rhode Island	Within 48 hours	Death
	Within 10 days	Disability of 3 days or more
	Within 2 years of injury	Any claim resulting in medical expenses
South Carolina	Within 10 days[22]	All injuries
South Dakota	Within 10 days	All injuries[23]
Tennessee	Within 14 days	All injuries requiring medical attention
Texas	Within 8 days[22]	Disability of more than 1 day, or occupational illnesses
Utah	Within 1 week	All injuries
Vermont	Within 72 hours[22]	Disability of 1 day or more requiring medical care
Virgin Islands	Within 8 days	Injury or disease
Virginia	Within 10 days[22]	All injuries
Washington	Immediately	All injuries
West Virginia	Within 5 days	All injuries
Wisconsin	Within 7 days	Disability beyond 3-day waiting period
Wyoming	Within 10 days	All injuries
FECA	Immediately	All injuries
LHWCA	10 days	Injuries that cause loss of 1 or more shifts of work or death

[1] In many states, except for initial reports, the insured's company relieves the *employer* of the responsibility of reporting. However, a *physician* may render progress, suppplemental, and final medical reports weekly and monthly, depending on the nature of the industrial accident. In some states (Colorado, Guam, Kansas, Nebraska), a failure to report tolls (suspends) time limits for claims. When a time limit is "tolled," it stops running. The time limit resumes when the report is filed.

[2] *American Samoa.* Employer must also notify Commissioner upon first payment and suspension of payment and within 16 days after final payment.

[3] *California.* To division of Occupational Safety and Health. Within 5 days of employer's notice or knowledge of employee death, employer must report death to the Department of Industrial Relations.

[4] *Colorado. (a)* Failure to report tolls time limit for claims. *(b)* Disability of less than 3 days must be reported to insurer.

[5] *Delaware.* Supplemental report upon termination of disability.

[6] *Florida.* Report to carrier within 7 days, if injury caused employee to lose 7 or more work days. Supplemental report within 30 days after final payment.

[7] *Georgia.* Supplemental report on first payment and suspension of payment and within 30 days after final payment.

[8] *Guam.* Failure to report tolls limits for claims.

[9] *Idaho.* Supplemental report required after 60 days or upon termination of disability.

[10] *Indiana.* Supplemental report within 10 days after termination of compensation period.

[11] *Kansas.* Failure to report tolls time limit for claims. Childress v. Childress Painting Co., 1979.

[12] *Kentucky.* Supplemental report required after 60 days or upon termination of disability.

[13] *Louisiana.* Employers with more than 10 employees must also report, within 90 days, death, any nonfatal occupational illness or injury causing loss of consciousness, restriction of work or motion, job transfer, or medical treatment other than first aid. Violation of confidentiality of any record, subject to $500 fine.

[14] *Maine.* Must report asbestosis, mesothelioma, silicosis, and exposure to heavy metals no later than 30 days from date of diagnosis.

[15] *Missouri.* Supplemental report within 1 month after original notice to Division.

[16] *Montana.* Insurance carrier also required to report (by rule).

[17] *Nebraska.* Report may be made by insurance carrier or employer. Failure to report tolls time limits.

[18] *Nevada.* For minor injuries not requiring medical treatment, the employee may file a "Notice of Injury," which must be retained by the employer for 3 years.

[19] *New Jersey.* Uninsured employers are required to report compensable injuries only. If insured, carrier is also required to make report.

[20] *North Carolina.* Supplemental report required after 60 days or upon termination of disability.

[21] *Oregon.* Insurers to send disabling claims to Workers' Compensation Department within 21 days of employer knowledge.

[22] *South Carolina, Texas, Vermont, and Virginia.* Supplemental report required after 60 days or upon termination of disability.

[23] *South Dakota.* Any injury that requires treatment other than first aid or that incapacitates employee for at least 7 calendar days.

TABLE 14-2
Minimum Number of Employees for State Workers' Compensation Laws

No. of Employees				
1		3	4	5
Alaska	Nebraska	American Samoa	Florida	Alabama
Arizona	Nevada	Arkansas	Rhode Island	Mississippi
California	New Hampshire	Georgia	South Carolina	Missouri
Colorado	New Jersey	Michigan		Tennessee
Connecticut	New York	New Mexico		
Delaware	North Dakota	North Carolina		
District of Columbia	Ohio	Virginia		
Guam	Oklahoma			
Hawaii	Oregon			
Idaho	Pennsylvania			
Illinois	Puerto Rico			
Indiana	South Dakota			
Iowa	Texas			
Kansas	Utah			
Kentucky	Vermont			
Louisiana	Virgin Islands			
Maine	Washington			
Maryland	West Virginia			
Massachusetts	Wisconsin			
Minnesota	Wyoming			
Montana				

TABLE 14–3
Waiting Period for Income Benefits; Medical Benefits*

Jurisdiction	Waiting Period (days)	Jurisdiction	Waiting Period (days)
Alabama	3	Nebraska	7
Alaska	3	Nevada	5
American Samoa	3	New Hampshire	3
Arizona	7	New Jersey	7
Arkansas	7	New Mexico	7
California	3	New York	7
Colorado	3	North Carolina	7
Connecticut	3	North Dakota	5
Delaware	3	Ohio	7
District of Columbia	3	Oklahoma	3
Florida	7	Oregon	3
Georgia	7	Pennsylvania	7
Guam	3	Puerto Rico	0
Hawaii	3	Rhode Island	3
Idaho	5	South Carolina	7
Illinois	3	South Dakota	7
Indiana	7	Tennessee	7
Iowa	3	Texas	7
Kansas	7	Utah	3
Kentucky	7	Vermont	3
Louisiana	7	Virgin Islands	1
Maine	7	Virginia	7
Maryland	3	Washington	3
Massachusetts	5	West Virginia	3
Michigan	7	Wisconsin	3
Minnesota	3	Wyoming	3
Mississippi	5	FECA	3
Missouri	3	LHWCA	3
Montana	6		

* These are statutory provisions for waiting periods. Statutes provide that a waiting period must elapse during which income benefits are not payable. This waiting period affects only compensation, since medical and hospital care are provided immediately.

WAITING PERIODS

The laws state that a waiting period must elapse before income benefits are payable. This waiting period affects only compensation because medical and hospital care are provided immediately. To find the waiting period of your state, see Table 14–3.

TYPES OF STATE COMPENSATION BENEFITS

The five principal types of state compensation benefits that may apply in ordinary cases are

1. *Medical treatment.* This includes hospital, medical and surgical services, medications, and prosthetic devices. Treatment may be rendered by a licensed physician, osteopath, dentist, or chiropractor.
2. *Temporary disability indemnity.* This is in the form of weekly cash payments made directly to the injured or ill.
3. *Permanent disability indemnity.* This may consist of either weekly or monthly cash payments based on a rating of percentages of permanent disability or a lump sum award. California has a unique system of permanent disability evaluation that requires a separate determination by the disability rating bureau in San Francisco. No other state has this system.
4. *Death benefits for survivors.* This consists of cash payments to dependents of employees who are fatally injured. In some states, a burial allowance is also given.
5. *Rehabilitation benefits.* In cases of severe disa-

bilities, this can be either medical or vocational rehabilitation.

TYPES OF STATE CLAIMS

There are three types of state workers' compensation claims: nondisability claims, temporary disability claims, and permanent disability claims. Each type will be discussed in detail for a clear understanding of the process that each one requires.

NONDISABILITY CLAIM

This is the simplest type of claim, and it is easily adjusted. Generally, a nondisability claim is considered a minor injury in which the patient is seen by the doctor but is able to continue working. The laws clearly state that the injured person must promptly report the industrial injury or illness to his or her employer or immediate supervisor. The employer sends in an Employer's Report of Occupational Injury or Illness Form (Fig. 14–1) to the insurance company. In different states, the time limit on submission of this form varies from immediately to as long as 30 days (see Table 14–1). Many states have adopted the form shown in Figure 14–1 to meet the requirements of the Federal Occupational Safety and Health Act of 1970 (see pp. 344–345) as well as for their state statistical purposes.

Medical Service Order

In addition to the employer's report, the employer may complete and sign a medical service order, giving this to the injured employee to take to the physician's office (Fig. 14–2). This authorizes the physician to treat the injured employee. Photocopy the form, retaining the copy for the physician's files, and attach the original to the Doctor's First Report of Occupational Injury or Illness (preliminary report). An employer may prefer to write the service order on his or her business letterhead, billhead, or a piece of scratch paper. Authorizations may also be obtained over the telephone.

If a patient arrives for an appointment without written authorization, telephone the employer and ask that the authorized person fax the permission for treatment. Subsequently, if payment is not received or the claim is disputed, it may be easier to collect if a copy of the written authorization is included when sending collection follow-up correspondence.

If an appointment was arranged by the employer or insurance company and was not canceled 72 hours before the appointment time, a charge can be made. This policy may vary depending on state laws, so check with the insurance company.

If outside testing or treatment is necessary, obtain authorization from the employer or insurance company. When this is done by telephone, state the name of the procedure or test and the medical necessity for it. Obtain the name and title of the person (adjuster) giving authorization and write this on the order form as well as the date since no authorization numbers are issued in workers' compensation cases.

First Treatment Medical Report

After the physician sees the injured person, he or she sends in a completed First Treatment Medical Report (Fig. 14–3) or a Doctor's First Report of Occupational Injury or Illness form (used in California; see Fig. 14–15) as soon as possible. Because this time limit also varies from state to state, refer to Table 14–1 for the requirements of your state. Failure to file the report can be a misdemeanor. Copies of the form, which is a legal document, go to the insurance carrier and the state. Some physicians even send a copy to the employer. Because this is a legal document, each copy *must be signed in ink* by the physician. The insurance company waits for the physician's report and bill, which should state that the patient has been discharged and that no further treatment is necessary. The insurance company pays the medical bill to the physician and closes the case.

TEMPORARY DISABILITY CLAIM

Temporary disability occurs when a worker has a work-related injury or illness and is unable to perform the duties of his or her occupation. The time period of temporary disability can extend from the date of injury until the worker either returns to full duty without residual rateable disability (discussed later), returns to modified work, or has rateable residual disability that the physician states is permanent and stationary.

State laws mandate that there must be a waiting period before temporary disability (TD) (salary replacement) can begin. See Table 14–3 to determine the waiting period for your state. The insurance adjuster's most important function in adjusting the claim is to put up the proper reserves. In other words, the adjuster must predict in advance how much money will be needed during the course of

State of California
EMPLOYER'S REPORT OF OCCUPATIONAL INJURY OR ILLNESS

Please complete in triplicate (type, if possible). Mail two copies to:

Insurance Carrier Name and Address

OSHA Case No. #18
☐ Fatality

Any person who makes or causes to be made any knowingly false or fraudulent material statement or material representation for the purpose of obtaining or denying workers' compensation benefits or payments is guilty of a felony.

NOTICE: California law requires employers to report within **five days** of knowledge every occupational injury or illness which results in lost time beyond the date of the incident ***OR*** requires medical treatment beyond first aid. If an employee subsequently dies as a result of a previously reported injury or illness, the employer must file within **five days** of knowledge an amended report indicating death. In addition, every serious injury/illness, or death must be reported **immediately** by telephone or telegraph to the nearest office of the California Division of Occupational Safety and Health.

EMPLOYER

1. FIRM NAME: TOWER TRUCKING, INC.
1A. POLICY NUMBER: 272745-9X
2. MAILING ADDRESS (Number and Street, City, ZIP): 1250 FOLSOM ST. WOODLAND HILLS, XY 12345
2A. PHONE NUMBER: 015-552-8500
3. LOCATION, IF DIFFERENT FROM MAILING ADDRESS (Number and Street, City, ZIP):
3A. LOCATION CODE:
4. NATURE OF BUSINESS, e.g., painting contractor, wholesale grocer, sawmill, hotel, etc.: TRUCKING
5. STATE UNEMPLOYMENT INSURANCE ACCT. NO.: 3369418-8
6. TYPE OF EMPLOYER: ☒ PRIVATE ☐ STATE ☐ CITY ☐ COUNTY ☐ SCHOOL DIST. ☐ OTHER GOVERNMENT - SPECIFY ____

EMPLOYEE

7. EMPLOYEE NAME: JAMES SMITH
8. SOCIAL SECURITY NUMBER: 647-01-8818
9. DATE OF BIRTH (mm/dd/yy): 4-11-40
10. HOME ADDRESS (Number and Street, City, ZIP): 1985 UNION ST. WOODLAND HILLS, XY 12345
10A. PHONE NUMBER: 013-346-3787
11. SEX: ☒ MALE ☐ FEMALE
12. OCCUPATION (Regular job title—NO initials, abbreviations or numbers): TRUCKER
13. DATE OF HIRE (mm/dd/yy): 1-20-61
14. EMPLOYEE USUALLY WORKS: 8 hours per day; 5 days per week; 40 total weekly hours
14A. EMPLOYMENT STATUS (check applicable status at time of injury): ✓ regular full-time ____ part-time ____ temporary ____ seasonal
14B. Under what class code of your policy were wages assigned? 7219
15. GROSS WAGES/SALARY: $ 500.00 per week
16. OTHER PAYMENTS NOT REPORTED AS WAGES/SALARY (e.g., tips, meals, lodging, overtime, bonuses, etc.)? ☐ YES, $ ____ per ____ ☒ NO

INJURY OR ILLNESS

17. DATE OF INJURY OR ONSET OF ILLNESS (mm/dd/yy): 12-18-9X
18. TIME INJURY/ILLNESS OCCURRED: 9:00 A.M. ____ P.M.
19. TIME EMPLOYEE BEGAN WORK: 8:00 A.M. ____ P.M.
20. IF EMPLOYEE DIED, DATE OF DEATH (mm/dd/yy):
21. UNABLE TO WORK FOR AT LEAST ONE FULL DAY AFTER DATE OF INJURY? ☐ YES ☐ NO
22. DATE LAST WORKED (mm/dd/yy): 12-18-9X
23. DATE RETURNED TO WORK (mm/dd/yy):
24. IF STILL OFF WORK, CHECK THIS BOX ☒
25. PAID FULL WAGES FOR DAY OF INJURY OR LAST DAY WORKED? ☒ YES ☐ NO
26. SALARY BEING CONTINUED? ☐ YES ☒ NO
27. DATE OF EMPLOYER'S KNOWLEDGE/NOTICE OF INJURY/ILLNESS (mm/dd/yy): 12-18-9X
28. DATE EMPLOYEE WAS PROVIDED EMPLOYEE CLAIM FORM (mm/dd/yy): 12-18-9X
29. SPECIFIC INJURY/ILLNESS AND PART OF BODY AFFECTED, MEDICAL DIAGNOSIS, if available, e.g., second degree burns on right arm, tendonitis of left elbow, lead poisoning.: FRACTURED RIBS, CONTUSIONS, CUTS ON FACE
30. LOCATION WHERE EVENT OR EXPOSURE OCCURRED (Number, Street, City): HWY 280, NEAR CRYSTAL SPRINGS
30A. COUNTY: SAN MATEO
30B. ON EMPLOYER'S PREMISES? ☐ YES ☒ NO
31. DEPARTMENT WHERE EVENT OR EXPOSURE OCCURRED, e.g., shipping department, machine shop.:
32. OTHER WORKERS INJURED/ILL IN THIS EVENT? ☐ YES ☒ NO
33. EQUIPMENT, MATERIALS AND CHEMICALS THE EMPLOYEE WAS USING WHEN EVENT OR EXPOSURE OCCURRED, e.g., acetylene, welding torch, farm tractor, scaffold.:
34. SPECIFIC ACTIVITY THE EMPLOYEE WAS PERFORMING WHEN EVENT OR EXPOSURE OCCURRED, e.g., welding seams of metal forms, loading boxes onto truck.: DRIVING TRUCK, GOING SOUTH TO MAKE A DELIVERY
35. HOW INJURY/ILLNESS OCCURRED. DESCRIBE SEQUENCE OF EVENTS. SPECIFY OBJECT OR EXPOSURE WHICH DIRECTLY PRODUCED THE INJURY/ILLNESS, e.g., worker stepped back to inspect work and slipped on scrap material. As he fell, he brushed against fresh weld, and burned right hand. USE SEPARATE SHEET IF NECESSARY.: A SMALL CAR CUT IN FRONT OF MR. SMITH'S TRUCK AND FORCED HIM TO SWERVE OFF THE HWY. AND HIT A GUARD RAILING
36. NAME AND ADDRESS OF PHYSICIAN (Number and Street, City, ZIP): JAMES HASSE, MD 4567 BROAD AVE., WOODLAND HILLS, XY 12345
36A. PHONE NUMBER: 013-486-9002
37. IF HOSPITALIZED AS AN INPATIENT, NAME AND ADDRESS OF HOSPITAL (Number and Street, City, ZIP): COLLEGE HOSPITAL 4500 BROAD AVE., WOODLAND HILLS, XY 12345
37A. PHONE NUMBER: 013-487-6789

DO NOT USE THIS COLUMN: Case No. | Ownership | Industry | Occupation | Sex | Age | Daily hours | Days per week | Weekly hours | Weekly wage | County | Nature of injury | Part of body | Source | Event | Sec. Source | Extent of Injury

Completed by (type or print)	Signature	Title	Date
THOMAS TOWER	Thomas Tower	PRESIDENT	12-18-9X

FORM 5020 (REV. 6)
1992

FILING OF THIS REPORT IS NOT AN ADMISSION OF LIABILITY

FIGURE 14–1
Employer's Report of Occupational Injury of Illness. This form complies with OSHA requirements as well as California State Workers' Compensation laws.

STATE COMPENSATION INSURANCE FUND
P.O. Box S, Ventura, California 93001

Medical Service Order

Dr./Clinic Max Gluteus, MD

Address 4567 Broad Avenue, Woodland Hills, XY 12345

We are sending Mrs. Ima Hurt
to you for treatment in accordance with the terms of the Workers' Compensation Laws. Please submit your report to the State Compensation Insurance Fund at once. Compensation cannot be paid without complete medical information.

Employer The Conk Out Company

Signature U.R. Wright Date 4-3-9x
If patient is able to return to work today or tomorrow, please show date and time below—sign and give to patient to return to employer. If there are any work restrictions indicate on the back of this form. Please submit your usual first report in any case.

Date/Time ____________ By ____________

SCIF FORM 358 (REV. 3-75) 13 32053-218 3-75 50M ① ◊ OSP

FIGURE 14–2
Medical Service Order.

the claim and calculate as accurate a reserve as possible. This is frequently a difficult task, since a seemingly minor back strain may ultimately require fusion, or a small cut may become gangrenous and lead to an amputation. The insurance carrier wants to provide the best possible medical care for the patient. If a specialist is required on a case, the patient will be immediately referred to the specialist.

Compensation benefits are not subject to income tax. Usually workers' compensation weekly TD payments are based on the employee's earnings at the time of the injury.

In a TD case, a *supplemental report* is sent to the insurance carrier after 2 to 4 weeks of treatment to give information on the current status of the patient. If there is a significant change in the prognosis, a detailed progress report (sometimes called a *re-examination report*) is sent to the insurance carrier. TD is ended when the physician tells the insurance carrier that the patient is able to return to work. Sometimes a Doctor's Final Report (see Fig. 14–8) is required at the time of discharge. When the patient resumes work, the insurance carrier closes the case, and the TD benefits cease.

Sometimes a patient is released to modified work to effect a transition between the period of inactivity due to disability and a return to full duty, especially when heavy work is involved. Increasing numbers of employers are developing work-hardening programs in which an employee is returned to the company and placed in a different department or division so he or she is gainfully employed while not using the injured body part.

Vocational Rehabilitation

Many states provide rehabilitation in the form of retraining, education, and job guidance and placement, to assist an injured individual in finding work before temporary disability compensation benefits expire. In any successful rehabilitation program, the employer, insurance carrier, physician, physical therapist, supervisor, and personnel department must act as a team with the common goal of getting an injured employee back to light duty or regular work as soon as possible. It is felt that the longer a person remains out of work, the less chance there is that he or she will return to the workplace. The employer and insurance adjuster must keep in communication with rehabilitation center therapists to determine when the injured person will be able to resume some form of work. The physician may sug-

printed on recycled paper

NEBRASKA WORKERS' COMPENSATION COURT

First Treatment Medical Report

(Must be filed with Compensation Court & Employer within 14 days of first treatment)

TYPE OR PRINT

(Shaded sections are not required)

PATIENT & INSURED (SUBSCRIBER) INFORMATION

1. PATIENT'S NAME (First name, middle initial, last name)	2. PATIENT'S DATE OF BIRTH	3. INSURED'S NAME (Employer)
Lester M. Task	05 | 06 | 60	Jonas Construction Company
4. PATIENT'S ADDRESS (Street, City, State, ZIP Code)	5. PATIENT'S SEX	6. INSURED'S I.D. NO. (Include any letters)
5400 Holly Street Woodland Hills, XY 12345	[X] MALE [ ] FEMALE	B 785700
	7. PATIENT'S RELATIONSHIP TO INSURED [X] SELF [ ] SPOUSE [ ] CHILD [ ] OTHER	8. INSURED'S GROUP NO. (Or Group Name) 5601
9. OTHER HEALTH INSURANCE COVERAGE – Enter Name of Policyholder and Plan Name and Address and Policy or Medical Assistance Number	10. WAS CONDITION RELATED TO: A. PATIENT'S EMPLOYMENT [X] YES [ ] NO B. AN AUTO ACCIDENT [ ] YES [ ] NO	11. INSURED'S ADDRESS (Street, City, State, ZIP Code) 300 Main Street Woodland Hills, XY 12345
12. PATIENT'S OR AUTHORIZED PERSON'S SIGNATURE I Authorize the Release of any Medical Information Necessary to Process this Claim SIGNED	12A. PATIENT'S SOCIAL SECURITY NO. 578 | 03 | 1921 DATE 11-8-9X	13. I AUTHORIZE PAYMENT OF MEDICAL BENEFITS TO UNDERSIGNED PHYSICIAN OR SUPPLIER FOR SERVICE DESCRIBED BELOW SIGNED (Insured or Authorized Person)

PHYSICIAN OR SUPPLIER INFORMATION

14. DATE OF:	ILLNESS (FIRST SYMPTOM OR INJURY (ACCIDENT)	15. DATE FIRST CONSULTED YOU FOR THIS CONDITION	16. HAS PATIENT EVER HAD SAME OR SIMILAR SYMPTOMS?
11-8-9X		11-8-9X	[ ] YES [X] NO
17. DATE PATIENT ABLE TO RETURN TO WORK	18. DATES OF TOTAL DISABILITY FROM 11-8-9X	THROUGH 12-8-9X	DATES OF PARTIAL DISABILITY FROM THROUGH
19. NAME OF REFERRING PHYSICIAN			20. FOR SERVICES RELATED TO HOSPITALIZATION GIVE HOSPITALIZATION DATES ADMITTED 11-8-9X DISCHARGED 11-10-9X
21. NAME & ADDRESS OF FACILITY WHERE SERVICES RENDERED (If other than home or office) Community Hospital, 400 Oak St., Woodland Hills, XY 12345			22. WAS LABORATORY WORK PERFORMED OUTSIDE YOUR OFFICE? [ ] YES [X] NO CHARGES:

23. DIAGNOSIS OR NATURE OF ILLNESS OR INJURY, RELATE DIAGNOSIS TO PROCEDURE IN COLUMN D BY REFERENCE TO NUMBERS 1, 2, 3, ETC. OR DX CODE

1. fracture of right patella 822.1
2.
3.
4.

24. A DATE OF SERVICE	B* PLACE OF SERVICE	C PROCEDURE CODE (IDENTIFY:)	FULLY DESCRIBE PROCEDURES, MEDICAL SERVICE OR SUPPLIES FURNISHED FOR EACH DATE GIVEN (EXPLAIN UNUSUAL SERVICES OR CIRCUMSTANCES)	D DIAGNOSIS CODE	E CHARGES	F
11-8-9X	1	99222	Initial hospital care	1	125 00	
11-8-9X	1	27524	Open TX patellar fracture with internal fixation	1	600 00	

24A. HISTORY. GIVE BRIEF DESCRIPTION OF WHAT OCCURRED. PATIENT'S ACCOUNT OF ACCIDENT.

Patient was up on a scaffold at a construction site about and fell off of it about 8 feet hitting the ground with the right knee.

25. SIGNATURE OF PHYSICIAN OR SUPPLIER	26. ACCEPT ASSIGNMENT GOVERNMENT CLAIMS ONLY) [ ] YES [ ] NO	27. TOTAL CHARGE	28. AMOUNT PAID	29. BALANCE DUE
SIGNED Gregory T. Getwell, MD DATE 11-8-9X	PHYSICIAN'S SOCIAL SECURITY NO.	725.00		725 | 00
32. YOUR PATIENT'S ACCOUNT NO.	33. YOUR EMPLOYER I.D. NO. 95-3208976	31. PHYSICIAN'S OR SUPPLIER'S NAME, ADDRESS, ZIP CODE & TELEPHONE NO. Gregory T. Getwell, MD 60 North State Street Woodland Hills, XY 12345 I.D. NO. A123456 013-459-0087		

*PLACE OF SERVICE CODES

1—(IH) – INPATIENT HOSPITAL
2—(OH) – OUTPATIENT HOSPITAL
3—(O) – DOCTOR'S OFFICE
4—(H) – PATIENT'S HOME
5— – DAY CARE FACILITY (PSY)
6— – NIGHT CARE FACILITY (PSY)
7—(NH) – NURSING HOME
8—(SNF) – SKILLED NURSING FACILITY
9— – AMBULANCE
O—(OL) – OTHER LOCATIONS
A—(IL) – INDEPENDENT LABORATORY
B— – OTHER MEDICAL/SURGICAL FACILITY

NWCC FORM 45 (Rev. 86)

reference initials

FIGURE 14-3

First Treatment Medical Report form used in Nebraska. This form follows the format of the Health Insurance Claim Form HCFA-1500 developed by the American Medical Association Council on Medical Service (see Chapter 6).

gest a rehabilitation center that provides good care, or the employer may have an in-house program.

One form of rehabilitation is the use of sports medicine to train the injured worker. Another method, called *work hardening*, is an individualized program of therapy using simulated or real work tasks to build up strength and improve the worker's endurance toward a full day's work. In some cases, job or worksite modifications may be instituted to get the employee back to gainful employment. Injured individuals may also be retrained into another career field if their disability prevents them from returning to their former occupation.

PERMANENT DISABILITY CLAIM

In this type of claim the patient or injured party is usually on TD benefits for a time and then is unable to return to his or her former occupation. The physician states in the report that the patient has residual disability that will hamper his or her opportunity to compete in the open job market. Examples of residual disability include loss of a hand, an eye, or a leg; neurologic problems; and so on. The permanent disability (PD) rating depends on the severity of the injury, the age of the injured person, and the patient's occupation at the time of the injury. The older the person, the greater the PD benefit will be. One might think that a younger person deserves higher compensation because he or she will be disabled for a longer portion of his working career. However, the workers' compensation laws assume that a young person has a better chance of being rehabilitated into another occupation.

In a PD claim, the physician's final report must include the words "permanent and stationary" (P and S). This phrase means that the physician is unable to do anything more for the patient and that the patient will be hampered by the disability to some extent for the rest of his or her life. The case is rated for PD, and a settlement is made called a *compromise and release* (C and R). This is an agreement between the injured party and the insurance company on a total sum. The case can then be closed.

However, reasons that may delay closing a workers' compensation case are

1. Unanswered questions or incomplete answers to data required on workers' compensation forms by either the employee, employer, or physician.
2. Vague terminology used by the physician in medical reports.
3. Omitted signatures from forms or written reports by either the employee, employer, or physician.
4. Incorrect billing by the physician's office.
5. Inadequate progress reports—i.e., the physician fails to send in a medical report routinely to update the insurance carrier when the injured employee is seen in subsequent visits.

RATING

Final determination of the issues involving settlement of an industrial accident is known as *adjudication*, or the rating of a case. A physician does not rate disability but renders a professional opinion on whether the injured individual has temporary or permanent disability that prevents him or her from gainful employment. Rating itself is carried out by the state's industrial accident commission or workers' compensation board. Wage loss, earning capacity, and physical impairment are three categories that may be taken into consideration to rate partial, permanent partial, or total disabilities. In addition, permanent partial disabilities may be rated by using a scheduled or nonscheduled injury award system. This system is based on the number of weeks of compensation for loss of body parts, such as 288 weeks for the loss of a leg. Scheduled injuries may include loss of a body part, disfigurement, permanent hearing loss, and so on. Nonscheduled injuries are more general, such as disability due to injury to the back or neck.

If an injured person is dissatisfied with the rating after the case has been declared P and S, he or she may appeal the case (by petition) to the Workers' Compensation Appeals Board or the Industrial Accident Commission.

Surveillance

In rating a case, *sub rosa films* are sometimes provided to document the extent of a patient's permanent disability. Sub rosa means "under the rose." In ancient times, the rose was a symbol of silence or secrecy. Videotapes are made over a period of 2 to 3 days without the patient's knowledge. This surveillance is expensive and is used as a last resort, especially in cases where a person receiving workers' compensation benefits is suspected of making exaggerated complaints. It is also used in cases when a worker has been off work for a long period of time and is supposedly unable to perform any work activity, not even light duty.

Investigators have been known to carry a camera in a gym bag and videotape a supposedly disabled claimant bench pressing at the gym. Patients have also been videotaped going into the physician's office for an appointment wearing a neck brace and removing the brace on returning to their car.

FRAUD AND ABUSE

In the 1990s, increases in fraudulent workers' compensation claims have been noted throughout many large metropolitan cities. These problems have involved employers, employees, insurers, medical providers, and lawyers. An increasing number of states have enacted some kind of antifraud legislation and stiffened penalties for workers' compensation fraud, making it a felony. Some states require reporting suspected insurance fraud and have revised their forms to incorporate wording in regard to fraudulent statements. For an example, see Figure 14–4.

Notify the insurance carrier of any suspicious situation so that action can be taken to have the case investigated further by one of their own divisions or the district attorney's office. For further information on fraud and abuse in the medical setting, see Chapter 2.

Some signs of fraud and abuse to be alert to in the context of the various perpetrators follow.

EMPLOYEE

- Misses the first physician's visit
- Cannot describe the pain or is overly dramatic, such as an employee who comes into the physician's office limping on the left leg, suddenly starts limping on the right leg, and then goes back to limping on the left leg
- Delays in reporting the injury
- Does not report Friday's injury until Monday morning
- First reports an injury to a legal or regulatory agency
- Reports an injury after missing several days of work
- Changes physicians frequently
- Is a short-term worker
- Has a curious claim history
- Fabricates an injury
- Exaggerates a work-related injury to obtain larger benefits, such as an injured employee who has a back pain and claims inability to bend over or lift. Surveillance cameras capture the individual at work on weekends repairing cars in the driveway at home—a task he is supposedly unable to perform
- Blames an injury that occurred off the job on the employer

EMPLOYER

- Misrepresents the annual payroll to get lower premium rates
- Misrepresents the number of workers employed
- Gives a false address with the least expensive premium rates
- Falsely classifies the job duties of workers (as not hazardous), such as stating the job title as a clerical worker when, in fact, the employee is using a lathe every day

INSURER

- Refuses to pay valid medical claims
- Forces the injured worker to settle by using unethical tactics. An insurance agent told an employee that he had a back sprain. Relying on that information, the worker settled the case. Later, a myelogram revealed a herniated intervertebral disk. The patient was left with a permanent partial disability.

MEDICAL PROVIDER

- Orders or performs unnecessary tests
- Renders unnecessary treatment
- Charges the insurance carrier for services never rendered
- Participates in a provider mill scheme (see explanation under "lawyer")
- Makes multiple referrals from a clinic practice regardless of type of injury
- Sends medical reports that look photocopied with the same information typed in (e.g., employer's address, description of injury) or that read almost identical to other reports
- Sends in many claims in which injuries are of a subjective nature, such as stress, emotional distress, headaches, inability to sleep
- Sends in claims from one employer showing several employees with similar injuries, using the same physicians and/or attorneys

State of California
Department of Industrial Relations
DIVISION OF WORKERS' COMPENSATION

Estado de California
Departamento de Relaciones Industriales
DIVISION DE COMPENSACIÓN AL TRABAJADOR

EMPLOYEE'S CLAIM FOR WORKERS' COMPENSATION BENEFITS

If you are injured or become ill because of your job, you may be entitled to workers' compensation benefits.

Complete the "**Employee**" section and give the form to your employer. Keep the copy marked "**Employee's Temporary Receipt**" until you receive the dated copy from your employer. You may call the Division of Workers' Compensation at **1-800-736-7401** if you need help in filling out this form or in obtaining your benefits. An explanation of workers' compensation benefits is included on the back of this form.

You should also have received a pamphlet from your employer describing workers' compensation benefits and the procedures to obtain them.

Any person who makes or causes to be made any knowingly false or fraudulent material statement or material representation for the purpose of obtaining or denying workers' compensation benefits or payments is guilty of a felony.

PETICION DEL EMPLEADO PARA BENEFICIOS DE COMPENSACIÓN DEL TRABAJADOR

Si Ud. se ha lesionado o se ha enfermado a causa de su trabajo, Ud. tiene derecho a recibir beneficios de compensación al trabajador.

*Complete la sección "**Empleado**" y entregue la forma a su empleador. Quédese con la copia designada "**Recibo Temporal del Empleado**" hasta que Ud. reciba la copia fechada de su empleador. Si Ud. necesita ayuda para completar esta forma o para obtener sus beneficios, Ud. puede hablar con la Division de Compensación al Trabajador llamando al **1-800-736-7401**. En la parte de atrás de esta forma se encuentra una explicación de los beneficios de compensación al trabajador.*

Ud. también debería haber recibido de su empleador un folleto describiendo los beneficios de compensación al trabajador lesionado y los procedimientos para obtenerlos.

Toda aquella persona que a propósito haga o cause que se produzca cualquier declaración o representación material falsa o fraudulenta con el fin de obtener o negar beneficios o pagos de compensación a trabajadores lesionados es culpable de un crimen mayor "felonía".

Employee: ***Empleado:***

1. Name. *Nombre.* Ima B. Hurt — Today's Date. *Fecha de Hoy.* 4-3-9X
2. Home Address. *Dirección Residencial.* 300 East Central Avenue
3. City. *Ciudad.* Woodland Hills — State. *Estado.* XY — Zip. *Código Postal.* 12345-0001
4. Date of Injury. *Fecha de la lesión(accidente).* 4-3-9X — Time of Injury. *Hora en que ocurrió.* ____ a.m. 4:00 p.m.
5. Address and description of where injury happened. *Dirección/lugar dónde occurió el accidente.* ABC Printing Company, 45 South Gorman Street, Woodland Hills, XY 12345 injured in stock room
6. Describe injury and part of body affected. *Describa la lesión y parte del cuerpo afectada.* a ream of paper fell off of shelf injuring left hand near the left finger
7. Social Security Number. *Número de Seguro Social del Empleado.* 120 23 6542
8. Signature of employee. *Firma del empleado.* Ima B. Hurt

Employer—complete this section and give the employee a copy immediately as a receipt.
Empleador—complete esta sección y déle inmediatamente una copia al empleado como recibo.

9. Name of employer. *Nombre del empleador.* ABC Printing Company
10. Address. *Dirección.* 45 South Gorman Street, Woodland Hills, XY 12345
11. Date employer first knew of injury. *Fecha en que el empleador supo por primera vez de la lesión o accidente.* 4-3-9X
12. Date claim form was provided to employee. *Fecha en que se le entregó al empleado la petición.* 4-3-9X
13. Date employer received claim form. *Fecha en que el empleado devolvió la petición al empleador.* 4-3-9X
14. Name and address of insurance carrier or adjusting agency. *Nombre y dirección de la compañía de seguros o agencia administradora de seguros.* State Compensation Insurance Fund, 669 County Square Drive, Ventura, CA 93001
15. Insurance Policy Number. *El número de la póliza del Seguro.* B 12345
16. Signature of employer representative. *Firma del representante del empleador.* J. D. Hawkins
17. Title. *Título.* Owner — 18. Telephone. *Teléfono.* 013-430-3488

Employer: You are required to date this form and provide copies to your insurer or claims administrator and to the employee, dependent or representative who filed the claim within **one working day** of receipt of the form from the employee.

SIGNING THIS FORM IS NOT AN ADMISSION OF LIABILITY

Empleador: *Se requiere que Ud. feche esta forma y que provéa copias a su compañía de seguros, administrador de reclamos, o dependiente/representante de reclamos y al empleado que hayan presentado esta petición dentro del plazo de **un día hábil** desde el momento de haber sido recibida la forma del empleado.*

EL FIRMAR ESTA FORMA NO SIGNIFICA ADMISION DE RESPONSABILIDAD

Original (Employer's Copy)
DWC Form 1 (REV. 1/94)

ORIGINAL (Copia del Empleador)
DWC Forma 1 (REV. 1/94)

FIGURE 14-4

Employee's Claim for Workers' Compensation Benefits. Notice the insert regarding fraudulent material.

14

LAWYER

- Overbills clients
- Participates in a medical provider mill scheme. An individual is solicited while in the unemployment line by a recruiter known as a "capper." The capper tells the worker it is possible to obtain more money on disability than through unemployment. The worker is referred to an attorney and a "provider mill" clinic, which help the individual fabricate a claim by claiming stress or an on-the-job injury.

OCCUPATIONAL SAFETY AND HEALTH ADMINISTRATION (OSHA) ACT OF 1970

BACKGROUND

Congress has established an office known as the Occupational Safety and Health Administration (OSHA) to protect employees against on-the-job health and safety hazards. This program includes tougher health and safety standards and a sensible complaint procedure enabling individual workers to trigger enforcement measures. The Act provides that if a state submits an OSHA plan and it is approved by the government, then the state may assume responsibility for carrying out OSHA policies and procedures and is excluded from federal jurisdiction.

Work standards are designed to minimize exposure to on-the-job hazards such as faulty machinery, noise, dust, and toxic chemical fumes. Employers are required by law to meet these health and safety standards. Failure to do so can result in fines against the employer that could run into thousands of dollars.

COVERAGE

The law applies to almost all businesses, large or small. It applies to heavy, light, and service industries, nonprofit and charitable institutions, churches' secular activities in hospitals, farmers, and retailers. Employees of state and local governments are also covered. Federal employees, a farmer's immediate family, church employees engaged in religious activities, independent contractors, and household domestic workers are *not* covered.

REGULATIONS

Specific regulations that affect the medical setting are those aimed at minimizing exposure to hepatitis B virus (HBV), human immunodeficiency virus (HIV), and other bloodborne pathogens. Any worker who comes in contact with human blood and infectious materials must receive proper information and training and use universal precautions to avoid injury. Vaccinations must be provided for those who become exposed to hepatitis B, and comprehensive records must be maintained. For fact sheets, booklets, and guidelines on bloodborne pathogens, contact the nearest OSHA office or write to OSHA Publications Office, 200 Constitution Avenue, N.W., Room N3101, Washington, D.C. 20210.

In many work settings, chemicals and hazardous substances are used that impose dangers. Employers are required to obtain or develop material safety data sheets (MSDS) for each hazardous chemical used or produced. A compliance kit is available from the Superintendent of Documents, U.S. Government Printing Office, Washington, D.C. 20402.

FILING A COMPLAINT

To file a complaint, the proper form is obtained from the federal Division of Industrial Safety or a state OSHA office and completed by the employee. It is against the law for an employer to take any adverse action against an employee who files such a complaint.

INSPECTION

A compliance officer (inspector) may call for an appointment or may be sent unannounced to the place of employment, and the employer may be cited for specific violations of the law. A court warrant may be required to search a company's premises if the employer does not consent to OSHA entry. A business may be fined, or depending on the violation, criminal penalties may be imposed.

RECORDKEEPING, POSTING, AND REPORTING

Employers must keep records of their employees' work-related injuries and illnesses on OSHA Form No. 200. Forms may be obtained from the OSHA office or from any office of the U.S. Department of Labor. This document must be on file at the work place and available to employees and OSHA compliance officers on request. Form 200 must be retained in the file for 5 years. After 6 days, a case recorded on Form 200 must have a supplementary record, OSHA Form 101, completed and kept in the files. Some states have modified their workers' compensation forms so they may be used as substitutes for Form 101. Certain low-hazard industries are exempt from having to complete and retain Forms 200 and 101. Companies with under 11 employees must complete safety survey OSHA Form 200-S. An accident that results in the death or hospitalization of five or more employees must be reported to OSHA. Companies are also required to display OSHA posters to inform employees of their job safety rights.

SPECIAL CIRCUMSTANCES

THIRD PARTY SUBROGATION

The legal term *subrogation* means "to substitute" one person for another. When applied to workers' compensation cases, it means a transfer of the claims and rights of the original creditor. In a compensation case involving third-party subrogation, the participants are the patient, the insurance carrier, and a third party responsible for the injury.

Imagine, for example, that a secretary is going to the bank to deposit some money for her employer. While she is on the errand, her car is rear-ended by another automobile and she is injured. In such a case there is no question of fault and no question of cause. The secretary was hurt during the performance of her work, and the workers' compensation insurance carrier is liable. The carrier must adjust the claim, provide all medical treatment, and pay all TD and PD benefits.

However, the insurance carrier does have legal recourse. It may send a representative to visit with the secretary, explain to her that she has a good subrogation case, and encourage her to seek the advice of an attorney and sue the third party in civil court.* If the secretary agrees to sue, the insurance carrier puts in a demand for repayment of all the money that it has paid out. This is called a *lien* and is discussed in more detail in the next section. If an award is made to the secretary when the case is settled, the insurance carrier is reimbursed for all that it has paid and the secretary then receives the balance.

In some states, such as California, the patient is legally prevented from collecting twice. If the patient's attorney should call the physician's office for information, it is only ethical and legal to ask permission from the insurance carrier before giving out any medical information since the contract exists between the physician and the insurance carrier, not the physician and the patient (see p. 358).

If a case is taken to court, the physician may be expected to testify as an expert witness. A written agreement from the patient's lawyer should be obtained stating exactly what compensation the physician will receive for research (preparation), time spent waiting to testify (if appointments must be cancelled), and actual testimony time. In some cases, the physician may want to ask for an advance partial payment. If the physician is subpoenaed, he or she must appear in court regardless of whether an agreement exists.

* This is sometimes referred to as *litigation,* which is the process of carrying on a lawsuit.

MEDICAL TESTIMONY

In the event of an accident case with third party liability, the physician may have to testify as an expert witness, take time to give a deposition, or attend a pretrial conference. It is important that there be a clear understanding of the terms of testimony and payment (Fig. 14–5). The correct CPT code for this is 99075 (medical testimony). This medical testimony agreement should be signed by the physician and then sent to the attorney. The attorney should return the original to the physician, retaining a copy for his or her files. This agreement should eliminate any future misunderstandings.

DEPOSITIONS

A deposition is a proceeding in which an attorney asks a witness questions regarding a case, and the witness answers under oath but not in open court. In a workers' compensation case, depositions are usually taken for permanent disability cases from the physician and the injured party by the attorney representing the workers' compensation insurance company. If the witness is the defendant, his or her attorney is also present. Direct and cross-examination may be done by both attorneys.

Depositions may be taken to find out additional information, the physician's version of the facts, the patient's version of the facts, what kind of witness the physician and patient will be, and so on.

When a case involves an independent medical examiner (IME), a deposition may be taken of his or her testimony. An IME is a physician who is hired by the insurance company or appointed by the referee or appeals board to examine an individual, in-

MEDICAL TESTIMONY AGREEMENT

AGREEMENT made this ______ day of ________, 19xx, between ________________________________ herein referred to as attorney, and ____, of __________________, ____________, ______________ ____________, a licensed
(street address) (city) (state) (ZIP code)

In consideration of their mutual covenants set forth herein, the parties agree as follows:

1. The doctor will give medical testimony in the case of:
____
as a treating physician or as an expert witness (delete the unwanted phrase).

2. The doctor agrees to appear promptly when called and to present his medical testimony in a well-prepared professional manner.

3. The doctor will be compensated for time away from the practice of his or her medical duties in accordance with the following:

(a) $________ per hour for reports and preparation of medical testimony.
(b) $________ per hour for pre-trial conferences.
(c) $________ per hour for court appearance, including travel time to and from the office.
(d) $________ per hour for deposition.
(e) $________ per hour for being on call with cancellation of appointments but not appearing in court.

4. The doctor will appear in court on ______ hour's notice from the attorney, unless prior arrangements have been made for the exact time of appearnce.

5. The doctor will be compensated on completion of his or her medical testimony and payment will not be contingent upon the outcome of the case. However, if the case is settled before reaching the court, the doctor will be compensated for being on call as noted above.

This contract shall be binding upon the parties.

IN WITNESS WHEREOF, the said parties hereto have subscribed their respective signatures.

____
(physician)

____
(attorney)

Date: ___________________________

FIGURE 14–5
Example of a medical testimony agreement between physician and attorney. This is signed by the physician and sent to the attorney for signature. A copy is retained by the attorney, and the original is kept by the physician.

dependent from the attending physician. An IME renders an unbiased opinion regarding the degree of disability of an injured worker.

The session may be recorded on a stenotype machine, in shorthand, by videotape, or by audiotape. Exhibits may be entered into evidence. The witness is allowed to read the transcript and make corrections or changes. The witness may be asked to sign the transcript but can waive signature if his or her attorney does not wish this to be done. The deposition is used when the case comes to trial.

Video depositions are used in several instances. For example, if a plaintiff in a case is terminally ill and the plaintiff's attorney wishes to preserve the plaintiff's testimony, a video deposition may be used as substantive evidence. Or, if a witness cannot be present at the trial, a video deposition may be taken. In a case in which a witness may be in Arizona and cannot appear in Pennsylvania, the attorney takes the deposition in Arizona and proves to the court that the witness is beyond its jurisdiction. The same is true for a physician defendant who is not available for some reason.

Another use for a deposition is to impeach a witness on cross-examination. If the witness takes the stand and the testimony is inconsistent with the deposition, the attorney will make this known to the jury.

LIENS

The word *lien* derives from the same origin as the word *liable,* and the right of lien expresses legal claim on the property of another for the payment of a debt (Fig. 14–6). Liens are sometimes called encumbrances and may be filed for a number of reasons. Suppose an attorney advises a client not to pay

TO: Attorney____________________

____

____

REQUEST FOR ALLOWANCE OF LIEN

ASSIGNMENT AND AUTHORIZATION

WHEREAS, I have a right or cause of action arising out of personal injury, to wit:

I, ____________________ (patient's name) hereby authorize ____________________ (physician's name),

to furnish, upon request, to my attorneys, ____________________, any and all medical records, or reports of examination, diagnosis, treatment, or prognosis but not necessarily limited to those items as set forth herein, in addition to an itemized statement of account for services rendered therefore or in connection therewith, which my attorney may from time to time request in connection with the injuries described above and sustained by me on the________day of__________, 19__.

I, hereby irrevocably authorize and direct my said attorney set forth herein to pay to________________ (physician's name) all charges for attendance in court, if required as an expert witness whether he testifies or not; reports or other data supplied by him; depositions given by said doctor; medical services rendered or drugs supplied; and any other reasonable and customary charges incurred by my attorney as submitted by________________ (physician's name) and in connection with said injury. Said payment or payments are to be made from any money or monies received by my attorney whether by judgment, decree or settlement of this case, prior to disbursement to me and payment of the amount as herein directed shall be the same as if paid by me. This authorization to pay the within doctor shall constitute and be deemed as assignment of so much of my recovery I receive. It is agreed that nothing herein relieves me of the primary responsibility and obligation of paying my doctor for services rendered, and I shall at all times remain personally liable for such indebtedness unless released by the within doctor or by payment disbursed by my attorney.

I accept the above assignment:

Dated:____________________ ____________________ Patient

Dated:____________________ ____________________ Attorney

FIGURE 14-6

Patient's authorization to release information to an attorney and to grant lien to the physician against proceeds of settlement in connection with accident, industrial, or third party litigation cases.

the physician until after the trial. Or what happens if payment is not made for the physician's courtroom testimony when a case is lost or medical reports are ordered and an attorney neglects to pay for them? If no lien has been signed, once the case has been settled and the money has been received, the settlement belongs to the patient. At this point what he or she does with the money is solely up to the patient. What happens if the patient forgets about the physician's bill?

A case in point is a physician who had an oral agreement covering the fee. The patient was unable to pay for medical treatment except on legal monetary recovery. When the patient settled, the proceeds went almost entirely to welfare agencies because the patient was on Medicaid. The physician sued the patient's attorney and lost. If the physician had gotten a written assignment of the proceeds, the lawyer could have been held liable for the fee.

Some patients may be persuaded to pay before a legal settlement is made or at least to make payments until a settlement is reached.

The advantages of filing a lien are as follows:

1. It is a source of protection in the event of litigation.
2. It ensures that payment for previously rendered medical services will be received when the attorney and patient have reached a settlement with the insurance company in an accident case.
3. It avoids harassment in trying to collect the bill.
4. It is an inexpensive method of collecting the fee. The physician can file suit and try to get a judgment against the patient, but this is relatively expensive in comparison with filing a lien.
5. It is a written agreement and will be recognized in court.
6. The physician will collect the full fee. If the physician assigns such a delinquent account to a collection agency, he or she may lose as much as 50% of the fee when it is collected.
7. If the physician wishes to bill more than what is allowed for a given service or services, a lien can be filed and the judge will determine whether it is reasonable.

When you fill out a lien form, specify a time limit, because litigation may take several years before settlement is reached. At the end of the time limit, the lien becomes null and void. If the patient's financial status has changed, you might be able to collect because you can now bill the patient. If not, file an amended or subsequent lien stating the actual balance of the patient's account. Type the word "amended" on the new lien below the Workers' Compensation Appeals Board case number. Protect the physician's fee by asking the attorney to sign the lien, thereby indicating that he or she will pay the physician directly from any money received in a settlement. This makes the attorney responsible for the fee. The patient's file must be placed in a Hold for Settlement category until the case comes up in court. In some states, the physician's fee owed by the patient constitutes a first lien against any such money settlement, and the attorney must first satisfy the lien of the physician before the patient or attorney receives any money from the settlement. Check the laws of your state. Call the office of the patient's attorney at least quarterly for an update.

If there is a third party litigation involved in an industrial case or a decision has not been reached as to whether an accident is due to industrial or nonindustrial causes, file both a regular lien and a workers' compensation lien. In most states, a special lien form for workers' compensation filing is available and should be used. A copy of the lien should be completed and sent to all concerned parties:

- Appeals board
- Employer of the patient
- Employee (the patient)
- Insurance carrier
- Physician's files (lien claimant or one who is filing for the lien)

The patient/employee consents to the lien by his or her signature. Do not accept a lien form unless it is also signed by the patient's attorney. Check with your local Division of Industrial Accidents for forms pertinent to filing a lien and instructions on the formalities, number of copies required, and where they are to be sent.

SECOND-INJURY FUND (SUBSEQUENT INJURY FUND)

This fund was established to meet problems arising when an employee has a pre-existing injury or condition and is subsequently injured at work. The pre-existing injury combines with the second injury to produce disability that is greater than that caused by the latter alone. For example, an individual loses a left thumb while working a lathe. Then, 2 years later, he or she loses the left index finger. A question could arise of whether the second injury added to a pre-existing condition or was related to the prior injury. The case illustrates that the existence of the former injury or disability substantially increased the disability caused by the latter injury.

Two functions of the fund are (1) to encourage hiring of the physically handicapped and (2) to allocate more equitably the costs of providing benefits to such employees. Second-injury employers pay compensation related primarily to the disability caused by the second injury, even though the employee receives benefits relating to the combined disability; the difference is made up from the second-injury fund, also known as the subsequent injury fund.

UNEMPLOYMENT COMPENSATION DISABILITY AND WORKERS' COMPENSATION

As mentioned in Chapter 15, five states have state disability insurance (unemployment compensation disability insurance): California, Hawaii, New Jersey, New York, and Rhode Island, along with Puerto Rico. If a recipient is collecting benefits from a workers' compensation insurance carrier and the amount that the compensation carrier pays is less than that allowed by the unemployment compensation disability insurance program, then the state disability program will pay the balance.

MEDICAL REPORTS

In most states, the first report of an industrial injury submitted by the employer and the physician is required by law (see Figs. 14–1, 14–3, and 14–16). However, subsequent progress or supplemental reports may be narrative and are not necessarily completed on the special forms available in most states (Figs. 14–7 to 14–9). The insurance carrier authorizing the examination should be furnished with the report in triplicate or quadruplicate, depending on its needs. A copy should always be retained for the physician's files.

A report should be sent to the insurance carrier primarily after each hospitalization to update the progress of a case. A surgeon's final report should be sent in, after the patient is discharged, indicating any impairment, permanent disability, and total expenses incurred.

CONFIDENTIALITY

There is a difference in the confidentiality of certain records in industrial cases. In most states, insurance claims adjusters have unlimited access to the injured employee's medical records pertaining only to an industrial case. Some states allow employers similar access.

DOCUMENTATION

Documentation must always show the necessity for the procedures performed. If there is not an accurate diagnostic code to explain the patient's condition, a report should be sent in describing the details of the diagnosis.

RECORDKEEPING

If a private patient comes to the office with an industrial injury, set up a separate medical record and financial record (ledger) for the work-related injury. Never mix a private medical record with an industrial case because the workers' compensation case may go to court. Some medical practices use a colored file folder for the industrial medical record, making filing of any insurance claims easier for the insurance billing specialist. If this should occur, it is easy to pull the industrial medical record and ledger quickly without having to dig through the patients' previously unrelated private medical records.

TERMINOLOGY

It is important to become familiar with some medical terms used in accidents as well as industrial injury reports. Figure 14–10 illustrates the use of some anatomic terms referring to directional words. Figure 14–11 shows commonly used terms for range of motion for upper and lower extremities. Figures 14–12 and 14–13 give pertinent anatomic words commonly used in reports about injuries. Carefully study the illustrations and look up the definitions to the words in the dictionary and learn how to spell them.

If the physician prefers to submit a narrative letter, the medical report should include the following:

1. Complete *history* of the accident, injury, or illness. The physician should state whether there is a causal connection between the accident and conditions that may appear subsequently but are not obvious sequelae. If facts were obtained by reviewing prior records or x-ray films, the source should be mentioned. When a history is obtained through an interpreter, be sure to include that person's name.
2. The patient's *present complaints;* sometimes given as *subjective* complaints.
3. The patient's *past history* and whether the employee has a pre-existing defect that might entitle him or her to benefits from the subsequent injury fund or represent the actual cause of the present condition.
4. Complete *medical findings* on examination; sometimes given as *objective* findings.

Text continued on page 353

ATTENDING PHYSICIAN'S REPORT

Employee: Mrs. Ima B. Hurt   Claim Number: 120 23 6542

Employer: The Conk Out Company   Date of Injury(ies): 4-3-9x   Date of Next Exam: ______

Date of This Exam: 5-5-9x   Patient Social Security No.: 120 23 6542

Current Diagnosis: (Include ICD•9 Code) sprain left metacarpal phalangeal joint of fifth finger 842.12

PATIENT STATUS

Since the last exam, this patient's condition has:

- ☒ improved as expected.
- ☐ improved, but slower than expected.
- ☐ not improved significantly.
- ☐ worsened.
- ☐ plateaued, no further improvement is expected.
- ☐ has been determined to be non-work related.

Briefly, describe any change in objective or subjective complaint:

Considerable pain left little finger and some restriction of motion

TREATMENT

Treatment plan: (only list changes from prior status)   ☐ No change   ☐ Patient is/was discharged from care on ______

Est. Discharge Date: 5-19-9x   Medications: Tylenol for pain

Therapy: Type hand exercises   Times per week 3   Estimated Date of Completion 5-19-9x

Diagnostic Studies: ______

Hospitalization/Surgery: ______

Consult/Other Service: ______

WORK STATUS

The patient has been instructed to:

- ☐ return to full duty with no limitations or restrictions.
- ☐ remain off the rest of the day and return to work tomorrow:
  ____ with no limits or restrictions.   ____ with limits listed below.
- ☒ return to work on 5-19-9x
  work limitations: ______
- ☐ remain off work until ______

Estimated date patient can return full duty: 5-19-9x

DISABILITY STATUS

- ☐ Patient discharged as cured.

Please supply a brief narrative report if any of the below apply:

- ☐ Patient will be permanently precluded from engaging in his/her usual and customary occupation.
- ☐ Patient's condition is permanent and stationary.
- ☐ Patient will have permanent residuals   ☐ Patient will require future medical care.

Physician Name: Martin Feelgood, MD   Address: 4567 Broad Avenue, Woodland Hills, XY 12345

Date: May 5, 199x   Telephone: (013) 482-9006

Signature: Martin Feelgood, MD

reference initials

FIGURE 14–7
Physician's Supplemental Report form.

STATE COMPENSATION INSURANCE FUND

669 COUNTY SQUARE DRIVE,VENTURA, CALIFORNIA 93003

DOCTOR'S FINAL (OR MONTHLY) REPORT AND BILL

Monthly itemized bills required on all cases under continuing treatment.
Services beginning late in month and extending into succeeding month may be itemized on one statement.

CASE No. 120 23 6542

EMPLOYEE Mrs. Ima B. Hurt
DATE OF INJURY April 3, 199x
EMPLOYER The Conk Out Company

SERVICES FOR MONTH OF April 19 9x

Patient refused treatment ______ 19 ___
Patient stopped treatment without orders ______ 19 ___
Patient entered hospital ______ 19 ___
Further treatment anticipated? X (Yes) ___ (No)

Patient able to return to work May 19, 19 9x
Patient discharged as cured ______ 19 ___
Condition at time of last visit ______

Any other charges authorized such as Drugs? ___ (Check) Hospital? ___ (Check)

Code: O—Office; V—Home Visit; H—Hospital Visit; N—Night Visit; S—Operation; X—X-ray.

Month	1	2	3	4	5	6	7	8	9	10	11	12	13	14	15	16	17	18	19	20	21	22	23	24	25	26	27	28	29	30	31
May			0																												

		RVS CODE	TOTALS
First aid treatment (describe)		#	$
Office Visits	5-31-9x Office visit	# 99203	$ 80.00
Home Visits		#	$
Hospital Visits		#	$
Operations		#	$
MATERIAL (Itemize at cost)	AP & lat films lt hand	# 73120	$ 70.00
	Splint	99070	35.00

Any charges shown above which are in excess of the scheduled fee must be explained regarding nature of such services, indicating the date rendered. TOTAL $ 185.00

Make check payable to:

Doctor Martin Feelgood, MD

Address 4567 Broad Avenue (Street)

Woodland Hills, XY 12345 (City) (Zip)

Signature *Martin Feelgood, MD*

Date April 5, 199x

Internal Revenue Code Section 6109 requires you to furnish your Internal Revenue Service Employer Identification Number or Social Security Number. Please enter the Identification Number here 95-3664021

LEAVE BLANK
APPROVED
(Dollars) (Cents)
BY ______
DATE ______

IMPORTANT.—
Bills Must Be Submitted in Duplicate
MAIL ADDRESS: P.O. BOX S, VENTURA, CALIFORNIA 93002

SCIF FORM 60 REV 5 78

FIGURE 14–8
Doctor's Final or Monthly Report and Bill form.

14

REPORT OF DENTAL INJURY

STATE COMPENSATION INSURANCE FUND

- Authorization should be obtained for all treatment other than ordinary first aid or emergency care.
- Under the Worker's Compensation Laws employers are only liable for repair or replacement of teeth actually damaged or lost due to occupational injuries.
- Mail report immediately after seeing patient for first time.

Claim No. ________________

- Attending Physician or Dentist - If you have not already done so, you must also send us a completed Doctor's First Report of Occupational Injury or Illness (SCIF Form 3111) within 5 days of your initial examination.

1. EMPLOYER ______________________________

2. Address ______________________________

3. EMPLOYEE (First name, middle initial, last name) ______________________ Social Security No. ____________

4. Address ______________________ City ______________ Zip ________

5. Date injured ______________ Hour ______ M. Date of your first examination ____________

6. ACCIDENT OR EXPOSURE: Did employee notify employer of this injury? ______ Employee's statement of cause of injury or illness?

____

7. PRIOR HISTORY:

Briefly comment on condition of oral cavity prior to present injury. Include comments on oral hygiene, periodontal disease, teeth missing, dental caries, and teeth filled, crowned, or replaced by bridges or plates.

____

8. NATURE AND EXTENT OF INJURY:

Give nature and extent of present injury. Include all objective findings, subjective complaints and diagnoses, outline on dental chart injuries caused by present occupational injury.

____

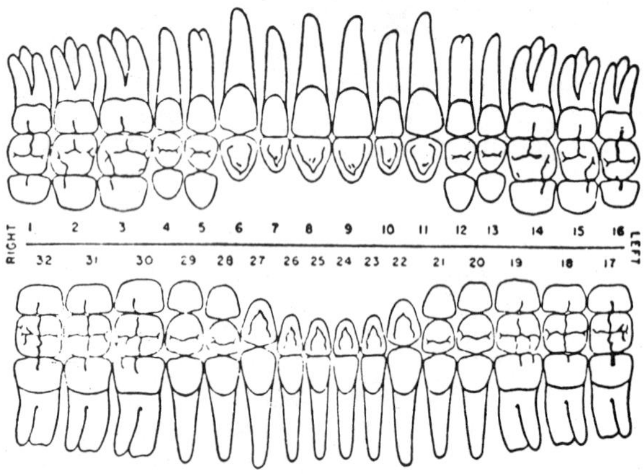

9. REPAIR, REPLACEMENT OF TREATMENT REQUIRED:

Indicate the types of materials to be used in fillings, crowns, partial and full dentures. Name the teeth to be replaced and those to be clasped in partial dentures. Name the type of prosthetic appliances to be used on abutment teeth, the type of pontics, and name the teeth being replaced by the bridges.

Note: Payment will be made only for care required because of the industrial injury.

____

10. COST:

____

Total $________

11. This report will be considered a request for authorization to undertake the described dental repair at the cost specified. You are requested to obtain authorization for all elective procedures. Submit an itemized bill. IN DUPLICATE, when work is completed.

Name ______________________ (Print or Type) Degree ____________ {PERSONAL SIGNATURE} ______________________

Date of report ______________ Address ______________________ Tel. No. ____________

Any person who makes or causes to be made any knowingly false or fraudulent material statement or material representation for the purpose of obtaining or denying workers' compensation benefits or payments is guilty of a felony.

SCIF 3071 (REV. 7-93)

FIGURE 14–9
Report of Dental Injury form.

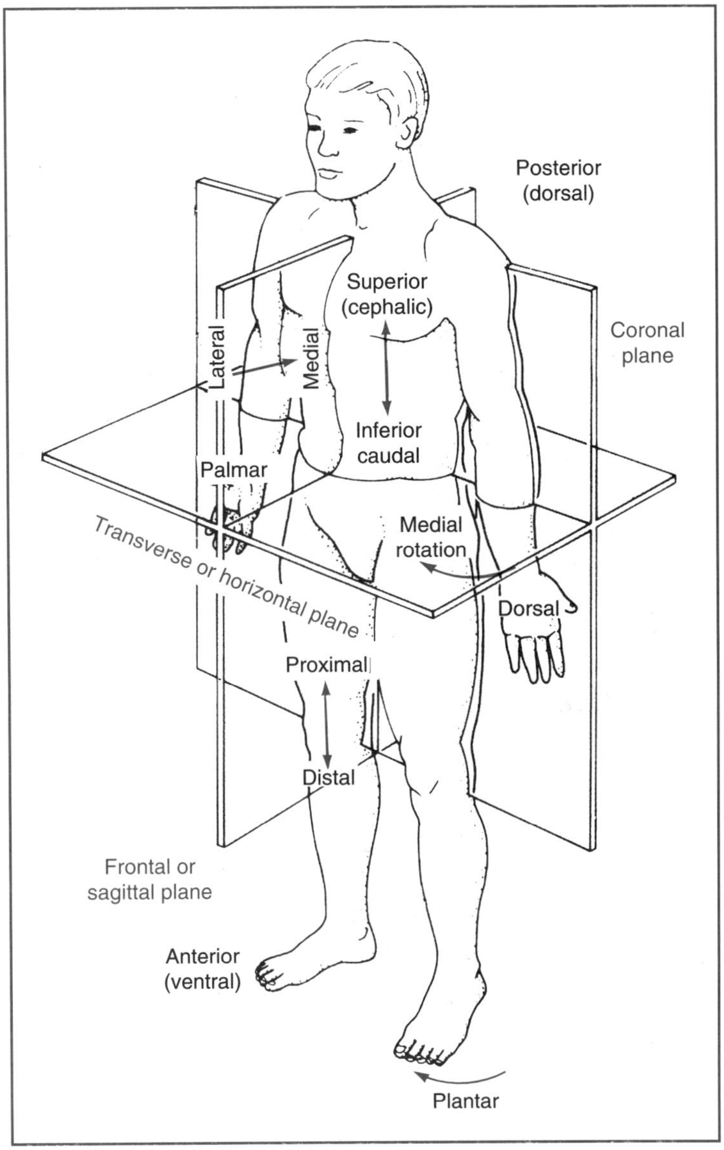

FIGURE 14-10
Directional terminology used in workers' compensation reports. This diagram illustrates the use of some anatomic terms referring to position and movement. (Reprinted with permission from Chabner, D. E.: *Medical Terminology: A Short Course.* Philadelphia, W.B. Saunders Company, 1991, p. 36.)

5. Report of *laboratory* or *x-ray* findings.
6. Complete *diagnosis.*
7. Opinion as to *relationship,* if any, between the injury or disease and the condition diagnosed.
8. The planned scope, course, and duration or recommended *treatment.*
9. The patient's *disability* and *prognosis,* including:
   a. Period during which the patient has been unable to work because of the injury or illness.
   b. Opinion as to probable further temporary disability and a statement as to when the patient will be able to return to work or has returned to work.
   c. Statement indicating whether the condition is currently permanent and stationary, as well as the probability of future permanent disability.
   d. When a patient has multiple complaints but no clinical objective findings, the physician may state, for example: "All objective tests for organic pathology are negative. There is obviously a strong functional or emotional overlay."

14

An evaluation of subjective factors should be given. *Subjective* refers to statements made by the patient about symptoms and how he or she feels. Subjective disability can best be evaluated by

- A description of the activity that produces the disability,
- The duration of the disability,

Text continued on page 358

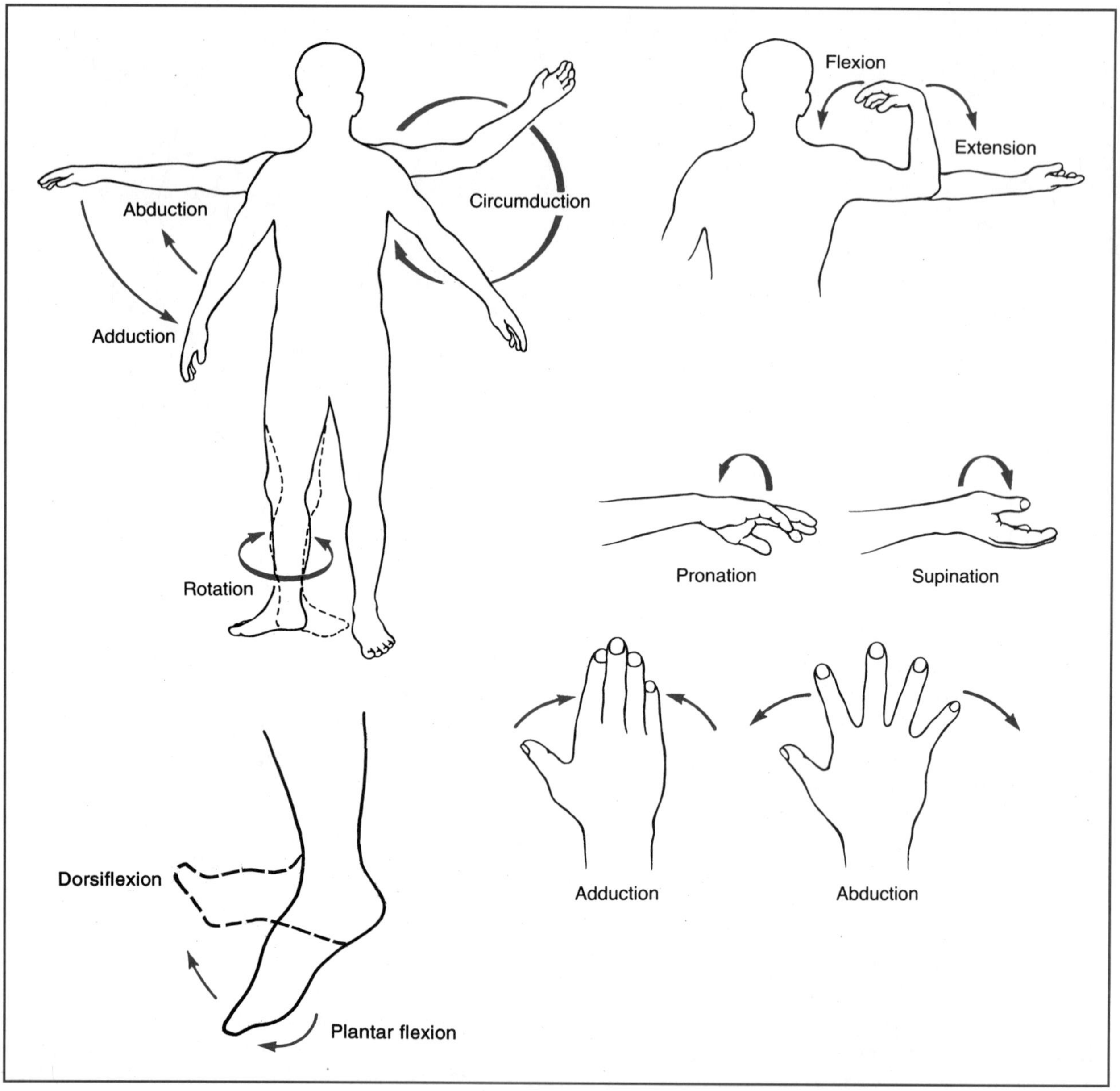

FIGURE 14–11
Range of motion for upper and lower extremities, including commonly used dictated terms. (Reprinted with permission from Sloane, S., and Fordney, M. T.: *Saunders Manual of Medical Transcription*. Philadelphia, W.B. Saunders Company, 1994.)

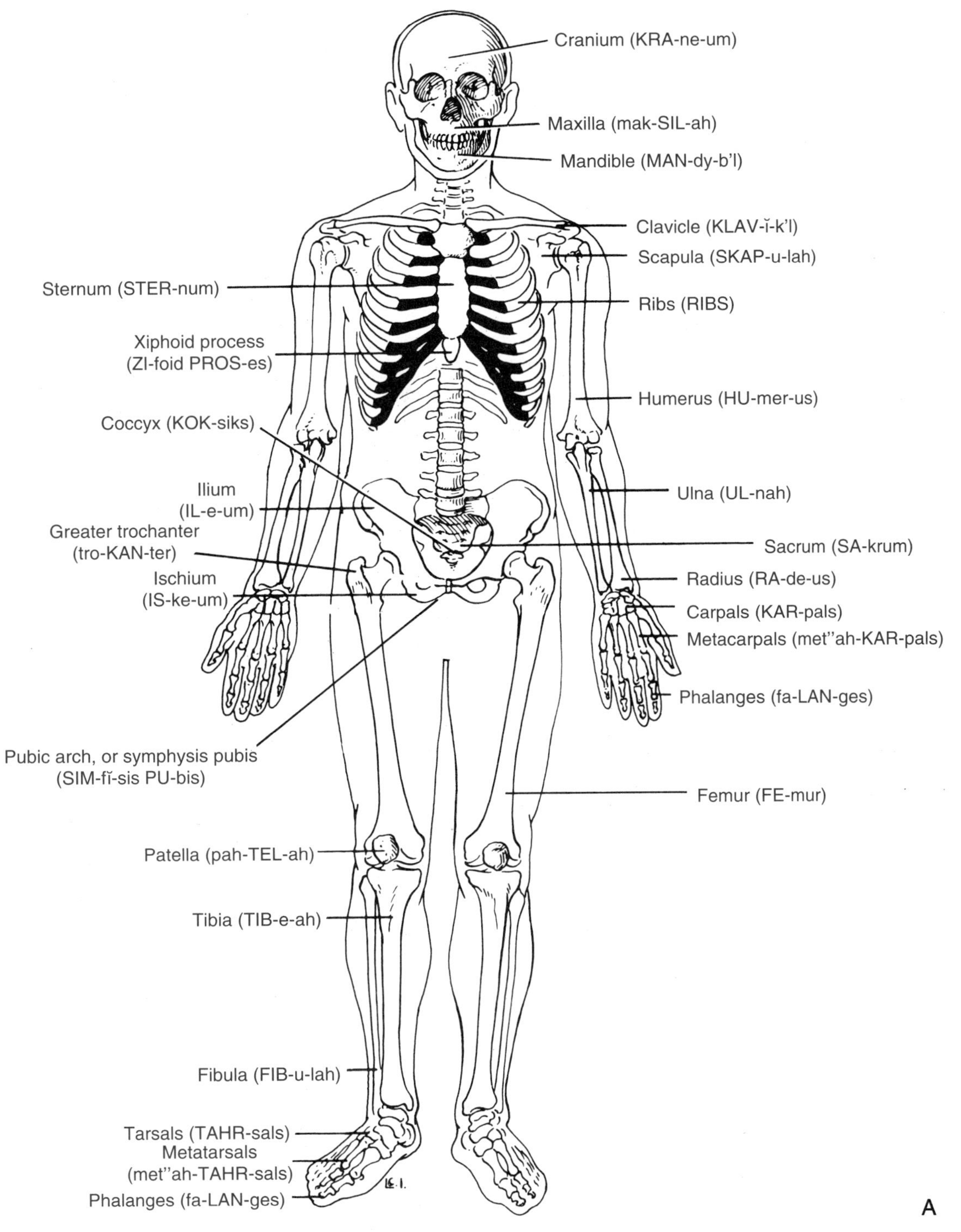

FIGURE 14–12

A and *B*, Terminology pertinent to the skeletal anatomy commonly used in reports on injury cases. (Reprinted with permission from Chabner, D. E.: *The Language of Medicine,* 4th ed. Philadelphia, W.B. Saunders Company, 1991, p. 501.)

Illustration continued on following page

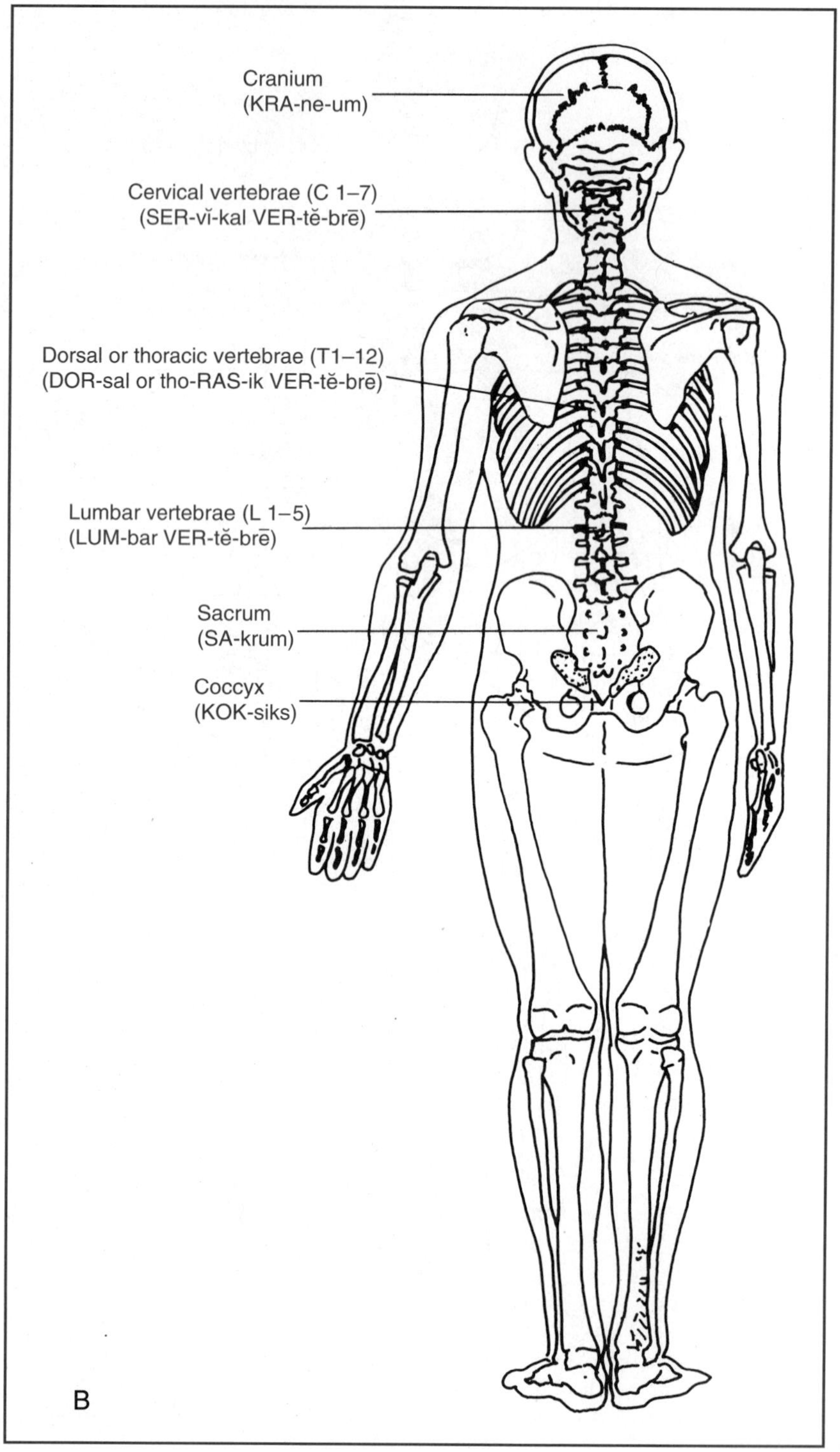

FIGURE 14–12 *Continued*

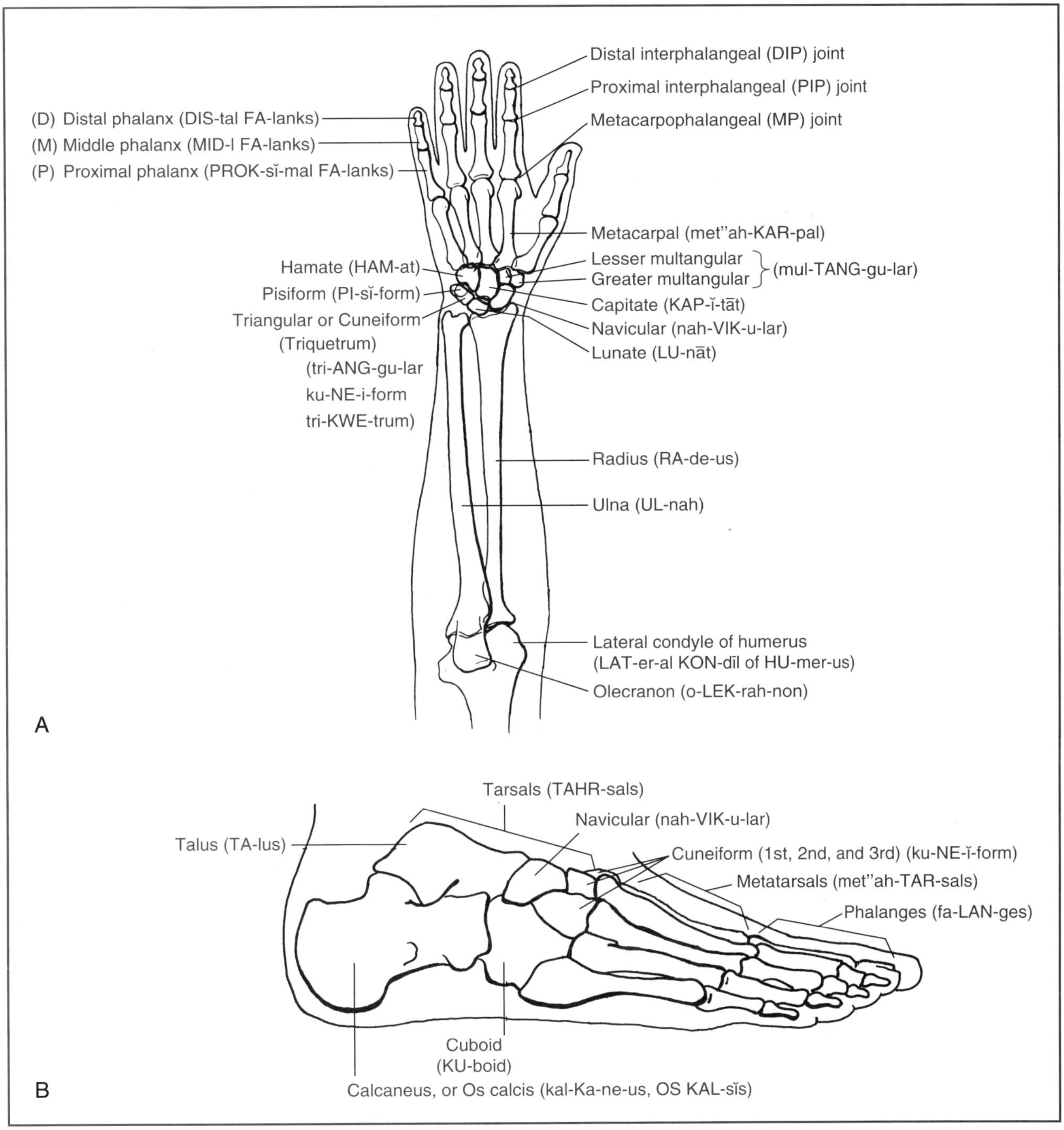

FIGURE 14-13

Terminology pertinent to the hand *(A)* and the foot *(B)*, indicating the common medical terms seen in reports on injury cases. (*A*, Redrawn from Marble, H. C.: *The Hand; A Manual and Atlas for the General Surgeon*. Philadelphia, W. B. Saunders Company, 1960; *B*, redrawn from Chabner, D. E.: *The Language of Medicine*, 4th ed. Philadelphia, W.B. Saunders Company, 1991.)

- The activities that are precluded by, and those that can be performed with, the disability,
- The means necessary for relief.

The following definitions were developed as examples of interpretations of *subjective* complaints:

1. A *severe pain* would preclude the activity causing the pain.
2. A *moderate pain* could be tolerated but would cause marked handicap in the performance of the activity precipitating the pain.
3. A *slight pain* could be tolerated but would cause some handicap in the performance of the activity precipitating the pain.
4. A *minimal or mild pain* would constitute an annoyance but would cause no handicap in the performance of the particular activity. It would be considered a nonratable permanent disability.

INFORMATION TO BE INCLUDED IN DETAILED PROGRESS OR RE-EXAMINATION REPORTS

1. Date of most recent examination
2. Present condition and progress since last report
3. Measurements of function
4. X-ray or laboratory report since last examination
5. Treatment (give type and duration)
6. Work status (patient working or estimated date of return to work)
7. Permanent disability to be anticipated

BILLING CLAIMS

FINANCIAL RESPONSIBILITY

As discussed in Chapter 2, the contract for treatment in a personal illness or injury case is between the physician and the patient who is responsible for the entire bill. However, when a business is self-insured, a person is under a state program for care, or an individual is being treated as a workers' compensation case, the financial responsibility exists between the physician and insurance company or state program. As long as treatment is authorized by the insurance carrier who retains the physician, the insurance company is responsible for payment. You cannot collect a copayment amount or balance bill the patient for any amount not covered by the workers' compensation fee schedule. If an injured worker refuses to accept the physician retained by the insurance company for the employer, then the patient is responsible for the cost of medical treatment. Some states have a medical program where employers can reduce their workers' compensation rates by paying the first $1000 in medical bills. This is similar to a deductible for the employer's policy. In this situation, send the statement to the employer for payment.

Sometimes while examining an injured worker the physician may discover that the patient has high blood pressure. The physician may bill the workers' compensation carrier for the examination but needs to code the claim carefully with regard to the treatment of the injury. If treatment is initiated for the patient's high blood pressure, then this becomes the financial obligation of the patient and not the workers' compensation carrier. Always obtain health insurance information in case you need to bill for services provided that are not work related or if the injury or illness is declared nonindustrial. To assist in informing patients of financial responsibility for nonrelated illness, have the worker sign an agreement for nonrelated medical expenses, as shown in Figure 14–14.

FEE SCHEDULES

Some states have developed and adopted workers' compensation fee schedules, whereas other states pay medical claims based on the Medicare fee schedule plus a certain percentage. Fee schedules assist with the following:

1. They limit the fees providers can charge for standard medical procedures paid by workers' compensation companies.
2. They limit the amount that providers will be paid.
3. They make the allowable charges and procedures more consistent.
4. They provide procedures to follow in case of a fee dispute.

Most states have some type of medical fee schedule. Some schedules list maximum reimbursement levels for physicians and other nonhospital providers. Generally, however, the physician is expected to accept payment by the insurance company as payment in full when based on a fee schedule. If the fee charged is more than the amount listed, the following factors may be considered:

- provider's medical training, qualifications, and time in practice
- nature of services provided

WORKERS' COMPENSATION AGREEMENT

Patient's Name________________________________Soc. Sec. #___________

Address______________________________________Tel. No.____________

WC Insurance Carrier_________________________________

Address_____________________________ Telephone No._____________

Date of illness_________________Date of first visit__________________

Emergency Yes_____ No _____

Is this condition related to employment? Yes_____ No _____

If accident: Auto_____ Other ___________________________

Where did injury occur?___________________________________

How did injury happen?____________________________________

Employee/employer who verified this information_______________

Employer's name and address______________________________________

Employer's telephone No.______________________

In the event the claim for workers' compensation is declared fraudulent for this illness or condition or it is determined by the Workers' Compensation Board that the illness or injury is not a compensable workers' compensation case, I, ___________________, hereby agree to pay the physician's fee for services rendered.

I have been informed that I am responsible to pay for any services rendered by Dr.__________________with regard to the discovery and treatment of any condition not related to the workers' compensation injury or illness. I agree to pay for all services not covered by workers' compensation and all charges for treatment and personal items unrelated to my workers' compensation illness or injury.

Signed___________________________ Date______________________

FIGURE 14–14

Workers' compensation agreement to pay the physician's fees if the case is declared not work related or if an illness is discovered and treated that is not work related.

14

- fees usually charged by the provider
- fees usually charged by others in the region where services were given
- other aspects of the economics of the provider's practice that are relevant
- any unusual circumstances in the case

If documentation is sent validating the fee, sometimes the insurance carrier will pay the additional amount.

Types of Fee Schedules

Percentile of charge schedule, which is designed to set fees at a percentile of the providers' usual and customary fee.

Relative value scale schedule, which takes into account the time, skills, and extent of the service provided by the physician. Each procedure is rated on how difficult it is, how long it takes, the training a physician must have to perform it, and expenses the physician incurs, including the cost of malpractice insurance. Many of the fee schedules are similar to the CPT format as far as sections (i.e., Evaluation and Management; Anesthesia; Surgery; Radiology, Nuclear Medicine and Diagnostic Ultrasound; Pathology and Laboratory; and Medicine). Sometimes a schedule may include modifiers and code numbers not listed in the CPT code book. A *conversion factor* of so many dollars and cents is used for each of the sections of the fee schedule. Conversion factors may be adjusted to reflect regional differences and in some states are recalculated on an annual basis. The 1994 conversion factors for workers' compensation in California are

$7.15/unit	Evaluation and Management section
$6.15/unit	Medicine section
$34.50/unit	Anesthesia section
$153.00/unit	Surgery section
$12.50/unit	Radiology section (total unit value column)
$1.95/unit	Professional component
$1.50/unit	Technical component
$1.50/unit	Pathology section technical component

With regard to enforcement of fee schedules, three methods are seen in states across the nation. In some states, the state agency or state fund responsible for overseeing workers' compensation performs bill reviews. In other states, the payer (employer or insurance carrier) does bill reviews. A number of states combine the practices by requiring bill review by payers and in addition provide a state agency to conduct compliance audits.

HELPFUL BILLING TIPS

The following are helpful hints for billing workers' compensation claims.

1. Whenever a patient comes in for an appointment for care of an injury, the individual registering and verifying insurance information should *always* ask whether the injury occurred within the scope of employment. This will prevent filing initial claims with the wrong insurance carrier.
2. Educate the patient with regard to your billing policies for workers' compensation cases by having them complete the form shown in Figure 14–14.
3. Ask the patient to obtain the claim number of their case when he or she comes in for the initial visit.
4. Document in a telephone log or patient's record all data for authorization of examination and diagnostic studies, e.g., data, name of individual who authorizes, response, and so forth.
5. Verify if prior authorization is required before a surgical procedure is performed.
6. Obtain the workers' compensation fee schedule for your state.
7. Use appropriate five-digit code numbers and modifiers to ensure prompt and accurate payment for services rendered.
8. Complete the Doctor's First Report of Occupational Injury of Illness form for your state and submit it within the time limit shown in Table 14–1.
9. Submit a monthly itemized statement or bill on the termination of treatment for nondisability claims.
10. Any charges in excess of the fee schedule should be clearly defined by the physician. Attach any x-ray reports, operative reports, discharge summaries, pathology reports, and so forth to clarify such excess charges or when *by report* (BR) is shown for a code selected from the workers' compensation procedure code book.
11. Drugs and dressings furnished by the physician should be itemized in detail and charged at cost.
12. If you have a question regarding the fee, call the insurance carrier and talk with the adjuster who is familiar with the patient's case.
13. For booklets, bulletins, forms, and legislation information, write to the workers' compensation state plan office in your state. See Appendix A for the address.

14. For information about federal benefits, contact the following:
    Department of Labor
    Employment Standards Administration
    Washington, D.C. 20210
    and direct your inquiry to one of these departments:
    Division of Coal Mine Workers' Compensation
    Division of Federal Employees' Compensation
    Division of Longshore and Harbor Workers' Compensation

ELECTRONIC CLAIMS SUBMISSION

See Chapter 7 for information on workers' compensation claims processed via Electronic Data Systems, Inc. (EDS) and Insurance Value-Added Network Services (IVANS).

OUT-OF-STATE CLAIMS

When billing for an out-of-state claim, insurance billing specialists must treat all workers' compensation regulations from the jurisdiction (state) where the claim originated and remains as an open case. Sometimes a patient may seek care from a physician in an adjacent state because he or she feels the physician provides a higher quality of care or the patient needs a specialized type of surgery, expensive diagnostic tests, or treatment. It is important that referral requirements be met before the patient is seen, e.g., written referral or preauthorization from the managing doctor with a copy to the workers' compensation carrier. Nine states hold the injured employee responsible for unauthorized care (Alabama, Alaska, Arkansas, New Jersey, North Dakota, Ohio, Washington, West Virginia, and Wisconsin).

Obtain the out-of-state fee schedule to determine the proper procedure codes, modifiers, and amounts for billing the claim. Find out whether ICD-9-CM diagnostic codes are acceptable. Ask whether the claimant's jurisdiction accepts the HCFA-1500 claim form or another form. Determine whether other documents, e.g., the operative report, should be submitted with the bill. When a patient crosses a state line for treatment, he or she may be liable for some balance billing, and the patient should be informed of this fact.

INSTRUCTIONS FOR COMPLETING THE DOCTOR'S FIRST REPORT OF OCCUPATIONAL INJURY OR ILLNESS (Fig. 14–15 for *Workbook* Assignment 50)

Type an original and make three or four copies. This form must be submitted anywhere from immediately to within 5 days after the patient has been seen by the physician, depending on state law. Distribute copies as follows:

Original to the insurance carrier (unless more copies are required)
One copy to the state
One copy to the patient's employer
One copy retained for the physician's files in the patient's workers' compensation file folder

In some states, attending physicians may file a single report directly to the insurer or self-insured employer within a specified number of days from initial treatment. The insurer or self-insured employer, in turn, is required to send a report to the state agency. This cuts down on paperwork and postage. Refer to Table 14–1 to find out the time limit in your state during which the physician must submit the initial report.

Element 1 ■ Enter the insurance carrier's complete name, street address, city, state, and ZIP code.

Element 2 ■ List the employer's full name. If the policy number is known, list it also on this line, since some insurance carriers file by employer and then by policy number. Sometimes the employer's telephone number is required on this line.

Element 3 ■ Give the employer's street address, city, state, and ZIP code.

Element 4 ■ List the type of business the company is involved in, such as manufacturing shoes, building construction, retailing men's clothes, and so forth.

Element 5 ■ State the patient's complete first name, middle initial, and last name.

Element 6 ■ Check the appropriate box to indicate whether the patient is male or female.

Element 7 ■ Type the patient's birth date in this box.

Element 8 ■ List the patient's street address, city, state, and ZIP code.

Element 9 ■ List the patient's home telephone number.

Element 10 ■ Give the title of the patient's occupation. It is important to be accurate in listing the occupation so that the insurance carrier may be cer-

14

STATE OF CALIFORNIA

DOCTOR'S FIRST REPORT OF OCCUPATIONAL INJURY OR ILLNESS

Within 5 days of your initial examination, for every occupational injury or illness, send two copies of this report to the **employer's workers' compensation insurance carrier** or the **self-insured employer.** Failure to file a timely doctor's report may result in assessment of a civil penalty. **In the case of diagnosed or suspected pesticide poisoning,** send a copy of this report to Division of Labor Statistics and Research, P.O. Box 420603, San Francisco, CA 94142-0603, and notify your local health officer by telephone within 24 hours.

PLEASE DO NOT USE THIS COLUMN: Case No. / Industry / County / Age / Hazard / Disease / Hospitalization / Occupation / Return Date/Code

1. **INSURER NAME AND ADDRESS**
   Best Insurance Company, 1100 Fine Street, Happiness, XY 12345
2. **EMPLOYER NAME**
   The Conk Out Company Policy #3452-9X
3. Address No. and Street City Zip
   3300 Debilitated Street Repair, XY 12345
4. Nature of business (e.g., food manufacturing, building construction, retailer of women's clothes)
   plumbing repair
5. **PATIENT NAME** (first name, middle initial, last name)
   Ima B. Hurt
6. Sex ☐ Male ☒ Female
7. Date of Birth Mo. Day Yr. 3-4-66
8. Address: No. and Street City Zip
   3300 Broke Street, Fractured, XY 12345
9. Telephone number (013) 476-9899
10. Occupation (Specific job title)
    clerk typist
11. Social Security Number 023- 45 - 6789
12. Injured at: No. and Street City County
    3300 Debilitated Street, Repair, XY 12345 Humboldt
13. Date and hour of injury or onset of illness Mo. Day Yr. 4-3-9X ______ a.m. Hour 2:00 p.m.
14. Date last worked Mo. Day Yr. 4-3-9X
15. Date and hour of first examination or treatment Mo. Day Yr. 4-3-9X ______ a.m. Hour 4:00 p.m.
16. Have you (or your office) previously treated patient? ☐ Yes ☒ No

Patient please complete this portion, if able to do so. Otherwise, doctor please complete immediately. Inability or failure of a patient to complete this portion shall not affect his/her rights to workers' compensation under the California Labor Code.

17. **DESCRIBE HOW THE ACCIDENT OR EXPOSURE HAPPENED** (Give specific object, machinery or chemical. Use reverse side if more space is required.)
    Patient states, "lifted corner of wordprocessor to dust desk, temporarily lost control, and wordprocessor came down on my left little finger."
18. **SUBJECTIVE COMPLAINTS** (Describe fully. Use reverse side if more space is required.)
    Pain and some slight swelling of left little finger.
19. **OBJECTIVE FINDINGS** (Use reverse side if more space is required.)
    A. Physical examination
    Pain and some slight swelling of left little finger.
    B. X-ray and laboratory results (State if none or pending.) AP and lat. films left hand reveal hairline fracture
20. **DIAGNOSIS** (if occupational illness specify etiologic agent and duration of exposure.) Chemical or toxic compounds involved? ☐ Yes ☒ No
    Fracture distal interphalangeal joint 5th phalanx ICD-9 Code 923.3
21. Are your findings and diagnosis consistent with patient's account of injury or onset of illness? ☒ Yes ☐ No If "no", please explain.
22. Is there any other current condition that will impede or delay patient's recovery? ☐ Yes ☒ No If "yes", please explain.
23. **TREATMENT RENDERED** (Use reverse side if more space is required.)
    Examination, x-rays, applied splint to left hand, advised restricted use of left hand and return in one week for recheck.
24. If further treatment required, specify treatment plan/estimated duration.
    Physical therapy 3 X 4 *(3 times a week for 4 weeks)*
25. If hospitalized as inpatient, give hospital name and location Date admitted Mo. Day Yr. Estimated stay
26. **WORK STATUS**—Is patient able to perform usual work? ☐ Yes ☒ No
    If "no", date when patient can return to: Regular work 5 / 19 / 9X
    Modified work ___/___/___ Specify restrictions ______

Doctor's Signature *Martin Feelgood, MD* 4-5-9X CA License Number A 12345
Doctor Name and Degree (please type) Martin Feelgood, MD IRS Number 95-3664021
Address 4567 Broad Avenue, Woodland Hills, XY 12345 Telephone Number (013) 486-9002

FORM 5021 (REV. 4) 1992

Any person who makes or causes to be made any knowingly false or fraudulent material statement or material representation for the purpose of obtaining or denying workers' compensation benefits or payments is guilty of a felony.

reference initials

FIGURE 14-15
Doctor's First Report of Occupational Injury or Illness form, used in California.

tain the patient was doing the job for which he or she was insured.

Element 11 ▪ Give the patient's Social Security number. Some insurance carriers use the Social Security number as the industrial case number.

Element 12 ▪ The exact location where the patient was injured should be given. Many times the injury may occur off the premises of the company or factory, depending on the type of job on which the employee was working. List the county where the patient was injured.

Element 13 ▪ Enter the date the patient was injured and give the exact or approximate time of the injury.

Element 14 ▪ State the date the patient last worked. It is important to list this so that the insurance carrier will know whether the patient is still working or has been disabled and cannot return to work.

Element 15 ▪ Enter the date of the physician's first examination. It is important for the insurance carrier to know how soon after the accident the patient sought medical attention. List, as nearly as possible, the time the physician saw the patient.

Element 16 ▪ Check the appropriate box indicating whether the physician has previously treated the patient.

Element 17 ▪ Answers to these questions regarding medical findings may be found in the patient's medical record, or the physician may dictate this information to the assistant. This should be in the patient's own words.

Element 18 ▪ Subjective complaints.

Element 19 ▪ Objective findings.

Element 20 ▪ Diagnosis and ICD-9-CM code number.

Element 21 ▪ Check the appropriate box (Yes or No) to indicate whether the findings and diagnosis are consistent with the history of injury or onset of illness.

Element 22 ▪ Check the appropriate box (Yes or No) to indicate whether there is any other current condition that will impede or delay the patient's recovery.

Element 23 ▪ Give a description of what treatment was rendered.

Element 24 ▪ Indicate whether further treatment is required. Indicate whether physical therapy is required.

Element 25 ▪ If the patient is to be hospitalized, give the name and location of the hospital, the admission date, and the estimated stay.

Element 26 ▪ Check the appropriate box (Yes or No) to indicate whether the patient is able to work as usual. If the answer is No, give the date when it is estimated that the patient will be able to return to regular or modified work. It is very important for the insurance company to anticipate how much future treatment will be required so that money may be set aside for temporary disability benefits, medical benefits, and, if necessary, permanent disability benefits. If the estimated date of return to work should change after the form is submitted, a supplemental report or progress note should be sent to the insurance carrier to change the date of the disability.

If not preprinted at the bottom of the form, type in the physician's name and degree (e.g., M.D., D.C., and so on), complete address, telephone number, state license number, and IRS number. Indicate the date the report is submitted. The insurance billing specialist should type reference initials in the lower left-hand corner of the form. This form *must be signed in ink* by the physician. Any carbon copies or photocopies must also be signed in ink. A stamped signature will *not* be accepted if the case goes into litigation or is presented for a permanent disability rating. Only those documents considered as original medical records are acceptable, and this means a handwritten signature by the attending physician.

DELINQUENT CLAIMS

If a workers' compensation claim becomes 45 days delinquent, the insurance billing specialist should send a letter to the insurance carrier (Fig. 14–16).

After receiving a response from the insurance carrier, it may be necessary to send subsequent letters to the employer. For example, if the insurance company notifies the physician's office that the employer's preliminary report of injury has not been received, then send a letter to the employer (Fig. 14–17).

If the employer does not respond to the letter requesting the Employer's Report of Work Injury after 30 days have elapsed from the date of the letter, send a letter to the Workers' Compensation Board or Industrial Accidents Commission in your state (Fig. 14–18).

Refer to Chapter 8 for additional information on following up on delinquent claims.

Max Gluteus, MD
4567 Broad Avenue
Woodland Hills, XY 12345
013/486-9002

June 1, 199x

Best Insurance Company
1100 Fine Street
Happiness, XY 12345

Dear Madam or Sir:

Re: Case No.: 120 23 6542
Injured: Mrs. Ima B. Hurt
Date of Injury: April 3, 199x
Employer: The Conk Out Company
Amount: $75.00

Our records indicate that our final statement for the above case dated April 5, 199x remains unpaid.

Your cooperation in furnishing us the present status of this statement will be appreciated. A notation on the bottom of this letter will be sufficient.

Very truly yours,

______________________, MD

ref initials

_____No Employer's Report on file.
_____No Doctor's First Report on file.
_____Did not receive itemized billing statement.
_____Payment was made. Check No.______Date______________
_____Other reason(s)________________________________

FIGURE 14–16
If a workers' compensation claim becomes 45 days delinquent, the insurance billing specialist should send this letter to the insurance carrier.

Max Gluteus, MD
4567 Broad Avenue
Woodland Hills, XY 12345
013/486-9002

June 15, 199x

The Conk Out Company
3300 Debilitated Street
Repair, XY 12345

Dear Madam or Sir:

Re: Case No.: 120 23 6542
Injured: Mrs. Ima B. Hurt
Date of Injury: April 3, 199x

I have been informed by your workers' compensation insurance carrier that they have not as yet received the employer's report in regard to the above injured person.

Unless you have already done so, may I ask your cooperation in completing and sending this report so that the case may be closed.

Should you have any questions or if I can be of assistance to you in any way, please do not hesitate to call on me.

Very truly yours,

__________________________,MD

ref initials

FIGURE 14-17
If the insurance company notifies the physician's office that the employer's preliminary report of injury has not been received, send this letter to the employer.

Max Gluteus, MD
4567 Broad Avenue
Woodland, Hills, XY 12345
013/486-9002

July 15, 199x

Division of Industrial Accidents
Los Angeles State Office Building
107 South Broadway, Room 4107
Los Angeles, CA 90012

Dear Madam or Sir:

Re: Failure of employer to follow Section No. 3760

Your office is being solicited to help secure an Employer's Report of Work Injury from the employer listed below.

Case No.:	120 23 6542
Name of Employer:	The Conk Out Company
Address:	3300 Debilitated Street Repair, XY 12345
Name of Injured:	Mrs. Ima B. Hurt
Address:	23 Broke Street Fractured, XY 12345
Date of Injury:	April 3, 199x
Name of Insurance Carrier:	Best Insurance Company
Amount of Unpaid Bill:	$75.00

Your cooperation in this matter will be greatly appreciated. If you need further information, please feel free to contact my office.

Sincerely yours,

__________________________, MD

ref initials

FIGURE 14–18
If the employer does not respond to your letter requesting the Employer's Report of Work injury after 30 days have elapsed from the date of the letter, send this letter to the Workers' Compensation Board or Industrial Accident Commission in your state.

A REQUEST FOR SICK LEAVE

To end this chapter with a bit of levity, here is a report from the *Toronto Star* of a true incident.

One hour after beginning a new job which involved moving a pile of bricks from the top of a two-story house to the ground, a construction worker in Peterborough, Ontario, suffered an accident which hospitalized him. He was instructed by his employer to fill out an accident report. It read:

"Thinking I could save time, I rigged a beam with a pulley at the top of the house, and a rope leading to the ground. I tied an empty barrel on one end of the rope, pulled it to the top of the house, and then fastened the other end of the rope to a tree. Going up to the top of the house, I filled the barrel with bricks.

"Then I went down and unfastened the rope to let the barrel down. Unfortunately, the barrel was now heavier than I, and before I knew what was happening, the barrel jerked me up in the air.

"I hung on to the rope, and half-way up I met the barrel coming down, receiving a severe blow on the left shoulder. I then continued on up to the top, banging my head on the beam and jamming my fingers in the pulley.

"When the barrel hit the ground, the bottom burst, spilling the bricks. As I was now heavier than the barrel, I started down at high speed. Halfway down, I met the empty barrel coming up, receiving several cuts and contusions from the sharp edges.

"At this point I must have become confused, because I let go of the rope. The barrel came down, striking me on the head, and I woke up in the hospital.

"I respectfully request sick leave."

TO THE STUDENT

For further knowledge and understanding, the key terms at the beginning of the chapter appear in the Glossary at the end of this textbook so you can look up the pertinent terms. You are now ready to complete the review questions and Assignments 50 through 52 in the *Workbook*. The assignments will give you hands-on experience in completing workers' compensation insurance claim forms and reports, as well as enhanced proficiency in procedural and diagnostic coding.

After completing the *Workbook* assignments, you may want additional practice on the concepts you have learned. Case 5 is not a workers' compensation scenario but is a private insurance accident case and is available on your computer disk.

Objectives*

THE INSURANCE BILLING SPECIALIST WILL BE ABLE TO:

- Describe benefits and exclusions contained in individual and group disability income insurance.
- Define terminology and abbreviations pertinent to disability insurance and disability benefit programs.
- Name federal disability benefit programs.
- State eligibility requirements, benefits, and limitations of SSDI and SSI.
- Differentiate between SSDI and SSI.
- Explain disability benefit programs for disabled active military personnel, veterans, and their dependents.
- Name states that have state disability insurance plans.
- State eligibility requirements, benefits, and limitations of state disability plans.
- Explain voluntary plans of disability insurance.
- Recognize forms used for processing state disability plans.
- Explain topics and contents of a medical history report.
- Define the words *temporary disability* and *permanent disability*, as related to each type of disability program.
- List guidelines to follow for federal, state, individual, and group disability claim procedures.

Key Terms

accidental death and dismemberment
armed services disability
Civil Service Retirement System (CSRS)
consultative examiner (CE)
cost-of-living adjustment
Disability Determination Services (DDS)
disability income insurance
double indemnity
elimination period
Federal Employees Retirement System (FERS)
future purchase option
hearing
long-term disability insurance
nonoccupational policy
partial disability
reconsideration
regional office (RO)
short-term disability income insurance
Social Security Administration (SSA)
Social Security Disability Insurance (SSDI) program
State Disability Insurance (SDI)
supplemental benefits
Temporary Disability Insurance (TDI)
total disability
Unemployment Compensation Disability (UCD)
Veterans Administration Disability program
Veterans Administration (VA) Outpatient Clinics
voluntary disability insurance
waiver of premium

*Performance objectives and exercises for hands-on practical experience for this chapter appear in the *Workbook*.

CHAPTER 15

Disability Income Insurance and Disability Benefit Programs

Introduction

Not everyone has disability insurance, but when working with patients who have it, you may encounter some interesting and unique accidents, injuries, or illnesses. After reading these extracts or direct quotations from disability insurance claim applications, you may ask "How in the world could something like this happen?" The following gems become quotable quotes and show just how funny some situations can appear.

Describe how your disability occurred:

"A hernia, from pulling cork out of bottle."

"Put tire patch on Playtex girdle and it caused infection on right thigh."

"While waving goodnight to friends, fell out a two-story window."

"Back injury received from jumping off a ladder to escape being hit by a train."

One victim described graphically an experience most of us have had: "Getting on a bus, the driver started before I was all on." Can you hear them asking at the hospital, "Was this your assigned seat?"

"I dislocated my shoulder swatting a fly." Have you ever dislocated a shoulder at this sport—I have—I knocked over two table lamps, several highballs, and skinned an elbow.

Funny misspellings on insurance forms:	**What it should have been:**
yellow "jonders"	yellow jaundice
"goalstones"	gallstones
"limp glands"	lymph glands
"falls teeth"	false teeth
"high pretension"	hypertension
"Pabst smear"	Pap smear
"wrecktum"	rectum

Unique accident:

The patient was under the kitchen sink repairing a leak when the family cat came along, watched for awhile, then playfully—but painfully—reached up and clawed him. Startled, the man threw his head back, cracked it on the bottom of the sink, and was knocked out cold. He came to as he was being carried out on a stretcher and explained to the attendants what had happened. One stretcher bearer laughed so hard, he relaxed his hold and the patient fell to the ground and broke his arm.

Because you have come to the end of your course on insurance billing and have learned a great deal, you may feel a bit bogged down by the many rules and regulations and their everchanging nature. The introduction to this chapter may add a bit of levity to your perspective on the world of disability insurance.

This chapter introduces various types of disability income insurance plans as well as a number of disability benefit programs. The first topic, which is *disability income insurance,* is a form of health insurance providing periodic payments under certain conditions when the insured is unable to work because of illness, disease, or injury—not as a result of work-related accidents or conditions.

A second section describes six major programs administered by the U.S. government related to industrial accidents and disability benefit programs unrelated to work injuries.

The third part of the chapter deals with nonindustrial state disability programs administered in six states, as well as voluntary disability insurance plans.

Specific administrative guidelines for federal, state, individual, and group disability claim procedures are presented at the end of the chapter.

History

Before the late 1800s, disability income insurance provided only accident protection. Some life insurance contracts had disability income riders attached to them offering limited benefits. Insurance companies in the early 1880s began selling disability income policies offering coverage for accident and illness. Then in the early 1900s, the Paul Revere Life Insurance Company introduced the first noncancelable disability income policy. This meant that the contract would be in force for a certain period of time and guaranteed that the premium would not be increased. In 1956, Congress enacted legislation providing for disability income protection under the Social Security program for disabled individuals over the age of 50 years. This program was expanded by 1965 to cover workers without regard to age as long as certain eligibility standards were met.

Today, disability income insurance is available from private insurance companies (individual policies) and employer-sponsored plans (group policies). Government-funded and state benefit programs are also available for disabled persons. This chapter will discuss all these plans and programs and the role of the insurance billing specialist.

Disability Income Insurance

INDIVIDUAL

Disability income insurance is coverage that provides a specific monthly or weekly income when an individual becomes unable to work, temporarily or totally, because of an illness or injury. The disability is *not* work related. With workers' compensation insurance, however, the illness or accident *must be* work related. Disability income policies *do not* provide medical expense benefits. For individuals who are self-employed, this insurance is particularly important because a business could not meet its financial obligations if the owner became injured or too ill to work. For example, if an individual is self-employed with a home-based business, repetitive stress injuries (RSIs) would not allow that individual to use the computer for several months. The main purpose of these policies is to provide some benefits while the person is not able to work. To collect benefits, the individual must meet the policy's criteria of what constitutes partial, temporary, or total disability. These policies terminate when the individual retires or reaches a certain age, usually 65 years.

Waiting Period

Basic terminology used with this type of coverage is as follows: The time period from the beginning of disability to receiving the first payment of benefits is called an *elimination period* or *waiting period.* During this initial period, a disabled individual is not eligible to receive benefits even though he or she is unable to work.

Benefit Period

A *benefit period* is the maximum amount of time that benefits will be paid to the injured or ill person for the disability (i.e., 2-year, 5-year, to age 65, or lifetime). Benefits paid to the insured disabled person are called *indemnity* and can be received daily, weekly, monthly, or semiannually depending on the policy.

Disability

The definition of *total disability* that is stated in each policy varies from one to the other as there is no standard definition. An example of a liberal definition might read: "The insured must be unable to perform the major duties of his or her specific occupation." Social Security has a restrictive definition that you will read later in this chapter; see page 373.

The terms *residual disability* and *partial disability* are defined as "when an illness or injury prevents an insured person from performing *one or more* of the functions of his or her regular job"—in other words, when a person cannot perform all of the job duties. *Temporary disability* exists when a person cannot perform *all* the functions of his or her regular job for a limited period of time. Benefits are not taxable if premiums are paid by the individual.

Clauses

If a policy is *guaranteed renewable,* this means the insurer is required to renew the policy as long as premium payments are made for a specified number of years or to age 60, 65, or 70 or for life. However, the premium may be increased when it is renewed. If the policy has a *noncancelable clause,* this means the premium cannot be increased.

A *waiver of premium,* if included in the insurance contract, means that while disabled, the employee does not have to pay any premiums, and these are paid by the policy. Usually this provision is used as a total and permanent disability benefit and may be available in certain other cases.

Benefits

Premiums and benefits hinge on several risk factors, such as age, gender, health history and physical state, income, and occupational duties. Some policies include residual or partial disability income benefits.

Residual benefits pay a partial benefit when the insured is not totally disabled. If one becomes partially disabled or can work only part-time or in a limited capacity, the residual benefits make up the difference between what an individual can make now and what he or she would have made working full-time.

Supplemental benefits may consist of insurance provisions that will

1. Increase monthly indemnity (*future purchase option* or *cost-of-living adjustment*)
2. Distribute a percentage of the policy premiums if an individual keeps a policy in force for 5 or 10 years or does not file any claims.

An *accidental death and dismemberment* benefit is written into some contracts. This offers the insured person protection when loss of sight or loss of limb(s) occurs. In some policies, such as life insurance, if an unintended, unexpected, and unforeseeable accident occurs resulting in death, a special provision known as *double indemnity* applies. This feature provides for twice the face amount of the policy to be paid if death results from accidental causes.

Exclusions ▪ These are provisions written into the insurance contract denying coverage or limiting the scope of coverage. Examples are pre-existing conditions; disability due to war, riot, self-inflicted injury, or attempted suicide; disability while legally intoxicated or under the influence of narcotics unless prescribed by a licensed physician; that arising from normal pregnancy, during the act of committing a felony, or if benefits are being received under workers' compensation or a government program. The phrase *legally intoxicated* means intoxication in an individual who has a certain amount of alcohol in the blood when tested that exceeds limits set down by state law.

AIDS and HIV ■ States have statutes governing questions that can and cannot be asked on insurance and other forms regarding AIDS and HIV testing; therefore, *each* state has developed its own claim and filing insurance forms. If a private insurance company wishes to test an applicant, a consent/notice form including acceptance of pre- and post-test counseling must be signed.

GROUP

Some employers elect to offer group disability income insurance as a fringe benefit. These contracts are drawn up between the insurer and the employer. Premiums may be paid by the employer with or without contributions from the employee. Employees hold certificates of insurance and are covered under the employer's policy, so they are not called policyholders. Monthly benefits are usually paid directly to the employee and are taxable if the employee is not making any contribution toward the premiums. When the employee leaves the company the insurance terminates, unless the employee is disabled. A few group policies allow conversion to a limited benefit individual policy.

Benefits vary from one plan to another but usually cover short-term disabilities (13 weeks to 24 months) or long-term disabilities (to age 65). To qualify for benefits, an individual must be unable to perform the major duties of his or her occupation during the initial period of disability (i.e., the first 2 years). Benefits cease when the employee returns to work even part time. These policies offer the worker partial disability income benefits to motivate a disabled individual to return to work on a part-time basis.

Disabilities commonly excluded from coverage include

- Illness or injury requiring medical treatment 3 months preceding the date of coverage
- Disabilities due to war
- Self-inflicted injury
- Attempted suicide
- Mental or nervous conditions
- Medical problems from normal pregnancy
- When disability benefits are being received under a government program

Federal Disability Programs

WORKERS' COMPENSATION

The federal government has a number of programs that cover workers from loss of income because of work-related disability. Government employees receive protection under the Federal Employees Compensation Act (FECA). Special groups of workers—miners, maritime workers, railroad employees—receive protection under the Black Lung Benefits Act, Longshoreman's and Harbor Workers' Compensation Act, and Railroad Retirement Act. These programs were mentioned in Chapter 14, because work-related disabilities fall under workers' compensation laws. When an individual is eligible under more than one program, coordination of benefits is used so that a worker cannot receive benefits that result in an amount greater than what the person receives when working. *Coordination of benefits* is a provision preventing double payment for expenses by making one of the programs primary payer and assuring that no more than 100% of the costs are covered.

DISABILITY BENEFIT PROGRAM

Major government disability programs are:

- Social Security Disability Insurance (SSDI) program
- Supplemental Security Income (SSI)
- Civil Service Retirement System (CSRS)
- Federal Employees Retirement System (FERS)
- Veterans Administration Disability program
- Armed Services Disability

The Social Security Administration (SSA) manages two programs that pay monthly disability benefits to people under age 65 who cannot work for at least a year because of a severe disability: SSDI and SSI. Medical requirements are the same for both programs.

Social Security Disability Insurance Program

Background ■ In 1935, the Social Security Act, the Old-Age, Survivors, Disability and Health Insurance Program (OASDHI), was enacted, providing benefits for death, retirement, disability, and medical care. Then in 1956, Congress decided to establish a program for long-term disability known as Social Security Disability Insurance (SSDI) under Title II of the Social Security Act. This is an entitlement, not welfare, program providing monthly benefits to workers and those self-employed who meet certain conditions.

Disability ▪ Disability under Social Security has a strict definition:

"Inability to engage in any substantial gainful activity by reason of any medically determinable physical or mental impairment which can be expected to result in death or which has lasted or can be expected to last for a continuous period of not less than 12 months."

Eligibility ▪ Eligibility requirements for SSDI are as follows:

- Disabled workers under age 65 years and their families;
- Individuals who become disabled before age 22 years, if a parent (or in certain cases, a grandparent) who is covered under Social Security retires, becomes disabled, or dies;
- Disabled widows or widowers, age 50 years or over, if the deceased spouse worked at least 10 years under Social Security;
- Disabled surviving divorced spouses over age 50 years, if the ex-spouse was married to the disabled person for at least 10 years;
- Blind workers whose vision in the better eye cannot be corrected to better than 20/200, or whose visual field in the better eye, even with corrective lenses, is 20 degrees or less.

Workers must be fully insured in accordance with standards set by the Social Security administration, i.e., age, number of quarters worked, and amount of wages earned per quarter. Claims processing for eligibility may take up to 2 months.

When an individual becomes age 65, the benefits convert to retirement benefits. After 24 months of disability payments, the disabled individual also becomes eligible for Medicare.

Supplemental Security Income

Eligibility ▪ The Supplemental Security Income (SSI) program is under Title XVI of the Social Security Act and provides disability payments to needy people (adults and children) with limited income and few resources. No prior employment is needed. Many SSI recipients qualify for Medicaid, a state assistance program. SSI disability payments can be made to

- Disabled persons under age 65 years who have very limited income and resources;
- Disabled children under age 18 years, if the disability compares in severity with one that would keep an adult from working and has lasted or is expected to last at least 12 months or result in death;
- Blind adults or children who, in the better eye, with the use of corrective lenses, have a visual acuity no better than 20/200 or have a visual field of 20 degrees or less.

Application

To establish disability under SSDI or SSI, an individual calls or visits any Social Security office and completes application forms with the help of a social worker. Then, a determination process is set into action. A physician may be involved in the determination process in one of three ways: as a treating source who provides medical evidence on behalf of his or her patient, as a consultative examiner (CE) who is paid a fee and examines and/or tests the applicant, or as a full- or part-time medical or psychologic consultant reviewing claims for the state or regional offices (ROs).

In addition to a medical report from one of these sources, other criteria taken into consideration are the individual's age and vocational and educational factors that may contribute to the person's ability to work. It is possible that a person may be eligible for disability payments under one government program and not eligible under Social Security since the rules differ.

Social Security disability programs are designed to give long-term protection to individuals totally disabled, using Social Security criteria, and unable to do any type of work in the national economy, whereas short-term disability may be provided through workers' compensation, insurance, savings, and investments. If the applicant has reports from another agency, they may be used to determine whether a person is disabled for Social Security purposes. Many SSA state agencies have a division known as Disability Determination Services (DDS). The physician does not make the disability determination. Determination of disability is made by a DDS team composed of a physician/psychologist and disability examiner (DE).

Work Incentives

Special rules allow disabled or blind people presently receiving Social Security or SSI to work and still receive monthly benefits as well as Medicare or Medicaid. These are called "work incentives," and the rules are different for Social Security beneficiaries and SSI recipients.

Appeals Process

If a claimant does not agree with the determination of disability, a four-level appeals process is available:

1. A *reconsideration,* which is a complete review of the claim by a medical or psychologic consultant/disability examiner team that did not take part in the original disability determination.
2. A *hearing* before an administrative law judge (ALJ) who had no part in the initial or reconsideration determinations of the claim. The hearing is held within 75 miles of the claimant's home. The claimant and his or her representative are permitted to present their case in person and to present a written statement. They also are permitted to review information the ALJ will use to make a decision and to question any witnesses.
3. A *review by the Appeals Council,* which considers all requests for review, but it may deny a request if it believes the decision by the ALJ was correct. If the Appeals Council decides the case should be reviewed, it will either make a decision on the case or return it to an ALJ for further review.
4. A *review by the federal court,* for which the claimant may file an action where he or she resides.

From time to time, disability cases are reviewed to be sure the individuals are still disabled. The frequency depends on the nature and severity of the impairment, the likelihood of improvement, rehabilitation, ability to work, and so on.

Civil Service and Federal Employees Disability Benefits

Federal employees who work in civil service fall under the Civil Service Retirement System (CSRS). This system has provisions for those who become totally disabled, and benefits are payable for life. Five years of service are required before benefits are payable under this system. Eighteen months of service are required under the Federal Employees Retirement System (FERS). This program is a combination of federal disability and Social Security disability. Both portions of the program must be applied for by the worker. The disability cannot be work related for this program.

An example is an individual who works for the Internal Revenue Service performing clerical and filing job duties and has an automobile accident on the weekend. The head injuries are so severe that the person is unable to return to gainful employment at any job.

Armed Services Disability Benefits

Individuals covered under this program must be members of the armed services on active duty. If a disability occurs or is aggravated while serving in the military service, monthly benefits are payable for life. Benefits are based on years of service, base pay, and severity of disability. This, too, is subject to review.

Veterans Administration Disability Benefits

Policies and Guidelines

The Veterans Administration (VA) is authorized by law to provide a wide range of benefits to those who have served their country in the armed forces, and to their dependents. If a veteran who is honorably discharged files a claim for a service-connected disability within 1 year of sustaining that injury, he or she is eligible for outpatient treatment at VA expense and is issued a VA Outpatient Clinic card (Fig. 15–1). Usually a veteran seeks care at the nearest VA outpatient clinic. However, when a VA facility is not within reasonable distance, when the veteran is too ill to travel to the nearest location, or when the condition needs prompt attention, the veteran can apply for and be granted medical care through the Home Town Care Program and then seek care by a private physician.

Payment for services rendered can be made only for a service-connected disability, and any other professional service that is not related to the service disability must be paid for by the veteran out of his or her own pocket. In regard to the service-connected disability, the physician must accept what the VA pays as payment in full and cannot bill the patient for any additional charges, even if there is a balance after the VA pays the claim. If the treatment is likely to cost more than $40 per month, the physician must obtain prior authorization from the nearest VA facility. A separate ledger card must be prepared for VA benefits if the physician is also treating the patient for ailments other than the service-connected disability.

Non–Service-Connected Disability

Certain veterans with non–service-connected disabilities who are in receipt of house-bound or aid-

BILLING AND REPORTS. Bill the Station of Jurisdiction monthly. Please itemize your usual statement to include (1) patient's name; (2) identification number, (3) condition treated; (4) treatment and dates rendered; and (5) your usual and customary fee. Bills for auxiliary medical services must reflect the name of the prescribing doctor of medicine or osteopathy. Submit a brief treatment report only when the cost of urgent treatment causes the $30.00 limitation to be exceeded, or when a significant clinical change in a disability occurs.

PAYMENT. Payment by the VA for services rendered is payment in full.

IMPORTANT: Direct inquiries and any change of address to the Station of Jurisdiction. 752

Station of Jurisdiction:

VETERANS ADMINISTRATION
OUTPATIENT C 9044/136A6
428 SOUTH HILL ST.
LOS ANGELES CA 90013

FOLD

VA OUTPATIENT MEDICAL TREATMENT INFORMATION CARD

E. Z. Slipdisk
Beneficiary's Name

012-34-5678
Identification No.

DISABILITY FOR WHICH TREATMENT IS AUTHORIZED—VALID UNTIL CANCELLED BY VA

X P. O. HERNIATED NUC. PULPOSUS

VA FORM 10-1174, FEB 1971

Front

PLEASE READ CAREFULLY

TO VETERAN—You are authorized to obtain treatment within a reasonable distance from your permanent or temporary residence for the disability shown. When treatment is required, select a doctor of medicine or osteopathy who is licensed in the State in which treatment will be rendered. This card constitutes an agreement to provide care to you as a VA beneficiary within the limitations stated. Please alert the doctor to the instructions printed on the card and be sure he has your NAME, IDENTIFICATION NO. and the ADDRESS OF THE STATION OF JURISDICTION. If a specific therapy is authorized in lieu of listing disabilities, this card authorizes ONLY that therapy. IT MAY NOT BE USED TO OBTAIN OTHER MEDICAL SERVICES, SURGICAL PROCEDURES, NON-VA HOSPITALIZATION, OR PROSTHETIC APPLIANCES. Prescriptions of a recurring nature and others not needed at once should be brought or mailed to the VA station of jurisdiction. They will be filled promptly. When it is necessary to obtain medication immediately, PLEASE REQUEST THE PRIVATE PHARMACIST TO BILL THE STATION OF JURISDICTION SHOWN ON THIS CARD.

The VA may reimburse local, round trip, travel expenses between your permanent or temporary residence and the place treatment is obtained. A mileage allowance will be paid in lieu of actual and necessary expenses of travel (including lodging and subsistence). Your one-time, written request for travel expenses, when received within 30 days from the the date you first obtain medical services, will be approved to be effective with the first visit. A claim received after that 30-day-period will be effective from the date received. Generally, travel expenses are paid for a 3-months period.

TO PHYSICIAN—The beneficiary named on this card is authorized OUTPATIENT TREATMENT for the disabilities shown by a doctor of medicine or osteopathy licensed in the State in which medical services are rendered. When treatment of these conditions requires eyeglasses, hearing aids, other prostheses, home nursing services and/or dental services, notify the Station of Jurisdiction. Items or services of this nature will be provided by the Veterans Administration. Please request additional medical or other information from the Station of Jurisdiction, if required.

MEDICAL SERVICES includes prescription and referral for auxiliary medical services when required. All routine treatment may not exceed a total cost of $30.00 per month without prior VA approval.

PHARMACY SERVICES: Please have Rxs filled by VA unless needed at once. Veteran may obtain stat Rx from private pharmacy if you certify Rx, "The VA has authorized me to treat the disability for which this prescription is written."

Back

FIGURE 15-1
Sample Veterans Administration outpatient clinic card.

in-attendance benefits are eligible for treatment by a private physician if they are unable to travel to a VA facility owing to geographic inaccessibility. Their identification card, benefits, and claims procedures are identical to those of veterans with service-connected disabilities receiving outpatient medical care.

Benefits

The following is a general list of veterans' medical benefits. Each benefit requires that certain criteria be met. These criteria are everchanging and will not be mentioned here. A complete up-to-date booklet listing all the benefits is available.*

- Hospital care in a VA hospital
- Nursing home care in a VA facility
- Domiciliary care
- Outpatient medical treatment at a VA facility or by a private physician
- Emergency treatment in a hospital for a service-connected condition
- Prescription drugs and medication issued by a VA pharmacy or other participating pharmacy. Only bona fide emergency prescriptions can be filled by a private pharmacy
- Certain medical equipment, such as oxygen, prosthetics, and so on
- Travel expenses when receiving VA medical care
- Outpatient dental treatment (if the veteran files a claim within 90 days from the date that he or she was discharged from the service)
- Agent Orange or nuclear radiation exposure
- Alcohol and drug dependence outpatient care
- Readjustment counseling services

Emergency Outpatient Treatment

Veterans eligible for outpatient treatment and not in the fee basis program may obtain any outpatient

* *Federal Benefits for Veterans and Dependents.* Department of Veterans Affairs, Washington, D.C. 20420. The booklet is published annually and is available for a small fee from the Superintendent of Documents, U.S. Government Printing Office, Mail Stop: SSOP, Washington, D.C. 20402-9328.

medical care to which they are entitled only from a VA facility. The specific instances in which these veterans may obtain treatment from a private physician are (1) when treatment is an emergency, or (2) when the VA outpatient clinic is notified within 15 days of the treatment rendered. In such cases, the treating physician must submit evidence of an emergency (i.e., detailed justification on the invoice) to the VA outpatient clinic. Form 10-583, Claim for Payment of Cost of Unauthorized Medical Services (Fig. 15–2), generally used for hospital emergency care, also can be used for professional care if the doctor is billing after the 15-day period has elapsed. The fee consultant physician of the VA outpatient clinic makes the final decision as to whether an emergency existed.

Veterans Administration Installations

For information or assistance on veterans' benefits, write or call one of the regional offices listed in Appendix A. Many states have toll-free telephone services to the VA from communities in the state. Consult the local telephone directory or information assistance operator for the latest listing of these numbers.

State Disability Insurance

BACKGROUND

In 1944, Rhode Island began a State Disability Insurance (SDI) program that proved successful. This form of insurance is part of an employment security program that provides temporary cash benefits for workers suffering a wage loss due to off-the-job illness or injury. It can be referred to as unemployment compensation disability (UCD) or temporary disability insurance (TDI). California became the second state to add nonindustrial disability coverage to the Social Security protection afforded to its citizens by appending Article 10 to the Unemployment Insurance Act. This became law on May 21, 1946, and when the legislation took effect on December 1, 1946, this article diverted the 1% tax formerly paid by workers for unemployment insurance to a disability insurance fund. New York and New Jersey soon followed with similar programs. Two decades later, in 1969, Puerto Rico and Hawaii passed nonindustrial disability insurance laws.

As of 1996, nonindustrial disability insurance programs exist in only five states and Puerto Rico. In each area, the law is known by a different name:

■ New Jersey	California Unemployment Insurance Code
■ Hawaii	Temporary Disability Insurance Law
■ California	Temporary Disability Benefits Law
■ New York	Disability Benefits Law
■ Puerto Rico	Disability Benefits Act
■ Rhode Island	Temporary Disability Insurance Act

FUNDING

Usually a small percentage is deducted from employees' paychecks each month, or the employer may elect to pay all or part of the cost of the plan as a fringe benefit for employees. The money is then sent in quarterly installments to the state and put into a special fund.

ELIGIBILITY

To receive state disability insurance benefits, an employee must be

- employed full- or part-time
- suffering a loss of wages because of disability
- under the care and treatment of a physician who certifies the employee is disabled
- disabled at least 7 or 8 calendar days or hospitalized as an inpatient
- filing a claim within the time limit
- eligible for benefits depending on the amount withheld during a previous period before disability began
- employed or actively looking for work when disability begins

Certain types of workers are not covered: employees of school districts, community college districts, and churches; state workers; federal employees; interstate railroad workers; nonprofit organization employees; and domestic workers. If the worker was employed at the time of disability, benefits are not subject to federal income tax. An employee who retires is no longer eligible for the insurance. A worker may file a claim with the state seeking exemption from program participation on religious grounds.

BENEFITS

Weekly benefits are determined by the wages earned in a base period or based on a percentage of

Form Approved
Budget Bureau No. 76-R0352

VETERANS ADMINISTRATION

CLAIM FOR PAYMENT OF COST OF UNAUTHORIZED MEDICAL SERVICES

Each person, firm or institution claiming payments or reimbursements must complete this form. No carbon paper necessary. Please use typewriter or ball point pen, and submit both copies.

1A. VETERAN'S LAST NAME - FIRST - MIDDLE INITIAL	1B. CLAIM NO. C-	1C. SOCIAL SECURITY NO.

1D. PRESENT ADDRESS *(Include ZIP Code)*

2. NAME AND ADDRESS OF PERSON, FIRM OR INSTITUTION MAKING CLAIM *(Leave blank if same as above)*

3. STATEMENT OF CIRCUMSTANCES UNDER WHICH THE SERVICES WERE RENDERED *(Include diagnosis, symptoms, whether emergency existed, and reason VA facilities were not used)*

4. AMOUNT CLAIMED $	*Attach bills or receipts showing services furnished, dates, and charges*

5. COMPLETE A OR B, AS APPROPRIATE

A. Amount claimed does not exceed that charged the general public for similar services, and payment has not been received. SIGNATURE AND TITLE OF PROVIDER OF SERVICE, AND DATE	B. I certify that the amount claimed has been paid and reimbursement has not been received. SIGNATURE OF VETERAN OR REPRESENTATIVE, AND DATE

FOR VETERANS ADMINISTRATION USE ONLY

6. ACTION

☐ APPROVED $ ____________

Treatment was provided in an emergency for a service-connected or adjunct disability, any disability of a veteran who has a total disability permanent in nature from a service-connected disability, or for any illness, injury, or dental condition in the case of a veteran eligible under Chapter 31 (Vocational Rehabilitation) Title 38, U.S. Code. VA facilities were not feasibly available and delay would have been hazardous.

☐ DISAPPROVED

7. SIGNATURE, CHIEF, MEDICAL ADMINISTRATION SERVICE	8. DATE	9. ADMINISTRATIVE VOUCHER NO.

VA FORM MAY 1974 **10-583** SUPERSEDES VA FORM 10-583, FEB 1966, AND WHICH WILL NOT BE USED.

FIGURE 15–2
Veterans Administration Form 10-583, Claim of Payment of Cost of Unauthorized Medical Services.

15

average weekly wages (Table 15–1). Benefits begin after the seventh consecutive day of disability. However, in California, if the disability extends to 22 calendar days (or beyond), benefits are paid from the first day of the disability. There is no provision under the law for hospital or other medical benefits except in Hawaii and Puerto Rico, where hospital benefits are payable under a prepaid health care program if the employee meets certain eligibility requirements.

Limited Benefits ▪ In some states, a patient may qualify for benefits if he or she is a resident of an approved alcoholic recovery facility or an approved drug-free residential facility.

Reduced Benefits ▪ An individual may be entitled to only partial benefits if receiving certain types of income, such as

Sick leave
Vacation
Wages paid by employer

TABLE 15–1
State Disability Information Summary

State	Name of State Law	Maximum Benefit Period (wk)	Time Limit for Filing Claims	1996 Deductions from Salary (%)	Benefits
California	California Unemployment Insurance Code	52	49 days from disability	1.2–1.3	Based on earnings in a 12-mo base period, which begins approximately 18 mo before disability
Hawaii	Temporary Disability Insurance Law	26	90 days from disability	0.5	Based on 55% of average weekly wage
New Jersey	Temporary Disability Benefits Law	26	30 days from disability	0.5	Based on average weekly wage
New York	Disability Benefits Law	26	30 days from disability	0.5 (max. 60 cents/wk)	Based on 50% of average weekly wage (max. $170/wk)
Puerto Rico	Disability Benefits Act	26	3 months from disability	0.3 employee and 0.3 employer	Based on wages earned during base year
Rhode Island	Temporary Disability Insurance Act	30	1 year from disability	1.1	Based on 4.62% of wages in the base period quarter in which wages were the highest

Insurance settlement for the disability
Workers' compensation benefits
Unemployment benefits

TIME LIMITS

A claim for disability insurance should be filed within the time limit of the state laws, but there is usually a grace period of 7 to 8 days after the deadline (see Table 15–1). After the claim is approved, basic benefits become payable with the eighth day of disability or the first day of hospital confinement, whichever comes first. In California, benefits are paid from day 1 if the disability extends to 22 calendar days or more. A person may continue to draw disability insurance for a maximum of 26 weeks in Hawaii, New Jersey, New York, Puerto Rico, and Rhode Island and 52 weeks in California on the same illness or injury or overlapping disabilities. An employee is also entitled to disability benefits 15 days after recovery from a previous disability or illness. In other words, if a patient is discharged by the physician to return to work and is on the job 15 calendar days and then becomes ill with the *same* ailment, he or she may file a new claim.

MEDICAL EXAMINATIONS

The claimant may be required to submit to an examination or examinations by an independent medical examiner (IME) to determine any mental or physical disability. Fees for such examinations are paid by the state department handling disability insurance. Codes for billing these medical examinations may be found in the Special Evaluation and Management Services section of *Current Procedural Terminology* (CPT), codes 99450 to 99456.

LIMITATIONS

There are many restrictions on disability insurance. A few of the major situations in which a claim could possibly be denied are listed here.

1. *Pregnancy-related disability,* unless the pregnancy is complicated (e.g., cases in which the patient has diabetes, varicose veins, ectopic pregnancy, or cesarean section). *Exceptions:* California, Hawaii, New Jersey, and Rhode Island have maternity benefits that may be applied for at the time the physician tells the patient to stop working.
2. *Conditions covered by workers' compensation,* unless the rate is less than the disability insurance rate. In that case, the state pays the difference between the two rates.
3. If the applicant is receiving *unemployment insurance benefits over a certain specified amount. Exception:* If the applicant is on unemployment insurance and then becomes ill or injured, he or she is put on temporary disability insurance until able to go for a job interview.
4. *Disabilities beginning during a trade dispute.* If an employee is on strike and is injured while walking a picket line, he or she is not eligible for benefits. However, if the union is on strike and an individual member remains at home and then becomes ill or injured, he or she can claim disability and will receive benefits.
5. *Confinement by court order or certification in a public or private institution* as an alcoholic, drug addict, or sexual psychopath or whenever legal custody is the cause of unemployment.
6. *If the employing company has a voluntary disability plan and is not paying into a state fund.*
7. If the employee or company has a *religious exemption certificate* on file and is not paying into a state fund.

VOLUNTARY DISABILITY INSURANCE PLAN

Persons residing and working in states that do not have state disability insurance programs may elect to contact a local private insurance carrier to arrange for coverage. If these persons become ill or disabled, they receive a fixed weekly or monthly income, usually for approximately 6 months. If the disability or illness is permanent and the individual is unable to return to work, there is sometimes a small monthly income for the duration of the person's life. Some of the state laws provide that a "voluntary plan" may be adopted instead of the "state plan" if a majority of company employees consent to private coverage.

Instructions and Procedures for Claims Submission

15

DISABILITY INCOME CLAIMS

When the insurance billing specialist is handling disability income claim forms, he or she should note that the insured (claimant) is responsible to notify the insurance company of a disability. A proof of loss form is completed to establish disability.

Information required:

- When and how the disability occurred
- When the disabled is expected to be well enough to work
- Name of treating physician
- Why the disability prevents the insured from work

The report must show that the patient's disability meets the policy's definition of disability, or benefits will be denied. Because the definition of disability varies among policies, the critical issues are the content and wording on the claim form.

A portion of this form is usually completed by the attending physician. It asks for the following:

Medical history
Subjective symptoms (patient's own words about his or her chief complaints)
Objective findings on physical examination (e.g., rashes, lacerations, abrasions, contusions, and so forth)
Severity of the illness or injury (range of motion tests)
Diagnosis
Medication and treatment dates
Dates of disability
Prognosis (outcome of the disease or injury)
How long disability is expected to last
Names of any other treating physician
Performance of job duties
Photocopies of laboratory tests, x-ray studies, hospital discharge report

This information helps verify the disability. In some cases, the physician may wish to dictate a medical report and attach it to the claim form instead of completing a portion of the form. The insurance billing specialist must be prepared to extract data from source documents, such as medical and financial records, to complete the claim form. Always ask the patient to sign an authorization form to release medical information.

Reasons for denial of benefits are improper choice of words or inadequate medical information. If the insurance billing specialist has abstracted data from the patient record to insert on the form, ask the physician to read the information carefully before signing the document.

The insurance company may request information from other places to justify payment of benefits, such as employer's records, employee's wage statements and/or tax forms, or the attending physician's medical records. A company representative may interview the insured if conflicting information exists.

If disability continues, additional claim forms may need to be completed monthly, or less frequently, by the insured and attending physician. Other sources of information may be requested, e.g., records from medical specialists or Social Security records.

If the validity of the case is in question, an IME may be asked by the insurance company to examine the disabled individual. If the claimant neglects to return claim forms, refuses telephone calls, misses appointments, or engages in questionable activities, then the insurance company will discreetly engage in surveillance of the insured through the services of a professional investigation firm.

FEDERAL DISABILITY CLAIMS

The Social Security Administration division called Disability Determination Services (DDS) has a teledictation service so the physician or psychologist can telephone in a medical report instead of completing a medical report form. The service is available at any time, including nights and weekends. A typed transcript is sent to the physician to review, sign, and return to the SSA state agency, or a report may be typed on the physician's stationery. The physician may photocopy relevant portions of the patient's chart and submit that information, but it should be legible. Be sure the patient has signed an authorization to release information. Copies of consultation reports and hospital summaries are also helpful. By law, only recent data no more than 1 year old are allowed.

A medical report must include

Relevant medical history, past history, social history, and family history
Subjective complaints (patient's symptoms)
Objective findings on physical examination (e.g., results of physical or mental status examination, blood pressure)
Laboratory and x-ray findings
Diagnostic studies (treadmill tests, pulmonary function tests, tracings, and so on)
Diagnosis (statement of disease or injury based on signs and symptoms)
Treatment prescribed, with response and prognosis
Medical source statement based on medical findings, describing the individual's ability to perform work-related activities, such as standing, sitting, lifting, carrying, walking, handling ob-

NOTE: If you need assistance in a language other than English, write that language here ______

CLAIM STATEMENT OF EMPLOYEE

COMPLETE *ALL* ITEMS. IF INCOMPLETE, THIS FORM WILL BE RETURNED, CAUSING A DELAY IN BENEFIT PAYMENTS

1. Print your full name: FIRST INITIAL LAST

Mr. [ ] Mrs. [ ] Miss [X] Ms. [ ] MARCIA M. MONROE

Other Names Used:

3501 Maple Street, Woodland Hills, XY 12345

Your Mailing Address: STREET ADDRESS, P.O. BOX OR RFD APT. NO. CITY OR TOWN STATE AND ZIP CODE

Your Home Address: (if different from mailing address) STREET ADDRESS, OR SPECIFIC DIRECTIONS TO YOUR HOME IF P.O. BOX OR RFD

2. **IMPORTANT: Enter your Social Security Account Number**

5 4 0 2 1 9 8 8 1

2A. If you have used another Social Security number, enter that number here

_ _ _ _ _ _ _ _ _

3. What was the first day you were too sick to perform all the duties of your regular or customary work, even if it was a Saturday, Sunday, holiday, or a normal day off?

MONTH 10 DAY 10 YEAR 9x

MALE [ ] FEMALE [X] Birthdate Mo. Day Yr. 03 / 04 / 52

4. What was the last day you worked? MONTH 10 DAY 9 YEAR 9x

5. Employer's Business Name: A and B Company Telephone Number (013) 487-9980

Employer's Business Address: NUMBER AND STREET 3498 White Street, CITY Woodland Hills, STATE AND ZIP CODE XY 12345

6. Your occupation with this employer. secretary Your Badge or Payroll number: 4399

7. What is your usual occupation? secretary

8. Were you an employer or self-employed individual? Yes ☐ No ☒

9. Did you lose any time from work because of this illness or injury during the two weeks before the last day you worked as shown in item (4) above? Yes ☐ No ☒

10. Did you stop work because of sickness or injury? If "No," please give reason: Yes ☒ No ☐

11. Have you filed for or received UNEMPLOYMENT INSURANCE benefits between the last day you worked and the first day you became disabled? Yes ☐ No ☒

12. Has, or will your employer continue your pay, by means of sick leave, vacation, pension, gift or other means? Yes ☐ No ☒

13. Was this disability caused by your work? If "Yes," describe HOW: Yes ☐ No ☒

Are you claiming or receiving WORKERS' COMPENSATION Benefits for any on-the-job injuries or illnesses during the period covered by this claim? Yes ☐ No ☒

14. Have you recovered from your disability? If "Yes," enter date of recovery? Yes ☐ No ☒

15. Have you returned to work for any day, part-time or full-time after the beginning date of your disability as shown in item (3) above? If "Yes," please enter such dates: Yes ☐ No ☒

16. I hereby claim benefits and certify that for the period covered by this claim I was unemployed and disabled, that the foregoing statements including any accompanying statements are to the best of my knowledge and belief true, correct and complete. I hereby authorize my attending physician, practitioner, hospital and employer to furnish and disclose all facts concerning my disability and wages or earnings that are within their knowledge and to allow inspection of and provide copies of any hospital records concerning my disability that are under their control. I understand this authorization is granted for a period of 18 months from the date of my signature or the effective date of the claim, whichever is later. I agree that a photocopy of this release shall be as valid as the original.

Claim signed on: MONTH 10 DAY 19 YEAR 9x

Claimant's signature: (DO NOT PRINT)

Telephone Number (013) 487-9980

Under Section 2101 of the California Unemployment Insurance Code, it is a violation to wilfully make a false statement or knowingly conceal a material fact in order to obtain the payment of any benefits, such violation being punishable by imprisonment and/or by a fine not exceeding $20,000 or both.

If your signature is made by mark (X) it must be attested by two witnesses with their addresses.

SIGNATURE-WITNESS SIGNATURE-WITNESS

ADDRESS ADDRESS

If an authorized agent is filing for benefits for an INCAPACITATED or DECEASED claimant, or a spouse is filing for a MENTALLY INCAPACITATED individual, contact the office below for the required forms and instructions.

15

FIGURE 15–3

Form DE 2501, Claim Statement of Employee. This is a two-part form, and this side is completed by the claimant.

DOCTOR'S CERTIFICATE

Certification may be made by a licensed medical or osteopathic physician and surgeon, chiropractor, dentist, podiatrist, optometrist, designated psychologist or an authorized medical officer of a United States Government facility. Certification may also be made by a licensed nurse-midwife or nurse practitioner for the purposes of disability related to normal pregnancy or childbirth. All items on this sheet must be completed legibly.

Patient File No.	Name MARCIA M. MONROE	Social Security Number 540-21-9881

17. I attended the patient for the present medical problem from: MONTH DAY YEAR 10-19-9x To MONTH DAY YEAR present At intervals of: one visit to date

18. Are you completing this form for the sole purpose of referral or recommendation to an alcoholic recovery home or drug-free residential facility? Yes ☐ No ☒ If yes, please enter facility name and address in item #28.

19. History: cough of 2 weeks duration, chest pain, 100°F
State the nature, severity and the bodily extent of the incapacitating disease or injury.
Findings: bilateral pneumonitis
Diagnosis: bilateral pneumonitis
Type of treatment and/or medication rendered to patient: examination, x-rays and prescribed antibiotics

20. Diagnosis confirmed by: **(Specify type of test or X-ray)** AP and lateral chest x-rays

21. Is this patient now pregnant or has she been pregnant since the date of treatment as reported above? Yes ☐ No ☒ If "Yes", date pregnancy terminated or future EDC.
Is the pregnancy normal? Yes ☐ No ☐ If "No," state the abnormal and involuntary complication causing maternal disability:

22. Operation Date performed DNA Or to be performed ______ Type of operation:

23. Has the patient at any time during your attendance for this medical problem, been incapable of performing his or her regular work? Yes ☒ No ☐ If "Yes" the disability commenced on: 10-10-9x

24. APPROXIMATE date, based on your examination of patient, disability (if any) should end or has ended sufficiently to permit the patient to resume regular or customary work. Even if considerable question exists, make SOME "estimate." This is a requirement of the Code, and the claim will be delayed if such date is not entered. Such answers as "Indefinite" or "don't know" will not suffice. (ENTER DATE) 11-19-9x

25. Based on your examination of patient, is this disability the result of "occupation" either as an "industrial accident" or as an "occupational disease"?
Yes ☐ No ☒ (This should include aggravation of pre-existing conditions by occupation.)

26. Have you reported this OR A CONCURRENT DISABILITY to any insurance carrier as a Workers' Compensation Claim?
Yes ☐ No ☒ If "Yes," to whom? (Name of carrier or firm)

27. Further comments (if indicated):

28. Was or is patient confined as a registered bed patient in a hospital? Yes ☐ No ☒
Was patient treated in the surgical unit of a hospital or surgical unit? Yes ☐ No ☒
Was or is patient a resident in an alcoholic recovery home or drug-free residential facility? If "Yes," please provide name and address: Yes ☐ No ☒

29. Date and hour entered as a registered bed patient and discharged pursuant to your orders:

ENTERED	STILL CONFINED	DISCHARGED
on , 19 , at A.M. P.M.	on , 19	on , 19 , at A.M. P.M.

30. Would the disclosure of this information to your patient be medically or psychologically detrimental to the patient?
Yes ☐ No ☒

I hereby certify that, based on my examination, the above statements truly describe the patient's disability (if any) and the estimated duration thereof, and that I am a M. D. (TYPE OF DOCTOR) licensed to practice by the State of California

▶ David W. Smith, MD
PRINT OR TYPE DOCTOR'S NAME AS SHOWN ON LICENSE
▶ ______
SIGNATURE OF ATTENDING DOCTOR

▶ 4567 Broad Ave., Woodland Hills, XY 12345
NO. AND STREET CITY ZIP CODE
▶ C 14020 (013) 486-9002 10-20-9x
STATE LICENSE NUMBER TELEPHONE NO. DATE OF SIGNING THIS FORM

"Under Section 2116 of the California Unemployment Insurance Code, it is a violation for any individual who, with the intent to defraud, falsely certifies the medical condition of any person in order to obtain disability insurance benefits, whether for the maker or for any other person, and is punishable by imprisonment and/or a fine not exceeding twenty thousand dollars.

reference initials

FIGURE 15–4
Form DE 2501, Doctor's Certificate. This side is completed by the attending physician and submitted within a set period of time from the beginning date of disability to initiate benefits. If the patient is seen by a second physician, this form is mailed to the claimant to secure the certification of a new physician or to clarify a specific claimed period of disability.

NOTICE OF FINAL PAYMENT

The information contained in your claim for Disability Insurance indicates that you are now able to work, therefore, this is the final check that you will receive on this claim.

IF YOU ARE ***STILL*** DISABLED: You should complete the Claimant's Certification portion of this form and contact your doctor immediately to have him/her complete the Physician's Supplementary Certificate below.

IF YOU BECOME DISABLED ***AGAIN:*** File a new Disability Insurance claim form.

IF YOU ARE UNEMPLOYED AND AVAILABLE FOR WORK: Report to the nearest Unemployment Insurance office of the Department for assistance in finding work and to determine your entitlement to Unemployment Insurance Benefits.

This determination is final unless you file an appeal within twenty (20) days from the date of mailing of this notification. You may appeal by giving a detailed statement as to why you believe the determination is in error. All communications regarding this Disability Insurance claim should include your Social Security Account Number and be addressed to the office shown.

CLAIMANT'S CERTIFICATION

I certify that I continue to be disabled and incapable of doing my regular work, and that I have reported all wages, Workers' Compensation benefits and other monies received during the claim period to the Employment Development Department.

ENTER YOUR SOCIAL SECURITY NUMBER ________ ____ ________

Sign Your Name ______________________ **Date Signed** ______________________

PHYSICIAN'S SUPPLEMENTARY CERTIFICATE

Department Use Only	

1. Are you still treating patient?________ Date of last treatment ______________, 19 ____.
2. What present condition continues to make the patient disabled?

   ____

   ____

   ____

3. Date patient recovered, or will recover sufficiently (even if under treatment) to be able to perform his/her regular and customary work ______________, 19 ____. Please enter a specific or estimated recovery date.
4. Would the disclosure of this information to your patient be medically or psychologically detrimental to the patient?

   Yes ☐ No ☐

I hereby certify that the above statements in my opinion truly describe the claimant's condition and the estimated duration thereof.

______________, 19 ____. Doctor's Signature ______________________
Date

Phone Number ______________________

DE 2525XX Rev. 13 (3-86) — Versión en español en el dorso —

FIGURE 15–5

Notice of Final Payment/Physician's Supplementary Certificate Form DE 2525XX. This form indicates that the period of disability is "closed" or terminated with the accompanying check, based on information in the claim records. Benefits will cease unless the reverse side of the form is completed by the claimant's physician, extending the duration of disability. This form is pink. One side of the form is in English and the other is in Spanish.

15

jects, hearing, speaking, and traveling regardless of the impairment. For cases of mental impairment, the statement should present the individual's capacity for understanding and memory, sustained concentration and persistence, social interaction, and adaptation

VETERANS ADMINISTRATION DISABILITY OUTPATIENT CLINIC CLAIMS

The processing of invoices from fee physicians is a somewhat lengthy procedure as required by VA regulations and involves several steps in different

STATE OF CALIFORNIA
EMPLOYMENT DEVELOPMENT DEPARTMENT

FOR DEPT. USE ONLY

REFER TO

4920 — Our File No.
Marcia M. Monroe — Your Patient
— Regular or Customary Work

REQUEST FOR ADDITIONAL MEDICAL INFORMATION

David W. Smith, MD
4567 Broad Avenue
Woodland Hills, XY 12345

The original basic information and estimate of duration of your patient's disability have been carefully evaluated. At the present time, the following additional information based upon the progress and present condition of this patient is requested. This will assist the Department in determining eligibility for further disability insurance benefits. Return of the completed form as soon as possible will be appreciated.

WM. C. SCHMIDT, M.D., MEDICAL DIRECTOR

CLAIMS EXAMINER

DOCTOR: Please complete either Part A or B, date and sign.

PART A IF YOUR PATIENT HAS RECOVERED SUFFICIENTLY TO BE ABLE TO RETURN TO HIS/HER REGULAR OR CUSTOMARY WORK LISTED ABOVE, PLEASE GIVE THE DATE, ____________ 19 ___.

PART B THIS PART REFERS TO PATIENT WHO IS STILL DISABLED.

Are you still treating the patient? YES ☒ NO ☐ November 15, 19 9x. (DATE OF LAST TREATMENT)

What are the medical circumstances which continue to make your patient disabled?

bilateral pneumonitis

What is your present estimate of the date your patient will be able to perform his/her regular or customary work listed above? Date November 30, 19 9x.

Further Comments: ____________

Would the disclosure of this information to your patient be medically or psychologically detrimental to the patient? YES ☐ NO ☒

Date November 17, 19 9x

David W. Smith, M.D.
DOCTOR'S SIGNATURE

SE
David W. Smith, MD

ENCLOSED IS A STAMPED PREADDRESSED ENVELOPE FOR YOUR CONVENIENCE.

DE 2547 Rev. 18 (8-84)

FIGURE 15-6

Request for Additional Medical Information Form DE 2547. This form is mailed to the physician when the normal expectancy date of the disability is reached, provided that the physician has requested a longer-than-normal duration without complications as indicated.

STATE OF CALIFORNIA

EMPLOYMENT DEVELOPMENT DEPARTMENT

P.O. Box 1529, Santa Barbara, CA 93102
(805) 963-9611

For Dept. Use Only	

REFER TO

4920 - Our File No.
Marcia M. Monroe - Your Patient
- Regular Work

MEDICAL INQUIRY

David W. Smith, MD
4567 Broad Avenue
Woodland Hills, XY 12345

A review of the medical certificate received in conjunction with a claim for disability insurance benefits filed by your patient, named above, reveals that some additional information is needed in order to evaluate the claim properly. Your cooperation in answering the question or questions below and returning the form in the enclosed stamped and addressed envelope will be appreciated.

WM. C. SCHMIDT, MD, MEDICAL DIRECTOR

CLAIMS EXAMINER

What is the name and address of the facility that took the x-rays on this patient?

Speedy Radiology Service
4598 Main Street
Woodland Hills, XY 12345

Would the disclosure of this information to your patient be medically or psychologically detrimental to the patient: Yes [ ] No [X]

October 24 1988 — Date

David W. Smith MD — Doctor's Signature

SE

David W. Smith, MD

DE 2547A Rev. 10 (9-84)

FIGURE 15-7

Medical Inquiry Form DE 2547A. This form is mailed to the physician at any time during the life of the claim if any questions need to be answered or if the physician has failed to enter a prognosis date.

15

VA agencies. To keep the delay in payment to a minimum, fee physicians are urged to bill the VA on a monthly basis. To insure prompt processing, invoices should contain the following information:

1. Patient's name as shown on the I.D. card, VA Form 10-1174 (see Fig. 15–1)
2. Patient's Social Security number
3. Condition treated must be shown on every invoice, since this is the basis for approval of payment. Diagnosis treated must be listed on the I.D. card or authorized by the statement "for any condition." Abstract the diagnosis exactly as it is stated on the I.D. card.
4. Treatment given and dates rendered
5. Physician's usual and customary fee
6. Name and address of fee physician and his or her Social Security or Federal Taxpayer I.D. number. If the I.D. number is assigned to a group and the physician desires to be paid individually, the VA outpatient clinic must be so advised.

Fee physicians, as well as veterans, are urged to read the instructions on the I.D. card carefully. This is sometimes neglected and can lead to misunderstanding.

If the physician does not wish to bill the VA outpatient clinic, the patient can pay the physician and then be reimbursed, but the veteran must carefully follow the instructions on the back of the VA Outpatient Clinic card.

STATE DISABILITY CLAIMS

Residents of a state that provides unemployment compensation disability may call or write to the nearest office that handles state disability insurance to obtain a claim form and insurance pamphlet. A list of offices and addresses for each state is provided in Appendix A.

In some states, the claim form is in three parts and must be completed by the claimant, employer, and physician; in others, the form is in two parts and is completed by the claimant and physician only (Figs. 15–3 and 15–4). In either case, the claim must be documented by a physician before the applicant may begin receiving benefits. Carefully read all information from the state disability insurance office and follow the directions. Provide the data requested and have the physician and patient sign the forms. Send in the form within the stated time limits.

After the claim has been completed by all parties concerned, it is submitted to the nearest local office for processing. The most important item on the claim form is the claimant's Social Security number; without it the claim cannot be researched properly to establish wages earned in the base period.

For examples of the different forms involved in the processing of disability insurance, California has been selected as the model state. To establish a claim, the First Claim for Disability Insurance Form DE 2501 must be completed by both the patient (see Fig. 15–3) and the attending physician (see Fig. 15–4). If an extension of disability is required, the Physician's Supplementary Certificate Form DE 2525XX must be completed by the physician (Fig. 15–5). This accompanies the last check issued to the patient. For additional medical information that might be required, Forms DE 2547 and DE 2547A are sometimes sent to the attending physician for completion (Figs. 15–6 and 15–7).

Remember that all follow-up correspondence should include the patient's name and Social Security number. The insurance billing specialist should promptly report any change of address, telephone number, return to work, or recovery date to the state disability insurance office. Patients must report any income received to the state disability insurance office, because this may affect benefits.

TO THE STUDENT

For further knowledge and understanding, the key terms at the beginning of the chapter appear in the Glossary at the end of this textbook so you can look up the pertinent terms. You are now ready to complete the review questions and Assignments 53 through 57 in the *Workbook*. These assignments will provide you with hands-on experience in working with patient histories and completing disability insurance claim forms described in this chapter.

UNIT

4

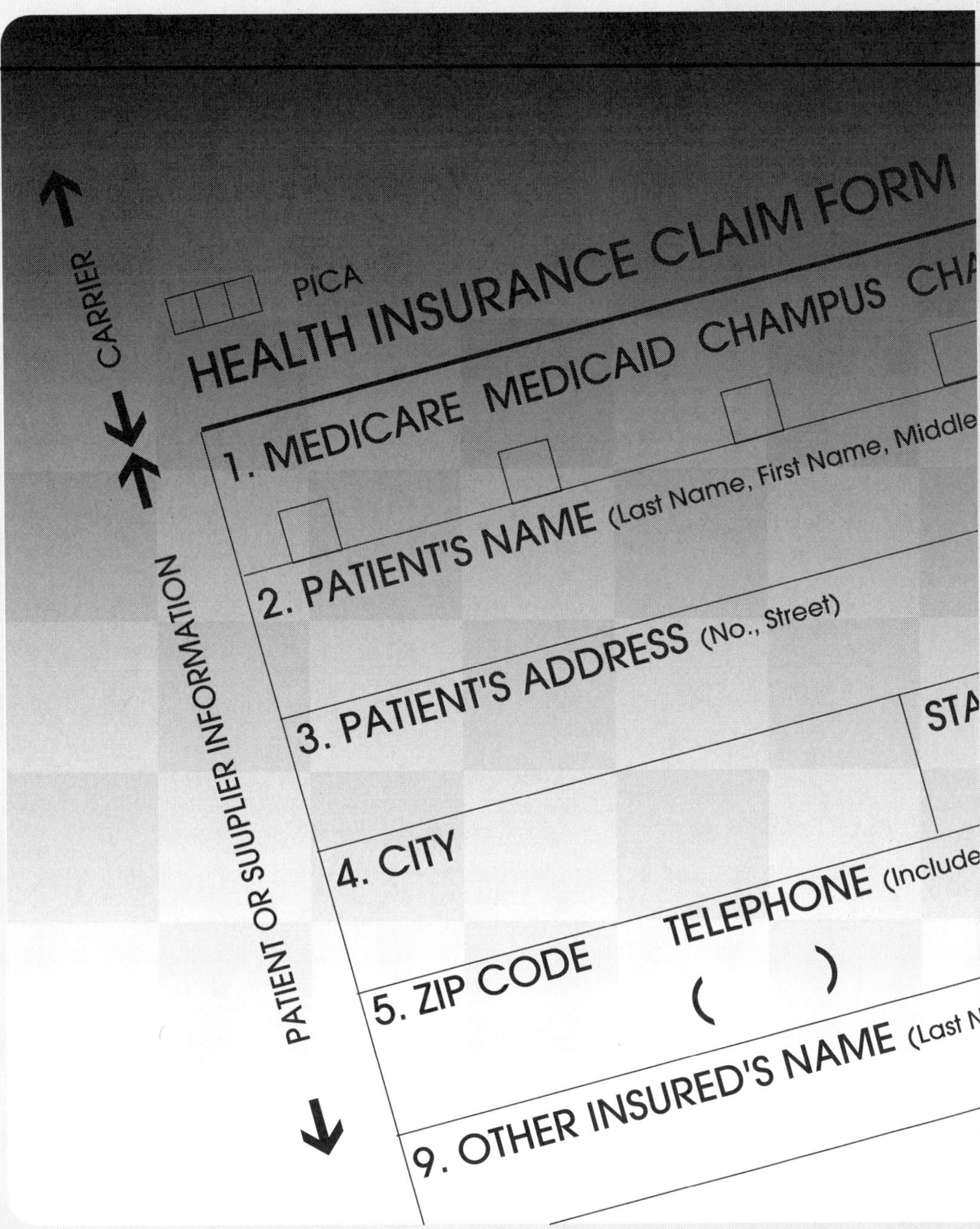

Inpatient and Outpatient Billing

Objectives*

THE INSURANCE BILLING SPECIALIST WILL BE ABLE TO:

- Define common terms related to hospital billing and diagnosis-related groups.
- State reimbursement methods made to hospitals under managed care contracts.
- List six instances of verbal breaching of confidentiality in a hospital setting.
- Identify categories of therapeutic, diagnostic, and prophylactic procedures in ICD-9-CM Volume 3.
- Complete insurance claims in both hospital inpatient and outpatient settings to minimize their chance of rejection by insurance carriers.
- Explain the basic steps in processing an inpatient hospital stay, from billing through the receipt of payment.
- State when the Uniform Bill UB-92 claim form may and may not be used.
- Recognize general guidelines for completing the Uniform Bill UB-92 claim form.
- Describe the history of diagnosis-related groups.
- List the purpose of diagnosis-related groups.
- Identify how payment is made based on diagnosis-related groups.
- Define the role of the insurance billing specialist when working with diagnosis-related groups.

Key Terms

admission review
ambulatory patient groups (APGs)
ambulatory visit groups (AVGs)
appropriateness evaluation protocol (AEP)
capitation
case rate
charges
clinical outlier
coding
comorbidity
complication
cost outlier
cost outlier review
day outlier review
diagnosis-related groups (DRGs)
discharge face sheet
discharge status
DRG creep
DRG rate
elective surgery
grouper
inpatient
International Classification of Diseases, Ninth Revision, Clinical Modification (ICD-9-CM)
looping
low-volume DRGs
major diagnostic categories (MDCs)
outpatient
outliers (atypical cases)
percentage of revenue
per diem
preadmission testing (PAT)
principal diagnosis
principal procedure
procedure review
professional review organizations (PROs)
readmission review
stop loss
transfer
transfer review
Uniform Bill (UB-92) claim form
utilization review (UR)

*Performance objectives and exercises for hands-on practical experience for this chapter appear in the *Workbook*.

CHAPTER 16

Hospital Billing

Introduction

Because jobs are available in the medical records and financial departments of hospitals for individuals with knowledge and experience in coding and insurance claims completion, this chapter will focus on hospital insurance billing.

A hospital facility (the employer) is larger than a clinic or private physician's office, so there is more chance for advancement. An individual may be hired as a file clerk and advance from junior to senior clerk, insurance clerk, or insurance patient representative. He or she may advance to an administrative position or decide to establish a privately owned billing office. Most hospital facilities have policies that encourage career growth by promoting from within. Refer to Chapter 1, A Career as an Insurance Billing Specialist, for details on educational and training requirements, professionalism, and ethics; the job description of a patient service representative; and so on. Figure 16–1 provides a generic job description for an individual in a hospital billing department.

Because of the diversity in reimbursement methods, it is very important that the insurance billing specialist has basic knowledge of insurance programs and knows how to correctly process each insurance claim. This is essential for obtaining maximum reimbursement from the insurance company and then collecting whatever payment is necessary from the patient. To remain an asset to employers, an insurance billing specialist must continually update his or her knowledge of coding and insurance program policies by attending seminars, workshops, and classes.

Position Description

Title: Patient Service Representative
Department: Business Office
Reports to: Patient Accounts Manager

Job Number: 215
Effective Date: 3/1/89
Revision Date: 11/1/93

Primary Function:

To promptly file hospital inpatient and outpatient claims with third-party payers, following up in a timely and efficient manner, to assure maximum reimbursement is received for services provided. To assist the public in obtaining full benefits from their coverage and in understanding billing procedures, always maintaining good public relations.

Principal Responsibilities:

1. Processes claims within assigned responsibility in a timely and efficient manner, performing all associated duties in order to assure completeness and correctness of all claims information, facilitating maximum reimbursement.
   a. Analyzes, update and corrects claim data according to established procedure.
   b. Inputs data accurately, efficiently and consistently.
   c. Performs work as scheduled, prioritizing as required for maximizing cash flow.
   d. Demonstrates thorough knowledge of third-party payers' claims requirements, UB-92 requirements by payer, computer capabilities as related to claims production, and admitting/medical records input as it affects claims.
2. Handles phone, mail and personal inquiries from and regarding patient accounts.
   a. Assists each person promptly, efficiently and courteously.
   b. Follows through on all issues identified as requiring action as a result of inquiry.
   c. Performs duties with a minimum of supervision, exhibits innovation and good judgment as well as thorough knowledge of ethical and legal billing procedures.
3. Performs related business office responsibilities as assigned by patient accounts manager.
   a. Follows hospital and department policies and procedures.
   b. Observes confidentiality in all matters.
   c. Maintains all documentation and records in accordance with federal and state regulations.
   d. Maintains good interdepartmental relations.
4. Provides coverage for A/R specialist 2 position for vacation and illness.
   a. Demonstrates knowledge of and ability to perform all duties and functions.
5. Participates in educational opportunities offered by hospital for job and personal development.
   a. Attends classes, workshops and seminars relating to billing/collection functions.
   b. Participates actively in such seminars, classes and workshops.
   c. Takes advantage of opportunities for personal growth and development as offered.
6. Takes an active role in facilitating team approach to functions within the department.
   a. Attends departmental meetings.
   b. Actively participates as team member in resolution of problems as they are identified.
   c. Analyzes current procedures, bringing suggestions for improvement to the attention of team members and supervisor for consideration.

Direction of Others:

Provides some direction to student learner. Number of persons supervised —1.

Qualifications:

High school graduation with 1-3 years experience in claims processing, business or accounting. Experience in health care field desirable.

Physical Qualifications:

These requirements may be met with the aid of mechanical devices and are those minimally necessary for safe completion of duties. They are not intended to discriminate against handicapped persons, only to insure safe working conditions for all persons.

1. Must be able to enter data into a computer and effectively operate a 10-key adding matching.
2. Must be able to communicate in a pleasant and tactful manner to other employees and patients.
3. Must pass a pre-employment physical examination.

Working Conditions:

Normal office working conditions.

Department approval: ______________________ Date: __________

Administrative approval: ______________________ Date: __________

Human resources approval: ______________________ Date: __________

FIGURE 16–1

Job description for Patient Service Representative (hospital biller) from The Health Care Biller (newsletter) August 1995. Reprinted courtesy of Aspen Publishers, Inc., Frederick, Maryland

REIMBURSEMENT METHODS

Generally, a hospital bill for inpatient care will be much larger than the bill for services rendered in a physician's office. Hospitals use and maintain highly sophisticated, expensive equipment; are located in large facilities; and employ large numbers of personnel, many of whom are state licensed and specialized. Salaries and operating costs must be recovered through patient billing. Usually, individuals are admitted to hospitals for health problems that require major surgery, resulting in considerable expense to the patient. Working parents with families, the elderly, and jobless persons, even those who have insurance have found it increasingly difficult to pay their share of the hospital bills.

Growing numbers of the population are now served by a variety of managed health care programs. All of these programs operate under varying contracts, policies, and guidelines depending on the state and federal laws. In negotiating a reimbursement arrangement, the managed care plan administrator tries to obtain discounts for participation by a hospital in the plan in exchange for an increased volume of patients. These programs use any one or a combination of various payment methods. If you do not understand the terminology presented here, read Chapter 9, Managed Care Systems and Special Plans, in which examples are given. A partial list of some reimbursement methods follows:

Charges ■ In a managed care plan, the dollar amount owed to a participating provider for health care services rendered to a plan member, according to a fee schedule set by the managed care plan. This is the most expensive and least desirable type of reimbursement contract, so not many of these contracts exist.

Discounts in the form of sliding scale ■ For example, a 10% reduction in charges for 0 to 500 total bed days per year with incremental increases in the discount up to a maximum percentage. Timeliness of payment may also be included to encourage a hospital to join a plan (e.g., an additional 4% discount for paying a clean claim within 14 days of receipt); on the other hand, a hospital may demand a penalty for clean claims not processed within 30 days.

Flat rate ■ A single charge per hospital admission paid by the managed care plan.

Fee schedule ■ A comprehensive listing, under a fee-for-service (FFS) arrangement, or discounted FFS, that states fee maximums paid by the health plan within the period of the managed care contract. Usually the fee schedule is based on CPT codes. For industrial cases, whether managed care or not, this may be called a workers' compensation fee schedule. This document may also be known as a fee maximums schedule or fee allowance schedule.

Per diem ■ A single charge for a day in the hospital regardless of actual charges or costs incurred (e.g., a plan that pays $800 for each day regardless of the actual cost of service).

Sliding scales for discounts and per diems ■ Based on total volume, this is a reimbursement method in which an interim per diem is paid for each day in the hospital. For example, a lump sum is either added to or withheld from the payment due at the end of each year to adjust for actual hospital use.

Differential by day in hospital ■ Most hospitalizations are more expensive on the first day. This type of reimbursement method may be combined with a per diem arrangement where the first day is paid at a higher rate (e.g., the first day may be paid at $1,000 and each subsequent day at $500).

Diagnostic-related groups (DRGs) ■ A classification system that categorizes patients who are medically related with respect to diagnosis and treatment and are statistically similar in length of hospital stay. Medicare, Blue Cross, and some private hospital insurance payments are based on fixed dollar amounts determined by DRGs. DRGs are discussed in detail later in the chapter.

Differential by service type ■ Service types are defined in the contract (e.g., medicine, surgery, intensive care, neonatal intensive care, psychiatry, obstetrics, and so on). The hospital receives a flat per-admission reimbursement for the service to which the patient is admitted. If services are mixed, a prorated payment may be made (e.g., 50% for intensive care and 50% for medicine).

Case rate ■ An averaging after a flat rate has been given to certain categories of procedures (e.g., normal vaginal delivery is $1,800 and cesarean section is $2,300). Utilization is expected to be 80% vaginal and 20% cesarean section; therefore, the case rate is $1900. Specialty procedures may also be given a case rate (e.g., coronary artery bypass graft surgery or heart transplantation). *Bundled case rate* means an all-inclusive rate is paid for both institutional and professional services; for example, for coronary artery bypass graft surgery, a rate is used to pay all who provide services connected with that procedure. Bundled case rates are seen in teaching facilities in which a faculty practice plan works closely with the hospital.

Bed leasing ■ A managed care plan leases beds from a facility (e.g., payment to the hospital of $300 per bed for 20 beds regardless of whether those beds are used).

16

Capitation or percentage of revenue ■ *Capitation* means reimbursement to the hospital on a per-member per-month basis to cover costs for the members of the plan. *Percentage of revenue* means a fixed percentage of the collected premium rate paid to the hospital to cover services.

Ambulatory patient groups (APGs) ▪ Modifications of ambulatory visit groups (AVGs), which is an outpatient classification scheme developed by Health Systems International. This method is based on procedures rather than on diagnoses. Services associated with a specific procedure or visit are bundled into the APG reimbursement. More than one APG may be billed if more than one procedure is performed, but discounts may be applied to any additional APGs.

Ambulatory surgery categories ▪ Hospitals with ambulatory surgery services (outpatient or day surgery cases) use ambulatory surgery categories (ASCs) which are derived from the surgery section of CPT. ASCs use disease and procedural coding classification systems to supply the input to the computer program to assign ASCs.

Periodic interm payments (PIPs) and cash advances ▪ Methods in which the plan advances cash to cover expected claims to the hospital. The fund is replenished periodically. Insurance claims may be applied to the cash advance or paid outside of it.

Withhold ▪ Method by which part of the plan's payment to the hospital may be withheld or set aside in a bonus pool. If the hospital meets or exceeds the criteria set down, then the hospital receives its withhold or bonus; also called *risk pools, withhold pools, bonus pools,* or *capitation pools.*

Stop loss ▪ A form of reinsurance in which the managed care program limits the losses on an individual highly expensive hospital claim (e.g., a plan may have stop-loss reinsurance for cases that exceed $100,000 for the year). After a case reaches $100,000, the plan may receive 80% of expenses in excess of $100,000 from the reinsurance company for the remainder of the year.

Medicolegal

CONFIDENTIALITY

The patient record and any photographs are legal documents and must be kept confidential (see Chapter 2). They may not be released unless a patient has signed an authorization form to release the information. An exception is when a medical record is subpoened by the court. Chapter 2 contains information on confidentiality when facsimile communication is used. In a hospital or office setting, however, verbal breaches of confidentiality may occur that could result in an insurance billing specialist being held liable and the facility being sued. New employees should be given a confidentiality orientation and asked to sign a confidentiality statement. This statement should emphasize that in the event of a violation, the employee may be subject to immediate termination. Any one of the following scenarios in which the patient's right to privacy has been breached may be encountered by an insurance billing specialist.

Example 1. A coding clerk overhears two hospital employees discussing a patient by name. Because the clerk had been working on the medical record of that patient and is now familiar with the patient's history, he or she realizes that the information being discussed is not accurate. The coding clerk then interrupts, making a comment about the patient's diagnosis.

Comment: Information should not be discussed with coworkers or other hospital employees and must never be related to anyone other than a person who has a valid need to provide care for the patient.

Example 2. A Marilyn Monroe impersonator is discharged from the hospital after receiving plastic surgery. Over dinner at home, an insurance billing specialist relates the diagnosis and name of the surgery to his or her spouse.

Comment: Never discuss confidential information about patients to family or friends.

Example 3. An insurance billing specialist working at home has a sister who was hospitalized to undergo major surgery and wants to help his or her parents better understand the medical condition. The specialist calls a friend in the hospital billing department and asks that person to make photocopies of a document in the medical record.

Comment: Remember that all medical reports are confidential, so the employee must deny the request unless the sister signs a release of information that would authorize her family to have copies of the document.

Example 4. In reviewing an insurance claim before it is mailed, the insurance billing specialist realizes that he or she knows the individual, who has a diagnosis that indicates a mental condition. The specialist discusses this with a coworker.

Comment: This is a violation because a hospital employee must never give anyone information on a patient's diagnosis.

Example 5. A physician in private practice calls via cellular telephone to the billing clerk to answer a question about the diagnosis to be listed on a patient's insurance claim.

Comment: Cellular transmission may be intercepted

by anyone with inexpensive eavesdropping equipment. In this scenerio, a traditional telephone line must be used when relating confidential information about a patient's diagnosis. The physician should verify if he or she is speaking to the billing clerk.

Example 6. An experienced insurance billing specialist applies for a job. At an interview, he or she presents some samples of typed insurance claims that include hospital and patient names.

Comment: This indicates that the prospective employee has taken data from a former employer's facility and violated the patient's confidentiality by not removing the names in the samples.

When work is done in a sensitive area of a facility, document shredders should be used to prevent violations of confidentiality. Know and adhere to hospital policies and guidelines in regard to use of the computer, such as the following:

1. Downloading computer data from one department to another
2. Length of time that documents may be retained on computer hard drives by employees
3. Procedures on deletion of confidential information and how this is verified
4. Data archival procedures
5. Policies for use of the modem, fax, or cellular telephone
6. Use of passwords and other encryption methods

Billing Errors

Many times, patients receive hospital bills, are stunned by the total balance due, and are unable to make sense of specific items, abbreviations, or codes on itemized billing statements. A brief hospital stay may translate into hundreds of individual charges. A patient has the right to examine and question a detailed statement, as mentioned in the Patient's Bill of Rights—a nationally recognized code of conduct published by the American Hospital Association. If the bill lumps charges together under broad categories such as pharmacy, surgical supplies, and radiology and the patient requests an itemized invoice, then it should be provided at no cost to the patient. In fact, consumer advocates and policies governing the Medicare program encourage consumers to scrutinize their hospital bills for mistakes. If the charges seem exorbitant, the hospital may receive a call or letter from the patient asking for an explanation of the charges. Sometimes, hospital billing personnel, a hospital patient representative or advocate, the attending physician, and/or his or her staff may be able to satisfactorily explain a confusing charge.

DUPLICATE STATEMENTS

Duplicate billings, which may confuse the patient, can occur when a patient receives both inpatient and outpatient preadmission tests or services. Perhaps a test was canceled and rescheduled, and a charge is shown for the canceled test. Or several physicians may have consulted on a case and each ordered the same test or therapy. Possibly, a technician took the incorrect amount of blood or produced an unclear radiograph, submitting a charge for the service performed in error as well as for the correct service and thereby generating two charges for one test. These examples are hospital personnel errors, and patients should not have to pay for such mistakes.

DOUBLE BILLING

Another example involving a violation of Medicare policy is double billing, which results when a patient undergoes routine outpatient testing for a specific diagnosis and then develops unanticipated problems related to that diagnosis, requiring hospital admission. Outpatient personnel may not be aware that the patient was later admitted, and inpatient personnel may not know that the patient had undergone outpatient testing within the previous 72 hours. Under Medicare policy, a hospital may be fined because it would be in violation of a 72-hour outpatient billing rule. Such charges must be bundled into the inpatient DRG payment. Therefore, it is imperative that hospital billing personnel either review claims involving outpatient testing, with subsequent admission of the same patient, spot-check registration, and outpatient dates with registrars, or use computer software that screens claims for potential double-billing problems.

PHANTOM CHARGES

Physicians order admission procedures for each patient who enters the hospital. If a patient has refused some of these tests, make sure that the charges were deleted from the financial records before the bill is sent out. Similarly, if, for example, a patient refuses to take sleeping pills or takes only a few aspirin, he or she should not be charged for refused medication or a bottle of aspirin. The hospital may offer a standard kit of supplies on admission or, when appropriate, a new-mother packet. If the patient does not accept some of these supplies, he or she should not have to pay for them. If a patient requests a semiprivate room but is sent to a private room because all semiprivate rooms are occupied, the patient should not be billed at the higher rate. Phantom charges may appear if a scheduled test is canceled by a physician or if the patient is released early, making it imperative to check the dates and times of admission and discharge.

POSTING ERRORS

Code errors may occur when data are transferred from a master list to the bill and an incorrect key is punched by the individual entering the data ($79.90 for a drug or service instead of $7.99). A bill should never show unexplained codes or items without descriptions. Errors may be made when entries are transferred from a patient's medical record to a bill because of illegible handwriting on the patient's chart or a typographic error by the typist. Also, charges that should appear on a patient's itemized statement may be missing because the charges were transferred to the wrong patient's bill. This requires a review of the patient's medical records. When a charge cannot be accounted for by a review of the patient's record or by talking to the attending physician, the charge should be deleted from the bill.

Hospital Billing Process

The insurance billing office is often part of the hospital's business office and is placed near the admission department, hospital cashier, and main lobby (entry/exit) of the hospital because patients need easy access. In some facilities, the financial department may have grown so large that it has been relocated to a building at another site.

The inpatient billing process involves many people and departments in the hospital. Figure 16–2 shows how the billing process flows from beginning to end. An admitting clerk interviews the patient and obtains personal and insurance information as well as admitting diagnosis. He or she then has the patient sign various legal documents (e.g., consent form for an invasive procedure, insurance assignment form, blanket form for routine hospital procedures, arbitration agreement, and/or responsibility for payment form). There is no law requiring that a person give his or her real name on admission. In fact, celebrities often give fictitious names. If laboratory tests and/or x-rays were not performed on a preadmission basis, the patient is sent to these departments to have tests performed. Next, the patient is taken to his or her hospital room, and as the patient receives medical services, the attending physician and nurses enter daily progress notations on the patient's medical record. The physician dictates necessary medical and surgical reports, ending with a discharge summary that is sometimes known as the *clinical resume* or *final progress note*. This document includes the course of treatment during the hospital stay, laboratory and x-ray studies, consultations, hospital course, patient's history and physical examination, admission and discharge diagnoses, operations performed, condition of patient at the time of discharge, instructions for continuing care and follow-up treatment, and postoperative office visit date. Charges may be compiled via computer from all hospital departments that furnished services to the patient. For institutional facilities (e.g., inpatient and outpatient departments, rural health clinics, chronic dialysis services, and adult day health care), the information is organized and printed onto a hospital Uniform Bill claim form, the UB-92. An insurance billing specialist and/or coding specialist *must always* review the information for accuracy, referring, if necessary, to the patient's admission sheet and medical record and manually entering special information that may have been omitted. The UB-92 claim form is then sent to the appropriate insurance company to obtain payment. For physicians' professional outpatient claims, the HCFA-1500 Claim Form is used. Mail the claim form to the insurance carrier for payment; retain a copy for the files. Document the patient's file with the date mailed and the address to which the insurance claim was filed. If errors are not caught, the claim may be rejected or delayed, leading to slow payment or nonpayment. For a list of common reasons why claims are rejected or delayed, see Chapter 6, The Health Insurance Claim Form.

ELECTRONIC DATA INTERCHANGE

As early as the 1980s, large hospitals began submitting electronic claims for payment to third party payers instead of printing out the UB-92 claim form; this is called electronic data interchange (EDI). This method of claim submission reduces the cost to the hospital of doing business. Use of computer software assists the data entry operator in checking for errors before forwarding the claim to the proper claims office; payment activity can also be tracked. Medicare, Medicaid, the Blue Plans, group health

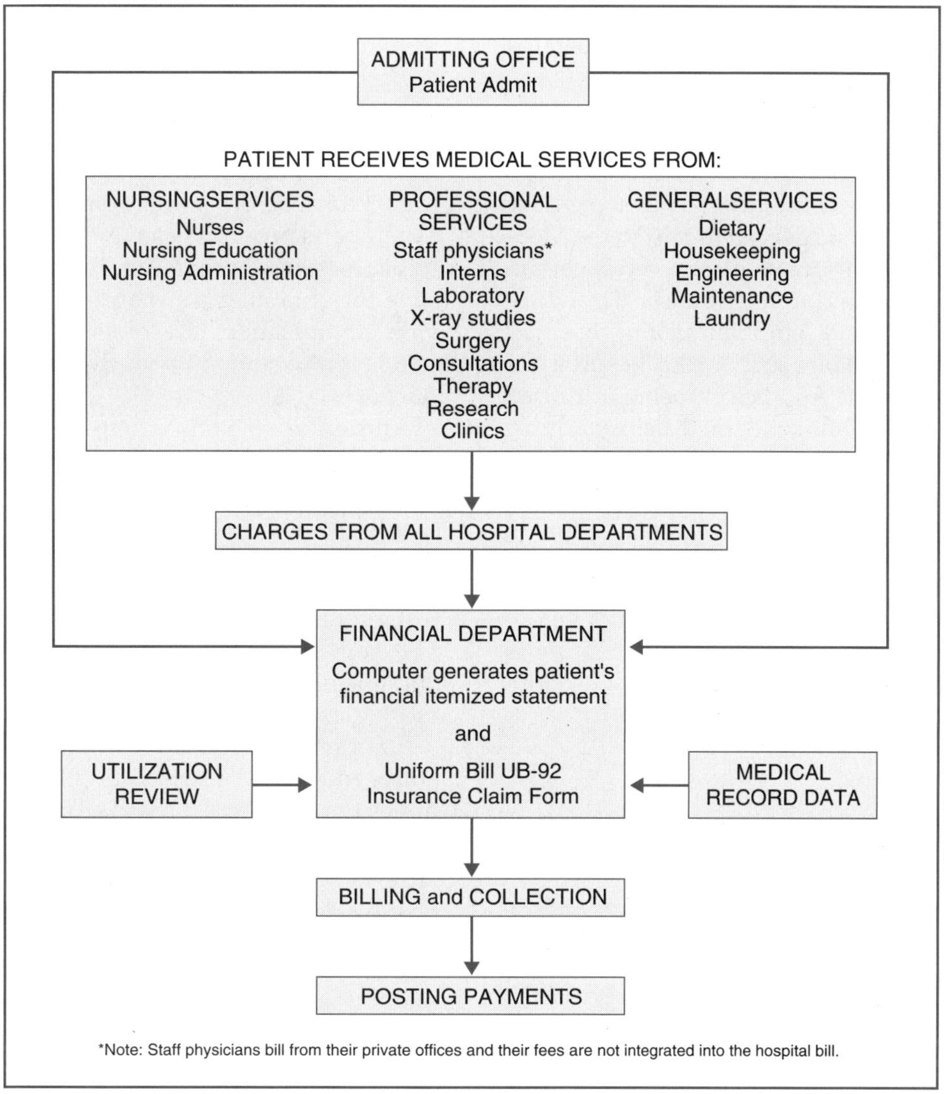

FIGURE 16–2
Basic flow of the hospital billing process for an inpatient.

carriers, many health maintenance organizations (HMOs), and some workers' compensation carriers use EDI. For detailed information on this topic, refer to Chapter 7, Electronic Data Interchange.

PAYMENTS

On receipt of payment from insurance plans, managed care programs, or patients that is to be applied to outstanding accounts, standard bookkeeping procedures and posting entries are used. Financial management for managed care programs is discussed and shown in figures in Chapter 9, Managed Care Systems and Special Plans.

Outpatient Insurance Claims

The term *outpatient* is used when an individual receives medical service from the hospital and goes home on the same day. If an individual has an accident, injury, or acute illness, he or she may seek the services of medical personnel in the emergency department of the hospital. When seen in this department, a patient is considered an outpatient unless he or she is admitted for an overnight hospital stay. Many elective surgeries are done on an outpatient basis. *Elective surgery* indicates a surgical procedure that can be scheduled in advance, is not an emergency, and is discretionary on the part of the physician and patient. Elective procedures are those that are deferrable, which means that the patient will not experience serious consequences if the operation is postponed or there is failure to undergo the operation. Some insurance policies require a second opinion for elective surgery. If the patient does not seek a second opinion and chooses to undergo surgery, the insurance company may not pay. See Chapter 12 for elective surgery in regard to the Medicare program. Patients may also receive certain types of therapy on an outpatient basis. To reduce inpatient expenses and eliminate extra hospital days, a patient is usually sent to the hospital for preadmission testing (PAT) before being admitted for major surgery. When scheduled before admission, these charges are usually included on the inpatient bill. Preadmission tests must be performed from 12 to 72 hours before admission, depending on the policies of the plan. Preadmission tests may include laboratory studies, chest x-rays, or electrocardiography. If a patient is admitted 48 hours before a scheduled procedure and only routine testing is done, the hospital could be in jeopardy for the entire hospital bill or for the portion relating to the days before surgery.

Inpatient Insurance Claims

A patient is considered an *inpatient* on admission to the hospital for an overnight stay, and a medical record number is assigned and a patient record is begun. If the patient receives medication, medical supplies, and therapy; undergoes laboratory tests and surgery; and so on, then each hospital department posts the charges to the patient's bill via a computer terminal.

PRIVATE INSURANCE (GROUP OR INDIVIDUAL)

It is the responsibility of the outpatient and inpatient admitting personnel to obtain complete and accurate information during the initial registration of the patient. The patient must provide a current insurance card or cards and, if necessary, claim forms. Obtain photocopies of the front and back of all cards. Some hospital facilities employ an insurance verification clerk. He or she has the responsibility of contacting the insurance company or the insured individual's employer to verify the type of insurance. The clerk must also call the insurance company to verify eligibility and benefits and to determine whether prior authorization is needed.

BLUE PLANS

There are three instances in which a patient is admitted to the hospital:

Admission to Participating Hospital ▪ An attending participating physician contacts the Blue Plan at least 3 days before admission to give notification of a member's proposed elective admission. If a preadmission review is required, the physician is responsible for obtaining prior authorization from the review organization. The physician calls the hospital to relay information about the patient for admitting purposes.

Admission to Nonparticipating Hospital ▪ An attending physician should call the designated review organization for admission in a nonemergency situation. Within 1 working day of approval requests for prior authorization, the review organization calls the physician and hospital and assigns a control number that certifies approval of the admission. The review organization furnishes the physician and hospital with an approved preadmission/referral request form.

Emergency Admission ▪ A patient is seen in the emergency department, and the physician determines that it is necessary to admit the patient to the hospital. Emergency admissions do not need prior authorization, but the hospital utilization review staff member must notify the insurance plan within the next working day to inform them of the admission. The plan authorizes the first days of the admission automatically and approves subsequent days based on utilization review. The review organization determines the emergency status and may send written notification to the hospital and physician. Emergency department charges are billed with charges for the inpatient stay on the UB-92 claim form.

WORKERS' COMPENSATION

In a workers' compensation case, the patient will not have an insurance card. When seen on an emergency basis, an employer's report of injury must be completed and sent to the insurance company and state industrial accident board before a hospital's or physicians' insurance claims can be submitted. A case number is assigned. Appropriate information relating to the injured patient, the industrial accident, the insurance carrier, and the employer must be obtained. See Chapter 14, Workers' Compensation, for further details on this subject.

MANAGED CARE

There may be restrictions and various policies and procedures to follow when a patient has a managed care (HMO, preferred provider organization [PPO]) type of insurance coverage. Obtain photocopies of the front and back of the identification card. General guidelines are as follows:

Emergency Outpatient Admission

1. Hospital *with* contract: Notify managed care program within 48 hours or the next working day and obtain authorization number. Patient may have a deductible and copay requirement.
2. Hospital *without* contract: Notify managed care program of emergency admission on the next working day and obtain authorization number; if required, prepare the patient for transfer to a contracting hospital. The patient may have the option of staying and paying the deductible, copay, or entire bill and not file with the managed care plan. The managed care plan will not cover any charges. However, some plans with deductibles and copays may cover certain charges.

Nonemergency Inpatient Admission

1. Hospital *with* contract: Patient must be referred by his or her primary care physician and must obtain authorization for length of hospital stay. Patient may have a copay requirement.
2. Hospital *without* contract: Patient may be responsible for a higher deductible and copay.

For information on this subject, see Chapter 9, Managed Care Systems and Special Plans.

MEDICARE

Obtain photocopies of the front and back of the patient's identification cards for Medicare and any supplemental or secondary insurance policies. When billing a secondary insurance company for Medicare Part A or B, use a copy of the UB-92 claim form, complete the Benefits Due portion (i.e., deductible and/or coinsurance), and send a copy of the Remittance Advice (RA) to the supplemental or secondary insurance company for payment. For detailed data on this program, see Chapter 12, Medicare.

MEDICAID

Obtain photocopies of the front and back of the patient's identification card or verify eligibility via touchtone telephone, modem, or specialized Medicaid terminal equipment. Patients who receive both Medicare and Medicaid benefits are considered to have crossover claims. The claim form will be processed automatically by Medicaid (in California, Medi-Cal) after processing is completed by Medicare. For additional information, see Chapter 11, Medicaid and Other State Programs.

CHAMPUS, CHAMPVA, AND TRICARE

Obtain photocopies of the front and back of the patient's identification card or verify eligibility via touchtone telephone or modem. For additional information, see Chapter 13, CHAMPUS, CHAMPVA, and TRICARE.

Diagnostic Coding

The *International Classification of Diseases, Ninth Revision, Clinical Modification* (ICD-9-CM) Volumes 1, 2, and 3 are used to list diagnostic codes on hospital insurance claims. Some editions of ICD-9-CM may contain all three volumes in one book. Chapter 5, Diagnostic Coding, gives basic information and instructions on how to use Volumes 1 and 2.

ICD-9-CM VOLUME 3 PROCEDURES: TABULAR LIST AND ALPHABETIC INDEX

ICD-9-CM Volume 3, which is not used in physicians' offices for coding, is used in the hospital setting. This volume combines both the alphabetic and tabular lists for the classification of surgical and nonsurgical procedures and miscellaneous therapeutic and diagnostic procedures.

TABULAR LIST

The Tabular List is divided into chapters that relate to operations or procedures for anatomic sites, with the last chapter referring to miscellaneous diagnostic, therapeutic, and prophylactic procedures. Procedure codes are two digits at the category code level with two digits beyond the decimal point. These digits differentiate between unilateral or bilateral, between surgical approach or techniques, and among condition types (e.g., indirect and direct hernia). No alphabetic characters are used. When a three-digit code is followed by a fourth digit, all four digits must be listed. Chapter categories are as follows:

Chapter 1	Operations on the Nervous System	Codes 01–05
Chapter 2	Operations on the Endocrine System	Codes 06–07
Chapter 3	Operations on the Eye	Codes 08–16
Chapter 4	Operations on the Ear	Codes 18–20
Chapter 5	Operations on the Nose, Mouth, and Pharynx	Codes 21–29
Chapter 6	Operations on the Respiratory System	Codes 30–34
Chapter 7	Operations on the Cardiovascular System	Codes 35–39
Chapter 8	Operations on the Hemic and Lymphatic Systems	Codes 40–41
Chapter 9	Operations on the Digestive System	Codes 42–54
Chapter 10	Operations on the Urinary System	Codes 55–59
Chapter 11	Operations on the Male Genital System	Codes 60–64
Chapter 12	Operations on the Female Genital System	Codes 65–71
Chapter 13	Obstetrical Procedures	Codes 72–75
Chapter 14	Operations on the Musculoskeletal System	Codes 76–84
Chapter 15	Operations on the Integumentary System	Codes 85–86
Chapter 16	Miscellaneous Diagnostic and Therapeutic Procedures	Codes 87–99

ALPHABETIC INDEX

The Alphabetic Index is arranged by procedure (e.g., incision, excision, graft, implant) and not anatomic site. It is used to locate the main entry. Read any notations that appear under the main term, which appears in bold type. A main term may be followed by modifiers (i.e., a series of subterms in parentheses) that give differences in site or surgical technique.

Example:
Amputation (cineplastic) (closed flap) (guillotine) (kineplastic) (open) 84.91

An operation named for a person is termed an *eponym*. Such names are listed both as main terms and under the main term "operation." The description of the procedure or anatomic site follows the eponym.

Example:
Operation
Billroth II (partial gastrectomy with gastroduodenostomy) 43.6

SPECIAL POINTS TO REMEMBER IN VOLUME 3

Basic steps in coding from Volume 3 are:

- Locate the main term (procedure or condition) in the Alphabetic Index.
- Read the modifier (descriptive notation relating to the condition).
- Obtain the code number and refer to the Tabular List (Volume 3) to verify that the code number selected matches the classification of the procedure. Never code based on only the Alphabetical Index because important instructions may appear in the Tabular List.
- Note any exclusions, inclusions, notes concerning fifth digits, colons, and any other information that may affect the choice of codes. Note "code also" and "omit code" instructions. Then, select the appropriate code number. Use fourth and/or fifth digit codes if necessary. If necessary, use two or more code numbers to completely describe a diagnosis or procedure.

Example:
Diagnosis: Complete vaginal hysterectomy with bilateral salpingectomy

Code	Description
68.5	Vaginal hysterectomy
66.51	Removal of both fallopian tubes at same operative episode

DIAGNOSTIC CODING HANDY HINTS

Be sure the code for the principal diagnosis is listed first, because this is the most important code. The principal diagnosis code represents the significant reason that a patient is admitted to the hospital. If the person initially came in for a heart transplantation, heart disease would be the principal diagnosis. However, if the heart transplant patient went home and then came into the hospital with pneumonia, pneumonia would be the principal diagnosis. Subsequent diagnostic codes should be for any current coexisting conditions that are documented in the record. Do not include codes for conditions that were previously treated and no longer exist.

Procedural Coding

CURRENT PROCEDURAL TERMINOLOGY

An up-to-date edition of *Current Procedural Terminology* (CPT), the code book published by the American Medical Association, is used to list procedural codes on hospital insurance claims for hospital services and medical supplies. Chapter 4, Procedural Coding, gives basic information and instruction on how to use the code book.

PROCEDURAL CODING HOSPITAL BILLING HANDY HINTS

Although physicians make daily hospital visits to their patients, perform surgeries, discharge patients from the hospital, and are called to the hospital to provide consultation on cases, these services are billed as professional services by the physician and not by the hospital billing department. Only services provided by the hospital should be coded by the hospital.

HEALTH CARE FINANCE ADMINISTRATION COMMON PROCEDURE CODING SYSTEM

The Health Care Finance Administration Common Procedure Coding System (HCPCS; pronounced "hick-picks") is used to list procedural codes for Medicare patients on hospital insurance claims that are not in the CPT code book. Chapter 12, Medicare, gives basic information on the three levels of this code system.

Hospital Billing Claim Form

UNIFORM BILL INPATIENT AND OUTPATIENT CLAIM FORM

In 1982, the UB-82 claim form was developed for hospital claims and was printed in green ink. A need was seen to update this form, so a revision was issued in 1992. The UB-92 claim form is also known as the HCFA-1450. This form is considered a summary document supported by an itemized or detailed bill. It is used by institutional facilities (e.g., inpatient and outpatient departments, rural health clinics, chronic dialysis services, and adult day health care) to submit claims for inpatient and outpatient services. This claim form is printed in red ink on white paper for processing with optical scanning equipment. Figure 16–3 illustrates a completed UB-92 claim form. Dates of service and monetary values are entered without spaces or decimal points (e.g., $200.00 should be shown as 20000, and June 23, 1995 should be shown as 062395). Dates of birth are entered using two sets of two-digit numbers for the month and day and a four-digit number for the year (e.g., June 23, 1995, should be shown as 06231995). (For information on how to complete the HCFA-1500 Claim Form for professional services, see Chapter 6, The Health Insurance Claim Form.)

INSTRUCTIONS FOR COMPLETING THE UB-92 CLAIM FORM

Only general guidelines are mentioned here. Always refer to the medical hospital manual and, if available, your local UB-92 manual to determine whether there are billing guidelines that pertain to your region. The following item numbers and descriptions correspond to Figure 16–3, which shows a completed UB-92 claim form.

Block 1 ▪ On the first three lines, enter the provider name, address, city, state, and zip code. On the fourth line, enter telephone number, fax number, or county code applicable to the provider. **Medicare, Medicaid,** and **Medi-Cal:** The fourth line is optional. **CHAMPUS:** The fourth line is required.

Block 2 ▪ Leave blank.

Block 3 ▪ Patient control number: This is an optional block that can be used to identify an individual patient account. Enter the patient's medical record number or account number.

Block 4 ▪ Enter the appropriate three-digit bill code as specified in the UB-92 Manual Billing Procedures. For example, inpatient billing code is 11X and outpatient billing code is 13X. The facility may

16

APPROVED OMB NO. 0938-0279

COLLEGE HOSPITAL
4500 BROAD AVENUE
WOODLAND HILLS, XY 12345-0001
013-487-6789

2

3 PATIENT CONTROL NO.: 1150748-001
4 TYPE OF BILL: 112

5 FED. TAX NO.: 95-1690976
6 STATEMENT COVERS PERIOD FROM: 082196 THROUGH: 090396
7 COV D.: 12
8 N-C D. 9 C-I D. 10 L-R D. 11

12 PATIENT NAME: SOUZA, JAMES
13 PATIENT ADDRESS: 1402 12TH PLACE WOODLAND HILLS XY 12345

14 BIRTHDATE	15 SEX	16 MS	ADMISSION 17 DATE	18 HR	19 TYPE	20 SRC	21 D HR	22 STAT	23 MEDICAL RECORD NO.	CONDITION CODES 24	25	26	27	28	29	30	31
08211994	M	S	082196	19	2	4	11	30	1150748	C1							04101

32 OCCURRENCE CODE DATE · 33 OCCURRENCE CODE DATE · 34 OCCURRENCE CODE DATE · 35 OCCURRENCE CODE DATE · 36 OCCURRENCE SPAN CODE FROM THROUGH · 37 A B C

38
SOUZA, MARIA
1402 12TH PLACE
WOODLAND HILLS XY 12345

39 VALUE CODES CODE: a 01 AMOUNT: 804 00
40 VALUE CODES CODE AMOUNT
41 VALUE CODES CODE AMOUNT

	42 REV. CD.	43 DESCRIPTION	44 HCPCS / RATES	45 SERV. DATE	46 SERV. UNITS	47 TOTAL CHARGES	48 NON-COVERED CHARGES	49
1	175	NEONATAL ICU	1844.00		14	25816 00		
2	250	PHARMACY				4083 20		
3	258	IV SOLUTIONS-PHARMACY				3387 90		
4	270	MED-SUR SUPPLIES				15606 71		
5	300	LABORATORY				12958 40		
6	310	PATHOLOGY LAB				47 10		
7	320	OX X-RAY				950 00		
8	360	OR SERVICES				1800 00		
9	370	ANESTHESIA				1392 37		
10	390	BLOOD/STOR-PROC				630 30		
11	402	RADIOLOGY ULTRASOUND				808 00		
12	410	RESPIRATORY SVC			22	8682 70		
13	481	CARDIAC CATH LAB				1139 60		
14	920	OTHER DX SVS				36 00		

50 PAYER	51 PROVIDER NO.	52 REL INFO	53 ASG BEN	54 PRIOR PAYMENTS	55 EST. AMOUNT DUE	56
A FOUNDATION HEALTH PLAN		Y	Y		77338 28	

57 DUE FROM PATIENT ▶

58 INSURED'S NAME	59 P.REL	60 CERT. - SSN - HIC. - ID NO.	61 GROUP NAME	62 INSURANCE GROUP NO.
A SOUZA, MARIA	03	61807576810	ALDEN TERRACE	CA00446

63 TREATMENT AUTHORIZATION CODES	64 ESC	65 EMPLOYER NAME	66 EMPLOYER LOCATION
A 85092/3327	1	ALDEN TERRACE CONV	105 MAIN RD WOODLAND HILLS XY 12345

67 PRIN. DIAG. CD.: 7566 · OTHER DIAG. CODES 68–75 · 76 ADM. DIAG. CD.: 7566 · 77 E-CODE · 78

79 P.C.: 9 · 80 PRINCIPAL PROCEDURE CODE: 537 DATE: 082296 · 81 OTHER PROCEDURE CODE DATE

82 ATTENDING PHYS. ID: 167803740 SMITH JOHN
83 OTHER PHYS. ID
OTHER PHYS. ID

84 REMARKS

85 PROVIDER REPRESENTATIVE: X John Smith MD
86 DATE: 091296

I CERTIFY THE CERTIFICATIONS ON THE REVERSE APPLY TO THIS BILL AND ARE MADE A PART HEREOF.

UB-92 HCFA-1450 OCR/ ORIGINAL

FIGURE 16–3
Scannable (red ink) Uniform Bill insurance claim form. This form is also known as the UB-92 and is shown completed to an insurance company. Third party payers, state, and local guidelines vary and may not always follow the visual guide presented here.

assign a number for the "X." **Medicare:** Required. **Medi-Cal:** Optional.

Block 5 ▪ Enter the facility's provider federal tax number. This number is also called a tax identification number (TIN) or an employer identification number (EIN). **Medicare** and **Medi-Cal:** Not required. **Commercial insurers** and **CHAMPUS:** Required. **Blue Cross** and some **Medicaid programs:** A number in this field may be required.

Block 6 ▪ Enter beginning and ending dates of service for the period shown on the bill (e.g., 01049X to 01069X). **Medicare** and **third party payers:** Required. **Medi-Cal:** Not required.

Block 7 ▪ Enter the number of inpatient days. **Medicare:** Required. **Medicaid, commercial carriers,** and **Blue Plans:** Depending on plan or state policies, may be required. **Medi-Cal:** Not required. **CHAMPUS:** Not required.

Block 8 ▪ Enter the days of care not covered by the primary insurance carrier. **Medicare:** Required. **Medicaid, Commercial carriers,** and **Blue Plans:** Depending on plan or state policies, may be required. **Medi-Cal** and **CHAMPUS:** Not required.

Block 9 ▪ **Medicare:** Enter inpatient days occurring after the 60th day and before the 91st day of one illness. **Medicare/Medicaid, Medicare/supplemental insurance,** and **Medicare/Blue Plans:** Required. **Medi-Cal** and **CHAMPUS:** Not required.

Block 10 ▪ Under Medicare, each beneficiary has a lifetime reserve of 60 additional days of inpatient hospital services after using 90 days of inpatient hospital services during a spell of illness. **Medicare:** Required. **Medicare/Medicaid, Medicare/supplemental insurance,** and **Medicare/Blue Plans:** Must be completed for patients. **Medicaid, Medi-Cal,** and **CHAMPUS:** Not required.

Block 11 ▪ Leave blank.

Block 12 ▪ Enter the patient's last name, first name, and middle initial. Avoid nicknames or aliases.

Block 13 ▪ Patient address: Enter the patient's street address, city, state, and zip code. **Medicare, Blue Plans, third party payers, CHAMPUS,** and **some Medicaid programs:** Required. **Medi-Cal:** Not required.

Block 14 ▪ Birthdate: Enter the patient's date of birth in an eight-digit format (e.g., June 1, 1995, becomes 06011995). **Medicare** and **third party payers:** Required.

Block 15 ▪ Use the capital "M" for male and "F" for female. **Medicare** and **third party payers:** Required.

Block 16 ▪ **CHAMPUS, third party payers,** and **some Blue Plans:** Marital status of the patient on date of registration as an inpatient or outpatient or at the start of care is entered. **Medicare, Medicaid, and Medi-Cal:** Not required. S indicates single; M, married; D, divorced; W, widowed; X, legally separated; and U, unknown.

Block 17 ▪ Enter admission or start of care date. **Medicare** and **third party payers:** Required. **Medi-Cal:** Not required.

Block 18 ▪ Enter the hour during which the patient was admitted for inpatient or outpatient care (e.g., midnight is 00 and noon is 12, 1 to 1:59 A.M. is 01, 1 to 1:59 P.M. is 13, and 11:59 is shown as 23). **Medicare, CHAMPUS, third party payers, some Blue Plans,** and **Medicare/Medicaid:** Required. **Medicare/Medi-Cal:** Not required. **Blue Plans:** Depending on specific plan, may be required.

Block 19 ▪ Enter the code indicating the priority of the inpatient admission. **Medicare, third party payers, CHAMPUS** and **some Medicaid programs:** Required when inpatient claim is submitted. **Medi-Cal:** Not required. 1 indicates emergency; 2, urgent; 3, elective; 4, newborn; and 9, information not available.

Block 20 ▪ Enter the code indicating the source of the admission or outpatient service. **Medicare, third party payers,** and **CHAMPUS:** Required. **Medicaid:** May be required. **Blue Plans:** Depending on contract requirements, may be required. **Medi-Cal:** Not required. Codes are as follows:

- 1 Physician referral
- 2 Clinic referral
- 3 Health maintenance organization (HMO) referral
- 4 Transfer from a hospital
- 5 Transfer from a skilled nursing facility (SNF)
- 6 Transfer from another health care facility
- 7 Emergency department
- 8 Court/law enforcement
- 9 Information not available
- 0 Transfer from psychiatric, substance abuse, or rehabilitation hospital
- A Transfer from a rural primary care hospital
- B–Z Reserved for national assignment

Newborn codes:

- 1 Normal delivery
- 2 Premature delivery
- 3 Sick baby
- 4 Extramural birth
- 5–8 Reserved for national assignment
- 9 Information not available

16

Block 21 ▪ Enter hour when patient was discharged from inpatient care (e.g., midnight is 00 and noon is 12, 1 to 1:59 A.M. is 01, 1 to 1:59 P.M. is 13, and 11:59 is shown as 23). **Medicare** or **Medi-Cal:**

Not required. **Third party payers** and **CHAMPUS:** Required. **Medicaid:** May be required. **Blue Plans:** Depending on contract requirements, may be required.

Block 22 ▪ Enter a code indicating the patient's disposition as of the ending date of service for the period of care reported. **Medicare, Medicaid, Blue Plans,** and **third party payers:** Required for inpatient claims. **Medi-Cal:** Not required. Codes are:

01	Discharged to home or self-care (routine discharge)
02	Discharged/transferred to another short-term general hospital for inpatient care
03	Discharged/transferred to SNF
04	Discharged/transferred to an intermediate care facility
05	Discharged/transferred to another type of institution for inpatient care or referred for outpatient services to another institution
06	Discharged/transferred to home under care of organized home health service organization
07	Left against medical advice or discontinued care
08	Discharged/transferred to home under care of home intravenous provider
09	Admitted as an inpatient to this hospital
10–19	Discharge to be defined at state level, if necessary
20	Expired
21–29	Expired, to be defined at state level, if necessary
30	Still a patient or expected to return for outpatient services
31–39	Still a patient to be defined at state level, if necessary
40	Expired at home (for hospice care)
41	Expired in a medical facility such as a hospital, an SNF, an intermediate care facility, or a free-standing hospice (for hospice care)
42	Expired, place unknown (for hospice care)
43–49	Reserved for national assignment
50	Discharged to hospice—home
51	Discharged to hospice—medical facility
52–99	Reserved for national assignment

Block 23 ▪ Enter the number given by the provider to the patient's medical record. **Medicare, CHAMPUS,** and **third party payers:** Required. **Some Medicaid programs:** May be required. **Some Blue Plans:** Depending on contract requirements, may be required.

Blocks 24–30 ▪ Condition codes: This helps determine patient eligibility and benefits and helps determine benefits from primary or secondary insurance coverage. Codes are:

01	Military service related
02	Condition is employment related
03	Patient covered by insurance not reflected here
04	Patient is HMO enrollee
05	Lien has been filed
06	End-stage renal disease (ESRD) patient in first 18 months of entitlement covered by employer group health insurance
07	Treatment of nonterminal condition for hospice patient
08	Beneficiary would not provide information concerning other insurance coverage
09	Neither patient nor spouse is employed
10	Patient and/or spouse is employed, but no employer group health plan (EGHP) coverage exists
11	Disabled beneficiary, but no large group health plan (LGHP) coverage exists
12–14	Reserved for third party payer only
15	Clean claim delayed in HCFA's processing system
16	Skilled Nursing Facility (SNF) transition exemption
17	Patient more than 100 years old
18	Maiden name is retained
19	Child retains mother's name
20	Beneficiary requested billing
21	Billing for denial notice
22	Patient on multiple drug regimen
23	Home caregiver available
24	Home intravenous patient also receiving home health agency (HHA) services
25	Reserved for national assignment
26	Veterans Affairs–eligible patient chooses to receive services in Medicare-certified facility
27	Patient referred to a sole community hospital for a diagnostic laboratory test
28	Patient and/or spouse's EGHP is secondary to Medicare

29	Disabled beneficiary and/or family member's LGHP is secondary to Medicare
30	Reserved for national assignment
31	Patient is student (full-time day)
32	Patient is student (cooperative/work study program)
33	Patient is student (full-time night)
34	Patient is student (part-time)
35	Reserved for national assignment
36	General care patient in a special unit
37	Ward accommodation at patient's request
38	Semiprivate room not available
39	Private room medically necessary
40	Same-day transfer
41	Partial hospitalization
42–45	Reserved for national assignment
46	CHAMPUS Nonavailability Statement on file
47	Reserved for CHAMPUS
48	Claims submitted by a CHAMPUS-authorized psychiatric residential treatment center (RTC) for children and adolescents
49–54	Reserved for national assignment
55	SNF bed not available
56	Medical appropriateness. SNF admission was delayed more than 30 days after hospital discharge
57	SNF readmission
58–59	Reserved for national assignment
60	Operating cost day outlier
61	Operating cost outlier
62	Periodic interim payment (PIP) bill
63	Payer-only code
64	Other than clean claim
65	Non–prospective payment system bill
66	Provider does not wish cost outlier payment
67	Beneficiary elects not to use lifetime reserve (LTR) days
68	Beneficiary elects to use lifetime reserve (LTR) days
69	Reserved for national assignment
70	Self-administered erythropoietin (EPO) for home dialysis patient
71	Full care in dialysis unit
72	Self-care in dialysis unit
73	Self-care in dialysis training
74	Patient receiving dialysis services at home
75	Home dialysis—100% payment
76	Backup in-facility dialysis
77	Provider accepts or is obligated/required due to a contractural arrangement or law to accept payment by a primary payer as payment in full
78	New coverage not implemented by HMO
79	Comprehensive outpatient rehabilitation facility services provided offsite
80–99	Reserved for state assignment
A0	CHAMPUS External Partnership Program
A1	Early Periodic Screening Diagnosis Treatment/Child Health Assurance Program (EPSDT/CHAP)
A2	Physically handicapped children's program
A3	Special federal funding
A4	Family planning
A5	Disability
A6	Pneumonococcal pneumonia vaccine (PPV) services should be reimbursed under a special Medicare program provision, 100% payment
A7	Induced abortion—danger to life
A8	Induced abortion—victim rape/incest
A9	Second-opinion surgery
B0–B9	Reserved for national assignment
C0	Reserved for national assignment
C1	Approved as billed
C2	Automatic approval as billed based on focused review
C3	Partial approval
C4	Admission/services denied
C5	Postpayment review applicable
C6	Admission preauthorization
C7	Extended authorization
C8–C9	Reserved for national assignment
D0	Change to service dates
D1	Change to charges
D2	Change in revenue codes/HCPCS
D3	Second or subsequent interim prospective payment system bill
D4	Change in grouper input
D5	Cancel to correct health insurance claim number (HICN) or provider identification number
D6	Cancel only to repay a duplicate or Office of the Inspector General (OIG) overpayment
D7	Change to make Medicare the secondary payer
D8	Change to make Medicare the primary payer

D9	Any other change
E0	Change in patient status
E1–L9	Reserved for national assignment
M0	All-inclusive rate for outpatient services (payer-only code)
M1	Roster billed influenza virus vaccine (payer only code)
M2	HHA payment significantly exceeds total charges (payer only code)
M3–M9	Reserved for payer assignment
N0–W9	Reserved for national assignment
X0–Z9	Reserved for state assignment

Block 31 ▪ Reserved for national assignment.

Blocks 32–35 ▪ Occurence codes and dates are used to identify significant events relating to a bill that may affect payer processing (i.e., determination of liability, coordination of benefits, administer subrogation clauses in benefit programs). **Medicare** or **third party payers:** Required. Codes are as follows:

01	Accident
02	No-fault insurance involved, including auto accident and other
03	Accident—tort liability
04	Accident—employment related
05	Other accident
06	Crime victim
07–08	Reserved for national assignment
09	Start of infertility treatment cycle
10	Last menstrual period
11	Onset of symptoms/illness
12	Date of onset for a chronically dependent individual (CDI) (HHA claims only)
13–16	Reserved for national assignment
17	Date outpatient occupational therapy plan established or last reviewed
18	Date of retirement of patient/beneficiary
19	Date of retirement of spouse
20	Guarantee of payment began
21	Utilization review (UR) notice received
22	Date active care ended
23	Reserved for national assignment
24	Date insurance denied
25	Date benefits terminated by primary payer
26	Date SNF bed available
27	Date home health plan established or last reviewed (HHA)
28	Date comprehensive outpatient rehabilitation facility (CORF) plan established or last reviewed
29	Date outpatient physical therapy plan established or last reviewed
30	Date outpatient speech pathology plan established or last reviewed
31	Date beneficiary notified of intent to bill (accommodations)
32	Date beneficiary notified of intent to bill (diagnostic procedures or treatments)
33	First day of the Medicare coordination period for end-stage renal disease beneficiaries covered by an EGHP
34	Date of election of extended care services
35	Date treatment started for physical therapy
36	Date of inpatient hospital discharge for covered transplant patient
37	Date of inpatient hospital discharge for noncovered transplant patient
38	Date treatment started for home intravenous therapy
39	Date discharged on a continuous course of intravenous therapy
40	Scheduled date of admission
41	Date of first test for preadmission testing
42	Date of discharge (hospice only)
43	Scheduled date of cancelled surgery
44	Date treatment started for occupational therapy
45	Date treatment started for speech therapy
46	Date treatment started for cardiac rehabilitation
47–49	Payer codes
50–69	Reserved for state assignment
70–99	Reserved for occurrence span codes
A0	Reserved for national assignment
A1	Birthdate—insured A
A2	Effective date—insured A policy
A3	Benefits exhausted
A4–A9	Reserved for national assignment
B0	Reserved for national assignment
B1	Birthdate—insured B
B2	Effective date—insured B policy
B3	Benefits exhausted
B4–B9	Reserved for national assignment
C0	Reserved for national assignment
C1	Birthdate—insured C
C2	Effective date—insured C policy
C3	Benefits exhausted
C4–C9	Reserved for national assignment
D0–D9	Reserved for national assignment
E0	Reserved for national assignment
E1	Birthdate—insured D
E2	Effective date—insured D policy

E3	Benefits exhausted
E4–E9	Reserved for national assignment
F0	Reserved for national assignment
F1	Birthdate—insured E
F2	Effective date—insured E policy
F3	Benefits exhausted
F4–F9	Reserved for national assignment
G0	Reserved for national assignment
G1	Birthdate—insured F
G2	Effective date—insured F policy
G3	Benefits exhausted
G4–G9	Reserved for national assignment
H0–I9	Reserved for national assignment
J0–L9	Reserved for national assignment
M0–Z9	See Block 36 occurrence span codes

Block 36 ■ Enter code identifying occurrence that happened over a span of time. Codes are as follows:

70	Qualifying stay dates (for SNF use only)
71	Prior stay dates
72	First/last visits
73	Benefit eligibility period
74	Noncovered level of care/leave of absence (LOA)
75	SNF level of care
76	Patient liability period
77	Provider liability
78	SNF prior stay dates
79	Provider liability—no utilization (payer code)
80–99	Reserved for state assignment
M0	Peer review organization/utilization review (PRO/UR) approved stay dates (partial approval)
M1–W9	Reserved for national assignment
X0–Z9	Reserved for state assignment

Block 37 ■ For adjustment claims, enter the internal control number (ICN) or document control number (DCN) assigned to the original bill by the payer or the payer's intermediary. **Medicare:** Required. **Third party payers** and **Medi-Cal:** Not required. **Medicaid:** May be required. **Some Blue Plans:** Depending on contract requirements, may be required. **CHAMPUS:** For reporting claim changes.

Block 38 ■ Enter the name and address of the party responsible for the bill. **Third party payers:** Required. **Blue Plans, CHAMPUS, Medicare, Medicaid,** and **Medi-Cal:** Not required.

Blocks 39–41 ■ Enter the value codes and amounts of the patient's share of cost for the following:

01	Most common semiprivate room rate
02	Hospital has no semiprivate rooms
03	Reserved for national assignment
04	Inpatient professional component charges that are billed combined
05	Professional component included in charges and billed separately to carrier
06	Medicare blood deductible amount
07	Reserved for national assignment
08	Medicare lifetime reserve amount in the first calendar year
09	Medicare coinsurance amount in the first calendar year
10	Medicare lifetime reserve amount in the second calendar year
11	Medicare coinsurance amount for second calendar year
12	Working aged beneficiary/spouse with EGHP
13	End-stage renal disease beneficiary in a Medicare coordination period for an EGHP
14	No-fault insurance, including auto or other
15	Workers' compensation
16	Public health service (PHS) or other federal agency
17	Outlier amount
18	Disproportionate share amount
19	Indirect medical education amount
20	Total prospective payment system capital payment amount
25–29	Reserved for national assignment—Medicaid
30	Preadmission testing
31	Patient liability amount
32–36	Reserved for national assignment
37	Pints of blood furnished
38	Blood deductible pints
39	Pints of blood replaced
40	New coverage not implemented by HMO (for inpatient claims only)
41	Black lung
42	Veterans' Affairs
43	Disabled beneficiary under age 65 with LGHP
44	Amount provider agreed to accept from primary payer when this amount is less than total charges but greater than the primary insurer's payment
45	Accident hour
46	Number of grace days
47	Any liability insurance
48	Hemoglobin reading
49	Hematocrit reading
50	Physical therapy visits

51	Occupational therapy visits
52	Speech therapy visits
53	Cardiac rehabilitation visits
54–55	Reserved for national assignment
56	Skilled nurse—home visit hours (HHA only)
57	Home health aide—home visit hours (HHA only)
58	Arterial blood gas (PO_2/PA_2)
59	Oxygen saturation (O_2 sat/oximetry)
60	HHA branch metropolitan statistical area (MSA)
61–66	Reserved for national assignment
67	Peritoneal dialysis
68	EPO—drug
70	Interest amount
71	Funding of ESRD networks
72	Flat-rate surgery charge
73	Drug deductible
74	Drug coinsurance
75	Gramm-Rudman-Hollings reduction—for payers use only
76	Provider's interim rate
77–79	Payer codes
80–99	Reserved for state assignment
A1	Deductible payer A
B1	Deductible payer B
C1	Deductible payer C
E1	Deductible payer D
F1	Deductible payer E
G1	Deductible payer F
A2	Coinsurance payer A
B2	Coinsurance payer B
C2	Coinsurance payer C
E2	Coinsurance payer D
F2	Coinsurance payer E
G2	Coinsurance payer F
A3	Estimated responsibility payer A
B3	Estimated responsibility payer B
C3	Estimated responsibility payer C
D3	Estimated responsibility payer D
F3	Estimated responsibility payer E
G3	Estimated responsibility payer F
A0	Reserved for national assignment
A4–A9	Reserved for national assignment
B0	Reserved for national assignment
B4–B9	Reserved for national assignment
C0	Reserved for national assignment
C4–C9	Reserved for national assignment
D0–D2	Reserved for national assignment
D4–D9	Reserved for national assignment
E0	Reserved for national assignment
E4–E9	Reserved for national assignment
F0	Reserved for national assignment
F4–F9	Reserved for national assignment
G0	Reserved for national assignment
G4–G9	Reserved for national assignment
X0–Z9	Reserved for national assignment

Block 42 ■ Enter a three- or four-digit code corresponding to each narrative description or standard abbreviation that identifies a specific accommodation, ancillary service, or billing calculation related to services billed. Revenue code 001 must be the final entry on all bills. Revenue codes are an important factor when payment is considered by managed care contractors. Billing guidelines for revenue codes are extensive, so refer to the UB-92 manual for detailed information. **Medicare:** Required. **Medi-Cal:** Not required for outpatient services except when code 001 is used to indicate Total Charge line.

Block 43 ■ This optional block helps separate and identify descriptions of each service. The description must identify the particular service code indicated in the HCPCS/Rates field (Block 44). **Blue Plans, third party payers,** and **CHAMPUS:** Required. **Medicare:** Not required. **Some Medicaid programs:** Depending on contract requirements, may be required.

Block 44 ■ Enter the applicable CPT or HCPCS code number and modifier. **Medicare:** Required. **Third party payers** or **Medicaid:** Depending on contract requirements, may be required. When billing for recipients with both Medicare/Medi-Cal, bill Medi-Cal for only those services listed in the Medicare noncovered section. All other services must be billed to Medicare first.

Block 45 ■ Enter the date the service was rendered for outpatient in six-digits (e.g., 062395). See the patient's itemized bill for dates. **Medicare** and **Medicaid:** Required. **Some Blue Plans** and **third party payers:** Depending on contract requirements, may be required.

Block 46 ■ Enter the actual number of times a single procedure was provided for the date of service. This may be seen on the patient's itemized bill. Although this is a seven-digit Block, Medi-Cal allows only three digits in this Block. If billing for more than 99, divide the units onto two or more lines. **Medicare:** Complete for billing.

Block 47 ■ Enter the total charge. **Medicare** or **third party payers:** Required.

Example: $100 should be entered 100 00

47 TOTAL CHARGES	
100	00

Block 48 ■ Enter total noncovered charges for the primary payer pertaining to a particular revenue code. Personal items are not covered. **Medicare, third party payers, Medicaid,** and **Blue Plans:** Required. **CHAMPUS** or **Medi-Cal:** Not required.

Block 49 ■ Reserved for national assignment.

Block 50 ■ Enter name and number identifying each payer organization from which the provider may expect some payment for the bill. Line 50A is used to report the primary payer. Line 50B is used for the secondary payer. Line 50C is used for the tertiary payer. **Medicare, third party payers, Blue Plans, Medicaid,** and **CHAMPUS:** Required. **Medi-Cal:** Enter "O/P MEDI-CAL" to indicate the type of claim and payer. **Blue Plans:** Refer to the UB-92 manual for a list of the Blue Plan code numbers.

Block 51 ■ Enter the national provider identifier when services are provided by an outside or independent contractor, e.g., laboratory tests. **Medicare, Blue Plans, Medicaid,** and **third party payers:** Required. **CHAMPUS:** Requires the zip code of the physical location of the provider plus the four-digit subidentification number.

Block 52 ■ Enter code indicating if provider has patient's signature on file permitting release of data. **Medicare:** Required. **Medi-Cal:** Not required. **Some Blue Plans** and **Medicaid:** Depending on contract requirements, may be required. Y indicates yes; R, restricted or modified release; and N, no release.

Block 53 ■ Enter Y (yes, benefits assigned) or N (benefits not assigned). **Third party payers** and **CHAMPUS:** Required. **Some Blue Plans:** Depending on contract requirements, may be required. **Medicare, Medicaid,** and **Medi-Cal:** Not required.

Block 54 ■ Enter the amount of payment received from other coverage on the same line as the other coverage "payer" (Block 50) (e.g., $100 should be entered as 100 00. *Do not* enter Medicare payments in this block; leave blank if not applicable. **Medicare, Medicaid,** and **Medi-Cal:** Required. **Blue Plans:** Depending on contract requirements, may be required.

Block 55 ■ Enter the estimated amount due (difference between "Total Charges" and any deductions, i.e., patient's share of cost and/or other coverage). **Third party payers, CHAMPUS, Medicaid,** and **Medi-Cal:** Required. **Some Blue Plans:** Depending on contract requirements, may be required. **Medicare:** Not required.

Blocks 56–57 ■ Reserved for state assignment.

Block 58 ■ Enter name of the patient or insured individual. **Medicare, Medicaid, Blue Plans, CHAMPUS,** and **third party payers:** Required. If billing for an infant, use the mother's name. If billing for an organ donor, enter the recipient's name and the patient's relationship to the recipient in Block 59. Otherwise, leave blank.

Block 59 ■ Enter code number indicating relationship of the patient to the insured individuals identified in Block 58. **Medicare, Medicaid, Blue Plans, CHAMPUS,** and **third party payers:** Required. Codes are:

01	Patient is the insured
02	Spouse
03	Natural child/insured has financial responsibility
04	Natural child/insured does not have financial responsibility
05	Stepchild
06	Foster child
07	Ward of the court
08	Employee
09	Unknown
10	Handicapped dependent
11	Organ donor
12	Cadaver donor
13	Grandchild
14	Niece/nephew
15	Injured plaintiff
16	Sponsored dependent
17	Minor dependent of a minor dependent
18	Parent
19	Grandparent
20	Life partner
21–99	Reserved for national assignment

Block 60 ■ Enter the insured's identification number assigned by the payer organization (i.e., Social Security number or health insurance claim I.D. number). Required by all programs.

Block 61 ■ Enter the group name or plan through which the health insurance coverage is provided to the insured. **Medicare** and **third party payers:** Required. **CHAMPUS:** Enter the sponsor's branch of service (e.g., USA, USAF). **Medi-Cal:** Not required.

Block 62 ■ Enter the insurance group number. **Medicare** and **third party payers:** Required. **CHAMPUS:** Enter the sponsor's military status and pay grade codes. **CHAMPVA:** Enter the veteran's military status code (e.g., "ACT" for active or "RET" for retired). **Medi-Cal:** Not required.

Block 63 ■ Enter the treatment authorization code (TAR). **Medicare, third party payers, Blue Plans,** and **CHAMPUS:** Required. **Medi-Cal:** For services requiring a TAR, enter the 11-digit TAR control number. It is not necessary to attach a copy of the TAR to the claim.

Block 64 ■ Enter the employment status code. **Medicare** and **third party payers:** Required. **Some Blue Plans:** Depending on contract requirements, may be required. **Some Medicaid programs:** May be required. **Medi-Cal:** Not required. **CHAMPUS:** Enter the code that describes the employment status of the individual identified in Block 58. Codes are:

1	Employed full-time
2	Employed part-time
3	Not employed
4	Self-employed
5	Retired
6	On active military duty
7–8	Reserved for national assignment
9	Unknown

Block 65 ▪ Enter the employer's name for the individual in Block 58. **Medicare, CHAMPUS,** and **third party payers:** Required. **Some Blue Plans:** Depending on contract requirements, may be required. **Medicaid:** May be required. **Medi-Cal:** Not required.

Block 66 ▪ Enter the employer's location of the insured individual identified in Block 58. **Medicare, CHAMPUS,** and **third party payers:** Required. **Some Blue Plans:** Depending on contract requirements, may be required. **Some Medicaid programs:** May be required. **Medi-Cal:** Not required.

Block 67 ▪ Enter all letters and/or numbers of the ICD-9-CM code for the principal diagnosis, including fourth and fifth digits. Do not enter a decimal point when entering the code. Required for all programs.

Blocks 68–75 ▪ The primary code should be entered next. Enter all letters and/or numbers of the secondary ICD-9-CM code. Required for all programs. Blocks 69–81, **Medi-Cal:** Not required.

Block 76 ▪ Enter admitting diagnosis code, including fourth and fifth digits. Required for all programs.

Block 77 ▪ If there is an external cause of injury, poisoning, or adverse effect, enter the diagnostic E code, including the third and fourth digits. **Medicare** and **third party payers:** Not required.

Block 78 ▪ Reserved for state assignment.

Block 79 ▪ Enter coding system used. **Third party payers, Medicaid,** and **CHAMPUS:** Required. **Some Blue Plans:** Depending on contract requirements, may be required. **Medicare:** Not required. Codes are:

1–3	Reserved for state assignment
4	CPT procedure codes
5	HCPCS codes
6–8	Reserved for national assignment
9	ICD-9-CM diagnostic codes

Block 80 ▪ Enter the procedure code for principal procedure and date performed. **Medicare, Medicaid, Blue Plans, CHAMPUS,** and **third party payers:** Required.

Block 81 ▪ Enter one or two additional major procedure codes and dates performed to identify significant procedures other than the principal procedure and corresponding dates when procedures were performed. **Medicare, Blue Plans, third party payers,** and **CHAMPUS:** Required. **Medicaid:** Depending on contract requirements, may be required.

Block 82 ▪ Enter the name and/or national provider identifier (NPI) for the referring or prescribing physician. This Block is mandatory for radiologists. If the physician is not a Medicaid or Medi-Cal provider, enter the state license number. Do not use a group provider number. Required by all programs.

Block 83 ▪ Enter the name and/or identification number of the licensed physician other than the attending physician. Required for all programs. **Medi-Cal:** On the top line of Block 83, enter the individual nine-digit Medi-Cal provider number for the physician actually providing services. Do not use a group provider number or state license number.

Block 84 ▪ Use this area for procedures that require additional information, justification, or an emergency certification statement. If it will not fit in this area, attach the statement to the claim. Required for all programs.

Block 85 ▪ Provider or authorized signer must sign and date claim. **Blue Cross:** Does not require a provider representative signature on hard-copy claims, but a provider representative may elect to sign or use a facsimile signature. **Medicare:** A stamped signature is acceptable. For other programs, a facsimile signature may be acceptable after approval. A provider representative signature is not possible on electronic claims.

Block 86 ▪ Insert the date the claim is submitted to the insurance company or fiscal intermediary. Required for all programs.

Diagnosis-Related Groups

HISTORY

The concept of diagnosis-related groups (DRGs) was developed by Professors John D. Thompson and Robert B. Fetter at Yale University and tested in New Jersey from 1977 to 1979. The goal was to develop a scheme of patient classification to be used in utilization review (UR).* Soon other applications were found in such areas as budgeting, planning, and reimbursement.

* Review of hospital admissions to determine whether they are justified; this is discussed later in the chapter.

Because of inconsistencies and inadequacies in the original concept, a second set of DRGs was developed and has been used in New Jersey since 1982. Under the Medicare Prospective Payment System (PPS), the DRGs were implemented nationwide for all hospitalizations after the Tax Equity and Fiscal Responsibility Act of 1982 (TEFRA) was passed. The purpose of a DRG-based system of Medicare reimbursement is to hold down rising health care costs. Therefore, Medicare reimbursement as a whole is expected to decrease significantly under the DRG payment system.

THE DRG SYSTEM

The DRG system is a patient classification scheme that categorizes patients who are medically related with respect to diagnosis and treatment and who are statistically similar in length of hospital stay. This system changed hospital reimbursement from a fee-for-service system to a lump-sum, fixed-fee payment based on the diagnoses rather than on time or services rendered. The fees were fixed by a research team, which determined a national "average" fee for each of the principal discharge diagnoses. The classifications were formed from more than 10,000 ICD-9-CM codes that were divided into 25 basic major diagnostic categories (MDCs). These diagnoses were assigned a specific DRG number from 001 to 495 and specific values commensurate with geographic areas, types of hospitals, depreciation values, teaching status, and other specific criteria. Six variables are responsible for DRG classifications:

- Principal diagnosis
- Secondary diagnosis
- Surgical procedures
- Comorbidity and complications
- Age and sex
- Discharge status

Let's take an example of the case of a patient with chronic bronchitis who is admitted to the hospital with pneumonia; his medical record shows that he has had emphysema for many years. Refer to Figure 16–4, which lists chronic obstructive lung disease as the principal diagnosis, with pneumonia as a secondary diagnosis (inaccurate DRG assignment). This would entitle the hospital to receive $2,723.66. However, if pneumonia was listed as the principal diagnosis with two secondary diagnoses, emphysema and chronic bronchitis, then the hospital would be entitled to $3,294.17—$570 more with the use of the correct DRG assignment.

Cases that cannot be assigned to an appropriate DRG because of atypical situations are called *cost outliers*. These atypical situations are as follows:

1. Clinical outliers:
   a. Unique combinations of diagnoses and surgeries causing high costs. These are more common than day outliers.

SAMPLE CASE HISTORY			
CORRECT DRG ASSIGNMENT		INACCURATE DRG ASSIGNMENT	
MDC 4: Respiratory System		MDC 4: Respiratory System	
Principal Diagnosis	Pneumonia (ICD9CM-486)	Principal Diagnosis	COPD (ICD9CM-496)
Secondary Diagnosis	Emphysema (ICD9CM-492.8)	Secondary Diagnosis	Pneumonia (ICD9CM-486)
Secondary Diagnosis	Chronic Bronchitis (ICD9CM-491.2)	Principal Operative Procedure	None
Principal Operative Procedure	None	Principal Operative Procedure	None
Secondary Operative Procedure	None	Secondary Operative Procedure	None
Age	69 Years	Age	69 Years
Discharge Status	Routine	Discharge Status	Routine
Sex	Male	Sex	Male
Length of Stay	15 Days	Length of Stay	15 Days
DRG	89	DRG	88
Trim Points	4–22 Days	Trim Points	3–19 Days
Rate	$3,294.17	Rate	$2,723.66

FIGURE 16–4
Sample case history showing correct and incorrect DRG assignment and the difference in payment between the two.

   b. Very rare conditions
2. Long length of stay (LOS), referred to as *day outlier**
3. Death
4. Leaving against medical advice
5. Admitted and discharged on the same day
6. Low-volume DRGs

The current federal plan for outliers is the full DRG rate plus an additional payment for the services provided. Coding that is inappropriately altered to obtain a higher payment rate is called *DRG creep.*

As you recall from Chapter 4, the primary diagnosis is that illness or injury that prompts the office visit or service, and the primary diagnosis is used for all billings from physicians' offices. For a hospitalized patient, the principal diagnosis is that illness or injury that effected hospitalization, and the principal diagnosis is used for billings from the hospital. The principal diagnosis is the most important factor in the assignment of the DRG number, because this determines the payment received by the health care facility.

The amount may be increased by documenting in the patient's medical record any comorbid conditions or complications. When referring to DRGs, the abbreviation CC is used to indicate such complications and/or comorbidities (not the more common interpretation found in patient charting, Chief Complaint). *Comorbidity* is defined as a pre-existing condition that will, because of its effect on the specific principal diagnosis, require more intensive therapy or cause an increase in LOS by at least 1 day in approximately 75% of cases.

If a patient is admitted because of two or more conditions and the physician fails to indicate the "most resource-intensive" or "most specific" diagnosis as the principal diagnosis, the DRG assessment will be incorrect, resulting in decreased reimbursement to the health care facility. It is the responsibility of the attending physician to decide on a principal diagnosis based on his or her best judgment.

Example: A patient has had congestive heart failure for several years and is admitted with a principal diagnosis of anterior wall myocardial infarction (MI). While hospitalized, the patient suffers atrial fibrillation.

Principal diagnosis:	410.1	anterior wall myocardial infarction
Comorbid condition (CC):	428.0	congestive heart failure
Complication:	427.31	atrial fibrillation

Example: A patient has had chronic obstructive pulmonary disease (COPD) for the last 6 months and is admitted with a principal diagnosis of anterior wall myocardial infarction (MI). While hospitalized, the patient suffers respiratory failure.

Principal diagnosis:	410.1	anterior wall myocardial infarction
Comorbid condition:	496	chronic obstructive pulmonary disease
Complication:	799.1	respiratory failure

Both examples would warrant additional payment because of comorbid conditions and complications.

The *grouper,* which is the computer program that assigns DRGs, does not consider any differences between chronic and acute conditions. The following information is abstracted from inpatient data by the grouper to assign appropriate DRGs to discharged patients: patient's age, sex, principal diagnosis, principal procedures performed, and discharged status. *Looping* is the grouper process of searching all listed diagnoses for the presence of any comorbid condition or complication or searching all procedures for OR (operating room) procedures or more specific procedures.

DRG/ICD-9-CM Code Book is a good reference and code book presented in an easy-to-use binder and containing Volumes 1, 2, and 3 of ICD-9-CM. Sections are color-highlighted for maximum payment. Refer to Appendix B to locate publishers of ICD-9-CM code books.

DIAGNOSIS-RELATED GROUPS AND THE MEDICAL ASSISTANT/INSURANCE BILLING SPECIALIST

Even though DRGs affect Medicare hospital payments, it is important to stress the role of the medical assistant in a physician's office when communicating the admitting diagnosis to the hospital. This can greatly affect the DRG assignment. The medical assistant should remember the following points:

1. When calling the hospital to admit a patient,

* Day outliers are to be eliminated.

you may be asked the admitting diagnosis. It is important to be sure to give all of the diagnoses if there are more than one so the hospital personnel can then use their expertise in listing the primary and secondary diagnoses.

2. After the Medicare patient is admitted, a hospital representative may call you and question the tests, LOS, or treatments ordered by the attending physician. The hospital needs this information to justify a higher-than-average bill to Medicare. As mentioned previously, these cost outlier cases can also be affected by the patient's death, if the patient is admitted and discharged on the same day, if the patient leaves against medical advice, by clinical outliers, by long LOS, or by low-volume DRGs.
3. Ask the physician to review the treatment or procedure in question.
4. Get to know the hospital coordinator on a first-name basis so that when the physician or patients have DRG-related questions, you can call on this hospital expert.

When the DRG system is implemented by other third party payers and/or segments of the population other than Medicare patients, you should contact them locally to assist you. It is important that records and hospital insurance claims contain the correct *principal diagnosis*, the patient's *age*, *discharge diagnosis*, *detailed facts to support the principal diagnosis and complications*, and *medical data to justify all procedures performed*.

HANDY HINTS FOR THE PHYSICIAN'S PRACTICE

Before Admission

1. Use outpatient and preadmission testing for patients with elective admissions to the hospital. Order these tests at least 24 hours prior to admission (and not more than 72 hours before admission for complete blood count and urinalysis on elective admissions) for sufficient time to identify additional medical problems. Find out which regular procedures Medicare approves as inpatient procedures and which must be done as outpatient procedures. Usually, preadmission testing is done to eliminate extra hospital days and, if done 48 to 72 hours before admission, is not included on the inpatient bill. However, the same testing done 24 hours before admission is included on the inpatient bill. Preadmission tests might include laboratory studies, chest x-rays, or electrocardiography. Some procedures may be approved on an inpatient basis if adequate proof of their necessity is given.

   If preadmission testing is performed, the physician can easily complete a report, or at least a comprehensive admitting note, before admission. If the patient is admitted 48 hours before a scheduled procedure and only routine testing is done, the hospital could be in jeopardy for the physician's bill pertaining to that period. The preadmission report should contain the following:

   a. Outpatient treatment, tests, and/or x-rays done before admission (e.g., minor surgery, electrocardiogram, chest x-ray, complete blood count and differential, urinalysis, and so on).
   b. An explanatory note of the work-up done. Avoid the statement "admission for work-up only."
   c. The patient's lack of response to treatment.
   d. Why the patient needs hospital admission.
   e. Admitting diagnosis. Avoid listing symptoms when possible; avoid using words such as weakness, shortness of breath, dizziness, impaction, low blood count, debilitated condition, disposition problem, confusion, etiology unknown, organic brain syndrome, inability to retain food, and so on.

      Avoid using the hospital for surgical or medical consultations that could be done in the specialist's office unless the patient physically requires admission. This necessity should be documented. If a patient is admitted for consultation only, the entire payment for hospital admission will be denied as well as any physician fees involved. Some private insurance companies require second opinions on some admissions. Patients under the Medicare program who have supplementary insurance coverage, such as Blue Cross/Blue Shield, also require second opinions. This is a cost-saving measure imposed by insurance companies.
2. Use short-stay surgery when medically appropriate.
3. Find out whether the physician's supplementary services (laboratory, x-rays, and other diagnostic tests) are considered customary for the type of illness under the DRG codes and, if not, what facts are needed to have such services covered under a DRG cost outlier.
4. For case management, Social Services personnel can visit patients at home to assist them and their families with home care or placement on a fee-for-service basis.

DRG WORKSHEET

Patient's Name Dennis Kolar Age 90

Patient's # 238 Adm. Date 6/1/9X Discharged 6/16/9X

This will NOT become part of the permanent medical record. Please add, delete, change, or correct any of the information listed below. These are working diagnoses which will be used to assign a DRG. Please refer any questions to the Utilization Review Coordinator or call the DRG Hotline.

TENTATIVE "PRINCIPAL DIAGNOSIS" (conditions after study determined to be the reason for admission)

Date Added		ICD-9
6/1	1. Hemophilus Pneumonia	482.2
	2.	
	3.	

ADDITIONAL DIAGNOSES, CO-MORBID CONDITIONS AND COMPLICATIONS

Date Added		ICD-9
6/3	1. Benign Prostatic Hypertrophy with	600.
	2. Urinary Retention	788.2
	3. Senile Dementia	290.0
	4.	
	5.	
	6.	
	7.	

PROCEDURES

Date Added		CPT-4
6/11	1. TURP	52601
	2.	

THIS SECTION TO BE COMPLETED BY UTILIZATION REVIEW

REVIEW DATE	DATE DRG CALCULATED	DRG NUMBER	DAYS IN	TARGET LOS	DRG TARGET CHARGES	ACTUAL CHARGES TO DATE
6/2	6/2	89	1	9	6284	476
6/4			4			2178
6/7			7			3462
6/10			10			5355
6/12	6/12	468	12	11	11,987	6547
6/14			14			9579
6/16	6/16	468	15	11	11,987	11,531

Discharged

YOUR SUPPORT IS GREATLY APPRECIATED

FIGURE 16–5
Example of a DRG Worksheet and the information it contains.

During Admission

1. Involve Social Services early.
2. Reduce the LOS when possible by using Home Health Services.
3. Minimize intensive care unit days within medical feasibility.
4. Consider transferring the patient to a skilled nursing facility or an acute rehabilitation center when appropriate.
5. Order tests, therapy, and consultations as early as possible.

DIAGNOSTIC RELATED GROUPS AND MEDICAL RECORDS

The most important job of the medical assistant when helping the physician with DRGs is medical records completion. A DRG worksheet is supplied by most hospitals and can be of great assistance in the office (Fig. 16–5). Record *all* diagnoses on the worksheet and indicate whether conditions are

DISCHARGE FACE SHEET

	Discharge Date	Time

Name & Address SS #, Medicare #, Phone Adm. Date Time Room/Bed /Sex M/S R M/R No.

Employer	Birthdate Age Place
	Adm Dr/Prm Dr/Diagnosis T/S Pat Type
Emergency Notification Relat Phone	
Spouse/Parent Name Address	Allergies
Name & Address SS # /Reltn/Phone	Guar/Spouse Employer Length/Occ/Phone
Ins #1 Carrier	Admit Orders

Principal Diagnosis: (diagnosis which, after study, was chiefly responsible for hospitalization).	ICD-9-CM CODE
Complications/Comorbidity	
Principal Procedure	
Other Procedures	
Cause of Death:	

Consultation: ☐ Yes ☐ No ☐ Died under 48 Hrs. Autopsy: ☐ Yes ☐ No HOSPITAL DAYS

☐ Died Over 48 Hrs. __________

____________________________ M.D.

Medical Records Chart Reviewed and Approved by—Attending Physician

FIGURE 16–6
Discharge face sheet showing general information required on the discharge of a patient from the hospital.

acute, chronic, or both. Once the physician signs the DRG worksheet, thereby agreeing with the documentation, the medical assistant can use it as an aid in completing medical records.

Hospitals receive reimbursement only after the discharge face sheet (discharge summary or discharge abstract) is completed and signed by the physician (Fig. 16–6). Hospital charts should be completed within 3 to 4 days after the patient is discharged or a cash flow problem will result for the hospital. The medical assistant can help by scheduling the physician's time so that medical records can be completed.

The physician should be made aware that certain diagnoses that are signed out as principal diagnoses are subject to 100% review by the review agency. The physician should avoid using the following as principal diagnoses:

16

1. Arteriosclerotic heart disease (ASHD). This is

acceptable as a diagnosis only when cardiac catheterization and/or open heart surgery is performed.
2. Diabetes mellitus without complications.
3. Right or left bundle branch block.
4. Coronary atherosclerosis.

Check periodically with your local hospital medical record department personnel to find out whether new items have been added to this list.

OUTPATIENT CLASSIFICATIONS

Ambulatory Patient Groups

Ambulatory patient groups (APGs) are a modification of ambulatory visit groups (AVGs) that were developed as an outpatient classification scheme by Health Systems International (HSI). Originally, there was a total of 571 AVGs designed to group outpatients, which has been reduced to approximately 297 APGs. APGs are based on patient classifications (ICD-9-CM diagnoses, CPT procedures, age, and sex) rather than disease classifications. APGs are applied to ambulatory surgery, emergency department, clinic, and physician office services. They do not apply to telephone contacts, house visits, home health nursing visits, free-standing rehabilitation facilities, or inpatient services. The development process for APGs is similar to that used for DRGs. The procedure code is the primary axis of classification, not the diagnosis code.

The General Accounting Office (GAO) has ordered Congress to begin conversion of surgical, radiology, and other diagnostic services to an APG system by January 1, 1996. Ambulatory surgery categories (ASCs) mentioned at the beginning of this chapter are part of this system. In the future, refer to the *Federal Register* for guidelines and policies on this topic.

Ambulatory Care Groups

Ambulatory care groups (ACGs) were developed by researchers at Johns Hopkins for ambulatory care patients. Patients were grouped into 34 diagnostic categories according to age, sex, and ICD-9-CM codes, and those categories subsequently were broken down into 51 ACGs. These treatment-monitoring guidelines consider a patient's illness over a period of time and define major and minor, stable and unstable, acute or chronic conditions. The ACGs include several diagnoses that require the same treatment. Each patient may fall into one or more categories. This system is not used but is in the research phase. It may help in monitoring practice guidelines, quality of care, and reimbursements.

UTILIZATION REVIEW

Each hospital has a utilization review department that conducts an admission review on all cases to determine whether admissions are justified. If the admission is found to be necessary, it is certified. At the time of the initial admission review, the physician establishes a tentative diagnosis so that a tentative DRG can be assigned. The tentative DRG is assigned based on (1) admission diagnosis, (2) scheduled procedures, (3) age, and (4) known secondary diagnoses. The DRG is assigned using an automated system called the DRG grouper. If any factors that affect the DRG assignment change or are added, the new information is entered into the DRG grouper, and the case is assigned to the new DRG. Interim reviews and discharge planning are also done on inpatients.

There also are utilization review companies that provide utilization review and case management services for self-insured employers, third party administrators, and insurance companies. They furnish data to the person who buys their services to achieve saving dollars; they also generate reports on how much money has been saved.

Peer Review Organization

Under the prospective payment system (PPS), responsibility for maintaining quality of care is delegated to peer review organizations, sometimes referred to as professional review organizations (PROs). The Peer Review Improvement Act of 1982 authorized the establishment of PROs in geographic areas across the nation. PROs are composed of licensed doctors of medicine or osteopathy actively engaged in the practice of medicine or surgery. Working under federal guidelines, these physicians evaluate other physicians regarding quality of professional care as well as other factors. The PROs are responsible for the following:

1. *Admission review* for appropriateness and necessity of admissions.
2. *Readmission review* on patients readmitted within 7 days with problems related to the first admission to determine whether the first discharge was premature and/or the second admission is medically necessary.

3. *Procedure review* of diagnostic and therapeutic procedures in cases in which past abuses have been found, to determine appropriateness.
4. *Day outlier review* for additional Medicare reimbursement.
5. *Cost outlier review* for necessity of admission and to determine whether all services rendered were medically necessary and appropriate.
6. *DRG validation* to find out whether the diagnostic and procedural information affecting DRG assignment is substantiated by the clinical information in the patient's chart.
7. *Transfer review* in cases involving a transfer to a distinct part or unit of the same hospital.

Hospitals contract with a PRO for Medicare reimbursement. If a hospital does not have a PRO contract, it will not receive payment from Medicare.

In some cases, the patient may be denied admission to a specific hospital. For example, if an acute care general hospital does not operate a coronary care unit (CCU) and the patient's condition calls for this service, then the patient will be sent to a hospital that does operate a CCU. However, it may not be a hospital that the family traditionally uses.

Appropriateness Evaluation Protocols

Appropriateness evaluation protocols (AEPs) must also be met. These criteria are used by the review agency for admission screening. The Medicare PPS requires that all patients meet at least one severity of illness (SI) or one intensity of service (IS), unless otherwise indicated, to be certified for reimbursement. Within the first 24 hours, the documentation on the medical record must reflect how the patient meets these criteria. A list of AEPs is provided here.

APPROPRIATENESS EVALUATION PROTOCOL CRITERIA FOR ADMISSION CERTIFICATION

An admission may be certified if one of the following criteria is met:

SEVERITY OF ILLNESS (SI)

1. Sudden onset of unconsciousness or disorientation (coma or unresponsiveness).
2. Pulse rate <50 or >140.
3. Systolic blood pressure <80 or >200. Diastolic blood pressure <60 or >120.
4. Sudden onset of loss of sight or hearing.
5. History of persistent fever $\geq 100°F$ (orally) or 101°F (rectally) for more than 5 days or with white blood cell count $>15{,}000/mm^3$.
6. Sudden onset of motor function loss of any body part.
7. Active, uncontrolled bleeding.
8. Electrolyte or blood gas abnormality of serum K^+: <2.5, >6.0; serum Na^+ <123, >156; CO_2 <20 mEq/L, >36 mEq/L (new findings).
9. Acute or progressive sensory, motor, circulatory, or respiratory embarrassment sufficient to incapacitate the patient (one of the IS criteria must also be met).
10. Electrocardiographic evidence of acute ischemia with suspicion of new myocardial infarction.
11. Wound dehiscence or evisceration.

INTENSITY OF SERVICE (IS)

12. Administration and monitoring of intravenous medications and/or fluid replacement (does not include tube feeding).
13. Surgery or procedure scheduled within 24 hours requiring general or regional anesthesia with use of equipment and facilities available only in a hospital.
14. Vital sign monitoring at least every 2 hours, including telemetry and bedside cardiac monitoring.
15. Use of chemotherapeutic agents that require continuous observation for a life-threatening toxic reaction.
16. Treatment in intensive/coronary care unit.
17. Administration of intramuscular antibiotics at least every 8 hours.
18. Intermittent or continuous respirator use at least every 8 hours.
19. Documentation on the medical record by the attending physician that the patient has been unsuccessfully treated as an outpatient *with* further documentation of how the patient is now to be treated as an inpatient.

16

TO THE STUDENT

Study Chapter 16 and then answer the review questions to reinforce the theory learned in this chapter of the text and to help prepare you for a future test. In addition, refer to the Workbook Assignments 58 and 61 to gain hands-on experience in analyzing and editing information from computer generated UB-92 claim forms for inpatient and outpatient hospital billing. Assignment 62 will assist you in further enhancing your diagnostic coding skills in relation to DRGs. These problems will point out the value of coding properly versus improperly regarding proper diagnostic sequence, indicating the variance in payment.

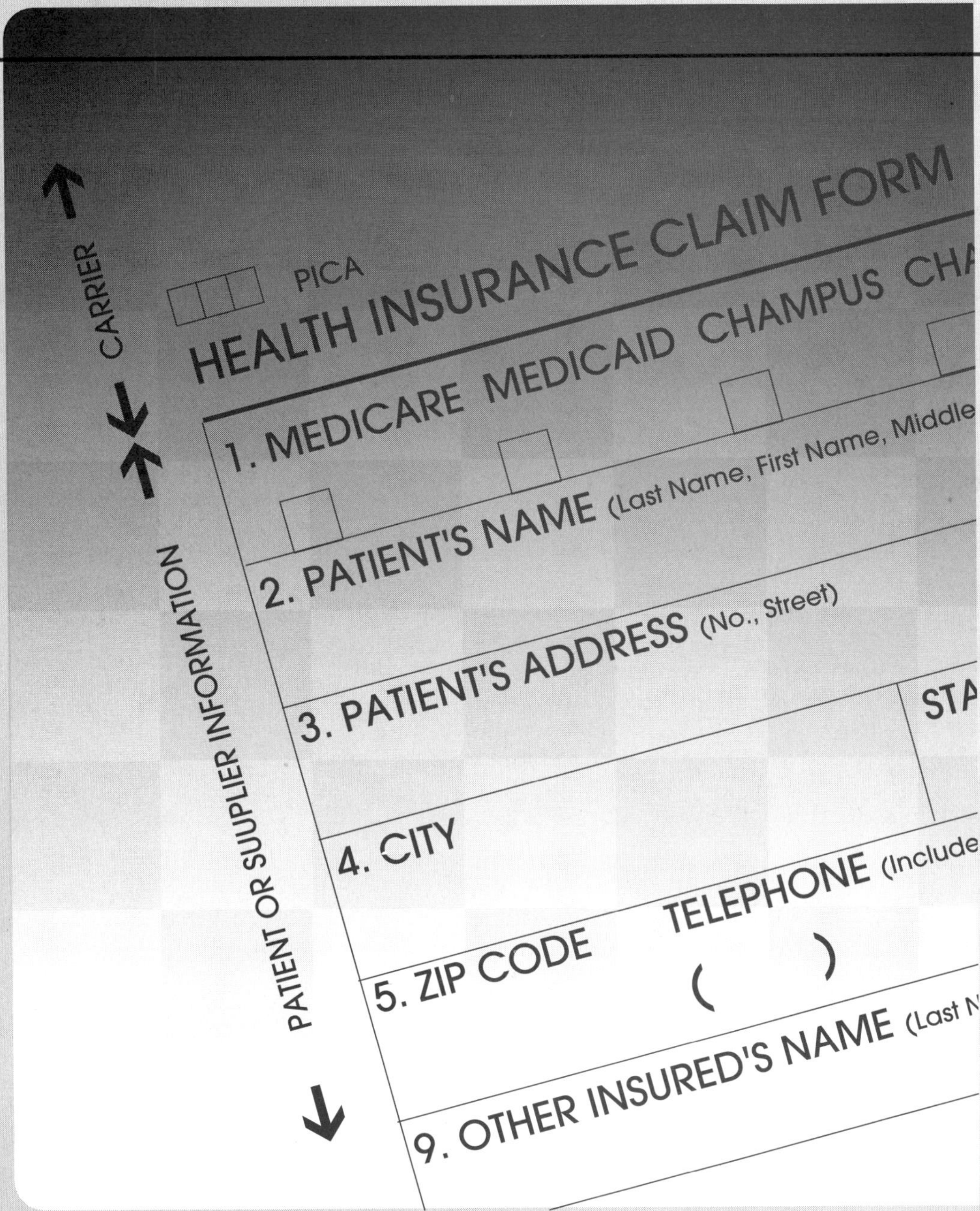

UNIT 5

Employment

Objectives*

THE INSURANCE BILLING SPECIALIST WILL BE ABLE TO:

- Prepare to find a position as an insurance billing specialist, claims assistance professional, or electronic claims processor.
- Conduct a job search by listing prospective employers.
- Compose a letter of introduction to accompany the resume.
- Analyze education and experience to prepare a resume.
- Identify illegal interview questions.
- Prepare responses to interview questions.
- Assess responsibilities assigned to insurance billing and coding specialists, electronic claims processors, and claims assistance professionals.
- Contact computerized job search data bases for on-line services.
- Explore the business aspects of self-employment.
- Search on-line for employment opportunities.

Key Terms

alien
application form
Certified Claims Assistance Professional (CCAP)
Certified Coding Specialist (CCS)
Certified Electronic Claims Professional (CECP)
Certified Procedural Coder (CPC)
chronologic resume
Claims Assistance Professional (CAP)
coding specialist
combination resume
cover letter
electronic claims processor (ECP)
employment agency
free-lancer
functional resume
insurance billing specialist
interview
portfolio
resume
self-employment

* Performance objectives and exercises for hands-on practical experience for this chapter appear in the *Workbook*.

CHAPTER 17

Seeking a Position as an Insurance Billing Specialist

Employment Opportunities

Employment opportunities throughout the United States are available for insurance billing specialists who attain coding skills, knowledge of insurance programs, and expertise in completing insurance claims accurately. The increase in the volume of paperwork associated with insurance claims, medical recordkeeping, and state and government agencies means a corresponding increase in the need for an insurance billing specialist. Because an individual can choose a number of different types of positions, this chapter provides information on each.

Examples of generic job descriptions are shown in Figures 17–1 to 17–4 to illustrate what job duties, skills, and requirements might be encountered for various insurance billing and coding positions. Job descriptions assist managers, supervisors, and employers in recruiting, supervising, and evaluating individuals in these positions for salary upgrades. Companies have had to readdress their job functions because of the Americans with Disabilities Act.

GENERIC JOB DESCRIPTION FOR ENTRY LEVEL INSURANCE BILLING SPECIALIST

Knowledge, skills, and abilities:

1. Minimum education level consists of certificate from one-year insurance billing course, associate degree, or equivalent in work experience and continuing education.
2. Knowledge of basic medical terminology, anatomy and physiology, diseases, surgeries, medical specialties, and insurance terminology.
3. Ability to operate word processing, computer, photocopy, and calculator equipment.
4. Written and oral communication skills including grammar, punctuation, and style.
5. Ability and knowledge to use procedure code books.
6. Ability and knowledge to use diagnostic code books.
7. Ability to type or keyboard 45 to 60 wpm.
8. Ability to work independently.
9. Certified Procedural Coder (CPC) or Certified Coding Specialist (CCS) status preferred.

Working conditions:
Medical office setting. Sufficient lighting.

Physical demands:
Prolonged sitting, standing, and walking, using typewriter, wordprocessor, or computer equipment. Some stooping, reaching, climbing, and bending. Occasional lifting of ____lbs. to a height of 5 feet. Hearing and speech capabilities necessary to communicate with patients and staff in person and on telephone. Vision capable of viewing computer monitors, calculators, charts, forms, text, and numbers for prolonged periods.

Salary:
Employer would list range of remuneration for the position.

Job responsibilities:	**Performance standards:**
1. Abstracts medical information from patient records.	1.1 Uses knowledge of medical terminology, anatomy and physiology, diseases, surgeries, and medical specialties. 1.2 Consults reference materials to clarify meanings of words. 1.3 Meets accuracy and production requirements adopted by employer. 1.4 Verifies with physician any vague information for accuracy.
2. Exhibits an understanding of ethical and medicolegal responsibilities related to insurance billing programs.	2.1 Observes policies and procedures related to confidentiality, medical records, release of information, retention of records, statute of limitations for claim submission. 2.2 Meets standards of professional etiquette and ethical conduct. 2.3 Recognizes and reports problems involving fraud, abuse, embezzlement, and forgery to appropriate individuals.

FIGURE 17-1
Generic job description for an insurance billing specialist.

3. Operates word processing, computers, or typewriter equipment to complete insurance claims.	3.1 Operates equipment skillfully and efficiently. 3.2 Evaluates condition of equipment and reports need for repair or replacement.
4. Follows employer's policies and procedures.	4.1 Punctual work attendance and is dependable. 4.2 Answers routine inquiries related to account balances and dates insurance forms submitted.
5. Completes and submits insurance claims accurately.	5.1 Updates insurance registration and account information 5.2 Processes payments and posts to accounts accurately. 5.3 Handles correspondence related to insurance claims. 5.4 Reviews encounter forms for accuracy before submission to data entry. 5.5 Inserts data on insurance claims accurately. 5.6 Codes procedures and diagnoses accurately. 5.7 Telephones insurance companies with regard to delinquent claims. 5.8 Traces insurance claims. 5.9 Files appeals for denied claims. 5.10 Documents data from patients accurately. 5.11 Maintains separate insurance files.
6. Enhances knowledge and skills to keep up to date.	6.1 Attends continuing education activities. 6.2 Obtains current knowledge applicable to state and federal programs as they relate to insurance claim submission. 6.3 Keeps abreast of current changes in coding requirements from Medicare, Medicaid, and other third-party payers. 6.4 Assists with updating fee schedules and encounter forms with current codes. 6.5 Assists in the research of proper coding techniques to maximize reimbursement.
7. Employs interpersonal expertise to provide good working relationships with patients, employer, employees, and insurance companies.	7.1 Works with employer and employees cooperatively as a team. 7.2 Communicates effectively with patients and insurance companies regarding payment policies and financial obligations. 7.3 Executes job assignments with diligence and skill. 7.4 Assists staff with coding and reimbursement problems. 7.5 Assists other employees when needed. 7.6 Assists with giving fee estimates to patients when necessary.

FIGURE 17-1 *Continued*

GENERIC JOB DESCRIPTION FOR A CLAIMS ASSISTANCE PROFESSIONAL

Knowledge, skills, and abilities:
1. Minimum education level consists of certificate from one-year insurance billing course, associate degree, or equivalent in work experience and continuing education.
2. Knowledge of basic medical terminology, anatomy and physiology, diseases, surgeries, medical specialties, and insurance terminology.
3. Ability to operate typewriter, word processing, or computer equipment as well as photocopy and calculator equipment.
4. Written and oral communication skills including grammar, punctuation, and style.
5. Ability and knowledge to use procedure code books.
6. Ability and knowledge to use diagnostic code books.
7. Ability to type or keyboard 45 to 60 wpm.
8. Ability to work independently.
9. Certified Claims Assistance Professional (CCAP) status preferred.

Working conditions:
Home office setting. Sufficient lighting and space to allow for at least 3 or more people.

Physical demands:
Prolonged sitting, standing, and walking, using typewriter, wordprocessor, or computer equipment. Some stooping, reaching, climbing, and bending. Occasional lifting of ____lbs. to a height of 5 feet. Hearing and speech capabilities necessary to communicate with clients in person and on telephone. Vision capable of viewing computer monitors, calculators, charts, forms, text, and numbers for prolonged periods.

Salary:
Client would pay a percentage of reimbursement or annual, hourly, or per claim fee.

Job responsibilities:	**Performance standards:**
1. Files secondary insurance claims and maintains insurance files.	1.1 Completes accurately and submits secondary insurance claims.
2. Tracks insurance claim payments received by clients.	2.1 Maintains files and traces insurance claims for clients.
3. Exhibits an understanding of ethical and medicolegal responsibilities to insurance billing programs.	3.1 Observes policies and procedures related to confidentiality of medical records, release of information, retention of records, and statute of limitations for claim submission.

FIGURE 17-2
Generic job description for a claims assistance professional (CAP).

There are two ways to work—either employed by someone or self-employed. In this career field, some of the choices are

- Insurance billing specialist
- Electronic claims processor
- Medicare or Medicaid billing specialist
- Claims assistance professional
- Coding specialist (free-lance or employed)

In addition to the skills necessary for performance on the job, you must sharpen your job-seeking techniques. Individuals must

- Be motivated and interested in finding a job
- Communicate effectively in an interview
- Enjoy good health
- Be mature
- Have good grooming and manners

	3.2 Meets standards of professional etiquette and ethical conduct. 3.3 Recognizes and reports problems involving fraud, abuse, embezzlement, and forgery to appropriate individuals.
4. Knowledge of medical terminology.	4.1 Explains data on insurance claim forms.
5. Knowledge of procedure and diagnostic code requirements as well as health insurance terminology.	5.1 Understands procedural and diagnostic codes and checks to see if correct codes were used.
6. Operates word processing, computers, or typewriter equipment to complete and submit secondary insurance claims.	6.1 Operates equipment skillfully and efficiently. 6.2 Evaluates condition of equipment and negotiates repair or replacement.
7. Employs interpersonal expertise to provide good working relationships with clients, medical office personnel, and insurance companies.	7.1 Works with clients, medical office personnel, and insurance companies with efficiency, diligence, and skill. 7.2 Communicates effectively with clients and insurance companies regarding payment policies. 7.3 Answers routine inquiries related to status of clients' accounts and dates insurance forms submitted.
8. Assists clients in challenging insurer's denials of payment of claims.	8.1 Handles correspondence related to denial of insurance payment. 8.2 Telephones insurance companies and medical offices with regard to delinquent claims.
9. Interacts with health personnel to render additional information to appeal a denied claim and obtains payment for clients depending on terms of the health insurance policy or program.	9.1 Files appeals for denied claims.
10. Enhances knowledge and skills to keep up to date.	10.1 Attends continuing education activities. 10.2 Obtains current knowledge applicable to private insurance and the Medicare program related to insurance claim submission and payments. 10.3 Keeps abreast of current changes in coding requirements from Medicare, Medicaid, and other third-party payers.

FIGURE 17–2 *Continued*

Some hospital facilities prefer credentialed coders and advertise for a Certified Procedural Coder (CPC), Certified Coding Specialist (CCS), or Certified Electronic Claims Processor (CECP). When trying to obtain clients, claims assistance professionals (CAPs) find it advantageous to be able to advertise that they are Certified Claims Assistance Professionals (CCAPs). Becoming certified is certainly an essential goal if one seeks career advancement and professionalism. For further information on certification, refer to Chapter 1.

Text continued on page 428

GENERIC JOB DESCRIPTION FOR AN ELECTRONIC CLAIMS PROCESSOR

Knowledge, skills, and abilities:

1. Minimum education level consists of certificate from one-year insurance billing course, associate degree, or equivalent in work experience and continuing education.
2. Knowledge of basic medical terminology, anatomy and physiology, diseases, surgeries, medical specialties, and insurance terminology.
3. Ability to operate computer, modem, and printer as well as photocopy and calculator equipment.
4. Written and oral communication skills including grammar, punctuation, and style.
5. Ability and knowledge to use procedure code books.
6. Ability and knowledge to use diagnostic code books.
7. Ability to keyboard 45 to 60 wpm.
8. Ability to work independently.
9. Certified Electronic Claims Processor (CECP) status preferred.

Working conditions:
Medical office setting. Sufficient lighting.

Physical demands:
Prolonged sitting, standing, and walking, using computer equipment. Some stooping, reaching, climbing, and bending. Occasional lifting of ____lbs. to a height of 5 feet. Hearing and speech capabilities necessary to communicate with patients and staff in person and on telephone. Vision capabilities necessary to view computer monitors, calculators, charts, forms, text, and numbers for prolonged periods.

Salary:
Employer would list range of remuneration for the position.

Job responsibilities:	**Performance standards:**
1. Acts as a link between the medical provider or facility and insurance companies.	1.1 Uses knowledge of medical terminology, anatomy and physiology, diseases, surgeries, and medical specialties. 1.2 Understands computer applications and equipment required to convert and transmit patient billing data electronically. 1.3 Consults reference materials to clarify meanings of words. 1.4 Meets accuracy and production requirements adopted by employer. 1.5 Verifies with physician any vague information for accuracy. 1.6 Reduces volume of paperwork and variety of claim forms providers need to submit claims for payment.
2. Converts patient billing data into electronically readable formats.	2.1 Inputs data and transmits insurance claims accurately, either directly or through a clearinghouse. 2.2 Answers routine inquiries related to account balances and dates insurance data transmitted to insurance carriers.

FIGURE 17–3
Generic job description for an electronic claims processor (ECP).

	2.3 Updates and maintains software applications with requirements of clearinghouses and insurance carriers.
3. Uses software that eliminates common claim filing errors, provides clean claims to insurance carriers, expedites payments to providers or facilities, and follows up on delinquent or denied claims.	3.1 Codes procedures and diagnoses accurately. 3.2 Telephones insurance companies about delinquent claims. 3.3 Traces insurance claims. 3.4 Files appeals for denied claims.
4. Exhibits an understanding of ethical and medicolegal responsibilities related to insurance billing programs and plans.	4.1 Observes policies and procedures related to confidentiality, medical records, release of information, retention of records, and statute of limitations for claim submission. 4.2 Meets standards of professional etiquette and ethical conduct. 4.3 Recognizes and reports problems involving fraud, abuse, embezzlement, and forgery to appropriate individuals.
5. Operates computer equipment to complete insurance claims.	5.1 Operates equipment skillfully and efficiently. 5.2 Evaluates condition of equipment and reports need for repair or replacement.
6. Follows employer's policies and procedures.	6.1 Must have punctual work attendance and be dependable.
7. Enhances knowledge and skills to keep up to date.	7.1 Attends continuing education skills activities. 7.2 Obtains current knowledge applicable to state and federal programs as they relate to transmission of insurance claims. 7.3 Keeps abreast of current changes in coding requirements from Medicare, Medicaid, and other third-party payers. Assists in the research of proper coding techniques to maximum reimbursement.
8. Employs interpersonal expertise to provide good working relationships with patients , employer, employees, and insurance companies.	8.1 Works with employer and employees cooperatively as a team. 8.2 Communicates effectively with patients and insurance companies regarding payment policies and financial obligations. 8.3 Executes job assignments with diligence and skill. 8.4 Assists staff with coding and reimbursement problems. 8.5 Assists other employees when needed. 8.6 Assists with giving fee estimates to patients when necessary.

FIGURE 17-3 *Continued*

Generic Job Description for Coders

POSITION DESCRIPTION

POSITION TITLE:
Health Information/Medical Record Technician; Coder & Specialist for an acute and/or ambulatory care setting.

DEPARTMENT:
Health Information/Medical Record.

JOB SUMMARY:
Codes information from the medical records of patients to generate a clinical patient care database for the facility. Assures the maintenance and accuracy of diagnostic and procedural statistics for the facility as well as optimum appropriate reimbursement from third party payers, by the timely coding of diagnoses and procedures using the required classification systems.

SPECIFIC RESPONSIBILITIES:
Reviews and screens the entire medical record to abstract medical, surgical, laboratory, pharmaceutical, demographic, social and administrative data from the medical record in a timely manner.
Ensures providers that all diagnoses and procedures that may impact the facility's reimbursement are identified and attested to by the physician, if appropriate, sequenced correctly, and coded in an accurate and ethical manner for optimum reimbursement.
Determines correct codes for routine, and/or new or unusual diagnoses and procedures not clearly listed in ICD-9-CM and CPT.
Consults with physicians for clarifications of clinical data when encountering conflicting or ambiguous information.
Keeps abreast of regulatory changes affecting coded information required by the Health Care Financing Administration, the Office of Statewide Health Planning Department, and others, as appropriate; and applies current Uniform Hospital Discharge Data Set (UHDDS) definitions for code selection.
Maintains knowledge of current information related to third party reimbursement regulations and seeks continuing education in all phases of coding acumen.
Participants in the Coding Team's regular meetings with the objective of solving problems, brain-storming, educating physicians and others as to the coding policies and procedures of the facility, as well as promoting consistency of data collected.
Achieves a balance in quality and quantity, with a goal of maintaining both elements at a prescribed level of efficiency.
Abides by AHIMA's established code of ethical principles to safeguard the public and contribute within the scope of the profession to quality and efficiency in health care, thus promoting ethical conduct.

OTHER SPECIFIC OR POTENTIAL DUTIES/ RESPONSIBILITIES FOR THIS POSITION:
Identifies any loss of revenue by failure to charge for any procedures, supplies, injections or other services, and then submits the missed charges.
Verifies all fee sheets to assure that all charges, appropriate modifiers, dates of injury, E code(s) as well as referring physicians' license numbers (when required) have been documented.
Assigns Diagnosis-Related Groups (DRGs) after identifying not only the principal diagnosis (reason for admission) but also significant complications and/or comorbidities as well as operating room procedures following comparison of relative weights in the DRG GROUPER software, and selection of the highest reimbursement allowable among alternative principal diagnoses documented in the record.
Identifies and abstracts information from medical records for special studies and audits, internal and external.
Assists physicians, ancillary, and administrative personnel with retrieving patient care information for research, planning and marketing projects. Answers questions regarding DRGs as well as disease and procedure classification systems.

FIGURE 17-4
Generic job description for a coder. (From Stewart, S. P.: Generic job description for coders. J CHIA, 1992. Reprinted with permission from California Health Information Association, Fresno, California.)

Generates reports using a computer report-writer to retrieve coded and abstracted information from the provider's data processing system.

Orients and instructs new personnel and/or students from health information/medical record technology/administration programs, on unit operations, coding and abstracting activities.

DESCRIPTION OF SKILLS:

I. TECHNICAL SKILLS REQUIRED:

A. Experience with and knowledge of instructional notations and conventions of ICD-9-CM and CPT HCPCS classification systems; and ability to follow the detailed guidelines related to their use in assigning single, and sequencing multiple, diagnosis and procedure codes for appropriate reimbursement and data collection.

B. Ability to read handwritten and transcribed documents in the medical record, interpret information, and enter complete and accurate data into an on-line computer system.

C. Comprehensive knowledge of medical diagnostic and procedural terminology required.

D. College level understanding of disease processes, anatomy and physiology necessary for assigning accurate numeric and alpha-numeric codes.

E. Knowledge of federal, state and local government regulations and requirements which pertain to patient care information.

F. Knowledge of legalities and confidentiality issues involved with release of clinical or billing information.

G. Knowledge of third party payer reimbursement requirements and an understanding of relative values for multi-medical specialties, encounters, and procedures in acute care and ambulatory care settings.

II. DECISION-MAKING/ RESEARCH SKILLS REQUIRED:

A. Ability to query, analyze and determine the type of data needed to meet the request for information.

B. Ability to communicate technical and clinical information concerning patient care and classification systems at different levels; i.e., physicians, ancillary, and administrative personnel.

C. Ability to apply policies and procedures regarding data security and confidentiality to protect the inappropriate release of information

D. Ability to exercise judgement with minimal supervision.

III. ORGANIZATIONAL SKILLS REQUIRED:

A. Ability to assume responsibility for compilation of clinical data related to inpatient and outpatient encounters including diagnoses, procedures, physicians and services.

B. Remains current with periodic updates of all coding manuals and guidelines in accordance with federal, state and local regulations.

C. Ability to manage time schedules, deadlines, multiple requests and priorities, and to maintain productivity.

IV. INTERPERSONAL SKILLS REQUIRED:

A. Communicates effectively, orally and in writing, with physicians, nurses and peers (both inter- and intra- departmentally) and with external organizations.

B. Communicates medical information with consideration of ethical and professional standards.

C. Upholds standards of confidentiality regarding patients, personnel and physicians.

V. EDUCATION AND EXPERIENCE REQUIRED:

A. High School Diploma.

B. Completion of an accredited program for coding certification or an accredited health information medical record technology program. A Certified Coder, an Accredited Record Technician, a Coder Specialist or a Registered Record Administrator preferred, with current affiliation with the American Health Information Management Association.

C. Continuing education in health information management is required. ■

FIGURE 17-4 *Continued*

Job Search

INSURANCE BILLING SPECIALIST

There are several ways to seek employment. The applicant may wish to be employed by a physician, hospital, or other medical facility, may choose to be self-employed, or may even choose some type of combination situation. Here are suggested ways to search for a job:

1. Join a professional organization, as mentioned in Chapter 1, to network with others in the same career field and to hear about job openings or in case someone needs help because of an overabundance of work. Put a notice about your availability in the chapter newsletter.
2. Attend meetings and workshops in this career field to keep up to date and network with others.
3. If you have just completed a course at a community college or trade school, contact the school placement personnel, complete the necessary paperwork to be placed on file, and leave a resume.
4. Spread the word to classmates, instructors, school counselors, relatives, and friends who work in medical settings who might hear of openings in medical facilities.
5. Pharmaceutical representatives visit physicians' offices and hospitals and may be good contacts.
6. Visit public and private employment agencies as well as state and federal government offices and agencies. Before signing up with an agency, ask whether the employer or the applicant pays the agency fee.
7. Look for part-time employment that might lead to a permanent full-time position.
8. Frequently check bulletin boards in personnel offices of hospitals and clinics for posted job offerings.
9. Go to your local medical society to see if it has a provision for supplying leads.
10. Consult the *Yellow Pages* of the telephone directory or medical society roster for names of professional offices and hospitals to contact with an introductory telephone call or letter.
11. Send a blind mailing of the resume, including a cover letter, to possible prospects. A blind mailing means to send information to employers that you do not know personally and who have not advertised for a job opening. This may result in a positive response with either a request to complete an application form or an invitation for an interview.
12. Go to the local library and look through Dunn and Bradstreet's *Million Dollar Directory* and the *Middle Market Directory* for information on potential employers in many cities.
13. Visit the Chamber of Commerce and ask for some of their publications that contain membership directories, names of major professional employers in specific areas, and brochures describing regional facts.
14. Subscribe to the principal newspaper of the city where employment is desired. Read Help Wanted ads in the classified section. Positions to interest you might be listed as Insurance Billing specialist, Reimbursement Manager, Insurance Claims Manager, Insurance Coordinator, Insurance Biller, Coding/Reimbursement Specialist, Reimbursement Coordinator, Coder/Abstracter, Electronic Claims Processor, and so on.
15. Register with a computerized job search company. An individual with a computer and modem can access on-line services. A firm in Irvine, California, American Computerized Employment Service,* has entered the job placement field with a trademarked system called TeleRecruiting. Job candidates may register without charge and complete an extensive profile questionnaire listing experience, skills, job-related factors, maximum commuting distance, and flex-time requirements. The firm acts as a liaison between employers and applicants. Employers use a touch-tone telephone to access the computer and search for candidates. They pay either an annual subscription, pay-per-search, or package search fee.

ON-LINE JOB SEARCH

Because of the vast communication available via the Internet's World Wide Web, newspaper and magazine classified advertisements may become things of the past. Many resources on the Internet incorporate text, sound, graphics, animation, and video. It is possible to contact employers across the nation who are offering jobs to health care workers. There are several ways to gain access to the Internet. Your school may allow you to access the Internet on campus. If you have a computer at home, you may wish to subscribe to either a commercial on-line ser-

---

*American Computerized Employment Service, 17801 Main Street, Suite A, Irvine, California 92714; telephone (714) 250-0221.

vice (America Online, Prodigy, CompuServe) with Internet access or an Internet service in your locale.

Once online, go to a Web index, such as Yahoo (www.yahoo.com/), that lists different options to explore. One of the resources will be Career Magazine (www.careermag.com/careermag/), which lets you browse through hundreds of national job openings in a variety of fields. Check out America's Job Bank (http://www.ajb.dni.us) and E-Span Employment Database Search (www.espan.com/), which have job postings that you can browse according to field, location, and career type. Go to PracticeNet (http://www.practice-net.com), which provides descriptions of medical practice opportunities. This 24-hour service names the recruiter, location, and an 800 number to contact. MedSearch America is another health employment service that posts jobs for hospitals, health maintenance organizations (HMOs), and pharmaceutical companies. Job seekers can send their resumes via E-mail for free online posting. MedSearch has two online addresses (hhtp://ww.medsearch.com and gopher://gopher.medsearch.com). You may want to post your resume in an on-line resume bank on the Internet.

If you subscribe monthly to a commercial online service (America Online, CompuServe, Prodigy), you can network by posting a notice on a bulletin board with your resume or a note that you are looking for a particular type of position in a given locale.

If you wish to read about career options on the Internet, obtain a book by Joyce Lain Kennedy entitled *Hook Up, Get Hired! The Internet Job Search Revolution* published by John Wiley & Sons, New York.

ELECTRONIC RESUME

Once a medical position has been discovered, some basic steps to go online with a resume are:

- Compose a resume using a word processor with accurate spelling features and then save in a job search file.
- Discard traditional resume-writing techniques, such as focusing on action verbs. Instead think descriptive nouns, such as medical biller, education, experience, skills, knowledge, and abilities.
- Avoid the use of decorative graphics and complex typefaces, underlining, or italics.
- Forget the one-page rule; electronic resumes may be three or four pages.
- Refer to the word processor manual to convert the cover letter and resume to ASCII (American Standard Code for Information Interchange; pronounced AS-kee) to plain text, which can be read by most personal computers.
- Study online guides presenting special procedures for sending E-mail and files. Some E-mail programs allow binary files to be sent whereas others allow only ASCII text files.
- Using the wordprocessing software "copy and paste" feature, enter the information into E-mail or "attach a file" to the E-mail message.
- It is not necessary to post a letter of introduction when posting a resume to a bulletin board.
- To post a resume on-line, upload the resume using the file-transfer feature of the software following the computer manual directions. When sending the resume over an online service to a recipient on the same online service or from a computer to a dial direct bulletin board, the ASCII file is all that is required.

If the file is sent across the Internet, it should be doctored up in a technical form—encoded by the sender and decoded by the receiver. Take the following steps to prepare a plain ASCII text file.

1. Create the message using WordPerfect or Word software. Make certain all lines are no more than 65 characters in length. Put a space at the beginning of each blank line between paragraphs.
2. Referring to the word processing software manual for directions, proofread the resume and save it as plain ASCII text.
3. To upload the ASCII text to a bulletin board, log onto the board and go to the message Menu following the bulletin board's directions.
4. Select or type "All" or "Resume posting" from the bulletin board's message Menu for the recipient and subject.
5. Upload the resume following the software manual's directions for the communications program being used.
6. Depending on the bulletin board, a "Message Edit" menu or the next available line will appear issuing message-editing commands. Customize the resume by typing in additional information related to the specific job.

CLAIMS ASSISTANCE PROFESSIONAL

If you wish to establish self-employment as a claims assistance professional in addition to some of the aforementioned positions, contact local hospitals to see whether they have patients who require insurance help and small employers to see whether they need assistance in controlling health insurance costs. Develop a well-organized marketing plan: obtain business cards, print some flyers, and place advertisements in newspapers, *Yellow Pages*, and cable television. Attend local meetings for Medicare recipients. Join local volunteer service organizations and the Chamber of Commerce to network with others. Obtain a copy of the *Claims Assistance Professional Manual* as well as marketing brochures published by the National Association of Claims Assistance Professionals, Inc., and read the section on Marketing, which has many suggestions. See Appendix B for the address. Contact the LEADS Club at (800) 783-3761 or The National Association of Female Executives at (800) 669-1002 for potential client leads and networking.

ELECTRONIC CLAIMS PROFESSIONAL

For those wishing to establish their own business as an Electronic Claims Professional, obtain marketing brochures as well as copies of two publications: *Entrepreneurial Basics* and *Electronic Claims Professional Manual* published by the National Association of Claims Assistance Professionals, Inc., which devotes an entire chapter to ways of assessing the competition. See Appendix B for the address.

APPLICATION

When visiting a potential employer, ask for an application form to complete in case the facility keeps potential job applicants on file (Fig. 17–5). Study each question carefully before answering, since the employer may evaluate the application itself to determine whether the applicant can follow instructions. Furnish as much information as possible, and if a question does not apply or cannot be answered, insert "no," "none," "NA" (not applicable), or "DNA" (does not apply). Always allow at least 2 days when making an appointment for an interview so you will have time to prepare. In completing an application form, follow these guidelines:

1. Read the whole application form, since some instructions may appear on the last page or last line.
2. Read the fine print and instructions: "Please print," "Put last name first," or "Complete in your own handwriting." This indicates ability to follow directions or instructions.
3. Print if your handwriting is poor, and abbreviate only when there is lack of space.
4. Complete the application in ink unless pencil is specified.
5. Refer to data from a portfolio or resume that has been checked for accuracy; use this information to copy onto each new application form. Be neat.
6. List correct dates of previous employment so that if the employer should seek to verify this, it will be accurate. If a question is presented asking the reason for leaving a position, leave it blank and discuss this during the interview.
7. Name specific skills (e.g., CPT coding, ICD-9-CM coding, knowledge of insurance programs, completing the HCFA-1500 claim form, typing or keyboarding (number of) words per minute, speaking a second language (e.g., Spanish, Italian, Japanese), and so on (see p. 437 for additional skills to list).
8. When a question is asked about salary amount, write in "negotiable" or "flexible" and then discuss this during the interview if it is brought up.
9. Sign the application after completion.
10. Reread the entire form, word for word, to find any errors of omission or commission to avoid having to apologize during an interview for a mistake.

LETTER OF INTRODUCTION

Individuals spend days in perfecting a resume but throw together a *letter of introduction* or *cover letter* in minutes; this is a mistake. The main goal of the cover letter is to get the employer to take notice of the potential employee and resume so an interview appointment can be made. Letters should be typed, addressed to a specific person, and customized to each potential employer. If the advertisement gives a telephone number, call and ask for the name of the person doing the interviewing so the letter can include that person's name. When the name is unknown, use "Dear Sir or Madam" or "To Whom It May Concern," or a less formal "Hello" or "Good Morning."

Do not repeat everything in the resume. Begin with an attention-grabber, and get right to the point so the employer knows what is wanted and why. The letter should explain how the applicant's qualifications and skills would benefit the employer. Use key words that appear in the "position wanted" ad. End the letter by requesting an interview and be sure to enclose a resume. Always include a tele-

APPLICATION FOR POSITION / Medical or Dental Office
AN EQUAL OPPORTUNITY EMPLOYER

(In answering questions, use extra blank sheet if necessary)

No employee, applicant, or candidate for promotion, training or other advantage shall be discriminated against (or given preference) because of race, color, religion, sex, age, physical handicap, veteran status, or national origin.

PLEASE READ CAREFULLY AND WRITE OR PRINT ANSWERS TO ALL QUESTIONS. DO NOT TYPE.

Date of Application

A. PERSONAL INFORMATION

Name - Last | First | Middle | Social Security No. | Area Code/Phone No. ( )

Present Address: - Street | (Apt #) | City | State | Zip | How Long At This Address?:

Previous Address: - Street | City | State | Zip | From: | To: | Person to notify in case of Emergency or Accident - Name: | Address: | Telephone:

B. EMPLOYMENT INFORMATION

For What Position Are You Applying?: ☐ Full-Time ☐ Part-Time ☐ Either | Date Available For Employment?: | Wage/Salary Expectations:

List Hrs./Days You Prefer To Work | List Any Hrs./Days You Are Not Available: (Except for times required for religious practices or observances) | Can You Work Overtime, If Necessary? ☐ Yes ☐ No

Are You Employed Now?: ☐ Yes ☐ No | If So, May We Inquire Of Your Present Employer?: ☐ No ☐ Yes, If Yes: Name Of Employer: Phone Number: ( )

Have You Ever Been Bonded? ☐ Yes ☐ No | If Required For Position, Are You Bondable? ☐ Yes ☐ No ☐ Uncertain | Have You Applied For A Position With This Office Before? ☐ No ☐ Yes If Yes, When?:

Referred By / Or Where Did You Learn Of This Job?:

Can You, Upon Employment, Submit Verification Of Your Legal Right To Work In The United States?: ☐ Yes ☐ No
Submit Proof That You Meet Legal Age Requirement For Employment? ☐ Yes ☐ No

Language(s) Applicant Speaks or Writes (If Use Of A Language Other Than English is Relevant To The Job For Which The Applicant Is Applying:

C. EDUCATIONAL HISTORY

Name & Address Of Schools Attended (Include Current)	Dates From	Dates Thru	Highest Grade/Level Completed	Diploma/Degree(s) Obtained/Areas of Study
High School				
College				Degree/Major
Post Graduate				Degree/Major
Other				Course/Diploma/License/ Certificate

Specific Training, Education, Or Experiences Which Will Assist You In The Job For Which You Have Applied.

Future Educational Plans

D. SPECIAL SKILLS

CHECK BELOW THE KINDS OF WORK YOU HAVE DONE:		☐ MEDICAL INSURANCE FORMS	☐ RECEPTIONIST
☐ BLOOD COUNTS	☐ DENTAL ASSISTANT	☐ MEDICAL TERMINOLOGY	☐ TELEPHONES
☐ BOOKKEEPING	☐ DENTAL HYGIENIST	☐ MEDICAL TRANSCRIPTION	☐ TYPING
☐ COLLECTIONS	☐ FILING	☐ NURSING	☐ STENOGRAPHY
☐ COMPOSING LETTERS	☐ INJECTIONS	☐ PHLEBOTOMY (Draw Blood)	☐ URINALYSIS
☐ COMPUTER INPUT	☐ INSTRUMENT STERILIZATION	☐ POSTING	☐ X-RAY
OFFICE EQUIPMENT USED: ☐ COMPUTER	☐ DICTATING EQUIPMENT	☐ WORD PROCESSOR	☐ OTHER:
Other Kinds Of Tasks Performed Or Skills That May Be Applicable To Position:		Typing Speed	Shorthand Speed

ORDER # 72-110 • © 1976 BIBBERO SYSTEMS, INC. • PETALUMA, CA. • (REV. 1/95)
TO REORDER CALL TOLL FREE: (800) BIBBERO (800-242-2376) OR FAX (800) 242-9330 MFG IN U.S.A.

(PLEASE COMPLETE OTHER SIDE)

FIGURE 17-5
Application for Position/Medical or Dental Office form. (Reprinted with permission from Bibbero Systems, Inc., Petaluma, California. Phone: 800-242-2376, FAX: 800-242-9330.)

17

E. EMPLOYMENT RECORD

LIST MOST RECENT EMPLOYMENT FIRST | **May We Contact Your Previous Employer(s) For A Reference?** ☐ Yes ☐ No

		Worked Performed. Be Specific:
1) Employer		
Address Street City State Zip Code		
Phone Number ( )		
Type of Business	Dates Mo. Yr. From Mo. Yr. To	
Your Position	Hourly Rate/Salary Starting Final	
Supervisor's Name		
Reason For Leaving		

		Worked Performed. Be Specific:
2) Employer		
Address Street City State Zip Code		
Phone Number ( )		
Type of Business	Dates Mo. Yr. From Mo. Yr. To	
Your Position	Hourly Rate/Salary Starting Final	
Supervisor's Name		
Reason For Leaving		

		Worked Performed. Be Specific:
3) Employer		
Address Street City State Zip Code		
Phone Number ( )		
Type of Business	Dates Mo. Yr. From Mo. Yr. To	
Your Position	Hourly Rate/Salary Starting Final	
Supervisor's Name		
Reason For Leaving		

F. REFERENCES — FRIENDS / ACQUAINTANCES NON-RELATED

(1) Name | Address | Telephone Number | (☐ Work ☐ Home) | Occupation | Years Acquainted

(1) Name | Address | Telephone Number | (☐ Work ☐ Home) | Occupation | Years Acquainted

Please Feel Free To Add Any Information Which You Feel Will Help Us Consider You For Employment

READ THE FOLLOWING CAREFULLY, THEN SIGN AND DATE THE APPLICATION

"I certify that all answers given by me on this application are true, correct and complete to the best of my knowledge. I acknowledge notice that the information contained in this application is subject to check. I agree that, if hired, my continued employment may be contingent upon the accuracy of that information. If employed, I further agree to comply with Company/Office rules and regulations."

Signature: ______________________ Date: __________

FIGURE 17–5 *Continued*

phone number and the time of day when you are available.

Reread the letter for typos and errors in grammar, punctuation, and spelling. Avoid the use of "I" in the sentence structure (Fig. 17–6).

RESUME

A *resume* is a data sheet designed to sell job qualifications to prospective employers. A resume may be *chronologic,* giving recent experiences first with dates and descriptive data for each job; *functional,* stating the qualifications or skills an individual is able to perform; or *combination* style, summarizing the applicant's job skills as well as educational and employment history. Combination style is the best choice for an insurance billing specialist (Fig. 17–7).

The ideal length for a resume is one page. It can be typed on a 10- by 14-inch page and reduced to letter size. The resume should be typed, not handwritten, on high-quality, wrinkle-free bond off-white or white paper; single spaced internally with double spacing between main headings; and balanced spacing for all four margins. Laser-printed resumes give a professional appearance.

Under the Civil Rights Act of 1964, enforced by the Equal Employment Opportunity Commission, information about height, weight, birthdate, marital status, Social Security number, and physical condition may be omitted. Listing these, however, can sometimes enhance landing a job. Additional items to omit are salary requirements, reason for leaving jobs, date of resume preparation, date available to begin work, references, and vague references to time gaps. Hobbies and outside interests that would relate to the profession might be included. Membership and/or leadership positions held in profes-

Street Address
City, State, ZIP code
Date of letter

John Doe, MD or
Personnel Director
Street Address
City, State, ZIP code

Dear Dr. Doe:

Paragraph 1: Explain where you heard about the position and say you are writing for a position as an insurance billing specialist.

Paragraph 2: Name two or more qualifications of great interest to the prospective employer. State reasons you are interested in this specialty, location, or type of work. Mention if experienced or trained for this career field.

Paragraph 3: Refer the reader to the resume or application form enclosed.

Paragraph 4: Close the letter by asking for an interview and suggesting a date and time or that you will call for an appointment. If requesting further information about the job opening, enclose a self-addressed, stamped envelope as a courtesy. Do not end the letter with a vague statement but give the reader a specific action to take.

Sincerely yours,

(handwritten signature)

Type name

Enclosure

FIGURE 17–6
Suggested content for a letter of introduction to accompany a resume.

WRITING A RESUME	
It is optional to type RESUME or CURRICULUM VITAE. Every personnel manager knows what a resume looks like.	**RESUME**
	John M. Velasquez 1234 Martin Streeet Woodland Hills, XY 12345-0000 (013) 439-9800
One error can kill your chances for a job. Carefully proofread.	**QUALIFICATIONS:**
Summary gives the reader reason why resume is of interest.	Insurance billing specialist with 3 years of experience. Major skills include keyboarding 60 wpm, knowledge of medical terminology, ability to code diagnoses and procedures proficiently, ability to operate computer, photocopy, and calculator equipment, and preparing for certification.
Cover letter can explain why no job was held in years because a person had to raise a family or was ill. Resume does not need to mention this job because work was not in medical field.	**EMPLOYMENT:** EASTERN AIRLINES, Orlando, Florida RECEPTIONIST - 1983-1986
This section not only gives job titles but emphasizes accomplishments as well.	ST. JOHN'S OUTPATIENT CLINIC, Woodland Hills, XY INSURANCE BILLING SPECIALIST - February, 1992 to August, 1995 Began as a part time billing clerk and worked into a full time position developing skills in diagnostic and procedural coding and insurance claims completion. Won a bonus for keeping delinquent claims affecting accounts receivable total below previous year's total.
Shows recent education to learn personal computers. Employers sense extra initiative and new skills.	**EDUCATION:** ABC High School, Woodland Hills, XY, Graduated 1989, Diploma awarded. VOCATIONAL BUSINESS SCHOOL, Woodland Hills, XY (1990) Certificate awarded for personal computer word processing and spread sheet programs.
Although no degree was awarded, listing the number of credits earned and highlighting some business and medical courses may help broaden an employer's interest.	MONTANA STATE UNIVERSITY, Woodland Hills, XY (1992) 24 credits (1990-92) Medical classes including insurance, medical terminology, anatomy and physiology, and other core courses.
Listing skills is vital when applying for work as an insurance billing specialist.	**SKILLS:** Type 60 words per minute. Knowledge of medical terminology, diseases, surgeries, and insurance terminology. Ability and knowledge to use procedure and diagnostic code books. Able to operate computer, photocopy, and calculator equipment. Ability to speak Spanish fluently. Excellent proofreader. Good oral and writing communication skills, including grammar, punctuation, and style. *(List skills that would be valuable in the employment you are seeking.)*
It is not necessary to list references.	**REFERENCES:** Furnished upon request.

FIGURE 17–7
Example of the combination-format resume stressing education and skills. Personal data may be excluded as a result of the Civil Rights Act of 1964, enforced by the EEOC.

sional organizations related to the medical field might be mentioned. A photograph might be included only if it will be of value to the interviewer for recall purposes.

The format may include the following:

Title ■ Resume, Personal Data Sheet, Biographic Sketch, or Curriculum Vitae.

Heading ■ At the beginning of the resume, the applicant's name, address, and telephone number are typed.

Summary ■ This may be a statement as to why the employer would be interested. Use action words as shown in Figure 17–7 and avoid the personal pronoun.

INTERVIEW EVALUATION AND REFERENCE INVESTIGATION FORM, MEDICAL or DENTAL OFFICE

SUMMARY OF EVALUATION	
POINTS FROM APPLICATION AND INTERVIEW	
POINTS FROM REFERENCES	
TOTAL POINTS	
OVERALL IMPRESSION	

NAME OF APPLICANT	DATE

RATING: GOOD – 2 POINTS
FAIR – 1 POINT
POOR – 0 POINTS

POSITION APPLIED FOR:			
FROM APPLICATION FOR POSITION, GAUGE APPLICANT IN FOLLOWING AREAS	GOOD	FAIR	POOR
APPLICATION SECTION REFERENCE: 1. STABILITY (REMAINED IN ONE PLACE OF RESIDENCE AND ONE JOB FOR A REASONABLE LENGTH OF TIME) ?			
2. HEALTH?			
3. THE PROPER EDUCATIONAL BACKGROUND TO FILL THE POSITION?			
4. LEGIBLE HANDWRITING?			
5. AN EMPLOYMENT HISTORY THAT POINTS TOWARDS DEPENDABILITY?			
6. LIMITATION ON WORKING HOURS?			
7. THE PROPER EXPERIENCE AND / OR SKILLS TO FILL THE POSITION?			
8. SALARY REQUIREMENT COMMENSURATE WITH POSITION?			
FROM THE PERSONAL INTERVIEW – (SHOULD BE SPECIFIC QUALITIES – OBJECTIVE)			
9. SUFFICIENT CAPABILITY TO HANDLE ANY SITUATION THAT MAY ARISE WHEN ALONE IN OFFICE?			
10. AN APPROPRIATE ATTITUDE TOWARDS WORK?			
11. AN APPROPRIATE VOICE, DICTION, GRAMMAR?			
12. POISE?			
13. SELF CONFIDENCE (NOT OVER-CONFIDENCE)?			
14. TACT?			
15. SUFFICIENT MATURITY FOR JOB?			
16. AN ABILITY TO EXPRESS ONESELF WELL?			
17. AN INITIATIVE OR INTEREST IN LEARNING?			
18. ABILITY TO WORK WITH OTHERS IN OFFICE?			
19. APPROPRIATE APPEARANCE (NEAT, CLEAN; SUITABLE TO BUSINESS)			
20. ENERGY, VITALITY & PERCEIVED ABILITY TO HANDLE PRESSURE OF POSITION?			
21. EAGERNESS TO OBTAIN THE POSITION IN QUESTION?			
COLUMNAR TOTALS			
	GRAND TOTAL		

DIRECTIONS FOR USE OF FORM:

1. Look over your ratings. A zero score on any one VITAL question should automatically eliminate applicant. Add up the total rating points and enter in the SUMMARY OF EVALUATION BLOCK in the upper right-hand corner of this page.
2. After finishing all interviews, choose the "best bets" and check their references using the reverse side of this form.
3. Enter, as above, the results of your reference check and then your overall impression. (E – Excellent, G – Good, F – Fair, P – Poor)

(PLEASE TURN OVER)

FIGURE 17–8

Example of an Interview Evaluation and Reference Investigation form. (Reprinted with permission from Bibbero Systems, Inc., Petaluma, California. Phone: 800-242-2376, FAX: 800-242-9330.)

NOTES:

	REFERENCE INVESTIGATION		
1.	OFFICE CONTACTED	PHONE: ( )	DATE
	PERSON CONTACTED		
	HOW LONG HAVE YOU KNOWN THIS PERSON?		
	BETWEEN WHAT DATES WAS THIS PERSON EMPLOYED BY YOU? FROM	TO	
	WHAT TYPE OF WORK DID THIS PERSON DO FOR YOU?	TITLE OF POSITION:	SATISFACTORILY ?
	WAS THIS PERSON CONSISTENTLY COOPERATIVE?	WHAT WERE SHORT COMINGS?	
	DID THIS PERSON GET ALONG WELL WITH OTHERS?		
	WAS THIS PERSON TRUSTWORTHY / DEPENDABLE ?		ATTENDANCE RECORD:
	WHY DID THIS PERSON LEAVE YOUR EMPLOY?		SALARY LEVEL:
	WOULD YOU REHIRE THIS PERSON?		
	NOTES:		
			RATING:
2.	OFFICE CONTACTED	PHONE: ( )	DATE
	PERSON CONTACTED		
	HOW LONG HAVE YOU KNOWN THIS PERSON?		
	BETWEEN WHAT DATES WAS THIS PERSON EMPLOYED BY YOU? FROM	TO	
	WHAT TYPE OF WORK DID THIS PERSON DO FOR YOU?	TITLE OF POSITION:	SATISFACTORILY ?
	WAS THIS PERSON CONSISTENTLY COOPERATIVE?	WHAT WERE SHORT COMINGS?	
	DID THIS PERSON GET ALONG WELL WITH OTHERS?		
	WAS THIS PERSON TRUSTWORTHY / DEPENDABLE ?		ATTENDANCE RECORD:
	WHY DID THIS PERSON LEAVE YOUR EMPLOY?		SALARY LEVEL:
	WOULD YOU REHIRE THIS PERSON?		
	NOTES:		
			RATING:
3.	OFFICE CONTACTED	PHONE: ( )	DATE
	PERSON CONTACTED		
	HOW LONG HAVE YOU KNOWN THIS PERSON?		
	BETWEEN WHAT DATES WAS THIS PERSON EMPLOYED BY YOU? FROM	TO	
	WHAT TYPE OF WORK DID THIS PERSON DO FOR YOU?	TITLE OF POSITION:	SATISFACTORILY ?
	WAS THIS PERSON CONSISTENTLY COOPERATIVE?	WHAT WERE SHORT COMINGS?	
	DID THIS PERSON GET ALONG WELL WITH OTHERS?		
	WAS THIS PERSON TRUSTWORTHY / DEPENDABLE ?		ATTENDANCE RECORD:
	WHY DID THIS PERSON LEAVE YOUR EMPLOY?		SALARY LEVEL:
	WOULD YOU REHIRE THIS PERSON?		
	NOTES:		
			RATING:

INTERVIEWER ______________________ DATE: ______________________

FIGURE 17–8 *Continued*

Education ■ Name high school, college, and any business school attended, city and state, degree, and date received. List in reverse chronologic order. Grade average and awards or scholastic honors may be included.

Professional Experience ■ Name all employers in reverse chronologic order with addresses, telephone numbers, and dates of employment. Include summer, full-time, part-time, and temporary jobs as well as volunteer work.

Skills ▪ Mention typing or keyboarding words per minute, computer equipment operated, accurate procedure and diagnostic coding, expertise in insurance claims completion and submission, knowledge of medical terminology, bookkeeping (posting charges, payments, and adjustments to accounts receivable journal), experience in preparing appeals for denied claims, resubmittal of delinquent claims, ability to explain insurance programs and plans (i.e., benefits, requirements, and submission of claims) to patients, ability to abstract from patient's charts and ledgers, and review insurance payments. If you are fluent in another language, insert this information. Telephone skills might also be mentioned.

References ▪ Type in the phrase "Furnished upon request." Be sure to contact the persons referenced *before* an interview if you wish them to serve in this capacity.

Final Details ▪ It is acceptable to fax a resume to an employer who advertises a job opening but gives no guidelines on how to submit the resume. In a competitive employment market where time is of the essence, it is wise to use every advantage possible.

Proofread the resume carefully for spelling, punctuation, grammatic, and typographic errors. Ask a friend or professional individual with excellent English skills to read and critique it.

INTERVIEW

It is important to make the best impression possible to the prospective employer as soon as you walk through the door. Hiring depends on positive qualities. Concentrate on good grooming and a fresh, relaxed appearance. Display a warm, positive attitude. Use proper grammar and avoid using slang. Maintain eye contact.

A female applicant should wear a clean skirt, dress, or tailored suit and nylon stockings with low-heeled pumps. A man should wear a clean dark gray or navy suit, plain socks, and well-shined shoes. Men should avoid a lot of facial hair, long hair, earrings, and heavy aftershave lotion. Women should have a conservative hair style, wear jewelry sparingly, and avoid heavy makeup, low-cut necklines, sleeveless dresses, strong perfume, and dark or bright nail polish. Do not smoke or chew gum. Use a proper deodorant. Eliminate nervous habits. It has been found that when applicants have similar skills and education, the decision to hire has been based on physical appearance at the interview.

Role playing is a good method to use to prepare for an interview. Give a friend a list of questions to ask you, then try to answer the questions spontaneously without stumbling. Videotape or audio tape the session, if possible, to see and/or hear what the employer will experience.

Figure 17–8 is an example of an interview evaluation and reference investigation form. This form points out the areas an interviewer observes and how impressions are rated.

Research beforehand to know whether the salary (when offered) is acceptable. If you wish to ask questions about fringe benefits, do not appear to be too interested in them.

Choose the right time for the interview and arrive promptly. It has been found that late Monday and Friday afternoons between 4:00 P.M. and 5:00 P.M. are not good times for interviews since Mondays are usually catch-up, heavily scheduled days and Fridays are getaway days. Research has proved that the likelihood of hiring the last person interviewed for a position is greater than of hiring those interviewed first.

Questions an interviewer might ask about personal life (marital status), family planning, provision for child care, religious preference, club memberships, height, weight, dependents, age (birthdate), ethnic background, maiden name, native language, physical or psychiatric problems, whether a spouse is employed and the earnings, credit rating, home and automobile ownership, family planning, and pregnancy are illegal and do not have to be answered. If an employer wishes to know whether an applicant smokes, this is not considered discriminatory. Three suggestions for handling an illegal question are

1. Answer the question and ignore the fact you know it is illegal.
2. Answer with "I think the question is not relevant to the requirements of this position."
3. Refuse to answer and contact the nearest Equal Employment Opportunity Commission office.

Shake the interviewer's hand at the conclusion of the meeting. Ask how long it will be before a job offer or a denial is forthcoming and then leave with a "thank you." If the job is offered at the interview and the applicant is not sure about accepting, ask "How soon do you need to know?" This will give time for thinking before making a commitment.

Portfolio

Prepare in advance for the interview by organizing a portfolio. Assemble letters of recommendation (from former employers, teachers, family physician, professional friends, community leaders), school di-

Street Address
City, State, ZIP code
Date of letter

John Doe, MD or
Personnel Director
Street Address
City, State, ZIP code

Dear Dr. Doe:

Thank you for spending your valuable time yesterday to interview me for the insurance billing specialist position in your clinic.

I hope that you will allow me the opportunity to prove my abilities as I feel that I am able to perform the work with expertise. Meeting your staff was most enjoyable and I would certainly enjoy working with them as a team.

Please let me hear from you in the near future (439-9807).

Sincerely yours,

(handwritten signature)

Type name

FIGURE 17–9
Example of a thank-you letter sent after an interview.

plomas or degrees, transcripts, certificates, names and addresses of references, extra copies of the resume, Social Security card, timed typing test certified by an instructor, some neatly typed insurance claim forms with evidence of coding skills, and any other items related to prior education and work experience.

Alien ■ Any alien employee must have on file with his or her employer an Employment Eligibility Verification Form I-9. This form can be obtained by writing the Immigration and Naturalization Service (INS) at 425 I Street, N.W., Washington, D.C. 20536. Within 3 days of hiring an alien, the employee must show one of the following: a naturalization certification (citizen papers), an alien registration receipt card, a temporary resident receipt card, or an employment authorization card. One of these items should be in the portfolio in the event it is requested by the prospective employer during the interview.

After the Interview

Write a follow-up letter indicating thanks for the interview and restating interest in the position (Fig. 17–9). This keeps the applicant's name before the potential employer. If no response is heard within the time frame given, telephone to express continued interest in the position.

Self-Employment or Free-Lancing

SETTING UP AN OFFICE

When an individual wishes to be his or her own boss (self-employed), it is usually wise to get some experience in the chosen career before undertaking this task. Preferably an individual should begin as an insurance billing specialist and then proceed to becoming an electronic claims processor. For the individual who wants to work as a claims assistance professional, some experience in public relations as well as having a strong insurance background is desirable. For coding specialists, it is vital to have inpatient hospital, outpatient hospital, and physician billing experience in several specialties before becoming a code expert.

One must have something to offer clients when marketing and selling one's services and skills. Only with years of experience can this knowledge and expertise be gained. Full-time commitment, hard work, dedication, and many long hours to obtain clients will be encountered when beginning a business.

In addition, money is needed for equipment, computer software, overhead, taxes, stationery, preprinted statements, HCFA-1500 claim forms, and myriad other expenses. It is vital to have sufficient funds to run the business for a period of 6 months to a year. It is imperative that this be accrued before vacating a full-time job. This will help eliminate a lot of fear and anxiety over not having enough business clients. A common reason for business failure is running out of the money necessary to keep the business going. It may take a year or more to begin seeing a profit, so one must be patient. If you work for a while prior to striking out independently, contacts will be made on the job that will often help build clientele.

Networking is extremely important when one tries to establish a successful business. Many times it is who the individual knows that may get a foot in the potential client's door. Networking may open up many opportunities.

An insurance billing specialist can work for the medical professional from home to reduce overhead and have flexible hours. Working at home requires self-discipline. Developing a schedule and sticking to it is essential to good time management. It takes additional hours to advertise, obtain clients, bill, and perform the bookkeeping tasks. Figure 17–10 is a checklist of tasks that must be done to establish a new business.

Publications available about starting your own claims processing or medical billing service are listed in Appendix B.

FINANCES

If an individual has had no experience or is not strong in marketing skills and small business accounting, courses may be taken to instill some confidence in these areas. Attend workshops and lectures on starting a business that are offered by financial institutions, universities, community colleges, or private institutions.

It would be wise to seek the services of a lawyer, accountant, or both to go about legally establishing a business and making appropriate selection of the tax options involved. Establish detailed financial records from the very beginning, even if an accountant is to be hired. Obtain simplified bookkeeping software for use on the computer. Expert advice is essential and will help develop a successful business; without it, a business could fail.

Establishing a business in a home may result in some deductions, so obtain the IRS publication No. 587 entitled "Business Use of Your Home." Self-employment tax on net income is due each year. Quarterly estimated tax payments are required once the net income amounts to $500 or more. Keep receipts and complete records of income and expenses, as these are extremely important for Internal Revenue Service (IRS) purposes.

Paycheck stubs, copies of hours worked, and identifying data on hospitals or clients must be retained for the period of time stipulated by the IRS. Record retention schedules follow:

Bank statements	3 years
Canceled checks	permanently
Expired contracts	7 years
Financial statements	permanently
General correspondence	2 years
Payroll records and summaries	7 years
Tax returns, worksheets, and other tax documents	permanently

Keep a record of business travel expenses and document mileage. Travel log books are available at stationery stores.

EQUIPMENT

When setting up a business at home or in a small office, certain items must be purchased. Necessary equipment to consider is a computer, modem, printer, telephone answering machine, fax machine, office furniture, filing cabinet, and calculator. It is imperative to install a separate telephone line for clients or patients calling in. For transmitting claims electronically, a telephone line will be needed. An optional item might be a postage meter. Research equipment costs and maintenance options before purchase or lease and find out how much it costs for service contracts.

It is possible to obtain a low-interest government Small Business Administration (SBA) loan for starting a business. Loans are also available to physically challenged persons who qualify.

INSURANCE

Business owners find it necessary to protect income and property from unexpected loss. If the business grows and employees are hired, workers' compensation insurance must be obtained. Some types of insurance to investigate are

NEW BUSINESS CHECKLIST

___ 1. Decide what address you will use, since you may wish to obtain a post office box number instead of using your home address.

___ 2. Obtain a business license from the business license section of your city hall. Regulations vary in each city licensing office. You might have to obtain a home occupation permit from the planning department and have it signed by your landlord if you are renting. The city may have guidelines on hours of business, pedestrian and vehicular activity, noise, and so forth in the residential area.

___ 3. File a fictitious business name (Doing Business As—DBA) at the county clerk's office by obtaining the proper form for completion. If you use your given name, you do not have to file a fictitious business name.

___ 4. Publish the fictitious name in a local newspaper.

___ 5. If you have employees, contact the Internal Revenue Service (IRS) for an employer identification number and/or tax information. Obtain the booklet *Tax Guide for Small Business* No. 334 to determine business expenses that are deductible. Depending on how you set up your business, some possible tax breaks are as follows: depreciation of office equipment; declaring a room of your home as an office; subscriptions to professional publications; dues to professional associations; expenses associated with your automobile; telephone, photocopying, office supplies (stationery, books, typewriter ribbons, and so on); promotion and advertising (postage, meals with business associates, and so on); and any expenses pertaining to meetings, conventions, workshops, or seminars (registration fees, lodging, meals, transportation, parking, and so forth).

___ 6. If you have no employees, contact the Franchise Tax Board for the form used for estimating state withholding taxes for yourself. This must be filed quarterly. If you build up your business and have employees, obtain the proper forms and information for employees (state income tax, and state disability and unemployment insurance).

___ 7. Obtain the insurance that you need: health insurance, disability insurance, life insurance, liability insurance, worker's compensation (if you have employees), and so forth. Insurance is available to protect you against loss of material called "Release of Information Insurance" or "Errors and Omissions Insurance" with a "Hold Harmless" clause. You might want to consider a retirement IRA or Keogh plan.

___ 8. Contact the telephone company for phone and fax equipment and lines. Do this early because there is often a delay in hook-up. You might consider using your existing telephone number and switching to a business listing. This allows you to be listed in the *Yellow Pages* of your telephone directory.

___ 9. Open a bank account. If you want your telephone number on your checks, put the checks on hold until the telephone is confirmed. Some banks require a business license and Doing Business As documents to open an account. Take these documents with you to the bank.

___ 10. Order business cards, stationery, billing forms, and reference books. Design a logo for the business.

___ 11. Begin to advertise your business by some of the following methods: newspaper, radio, flyers, announcements, signs, word of mouth, and letters to prospects (hospitals, clinics, and physician's offices).

Additional points to consider if expanding to a location outside of a home:

___ 12. Check the zoning of the location at your city hall's planning department or, if you are in the county, the county's planning department. Sign a lease contingent on proper zoning and on meeting all federal, state, county, and city building safety and health requirements. Inquire about parking and sign restrictions at the planning department. Find out if you need any permits (building permit, certificate of occupancy, health permit, and so forth). City and county offices may require a sign permit for new signs and changes on old ones.

___ 13. If you have opened an office at a location, make a deposit for water, gas, and electricity. Rent, renovation, and janitorial or trash services must be considered.

___ 14. Call the assessor's office and ask to be put on the mailing list for business property tax (inventory tax).

___ 15. Contact the various inspectors: health, building, and safety, and sign to have all completed work inspected and the necessary permits signed off.

FIGURE 17–10

New business checklist. (Modified from Diehl, M. O., and Fordney, M. T.: *Medical Keyboarding, Typing, and Transcribing Techniques and Procedures*. Philadelphia, W. B. Saunders Company, 1997.)

- Property insurance in case of fire, theft, or a disaster
- Disability insurance if one becomes unable to work because of illness or injury
- Health insurance
- Life insurance
- Business interruption insurance. (In case of fire, it would take time and money to recreate data. Backed up data should be stored off site.)
- Professional liability insurance

MARKETING, ADVERTISING, PROMOTION, AND PUBLIC RELATIONS

It is always wise to rent a post office box. Never use a home address because this encourages patients who might visit at inconvenient hours. In some regions, business licenses are not issued for residential areas if clients come to the door. To get around this issue, a post office box becomes essential.

Here are ways to market a business:

- Obtain professionally printed stationery and business cards.
- Pass out business cards at professional meetings, as this advertises availability and services.
- Develop a logo for the company.
- Proofread everything before printing and have someone else proofread too. When items are not professionally assembled or misspellings are seen, a potential client receives a negative image of the company.
- Develop a professional flyer and distribute it to medical facilities and physicians' offices. Then follow up with a telephone call to offer services personally and let potential clients know your availability.
- Advertise in the journal or newsletter of the county medical society and state medical association.
- Put an ad in the *Yellow Pages*.
- Network with members of professional organizations.
- Network via computer using the Internet World Wide Web, Prodigy, CompuServe, American On Line, and Genie bulletin boards for this career field.
- Check with established businesses to determine whether they are overloaded with work, the owner needs a vacation, or help is needed in a temporary situation because of illness.

Insurance billing and coding specialists market to those who will use these services in the community, such as physicians (family practitioners, surgeons, psychiatrists, psychologists, physical therapists), small hospitals, clinics, laboratories, podiatrists, and chiropractors. However, claims assistance professionals' target audience is the consumer and Medicare recipients. Marketing suggestions were made at the beginning of this chapter for CAPs.

Convince clients that the service is better and can do more for their business than what they presently have—save them money! Stress being reliable, committed, efficient, and professional, and offer them something they cannot do for themselves.

CONTRACTS OR AGREEMENTS

Some facilities, such as an acute care hospital, require a contract and may even have their legal department review it. This can help eliminate misunderstandings. Put everything in writing (e.g., services, per claim rate, coverage arrangements due to illness or absence, and so on). If there is any change in the terms of the agreement, write a letter outlining the new terms. Some contracts may include a statement on confidentiality assuring the contracting hospital that all patient data will be handled in a confidential manner. Long-term contracts are preferred over short-term ones, so it is important to put in dates of validity. When the contract expires, renegotiation is in order.

If an agreement is done verbally, write down the basic terms of the agreement and retain this record in the files.

DOCUMENTATION

If you are hired as a coding specialist, keep written records of the numbers of hours worked, the quantity of work done each day, and the corrections applied to the work by officials in the contracting hospital. Retain any written coding guideline from the contracting hospital.

STATEMENTS AND PRICING

A variety of methods are used to price services, such as a percentage of reimbursement or an annual, hourly, or per claim fee. Deciding on which method depends on the type of client being served and the work to be done. Claims assistance professionals bill in 15-minute increments. Telephone other billing and insurance services in the area to see how they are charging.

NETWORKING

Join as many organizations as possible, because when you are self-employed, it can be difficult to keep abreast of ongoing changes in the insurance industry. Many of the professional organizations publish monthly newsletters and/or quarterly journals, offer certification, and plan national conventions, state conferences, and regional meetings. In addition to the organizations mentioned in Chapter 1, some additional ones to contact are

American Guild of Patient Account Management (AGPAM)
1101 Connecticut Avenue, N. W., Suite 700
Washington, D.C. 20036

Health Care Management Association of Southern California
P.O. Box 27771
Santa Ana, CA 92799

Healthcare Financial Management Association (HFMA)
Two Westbrook Corporate Center, Suite 700
Westchester, IL 60154-5700

TO THE STUDENT

For further knowledge and understanding, the key terms at the beginning of the chapter appear in the Glossary at the end of this textbook so you can look up the pertinent terms. You are now ready to complete the review questions and Assignments 62 through 66 in the *Workbook.* The assignments will give you hands-on experience in completing an application for a position as an insurance billing specialist, preparing and typing a resume, composing a cover letter to go with the resume, having someone evaluate you during an interview, and typing a follow-up thank you letter after being interviewed.

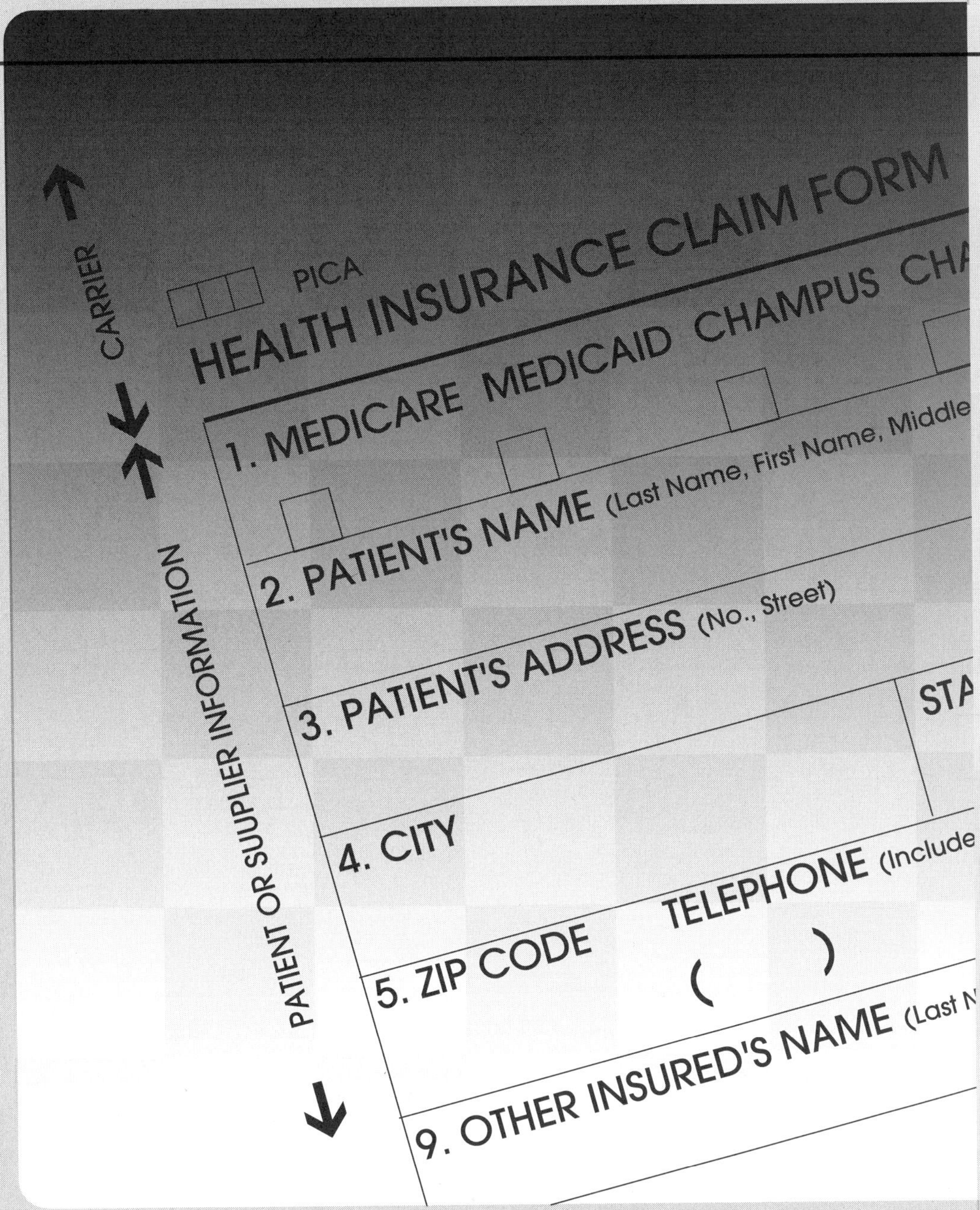

CARRIER
PICA
HEALTH INSURANCE CLAIM FORM
1. MEDICARE MEDICAID CHAMPUS
2. PATIENT'S NAME (Last Name, First Name, Middle
3. PATIENT'S ADDRESS (No., Street)
4. CITY
5. ZIP CODE
TELEPHONE
9. OTHER INSURED'S NAME
PATIENT OR SUUPLIER INFORMATION

Appendices

APPENDIX A

Addresses for Submitting Claims and Other Information

The list of names and addresses presented here for each state has been compiled for your use in submitting insurance claim forms to Blue Cross/Blue Shield plans and state and federal programs. In addition, insurance commissioners' state offices are included for when a question, problem, or complaint arises that needs to be resolved. Addresses for state boards of medical examiners are given in case medicolegal information is sought at a state level. State addresses for workers' compensation are given here in case there is need to obtain forms and guidelines for claims or for cases that are being settled or appealed. Insurance companies across the nation handle workers' compensation insurance; they are too numerous to include in this textbook. Federal workers' compensation district office addresses for each state may be used when submitting insurance claims for a federal worker injured while working.

The information contained in this Appendix has been reorganized so the reader can locate information quickly and easily. Look for the name of your state and then check the subheadings, which are arranged alphabetically, for the program or plan name and address.

The list of names and addresses in this Appendix has been compiled from state and federal references published in 1996. Because fiscal intermediaries (insurance carriers) for state and federal programs (CHAMPUS, CHAMPVA, Medicaid, Medicare) change as contracts expire, it is always wise to use the telephone directory and call to verify addresses when in doubt as to their accuracy.

This textbook will be revised every 2 years, and these lists will continue to be updated as necessary.

Alabama

BLUE CROSS & BLUE SHIELD

Corporate Headquarters
450 Riverchase Parkway, East
P. O. Box 995
Birmingham, AL 35298

CHAMPUS/TRICARE CLAIM OFFICE

Wisconsin Physicians Service
P. O. Box 202000
Florence, SC 29502-2000

CHAMPVA CLAIM OFFICE

CHAMPVA Center
4500 Cherry Creek Drive, South
Box 65024
Denver, CO 80206-9024

INSURANCE COMMISSIONER STATE OFFICE

Insurance Commissioner
135 S. Union Street, #200
Montgomery, AL 36130

MATERNAL AND CHILD HEALTH PROGRAM

Children's Rehabilitation Services
2129 E. South Boulevard
P. O. Box 11586

Montgomery, AL 36111-0586
Family Health Services
434 Monroe Street
Montgomery, AL 36130-1701

MEDICAID FISCAL AGENT
Electronic Data Systems Corporation
P. O. Box 105013
Tucker, GA 30085

MEDICARE DURABLE MEDICAL EQUIPMENT
Palmetto Government Benefits Administrators
Medicare DMERC Operations
P. O. Box 100141
Columbia, SC 29202-3141

MEDICARE FISCAL AGENT OR CARRIER
Medicare/Blue Cross–Blue Shield of Alabama
P. O. Box 83140
Birmingham, AL 35292

MEDICARE RAILROAD RETIREE CARRIER
The MetraHealth Insurance Company
Railroad Medicare Service Center
P. O. Box 10066
Augusta, GA 30999-0001

STATE BOARD OF MEDICAL EXAMINERS
Alabama State Board of Medical Examiners
848 Washington Avenue
P. O. Box 946
Montgomery, AL 36101-0946

VETERANS ADMINISTRATION INSTALLATION
Alabama Medical Centers:
Birmingham 35233 (700 S. 19th Street)
Montgomery 36109 (215 Perry Hill Road)
Tuscaloosa 35404 (3701 Loop Road East)
Tuskegee 36083 (2400 Hospital Road)

WORKERS' COMPENSATION FEDERAL DISTRICT OFFICE
Office of Workers' Compensation Programs
214 N. Hogan Street, Suite 1006
Jacksonville, FL 32202

WORKERS' COMPENSATION STATE PLAN OFFICE
Workmen's Compensation Division
Department of Industrial Relations
Industrial Relations Building
Montgomery, AL 36131

Alaska

BLUE CROSS & BLUE SHIELD
Blue Cross of Washington and Alaska
P. O. Box 327
Seattle, WA 98111-0327

CHAMPUS CLAIM OFFICE
Palmetto Government Benefits Administrators
P. O. Box 870020
Surfside Beach, SC 29587-8720

CHAMPVA CLAIM OFFICE
CHAMPVA Center
4500 Cherry Creek Drive, South
Box 65024
Denver, CO 80206-9024

INSURANCE COMMISSIONER STATE OFFICE
Division of Insurance
P. O. Box 110805
Juneau, AK 99811-0805

Division of Insurance
3601 C Street, Suite 1324
Anchorage, AK 99503-5948

MATERNAL AND CHILD HEALTH PROGRAM
Alaska Department of Health & Social Services
Maternal Child and Family Health
1231 Gambell Street
Anchorage, AK 99501-4627

Special Needs Programs Administration
Alaska Department of Health & Social Services
Division of Public Health
1231 Gambell Street
Anchorage, AK 99501-4627

MEDICAID FISCAL AGENT
First Health (EC)
P. O. Box 240807
Anchorage, AK 99524

MEDICARE DURABLE MEDICAL EQUIPMENT
Connecticut General Life Insurance
DMERC-CIGNA Medicare
P. O. Box 690
Nashville, TN 37320

MEDICARE FISCAL AGENT OR CARRIER
Medicare/Blue Cross Blue Shield of North Dakota
4510 13th Avenue, S.W.
Fargo, ND 58121-0001

MEDICARE RAILROAD RETIREE CARRIER
The MetraHealth Insurance Company
Railroad Medicare Service Center
P. O. Box 30050
Salt Lake City, UT 84130-0050

STATE BOARD OF MEDICAL EXAMINERS
Alaska State Medical Board
3601 C Street, Suite 722
Anchorage, AK 99503-5986

VETERANS ADMINISTRATION INSTALLATION
Alaska Outpatient Clinic and Regional Office
2925 De Barr Road
Anchorage, AK 99508-2989

WORKERS' COMPENSATION FEDERAL DISTRICT OFFICE
Office of Workers' Compensation Programs
1111 Third Avenue, Suite 615
Seattle, WA 98101-3212

WORKERS' COMPENSATION STATE PLAN OFFICE
Division of Workers' Compensation
Department of Labor
P. O. Box 25512
Juneau, AK 99802-5512

American Samoa

INSURANCE COMMISSIONER STATE OFFICE
Insurance Commissioner
Office of the Governor
Pago Pago, AS 96799

MATERNAL AND CHILD HEALTH PROGRAM
Department of Public Health
LBJ Tropical Medical Center
Government of American Samoa
Pago Pago, AS 96799

MEDICARE DURABLE MEDICAL EQUIPMENT
Connecticut General Life Insurance
DMERC-CIGNA Medicare
P. O. Box 690
Nashville, TN 37320

MEDICARE FISCAL AGENT OR CARRIER
Medicare/Aetna Life Insurance Company
P. O. Box 860
Honolulu, HI 96808

MEDICARE RAILROAD RETIREE CARRIER
Medicare Part B claims are handled by claim service centers. For the address and toll-free number of the office nearest you, call the Railroad Retirement Board listed in your telephone directory under U.S. Government.

WORKERS' COMPENSATION STATE PLAN OFFICE
Workmen's Compensation Commission
Office of the Governor
Government of American Samoa
Pago Pago, AS 96799

Arizona

BLUE CROSS & BLUE SHIELD
Blue Cross & Blue Shield of Arizona, Inc.
P. O. Box 13466
Phoenix, AZ 85002-3466

CHAMPUS CLAIM OFFICE
Palmetto Government Benefits Administrators
P. O. Box 870020
Surfside Beach, SC 29587-8720

Beginning April, 1997, TriWest Healthcare Alliance will be the fiscal intermediary. Read your CHAMPUS bulletin for the address information.

CHAMPVA CLAIM OFFICE
CHAMPVA Center
4500 Cherry Creek Drive, South
Box 65024
Denver, CO 80206-9024

INSURANCE COMMISSIONER STATE OFFICE
Department of Insurance
2910 North 44th Street, Suite 210
Phoenix, AZ 85018-7256

MATERNAL AND CHILD HEALTH PROGRAM
Arizona Department of Public Health Services
Children with Special Health Care Needs
1740 W. Adams Street, Room 310
Phoenix, AZ 85007

Office of Women's and Children's Health
Arizona Department of Health
411 N. 24th Street, Birch Hall
Phoenix, AZ 85008

MEDICAID FISCAL AGENT
Arizona Health Care Cost Containment System
P. O. Box 25520
Phoenix, AZ 85002

MEDICARE DURABLE MEDICAL EQUIPMENT
Connecticut General Life Insurance
DMERC-CIGNA Medicare
P. O. Box 690
Nashville, TN 37320

MEDICARE FISCAL AGENT OR CARRIER
Medicare/Blue Cross Blue Shield of North Dakota
4510 13th Avenue, S.W.
Fargo, ND 58121-0001

MEDICARE RAILROAD RETIREE CARRIER
The MetraHealth Insurance Company
Railroad Medicare Service Center
P. O. Box 30050
Salt Lake City, UT 84130-0050

STATE BOARD OF MEDICAL EXAMINERS
Arizona Board of Osteopathic Examiners in Medicine & Surgery
141 E. Palm Lane, Suite 205
Phoenix, AZ 85004

Arizona State Board of Medical Examiners
1651 E. Morten Avenue, Suite 210
Phoenix, AZ 85020

VETERANS ADMINISTRATION INSTALLATION
Arizona Medical Centers:
Phoenix 85012 (650 E. Indian School Road)
Tucson 85723 (3601 S. 6th Avenue)
Prescott 86313 (500 Highway 89, North)

WORKERS' COMPENSATION FEDERAL DISTRICT OFFICE
Office of Workers' Compensation Programs
71 Stevenson Street, 2nd Floor (94105)
P. O. Box 193769
San Francisco, CA 94119-3769

WORKERS' COMPENSATION STATE PLAN OFFICE
Industrial Commission
800 W. Washington
P. O. Box 19070
Phoenix, AZ 85005-9070

Arkansas

BLUE CROSS & BLUE SHIELD
Arkansas Blue Cross and Blue Shield
P. O. Box 2181
Little Rock, AR 72203

CHAMPUS/TRICARE CLAIM OFFICE
c/o Foundation Health Federal Services
Wisconsin Physicians Service
P. O. Box 8999
Madison, WI 53708

CHAMPVA CLAIM OFFICE
CHAMPVA Center
4500 Cherry Creek Drive, South
Box 65024
Denver, CO 80206-9024

INSURANCE COMMISSIONER STATE OFFICE
Insurance Commissioner
1123 S. University Avenue,
Suite 400, University Tower Building
Little Rock, AR 72204-1699

MATERNAL AND CHILD HEALTH PROGRAM
Section of Maternal and Child Health
Arkansas Department of Human Services
4815 W. Markham, Slot 41
Little Rock, AR 72205

Children's Medical Services
Department of Human Services
P. O. Box 1437, Slot 526
Little Rock, AR 72203

MEDICAID FISCAL AGENT
Electronic Data Systems (EC)
P. O. Box 8036
Little Rock, AR 72203

MEDICARE DURABLE MEDICAL EQUIPMENT
Palmetto Government Benefits Administrators
Medicare DMERC Operations
P. O. Box 100141
Columbia, SC 29202-3141

MEDICARE FISCAL AGENT OR CARRIER
Medicare/Arkansas Blue Cross and Blue Shield
P. O. Box 1418
Little Rock, AR 72203-1418

MEDICARE RAILROAD RETIREE CARRIER
The MetraHealth Insurance Company
Railroad Medicare Service Center
P. O. Box 30050
Salt Lake City, UT 84130-0050

STATE BOARD OF MEDICAL EXAMINERS
Arkansas State Medical Board
2100 Riverfront Drive, Suite 200
Little Rock, AR 72202-1793

VETERANS ADMINISTRATION INSTALLATION
Arkansas Medical Centers:
Fayetteville 72703 (1100 N. College Avenue)
Little Rock 72205 (4300 W. 7th Street)

WORKERS' COMPENSATION FEDERAL DISTRICT OFFICE
Office of Workers' Compensation Programs
525 Griffin Street
Dallas, TX 75202

WORKERS' COMPENSATION STATE PLAN OFFICE
Workers' Compensation Commission
Fourth & Spring Streets
P. O. Box 950
Little Rock, AR 72203

California

BLUE CROSS & BLUE SHIELD
Blue Shield of California (California Physician Service)
Two N. Point (94133)
P. O. Box 7168
San Francisco, CA 94120

Blue Cross of California
21555 Oxnard Street
Woodland Hills, CA 91367

P. O. Box 70000 (mailing address)
Van Nuys, CA 91470

CALIFORNIA MEDICAL SERVICES
(Known in other states as Maternal and Child Health Program)
California Children's Service Branch
California State Department of Health
714 "P" Street, Room 323
Sacramento, CA 95814

Maternal & Child Health
California State Department of Health
714 "P" Street, Room 750
Sacramento, CA 95814

CHAMPUS/TRICARE CLAIM OFFICE
Palmetto Government Benefits Administrators
CHAMPUS Claims
P. O. Box 870001
Surfside Beach, SC 29587-8701

CHAMPVA CLAIM OFFICE
CHAMPVA Center
4500 Cherry Creek Drive, South
Box 65024
Denver, CO 80206-9024

INSURANCE COMMISSIONER STATE OFFICE
Commissioner of Insurance
300 Capital Mall, Suite 1500
Sacramento, CA 95814

MEDI-CAL FISCAL AGENT
Medi-Cal Fiscal Intermediary
P. O. Box 15700
Sacramento, CA 95852-1700

MEDICARE DURABLE MEDICAL EQUIPMENT
Connecticut General Life Insurance
DMERC-CIGNA Medicare
P. O. Box 690
Nashville, TN 37320

MEDICARE FISCAL AGENT OR CARRIER
Counties of Los Angeles, Orange, San Diego, Ventura, Imperial, San Luis Obispo, Santa Barbara:
Medicare/Transamerica Occidental Life Insurance Company*
P. O. Box 30540
Los Angeles, CA 90030-0540

Rest of State:
Medicare Claims Department
Blue Shield of California
Chico, CA 95976

MEDICARE RAILROAD RETIREE CARRIER
The MetraHealth Insurance Company
Railroad Medicare Service Center
P. O. Box 30050
Salt Lake City, UT 84130-0050

STATE BOARD OF MEDICAL EXAMINERS
Medical Board of California
(formerly Board of Medical Quality Assurance)
1426 Howe Avenue, Suite 54
Sacramento, CA 95825-3236

Osteopathic Medical Board of California
2720 Gateway Oaks Drive, Suite 350
Sacramento, CA 95833

*This office has professional relations field representatives (San Luis Obispo to San Diego—nine counties) for the purpose of interpreting Medicare policies and procedures. These representatives make personal calls at physicians' offices, conduct seminars for doctors and medical assistants, and speak to hospital staff and at local medical society meetings.

UNEMPLOYMENT COMPENSATION DISABILITY & STATE DISABILITY OFFICES
Bakersfield
1401 South H, 93304-4512
P. O. Box 1633, 93302-1633

Chico
645 Salem, 95928-5576
P. O. Box 8190, 95927-8190

Culver City
3861 Sepulveda, 90230-4605
P. O. Box 3875, 90231-3875

Eureka
415 4th, Suite C, 95501-1001
P. O. Box 4986, 95502-4986

Fresno
2550 Mariposa, Room 1080A, 93721-2270
P. O. Box 32, 93707-0032

Glendale
710 South Central, 91203-2532
P. O. Box 990, 91209-0990

Long Beach
1315 Pine, 2nd Floor, 90813-3189
P. O. Box 469, 90801-0469

Los Angeles
221 North Figueroa, 2nd Floor, 90012-2601
P. O. Box 3096, 90051-1096

Oakland
7700 Edgewater Road, Suite 210, 94621-3018
P. O. Box 1857, 94604-1857

Redding
615 Locust, 96001-2711
P. O. Box 1898, 96099-1898

Riverside
1120 Palmyrita, Suite 280, 92507-1708
P. O. Box 59903, 92517-1903

Sacramento
5009 Broadway, 95820-1613
P.O. Box 13140, 95813-3140

San Bernardino
371 W. 3rd Street, Room 101, 92401-1818
P. O. Box 781, 92402-0781

San Diego
8977 Activity Road, Building B, 92126-3287
P. O. Box 831, 92112-0831

San Francisco
745 Franklin, Room 202, 94102-3287
P. O. Box 3534, 94119-3534

San Gabriel Valley
17171 East Gale Avenue, City of Industry, 91745-1810
P. O. Box 60006, 91716-0006

San Jose
297 W. Hedding Street, 95110-1628
P. O. Box 637, 95106-0637

Santa Ana
28 Civic Center Plaza, 7th Floor, 92701-4024
P. O. Box 1466, 92702-1466

Santa Barbara
128 E. Ortega, 93101-1529
P. O. Box 1529, 93102-1529

Santa Rosa
50 D, Room 325, 95404-4757
P. O. Box 700, 95402-0700

Stockton
528 N. Madison, 95202-1917
P. O. Box 201006, 95201-9006

Woodland Hills
21210 Erwin, 91367-3714
P. O. Box 4256, 91365-4256

VETERANS ADMINISTRATION INSTALLATION

California Medical Centers:
Fresno 93703 (2615 E. Clinton Avenue)
Livermore 94450 (4951 Arroyo Road)
Loma Linda 92357 (11201 Benton Street)
Long Beach 90822 (5901 E. 7th Street)
Palo Alto 94304 (3801 Miranda Avenue)
San Diego 92161 (3350 La Jolla Village Drive)
San Francisco 94121 (4150 Clement Street)
Sepulveda 91343 (1611 Plummer Street)
West Los Angeles 90073 (Wilshire & Sawtelle Blvds)

WORKERS' COMPENSATION FEDERAL DISTRICT OFFICE

Office of Workers' Compensation Programs
71 Stevenson Street, 2nd Floor (94105)
P. O. Box 193769
San Francisco, CA 94119-3769

WORKERS' COMPENSATION STATE PLAN OFFICES

Department of Workers' Compensation
(formerly Division of Industrial Accidents)
455 Golden Gate Avenue, Room 5182
San Francisco, CA 94102

Workers' Compensation Appeals Board
455 Golden Gate Avenue, Room 2181
San Francisco, CA 94102

Canada

BLUE CROSS & BLUE SHIELD

Alberta Blue Cross Plan
10009-108th Street
Edmonton, AB T5J 3C5

British Columbia
Medical Services Association
P. O. Box 9300
Vancouver, BC V6B 5M1

Manitoba Blue Cross Plan
P. O. Box 1046
Winnipeg, MB R3C 2X7

Blue Cross of Atlantic Canada (New Brunswick)
P. O. Box 220
Moncton, NB EIC 8L3

Blue Cross in Ontario (New Brunswick)
P. O. Box 220
Moncton, NB EIC 8L3

Blue Cross in Ontario
P. O. Box 2000
Etobicoke, ON M9C 5P1

Quebec Blue Cross
550 Sherbrooke Street, West
Montreal, PQ H3A 1B9

Saskatchewan-Group Medical Services
1992 Hamilton Street
Regina, SK S4P 2C6

CHAMPUS CLAIM OFFICE

P. O. Box 7985
Madison, WI 53707-7985

CHAMPVA CLAIM OFFICE

CHAMPVA Center
4500 Cherry Creek Drive, South
Box 65024
Denver, CO 80206-9024

Colorado

BLUE CROSS & BLUE SHIELD

Blue Cross and Blue Shield of Colorado
700 Broadway
Denver, CO 80273

CHAMPUS CLAIM OFFICE

Palmetto Government Benefits Administrators
P. O. Box 870020
Florence, SC 29587-8720

Beginning April, 1997, TriWest Healthcare Alliance will be the fiscal intermediary. Read your CHAMPUS bulletin for the address information.

CHAMPVA CLAIM OFFICE

CHAMPVA Center
4500 Cherry Creek Drive, South
Box 65024
Denver, CO 80206-9024

INSURANCE COMMISSIONER STATE OFFICE

Commissioner of Insurance

1560 Broadway, Suite 850
Denver, CO 80202

MATERNAL AND CHILD HEALTH PROGRAM
Family/Community Health Services
Colorado Department of Health Services
4300 Cherry Creek Drive, South
Denver, CO 80222-1530

Health Care Program for Children with Special Needs
Colorado Department of Public Health and Environment
4300 Cherry Creek Drive, South
Denver, CO 80222-1530

MEDICAID FISCAL AGENT
Blue Cross and Blue Shield
P. O. Box 17330
Denver, CO 80217

MEDICARE DURABLE MEDICAL EQUIPMENT
Palmetto Government Benefits Administrators
Medicare DMERC Operations
P. O. Box 10041
Columbia, SC 29202-3141

MEDICARE FISCAL AGENT OR CARRIER
Medicare/Blue Cross and Blue Shield of Colorado
Coordination of Benefits
P. O. Box 173550
Denver, CO 80217

MEDICARE RAILROAD RETIREE CARRIER
The MetraHealth Insurance Company
Railroad Medicare Service Center
P. O. Box 30050
Salt Lake City, UT 84130-0050

STATE BOARD OF MEDICAL EXAMINERS
1560 Broadway, Suite 1300
Denver, CO 80220

VETERANS ADMINISTRATION INSTALLATION
Colorado Medical Centers:
Denver 80220 (1055 Clermont Street)
Grand Junction 81501 (2121 North Avenue)
Fort Lyon 81038 (C Street)

WORKERS' COMPENSATION FEDERAL DISTRICT OFFICE
Office of Workers' Compensation Programs
1801 California Street, Suite 915
Denver, CO 80202-2614

WORKERS' COMPENSATION STATE PLAN OFFICE
Division of Workers' Compensation
1515 Arapahoe Street
Denver, CO 80202

Industrial Claims Appeal Office
1515 Arapahoe Street
Denver, CO 80202

Connecticut

BLUE CROSS & BLUE SHIELD
Blue Cross & Blue Shield of Connecticut, Inc.
P. O. Box 504
North Haven, CT 06473

CHAMPUS CLAIM OFFICE
UNISYS Corporation
P. O. Box 3066
Columbus, IN 47202-3066

CHAMPVA CLAIM OFFICE
CHAMPVA Center
4500 Cherry Creek Drive, South
Box 65024
Denver, CO 80206-9024

INSURANCE COMMISSIONER STATE OFFICE
Insurance Commissioner
P. O. Box 816
Hartford, CT 06142-0816

MATERNAL AND CHILD HEALTH PROGRAM
Department of Public Health Services
Family Health Services Division
410 Capitol Avenue, MS 11FHS
Hartford, CT 06134-0308

CSCHN
Department of Public Health and Addiction Services
999 Asylum Avenue
Hartford, CT 06105

MEDICAID FISCAL AGENT
Electronic Data Systems Corporation
P. O. Box 2941
Hartford, CT 06104

MEDICARE DURABLE MEDICAL EQUIPMENT
MetraHealth, Inc
320 S. Pennsylvania Boulevard, Suite 339
Wilkes-Barre, PA 18701-2215

MEDICARE FISCAL AGENT OR CARRIER
Medicare/The Travelers Companies
538 Preston Avenue
P. O. Box 9000
Meriden, CT 06454-9000

MEDICARE RAILROAD RETIREE CARRIER
The MetraHealth Insurance Company
Railroad Medicare Service Center
P. O. Box 10066
Augusta, GA 30999-0001

STATE BOARD OF MEDICAL EXAMINERS
Connecticut Department of Health Services
P. O. Box 340308
Hartford, CT 06134-0308

VETERANS ADMINISTRATION INSTALLATION
Connecticut Health System
Newington 06111 (555 Willard Avenue)
West Haven 06516 (W. Spring Street)

WORKERS' COMPENSATION FEDERAL DISTRICT OFFICE
Office of Workers' Compensation Programs
JFK Federal Building, Room E260
Boston, MA 02203

WORKERS' COMPENSATION STATE PLAN OFFICE
Workers' Compensation Commission
210 Alaska Street, 4th Floor
Hartford, CT 06106

Delaware

BLUE CROSS & BLUE SHIELD
Blue Cross & Blue Shield of Delaware, Inc.
P. O. Box 1991
Wilmington, DE 19899

CHAMPUS CLAIM OFFICE
UNISYS Corporation
P. O. Box 3076
Columbus, IN 47202-3076

CHAMPVA CLAIM OFFICE
CHAMPVA Center
4500 Cherry Creek Drive, South
Box 65024
Denver, CO 80206-9024

INSURANCE COMMISSIONER STATE OFFICE
Insurance Commissioner
841 Silver Lake Boulevard
Dover, DE 19904

MATERNAL AND CHILD HEALTH PROGRAM
Family Health Services
Community Health Care Access
Division of Public Health
P. O. Box 637
Dover, DE 19903

MEDICAID FISCAL AGENT
Electronic Data Systems Corporation
Continental American Building
300 Continental Drive, Suite 250
Newark, DE 19713

MEDICARE DURABLE MEDICAL EQUIPMENT
MetraHealth, Inc.
320 S. Pennsylvania Boulevard, Suite 339
Wilkes-Barre, PA 18701-2215

MEDICARE FISCAL AGENT OR CARRIER
Medicare/Pennsylvania Blue Shield
P. O. Box 890200
Camp Hill, PA 17089-0200

MEDICARE RAILROAD RETIREE CARRIER
The MetraHealth Insurance Company
Railroad Medicare Service Center
P. O. Box 10066
Augusta, GA 30999-0001

STATE BOARD OF MEDICAL EXAMINERS
Delaware Board of Medical Practice
P. O. Box 1401
(861 Silver Lake Boulevard, Cannon Building, Suite 203)
Dover, DE 19903

VETERANS ADMINISTRATION INSTALLATION
Medical Center:
Wilmington 19805 (1601 Kirkwood Highway)

WORKERS' COMPENSATION FEDERAL DISTRICT OFFICE
Office of Workers' Compensation Programs
3535 Market Street
Philadelphia, PA 19104

WORKERS' COMPENSATION STATE PLAN OFFICE
Industrial Accident Board
Carvel State Office Building
820 N. French Street, 6th Floor
Wilmington, DE 19801

District of Columbia

BLUE CROSS & BLUE SHIELD
Blue Cross and Blue Shield of the National Capital Area
550 12th Street, S.W.
Washington, DC 20065

CHAMPUS CLAIM OFFICE
Palmetto Government Benefits Administrators
P. O. Box 100502
Florence, SC 29501-0502

CHAMPVA CLAIM OFFICE
CHAMPVA Center
4500 Cherry Creek Drive, South
Box 65024
Denver, CO 80206-9024

INSURANCE COMMISSIONER STATE OFFICE
Insurance Administration
441 4th Street, N.W.
8th Floor North
Washington, DC 20001

MATERNAL AND CHILD HEALTH PROGRAM
Office of Maternal and Child Health
Healthy Start Program
800 9th Street, S.W., 3rd Floor
Washington, DC 20024-2480

MEDICAID FISCAL AGENT
First Health

P. O. Box 37443 N.W.
Washington, DC 20001

MEDICARE DURABLE MEDICAL EQUIPMENT
AdminaStar Federal Incorporated
P. O. Box 7078
Indianapolis, IN 46206-0240

MEDICARE FISCAL AGENT OR CARRIER
Medicare/Pennsylvania Blue Shield
P. O. Box 890100
Camp Hill, PA 17089-0100

MEDICARE RAILROAD RETIREE CARRIER
The MetraHealth Insurance Company
Railroad Medicare Service Center
P. O. Box 10066
Augusta, GA 30999-0001

STATE BOARD OF MEDICAL EXAMINERS
District of Columbia Board of Medicine
614 H Street, N.W., Room 108
Washington, DC 20001

VETERANS ADMINISTRATION INSTALLATION
District of Columbia Medical Center:
Washington, DC 20422 (50 Irving Street, N.W.)

WORKERS' COMPENSATION FEDERAL DISTRICT OFFICE
Office of Workers' Compensation Programs
800 N. Capitol Street, N.W., Room 800
Washington, DC 20211

WORKERS' COMPENSATION STATE PLAN OFFICE
Department of Employment Services
Office of Workers' Compensation
1200 Upshur Street, N.W.
Washington, DC 20011

Florida

BLUE CROSS & BLUE SHIELD
532 Riverside Avenue (32202)
P. O. Box 1798
Jacksonville, FL 32231-0014

CHAMPUS/TRICARE CLAIM OFFICE
Wisconsin Physicians Service
P. O. Box 202000
Florence, SC 29502-2000

CHAMPVA CLAIM CENTER
CHAMPVA Center
4500 Cherry Creek Drive, South
Box 65024
Denver, CO 80206-9024

INSURANCE COMMISSIONER STATE OFFICE
Insurance Commissioner
Plaza Level Eleven–The Capitol
Tallahassee, FL 32399-0300

MATERNAL AND CHILD HEALTH PROGRAM
Children's Medical Services
Building 5, Room 127
1317 Winewood Boulevard
Tallahassee, FL 32399-0700

Health Program
Policy and Development
Family Health Services
1317 Winewood Boulevard
Tallahassee, FL 32399-0700

MEDICAID FISCAL AGENT
Consultec Inc.
P. O. Box 7072
Tallahassee, FL 32301

MEDICARE DURABLE MEDICAL EQUIPMENT
Palmetto Government Benefits Administrators
Medicare DMERC Operations
P. O. Box 100141
Columbia, SC 29202-3141

MEDICARE FISCAL AGENT OR CARRIER
Medicare/Blue Cross and Blue Shield of Florida, Inc.
P. O. Box 2360
Jacksonville, FL 32231

MEDICARE RAILROAD RETIREE CARRIER
The MetraHealth Insurance Company
Railroad Medicare Service Center
P. O. Box 10066
Augusta, GA 30999-0001

STATE BOARD OF MEDICAL EXAMINERS
Florida Board of Medicine
Northwood Centre #60
1940 N. Monroe Street
Tallahassee, FL 32399-0775

Florida Board of Osteopathic Medical Examiners
Northwood Centre
1940 N. Monroe Street
Tallahassee, FL 32399-0775

VETERANS ADMINISTRATION INSTALLATION
Florida Medical Centers:
Bay Pines 33504 (1000 Bay Pines Blvd., North)
Gainesville 32608 (1601 Southwest Archer Road)
Lake City 32055 (801 S. Marion Street)
Miami 33125 (1201 N.W. 16th Street)
Tampa 33612 (13000 Bruce B. Downs Blvd.)
West Palm Beach 33410 (7305 N. Military Trail)

WORKERS' COMPENSATION FEDERAL DISTRICT OFFICE
Office of Workers' Compensation Programs
214 N. Hogan Street, Suite 1006
Jacksonville, FL 32202

WORKERS' COMPENSATION STATE PLAN OFFICE
Division of Workers' Compensation
Department of Labor and Employment Security
301 Forrest Building
2728 Centerview Drive
Tallahassee, FL 32399-0680

Georgia

BLUE CROSS & BLUE SHIELD
Blue Cross and Blue Shield of Georgia, Inc.
P. O. Box 4445
Atlanta, GA 30302-4445

CHAMPUS/TRICARE CLAIM OFFICE
Palmetto Government Benefits Administrators
P. O. Box 202000
Florence, SC 29502-2000

CHAMPVA CLAIM OFFICE
CHAMPVA Center
4500 Cherry Creek Drive, South
Box 65024
Denver, CO 80206-9024

INSURANCE COMMISSIONER STATE OFFICE
Insurance Commissioner
2 Martin Luther King Jr. Drive
Atlanta, GA 30334

MATERNAL AND CHILD HEALTH PROGRAM
Family Health Branch
2 Peachtree Street, N.E., Suite 8-113
Atlanta, GA 30303

MEDICAID FISCAL AGENT
Electronic Data Systems Corporation
P. O. Box 105013
Tucker, GA 30085

MEDICARE RAILROAD RETIREMENT
The MetraHealth Insurance Company
Railroad Medicare Service Center
P. O. Box 10066
Augusta, GA 30999-0001

MEDICARE DURABLE MEDICAL EQUIPMENT
Palmetto Government Benefits Administrators
Medicare DMERC Operations
P. O. Box 100141
Columbia, SC 29202-3141

MEDICARE FISCAL AGENT OR CARRIER
Medicare/Blue Cross Blue Shield of Alabama
P. O. Box 83140
Birmingham, AL 35292

STATE BOARD OF MEDICAL EXAMINERS
166 Pryor Street, S.W.
Atlanta, GA 30303-3465

VETERANS ADMINISTRATION INSTALLATION
Georgia Medical Centers:
Augusta 30904 (1 Freedom Way)
Decatur 30033 (1670 Clairmont Road)
Dublin 31021 (1826 Veterans Blvd.)

WORKERS' COMPENSATION FEDERAL DISTRICT OFFICE
Office of Workers' Compensation Programs
214 N. Hogan Street, Suite 1006
Jacksonville, FL 32202

WORKERS' COMPENSATION STATE PLAN OFFICE
Board of Workers' Compensation
South Tower, Suite 1000
One CNN Center
Atlanta, GA 30303-2788

Guam

INSURANCE COMMISSIONER STATE OFFICE
Insurance Commissioner
Government of Guam
378 Chalan San Antonio
Tamuning, Guam 96911

MATERNAL AND CHILD HEALTH PROGRAM
Department of Public Health & Social Services
Bureau of Family Health and Nursing Services
P. O. Box 2816
Agana, GU 96910

MEDICARE DURABLE MEDICAL EQUIPMENT
Connecticut General Life Insurance
DMERC-CIGNA Medicare
P. O. Box 690
Nashville, TN 37320

MEDICARE FISCAL AGENT OR CARRIER
Medicare/Aetna Life Insurance Company
P. O. Box 3947
Honolulu, HI 96812

MEDICARE RAILROAD RETIREE CARRIER
Medicare Part B claims are handled by claim service centers. For the address and toll-free number of the office nearest you, call the Railroad Retirement Board listed in your telephone directory under U.S. Government.

STATE BOARD OF MEDICAL EXAMINERS
Guam Board of Medical Examiners
Department of Public Health Center
1304 E. Sunset Boulevard, Tiyan
Barrigada, GU 96913

VETERANS ADMINISTRATION INSTALLATION
Agana 96910 (222 Chalan Santo Papast Reflection Center, Suite 102)

WORKERS' COMPENSATION STATE PLAN OFFICE
Workers' Compensation Commission
Department of Labor
Government of Guam
P. O. Box 9970
Tamuning, GU 96930-2970

Hawaii

BLUE CROSS & BLUE SHIELD
Blue Cross & Blue Shield of Hawaii
818 Keeaumoku Street (96814)
P. O. Box 860
Honolulu, HI 96808-0860

CHAMPUS/TRICARE CLAIM CENTER
Palmetto Government Benefits Administrators
P. O. Box 870001
Surfside Beach, SC 29587-8701

CHAMPVA CLAIM OFFICE
CHAMPVA Center
4500 Cherry Creek Drive, South
Box 65024
Denver, CO 80206-9024

INSURANCE COMMISSIONER STATE OFFICE
Insurance Commissioner
250 S. King Street, 5th Floor
Honolulu, HI 96811-3614

MATERNAL AND CHILD HEALTH PROGRAM
Department of Health
Children with Special Needs Branch
714 Sunset Avenue
Honolulu, HI 96816

Family Health Services
Hawaii Department of Health
3652 Kilauea Avenue
Honolulu, HI 96816

MEDICAID FISCAL AGENT
Hawaii Medical Service Association (EC)
P. O. Box 1220
Honolulu, HI 96807

MEDICARE DURABLE MEDICAL EQUIPMENT
Connecticut General Life Insurance
DMERC-CIGNA Medicare
P. O. Box 690
Nashville, TN 37320

MEDICARE FISCAL AGENT OR CARRIER
Medicare/Blue Cross Blue Shield of North Dakota
4510 13th Avenue, S.W.
Fargo, ND 58121-0001

MEDICARE RAILROAD RETIREMENT
The MetraHealth Insurance Company
Railroad Medicare Service Center
P. O. Box 30050
Salt Lake City, UT 84130-0050

STATE BOARD OF MEDICAL EXAMINERS
Hawaii Board of Medical Examiners
Department of Commerce & Consumer Affairs
1010 Richards Street (98613)
P. O. Box 3469
Honolulu, HI 96801

TEMPORARY DISABILITY INSURANCE
Department of Labor & Industrial Relations
Disability Compensation Division

Hawaii
State Office Building
75 Aupuni Street
Hilo, HI 96720

Kauai
State Office Building
3060 Eiwa Street
Lihue, HI 96766

Maui
State Office Building, #2
2264 Aupuni Street
Wailuku, HI 96793

Oahu
830 Punchbowl Street, Suite 210
P. O. Box 3769
Honolulu, HI 96812-3769

West Hawaii
Ashikawa Building
P. O. Box 49
Kealakekua, HI 96750

VETERANS ADMINISTRATION INSTALLATION
Hawaii Medical Center and Regional Office:
Honolulu 96850 (P. O. Box 50188, 300 Ala Moana Blvd., Room 1004)
Medical Office: (808) 566-1000
Regional Office: From Oahu: (808) 566-1000
From Hawaiian neighbor Islands, 1-800-827-1000
From Guam, 475-8387
From American Samoa, 1-1-800-844-7928

WORKERS' COMPENSATION STATE PLAN OFFICE
Disability Compensation Division
Department of Labor and Industrial Relations
P. O. Box 3769
Honolulu, HI 96812

Labor and Industrial Relations Appeals Board
888 Mililani Street, Room 400
Honolulu, HI 96813

WORKERS' COMPENSATION FEDERAL DISTRICT OFFICE
Office of Workers' Compensation Programs
71 Stevenson Street, 2nd Floor (94105)
P. O. Box 193769
San Francisco, CA 94119-3769

Idaho

BLUE CROSS & BLUE SHIELD
Blue Shield of Idaho
(Medical Service Bureau of Idaho, Inc.)
P. O. Box 1106
Lewiston, ID 83501

Blue Cross of Idaho Health Services, Inc.
1501 Federal Way (83705)
P. O. Box 7408
Boise, ID 83707

CHAMPUS CLAIM OFFICE
For zip codes 83854 and 83876
Foundation Health Federal Services
P. O. Box 419010
Rancho Cordova, CA 94741-9010

Except zip codes 83854 and 83876
Palmetto Government Benefits Administrators
P. O. Box 870020
Surfside Beach, SC 29587-8720

Northern Idaho
(Benewah, Bonner, Boundary, Kootenai, Shoshone, and Latah Counties)
Foundation Health Federal Services
c/o WPS/Tricare
P. O. Box 419010
Rancho Cordova, CA 94741-9010

Beginning April, 1997, TriWest Healthcare Alliance will be the fiscal intermediary. Read your CHAMPUS bulletin for the address information.

CHAMPVA CLAIM OFFICE
CHAMPVA Center
4500 Cherry Creek Drive, South
Box 65024
Denver, CO 80206-9024

INSURANCE COMMISSIONER STATE OFFICE
Director of Insurance
700 W. State Street
Boise, ID 83720

MATERNAL AND CHILD HEALTH PROGRAM
Children's Special Health Program
Idaho Department of Health and Welfare
450 W. State Street
P. O. Box 83720
Boise, ID 83720-0036

Public Health Services
Idaho Department of Health and Welfare
450 W. State Street, P. O. Box 83720
Boise, ID 83720-0036

MEDICAID FISCAL AGENT
Electronic Data Systems (EC)
P. O. Box 26
Boise, ID 83707

MEDICARE DURABLE MEDICAL EQUIPMENT
Connecticut General Life Insurance
DMERC-CIGNA Medicare
P. O. Box 690
Nashville, TN 37320

MEDICARE FISCAL AGENT OR CARRIER
Connecticut General Life Insurance Company
3150 N. Lakeharbor Lane, Suite 254
P. O. Box 8048
Boise, ID 83707-6219

MEDICARE RAILROAD RETIREE CARRIER
The MetraHealth Insurance Company
Railroad Medicare Service Center
P. O. Box 30050
Salt Lake City, UT 84130-0050

STATE BOARD OF MEDICAL EXAMINERS
Idaho State Board of Medicine
P. O. Box 83720
280 N. 8th, Suite 202, Statehouse Mail
Boise, ID 83720-0058

VETERANS ADMINISTRATION INSTALLATION
Idaho Medical Center:
Boise 83702 (500 W. Fort Street)

WORKERS' COMPENSATION FEDERAL DISTRICT OFFICE
Office of Workers' Compensation Programs
1111 Third Avenue, Suite 615
Seattle, WA 98101-3212

WORKERS' COMPENSATION STATE PLAN OFFICE
Industrial Commission
317 Main Street
Boise, ID 83720

Illinois

BLUE CROSS & BLUE SHIELD
Blue Cross and Blue Shield of Illinois
P. O. Box 1364
Chicago, IL 60690

CHAMPUS CLAIM CENTER
UNISYS Corporation
P. O. Box 3054
Columbus, IN 47202-3054

CHAMPVA CLAIM OFFICE
CHAMPVA Center
4500 Cherry Creek Drive, South
Box 65024
Denver, CO 80206-9024

INSURANCE COMMISSIONER STATE OFFICE
Director of Insurance
320 W. Washington Street
Springfield, IL 62767

100 West Randolph Street
Suite 15-100
Chicago, IL 60601

MATERNAL AND CHILD HEALTH PROGRAM
Division of Family Health
Illinois Department of Public Health
535 W. Jefferson Street
Springfield, IL 62761

Division of Specialized Care for Children
University of Illinois/Chicago, Administration Office
2815 W. Washington, Suite 300
Springfield, IL 62794-9481

MEDICAID FISCAL AGENT
Department of Public Aid (Hospital)
P. O. Box 19105
Springfield, IL 62794

MEDICARE DURABLE MEDICAL EQUIPMENT
AdminaStar Federal Incorporated
P. O. Box 7078
Indianapolis, IN 46206-0240

MEDICARE FISCAL AGENT OR CARRIER
Medicare Claims/Health Care Service Corporation
P. O. Box 4422
Marion, IL 62959

MEDICARE RAILROAD RETIREE CARRIER
The MetraHealth Insurance Company
Railroad Medicare Service Center
P. O. Box 10066
Augusta, GA 30999-0001

STATE BOARD OF MEDICAL EXAMINERS
Illinois Department of Professional Regulation
100 W. Randolph Street, #9-300
Chicago, IL 60601

VETERANS ADMINISTRATION INSTALLATION
Illinois Medical Centers:
Chicago 60611 (Lakeside, 333 E. Huron Street)
Chicago 60680 (Westside, 820 S. Damen Avenue, P. O. Box 8195)
Danville 61832 (1900 E. Main Street)
Hines 60141 (Roosevelt Road & 5th Avenue)
Marion 62959 (2401 W. Main Street)
North Chicago 60064 (3001 Green Bay Road)

WORKERS' COMPENSATION FEDERAL DISTRICT OFFICE
Office of Workers' Compensation Programs
230 S. Dearborn Street, 8th Floor
Chicago, IL 60604

WORKERS' COMPENSATION STATE PLAN OFFICE
Industrial Commission
100 W. Randolph Street, Suite 8-200
Chicago, IL 60601

Indiana

BLUE CROSS & BLUE SHIELD
Anthem Blue Cross and Blue Shield
120 Monument Circle
Indianapolis, IN 46204

CHAMPUS CLAIM OFFICE
UNISYS Corporation
P. O. Box 3056
Columbus, IN 47202-3056

CHAMPVA CLAIM OFFICE
CHAMPVA Center
4500 Cherry Creek Drive, South
Box 65024
Denver, CO 80206-9024

INSURANCE COMMISSIONER STATE OFFICE
Commissioner of Insurance
311 W. Washington Street, Suite 300
Indianapolis, IN 46204-2787

MATERNAL AND CHILD HEALTH PROGRAM
Children's Special Health Care Services
Indiana State Department of Health
1330 W. Michigan Street
Indianapolis, IN 46206-1964

State Department of Health CSHCS/MCH/WIC
2 N. Meridian, Suite 700
Indianapolis, IN 46204

MEDICAID FISCAL AGENT
Electronic Data Systems
P. O. Box 68765
Indianapolis, IN 46268

MEDICARE DURABLE MEDICAL EQUIPMENT
AdminaStar Federal Incorporated
P. O. Box 7078
Indianapolis, IN 46206-0240

MEDICARE FISCAL AGENT OR CARRIER
Medicare Part B/AdminaStar Federal
P. O. Box 7073
Indianapolis, IN 46207

MEDICARE RAILROAD RETIREE CARRIER
The MetraHealth Insurance Company
Railroad Medicare Service Center
P. O. Box 10066
Augusta, GA 30999-0001

STATE BOARD OF MEDICAL EXAMINERS
Indiana Health Professions Bureau
402 W. Washington Street, Room 041
Indianapolis, IN 46204

VETERANS ADMINISTRATION INSTALLATION
Indiana Medical Centers:
Fort Wayne 46805 (2121 Lake Avenue)
Indianapolis 46202 (1481 W. 10th Street)
Marion 46952 (E. 38th Street)

WORKERS' COMPENSATION FEDERAL DISTRICT OFFICE
Office of Workers' Compensation Programs
1240 E. Ninth Street, Room 851
Cleveland, OH 44199

WORKERS' COMPENSATION STATE PLAN OFFICE
Workers' Compensation Board
402 W. Washington Street, Room W196
Indianapolis, IN 46204

Iowa

BLUE CROSS & BLUE SHIELD
Blue Cross and Blue Shield of Iowa
636 Grand Avenue
Des Moines, IA 50309

CHAMPUS CLAIM OFFICE
Palmetto Government Benefits Administrators
P. O. Box 100598
Florence, SC 29501-0598

Beginning April, 1997, TriWest Healthcare Alliance will be the fiscal intermediary. Read your CHAMPUS bulletin for the address information.

CHAMPVA CLAIM OFFICE
CHAMPVA Center
4500 Cherry Creek Drive, South
Box 65024
Denver, CO 80206-9024

INSURANCE COMMISSIONER STATE OFFICE
Insurance Commissioner
Lucas State Office Building, 6th Floor
Des Moines, IA 50319

MATERNAL AND CHILD HEALTH PROGRAM
Family Services Bureau
Iowa Department of Public Health
321 East 12th Street, Lucas Building
Des Moines, IA 50319-0075

Child Health and Specialty Clinics
247 Hospital School
Iowa City, IA 52242-1011

MEDICAID FISCAL AGENT
Paramax Corporation (EC)
P. O. Box 10309
Des Moines, IA 50306

MEDICARE DURABLE MEDICAL EQUIPMENT
Connecticut General Life Insurance
DMERC-CIGNA Medicare
P. O. Box 690
Nashville, TN 37320

MEDICARE FISCAL AGENT OR CARRIER
Medicare/IASD Health Services Corporation
(Blue Cross & Blue Shield of Iowa)
636 Grand Avenue
Des Moines, IA 50309

MEDICARE RAILROAD RETIREE CARRIER
The MetraHealth Insurance Company
Railroad Medicare Service Center
P. O. Box 30050
Salt Lake City, UT 84130-0050

STATE BOARD OF MEDICAL EXAMINERS
Iowa State Board of Medical Examiners
Executive Hills West
1209 E. Court Avenue
Des Moines, IA 50319-0180

VETERANS ADMINISTRATION INSTALLATION
Iowa Medical Centers:
Des Moines 50310 (30th & Euclid Avenue)
Iowa City 52246 (Highway 6, West)
Knoxville 50138 (1515 W. Pleasant Street)

WORKERS' COMPENSATION FEDERAL DISTRICT OFFICE
Office of Workers' Compensation Programs
911 Walnut Street
Kansas City, MO 64106

WORKERS' COMPENSATION STATE PLAN OFFICE
Division of Industrial Services
Department of Employment Services
1000 E. Grand Avenue
Des Moines, IA 50319

Kansas

BLUE CROSS & BLUE SHIELD
Blue Cross and Blue Shield of Kansas, Inc.
P. O. Box 239
Topeka, KS 66601-0239

CHAMPUS CLAIM OFFICE
Wisconsin Physicians Service
P. O. Box 8932
Madison, WI 53708-8932

Beginning April, 1997, TriWest Healthcare Alliance will be the fiscal intermediary. Read your CHAMPUS bulletin for the address information.

CHAMPVA CLAIM OFFICE
CHAMPVA Center
4500 Cherry Creek Drive, South
Box 65024
Denver, CO 80206-9024

INSURANCE COMMISSIONER STATE OFFICE
Commissioner of Insurance
420 S.W. 9th Street
Topeka, KS 66612

MATERNAL AND CHILD HEALTH PROGRAM
Bureau of Children, Youth and Families
Kansas Department of Health & Environment
900 S.W. Jackson, 10th Floor, 1052 LSOB
Topeka, KS 66612-1290

Services for CSHCN Section
Kansas Department of Health & Environment
900 S.W. Jackson, 10th Floor, 1005 N, LSOB
Topeka, KS 66612-1290

MEDICAID FISCAL AGENT
Electronic Data Systems Federal Corporation (EC)
P. O. Box 4646
Topeka, KS 66604

MEDICARE DURABLE MEDICAL EQUIPMENT
Connecticut General Life Insurance
DMERC-CIGNA Medicare
P. O. Box 690
Nashville, TN 37320

MEDICARE FISCAL AGENT OR CARRIER
Counties of Johnson and Wyandotte:
Medicare/Blue Cross and Blue Shield of Kansas, Inc.
P.O. Box 419840
Kansas City, MO 64141-6840

Rest of State:
Medicare/Blue Cross and Blue Shield of Kansas, Inc.
P. O. Box 239
1133 S.W. Topeka Blvd.
Topeka, KS 66629-0001

MEDICARE RAILROAD RETIREE CARRIER
The MetraHealth Insurance Company
Railroad Medicare Service Center
P. O. Box 30050
Salt Lake City, UT 84130-0050

STATE BOARD OF MEDICAL EXAMINERS
Kansas State Board of Healing Arts
235 S.W. Topeka Blvd.
Topeka, KS 66603-3068

VETERANS ADMINISTRATION INSTALLATION
Kansas Medical Centers:
Leavenworth 66048 (4101 S. 4th Street)
Topeka 66622 (2200 Gage Blvd.)
Wichita 67218 (5500 E. Kellogg)

WORKERS' COMPENSATION FEDERAL DISTRICT OFFICE
Office of Workers' Compensation Programs
911 Walnut Street
Kansas City, MO 64106

WORKERS' COMPENSATION STATE PLAN OFFICE
Division of Workers' Compensation
Department of Human Resources
800 S.W. Jackson Street, Suite 600
Topeka, KS 66612-1227

Kentucky

BLUE CROSS & BLUE SHIELD
Anthem Blue Cross & Blue Shield
9901 Linn Station Road
Louisville, KY 40223

CHAMPUS CLAIM OFFICE
Palmetto Government Benefits Administrators
(Except Fort Campbell area)
P. O. Box 100598
Florence, SC 29501-0598

Wisconsin Physicians Service
(Fort Campbell area only)
P. O. Box 7889
Madison, WI 53707-7889

CHAMPVA CLAIM OFFICE
CHAMPVA Center
4500 Cherry Creek Drive, South
Box 65024
Denver, CO 80206-9024

INSURANCE COMMISSIONER STATE OFFICE
Insurance Commissioner
215 West Main Street
Frankfort, KY 40602

MATERNAL AND CHILD HEALTH PROGRAM
Division of Maternal/Child Health
Department for Health Services
275 E. Main Street, HSB 2R
Frankfort, KY 40621-0001

Kentucky Commission for CSHCN
982 Eastern Parkway
Louisville, KY 40217

MEDICAID FISCAL AGENT
Electronic Data Systems (EC)
P. O. Box 2018
Frankfort, KY 40602

MEDICARE DURABLE MEDICAL EQUIPMENT
Palmetto Government Benefits Administrators
Medicare DMERC Operations
P. O. Box 100141
Columbia, SC 29202-3141

MEDICARE FISCAL AGENT OR CARRIER
Medicare-Part B/Blue Cross & Blue Shield of Kentucky, Inc.
100 E. Vine Street
Lexington, KY 40507

MEDICARE RAILROAD RETIREE CARRIER
The MetraHealth Insurance Company
Railroad Medicare Service Center
P. O. Box 10066
Augusta, GA 30999-0001

STATE BOARD OF MEDICAL EXAMINERS
Kentucky Board of Medical Licensure
The Hurstbourne Office Park
310 Whittington Parkway, Suite 1B
Louisville, KY 40222

VETERANS ADMINISTRATION INSTALLATION
Kentucky Medical Centers:
Lexington 40511 (Leestown Road)
Louisville 40206 (800 Zorn Avenue)

WORKERS' COMPENSATION FEDERAL DISTRICT OFFICE
Office of Workers' Compensation Programs
214 N. Hogan Street, Suite 1006
Jacksonville, FL 32202

WORKERS' COMPENSATION STATE PLAN OFFICE
Department of Workers' Claims
Perimeter Park West
1270 Louisville Road, Building C
Frankfort, KY 40601

Louisiana

BLUE CROSS & BLUE SHIELD
Blue Cross & Blue Shield of Louisiana
P. O. Box 98029
Baton Rouge, LA 70898-9029

CHAMPUS/TRICARE CLAIM OFFICE
Palmetto Government Benefits Administrators
(New Orleans area)
P. O. Box 202000
Florence, SC 29502-2000

Foundation Health Federal Services
(Except New Orleans area)
c/o WPS/Tricare
P. O. Box 8999
Madison, WI 53708

CHAMPVA CLAIM OFFICE
CHAMPVA Center
4500 Cherry Creek Drive, South
Box 65024
Denver, CO 80206-9024

INSURANCE COMMISSIONER STATE OFFICE
Insurance Commissioner
P. O. Box 94214
Baton Rouge, LA 70801-9214

MATERNAL AND CHILD HEALTH PROGRAM
Children's Special Health Services
Office of Public Health
P. O. Box 60630
New Orleans, LA 70160

MATERNAL AND CHILD HEALTH SECTION
Office of Public Health
P. O. Box 60630
New Orleans, LA 70160

MEDICAID FISCAL AGENT
Paramax Corporation (EC)
P. O. Box 91020
Baton Rouge, LA 70821

MEDICARE DURABLE MEDICAL EQUIPMENT
Palmetto Government Benefits Administrators
Medicare DMERC Operations
P. O. Box 100141
Columbia, SC 29202-3141

MEDICARE FISCAL AGENT OR CARRIER
Arkansas Blue Cross & Blue Shield, Inc.
Medicare Administration
P. O. Box 83830
Baton Rouge, LA 70884-3830

MEDICARE RAILROAD RETIREE CARRIER
The MetraHealth Insurance Company
Railroad Medicare Service Center
P. O. Box 30050
Salt Lake City, UT 84130-0050

STATE BOARD OF MEDICAL EXAMINERS
Louisiana State Board of Medical Examiners
P. O. Box 30250
1630 Camp Street
New Orleans, LA 70190-0250

VETERANS ADMINISTRATION INSTALLATION
Louisiana Medical Centers:
Alexandria 71301 (Shreveport Highway)
New Orleans 70146 (1601 Perdido Street)
Shreveport 71101 (510 E. Stoner Avenue)

WORKERS' COMPENSATION FEDERAL DISTRICT OFFICE
Office of Workers' Compensation Programs
525 Griffin Street
Dallas, TX 75202

WORKERS' COMPENSATION STATE PLAN OFFICE
Department of Labor
Office of Workers' Compensation Administration
P. O. Box 94040
Baton Rouge, LA 70804-9040

Maine

BLUE CROSS & BLUE SHIELD
Blue Cross and Blue Shield of Maine

2 Gannett Drive
South Portland, ME 04106-6911

CHAMPUS CLAIM OFFICE
UNISYS Corporation
P. O. Box 3064
Columbus, IN 47202-3064

CHAMPVA CLAIM OFFICE
CHAMPVA Center
4500 Cherry Creek Drive, South
Box 65024
Denver, CO 80206-9024

INSURANCE COMMISSIONER STATE OFFICE
Superintendent of Insurance
State House Station #34
Augusta, ME 04333-0034

MATERNAL AND CHILD HEALTH PROGRAM
Division of Community and Family Health
Department of Human Services
State House Station #11
Augusta, ME 04333-0011

MEDICAID FISCAL AGENT
Medical Assistance Claims Processing
M500 Department of Human Services
Claims Review–Station 11
Augusta, ME 04333

MEDICARE DURABLE MEDICAL EQUIPMENT
MetraHealth, Inc.
320 S. Pennsylvania Boulevard, Suite 339
Wilkes-Barre, PA 18701-2215

MEDICARE FISCAL AGENT OR CARRIER
For Assigned Claims:
Medicare/C and S Administrative Services
P. O. Box 1000
Hingham, MA 02044-9191

For Nonassigned Claims:
P. O. Box 222
Hingham, MA 02044-9193

MEDICARE RAILROAD RETIREE CARRIER
The MetraHealth Insurance Company
Railroad Medicare Service Center
P. O. Box 10066
Augusta, GA 30999-0001

STATE BOARD OF MEDICAL EXAMINERS
Maine Board of Osteopathic Licensure
State House Station #142
Augusta, ME 04333-0142

Maine Board of Licensure in Medicine
State House Station #137
Two Bangor Street
Augusta, ME 04333-0137

VETERANS ADMINISTRATION INSTALLATION
Maine Medical Center:
Togus 04330 (Route 17 East)

WORKERS' COMPENSATION FEDERAL DISTRICT OFFICE
Office of Workers' Compensation Programs
JFK Federal Building, Room E260
Boston, MA 02203

WORKERS' COMPENSATION STATE PLAN OFFICE
Workers' Compensation Commission
Deering Building
State House Station #27
Augusta, ME 04333-0027

Maryland

BLUE CROSS & BLUE SHIELD
Blue Cross and Blue Shield of Maryland, Inc.
10455 Mill Run Circle
P. O. Box 1010
Owings Mills, MD 21117

CHAMPUS CLAIM OFFICE
Palmetto Government Benefits Administrators
P. O. Box 100502
Florence, SC 29501-0502

CHAMPVA CLAIM OFFICE
CHAMPVA Center
4500 Cherry Creek Drive, South
Box 65024
Denver, CO 80206-9024

INSURANCE COMMISSIONER STATE OFFICE
Insurance Commissioner
501 St. Paul Place, 7th Floor
Baltimore, MD 21202

MATERNAL AND CHILD HEALTH PROGRAM
Specialty Care, Office of Children's Health
Department of Health and Mental Hygiene
201 W. Preston Street
Baltimore, MD 21201

Maternal Health and Family Planning
Department of Health and Mental Hygiene
201 W. Preston Street, Room 318
Baltimore, MD 21201

MEDICAID FISCAL AGENT
Medical Care Operations Administration
P. O. Box 1935
Baltimore, MD 21203

MEDICARE DURABLE MEDICAL EQUIPMENT
AdminaStar Federal Incorporated
P. O. Box 7078
Indianapolis, IN 46206-0240

MEDICARE FISCAL AGENT OR CARRIER
Counties of Montgomery and Prince George's:
Medicare/Pennsylvania Blue Shield
P. O. Box 890100
Camp Hill, PA 17089-0100

Rest of State:
Blue Cross and Blue Shield of Maryland, Inc.
1946 Greenspring Drive
Timonium, MD 21093

MEDICARE RAILROAD RETIREE CARRIER
The MetraHealth Insurance Company
Railroad Medicare Service Center
P. O. Box 10066
Augusta, GA 30999-0001

STATE BOARD OF MEDICAL EXAMINERS
Maryland Board of Physician Quality Assurance
4201 Patterson Avenue, 3rd Floor
P. O. Box 2571
Baltimore, MD 21215-0095

VETERANS ADMINISTRATION INSTALLATION
Maryland Medical Centers:
Baltimore 21201 (Prosthetic Assessment Information Center, 103 E. Gay Street)
Baltimore 21201 (10 N. Greene Street)
Fort Howard 21052 (N. Point Road)
Perry Point 21902

WORKERS' COMPENSATION FEDERAL DISTRICT OFFICE
Office of Workers' Compensation Programs
800 N. Capitol Street, N.W., Room 800
Washington, DC 20211

WORKERS' COMPENSATION STATE PLAN OFFICE
Workers' Compensation Commission
6 N. Liberty Street
Baltimore, MD 21201

Massachusetts

BLUE CROSS & BLUE SHIELD
Blue Cross and Blue Shield of Massachusetts, Inc.
100 Summer Street
Boston, MA 02110

CHAMPUS CLAIM OFFICE
UNISYS Corporation
P. O. Box 3063
Columbus, IN 47202-3063

CHAMPVA CLAIM CENTER
CHAMPVA Center
4500 Cherry Creek Drive, South
Box 65024
Denver, CO 80206-9024

INSURANCE COMMISSIONER STATE OFFICE
Commissioner of Insurance
470 Atlantic Avenue, 6th Floor
Boston, MA 02210-2223

MATERNAL AND CHILD HEALTH PROGRAM
Bureau of Family & Community Health
Massachusetts Department of Public Health
250 Washington Street, 5th Floor
Boston, MA 02108-4619

MEDICAID FISCAL AGENT
Paramax Corporation
P. O. Box 9102
Somerville, MA 02145

MEDICARE DURABLE MEDICAL EQUIPMENT
MetraHealth, Inc.
320 S. Pennsylvania Boulevard, Suite 339
Wilkes-Barre, PA 18701-2215

MEDICARE FISCAL AGENT OR CARRIER
For Nonassigned Claims:
Medicare/C & S Administrative Services
P. O. Box 1000
Hingham, MA 02044-9191

For Assigned Claims:
Medicare/C & S Administrative Services
P. O. Box 2222
Hingham, MA 02044-9193 and -7030

MEDICARE RAILROAD RETIREE CARRIER
The MetraHealth Insurance Company
Railroad Medicare Service Center
P. O. Box 10066
Augusta, GA 30999-0001

STATE BOARD OF MEDICAL EXAMINERS
Massachusetts Board of Registration in Medicine
Ten West Street, 3rd Floor
Boston, MA 02111

VETERANS ADMINISTRATION INSTALLATION
Massachusetts Medical Centers:
Bedford 01730 (200 Spring Road)
Boston 02130 (150 S. Huntington Avenue)
Brockton 02401 (940 Belmont Street)
Northampton 01060 (421 N. Main Street)
West Roxbury 02132 (1400 VFW Parkway)

WORKERS' COMPENSATION FEDERAL DISTRICT OFFICE
Office of Workers' Compensation Programs
JFK Federal Building, Room E 260
Boston, MA 02203

WORKERS' COMPENSATION STATE PLAN OFFICE
Department of Industrial Accidents
600 Washington Street, 7th Floor
Boston, MA 02111

Michigan

BLUE CROSS & BLUE SHIELD
Blue Cross and Blue Shield of Michigan
600 Lafayette East
Detroit, MI 48226-2998

CHAMPUS CLAIM OFFICE
UNISYS Corporation
P. O. Box 3053
Columbus, IN 47202-3053

CHAMPVA CLAIM OFFICE
CHAMPVA Center
4500 Cherry Creek Drive, South
Box 65024
Denver, CO 80206-9024

INSURANCE COMMISSIONER STATE OFFICE
Commissioner of Insurance
Insurance Bureau
611 West Ottawa Street
2nd Floor North
Lansing, MI 48933

MATERNAL AND CHILD HEALTH PROGRAM
Bureau of Child & Family Services
Michigan Department of Public Health
3423 N. Martin Luther King Jr. Blvd.
Lansing, MI 48909

DSCC/Children's Special Health Care Services
Michigan Department of Public Health
3423 N. Logan Street
P. O. Box 30195
Lansing, MI 48909-0195

MEDICAID FISCAL AGENT
Medical Service Administration
P. O. Box 30037
Lansing, MI 48909

MEDICARE DURABLE MEDICAL EQUIPMENT
AdminaStar Federal Incorporated
P. O. Box 7078
Indianapolis, IN 46206-0240

MEDICARE FISCAL AGENT OR CARRIER
Medicare Part B
Blue Cross & Blue Shield of Michigan
P. O. Box 2201
Detroit, MI 48231-2201

MEDICARE RAILROAD RETIREE CARRIER
The MetraHealth Insurance Company
Railroad Medicare Service Center
P. O. Box 10066
Augusta, GA 30999-0001

STATE BOARD OF MEDICAL EXAMINERS
Michigan Board of Medicine
611 W. Ottawa Street, 4th Floor, 48933
P. O. Box 30018
Lansing, MI 48909-7518

Michigan Board of Osteopathic Medicine & Surgery
611 W. Ottawa Street, 4th Floor, 48933
P. O. Box 30018
Lansing, MI 48909-7518

VETERANS ADMINISTRATION INSTALLATION
Michigan Medical Centers:
Allen Park 48101 (Southfield & Outer Drive)
Ann Arbor 48105 (2215 Fuller Road)
Battle Creek 49016 (5500 Armstrong Road)
Iron Mountain 49801 (H Street)
Saginaw 48602 (100 Weiss Street)

WORKERS' COMPENSATION FEDERAL DISTRICT OFFICE
Office of Workers' Compensation Programs
1240 E. Ninth Street, Room 851
Cleveland, OH 44199

WORKERS' COMPENSATION STATE PLAN OFFICE
Board of Magistrates
201 N. Washington Square
P. O. Box 30016
Lansing, MI 48909

Bureau of Workers' Disability Compensation
Department of Labor
201 N. Washington Square
P. O. Box 30016
Lansing, MI 48909

Workers' Compensation Appellate Commission
Department of Labor
7150 Harris Drive
P. O. Box 30015
Lansing, MI 48909

Minnesota

BLUE CROSS & BLUE SHIELD
Blue Cross and Blue Shield of Minnesota
3535 Blue Cross Road (55122)
P. O. Box 64560
St. Paul, MN 55164-0560

CHAMPUS CLAIM OFFICE
Palmetto Government Benefits Administrators
P. O. Box 100598
Florence, SC 29501-0598

Beginning April, 1997, TriWest Healthcare Alliance will be the fiscal intermediary. Read your CHAMPUS bulletin for the address information.

CHAMPVA CLAIM OFFICE
CHAMPVA Center
4500 Cherry Creek Drive, South
Box 65024
Denver, CO 80206-9024

INSURANCE COMMISSIONER STATE OFFICE
Commissioner of Commerce
133 E. 7th Street
St. Paul, MN 55101

MATERNAL AND CHILD HEALTH PROGRAM
Division of Family Health
Minnesota Department of Health
717 S.E. Delaware Street
P. O. Box 9441
Minneapolis, MN 55440-9441

Department of Health
Children with Special Health Needs
717 S.E. Delaware Street
P. O. Box 9441
Minneapolis, MN 55440-9441

MEDICAID FISCAL AGENT
Department of Human Services (EC)
444 Lafayette Road
St. Paul, MN 55155

MEDICARE DURABLE MEDICAL EQUIPMENT
AdminaStar Federal Incorporated
P. O. Box 7078
Indianapolis, IN 46206-0240

MEDICARE FISCAL AGENT OR CARRIER
Counties of Anoka, Dakota, Fillmore, Goodhue, Hennepin, Houston, Olmsted, Ramsey, Wabasha, Washington, Winona:
Medicare/The Travelers Insurance Company
8120 Penn Avenue, South
Bloomington, MN 55431

Rest of State:
Medicare/Blue Cross & Blue Shield of Minnesota
P. O. Box 64357
St. Paul, MN 55164

MEDICARE RAILROAD RETIREE CARRIER
The MetraHealth Insurance Company
Railroad Medicare Service Center
P. O. Box 30050
Salt Lake City, UT 84130-0050

STATE BOARD OF MEDICAL EXAMINERS
Minnesota Board of Medical Practice
2700 University Avenue West, Suite 106
St. Paul, MN 55144-1080

VETERANS ADMINISTRATION INSTALLATION
Minnesota Medical Centers:
Minneapolis 55417 (One Veterans Drive)
St. Cloud 56303 (4801 8th Street, North)

WORKERS' COMPENSATION FEDERAL DISTRICT OFFICE
Office of Workers' Compensation Programs
230 S. Dearborn Street, 8th Floor
Chicago, IL 60604

WORKERS' COMPENSATION STATE PLAN OFFICE
Workers' Compensation Court of Appeals
25 Constitution Avenue, Suite 405
St. Paul, MN 55155

WORKERS' COMPENSATION DIVISION
Department of Labor and Industry
443 Lafayette Road
St. Paul, MN 55155

Mississippi

BLUE CROSS & BLUE SHIELD
Blue Cross and Blue Shield of Mississippi
P. O. Box 1043
Jackson, MS 39215-1043

CHAMPUS/TRICARE CLAIM OFFICE
Palmetto Government Benefits Administrators
P. O. Box 202000
Florence, SC 29502-2000

CHAMPVA CLAIM OFFICE
CHAMPVA Center
4500 Cherry Creek Drive, South
Box 65024
Denver, CO 80206-9024

INSURANCE COMMISSIONER STATE OFFICE
Commissioner of Insurance
1804 Walter Sillers Building
Jackson, MS 39205

MATERNAL AND CHILD HEALTH PROGRAM
Bureau of Health Services
Mississippi State Health Department
2423 N. State Street
P. O. Box 1700
Jackson, MS 39215-1700

Children and Adolescent Health
Mississippi State Health Department
2423 N. State Street
P. O. Box 1700
Jackson, MS 39215-1700

MEDICAID FISCAL AGENT
First Health Services (EC)
P. O. Box 23076
Jackson, MS 39225

MEDICARE DURABLE MEDICAL EQUIPMENT
Palmetto Government Benefits Administrators
Medicare DMERC Operations
P. O. Box 100141
Columbia, SC 29202-3141

MEDICARE FISCAL AGENT OR CARRIER
Medicare/The Travelers Insurance Company
P. O. Box 22545
Jackson, MS 39225-2545

MEDICARE RAILROAD RETIREE CARRIER
The MetraHealth Insurance Company
Railroad Medicare Service Center
P. O. Box 10066
Augusta, GA 30999-0001

STATE BOARD OF MEDICAL EXAMINERS
Mississippi State Board of Medical Licensure
2688-D Insurance Center Drive
Jackson, MS 39216

VETERANS ADMINISTRATION INSTALLATION
Mississippi Medical Centers:
Biloxi 39531 (400 Veterans Avenue)
Jackson 39216 (1500 E. Woodrow Wilson Drive)

WORKERS' COMPENSATION FEDERAL DISTRICT OFFICE
Office of Workers' Compensation Programs
214 N. Hogan Street, Suite 1006
Jacksonville, FL 32202

WORKERS' COMPENSATION STATE PLAN OFFICE
Workers' Compensation Commission
1428 Lakeland Drive
P. O. Box 5300
Jackson, MS 39296-5300

Missouri

BLUE CROSS & BLUE SHIELD
Blue Cross and Blue Shield of Kansas City
P. O. Box 419169
Kansas City, MO 64141-6169

Alliance Blue Cross Blue Shield
1831 Chestnut Street
St. Louis, MO 63103-2275

CHAMPUS CLAIM OFFICE
Wisconsin Physicians Service
P. O. Box 8932
Madison, WI 53708-8932

Beginning April, 1997, TriWest Healthcare Alliance will be the fiscal intermediary. Read your CHAMPUS bulletin for the address information.

CHAMPVA CLAIM OFFICE
CHAMPVA Center
4500 Cherry Creek Drive, South
Box 65024
Denver, CO 80206-9024

INSURANCE COMMISSIONER STATE OFFICE
Department of Insurance
301 W. High Street
6 North
Jefferson City, MO 65102-0690

MATERNAL AND CHILD HEALTH PROGRAM
Bureau of Special Health Care Needs
Missouri Department of Health
1730 E. Elm Street
P. O. Box 570
Jefferson City, MO 65102-0570

Division of Maternal, Child & Family Health
Missouri Department of Health
1730 E. Elm Street
P. O. Box 570
Jefferson City, MO 65102-0570

MEDICAID FISCAL AGENT
GTE Data Services (EC)
P. O. Box 5600
Jefferson City, MO 65102

MEDICARE DURABLE MEDICAL EQUIPMENT
Connecticut General Life Insurance
DMERC-CIGNA Medicare
P. O. Box 690
Nashville, TN 37320

MEDICARE FISCAL AGENT OR CARRIER
Counties of Andrew, Atchison, Bates, Benton, Buchanan, Caldwell, Carroll, Cass, Clay, Clinton, Daviess, DeKalb, Gentry, Grundy, Harrison, Henry, Holt, Jackson, Johnson, Lafayette, Livingston, Mercer, Nodaway, Pettis, Platte, Ray, St. Clair, Saline, Vernon, Worth:
Medicare/Blue Cross & Blue Shield of Kansas, Inc.
P. O. Box 41980
Kansas City, MO 64141-6840

Rest of State:
General American Life Insurance Company
P. O. Box 505
St. Louis, MO 63166

MEDICARE RAILROAD RETIREE CARRIER
The MetraHealth Insurance Company
Railroad Medicare Service Center
P. O. Box 30050
Salt Lake City, UT 84130-0050

STATE BOARD OF MEDICAL EXAMINERS
Missouri State Board of Registration for the Healing Arts
3605 Missouri Boulevard (65109)
P. O. Box 4
Jefferson City, MO 65102

VETERANS ADMINISTRATION INSTALLATION
Missouri Medical Centers:
Columbia 65201 (800 Hospital Drive)
Kansas City 64128 (4801 Linwood Blvd.)
Poplar Bluff 63901 (1500 N. Westwood Blvd.)
St. Louis 63106 (John Cochran Division, 915 N. Grand Boulevard)
St. Louis 63125 (Jefferson Barracks Division)

WORKERS' COMPENSATION FEDERAL DISTRICT OFFICE
Office of Workers' Compensation Programs
911 Walnut Street
Kansas City, MO 64106

WORKERS' COMPENSATION STATE PLAN OFFICE
Division of Workers' Compensation
Department of Labor and Industrial Relations
3315 W. Truman Blvd.
P. O. Box 58
Jefferson City, MO 65102

Labor and Industrial Relations
3315 W. Truman Blvd.
P. O. Box 599
Jefferson City, MO 65102

Montana

BLUE CROSS & BLUE SHIELD
Blue Cross and Blue Shield of Montana, Inc.
P. O. Box 4309
Great Falls, MT 59604-4309

CHAMPUS CLAIM OFFICE
Palmetto Government Benefits Administrators
P. O. Box 870020
Surfside Beach, SC 29587-8720

CHAMPVA CLAIM OFFICE
CHAMPVA Center
4500 Cherry Creek Drive, South
Box 65024
Denver, CO 80206-9024

Beginning April, 1997, TriWest Healthcare Alliance will be the fiscal intermediary. Read your CHAMPUS bulletin for the address information.

INSURANCE COMMISSIONER STATE OFFICE
Commissioner of Insurance
126 N. Sanders
Mitchell Building, Room 270
Helena, MT 59601

MATERNAL AND CHILD HEALTH PROGRAM
Children's Special Health Services
Department of Public Health and Human Services
Cogswell Building
P. O. Box 202951
Helena, MT 59620

Family/Maternal/Child Health Bureau
Department of Public Health and Human Services
Cogswell Building
P. O. Box 202951
Helena, MT 59620

MEDICAID FISCAL AGENT
Consultec, Inc. (EC)
P. O. Box 8000
Helena, MT 59604

MEDICARE DURABLE MEDICAL EQUIPMENT
Connecticut General Life Insurance
DMERC-CIGNA Medicare
P. O. Box 690
Nashville, TN 37320

MEDICARE FISCAL AGENT OR CARRIER
Medicare/Blue Cross and Blue Shield of Montana, Inc.
2501 Beltview
P. O. Box 4310
Helena, MT 59604

MEDICARE RAILROAD RETIREE CARRIER
The MetraHealth Insurance Company
Railroad Medicare Service Center
P. O. Box 30050
Salt Lake City, UT 84130-0050

STATE BOARD OF MEDICAL EXAMINERS
Montana Board of Medical Examiners
Arcade Building, Lower Level
111 N. Jackson
P. O. Box 200513
Helena, MT 59620-0513

VETERANS ADMINISTRATION INSTALLATION
Montana Regional and Medical Office Center:
Fort Harrison 59636 (William Street off Highway 12 W.)

Montana Medical Center:
Miles City 59301 (210 S. Winchester)

WORKERS' COMPENSATION FEDERAL DISTRICT OFFICE
Office of Workers' Compensation Programs
1801 California Street, Suite 915
Denver, CO 80202-2614

WORKERS' COMPENSATION STATE PLAN OFFICE
Employment Relations Division
P. O. Box 8011
Helena, MT 59604-8011

State Fund Insurance Company
P. O. Box 4759
Helena, MT 59604-4759

Workers' Compensation Court
P. O. Box 537
Helena, MT 59624

Nebraska

BLUE CROSS & BLUE SHIELD
Blue Cross and Blue Shield of Nebraska
P. O. Box 3248
Main Post Office Station
Omaha, NE 68180-0001

CHAMPUS CLAIM OFFICE
Palmetto Government Benefits Administrators
P. O. Box 870020
Surfside Beach, SC 29587-8720

Beginning April, 1997, TriWest Healthcare Alliance will be the fiscal intermediary. Read your CHAMPUS bulletin for the address information.

CHAMPVA CLAIM OFFICE
CHAMPVA Center
4500 Cherry Creek Drive, South
Box 65024
Denver, CO 80206-9024

INSURANCE COMMISSIONER STATE OFFICE
Director of Insurance
941 "O" Street, Suite 400
Lincoln, NE 68508

MATERNAL AND CHILD HEALTH PROGRAM
Section of Family Health
Nebraska Department of Social Services
301 Centennial Mall South, 3rd Floor
P. O. Box 95007
Lincoln, NE 68509-5007

Medically Handicapped Children's Program
Nebraska Department of Social Services
301 Centennial Mall South, 5th Floor
Lincoln, NE 68509-5026

MEDICAID FISCAL AGENT
Department of Social Services (EC)
301 Centennial Mall South, 5th Floor
P. O. Box 9502
Lincoln, NE 68509

MEDICARE DURABLE MEDICAL EQUIPMENT
Connecticut General Life Insurance
DMERC-CIGNA Medicare
P. O. Box 690
Nashville, TN 37320

MEDICARE FISCAL AGENT OR CARRIER
The carrier for Nebraska is Blue Cross and Blue Shield of Kansas, Inc. Claims, however, should be sent to:
Medicare Part B
Blue Cross/Blue Shield of Nebraska
P. O. Box 3106
Omaha, NE 68103-0106

MEDICARE RAILROAD RETIREE CARRIER
The MetraHealth Insurance Company
Railroad Medicare Service Center
P. O. Box 30050
Salt Lake City, UT 84130-0050

STATE BOARD OF MEDICAL EXAMINERS
Nebraska Department of Health
301 Centennial Mall South
P. O. Box 94986
Lincoln, NE 68509-4986

VETERANS ADMINISTRATION INSTALLATION
Nebraska Medical Centers:
Grand Island 68803 (2201 N. Broadwell)
Lincoln 68510 (600 S. 70th Street)
Omaha 68105 (4101 Woolworth Avenue)

WORKERS' COMPENSATION FEDERAL DISTRICT OFFICE
Office of Workers' Compensation Programs
911 Walnut Street
Kansas City, MO 64106

WORKERS' COMPENSATION STATE PLAN OFFICE
Workers' Compensation Court
State House, 12th Floor
P. O. Box 98908
Lincoln, NE 68509-8908

Nevada

BLUE CROSS & BLUE SHIELD
Blue Cross and Blue Shield of Nevada
5250 S. Virginia Street (89502)
P. O. Box 10330
Reno, NV 89520-0330

CHAMPUS CLAIM OFFICE
Palmetto Government Benefits Administrators
P. O. Box 870020
Surfside Beach, SC 29587-8720

Beginning April, 1997, TriWest Healthcare Alliance will be the fiscal intermediary. Read your CHAMPUS bulletin for the address information.

CHAMPVA CLAIM OFFICE
CHAMPVA Center
4500 Cherry Creek Drive, South
Box 65024
Denver, CO 80206-9024

INSURANCE COMMISSIONER STATE OFFICE
Commissioner of Insurance
1665 Hot Springs Road, Suite 152
Carson City, NV 89710

MATERNAL AND CHILD HEALTH PROGRAM
Family Health Services
Nevada State Health Division
505 E. King Street, Room 200
Carson City, NV 89710

MEDICAID FISCAL AGENT OR CARRIER
Blue Cross & Blue Shield of Nevada
P. O. Box 12727
Reno, NV 89510

MEDICARE DURABLE MEDICAL EQUIPMENT
Connecticut General Life Insurance
DMERC-CIGNA Medicare
P. O. Box 690
Nashville, TN 37320

MEDICARE FISCAL AGENT OR CARRIER
Medicare/Blue Cross Blue Shield of North Dakota
4510 13th Avenue, S.W.
Fargo, ND 58121-0001

MEDICARE RAILROAD RETIREE CARRIER
The MetraHealth Insurance Company
Railroad Medicare Service Center
P. O. Box 30050
Salt Lake City, UT 84130-0050

STATE BOARD OF MEDICAL EXAMINERS
Nevada State Board of Medical Examiners
1105 Terminal Way, Suite 301 (89502)
P. O. Box 7238
Reno, NV 89510

Nevada State Board of Osteopathic Medicine
2950 E. Flamingo Road, Suite E-3
Las Vegas, NV 89121-5208

VETERANS ADMINISTRATION INSTALLATION
Nevada Medical Center:
Reno 89520 (1000 Locust Street)
Las Vegas 89102 (1703 W. Charleston)

WORKERS' COMPENSATION FEDERAL DISTRICT OFFICE
Office of Workers' Compensation Programs
71 Stevenson Street, 2nd Floor (94105)
P. O. Box 193769
San Francisco, CA 94119-3769

WORKERS' COMPENSATION STATE PLAN OFFICE
Division of Industrial Relations
400 W. King Street
Carson City, NV 89710

State Industrial Insurance System
515 E. Musser Street
Carson City, NV 89714

New Hampshire

BLUE CROSS & BLUE SHIELD
Blue Cross and Blue Shield of New Hampshire
3000 Goffs Falls Road
Manchester, NH 03111-0001

CHAMPUS CLAIM OFFICE
UNISYS Corporation
P. O. Box 3067
Columbus, IN 47202-3067

CHAMPVA CLAIM OFFICE
CHAMPVA Center
4500 Cherry Creek Drive, South
Box 65024
Denver, CO 80206-9024

INSURANCE COMMISSIONER STATE OFFICE
Insurance Commissioner
169 Manchester Street
Concord, NH 03301

MATERNAL AND CHILD HEALTH PROGRAM
Maternal and Child Health
Division of Public Health Services
6 Hazen Drive
Concord, NH 03301

Office of Family & Community Health
New Hampshire Division of Public Health Services
6 Hazen Drive
Concord, NH 03301

MEDICAID FISCAL AGENT
Electronic Data Systems Federal Corporation (EC)
P. O. Box 2001
Concord, NH 03302

MEDICARE DURABLE MEDICAL EQUIPMENT
MetraHealth, Inc.
320 S. Pennsylvania Boulevard, Suite 339
Wilkes-Barre, PA 18701-2215

MEDICARE FISCAL AGENT OR CARRIER
Medicare/C and S Administrative Services
P. O. Box 1000
Hingham, MA 02044-9191

MEDICARE RAILROAD RETIREE CARRIER
The MetraHealth Insurance Company
Railroad Medicare Service Center
P. O. Box 10066
Augusta, GA 30999-0001

STATE BOARD OF MEDICAL EXAMINERS
New Hampshire Board of Medicine
2 Industrial Park Drive, Suite 8
Concord, NH 03301-8520

New Hampshire Board of Registration in Medicine
Health & Welfare Building
6 Hazen Drive
Concord, NH 03301

VETERANS ADMINISTRATION INSTALLATION
New Hampshire Medical Center:
Manchester 03104 (718 Smyth Road)

WORKERS' COMPENSATION FEDERAL DISTRICT OFFICE
Office of Workers' Compensation Programs
JFK Federal Building, Room E260
Boston, MA 02203

WORKERS' COMPENSATION STATE PLAN OFFICE
Department of Labor
Division of Workers' Compensation
State Office Park South
95 Pleasant Court
Concord, NH 03301

New Jersey

BLUE CROSS & BLUE SHIELD
Blue Cross and Blue Shield of New Jersey, Inc.
3 Penn Plaza, East
Newark, NJ 07105

CHAMPUS CLAIM OFFICE
UNISYS Corporation
P. O. Box 3052
Columbus, IN 47202-3052

CHAMPVA CLAIM OFFICE
CHAMPVA Center
4500 Cherry Creek Drive, South
Box 65024
Denver, CO 80206-9024

INSURANCE COMMISSIONER STATE OFFICE
Commissioner
Department of Insurance
20 West State Street, CN325
Trenton, NJ 08625

MATERNAL AND CHILD HEALTH PROGRAM
Adm MCHS-Family Health Services
New Jersey Department of Health-CN 364
50 E. State Street
Trenton, NJ 08625-0364

Special Child Health Services
New Jersey Department of Health-CN 364
363 W. State Street
Trenton, NJ 08625-0364

MEDICAID FISCAL AGENT
Paramax Corporation (EC)
Unisys, CN 4808
Trenton, NJ 08650

MEDICARE DURABLE MEDICAL EQUIPMENT
MetraHealth, Inc.
320 S. Pennsylvania Boulevard, Suite 339
Wilkes-Barre, PA 18701-2215

MEDICARE FISCAL AGENT OR CARRIER
Medicare/Pennsylvania Blue Shield
P. O. Box 400010
Harrisburg, PA 17140-0010

MEDICARE RAILROAD RETIREE CARRIER
The MetraHealth Insurance Company
Railroad Medicare Service Center
P. O. Box 10066
Augusta, GA 30999-0001

STATE BOARD OF MEDICAL EXAMINERS
New Jersey State Board of Medical Examiners
140 E. Front Street, 2nd Floor
Trenton, NJ 08608

TEMPORARY DISABILITY INSURANCE
New Jersey Department of Labor
Division of Temporary Disability Insurance
CN 387
Trenton, NJ 08625-0387

VETERANS ADMINISTRATION INSTALLATION
New Jersey Medical Centers:
East Orange 07019 (Tremont Avenue)
Lyons 07939 (Valley & Knollkroft Road)

WORKERS' COMPENSATION FEDERAL DISTRICT OFFICE
Office of Workers' Compensation Programs
201 Varick Street, Room 750
P. O. Box 566
New York, NY 10014

WORKERS' COMPENSATION STATE PLAN OFFICE
Department of Labor
Division of Workers' Compensation
CN 381
Trenton, NJ 08625-0381

New Mexico

BLUE CROSS & BLUE SHIELD
Blue Cross and Blue Shield of New Mexico
P. O. Box 27630
Albuquerque, NM 87125-7630

CHAMPUS CLAIM OFFICE
Palmetto Government Benefits Administrators
P. O. Box 870020
Surfside Beach, SC 29587-8720

Beginning April, 1997, TriWest Healthcare Alliance will be the fiscal intermediary. Read your CHAMPUS bulletin for the address information.

CHAMPVA CLAIM OFFICE
CHAMPVA Center
4500 Cherry Creek Drive, South
Box 65024
Denver, CO 80206-9024

INSURANCE COMMISSIONER STATE OFFICE
Superintendent of Insurance
P. O. Drawer 1269
Santa Fe, NM 87504-1269

MATERNAL AND CHILD HEALTH PROGRAM
Children's Medical Services
New Mexico Department of Health
1190 St. Francis Drive
P. O. Box 26110
Santa Fe, NM 87502

Maternal & Child Health Bureau
New Mexico Department of Health and Environment
1190 St. Francis Drive
P. O. Box 26110
Santa Fe, NM 87502

MEDICAID FISCAL AGENT
First Health
P. O. Box 25118
Santa Fe, NM 85704

MEDICARE DURABLE MEDICAL EQUIPMENT
Palmetto Government Benefits Administrators
Medicare DMERC Operations
P. O. Box 10041
Columbia, SC 29202-3141

MEDICARE FISCAL AGENT OR CARRIER
Medicare/Arkansas Blue Cross Blue Shield
P. O. Box 1418
Little Rock, AR 72203-1418

MEDICARE RAILROAD RETIREE CARRIER
The MetraHealth Insurance Company
Railroad Medicare Service Center
P. O. Box 30050
Salt Lake City, UT 84130-0050

STATE BOARD OF MEDICAL EXAMINERS
New Mexico State Board of Medical Examiners
Lamy Building, 2nd Floor
491 Old Santa Fe Trail
Santa Fe, NM 87501

New Mexico Board of Osteopathic Medical Examiners
725 St. Michaels Drive (87501)
P. O. Box 25101
Santa Fe, NM 87504

VETERANS ADMINISTRATION INSTALLATION
New Mexico Medical Center:
Albuquerque 87108 (2100 Ridgecrest Drive, S.E.)

WORKERS' COMPENSATION FEDERAL DISTRICT OFFICE
Office of Workers' Compensation Program
525 Griffin Street
Dallas, TX 75202

WORKERS' COMPENSATION STATE PLAN OFFICE
Workers' Compensation Administration
1820 Randolph Road, S.E.
P. O. Box 27198
Albuquerque, NM 87125-7198

New York

BLUE CROSS & BLUE SHIELD
Blue Cross & Blue Shield of Central New York, Inc.
P. O. Box 4809
Syracuse, NY 13221-4809

Blue Cross & Blue Shield of the Rochester Area
Finger Lakes Health Insurance Co., Inc.
150 E. Main Street
Rochester, NY 14647

Blue Cross & Blue Shield of Utica-Watertown, Inc.
12 Rhoads Drive, Utica Business Park
Utica, NY 13502-6398

Blue Cross & Blue Shield of Western New York, Inc.
P. O. Box 80
Buffalo, NY 14240-0080

Empire Blue Cross & Blue Shield
P. O. Box 345
New York, NY 10163-0345

CHAMPUS CLAIM OFFICE
UNISYS Corporation:

For Zip Codes 10000-12999:
P. O. Box 3051
Columbus, IN 47202-3051

For Zip Codes 13000-14999:
P. O. Box 3050
Columbus, IN 47202-3050

CHAMPVA CLAIM OFFICE
CHAMPVA Center
4500 Cherry Creek Drive, South
Box 65024
Denver, CO 80206-9024

DISABILITY BENEFITS BUREAU
Workers' Compensation Board
Disability Benefits Bureau
100 Broadway—Menands
Albany, NY 12241

INSURANCE COMMISSIONER STATE OFFICE
Superintendent of Insurance
160 W. Broadway
New York, NY 10013-3393

Agency Building One
Empire State Plaza
Albany, NY 12257

MATERNAL AND CHILD HEALTH PROGRAM
State Department of Health
Center for Community Health
Empire State, Corning Tower Building, Room 612
Albany, NY 12237

MEDICAID FISCAL AGENT
Computer Sciences Corporation (EC)
P. O. Box 4444
Albany, NY 12204

MEDICARE DURABLE MEDICAL EQUIPMENT
MetraHealth, Inc.
320 S. Pennsylvania Boulevard, Suite 339
Wilkes-Barre, PA 18701-2215

MEDICARE FISCAL AGENT OR CARRIER
Counties of: Nassau, Suffolk
Medicare B/Empire Blue Cross and Blue Shield
P. O. Box 2280
Peekskill, New York 10566

Counties of: Bronx, Columbia, Delaware, Greene, Kings, New York, Orange, Putnam, Richmond, Rockland, Suffolk, Ulster, Westchester
Medicare B/Empire Blue Cross and Blue Shield
P. O. Box 2280
Peekskill, New York 10566

County of: Queens
Medicare/Group Health, Inc.
P. O. Box 1608, Ansonia Station
New York, New York 10023

Rest of State:
Blue Shield of Western New York
Upstate Medicare Division-Part B
7-9 Court Street
Binghamton, New York 13901-3197

MEDICARE RAILROAD RETIREE CARRIER
The MetraHealth Insurance Company
Railroad Medicare Service Center
P. O. Box 10066
Augusta, GA 30999-0001

STATE BOARD OF MEDICAL EXAMINERS
New York State Board for Medicine
Cultural Education Center, Room 3023
Empire State Plaza
Albany, NY 12230

New York State Board for Professional Medical Conduct
New York State Department of Health
Office of Professional Medical Conduct
Room 438, Corning Tower Building
Albany, NY 12237-0756

TEMPORARY DISABILITY INSURANCE
Workers' Compensation Board
Disability Benefits Bureau
100 Broadway (Menands)
Albany, NY 12241

VETERANS ADMINISTRATION INSTALLATION
New York Medical Centers:
- Albany 12208 (113 Holland Avenue)
- Batavia 14020 (222 Richmond Avenue)
- Bath 14810 (Veterans Avenue)
- Bronx 10406 (130 W. Kingsbridge Road)
- Brooklyn 11209 (800 Poly Place)
- Buffalo 14215 (3495 Bailey Avenue)
- Canandaigua 14424 (Fort Hill Avenue)
- Castle Point 12511 (Route 9D)
- Montrose 10548 (Route 9A)
- New York City 10010 (423 E. 23rd Street)
- Northport 11749 (79 Middleville Road)
- Syracuse 13210 (800 Irvine Avenue)

WORKERS' COMPENSATION FEDERAL DISTRICT OFFICE
Office of Workers' Compensation Programs
201 Varick Street, Room 750
P. O. Box 566
New York, NY 10014

WORKERS' COMPENSATION STATE PLAN OFFICE
Workers' Compensation Board
180 Livingston Street
Brooklyn, NY 11248

North Carolina

BLUE CROSS & BLUE SHIELD
Blue Cross and Blue Shield of North Carolina
P. O. Box 2291
Durham, NC 27702

CHAMPUS CLAIM OFFICE
Palmetto Government Benefits Administrators
P. O. Box 100502
Florence, SC 29501-0502

CHAMPVA CLAIM OFFICE
CHAMPVA Center
4500 Cherry Creek Drive, South
Box 65024
Denver, CO 80206-9024

INSURANCE COMMISSIONER STATE OFFICE
Commissioner of Insurance
Dobbs Building
430 N. Salisbury Street
Raleigh, NC 27603

MATERNAL AND CHILD HEALTH PROGRAM
Children & Youth Section
Division of Maternal & Child Health
Department of Environment, Health, and Natural Resources
P. O. Box 27687
Raleigh, NC 27611-7687

Division of Maternal and Child Health
Department of Environment, Health, and Natural Resources
P. O. Box 27687
Raleigh, NC 27611-7687

MEDICAID FISCAL AGENT
Electronic Data Systems Federal Corporation (EC)
P. O. Box 30968
Raleigh, NC 27622

MEDICARE DURABLE MEDICAL EQUIPMENT
Palmetto Government Benefits Administrators
Medicare DMERC Operations
P. O. Box 100141
Columbia, SC 29202-3141

MEDICARE FISCAL AGENT OR CARRIER
Connecticut General Life Insurance Company
P. O. Box 671
Nashville, TN 37202

MEDICARE RAILROAD RETIREE CARRIER
The MetraHealth Insurance Company
Railroad Medicare Service Center
P. O. Box 10066
Augusta, GA 30999-0001

STATE BOARD OF MEDICAL EXAMINERS
North Carolina Medical Board
203 Front Street (27609)
P. O. Box 20007
Raleigh, NC 27619-0007

VETERANS ADMINISTRATION INSTALLATION
North Carolina Medical Centers:
Asheville 28805 (1100 Tunnel Road)
Durham 27705 (508 Fulton Street)
Fayetteville 28301 (2300 Ramsey Street)
Salisbury 28144 (1601 Brenner Avenue)

WORKERS' COMPENSATION FEDERAL DISTRICT OFFICE
Office of Workers' Compensation Programs
214 N. Hogan Street, Suite 1006
Jacksonville, FL 32202

WORKERS' COMPENSATION STATE PLAN OFFICE
Industrial Commission
Dobbs Building
430 N. Salisbury Street
Raleigh, NC 27611

North Dakota

BLUE CROSS & BLUE SHIELD
Blue Cross/Blue Shield of North Dakota
4510 13th Avenue, S.W.
Fargo, ND 58121-0001

CHAMPUS CLAIM OFFICE
Palmetto Government Benefits Administrators
P. O. Box 870020
Surfside Beach, SC 29587-8720

Beginning April, 1997, TriWest Healthcare Alliance will be the fiscal intermediary. Read your CHAMPUS bulletin for the address information.

CHAMPVA CLAIM OFFICE
CHAMPVA Center
4500 Cherry Creek Drive, South
Box 65024
Denver, CO 80206-9024

INSURANCE COMMISSIONER STATE OFFICE
Commissioner of Insurance
600 East Boulevard Avenue
Bismarck, ND 58505-0320

MATERNAL AND CHILD HEALTH PROGRAM
Children's Special Health Services
State Department of Health
600 E. Boulevard Avenue
Bismarck, ND 58505-0269

Division of Maternal and Child Health
State Health Department
600 E. Boulevard Avenue
Bismarck, ND 58505-0251

MEDICAID FISCAL AGENT
Department of Human Services (EC)
600 E. Boulevard Avenue
Bismarck, ND 58505

MEDICARE DURABLE MEDICAL EQUIPMENT
Connecticut General Life Insurance
DMERC-CIGNA Medicare
P. O. Box 690
Nashville, TN 37320

MEDICARE FISCAL AGENT OR CARRIER
Medicare/Blue Shield of North Dakota
4510 13th Avenue, S.W.
Fargo, ND 58121-0001

MEDICARE RAILROAD RETIREE CARRIER
The MetraHealth Insurance Company
Railroad Medicare Service Center
P. O. Box 30050
Salt Lake City, UT 84130-0050

STATE BOARD OF MEDICAL EXAMINERS
North Dakota State Board of Medical Examiners
City Center Plaza
418 E. Broadway, Suite 12
Bismarck, ND 58501

VETERANS ADMINISTRATION INSTALLATION
North Dakota Medical Center
2101 Elm Street
Fargo, ND 58102

WORKERS' COMPENSATION FEDERAL DISTRICT OFFICE
Office of Workers' Compensation Programs
1801 California Street, Suite 915
Denver, CO 80202-2614

WORKERS' COMPENSATION STATE PLAN OFFICE
Workers' Compensation Bureau
500 E. Front Avenue
Bismarck, ND 58504-5685

Ohio

BLUE CROSS & BLUE SHIELD
Blue Cross and Blue Shield of Ohio
2060 E. Ninth Street
Cleveland, OH 44115-1355

Anthem Blue Cross and Blue Shield
1351 William Howard Taft Road
Cincinnati, OH 45206

CHAMPUS CLAIM OFFICE
Palmetto Government Benefits Administrators
P. O. Box 100598
Florence, SC 29501-0598

CHAMPVA CLAIM OFFICE
CHAMPVA Center
4500 Cherry Creek Drive, South
Box 65024
Denver, CO 80206-9024

INSURANCE COMMISSIONER STATE OFFICE
Director of Insurance
2100 Stella Court
Columbus, OH 43215

MATERNAL AND CHILD HEALTH PROGRAM
Division of Family and Community Health Services
Ohio Department of Public Health
246 N. High Street
P. O. Box 118
Columbus, OH 43266-0118

Ohio Department of Public Health
Bureau for Children with Medical Handicaps
P. O. Box 1603
Columbus, OH 43216-1603

MEDICAID FISCAL AGENT
Electronic Data Systems Federal Corporation (EC)
P. O. Box 1461
Columbus, OH 43266

MEDICARE DURABLE MEDICAL EQUIPMENT
AdminaStar Federal Incorporated
P. O. Box 7078
Indianapolis, IN 46206-0240

MEDICARE FISCAL AGENT OR CARRIER
Medicare/Nationwide Mutual Insurance Company
P. O. Box 57
Columbus, OH 43216

MEDICARE RAILROAD RETIREE CARRIER
The MetraHealth Insurance Company
Railroad Medicare Service Center
P. O. Box 10066
Augusta, GA 30999-0001

STATE BOARD OF MEDICAL EXAMINERS
Ohio State Medical Board
77 S. High Street, 17th Floor
Columbus, OH 43266-0315

VETERANS ADMINISTRATION INSTALLATION
Ohio Medical Centers:
Brecksville 44141 (10000 Brecksville Road)
Chillicothe 45601 (17273 State Route #104)
Cincinnati 45220 (3200 Vine Street)
Cleveland 44106 (10701 East Blvd.)
Dayton 45428 (4100 W. 3rd Street)

WORKERS' COMPENSATION FEDERAL DISTRICT OFFICE
Office of Workers' Compensation Programs
1240 E. Ninth Street, Room 851
Cleveland, OH 44199

WORKERS' COMPENSATION STATE PLAN OFFICE
Industrial Commission
30 W. Spring Street
Columbus, OH 43266-0581

Bureau of Workers' Compensation
30 W. Spring Street
Columbus, OH 43266-0581

Oklahoma

BLUE CROSS & BLUE SHIELD
Blue Cross and Blue Shield of Oklahoma
P. O. Box 3283
Tulsa, OK 74102-3283

CHAMPUS/TRICARE CLAIM OFFICE
Foundation Health Federal Services
c/o Wisconsin Physicians Service
P. O. Box 8999
Madison, WI 53708

CHAMPVA CLAIM OFFICE
CHAMPVA Center
4500 Cherry Creek Drive, South
Box 65024
Denver, CO 80206-9024

INSURANCE COMMISSIONER STATE OFFICE
Insurance Commissioner
1901 North Walnut
Oklahoma City, OK 73105

MATERNAL AND CHILD HEALTH PROGRAM
Family Support Services
Department of Human Services
P. O. Box 25352
Oklahoma City, OK 73125

Child Health and Guidance Service
Oklahoma State Department of Health
1000 N.E. Tenth Street
P. O. Box 53551
Oklahoma City, OK 73117-1299

MEDICAID FISCAL AGENT
Paramax Corporation (EC)
P. O. Box 54740
Oklahoma City, OK 73154

MEDICARE DURABLE MEDICAL EQUIPMENT
Palmetto Government Benefits Administrators

Medicare DMERC Operations
P. O. Box 100141
Columbia, SC 29202-3141

MEDICARE FISCAL AGENT OR CARRIER
Medicare/Arkansas Blue Cross Blue Shield
P.O. Box 1418
Little Rock, AR 72203-1418

MEDICARE RAILROAD RETIREE CARRIER
The MetraHealth Insurance Company
Railroad Medicare Service Center
P. O. Box 30050
Salt Lake City, UT 84130-0050

STATE BOARD OF MEDICAL EXAMINERS
Oklahoma State Board of Medical Licensure & Supervision
5104 N. Francis, Suite C (73118)
P. O. Box 18256
Oklahoma City, OK 73154-0256

Oklahoma State Board of Osteopathic Examiners
4848 N. Lincoln Boulevard, Suite 100
Oklahoma City, OK 73105-3321

VETERANS ADMINISTRATION INSTALLATION
Oklahoma Medical Centers:
Muskogee 74401 (Honor Heights Drive)
Oklahoma City 73104 (921 N.E. 13th Street)

WORKERS' COMPENSATION FEDERAL DISTRICT OFFICE
Office of Workers' Compensation Programs
525 Griffin Street
Dallas, TX 75202

WORKERS' COMPENSATION STATE PLAN OFFICE
Oklahoma Workers' Compensation Court
1915 N. Stiles
Oklahoma City, OK 73105

Oregon

BLUE CROSS & BLUE SHIELD
Blue Cross and Blue Shield of Oregon
P. O. Box 1271
Portland, OR 97207

CHAMPUS/TRICARE CLAIM OFFICE
Foundation Health Federal Services
P. O. Box 419010
Rancho Cordova, CA 94741

CHAMPVA CLAIM OFFICE
CHAMPVA Center
4500 Cherry Creek Drive, South
Box 65024
Denver, CO 80206-9024

INSURANCE COMMISSIONER STATE OFFICE
Director of Insurance
350 Winter Street, N.E.
Room 200
Salem, OR 97310-0700

MATERNAL AND CHILD HEALTH PROGRAM
Oregon State Health Division
800 N.E. Oregon Street #21, Suite 850
Portland, OR 97232

Child Development and Rehabilitation Center
Oregon Health Sciences University
P. O. Box 574
Portland, OR 97207

MEDICAID FISCAL AGENT
Department of Human Resources (EC)
203 Public Service Building
Salem, OR 97310

MEDICARE DURABLE MEDICAL EQUIPMENT
Connecticut General Life Insurance
DMERC-CIGNA Medicare
P. O. Box 690
Nashville, TN 37320

MEDICARE FISCAL AGENT OR CARRIER
Medicare/Blue Cross Blue Shield of North Dakota
4510 13th Avenue, S.W.
Fargo, ND 58121-0001

MEDICARE RAILROAD RETIREE CARRIER
The MetraHealth Insurance Company
Railroad Medicare Service Center
P. O. Box 30050
Salt Lake City, UT 84130-0050

STATE BOARD OF MEDICAL EXAMINERS
Oregon Board of Medical Examiners
620 Crown Plaza
1500 S.W. First Avenue
Portland, OR 97201-5826

VETERANS ADMINISTRATION INSTALLATION
Oregon Medical Centers:
Portland 97207 (3710 S.W. U.S. Veterans Hospital Road)
Roseburg 97470 (913 N.W. New Gaden Valley Blvd.)

WORKERS' COMPENSATION FEDERAL DISTRICT OFFICE
Office of Workers' Compensation Programs
1111 Third Avenue, Suite 615
Seattle, WA 98101-3212

WORKERS' COMPENSATION STATE PLAN OFFICE
Department of Consumer and Business Services
21 Labor and Industries Building
Salem, OR 97310

Workers' Compensation Board
2250 McGilcrist, S.E.
Salem, OR 97310

Pennsylvania

BLUE CROSS & BLUE SHIELD
Blue Cross of Northeastern Pennsylvania
70 N. Main Street
Wilkes-Barre, PA 18711

Blue Cross of Western Pennsylvania
120 Fifth Avenue
Pittsburgh, PA 15222-3099

Capital Blue Cross
2500 Elmerton Avenue
Harrisburg, PA 17110

Independence Blue Cross
1901 Market Street
Philadelphia, PA 19103

Or—Checks Only:
P. O. Box 13400
Philadelphia, PA 19107

Pennsylvania Blue Shield
P. O. Box 890089
Camp Hill, PA 17089-0089

CHAMPUS CLAIM OFFICE
Zip Codes: 15001-15299 and 19001-19199:
UNISYS Corporation
P. O. Box 3074
Columbus, IN 47202-3074

For all other zip codes:
UNISYS Corporation
P. O. Box 3075
Columbus, IN 47202-3075

CHAMPVA CLAIM OFFICE
CHAMPVA Center
4500 Cherry Creek Drive, South
Box 65024
Denver, CO 80206-9024

INSURANCE COMMISSIONER STATE OFFICE
Insurance Commissioner
1326 Strawberry Square, 13th Floor
Harrisburg, PA 17120

MATERNAL AND CHILD HEALTH PROGRAM
Division of Maternal and Child Health
Pennsylvania Department of Health
Room 725, Health and Welfare Building
P. O. Box 90
Harrisburg, PA 17108

Pennsylvania Department of Health
Division of CSCHN
Room 714, Health and Welfare Building
P. O. Box 90
Harrisburg, PA 17108

MEDICAID FISCAL AGENT
Provider Relations (Non-Hospital)
P. O. Box 8046
Harrisburg, PA 17105

MEDICARE DURABLE MEDICAL EQUIPMENT
MetraHealth, Inc.
320 S. Pennsylvania Boulevard, Suite 339
Wilkes-Barre, PA 18701-2215

MEDICARE FISCAL AGENT OR CARRIER
Medicare/Pennsylvania Blue Shield
P. O. Box 890065
Camp Hill, PA 17089-0065

MEDICARE RAILROAD RETIREE CARRIER
The MetraHealth Insurance Company
Railroad Medicare Service Center
P. O. Box 10066
Augusta, GA 30999-0001

STATE BOARD OF MEDICAL EXAMINERS
Pennsylvania State Board of Medicine
116 Pine Street (17101)
124 Pine Street—for Express Mail
P. O. Box 2649
Harrisburg, PA 17105-2649

Pennsylvania State Board of Osteopathic Medicine
116 Pine Street (17105)
124 Pine Street—for Express Mail
P. O. Box 2649
Harrisburg, PA 17105-2649

VETERANS ADMINISTRATION INSTALLATION
Pennsylvania Medical Centers:
Altoona 16602 (2907 Pleasant Valley Blvd.)
Butler 16001 (325 New Castle Road)
Coatesville 19320 (1400 Black Horse Hill Road)
Erie 16504 (135 E. 138th Street)
Lebanon 17042 (1700 S. Lincoln Avenue)
Philadelphia 19104 (University & Woodland Avenues)
Pittsburgh 15206 (7180 Highland Drive)
Pittsburgh 15240 (University Drive C)
Wilkes-Barre 18711 (1111 E. End Blvd.)

WORKERS' COMPENSATION FEDERAL DISTRICT OFFICE
Office of Workers' Compensation Programs
3535 Market Street
Philadelphia, PA 19104

WORKERS' COMPENSATION STATE PLAN OFFICE
Bureau of Workers' Compensation
Department of Labor and Industry
1171 S. Cameron Street, Room 103
Harrisburg, PA 17104-2501

Workers' Compensation Appeal Board
1171 S. Cameron Street, Room 305
Harrisburg, PA 17104-2511

Puerto Rico

BLUE CROSS & BLUE SHIELD
Triple-S
P. O. Box 363628
San Juan, PR 00936-3628

La Cruz Azul de Puerto Rico
P. O. Box 366068
San Juan, PR 00936-6068

CHAMPUS CLAIM OFFICE
Wisconsin Physicians Service
P. O. Box 7985
Madison, WI 53707-7985

CHAMPVA CLAIM OFFICE
CHAMPVA Center
4500 Cherry Creek Drive, South
Box 65024
Denver, CO 80206-9024

INSURANCE COMMISSIONER STATE OFFICE
Commissioner of Insurance
Fernandez Juncos Station
1607 Ponce de Leon Avenue
Santurce, PR 00910

MATERNAL AND CHILD HEALTH PROGRAM
CSHCN Director
Puerto Rico Department of Health
Call Box 70184
San Juan, PR 00936-8184

Maternal Child Health Director
Puerto Rico Department of Health
Call Box 70184
San Juan, PR 00936-8184

MEDICARE DURABLE MEDICAL EQUIPMENT
Palmetto Government Benefits Administration
P. O. Box 100141
Columbia, SC 29202-3141

MEDICARE FISCAL AGENT OR CARRIER
Medicare/Seguros de Servicio de Salud de Puerto Rico
Call Box 71391
San Juan, PR 00936

MEDICARE RAILROAD RETIREE CARRIER
The MetraHealth Insurance Company
Railroad Medicare Service Center
P. O. Box 10066
Augusta, GA 30999-0001

STATE BOARD OF MEDICAL EXAMINERS
Puerto Rico Board of Medical Examiners
Call Box 13969—(Kennedy Avenue, ILA Building, Hogar del Obrero Portuario, Piso & Puerto Nuevo 00920)
San Juan, PR 00908

TEMPORARY DISABILITY INSURANCE
Department of Labor and Human Resources
Bureau of Employment Security
Disability Insurance Program
Prudencio Rivera Martinez Building
505 Munoz Rivera Avenue
Hato Rey, PR 00918

VETERANS ADMINISTRATION INSTALLATION
Puerto Rico Medical Center:
San Juan 00927 (1 Veterans Plaza)

WORKERS' COMPENSATION FEDERAL DISTRICT OFFICE
Office of Workers' Compensation Programs
201 Varick Street, Room 750
P. O. Box 566
New York, NY 10014

WORKERS' COMPENSATION STATE PLAN OFFICE
Corporation of the State Insurance Fund
G.P.O. Box 365028
San Juan, PR 00936-5028

Industrial Commissioner's Office
G.P.O. Box 4466
San Juan, PR 00936

Rhode Island

BLUE CROSS & BLUE SHIELD
Blue Cross & Blue Shield of Rhode Island
444 Westminster Street
Providence, RI 02903-3279

CHAMPUS CLAIM OFFICE
UNISYS Corporation
P. O. Box 3065
Columbus, IN 47202-3065

CHAMPVA CLAIM OFFICE
CHAMPVA Center
4500 Cherry Creek Drive, South
Box 65024
Denver, CO 80206-9024

INSURANCE COMMISSIONER STATE OFFICE
Insurance Commissioner
233 Richmond Street
Providence, RI 02903-4233

MATERNAL AND CHILD HEALTH PROGRAM
Medical Director
Division of Family Health
Rhode Island Department of Health
Three Capitol Hill, Room 302
Providence, RI 02908-5097

MEDICAID FISCAL AGENT
Electronic Data Systems Federal Corporation
P. O. Box 2009
Warwick, RI 02887

MEDICAID RHODE ISLAND
Department of Human Services
600 New London Avenue
Cranston, RI 02920

MEDICARE DURABLE MEDICAL EQUIPMENT
MetraHealth, Inc.
320 S. Pennsylvania Boulevard, Suite 339
Wilkes-Barre, PA 18701-2215

MEDICARE FISCAL AGENT OR CARRIER
Medicare/Blue Cross and Blue Shield of Rhode Island
Inquiry Department
444 Westminster Street
Providence, RI 02903-3279

MEDICARE RAILROAD RETIREE CARRIER
The MetraHealth Insurance Company
Railroad Medicare Service Center
P. O. Box 10066
Augusta, GA 30999-0001

STATE BOARD OF MEDICAL EXAMINERS
Rhode Island Board of Licensure & Discipline
Department of Health
3 Capitol Hill, Room 205
Cannon Building
Providence, RI 02908-5097

TEMPORARY DISABILITY INSURANCE
Department of Employment and Training
Temporary Disability Insurance Division
P. O. Box 1028
Providence, RI 02901-1028

VETERANS ADMINISTRATION INSTALLATION
Rhode Island Medical Center:
Providence 02908 (830 Chalkstone Avenue)

WORKERS' COMPENSATION FEDERAL DISTRICT OFFICE
Office of Workers' Compensation Programs
JFK Federal Building, Room E260
Boston, MA 02203

WORKERS' COMPENSATION STATE PLAN OFFICE
Department of Labor
Division of Workers' Compensation
610 Manton Avenue
P. O. Box 3500
Providence, RI 02909

Workers' Compensation Court
1 Dorrance Plaza
Providence, RI 02903

South Carolina

BLUE CROSS & BLUE SHIELD
Blue Cross and Blue Shield of South Carolina
I-20 East at Alpine Road
Columbia, SC 29219

CHAMPUS/TRICARE CLAIM OFFICE
Palmetto Government Benefits Administrators
P. O. Box 202000
Florence, SC 29502-2000

CHAMPVA CLAIM OFFICE
CHAMPVA Center
4500 Cherry Creek Drive, South
Box 65024
Denver, CO 80206-9024

INSURANCE COMMISSIONER STATE OFFICE
Director, Department of Insurance
1612 Marion Street
P. O. Box 100105
Columbia, SC 29202-3105

MATERNAL AND CHILD HEALTH PROGRAM
Bureau of Maternal and Child Health
Department of Health & Environmental Control
Mills/Jarrett Complex
Box 101106
Columbia, SC 29211

Division of Children's Rehabilitative Services
Department of Health & Environmental Control
Mills/Jarrett Complex
Box 101106
Columbia, SC 29211

MEDICAID FISCAL AGENT
Department of Human Services (EC)
P. O. Box 1412
Columbia, SC 29202

MEDICARE DURABLE MEDICAL EQUIPMENT
Palmetto Government Benefits Administrators
Medicare DMERC Operations
P. O. Box 100141
Columbia, SC 29202-3141

MEDICARE FISCAL AGENT OR CARRIER
Medicare Part B
Blue Cross and Blue Shield of South Carolina
P. O. Box 100190
Columbia, SC 29202

MEDICARE RAILROAD RETIREE CARRIER
The MetraHealth Insurance Company
Railroad Medicare Service Center
P. O. Box 10066
Augusta, GA 30999-0001

STATE BOARD OF MEDICAL EXAMINERS
South Carolina State Board of Medical Examiners
3600 Forest Drive, 29204
P. O. Box 11289
Columbia, SC 29211-1289

VETERANS ADMINISTRATION INSTALLATION
South Carolina Medical Centers:
Charleston 29401 (109 Bee Street)
Columbia 29209 (Gamers Ferry Road)

WORKERS' COMPENSATION FEDERAL DISTRICT OFFICE
Office of Workers' Compensation Programs
214 N. Hogan Street, Suite 1006
Jacksonville, FL 32202

WORKERS' COMPENSATION STATE PLAN OFFICE
Workers' Compensation Commission
1612 Marion Street
P. O. Box 1715
Columbia, SC 29202

South Dakota

BLUE CROSS & BLUE SHIELD
Blue Cross/Blue Shield of South Dakota
1601 W. Madison Street
Sioux Falls, SD 57104

CHAMPUS CLAIM OFFICE
Palmetto Government Benefits Administrators
P. O. Box 870020
Surfside Beach, SC 29587-8720

Beginning April, 1997, TriWest Healthcare Alliance will be the fiscal intermediary. Read your CHAMPUS bulletin for the address information.

CHAMPVA CLAIM OFFICE
CHAMPVA Center
4500 Cherry Creek Drive, South
Box 65024
Denver, CO 80206-9024

INSURANCE COMMISSIONER STATE OFFICE
Director of Insurance
500 E. Capitol
Pierre, SD 57501-3940

MATERNAL AND CHILD HEALTH PROGRAM
Children's Special Health Services
South Dakota Department of Health
445 E. Capitol
Pierre, SD 57501-3185

Office of Family Health
South Dakota Department of Health
445 E. Capitol
Pierre, SD 57501

MEDICAID FISCAL AGENT
Department of Social Services (EC)
Office of Medicaid/Richard F. Kneip Building
700 Governors Drive
Pierre, SD 57501

MEDICARE DURABLE MEDICAL EQUIPMENT
Connecticut General Life Insurance
DMERC-CIGNA Medicare
P. O. Box 690
Nashville, TN 37320

MEDICARE FISCAL AGENT OR CARRIER
Medicare Part B/Blue Shield of North Dakota
4510 13th Avenue, S.W.
Fargo, ND 58121-0001

MEDICARE RAILROAD RETIREE CARRIER
The MetraHealth Insurance Co.
Railroad Medicare Service Center
P. O. Box 30050
Salt Lake City, UT 84130-0050

STATE BOARD OF MEDICAL EXAMINERS
South Dakota State Board of Medical & Osteopathic Examiners
1323 S. Minnesota Avenue
Sioux Falls, SD 57105

VETERANS ADMINISTRATION INSTALLATION
South Dakota Medical Centers:
Fort Meade 57741 (I-90/Highway 34)
Hot Springs 57747 (Off 5th Street)
Sioux Falls 57117 (2501 W. 22nd Street)

WORKERS' COMPENSATION FEDERAL DISTRICT OFFICE
Office of Workers' Compensation Programs
1801 California Street, Suite 915
Denver, CO 80202-2614

WORKERS' COMPENSATION STATE PLAN OFFICE
Division of Labor and Management
Department of Labor
Kneip Building, Third Floor
700 Governors Drive
Pierre, SD 57501-2277

Tennessee

BLUE CROSS & BLUE SHIELD
Blue Cross and Blue Shield of Memphis
(Memphis Hospital Service & Surgical Association, Inc.)
85 N. Danny Thomas Blvd.
Memphis, TN 38103

Blue Cross and Blue Shield of Tennessee
801 Pine Street
Chattanooga, TN 37402

CHAMPUS/TRICARE CLAIM OFFICE
Palmetto Government Benefits Administrators
P. O. Box 202000
Florence, SC 29502-2000

CHAMPVA CLAIM OFFICE
CHAMPVA Center
4500 Cherry Creek Drive, South
Box 65024
Denver, CO 80206-9024

INSURANCE COMMISSIONER STATE OFFICE
Commissioner of Insurance
500 James Robertson Parkway
Nashville, TN 37243-0565

MATERNAL AND CHILD HEALTH PROGRAM
Maternal and Child Health
Tennessee Department of Health
426 5th Avenue, N.
5th Floor, Cordell Hull Building
Nashville, TN 37247-4701

MEDICAID FISCAL AGENT
Medicaid Tennessee
P. O. Box 460
Nashville, TN 37202

MEDICARE DURABLE MEDICAL EQUIPMENT
Palmetto Government Benefits Administrators
Medicare DMERC Operations
P. O. Box 100141
Columbia, SC 29202-3141

MEDICARE FISCAL AGENT OR CARRIER
Connecticut General Life Insurance Company
P. O. Box 1465
Nashville, TN 37202

MEDICARE RAILROAD RETIREE CARRIER
The MetraHealth Insurance Company
Railroad Medicare Service Center
P. O. Box 10066
Augusta, GA 30999-0001

STATE BOARD OF MEDICAL EXAMINERS
Tennessee State Board of Medical Examiners
283 Plus Park Boulevard
Nashville, TN 37247-1010

Tennessee State Board of Osteopathic Examiners
287 Plus Park Boulevard
Nashville, TN 37247-1010

VETERANS ADMINISTRATION INSTALLATION
Tennessee Medical Centers:
Memphis 38104 (1030 Jefferson Avenue)
Mountain Home 37684 (Sidney & Lamont Street)
Murfreesboro 37129 (3400 Lebanon Road)
Nashville 37212 (1310 24th Avenue, South)

WORKERS' COMPENSATION FEDERAL DISTRICT OFFICE
Office of Workers' Compensation Program
214 N. Hogan Street, Suite 1006
Jacksonville, FL 32202

WORKERS' COMPENSATION STATE PLAN OFFICE
Workers' Compensation Division
Department of Labor
710 James Robertson Parkway
Gateway Plaza, Second Floor
Nashville, TN 37243-0661

Texas

BLUE CROSS & BLUE SHIELD
Blue Cross and Blue Shield of Texas, Inc.
P. O. Box 655730
Dallas, TX 75265-5730

CHAMPUS CLAIM OFFICE
Foundation Health Federal Services
(except the southwestern corner of the state that includes El Paso)
c/o WPS/Tricare
P. O. Box 8999
Madison, WI 53708

Beginning April, 1997, TriWest Healthcare Alliance will be the fiscal intermediary. Read your CHAMPUS bulletin for the address information.

CHAMPVA CLAIM OFFICE
CHAMPVA Center
4500 Cherry Creek Drive, South
Box 65024
Denver, CO 80206-9024

INSURANCE COMMISSIONER STATE OFFICE
State Insurance Commissioner
333 Guadalupe Street
P. O. Box 149104
Austin, TX 78714-9091

MATERNAL AND CHILD HEALTH PROGRAM
Bureau of Women and Children
Texas Department of Health
1100 W. 49th Street
Austin, TX 78756

MEDICAID FISCAL AGENT
National Heritage Insurance Company
P. O. Box 200555
Austin, TX 78720

MEDICARE DURABLE MEDICAL EQUIPMENT
Palmetto Government Benefits Administrators
P. O. Box 100141
Columbia, SC 29202-3141

MEDICARE FISCAL AGENT OR CARRIER
Medicare/Blue Cross & Blue Shield of Texas, Inc.
P. O. Box 660031
Dallas, TX 75266-0031

MEDICARE RAILROAD RETIREE CARRIER
The MetraHealth Insurance Company
Railroad Medicare Service Center
P. O. Box 30050
Salt Lake City, UT 84130-0050

STATE BOARD OF MEDICAL EXAMINERS
Texas State Board of Medical Examiners
333 Guadalupe, Tower 3, Suite 610 (78701)
P. O. Box 2018
Austin, TX 78768-2018

VETERANS ADMINISTRATION INSTALLATION
Texas Medical Centers:
Amarillo 79106 (6010 Amarillo Blvd., West)
Big Spring 79720 (2400 S. Gregg Street)
Bonham 75418 (1201 E. Ninth)
Dallas 75216 (4500 S. Lancaster Road)
Houston 77030 (2002 Holcombe Boulevard)
Kerrville 78028 (3600 Memorial Blvd.)
Marlin 76661 (1016 Ward Street)
San Antonio 78284 (7400 Merton Minter Blvd.)
Temple 76504 (1901 S. First)
Waco 76711 (4800 Memorial Drive)

WORKERS' COMPENSATION FEDERAL DISTRICT OFFICE
Office of Workers' Compensation Program
525 Griffin Street
Dallas, TX 75202

WORKERS' COMPENSATION STATE PLAN OFFICE
Workers' Compensation Commission
Southfield Building
4000 South IH 35
Austin, TX 78704

Utah

BLUE CROSS & BLUE SHIELD
Blue Cross and Blue Shield of Utah
P. O. Box 30270
Salt Lake City, UT 84130-0270

CHAMPUS CLAIM OFFICE
Palmetto Government Benefits Administrators
P. O. Box 870020
Surfside Beach, SC 29587-8720

Beginning April, 1997, TriWest Healthcare Alliance will be the fiscal intermediary. Read your CHAMPUS bulletin for the address information.

CHAMPVA CLAIM OFFICE
CHAMPVA Center
4500 Cherry Creek Drive, South
Box 65024
Denver, CO 80206-9024

INSURANCE COMMISSIONER STATE OFFICE
Commissioner of Insurance
3110 State Office Building
Salt Lake City, UT 84114

MATERNAL AND CHILD HEALTH PROGRAM
Children's Special Health Services
Utah Department of Health
P. O. Box 144610
Salt Lake City, UT 84114-4610

Community & Family Health Services Division
Utah Department of Health
P. O. Box 144100
Salt Lake City, UT 84116-4100

MEDICAID FISCAL AGENT
Bureau of Medicaid Claims Processing (EC)
P. O. Box 16520
Salt Lake City, UT 84116

MEDICARE DURABLE MEDICAL EQUIPMENT
Connecticut General Life Insurance
DMERC-CIGNA Medicare
P. O. Box 690
Nashville, TN 37320

MEDICARE FISCAL AGENT OR CARRIER
Medicare/Blue Shield of Utah
P. O. Box 30269
Salt Lake City, UT 84130-0269

MEDICARE RAILROAD RETIREE CARRIER
The MetraHealth Insurance Company
Railroad Medicare Service Center
P. O. Box 30050
Salt Lake City, UT 84130-0050

STATE BOARD OF MEDICAL EXAMINERS
Utah Department of Commerce
Division of Occupational & Professional Licensing
Heber M. Wells Building, 4th Floor
160 E. 300 South (84111)
P. O. Box 146741
Salt Lake City, UT 84114-6741

VETERANS ADMINISTRATION INSTALLATION
Utah Medical Center:
Salt Lake City 84148 (500 Foothill Drive)

WORKERS' COMPENSATION FEDERAL DISTRICT OFFICE
Office of Workers' Compensation Program
1801 California Street, Suite 915
Denver, CO 80202-2614

WORKERS' COMPENSATION STATE PLAN OFFICE
Industrial Commission
P. O. Box 146600
Salt Lake City, UT 84114-6600

Vermont

BLUE CROSS & BLUE SHIELD
Blue Cross and Blue Shield of Vermont
P. O. Box 186
Montpelier, VT 05601

CHAMPUS CLAIM OFFICE
UNISYS Corporation
P. O. Box 3068
Columbus, IN 47202-3068

CHAMPVA CLAIM OFFICE
CHAMPVA Center
4500 Cherry Creek Drive, South
Box 65024
Denver, CO 80206-9024

INSURANCE COMMISSIONER STATE OFFICE
Commissioner of Banking, Insurance, and Securities
89 Main Street, Drawer 20
Montpelier, VT 05620-3101

MATERNAL AND CHILD HEALTH PROGRAM
Children with Special Health Care Needs
Vermont Department of Health
108 Cherry Street
P. O. Box 70
Burlington, VT 05402

Maternal and Child Health
Vermont Department of Health
108 Cherry Street
P. O. Box 70
Burlington, VT 05402

MEDICAID FISCAL AGENT
Electronic Data Systems Federal Corporation (EC)
P. O. Box 1102
South Burlington, VT 05402

MEDICARE DURABLE MEDICAL EQUIPMENT
MetraHealth, Inc.
320 S. Pennsylvania Boulevard, Suite 339
Wilkes-Barre, PA 18701-2215

MEDICARE FISCAL AGENT OR CARRIER
Assigned claims:
Medicare/C and S Administrative Services
P. O. Box 1000
Hingham, MA 02044-9191

Non-Assigned claims:
P. O. Box 222
Hingham, MA 02044-9193

MEDICARE RAILROAD RETIREE CENTER
The MetraHealth Insurance Company
Railroad Medicare Service Center
P. O. Box 10066
Augusta, GA 30999-0001

STATE BOARD OF MEDICAL EXAMINERS
Vermont Board of Medical Practice
109 State Street
Montpelier, VT 05609-1106

Vermont Board of Osteopathic Physicians and Surgeons
109 State Street
Montpelier, VT 05609-1106

VETERANS ADMINISTRATION INSTALLATION
Vermont Medical Center:
White River Junction 05009 (N. Hartland Road)

WORKERS' COMPENSATION FEDERAL DISTRICT OFFICE
Office of Workers' Compensation Programs
JFK Federal Building, Room E260
Boston, MA 02203

WORKERS' COMPENSATION STATE PLAN OFFICE
Department of Labor and Industry
National Life Building
Drawer 20
Montpelier, VT 05620-3401

Virgin Islands

CHAMPVA CLAIM OFFICE
CHAMPVA Center
4500 Cherry Creek Drive, South
Box 65024
Denver, CO 80206-9024

INSURANCE COMMISSIONER STATE OFFICE
Director
Lieutenant Governor's Office
Kongens Garde No. 18
St. Thomas, VI 00802

MATERNAL AND CHILD HEALTH PROGRAM
Department of Health MCH and CSHCN
Elaineco Building Complex
St. Thomas, VI 00802

Maternal and Child Health and Children with Special Health Care Needs
3500 Estate Richmond, Christiansted
St. Croix, VI 00820

MEDICARE DURABLE MEDICAL EQUIPMENT
Palmetto Government Benefits Administrators
P. O. Box 100141
Columbia, SC 29202-3141

MEDICARE FISCAL AGENT OR CARRIER
Medicare/Seguros de Servicio de Salud de Puerto Rico
Call Box 71391
San Juan, PR 00936

MEDICARE RAILROAD RETIREE CARRIER
Medicare Part B Claims are handled by claim service centers. For the address and toll-free number of the office nearest you, call the Railroad Retirement Board listed in your telephone directory under U. S. Government.

STATE BOARD OF MEDICAL EXAMINERS
Virgin Islands Board of Medical Examiners
Virgin Islands Department of Health
48 Sugar Estate
St. Thomas, VI 00802

VETERANS ADMINISTRATION INSTALLATION
For Information on VA benefits call 1-800-827-1000

WORKERS' COMPENSATION STATE PLAN OFFICE
Department of Labor
Workers' Compensation Division
3012 Vitraco Mall
Christiansted
St. Croix, VI 00820

WORKERS' COMPENSATION FEDERAL DISTRICT OFFICE
Office of Workers' Compensation Programs
201 Varick Street, Room 750
P. O. Box 566
New York, NY 10014

Virginia

BLUE CROSS & BLUE SHIELD
Trigon Blue Cross/Blue Shield
2015 Staples Mill Road (25230)
P. O. Box 27401
Richmond, VA 23279

CHAMPUS CLAIM OFFICE
Palmetto Government Benefits Administrators
P. O. Box 100502
Florence, SC 29501-0502

CHAMPVA CLAIM OFFICE
CHAMPVA Center
4500 Cherry Creek Drive, South
Box 65024
Denver, CO 80206-9024

INSURANCE COMMISSIONER STATE OFFICE
Commissioner of Insurance
1300 E. Main Street
Richmond, VA 23219

MATERNAL AND CHILD HEALTH PROGRAM
Children's Specialty Services
Virginia Department of Health
1500 E. Main Street, Suite 135
P. O. Box 2448
Richmond, VA 23218-2448

Women and Infants Health
Virginia Department of Health
1500 E. Main Street, Suite 137
Richmond, VA 23218-2448

MEDICAID FISCAL AGENT
The Computer Company (EC)
DMAS P. O. Box 27444
Richmond, VA 23261

MEDICARE DURABLE MEDICAL EQUIPMENT
AdminaStar Federal Incorporated
P. O. Box 7078
Indianapolis, IN 46206-0240

MEDICARE FISCAL AGENT OR CARRIER
Counties of Arlington, Fairfax:
Cities of Alexandria, Fairfax, Falls Church:
Medicare/Pennsylvania Blue Shield
P. O. Box 890100
Camp Hill, PA 17089-0100

Rest of State:
Medicare/The Travelers Insurance Company
P. O. Box 26463
Richmond, VA 23261

MEDICARE RAILROAD RETIREE CARRIER
The MetraHealth Insurance Company
Railroad Medicare Service Center
P. O. Box 10066
Augusta, GA 30999-0001

STATE BOARD OF MEDICAL EXAMINERS
Virginia Board of Medicine
6606 W. Broad Street, 4th Floor
Richmond, VA 23230-1717

VETERANS ADMINISTRATION INSTALLATION
Virginia Medical Centers:
Hampton 23667 (100 Emancipation Drive)
Richmond 23249 (1201 Broad Rock Road)
Salem 24153 (1970 Roanoke Blvd.)

WORKERS' COMPENSATION FEDERAL DISTRICT OFFICE
Office of Workers' Compensation Programs
800 N. Capitol Street, N.W., Room 800
Washington, DC 20211

WORKERS' COMPENSATION STATE PLAN OFFICE
Workers' Compensation Commission
1000 DMV Drive
P. O. Box 1794
Richmond, VA 23214

Washington

BLUE CROSS & BLUE SHIELD
Blue Cross of Washington and Alaska

Blue Shield in North Central Washington
Blue Cross and Blue Shield of Alaska
P. O. Box 327
Seattle, WA 98111-0327

King County Medical Blue Shield
P. O. Box 21267
Seattle, WA 98111-3267

Medical Service Corporation of Eastern Washington
P. O. Box 3048
Spokane, WA 99220

Pierce County Medical Bureau, Inc.
P. O. Box 2354
Tacoma, WA 98401

Skagit County Medical Bureau
P. O. Box 699
Mount Vernon, WA 98273

Washington Physicians Service, Inc.
P. O. Box 2010
Seattle, WA 98111

Whatcom Medical Bureau
P. O. Box 9753
Bellingham, WA 98227-9753

CHAMPUS/TRICARE CLAIM OFFICE
Foundation Health Federal Services
P. O. Box 419010
Rancho Cordova, CA 94741

CHAMPVA CLAIM OFFICE
CHAMPVA Center
4500 Cherry Creek Drive, South
Box 65024
Denver, CO 80206-9024

INSURANCE COMMISSIONER STATE OFFICE
Insurance Commissioner
Insurance Building—Capitol Campus
P. O. Box 40255
Olympia, WA 98504-0255

MATERNAL AND CHILD HEALTH PROGRAM
Maternal and Child Health
State Department of Health
P. O. Box 47880
Olympia, WA 98504-7880

State Department of Health
Community and Family Health
P. O. Box 47880, Industrial Center, Building 8
Olympia, WA 98504-7880

MEDICAID FISCAL AGENT
Department of Social & Health Services
Office of Provider Services
P. O. Box 1956
Olympia, WA 98507

MEDICARE DURABLE MEDICAL EQUIPMENT
Connecticut General Life Insurance
DMERC-CIGNA Medicare
P. O. Box 690
Nashville, TN 37320

MEDICARE FISCAL AGENT OR CARRIER
Blue Cross Blue Shield of North Dakota
4510 13th Avenue, S.W.
Fargo, ND 58121-0001

MEDICARE RAILROAD RETIREE CARRIER
The MetraHealth Insurance Company
Railroad Medicare Service Center
P. O. Box 30050
Salt Lake City, UT 84130-0050

STATE BOARD OF MEDICAL EXAMINERS
Washington Medical Quality Assurance Commission
1300 S.E. Quince Street
P. O. Box 47866
Olympia, WA 98504-7866

WASHINGTON STATE BOARD OF OSTEOPATHIC MEDICINE AND SURGERY
1300 S.E. Quince Street
P. O. Box 47866
Olympia, WA 98504-7866

VETERANS ADMINISTRATION INSTALLATION
Washington Medical Centers:
Seattle 98108 (1660 S. Columbian Way)
Spokane 99205 (4815 N. Assembly Street)
Tacoma 98493 (9900 Veterans Drive, S.W., American Lake)
Walla Walla 99362 (77 Wainwright Drive)

WORKERS' COMPENSATION FEDERAL DISTRICT OFFICE
Office of Workers' Compensation Programs
1111 Third Avenue, Suite 615
Seattle, WA 98101-3212

WORKERS' COMPENSATION STATE PLAN OFFICE
Board of Industrial Insurance Appeals
2430 Chandler Court, S.W.
P. O. Box 42401
Mail Stop FN 21
Olympia, WA 98504

Department of Labor and Industries
Headquarters Building
7273 Linderson Way, S.W., 5th Floor
Olympia, WA 98504

West Indies

CHAMPUS CLAIM OFFICE
Wisconsin Physicians Service

P. O. Box 7985
Madison, WI 53707-7985

CHAMPVA CLAIM OFFICE
CHAMPVA Center
4500 Cherry Creek Drive, South
Box 65024
Denver, CO 80206-9024

West Virginia

BLUE CROSS & BLUE SHIELD
Mountain State Blue Cross & Blue Shield, Inc.
P. O. Box 1948
Parkersburg, WV 26102

CHAMPUS CLAIM OFFICE
Palmetto Government Benefits Administrators
P. O. Box 100598
Florence, SC 29501-0598

CHAMPVA CLAIM OFFICE
CHAMPVA Center
4500 Cherry Creek Drive, South
Box 65024
Denver, CO 80206-9024

INSURANCE COMMISSIONER STATE OFFICE
Insurance Commissioner
2019 Washington Street, East
P. O. Box 50540
Charleston, WV 25305-0540

MATERNAL AND CHILD HEALTH PROGRAM
Director of Maternal and Child Health
West Virginia Department of Health
1411 Virginia Street, East
Charleston, WV 25301-3013

Handicapped Children's Services
1116 Quarrier Street, East
Charleston, WV 25301

MEDICAID FISCAL AGENT
Department of Human Services (EC)
7012 MacCorkle Avenue, S.W.
Charleston, WV 25304

MEDICARE DURABLE MEDICAL EQUIPMENT
AdminaStar Federal Incorporated
P. O. Box 7078
Indianapolis, IN 46206-0240

MEDICARE FISCAL AGENT OR CARRIER
Medicare/Nationwide Mutual Insurance Co.
P. O. Box 57
Columbus, OH 43216

MEDICARE RAILROAD RETIREE CARRIER
The MetraHealth Insurance Company
Railroad Medicare Service Center
P. O. Box 10066
Augusta, GA 30999-0001

STATE BOARD OF MEDICAL EXAMINERS
West Virginia Board of Medicine
101 Dee Drive
Charleston, WV 25311

West Virginia Board of Osteopathy
334 Penco Road
Weirton, WV 26062

VETERANS ADMINISTRATION INSTALLATION
West Virginia Medical Centers:
Beckley 25801 (200 Veterans Avenue)
Clarksburg 26301 (1 Medical Center Drive)
Huntington 25704 (1540 Spring Valley Drive)
Martinsburg 25410 (Route 9)

WORKERS' COMPENSATION FEDERAL DISTRICT OFFICE
Office of Workers' Compensation Programs
3535 Market Street
Philadelphia, PA 19104

WORKERS' COMPENSATION STATE PLAN OFFICE
Bureau of Employment Program
Workers' Compensation Division
Executive Offices
601 Morris Street
Charleston, WV 25332-1416

Workers' Compensation Appeal Board
601 Morris Street, Room 303
Charleston, WV 25301

Wisconsin

BLUE CROSS & BLUE SHIELD
Blue Cross & Blue Shield United of Wisconsin
P. O. Box 2025
Milwaukee, WI 53201

CHAMPUS CLAIM OFFICE
Palmetto Government Benefits Administrators
P. O. Box 100598
Florence, SC 29501-0598

CHAMPVA CLAIM OFFICE
CHAMPVA Center
4500 Cherry Creek Drive, South
Box 65024
Denver, CO 80206-9024

INSURANCE COMMISSIONER STATE OFFICE
Commissioner of Insurance
121 E. Wilson
Madison, WI 53702

MATERNAL AND CHILD HEALTH PROGRAM
Children with Special Health Care Needs

Wisconsin Department of Health and Social Services
1414 E. Washington Avenue, Room 167
Madison, WI 53707-3044

MEDICAID FISCAL AGENT
Electronic Data Systems Corporation (EC)
6406 Bridge Road
Madison, WI 53784

MEDICARE DURABLE MEDICAL EQUIPMENT
AdminaStar Federal Incorporated
P. O. Box 7078
Indianapolis, IN 46206-0240

MEDICARE FISCAL AGENT OR CARRIER
Medicare/WPS
Box 1787
Madison, WI 53701

MEDICARE RAILROAD RETIREE CARRIER
The MetraHealth Insurance Company
Railroad Medicare Service Center
P. O. Box 30050
Salt Lake City, UT 84130-0050

STATE BOARD OF MEDICAL EXAMINERS
Wisconsin Medical Examining Board
1400 E. Washington Avenue
P. O. Box 8935
Madison, WI 53703

VETERANS ADMINISTRATION INSTALLATION
Wisconsin Medical Centers:
Madison 53705 (2500 Overlook Terrace)
Milwaukee 53295 (5000 W. National Avenue)
Tomah 54660 (500 E. Veterans Street)

WORKERS' COMPENSATION FEDERAL DISTRICT OFFICE
Office of Workers' Compensation Programs
230 S. Dearborn Street, 8th Floor
Chicago, IL 60604

WORKERS' COMPENSATION STATE PLAN OFFICE
Labor and Industry Review Commission
P. O. Box 8126
Madison, WI 53708

Workers' Compensation Division
Department of Industry, Labor, and Human Relations
201 E. Washington Avenue, Room 161
P. O. Box 7901
Madison, WI 53707

Wyoming

BLUE CROSS & BLUE SHIELD
Blue Cross and Blue Shield of Wyoming
P. O. Box 2266
Cheyenne, WY 82003-2266

CHAMPUS CLAIM OFFICE
Palmetto Government Benefits Administrators
P. O. Box 870020
Surfside Beach, SC 29587-8720

Beginning April, 1997, TriWest Healthcare Alliance will be the fiscal intermediary. Read your CHAMPUS bulletin for the address information.

CHAMPVA CLAIM OFFICE
CHAMPVA Center
4500 Cherry Creek Drive, South
Box 65024
Denver, CO 80206-9024

INSURANCE COMMISSIONER STATE OFFICE
Commissioner of Insurance
Herschler Building
122 W. 25th Street
Cheyenne, WY 82002-0440

MATERNAL AND CHILD HEALTH PROGRAM
Division of Public Health
Hathaway Building, Room 465
Cheyenne, WY 82002-0480

Maternal and Child Health
Division of Public Health
Hathaway Building, Room 462
Cheyenne, WY 82002-0480

MEDICAID FISCAL AGENT
Division of Health & Medical Service
P. O. Box 906
Cheyenne, WY 82003

MEDICARE DURABLE MEDICAL EQUIPMENT
Connecticut General Life Insurance
DMERC-CIGNA Medicare
P. O. Box 690
Nashville, TN 37320

MEDICARE FISCAL AGENT OR CARRIER
Blue Cross and Blue Shield of North Dakota
P. O. Box 628
Cheyenne, WY 82003

MEDICARE RAILROAD RETIREE CARRIER
The MetraHealth Insurance Company
Railroad Medicare Service Center
P. O. Box 30050
Salt Lake City, UT 84130-0050

STATE BOARD OF MEDICAL EXAMINERS
Wyoming Board of Medicine
Colony Building
211 West 19th Street, 2nd Floor
Cheyenne, WY 82002

VETERANS ADMINISTRATION INSTALLATION
Wyoming Medical Centers:

Cheyenne 82001 (2360 E. Pershing Blvd.)
Sheridan 82801 (1898 Fort Road)

WORKERS' COMPENSATION FEDERAL DISTRICT OFFICE
Office of Workers' Compensation Programs
1801 California Street, Suite 915
Denver, CO 80202-2614

WORKERS' COMPENSATION STATE PLAN OFFICE
Workers' Compensation Division
Department of Employment
East Wing, Herschler Building
122 W. 25th Street, 2nd Floor
Cheyenne, WY 82002-0700

APPENDIX B

Reference List of Audiotapes, Books, Newsletters, Periodicals, Software, and Videotapes

At the end of each reference is a bracketed number. At the end of this Appendix, you will find the number under "Names and Addresses of Resources."

Index

Automation
Billing
Billing Services, Software and Systems Vendors and Consultants
Blue Cross and Blue Shield
Certification
CHAMPUS
Charges
Claims Assistance Professionals
Coding
Delinquent and Denied Claims
Diagnosis-Related Groups
Diagnostic and Procedure Handbooks for Terminology (DPT)
Dictionaries and Glossaries
Disability Benefit Programs
Disability Income Insurance
Documentation, Medical
Education and Training
Electronic Data Interchange
Ethics
Fees, Reimbursement, Charges
Fraud and Abuse
HCFA-1500 Claim Form
HCFA Common Procedure Coding System (HCPCS)
Health Insurance
Health Maintenance Organizations/Preferred Provider Organizations
Hospital Insurance Claims
Insurance Directories
Law and Ethics
Managed Care
Medicaid
Medical Management
Medicare
Preferred Provider Organizations
Reimbursement
Relative Value Studies
Self-Employment
Videotapes
Workers' Compensation
Workshops and Seminars

Resource List

AUTOMATION

See *Electronic Data Interchange.*

BILLING

See also *Fees, Reimbursement, Charges.*

Books

Insurance Career Development Center, *A Guide to Medical Billing,* Volume 1 of 3, Mosby-Year Book, Inc., St. Louis, Missouri, 1994 [59]

Newsletters

Health Care Biller, Aspen Publishers, Inc., Frederick, Maryland, monthly publication [15]

Reference Guides

Health Care Billing: A Guide to Billing Office Policies & Practices (Health Care Billing Manual), Aspen Publishers, Inc., Frederick, Maryland, 1994 [15]

Reports

"Countdown to UB-92," Aspen Publishers, Inc., Frederick, Maryland [15]

"40 Tips Health Care Billers Can't Live Without," Aspen Publishers, Inc., Frederick, Maryland [15]

BILLING SERVICES, SOFTWARE AND SYSTEMS VENDORS, AND CONSULTANTS

Conomikes Associates, Inc., Los Angeles, California [24]

Medical Software, *Systems & Services Directory,* Practice Management Information Corporation, Los Angeles, California [63]

BLUE CROSS AND BLUE SHIELD

Newsletters for Physicians

Obtain from Blue Cross/Blue Shield. See Appendix A for address in your state.

CERTIFICATION

American Academy of Procedural Coders, *Certified Procedural Coder/CPC-Hospital Outpatient, Independent Study Programs,* American Academy of Procedural Coders, Salt Lake City, Utah [3]

American Academy of Procedural Coders, *Certified Procedural Coder Examination Study Guide,* American Academy of Procedural Coders, Salt Lake City, Utah [3]

American Guild of Patient Account Management Certification Study Guide for CPAM/CCAM Exams, American Guild of Patient Account Management, Washington, D.C. [8]

American Health Information Management Association, *Certified Coding Specialist Certification Guide,* Professional Examination Service, New York, New York [10]

Candidate Handbook for Certification Examinations for Claims Assistance Professionals and Electronic Claims Professionals, National Association of Claims Assistance Professionals, Downers Grove, Illinois [60]

Ramirez, Doris, *CPC Exam Prep Program,* Professional Practice Builders, San Mateo, California [65]

CHAMPUS

Bulletins

Obtain from state intermediary. See Appendix A for address in your state.

Newsletters

Understanding CHAMPUS, Volume 1, Commerce Clearing House, Inc., Chicago, Illinois, updated as needed [22]

CHARGES

See *Fees, Reimbursement, Charges.*

CLAIMS ASSISTANCE PROFESSIONALS

Books

Claims Assistance Professional Basics, National Association of Claims Assistance Professionals, Downers Grove, Illinois, 1992 [60]

Clement and Associates, *Medical Claims Processing* (self-employment book), Entrepreneur, Cleveland, Ohio, 1988 [32]

PROClaimer Analyst Newsletter, Strategic Decisions Plus, Silverthorne, Colorado, monthly [75]

CODING

Books, Diagnostic and Procedural

Adams, Wanda, *Adams' Guide to Coding and Reimbursement,* Mosby-Year Book, Inc., St. Louis, Missouri, 1994 [59]
American Academy of Orthopaedic Surgeoms, *Common Orthopaedic Procedures and Diagnostic Codes; A Reference Guide,* Rosemont, Illinois [1]
American Academy of Orthopaedic Surgeons, *CPT Guidebook,* Rosemont, Illinois [1]
American Academy of Orthopaedic Surgeons, *Orthopaedic ICD-9-CM Expanded,* Rosemont, Illinois [1]
American Academy of Pediatrics, *CPT-4 Teaching Manual,* Elk Grove Village, Illinois [2]
American College of Emergency Physicians, *Diagnosis Coding,* Dallas, Texas [5]
American College of Emergency Physicians, *Procedure Coding,* Dallas, Texas [5]
American College of Rheumatology, *ICD-9 Chart; Effective CPT Coding for Rheumatology Practices,* Atlanta, Georgia [7]
American Health Consultants, Inc., *Key Questions in Cardiopulmonary Coding,* Atlanta, Georgia [9]
American Health Consultants, Inc., *Key Questions in Medicare Coding,* Atlanta, Georgia [9]
American Health Consultants, Inc., *Key Questions in Oncology Coding,* Atlanta, Georgia [9]
American Health Consultants, Inc., *Key Questions in Orthopaedic Coding,* Atlanta, Georgia [9]
American Health Consultants, Inc., *Key Questions in Surgical Coding,* Atlanta, Georgia [9]
American Medical Association, *Current Procedural Terminology (CPT),* Chicago, Illinois, available in computer software, magnetic tape, published annually [12]
American Physical Therapy Association and St. Anthony Publishing, Inc., *Coding and Payment Guide for the Physical Therapist, CPT, HCPCS Level II, ICD-9-CM,* St. Anthony Publishing, Inc., Washington, D.C. [72]
American Psychiatric Press, Inc., *Diagnostic & Statistical Manual of Mental Disorders,* Third Edition (DSM-III-R), American Psychiatric Press, Inc., Washington, D.C., 1987 [13]
American Society for Parenteral and Enteral Nutrition, *Companion to CPT-4 ASPEN Guide to Physician Codes for Nutrition Support Services,* Silver Spring, Maryland [14]
Bradford, Billie C., *ICD-9-CM Coding for Physicians Offices,* McGraw-Hill Healthcare Management Group, New York, New York [50]
Channel Publishing, Ltd., *Generic Hospital ICD-9-CM,* Volumes 1, 2, and 3 (paperback), Reno, Nevada, updated annually [19]
Channel Publishing, Ltd., *Annual Hospital Version, The Educational Annotation of ICD-9-CM,* Volumes 1, 2, and 3, Reno, Nevada, updated annually [19]
Channel Publishing Ltd., *Annual Physician Version, The Educational Annotation of ICD-9-CM,* Volumes 1 and 2, Reno, Nevada, updated annually [19]
Channel Publishing, Ltd., *Post Binder Hospital Version, The Educational Annotation of ICD-9-CM,* Volumes 1, 2, and 3, Reno, Nevada, updated annually [19]
Channel Publishing, Ltd., *Soft Cover Hospital Version, The Educational Annotation of ICD-9-CM,* Volumes 1, 2, and 3, Reno, Nevada, updated annually [19]
Channel Publishing, Ltd., *Soft Cover Physician Version, The Educational Annotation of ICD-9-CM,* Volumes 1 and 2 (soft cover), Reno, Nevada [19]
ChartCare Solutions, *Chiropractic Code Book* (excerpts from CPT, HCPCS, and ICD-9-CM with RVUs), Phoenix, Arizona, updated annually [20]
Commission on Professional Hospital Activities, *Compendium of ICD-9-CM for Ob-Gyn, Cardiology, Neurology, Ophthalmology, Urology, Orthopedics,* Ann Arbor, Michigan [23]
Context Software Systems, *ICD-9-CM, International Classification of Diseases, 9th Revision, Clinical Modification* (color coded), McGraw-Hill Healthcare Management Group, New York, New York, updated annually [50]
HCIA Inc., *ICD-9-CM Code Book,* Volumes 1, 2, & 3, HCIA Inc., Baltimore, Maryland [90]
Healthcare Management Advisors, Inc., *Coding for Quality, CPT Coding for Outpatient Surgery, a Comprehensive Guide,* Atlanta, Georgia, updated periodically [38]
Holt, R. B., *ICD-9-CM to CPT Radiology Cross Code,* Sandy, Utah [40]
Hunt, William J., *ENT Diagnosis Code, CPT, ICD-9-CM Diagnosis and Procedures,* West Palm Beach, Florida [42]
Jorwic, Therese M., *ICD-9-CM Coding Handbook for Physician Practices* (looseleaf manual), Aspen Publishers, Inc., Frederick, Maryland, updated annually [15]
KFC Medical Systems, Inc., *ICD-9 Coding Utility for Medical Billing* (software program), Long Beach, California [46]
Knaus, Gary M., *Getting Paid for What You Do; Coding for Optimal Reimbursement,* McGraw-Hill Healthcare Management Group, New York, New York, 1993 [50]
Kotoski, Gabrielle M., *Coding Answers for Optimal Physician Payment,* Aspen Publishers, Inc., Frederick, Maryland, 1994 [15]
Kotoski, Gabrielle M., *CPT Coding Made Easy; A Technical Guide,* Volumes 1 and 2, Aspen Publishers, Frederick, Maryland [15]
Medical Business Resource Center, *Ambulatory Facility Coding,* Phoenix, Arizona (Catalog #214) [52]
Medical Business Resource Center, *CPT Coding, E & M, RBRVS,* Phoenix, Arizona (Catalog #201) [52]
Medical Business Resource Center, *CPT Coding–Operative Reports,* Phoenix, Arizona (Catalog #204) [52]
Medical Business Resource Center, *CPT Coding–Paraprofessional, HCPCS,* Phoenix, Arizona (Catalog #203) [52]
Medical Business Resource Center, *CPT Coding–Surgical,* Phoenix, Arizona (Catalog #202) [52]
Medical Business Resource Center, *ICD-9 Coding–Introduction,* Phoenix, Arizona (Catalog #211) [52]
Medical Business Resource Center, *ICD-9 Coding–Late Effects, V Codes,* Phoenix, Arizona (Catalog #212) [52]
Medical Business Resource Center, *ICD-9 Coding–Special Tables, E Codes,* Phoenix, Arizona (Catalog #213) [52]
Medical Business Resource Center, *Introduction to Coding,* Phoenix, Arizona (Catalog #200) [52]
Medical Business Resource Center, *Medical Terminology–Basic,* Phoenix, Arizona (Catalog #229/230) [52]
Medical Business Resource Center, *Medical Terminology–Body Systems,* Phoenix, Arizona (Catalog #231) [52]
Medical Business Resource Center, *Medical Terminology–Body Systems II,* Phoenix, Arizona (Catalog #232) [52]
Medical Learning Incorporated, *Interventional Radiology Coder,* St. Paul, Minnesota. This company publishes code books for ambulatory surgery procedures, emergency services, and laboratory tests. [89]

Medicode, Inc., *Code It Right; A Guide to Selecting CPT, ICD-9, and HCPCS Codes,* Med-Index Publishing Division, Salt Lake City, Utah, 1993 [57]

Medicode, Inc., *Coders' Desk Reference,* Med-Index Publishing Division, Salt Lake City, Utah, 1995 [57]

Medicode, Inc., *CPT, ICD-9, and HCPSC Coding Illustrated: The Eyeball; Lower Face: Skeletal Structures and Definitions; Lower Face: Soft Tissue; Peripheral Vascular System; Uterus, Tubes and Ovaries: Nonpregnant,* Med-Index Publishing Division, Salt Lake City, Utah, 1994 [57]

Medicode, Inc., *Emergency: A Coding and Reimbursement Guide for Emergency Services,* Med-Index Publishing Division, Salt Lake City, Utah [57]

Medicode, Inc., *ICD-9-CM,* Volumes 1 and 2 (for physicians); Volume 3 (for hospitals), Med-Index Publishing Division, Salt Lake City, Utah, updated annually [57]

Practice Management Information Corporation, *CPT and HCPCS Coding Made Easy! A Comprehensive Guide to CPT and HCPCS Coding for Health Care Professionals,* Los Angeles, California, 1992 [63]

Practice Management Information Corporation, *CPT Coding Tool,* Los Angeles, California, 1992 [63]

Practice Management Information Corporation, *E/M Coding Made Easy,* Los Angeles, California, 1993 [63]

Practice Management Information Corporation, *ICD-9-CM Coding Made Easy! A Comprehensive Coding Guide for Health Care Professionals,* Los Angeles, California, 1989 [63]

Practice Management Information Corporation, *ICD-9-CM International Classification of Diseases, 9th Revision, Clinical Modification,* Volumes 1 and 2, Volumes 1, 2 and 3, or Binder Version or Hard Bound Version, Los Angeles, California [63]

Society of Thoracic Surgeons, *Using CPT for Cardiothoracic Reimbursement: A Manual for Surgeons and Insurance Billing Specialists,* Chicago, Illinois [68]

St. Anthony Publishing, Inc., *Coding and Payment Guide for the Physical Therapist,* Washington, D.C. [72]

St. Anthony's Clinical Coder for Cardiology: The Color-Coded Guide to Medicare Coding and Billing, Under RBRVS, St. Anthony Publishing, Inc., Washington, D.C. [72]

St. Anthony's Clinical Coder for Family Practice: The Color-Coded Guide to Medicare Coding and Billing, Under RBRVS, St. Anthony Publishing, Inc., Washington, D.C. [72]

St. Anthony's Clinical Coder for General Surgery: The Color-Coded Guide to Medicare Coding and Billing, Under RBRVS, St. Anthony Publishing, Inc., Washington, D.C. [72]

St. Anthony's Clinical Coder for Ophthalmology: The Color-Coded Guide to Medicare Coding and Billing, Under RBRVS, St. Anthony Publishing, Inc., Washington, D.C. [72]

St. Anthony's Clinical Coder for Orthopaedics: The Color-Coded Guide to Medicare Coding and Billing, Under RBRVS, St. Anthony Publishing, Inc., Washington, D.C. [72]

St. Anthony's Coding Companion for OB/GYN, St. Anthony Publishing, Inc., Washington, D.C. [72]

St. Anthony's Coding Companion for Orthopaedics, St. Anthony Publishing, Inc., Washington, D.C. [72]

St. Anthony's Color-Coded Annotated ICD-9-CM Code Book, St. Anthony Publishing, Inc., Washington, D.C. [72]

St. Anthony's Color-Coded Guide to Ambulatory Surgery Center Payment Groups, St. Anthony Publishing, Inc., Washington, D.C. [72]

St. Anthony's Color-Coded ICD-9-CM Code Book for Outpatient Services, St. Anthony Publishing, Inc., Washington, D.C. [72]

St. Anthony's Color-Coded ICD-9-CM Code Book for Physician Payment, Professional Edition, Volumes 1, 2, and 3, updated annually, binder or soft bound, St. Anthony Publishing, Inc., Washington, D.C. [72]

St. Anthony's Guide to Code Linkage, St. Anthony Publishing, Inc., Washington, D.C. [72]

St. Anthony's Guide to E/M Coding and Documentation, St. Anthony Publishing, Inc., Washington, D.C. [72]

St. Anthony's ICD-9-CM Code Book for Home Health Services, Nursing Homes & Hospices, St. Anthony Publishing, Inc., Washington, D.C. [72]

St. Anthony's ICD-9-CM Code Book for Outpatient Services, Volumes 1, 2, and 3, St. Anthony Publishing, Inc., Washington, D.C. [72]

St. Anthony's ICD-9-CM Code Book for Physician Payment, Combined Volumes 1 and 2, in 3-hole binder with indexes and color coded for maximum reimbursement, St. Anthony Publications, Inc., Washington, D.C. [72]

St. Anthony's ICD-9-CM Ob/Gyn, St. Anthony Publishing, Inc., Washington, D.C. [72]

St. Anthony's ICD-9-CM Ophthalmology, St. Anthony Publishing, Inc., Washington, D.C. [72]

St. Anthony's ICD-9-CM Orthopaedics, St. Anthony Publishing, Inc., Washington, D.C. [72]

St. Anthony's ICD-9-CM Specialty Code Book, St. Anthony Publishing, Inc., Washington, D.C. [72]

St. Anthony's Quick Check for Physician Coding: ICD-9-CM and CPT Questions and Answers, St. Anthony Publishing, Inc., Washington, D.C. [72]

St. Anthony's Reimbursement Guide for Radiology Services: The Coding, Billing and Coverage Guide, St. Anthony Publishing, Inc., Washington, D.C. [71]

St. Anthony's 3-in-1 Code Book for Cardiology, St. Anthony Publishing, Inc., Washington, D.C. [72]

St. Anthony's 3-in-1 Code Book for Cardiovascular and General Surgery, St. Anthony Publishing, Inc., Washington, D.C. [72]

St. Anthony's 3-in-1 Code Book for Dermatology, Plastic and Reconstructive Surgery, St. Anthony Publishing, Inc., Washington, D.C. [72]

St. Anthony's 3-in-1 Code Book for ENT, St. Anthony Publishing, Inc., Washington, D.C. [72]

St. Anthony's 3-in-1 Code Book for Gynecology, Obstetrics, and Urology, St. Anthony Publishing, Inc., Washington, D.C. [72]

St. Anthony's 3-in-1 Code Book for Oncology and Hematology, St. Anthony Publishing, Inc., Washington, D.C. [72]

St. Anthony's 3-in-1 Code Book for Ophthalmology, St. Anthony Publishing, Inc., Washington, D.C. [72]

St. Anthony's 3-in-1 Code Book for Orthopaedics and Neurosurgery, St. Anthony Publishing, Inc., Washington, D.C. [72]

Schmidt, Chester W., Jr., *CPT Handbook for Psychiatrists,* American Psychiatric Press, Inc., Washington, D.C., 1993 [13]

Society of Cardiovascular and Interventional Radiology, The, *The Interventional Radiology Coding User's Guide,* published annually, Fairfax, Virginia [88]

Uniack, Ann G., *ICD-9-CM Coding in a SNAP,* alphabetical listing of over 1700 commonly used diagnosed codes, Skilled Nursing Assessment Programs (SNAP), San Anselmo, California, updated annually [86]

Unicor Medical, Inc., *Easy Coder,* Montgomery, Alabama. Easy coder books are available for the following specialties: cardiology, dermatology, ears/nose/throat, family practice, internal medicine, obstetrics/gynecology, ophthalmology, orthopedics, psychiatry, and urology [76]

United Communications Group, *National Correct Coding Primer,* Washington, D.C. [77]

World Health Organization, *ICD-10, The International Statistical Classification of Diseases and Related Health Problems, Tenth Revision,* Volume 1, World Health Organization, Geneva, 1992, distributed by Medicode, Inc., Med-Index Publishing Division, Salt Lake City, Utah [57]

Code Cards

Zupko, Karen, & Associates, *"Code-Its,"* compiled list of most common ICD-9-CM codes in each specialty. Request specialty—family practice, cardiology, ears/nose/throat, obstetrics/gynecology, urology, pediatrics, podiatry, cardiovascular surgery, ophthalmology (laminated cards), Karen Zupko & Associates, Chicago, Illinois [85]

Code Journals

CPT Assistant (four issues), American Medical Association, Chicago, Illinois [11]

Code Hotlines

Hotlines for Coding and Billing, St. Anthony's Hotline, (703) 836-9471 [72]

Code Newsletters

American Academy of Procedural Coders, *AAPC News,* Salt Lake City, Utah [3]

American Health Consultants, Inc., *Physicians Payment Update,* Atlanta, Georgia. Includes center section specific to coding strategies [9]

Group Health Management Corporation, *The Coding Connection,* Tucson, Arizona [36]

Medicode, Inc., *Reimbursement Update,* Med-Index Publishing Division, Salt Lake City, Utah [57]

St. Anthony Publishing, Inc., *Current Procedural Terminology (CPT),* Washington, D.C., published annually [72]

St. Anthony's Cardiovascular Coding Newsletter, St. Anthony Publishing, Inc., Washington, D.C. [72]

St. Anthony's Coding for General Surgery Reimbursement Newsletter, St. Anthony Publishing, Inc., Washington, D.C. [72]

St. Anthony's Coding for Ob/Gyn Reimbursement Newsletter, St. Anthony Publishing, Inc., Washington, D.C. [72]

St. Anthony's Coding for Ophthalmology Reimbursement Newsletter, St. Anthony Publishing, Inc., Washington, D.C. [72]

St. Anthony's Coding for Orthopaedic Reimbursement Newsletter, St. Anthony Publishing, Inc., Washington, D.C. [72]

St. Anthony's Color-Coded Guide to E/M Coding, St. Anthony Publishing, Inc., Washington, D.C. [72]

St. Anthony's Guide to E/M Coding and Documentation, St. Anthony Publishing, Inc., Washington, D.C. [72]

St. Anthony's CPT Coding for Physician Reimbursement (diagnostic and procedure coding, guidelines for billing, claims monitoring for physicians offices), St. Anthony Publishing, Inc., Washington, D.C., monthly [72]

St. Anthony's CPT 1994 Companion: A Guide to Medicare Billing, St. Anthony Publishing, Inc., Washington, D.C., 1994 [72]

St. Anthony's Hospital Fast Payment Report Newsletter, St. Anthony Publishing, Inc., Washington, D.C. [72]

St. Anthony's ICD-9-CM Coding for Reimbursement, St. Anthony Publishing, Inc., Washington, D.C. [72]

St. Anthony's Radiology Advisor, St. Anthony Publishing, Inc., Washington, D.C. [71]

Unicor Medical, Inc., *Coding News,* Montgomery, Alabama [76]

Wentworth Worldwide Media, *How to Get Paid.* Lancaster, Pennsylvania (features Medicare, coding, and third-party payer information, monthly) [80]

Code Research and Review Services

St. Anthony's Operative Report and Coding, Research and Review Service, St. Anthony Publishing, Inc., Washington, D.C. [72]

Code Software

ADP Business Assessments, *MCSS CPT and HCPCS Software,* distributed by MedSmart, Libertyville, Illinois [58]

ADP Business Assessments, *MCSS CPT and ICD-9 and HCPCS Software,* distributed by MedSmart, Libertyville, Illinois [58]

ADP Business Assessments, *MCSS CPT and ICD-9 Software,* distributed by MedSmart, Libertyville, Illinois [58]

ADP Business Assessments, *MCSS ICD-9 Software,* distributed by MedSmart, Libertyville, Illinois [58]

ADP Business Assessments, *Medical Code Software System,* MCSS Automated Code Finder (searches CPT, ICD-9, and HCPCS), MCSS CPT Software, distributed by MedSmart, Libertyville, Illinois [58]

American Medical Association, *ICD-9-CM* (floppy disk), Chicago, Illinois [11]

Channel Publishing, Ltd., *InfoCoder* (ICD-9-CM encoder), Reno, Nevada [19]

Code Master Corporation, *Code Master Plus,* Chicago, Illinois [84]

Context Software Systems, *Claims Editor,* Context Software Systems, Inc., Burr Ridge, Illinois [25]

Context Software Systems, *Codelink for Ophthalmology,* McGraw-Hill Healthcare Management Group, New York, New York [50]

Context Software Systems, *Codelink for Oral & Maxillofacial Surgery,* McGraw-Hill Healthcare Management Group, New York, New York [50]

Context Software Systems, *Codelink for Orthopaedics,* McGraw-Hill Healthcare Management Group, New York, New York [50]

Context Software Systems, *Codelink Software* (CPT,

HCPCS, and ICD-9-CM codes), McGraw-Hill Healthcare Management Group, New York, New York [50]

Context Software Systems, *Diagnostic ICD-9-Code Software*, McGraw-Hill Healthcare Management, New York, New York, 1994 [50]

Context Software Systems, Inc., *CODELINK*, Burr Ridge, Illinois [25]

DiagnostIC Data, Inc., *Code-Search*, West Hartford, Connecticut [29]

Dr. P's Software, Inc., *QuickCODE*, Springfield, Missouri [31]

Idea Planners, Inc., *Medcoder*, Clearwater, Florida [43]

Medicode, Inc., *OMS Cross Coder* (CPT and ICD-9 Codes), Med-Index Publishing Division, Salt Lake City, Utah [57]

SRC Systems, *Omnicoder and ICD coder*, San Antonio, Texas [70]

Unicor Medical, Inc., *Alpha II ICD-9 Coder*, Montgomery, Alabama [76]

United Communications Group, *RBRVS FEECALC*, calculates physicians' payments under the Medicare RBRVS fee schedule, Rockville, Maryland, upgraded periodically [77]

Wasserman Medical Publishers Limited, *ICD-9-CM Volume I, Software and HCPCS Level II Software*, West Allis, Wisconsin [79]

DELINQUENT AND DENIED CLAIMS

Collections from Insurance Carriers

Berry, Michael J., *Collections Made Easy! A Comprehensive Guide for Medical and Dental Professionals*, Practice Management Information Corporation, Los Angeles, California [63]

DIAGNOSIS-RELATED GROUPS

St. Anthony's Clinical Coder, St. Anthony Publishing, Inc., Washington, D.C. [72]

St. Anthony's DRG Optimizer, St. Anthony Publishing, Inc., Washington, D.C. [72]

St. Anthony's DRG Working Guidebook, St. Anthony Publishing, Inc., Washington, D.C. [72]

DIAGNOSTIC AND PROCEDURE HANDBOOKS FOR TERMINOLOGY

These medical books may be of assistance as references for researching medical terminology when doing diagnostic and procedural coding.

Golish, Joseph A. (Ed.), *Diagnostic and Procedure Handbook*, Lexi-Comp, Hudson, Ohio, 1992 [47]

The Merck Manual of Diagnosis and Therapy, Merck Sharp and Dohme Research Laboratories, Rahway, New Jersey, 1992, distributed by MedSmart, Libertyville, Illinois [58]

DICTIONARIES AND GLOSSARIES

Dorland's Illustrated Medical Dictionary, W. B. Saunders Company, Philadelphia, Pennsylvania, 1994 [66]

Health Insurance Terminology: A Glossary of Health Insurance Terms, Health Insurance Association of America, Washington, D.C. [39]

Stedman's Medical Dictionary, Williams & Wilkins, Baltimore, Maryland, 1995 [82]

Thomas, Clayton L. (Ed.), *Taber's Cyclopedic Medical Dictionary*, F. A. Davis Company, Philadelphia, Pennsylvania, 1985 [27]

DISABILITY BENEFIT PROGRAMS

Booklets and Pamphlets

Obtain from the state disability programs for the following states: California, Hawaii, New Jersey, New York, Puerto Pico, and Rhode Island. See Appendix A for state addresses.

Newsletters

Unemployment Insurance Reports with Social Security, Commerce Clearing House, Inc., Chicago, Illinois, weekly [22]

DISABILITY INCOME INSURANCE

Disability Income Insurance: An Overview of Income Protection Insurance, Health Insurance Association of America, Washington, D.C. [39]

DOCUMENTATION, MEDICAL

Kotoski, Gabrielle M., *Physician Documentation for Reimbursement*, Aspen Publishers, Inc., Frederick, Maryland, 1994 [15]

Medical Documentation; Streamlining an Essential Clinical Process, Medicode, Inc., Med-Index Publishing Division, Salt Lake City, Utah [57]

EDUCATION AND TRAINING

Audiocassette Tapes

Individual Health Insurance, Parts A and B, Group Life & Health Insurance, Parts A, B, and C, Long-Term Care, Health Insurance Association of America, Washington, D.C. [39]

Walsh, John, *Medicare: Surgery Coding for Dollars*, National Healthcare Seminars, Novato, California [61]

Books

American Health Information Management Association, *Coding Curriculum Guide,* New York, New York [10]

Anderson, Ellen, Nicholas, Toula, and Rogers, Vickie, *CPT: Beyond the Basics* (self-study), four lessons, American Health Information Management Association, New York, New York [10]

Anderson, Ellen, and Nicholas, Toula, *ICD-9-CM: Beyond the Basics* (self-study), four lessons, American Health Information Management Association, New York, New York [10]

Buck, Carol J., *Step-by-Step Medical Coding,* W. B. Saunders Company, Philadelphia, Pennsylvania [66]

California Health Information Association, *Module II, The Advanced Coder,* Fresno, California [17]

California Health Information Association, *Steps to Coding with ICD-9-CM for Long Term Care,* Fresno, California, 1993 [17]

California Health Information Association, *Steps to Coding with ICD-9-CM Module I. The Beginning Coder,* Fresno, California [17]

Covell, Alice G., *Coding Workbook for the Physician's Office,* Delmar Publishers, Inc., Albany, New York, Published annually [28]

Holloway, J. A., & Associates, Inc., *Basic ICD-9-CM for Physicians' Offices,* American Health Information Management Association, New York, New York [10]

Holloway, J. A. & Associates, Inc., *Introduction to CPT for the Physician Coder,* American Health Information Management Association, New York, New York [10]

Medical Learning Incorporated, *CPT Coding Workbook for the Student,* St. Paul, Minnesota [89]

Med-Index Self-Tests (Coding Instructions), Medicode, Inc., Med-Index Publishing Division, Salt Lake City, Utah [57]

Morin-Spatz, Patricia, *Case Study Workbook* (for advanced coder), MedBooks, Houston, Texas, 1993 [51]

Morin-Spatz, Patricia, *CP "Teach,"* Instructors Manual, Med-Books, Houston, Texas, 1993 [51]

Morin-Spatz, Patricia, *CP "Teach,"* Workbook, MedBooks, Houston, Texas, 1994 [51]

Morin-Spatz, Patricia, *CP "Teach"—Expert Coding Made Easy!,* Textbook, MedBooks, Houston, Texas, 1993 [51]

Moss, Edna, *Basic Keyboarding for the Medical Office Assistant,* Delmar Publishers, Inc., Albany, New York, 1995 [28]

Nicholas, Toula, *Basic ICD-9-CM Coding Handbook,* American Health Information Management Association, New York, New York, 1994 [10]

Nicholas, Toula, *CPT/HCPCS Basic Coding Handbook,* American Health Information Management Association, New York, New York [10]

Renfro, Joy, *Coding Skills for the Medical Assistant,* American Association of Medical Assistants, Chicago, Illinois, 1993 [4]

Soerries, Sandra, *Multispecialty Medical Coding Workbook,* Soerries Enterprises, Oak Grove, Missouri, updated annually [69]

Courses

See also *Videotapes* and *Workshops and Seminars.*

Soerries, Sandra, *Evaluation and Management Training* (2-hour training session), Soerries Enterprises, Oak Grove, Missouri [69]

Soerries, Sandra, *Multispecialty Medical Coding Workbook,* Soerries Enterprises, Oak Grove, Missouri, updated annually [69]

Soerries, Sandra, *S.O.S. for the Medical Office* (12-hour training session), Soerries Enterprises, Oak Grove, Missouri [69]

St. Anthony Publishing, Inc., *CPT-4 Clinic: Basic Procedural Coding,* Washington, D.C. [72]

St. Anthony Publishing, Inc., *ICD-9-CM Clinic: Basic Diagnostic Coding,* Washington, D.C. [72]

St. Anthony Publishing, Inc., *Physician Reimbursement Clinic: Managing Payment, Billing & Coding in the RBRVS Era,* Washington, D.C. [72]

St. Anthony Publishing, Inc., *St. Anthony's Basic ICD-9-CM Coding: Self-Directed Training for the Physician Office Professional* (four audiocassette tapes and workbook), Washington, D.C. [72]

St. Anthony Publishing, Inc., *The 3-in-1 Coding Workshop: ICD-9-CM, CPT, and HCPCS Level II,* Washington, D.C. [72]

Strategic Decisions Plus, *Electronic Medical Claims,* Silverthorne, Colorado [75]

ELECTRONIC DATA INTERCHANGE

Books

Automated Medical Payments Directory, Faulkner & Gray, Inc., Chicago, Illinois, updated annually [33]

Compliance Guide to Electronic Health Care Payments, A Practical Reference to Legislation, Codes, Regulations, and Industry Standards, Faulkner & Gray, Inc., Chicago, Illinois, 1994 [33]

Electronic Claims Professional Basics, National Association of Claims Assistance Professionals, Downers Grove, Illinois, 1992 [60]

Electronic Billing Software: Who's Out There Selling? (about electronic claims processing) Aspen Publishers, Inc., Frederick, Maryland [15]

Electronic Medical Claims Presentation Manual, Strategic Decisions Plus, Silverthorne, Colorado [75]

Claims Processing Bulletin Board Services

Claims Wizard Software, InfoAlliance, Madison, Wisconsin [45]

Computer Bulletin Board for Claims Professionals, InfoAlliance, Madison, Wisconsin [45]

ETHICS

See also *Law and Ethics.*

Code of Medical Ethics, Current Opinions with Annotations, American Medical Association, Chicago, Illinois, 1994 [11]

Reports of the Council on Ethical & Judicial Affairs, American Medical Association, Chicago, Illinois, 1994 [11]

FEES, REIMBURSEMENT, CHARGES

Aspen Publishers, Inc., *Reimbursement Advisor,* Frederick, Maryland, monthly newsletter [15]
Cambridge Health Economics Group, *What Are My Fees? A Physician's Guide to the Complete National Medicare Fee Schedule,* McGraw-Hill Healthcare Management Group, New York, New York [50]
Davis, James R., *Reimbursement Manual for the Medical Office, A Comprehensive Guide to Coding, Billing and Fee Management,* Practice Management Information Corporation, Los Angeles, California, 1992 [63]
Fox, Thomas C., Carol Colborn, Carl Krasik, and Joseph W. Metro, *Health Care Financial Transactions Manual,* Clark Boardman Callaghan, Deerfield, Illinois, revised periodically [21]
HealthCare Consultants of America, Inc., *"Fees on Disk" Software.* Specialties: Cardiology, Dermatology, Family/General Practice, Internal Medicine, Ob/Gyn/Surgery, Augusta, Georgia [37]
Lyle, James R., and Torras, Hoyt W., *1994 Physicians' Fee & Coding Guide, A Comprehensive Fee and Coding Reference,* HealthCare Consultants of America, Augusta, Georgia, updated annually [37]
McGraw-Hill Healthcare Management Group, *RVP Fees: Primary Care,* (software program), New York, New York [50]
McGraw-Hill Healthcare Management Group, *RVP Fees, Version 3.1* (software program), New York, New York [50]
McGraw-Hill Healthcare Management Group, *What Are My Fees? A Physician's Guide to the Complete Local Medicare Fee Schedule,* New York, New York [50]
Medicode, Inc., *Physician Fee Analyzer Plus,* Med-Index Publishing Division, Salt Lake City, Utah [57]
Medicode, Inc., *Reimbursement Strategies; Master the Payment Cycle Today,* Med-Index Publishing Division, Salt Lake City, Utah, 1992 [57]
Practice Management Information Corporation, *Physician Fees: A Comprehensive Guide for Fee Schedule Review and Management,* Los Angeles, California, updated annually [63]
St. Anthony Publishing, Inc., "Medirisk Physician Fee Schedules," Washington, D.C. (reports are available for 30 specialties and all geographic regions) [72]
Wasserman Medical Publishers Limited, *Physicians' Fee Reference* (available in book and on disk), West Allis, Wisconsin, updated annually [79]
Zimmerman & Associates, *Health Care Billing Manual,* Aspen Publishers, Inc., Frederick, Maryland [15]

FRAUD AND ABUSE

See also *Videotapes.*

"Consumer Fraud—Medicare and Home Medical Equipment" (pamphlet), United States Government Printing Office, Washington, D.C., 1992:332.525 [78]

HCFA-1500 CLAIM FORM

St. Anthony's Claims Administrator, The HCFA 1500 from Submission to Payment, St. Anthony's Publishing, Inc., Washington, D.C. [72]

HCFA COMMON PROCEDURE CODING SYSTEM (HCPCS)

Context Software Systems, *HCPCS Level II, National Codes,* McGraw-Hill Healthcare Management Group, New York, New York, published annually [50]
Medicode, Inc., *HCPCS, Medicare's National Level II Codes,* Med-Index Publishing Division, Salt Lake City, Utah [57]
Practice Management Information Corporation, *HCPCS, HCFA Common Procedure Coding System,* spiral-bound version or binder version (annual publication), Los Angeles, California [63]
St. Anthony Publishing, Inc., *HCPCS Level II Codes,* Washington, D.C., published annually [72]
St. Anthony's HCPCS Report Newsletter, St. Anthony Publishing, Inc., Washington, D.C. [72]
U.S. Government Printing Office, *HCPCS Common Procedure Coding System* (non-CPT-4 portion). Order document number 01706000307-3 from U.S. Government Printing Office, Washington, D.C. [78]
Wasserman Medical Publishers, Limited, *HCPCS Level II Code Book,* West Allis, Wisconsin, updated annually [79]

HEALTH INSURANCE

Books

Collins, Rhoda, *From Patient to Payment: Insurance Procedures for the Medical Office,* Glencoe, Macmillan/McGraw-Hill, Columbus, Ohio, 1993 [35]
Health Insurance Association of America, *The Business of Insurance,* Washington, D.C., 1993 [39]
Insurance Career Development Center, *A Guide to Health Claims Examining,* (Volume 3 of multivolume set), Mosby-Year Book, Inc., St. Louis, Missouri, 1994 [59]
Long, Dani L., and Morton, Gene A., *Principles of Life & Health Insurance,* FLMI Insurance Education Program, Life Management Institute LOMA, National Association of Claims Assistance Professionals, Downers Grove, Illinois, 1988 [60]
National Association of Claims Assistance Professionals, *Insurance Basics,* Downers Grove, Illinois, 1992 [60]
Rowell, JoAnn C., *Understanding Medical Insurance: A Step by Step Guide,* Delmar Publishers, Inc., Albany, New York, 1994 [28]

HEALTH MAINTENANCE ORGANIZATIONS/PREFERRED PROVIDER ORGANIZATIONS

See *Managed Care.*

HOSPITAL INSURANCE CLAIMS

UB-92 Edition: A Guide to Medicare Billing, St. Anthony Publishing, Inc., Washington, D.C. [72]

INSURANCE DIRECTORIES

Health Insurance Carrier Directory, A Comprehensive Guide to Insurance Carriers & Claims Processing, binder or spiral-bound versions, Practice Management Information Corporation, Los Angeles, California, annual publication [63]

Insurance Directory, Medicode, Inc., Med-Index Publishing Division, Salt Lake City, Utah, updated annually [57]

Physicians' Insurance Reference, Wasserman Medical Publishers, Limited, West Allis, Wisconsin, updated annually [79]

LAW AND ETHICS

See also *Ethics*.

Books

Cacioppo, Paul P., *Health Care Fraud and Abuse*, Clark Boardman Callaghan, Deerfield, Illinois, (revised annually) [21]

Flight, Myrtle R., *Law, Liability & Ethics for Medical Office Personnel*, Delmar Publishers, Inc., Albany, New York [28]

Judson, Karen, and Blesie, Sharon, *Law & Ethics for Health Occupations*, Glencoe, Macmillan/McGraw-Hill, Columbus, Ohio, 1993 [35]

Newsletters

Flight, Myrtle R., *Legal Issues for the Medical Office*, provides timely information on legal issues that arise in the daily functioning of a medical office, Canton, Massachusetts, monthly [34]

In Confidence, American Health Information Management Association, New York, New York, (6 issues/year) [10]

Patient Confidentiality, Alphabetical Guide to the Release of Medical Information, Medicode, Inc., Med-Index Publishing Division, Salt Lake City, Utah, updated annually [57]

Software

Black, Henry Campbell, *Black's Law Dictionary*, Electronic Edition, 3.5" or 5.25" disks, West Information Publishing Group, Eagan, Minnesota [81]

MANAGED CARE

American Medical Association, *Criteria for Participating in Managed Care Systems; How to Evaluate a Managed Care System Contract*, Chicago, Illinois [11]

American Medical Association, *Doctors Resource Service (DRS)* (publication, video cassette, audiocassette), Paterson, New Jersey, mailed every 6 weeks [12]

Conomikes Associates, Inc., *Conomikes Managed Care Handbook*, Los Angeles, California [24]

Kongsvedt, Peter R., *The Managed Health Care Handbook*, Aspen Publishers, Inc., Frederick, Maryland, 1996 [15]

Lyle, James R., and Torras, Hoyt W., *Physician's Guide to Managed Care, A Comprehensive Guide to Managed Competition, Managed Care, and Global Budgeting*, HealthCare Consultants of America, Inc., Augusta, Georgia, 1993 [37]

Managed Care Information Center, *Managed Care Resource Guide*, Wall Township, New Jersey, quarterly [48]

Medical Economics, *HMO/PPO Directory*, Medical Economics Publishing, Montvale, New Jersey, published annually [53]

Medical Management Institute, *Negotiating Managed Care Contracts*, McGraw-Hill Health Care Management Group, New York, New York, 1994 [50]

Nash, David B., *The Physician's Guide to Managed Care*, Aspen Publishers, Inc., Frederick, Maryland, 1993 [15]

Practice Management Information Corporation, *The Managed Care Handbook, A Comprehensive Guide to Preparing Your Practice for the Managed Care Revolution*, Los Angeles, California [63]

Richards, Carol K., *Managing Managed Care for the Physician's Office*, American Association of Medical Assistants, Chicago, Illinois, 1991 [4]

Newsletters

CCH Monitor, The Newsletter of Managed Care, Commerce Clearing House, Inc., Chicago, Illinois, biweekly [22]

CCH Pulse, The Health Care Reform Newsletter, Commerce Clearing House, Inc., Chicago, Illinois, bimonthly [22]

Physician's Managed Care Report, American Health Consultants, Inc., Atlanta, Georgia, monthly [9]

MEDICAID

Bulletins

Obtain from the State Intermediary. See Appendix A for the address in your state.

CD-ROM

The Medicare and Medicaid Guide, Volumes 1 through 5 updated weekly and CD-ROM updated monthly, Commerce Clearing House, Inc., Chicago, Illinois [22]

The Medicare/Medicaid Library (CD-ROM monthly subscription with modem access to Bulletin Board service, which contains updates to Federal Register), Information Handling services (IHS) Regulatory Products, Englewood, Colorado [45]

Newsletters

California Medi-Cal Guide, Commerce Clearing House, Inc., Chicago, Illinois, monthly [22]

MEDICAL MANAGEMENT

Books

Managing Medical Office Personnel, A Comprehensive Guide to Personnel Management in the Medical Practice, Practice Management Information Corporation, Los Angeles, California [63]

Newsletters

American Health Consultants, Inc., *Physician's Marketing & Management,* Atlanta, Georgia, monthly [9]
California Health Information Association, *Journal of CHIA,* Fresno, California. (Includes articles on coding, reimbursement, and legal issues. Directed to hospitals and ambulatory surgery centers), monthly [17]
Conomikes Reports on Medical Practice Management, Conomikes Associates, Inc., Los Angeles, California, monthly [24]
MCA Publications, *The Physician's Advisory,* Syracuse, New York, monthly [49]
Medical Office Manager, Atlanta, Georgia [56]
Uncommon Sense, Practice Performance Publishing, Inc., Long Beach, California, monthly [64]
Wentworth Worldwide Media, *The Doctor's Office,* Lancaster, Pennsylvania, monthly [80]

MEDICARE

Books

American Health Consultants, *Key Questions in Medicare Coding,* Atlanta, Georgia [9]
American Medical Association, *Medicare RBRVS: The Physicians' Guide Book,* Chicago, Illinois, 1994 [11]
Bear, Philip L., *The ProSTAT Guide to Medicare,* Medicode, Inc., Med-Index Publishing Division, Salt Lake City, Utah [57]
Commerce Clearing House and the American Medical Association Physicians' Medicare Guide, Commerce Clearing House, Inc., Chicago, Illinois, every other month [22]
Context Software Systems, Inc., *Medicare Rules & Regulations,* Volumes 1 through 8, McGraw-Hill HealthCare Management Group, New York, New York, updated as necessary [50]
Guide to RBRVS for Primary Care Physicians, HealthCare Consultants of America, Inc., Augusta, Georgia, (also other RVS fee guides and insurance publications) [37]
Knaus, Denise L., *The Medicare Coverage Issues Manual,* McGraw-Hill HealthCare Management Group, New York, New York [50]
Knaus, Denise L., *The Medicare Survival Guide,* McGraw-Hill HealthCare Management Group, New York, New York [50]
Lyle, James R., and Torras, Hoyt W., *Make Medicare Work for You* (updated to include RBRVS), HealthCare Consultants of America, Inc., Augusta, Georgia, 1992 [37]
Medicare at a Glance: How Carriers Scrutinize Your Procedural Coding, Medicode, Inc., Med-Index Publishing Division, Salt Lake City, Utah [57]
Medicare Rules & Regulations, A Survival Guide to Policies, Procedures and Payment Reform, Practice Management Information Corporation, Los Angeles, California, 1994 [63]
St. Anthony's Color-Coded Medicare Coverage Manual, St. Anthony Publishing, Inc., Washington, D.C. (with color-coded prompts) [72]
St. Anthony's CPT '95 Companion: A Guide to Medicare Billing, St. Anthony Publishing, Inc., Washington, D.C. [72]
St. Anthony's Guide to Ambulatory Surgery Center Payment Groups, St. Anthony Publishing, Inc., Washington, D.C. [72]
St. Anthony's Medicare Secondary Payer Billing and Reimbursement Guide, St. Anthony Publishing, Inc., Washington, D.C. [72]
United Communications Group, *Part B Answer Book, Medicare Billing Rules from A to Z,* Rockville, Maryland, updated quarterly [77]
United Communication Group, *Part B Pocket Billing Guide,* Rockville, Maryland, updated quarterly [77]

Bulletins

Obtain from the State intermediary. See Appendix A to obtain the address for your state.

CD-ROM

The Medicare and Medicaid Guide, Volumes 1 through 5 updated weekly and CD-ROM updated monthly, Commerce Clearing House, Inc., Chicago, Illinois [22]
The Medicare/Medicaid Library, IHS Regulatory Products, Englewood, Colorado [44]

Newsletters

Conomikes Medicare Hotline, Conomikes Reports, Inc., Los Angeles, California, monthly [24]
Medicare Review, Shannon Publications, Inc., Dallas, Texas, monthly [67]
Part B News, United Communications Group, Rockville, Maryland, bimonthly [77]
Physicians' Medicare Guide Newsletter, Commerce Clearing House, Inc., Chicago, Illinois, every other month [22]

PREFERRED PROVIDER ORGANIZATIONS

See *Managed Care.*

REIMBURSEMENT

See *Fees, Reimbursement, Charges.*

RELATIVE VALUE STUDIES

Relative Value Studies, Inc., *St Anthony's Complete RBRVS,* St. Anthony Publishing, Inc., Washington, D.C., updated annually [72]

Relative Value Studies with Regard to Radiology, American College of Radiology, Reston, Virginia (write for information) [6]

Resource-Based Relative Value Scale (RBRVS), Physicians Fee Schedule, Addendum E, page 63852, Federal Register, Stock No. 069-001-00063-7, Superintendent of Documents, U.S. Government Printing Office, Washington, D.C., December 2, 1993 [78]

SELF-EMPLOYMENT

Audiotapes

Electronic Medical Claims Marketing Strategies, Strategic Decisions Plus, Silverthorne, Colorado [75]

Books

Benzel, Rick, *Health Service Business on Your Home-Based P/C,* Windcrest/McGraw-Hill, Blue Ridge Summit, Pennsylvania [83]. May be purchased from Oxford Medical Systems, Cincinnati, Ohio [62]

Magazines

Home Office Computing, Home Office Computing, Boulder, Colorado, monthy [41]

Marketing

Brochure Collection (24 sample pieces), Strategic Decisions Plus, Silverthorne, Colorado [75]

Newsletters

PRO Claimer Analyst, Strategic Decisions Plus, Silverthorne, Colorado, monthly [75]

Software

Eazy Quote, Strategic Decisions Plus, Silverthorne, Colorado [75]

Power Leads for Medical Claims Businesses, InfoAlliance, Madison, Wisconsin [44]

VIDEOTAPES

Blue Shield of California, Fraud & Abuse Unit, "Medicare Part B: Putting an End to Fraud & Abuse," 8 Minutes, Chico, California [16]

Blue Shield of California, Fraud & Abuse Unit, "Understanding Limiting Charges, Benefits of Medicare Part B Beneficiaries," 8 Minutes, Chico, California [16]

Channel Publishing, Ltd., "Beginning ICD-9-CM," 2-Hour videotape, binder, and workbook, Reno, Nevada [19]

ChartCare Solutions, "E & M Coding & Documentation," Phoenix, Arizona [20]

Health Insurance Association of America, "Fighting Fraud," Washington, D.C. [39]

Health Insurance Association of America, "Protecting Tomorrow: Long-Term Care," Washington, D.C. [39]

Health Insurance Association of America, "The Case for Case Management," Washington, D.C. [39]

Healthcare Management Advisors, Inc., "Coding for Quality," ICD-9-CM Level 1 (26 videotapes); Introduction to CPT (3 videotapes), Atlanta, Georgia [38]

HealthMarket International, "ICD-10," HealthMarket International, Ann Arbor, Michigan [87]

WORKERS' COMPENSATION

Guides to the Evaluation of Permanent Impairment, American Medical Association, Chicago, Illinois, 1994 [11]

Milliman and Robertson, Inc., *Healthcare Management Guidelines Return-to-Work Planning,* distributed by St. Anthony Publishing, Inc., Washington, D.C., 1994 [72]

Official California Workers' Compensation Medical Fee Schedule, California Medical Fee Schedule, State of California, San Francisco, California [74]

WORKSHOPS AND SEMINARS

American Health Information Management Association [10]

Conomikes Reports, Inc., Los Angeles, California [24]

Medical Management Institute, Alpharetta, Georgia [55]

Medical Management Information Services, Inc., Long Beach, California [54]

Medicode, Inc., *The Reimbursement Manager Training Program (RMTP),* Med-Index Publishing Division, Salt Lake City, Utah [57]

National Healthcare Seminars, Novato, California [61]

St. Anthony's Seminars, Springfield, Virginia [73]
Advanced Cardiovascular Coding
Ambulatory Surgery Coding Clinic
Ambulatory Training Series
Cardiovascular Coding Workshop
CPT-4 Hospital Clinic
Emergency Medicine Workshop
Ob/Gyn Coding Workshop
Ophthalmology Coding Workshop
Orthopaedic Coding Workshop
Physician Billing & Reimbursement

Radiology Coding & Reimbursement
Three-in-One Coding Clinic
United Communications Group, Rockville, Maryland [27]

See also *Education and Training; Courses,* which offer prior approval and continuing education units.

Names and Addresses of Resources

1. American Academy of Orthopaedic Surgeons
   6300 N. River Road
   Rosemont, IL 60018-4226
   (800) 346-AAOS or (800) 626-6726
   (708) 823-7186
   FAX: (708) 823-8125
2. American Academy of Pediatrics
   141 N.W. Point Boulevard
   P. O. Box 927
   Elk Grove Village, IL 60009-0927
   (708) 228-5005
   (800) 433-9016
3. American Academy of Procedural Coders
   145 West Crystal Avenue
   Salt Lake City, UT 84115
   (800) 626-CODE
4. American Association of Medical Assistants
   20 N. Wacker Drive, Suite 1575
   Chicago, IL 60606
   (800) 228-2262
5. American College of Emergency Physicians
   P. O. Box 619911
   Dallas, TX 75261
   (800) 798-1822
6. American College of Radiology RVS
   1891 Preston White Drive
   Reston, VA 22090
7. American College of Rheumatology
   60 Executive Park South, Suite 150
   Atlanta, GA 30329
   (404) 633-3777
8. American Guild of Patient Account Management
   National Certification Examination Program
   1101 Connecticut Avenue, N.W., Suite 700
   Washington, DC 20036
9. American Health Consultants, Inc.
   3525 Piedmont Road, N.E., Building 6, Suite 400 (30305)
   P. O. Box 740060, Department 1203
   Atlanta, GA 30374-9822
10. American Health Information Management Association
    Attention: AHIMA Coordinator
    Professional Examination Service
    475 Riverside Drive
    New York, NY 10115
    (212) 870-3136
11. American Medical Association
    515 N. State Street
    P. O. Box 10946
    Chicago, IL 60610-0946
    (800) 621-8335
12. American Medical Association
    Doctors Resource Service
    Department CRAD41
    P. O. Box 9025
    Paterson, NJ 07509-9912
    (800) AMA-1066
13. American Psychiatric Press, Inc.
    1400 K Street, N.W.
    Washington, DC 20005
14. American Society for Parenteral and Enteral Nutrition
    8630 Fenton Street, Suite 412
    Silver Spring, MD 20910-3805
    (301) 587-6315
15. Aspen Publishers, Inc.
    P. O. Box 990
    Frederick, MD 21705-9727
    (800) 638-8437
16. Blue Shield of California
    Fraud & Abuse Unit
    P. O. Box 2807
    Chico, CA 95927
    (916) 896-7055
17. California Health Information Association
    5108 E. Clinton Way, Suite 113
    Fresno, CA 93727-8509
    (800) 247-8907
18. California Medical Fee Schedule
    Department 05445
    P. O. Box 39000
    San Francisco, CA 94139
19. Channel Publishing, Ltd.
    4750 Longley Lane, Suite 110
    Reno, NV 89502
    (800) 248-2882
20. ChartCare Solutions
    7803 N. 12th Avenue
    Phoenix, AZ 85021
    (800) 449-1272
21. Clark Boardman Callaghan
    155 Pfingsten Road
    Deerfield, IL 60015-4998
    (800) 221-9428
22. Commerce Clearing House, Inc.
    4025 West Peterson Avenue (60646)
    P. O. Box 5490
    Chicago, IL 60680-9882
    (800) 835-5224
23. Commission on Professional Hospital Activities (CPHA)
    P. O. Box 1809
    Ann Arbor, MI 48106
    (313) 769-6511
24. Conomikes Associates, Inc.
    6033 West Century Boulevard, Suite 990
    Los Angeles, CA 90045
    (800) 421-6512
25. Context Software Systems, Inc.
    241 S. Frontage Road, Suite 38
    Burr Ridge, IL 60521
    (708) 654-8800
    (800) 783-3378
26. Covell and Harwood, Consultants
    1503 S. Burdick Street
    Kalamazoo, MI 49001-2701
27. F. A. Davis Company/Publishers
    1915 Arch Street
    Philadelphia, PA 19103
    (800) 323-3555

28. Delmar Publishers, Inc.
3 Columbia Circle Drive
P. O. Box 15015
Albany, NY 12212-5015
(800) 347-7707
29. DiagnostIC Data, Inc.
20 Balfour Drive
West Hartford, CT 06117
(800) 999-6405
30. The Doctor's Office
P. O. Box 10488
Lancaster, PA 17605-0488
31. Dr. P's Software, Inc.
3525 S. National, Suite 110
Springfield, MO 65807
32. Entrepreneur
6001 D Landerhaven
Cleveland, OH 44124
(216) 449-8022
33. Faulkner & Gray, Inc.
P. O. Box 87271
Chicago, IL 60680-9748
(800) 826-3115
34. Myrtle R. Flight, Attorney at Law
Two Harrison Road
Canton, MA 02021
35. Glencoe, Macmillan/McGraw-Hill
P. O. Box 508
Columbus, OH 43216
(800) 334-7344
36. Group Health Management Corporation
P. O. Box 12929
Tucson, AZ 85732
(602) 747-0010
37. HealthCare Consultants of America, Inc.
609 Fifteenth Street
Augusta, GA 30901
(800) 253-4945
(706) 724-2078
FAX: (706) 722-9869
38. Healthcare Management Advisors, Inc.
1091-C Cambridge Square
Atlanta, GA 30201-1844
(800) 875-8HMA
39. Health Insurance Association of America
1025 Connecticut Avenue, N.W.
Washington, DC 20036-3998
(202) 223-7539
40. Dr. R. B. Holt
2182 E. Sublette Place
Sandy, UT 84093-1056
41. Home Office Computing
P. O. Box 51344
Boulder, CO 80321-1344
42. William J. Hunt, M.D.
3540 Forest Hill Boulevard
West Palm Beach, FL 33406
43. Idea Planners, Inc.
2075 San Marino Way, North
Clearwater, FL 34623
(813) 442-6506
44. InfoAlliance
6701 Seybold, Suite 219
Madison, WI 53719
(608) 277-2990
45. Information Handling Services (IHS) Regulatory Products
6160 S. Syracuse Way
Englewood, CO 80110
(303) 267-0543
(800) 525-5539
46. KFC Medical Systems, Inc.
713 St. Louis Avenue
Long Beach, CA 90804
(213) 434-7224
47. Lexi-Comp
Hudson, OH
(800) 837-LEXI
48. Managed Care Information Center
3100 Highway 138
Wall Township, NJ 07719-1442
(908) 681-1133
FAX: (908) 681-0490
49. MCA Publications
P. O. Box 6093
Syracuse, NY 13217
(610) 828-3888
50. McGraw-Hill Healthcare Management Group
1221 Avenue of the Americas
New York, NY 10020
51. MedBooks
P. O. Box 670308
Houston, TX 77267-0308
(800) 443-7397
52. Medical Business Resource Center
1221 E. Osborn Road, Suite 101
Phoenix, AZ 85014
53. Medical Economics Publishing
5 Paragon Drive
Montvale, New Jersey 07645
(800) 432-4570
54. Medical Management Information Services, Inc.
6475 E. Pacific Coast Highway, Suite 409 (90802)
P. O. Box 33-409
Long Beach, CA 90801
(310) 596-1186
55. Medical Management Institute
1125 Cambridge Square
Alpharetta, Georgia 30201
(800) 334-5724
56. Medical Office Manager
P. O. Box 500845
Atlanta, GA 31150
(404) 319-8105
57. Medicode, Inc.
Med-Index Publishing Division
5225 Wiley Post Way, Suite 500 (84116-2889)
P. O. Box 526180
Salt Lake City, UT 84152-6180
(800) 999-4614
58. MedSmart
1590 S. Milwaukee Avenue, Suite 212
Libertyville, IL 60048
(800) 50-SMART
59. Mosby–Year Book, Inc.
11830 Westline Industrial Drive
St. Louis, MO 63146
(800) 633-6699
FAX: (314) 432-1380
60. National Association of Claims Assistance Professionals
5329 South Main Street, Suite 102
Downers Grove, IL 60515-4845
61. National Healthcare Seminars

258 Ignacio Valley Circle
Novato, CA 94949
(415) 883-3541

62. Oxford Medical Systems
230 Northland Boulevard, Suite 223
Cincinnati, OH 45246
63. Practice Management Information Corporation
8330 W. Third Street
Los Angeles, CA 90048
(800) MED-SHOP
64. Practice Performance Publishing, Inc.
2508 E. Willow, Suite 302
Long Beach, CA 90806
(310) 595-1728
65. Professional Practice Builders
2000 Ticonderoga Drive
San Mateo, CA 94402
(415) 573-0109
66. W. B. Saunders Company
6277 Sea Harbor Drive
Orlando, FL 32821-9989
(800) 545-2522
FAX: (800) 874-6418
67. Shannon Publications, Inc.
Northcreek Place 1
9441 LBJ Freeway, Suite 510, Box 2
Dallas, TX 75243-9940
(800) 578-4888
68. Society of Thoracic Surgeons
401 N. Michigan Avenue
Chicago, IL 60611-4267
(312) 644-6610
69. Soerries Enterprises
8318 S. Outer Belt Road
Oak Grove, MO 64075
(816) 690-8996
70. SRC Systems
14785 Omicron Drive
Texas Research Park
San Antonio, TX 78245-3201
(210) 677-6010
71. St. Anthony Publishing, Inc.
11410 Isaac Newton Square
Reston, VA 22090
(703) 904-3900
(800) 632-0123
72. St. Anthony Publishing, Inc.
P. O. Box 14212
Washington, DC 20044-4212
(800) 632-0123
FAX: (703) 706-5830
73. St. Anthony's Seminars
5224 Juliette Street
Springfield, VA 22151
(800) 632-0123
74. State of California
Department of Industrial Relations
Division of Workers' Compensation
455 Golden Gate Avenue, Room 5182
San Francisco, CA 94102
75. Strategic Decisions Plus
P. O. Box 2108
Silverthorne, CO 80498
(303) 262-9290
76. Unicor Medical, Inc.
4160 Carmichael Road, Suite 101
Montgomery, AL 36106
(800) 825-7421
(205) 260-8150
77. United Communications Group
11300 Rockville Pike, Suite 1100 (20852)
P. O. Box 90608
Washington, DC 20077-7637
(800) 929-4824
78. United States Government Printing Office
Superintendent of Documents
Washington, DC 20402
79. Wasserman Medical Publishers, Limited
3036 S. 92nd Street
P. O. Box 27365
West Allis, WI 53227
(800) 669-3337
80. Wentworth Worldwide Media
1866 Colonial Village Lane
P. O. Box 10488
Lancaster, PA 17605-0488
(800) 331-5196
81. West Information Publishing Group
620 Opperman Drive
P. O. Box 64526
Eagan, MN 55123-1396
(800) 328-9352
82. Williams & Wilkins
P. O. Box 1496
Baltimore, MD 21298-9724
(800) 638-0672
83. Windcrest/McGraw-Hill
Blue Ridge Summitt, PA 17294-0850
84. Code Master Corporation
10 South Riverside Plaza
Chicago, Illinois
(800) 634-4255
85. Karen Zupko & Associates
980 N. Michigan Avenue, #1325
Chicago, IL 60611
(312) 642-5616
86. Skilled Nursing Assessment Programs (SNAP)
P. O. Box 574
San Anselmo, CA 94979
(415) 454-5752
Fax: (415) 453-6029
87. Health Market International
4885 Lone Oak Court
Ann Arbor, MI 48108
(313) 665-1360
88. The Society of Cardiovascular and Interventional Radiology
10201 Lee Highway, Suite 500
Fairfax, VA 22030
(703) 691-1805
89. Medical Learning Incorporated
245 East Sixth Street, Suite 502
St. Paul, MN 55101
(800) 252-1578
Fax: 612-224-4694
90. HCIA Inc.
300 East Lombard Street
Baltimore, MD 21202
(800) 568-3282

APPENDIX C

Medi-Cal

Objectives

THE INSURANCE BILLING SPECIALIST WILL BE ABLE TO:

- Understand the benefits and nonbenefits of Medi-Cal.
- Define abbreviations inherent to Medi-Cal.
- Minimize the number of insurance forms rejected because of improper completion.
- List important information to obtain from the patient's Medi-Cal identification card.
- State how to verify a patient's Medi-Cal eligibility.
- Explain how to identify patients covered by prepaid health plans.
- List basic Medi-Cal claim procedure guidelines.
- State how to process Medi-Cal patients who have additional coverage.
- List when it is necessary to use and how to complete a Treatment Authorization Request Form.
- Describe the time limit and state exceptions for submitting Medi-Cal claims.
- Complete the UB-92 Outpatient Claim Form.
- Explain entries shown on a Remittance Advice Details document.
- Identify information on a Resubmission Turnaround Document.
- State when to use and how to complete a Claims Inquiry Form.

Key Terms and Abbreviations

In addition to the key terms given in Chapter 11, Medicaid and Other State Programs, the following abbreviations are emphasized for study from Appendix C.

Abbreviation	Expansion
AB	Aid to the Blind
A/R	accounts receivable
AEVS	automated eligibility verification system
AFDC	Aid to Families with Dependent Children
ATD	Aid to the (permanently) Disabled
BIC	benefits identification card
Cal-MAP	California Medical Assistance Program
CCN	claim control number
CCS	California Children's Services
CERTS	claims and eligibility real-time system
CHDP	Child Health and Disability Prevention Program
CIF	Claims Inquiry Form
CMC	computer media claims
CMSP	County Medical Services Program
CNN	claim control number
CPSP	Comprehensive Perinatal Services Program
DME	durable medical equipment
EDS	Electronic Data Systems Corporation
EFT	electronic funds transfer
EVC	eligibility verification confirmation
GHPP	Genetically Handicapped Persons Program
ICF	intermediate care facility
MI	medically indigent
MN	medically needy
OASHDI	Old Age Survivors, Health and Disability Insurance Program
PE	presumptive eligibility
PHP	prepaid health plan
POE	proof of eligibility
POS	point of service device
PTN	Provider Telecommunications Network
RAD	Remittance Advice Details (formerly EOB/RA)
RTD	Resubmission Turnaround Document
SNF	skilled nursing facility
SOC	share of cost
SSN	Social Security number
TAR	Treatment Authorization Request Form
VDTS	Voice Drug TAR System

APPENDIX C

Medi-Cal

Introduction

For information on the history of Medicaid and basic knowledge about how the welfare system works, read Chapter 11, Medicaid and Other State Programs, before reading Appendix C. As mentioned in Chapter 11, in California the Medicaid program is known as Medi-Cal and as Cal-MAP. Medi-Cal is administered by the California State Department of Health, a department of the California State Human Relations Agency. Medi-Cal became effective on March 1, 1966. The information in this Appendix is a brief overview of the Medi-Cal program with basic guidelines for most regions in California. For additional detailed information and for data on Solano, San Mateo, and Santa Barbara counties, which have different guidelines, always refer to an updated *Medi-Cal Provider Manual for Medical Services,* which will contain the latest program policies and procedures supplied by the current fiscal intermediary. Abbreviations are used quite frequently during lectures and on documentation relating to the Medi-Cal program. To assist you in their interpretation, a list is compiled at the beginning of this Appendix.

MEDI-CAL REFORM

An increasing number of regions in California offer PHPs to individuals eligible for Medi-Cal. This is indicated by *Other Coverage* alpha codes, that is, CHAMPUS (C), Kaiser (K), Ross Loos/CIGNA (R), and any other PHP/(HMO) (P). Individuals covered under those plans must seek treatment from facilities contracted under the PHP, except in emergencies. Otherwise, services will not be reimbursed by Medi-Cal. If service is not available through contracted facilities and the patient seeks care outside of the plan, a denial letter from the health plan must accompany the Medi-Cal claim.

ELIGIBILITY

Individuals in the following groups are entitled to benefits under the Medi-Cal program:

- Californians who qualify for OASHDI program benefits
- AFDC
- AB
- ATD
- MN persons whose incomes are above the assistance level but who are unable to provide mainstream medical care and are eligible as MI. Some of these patients have a liability to meet each month called SOC.

BENEFITS

The basic medical benefits provided under Medi-Cal include the following:

1. Physician services
2. Inpatient or outpatient hospital services in any approved hospital
3. Laboratory and x-ray services
4. Nursing home services
5. Home health care
6. Private duty nursing
7. Outpatient clinic services
8. Dental services (through Delta Dental, called Denti-Cal)
9. Hearing aids
10. Drugs and medical supplies
11. Optometric services and eye appliances
12. Physical therapy and other diagnostic, preventive, or rehabilitative services and equipment
13. Medi-Cal also pays the full deductible under Medicare Part A and buys into Medicare Part B by paying the monthly premiums for those who are over 65, disabled, or blind. These persons are called Medicare/Medi-Cal recipients; see Chapter 12, Medicare.
14. Obstetric services. The CPSP offers a wide range of services to pregnant Medi-Cal recipients from conception through 60 days after the month of delivery. In addition to maternity services, certified providers may be reimbursed for nutritional, psychosocial and health education services, case coordination, client orientation, and vitamin and mineral supplements. A federal/state program designed to ease access to prenatal care is called PE. It allows the provider to offer immediate temporary coverage for prenatal care to low-income pregnant women pending a formal Medi-Cal application.

FISCAL INTERMEDIARIES

Two fiscal intermediaries are contracted by the state to receive and audit claims for payment of medical services and to make payments to providers of services. When the contract expires, these intermediaries may change, but at the present they are EDS Corporation in Sacramento, California, for hospital billing and professional services and Delta Dental (formerly California Dental Services) for dental services under Denti-Cal. For the address of EDS, refer to Appendix A.

IDENTIFICATION CARD

The State of California Department of Health Services issues a plastic BIC to each Medi-Cal recipient when the individual is declared eligible for benefits (Fig. C–1). County welfare departments may issue paper Medi-Cal cards in exceptional cases for temporary use (i.e., retroactive eligibility). Solano, San Mateo, and Santa Barbara counties issue monthly cards with labels and will implement plastic BICs at a later date. It is the provider's responsibility to verify that the person to receive care is eligible for the month service is rendered and is, indeed, the individual to whom the card was issued. Match the name and signature on the BIC against the signature on a valid California driver's license, a California identification card issued by the Department of Motor Vehicles, another acceptable picture identification card, or another credible document of identification. Eligibility, which is verified at the first of the month, is valid for the entire month of service. The insurance billing specialist should keep the verification number in the recipient's file and use it as proof of eligibility for the entire month. A person may have a Medi-Cal card, but this does not indicate proof of eligibility. Four methods by which to verify eligibility and perform SOC and Medi-Service transactions are listed here. SOC is the amount of money that must be paid by the patient each month before any Medi-Cal benefits will begin. Medi-Services are certain services supplied by chiropractors, psychologists, acupuncturists, podiatrists, occupational therapists, speech pathologists, and audiologists. Most recipients eligible for Medi-Cal are allowed two Medi-Services per calendar month. These services should be reserved using a POS device.

ELIGIBILITY VERIFICATION

- Use of a POS device. An EVC number on a printout from the POS device verifies that an inquiry was re-

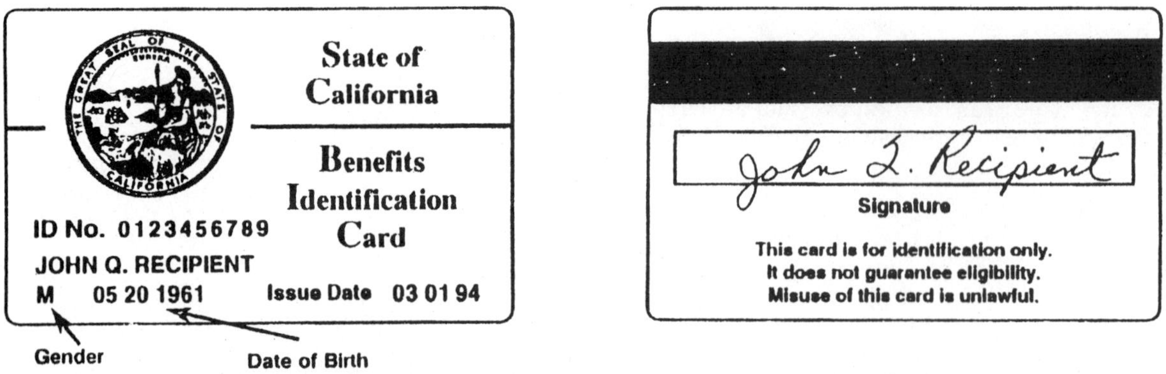

FIGURE C–1
Medi-Cal Sample Plastic Benefits Identification Card (BIC). This is a white card with blue letters on the front and black letters on the back.

ceived and eligibility information was transmitted. When a Medi-Cal recipient is limited to receive certain medical services, a restriction message is returned from the Medi-Cal host computer after verification of eligibility. Document that the services relate to the applicable restriction (i.e., date of service and name of provider who prescribed limited services). Never bill Medi-Cal for the SOC that a patient pays but do enter it into the POS system. This will clear the SOC and let Medi-Cal know that the patient has paid, allowing the recipient to become eligible for Medi-Cal benefits. Figure C–2 illustrates SOC and Medi-Service printouts from the POS device.

- Use of the CERTS software. An EVC number on a printout from the software verifies that an inquiry was received and eligibility information was transmitted.
- Have existing software modified by a vendor, or purchase a vendor-supplied software package capable of performing the transactions. An EVC number verifies that an inquiry was received and eligibility information was transmitted.
- Use a telephone to obtain AEVS. An EVC number verifies that an inquiry was received and eligibility information was transmitted. However, this system is not able to perform SOC or Medi-Service transactions.

Receipt of an EVC number does not guarantee claim payment. Carefully review all information returned with the eligibility response to ensure that services are covered under the recipient eligibility.

COPAYMENT

Current law requires Medi-Cal recipients to make a nominal copayment for most outpatient services, some emergency department services, and some prescribed drugs. Copayment is never required for the following:

- Any person 18 years of age or under
- Any woman receiving perinatal care
- Any child in AFDC foster care
- Any person who is an inpatient in a health facility (e.g., hospital, skilled nursing facility, intermediate care facility)
- Any service for which payment by Medi-Cal is $10 or less.
- Emergency services or family planning services and supplies; the health care provider has the option to collect or not collect copayment at the time at which service is rendered. Figure C–3 lists classifications, fees, and exclusions.

Prior Approval

TREATMENT AUTHORIZATION REQUEST

A TAR Form 50-1 (see Chapter 11, Fig. 11–2) is used to obtain prior approval from the Medi-Cal field office consultant for certain procedures and services. To find out whether a particular service is a benefit or nonbenefit, refer to the *Medi-Cal Medical Services Provider Manual* TAR nonbenefit list. This list indicates which services require a TAR or are not a benefit. Some, but not all, of the TAR-required services are as follows:

- Long-term care facility services
- Some vision services
- Inpatient hospital services
- Home health agency services
- Chronic hemodialysis services
- Some transportation services
- Some DME, medical supplies, or prosthetic/orthotic appliances
- Hearing aids
- Some pharmacy services
- Some surgical procedures

Response to a TAR takes approximately 10 to 15 days. A TAR Transmittal Form MC3020 may be completed to help track submitted TARs or to appeal a TAR. If the request for hospitalization of a patient is approved, a copy of the approved TAR should be sent to the hospital before admission of the patient. Check with the field office to determine if and when faxed TARs will be accepted because policies vary from one office to another.

In some cases, it is not possible to obtain a TAR in advance of hospital admission or initiation of a treatment program. In these cases, authorization may be obtained by telephone or fax. Call the local department of health services field office to receive approval, and then complete and submit a TAR Form 50-1 to the field office, indicating that it was already authorized by including

- Date authorized
- Name of person who gave authorization
- Approximate time of day at which authorization was given
- Verbal number stated by the field office

Do not bill the fiscal intermediary with the verbal TAR number.

INSTRUCTIONS FOR COMPLETING A TREATMENT AUTHORIZATION REQUEST FORM 50-1

The following item numbers and descriptions correspond to Chapter 11, Figure 11–2.

1. Leave blank. The fiscal intermediary inserts a CNN in this box.
   - Verbal Control Number is generally left blank unless this number is obtained by telephone.
2. Enter an X in the appropriate boxes to show Drug or Other, Retroactive Request, and/or Medicare eligibility status. It is optional to list the provider's telephone number.
   - Enter the provider's name and complete address.
3. Enter the nine-digit Medi-Cal rendering provider number. When requesting authorization for an elective hospital admission, the hospital provider number must be entered in this box.

POS DEVICE

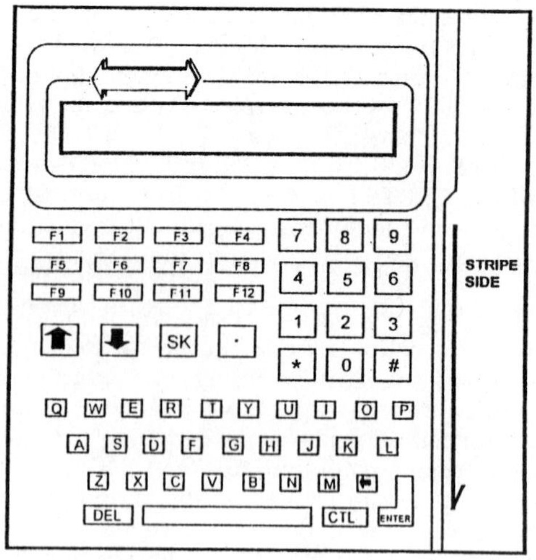

POS DEVICE: SHARE OF COST PRINTOUT

EDS TRAINING 3213 PROSPECT PARK TERMINAL

94-02-15
01:44:35

PROVIDER NUMBER:
HSC30175G

TRANSACTION TYPE: SHARE OF COST

RECIPIENT ID:
607357101

YEAR & MONTH OF BIRTH:
1964-10

DATE OF ISSUE:
94-02-01

DATE OF SERVICE:
94-02-15

CASE NUMBER:

PROCEDURE CODE:
90945

PATIENT APPLIED AMOUNT:
$50.00

TOTAL BILLED AMOUNT:
$100.00

LAST NAME: JOHNSO.
AMOUNT DEDUCTED: $50.00
SHARE OF COST HAS BEEN MET.

POS DEVICE: MEDI-SERVICE PRINTOUT

EDS 10050 OLSON DRIVE TERMINAL T309006

94-02-15
17:16:36

PROVIDER NUMBER:
HSC30175G

TRANSACTION TYPE: MEDI-SERVICES

RECIPIENT ID:
607357101

YEAR & MONTH OF BIRTH:
1966-12

DATE OF ISSUE:
94-02-01

DATE OF SERVICE:
94-02-15

PROCEDURE CODE:
A2000

LAST NAME: JOHNSO. MEDI SVC
RESERVATION APPLIED.

FIGURE C–2
Point of service (POS) device and two examples of printouts: share of cost and Medi-Service.

Medi-Cal Copayment Criteria

<table>
<tr><th>Services Subject to Copayment</th><th>Copayment Fee</th><th>Exceptions to Fee</th></tr>
<tr><td>NONEMERGENCY SERVICES PROVIDED IN AN EMERGENCY ROOM

A nonemergency service is defined as "any service not required for alleviation of severe pain or the immediate diagnosis and treatment of severe medical conditions which, if not immediately diagnosed and treated, would lead to disability or death." Such services provided in an emergency room are subject to copayment.</td><td>$5.00</td><td rowspan="3">1 Persons age 18 or under.

2. Any woman during pregnancy and the postpartum period (through the end of the month in which the 60-day period following termination of pregnancy ends)

3. Persons who are inpatients in a health facility (hospital, skilled nursing facility or intermediate care facility)

4. Any child in AFDC-Foster care

5. Any service for which the program's payment is $10 or less

6. Any hospice patient

7. Family planning services and supplies</td></tr>
<tr><td>OUTPATIENT SERVICES

Physician, optometric, chiropractic, psychology, speech therapy, audiology, acupuncture, occupational therapy, podiatric, surgical center, hospital or outpatient clinic, physical therapy.</td><td>$1.00</td></tr>
<tr><td>DRUG PRESCRIPTIONS

Each drug prescription or refill.</td><td>$1.00</td></tr>
</table>

FIGURE C-3
Medi-Cal copayment criteria.

The hospital name may be placed in the Medical Justification area.

4. Enter the patient's last name, first name, middle initial, address, and telephone number.
5. Enter the recipient's Medi-Cal identification number from the BIC. The county code and aid code must be entered above this box. Do not use any characters (dashes, hyphens, special characters) in the remaining blank positions of the Medi-Cal ID field or in the Check Digit box.
6. If the patient's Medi-Cal eligibility is not yet established and the Medi-Cal number is not known, insert the letter P to indicate "pending."
7. Use an M for male or F for female, obtained from the BIC. Enter the patient's age in the AGE box.
8. Enter the recipient's date of birth in six-digit format. If not available, enter the year of the recipient's birth preceded by "0101."

   ■ Patient's status: Enter an X if patient is to receive services at home, board and care, acute hospital, inpatient in a nursing facility level A (ICF), or nursing facility level B (SNF). Enter the name of the facility in the Medical Justification area of the form.

   ■ Diagnosis: Enter the description of the diagnosis and its code from the ICD-9-CM code book.

   ■ Medical justification: Provide sufficient supporting information for the consultant to determine whether the service is medically justified. If necessary, attach documentation. Enter the name of the hospital or nursing facility. Requests by nonmedical providers must include the name and telephone number of the prescriber (placed in the lower left corner of this box).

9. Leave blank. Consultant will indicate if the service line item is authorized.

   ■ Authorized: Leave blank. Consultant will indicate the number of times the procedure, item, or days have been authorized.

10. Approved Units and Units of Service boxes: Leave blank.

    ■ Specific Services Requested: Indicate the name of the procedure, item, or service requested.

11. Enter the procedure code (five-character HCPCS or five-digit CPT with two-digit modifier when necessary). When requesting hospital

days, the stay must be requested on the first line of the TAR with the provider entering the word "DAY(S)."

12. Enter the number of times a procedure or service is requested or the number of hospital days requested. Indicate the dollar amount of the provider's usual and customary charge for the service(s) requested.

32A. If applicable, enter the name and address of the patient's authorized representative, representative payee, conservator over the person, legal representative, or other representative handling the recipient's medical and personal affairs.

33–36. Leave blank. Consultant's determination and comments will be entered in this section. The TAR must show the consultant's signature. The Comments/Explanation lines list the approved procedures or any further information the provider must submit with the HCFA-1500 claim.

37–38. Leave blank. Consultant will indicate valid dates of authorization.

39. Leave blank. Medi-Cal field office consultant will enter a two-digit prefix and a one-digit suffix to the preimprinted eight-digit number. This 11-digit number must be entered on the HCFA-1500 claim form when the service is billed, indicating prior authorization has been obtained. PI means pricing information and is to be left blank. *Do not attach a copy of the TAR to the HCFA-1500 claim form.*

- Signature of Physician or Provider: The provider or authorized representative must sign and date the form.

40–43. Leave blank.

TELECOMMUNICATIONS NETWORKS

The PTN is an automated voice-response system that allows the provider to use the telephone to obtain summary checkwrite, claim, and prior authorization (TAR) information for services rendered through the Medi-Cal program, CMSP, CHDP, CCS, and GHPP. The provider must use the PTN as the primary source of checkwrite (issuing of Medi-Cal payment check), claim, and TAR information. Providers are automatically enrolled in the PTN and assigned a seven-digit PIN that must be used to access the PTN on a touch-tone telephone. A VDTS is also available, which is an automated voice-response system that allows the provider to dictate and record requests for drug TARs and inquire on the continuing care status of a patient by using touch-tone and voice-activated prompts. VDTS is linked to the Medi-Cal Drug Units to permit the processing of TARs after completion of a recording. VDTS can *only* be used to request *urgent* and *initial* drug TARs, to inquire about the status of previously entered drug TARs, or to inquire whether a patient is receiving continual care with a drug.

TIME LIMIT

Medi-Cal claims must be submitted within 2 months or 60 days from the end of the month of service, or the physician will not receive reimbursement. The following exceptions have a 1-year time limit:

- Retroactive eligibility
- Patient has not informed the physician that he or she is on Medi-Cal
- Dental bills
- Obstetric bills
- Completion of treatment plan
- Patient has other insurance coverage (physician may elect to bill the other insurance carrier)

Claims Procedure

HEALTH INSURANCE HCFA-1500 CLAIM FORM

After verifying Medi-Cal eligibility using one of the aforementioned methods, complete an HCFA-1500 Claim Form and mail it to the fiscal intermediary. Basic instructions on how to complete the HCFA-1500 Claim Form are given in Chapter 6. A summary of requirements for the Medi-Cal program is given here.

FIELD REQUIREMENTS FOR THE HCFA-1500 CLAIM FORM FOR THE MEDI-CAL PROGRAM

Field No.	Requirement
1–3	Required
4	If applicable
5	Optional
6	If applicable
7–9a–d	Not required
10a	If applicable
10b and 10c	Not required
11a–c	Not required
11d	If applicable
12	Not required
13	Not required (can place EVC No. here)
14	If applicable
15 and 16	Not required
17 and 17a	If applicable
18	If applicable
19	Remarks
20	If applicable
21.1 and 21.2	If applicable
21.3 and 21.4	Not required
22	Required
23	If applicable
24a and 24b	Required
24c	Not required
24d	Required
24e	Not required
24f and 24g	Required
24h–k	If applicable
25	Not required
26	Optional

27	Not required
28	Required
29	If applicable
30 and 31	Required
32	If applicable
33	Required

Figure C–4 illustrates the HCFA-1500 Claim Form and Medi-Cal required fields. Use basic guidelines for completing a claim to be processed by optical scanning equipment. (These guidelines are stated in Chapter 6, pages 142–143.) The HCFA-1500 Claim Form must contain the bar codes at the top of the form because this sensor block triggers equipment to assign a claim number. To delete specific information on the HCFA-1500 Claim Form, draw a thin black line through the entire line but do not obliterate. There is no need to write "See Attachments" because the equipment stamps the same assigned claim number on all accompanying sheets until the equipment recognizes another bar code. Use white paper tape or dry line tape to block out and correct a typed error. Keep the small printout from the POS device for the physician's records and, in general, do not use it as an attachment. If for some reason you need to send it to the fiscal intermediary, attach it to a standard-size sheet of paper.

UB-92 OUTPATIENT CLAIM FORM

The UB-92 Claim Form is used by institutional facilities (e.g., inpatient and outpatient departments, rural health clinics, chronic dialysis services, and adult day health care) to submit claims for outpatient services. Figure C–5 illustrates a complete UB-92 Claim Form. Dates of service and monetary values are entered without spaces (i.e., $200.00 should be shown as 20000, and June 23, 1995, should be shown as 062395). Dates of birth are entered using two sets of two-digit numbers for the month and day and a four-digit number for the year (i.e., June 23, 1995, should be shown as 06231995). Additional information about the UB-92 claim form may be found in Chapter 16.

INSTRUCTIONS FOR COMPLETING THE UB-92 CLAIM FORM

Figure B–5 shows a correctly completed UB-92 Claim Form. The following item numbers and descriptions correspond to Figure C–5.

1. Enter the provider name, address, and ZIP code. A telephone number is optional.
2. Leave blank.
3. Patient Control Number: This is an optional field for ease in identifying a recipient of RTDs and RADs. Enter the patient's medical record number or account number.
4. Enter the appropriate Type of Bill code as specified in the UB-92 Manual of Billing Procedures. This is optional when billing Medi-Cal.

5–11. Not required by Medi-Cal.

12. Enter the patient's last name, first name, and middle initial. Avoid nicknames or aliases.
13. Patient Address: Not required by Medi-Cal.
14. Birthdate: Enter the patient's date of birth in an eight-digit format (e.g., June 1, 1995, becomes 06011995).
15. Use M for male or F for female.

16–23. Not required by Medi-Cal.

24–30. The claims processing system ignores all condition codes not applicable to Medi-Cal. Condition codes used to identify conditions relating to this bill that may affect payer processing are:

80	Other coverage
81	Emergency certification
82	Outside laboratory
A1	CHDP screening-related
A3	Family planning/sterilization
A4	Family planning/other

31. Not required by Medi-Cal.

32–35A–B. Occurrence codes and dates used to identify significant events relating to a bill that may affect payer processing are as follows:

Billing Limit Exception Codes

X0	After 6-month limitation (no reason)
X1	Proof of eligibility (POE) unknown
X2	Medicare/other coverage
X3	TAR approval delay
X4	California Department of Health Services (DHS) delay
X5	Delivery delay
X6	Fire, flood, disaster
X7	Theft, sabotage
X8	Decisions, appeals
X9	Late charges (inpatient only)

Medicare Status Codes

Y0	Under 65, does not have Medicare coverage
Y1	Benefits exhausted
Y2	Utilization committee denial or physician noncertification
Y3	No prior hospital stay
Y4	Facility denial
Y5	Noneligible provider
Y6	Noneligible recipient
Y7	Medicare benefits denied or cut short by Medicare intermediary
Y8	Noncovered services
Y9	Professional standards review organization (PSRO) denial
Z1	Medi/Medi Charpentier: benefit limitations
Z2	Medi/Medi Charpentier: rates limitations
Z3	Medi/Medi Charpentier: both rates and benefit limitations

36–38. Not required by Medi-Cal.

39–41A–D. Enter the value codes and amounts of the patient's share of cost for the following:

PLEASE DO NOT STAPLE IN THIS AREA

APPROVED OMB 0938 0008

CARRIER ↑

PICA

HEALTH INSURANCE CLAIM FORM

PICA

1\. MEDICARE (Medicare #) MEDICAID (Medicaid #) CHAMPUS (Sponsor's SSN) CHAMPVA (VA File #) GROUP HEALTH PLAN (SSN or ID) FECA BLK LUNG (SSN) OTHER (ID)

1a. INSURED'S I.D. NUMBER (FOR PROGRAM IN ITEM 1)
MEDI-CAL ID NUMBER

2\. PATIENT'S NAME (Last Name, First Name, Middle Initial)
PATIENT'S COMPLETE NAME

3\. PATIENT'S BIRTH DATE MM DD YY SEX
DATE OF BIRTH M ☐ SEX F ☐

4\. INSURED'S NAME (Last Name, First Name, Middle Initial)
MOTHER'S NAME FOR NEWBORN

5\. PATIENT'S ADDRESS (No., Street)
PATIENT'S COMPLETE ADDRESS

6\. PATIENT RELATIONSHIP TO INSURED
Self ☐ Spouse ☐ Child ☐ Other ☐

7\. INSURED'S ADDRESS (No., Street)
N/A

CITY
PATIENT'S CITY

STATE
ST

8\. PATIENT STATUS N/A
Single ☐ Married ☐ Other ☐

CITY
N/A

STATE
N/A

ZIP CODE
PATIENT'S ZIP

TELEPHONE (Include Area Code)
( ) PATIENT'S PHONE

Employed ☐ Full-Time Student ☐ Part Time Student ☐

ZIP CODE
N/A

TELEPHONE (INCLUDE AREA CODE)
( ) N/A

9\. OTHER INSURED'S NAME (Last Name, First Name, Middle Initial)
N/A

10\. IS PATIENT'S CONDITION RELATED TO:

11\. INSURED'S POLICY GROUP OR FECA NUMBER
N/A

a. OTHER INSURED'S POLICY OR GROUP NUMBER
N/A

a. EMPLOYMENT? (CURRENT OR PREVIOUS)
☐ YES ☐ NO

a. INSURED'S DATE OF BIRTH MM DD YY SEX
N/A M ☐ F ☐

b. OTHER INSURED'S DATE OF BIRTH MM DD YY SEX
N/A M ☐ N/A F ☐

b. AUTO ACCIDENT? PLACE (State)
N/A ☐ YES ☐ NO N/A

b. EMPLOYER'S NAME OR SCHOOL NAME
N/A

c. EMPLOYER'S NAME OR SCHOOL NAME
N/A

c. OTHER ACCIDENT?
N/A ☐ YES ☐ NO

c. INSURANCE PLAN NAME OR PROGRAM NAME
N/A

d. INSURANCE PLAN NAME OR PROGRAM NAME
N/A

10d. RESERVED FOR LOCAL USE
PATIENT'S SHARE OF COST

d. IS THERE ANOTHER HEALTH BENEFIT PLAN?
OTHER COVERAGE/DOLLAR AMOUNT
☐ YES ☐ NO *If yes, return to and complete item 9 a-d.*

READ BACK OF FORM BEFORE COMPLETING & SIGNING THIS FORM.

12\. PATIENT'S OR AUTHORIZED PERSON'S SIGNATURE I authorize the release of any medical or other information necessary to process this claim. I also request payment of government benefits either to myself or to the party who accepts assignment below.

SIGNED N/A DATE N/A

13\. INSURED'S OR AUTHORIZED PERSON'S SIGNATURE I authorize payment of medical benefits to the undersigned physician or supplier for services described below.

SIGNED POE LABEL

PATIENT AND INSURED INFORMATION

14\. DATE OF CURRENT: MM DD YY ILLNESS (First symptom) OR INJURY (Accident) OR PREGNANCY (LMP)
DATE OF ONSET

15\. IF PATIENT HAS HAD SAME OR SIMILAR ILLNESS, GIVE FIRST DATE MM DD YY
N/A

16\. DATES PATIENT UNABLE TO WORK IN CURRENT OCCUPATION
FROM MM DD YY N/A TO MM DD YY

17\. NAME OF REFERRING PHYSICIAN OR OTHER SOURCE
NAME OF REFERRING PROVIDER

17a. I.D. NUMBER OF REFERRING PHYSICIAN
REFERRING NPI

18\. HOSPITALIZATION DATES RELATED TO CURRENT SERVICES
FROM MM DD YY FROM DOS TO MM DD YY THRU DOS

19\. RESERVED FOR LOCAL USE
REMARKS/EMERGENCY CERTIFICATION STATEMENT

20\. OUTSIDE LAB? OUTSIDE LAB $ CHARGES
☐ YES ☐ NO N/A N/A

21\. DIAGNOSIS OR NATURE OF ILLNESS OR INJURY (RELATE ITEMS 1,2,3 OR 4 TO ITEM 24E BY LINE)

1\. PRIMARY ICD 9-CM 3. N/A

2\. SECONDARY ICD 9-CM 4. N/A

22\. MEDICAID RESUBMISSION CODE MEDICARE STATUS CODE ORIGINAL REF. NO. N/A

23\. PRIOR AUTHORIZATION NUMBER
TAR CONTROL NUMBER

24 A DATE(S) OF SERVICE From MM DD YY	To MM DD YY	B Place of Service	C Type of Service	D PROCEDURES, SERVICES, OR SUPPLIES (Explain Unusual Circumstances) CPT/HCPCS	MODIFIER		E DIAGNOSIS CODE	F $ CHARGES	G DAYS OR UNITS	H EPSDT Family Plan	I EMG	J COB	K RESERVED FOR LOCAL USE
1 DATE OF SERVICE FROM	DATE OF SERVICE THRU	POS	N/A	PRO-CEDURE CODE	MOD	N/A	N/A	SERVICE CHARGES	QUANTITY	FP/CHDP	EMERCERT	BILLLINGLIMIT	RENDERING NPI
2													
3													
4													
5													
6													

25\. FEDERAL TAX I.D. NUMBER SSN EIN
N/A ☐ ☐

26\. PATIENT'S ACCOUNT NO.
PATIENT ACCOUNT NUMBER

27\. ACCEPT ASSIGNMENT? (For govt. claims, see back)
☐ YES ☐ NO N/A

28\. TOTAL CHARGE
$ TOTAL CHARGES

29\. AMOUNT PAID
$ TOTAL DEDUCTIONS

30\. BALANCE DUE
$ NET AM'T BILLED

31\. SIGNATURE OF PHYSICIAN OR SUPPLIER INCLUDING DEGREES OR CREDENTIALS (I certify that the statements on the reverse apply to this bill and are made a part thereof.)
SIGNATURE OF PROVIDER OR PERSON AUTHORIZED DATE
SIGNED DATE

32\. NAME AND ADDRESS OF FACILITY WHERE SERVICES WERE RENDERED (If other than home or office)
MEDI-CAL FACILITY PROVIDER NUMBER

33\. PHYSICIAN'S, SUPPLIER'S BILLING NAME, ADDRESS, ZIP CODE & PHONE #
PROVIDER NAME
ADDRESS
CITY, STATE, ZIP
PROVIDER PHONE NUMBER
MEDI-CAL
PIN# PROVIDER #/CD GRP# N/A

PHYSICIAN OR SUPPLIER INFORMATION

(APPROVED BY AMA COUNCIL ON MEDICAL SERVICE 8/88) *PLEASE PRINT OR TYPE* FORM HCFA-1500 (12-90) FORM OWCP-1500 FORM RRB-1500

REORDER FROM STANDARD REGISTER FORM NO. HC0901B-2

FIGURE C–4
HCFA-1500 claim form illustrating Medi-Cal required fields.

DIALYSIS TREATMENT CENTER
14562 MAIN STREET
ANYTOWN, CA 98523

3 PATIENT CONTROL NO: ROBIN765

5 FED. TAX NO | 6 STATEMENT COVERS PERIOD FROM THROUGH | 7 COV D | 8 N-C D | 9 C-I D | 10 L-R D | 11

12 PATIENT NAME: ROBINSON, MYRA

13 PATIENT ADDRESS: 500 PARK AVE., ANYTOWN, CA 95823

14 BIRTHDATE: 05 26 1970 | 15 SEX: F | 16 MS | ADMISSION 17 DATE 18 HR 19 TYPE 20 SRC | 21 D HR | 22 STAT | 23 MEDICAL RECORD NO | CONDITION CODES 24: Y0 | 25 | 26 | 27 | 28 | 29 | 30 | 31

32–35 OCCURRENCE CODE DATE | 36 OCCURRENCE SPAN CODE FROM THROUGH | 37 A B C

38 | 39–41 VALUE CODES CODE AMOUNT (a b c d)

42 REV. CD	43 DESCRIPTION	44 HCPCS / RATES	45 SERV DATE	46 SERV UNITS	47 TOTAL CHARGES	48 NON COVERED CHARGES	49
	CHRONIC HEMODIALYSIS AND ROUTINE LAB 11/4, 11/8, 11/12, 11/15, 11/19, 11/22, 11/26, 11/29/94	Z6004	11 04 94 11 29 94	8	1104 00		
001	TOTAL CHARGES				1104 00		

50 PAYER: O/P MEDI-CAL 8 | 51 PROVIDER NO: CDC90009F2 | 52 REL INFO | 53 ASG BEN | 54 PRIOR PAYMENTS | 55 EST. AMOUNT DUE: 1104 00 | 56

57 DUE FROM PATIENT ▶

58 INSURED'S NAME | 59 P REL | 60 CERT - SSN - HIC - ID NO: 5678976521 | 61 GROUP NAME | 62 INSURANCE GROUP NO

63 TREATMENT AUTHORIZATION CODES: 12398765421 | 64 ESC | 65 EMPLOYER NAME | 66 EMPLOYER LOCATION

67 PRIN DIAG CD: 582 | 68–75 OTHER DIAG CODES | 76 ADM. DIAG. CD | 77 E CODE | 78

79 P C | 80 PRINCIPAL PROCEDURE CODE DATE | 81 OTHER PROCEDURE CODE DATE

82 ATTENDING PHYS ID: 00A000099

83 OTHER PHYS ID

OTHER PHYS ID

84 REMARKS

85 PROVIDER REPRESENTATIVE: X Jane Doe | 86 DATE: 12 05 94

I CERTIFY THE CERTIFICATIONS ON THE REVERSE APPLY TO THIS BILL AND ARE MADE A PART HEREOF.

UB-92 HCFA-1450

FIGURE C–5

Example of a completed UB-92 claim form illustrating a billing for monthly dialysis fee using the "from-through" format. The dates that the patient came in for dialysis are listed in the Description on the paper claim or the Remarks Record of the claim when electronically transmitted. The physician would bill his or her fees separately on the HCFA-1500 claim form when this code is billed by the facility.

Code	Description
06*	Blood deductible amount
23	Share of cost
38*	Blood deductible pints
A1*	Medicare deductible
B1*	Medicare deductible
A2*	Medicare coinsurance
B2*	Medicare coinsurance

(* For crossovers only.)

42. The revenue code is not required by Medi-Cal for outpatient services except when code 001 is used to indicate Total Charge line.
43. This optional field helps separate and identify descriptions of each service. The description must identify the particular service code indicated in the HCPCS/Rates field (Box 44).
44. Enter the applicable CPT or HCPCS code number and modifier. When billing for recipients with both Medicare/Medi-Cal, bill Medi-Cal for only those services listed in the Medicare noncovered section. All other services must be billed to Medicare first.
45. Enter the date the service was rendered in six-digit (e.g., 062395).
46. Enter the actual number of times a single procedure was provided for the Date of Service. Although this is a seven-digit field, Medi-Cal allows only three digits in this field. If billing for more than 99, divide the units on two or more lines.
47. Enter the total charge (e.g., $100 should be entered as 10000).

48–49. Not required by Medi-Cal.

50A–C. Enter "O/P MEDI-CAL" to indicate the type of claim and payer.

Code	Place of Service
1	Office
2	Home
3	Inpatient hospital
4	Nursing facility level B (SNF)
5	Outpatient hospital
6	Independent laboratory
7	Other (describe in *Remarks*)
8	Independent kidney treatment center
9	Clinic
A	Surgery clinic
B	Emergency department
C	Nursing facility level A (ICF)
F	Subacute care facility
G	Intermediate care facility–developmentally disabled (ICF/DD)
H	Intermediate care facility–developmentally disabled, habilitative (ICF/DD-H)
I	Intermediate care facility–developmentally disabled, nursing (ICF/DD-N)
M	Pediatric subacute care

51A–C. Enter the Medi-Cal nine-character provider number. Check digit is not a required item.

52–53. Not required by Medi-Cal.

54A–B. Enter the amount of payment received from other coverage on the same line as the other coverage "payer" (Box 50) (i.e., $100 should be entered as 10000). *Do not* enter Medicare payments in this box. Leave blank if not applicable.

55A–C. Enter the difference between "Total Charges" and any deductions (i.e., patient's share of cost and/or other coverage).

56–57. Not required by Medi-Cal.

58–59A–C. If billing for an infant using the mother's identification number or for an organ donor, enter the Medi-Cal recipient's name and the patient's relationship to the recipient in Box 59 (03 = child and 11 = donor). Otherwise, leave blank.

60A–C. Enter the 10-character recipient identification number as it appears on the BIC or paper Medi-Cal identification card.

61–62. Not required by Medi-Cal.

63A–C. For services requiring a TAR, enter the 11-digit TAR Control Number. It is not necessary to attach a copy of the TAR to the claim.

64–66. Not required by Medi-Cal.

67. Enter all letters and/or numbers of the ICD-9-CM code for the primary diagnosis, including the fourth and fifth digits. Do not enter a decimal point when entering the code.
68. Enter all letters and/or numbers of the secondary ICD-9-CM code.

69–81. Not required by Medi-Cal.

82. On the top line of Box 82, enter the National provider identifier (NPI) for the referring or prescribing physician. This field is mandatory for radiologists. If the physician is not a Medi-Cal provider, enter the state license number. Do not use a group provider number.

83A. On the top line of Box 83A, enter the national provider identifier (NPI) number for the physician actually providing services. Do not use a group provider number or state license number.

84. Remarks: Use this area for procedures that require additional information, justification, or an Emergency Certification Statement. If it will not fit in this area, attach the statement to the claim.

85–86. The claim must be signed and dated by the provider or a representative assigned by the provider. Stamps, initials, or facsimiles are not acceptable.

COMPUTER MEDIA CLAIMS

In the Medi-Cal program, claims via electronic media or modem are called CMC. Claims may be submitted on tape, on-line through the POS network, or via computer with modem over telephone lines. A variety of computer software formats are acceptable. The *Medi-Cal CMC Tech-*

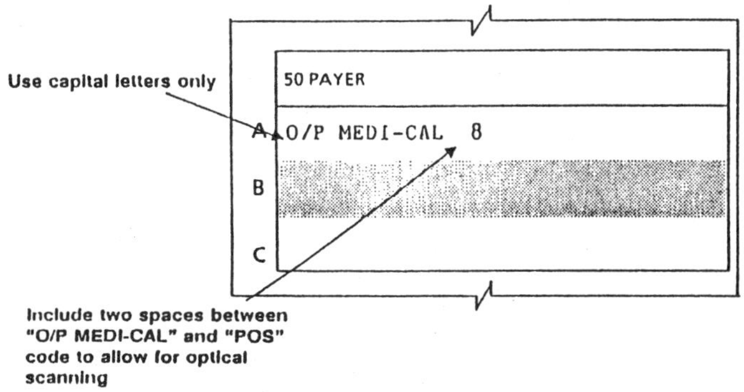

nical Manual contains the latest specifications to update existing systems.

REMITTANCE ADVICE DETAILS

Formerly known as Explanation of Benefits and Remittance Advice (EOB/RA), an RAD accompanies all Medi-Cal payment checks to the physician. Five categories of adjudicated claims appear on an RAD: adjustments, approvals, denials, suspends, and A/R transactions. A claim requiring special handling or correction of errors is placed in temporary suspense and may be referred to as a *suspend*. Four categories of adjudicated claims are shown in Chapter 11, Figure 11–4, illustrating the Medi-Cal resolution process.

An electronic RAD is an automated form of the Medi-Cal RA data for providers who have individual agreements with the fiscal intermediary. The State Controller's Office also sends a hard copy of the RAD.

Providers receiving RADs should reconcile each claim transaction to their records. Post claim payments to the patient's ledger card. Review denied claims to ensure they are correct. Suspends should be referenced to determine whether an RTD was issued. Post negative adjustments as debits to the patient's ledger card. Post accounts receivable transactions to the appropriate Suspense account. It is important that each claim being reported, or not reported, be accounted for; that the necessary follow-up is performed; and that all of the rules governing timelines be followed. For translations of the RAD codes and billing tips on how to correct denied claims, refer to the *Medi-Cal Medical Services Provider Manual.*

ADJUSTMENTS

When overpayments or underpayments occur, an adjustment is initiated, and two lines appear on the RAD. The first line indicates a "take back" of the original payment (original CCN); the second line reflects the correct payment of the claim (new CCN). The net amount between the two lines is the adjustment. CCNs are assigned to identify and track claims as they move through the claims processing system.

APPROVALS

If an original claim or a previously denied claim is approved for payment, it is listed on the RAD. If a reduction in the billed amount is warranted, the explanation will be given via a three-digit code.

DENIALS

Denial of claims is shown only on the RAD. If a physician believes that the claim was incorrectly denied, he or she should submit a CIF for reconsideration of the claim. Until the claim is resubmitted for processing, it is no longer in the system. When the claim is resubmitted, it will be given a new CCN and be processed as a new claim in the system.

SUSPENDS

Claims in suspense for 30 days or more are listed. There are several general explanation codes for suspended claims. Such a listing does not explain the reason but rather lets the physician know that the claim was received by the fiscal intermediary. *Do not* send CIFs for claims that have been temporarily suspended.

A/R TRANSACTIONS

These are miscellaneous transactions as a result of cost settlements, state audits, or refund checks received by the fiscal intermediary. A three-digit code indicates the reason for the A/R transaction. A/R transactions show when it is necessary to recover funds from a provider or, in certain situations, to pay funds to a provider. The AR system is used in financial transactions pertaining to:

- Recoupment of interim payments
- Withholds against payments to providers according to state instructions
- Payments to providers according to state instructions

Amounts may be either positive (+) or negative (−) amounts that correspond to the increase or decrease in the amount of the Medi-Cal warrant (check). The adjustment refers to previously paid claims that may be adjusted if an error in payment occurred. An adjustment may be initiated by the provider, fiscal intermediary, or state.

ELECTRONIC FUNDS TRANSFER

Through EFT, providers may have their payments deposited directly into their bank accounts, and paper warrants will not be generated. However, the provider will receive a RAD document. This system will be phased-in to enrollees, so it is important to keep abreast of the latest information through Medi-Cal bulletins.

Resubmission Turnaround Document

The fiscal intermediary sends an RTD 65-1 to providers when the submitted claim form has questionable or missing information. This document eliminates the need for providers to resubmit the entire claim form to correct a limited number of errors. The RTD must be completed and returned to the fiscal intermediary by the date specified on the RTD.

INSTRUCTIONS FOR COMPLETING THE RESUBMISSION TURNAROUND DOCUMENT

Part A of the RTD (Fig. C–6) describes the information that requires correction, and part B corrects the suspended claim. To complete an RTD, either type or handwrite the correct data on the appropriate line in the Correct Information section of Part B. The data should be entered exactly as required on the claim form (i.e., no dashes, all dates in six-digit format). If a line is correct, it is not necessary to repeat the data; leave blank that line of the Correct Information section. Providers must return part B of the RTD to the fiscal intermediary, but *do not* mail RTDs in the same envelope with claims. Refer to the *Medi-Cal Medical Services Provider Manual* for the address. Figure C–6 shows a correctly completed RTD. (The following item numbers and descriptions correspond to Figure C–8.) The top of the form contains instructions for completing the form.

1. Information: the name of the claim form box in question.
2. Submitted information: questionable or missing information on the claim as entered into the Medi-Cal system.
3. Service Code: procedure code, medical supply type code, or manufacturer billing code and drug code for the services being billed.
4. Error code: See Item 7. RTD error codes are *not* the same as the remittance advice denial codes. Note that 325 indicates that the modifier submitted is incorrect as shown in figure.
5. Date of Service: date the service was rendered.
6. Corrected Information: If the information in Item 2 needs to be corrected, the correct information may be noted here for the provider's records. The actual correction of the information that is sent to the fiscal intermediary is entered in Item 21.
7. Error Description: This is the full explanation of the code that appears in Item 4. Compare this with your copy of the claim to assist you in identifying the error; the error description will be helpful.
8. Provider Name and Address.
9. Provider Number.
10. Final Notice: this is for the fiscal intermediary's use only.
11. Date of Notice.
12. Number of pages in RTD.
13. Service Date(s)/Provider Reference Number.
14. Preprinted information that identifies the patient, Medi-Cal identification number, medical records number, total charges, and specific CCN.
15. Correspondence Reference Number: leave blank.
16. Provider's Number.
17. Provider's Name.
18. Patient's Medi-Cal identification number entered by the provider on the original claim.
19. Patient's Name.
20. Leave blank.
21. Enter correct information (Part B of the RTD) in the numbered box that corresponds with the error line in the Information Block (Item 1 in Part A). If the information in part A is correct, leave the corresponding line blank. When entering correct information, enter all characters (numbers and letters) exactly as they would be entered on the claim. Corrected information on the RTD must be the same alpha or numeric format required on the claim form (i.e., date of birth: June 6, 1968 would be entered as 060668). Claims cannot be processed if the corrected information is not accurate or is not shown in the required format.
22. Signature: All RTDs must be signed and dated by the provider or an authorized representative.
23. If a claim requires POE, this will show as an error description (Item 7) indicating that the POE label is missing or invalid on original claim.

Claims Inquiry Form

A CIF 60-1 is used for tracing a claim, resubmitting a claim after a denial, or requesting an adjustment for underpaid or overpaid claims (Fig. C–7). This form may also be used to request SOC reimbursement for a previously paid claim, but such cases must be submitted separately. CIFs should be submitted within 6 months from the date of the RAD.

Providers wishing to refund an incorrect payment may complete a CIF, noting the overpayment, and forward the refund to the fiscal intermediary. Attach a photocopy of the RAD. This form is used to trace claims, make corrections or adjustments, and make supplemental requests. It should be mentioned that if an overpayment is received and an insurer presses the provider of service for a refund, the insurance plan can always recoup the money re-

RESUBMISSION TURNAROUND DOCUMENT

INSTRUCTIONS: Listed in Section "A" are error(s) found on the original claim. To expedite payment, type the correct information in the numbered Box of Section "B" that corresponds to numbered line in Section "A", sign and date the form, and return Section "B" (bottom portion) to F.I. Please respond promptly as the claim cannot be paid unless your corrections are received by August 30, 1990 See your provider manual for assistance regarding the completion of this form.

	INFORMATION BLOCK	SUBMITTED INFORMATION	SERVICE CODE	ERROR CODE	BEG DOS	PATIENT NAME	COR INFO
1	RECIPIENT ID	1234567899		325	90/06/01	Smith, Mike	
2	RECIPIENT SEX	F		325	90/06/01	Smith, Mike	
3	DATE OF BIRTH	060151	(3)	325	90/06/15	Smith, Mike	(6)
4	(1)			(4)	(5)		
5		(2)					
6							

ERROR DESCRIPTION

(7) 325 – RECIPIENT SEX AND DATE OF BIRTH DOES NOT MATCH REHF POE LABEL REQUIRED

PROVIDER NAME AND ADDRESS

MEDICAL GROUP
1223 PROFESSIONAL DRIVE
SACRAMENTO, CA 98765
(8)

(9) PROVIDER NUMBER ZZZ12345Z (10) FINAL NOTICE

DATE June 30, 1990 (11) PAGE (12) 1 OF 1

SERVICE DATE(S) / PROVIDER REFERENCE NO. (13) June 15, 1990

RETAIN THIS PORTION

PATIENT NAME	MEDI-CAL ID NUMBER	MEDICAL RECORDS NO.	TOTAL CHARGES	CLAIM CONTROL NUMBER
(14) SMITH, MIKE	1234567899	12345	$1575.00	017062609702

DETACH AND RETURN TO APPROPRIATE F.I.

DO NOT STAPLE IN BAR AREA

CORRESPONDENCE REFERENCE NUMBER - F.I. USE ONLY (15)

4

PROVIDER NUMBER (16) ZZZ12345Z FINAL NOTICE June 30, 1990

PROVIDER NAME MEDICAL GROUP (17)

PATIENT MEDI-CAL ID NO. 1234567899 (18)

PATIENT NAME SMITH, MIKE (19)

This is to certify that the corrected information is true, accurate, and complete and that the provider has read, understands, and agrees to be bound by and comply with the statements and conditions contained on the back of this form.

(22)

Signature of provider or person authorized by provider to bind provider by above signature to statements and conditions contained on this form. DATE

F.I. USE ONLY

CCN 017062609702 N CLAIM TYPE 05 PAGE 1 OF PAGES 1

SUBMITTED INFORMATION	ERROR CODE	LINE	FIELD	LABEL
1234567899	325	00	002	☐
F (20)	325	00	003	☐
	325	00	004	☐
				☐
				☐
				☐

CORRECT INFORMATION MUST BE ENTERED ON THE SAME LINE AS THE ERROR SHOWN IN SECTION "A"

CORRECT INFORMATION

1 (21)
2
3
4
5
6

IF SPECIFICALLY REQUESTED, PLACE LABEL IN THE BOX INDICATED ... THIS SPACE MAY ALSO BE USED FOR COMMENTS

(23)

1	2	3
4	5	6

FIGURE C-6

Example of a completed Medi-Cal Resubmission Turnaround Document (RTD) Form 65-1.

DO NOT STAPLE IN BAR AREA

(1) CORRESPONDENCE REFERENCE NUMBER • FOR CSC USE ONLY

FASTEN HERE

CLAIMS INQUIRY

COMPUTER SCIENCES CORPORATION
P.O. BOX 15300C
SACRAMENTO, CALIFORNIA 95813
TELEPHONE NO. 1-800-852-7682

READ INSTRUCTIONS ON REVERSE PRIOR TO COMPLETING AND SIGNING THIS FORM. DO NOT TYPE/MARK IN SHADED AREAS.

(2) DOCUMENT NUMBER
20953190

TYPEWRITER ALIGNMENT ELITE PICA

(3) PROVIDER NAME/ADDRESS

SUSAN SMITH MD
727 ELM BLVD
ANYTOWN CA 90101

(4) PROVIDER NO.
00A12121 0

(5) CLAIM TYPE
CHECK ONE BOX ONLY

- 01 PHARMACY
- 02 LTC
- 03 HOSPITAL INPATIENT
- 04 HOSPITAL OUTPATIENT/CLINIC
- 05 X PHYSICIAN/ALLIED
- 07 VISION

TYPEWRITER ALIGNMENT ELITE PICA

PLEASE FILL IN ALL APPLICABLE INFORMATION REQUESTED BELOW

(6) DELETE		(7) PATIENT'S NAME OR MEDICAL RECORD NO.	(8) PATIENT'S MEDI-CAL I.D. NO.	(9) CLAIM CONTROL NO.	LINE	(10) DATE OF SERVICE	(11) PROC./MOD DRUG CODE	(12) AMOUNT BILLED	(13) CROSS-OVER	(14) ATTACH-MENT
	01	BROWN	36543212345678	22010724045	01					X
	02	SMITH	19846830151602	22386897223	01					X
	03	VANDERBULL	12345678901234			09019X	90070	25.00		
	04									
	05									
	06									
	07									
	08									

REMARKS (CORRECTIONS OR ADDITIONAL INFORMATION NECESSARY TO RECONSIDER OR TRACE CLAIMS LISTED ABOVE)

LINE 1 - DENIED 347 - CORRECT FACILITY PROVIDER NUMBER IS HSC12345F

LINE 2 - OFFICE VISIT 90070 WAS INCORRECTLY BILLED AS 90730
AND WE WERE UNDERPAID. PLEASE ADJUST PAYMENT.
CORRECTED CLAIM COPY ATTACHED

LINE 3 - PLEASE TRACE.

This is to certify that the information contained above is true, accurate, and complete, and that the provider has read, understands, and agrees to be bound by and comply with the statements and conditions contained on the back of this form.

Cynthia Morris, Accts. Mgr. 11/12/9X

Signature of provider or person authorized by provider to bind provider by above signature to statements and conditions contained on this form. DATE

60-1 9/81

FIGURE C–7
Example of a completed Medi-Cal Claims Inquiry Form 60-1.

quested from the next check. This happens frequently with refunds due Medicare, Medicaid, and other government payers.

For denial and adjustment requests, complete a CIF and attach a legible copy of the corrected claim form, a copy of the RAD on which the claim is listed, and any other pertinent information.

A CIF may be used to trace claims submitted to the fiscal intermediary more than 45 days previously that have not appeared on the RAD as approved or denied and that are not indicated on the most recent RAD as suspended. When submitting a tracer, leave the CCN box blank. As many as eight claims may be listed on a single CIF when tracing. Do not attach claim copies or any other documentation to a tracer. The CIF request for tracing a claim will automatically review the recipient's history and generate a response letter showing the results of the review. Based on the information in the letter, a CIF may be resubmitted for denial reconsideration, adjustment, or proof of previous timely submission.

INSTRUCTIONS FOR COMPLETING THE CLAIMS INQUIRY FORM

The following are instructions for completing the CIF. Each line on the CIF corresponds to a single line on the HCFA-1500 Claim Form. Complete the lines on the CIF according to the type of inquiry you wish to make. Adjustment and denial reconsideration requests may be combined on one CIF. Tracer requests must be submitted separately.

It is important that the correct number of characters be entered in the spaces provided on the form. Any time a reference is made to a claim previously adjudicated, be certain to indicate the previous CCN and attach a copy of the corrected claim and RAD. *Do not* submit CIFs for claims that are listed under the Suspends heading on the RAD. Each numbered item refers to the numbers on the CIF (see Fig. C–7).

1. Correspondence Reference Number: leave blank. The fiscal intermediary will assign a number.
2. Document Number: a preimprinted number identifying the CIF.
3. Provider Name/Address: Enter provider name, street address, city, state, and ZIP code.
4. Provider Number: Enter the nine-character provider identification number, plus check digit, assigned by the Department of Health Services.
5. Claim Type: Enter an X in the box indicating the claim type. Check only one box.
6. Delete: Enter an X to delete the entire line.
7. Patient's Name or Medical Record Number: Enter up to the first 10 letters of the patient's last name or the first 10 characters of the patient's medical record number.
8. Patient's Medi-Cal Identification Number: Enter the recipient's identification number that appears on the RAD showing adjudication of that claim.
9. CCN: Enter the 13-digit number assigned by the fiscal intermediary to the claim line in question. This may be found on the RAD. If this line is blank, the inquiry will be considered a tracer request.
10. Date of Service: Enter the date in six-digit format (i.e., 06069X), on which the service was rendered. For block-billed claims, enter the "From" date of service.
11. Proc./Mod., Drug Code: Enter the appropriate procedure code, modifier, and drug or supply code if applicable. Long-term care and inpatient providers may leave this box blank.
12. Amount Billed: Enter the amount originally billed, using the two boxes to the right of the decimal point to reflect cents.
13. Attachment: Enter an X when attaching documentation and when resubmitting a denied claim. All CIFs should have attachments except when submitting a tracer.
14. Underpayment: Enter an X for an underpayment adjustment of a paid claim. *Do not* mark if the claim was denied.
15. Overpayment: Enter an X if all or part of the claim was overpaid. *Do not* mark if the claim was denied.
16. Signature: The provider or an authorized representative must sign the CIF.

APPEAL PROCESS

A provider with a grievance or complaint regarding payment of claims must direct this grievance or complaint to the fiscal intermediary within 90 days of the action causing the grievance or complaint. If the 90-day limit is not met, the appeal is subject to automatic denial. Appeals must be submitted using the Appeal Form 90-1 (Fig. C–8) and should include legible copies of supporting documentation (i.e., claim forms, RADs, CIFs, TARs, and so on). The fiscal intermediary will send an acknowledgment within 15 days of receipt and make a decision within 30 days from the date of the acknowledgment. If the appealed claim is approved for reprocessing, it will appear on a RAD. If the provider is not satisfied with the decision, a subsequent appeal may be made. If the provider is still not satisfied with the decision, then judicial remedy no later than 1 year after receipt of the decision may be undertaken.

Each numbered item refers to the numbers on the Appeal Form shown in Figure C–8.

1. Appeal Reference Number: Leave blank. The fiscal intermediary will assign a number.
2. Document Number: A preimprinted number that may be used when requesting information about the status of an appeal.
3. Provider Name/Address: Enter the provider's name, street address, city, state, and ZIP code.
4. Provider Number: Enter the provider's identification number. Without the correct provider number, appeal acknowledgment may be delayed.
5. Claim Type: Enter an X in the box indicating the claim type. Check only one box.
6. Statement of Appeal: For information purposes only.
7. Patient's Name or Medical Record Number: Enter up to the first 10 letters of the patient's last name or the first 10 characters of the patient's medical record number.
8. Patient's Medi-Cal ID Number/SSN: Enter the recipient's identification number that appears on the plastic BIC or paper Medi-Cal card.

DO NOT STAPLE IN BAR AREA

(1) APPEAL REFERENCE NUMBER

1

F.I. USE ONLY

FASTEN HERE

2

FIRST LEVEL APPEAL

READ INSTRUCTIONS ON REVERSE PRIOR TO COMPLETING AND SIGNING THIS FORM. DO NOT TYPE/MARK IN SHADED AREAS.

(2) DOCUMENT NUMBER
F0179869

TYPEWRITER ALIGNMENT
ELITE PICA

TYPEWRITER ALIGNMENT
ELITE PICA

(3) PROVIDER NAME/ADDRESS

3

HERBERT HARKER MD
1313 WALNUT AVENUE
SACRAMENTO, CA 95834

4

(4) PROVIDER NO: 00A123470 | CHECK DIGIT: 7

(5) CLAIM TYPE
CHECK ONE BOX ONLY

5

- 01 [ ] PHARMACY
- 02 [ ] LTC
- 03 [ ] HOSPITAL INPATIENT
- 04 [ ] HOSPITAL OUTPATIENT/ CLINIC
- 05 [X] PHYSICIAN/ ALLIED
- 07 [ ] VISION

(6)

6

AS PROVIDED BY THE CALIFORNIA ADMINISTRATIVE CODE, TITLE 22, SECTION 51015 (b-d). I AM SUBMITTING AN APPEAL OF MY CLAIM AS DEFINED BELOW. ENCLOSED ARE ALL THE PERTINENT DOCUMENTS CORRESPONDING TO THIS APPEAL, INCLUDING COPIES OF THE CLAIM, EOB/RA, CIFs, MEDICARE EOMB/RA AND ANY PREVIOUS CORRESPONDENCE WITH THE MEDI-CAL FISCAL INTERMEDIARY

PLEASE FILL IN ALL APPLICABLE INFORMATION REQUESTED BELOW

7 8 9 10 11 12

(7) PATIENT'S NAME OR MEDICAL RECORD NO.: CATLIN

(8) PATIENT'S MEDI-CAL I.D. NO./SSN: 346091231

	(9) DELETE	(10) CLAIM CONTROL NO	(11) DATE OF SERVICE	(12) EOB/RA CODE
01	[ ]	4121717612301	01 01 94	076
02	[ ]	4121717612302	01 01 94	401
03	[ ]	4131411232301	02 21 94	414
04	[ ]			
05	[ ]			
06	[ ]			
07	[ ]			
08	[ ]			
09	[ ]			
10	[ ]			
11	[ ]			
12	[ ]			
13	[ ]			
14	[ ]			

(13) REASON FOR APPEAL: (ENCLOSED ALL SUPPORTING DOCUMENTS, INCLUDING CLAIM COPY)

1. PLEASE SEE ATTACHED REPORT. WE SUBMITTED A CIF, BUT THE CLAIM WAS DENIED AGAIN FOR DOCUMENTATION. PLEASE RECONSIDER.
2. QUANTITY BILLED WAS 2, ONLY PAID 1. PLEASE ADJUST THIS UNDERPAYMENT.
3. BILLED IN ERROR, PLEASE RETRACT FAYMENT.

13

(14) COMMON APPEAL REASON
CHECK ONLY ONE (IF APPLICABLE)

14

- [ ] ELIGIBILITY (POE ATTACHED)
- [ ] TAR DENIAL (TAR ATTACHED)
- [ ] CROSSOVER (EOMB ATTACHED)
- [ ] ADJUSTMENT REQUEST (PAID WARRANT ATTACHED)

THIS IS TO CERTIFY THAT THE INFORMATION CONTAINED ABOVE IS TRUE, ACCURATE, AND COMPLETE AND THAT THE PROVIDER HAS READ, UNDERSTANDS, AND AGREES TO BE BOUND BY AND COMPLY WITH THE STATEMENTS AND CONDITIONS CONTAINED ON THE BACK OF THIS FORM.

15

(15) Joyce Johnson
SIGNATURE OF PROVIDER OR PERSON AUTHORIZED BY PROVIDER TO BIND PROVIDER BY ABOVE SIGNATURE TO STATEMENTS AND CONDITIONS CONTAINED ON THIS FORM

06-02-94
DATE

FORWARD TO APPROPRIATE F.I.

FORM 90-1 (7-90)

FIGURE C–8

Example of a completed Medi-Cal Appeal Form 90-1 to be used for denial resubmissions, underpayment reconsiderations, and overpayment returns.

Provider ID Number

Enter the provider ID number in Block 31.

31. SIGNATURE OF PHYSICIAN OR SUPPLIER INCLUDING DEGREES OR CREDENTIALS (I certify that the statements on the reverse apply to this bill and are made a part thereof.)	
00A121230	
SIGNED	DATE 9/15/9X

Recipient ID Number

Enter only one recipient ID number in either Block 9a or Block 32. Do not enter the same number in both blocks.

9a. OTHER INSURED'S POLICY OR GROUP NUMBER
521345678

OR

32. NAME AND ADDRESS OF FACILITY WHERE SERVICES WERE RENDERED (If other than home or office)
521345678

Crossover Billing Tips

Block 31: The provider ID number entered in this block will determine the provider to be paid.

Block 9a or 32: The Medi-Cal recipient ID number must be the recipient's nine-digit Social Security Number, Client Index Number, or the recipient's 14-digit Medi-Cal ID number.

A crossover claim may be suspended or denied if an incorrect Medi-Cal recipient number or multiple numbers are placed in either of these blocks, or if the Medi-Cal recipient ID number is placed in any block other than 9a or 32.

Block 32: If a number is preimprinted in this block and is in error, remove the name and address in this field, if applicable, before billing Medi-Cal. Be sure to remove the name and address by using self-adhesive correction tape. Do not use correction fluid.

FIGURE C-9
Medicare/Medi-Cal crossover billing tips for completing the HCFA-1500 claim form.

9. Delete: Enter an X to delete the corresponding line.
10. CCN: For adjudicated claims, enter the 13-digit number assigned by the fiscal intermediary to the claim line in question. This number appears on the RAD. When appealing a nonadjudicated claim (i.e., a traced claim that could not be located), the CCN field is not required.
11. Date of Service: In six-digit format (01029X), enter the date the service was rendered. For claims billed in a "From-Through" format, enter the "From" date of service.
12. RAD Code: When appealing an adjudicated claim, enter the RAD message code for the claim line (e.g., 072, 401, 010).
13. Reason for Appeal: Indicate the specific reason for filing an appeal. Remember to attach all supporting documentation.
14. Common Appeal Reasons: Check one of the boxes if applicable. Include a copy of the claim and supporting documents (e.g., TAR, RAD). Box 13 may be left blank if this box is used.
15. Signature: The provider or an authorized representative must sign.

MEDI-CAL AND OTHER COVERAGE

The physician must bill any other insurance carrier first and then Medi-Cal. Have the patient sign an assignment of benefits form for the other insurance. After payment is received from the other insurance carrier, include a copy of the other insurance EOB.

MEDI-CAL AND CHAMPUS

If a Medi-Cal patient is also covered by CHAMPUS, bill CHAMPUS first. Then bill Medi-Cal and attach the EOB to the claim form (see Chapter 13).

MEDI-CAL AND MEDICARE

Outpatient claims for recipients eligible for both Medicare and Medi-Cal coverage must always be billed to Medicare before Medi-Cal. These claims may be referred to as *crossover claims* because after processing by Medicare, claims are automatically crossed over to the Medi-Cal fiscal intermediary for final processing unless 100% of the claim was paid by Medicare. The claim must be assigned or it will not be crossed over. Hard-copy billing instructions for Medicare Part B crossover claims are different than the instructions for submitting straight Medi-Cal claims. When submitting a crossover claim, on the

HCFA-1500 Claim Form, enter an X in both the Medicaid and Medicare boxes of Block 1 to identify the claim as a crossover. Include the Medi-Cal provider identification number in Block 31 and the Medi-Cal recipient identification number in either Block 9a or Block 32 depending on the circumstances of the case (Fig. C–9).

TO THE STUDENT

Study Chapter 11 and Appendix C and then answer the review questions in the *Workbook* to reinforce the theories learned in these portions of the text and to help prepare you for a future test. Assignments 35 through 37 will give you experience in abstracting from case histories, posting to ledger cards, and completing forms pertinent to the Medicaid program in your state. For further knowledge and understanding, the key terms and abbreviations at the beginning of these chapters and this Appendix appear in the Glossary of this textbook so you can look up the pertinent terms.

After completing the *Workbook* assignments, you may want additional practice on the concepts you have learned. Medicaid Case 2 is available on your computer disk.

Glossary

Chapter number(s) is shown in parentheses after each term.

Abuse (2): Incidents or practices, not usually considered fraudulent, that are inconsistent with accepted sound medical business or fiscal practices.

Accident (14): An unexpected happening causing injury traceable to a definite time and place.

Accidental death and dismemberment (15): Insurance policy provision that protects the insured if he or she suffers loss of sight or loss of limb(s) or death by accident.

Actual charge (4): Physician's actual fee for his or her service at the time the insurance claim is submitted to the insurance company or government payer.

Adjudication (14): Final determination of the issues in an action according to which judgment is rendered.

Adjustments (10): Corrections or modifications reflecting changes in a previously submitted bill; for example, late charges.

Admission review (16): Review for appropriateness and necessity of admissions.

Admitting diagnosis (5): Initial identification of the condition or chief complaint for which the patient is treated.

Aid category (11): Designation within Supplemental Security Income or the State Social Services Department under which a person may be eligible for public assistance and/or medical assistance.

Alien (17): An individual belonging to another country or people; a foreigner.

Allowable charge (13): Amount on which CHAMPUS figures the patient's cost-share for covered care. This is based on 75 to 80% of the *allowable* charge.

Allowed amount (12): The amount Medicare will pay for a service. This is based on 80% of the *reasonable charge,* also known as the "approved charge."

Ambulatory patient groups (APGs) (16): Ambulatory patient goups are a modification of ambulatory visit groups (AVGs), developed as an outpatient classification scheme by Health Systems International (HSI).

Ambulatory visit groups (AVGs) (16): An outpatient classification scheme of 571 AVGs developed by Health Systems International (HSI).

American Academy of Procedural Coders (AAPC) (1): National association dedicated to promoting professional standards and recognition for procedural coders.

American Association for Medical Transcription (AAMT) (1): National association of medical transcriptionists with state associations and regional chapters; membership is limited to practicing or former transcriptionists and students in medical transcription programs.

American Association of Medical Assistants, Inc. (AAMA) (1): National association of medical assistants, medical assisting students, and medical assisting educators with both state and local chapters; recognized by the American Medical Association.

American Health Information Management Association (AHIMA) (1): National professional organization for promoting the art and science of medical record management and improving the quality of comprehensive health information for the welfare of the public.

American Medical Association (AMA) (1): National professional society of physicians.

Ancillary services (9): Supportive services other than routine hospital services provided by the facility, such as x-rays and laboratory tests.

Appeal (8): To request more payment by asking for a review of an insurance claim that has been paid or denied by an insurance company.

Applicant (3): Person applying for insurance coverage.

Application form (17): Request form to be completed with pertinent data when applying for employment.

Appropriateness evaluation protocol (AEP) (16): Nineteen criteria for admission under the prospective payment system, separated into two categories: severity of illness and intensity of illness. To allow a patient admission to an acute care facility, one criterion from each category must be met.

Arbitration (2): Legal method provided by statute in some states by which a patient and a physician may agree to resolve any controversy that may arise between them before an impartial panel (grievance committee).

Armed services disability (15): Disability occurring or aggravated while serving in military service.

Assignment (12): For Medicare, an agreement in which a patient assigns to the physician the right to receive payment from the fiscal intermediary. Under this agreement, the physician must agree to accept the program payment as payment in full except for 20% of the *reasonable (allowed or approved) charge* and the deductible. For CHAMPUS, providers who accept assignment agree to accept 75% or 80% of the CHAMPUS allowable charge as the full fee, collecting the deductible and 20% or 25% of the allowable charge from the patient.

Assignment of benefits (10): An agreement signed by the insured directing the carrier to pay benefits directly to the physician.

Assumption of risk (2): If one knowingly pursues a dangerous course, he or she cannot recover damages. If the patient has been informed of the risks and agrees to treatment, he or she cannot sue for damages unless there has been some other factor responsible for the trouble.

Asterisk procedures (4): RVS surgical procedure code number marked with an asterisk, which designates that the procedure may be billed following a different set of rules than unmarked surgical procedure code numbers.

Audit trail (7): Path left by a transaction when it is processed.

Authorized provider (13): Physician or other individual authorized provider of care or a hospital or supplier approved by CHAMPUS to provide medical care and supplies.

Back up (7): Duplicate data file; equipment designed to complete or redo the operation if the primary equipment fails.

Batch (7): Group of claims for different patients from one office submitted in one computer transmission.

Benefit period (12): Period of time for which payments for Medicare inpatient hospital benefits are available. A benefit period begins the first day an enrollee is given inpatient hospital care (nursing care or rehabilitation services) by a qualified provider and ends when the enrollee has not been an inpatient for 60 consecutive days. For disability insurance, it is the maximum amount of time that benefits will be paid to the injured or ill person for a disability.

Bit (7): Binary digit, either a 1 or 0.

Blanket contract (3): Comprehensive group insurance coverage through plans sponsored by professional associations for their members.

BlueCard program (10): An agreement among Blue Cross Plans through which a local plan may provide benefits for any out-of-area Blue Cross Plan subscriber.

Blue Cross (3): An independent, not-for-profit membership corporation providing protection against the costs of hospital care and, in some policies, protection against the costs of surgical and professional care.

Blue Cross and Blue Shield Association (BCBSA) (10): An organization founded to promote the betterment of public health and security; to secure the widest public acceptance of voluntary nonprofit prepayment of health services; and to provide national services to local Blue Cross and Blue Shield Plans. Contracts with the federal government as an administrative agency for federal health programs; sponsors and conducts programs on health care and prepayment issues.

Blue Cross and Blue Shield Plans (10): Independent, generally nonprofit community service organizations that contract with hospitals, physicians, and other health care providers to give prepaid health care services to their subscribers.

Blue Shield (3, 10): An independent, not-for-profit membership association providing protection against the costs of surgery and other items of medical care. Some policies also offer protection against the costs of hospital care.

Bonding (2): An insurance contract by which, in return for a stated fee, a bonding agency guarantees payment of a certain sum to an employer in the event of a financial loss to the employer by the act of a specified employee or by some contingency over which the employer has no control.

Breach of confidential communication (2): "Breach" means breaking or violation of a law or agreement. In the context of the medical office it means the unauthorized release of information about the patient.

Breach of contract (2): *See breach of confidential communication.* If a physician agrees to achieve a particular result for a patient and then fails to do so, he or she is liable for breach of contract even if he or she has used the highest degree of skill.

Breach of duty (2): A general term used for violation or omission of a legal or moral duty.

Buffing (9): Physicians justifying the transference of sick, high-cost patients to other physicians in a managed care plan.

Bug (7): An error in a program.

By report (BR) (14): A report must be submitted with the claim when the notation BR follows the procedure code description. This term is sometimes seen in workers' compensation fee schedules. Also see *Special Report.*

Byte (7): The number of bits used to represent one character.

Capitated payment (9): Annual fee paid by the insurer to the physician, hospital, or network providing health care to a patient.

Capitation (9, 16): System of payment used by managed care plans in which physicians and hospitals are paid a fixed, per capita amount for each patient enrolled over a stated period of time, regardless of the type and number of services provided; reimbursement to the hospital on a per-member/per-month basis to cover costs for the members of the plan.

Capitation fee (11): The fee the agency periodically pays to a contractor for each recipient enrolled under a contract for the provision of medical services under the state plan, whether or not the recipient receives the services during the period covered by the fee.

Carrier (10): An insurance company that underwrites policies that cover health care services. Within the context of the Medicare program, it refers to an entity (such as Blue Cross and/or Blue Shield) that contracts with the Health Care Financing Administration (HCFA) to process Medicare Part B claims. Also known as *fiscal agents.*

Carrier-direct system (7): Direct electronic transmission of insurance claims from the physician to the insurance company.

Case rate (16): An averaging after a flat rate is given to certain categories of procedures.

Categorically needy (11): Aged, blind, or disabled individuals or families and children who meet financial eligibility requirements for Aid to Families with Dependent Children, Supplemental Security Income, or an optional state supplement.

Central processing unit (CPU) (17): Brains of a computing device controlling the internal memory that directs the flow and processing of information.

Certificate number (10): Number that identifies the insured.

Certification (1): Statement issued by a board or association verifying that a person meets professional standards.

Certified Claims Assistance Professional (CCAP) (1, 17): Certification awarded to a person after appropriate training and by passing a certification examination administered by the National Association of Claims Assistance Professionals, Inc.

Certified Coding Specialist (CCS) (1, 17): Title received by a person after appropriate training and by passing a certification examination administered by the American Health Information Management Association.

Certified Electronic Claims Professional (CECP) (1, 17): Certification awarded to a person after appropriate training and by passing a certification examination administered by the National Association of Claims Assistance Professionals, Inc.

Certified Medical Assistant (CMA) (1): A title received by a person after appropriate training and by passing a certification examination administered by the American Association of Medical Assistants, Inc.

Certified Procedural Coder (CPC) (1, 17): Title received by a person after appropriate training and by passing a certification examination administered by the American Academy of Procedural Coders.

CHAMPUS (3, 13): The Civilian Health and Medical Program of the Uniformed Services, a government-sponsored program providing hospital and medical services for dependents of active service personnel, retired and reserve military personnel, families of active duty service members, and dependents of deceased members who died in active duty.

CHAMPUS supplemental insurance (13): Health benefit plans designed to supplement CHAMPUS benefits.

CHAMPUS/TRICARE (13): Three-option managed health care program offered to spouses and dependents of service personnel with uniform benefits and fees implemented nationwide by the Federal government.

CHAMPVA (3, 13): The Civilian Health and Medical Program of the Veterans Administration, a program for veterans with total, permanent, service-connected disabilities or surviving spouses and dependents of veterans who died from service-connected disabilities.

Charges (16): The dollar amount a hospital bills an outlier case based on the itemized bill.

Chronologic resume (17): A data sheet that outlines experience and education by dates.

Churning (9): Physicians seeing a high volume of patients—more than medically necessary—to increase revenue. May be seen in fee-for-service or managed care environments.

Civil law (2): Law that enforces private rights and liabilities, as distinguished from criminal law.

Civil Service Retirement System (CSRS) (15): Program for federal employees hired before 1984.

Claim (3): A billing sent to an insurance carrier. Also known as *encounter record.*

Claims Assistance Professional (CAP) (1, 17): A practitioner who works for the consumer and helps patients organize, complete, and file, and negotiate health insurance claims of all types to obtain maximum benefits as well as tell the patient what checks to write to providers to eliminate overpayment.

Claims processor (13): See *Fiscal agent.*

Claims-review type of foundation (9): A type of foundation that provides peer review by physicians to the numerous fiscal agents or carriers involved in its area.

Clean claim (6): A completed insurance claim form that contains all the necessary information without deficiencies so it can be processed and paid promptly.

Clearinghouse system (7): Insurance claims transmission to a clearinghouse, referred to as a third-party administrator (TPA), who redistributes the claims electronically to various insurance carriers.

Clinical outlier (16): Cases that cannot adequately be assigned to an appropriate DRG owing to unique combinations of diagnoses and surgeries, very rare conditions, or other unique clinical reasons. Such cases are grouped together into clinical outlier DRGs and, therefore, are considered *outliers.*

Closed panel program (9): A form of HMO that limits the patient's choice of personal physicians to those doctors practicing in the HMO group practice within the geographic location and/or facility. A physician must meet very narrow criteria in order to join a closed panel.

Coding (16): Transferring narrative description of diseases, injuries, and procedures into numeric designations.

Coding creep (4): Coding that is inappropriately altered to generate a higher reimbursement (e.g., an expanded problem or detailed history office visit is coded instead of a 5-minute minimal visit when the patient came in only for a blood pressure check).

Coding specialist (17): An individual whose expertise is in procedural and/or diagnostic coding.

Coinsurance (3): A cost-sharing requirement under a health insurance policy providing that the insured will assume a percentage of the costs for covered services; for Medicare, after application of the yearly cash deductible, the portion of the reasonable charges (20%) for which the beneficiary is responsible.

Combination code (5): Single five-digit code used to identify etiology and secondary process (manifestation) or complication of a disease.

Combination resume (16): Data sheet that combines specific dates of work experience with educational skills.

Comorbidity (16): An ongoing condition that exists along with the condition for which the patient is receiving treatment; in regard to DRGs, a pre-existing condition that, because of its presence with a certain principal diagnosis, will cause an increase in length of stay by at least 1 day in approximately 75% of cases. Also known as *substantial comorbidity.*

Competitive medical plan (CMP) (3): A type of managed care organization created by the 1982 TEFRA legislation for enrollment of Medicare beneficiaries into managed care plans.

Complementary benefits (10): Benefits designed to work together with those of another program. Medicare recipients, for example, may enroll in Blue Shield programs that pay bills not covered by Medicare.

Complication (16): Disease or condition arising during the course of, or as a result of, another disease modifying medical care requirements; for DRGs, a condition that arises during the hospital stay that prolongs the length of stay by at least 1 day in approximately 75% of cases. Also known as *substantial complication.*

Comprehensive type of foundation (9): A type of foundation that designs and sponsors prepaid health programs or set minimum benefits of coverage.

Compromise and release (C and R) (14): An agreement arrived at, whether in or out of court, for settling a workers' compensation case after the patient has been declared permanent and stationary.

Conditionally renewable (3): Insurance policy renewal provision that grants the insurer a limited right to refuse to renew a health insurance policy at the end of a premium payment period.

Consultative examiner (CE) (15): A physician who is paid a fee to examine and/or test a person for disability under either the SSDI or SSI program.

Continuing education (CE) (1): Formal education pursued by a working professional and intended to improve or maintain professional competence.

Contract (3): A legally enforceable agreement when relating to an insurance policy; for workers' compensation cases, an agreement involving two or more parties in which each is obligated to the other to fulfill promises made. (The contract exists between the physician and the insurance carrier.)

Control plan (10): A Blue Shield Plan that negotiates and administers a contract for an organization in its area that has other employees in other states. For example, the Michigan Blue Shield Plan has a national contract for workers in the automobile industry.

Conversion factor (4): The dollars and cents amount that is established for one unit as applied to a service rendered. This unit is then used to convert various procedures into fee-schedule payment amounts by multiplying the relative value unit by the conversion factor.

Cooperative care (13): Term used when a patient is seen by a civilian physician or hospital for services cost-shared by CHAMPUS.

Coordination of benefits (13): The coordination of the payment of CHAMPUS benefits with the payment of benefits made by the double coverage plan, so that there is no duplication of benefits paid between the double coverage plan and CHAMPUS. Likewise applies to disability programs.

Copayment (copay) (9): Patient's payment (i.e., 20% of a bill or $10 each visit) of a portion of the cost at the time the service is rendered. Also referred to as *coinsurance.*

Cost containment (9): Plan for reducing health care costs.

Cost-of-living adjustment (15): Disability insurance provision to increase monthly benefits.

Cost outlier (16): Typical case that has an extraordinarily high cost when compared with most discharges classified to the same DRG.

Cost outlier review (16): Review by a Professional Review Organization (PRO) for the necessity of a patient's hospital admission and to determine whether all services rendered were medically necessary. Cost outlier cases are recognized only if the case is not eligible for day outlier status.

Cost-share (13): The portion of the allowable charges for care on each claim that the patient pays and the portion that CHAMPUS pays.

Cover letter (17): Letter of introduction prepared to accompany a resume when seeking a job.

Covered services (11): Specific services and supplies for which Medicaid will provide reimbursement; these consist of a combination of mandatory and optional services within each state.

Crib sheet (4): Summary form listing key components of E/M codes.

Crossover claim (12): Bill for services rendered to a patient receiving benefits simultaneously from Medicare and Medicaid. Medicare pays first and then determines the amounts of unmet Medicare deductible and coinsurance to be paid by Medicaid.

***Current Procedural Terminology* (CPT) (4):** A reference procedural code book using a numerical system for procedures, established by the American Medical Association.

Customary charge (4): The amount that a physician usually charges the majority of her or his patients.

Data base (7): Any collection of data stored electronically.

Day outlier review (16): Review of potential day outliers (short or unusually long length of hospital stay) to determine the necessity of admission and number of days before the day outlier threshold is reached as well as the number of days beyond the threshold. The PRO determines the certification of additional days.

Debug (7): To remove errors from a software program or the computer itself.

Deductible (9): Specific dollar amount that must be paid by the insured before a medical insurance plan or government program begins covering health care costs.

Defense Enrollment Eligibility Reporting System (DEERS) (13): An electronic data base used to verify beneficiary eligibility.

Delinquent claim (8): Insurance claim submitted to an insurance company, for which payment is overdue.

Denied claim (8): Insurance claim submitted to an insurance company in which payment has been rejected due to a technical error or because of medical coverage policy issues.

Deposition (14): The process of taking a witness's sworn testimony out of court. This is usually done by an attorney.

Diagnosis-related groups (DRGs) (16): A patient classification system that categorizes patients who are medically related with respect to diagnosis and treatment and statistically similar in length of hospital stay. Medicare hospital insurance payments are based on fixed dollar amounts for a principal diagnosis as listed in DRGs.

Diagnostic cost groups (DCGs) (14): A system of Medicare reimbursement for HMOs with risk contracts in which enrollees are classified into various DCGs on the basis of each beneficiary's prior 12-month hospitalization history.

Diagnostic creep (16): Coding that is inappropriately altered to obtain a higher payment rate. Also known as *coding creep* and *DRG creep.*

Digital fax claim (6): Insurance claim sent to the insurance carrier via facsimile but never printed on paper. The fax is encoded while in electronic form via optical code reader and electronically entered into the claims processing system.

Dingy claims (6): Dingy claims happen when the Medicare contractor cannot process a claim for a particular service or bill type. The claims are held until the necessary system changes are implemented to pay the claim correctly.

Direct payment (10): In the context of Blue Shield, this phrase can have two meanings: (1) dues paid to a plan directly by subscribers rather than through payroll deductions; (2) payment to a physician directly by a Blue Shield plan.

Dirty claims (6): Claims submitted with errors or those requiring manual processing for resolving problems or rejection for payment.

Disability Determination Services (DDS) (15): A state Social Security division office that assesses a case for disability benefits.

Disability income insurance (3, 15): A form of health insurance that provides periodic payments to replace income when the insured is unable to work as a result of illness, injury, or disease.

Disabled (12): For purposes of enrollment under Medicare, individuals under 65 years of age who have been entitled to disability benefits under the Social Security Act or the railroad retirement system for at least 24 months are considered disabled and are entitled to Medicare.

Discharge face sheet (16): An admission summary prepared at the time of the patient's discharge from the hospital. Also known as *discharge summary* or *discharge abstract*.

Discharge status (16): Disposition of the patient on discharge.

Disenrollment (9): Member's voluntary cancellation of HMO membership.

Disk (7): A magnetic storage device made of rigid material (hard disk) or flexible plastic (floppy disk).

Documentation (4): Chronologic detailed recording of pertinent facts and observations about a patient's health as seen in chart notes and medical reports. For computer software, a user's guide to a program or piece of equipment.

Dollar rate (5): One or two factors used to calculate the payment under the DRG prospective payment system.

Double indemnity (15): A feature in some life and disability insurance policies that provides for twice the face amount of the policy to be paid if death results to the insured from accidental causes.

Down coding (4): Occurs when the coding system used on a claim does not match that used by the insurance company receiving the claim.

Down time (7): The period during which a computer is malfunctioning or not operating correctly.

DRG creep (16): See *Diagnostic creep*.

DRG rate (16): A fixed dollar amount based on an average of all patients in a specific DRG in the base year adjusted for inflation, economic factors, and bad debts.

DRG weight (5): An index number assigned to each DRG to reflect the relative cost for all hospitals for treating cases within that DRG.

E codes (5): A classification of ICD-9-CM coding for external causes of injury rather than disease. E codes are also used in coding adverse reactions to medications.

Early and Periodic Screening, Diagnosis, and Treatment (EPSDT) (11): The EPSDT program covers screening and diagnostic services to determine physical or mental defects in recipients under age 21 years and health care, treatment, and other measures to correct or ameliorate any defects and chronic conditions discovered. In New York, this is called the Child Health Assurance Program (CHAP).

Elective surgery (16): Surgical procedure that may be scheduled in advance, is not an emergency, and is discretionary on the part of the physician and patient.

Electronic claim (6): Insurance claim submitted to the insurance carrier via a central processing unit (CPU), tape diskette, direct data entry, direct wire, dial-in telephone, digital fax, or personal computer download or upload.

Electronic claims processor (ECP) (7, 17): Individual who converts insurance claims to standardized electronic format and transmits electronic insurance claims data to the insurance carrier or clearinghouse to help the physician receive payment. Sometimes referred to as electronic claims processor.

Electronic claims submission (ECS) (7): Insurance claims prepared on a computer and submitted via modem (telephone lines) to the insurance carrier's computer system. Also called *electronic media claims (EMC)*.

Electronic data interchange (EDI) (7): Process by which understandable data items are sent back and forth via computer linkages between two or more entities that function alternatively as sender and receiver.

Elimination period (15): See *Waiting period*.

Embezzlement (2): Willful act by an employee of taking possession of an employer's money.

Emergency (11): Severe, life-threatening, or potentially disabling condition that requires immediate attention.

Employer group health plan (EGHP) (12): A private, employment-originated health plan covering an individual who also has Medicare coverage due to being age 65 years or over. Medicare is secondary payer to such a plan.

Employers' liability insurance (14): Protects an employer against the claims for damages that arise out of the injuries to employees in the course of their work. This type of insurance provides protection in cases not covered by the state compensation law.

Employer supplemental insurance (6): A policy that a Medicare beneficiary has through a former employer.

Employment agency (17): Business organization that refers job applicants to potential employers.

Encounter form (7): Routing slip personalized to the practice of the physician.

Encounter record (6, 9): A new buzz term for "claim."

Encryption (7): To assign a code to represent data. This is done for the purpose of security.

End-stage renal disease (ESRD) (12): Individuals who have chronic kidney disease requiring dialysis or kidney transplant are considered to have ESRD. To qualify for Medicare coverage, an individual must be fully or currently insured under Social Security or the railroad retirement system or be the dependent of an insured person. Eligibility for Medicare coverage begins with the third month after the beginning of a course of renal dialysis. Coverage may begin sooner if the patient participates in a self-care dialysis training program or receives a kidney transplant without dialysis.

Eponyms (5): Conditions or procedures named after a person or place.

Ethics (1): Moral principles and standards in the ideal relationships between the physician and patient and also between physicians.

Etiology (5): The cause of disease.

Etiquette (1): Customs, rules of conduct, courtesy, and manners of the medical profession.

Exclusion (3): Limitations for certain conditions or circumstances for which the health insurance policy will not provide benefits.

Exclusive provider organization (EPO) (3): Type of managed health care plan in which subscriber members are eligible for benefits only when they use the services of a limited network of providers. EPOs are regulated under state health insurance laws. Such plans are for large clinics to participate in and combine fee-for-service PPO, and HMO benefits.

Explanation of Benefits (EOB) (10, 13): An explanation of services periodically issued to recipients or providers on whose behalf claims have been paid. Also known in Medicare, Medicaid, and some other programs as a *remittance advice*. In the CHAMPUS program, it is called a *summary payment voucher*.

Explanation of Medicare benefits (EOMB): See *Remittance Advice*.

Extraterritorial (14): When benefits under the state law apply to a compensable injury to an employee hired in one state but injured outside of that state.

Family planning services (11): Services that include diagnosis, treatment, drugs, supplies, and counseling for the purpose of enabling individuals to determine freely the number or spacing of their children. These services are furnished or prescribed by or under the supervision of a physician.

Federal Employee Health Benefits Progran (FEHBP) (10): A federal government health care insurance for federal employees of which there are three types of plans.

Federal Employee Program (FEP) (10): FEP is the acronym used within the Blue Cross/Blue Shield system. However, FEHBP (Federal Employees Health Benefits Program) is used by the federal government to describe the overall program of which FEP is a part.

Federal Employees Compensation Act (FECA) (14): Act instituted in 1908 providing benefits for on-the-job injuries to all federal employees.

Federal Employees Retirement System (FERS) (15): Program for federal employees hired after 1984 or those hired prior to 1984 who switched from CSRS to FERS.

Federal Tax Identification Number (10): A number issued by the Internal Revenue Service to a medical group or solo practice physician and used for income tax purposes.

Fee for service (9): Method of payment in which the patient pays the physician for each professional service performed from an established schedule of fees.

Fee schedule (14): A listing of established allowances for medical services and procedures. See also *Relative value study*.

Felony (2): A major crime, for which greater punishment is imposed than for a misdemeanor.

File (7): A collection of related data stored under a single title.

Fiscal agent (11): An organization under contract to the state to process claims for a state Medicaid program; insurance carrier handling claims from physicians and other suppliers of service for Medicare Part B; sometimes also referred to as *fiscal intermediary*.

Fiscal intermediary (FI) (12, 13): An organization under contract to the government that handles claims under Medicare Part A from hospitals, skilled nursing facilities, and home health agencies. For CHAMPUS and CHAMPVA, the insurance company that handles the claims for care received within a particular state or country. Also known as *fiscal agent, fiscal carrier,* and *claims processor*.

Fiscal year (11): The federal government's 12-month accounting period running from October 1 to September 30 of the following year.

Format (7): The organization or appearance of data.

Foundations for medical care (3, 9): An organization of physicians sponsored by a state or local medical association concerned with the development and delivery of medical services and the cost of health care.

Fraud (2): An intentional misrepresentation of the facts to deceive or mislead another.

Free-lancer (17): Independent individual who is self-employed and works for several clients.

Functional resume (17): Data sheet that highlights qualifications and skills.

Future purchase option (15): See *Cost-of-living adjustment*.

Gatekeeper (9): In the managed care system, this is the physician who controls patient access to specialists.

Global fee (4): A single fee that encompasses all services rendered before, during, and after a particular incident; e.g., billing for obstetric cases or certain surgical procedures.

Grievance committee (2): Impartial panel established by a local medical society to listen to and investigate patients' complaints in regard to medical care or excessive fees charged by a physician. Also seen in arbitration agreements.

Group model (9): Type of HMO in which many different health services are provided in a centrally located medical center. Physicians and staff of a group model HMO usually treat only HMO members.

Group practice (1): Association of three or more physicians or other health professionals who provide services, with income from the practice pooled and redistributed to the members of the group according to some prearranged plan.

Grouper (16): The computer software program that assigns DRGs of discharged patients using the following information: patient's age, sex, principal diagnosis, complications/comorbid conditions, principal procedure, and discharge status.

Guaranteed renewable (3, 15): A clause in an insurance policy that means the insurance company must renew the policy as long as premium payments are made. However, the premium may be increased when it is renewed. These policies may have age limits of 60, 65, or 70 years or may be renewable for life.

Hard copy (7): A printout from a printer via computer.

Hardware (7): The physical components of a computer system, e.g., display screen, hard disk.

HCFA-1500 claim form (6): Universal insurance claim form developed and approved by the American Medical Association Council on Medical Service and the Health Care Financing Administration. It is used by physicians and other professionals to bill outpatient services and supplies to CHAMPUS, Medicare and some Medicaid programs as well as some private insurance carriers and managed care plans.

Health and Human Services (HHS) (5): A governmental department given the task of developing a system of physician reimbursements based on DRGs; oversees the Medicare program.

Health benefits advisor (HBA) (13): An individual at military hospitals or clinics who is there to help CHAMPUS beneficiaries obtain medical care through the military and through CHAMPUS.

Health Care Financing Administration (HCFA) (12): Formerly known as the Social Security Administration, HCFA is that part of the Department of Health and Human Services that oversees Medicare, among other governmental health programs.

Health Care Financing Administration Common Procedure Coding System (HCPCS) (4): HCFA's Common Procedure Coding System. A national uniform coding structure for reporting physician/supplier services under the Medicare program. A coding system that includes CPT-4, national, and local codes. Pronounced "hick-picks."

Health insurance (3): A generic term applying to all types of insurance indemnifying or reimbursing for hospital and medical care costs or lost income arising from illness or injury. Also known as *accident and health insurance* or *disability income insurance*.

Health Maintenance Organization (HMO) (3, 9): A type of health care program in which enrollees receive benefits when they obtain services that are provided or authorized by selected providers, usually with a primary care physician "gatekeeper." In general, enrollees do not receive coverage for the services or providers who are not in the HMO network, except for emergency services.

Hearing (15): Second level of the appeal process for an individual applying for SSDI or SSI. This is a hearing before an administrative law judge who had no part in the initial or reconsideration disability determination.

High risk (3): A high chance of loss.

Home health agency (12): A public or private organization providing nursing services in patients' homes.

Hospice (12): A public agency or private organization primarily engaged in providing pain relief, symptom management, and supportive services to terminally ill patients and their families.

Hospital insurance (12): Known as Medicare Part A. A program providing basic protection against the costs of hospital and related posthospital services for individuals eligible under the Medicare program.

ICD-9-CM codes (5): The *International Classification of Diseases, Ninth Revision, Clinical Modification* is a numeric code system for diagnoses and procedures.

In-area (9): Within the geographic boundaries defined by an HMO as the area in which it will provide medical services to its members.

Incomplete claim (6): Any Medicare claim missing required information; such claims are identified to the provider so they may be resubmitted.

Idemnity (3): Benefits paid to insured while disabled.

Indemnity benefit contract (10): A contract that covers some or all of the actual expenses of providing covered services, but not more than the actual charges for a specific service.

Independent medical examiner (IME) (14): Physicians who make examinations of individuals, independent of the attending physician, and render an unbiased opinion regarding the degree of disability of a worker. IMEs are appointed by the referee or appeals board at state expense.

Independent (or *Individual*) Practice Association (IPA) (3, 9): A type of HMO in which a program administrator contracts with a number of physicians who agree to provide treatment to subscribers in their own offices for a fixed capitation payment per month. Also referred to as a *medical capitation plan.*

Individual responsibility program (IRP) (9): A program in some states in which physicians accept all patients but refuse to accept reimbursement from any third party, private or governmental. They bill the patient directly, and the patient then applies to the carrier or program for reimbursement.

Injury (14): In a workers' compensation policy, this term signifies any injury or disease sustained, arising out of, and in the course of employment, including injury to artificial members and medical braces of all types.

Inpatient (16): Term used when a patient is admitted to the hospital for overnight stay.

Inpatient Nonavailability Statement (INAS) (13): Certification from the uniformed service hospital that cannot provide medical inpatient care.

Input (7): That which goes into a computer memory bank.

Inquiry (8): See *Tracer.*

Insurance billing specialist (1, 17): A practitioner who carries out claims completion, coding, and billing responsibilities and may or may not perform managerial and supervisory functions; also known as an insurance claims processor or reimbursement specialist.

Insured (3): Individual or organization protected in case of loss under the terms of an insurance policy.

Intelligent character recognition (6): Same as *Optical character recognitions.*

Interactive transactions (7): Back and forth communication between user and computer.

Interface (7): The point at which two different systems are linked, e.g., computer to printer or modem.

Intermediate care facility (12): An institution furnishing health-related care and services to individuals who do not require the degree of care provided by hospitals or nursing facilities.

Internal control number (12): Unique many-digit identifying number which a carrier assigns to each Part B Medicare claim. Reference this number when communicating with the carrier about a specific claim.

***International Classification of Diseases, Ninth Revision, Clinical Modification* (ICD-9-CM) (5, 16):** A system for classifying diseases and operations to facilitate collection of uniform and comparable health information. This code book has been revised to ICD-10.

Interview (17): Meeting an individual face to face for evaluating and questioning a job applicant.

Invalid claim (6): Any Medicare claim that contains complete, necessary information but is illogical or incorrect (e.g., listing an incorrect provider number for a referring physician). Invalid claims are identified to the provider and may be resubmitted.

Invasion of privacy (2): Unwarranted exploitation of another's person or personal affairs with which one has no legitimate concern particularly, intrusion into another's affairs in such a way as to cause mental anguish or humiliation. *Example:* There should be no publication of a patient's medical case record and no showing of a photograph or motion picture from which the identity of the patient is determinable without the knowledge and authorization of the patient.

Italicized code (5): Diagnostic code in ICD-9-CM, Volume 1 Tabular list, that may never be sequenced as the principal diagnosis.

Itemized bill (10): A detailed list of all charges for services provided by a facility.

K (7): An expression for standard quantity measurement of disk or computer storage capacity.

Keypad (7): A device, separate or part of the keyboard, that contains keys to control mathematical functions.

Late effect (5): Inactive residual effect or condition produced after the acute phase of an illness or injury has ended.

Libel (2): Written or graphic statement to a third person that damages a person's reputation or subjects the person to ridicule.

Lien (14): A claim on the property of another as security for a debt. In litigation cases, it is a legal promise to satisfy a debt owed by the patient to the physician out of any proceeds received on the case.

Limited duty (14): Any work assignment given to temporarily disabled employees that is limited in scope of duties (e.g., no heavy lifting) and time (e.g., several weeks).

Limiting charge (12): A percentage limit on fees, specified by legislation, that nonparticipating physicians may bill Medicare beneficiaries above the fee schedule amount.

Litigation (2): A lawsuit.

Long-term disability insurance (15): A provision to pay benefits to a covered disabled person as long as he or she remains disabled, up to a specifed period exceeding 2 years.

Looping (16): The automated grouper (computer software program that assigns DRGs) process of searching all listed diagnoses for the presence of any comorbid condition or complication, or searching all procedures for OR procedures or other specific procedures.

Lost claim (8): Insurance claim that cannot be located after sending it to an insurer.

Low-volume DRGs (16): Diagnosis related groups with five or fewer patients in a hospital's base year.

Major diagnostic categories (MDCs) (16): Broad classifications of diagnoses. There are 83 coding system-oriented MDCs in the original DRGs, and 23 body system-oriented MDCs in the revised set of DRGs.

Managed care (9): Arrangements made by payers to promote cost-effective health care through establishing selective relationships with health care providers, developing coordinated delivery systems, and conducting medical management activities.

Managed care organization (MCO) (9): A generic term that refers to a managed care plan, e.g., HMO, PPO, and EPO. It is a group health plan that provides cost-effective health services to enrollees through contracts with selected providers.

Managed care system (MCS) (9): A self-administered, self-insured program that is an agreement between the employer and the employee. The employee may choose the provider. Once a procedure or service has been approved, the physician is free to charge his or her regular fee.

Manifestation (5): Signs and symptoms of an illness.

Maternal and Child Health Programs (MCHP) (3, 11): A state service organization to assist children under 21 years of age who have conditions leading to health problems.

Medicaid (MCD) (3, 11): A federally aided, state-operated and administered program that provides medical benefits for certain low-income persons in need of health and medical care. California's Medicaid program is known as *Medi-Cal.*

Medi-Cal (11): California's version of the nationwide program known as Medicaid. See *Medicaid.*

Medical necessity (12): Specific diagnostic or therapeutic requirements, for a specific service, provided to a specific Medicare beneficiary upon a specific occasion. Medical necessity MUST be established (via diagnostic and/or other information presented on the individual claim under consideration) before the carrier may make payment.

Medical record (2): Written or graphic information documenting facts and events during the rendering of patient care.

Medical record number (10): A facility's internal patient identification number issued by the medical records department of the hospital.

Medical service order (14): An authorization given to the physician, either written or verbal, to treat the injured employee.

Medically (or psychologically) necessary (13): Medical or psychologic services considered appropriate care and generally accepted by qualified professionals to be reasonable and adequate for the diagnosis and treatment of illness, injury, pregnancy, and mental disorders, or that are reasonable and adequate for well-baby care.

Medically needy (11): Persons in need of financial assistance and/or whose income and resources will not allow them to pay for the costs of medical care. Also called *medically indigent* in some states.

Medicare (3, 12): A nationwide health insurance program for persons age 65 years and over and certain disabled or blind persons regardless of income, administered by HCFA. Local Social Security offices take applications and supply information about the program.

Medicare/Medicaid case (12): Refers to an individual who receives medical and/or disability benefits from both Medicare and Medicaid programs. Sometimes referred to as a Medi-Medi case.

Medigap (MG) (12): A specialized insurance policy devised for the Medicare beneficiary that covers the deductible and copayment amounts typically not covered under the main Medicare policy written by a nongovernmental third-payer. Also known as *Medifill.*

Medigap policy (6): A health insurance policy offered by a private insurance company to persons on Medicare. It is designed to supplement Medicare benefits (fill in the gaps.) It may pay deductible, coinsurance amounts, and so forth. It does not include limited benefit coverage, such as "specified disease" or "hospital indemnity" coverage. It excludes a policy or plan offered by an employer or labor organization.

Member (3, 10): All persons covered under the Blue Cross/Blue Shield subscriber's contract, including (1) the subscriber or contract holder who is the person named on the membership identification card; and, (2) in the case of (a) two-person coverage, (b) one adult-one child coverage, or (c) family coverage, eligible family dependents enrolled under the subscriber's contract.

Memory (7): Storage in computer.

Military treatment facility (MTF) (13): All uniformed service hospitals. Also known as *military hospitals* or *uniformed service hospitals.*

Modem (7): MOdulator DEModulator unit, a device that converts data into signals for telephone transmission and then (at the receiving end) back again into data.

Modifier (4): In CPT coding, a two-digit add-on or five-digit number, representing the modifier, placed after the usual procedure code number. The two-digit modifier may be separated by a hyphen. In HCPCS Level 2 coding, one-digit or two-digit add-on alpha characters, placed after the usual Level 2 code number.

Example:

27372-51 (typed on one line)
OR
27372
09951 (typed on two lines)

National account (10): A company whose employees live in many parts of the country. The Blue Plans can provide these employees with uniform coverage despite their geographic dispersion.

National Association of Claims Assistance Professionals, Inc. (NACAP) (1): A national professional society for those that submit manual and/or electronic health insurance claims.

National codes (12): Alpha/numeric codes developed by HCFA. See *HCPCS.*

Negligence (2): Omission to do something a reasonable person would do under ordinary circumstances, or the doing of something that a reasonable person would not do under ordinary circumstances. (Negligence can work in two ways, involving action or omission.)

Network (7): Two or more interconnected computers.

Nonavailability Statement (13): When the uniformed services hospital cannot provide the inpatient care and the patient lives in a certain ZIP code near a military hospital, the patient must obtain this statement, signed by the commanding officer, before getting nonemergency inpatient care at a civilian hospital. INAS means inpatient nonavailability statement and ONAS means outpatient nonavailability statement.

Noncancelable clause or policy (3, 15): An insurance policy clause that means the insurance company cannot increase premium rates and must renew the policy until the insured reaches the age stated in the contract. Some disability income policies have noncancelable terms.

Nondisability (ND) claim (14): An on-the-job injury that requires medical care but does not result in loss of working time or income.

Nonoccupational policy (15): A contract that insures a person against off-the-job accident or sickness. It does not cover disability resulting from injury or sickness covered by workers' compensation. Group accident and sickness policies are frequently nonoccupational.

Nonparticipating provider (13): A provider who decides not to accept the CHAMPUS-determined allowable charge as the full fee for care. Payment goes directly to the patient in this case, and the patient must pay the bill in full.

Nonprivileged information (1): Information unrelated to the treatment of the patient. The patient's authorization is not required to disclose the data unless the record is in a specialty hospital or in a special service unit of a general hospital, such as the psychiatric unit.

Not elsewhere classifiable (NEC) (5): This term is used in the ICD-9-CM diagnostic coding system when the code lacks the information necessary to code the term in a more specific category.

Not otherwise specified (NOS) (5): Unspecified. Used in ICD-9-CM numeric code system for coding diagnoses.

Nursing facility (NF) (12): A specially qualified facility that has the staff and equipment to provide skilled nursing care and related services for patients who need medical or nursing care or rehabilitation services. Formerly known as *skilled nursing facility.*

Occupational illness (or disease) (14): One that is produced by hazards peculiar to the occupation carried on by the employee.

Occupational Safety and Health Administration (OSHA) (14): A federal agency that regulates and investigates safety and health standards of jobs.

Office of Federal Employee's Compensation (OFEC) (14): Office that oversees a program that provides workers' compensation for federal employees and others.

Office of Worker's Compensation Programs (OWCP) (14): This agency administers the Federal Employees' Compensation Act.

On-line system (7): 1. A system in which the input data enter the computer directly from the point of origin and in which output data are transmitted directly to where they are used. 2. A system that eliminates the need for human intervention between source recording and the ultimate processing by a computer.

Optical character recognition (OCR) (6): A device that can read typed characters at very high speed and convert them to digitized files that can be saved on disk. Also known as *intelligent character recognition* (ICR).

Optionally renewable (3): An insurance policy renewal provision in which the insurer has the right to refuse to renew the policy on a date and may add coverage limitations or increase premium rates.

Optometric service plan (9): A form of prepaid group vision care program.

Ordering physician (6): The physician ordering nonphysician services for a patient (e.g., diagnostic laboratory tests, pharmaceutical services, or durable medical equipment) when an insurance claim is submitted by a nonphysician supplier of services.

"Other" claims (6): Medicare claims not considered "clean" claims that require investigation or development on a prepayment basis (developed for Medicare Secondary Payer information).

Other health insurance (OHI) (13): Health care coverage for CHAMPUS beneficiaries through an employer, an association, or a private insurer. A student in the family may have a health care plan through school.

Outliers (atypical cases) (16): Patients displaying atypical characteristics relative to other patients in a DRG, i.e., short and long lengths of stay (day outlier), death, leaving against medical advice, admitted and discharged the same day, clinical outliers, and low-volume DRGs. Extraordinarily high costs are called *cost outliers.*

Out-of-area (9): Outside the geographic boundaries defined by the HMO as its service area. An HMO member may receive emergency services outside the HMO geographic limits.

Outpatient (16): Term used when an individual receives medical service from the hospital and goes home the same day.

Outpatient Nonavailability Statement (ONAS) (13): Certification from a uniformed service hospital that cannot provide medical outpatient care.

Output (7): Information transferred from internal memory storage to external storage.

Overpayment (8): More than the due amount paid by the insurer or paid by the patient.

Paper claim (6): An insurance claim submitted on paper, including those optically scanned and converted to an electronic form by the insurance carrier.

Partial disability (15): When an illness or injury prevents an insured person from performing one or more of the functions of his or her regular job.

Participating physician (9, 10): 1. A physician who provides services through an HMO. 2. A physician who has agreed to accept a Blue Shield Plan's payments for services to subscribers. Eighty per cent of practicing American physicians are participating physicians.

Participating physician program (12): A program under which individual physicians agree always to accept assignment on claims for Medicare-covered services. Medicare offers certain incentives to those who sign such agreements.

Participating provider (13): One who accepts CHAMPUS assignment. Payment in this case goes directly to the provider. The patient must still pay the cost-share, outpatient deductible, and the cost of care not covered by CHAMPUS. See *Assignment.*

Partnership program (13): A program that lets CHAM-

PUS-eligible individuals receive inpatient or outpatient treatment from civilian providers of care in a military hospital, or from uniformed services providers of care in civilian facilities.

Password (7): A combination of letters and numbers that each individual is assigned to access computer data.

Payments (8): Cash, checks, or money orders received for professional services rendered.

Peer review (8): Review of a patient's case done by a group of unbiased practicing physicians to judge the effectiveness and efficiency of professional care rendered. This is done to discover over- or misutilization of a plan's benefits.

Peer review organizations (PROs) (12): Groups of practicing physicians paid by the federal government to review hospital care of Medicare patients regarding effectiveness and efficiency.

Pending claim (6): Insurance claim held in suspense due to review or other reason. These claims may be cleared for payment or denied.

Percentage of revenue (16): Fixed percentage of the collected premium rate that is paid to the hospital to cover services.

Per diem (16): Single charge for a day in the hospital regardless of any actual charges or costs incurred.

Permanent and stationary (P & S) (14): A phrase used when a patient's condition has become stabilized and no improvement is expected. It is only after this declaration that a case can be rated for a compromise and release.

Permanent disability (PD) (14): An illness or injury that prevents a person from performing the functions of his or her regular job.

Personal insurance (3): Insurance plan issued to an individual (and/or his or her dependents). Also known as *individual contract.*

Petition (14): Commonly used to indicate an appeal; also means any request for relief other than an application.

Phantom billing (2): Billing for services not performed.

Physically clean claim (6): Insurance claims with no staples or highlighted areas. The bar code area has not been deformed.

Physician provider group (PPG) (9): A physician-owned business that has the flexibility to deal with all forms of contract medicine and still offer its own packages to business groups, unions, and the general public.

Point-of-service (POS) plan (9): An HMO consisting of a network of physicians and hospitals that provides an insurance company or an employer with discounts on its services. Sometimes referred to as *managed choice.*

Point-of-service (POS) product (10): A type of health benefit program in which enrollees receive the highest level of benefits when they obtain services from or at the direction of their designated primary care physician "gatekeepers." Enrollees may receive substantial, though reduced, benefits when they obtain care without gatekeeper approval from a provider of their own choosing.

Portfolio (17): A compilation of items that represents a job applicant's skills.

Preadmission testing (PAT) (16): Treatment, tests, and procedures done 48 to 72 hours prior to admission of a patient into the hospital. This is done to eliminate extra hospital days.

Preauthorization (3): Requirement in some health insurance plans to obtain permission for a service or procedure before it is done and to see whether the insurance program agrees it is medically necessary.

Precertification (3): To find out whether treatment (surgery, tests, hospitalization) is covered under a patient's health insurance policy.

Predetermination (3): To determine before treatment the maximum dollar amount the insurance company will pay for surgery, consultations, postoperative care, and so forth.

Pre-existing condition (3): An illness that began before the insurance policy was written.

Preferred provider organization (PPO) (3, 9): A type of health benefit program in which enrollees receive the highest level of benefits when they obtain services from a physician, hospital, or other health provider designated by their program as a "preferred provider." Enrollees may receive substantial, though reduced, benefits when they obtain care from a provider of their own choosing who is not designated as a "preferred provider" by their program.

Premium (12): A monthly fee that enrollees pay for Medicare Part B medical insurance. This fee is updated annually to reflect changes in program costs.

Prepaid group practice plan (9): A plan under which specified health services are rendered by participating physicians to an enrolled group of persons, with fixed periodic payments made in advance, by or on behalf of each person or family. If a health insurance carrier is involved, it contracts to pay in advance for the full range of health services to which the insured is entitled under the terms of the health insurance contract. Such a plan is one form of a *Health Maintenance Organization.*

Prepaid health plan (PHP) (9): A contract between an insurer and a subscriber or group of subscribers for a fixed periodic prepayment that provides certain health benefits rendered by participating physicians.

Prevailing charges (4): Those fees that are most frequently charged in an area by a specialty group of physicians. The top of this range establishes an overall limitation on the charges that a carrier, which considers prevailing charges in reimbursement, will accept as reasonable for a given service without special justification.

Primary care physician (PCP) (9): A physician (i.e., family practitioner, general practitioner, pediatrician, obstetrician/gynecologist, or general internist), who oversees the care of patients in a managed health care plan (HMO or PPO) and refers patients to see specialists (e.g., cardiologist, oncologists, surgeons) for services as needed. Also known as a *gatekeeper.*

Primary diagnoses (5): Initial identification of the condition or chief complaint for which the patient is treated for outpatient medical care.

Primary payer (12): Insurer or health care plan first responsible for making a coverage determination on claims for services provided to a Medicare beneficiary; with regard to coordination of benefits, the person or insurance carrier with first-ranking responsibility for payment of a patient's bill.

Principal diagnosis (5, 16): A condition established after study that is chiefly responsible for the admission of the patient to the hospital.

Principal procedure (16): A procedure performed for definitive treatment rather than for diagnostic or exploratory purposes or to take care of a complication. The principal procedure is that procedure most related to the principal diagnosis.

Prior approval (11): The evaluation of a provider request for a specific service to determine the medical necessity and appropriateness of the care requested for a patient. Also called *prior authorization* in some states.

Privileged communication (1): A confidential communication that may be disclosed only with the patient's permission. Without such permission, a doctor and staff are prohibited from divulging the information contained in such a communication.

Privileged information (1): Data related to the treatment and progress of the patient that can be released only when written authorization of the patient or guardian is obtained.

Procedure codes (4): The codes that describe each service the physician renders to a patient.

Procedure review (16): Review of diagnostic and therapeutic procedures to determine appropriateness.

Professional Association of Health Care Office Managers (PAHCOM) (1): A nationwide organization dedicated to providing a strong professional network for health care office managers.

Professional review organizations (PROs) (16): Groups of licensed physicians and osteopaths engaged in the practice of medicine or surgery in a particular area, formed to assure adequate review of the services provided by the various medical specialties and subspecialties in the area, as well as providing DRG validation; a group of physicians working with the government to review cases for hospital admission and discharge under government guidelines. Also known as *peer review.*

Program (7): See *Software.*

Prompt (7): A list of items displayed on a CRT from which the typist can choose the function to be performed. Also known as *menu.*

Prospective payment system (PPS) (12): A method of payment for Medicare hospital insurance based on DRGs (a fixed dollar amount for a principal diagnosis).

Provider (13): A person, organization, or institution enrolled and certified to provide health care services authorized under Medicaid, Medicare, or managed care programs. For CHAMPUS, the doctor, hospital, or other person or place that provides medical services and/or supplies.

Quality assurance (9): A formal set of PRO activities designed to assure the quality of services provided.

***Qui tam* action (2):** An action to recover a penalty, brought by an informer in a situation in which one portion of the recovery goes to the informer and the other portion to the state or government.

RAM (7): Random access memory, which allows data to be stored randomly and retrieved directly by specifying the address location.

Readmission review (16): Review of patients readmitted to a hospital within 7 days with problems related to the first admission, to determine whether the first discharge was premature and/or the second admission is medically necessary.

Reasonable fee (12): A charge is considered reasonable if it is deemed acceptable after peer review even though it does not meet the *customary* or *prevailing* criteria. This would include unusual circumstances or complications requiring additional time, skill, or experience in connection with a particular service or procedure.

Rebill (8): Sending another request for payment for an overdue bill to either the insurance company or patients.

Recertification (1): Renewal of certification after a specified time.

Recipient (11): A person certified by the local welfare department to receive the benefits of Medicaid under one of the specific aid categories; an individual certified to receive Medicare benefits.

Reconsideration (15): First level of appeal process for an individual applying for SSDI or SSI. It is a complete review of the claim by a medical or psychologic consultant/disability examiner team who did not take part in the original disability determination.

Referring physician (6): A physician requesting service for a patient when the insurance claim is submitted by the physician performing the service.

Regional health alliance (9): In a managed cooperation system, an agency that arranges insurance for businesses and individuals by negotiating with networks of physicians and hospitals.

Regional office (RO) (15): Social Security state office.

Registered Medical Assistant (RMA)(1): A title earned by completing appropriate training and by passing a registry examination administered by the American Medical Technologists (AMT).

Reimbursement specialist (1): See *Insurance billing specialist.*

Rejected claim (6, 8): Insurance claim submitted to insurance carrier that is discarded by the system due to a technical error (omission or erroneous information) or because it does not follow Medicare instructions. It is returned to the provider for correction or change so it may be processed properly for payment.

Relative value study (RVS) (4): Code book or list of procedure codes for professional services and procedures with unit values that indicate the relative value of one procedure over another.

Relative value unit (RVU) (12): Individual building block of RBRVS (resource based relative value scale). For each service, there are three RVUs: for work, practice expenses, and the cost of professional liability insurance.

Remittance advice (RA) (11, 12): An explanation of services periodically issued to recipients or providers on whose behalf claims have been paid by the Medicare or Medicaid program. Also known in some programs as an *Explanation of Benefits.*

Resource based relative value scale (RBRVS) (12): A system that ranks physician services by units; a Medicare fee schedule.

Respite care (12): Short-term hospice inpatient stay that may be necessary to give temporary relief to the person who regularly assists with home care of a patient.

***Respondeat superior* (2):** "Let the master answer." A physician is liable in certain cases for the wrongful acts of his or her assistant or employees.

Resume (17): Summary of education, skills, and work experience, usually in outline form.

Retrieve (7): The act of finding stored or filed information.

Review (8): To look over a claim to assess how much payment should be made.

ROM (7): Read-Only Memory. Data stored in ROM can be read but not changed. It usually contains a permanent program.

Secondary payer (SP) (12): The person or insurance carrier that pays benefits after the primary payer has discharged its obligation. Medicare is the secondary payer when a Medicare beneficiary has other insurance coverage through an employer group health plan or will obtain reimbursement owing to third-party liability.

Second-injury fund (14): See *Subsequent injury fund.*

Self-employment (17): To work for oneself, with direct control over work, services, and fees.

Service area (9): The geographic area defined by an HMO as the locale in which it will provide health care services to its members directly through its own resources or through arrangements with other providers in the area.

Service benefit contract (10): A contract that provides the covered services themselves rather than reimbursement for some or all of the expenses the subscriber incurs in obtaining covered services.

Share of cost (11): The amount the patient must pay each month before he or she can be eligible for Medicaid. Also known as *liability* or *spend down.*

Short-stay hospital (12): A hospital in which the average length of stay is less than 30 days. General and special hospitals are included in this category.

Short-term disability income insurance (15): A provision to pay benefits to a covered disabled person as long as he or she remains disabled, up to a specified period not exceeding 2 years.

Slanted brackets (5): Symbol used with a diagnostic code in ICD-9-CM, Volume 2, Alphabetic Index, indicating the code may never be sequenced as the principal diagnosis.

SOAP (4): An abbreviation for *S*ubjective complaints, *O*bjective findings, *A*ssessment of status, and diagnostic or therapeutic *P*lan; a method of structuring progress notes.

Social Security Administration (SSA) (15): Administers SSDI and SSI programs for disabled persons.

Social Security Disability Insurance (SSDI) (15): Entitlement program for disabled workers or self-employed individuals.

Soft copy (7): That which is displayed on a CRT screen.

Software (7): Instructions (programs) required to make hardware perform a specific task.

Special report (4): Documentation that must be submitted for specific CPT procedure codes and/or modifiers in determining medical appropriateness of service. Also see *By report.*

Sponsor (13): For the CHAMPUS program, the service person, either active duty, retired, or deceased, whose relationship makes the patient eligible for CHAMPUS.

Staff model (9): A type of HMO similar to the group model.

State Disability Insurance (SDI) (3, 15): See *Unemployment Compensation Disability.*

Statute of limitations (2): A time limit established for filing lawsuits.

Stop-loss (9, 16, 17): An agreement between a managed care company and a reinsurer in which absorption of prepaid patient expenses is limited; or limiting losses on an individual expensive hospital claim or professional services claim; form of reinsurance by which the managed care program limits the losses of an individual expensive hospital claim.

Subpoena (2): "Under penalty." A writ that commands a witness to appear at a trial or other proceeding and give testimony.

***Subpoena duces tecum* (2):** "In his possession." A subpoena that requires the appearance of a witness with his or her records. Sometimes the judge permits the mailing of records, and the physician is not required to appear in court.

Sub rosa films (14): Films made without the knowledge of the patient.

Subscriber (3, 10): The contract holder covered by a Blue Cross or Blue Shield Plan or affiliate, who either has coverage through his or her place of employment or who has purchased coverage directly from the Plan or affiliate.

Subsequent injury fund (SIF) (14): A special fund that assumes all or part of the liability for benefits provided to a worker because of the combined effect of a work-related impairment and a pre-existing condition.

Summary payment voucher (13): The document the fiscal agent sends to the provider and/or beneficiary, showing the service or supplies received, allowable charges, amount billed, the amount CHAMPUS paid, how much deductible has been paid, and the patient's cost share.

Supplemental benefits (15): Disability insurance provisions that allow benefits to the insured to increase the monthly indemnity or to receive a percentage of the policy premiums if an individual keeps a policy in force for 5 or 10 years or does not file any claims.

Supplemental insurer (12): An insurer whose policy is designed to supplement Medicare reimbursement and who, as such, is a secondary payer.

Supplemental Security Income (SSI) (11, 12): A program of income support for low-income aged, blind, and disabled persons established by Title XVI of the Social Security Act.

Supplemental medical insurance (SMI) (12): Also known as Medicare Part B. A voluntary insurance program for aged and disabled individuals who elect to enroll that provides insurance benefits for physician and other medical services in accordance with the provisions of Title XVIII of the Social Security Act.

Temporary disability (TD) (14): The recovery period following a work-related injury during which the employee is unable to work and the condition has not stabilized; a schedule of benefits payable for the temporary disability.

Temporary disability insurance (TDI) (15): See *Unemployment Compensation Disability.*

Terminal (7): An input/output device that can transmit entries to and obtain output from a computer system.

Tertiary care (9): Services provided by specialists—e.g., neurosurgeons, thoracic surgeons, and intensive care units.

Third party liability (14): Third party liability exists if an entity is liable to pay the medical cost for injury, disease, or disability of a person hurt during the performance of his or her occupation and the injury is caused by an entity not connected with the employer.

Third party payer (10): Insurance carrier who is not the physician or patient and who intervenes to pay hospital or medical bills as per prior contract with one of the first two parties; under Medicaid, third party liability exists if there is any entity (including other government programs or insurance) which is or may be liable to pay all or part of the medical cost of injury, disease, or disability of an applicant or recipient of Medicaid.

Third party subrogation (14): The legal process by which an insurance company seeks from a third party, who has caused a loss, recovery of the amount paid to the policyholder.

Time-sharing (7): Use of a computer device for two or more purposes, or by two or more users, at the same time.

Total disability (15): A term that varies in meaning from one disability insurance policy to another. An example of a liberal definition might read, "The insured must be unable to perform the major duties of his or her specific occupation."

Tracer (8): An inquiry made to an insurance company to locate the status of an insurance claim (i.e., claim in review, claim never received, and so forth).

Transfer (16): Moving a patient (1) from one inpatient area in a hospital to another in the same hospital; (2) from one hospital paid under prospective payment to another such hospital; or (3) from a hospital under prospective payment to a hospital in an approved statewide cost control program.

Transfer review (16): Review of transfers to different areas of the same hospital that are exempted from prospective payment.

Turfing (9): Transferring the sickest, high-cost patients to other physicians so the provider appears as a low-utilizer, in a managed care setting.

Unbundling (4): The practice of using numerous CPT codes to identify procedures normally covered by a single code; also known as itemizing, fragmented billing, exploding, or à la carte medicine; billing under Medicare Part B for nonphysician services to hospital inpatients furnished to the hospital by an outside supplier or another provider. Under the new law, unbundling is prohibited, and all nonphysician services provided in an inpatient setting will be paid as hospital services.

Unemployment Compensation Disability (UCD) (3, 15): Insurance that covers off-the-job injury or sickness and is paid for by deductions from a person's paycheck. This program is administered by a state agency and is sometimes also known as *State Disability Insurance.*

Uniform Bill (UB-92) claim form (16): Uniform Bill insurance claim form developed by the National Uniform Billing Committee for hospital inpatient billing and payment transactions.

Uniformed service hospitals (13): This includes all military hospitals and former Public Health Service hospitals that are now called "uniformed service treatment facilities" (in Baltimore, MD; Boston, MA; Seattle, WA; Portland, ME; Cleveland, OH; Houston, Galveston, Port Arthur, and Nassau Bay, TX; and Staten Island, NY).

Upcoding (4): Deliberate manipulation of CPT codes for increased payment.

Usual, customary, and reasonable (UCR) (4): A method used by insurance companies to establish their fee schedules. UCR uses the conversion factor method of establishing maximums; the method of reimbursement used under Medicaid by which state Medicaid programs set reimbursement rates using the Medicare method or a fee schedule, whichever is lower.

Utilization (9): Use of services.

Utilization review (UR) (9, 16): A process, based on established criteria, of reviewing and controlling the medical necessity for services and providers' use of medical care resources. Reviews are carried out by allied health personnel at predetermined times during the hospital stay to assess the need for the full facilities of an acute care hospital. In managed care systems, such as an HMO, reviews are done to establish medical necessity, thus curbing costs. Also called *utilization* or *management control.*

V codes (5): A classificaton of ICD-9-CM coding to identify health care encounters for reasons other than illness or injury and to identify patients whose injury or illness is influenced by special circumstances or problems.

Veterans Administration Disability program (15): Program for honorably discharged veterans who file claim for a service-connected disability.

Veterans Administration (VA) Outpatient Clinics (3, 15): A clinic where medical and dental services are rendered to veterans who have service-related disabilities.

Video display terminal (VDT) (7): A television-like screen attached to a computer or word processing terminal; also known as a cathode ray tube (CRT).

Virus (7): A destructive program that attaches and copies itself to other programs in a computer system. Some viruses destroy programs and data after a precise lapse of time.

Volume performance standard (VPS) (12): Desired growth rate for spending on Medicare Part B physician services, set each year by Congress.

Voluntary disability insurance (15): A majority of employees of an employer voluntarily consent to be covered by an insured or self-insured disability insurance plan instead of a state plan.

Waiting period (14): For disability insurance, the initial period of time when a disabled individual is not eligible to receive benefits even though unable to work; for workers' compensation, the days that must elapse before workers' compensation weekly income benefits become payable.

Waiver of premium (15): A disability insurance policy provision that an employee does not have to pay any premiums while disabled. Also known as *elimination period.*

Withhold (9): A portion of the monthly capitation payment to physicians retained by the HMO until the end of the year to create an incentive for efficient care. If the physician exceeds utilization norms, he or she will not receive it.

Work hardening (14): Individualized program of therapy using simulated or real job duties to build up strength and improve the worker's endurance to be able to work up to eight hours per day. Sometimes work site modifications are instituted to get the employee back to gainful employment.

Workers' Compensation Appeals Board (WCAB) (14): Board that handles workers' compensation liens and appeals.

Workers' Compensation (WC) Insurance (3, 14): A contract that insures a person against on-the-job injury or illness. The employer pays the premium for his or her employees.

Index

Note: Page numbers in *italics* refer to illustrations; page numbers followed by t refer to tables.

A

AAMA (American Association of Medical Assistants), 16
  code of ethics of, 11, *14*
AAMB (American Association of Medical Billers), 15
AAMT (American Association for Medical Transcription), 16
AAPC (American Academy of Procedural Coders), 16
Abbreviations, 502
  laboratory, 102t-103t, 104
Abdomen, terminology for regions of, 137
Abortion, coding of, 120
Abstraction, from medical record(s), 129, *130*, *131*
Abuse, in insurance claims, 30-34
  in Medicare, 290
  in workers' compensation, 342-344, *343*
Accident(s), 45
  report of, 333t-334t
  workers' compensation and, 330
Accidental death and dismemberment benefit, 371-372
Accounting, for managed care, 219
  records for, 27, 27t
Accounts receivable (A/R) transactions, in Medi-Cal, 513-514
ACGs (ambulatory care groups), 414
ACMPE (American College of Medical Practice Executives), 16-17
Acquired immunodeficiency syndrome (AIDS) testing, 372
  legal issues and, 129
Actual charge(s), 68
Add-on code(s), 90
Addresses, for submitting claims, 445-486
  of resources, 498-500
Adjudication, in workers' compensation, 341
Adjuster, 45
Adjustments, in Medi-Cal, 513
Administrative code(s), 90
Administrative law judge hearing, for Medicare, 195
  for SSI, 374
Admission, diagnosis-related groups and, 411-412
Admission review, 414
Admitting diagnosis, coding of, 120
Adverse effects, coding of, 114-115
Advertising, for insurance billing specialist, 441
AEP (appropriateness evaluation protocol), 415
AFDC. See *Aid to Families with Dependent Children (AFDC).*
Agent, fiscal, in Medi-Cal, 504
  in Medicare, 260
AGPAM (American Guild of Patient Account Management), 16
Agreements, for insurance billing specialist, 441
AHIMA. See *American Health Information Management Association (AHIMA).*
Aid to Families with Dependent Children (AFDC), health care reform and, 205-206
  Medicaid and, 249
AIDS (acquired immunodeficiency syndrome) testing, 372
  legal issues and, 129
Aliens, employment of, 438
  Medicaid and, 253
  Medicare and, 265
All-inclusive code(s), 94
Alphabet index, hospital billing and, 398
AMA (American Medical Association), code of ethics of, 8
  Committee on Medicolegal Problems, 36-39, *37*, *38*
  insurance claim form and, 125
  prevention commandments of, 36-39, *37*, *38*
Ambulatory care groups (ACGs), 414
Ambulatory patient groups (APGs), 392
  diagnosis-related groups and, 414
Ambulatory surgery. See *Outpatient treatment.*
American Academy of Procedural Coders (AAPC), 16
American Association for Medical Transcription (AAMT), 16
American Association of Medical Assistants (AAMA), 16
  code of ethics of, 11, *14*
American Association of Medical Billers (AAMB), 15
American College of Medical Practice Executives (ACMPE), 16-17
American Guild of Patient Account Management (AGPAM), 16
American Health Information Management Association (AHIMA), 4, *6*, *7*, 16
  code of ethics of, 11, *13*
  fax communication and, 23
  release of information and, 25, *26*
American Medical Association (AMA), code of ethics of, 8
  Committee on Medicolegal Problems, 36-39, *37*, *38*
  insurance claim form and, 125
  prevention commandments of, 36-39, *37*, *38*
American National Standards Institute (ANSI), 164
  electronic data and, 172
Ancillary services, 206
Anesthesia, modifier codes for, 96t, 97t
ANSI (American National Standards Institute), 164
  electronic data and, 172
APGs (ambulatory patient groups), 392
  diagnosis-related groups and, 414
Appeal process, 188-200, *189*
  for Blue Cross/Blue Shield, 189-190

Appeal process *(Continued)*
for CHAMPUS, 190, *191*
for Medicaid, 253
for Medi-Cal, 517, *518*, 519
for Medicare, 190-199, 192t, 290. See also *Medicare.*
for Medigap, 200
for Supplemental Security Income, 374
legal issues affecting, 35
Applicant, 44
Application, in job search, 430, *431-432*
insurance, *130*, 131
Appropriateness evaluation protocol (AEP), 415
Approval, in Medicaid, 251, *252*
in Medi-Cal, 513
prior, 505, 507-508
A/R (accounts receivable) transactions, in Medi-Cal, 513-514
Arbitration, 39
Armed Services disability benefits, 374
Assignment of benefits, 29, 45
in Form HCFA-1500, 59
Medicare and, 261, *264*
Assistant surgeon, modifier codes for, 99t-100t
Asterisk procedure, RVS coding and, 95
Audit, claims, 33-34
internal, 79-81, *79-81*
Audit trail, 35, *35*
Authorization, managed care and, 211, *212*
Medi-Cal and, 505, 507-508
prior. See *Preauthorization.*
signature, 29-30, *30*, *31*
Medicare and, 263-264
Automobile insurance coverage, Medicare and, 281-284, *282-283*

B

Back up, in electronic management, 174
Bankruptcy, managed care and, 221
Basic life services, codes for, 76
Batch, of claims, 159
Bed leasing, 391
Beneficiary representative, Medicare, 265-266
Benefit(s). See also *Coverage;* specific program.
accidental death and dismemberment, 371-372
assignment of, 29, 45
in Form HCFA-1500, 59
Medicare and, 261, *264*
Blue Cross/Blue Shield, 228
explanation of, 238, *239*
complimentary, 233
death, 336
disability, 371-372
state, 376-379, 378t
explanation of, 155-157, *156*
FEHBP, *243*, *244*, 245
HMO, 204
income continuation, 47
Medicaid, 250
Medi-Cal, 504
Medicare, 270-271
railroad retirement, 270-271
skilled nursing facility, 44
TRICARE, 321
VA, 375
workers' compensation, 330
state, 336-337
Bilateral procedure, modifier codes for, 97t
Billing, by self-employed insurance specialist, 441
double, 393
examples of, 51-52
fee-for-service, 205
in managed care, 219, *221*, *222*
for deceased patient, 284, *285-286*
for workers' compensation, 358-361, *359*
hospital, 388-416. See also *Hospital billing.*
Billing *(Continued)*
physician, 4, *6*
UB-92 form and, 509, *511*
Billing specialist, 2-17. See also *Insurance billing specialist.*
Birthday law, 45
Blanket contract, 47
Blanket-position bond, 34
Blue Cross/Blue Shield, 226-245
ambulatory surgery in, 234
benefits of, 228
explanation of, 238, *239*
central certification and processing in, 231
claims procedure in, 233-238, *236*, *240*
contracts for, 229
explanation of, 47-50
FEHBP and, 238-245. See also *Federal Employee Health Benefits Program (FEHBP).*
history of, 228
identification cards for, 231-233, *232*
inpatient treatment in, 396
managed care and, 207, 233
Medical Necessity Program of, 233
payment methods in, 229-230, 230t
physician participation in, 230-231
preadmission testing in, 234
purpose of, 228
review and appeal process for, 189-190
second opinions in, 234
special clauses of, 228
technology assessment and, 233-234
Bluecard program, 231
Bonding, 34
Buffing, 211
"Bug," in electronic data interchange, 168
Bundled code(s), 86-87
Burn(s), coding of, 120, *121*

C

C and R (compromise and release), in permanent disability claims, 341
California Chapter of International Billing Association, 17
California Relative Value Studies (CRVS), 67
Cancelable policy, 44
CAP. See *Claims assistance professional (CAP).*
Capitation, 21, 391-392
in managed care, 219-221, *223*
Career, as insurance billing specialist, 2-17. See also *Insurance billing specialist.*
Carrier agreement, in electronic data interchange, 164
Carrier-dealing prepayment organization, 281
Carrier-direct claims system, 161-162
Case, termination of, 39-40
Case management provisions, 45-47, *46*, *48*, *49*
Case rate, 391
Cash advance, 392
Categorically needy group, 249
CC (chief complaint), 77
CCAP (Certified Claims Assistance Professional), 15
CCS (Certified Coding Specialist), 15
CE (consultative examiner), 373
CECP (Certified Electronic Claims Professional), 15
Central processing unit (CPU), 160
Certification, in Blue Cross/Blue Shield, 231, 234
of insurance billing specialist, 15-17
Certified Claims Assistance Professional (CCAP), 15
Certified Coding Specialist (CCS), 15
Certified Electronic Claims Professional (CECP), 15
Certified Medical Assistant (CMA), 16
Certified Medical Billing Associate (CMBA), 17
Certified Medical Office Manager (CMOM), 16
Certified Medical Transcriptionist (CMT), 16
Certified Procedural Coder (CPC), 15
Challenged policy, 21

CHAMPUS, 296-327
  background of, 297-298
  benefits and coverage in, 300, *301-305*
  claims procedure in, 306-315
    dual coverage and, 313
    form for, *308*, 309-313
    Medicaid and, 313
    Medicare and, 313-315
    Medigap and, 313
    nonparticipating providers and, 309
    offices and, 306
    other insurance and, 313
    participating providers and, 306-309
    submission and, 313
    summary payment voucher for, 313, *314*
    third party liability and, 315, *316-320*
    workers' compensation and, 315
  Defense Enrollment Eligibility Reporting System for, 299
  eligibility for, 298-299
  explanation of, 50
  HMO and, 208-209
  hospital billing and, 397
  identification card for, *299*, 299-300, *300*
  managed care and, 207-208, 315-322, *322*
  Medicaid and, 253
  Medi-Cal and, 519
  nonavailability statement and, 305-306, *307*
  participating providers in, 299
  Privacy Act and, 305
  review and appeal process for, 190, *191*
  TRICARE standard, 327
CHAMPVA, background of, 298
  claims procedure in, 309, *310-311*
    form for, 309-313
    Medicare and, 315
  eligibility for, 300-305, *305*
  explanation of, 50
  hospital billing and, 397
  Medicaid and, 253
  nonavailability statement and, 305-306, *307*
  Privacy Act and, 305
Charge(s), 494. See also *Fee schedule; Payment(s).*
  actual, 68
  phantom, 393-394
  prevailing, 68
  reasonable, 68
    in Medicare, 262
Chief complaint (CC), 77
Chronologic resume, 433
Churning, 33
CIGNA Healthplans of California, 203
Circulatory system conditions, coding of, 118
Civil Monetary Penalties Law (CMPL), 267-269, *268*
Civil Service Retirement System (CSRS), 374
Civilian Health and Medical Program of Uniformed Services. See *CHAMPUS.*
Civilian Health and Medical Program of Veterans Administration. See *CHAMPVA.*
Claim(s), 45. See also *Insurance claim(s).*
  audits and review of, 33-34
  Blue Cross/Blue Shield, 233-238, *236*, *240*
    review and appeal process of, 189-190
  CHAMPUS, 306-315. See also *CHAMPUS.*
  CHAMPVA, 306, *308*
    form for, 309-313
  crossover, 275-276, 284, 287, 531-532
  delinquent, 181-183, 183t, 492
    in Blue Cross/Blue Shield, 238
    in workers' compensation, 363, *364-366*
  denied, 184-185, 492
    in Medi-Cal, 513
  dingy, 128
  dirty, 128
  disability, 379-380
Claim(s) *(Continued)*
    federal, 380-383
    permanent, 341
    temporary, 336t, 337-341
    Veterans Administration, 383-386
  electronic, 128. See also *Electronic data interchange (EDI).*
  FEHBP, 240, *241*, *242*
  form for, 399-408, *400*
  incomplete, 129
  invalid, 129
  lost, 183
  Maternal and Child Health Program, 256-257
  Medicaid, 250-253, *252*, *254*, *255*
  Medi-Cal, 508-514. See also *Medi-Cal.*
  Medicare, 190-199, 192t. See also *Medicare.*
  Medigap, 200
  nondisability, 337, *338-340*
  out-of-state, 361
  paper, 128
  pending, 181-183, 183t
    in Medi-Cal, 513
  rejected, 128-129, 184
  submitting, addresses for, 445-486
  TRICARE Extra, 325-327. See also *TRICARE Extra.*
  workers' compensation, billing and, 358-361, *359*
    delinquency and, 363, *364-366*
Claims assistance professional (CAP), 4
  job description for, *422-423*
  job search for, 429-430
  legal issues and, 19-20
Claims inquiry form, in CHAMPUS, 190, *191*
  in Medi-Cal, 514, *516*, 517, *518*, 519-520
    appeal process and, 517, *518*, 519
    CHAMPUS and, 519
    Medicare and, *519*, 519-520
Claims transfer. See *Crossover claims.*
Claims-review foundation for medical care, 210
Clause, of disability income insurance, 371
Clean claim, 128
Clearinghouse, 160
Clearinghouse claim system, 162, *163*
Clinical outlier, 409
Closed panel program, 204
CMA (Certified Medical Assistant), 16
CMBA (Certified Medical Billing Associate), 17
CMOM (Certified Medical Office Manager), 16
CMP (competitive medical plan), 50
CMPL (Civil Monetary Penalties Law), 267-269, *268*
CMT (Certified Medical Transcriptionist), 16
COBRA (Consolidated Omnibus Budget Reconciliation Act), 272-273, *273*, *274*
  group contracts and, 47
Code(s), add-on, 90
  administrative, 90
  all-inclusive, 94
  bundled, 86-87
  E, 114-115
  effective use of, 84-86, *85-87*
  monitoring of, 89, *89*
  symbols of, 82-83
  unbundling of, 88-89
  V, 115-116
Code cards, 491
Code hotlines, 491
Code journals, 491
Code modifier(s), in CPT, 83-84
  list of, 96-101t, 100-104
Code newsletters, 491
Code research and review services, 491
Code software, 491-492
Coder, certification of, 15-16
  job description for, *426-427*
  office for, 438
Coding, diagnostic, 106-122, 489-491. See also *Diagnostic coding.*
  down, 87-88

Coding *(Continued)*
in insurance claim problems, 185-186
electronic data interchange, 166-167, 167t
ethical, 9, *11-12*
laboratory, 104
Medicare, 104
tips in, 288-293, 289t
procedural, 64-104. See also *Procedural coding.*
responsibility for, 9, *12*
up, 88
Coinsurance, 60
Collection laws, 35
Combination code, 113
Combination resume, 433
Commissioner, insurance, 40
state, 178-180, *179*
Communication, fax, confidentiality and, 23, *24*
for electronic data interchange, 168-170, *170-172*
privileged, 11-14
Comorbidity, 410
Compensation, workers', 328-367. See also *Workers' compensation.*
Competitive medical plan (CMP), 50
Complaint form, 178, *179*
Complimentary benefit(s), 233
Comprehensive foundation for medical care, 210
Compromise and release (C and R), 341
Computer(s), confidentiality and, 172-174, *173*
electronic transmission of, 167-168, *168*
in electronic data interchange, 160-161, *161*, *162*
in eligibility verification, 166
in Medi-Cal claims, 512-513
Computer claims system, 161-163, *163*. See also *Electronic claims submission (ECS).*
Computer Matching and Privacy Protection Act, 305
Concurrent care, 69
coding of, 91
Conditionally renewable policy, 44
Confidentiality, 21-27
agreement for, 11, *14*
computer, 172-174, *173*
hospital billing and, 392-393
insurance billing specialist and, 11-15, *14*
medical records and, 21-25, *24*
disclosure of, 21-22, *22*
in workers' compensation, 349
release of information and, 25-27, *26*
retention and, 27, 27t
Confidentiality of Medical Information Act, 26
Consent for release of information, 25, *26*
Consolidated Omnibus Budget Reconciliation Act (COBRA), 272-273, *273*, *274*
group contracts and, 47
Consultation, 69
coding of, 89
criteria for, 74-75t
Consultative examiner (CE), 373
Contract(s). See also *Policy(ies).*
Blue Cross/Blue Shield, 229
for insurance billing specialist, 441
holder of, 44
insurance, 20-21
major medical, 44
managed care, 211
legal issues affecting, 21
patient/physician, 21
physician, 21
service benefit, 275
Contributory factors, 71
Conversion privilege, 47
Copayment(s), in Blue Cross/Blue Shield, 230
in managed care, 213
in Medicaid, 251
in Medi-Cal, 505, *507*
Copayments *(Continued)*
in Medicare, 281
in TRICARE, 322, *323-326*
Cost outlier, 409
Cost outlier review, 415
Counseling, 69
Cover letter, 430-433, *433*
Coverage. See also *Benefit(s).*
Medicaid, 289
Medicare, 270-274, *273*
data bank for, 289
of workers' compensation, 331-332
under OSHA Act of 1970, 344-345
CPC (Certified Procedural Coder), 15
CPT. See *Current procedural terminology (CPT).*
CPU (central processing unit), 160
Credit laws, 35
Crib sheet(s), in electronic data interchange, 166
in procedural coding, 81, *81*
Critical care, 69
coding of, 93
Crossover claims, 275-276, 284, 287, 531-532
CRVS (California Relative Value Studies), 67
CSRS (Civil Service Retirement System), 374
Current procedural terminology (CPT), 66-67, 82-94
codes in, administrative or add-on, 90
all-inclusive, 94
bundled, 86-87
down, 87-88
effective use of, 84-86, *85-87*
evaluation and management, 69-77
modifiers of, 83-84, 96-101t, 100-104
monitoring of, 89, *89*
symbols of, 82-83
unbundling of, 88-89
up, 88
for concurrent care, 91
for consultations, 89
for critical care, 93
for drugs and injections, 89-90
for emergency care, 93-94
for follow-up days, 91-92
for hospital billing, 399
for laceration repair, 94
for Medicare global package, 93
for multiple lesions, 94
for office visits, 89
for prolonged services, 93
for surgery, 90-93
Curriculum, medical insurance specialist, example of 1-year, 5
Custodial patient, 275
Customary fee, 68

D

Data, coding of, 9, *12*
electronic, 157-174. See also *Electronic data interchange (EDI).*
keying of, 166
Day outlier, 410
Day outlier review, 415
DCGs (diagnostic cost groups), 280
DDS (Disability Determination Service), 373
DE 2501 form, *381*, *382*, 386
DE 2547 form, *384*, *385*, 386
DE 2525XX form, *383*, 386
Death benefit(s), 336
Debugging, in electronic data interchange, 168
Deceased patient, billing for, 284, *285-286*
Deductibles, 213
Defense Enrollment Eligibility Reporting System (DEERS), 299
Deficit Reduction Act (DEFRA), 272
Delinquent claim(s), 181-183, 183t, 492
in Blue Cross/Blue Shield, 238

Delinquent claims *(Continued)*
in workers' compensation, 363, *364-366*
Delivery, coding of, 120
Denied claim(s), 184-185, 492
in Medi-Cal, 513
Dental injury, report of, 349, *352*
Dependents, 44
Deposition, workers' compensation and, 345-346
Detention, coding of, 93
Diabetes mellitus, coding of, 118-119
Diagnosis related groups (DRGs), 68-69, 408-414, 492
history of, 408-409
insurance billing specialist and, 410-411
medical records and, *412*, 412-414, *413*
outpatient classifications in, 414
physician's practice and, 411-412
Prospective Payment System and, 260-261
reimbursement and, 391
system of, *409*, 409-410
utilization review in, 414
Diagnostic coding, 106-122
E codes in, 114-115
for diseases, 108-109, 110t
for hospital billing, 397-399
for outpatient treatment and physician billing, 4, *6*
for signs, symptoms, and ill-defined conditions, 116-121
hints for, 114
instructions for, 109-114
physician's fee profile and, 121-122
V codes in, 115-116
Diagnostic cost groups (DCGs), 280
Diagnostic terminology, 129-137, 132t-136t, *137*
Differential, by day, 391
by service, 391
Dingy claim, 128
Directional terminology, *353*
Dirty claim, 128
Disability, 371
codes for, 76
explanation of, 50
partial, 371
permanent, 336
claim for, 341
residual, 371-372
Social Security, 373
subjective, 353
temporary, 336, 371
claim for, 336t, 337-341
total, 371
unemployment compensation, 349
Disability benefit programs, 492
Disability Determination Service (DDS), 373
Disability income insurance, 368-386, 492
claims procedures for, 379-386
federal, 380-383
state, *381-385*, 386
Veterans Administration outpatient, 383-386
explanation of, 50
federal, 372-376, *375*, *377*
history of, 370
individual, 370-372
state, 376-379, 378t
Disease, diagnostic coding of, 108-109, 110t
Documentation, for insurance billing specialist, 441
in procedural coding, 76-81
crib sheets in, 81, *81*
for evaluation and management services, 76-77
of history, 77-79
of internal audit, 79-81, *79-81*
of medical records, 77
in workers' compensation, 349
medical, 492
Double billing, 393
Double indemnity, 371
Down coding, 87-88
in insurance claim problems, 185-186
Down time, in electronic data interchange, 168
DRG. See *Diagnosis related groups (DRGs).*
DRG creep, 410
DRG validation, 415
Drug(s), coding of, 89-90
Duplicate statement, 393

E

E code(s), 114-115
Early and Periodic Screening, Diagnosis, and Treatment (EPSDT) service, 250
ECP (electronic claims processor), 162-163
job description for, *424-425*
job search for, 430
ECS (electronic claims submission), 159. See also *Electronic data interchange (EDI).*
in Blue Cross/Blue Shield, 237-238
in Medicare, 290
in workers' compensation, 361
EDI. See *Electronic data interchange (EDI).*
Education, and training, 492-493
for insurance billing specialist, 4, *5-7*
EFT (electronic funds transfer), 171
in Medi-Cal, 514
Elderly, employed, Medicare coverage of, 271-274
Elective surgery, 395
Electronic claim, 128
Electronic claims processor (ECP), 162-163
job description for, *424-425*
job search for, 430
Electronic claims submission (ECS), 159. See also *Electronic data interchange (EDI).*
in Blue Cross/Blue Shield, 237-238
in Medicare, 290
in workers' compensation, 361
Electronic data interchange (EDI), 157-174, 493
carrier agreements in, 164
completion of, 166-170, 167t, *168-172*
computer claims systems in, 161-163, *163*
computer in, 160-161, *161*, *162*
confidentiality in, 172-174, *173*
crib sheets for, 166
eligibility verification in, 166
encounter forms in, 165-166
for workers' compensation, 164
in hospital billing, 394-395
keying data for, 166
records management in, 174
remittance advice in, 171-172
signature requirements for, 164, *165*
statements of, 172
status review of, 170-171
Electronic funds transfer (EFT), 171
in Medi-Cal, 514
Electronic remittance notice, 170
Electronic resume, 429
Electronic signature, 29
Eligibility, computer verification of, 166
for CHAMPUS, 298-299
for CHAMPVA, 300-305, *305*
for HMO, 205
for Maternal and Child Health Program, 256
for Medicaid, *249*, 249-250
for Medi-Cal, 503
verification of, 504-505, *506*
for Medicare, 260
for SSDI, 373
for SSI, 373
for state disability insurance, 376
Elimination period, 45

Emancipated minor, 21
Embezzlement, 34-35, *35*
Emergency care, 69
  Blue Plans and, 396
  coding of, 93-94
  managed care and, 397
  of veterans, 375-376, *377*
Employed elderly, Medicare coverage of, 271-274
Employee, claim statement of, *381*, *382*, 386
  confidentiality agreement and, 11, *14*
  federal, disability benefits of, 374
  state workers' compensation and, 332, 335t
Employer liability, 20
Employer report of accident, 333t-334t
Employer supplemental insurance, 147
  Medicare and, 275
Encounter form, for managed care, 215-219, *218*
  in electronic data interchange, 165-166
Encryption, 172
EOB (explanation of benefits), 155-157, *156*
  in Blue Cross/Blue Shield, 238, *239*
  in FEHBP, *243*, *244*, 245
EPO (exclusive provider organization), 50
Eponym, claim forms and, 136
  diagnostic coding and, 113
EPSDT (Early and Periodic Screening, Diagnosis, and Treatment) service, 250
Equipment, for insurance billing specialist, 439
Errors and omissions insurance, 20
Established patient, 69
Ethics, 8-15, *9*, 493-494
  confidentiality in, 11-15, *14*
  laws and, 495
  preamble of, 8-11, *10-14*
Etiology, classification by, 112
Etiquette, for insurance billing specialist, 8
Evaluation and management (E/M), 69-77
  codes for, 69-71, *70*, 72t-75t
    in basic life and/or disability services, 76
    in unlisted procedures, 71-76
  documentation in, 76-77
Examiners, state boards of medical, 40
Exclusion, 45
Exclusive provider organization (EPO), 50
Explanation of benefits (EOB), 155-157, *156*
  in Blue Cross/Blue Shield, 238, *239*
  in FEHBP, *243*, *244*, 245
Expressed contract, 21
Extended benefits contract, 44
Extraterritorial compensation laws, 332

F

Fair hearing, Medicare, 195, *198*
  SSI, 374
Fax communication, confidentiality and, 23, *24*
  for electronic data interchange, 168-170, *170-172*
Fax signature stamp, 29, *31*
Federal Coal Mine Health and Safety Act, 331
Federal disability, 372-376, *375*, *377*
  claims for, 380-383
Federal Employee Health Benefits Program (FEHBP), 238-245
  benefits of, *243*, *244*, 245
  claims in, 240, *241*, *242*
    time limit for, 240-245
  identification card for, 240, *240*
  nonbenefits of, 238-240
Federal Employees' Compensation Act, 331
Federal Employees Retirement System (FERS), 374
Federal False Claims Amendments Act, 33
Federal Trade Commission (FTC), 178
Fee for service, 205, 494
Fee for service *(Continued)*
  in managed care, 219, *221*, *222*
Fee profile, physician's, 121-122
Fee reduction, appeal of, 188, *189*
Fee schedule, 67-68
  hospital billing and, 391
  in Blue Cross/Blue Shield, 230
  in workers' compensation, 358-360
FEHBP. See *Federal Employee Health Benefits Program (FEHBP).*
FERS (Federal Employees Retirement System), 374
Final report and bill, *351*
Financial responsibility, managed care and, 219-221, *220-223*
  patient/physician contracts and, 21
  workers' compensation and, 358, *359*
First treatment medical report, 337, *340*
Fiscal agents, in Medi-Cal, 504
  in Medicare, 260
Flat rate, 391
FMC (foundation for medical care), 210-211
  explanation of, 50
Follow-up days, coding of, 91-92
Foot, terminology of, *357*
Forgery, 33
Form(s), 124-157
  audit, 79, *80*
  CHAMPUS 1251, 306, *307*
  CHAMPUS DD 2527, 315, *316-320*
  CHAMPVA 10-7959A, 309, *310-311*
  claim, CHAMPUS, 190, *191*, *308*, 309-313
    FEHBP, 240, *241*, *242*
    Medicaid, 251-253, *254*
    Medi-Cal, 514-520, *516*, *518*, *519*
  consent for release of information, 25, *26*
  DE 2501, *381*, *382*, 386
  DE 2547, *384*, *385*, 386
  DE 2525XX, *383*, 386
  dental injury, 349, *352*
  encounter, for managed care, 215-219, *218*
    in electronic data interchange, 165-166
  explanation of benefits, 155-157, *156*
    Blue Shield, 238, *239*
    FEHBP, *243-244*, 245
  first treatment medical report, 337, *340*
  from medical records, 129, *130*, *131*
  HCA-1964, 192, *193*
  HCFA-1500. See *HCFA-1500 form.*
  HCFA-1660, 284, *285-286*
  HCFA-1965, 195, *198*
  HCFA-L 365, *282-283*, 284
  insurance application, 129, *130*, *131*
  insurance claims register, 55, *56*
  insurance complaint, 178, *179*
  insurance tracer, 181, *181*
  interview evaluation and reference investigation, *435-436*, *437*
  job application, 430, *431-432*
  Lifetime Beneficiary Claim Authorization and Information Release, for Medicare, 265
  Medicaid remittance advice, 253, *255*
  Medi-Cal appeal, 517, *518*
  medical inquiry, *384*, *385*, 386
  optically scanned, 142-143
  patient information, 56, *57*
    update of, *58*, 59
  physician's monthly report and bill, 349, *351*
  physician's supplemental report, 349, *350*
  precertification, 46, *47*
  predetermination, 47, *48*
  prior authorization, 251, *252*
  rejection or delay in, 140-142, *141*
  resubmission turnaround document, 514, *515*
  signature authorization, 29-30, *30*, *31*
    Medicare electronic, 164, *165*
  SSA-1696-U4, 195, *196-197*

Form(s) *(Continued)*
terminology in, 129-137, 132t-136t, *137*
treatment authorization request, 211, *212*
types of, 128-129
UB-92, 399-408, *400*
in Medi-Cal, 509, *511*, 512
VA 10-583, 376, *377*
Foundation for medical care (FMC), 210-211
explanation of, 50
Fraud, and abuse, 494
in insurance claims, 30-34
in Medicare, 290
in workers' compensation, 342-344, *343*
Free-lancing, as insurance billing specialist, 438-442, *440*
FTC (Federal Trade Commission), 178
Functional resume, 433
Funding, of disability insurance, 376
of workers' compensation, 332, 333t-334t

G

Gatekeeper, 206
Global fee, 95
Glossary of terms, 521-534
Grace period, 45
Group contract, 47
Group disability income insurance, 372
Group practice health plan, 203-204
Grouper, 410
Guaranteed renewable policy, 44-45
in disability income insurance, 371
Guarantor, 29

H

Hand, terminology of, *357*
Hardware, for electronic data interchange, 159
HCA-1964 form, 192, *193*
HCFA-1500 form, 125, *126*, *127*, 494
assignment of benefits and, 261, *264*
common errors on, 140, *141*
completion of, 143-155, *144*, *145*
in Blue Cross/Blue Shield, 234-237, *236*
in CHAMPUS, 306, *308*
in Medicaid, 284, *287*
in Medi-Cal, 508-509, *510*, *519*, 519-520
in Medicare, 276, *277*, *278*, 279t-280t
patient information and, 59, *60*
prior authorization and, 288, *288*
procedures for, 137-140
HCFA-1660 form, 284, *285-286*
HCFA-1965 form, 195, *198*
HCFA (Health Care Finance Administration), in Medicare appeals process, 195-199
HCFA-L 365 form, *282-283*, 284
HCPCS (Health Care Finance Administration Common Procedure Coding System), 66, 494
in hospital billing, 399
index of ranges for, *268*
Head crash, in electronic management, 174
Health Care False Claim Act, 34
Health Care Finance Administration (HCFA), common procedure coding system of, 66
in hospital billing, 399
index of ranges for, *268*
in Medicare appeals process, 195-199
Health care reform, 205-206
Health insurance, 42-62, 494
billing for, 51-52
choice of, 47
claims of, 52-61. See also *Insurance claim(s).*

Health insurance *(Continued)*
current information on, 61-62
history of, 44
policy for, 44-47
types of, 47-50
Health Insurance Association of America (HIAA), 125, *126*, *127*
Health Maintenance Organization Act, 204-205, 494
Health maintenance organization (HMO), 206
Blue Cross/Blue Shield and, 233
explanation of, 50
Medicare and, 276-281
Health plan, prepaid group practice, 203-204
triple option, 210
Hearing(s), CHAMPUS, 190
Medicare, 195, *198*
SSI, 374
HIAA (Health Insurance Association of America), 125, *126*, *127*
High-risk case, 47
Hippocrates, Oath of, 8, *9*
History, documentation of, 77-79
insurance company payment, 180
of present illness (HPI), 77
HIV (human immunodeficiency virus) testing, 372
HMO. See *Health maintenance organization (HMO).*
HMO Blue USA, 207
Honesty bond, 34
Hospital benefit(s), Medicare, 270
Hospital billing, 388-416
appropriateness evaluation protocols and, 415
CHAMPUS and, 397
claim form for, 399-408, *400*, 495
confidentiality and, 392-393
diagnosis related groups and. See also *Diagnosis related groups (DRGs).*
diagnostic coding in, 397-399
diagnostic-related groups and, 408-414
errors in, 393-394
inpatient claims and, 396-397
job description of, 389, *390*
outpatient claims and, 395-396
peer review and, 414-415
procedural coding in, 399
process of, 394-395, *395*
reimbursement methods in, 391-392
Hospital care, coding of, 93
HPI (history of present illness), 77
Human immunodeficiency virus (HIV) testing, 372
Hypertension, 118

I

IAIABC (International Association of Industrial Accident Boards and Commissions), 164
IBA (International Billing Association), 17
ICD-10 (*International Classification of Diseases, Tenth Revision*), 109
ICD-9-CM. See *International Classification of Diseases, Ninth Revision, Clinical Modification (ICD-9-CM).*
ICR (intelligent character recognition), 142-143
Identification card, for Blue Cross/Blue Shield, 231-233, *232*
for CHAMPUS/CHAMPVA, *299*, 299-300, *300*
for FEHBP, 240, *240*
for managed care, 213
for Medicaid, 250-251
for Medi-Cal, 504, *504*
for Medicare, *269*, 269-270
for TRICARE, 321, 322, *322*
Illness, occupational, first report of, 361-363, *362*
workers' compensation and, 330
severity of, in AEP, 415
Image, personal, 15
IME (independent medical examiner), 345-346
Implied contract, 21

Incentives, work, 373
Income continuation benefit, 47
Incomplete claim, 129
Incontestable policy, 21
Indemnity, 45
  double, 371
Indemnity benefit policy, 275
  Blue Cross/Blue Shield, 229
Independent medical examiner (IME), 345-346
Independent practice association (IPA), 206-207
  explanation of, 50
Individual contract, 47
Individual customary profile, 84
Individual disability income insurance, 370-372
Individual responsibility plan (IRP), 222
Information, privileged, 15
  release of, authorization for, 21-22, *22*
    confidentiality and, 25-27, *26*
Injection(s), coding of, 89-90
Injury(ies), coding of, 120-121
  dental, *352*
  occupational, 361-363, *362*
Inpatient treatment, CHAMPUS coverage for, 300, *301-305*
  claims for, 396-397
  evaluation and management codes for, 73t
  ICD-9-CM coding of, *7*
Insurance, disability income, 368-386. See also *Disability income insurance.*
  errors and omissions, 20
  for insurance billing specialist, 439-441
  health, 42-62. See also *Health insurance.*
Insurance billing, examples of, 51-52
Insurance billing specialist, 2-17, 418-442
  career advantages of, 5
  curriculum for, 4, *5*
  diagnosis-related groups and, 410-411
  education and training for, 4, *5-7*
  employment opportunities for, 419-427, *419-427*
  job description for, 389, *390*, *420-421*
  job search for, 428-438
    application in, 430, *431-432*
    as claims assistance professional, 429-430
    as electronic claims professional, 430
    electronic resume in, 429
    interview in, *435-436*, 437-438
    introduction letter in, 430-433, *433*
    objectives of, 502
    on-line, 428-429
    resume in, 433-437, *434*
  medical ethics and, 8-15, *9*. See also *Ethics.*
  medical etiquette for, 8
  personal qualifications of, 5-8
  professionalism and, 15-17
  self-employed, 438-442, *440*
Insurance claim(s), 52-61, 176-200
  audits and review of, 33-34
  forms for, 124-157
    benefit explanation and, 155-157, *156*
    completion of, 143-155, *144*, *145*
    from medical records, 129, *130*, *131*
    HCFA-1500 in, 137-140
    optically scanned, 142-143
    rejection or delay in, 140-142, *141*
    terminology in, 129-137, 132t-136t, *137*
    types of, 128-129
  fraud and abuse of, 30-34
  handling of, 56-61
    patient information sheet in, 56-60, *57*, *58*, *60*
    register for, 61
    submitting and tracing in, 60-61
  hospital, 399-408, 495
  inquiry of, electronic, 170-171
    rebilling and, 187
  legal issues affecting, 18-40. See also *Legal issue(s).*
Insurance claim(s) *(Continued)*
  management techniques for, 180-181, *181*, *182*
  problems with, 181-187
    delinquent claims in, 181-183, 183t
    denied claims in, 184-185
    down coding in, 185-186
    lost claims in, 183
    overpayment in, 187
    partial payment in, 186
    payment paid in, 186
    rejected claims in, 184
    two-party check in, 186-187
    types of, 181
  processing of, 52-56, *53-56*
  provisions of, 177
  rebilling of, 187-188, *189*
  register for, 55, *56*
  review and appeal process of, 188-200, *189*
    for Blue Cross/Blue Shield, 189-190
    for CHAMPUS, 190, *191*
    for Medicare, 190-199, 192t. See also *Medicare.*
    for Medigap, 199-200
  state insurance commissioner and, 178-180, *179*
Insurance commissioner, 40
  state, 178-180, *179*
Insurance complaint form, 178, *179*
Insurance directories, 495
Insurance policy. See *Policy(ies).*
Insurance Value-Added Network Services (IVANS), 164
Insured, 44
Intelligent character recognition (ICR), 142-143
Intensity of service (IS), in AEP, 415
Interactive transaction, 170
Interface, 160
Intermediary, fiscal, in Medi-Cal, 504
    in Medicare, 260
Internal audit, documentation of, 79-81, *79-81*
International Association of Industrial Accident Boards and Commissions (IAIABC), 164
International Billing Association (IBA), 17
International Classification of Diseases, Ninth Revision, Clinical Modification (ICD-9-CM), 4, *6*, *7*
  contents of, 109, 110t
  hospital billing and, 397-399
  in diagnostic coding, 108-109
  in procedural coding, 66
International Classification of Diseases, Tenth Revision (ICD-10), 109
Inter-Plan Teleprocessing Service (ITS), 231
Interview, *435-436*, 437-438
Intoxication, 114
Introduction letter, 430-433, *433*
Invalid claim, 129
IPA (independent practice association), 206-207
  explanation of, 50
IRP (individual responsibility plan), 222
IS (intensity of service), in AEP, 415
ITS (Inter-Plan Teleprocessing Service), 231
IVANS (Insurance Value-Added Network Services), 164

J

JCAHO (Joint Commission on Accreditation of Healthcare Organizations), 29
Job description, 419
  for claims assistance professional, *422-423*
  for coder, *426-427*
  for electronic claims processor, *424-425*
  for insurance billing specialist, *420-421*
  for patient service representative, 389, *390*
Job search, 428-438
  application in, 430, *431-432*
  for claims assistance professional, 429-430

Job search *(Continued)*
for electronic claims professional, 430
for insurance billing specialist, 428
interview in, *435-436*, 437-438
introduction letter in, 430-433, *433*
on-line, 428-429
resume in, 433-437, *434*
electronic, 429
Joint Commission on Accreditation of Healthcare Organizations (JCAHO), 29

K

Kaiser Permanente Medical Care Program, 204
Key terms, 502

L

Laboratory abbreviations, 102t-103t, 104
Laboratory test(s), managed care and, 213
modifier codes for, 100t
Laceration(s), repair of, coding of, 94
CPT coding of, 82
Late effects, coding of, 120-121
Law(s), credit and collection, 35
ethics and, 495
extraterritorial compensation, 332
workers' compensation, 330
Legal issue(s), 18-40
agreements in, 39
appeals in, 35
confidentiality in, 21-27. See also *Confidentiality*.
credit and collection laws in, 35
embezzlement in, 34-35, *35*
employer liability in, 20
insurance claims in, 29-30, *30*, *31*
fraud and abuse of, 30-34
insurance commissioners in, 40
insurance contracts in, 20-21
liability prevention in, 35-40, *37*, *38*. See also *Liability*.
medicolegal references in, 40
patient/physician contracts in, 21
physician and managed care contracts in, 21
state boards of medical examiners in, 40
statute of limitations in, 35
subpoena in, 28
Lesion(s), coding of, 94
Letter(s), for claim review, 181, *182*
for delinquent claims, 363, *364-366*
for fee estimation, 47, *49*
for fee reduction appeal, 188, *189*
for informed refusal, 213, *215*
for Medicare review request, 194, *194*
for patient discharge confirmation, 36, *38*
for payment authorization, 213, *214*
for withdrawal from case, 36, *37*
of introduction, 430-433, *433*
patient information, 215, *217*
thank-you, 438, *438*
LHWCA (Longshoremen's and Harbor Workers' Compensation Act), 331-332
Liability, employer, 20
prevention of, 35-40
American Medical Association Committee on Medicolegal Problems on, 36-39, *37*, *38*
physician/patient agreement in, 39
termination in, 39-40
third party, in CHAMPUS, 315, *316-320*
in Medicaid, 253
vicarious, 20
Liability insurance, Medicare and, 281-284, *282-283*
Liens, in workers' compensation, 346-348, *347*
Lifetime Beneficiary Claim Authorization and Information Release Form, for Medicare, 265
Longshoremen's and Harbor Workers' Compensation Act (LHWCA), 331-332
Looping, 410
Lost claim, 183

M

Macro, in electronic data interchange, 166
Major diagnostic categories (MDCs), 409
Major medical contract, 44
Malpractice, 35
Managed care, 202-224, 495
bankruptcy and, 221
Blue Cross/Blue Shield and, 233
CHAMPUS and, 207-209, 315-322, *322*
financial management of, 219-221, *220-223*
foundations for, 210-211
health maintenance organizations in, 206
history of, 203-206
individual practice association in, 206-207
inpatient treatment and, 397
legal issues affecting, 21
Medicaid and, 253
medical review of, 211
Medicare and, 209
optometric service plans in, 222
overpayment and, 187
physician provider groups in, 210
plan management in, 211-219
administration and, 213-219
contracts and, 211
guide for, 213
precertification and, 211-213, *212*, *214*, *215*
tests and, 213
point of service plans in, 209-210
preferred provider organizations in, 207
special plans in, 221-222
triple option health plan in, 210
workers' compensation and, 331
Managed care organization (MCO), 205
Management services organization (MSO), 3-4
Manager, medical office, 16
Mandated service, modifier codes for, 97t
Marketing, for insurance billing specialist, 441
Maternal and Child Health Program (MCHP), 256-257
explanation of, 50
McCarran Act, 178
MCHP (Maternal and Child Health Program), 256-257
explanation of, 50
MCO (managed care organization), 205
Medicaid, 246-256, 495-496
benefits of, 250
CHAMPUS and, 313
claim procedure in, 250-253, *252*, *254*, *255*
eligibility for, *249*, 249-250
explanation of, 50
hints for, 255-256
history of, 247-249
inpatient treatment and, 397
managed care programs and, 209
reform of, 248-249
Medicaid Qualified Medicare Beneficiaries (MQMB) program, 248
Medi-Cal, 248, 250, 503-520
benefits of, 504
claims inquiry form in, 514-520, *516*
appeal process and, 517-519, *518*
CHAMPUS and, 519
Medicare and, *519*, 519-520
claims procedure in, 508-514
adjustments and, 513

Medi-Cal *(Continued)*
approvals and, 513
A/R transactions and, 513-514
computer media and, 512-513
denials and, 513
EFT and, 514
HCFA-1500 form and, 508-509, *510*
remittance advice and, 513
suspends and, 513
UB-92 form and, 509, *511*, 512
copayments in, 505, *507*
eligibility for, 503
verification of, 504-505, *506*
fiscal intermediaries of, 504
identification card for, 504, *504*
prior approval in, 505, 507-508
reform of, 503
resubmission turnaround document in, 514, *515*
Medical assistant, diagnosis-related groups and, 410-411
ethics for, 11-15, *14*
Medical care, foundations for, 210-211
Medical ethics. See *Ethics.*
Medical etiquette, for insurance billing specialist, 8
Medical examiners, 40
Medical Group Management Association (MGMA), 16, 17
Medical Inquiry Form, *384*, *385*, 386
Medical management, 496
Medical Necessity Program, 233
Medical office manager, 16
Medical professional liability, 35-40, *37*, *38*
Medical record(s), abstracting from, 129, *130*, *131*
authentication of, 29
confidentiality and, 21-25, *22*, *24*
diagnosis-related groups and, *412*, 412-414, *413*
documentation of, *77*
electronic management of, 174
ethics for, 11, *13*
legal issues affecting, 18-40. See also *Legal issue(s).*
retention of, 27, 27t
Medical report(s), in workers' compensation, 349-358
confidentiality and, 349
documentation of, 349
information and, 358
recordkeeping and, 349
terminology and, 349-358, *353-357*
Medical review, 211
Medical Service Order, 337, *339*
Medical terminology, 129-137, 132t-136t, *137*
Medical testimony, in workers' compensation, 345, *346*
Medical transcriptionist, 16
Medically indigent (MI), 249
Medically needy class, 249
Medicare, 258-294, 496
abuse of, 290
aliens on, 265
automobile insurance coverage and, 281-284, *282-283*
beneficiary representative in, 265-266
billing for deceased patient in, 284, *285-286*
Blue Cross/Blue Shield and, claims in, 233
carrier-dealing prepayment organizations and, 281
CHAMPUS and, 313-315
CHAMPVA and, 315
coding for, 104
tips in, 288-293, 289t
confidential information and, 14
copayments in, 281
coverage in, 270-274, *273*
eligibility for, 260
explanation of, 50
fiscal intermediaries and agents in, 260
HCPCS for, 66
HMOs and, 276-281
inpatient treatment and, 397
liability insurance coverage and, 281-284, *282-283*
Medicare *(Continued)*
Lifetime Beneficiary Claim Authorization and Information Release Form for, 265
managed care programs and, 209
Medicaid and, 253, 284, *287*
Medi-Cal and, *519*, 519-520
overpayment and, 187
Part A, 261, *262*
Part B, 261-265, *263*, *264*, *265*
payments in, *266*, 266-270, *268*
prior authorization in, 288, *288*
Prospective Payment System of, 260-261
representative payee in, 265-266
review and appeal process for, 190-199, 192t
administrative law judge hearing in, 195
appeals council review in, 195
fair hearing in, 195, *198*
federal district court hearing in, 195
HCFA regional offices in, 195-199
inquiry in, 192
review in, 192-195, *193*, *194*, *196-197*
supplement insurance and, 274-276, *277*, *278*, 279t-280t
UB-92 form and, 521-524
utilization and quality control in, 284-288
Medicare Blue USA, 207
Medicare global package, coding of, 93
Medicare Secondary Payer (MSP), 275
claims for, 276
guidelines for, 275-276
Medicare Transaction System (MTS), 160
Medicare/Medicaid, 284, *287*
explanation of, 50
Medicolegal references, 40
Medigap, 147, 275
CHAMPUS and, 313
claims for, 276
guidelines for, 275-276
review and appeal process for, 200
Medi-Medi. See *Medicare/Medicaid.*
Member, 44
Metric system, in CPT, 85, *87*
MGMA (Medical Group Management Association), 16, 17
MI (medically indigent), 249
Microsurgery, codes for, 96t
Minimum assistant surgeon, codes for, 99t
Modifier code(s), 83-84
list of, 96t-101t, 100-104
Monthly report and bill, *351*
MQMB (Medicaid Qualified Medicare Beneficiaries) program, 248
MSHP (multiskilled health practitioner), 4
MSO (management services organization), 3-4
MSP (Medicare Secondary Payer), 275
guidelines for, 275-276
MTS (Medicare Transaction System), 160
Multiple lesions, coding of, 94
Multiple procedures, codes for, 97t
Multiskilled health practitioner (MSHP), 4

N

NACAP (National Association of Claims Assistance Professionals), certification and, 15
code of ethics of, 9, *10*
confidentiality and, 172
NAS (Nonavailability Statement), 305-306, *307*
in TRICARE Extra, 324
National Association of Claims Assistance Professionals (NACAP), certification and, 15
code of ethics of, 9, *10*
confidentiality and, 172
legal issues and, 20
National provider identification number, 272-274
NEC (not elsewhere classifiable), 111

Negligent diagnosis, 38
Neoplasm(s), coding of, 117-118
Network HMO, 206
Network provider, in TRICARE Extra, 322
Networking, for insurance billing specialist, 442
New patient, 69
Nonavailability Statement (NAS), 305-306, *307*
in TRICARE Extra, 324
Nonbenefit(s), in FEHBP, 238-240
Noncancellable policy, 45
Nondisability claim, 337, *338-340*
Nonparticipating physician, Medicare and, 262-263
Nonprivileged information, 14-15
NOS (not otherwise specified), 111
Not elsewhere classifiable (NEC), 111
Not otherwise specified (NOS), 111
Notary subpoena, 28

O

Oath of Hippocrates, 8, *9*
OBRA (Omnibus Budget Reconciliation Act), 271-272
Occupational illness, workers' compensation and, 330
Occupational injury, first report of, 361-363, *362*
Occupational Safety and Health Administration (OSHA), 344-345
OCR (optical character recognition), 142-143
Office manager, 16
Office of Inspector General (OIG), 33
Office visit(s), coding of, 89
emergency, 93-94
evaluation and management, 72t-73t
OIG (Office of Inspector General), 33
Omissions insurance, 20
Omnibus Budget Reconciliation Act (OBRA), 271-272
On-line job search, 428-429
Operating room, codes for, 99t
Optical character recognition (OCR), 142-143
Optionally renewable policy, 44
Optometric service plan, 222
OSHA (Occupational Safety and Health Administration), 344-345
Out-of-plan service, 280-281
Out-of-state claim, 361
Outpatient treatment, Blue Cross/Blue Shield and, 234
categories of, 392
CHAMPUS and, 300, *301-305*
diagnosis-related groups and, 414
diagnostic coding of, 4, *6*
emergency, 375-376, *377*
evaluation and management codes for, 72t-73t
hospital billing and, 395-396
Veterans Administration, 383-386
Overpayment, 187

P

PAHCOM (Professional Association of Health Care Office Managers), 16
Paper claim, 128
Parentheses, in CPT, 85, *86*
Partial disability, 371
Partial payment, 186
Participating provider, for CHAMPUS/CHAMPVA, 306-309
Password, in electronic management, 174
Past, family, and social histories (PFSH), 77
Patient information letter, for managed care, 215, *217*
Patient information sheet, 56-60, *57*, *58*, *60*
Patient service representative, 389, *390*
Patient/physician contract(s), 21
Payment(s), Blue Cross/Blue Shield, 229-230, 230t
hospital billing and, 395
Payments *(Continued)*
Medicare, *266*, 266-270, *268*
posting of, 290-293, *291-294*
of unauthorized medical services, 376, *377*
paid, 186
partial, 186
procedural coding and, 67-69
usual, customary, and reasonable, 68
in Blue Cross/Blue Shield, 229-230, 230t
PCM (primary care manager), 321-322
PE (physical examination), 77-78
Peer review, 188, 210
Peer review organization (PRO), 211
hospital billing and, 414-415
Medicare and, 284-288
Pending claim, 181-183, 183t
in Medi-Cal, 513
Per diem, 391
Percentage of revenue, 391-392
Percentile of charge schedule, 360
Periodic interm payment (PIP), 392
Permanent disability, 336
claim for, 341
Personal bond, 34
Personal image, 15
Phantom charge(s), 393-394
Physical examination (PE), 77-78
Physician(s), billing by, 4, *6*
contracts with, 21
diagnosis-related groups and, 411-412
fee profile of, 121-122
final report and bill of, *351*
in Blue Cross/Blue Shield, 230-231
in Medicare, 271
relative values for, 95
report of, for accident, 333t-334t
for workers' compensation, 361-363, *362*
supplemental, *350*
Physician provider group (PPG), 210
Physician/patient agreement, 39
Physician's Supplementary Certificate Form, *383*, 386
PIN (provider identification number), in Blue Cross/Blue Shield, 238
in Medicare, 272-274
"Ping-ponging," 32
PIP (periodic interm payment), 392
Point of service (POS), 204, 209-210
Blue Cross/Blue Shield and, 207, 233
explanation of, 50
Medi-Cal eligibility and, 504-505, *506*
Poisoning, 114
Policy(ies), 44-47. See also *Contract(s).*
cancelable, 44
challenged, 21
conditionally renewable, 44
guaranteed renewable, 44-45
in disability income insurance, 371
incontestable, 21
indemnity benefit, 275
Blue Cross/Blue Shield, 229
legal issues affecting, 20-21
limitations of, 45-47, *46*, *48*, *49*
noncancellable, 45
optionally renewable, 44
service benefit, 275
Blue Cross/Blue Shield, 229
Policyholder, 44
Portfolio, 437-438
POS. See *Point of service (POS).*
Position-schedule bond, 34
Postclaim agreement, 39
Posting error, 394
Postoperative management, codes for, 98t
PPG (physician provider group), 210

PPO (preferred provider organization), 207, 494
  Blue Cross/Blue Shield and, 207, 233
  explanation of, 50
PPS (Prospective Payment System), 260-261
Preadmission testing, 234
Preauthorization, 45
  in CHAMPUS, 305
  in managed care, 211-213, *212*, *214*, *215*
  in Medicare, 288, *288*
Precertification, 45-47, *47*
  in managed care, 211-213, *212*, *214*, *215*
  in Medicare, 288, *288*
  in TRICARE Extra, 323
Preclaim agreement, 39
Predetermination, 45-47, *48*
Preexisting conditions, 45
Preferred provider organization (PPO), 207, 494
  Blue Cross/Blue Shield and, 207, 233
  explanation of, 50
Pregnancy, coding of, 120
Premium, 45
Preoperative management, codes for, 98t
Prepaid group practice, 203-204
  health care reform and, 205
  model of, 206
Prepaid health plan, 47
  Medicare and, 276-281
Prevailing charge(s), 68
Prevailing profile, 84
Pricing, for insurance billing specialist, 441
Primary care manager (PCM), 321-322
Primary diagnosis, 107
Principle diagnosis, 107
Principles of Medical Ethics (AMA), 8
Prior approval, in Medicaid, 251, *252*
  in Medi-Cal, 505, 507-508
Prior authorization. See *Preauthorization.*
Privacy Act of 1974, 305
Private insurance, inpatient treatment and, 396
Privileged communication, 11-14
Privileged information, 15
PRO (peer review organization), 211
  hospital billing and, 414-415
  Medicare and, 284-288
Procedural coding, 64-104
  codes in, administrative or add-on, 90
    all-inclusive, 94
    bundled, 86-87
    down, 87-88
    effective use of, 84-86, *85-87*
    modifiers of, 83-84, 96t-101t, 100-104
    monitoring of, 89, *89*
    symbols for, 82-83
    unbundling of, 88-89
    up, 88-89
  current procedural terminology in, 66-67
  documentation in, 76-81
  for concurrent care, 91
  for consultations, 89
  for critical care, 93
  for drugs and injections, 89-90
  for emergency care, 93-94
  for evaluation and management, 69-76. See also *Evaluation and management (E/M).*
  for follow-up days, 91-92
  for hospital billing, 399
  for laceration repair, 94
  for Medicare, 104
  for Medicare global package, 93
  for multiple lesions, 94
  for office visits, 89
  for prolonged services, 93
  for surgery, 81-82, *82*, 90-91
  for surgical package, 92-93
Procedural coding *(Continued)*
  laboratory abbreviations in, 102t-103t, 104
  payment methods and, 67-69
  relative value studies in, 67, 95-100. See also *Relative value studies (RVS).*
  vocabulary in, 69
Procedure review, 415
Procedure(s), asterisk, 95
  bilateral, 97t
  multiple, 97t
  repeat, 99t
  unlisted, 71-76
  unrelated, 99t
Processing, of insurance claims, 52-56, *53-56*
Professional Association of Health Care Office Managers (PAHCOM), 16
Professional review organization. See *Peer review organization (PRO).*
Professionalism, 15-17
Progress report, workers' compensation and, 358
Prolonged service(s), coding of, 93
    modifier, 96t
Promotion, for insurance billing specialist, 441
Prompts, in electronic data interchange, 166
Prospective Payment System (PPS), 260-261
Provider identification number (PIN), in Blue Cross/Blue Shield, 238
  in Medicare, 272-274
Public relations, for insurance billing specialist, 441

Q

Quality assurance, in TRICARE Extra, 325
Quality control, in Medicare, 284-288
Qui tam action, 33

R

RA (remittance advice), 171-172
  in managed care, 219, *220*
  in Medicaid, 253, *255*
  in Medi-Cal, 513
Railroad retirement benefit(s), Medicare and, 270-271
Random access memory (RAM), 160
Range of motion, *354*
Rating, in state workers' compensation, 341-342
RBRVS (Resource-Based Relative Value Scale), 67, 266
Readmission review, 414
Read-only memory (ROM), 160
Reasonable charge(s), 68
  in Medicare, 262
Rebilling, 187-188, *189*
Recipient, 44
Reciprocity, in Medicaid, 251
Record(s), accounting, 27, 27t
  medical. See *Medical record(s).*
Reduced services, codes for, 98t
Re-examination report, workers' compensation and, 358
Reference, medicolegal, 40
Reference list, of audiotapes, books, newsletters, periodicals, software, and videotapes, 487-500
Referral(s), 69
  in Medicare, 271
  in TRICARE Extra, 323
Reform, health care, 205-206
  Medicaid, 248-249
  Medi-Cal, 503
  workers' compensation, 330-331
Register, insurance claims, 55, *56*, 61, 180
Registered Medical Assistant (RMA), 16
Rehabilitation benefit(s), of workers' compensation, 336-337

Reimbursement, 494
  hospital billing and, 391-392
Rejected claim, 128-129, 184
Relative value scale schedule, 360
Relative value studies (RVS), 66, 67
  conversion factors in, 95-100
  in Blue Cross/Blue Shield, 230
  modifier codes for, 100, 101t
Relative value unit (RVU), 266, 497
Remittance advice (RA), 171-172
  in managed care, 219, *220*
  in Medicaid, 253, *255*
  in Medi-Cal, 513
  in Medicare, 262, 290, 292-294
Repeat procedure, modifier codes for, 99t
Representative payee, Medicare, 265-266
Request for Hearing Form, 195, *198*
Residual disability, 371-372
Resource-Based Relative Value Scale (RBRVS), 67, 266
Resources, names and addresses of, 498-500
  reference list of, 487-498
Respondeat superior, 20, 35
Resubmission turnaround document (RTD), 514, *515*
Resume, 433-437, *434*
Review, medical, 211
  of systems, 77
Review process, 33-34, 188-200, *189*
  electronic, 170-171
  for Blue Cross/Blue Shield, 189-190
  for CHAMPUS, 190, *191*
  for Medicare, 190-199, 192t, 290. See also *Medicare.*
  for Medigap, 200
RMA (Registered Medical Assistant), 16
ROM (read-only memory), 160
ROS (review of systems), 77
Ross-Loos Medical Group, 203
RTD (resubmission turnaround document), 514, *515*
RVS. See *Relative value studies (RVS).*

S

SCC (Society for Clinical Coding), 16
Screen, 170
Second opinion, 234
Second-injury fund, 348
Self-employed insurance billing specialist, 438-442, *440*
Self-employment, 497
Self-insurance, workers' compensation and, 331
Semicolon, in CPT, 85, *85*
Seminars, workshops and, 497-498
Service benefit contract(s), 275
  Blue Cross/Blue Shield, 229
Severity of illness (SI), in AEP, 415
Signature, authorization of, 29-30, *30*, *31*
    Medicare and, 263
  in electronic data interchange, 164, *165*
Skeletal anatomy, terminology pertinent to, *355-356*
Skilled nursing facility, 44
Sliding scale, 391
Smart card, for eligibility verification, 166
SOAP notes, 77
Social Security Disability Insurance (SSDI), 372-373
Society for Clinical Coding (SCC), 16
Software, for electronic data interchange, 159
SSA-1696-U4 form, 195, *196-197*
SSDI (Social Security Disability Insurance), 372-373
SSI (Supplemental Security Income), 249, 373-374
Staff model, 206
Standby, coding of, 93
Stark I and II regulations, 271
State boards of medical examiners, 40
State disability insurance, 376-379
  explanation of, 50
State insurance commissioner, 178-180, *179*
State workers' compensation, 332-342
  benefits of, 336-337
  funding of, 332, 333t-334t
  minimum number of employees for, 332, 335t
  nondisability claims for, 337, *338-340*
  permanent disability claims for, 341
  rating in, 341-342
  temporary disability claims for, 336t, 337-341
  waiting periods for, 336, 336t
Statement, duplicate, 393
  in electronic data interchange, 172
  of ethical coding principles, 9, *11-12*
  of remittance, 219, *220*
Statute of limitations, 35
Sterilization, coding of, 117
Stop loss, 392
Storage, data, electronic management in, 174
Sub rosa films, in workers' compensation, 341
Subjective disability, 353
Subpoena, 28
Subrogation, third party, 345
Subscriber, 44
  Blue Cross/Blue Shield, 228
Subsequent-injury fund, 348
Summary Payment Voucher, for CHAMPUS, 313, *314*
Summary notice, Medicare. See *Remittance advice (RA), in Medicare.*
Superbill. See *Encounter form.*
Supplemental benefit(s), of disability income insurance, 371-372
Supplemental insurance, employer, 147
  Medicare, 274-276, *277*, *278*, 279t-280t
Supplemental report form, *350*
Supplemental Security Income (SSI), 373-374
Supplementary Certificate Form, Physician's, *383*, 386
Supplementary Security Income (SSI), 249
Surgeon, codes for, 99t
Surgery, ambulatory, categories of, 392
    in Blue Cross/Blue Shield, 234
  coding of, 90-93
    CPT, 81-82, *82*
    modifier, 98t
Surveillance, in workers' compensation, 341-342
Suspense file, 181-183, 183t
  in Medi-Cal, 513
Swipe card, for eligibility verification, 166
Symbol(s), in CPT, 82-83

T

Tabular list, hospital billing and, 397-398
TAR (treatment authorization request), 505, 507-508
Tax Equity and Fiscal Responsibility Act (TEFRA), 272
Technology Evaluation Center (TEC), 233-234
TEFRA (Tax Equity and Fiscal Responsibility Act), 272
Telecommunications network, Medi-Cal treatment authorization and, 508
Temporary disability, 336, 371
  claim for, 336t, 337-341
Termination of case, 39-40
Tertiary care, 213
Testimony, in workers' compensation, 345, *346*
Third party liability, in CHAMPUS, 315, *316-320*
  in Medicaid, 253
Third party subrogation, in workers' compensation, 345
Third-party administration (TPA), 162
Tickler file, 55, *55*, 180-181, *181*, *182*
Time limit(s), for receiving reimbursement, 183, 183t
  for submitting claims, 29, 45
    in FEHBP, 240-245
    in Medicaid, 251
    in Medi-Cal, 508
    in Medicare, 264

Time limit(s) *(Continued)*
in state disability insurance, 379
Total disability, 371
TPA (third-party administration), 162
Tracing insurance claim(s), 60-61, 176-200. See also *Insurance claim(s).*
Training, for insurance billing specialist, 4, *5-7*
Transcribed medical report, 29
Transfer review, 415
Treatment authorization request (TAR), 505, 507-508
TRICARE, 315-322, *322*
hospital billing and, 397
TRICARE Extra, 208, 322-327
claims procedure in, 325-327
copayments in, 322, *323-326*
identification card for, 322
network provider for, 322
Nonavailability Statement in, 324
quality assurance in, 325
referrals and precertification in, 323
TRICARE Prime, 208, 321
TRICARE Standard, 327
Triple option health plan, 210
Tumor(s), 117
Turfing, 211
Two-party check, 186-187

U

UB-92 form, 399-408, *400*
in Medi-Cal, 509, *511*, 512
UCD (unemployment compensation disability), 349
explanation of, 50
UCR (usual, customary, and reasonable) payment program, 68
in Blue Cross/Blue Shield, 229-230, 230t
Unbundling, 88-89
Unemployment compensation disability (UCD), 349
explanation of, 50
Uniform Bill insurance form, 399-408, *400*
in Medi-Cal, 509, *511*, 512
Unlisted procedure, codes for, 71-76
Unrelated procedure, codes for, 99t
Unusual anesthesia, codes for, 96t
Unusual services, codes for, 96t
Upcoding, 88
UR (utilization review), 211
diagnosis-related groups and, 408, 414
Medicare and, 284-288
Usual, customary, and reasonable (UCR) payment program, 68
in Blue Cross/Blue Shield, 229-230, 230t
Usual fee, 68
Utilization review (UR), 211
diagnosis-related groups and, 408, 414
Medicare and, 284-288

V

V code(s), 115-116
VDT (video display terminal), 160
Veterans Administration (VA), disability benefits of, 374-376, *375*, *377*
claims for, 383-386
outpatient clinics of, 50
Vicarious liability, 20
Video display terminal (VDT), 160
Videotapes, 497
Virus, computer, 173
Vocational rehabilitation, workers' compensation and, 339
Volume performance standard (VPS), 290
Voluntary disability insurance plan, 379
VPS (volume performance standard), 290

W

Waiting period, 45
for disability income insurance, 371
for workers' compensation, 336, 336t
Waiver, of benefits, 45
of premium, 371
Withhold, 206, 392
Work incentives, 373
Workers' compensation, 328-367, 497
benefits of, 330
billing claims in, 358-361, *359*
Blue Plans and, 396
CHAMPUS/CHAMPVA and, 315
coverage of, 331-332
delinquent claims in, 363, *364-366*
depositions and, 345-346
disability and, 372
doctor's report in, 361-363, *362*
electronic data interchange for, 164
explanation of, 50
fraud and abuse of, 342-344, *343*
history of, 329
liens in, 346-348, *347*
managed care and, 331
medical reports in, 349-358
confidentiality and, 349
documentation of, 349
information and, 358
recordkeeping and, 349
terminology and, 349-358, *353-357*
medical testimony in, 345, *346*
OSHA and, 344-345
purposes of, 330
reform of, 330-331
second-injury fund and, 348
self-insurance and, 331
state, 332-342
compensation benefits for, 336-337
funding of, 332, 333t-334t
minimum number of employees for, 332, 335t
nondisability claims for, 337, *338-340*
permanent disability claims for, 341
rating in, 341-342
temporary disability claims for, 336t, 337-341
waiting periods for, 336, 336t
third party subrogation in, 345
unemployment compensation and, 349
Workmen's Compensation Law of District of Columbia, 331
Workshops and seminars, 497-498

X

X-ray(s), managed care and, 213

Y

Year-end evaluation, in managed care, 219-221, *223*